WOMEN LATIN POETS

WITHDRAWN FROM
THE LIBRARY

UNIVERSITY OF
WINCHESTER

D1423969

KA 0308946 0

WOMEN LATIN POETS

Language, Gender, and Authority, from Antiquity to the Eighteenth Century

JANE STEVENSON

OXFORD

UNIVERSITY PRESS

OXFORD

UNIVERSITY PRESS

Great Clarendon Street, Oxford OX2 6DP

Oxford University Press is a department of the University of Oxford.
It furthers the University's objective of excellence in research, scholarship,
and education by publishing worldwide in

Oxford New York

Auckland Cape Town Dar es Salaam Hong Kong Karachi
Kuala Lumpur Madrid Melbourne Mexico City Nairobi
New Delhi Shanghai Taipei Toronto

With offices in

Argentina Austria Brazil Chile Czech Republic France Greece
Guatemala Hungary Italy Japan Poland Portugal Singapore
South Korea Switzerland Thailand Turkey Ukraine Vietnam

Oxford is a registered trade mark of Oxford University Press
in the UK and in certain other countries

Published in the United States
by Oxford University Press Inc., New York

© Jane Stevenson 2005

The moral rights of the author have been asserted
Database right Oxford University Press (maker)

First published 2005
First published in paperback, 2008

All rights reserved. No part of this publication may be reproduced,
stored in a retrieval system, or transmitted, in any form or by any means,
without the prior permission in writing of Oxford University Press,
or as expressly permitted by law, or under terms agreed with the appropriate
reprographics rights organization. Enquires concerning reproduction
outside the scope of the above should be sent to the Rights Department,
Oxford University Press, at the address above

You must not circulate this book in any other binding or cover
and you must impose this same condition on any acquirer

British Library Cataloguing in Publication Data

Data available

Library of Congress Cataloging in Publication Data

Stevenson, Jane, 1959–
Women Latin poets : language, gender, and authority, from antiquity to the
eighteenth century / Jane Stevenson.
p. cm.
Includes bibliographical references and index. (alk. paper)
1. Latin poetry, Medieval and modern–Women authors–History and criticism. 2. Latin
poetry–Women authors–History and criticism. 3. Women–Europe–Intellectual life. 4. Feminist
and literature–Europe. 5. Women and literature–Europe. 6. Authority in literature.
7. Sex role in literature. I. Title.

PA8050.S74 2005   871.009'9287–dc22   2004029384

Typeset by SPI Publisher Services, Pondicherry, India
Printed in Great Britain on acid-free paper by
Biddles Ltd, King's Lynn, Norfolk

ISBN 978–0–19–818502–4 (Hbk.)   978–0–19–922973–4 (Pbk.)

1 3 5 7 9 10 8 6 4 2

CATHEDRATICAE ORNATISSIMAE
MARGARET J. M. EZELL

UNIVERSITY OF WINCHESTER

871.
09   03089460

STE

Acknowledgements

The dedication of this book expresses my profound sense that, of all the many scholarly works which I consulted in its preparation, those of Professor Margaret Ezell were the most profoundly original: though learned women *per se* have not been her central concern, I have found her approach deeply illuminating, and have come to feel that I owe her an intellectual debt which I am more than happy to acknowledge.

I am also sincerely grateful for the generous help and assistance afforded to this project by a large number of individuals and institutions.

My first debt is to the libraries which have allowed me to consult manuscripts and rare books in their care, and granted me permission to cite or quote their texts: in Belgium, the Bibliothèque Royale, Brussels; in Denmark, the Kongelige Bibliotek, Copenhagen; in England, the University Library, Cambridge, the Cumbria County Record Office, Carlisle, the Public Record Office, Kew, the archive of Hatfield House, the Hertfordshire County Record Office, Hertford, the Northamptonshire Record Office, Northampton, the Nottinghamshire County Record Office, Nottingham, the Leicestershire County Record Office, Leicester, the British Library, London, the Library of the Society of Friends, London, the University of London Library, London, Dr Williams's Library, London, the Bodleian Library, Oxford, and the Warwickshire County Record Office, Warwick; in France, the Bibliothèque de l'Arsenal, Paris, Bibliothèque Mazarine, Paris, Bibliothèque Nationale de France, Paris, and Bibliothèque Sainte-Geneviève, Paris; in Germany, the Bayerische Staatsbibliothek, Munich, and the Herzog-August Bibliothek, Wolfenbüttel; in Italy, the Biblioteca civica Angelo Mai, Bergamo, the Archivio di stato, Biblioteca comunale dell'Archiginnasio, Bologna, the Biblioteca universitaria, Bologna, the Biblioteca comunale Ariosteia, Ferrara, the Biblioteca Laurentiana, Florence, the Biblioteca nazionale centrale, Florence, the Biblioteca Riccardiana, Florence, the Biblioteca Ambrosiana, Milan, the Archivio storico comunale, Modena, the Biblioteca Estense, Modena, the Biblioteca nazionale, Naples, the Biblioteca museo civico, Padua, the Biblioteca universitaria, Padua, the Biblioteca museo Bottacin, Padua, the Biblioteca universitaria, Pavia, the Biblioteca Roncioniana, Prato, the Biblioteca Classense, Ravenna, the Biblioteca nazionale centrale Vittorio Emanuele, Rome, the Biblioteca comunale Augusta, Perugia, the Biblioteca comunale degli Intronati, Siena, the Biblioteca Marciana, Venice, the Biblioteca comunale Bertolina, Verona; in the Netherlands, the Koniglijke Bibliotheek, The Hague, the Universiteitsbibliotheek, Leiden; in Scotland, the University Library, Aberdeen, the University Library, Edinburgh, the National Library of Scotland, Edinburgh; in Spain, the Biblioteca Nacional, Madrid, the Biblioteca Universitaria, Salamanca, the Instituto Interuniversitario de Estudios de Iberoamérica y Portugal,

Salamanca, the Archivio General, Simancas, and the Biblioteca del Colegia de Santa Cruz, Valladolid; in Sweden, the Kungliga Biblioteket, Stockholm, and the Universitetsbiblioteket, Uppsala; in the United States, the Houghton Library, Cambridge, and the Newberry Library, Chicago; in Vatican City, the Biblioteca apostolica.

I would like to record that the number of librarians and archivists in many countries who have gone out of their way to be helpful is both heartwarming and astonishing: in many cases they did not even give me their names, but I am grateful to them all the same, severally and collectively. I owe particular debts to the always-helpful Rare Books and Manuscripts librarians in the British Library and to the staff of Duke Humphrey's library, to Dr Jayne Ringrose in particular, but also to the other staff of the Cambridge University Library, the Rare Books librarians at the Koniglijke Bibliotheek in The Hague, Dr Z. Jagodzinski at the Polish Library, Hammersmith, a manuscripts librarian in the Biblioteca universitaria, Bologna, who gave me an amazing amount of her time but refused to give her name, Frau Dr Foohs and other staff of the Staatsbibliothek in Munich, Ángel Luis Redero Hernández in the Instituto Interuniversitario de Estudios de Iberoamérica y Portugal in Salamanca, A. César Castro of the Universidad Nacional Mayor de San Marcos, Lima, Peru, who kindly answered queries by email, the Rare Books librarian in the Universitetsbiblioteket in Uppsala, Dottoressa Margherita Carboni, the manuscripts librarian at the Biblioteca Marciana in Venice, and Dr Jacob Thomsen at the Kongelige Bibliotek, Copenhagen.

The University of Warwick was generous with travel grants, creative solutions, and various kinds of assistance during my time there, while several members of its administrative staff went out of their way for me in one sense or another: I would therefore like to thank Giles Carden, Nikki Muckle, Irene Blood, and Janet Bailey. The AHRB generously supported travel and research assistance, enabling me to visit Italy, France, Spain, Sweden, and Germany, as well as enabling me to draw on the talents of research assistants in three different countries—they have also been patient when it all took much longer than it was meant to.

Thanks are also due to a number of private individuals, friends, colleagues, and fellow members of the *respublica litterarum* who have answered questions, discussed ideas, sent references, offered insights, or helped in other ways over what is now a considerable period of time (including several of Oxford University Press's anonymous learned readers). The networks of support and friendship which I have suggested formed part of the experience of early modern learned women have certainly formed part of my own in writing this book. It is invidious to do anything but list those who have helped me in alphabetical order. I am grateful for all kinds of reasons to Marianne Alenius, Maria Rosa Antognazza, Ros Ballaster, Susan Bassnett, Jill Bepler, Titus Bicknell, Jim Binns, Louise Bourdua, Maisie Brown, Sylvia Brown, Patricia Brückmann, Abigail Brundin, Vicki Burke, Bernard Capp, Anna Carrdus, Laurie Churchill, Elizabeth Clarke, Marie-Louise Coolahan, Ceri Davies, Ruth Dawson, Ingrid de Smet, Stella Fletcher, Ed Foster, Paul Gehl, Joan Gibson, Gilbert Gigliotti, John Gilmore, Elisabet Göransson, Nick Graham,

Alastair Hamilton, Anthony Harvey, Yasmin Haskell, Fr. Bob Hendrie, Máire Herbert, Steve Hindle, Brenda Hosington, Howard Hotson, David Howlett, Arnold Hunt, Lorna Hutson, Josef Ijsewijn, Stephen Jaeger, James Knowles, Piotr Kuhiwczak, Margaret Lantry, Guy Lee, Henrique Leitao, Judi Loach, Roger Lonsdale, Richard Maber, Fr. Rupert McArdy, Peter Mack, Noel Malcolm, Michael Mallet, Jeremy Maule, Constant Mews, Shayne Mitchell, Dominic Montserrat, Cornelia Niekus Moore, Clara Mucci, Penny Murray, Christina Neagu, David Norbrook, Jane Ohlmeyer, Holt Parker, Georgina Paul, Frederik Pedersen, Andrew Pettegree, Ursula Phillips, Lee Piepho, Yopie Prins, Alison Rawles, Dom Daniel Rees, Jamie Reid Baxter, Alison Saunders, Wolfgang Schibel, Sabina Sharkey, Richard Sharpe, Alison Shell, Gabriela Signiori, Nigel Smith, Fr. Pavel St Grigoriev, Anne Thompson, Laura Tosi, Piotr Urbanski, Pieta van Beek, Lenka Vytlacilova, Mara Wade, Roger Walker, Michael Wyatt, Louise Yeoman, and Carla Zecher—and there are doubtless others I have forgotten to include, to whom I offer my apologies.

I owe a particular debt to my research assistants: Janet Fairweather in Cambridge, who also greatly improved the translations, Paul Gwynn in Rome, Carol Morley in London, and Mariska Roos in The Hague, and also the people who lived with me at various stages of this project, who offered help and encouragement both academic and personal, Andrew Biswell, Kate Chegdzoy, Siobhàn Keenan, Dominic Montserrat, David Morley, Winifred Stevenson—and above all, Peter Davidson, the first person to think that this was a project worth tackling. My cat Venetia contributed according to her lights by posting a dead rodent into a box-file full of irreplaceable Xeroxes (filed under 'A'; for 'A mouse'?): all subsequent feline intervention has thankfully been confined to quality assurance, which is to say, the creative rearrangement of piles of paper.

Parts of the thinking for this book were tried on a variety of audiences in the form of papers, and I would like to thank the participants for their responses: the Newberry Library, Chicago, seminar on Catholic culture in early modern England, the Centre for Early Modern Studies, University of Aberdeen, the eleventh congress of the International Association for Neo-Latin Studies, held in Cambridge, the Department of History, University of Edinburgh, the International Medieval Congress, University of Leeds, the seventeenth-century group at the University of Durham, the Women, Text and History seminar, Mansfield College, Oxford, the Boston/Tübingen International Association for the Study of the Classical Tradition, Tübingen, the Neo-Latin Seminar, University of Cambridge, the European Universities and Elites in the Renaissance conference at the University of Warwick's Centre for the Study of the Renaissance, the Friendship and Friendship Networks in the Middle Ages conference at King's College, London, and the Warwick Classics Seminar.

Contents

Abbreviations

Apuntes	Manuel Serrano y Santz, *Apuntes para una biblioteca de escritoras españolas desde el año 1401 al 1833*, 2 vols. in 4 (Madrid: Sucesores de Rivadeneyra, 1903–5)
Bandini Buti	Maria Bandini Buti, *Poetesse e scrittrici*, 2 vols. (Rome: Istituto editorie italiano, 1941–2)
CCCM	Corpus Christianorum Continuatio Medievalis
CCSL	Corpus Christianorum Series Latina
CIL	*Corpus Inscriptionum Latinarum*, ed. Theodor Mommsen et al., 24 vols. (Berlin: Georg Reimer, 1863–1995)
CLE	*Carmina Latina Epigraphica*, ed. Franz Bücheler, 3 vols. (Leipzig: Teubner, 1895)
Cosenza	Mario Emilio Cosenza, *Biographical and Bibliographical Dictionary of the Italian Humanists and of the World of Classical Scholarship in Italy, 1300–1800* (Boston: G. K. Hall, 1962–7)
CSEL	Corpus Scriptorum Ecclesiae Latinae
CSP	*Calendar of State Papers*
ECWW	Katharina M. Wilson, *Encyclopedia of Continental Women Writers*, 2 vols. (New York: Garland, 1991)
Erdmann	Axel Erdmann, *My Gracious Silence: Women in the Mirror of Sixteenth Century Printing in Western Europe* (Luzern: Gilhofer & Rauschberg, 1999)
ICL	D. Schaller and E. Könsgen, *Initia Carminum Latinorum Seculo Undecimo Antiquiorum* (Göttingen: Vandenhoeck & Ruprecht, 1977)
ICVMA	H. Walther, *Initia Carminum ac Versuum Medii Aevi Posterioris Latinorum: Alphabetisches Verzeichnis der Versenfänge mittelateinischer Dichtungen* (Göttingen: Vandenhoeck & Ruprecht, 1959; 2nd edn. 1969)
Iter Italicum	Paul Oskar Kristeller, *Iter Italicum: A Finding List of Uncatalogued or Incompletely Catalogued Humanist Manuscripts of the Renaissance in Italian and Other Libraries* (London: Warburg Institute; Leiden: E. J. Brill, 1963–96)
MGH	Monumenta Germaniae Historia
MLREL	Peter Dronke, *Medieval Latin and the Rise of European Love-Lyric*, 2 vols. (Oxford: Oxford University Press, 1968)
PG	J.-P. Migne (ed.), *Patrologia Graeca Cursus Completus* (Paris: J.-P. Migne, 1857–66)

PL	J.-P. Migne (ed.), *Patrologia Latina Cursus Completus* (Paris: J.-P. Migne, 1844–64)
PLRE i	A. H. M. Jones et al. (eds.), *The Prosopography of the Later Roman Empire, i: A.D. 260–395* (Cambridge: Cambridge University Press, 1971)
PLRE ii	J. R. Martindale (ed.), *The Prosopography of the Later Roman Empire, ii: A.D. 395–527* (Cambridge: Cambridge University Press, 1980)
SKGF	Jean M. Woods and Maria Fürstenwald, *Schriftstellerinnen, Künstlerinnen und gelehrte Frauen des deutschen Barock* (Stuttgart: Metzler, 1984)
WWMA	Peter Dronke, *Women Writers of the Middle Ages* (Cambridge: Cambridge University Press, 1984)
WWRR	Katharina M. Wilson, *Women Writers of the Renaissance and Reformation* (Athens: University of Georgia Press, 1987)

Prologue

The women's lives examined in this book span nearly two thousand years. There is a strong preponderance of aristocrats (though not all of them are aristocratic by any means), and they were active in all parts of Europe. Many of them were highly visible among the intellegentsia of their own milieux: most of them were subsequently forgotten on account of their anomalousness. So buried in oblivion are they that almost anyone would have an excuse for thinking this is a large book on a non-subject. With about four exceptions—Sulpicia, Proba, Hrotsvitha, and Hildegard are the usual names—guides to Latin literature, however apparently comprehensive, seldom mention women. For example, there is a *History of Anglo-Latin Literature*,[1] but not a single one of the forty-odd Englishwomen for whom there is some evidence of Latin verse production appears in its index, though Englishwomen have left a considerable amount of Latin in both verse and prose, and made some notable translations from that language—on which score, it is also notable that Henry Burrowes Lathrop's *Translations from the Classics into English, From Caxton to Chapman, 1477–1620*, though it includes an alphabetic list of translators, includes no women whatsoever, not even Elizabeth I.[2] The *History of Later Latin Literature* mentions Hrotsvitha, but not Hildegard or Proba;[3] and German-speakers are no better served by Ellinger's *Geschichte der neulateinischen Literatur*.[4] What is still more depressing is that surveys of Latin writers made in the last twenty years are not necessarily any more sensitive to the activities of women: the 1991 *Dictionnaire des auteurs grecs et latins de l'antiquité et du Moyen Âge*, for all the impression it gives of comprehensiveness, fails to include, for example, Julia Balbilla, some of whose Greek verse survives, or Cornificia.[5] Despite having the outstanding work of Dronke available to him, Josef Szövérffy's *Secular Latin Lyrics and Minor Poetic Forms of the Middle Ages*, published in 1992, is obtuse to the issue of gender, and names only one woman, Hrotsvitha. The result, of course, is that with the exception of the four women mentioned above,

---

[1] Leicester Bradner, *Musae Anglicanae* (New York: Modern Language Association of America, 1940).

[2] (Madison: University of Wisconsin Press, 1932), 319–24. Women are mentioned only as dedicatees.

[3] F. A. Wright and T. A. Sinclair, *A History of Later Latin Literature* (London: Routledge, 1931).

[4] Georg Ellinger, *Geschichte der neulateinischen Literatur Deutschlands in sechszehnten Jahrhundert*, 3 vols. (Berlin: W. de Gruyter, 1929–33).

[5] W. Buchwald, A. Hohlweg, and O. Prinz, trans. J.-D. Berger and J. Billen (Turnhout: Brepols, 1991). It mentions Cornificius but not Cornificia. Similarly, the only women Latinists mentioned by Michael Grant, *Greek and Latin Authors, 800 BC–AD 1000* (New York: H. W. Wilson Co., 1980), are Hrotsvitha (patronizingly handled) and Sulpicia.

and a few others (most notably Isotta Nogarola and Elizabeth Jane Weston) who have emerged into visibility in the last three decades, these writers are unknown, or have barely been studied.

One point which this work seeks to address is simply the size of the phenomenon. It has been stated as recently as 1993 that there were no more than 300 learned women active during the entire Christian era in Europe up to 1700.[6] This is a significant underestimate: defining 'learned' rather strictly as capable of translating from, or writing in, Latin, there is some kind of record of at least 300 in Italy alone in that timespan. Defining 'learned' extremely strictly, as able to write Latin verse, there are over 300 women Latin poets discussed in this book (to whom a smaller but significant number of women poets in Greek could be added). Using a more normal definition of 'learned' to mean widely read in at least two European languages and possibly conversant to some extent with Latin, I would hazard a guess that this estimate is out by a factor of ten or more. I am aware that, at some points, the book is in danger of becoming 'a river of names', but this seems unavoidable, since it is obviously necessary to demonstrate both that these women did exist, and that much of their work was published in near-contemporary editions or survives in manuscript, and is hence available for future study. I should perhaps also apologize in advance for including so few actual texts. This is due to considerations of space, since the book as it stands is already well over its agreed length, due to the large number and variety of women writers who have come to light in the course of research. The work of editing remains for another day, or for other scholars.

Part of the reason for their invisibility is that these writers do not fit with either the image of Latin, or the image of women. Consider, for example, the magisterial distaste of the future George Eliot, in 1854:[7]

We confess ourselves unacquainted with the productions of those awful women of Italy, who held professional chairs and were great in civil and canon law; we have made no researches into the catacombs of female literature, but we think we may safely conclude that they would yield no rivals to that which is still unburied.

This, besides being an indication that masculine impertinence as a discourse is not actually a monopoly of the male gender, is particularly interesting from a woman who was herself a good classicist (if she had not been, she would hardly have dared to compose so Latinate a sentence). She went on to laud the charming Mme de Staël for her possession of 'the small brain and vivacious temperament which permit the fragile system of woman to sustain the superlative activity required for intellectual creativeness'. Mary Ann Evans was not vivacious or fragile. She was plain and serious: five years later, she published her first novel, *Amos Barton*. It is evident from this passage that at 33 she had internalized the idea, prevalent in her

6 Gerda Lerner, *The Creation of a Feminist Consciousness from the Middle Ages to Eighteen-Seventy* (New York: Oxford University Press, 1993), 29.

7 George Eliot, 'Women in France: Madame de Sablé', in *Essays* (London: Routledge & Kegan Paul, 1963), 52–81 (p. 54).

own time, that in order to be acceptable, women writers needed above all to be charming. She feared the masculine ridicule which, in her own time, attended *femmes fortes*,[8] so far from finding such formidable spirits as Elena Piscopia and Novella d'Andrea comforting, it was necessary to her to set herself apart from them.[9] The reluctance of learned women to identify themselves as such will be a recurrent feature of this study, and accounts in part for the fact that they are so obscure: it is difficult for subsequent historians to count, or account for, individuals who were actively trying to avoid standing up to be counted.

In more recent times, littleness and vivacity have ceased to seem quite so essential to women's cultural production, but in poetry more generally, readers have been encouraged to look not for technical accomplishment, but for authenticity, self-revelation, and emotional honesty, qualities which are not central to neo-Latin verse, though far from unknown in it. Moreover, since almost all general works on Latin literature fail to mention the participation of women in Latin culture, students of women's literature and history have understandably tended to believe that the Latin tradition can have nothing to say to them.

Another possible reason for the invisibility of the women I discuss is that the early history of feminism laid so much stress on the significance of becoming articulate that it has been easy to shift from a belief (which I personally share) that education is important in bettering the lot of women, to a belief that if women even in small numbers wielded the language of power and attracted the respect which went with Latinity, something would necessarily have happened to improve the cultural position of women in general, and since it did not, they cannot have existed.

A third reason is the significant strand in feminist thinking which explicitly dismisses women educated like men on grounds of unrepresentativeness, voiced, for example, by Mary Wollstonecraft:[10]

I shall not lay any stress on the example of a few women who, from having received a masculine education, have acquired courage and resolution ... These ... may be reckoned exceptions, and are not all heroes as well as heroines exceptional to general rules?

This is an important point, but all the same, these 'heroines' have a significance of their own: they tested the boundaries of what women were deemed able to achieve, and were persistently brought into play by later women and their male defenders for precisely this reason.

The women Latinists of the Middle Ages are more happily situated with respect to contemporary scholarship than their sisters of later centuries, to a great extent on account of the mouldbreaking work of Peter Dronke, which is gratefully drawn on in this collection as far as that chronological period is concerned. I have been

---

[8] See Barbara Garlick, 'Radical Hens and Vociferous Ladies: Representation and Class in the Mid-Nineteenth Century', in Garlick et al. (eds.), *Stereotypes of Women in Power* (Westpart, Conn.: Greenwood Press, 1992), 157–80 (pp. 172–4).

[9] Deirdre David, *Intellectual Women and Victorian Patriarchy* (London: Macmillan, 1987), 177–88.

[10] *A Vindication of the Rights of Women* (London: J. Johnson, 1792).

deeply indebted to his work, both published and unpublished, since I was privileged to attend his revelatory course on medieval women Latinists in 1979: it is he more than any other single scholar who encouraged by example and ultimately led me to embark on explorations of women's activities in the Renaissance and early modern periods. The news, which came as this book was being completed, that despite all he has achieved there, Cambridge has decided to discontinue the teaching of medieval Latin, is an injury to the entire *respublica litterarum*.

One reason for engaging in a diachronic survey of this kind is that most of these women are, in their own contexts, exceptional; so much so, that they have not been set in a context of other women's writing at all.[11] Sulpicia has been little studied by classicists until very recently, because as the only woman poet of the Augustan age, she is hard to situate against her male contemporaries. Hildegard has been much studied, but mostly as an isolated phenomenon; yet the work of Herrad of Hohenburg, Willetrudis, and others helps one to assess the question of how her work emerges from its social context. While working on this collection, it became very clear that older commentators on any one poet, for example Olimpia Morata, tended to see her as unique, and therefore hard to discuss. As Gold remarks, even Hrotsvitha has been spoken of as 'a curious and unconnected phenomenon having neither roots nor influence . . . as we so often do to women of letters', despite the extensive evidence for the cultural participation of Ottonian women, particularly royal nuns.[12] This study attempts to demonstrate that learned women tended to emerge from milieux which, on closer examination, turn out to have produced several such, so their work may be compared and contrasted in useful ways. Moreover, very few Latin women poets can actually have believed themselves the only woman to venture into classical learning; rather, they were demonstrably encouraged and empowered by knowing of the achievements of others: we see this, for example, in the case of Elizabeth Jane Weston. In a number of cases, they cite other women's work to support their own activity, at other times, the existence of one woman poet is sometimes the stimulus which creates others. Olimpia Morata died childless, but there are explicit statements with which to demonstrate that she was a role model for more than one daughter of Renaissance Germany.

Throughout European history, precedent has been very important to women as a means of validating a variety of bold and unorthodox behaviour. At a time when even English men seldom travelled, Gregory Martin's guidebook to Rome, published in 1581, speaks approvingly of women treading in the steps of the great ladies of Christian antiquity—'thou shalt se how like they are to the old devout matrones'.[13] Having the example of St Jerome's friends Paula and Marcella to

---

11 Stephanie Merrim's *Early Modern Women's Writing and Sor Juana Inés de la Cruz* (Nashville: Vanderbilt University Press, 1999) is to be celebrated as a pioneering work, in that it locates Sor Juana de la Cruz in a context of other 17th-century women's cultural production.

12 Barbara Gold, 'Hrotsvitha Writes Herself', in Barbara K. Gold, Paul Allen Miller, and Charles Platter (eds.), *Sex and Gender in Medieval and Renaissance Texts* (New York: State University of New York Press, 1997), 41–70 (p. 43).

13 *Roma Sancta* (Reims(?), 1581), ed. G. B. Parks (Rome: Edizioni di storia e letteratura, 1969), 10.

point to gave him a way of explaining, even endorsing, contemporary women's actions. Similarly, Thomas Salter suggested that girls should read 'examples and lives of godly and vertuous Ladies ... out of the holy Scripture, and other histories both auncient and of late dayes' in order to 'pricke and incite their hartes, to follow vertue, and have vice in horror and disdaine'.[14] But such reading might also, and sometimes did, incite girls to active imitation of female literary models, or encourage them in other ways. For example, in the sphere of politics, Queen Elizabeth I was offered a model for a hugely successful woman ruler by Rasmus Glad's enormous Latin poem on the great late medieval Danish queen Margarethe, which was dedicated to her;[15] and in the sphere of religion, the writings of the medieval mystic Gertrude of Helfta exerted a direct influence on a number of Spanish religious thinkers who included Teresa of Avila and Luisa de Carvajal.[16]

It is, of course, true that few women have ever written in Latin, though it is a significant shift of perception to realize that they are numbered in hundreds rather than dozens. All the writers discussed here are exceptions, and one of the things that is interesting about them is that they demonstrate that in a very wide variety of contexts, elite culture in Europe has included individual women's voices while denying the rights of women in general. The twentieth-century women's movement has tended to see problems with this, reasonably enough. Adrienne Rich remarked caustically on the 'special woman' who allows herself to be 'lulled by that blandishment about being "different", more intelligent, more beautiful, more human, more committed to rational thinking, more humorous, more able to "write like a man" ... we have known that men would tolerate, even romanticise us as special, as long as our words didn't threaten their privilege of tolerating or rejecting us and our work'.[17]

All women Latin poets are 'special women' in Rich's highly negative sense; rather than *guerrillères* or 'intruders on the rights of men';[18] women implicitly or explicitly allowed a place which was liminal, neither that of women generally, nor that of men; but, in some nebulous way, 'above', 'beyond', or 'other' with respect to ordinary women, as Mary Wollstonecraft's remark also implies. But it is hard to see how a woman active in the sixteenth or seventeenth centuries, let alone earlier,

---

[14] Thomas Salter, *A Mirrhor Mete for All Mothers, Matrones, and Maidens, Intituled the Mirrhor of Modestie* (London: For E. White, 1579), in Suzanne Trill, Kate Chegdzoy, and Melanie Osborne (eds.), *Lay by your Needles Ladies, Take the Pen* (London: Arnold, 1997), 45.

[15] Margarethe (1372–1412), the daughter of King Valdemar IV of Denmark, became Queen Regent of Denmark from 1375, Queen Regent of Norway from 1380, Queen Regent (by election) of Sweden from 1387. At her death she was the undisputed mistress of all three kingdoms. Lisa Hopkins, *Women who Would be Kings* (London: Vision Press, 1991), 20–3. Glad's 6,666-line *Margaretica* was published in Frankfurt am Main, Sigismund Feyerabend, 1573.

[16] José Adriano Moreira de Freitas Carvalho, *Gertrudes de Helfta e Espanha: contribuição para estudo da historia da espiritualidade peninsular nos séculos xvi e xvii* (Oporto: Instituto Nacional de Investigação Científica, 1981).

[17] Adrienne Rich, 'When we Dead Awake: Writing as Re-vision', in *On Lies, Secrets and Silence: Selected Prose, 1966–1978* (New York: Norton, 1979), 38–9.

[18] A phrase coined by Anne Finch, Countess of Winchilsea: see Jane Stevenson and Peter Davidson (eds.), *Early Modern Women Poets, 1520–1700*, (Oxford: Oxford University Press, 2001) 259.

could have mounted any kind of opposition to this, beyond the insistence (which quite a number of them do make) that learned women are not so very uncommon. As Danielle Clarke observes, 'without institutional sites from which to challenge patriarchy all women were to some extent implicated in its demands and assumptions'.[19] Pre-modern women who argue for their right to a public role argue their case as individuals.[20] Feminism, an aspect of a more general secular egalitarianism, made no sense within the larger structures of European thinking until the twentieth century, and it seems profoundly unfair to castigate pre-modern women for not being shaped by modernity.[21] It is also hard to make a case for the view that all pre-modern women either should or necessarily did identify themselves primarily by gender when this cut across class lines, especially if we assume that the nature of this identification should be such that it would take precedence over other concerns such as filial obedience, aggrandizement of the family, or the love of God. Certainly, women Latin poets, though they sometimes argued for a larger place for women of their own kind, did not use their abilities to preach social revolution based on the need to make the position of men and women equal (though a few of them, on the other hand, were committed to spiritual equality and religious revolution, which is a rather different phenomenon).[22]

All the same, despite the limitations which they took for granted, what is to be seen in many of these poems is women taking control of the patterns of patriarchal discourse, and using not only the language, but the tropes and topoi of the classical tradition, to express themselves. There are some poems of intimate personal reflection in Latin written by women (the sixteenth-century Elizabeth Russell is a poet of striking emotional directness); there is also a surprising quantity of public, declamatory, political verse, written by women for whom politics are intimately entwined with their personal lives because they played active roles in the political life of their milieu (the verse of Radegund, Angela Nogarola, and Veronica Gàmbara would fall into this category). There is even one, Hrotsvitha's *Gesta Ottonis*, which is an Ottonian *Aeneid*: the commissioned epic of a rising dynasty. The kind of woman who wrote Latin poetry, in whichever century, was always one who was highly privileged: with one or two remarkable exceptions, she was also the daughter of a family which had formed a strongly positive view of women's education, and which can therefore be assumed to have been liberal and empowering by the standards of her times.

The hunt for these poets and their work has been in itself an extremely interesting and instructive exercise. Once I had left behind the relatively safe

---

[19] Danielle Clarke, *The Politics of Early Modern Women's Writing* (Harlow: Pearson Education Ltd, 2001), 2.

[20] See Merry Wiesner, 'Women's Defense of their Public Role', in Mary Beth Rose (ed.), *Women in the Middle Ages and the Renaissance* (Syracuse, NY: Syracuse University Press, 1986), 1–28 (p. 9).

[21] Hilda L. Smith, *Reason's Disciples: Seventeenth-Century English Feminists* (Urbana: University of Illinois Press, 1982), argues that women writers began to recognize that women's collective position needed to be challenged in the late 17th century.

[22] For example, Anna Maria van Schurman, a Labadist, and Mary Mollineux, née Southworth, a Quaker. Marie de Gournay is a notable exception to this general statement.

harbours provided by the *Initia Carminum* volumes of Schaller-Könsgen and Walther (extraordinarily erudite and inclusive guides to Latin verse writing before 1500) and the more specific but still useful volume of Bertalot, and had struck out into the uncharted seas of Renaissance and early modern Latin, I found that the treatment of women's Latin writings offered a series of problems which came up again and again. With the noble exception of Paul Oskar Kristeller's *Iter Italicum* (which focuses on Italian humanists with a less wide coverage of connected humanist circles, deals only with manuscripts, and was initially conceived as merely a supplement to Mazzatinti's *Inventari dei manoscritti*),[23] if there was a modern book which dealt with the Latin writing of a particular place or era, women were unlikely to be mentioned at all. A process of unconscious editing-out seems often to have taken place.

A different picture was given in Renaissance or early modern discussions of literature. By contrast, women were often well in evidence, though they seemed at first always to be the same ones: a stately list, beginning as often as not with Sappho and Corinna, and almost invariably including Cornificia, whose works disappeared from human knowledge some time in the fourth century. Furthermore, in these books, women's names and personal data tended to come unaccompanied by even a notional indication of where their work was to be found—a situation succinctly described by Abraham Cowley, in a poem which he wrote on the English poet Katherine Philips:[24]

> Of Female Poets, who had Names of old,
> Nothing is shown, but only Told,
> And all we hear of them perhaps may be
> Male-Flatt'ry only, and Male-Poetry.

For example, Abella is a less shadowy figure than many, since she has a death-date (1380), and is attested in the records of the medieval medical school of Salerno as the author of two treatises in Latin verse. It would have been most interesting to see Abella's work as specimens of the scientific treatise in Latin verse (a genre with an impeccable classical ancestry going back to texts such as Virgil's *Georgics*),[25] but she, like many other women Latin poets, continues at the time of writing to elude my grasp.

It became clear to me that there was an entire genre of books about learned ladies, which flourished between the fifteenth and the eighteenth centuries in most of the countries of Europe. These survive in greater numbers even than Ruth Kelso's major collection might suggest.[26] It also became clear that from the

---

[23] G. Mazzatinti, *Inventario dei manoscritti delle biblioteche d'Italia*, 97 vols. (Forlì: L. Bardandini, 1891–1911; Florence: L. Olschki, 1912–80).

[24] 'On the Death of Mrs Katherine Philips', in Abraham Cowley, *Poems*, ed. A. R. Walker (Cambridge: Cambridge University Press, 1905), 441–3.

[25] Now the subject of a major forthcoming study by Dr Yasmin Haskell.

[26] Ruth Kelso, *Doctrine for the Lady of the Renaissance* (Urbana: University of Illinois Press, 1978), lists 891 (pp. 327–424). See Jean Céard, 'Listes des femmes savantes au XVIe siècle', in Colette Nativel (ed.), *Femmes savantes, savoir des femmes* (Geneva: Droz, 1999), 85–94, Brenda Hosington, 'Learned

beginning of the sixteenth century until the eighteenth, almost all authors of any kind of general literary survey considered it *de rigueur* to include a chapter on women. Such books were, in turn, plundered by eighteenth- and nineteenth-century historians, many of whom, be it said, were highly intelligent people and among the leading scholars of their time.[27] The superficial impression of sameness which these books give turned out to be misleading, since their compositional method is accretive: though a given book may well redact the three facts known about (for example) Cornelia Adrichomia for the fifteenth time, it also often adds precious details about contemporary and near-contemporary women in the writer's own milieu.

It may trouble some readers that I use these works at all, given their uncritical nature. I was encouraged to do so by the fact that, in the case of women whose work I was subsequently able to find, the editors of these collections often turned out to have been well informed: the nearer the writer was to the woman he was describing, in time, space, and milieu, the more likely this was to be true: I have therefore included information on women whose work I have not traced, signalling its status as assertion. Unfortunately, though many of these writers were both painstaking and well intentioned, they were for the most part quite untroubled by thoughts of preserving their subjects' actual work: they were content, on the whole, to preserve names, in much the spirit of autograph-hunters or stamp-collectors (Simon Schama has pointed to 'the sheer Rabelaisian pleasure in compilation—the collector's list fetish—that was so marked a trait of humanist culture').[28] I have frequently had occasion to curse one or another admirer of learned women who notes that 'I have seen excellent poems by "x" ', but who fails to transmit even one. The first work of this kind to lay stress on collecting samples as well as names is that of Sarah Josepha Hale, whose *Woman's Record* is a mighty work of amateur scholarship, comparable with that of the earlier work of George Ballard, but far larger in scale.[29] The nature of the record has made this book rife with contradictions. Many women are *reported* as Latinate poetesses whose works cannot be traced; on the other hand, works by women survive whose authors do not appear in such collections, but which can be found by the simple, if laborious, exercise of working through catalogues and collections of manuscripts and early printed books.

Ladies: éloges de l'Anglaise savante', ibid. 95–106, Jean M. Woods, 'Das Gelarhte Frauenzimmer und die deutschen Frauenlexicon, 1631–1763', in Sebastian Neumeister and Conrad Wiedemann (eds.), *Res Publica Litteraria*, ii (Wiesbaden: Otto Harassowitz, 1987), 577–87.

[27] Giuseppe Ricuperati, 'The Renewal of the Dialogue between Italy and Europe: Intellectuals and Cultural Institutions from the End of the Seventeenth Century to the First Decades of the Eighteenth Century', in Dino Carpenetto and Giuseppe Ricuperati (eds.), *Italy in the Age of Reason* (London: Longman, 1987), 78–95, 80, 123.

[28] *The Embarrassment of Riches: An Interpretation of Dutch Culture in the Golden Age* (London: Collins 1987), 497. See Céard, 'Listes', 85.

[29] Sarah Hale was clearly unable to find work for all the women she cites, but the fact that she cared to try must be held to her credit, since she is one of the first to do so. Jean Buyze's *The Tenth Muse*, published in 1980, leans heavily on Sarah Hale, but represents an actual regression from her standards.

It is impossible to know the value of contemporary reports when these are not corroborated by surviving texts: as with Dr Johnson's notorious remark about women preachers and dogs walking on their hind legs, most collectors of such lists seem to have been so impressed by the concept of women's learning, or of learned women, that shades and nuances were of no interest to them. Any Latinate woman, however minuscule her oeuvre, tended to be hailed by well-intentioned men in her immediate social circle as a sister or rival to Sappho, and such descriptions are then passed on from book to book. Not one such collection that I have seen makes any serious attempt to engage critically with any woman's writing. We find that many women are 'as good as (or better than) Sappho', but we do not find that Luisa Sigea is judged better than her contemporary Catalina Paz, or vice versa. One such woman poet, Philippa Lazea, pleads that her correspondent Jean-Jacques Boissard, who had described her as 'the Illyrian Sappho', should instead 'count her in with his Alardus': i.e. treat her as a poet rather than a phenomenon. He did no such thing (though he does, unusually, judge the work of other women scholars). The critical assessment of these women is beginning only in our own time.

One of my principal purposes in this book is to open up the study of women's Latin as a subject: the volume therefore includes a checklist of Latin poetry by women which I have good reason to believe to exist (in most cases, because I have personally seen it) which includes call-numbers for printed books published before the twentieth century as well as manuscript classmarks, since these books are, in many cases, exceptionally rare, and are not covered in existing short-title catalogues. I also include 'ghosts': women to whom the attribution of Latin verse is near-contemporary and explicit, in the hopes that some of their work may yet come to light once the scholarly community has been alerted to the possibility that it exists. The checklist entries also include every manuscript and edition of each poet that I have been able to find: this is not mere pedantry, but an expression of the principle that the circulation and reception history of writing tells one important things about it. It is easy to assume that women Latinists and their work were treated with contempt and disappeared into instant oblivion since they are now having to be laboriously rediscovered, but the bibliography in some cases tells a different story; a history of modest visibility. Proba's *Cento*, most notably, was a consistently popular text for 1,300 years, and Hrotsvitha's works were published about twice a century from 1500 to the present day. Women's activity as writers of epigraphic verse in Latin was taken for granted from antiquity through to the eighteenth century. The manuscript history of some of the women Latinists of the Italian Renaissance shows that they were published or scribally published writers in their own time: for example, if the world of women's studies has forgotten Laurentia Strozzi, it is not for want of publication (two editions of her book of Latin hymns, in Florence and Paris), bio-bibliographical notices (one in the sixteenth, seven in the seventeenth century, in Italy, France, Belgium, and Germany), and even a mention in the frequently cited *Essay to Revive the Ancient Attainments of Gentlewomen* attributed to Bathsua Makin.[30]

---

[30] Yet in the most recent edition of the latter work, even her name is erased, and she appears as 'Lorentia Sforza'. Frances Teague, *Bathsua Makin: Woman of Learning* (Lewisburg, Pa.: Bucknell University Press, 1998), 125.

This is a preliminary survey, intended to open rather than close discussion of these writers and their work. All this being so, it is appropriate for me say with Hrotsvitha of Gandersheim: 'If anything has crept into [this book] the accuracy of which can be challenged, it is not my fault, unless it is a fault to have reproduced the statements of unreliable authorities.' Specialists in the study of the learning and literature of specific countries will doubtless find much to forgive—I am particularly uneasy about my very limited knowledge of Central Europe. However, it is my hope that this book will at least serve the purpose of establishing that the participation of women in elite culture before the modern period is a large enough subject to be worth studying, and act as a spur to further research. This has been a hard book to write, but an almost impossible one to finish. A project which in an ideal world would demand that its author should have gone everywhere and read everything can at best achieve the status of an interim report. It is to be hoped that others will revise and extend it in as many directions as possible.

The coverage offered in this survey is necessarily restricted to some extent by the amount of attention given by researchers in this century to the learned women of particular countries. The sources for Spain and Portugal, for example, are particularly clear, thanks to Manuel Serrano y Santz's *Apuntes*, so it is possible to get a good picture of women's participation in the intellectual culture of the Peninsula before the nineteenth century (though the location of texts is, sadly, a different matter). For Germany, there is an excellent bibliographical study covering the seventeenth and eighteenth centuries from Jean M. Woods and Maria Fürstenwald, while the activities of fifteenth- and sixteenth-century women humanists are far less easy to gauge. By contrast, Italy is quite well covered down to 1600 by Kristeller and Cosenza, and rather randomly served thereafter. For the British Isles, the fact that such basic aids as Pollard and Redgrave and Wing's short-title catalogues do not invariably list works in Latin or published abroad makes it hard to be certain of comprehensiveness, while the absence of equivalent short-title catalogues for Germany or Italy, to name only the countries most important to this study, means that there may still be works I have been compelled to cite at second hand which in fact survive, but in libraries I have not visited. *Caveat lector.*

All the data I have on women's poetry in Latin is in the Appendix. In the interests of economy, footnotes in the chapters refer to supporting material of all kinds, and to women's prose writing in Latin and their writing in other languages, but I do *not* repeat the data presented in the Appendix, to which readers are therefore referred. Publishers' names are given whenever they are available.

Introduction

In Aristotle's *Politics*, a work incalculably influential on European intellectual history, he makes the point that 'virtue', by which he means the capacity to rule oneself and hence to rule others, is 'without authority', or 'illegitimate' (*akuros*) in women.[1] Thus he suggests that although it may quite possibly exist, if it does, it is disallowed for purely social reasons to do with the maintenance of an existing social structure defined a priori as 'best' because 'natural'. The denial of any sort of public position to exceptional women is expedient in the same way that the denial of freedom to those who find themselves legally enslaved without being, as Aristotle defines them, 'natural slaves' is expedient, and is based on the principle of the greatest good for the greatest number. In this, he is challenging the view of his senior, Plato, who argues in *The Republic* that the rulers of his ideal state ('Guardians') might be either male or female.[2] The debate as to whether exceptional, or exceptionally positioned, women could take the same public roles as men, or whether all women were functionally interchangeable, therefore pre-dates the argument that men and women in general were created equal and could potentially occupy similar social spaces by almost two and a half millennia.

Though it is seldom explicitly addressed in succeeding centuries,[3] in practice, a thousand years after Plato wrote, by the fifth century AD, the point was pragmatically conceded, and certain individual women were allowed a liminal space either as rulers or in the republic of letters. The focus of this book, on the 'language of authority', purposely links the issues of authority in the sense of rule (over the self and over others) and authority in the sense of authorship: as I hope to demonstrate, the issue of women's writing in Latin is often closely connected with the issue of their participation in power.

The whole question of the Aristotelian public and the private sphere has been highlighted by Jürgen Habermas. He points out that in Athenian society, 'just as the wants of life and the procurement of its necessities were shamefully hidden within the *oikos* [the household, where women lived and worked], so the *polis* [the city considered as an arena for the interaction of citizens] provided an open field for honourable distinction: citizens indeed interacted as equals with equals, but each did his best to excel.'[4] This produces a 'classical' model for the interactions of human

---

[1] Aristotle, *Politics* 1. 13, trans. Carnes Lord (Chicago: University of Chicago Press, 1984), 53–4.

[2] Plato, *Republic* 5 451–6, trans. F. M. Cornford (Oxford: Clarendon Press, 1941), 145–51.

[3] One of the few pre-modern women to draw on Plato's arguments is the Swede Hedwig Charlotta Nordenflycht (1718–63), who argued both from modern philosophers and from Plato for an enhanced role for women. Elisabeth Møller Jensen, *Liv och verk* (Malmö: Bra Böcker, 2000), 208–9 (p. 209).

[4] Jürgen Habermas, *The Structural Transformation of the Public Sphere: An Inquiry into a Category of Bourgeois Society* (1962), trans. Thomas Burger (Brighton: Polity Press, 1989), 4.

beings within society—or at least, the interactions of men—as public and competitive. But one of the few of the competitive activities of the *polis* in which women took part was literature. As the later catalogues of learned women seldom tired of remembering, Pausanias claimed that the woman poet Corinna once bested Pindar in a poetic competition.[5] The fundamental question addressed by this book is therefore the extent to which all pre-modern European women belonged by definition within the *oikos* or its later equivalents: how, where, and in what circumstances personal qualities or descent allowed individual women to move in the public sphere.

The definition of 'public sphere' is by no means straightforward. Habermas used it in a specific sense focused on the holding of public offices, appropriate to his central focus on the nineteenth century. Women, unless they were heads of state, were almost invariably debarred from such functions before the twentieth century, but if the public sphere is defined more widely as the overlapping worlds of politics, legal rights and obligations, and the market, then women become visible as clearly a part of it to a much greater extent *c.* AD 500–1700.[6] Michelle Zimbalist Rosaldo has made the general point that 'women's status will be lowered in those societies where there is a firm differentiation between domestic and public spheres of activity'—a differentiation which was solidified in Europe only in the course of the eighteenth and nineteenth centuries.[7] If we examine earlier periods, in a number of contexts in medieval and early modern European history, women do hold public offices of one kind or another, mostly lowly.[8] They also function as heads of household to an extent which would have surprised Aristotle: in early modern England, roughly 20 per cent of households were headed by a *feme sole* (such households were generally poor and vulnerable).[9] But there are also other forms of social and political participation at higher social levels in which women are easily found, such as dispensing patronage, petitioning, entertaining, haranguing, gift-giving, writing, and disseminating ideas, activities which are liminal between the public and the private.[10] Schwoerer, to whom I am indebted for this formulation, also observes, 'Women's attitudes do not suggest a sharp dichotomy between, but rather the porosity of, public and private spheres. Interestingly, these developments invite modification of Habermas's ideas.'[11] In the Middle Ages, the

[5] *Description of Greece* 9. 22. 3, trans. Peter Levi, 2 vols. (Harmondsworth: Penguin, 1971), ii. 354.

[6] Mary Erler and Maryanne Kowaleski (eds.), *Women and Power in the Middle Ages* (Athens: University of Georgia Press, 1988), 3.

[7] M. Z. Rosaldo, 'A Theoretical Overview', in Michelle Zimbalist Rosaldo and Louise Lamphere (eds.), *Women, Culture and Society* (Stanford, Calif.: Stanford University Press, 1974), 36.

[8] See for example Merry Wiesner, 'Women's Defense of their Public Role', in Mary Beth Rose (ed.), *Women in the Middle Ages and the Renaissance* (Syracuse, NY: Syracuse University Press, 1986), 1–28.

[9] Bernard Capp, 'Separate Domains? Women and Authority', in Paul Griffiths, Adam Fox, and Steve Hindle (eds.), *The Experience of Authority in Early Modern England* (London: Macmillan, 1996), 117–45.

[10] David Cressy, 'Response: Private Lives, Public Performance, and Rites of Passage', in Betty S. Travitsky and Adele F. Seeff (eds.), *Attending to Women in Early Modern England* (Newark: University of Delaware Press/Associated University Presses, 1994), 187–97 (p. 187).

[11] Lois G. Schwoerer, 'Women's Public Political Voice in England, 1640–1740', in Hilda L. Smith (ed.), *Women Writers and the Early Modern British Political Tradition* (Cambridge: Cambridge University Press, 1998), 56–74 (pp. 57–8).

household, considered as a legal and economic unit and as the location of most production, was within the public sphere, and so, therefore, were many of women's activities: the increasingly clear-cut distinction between public and private over the subsequent centuries tended to restrict rather than enhance the position of women.[12] However, men's attitudes displayed in many specific instances also suggest that in medieval and early modern Europe, the intervention of some women in aspects of public life was accepted, or tolerated, despite the established rhetoric of exclusion which Hanley calls the 'defamation litany'.[13] Popular culture throughout late antique, medieval, and early modern Europe insisted on the universal stupidity, loquacity, sensuality, and moral short-sightedness of all women:[14] elite culture, in particular the intelligentsia, often took a more complex view, and some individuals, male and female, were active in challenging part, or even all, of the popular image of women.[15] MacLean observes that in sixteenth- and seventeenth-century France, despite all that was said about women's essential intellectual and moral incapacity,[16]

women's involvement in the public life of the Renaissance as members of guilds, prominent figures in religious administration, patrons of learning and polite society, queen regents and sovereigns, is well known to both contemporaries and posterity.

Such a discrepancy led some contemporaries to wonder whether women in general possessed more capacities than law and custom permitted to them, but it is far more often the case that writers interested in the subject assert the moral and intellectual equality of *some* women with men, which is basically a revival of the position argued by Plato in the *Republic*. The politically or intellectually capable woman was defined as an 'exceptional' woman, a categorization which prevented any need to rethink the position of women more generally.[17] For example, in Tiraqueau's treatise on marriage law, a compendium of early modern popular wisdom about women, he on the one hand assumes women's 'imbecility', inconstancy, lack of self-control, and so forth as the basic justification of the legal status quo, but at the same time feels impelled to produce counter-examples of women who were learned, constant, prudent, and wise, balancing the two merely by

[12] This was forcibly stated by Joan Kelly-Gadol, 'Did Women Have a Renaissance?', in Renate Bridenthal and Claudia Koonz (eds.), *Becoming Visible: Women in European History* (Boston: Houghton Mifflin, 1977), 137–64. Wiesner, 'Women's Defense of their Public Role', 5.

[13] Sarah Hanley, 'The Politics of Identity and Monarchic Government in France: The Debate over Female Exclusion', in Smith (ed.), *Women Writers*, 289–304 (p. 295).

[14] Though the widely distributed late medieval tale of the peasant man and woman who swap jobs for a day to find that she can do his work with ease and he cannot do hers at all points to a degree of recognition of women's abilities even at the most demotic level.

[15] Popular views of women often surface even with respect to women rulers: see, for example, Julia M. Walker (ed.), *Dissing Elizabeth: Negative Representations of Gloriana* (Durham, NC: Duke University Press, 1998).

[16] *Woman Triumphant* (Oxford: Clarendon Press, 1977), 22.

[17] Diana Robin, 'Women, Space and Renaissance Discourse', in Barbara K. Gold et al. (eds.), *Sex and Gender in Medieval and Renaissance Texts*, (New York: State University of New York Press, 1997), 165–88 (p. 168).

stating that 'there are a good many women who are above the nature of their sex'.[18] Another way of solving the problem, which was used by other pre-modern men, was to argue that the activity under dispute—whether it was writing, possessing an education, or inheriting an estate—was essentially private and thus should be open to women.[19]

Although it is Aristotle and not Plato who has dominated Western political thought, Western political developments created a world which neither philosopher would have approved. Once Rome became an empire, the passionate belief of the Roman army in the dynastic principle became crucial to political life: it is evidenced by the way that after the death of Augustus they successively promoted every male Julio-Claudian to the purple, regardless of capacity, or even sanity—they did not, however, promote Augustus' own daughter, or any other woman.[20] At the same time, Rome consistently encouraged strong kingship and dynasty formation in neighbouring 'barbarian' peoples, since this simplified the authorities with which they had to deal.[21] Inevitably, there were times when one royal line or another was reduced to representation by a widow or a daughter: the Roman authorities therefore supported such women, for example the British queen Cartimandua, when necessary.[22] From the mid-fifth century, the logic of this was followed through in the Roman Empire itself, and the dynastic principle occasionally put individual women into the public sphere *faute de mieux*, among the Romans themselves as well as among the societies influenced by them.

The second term which made this possible from the fifth century as it had not been before may have been the Roman Empire's adoption of Christianity: the principle that 'in Christ there is neither male nor female', and the fact that women could be, and sometimes were, spiritual leaders, going back to the Virgin Mary herself.[23] It is probably no accident that, as Berschin has recently observed, the earliest women to receive any kind of biography as people in their own right were found in Christian milieux (the first being Perpetua).[24] Something, at any rate, shifted the grounds of the concept of heritability in the fifth century. Thereafter,

---

[18] André Tiraqueau, *De Legibus Connubialibus* (Lyon: Guillaume Roville, 1560), 150ᵛ. This work even includes a list of learned women, pp. 183–92.

[19] Wiesner, 'Women's Defense of their Public Role', 5–6.

[20] 'A woman . . . might attain the heights in a monarchy, but that was something not to be tolerated in a democracy or a republic.' Tom Hilliard, 'On the Stage, Behind the Curtain: Images of Politically Active Women in the Late Roman Republic', in Barbara Garlick *et al.* (eds.), *Stereotypes of Women in Power* (Westport, Conn.: Greenwood Press, 1992), 37–64 (p. 38).

[21] E. A. Thompson, *Romans and Barbarians:, The Decline of the Western Empire* (Madison: University of Wisconsin Press, 1982), 40, Peter Brown, *The World of Late Antiquity* (London: Thames & Hudson, 1971), 123.

[22] The Romans sometimes supported women rulers, when it suited them, against the wishes or traditions of the people involved. See Thomas Charles-Edwards, 'Native Political Organization in Roman Britain and the Origin of Middle-Welsh *Brenhin*', in M. Mayrhofer et al. (eds.), *Antiquitates Indogermanicae: Gedenkschrift für Hermann Günters* (Innsbruck: Institut für Sprachwissenschaft der Universität Innsbruck, 1974), 33–45.

[23] Gillian Cloke, *'This Female Man of God'* (London: Routledge, 1995), 16–24.

[24] Walter Berschin, 'Radegundis and Brigit', in John Carey, Máire Herbert, and Pádraig Ó Riain (eds.), *Studies in Irish Hagiography: Saints and Scholars* (Dublin: Four Courts, 2001), 72–6.

once a dynasty had run out of sons, daughters, instead of being disallowed, were sometimes seriously considered as possible successors. Among many others, Theodosius the Great, Theodoric the Great, Alfred the Great, Otto the Great, William the Conqueror, Valdemar IV, and Henry VIII were dynasts who ran out of sons, and also the fathers of daughters who ruled (either as regents or in their own right) because the positive valuation attached to their blood outweighed the negative valuation attached to their gender.[25] There is clear evidence that their respective daughters, Pulcheria, Amalasuntha, Æthelflæd, Matilda, Adela, Margarethe, and Elizabeth, were all educated for rule, and for all except Æthelflæd, there is also clear evidence that their education included the study of Latin.[26]

Since the principle that women could function as decision-making rulers was established in late antiquity, the question of whether other kinds of exceptional women could occupy a position in the public sphere without disturbing existing ideas about 'women' as a category was one which could potentially be opened. For Habermas, the 'public sphere' consists not merely of a *politische Öffentlichkeit*, but also of a *literarische Öffentlichkeit*. Corinna of Tanagra is one of the few women of antiquity who demonstrably took a place in it, though Sappho was very probably another. Moving now from the Greek to the Roman and post-Roman world, there is a strong case for giving women's writing in Latin careful consideration in this context. Authority and linguistic competence are powerfully mutually related, since pre-modern government took place to a very great extent through the words of the ruler.[27] Since it is often assumed that women's writing is 'unofficial' (i.e. without recognition in the public sphere) because 'women always write in the vernacular', and hence do not claim, because they do not possess, the rights of individuals occupying the public linguistic domain of Latin—the language which in pre-modern Europe is *par excellence* the language of men talking about important things to other men—it seemed to me highly desirable to ask whether women, in fact, ever did occupy space in this realm, since it was obviously extremely difficult for any of them to do so, and what happened when they did.

Since certain exceptionally placed women took an active place in the public domain, whether as rulers or wielders of authority, they and their admirers were thus required to position themselves with respect to the 'defamation rhetoric' applied to women in general, and whatever version of the highly prescriptive

[25] See, for a view of this principle in the high Middle Ages, Lois Honeycutt, 'Female Succession and the Language of Power in the Writings of Twelfth-Century Churchmen', in John Carmi Parsons (ed.), *Medieval Queenship* (Stroud: Alan Sutton, 1993), 189–201. It continues to operate: Indira Gandhi, daughter of Jawaharlal Nehru, in India and Benazir Bhutto, daughter of Zulfikar Ali Bhutto, in Pakistan were educated at Oxford with the possibility of rule in mind (a cognate point is made by Phyllis Mack, *Visionary Women: Ecstatic Prophecy in Seventeenth-Century England* (Berkeley and Los Angeles: University of California Press, 1992), 301.

[26] Æthelflæd was known as 'The Lady of the Mercians': on Margarethe, see Prologue, n. 15.

[27] Maria Wyke, 'Augustan Cleopatras: Female Power and Poetic Authority', in Anton Powell (ed.), *Roman Poetry and Propaganda* (London: Bristol Classical Press, 1992), 98–140. John M. McManaman, *Funeral Oratory and the Cultural Ideals of Italian Humanism* (Chapel Hill: University of North Carolina Press, 1989), 113, describes eloquence as 'the art essential for public service', and shows it was praised in women.

narratives of what constituted woman's place was operative in their particular milieux. For example, in the British Isles in the sixteenth century, the rule of Mary, Queen of Scots and Elizabeth I was met with a variety of responses. John Knox's diatribe against the 'monstrous regiment' of women is by far the best known,[28] but in fact, there were also refutations of Knox in both England and Scotland, and university debates which took a far more positive line on women's rule.[29]

The most common strategy employed by women's defenders is denial: this particular woman is not like other women, hence the 'defamation litany' does not apply to her. Pamela Joseph Benson refines this basic position into two sub-arguments: (1) women are endowed with the cardinal virtues just like men. They suffer no special distinction due to their reproductive function. Therefore a virtuous woman is masculine without violating nature. (2) Women can be expected to be capable in a peculiarly female way because they are endowed with specifically female virtues and can be strong in a feminine way because of their reproductive functions. A woman who is masculine violates nature, though proponents of this position often praise feminine virtue as superior in kind.[30] What both these approaches have in common is that they posit 'all women' as the basic class with which they deal, and argue the intrinsic virtue or viciousness of 'women'.

But there is also a third approach, which is that the category of 'women' is divisible, just as the category of 'men' had always been assumed to be divisible. Some women need to be considered under a completely different heading, a reinvention of the argument of Plato: Tasso, for example, distinguishes *virtù feminile* (womanly virtue), and *virtù donnesca* (queenly, or gentlewomanly, virtue), the latter suitable for women rulers.[31] Women rulers were generally enjoined to be erudite, generous, courageous, and in many other ways to transcend the normal demands made on women, since women as ordinarily defined were legitimately, or

---

[28] *The First Blast of the Trumpet against the Monstrous Regiment of Women* (Geneva: J. Crespin, 1558).

[29] Knox's work may be contrasted with its refutations, John Aylmer's *An Harborowe for Faithfull and Trewe Subjectes, agaynste the Late Blowne Blaste, Concerning the Government of Wemen* (Strasborowe [London: J. Daye], 1559), Bishop John Leslie, *De Illustrium Feminarum in Republica Administranda* (Reims: Jean de Foigny, 1580), and a treatise by Henry Howard (1590): Amanda Shepherd, 'Henry Howard and the Lawful Regimentation of Women', *History of Political Thought*, 12 (1991), 589–603. On the universities, see J. W. Binns, *Intellectual Culture in Elizabethan and Jacobean England*, (Leeds: Francis Cairns, 1990), 77. A 36-line record of a thesis 'foeminam posse imperare', composed for the queen's visit to Oxford in 1566, survives. See also John Case, *Sphæra Civitatis* (Oxford: Jos. Barnesius, 1588), sig. C4v–5r.

[30] Pamela Joseph Benson, *The Invention of the Renaissance Woman* (University Park: Pennsylvania State University Press, 1992), 4.

[31] *Discorso della virtù feminile e donnesca* (Venice: Bernardo Giunta, 1582). The much earlier work of Durand de Champagne (s. xiii^ex–xiv), *Speculum Dominarum*, a manual of Christian morality for women in general but especially for queens and princesses, also addresses this theme. It was translated into French for Jeanne de Navarre and again for Marguerite de Navarre (Ruth Kelso, *Doctrine for the Lady of the Renaissance* (Urbana: University of Illinois Press, 1956), 360). See further the discussion of Francesco da Barberino in Ch. 5, and Anne de Beaujeu's instructions for her daughter, *A la requeste de treshaulte et puissante princesse ma dame Susanne de Bourbon* (Lyon: Le Prince, [?1534]).

even properly, un-learned, fiscally cautious, and timid—so in fact, women rulers had to be something much more like aristocratic men.[32] For example, the confessor of Queen Isabel of Spain insisted that Latin learning was part of her royal duty.[33] By the Renaissance, the idea that there were virtues and behaviours appropriate to different ranks and ages of men was generally accepted (e.g. physical courage is a major virtue for young men, a minor virtue for elderly ones);[34] but women were normally treated as a single category. However, many of the texts to be discussed here implicitly or explicitly take the view that there are some women whom it is not appropriate to confine within the social space accorded to 'woman' in general since heredity, or even talent, had given them the right to command themselves and others.

It is possible to find texts in which the category 'woman' is explicitly divided. One very early example is Brother Hermann's Life of the Countess Yolanda of Vianden, written in Middle High German shortly after 1283, which sums up her praiseworthy life in the following terms:[35]

Since I am to speak of woman, and have begun to do so, Yolanda could well be termed both 'woman' and 'female'. But there is sometimes a difference among women, and I had better write it down. Among 'females' are those undeserving of the name 'women'—women without women's nature. They are rare among women. A woman's name and nature are very holy and agreeable: God called His Mother 'Woman'. But 'females' are to observe here how good the name of 'woman' is, for all 'females' are not 'women'. Yolanda can be called 'woman' without any doubt. She had a pure and chaste heart.

Brother Hermann here offers the view that there are more 'women' (positive) than 'females' (negative), but it is more commonly the positive type which is seen as the rare bird—as, for example, in Giovanni Francesco Giuliani's much later, Italian, *Dialogue* of 1653:[36]

Soldier: And what difference does your excellency make between 'femine' and 'donne'?[37]
Doctor: Oh, a great difference, since 'femine' have a vile nature, and are dedicated to vice, and 'donne' are of a noble (*generoso*) nature, virtuous, brave, constant, skilful, and pious, far

---

[32] See, for example, Lodovico Dolce, *Della institution delle donne* (Venice: Gabriel Giolito, 1545), and Agrippa d'Aubigné, 'A mes filles touchant les femmes doctes de nostre siècle', in *Œuvres complétes*, ed. E. Réaume and F. de Caussade (Paris, 1843–92), i. 445–50.

[33] Peggy K. Liss, *Isabel the Queen* (New York: Oxford University Press, 1992), 125.

[34] Michel de Montaigne, 'On Experience', quoting 'Socrates', *The Essayes of Montaigne*, trans. John Florio [1603] (New York: The Modern Library, 1946) III. 13, 967.

[35] Bruder Hermann, *Leben der Gräfin Iolande von Vianden*, ed. John Meier (Wrocław: William Koebner, 1889), lines 5924–42, trans. Richard H. Lawson, *Brother Hermann's Life of the Countess Yolanda of Vianden* (Columbia, SC: Camden House, Inc., 1995), 69–70.

[36] Giovannni Francesco Giuliani, *Dialogo di un medico con un secretario et un palafreniere di un prencipe romane, nel quale si tratta di molte donne Illustri in arme, in lettere, e in santità* (Rome: Ignatio de Lazari, 1653), 23. 'Pall: E che differenza fà V.S. dalle femine alle donne? Med: O, ò, gran differenza, perche la femine sono d'animo vilissimo, e dedito al vitio, e le Donne sono d'animo generoso, invitto, intrepido, costante, virtuoso, e pio, lontane d'ogni atto indegno, e capriccio humane, mà prudente, e saggio, conforme alla giustitia divina e del mondo . . .'

[37] I leave these terms untranslated since, while 'femina' is unproblematic, 'donna' does not occupy the same semantic space as English 'lady', 'mistress', or 'noblewoman', or any other single word.

from any unworthy act or human caprice, but prudent and wise, conformable with divine and natural law . . .

There is a conceptual difference between subdividing 'women' into 'femine' and 'donne' (or however one chooses to put it) and the more familiar approach of dividing 'women' into 'women' and 'viragoes', which is to say, individuals who transcend womanhood to achieve a quasi-masculine standard of virtue. Though Brother Hermann and Giovanni Francesco Giuliani can have had few elements of their conceptual universe in common, they are both putting forward a concept of a kind of excellence which is proper to womanhood and clearly included within it, which is not quite the case with the problematic virago. However, Giuliani's category of 'donna' is obviously problematic for any aspirant to the status, since the standard erected is so high and was revocable—a single slip, and one could be redefined as a vile 'femina' at any moment—all the same, any ambitious woman would naturally aspire to it. This distinction had clear advantages for the male elite, since it allowed them to exploit women's talents when necessary, raised barriers against women making common cause with one other, and removed the need to rethink the position of women. It also had clear advantages for some individual women.

In practice, any woman who achieved, or was thrust into, a position of authority was required to negotiate her way through the same minefield, however her role was theorized by her admirers and supporters. She would have to demonstrate acceptable feminine behaviour; and she would be required to dress and in some respects behave like a woman: she could more easily usurp actual governance than the breeches which symbolized male authority;[38] though some women rulers made effective symbolic play with other masculine accoutrements such as swords and armour.[39] In the sixteenth century, neither Mary, Queen of Scots nor Henri III of France were successful rulers, but despite the latter's effeminacy, it was Mary who was presented by contemporaries as sexually monstrous.[40]

Female sovereigns are a special case. In a variety of other contexts explored in this book, it has also come to seem possible that there may sometimes be more to the liminality and contingency of women's public position than meets the eye. To be *akuros*, though intelligent and competent, is to have a particular kind of diplomatic usefulness when people, or groups, wish to negotiate without admitting that they are doing so: a variety of political writing in Latin by Renaissance Italian women may emerge from such contexts of preliminary exploration. That is, if

[38] The only partial exception who comes to mind is the massively eccentric ex-queen Christina of Sweden; but her form of 'rational dress', though masculine in appearance, did terminate in a skirt. Furthermore she did not adopt this attire while she was still a monarch.

[39] For example, Queen Elizabeth's semiotically complex dress worn when rallying her troops at Tilbury: see Carole Levin, *The Heart and Stomach of a King* (Philadelphia: University of Pennsylvania Press, 1994), 143–4, and Queen Isabel of Castile's appropriation of the sword of a king: Liss, *Isabel*, 97–8.

[40] Jenny Wormald, *Mary Queen of Scots: A Study in Failure* (London: Collins & Brown, 1991).

things start going wrong, an earlier oration or ode by a woman can be dismissed as 'feminine foolishness'; if they go well, there is a basis established for friendly contact. It would be worth investigating whether Anne of Denmark's correspondence and diplomatic contacts with foreign Catholic powers is not so much a defiance of her Protestant husband James I, but a usefully disownable aspect of his overall policies.[41] Dr William Denton makes the revealing comment in 1646, in the context of Civil War exiles in Paris,[42]

Women were never soe useful as now, and though you should be my agent and sollicitor of al the men I knowe...yett I am confident if you were here, you would doe as our sages doe, instruct your wife and leave her to act it with committees, their sexe intitles them to many privileges, and we find the comfort of them now more than ever.

However, women's approach to the 'language of authority' was fraught with complications. One of the most basic issues in the discussion of women's interaction with Latin is the vocabulary which is available to them; and women poets are marginalized out of existence by the language itself. Latin is a 'gendered' language; which is to say that in addition to obviously male and female objects requiring the pronouns 'he' and 'she', physically neutral objects, such as a pen or a book, also 'have gender'. Thus, *haec domina*, *hic dominus*, 'the mistress', 'the master'; but also *haec penna*, *hic stylus*, 'the (female) feather/pen', 'the (male) stylus'. Latin words fall into one or other of five 'declensions'; and one of the earliest rules that one learns about Latin nouns is that nouns of the first declension (words ending in -a, such as *domina* and *penna*) 'are feminine', those of the second ending in -us, like *dominus* and *stylus*, 'are masculine'. While this is a useful general rule, it is not strictly accurate. The match between sexual identity and grammatical gender is very loose. Crucially, a small group of common words relating to individuals are first declension *masculine*: they include *nauta*, a sailor, and *agricola*, a farmer, but also *poeta*, a poet. *Hic poeta*. This creates a uniquely Latin problem in talking about women who write poetry. If the Latin word for a poet had been **poetus*, then there would have been no problem about forming a feminine, [*haec*] *poeta*, in the same way that *coquus* (a [male] cook) is matched by *coqua* (a [female] cook). Most Latin terms for 'someone who does something' are third declension, and exist in a paired form: *lector/lectrix* (a reader, male/female), even *auctor/auctrix* (an author). But *poeta* is difficult. It can be 'feminized' only by borrowing Greek feminine endings and grafting them onto a word which looked female to start with, thus becoming *poetissa*, *poetria*, or *poetris*. 'The Muses female are', as the English poetess Martha

---

[41] Anne of Denmark is generally spoken of as empty-headed and frivolous, but she was highly educated, and the daughter of a notably intellectual mother (Leeds Barroll, *Anna of Denmark, Queen of England* (Philadelphia: University of Pennsylvania Press, 2001), 16). Linda Levy Peck, 'Women as Court Brokers: Queen Anne's Household', in her *Court Patronage and Corruption in Early Stuart England* (London: Routledge, 1993), 68–74. There is an undated Latin letter by Anne of Denmark to the Doge of Venice, Marino Grimani, in Leicester Record Office, DG7, Lit. 2, fo. 41, and another in Paris, Bibliothèque Nationale de France, Dupuy 33, fo. 147, to 'Gunterot'.

[42] Frances Parthenope and Margaret M. Verney (eds.), *Memoirs of the Verney Family during the Seventeenth Century*, 2 vols. (London: Longmans & Co., 1925), ii. 240.

Moulsworth pointed out,[43] but *poetae*, despite appearances, are male. Language itself subliminally excludes women.

However, I have kept the central focus on *poetissae*, women poets, in this book for a simple reason. The idea of 'knowing Latin' is an extremely fluid one. Across the two millennia considered in this study, it meant all kinds of things at different times, from sophisticated comprehension to bare literacy. The trajectory of pre-modern educational systems focused on reading first (mechanically defined as the ability to turn marks on the page into the appropriate noises), then on writing (defined as the physical ability to control a pen), then comprehension, then composition.[44] Medieval Europe contained boys—and perhaps girls—who could read aloud from the Vulgate with some fluency, without the faintest apprehension of what the words meant.[45] There were scribes who were marvellous penmen, working in complete ignorance of the contents of what they wrote.[46] Within this chaotic flux of 'knowledge' which, to one person, signifies control of mechanical skills, to another, sophisticated literary understanding, one clear criterion presented itself as beyond ambiguity. In any context, a woman who can write Latin verse has gone beyond even the fourth stage defined above, composition. She has been educated in the same way as the elite men of her milieu and there is no possible argument about this. Latin verse composition depends on a highly technical set of rules, because the intuitive perception of Latin metre faded out (one of the mysterious aesthetic turns of European culture) in late antiquity. Latin metrics has since then been an exercise in reconstruction. Nobody is, or has ever been, taught how to do this except as the culminating point of a Latin-based education.[47] Even prose Latin composition has to be taught; it does not follow automatically from comprehension.

The composition of Latin poetry in classical metres is a learned, highly specialized skill, entirely independent of the ability to comprehend or translate Latin texts. It was a defining ability of the educated elite from the Middle Ages to the twentieth century, not a mark of personal literary ambition. Sir Simonds d'Ewes recollected that as a schoolboy (educated by the father of Bathsua Makin, née Rainolds, and by Bathsua herself), he composed more than 2,800 Latin and Greek verses. Only the quantity is unusual.[48] Victor Hugo similarly associates 'college, and themes, and Latin verses'.[49] On the other hand, this skill is highly unusual in women. Any woman who has left an oeuvre of Latin verse, whatever its poetic merit, was by definition occupying a space normally regarded as belonging entirely

---

[43] Jane Stevenson and Peter Davidson (eds.), *Early Modern Women Poets, 1520–1700* (Oxford: Oxford University Press, 2001), 127.

[44] M. T. Clanchy, *From Memory to Written Record* (London: Edward Arnold, 1979), 175–201.

[45] Pierre Riché, *Education and Culture in the Barbarian West*, trans. J. J. Contreni (Columbia: University of South Carolina Press, 1976), 468.

[46] Clanchy, *From Memory to Written Record*, 181.

[47] *Aldhelm: The Poetic Works*, trans. Michael Lapidge and James L. Rosier (Ipswich: D. S. Brewer, 1985), 19–24.

[48] Françoise Waquet, *Latin: Or the Empire of a Sign*, trans. John Howe (London: Verso, 2000), 22.

[49] Ibid. 13.

to men, which is far harder to assess from more familiar 'feminine' texts such as letters or translations. Pre-modern women who wrote Latin verse implicitly challenge the socially defined parameters of 'female', just as, though on different grounds, black men who wrote Latin verse challenged the socially defined parameters of black people as childish, ineducable, and, consequently, natural slaves.[50]

One might 'learn Latin' for the sake of reading divine wisdom, since the Catholic Church resisted vernacular translation, or for communicating with people of other nations, or for a host of other reasons, many of them requiring only passive knowledge, but to have acquired the ability to write Latin verse directly argues not only an active competence in the language, but also an intentionality on the part of the subject's instructors that she or he should acquire such a competence. This book therefore, though it pays attention to women's Latin prose and indeed women's translation from Latin, focuses on poetry, since this clarifies the woman author's presence in the *literarische Öffentlichkeit* to such a marked extent. By focusing this study on women Latin poets, it is possible to assess whether and to what extent there were pre-modern women who really did receive an education comparable to that of a man. For those women of whom this can be said are apparently occupying the same authorial space as educated men, or, at the least, one more immediately contiguous to it than any other group of women writers could assume.

The second concept embodied in my title is 'the language of authority'. Before 1500, Latin is the language of the Church and the entire clerisy in the area geographically covered by the Western Roman Empire, and hence the language of official and permanent writing.[51] It is thus constituted as the language of authority. Moreover, in the Renaissance and subsequently, though the various European vernaculars were increasingly used in a variety of contexts, language was perceived in a context of linguistic hierarchies associated with gender: Latin was 'masculine', because of its order, logical structure, fixedness, permanence, and association with authority, while vernaculars were labile, unstable, ephemeral, and hence 'feminine'.[52] The fact that Chaucer was admired and revered as the first great poet in English caused Francis Kynaston to translate *Troilus and Criseyde* into

---

[50] There is a small number of very interesting black individuals who wrote Latin verse: Juan Latino's (*c.*1516–1594/7) 900-line *Austriad* was printed with some other verses in Granada by Hugo de Mena, 1573 (see Hans Werner Debrunner, *Presence and Prestige: Africans in Europe: A History of Africans in Europe before 1918* (Basel: Basler Afrika Bibliographien, 1979), 39–40). Francis Williams of Jamaica (*c.* 1700–1735), will be the subject of a forthcoming study by John Gilmore (Debrunner, *Presence and Prestige*, 120), and Jacobus Elisa Johannes Capitein (1717–47), included several Latin poems in his *Dissertatio Politico-theologica de Servitute Libertati Christianae non Contraria* (Leiden, 1742) (facsimile edn. in *The Agony of Asar*, trans. Grant Parker (Princeton: Markus Wiener; Jamaica: Ian Randle, 2001)).

[51] This basic fact is beyond argument: however, Michael Richter, in his *Studies in Medieval Language and Culture* (Dublin: Four Courts, 1995), offers some interesting nuances as to the extent and limits of the reign of Latin.

[52] Danielle Clarke, *The Politics of Early Modern Women's Writing* (Harlow: Pearson Education Ltd., 2001), 18. See also Patricia Parker, 'Virile Style', in L. Fradenburg and C. Freccero (eds.), *Premodern Sexualities* (New York: Routledge, 1996), 201–22.

Latin in the seventeenth century, lest it float away on the tide of linguistic change.[53] The whole question of the sociolinguistic position of the Latin language between 1500 and 1800 has been examined in Françoise Waquet's monumental *Latin: Or the Empire of a Sign*. The significance of Latin as a principal medium, or at least signal of membership, for elite culture down to the eighteenth century is a matter of common agreement, and Waquet provides an extraordinarily nuanced and complex account of how this operated in both theory and practice in the early modern period.

But it may also be helpful to think about 'authority'.[54] The resonance of 'authority' and 'authorship' is masculine. Cambridge University Press once invited me to sign a contract asserting my 'right of paternity (the right always to be identified as the author of the essay)'. It is a little disconcerting for a woman to be informed that she has become a father, but at the latter end of the twentieth century, it produced nothing more than a momentary dislocation, a rather acute version of the discomfort elicited by the grammatical use of 'he' as an impersonal form. Hélène Cixous has suggested that women have particular difficulties with 'coming to writing' even now, and struggle towards expression through their own guilt, fear, and sense of exclusion.[55] If this could be argued in the twentieth century, in a world awash with fiction and non-fiction by women which is regularly discussed in the academy and wins literary prizes, how could a pre-modern woman empower herself as a writer at all—let alone as a writer in Latin, the language of authority? In fact, as the following pages will show, a surprising number did so, mostly with the active support of their families. Not all writers acknowledge that there is a problem: Georges/Madeleine de Scudéry observe that 'even if Mercury and Apollo are of the other sex, Minerva and the Muses are of ours'.[56] However, there were also many women who found this stance impossible to maintain.

Another crucial question is that of authorities, in the sense of precedents. Authorities are used for authorization; a crucial strategy in all medieval writing, and common thereafter—Chaucer, for example, speaks in *Troilus and Criseyde* of 'myn auctour', or attributes the 'sentence' of his text to 'Lollio'.[57] Surtz, in his excellent book on Spanish women writers of the fifteenth century, formulates this in a way that few would quarrel with: 'needless to say, the written links in this chain of authority were all forged by males, whose textual male-bonding

[53] The first two volumes were published as *Amor Troilii et Creseidae Libri Duo Primi Anglico-latine* (Oxford: John Lichfield, 1635) (the rest is in Oxford, Bodleian Library, Add. C 287).

[54] See Jane Stevenson, 'Women and Classical Education in the Early Modern Period', in Yun Lee Too and Niall Livingstone (eds.), *Pedagogy and Power: Rhetorics of Classical Learning*, Ideas in Context (Cambridge: Cambridge University Press, 1998), 83–109.

[55] Women's strategies of 'coming to writing' in the modern world have been discussed theoretically by Hélène Cixous, *'Coming to Writing' and Other Essays*, ed. Deborah Jenson (Cambridge, Mass.: Harvard University Press, 1991), 1–58, esp. pp. 12, 20.

[56] [Georges] de Scudéry, *Les Femmes illustres, ou les harangues heroïques, avec les veritables portraits de ces heroines, tirés des medailles antiques*, 2 vols. (Paris: Augustine Courbé, 1654/5), i. 402.

[57] *Troilus and Criseyde*, II. 49, 'myn auctour shal I folwen, if I konne' (*The Works of Geoffrey Chaucer*, ed. F. N. Robinson, 2nd edn. (London: Oxford University Press, 1966), 402: see also I. 393–4, II. 18).

stretched diachronically back in time to classical antiquity.'[58] But 'textual bonding' is in fact not confined to men. Women *did* have a small and precious group of *auctrices* of their own which similarly stretched back to antiquity.[59] And with respect to women's intellectual history, the distinction between 'some' and 'none' has been of far greater significance to the aspirations of later generations than the distinction between 'some' and 'many'. The idea that it can be done at all is the crucial thing; and women can frequently be shown to have valued evidence that this was the case. Among many possible examples, Isotta Nogarola, one of the pioneer women Latinists of fifteenth-century Italy, was aware of Proba, whom she used to place herself in a tradition of women scholars,[60] and also of a whole litany of classical learned women.[61] Poliziano's acquaintance with another such pioneer, Cassandra Fedele, prompted him to research the earlier history of women poets and scholars (which he used to validate and context the achievement of his contemporary, Fedele), and his essay on the subject was widely read: its readers included the humanistically educated Mary, Queen of Scots, who gave a Latin oration on women's capacity for education, based on Poliziano, before Henri II and the French court.[62] In early sixteenth-century Augsburg, the scholarly Margarethe Welser cited Sidonius Apollinaris's commendation of wives' working on literature alongside their husbands in order to present herself as an example of a pre-existing phenomenon.[63] In eighteenth-century Italy, Luisa Gozzi Bergalli was seeking to trace a 'geography' and a 'genealogy' of Italian women poets as early as 1726;[64] in England, Mary Scott was looking for learned women fifty years later,[65] while in the nineteenth century, Elizabeth Barrett Browning famously sought 'grandmothers' for her poetic praxis, and, in an often-quoted passage, found none—but she did, however, find 'many learned women, not merely readers, but writers of the learned languages', a clause which is not quoted nearly so often.[66] As a serious poet, Barrett Browning saw herself as breaking new ground, but as a woman of

[58] Ronald E. Surtz, *Writing Women in Late Medieval and Early Modern Spain: The Mothers of St Teresa of Avila* (Philadelphia: University of Pennsylvania Press, 1995), 5–6.

[59] See Jane Stevenson, 'Female Authority and Authorisation Strategies in Early Modern Europe', in Danielle Clarke and Elizabeth Clarke (eds.), *This Double Voice: Gendered Writing in Early Modern England* (London: Palgrave; New York: St Martin's Press, 2000), 16–40.

[60] D. M. Robathon, 'A Fifteenth-Century Bluestocking', *Medievalia et Humanistica*, 2 (1944), 106.

[61] Listed in two letters to Guarini and Damiano Borgo, Florence, Biblioteca Riccardiana, 924 (N III 15), fos. 244ᵛ–47ᵛ, (fo. 247ʳ), and fo. 248ʳ⁻ᵛ, (fo. 248ʳ).

[62] *Angeli Politiani operum, tomus primus: epistoarum libros xii, ac miscellaneorum centuria* (Leiden: S. Gryphius, 1539), 84–6 bk. 3, no. 13.

[63] *Margartoe Velseriae, C. Peutingeri coniugis, ad Christophorum fratrem epistola, multa rerum antiquitatum cognitione insignis*, ed. H. A. Mertens (Augsburg: Klett and Franck, 1778), 16.

[64] Adriana Chemello, 'Literary Critics and Scholars, 1700–1850', in Letizia Panizza and Sharon Wood (eds.), *A History of Women's Writing in Italy* (Cambridge: Cambridge University Press, 2000), 137.

[65] She published *The Female Advocate* in 1774. See M. Ferguson, 'The Cause of my Sex: Mary Scott and the Female Literary Tradition', *Huntington Library Quarterly*, 50 (1987).

[66] 'Where are the poetesses? . . . I look everywhere for grandmothers.' *The Letters of Elizabeth Barrett Browning*, ed. F. C. Kenyon (New York: Macmillan, 1897), 231–2.

deep learning who regularly composed Greek odes for her parents' birthdays from the age of 13, even she was conscious of existing in a tradition.[67]

As far as Latin women writers are concerned, Proba, Sulpicia, and the pseudo-Sulpicia (then believed to be genuine) were in print before 1500. The most significant women writers of the Middle Ages also reached print very early. When Conrad Celtis discovered the primary manuscript of the tenth-century canoness Hrotsvitha of Gandersheim in 1494, he published it in a lavish folio at Nuremberg in 1501, causing great excitement within German humanist circles: some of the epigrams from members of Celtis's literary circle at Nuremberg actually portray her as a proto-humanist, because of her close study of the classical Latin playwright Terence.[68] In 1513, the leading French humanist printer Henri Estienne published a *Liber Trium Virorum et Trium Spiritalium virginum*, bringing to light mystical writings from high medieval women visionaries, Hildegard of Bingen, Elizabeth of Schönau, and Mechthild of Hackeborn (the latter, who had written in German, was translated into Latin). Among more recent writers, St Catherine of Siena (1334–80), one of only two women to be named a Doctor of the Church (the other is the sixteenth-century St Teresa of Jesus, whose works went straight into print shortly after her death), was first published in 1472, and many editions followed, including a Spanish translation, printed in 1511, and an English one in 1519. Far from being neglected, it will be clear from a glance at the Appendix (which makes no claims to comprehensiveness), some women's Latin verse, notably that of Sulpicia, the pseudo-Sulpicia, Proba, Eucheria, Hrotsvitha, and Hildegard, was edited over and over again.

This is not to say that to take an interest in learning was made easy for a pre-modern woman. Apart from the awkwardness of the word *poeta*, already discussed, another aspect of the way that Latin contrived to erect barriers against women includes the regular phrase for a 'learned lady': *docta puella*. *Doctus* means 'taught', i.e. educated; a *doctus puer* is a [well] taught boy. Due to the confusion of ignorance with innocence, the feminine form *docta* was also used to mean 'sexually initiated'. Thus *docta puella* can be an acknowledgement of learning and achievement, or a sly innuendo, depending on context; it is thus very difficult, perhaps impossible, entirely to remove a faintly ironic overtone (in the same way that an old mistress can never be exactly the same thing as an old master). The desire to know or to learn is, in women, readily equated with sexual curiosity ('know' often has a sexual meaning), or of course with the fatal curiosity of Eve. The complexities of *docta* bedevil women's attempts to become educated from the Augustan period onwards, but in the seventeenth century and later, the sociolinguistics of Latin create yet another complication for them: Latin itself, as it slipped from being the primary to the secondary language of culture, acquired erotic connotations. Early modern and

[67] Dierdre David, *Intellectual Women and Victorian Patriarchy*, (London: Macmillan, 1987), 23.

[68] *Hrosvite Illustris Virginis et Monialis Germano Gente Saxonica Orte Opera Nuper à Conrado Celte Inventa* (Nuremberg, Hieronymus Holtzel, 1501). See for instance Heinrich de Bunau's epigram on sig. a iiiᵛ. Celtis himself also wrote a poem on Hrotsvitha which, interestingly, links her with both Sappho and Proba: *Fünf Bücher Epigramme*, ed. Kark Hartfelder (1881; repr. Hildesheim: Olms, 1963), II. 69, p. 42.

subsequent Latin is sometimes precisely used to appeal over the 'innocent' heads of women, from man to man: the encyclopedist Pierre Bayle 'spiced many entries of his Dictionary with long (and often extremely funny) quotations, usually in Latin, dealing with sexual matters'.[69]

Clearly, this in itself presented a problem for women, since the female Latinate reader of Bayle, to look no further, was potentially familiar with things she 'should not' know. A late nineteenth-century 'decadent' writer, Joséphin Peladan, for example, depicts a coterie or private academy in a novel, *Vice suprême*, of 1884, in which a character reads from a work of moral theology on lust in which, as was normal, anything too obscene to be said in French was written in Latin (a habit which was not peculiar to France and which, to many boys, constituted the only good reason for learning Latin at all):

He read the Latin from the margin and the princess started to laugh to arouse people's curiosity.
'You are fortunate indeed to know Latin.'
'I want to learn it. It is the language of forbidden things'.

Similarly, Baudelaire wrote a Latin poem, *Franciscae meae Laudes*, in praise of a 'learned' mistress, in conscious pursuit of erotic mystification.[70]

Defences of Women

Returning now to the early modern period, alongside the Renaissance rediscovery of classical texts came an explosion of texts (mostly by men) about, and for, women, which praised women's virtue and their actual and potential abilities as rulers and creative artists. Ruth Kelso in her *Doctrine for the Lady of the Renaissance* and Glenda McLeod in her *Virtue and Venom* read them fairly literally.[71] Pamela Benson in *The Invention of the Renaissance Woman* takes a more subtle approach: Renaissance pro-woman tracts are rhetorical *adynata*,[72] exercises in proving the unprovable, or were written as rhetorical exercises or *jeux d'esprit*.[73] But unlike

---

[69] Carlo Ginzburg, *No Island is an Island: Four Glances at English Literature in World Perspective* (New York: Columbia University Press, 2000), 56.

[70] Both these examples are from Waquet, *Latin*, 255, as is evidence for the use of 'the obscurity of a learned language' (Gibbon's phrase) for obscene material, p. 115 (Byron comments drily on this in *Don Juan*, I. xliv–xlv).

[71] Kelso, *Doctrine*, Glenda McLeod, *Virtue and Venom: Catalogs of Women from Antiquity to the Renaissance* (Ann Arbor: University of Michigan Press, 1991).

[72] See generally, Rosalie Colie, *Paradoxia Epidemica* (Princeton: Princeton University Press, 1966), 102: 'the humanists amused themselves by writing paradoxes, specifically so called, in defence of women.' Speeches for or against topics were the core of Tudor education and fundamental to the fashioning of a humanist poetics. Arthur F. Kinney, *Humanist Poetics* (Amherst, Mass.: University of Massachusetts Press, 1986).

[73] Benson, *The Invention of the Renaissance Woman*, 2. Linda Woodbridge, *Women and the English Renaissance: Literature and the Nature of Womankind, 1540–1620* (Urbana: University of Illinois Press, 1984), argues that the formality of exchange within the *querelle des femmes* is an indication of the formality of the controversy: the same writer could pen both an attack on women and a defence. This

satiric or playful essays in praise of donkeys, folly, or baldness, rhetorical essays in praise of women carry a risk of perhaps unintended consequences: intellectually ambitious women themselves may absorb this rhetoric which is not aimed at them, but over their heads, and transform it into praxis. Whereas no donkey was liable to get ideas above its station from reading words in its praise, it is more than possible that women were encouraged by such works. Cornelius Agrippa's *Declamation on the Nobility and Preeminence of the Female Sex*, written in response to Johann Reuchlin and dedicated to Margaret of Austria (a Hapsburg, and a classic example of a woman ruling successfully as vicereine for a yet more powerful man), makes the essentially anti-Aristotelian point that the oppression of women rests on custom, and all customs are arbitrary.[74] This work may well, as Brenda Hosington suggests, have been written playfully, but most early commentators took it seriously and regarded it as genuinely a defence of women.[75] It circulated widely, and was translated into both French and English. Furthermore, when women such as Lucrezia Marinella, Marie de Gournay, or Anna Maria van Schurman entered the lists, we may see a movement from *serio ludere* to deadly earnest.[76] Agrippa's arguments were directly influential on Hélisienne de Crenne's defence of women, and probably on that of Aemilia Lanier.[77] Thus the *defensiones* and women themselves interact reciprocally: for example, Eleonora of Aragon was the dedicatee of Bartolomeo Goggio's *De Laudibus Mulierum*: she was also a mother with daughters to educate, and thus, since *De Laudibus* encouraged her to take herself and her children seriously, what may have been, to Goggio, merely a rhetorical exercise seems in practice to have had some effect in the real world of women and their choices.[78] Certainly, these daughters—Isabella and Beatrice d'Este—were educated to a very high standard. Beatrice in her turn was the dedicatee of Jacopo Foresti da Bergamo's *De Claris Mulieribus*, one of the most influential of all lists of learned women in the Italian Renaissance, and both women

certainly occurred: for example, Conor Fahy in Letizia Panizza (ed.), *Women in Italian Renaissance Culture and Society* (Oxford: European Humanities Research Centre, 2000), 442, points to Alessandro Piccolomini who wrote an *Oratione in lode delle donne*, delivered in the Academy of the Intronati no later than 1545, satirized by himself in his much better known dialoque *La Raffaelle, o della bella creanza delle donne*, first published in 1539.

[74] Cornelius Agrippa, *De Nobilitate et Praecellentia Foeminei Sexus* (Antwerp: Michael Hillenius, 1529), *On the Nobility and Preeminence of the Female Sex*, trans. Albert Rabil, Jr. (Chicago: University of Chicago Press, 1996), 94–5.

[75] In a paper read at the Eleventh International Congress of the Societas Internationalis Studii Neolatinis Provehendis, Cambridge, 30 July–5 Aug. 2000.

[76] This is demonstrated by Diane S. Wood. 'In Praise of Woman's Superiority: Heinrich Cornelius Agrippa's ' "De Nobilitate" (1529)', in Gold et al. (eds.), *Sex and Gender*, 189–206 (pp. 201–2).

[77] On de Crenne, see ibid. 200. The second section of Lanier's *Salve Deus Rex Judaeorum. Containing. 1 The Passion of Christ. 2 Eves Apologie in Defence of Women. 3 The Teares of the Daughters of Jerusalem. 4 The Salutation and Sorrow of the Virgine Marie. With divers other things not unfit to be read* (London: Valentine Simmes for Richard Bonian, 1611), uses the virtue of Pilate's wife as an argument for women, an argument which she probably took from Agrippa (*On The Nobility . . .*, trans. Rabil, 65).

[78] W. Gundersheimer, 'Bartolomeo Goggio: A Feminist in Renaissance Ferrara', *Renaissance Quarterly*, 23 (1980), 175–200.

received Latin letters from Cassandra Fedele, so they were obviously educated in Latin.[79]

The women who form the subject of this study were neither outlaws in their own time, nor, except in the remotest sense, a vanguard of social change. Their learning, their power, their exercise of authority, was accommodated within existing social structures. How this worked out in practice is the subject of the following chapters.

[79] *Cassandrae Fidelis Venetae Epistolae et Orationes Posthumae*, ed. Iac. Philippus Tomasinus (Padua: F. Bolzetti, 1676).

PART I

Antiquity and Late Antiquity

1. *Classical Latin Women Poets*

Very little writing by women survives among the Latin poetry of the late Republic and early Empire, but there is more than is generally known, and certainly what survives represents only a fraction of what was written. Phyllis Culham's statement that 'the study of women in ancient literature is the study of men's views of women and cannot become anything else' is understandable, but more pessimistic than is absolutely necessary.[1] In order to see how women participated in literary culture, it will be clearest to move forward generation by generation. Though so little survives, it is clear from the texts available that from the end of the Republic, literary circles often included women—not possibly fictitious mistresses of socially indeterminate or dubious status, but women identifiable as wives or connections of known poets.

Roman women, even of the elite, occupied a highly circumscribed and largely private place during the Republic and the early Empire. The limitations on their participation on public affairs is suggested by their language, since, according to Cicero, women tended to preserve old-fashioned standards of purity, because their speech habits were uncorrupted by modern idioms and pronunciations picked up through mixing with the city crowd.[2] Only three women from classical Rome are recorded as having made a public speech, the well-known Hortensia, frequently cited as an example for the women public orators of the Renaissance, Maesia Sentinas (who was also remembered, for example by Charles Gerbier),[3] and Gaia. Of the three, Hortensia and Maesia are described sympathetically as capable and brave, but Gaia as 'abounding in impudence'. The distinction seems to be that both Hortensia and Maesia spoke for themselves because there was no man to act for them, which was viewed as courageous, whereas Gaia did so from choice, which was seen as brazen.[4]

Complex considerations of caste and social position dictated whether a girl was taught to read, and encouraged to write, or whether 'she stayed at home, and spun wool'.[5] But in the Augustan period, education was part of an elite woman's social

[1] P. Culham, 'Ten Years after Pomeroy: Studies of the Image and Reality of Women in Antiquity', in M. B Skinner (ed.), *Rescuing Creusa: New Methodological Approaches to Women in Antiquity*, a special issue of *Helios*, NS 13.2 (1986), 9–30 (p. 15).

[2] Joseph Farrell, *The Latin Language and Latin Culture from Ancient to Modern Times* (Cambridge: Cambridge University Press, 2001), 65–6.

[3] C.G., *Eulogium Heroinum, or the Praise of Worthy Women* (London: T.M & A.C., 1650), 30–1: 'she with a manly, yet modest courage . . . with a loud voice and a becoming gesture and facundious suavity . . . pleaded her own cause.'

[4] Valerius Maximus, 8. 3. 1–3, discussed in Farrell, *Latin Language*, 67–74.

[5] The subject of a famous epitaph, which seems to draw a picture of an ideal Roman matron, *c.*150 BC (*CLE*, i, no. 52, p. 25).

resources.[6] Women of senatorial rank were educated: an appreciative audience for poetry, and sometimes poets themselves.[7] If we may take the Emperor Augustus own household as an example, for all the efforts he made to keep his daughter Julia chained to her wool-basket,[8] she acquired a reputation as a cultivated wit which lasted four centuries.[9] A single wistful hexameter attributed to 'a Vestal Virgin' is quoted by Seneca, *Controversiae* 6. 8, because it resulted in an accusation of unchastity:

> 'Happy are the married: may I die if it is not sweet to marry!'

This may be fictitious, but Seneca implies that there is nothing odd in the idea that a Vestal Virgin might be able to write verse. The Vestal Postumia was delated for unchastity because she was so witty she aroused suspicion, which may be the source of Seneca's story.[10] By the first century AD, it was possible for Musonius Rufus to argue that a daughter should receive the same education as a son, since it would train her mind in virtue and justice, and encourage chastity, self-control, and courage—though on the other hand, he advocated some limits to women's intellectual training: 'I do not mean that women should possess technical skill and acuteness in argument.'[11] These tropes, similarity up to a point, but a degree of difference which is focused on public speaking, will resurface again and again in Renaissance writings on women.

What keeps us from seeing Augustan poetry as a game for both sexes is the problem of texts and transmission. The massive attrition of time has destroyed most of what was written down in ancient Rome, even by writers who were widely admired by contemporaries. It is worth just stopping for a moment to register how many writers we know by name only, and the fact that so important a poet as Catullus survived antiquity in only one manuscript.[12] To a very great extent, the

---

[6] The first argument for the equal (moral) education of women was also raised in the classical period, by Gaius Musonius Rufus (*c*.AD 30–100). See *Musonius Rufus, the Roman Socrates*, ed. and trans. Cora E. Lutz (New Haven: Yale University Press, 1947), 47–9.

[7] Quintilian recommends this, so that mothers would be able to reinforce their sons' formal education (Quintilian, I. I. 6, ed. H. E. Butler 2 vols. (Cambridge, Mass.: Harvard University Press, 1920–1), i. 22). The association of writing with power is explored by Maria Wyke, 'Augustan Cleopatras: Female Power and Poetic Authority', in Anton Powell (ed.), *Roman Poetry and Propaganda* (London: British Classical Press, 1992), 98–140. Nikos Kokkinos, *Antonia Augusta: Portrait of a Great Roman Lady* (London: Routledge, 1992), 10, suggests that women of the highest rank were taught verse composition.

[8] Reported by Suetonius, *XII Caesares*, Augustus 64: see also 73.

[9] Macrobius, writing in the 4th century, records a variety of *bons mots*, *Saturnalia* 2. 5. 2 and 7 (ed. L. Janus, 2 vols. (Quedlinburg, 1848–52), ii. 245–7). See Amy Richlin, 'Julia's Jokes, Galla Placidia, and the Roman Use of Women as Political Icons', in Barbara Garlick et al. (eds.), *Stereotypes of Women in Power* (Westport, Conn.: Greenwood Press, 1992), 65–91.

[10] Livy, *Ab Urbe Condita* 4. 44. 11–12. S. F. Bonner, *Roman Declamation in the Late Republic and Early Empire* (Liverpool: Liverpool University Press, 1969), 33, suggests that Crassus' defence of the Vestal Licinia might be the source. Alternatively, Seneca is quoting a case which occurred during his lifetime. See Emily Hemelrijk, *Matrona Docta* (London: Routledge, 1999), 177, 339.

[11] Musonius Rufus, ed. and trans. Lutz: 'Should daughters receive the same education as sons?', 43–9.

[12] A single manuscript of Catullus (now lost) was discovered in Verona in 1300. Compare Tacitus: there is one 9th-century MS of *Annales* 1–6 (Florence, Biblioteca Laurentiana, plut. 68.1), one 11th-century MS of *Annales* 11–16 (Laurentiana 68.2), and 7–10 are lost.

survival of lyric poetry does not represent the considered judgement of the centuries, but random chance.[13] We cannot be certain that Catullus was a more esteemed poet than his contemporaries whom we do not have, Gallus, Varro, Valgius—or Cornificia—merely because his works still exist. Much of the poetry which Roman poets themselves hail as set to outlast the ages was irretrievably lost before AD 700.[14]

Apart from the probably mythical, and possibly divine, poet-prophetess Carmenta,[15] perhaps the first Roman woman we know anything about from her own mouth is Cornelia, mother of the demagogic politicians known as the Gracchi, who flourished in the second century BC: what are probably some of her letters survive, in which she insists on the respect due to her as a mother, and her own political involvement.[16] Cornelia is endlessly referred to by later women Latinists and their apologists, because she was a woman of achievement, but this achievement (principally the education of her sons) was entirely in the context of familial rather than personal ambition. She was held up to the admiration of posterity as a model matron because, in an often-told anecdote, she took the pride in her sons that lesser women took in their jewels.

The first Latin woman described as actually having written poetry is Sempronia, who flourished around 60 BC: '[Sempronia was] well educated in Greek and Latin literature . . . she could write poetry (*posse versus facere*) . . . she was in fact a woman of ready wit and considerable charm.'[17] And, of course, from the point of view of Sallust, her political enemy, who wrote this, her literary talents shed suspicion rather than lustre over her reputation; the implication is that ready wit is a suspicious attribute in a woman. However, a generation later, we have more direct evidence that aristocratic women were beginning to write verse.

Catullus, one of the first of the Latin poets to follow Hellenistic Greek models, was on friendly terms with a number of other poets with similar interests. They included an aristocratic young man, Cornificius, to whom he addressed several poems, including poem 38, asking for *consolatio*, which suggests a fairly close friendship. Cornificius was a *quaestor* at the time of the war between Pompey and Julius Caesar, and was proconsul of Africa when he was killed in 41 BC. Two lines of Cornificius' verse survive, one from a poem called *Glaucus*, quoted by

---

[13] Quintilian (10. 1. 93) suggests that if the judgement of antiquity had been the deciding factor, we would have the poems of Gallus and not Catullus. Ausonius and Sidonius demonstrate that at least part of the oeuvre of a number of poets who do not now survive (including two women) was still being read in the 4th and 5th centuries. Aldhelm in the 7th century quotes a lost poem by Lucan, *De Orpheo*, in his *De Metris et Enigmatibus* (*Opera*, ed. R. Ehwald (Berlin: Weidmann, 1919), 159).

[14] Catullus, poem 95, claims that Cinna's poem *Zmyrna* is destined to be read in distant parts of the world for many generations.

[15] Virgil, *Aeneid* 8. 339–41.

[16] There are two long fragments of letters to her son Caius, written in 124 BC: Judith P. Hallett, 'Women Writing in Rome and Cornelia, Mother of the Gracchi', in Laurie Churchill et al. (eds.), *Women Writing Latin from Roman Antiquity to Early Modern Europe* (New York: Routledge, 2002), i. 13–24. See also Hemelrijk, *Matrona Docta*, 193–6.

[17] Sallust, *Bellum Catilinae*, chs. 25. 2–5.

Macrobius in his *Saturnalia* 6. 4. 2 and 6. 5. 13. Cornificius' sister Cornificia was also a poet. Part of a monument to the sister and brother survives in Rome:[18]

> CORNIFICIA. Q.F. CAMERI
> Q. CORNIFICIUS. Q.F. FRATER
> PR. AUGUR

That is, 'Cornificia, daughter of Quintus, wife of Camerius, Quintus Cornificius, son of Quintus, her brother, praetor and augur'.This confirms Cornificius' status as the holder of a number of official positions (praetor, augur), and thus that the family was high-ranking. We know of Cornificia's poetic reputation only from the *Chronicle* of St Jerome (under 41 BC):

> Cornificius poeta a militibus desertus interiit,
> quos saepe fugientes galeatas lepores appellarat.
> Huius soror Cornificia, cuius insignia extant epigrammata.

Cornificius the poet perished, deserted by his soldiers, whom he had dubbed 'helmeted hares', because they so often ran away. His sister was Cornificia, whose famous epigrams survive.

Thus, some writings by Cornificia were still being read in the fourth century, when Jerome was writing, though they have subsequently been lost. Jerome describes her epigrams as *insignis*: famous, well known, excellent: a wholly positive word. He assumes that they are familiar to an educated reader, and he does not, it is worth observing, suggest that there is anything at all strange or inappropriate about an upper-class woman's writing poetry: since several of his female contemporaries did so (e.g. Paulina and Proba), this is hardly surprising. The fact that Cornificia wrote epigrams—a literary form strongly associated with the Alexandrian poetic school—may suggest that she was not merely socially proximate to Catullus, but actually a member of the Catullan avant-garde of Greek-influenced poets.

The epigraph also strengthens Cornificia's association with poets: Camerius, named as her husband, is perhaps the same Camerius who was another friend of Catullus, mentioned in his poem no. 55, again suggesting that she moved in literary circles. Though not a word of her work survives, she is one of the women writers whose names entered history, because Jerome's *Chronicle* was so widely read. Thus, for example, Boccaccio in *De Mulieribus Claris* devotes a chapter to the poet Cornificia, extrapolated from Jerome's note, which is copied by Christine de Pizan in *The Book of the City of Ladies* (I. 28. 1), among many others.[19]

Catullus' poem no. 35 is addressed to another friend and fellow poet, Caecilius: it speaks of the latter's girlfriend as 'a girl more scholarly than the muse Sappho' who has read the opening of his new poem with great appreciation. Propertius, a little later, also claimed to have a poetical girlfriend. 'I am not an assiduous lover for such nothings, but because . . . [Cynthia] challenges with her verse the writings

---

[18] *CIL*, vi. 1300 a.

[19] *Concerning Famous Women*, trans. Guido Guarino (New Brunswick, NJ: Rutgers University Press, 1963), 188.

of ancient Corinna, and does not think Erinna's songs the equal of her own.'[20] The mention of Cynthia brings us onto trickier ground. The essential fictionality of the Propertian *puella* has been carefully argued by Maria Wyke;[21] who suggests that this artistic prodigy should no more be taken as evidence for the social history of Roman *demi-mondaines* than Ovid's more obviously fictional limping muse/ mistress (the limp is a give-away: she has it because Ovid wrote in elegiac couplets, in which the second half of the distich is a foot shorter than the first).[22] But the fictionality of Cynthia does not necessarily imply that women who are referred to as part of the web of society (e.g. as fiancées, wives, or sisters), or who are referred to by their own names, are also fictions.

Catullus, Cornificia, and Sempronia belong to the last generation of the Roman Republic. The Battle of Actium, the crucial turning point in the Roman civil war, was fought in 31 BC, between Anthony and Cleopatra and Octavian, and the latter subsequently rose to power as Augustus, the first Roman emperor. A new world order, and a new generation of poets. The poets of the generation of Augustus fall into a number of groups, several of whom mention women contemporaries. Ovid (43 BC–AD 18) was one of these new poets: he is of course of incalculable import-ance to the history of women's writing for his *Heroides*—letters in the personae of famous women of antiquity.[23] He was a highly fashionable and much admired poet in Rome for some thirty years, until in AD 8 he was exiled for corrupting the morals of the Roman aristocracy. His poems from exile (the *Tristiae*) include one which tells us that his circle included at least one woman poet, Perilla. Sadly, nothing of her work has survived.

Go, greet Perilla, quickly-written letter, and be the trusty servant of my speech . . . Say to her, 'Are you also still devoted to our common pursuit of singing learned verse, though not in your father's way?'—for with your life, nature has given you modest ways and a rare dower of intelligence. I was the first to guide this to the spring of Pegasus, lest the stream of fertile water be sadly lost. I was the first to see this in the tender years of your girlhood, when, as father to daughter, I was your leader and companion. So, if the same fire remains in your breast, only the Lesbian bard will surpass your work. But I fear that my fate may now hold you back, that since my fall, your mind may be inactive. When it was possible, I used often to read your verse to myself, and mine to you, I was often your critic, often your teacher, now giving an ear to verses you had recently written, now making you blush if you stopped. (*Tristiae* 3. 7)

Whatever the precise relationship of Ovid and Perilla, the poem speaks of the fostering of a young protégée's poetic talent by an established poet.[24] It would be

---

[20] Propertius, *Elegiae* 2. 3, 16–17, 19, 21–2.

[21] Maria Wyke, 'Written Women: Propertius's *Scripta Puella*', *Journal of Roman Studies*, 77 (1987), 47–61: ' "Cynthia" is everywhere associated with Callimachus.'

[22] Maria Wyke, 'Reading Female Flesh: *Amores* 3. 1', in Averil Cameron (ed.), *History as Text* (London: Duckworth, 1989), 111–43.

[23] See articles by Danielle Clarke and Jane Stevenson in Danielle Clarke and Elizabeth Clarke (eds.), *This Double Voice* (London: Palgrave, 2000).

[24] E. Courtney, *The Fragmentary Latin Poets* (Oxford: Clarendon Press, 1993), 229, states: 'I would guess that she was a freedwoman of Ovid . . . I cannot see anything in favour of the view that she was Ovid's stepdaughter.'

perverse to see this relationship as imaginary: Ovid speaks to and of actual people in the poems written from Pontus.

Sulpicia

By far the most important Latin woman poet of antiquity is Sulpicia, a member of the circle of Tibullus.[25] Her *floruit* is in the last decades of the Roman republic, and she is now receiving increasingly serious critical attention as a poet. Where she was once dismissed as a writer of sweetly girlish ingenuousness (it is remarkable how often the word 'little', and variants thereon, appears in the older commentaries), she is now seen as 'an agile and distinctive poetic imagination'.[26] Here I want briefly to consider the social context of her writing, based on what we know of the circles in which she moved.

Sulpicia resembles the other classical women poets whose names we know in being part of a literary group. The reason why we have her verse at all is that, as good luck would have it, a volume of 'poems by friends and associates of M. Valerius Messalla Corvinus' was collected up and appended to the two books of Tibullus, the most distinguished of Messalla's literary protégés.[27] Thus some of Sulpicia's verse makes it into the Middle Ages, though only just: the tradition of Tibullus and his associates rests on a single manuscript which was at the Carolingian court in the eighth century, and it is unusual for works by members of a coterie to be preserved together with the oeuvre of its leading poet.[28] Some bare details of this woman's life can be reconstructed; as securely, at least, as the life of any other elegiac poet.[29] She was the daughter of a patrician, Servius Sulpicius Rufus, and of Valeria, the sister of the distinguished statesman Valerius Messalla

[25] I have not seen P. Rasi, *Una poetessa del secolo di Augusto* (Padua, 1913). Otto Gruppe, *Die römische Elegie* (Leipzig: O. Wigand, 1838), i. 27, denied her authorship of all the longer poems, an unargued assertion which commanded general, though not universal, acceptance thereafter until quite recently. Esther Bréguet, *Le Roman du Sulpicia: élégies IV, 2–12 du 'Corpus Tibullianum'* (Geneva, Georg, 1946), argues for the attribution of all the 'Sulpicia' poems to Ovid, as does R. S. Radford, 'Tibullus and Ovid', *American Journal of Philology*, 44 (1923), 1–26, while L. Herrmann, 'Reconstruction du Livret de Sulpicia', *Latomus*, 9 (1950), 35–47, attributes all the poems, including those in the third person, to Sulpicia. See also L. Herrmann, 'Un nouveau fragment de Sulpicia?', *Latomus*, 23 (1963), 322–3, for an attempt to add one further line to her oeuvre. Recent responses to her work include Matthew Santirocco, 'Sulpicia Reconsidered', *Classical Journal*, 74 (1979), 229–39, H. MacL. Currie, 'The Poems of Sulpicia', *Aufstieg und Niedergang der Römischen Welt*, 2. 30. 3 (1983), 1751–64, Stephen Hinds, 'The Poetess and the Reader: Further Steps towards Sulpicia', *Hermathena*, 143 (Winter 1987), 29–46, N. J. Lowe, 'Sulpicia's Syntax', *Classical Quarterly*, 38 (1988), 193–205, Holt Parker, 'Sulpicia, the *Auctor de Sulpicia* and the Authorship of III. 9 and III. 11 of the *Corpus Tibullianum*', *Helios*, 21 (1994), 39–62, Judith P. Hallett, 'The Eleven Elegies of the Augustan Poet Sulpicia', in Churchill et al. (eds.), *Women Writing Latin*, i. 45–66, Mathilde Skoie, *Reading Sulpicia* (Oxford: Oxford University Press, 2002).

[26] Lowe, 'Sulpicia's Syntax', 205.

[27] C. Davies, 'Poetry in the "Circle" of Messalla', *Greece and Rome*, 20 (1973), 25–35 (p. 25 n. 2).

[28] L. D. Reynolds et al. (eds.), *Texts and Transmission* (Oxford: Clarendon Press, 1983), 420–1.

[29] She gives her name as 'Sulpicia, filia Servi' in 3. 16. G. Provasi, 'Il ciclo tibulliano Sulpicia-Cerinto e le sue principali interpretazioni', *Rivista di filologia e di istruzione classica*, NS 15 (1937), 343–54 (pp. 349–50), discusses her identity.

Corvinus. This made Messalla Sulpicia's *avunculus* ('maternal uncle': an important relationship in Rome, as Hallett has shown),[30] and shows that she was an aristocratic young woman, whose family connections were of the highest respectability. Servius Sulpicius Rufus may have died circa 33/4 BC.[31] His daughter, her verse suggests, was inclined to pride herself on her family, so it may be worth noting that while her father enjoyed a modest literary reputation,[32] her grandfather (also Servius Sulpicius Rufus)[33] was a republican man of principle.[34] He was also closely coeval, and friendly, with his cousin Decimus Brutus, Caesar's murderer.[35]

However, the most important consequence of Sulpicia's orphaned state was that Messalla became her most important male relative: the fact that Messalla honoured this commitment and had an active concern for the welfare of his sister's children is clearly witnessed by his associating Sulpicia's brother, Postumius Sulpicius, with him when he took charge of the aqueducts in 11 BC.[36] It is highly likely that Sulpicia married M. Caecilius Cornutus, who was a member of the Arval College in 21–20 along with Messalla.[37] Cornutus appears to have been a protégé of Messalla's—hence, perhaps, an appropriate husband for an orphan niece.

If this identification, and the conclusions drawn from it, are acceptable, then they would provide a context for the last two lines of poem 3. 16,

> solliciti sunt pro nobis quibus illa dolori est
> ne cedam ignoto maxima causa toro.

They are distressed on my account, those to whom it is the greatest cause of grief, that I give way to an unworthy bed.

This poem, a stinging response to the unwelcome news (or rumour) that her lover has been caught with a prostitute, appears to cast in the teeth of 'Cerinthus' that he is of less aristocratic origin than herself,[38] and that there had been an element of condescension in her agreeing to marry him in the first place.[39]

---

[30] Judith Hallett, *Fathers and Daughters in Roman Society: Women and the Elite Family* (Princeton: Princeton University Press, 1984), 152–80, 325–8.

[31] Syme, *The Augustan Aristocracy*, 229.

[32] Quintilian, 10. 5. 4 and 10. 1. 116 and Horace, *Saturae* 1. 10. 86.

[33] He is last mentioned in 43 BC, and may have perished in the Proscriptions. Ronald Syme, *The Augustan Aristocracy* (Oxford: Clarendon Press, 1986), 206.

[34] Ibid. 26.

[35] Cicero, *Ad Familiares* 11. 7. 1.

[36] Syme, *The Augustan Aristocracy*, 299, based on Sextus Julius Frontinus, *De Aquis Urbis Romae*, 2. 99.

[37] Ronald Syme, *Some Arval Brethren* (Oxford: Clarendon Press, 1980), 1–2.

[38] The precise status of Sulpicia's grandfather is explored by Syme, *The Augustan Aristocracy*, 17. A daughter of what Syme describes as 'the decayed patriciate' might be, if anything, touchier on the subject of rank than one whose status was unassailable.

[39] Lowe, 'Sulpicia's Syntax', 202, offers the literal reading, 'They are worried for us [me], to whom it is the greatest grounds for sorrow, that I may not give way to a low bed.' The last clause most probably means, as Guy Lee translates it, 'that I may submit to a low-born bedmate', though (another ambiguity in a poem replete with multiple meanings) it might also mean 'that I yield [in the sense of being set aside in favour of] to a low bed'—i.e. that of the *scortum*.

Cornutus' forthcoming marriage is celebrated by Tibullus in 2. 2, and his son is also known to have become one of the Arval Brothers.[40] Membership of the Arval College suggests simultaneously patrician status, wealth, respectability, and conservatism: if Cornutus was deficient (as it seems) in patrician status, he was unlikely to be deficient in respectability and conservatism, and if Sulpicia was niece, wife, and eventually mother of *fratres Arvales* she was a very long way from the *demi-monde*. W. R. Johnson has described Messalla as '*Romanitas* incarnate'.[41] Her paternal ancestry has already been discussed. Moreover, her mother features in Seneca's list of wives of exemplary virtue.[42] So Sulpicia's immediate family circle is one of good old families of republican tendency; far more respectable than the actual court. It is therefore probable that her Cerinthus, if he existed at all, was none other than her fiancé, most probably M. Caecilius Cornutus.[43]

There is a question mark hanging over the attribution of poems to Sulpicia. The group of short poems (3. 13–18) are generally conceded to be hers. The longer poems about Sulpicia's life (3. 8–12), three of which are in the third person, two in the first, are widely held to be someone else's.[44] It is of course clear that the poems in the so-called 'Garland of Sulpicia' (the five longer poems) are influenced by the work of Tibullus and also by Propertius and Ovid,[45] as one would expect: poets working in a coterie (and the *clientes* of Messalla were certainly that) often do evolve together, and the stylistic traits of the most able, Tibullus in this case, exert a compelling influence on other members of the same circle. The adoption of a feminine persona by a male poet is far from unknown in Augustan poetry.[46] But there is a serious difference between writing a poem in the persona of a female contemporary disguised under a poetic name such as 'Arethusa', and writing in the

---

[40] Syme, *The Augustan Aristocracy*, 46–7. See further Marie-Therese Raepsaet-Charlier, *Prosopographie des femmes de l'ordre sénatorial Ier–IIe siècles* (Louvain: Peeters, 1987), 587.

[41] W. R. Johnson, 'Messalla's Birthday: The Politics of Pastoral', *Arethusa*, 23.1 (1990), 95–114: Messalla was 'a tough and resilient aristocrat . . . *Romanitas* incarnate' (p. 95). Tiberius took him as the model for his Latin style (Suetonius, *XII Caesares*, Tiberius 70).

[42] Seneca, *De Matrimonio* 77, ed. F. Haase, 3 vols. (Leipzig: Teubner, 1853), iii. 432.

[43] Susan Treggiari, *Roman Marriage: Iusti Coniuges from the Time of Cicero to the Time of Ulpian* (Oxford: Clarendon Press, 1991), 302–3. See also David F. Bright, *Haec Mihi Fingebam: Tibullus in his World* (Leiden: Brill, 1978), 7, who notes that 'several MSS' replace Cerinthus with Cornutus in 2. 2. 9 and 2. 3. 1. Gruppe, *Die römische Elegie*, i. 27, is the first to explore the identification of Cerinthus with Cornutus in detail, but see also Santirocco, 'Sulpicia Reconsidered', 236 and J. P. Boucher, 'A propos de Cérinthus et quelques autres pseudonymes dans la poésie augustéenne', *Latomus*, 35 (1976), 504–19 (pp. 504–8). On a different tack, Maria Wyke has stressed the fictionality of the 'elegiac woman' (discussed below): it is far from impossible that, similarly, Cerinthus is an entirely fictional 'elegiac man'.

[44] George Luck, *The Latin Love-Elegy* (New York: Barnes & Noble; London: Faber, 1959), 100–3. Gian Biagio Conte, *Latin Literature: A History*, trans. J. B. Solodow (Baltimore: Johns Hopkins University Press, 1994), 437. All sides of the debate may be found in n. 18 above.

[45] The lives of Propertius, Tibullus, and Ovid overlapped (on which see Peter White, *Promised Verse: Poets in the Society of Augustan Rome* (Cambridge, Mass.: Harvard University Press, 1993), 38–40). Propertius' first book of elegies was published *c.*29/28 BC, Tibullus' first book appeared soon after. They were contemporaries, moving in the same social circles, and also literary associates (*Tristia* 4. 10. 45, and see also *Epistulae ex Ponto* 2. 3. 67–82).

[46] Wyke, 'Reading Female Flesh: *Amores* 3. 1'.

persona of another member of the same social circle *who is also a poet*, using her own name. We could hardly imagine Ovid appropriating the voice of Propertius.[47]

Furthermore, if the first-person poems are not Sulpicia's own, the implied relationship between the (assumed to be male) author of 'The Garland' and Sulpicia herself becomes highly problematic. Sulpicia, as a poet, might reasonably resent being represented as a 'wooing lady' by a male acquaintance, but she was not merely a poet. She would also be entitled to resent this as a marriageable young lady of good family,[48] as would Messalla, a man who certainly could not be offended with impunity. Holt Parker has provided an extremely interesting possible resolution of the 'Garland of Sulpicia' problem, by suggesting that all the poems in the first person are by Sulpicia, while the three which are in the third person are by another hand. He points out that comparable anthologies do not automatically group their contents by author: they are more likely to group kindred themes together, or to alternate between authors. Another sorting principle, used by the compiler of the Catullus collection, is by length: here similarly, we have a group of poems of 20–5 lines followed by a group of poems of less than ten lines.[49] The acceptance of Holt Parker's thesis would dispose of the question of propriety raised above, since it is the two longer first-person poems which are the most problematic in this respect.

The three third-person poems about Sulpicia (3. 8, 10, 12) are like one another, very different from the first-person poems, and show several features which may suggest male authorship. All three are addressed to a deity. Poem 3. 8 describes Sulpicia as an object for the male gaze,[50] but also emphasizes status markers. As far as her personal attributes go, she is exquisitely beautiful, of course, and, thus far, she might be any *puella* celebrated by an elegiac poet. But she is also beautiful in robes of expensive and royal Tyrian dye or in a pure white dress (3. 8. 11–12); she has a thousand costumes, all of which suit her (3. 8. 13), she has a most elegant hairstyle (3. 8. 9–10) and she is the only worthy recipient of double-dyed Tyrian and Indian pearls (3. 8. 15–20). This Sulpicia is not an elegiac heroine, she is an aristocratic leader of fashion. Propertius, by contrast, insists on the irrelevance of hairdos and Coan silk to his Cynthia,[51] but then, he is not in the least interested in her public status. Even if Cynthia is in any sense a veridical portrait of Propertius' mistress, which is doubtful, her relation to Roman society is no part of his concern;

[47] A similar point is forcefully made by Parker in 'Sulpicia, the *Auctor de Sulpicia*, and the Authorship of III. 9 and III. 11', 43, 46.

[48] Evidence for the attitude taken to the chastity of elite women in the late Republic is ambiguous. See Catherine Edwards, *The Politics of Immorality in Ancient Rome* (Cambridge: Cambridge University Press, 1993), 36, 43–6, and A. E. Richlin, 'Approaches to the Sources on Adultery at Rome', *Women's Studies*, 8 (1981), 225–50 (this survey of the sources is more useful on the subject of marital than of pre-marital chastity).

[49] Parker, 'Sulpicia, the *Auctor de Sulpicia*, and the Authorship of III. 9 and III. 11', 42.

[50] As Hinds points out in 'The Poetess and the Reader', 34, the first line, 'Sulpicia est tibi culta tuis, Mars magne, kalendis', means 'Sulpicia has been decked out for you, great Mars, on your kalends', but could also mean 'Sulpicia has been worshipped by you, great Mars, on your kalends'. As the poem continues, 'Mars... is being invited to consider an enticing mortal alternative [to Venus]' (p. 31).

[51] Propertius, 1. 2. 1–2, 2. 1. 5–8.

she exists in his poetry only in relation to him.[52] She does not, as it were, have an uncle. Sulpicia is the name of a real woman, by no means a nonentity, and therefore to some extent, in a patriarchal world, a commodity. This poem, therefore, underlines and (probably) exaggerates her value, which is naturally and effectively expressed through her clothes.[53]

Poem 3. 12 is in some ways similar to 3. 8. Again, it celebrates Sulpicia making a public appearance in the context of worshipping a deity (perhaps we should remember that religious festivals represent perhaps the only opportunity, other than her wedding day, for a girl of good family to make an appearance in a public place).[54] In this poem also, Sulpicia is immaculately dressed and presented; a respectable young lady, publicly affianced to a suitable young man, whom she will marry next year (3. 12. 19–20). It is notable for its avoidance of any intrusion on her privacy: it captures an image of her as she appears decked for public admiration, and offers no titillating glimpses of her private self. The stance, as with 3. 8, is of an onlooker, his admiration of her charming appearance legitimized by the public context: both these poems describe a Sulpicia who is prepared to face the eyes of strange men, but is at the same time acting with total propriety. This appears to be a *genethliacum*, or birthday poem.[55] While it addresses the possibility that lovers may fall out of love, it is notably more discreet in alluding to Cerinthus' possible lukewarmness or infidelity than any of the first-person poems which treat this theme (3. 12. 8).

The last of the third-person poems, 3. 10, is also occasional, though its occasion is rather different; it was written for an illness of Sulpicia's, in a context in which Cerinthus is implicitly her acknowledged fiancé (3. 10. 24). All three, then, are wholly acceptable as representations of the niece of Messalla. They emphasize her status, and they represent her in decorous postures. It is the first-person 3. 9 which offers a wild fantasy of copulation in front of the hunters' nets and which, by its invocation of the legend of Venus and Adonis, represents Sulpicia as a 'wooing lady'. It is hard to imagine how anyone other than herself could have had the temerity to write such a poem about a well-connected girl. We cannot, of course, draw direct conclusions about her sexual *mores* from this or any other poem,

[52] Hence the gyrations of such commentaries as Georg Luck, 'The Woman's Role in Latin Love Poetry', in G.K. Galinsky (ed.), *Perspectives on Roman Poetry* (Austin: University of Texas Press, 1974), 15–31, which seek to reconcile the women of elegiac poetry with other kinds of evidence about Roman social relations.

[53] Several commentators note that the women of republican Rome used their wardrobes as a way of putting out public signals about their own and their families' social position. Livy, *Ab Urbe Condita* 34. 1–8 discusses the repeal of the Lex Oppia in 195 BC. A spokesman sympathetic to their viewpoint comments on the serious status implications of women's dress (34. 7. 8–9). See S. Dixon, 'Polybius and Roman Women and Property', *American Journal of Philology*, 106 (1985), 147–70.

[54] Note, for instance, that Virgil in the pageant of Roman history depicted on Aeneas' shield allows women to appear only as riding to a religious occasion in carriages, and chanting in temples (*Aeneid* 8. 665–6, 718).

[55] On *genethliaca* (birthday poems) see Currie, 'The Poems of Sulpicia', 1759, H. C. Bowerman, 'The Birthday as a Commonplace of Roman Elegy', *Classical Journal*, 12 (1916–17), 310–18, and Emanuele Cesaree, *Il carme natalizio nella poesia latino* (Palermo: 'Orfani Geneva', 1929).

especially since we cannot supply a chronology.[56] Some or all of these poems could have been written by Sulpicia as a married woman; and Martial's reaction to the second Sulpicia, to be discussed later, suggests that it was not necessarily considered improper among Roman *literati* for a wife to make it known that she enjoyed her husband's embraces.[57] As a young matron, Sulpicia would still be at her uncle's beck and call, since Cornutus was his *cliens*, i.e. dependent on his patronage.

The Latin love elegy involves the highly self-conscious adoption of a stance; a self-consistent mode of representing one's emotional state parallel to reality and overlapping with it to an unknown and unguessable extent. The other long first-person poem, 3. 11, is very similar to the shorter lyrics. It shares the rapturous absorption in love of 3. 9, with a warning note that she is ill disposed to tolerate any misconduct on her lover's part—her love is all-absorbing but, unlike that of Propertius or Catullus, conditional. Similarly, poem 3. 16, the angrily sarcastic (or playful) 'Gratum est securus multum quod iam tibi de me' ('I am so pleased that you allow yourself to be so confident in me'), raises the possibility that Cerinthus may care more for a prostitute than for Sulpicia, daughter of Servius: a preference not merely tasteless, but absurd. Sulpicia is not represented in any of these poems as an abjectly lovelorn damsel (unlike Tibullus or Propertius, both of whom emphasize their mistress's power over them even when she herself is unfaithful).[58]

I would suggest that this must be understood in terms of sexual politics: for a man, taking up a posture of abjection (however sincerely) is not to lose his social status and dignity.[59] Sulpicia insists on her control over the relationship, where her male counterparts insist on their lack of it. She is thus not imitating Tibullus or Propertius, and she is most certainly not playing at being Cynthia or Delia, since she makes no claim to be either sexually libertarian or even socially independent. She complains about having to go to the country, but does not claim that she can or will refuse. More significantly, she never implies that she has had lovers in the past, threatens to take another lover, or suggests that she might be unfaithful: only the third-person 3. 12 even raises this as a possibility, which may be another reason for

---

[56] Catullus' scorn for attempts to read the poet through his work expressed in poem 16. 1–6 is a position which was wholly inaccessible to women writers (and could be risky for men, as Ovid's career demonstrates).

[57] The younger Sulpicia is specifically remembered as a poet of married love. The idea that poetry and marriage are, for women at least, incompatible does not seem to be characteristic of late republican Rome.

[58] Tibullus, 1. 5, Propertius, 1. 1, 1. 4, 1. 16, among others: Luck, *The Latin Love-Elegy*, 122: 'the mistress becomes the *domina*, the lover her "slave" '. This is discussed by Frank O. Copley, '*Seruitium Amoris* in the Roman Elegists', *Transactions of the American Philological Association*, 78 (1947), 285–300, by R. O. A. M. Lyne, '*Seruitium Amoris*', *Classical Quarterly*, 29 (1979), 117–30, and by Ellen Greene, *The Erotics of Domination: Male Desire and the Mistress in Latin Love Poetry* (Baltimore: Johns Hopkins University Press, 1998). The *domina* represents a reversal of the socially expected norm: when Sulpicia reverses the reversal, in 3. 11. 3–4, the effect is profoundly disconcerting and almost perverse, since she is talking about something completely detached from the straightforward legal and social power of the male.

[59] Ovid, as well as undermining the realist texture of his predecessors' writing, undermines their abject posture in *Amores*: in 2. 7 he swears to his jealous mistress that he has no interest in her slave hairdresser Cypassis. In 2. 8 he writes to Cypassis, who is indeed his mistress.

suggesting that it is not her own work.[60] Thus in some important respects, the first-person poems in the 'Garland of Sulpicia' run against the grain of their nearest rivals and models, and with that of Sulpicia's short poems. In a culture which assumed that women were more, not less, prey to their emotions than men, it would be surprising to find a male poet representing a woman as more cool-headed about her passion than her male peer group and poetic models. In conclusion, then, I would support the thesis that the surviving oeuvre of Sulpicia consists of 3. 9, 3. 11, 3. 13–18, and one more poem, preserved epigraphically: nine in all.

Readings of elegy which seek to represent Cynthia, Delia, and Corinna as portraits of real people subsume Sulpicia's few poems into the composite portrait of the *docta puella*. This is particularly tempting because we *seem* to know so much more about 'Cynthia', since what one knows about a fictional character is explicit. But recent work, especially that of Maria Wyke, denies that Callimachean elegy has anything at all to tell us about the lives of real women;[61] in which case, reading back the *demi-mondaine* lifestyle of fictional *puellae* into the life of Sulpicia is a serious mistake. Moreover, in these poems, *Sulpicia* is an author, Cerinthus a construct. It is she who is in control of narrative strategy, so it is worth seeing what she has to say. Cerinthus, like Propertius' Cynthia, is unfaithful. Like her, he is silent; a silence which we take for granted when a man is writing about a woman, but which seems to demand explanation when a woman writes about a man.[62] Sulpicia adheres to the convention established by male poets (e.g. in 3. 7) that the poet is impassioned, and the commitment of the love-object less certain.[63] While the Cerinthus thus portrayed here could of course be read realistically as a less than absolutely devoted fiancé/husband, and it may seem that this is compatible with the social realities of Roman life, it is probably more to the point to think of these poems as a socially revealing attempt to reproduce the pattern of relationship between *erotes* and *eromenos* found in Propertius' Cynthia poems or Tibullus' Nemesis poems, but modifying the presentation of both participants in the light of the massive social inequality of men and women in late republican Rome.

It is at least arguable that the oeuvre of Sulpicia can be extended by one more poem of a quite different kind, and I should like to make the case here. The poem is an epitaph, in elegiacs, for a *lectrix* (reader-aloud) called Petale. This epigraphic poem was found in Rome, and announces that the inscription was raised over the ashes of the *lectrix* of Sulpicia (or of Sulpicia the *lectrix*). The possibility that this is another poem by our Sulpicia was first raised by Carcopino.[64] Obviously, it is a

---

[60] All this suggests that, far from identifying with the 'free' but déclassée Elegiac Woman, she is representing herself as the kind of girl Ovid says was *not* to read his *Ars Amatoria* (1. 31–2).

[61] Wyke, 'Written Women'.

[62] Sulpicia makes direct reference to Cerinthus' silence in 3. 11. 17–19: see Hinds, 'The Poetess and the Reader', 40.

[63] Similarly, E. S. Stigers, 'Sappho's Private World', *Women's Studies*, 8 (1981), 47–63, discusses the ways in which Sappho's stance as a poet diverges from that of male near-contemporaries such as Archilochus and Anacreon.

[64] J. Carcopino, 'Épitaphe en vers de la lectrice Petale', *Bulletin de la Société Nationale des Antiquaires de France* (1929), 84–6.

different type of poem from the 'Cerinthus' verses, but it is similarly in elegiacs. The memorialized woman, Petale, is associated with a Sulpicia who was sufficiently cultivated and wealthy to keep a servant specifically as a *lectrix*. She may have been Greek, as many highly skilled slaves were in late republican Rome: Petale (from Greek *petalon*)[65] is a name assigned to her, as the second line says, but her son Aglaos also has a Greek name. The poem lists the age, achievements, and virtues of the deceased in a conventional way, but the lack of any clauses referring to the grief of those she left behind produces a relatively impersonal effect, which would not be inappropriate for a mistress memorializing a valued servant whose role would necessarily have caused them to spend considerable time together.

> Sulpiciae cineres lectricis cerne viator
> Quoi servile datum nomen erat Petale
> Ter denos numero quattuor plus vixerat annos
> Natumque in terris Aglaon ediderat
> Omnia naturae bona viderat arte vigebat
> Splendebat forma, creverat ingenio
> Invida fors vita longinquom degere tempus
> Noluit hanc fatis defuit ipse colus.

> Passer-by. Observe the ashes of Sulpicia the lectrix/the lectrix of Sulpicia,
> to whom the slave-name 'Petale' had been given.
> She had lived thrice ten years plus four,
> and on earth, she had brought forth a son, Aglaos ('glorious');
> She had seen all the good things of nature, and was strong in artistry;
> she was splendid in beauty, and had grown [mature] in intellect.
> Envious Fortune was unwilling that she should spend a long time in life:
> the Fates' distaff itself failed them.

A number of linguistic features suggest that the Sulpicia who is the probable subject of this poem is connected with the Sulpicia who is author of the Cerinthus poems. The adverb *longinquom* ('a long while') is found in writers of the Republic, but falls out of use in Augustan poetry. *Quoi* for *cui* is also an archaic feature.[66] The masculine form *ipse colus* is used by Catullus and Propertius, whereas other classical writers treat the word as feminine.[67] The usage is thus peculiar to the first generation of elegiac poets, among whom the poet Sulpicia is numbered.

Insofar as it is possible to read any kind of poetic signature off such a tiny oeuvre, the epitaph is Sulpician. The ambiguities about naming in the two first lines suggest the same love of paradox as the use of *fama* in 3. 13: the dead woman is identified as Petale: clearly this is the name by which she would have been recognized and remembered. But the emphasis on this as a servile name implies she had a *non*-servile name, suggesting that Petale was manumitted on her deathbed,

---

[65] Petale appears as a slave-name in Propertius, 4. 7.

[66] The absence of these markers in the Cerinthus poems cannot really be brought in evidence, since they go back to a single MS witness which would almost certainly have been tidied up by scribal editing, whereas this poem displays the orthographic features of the generation in which it was composed.

[67] Catullus, 64. 311 'amictum...colum'; Propertius, 4. 9. 48 'Lydo...colo', and 4. 9. 48.

so she would at least die a free woman—and her free name would of course be Sulpicia, since it was normal to take the *nomen gentile* of the patron.[68] As Janet Fairweather has observed (pers. comm.), the fact that 'Sulpiciae' is the first word of the poem would normally suggest that it is the name of the person commemorated. The first line may therefore be saying, 'Passer-by, see here the ashes *of Sulpicia the lectrix of Sulpicia*,' emphasizing the similarity of their position as female dependants of Servius Sulpicius Rufus: a gesture of affection towards a slave who may have been very much a companion, or an ironic recognition of the contingent status of even a daughter of the elite?[69] Stephen Hinds has suggested a similar play with the ironies of women's identity in 3. 16. 4, 'you care for a *scortum* rather than for "Servi filia Sulpicia"; a prostitute is worlds apart from Sulpicia, but curiously, both are *servi filia*: "a slave's daughter/Servius's daughter" ' (an ambiguity increased, of course, by the absence of capitalization in Roman scripts).[70]

So if this is a poem by Sulpicia, then, it confirms what we otherwise know from her family history, that we would be quite wrong to assign to her the bohemian *demi-mondaine* status of the 'elegiac woman': like her own poems, and those of the 'amicus Sulpiciae', it implies that she is a wealthy upper-class girl: *lectrices* were only found in the houses of the unusually wealthy or the unusually literary.[71] The choice of a Greek woman for a servant who must have been very much a companion perhaps suggests the Philhellenism of cultivated circles in late republican Rome—it is perhaps just worth noticing that the literary reputation of Sulpicia's father was based on translating Greek verse.[72] With this sense of her social position goes a completely different attitude to her body and a perception of her value: Sulpicia is using a discourse of power, over herself, her social environment, and her lover, which is quite other than that constructed for women by the other elegiasts.

Sulpicia II and other poets of the early Empire

In the first century AD, the 'Silver Age' of Roman verse, Juvenal complains of women's learning in a satire which demonstrates the eternal principle that a woman's place is in the wrong: if she is not pig-ignorant, she will inevitably be pedantic:[73]

---

[68] Susan Treggiari, *Roman Freedmen during the Late Republic* (Oxford: Clarendon Press, 1969), 7. Daughters and manumitted women both carried the name of their father/*patronus*. In memorializing or listing a woman, it was proper to add *f.* to the genitive of the father's praenomen (as Sulpicia does in identifying herself as *filia Serui*) so as not to confuse her with a freedwoman (Hallett, *Fathers and Daughters*, 77–83, Orlando Patterson, *Freedom in the Making of Western Culture* (London: I. B. Tauris, 1991), 254–5. Martial speaks of manumitting his amanuensis Demetrius on the latter's deathbed (1. 150), 'so that he might not descend to the Stygian shades as a slave'.

[69] *Freedom*, 248. Patterson also suggests that the naming of women by their father's name only (a development of the late Republic) actually assimilated their position to that of freedwomen (p. 255). See also I. Kajanto, 'On the First Appearance of Women's Cognomina', *Acts of the VI International Congress of Greek and Latin Epigraphy* (Munich: Beck, 1973), 402–6.

[70] 'The Poetess and the Reader', 44–5.

[71] *CIL*, vi.4.2, no. 33473, 'Derceto Aureliae Virginis lectrix', and *CIL*, vi.2, no. 8786, 'Cnide lectrix', wife of Irenaeus, *cubicularius seruus* to Livia Drusi (Tiberius' daughter in-law).

[72] Quintilian, 10. 5. 4.

[73] Juvenal, *Satire* 6. 451–6.

I hate the woman who is continually poring over and studying Palaemon's treatise, who never breaks the rules or principles of grammar, and who quotes verses unknown to me, ancient stuff that men wouldn't bother with. Let her correct her girl-friend's verses—she ought to allow her husband to commit a solecism.

This suggests, however sarcastically, that women in Juvenal's milieu wrote verse. Lucian similarly mocks upper-class women's eagerness to be (or seem) learned:[74]

That is another thing women are keen about—to have educated men living in their households on a salary and following their litters. They count it as an embellishment if they are said to be cultured, to have an interest in philosophy, and to write songs that are hardly inferior to Sappho's.

Other women poets were believed in later centuries to have flourished in the 'Silver Age'. Edward Phillips in his *Theatrum Poetarum* of 1675, for example, lists 'Lucia: A Roman poetess sirnamed Mima, from her mimic or comical writings, mentioned by Plinie' among his women poets.[75] However, the only woman poet of the Silver Age to emerge from the shadows at all is another Sulpicia, active in the 90s AD. A surprising number of women of the *gens Sulpicia* were remembered for one reason or another;[76] and the existence of two poets suggests that the family may have maintained a tradition of educating their daughters. She is mentioned approvingly by Martial, who specifically memorializes her as a poet of married love:[77]

Let all maidens who want to please only one husband, read Sulpicia. Let all husbands, who would please only one wife, read Sulpicia. She does not describe the fury of Medea, or paint the feast of accursed Thyestes, nor does she believe in the existence of Scylla and Byblis, but she tells of chaste and affectionate loves, games, gratifications, and amusements. He who shall properly estimate her poems, will say that no one is more modest, no one more loving.

We have a couple of clues to her work here: that there was a fashion for mythological poetry among some contemporary poets, but that Sulpicia's own work deals with quotidian life. Two lines of this Sulpicia's poetry survive, in a scholarly note by a grammarian on a rare word (*cadurca*), which tend to confirm this picture. He quotes:

> si me cadurcis restitutis fasciis
> nudam Caleno concubantem proferat.

---

[74] Hemelrijk, *Matrona Docta*, 37, Lucian, 'On Salaried Poets in Great Houses' 36, Loeb Classical Library (Cambridge, Mass.: Harvard University Press, 1921), 470–3.

[75] Phillips, *Theatrum Poetarum*, (London: For Charles Smith, 1675), 244.

[76] In addition to the two poets, two other Sulpicias were sufficiently well remembered to feature in Boccaccio's *Concerning Famous Women*, chs. lxv and lxxxiii (trans. Guarino, 146–7, 186–7).

[77] (*Epigrams* 10. 35). There has been some recent work on Sulpicia II, which discusses this evidence fully: C. U. Merriam, 'The Other Sulpicia', Scholia, *Classical World*, 84.4 (Mar./Apr. 1991), 303–5, Holt Parker, 'Other Remarks on the Other Sulpicia', *Classical World*, 86 (1992–3), 89–95, Judith P. Hallett, 'Martial's Sulpicia and Propertius's Cynthia', *Classical World*, 86 (1992–3), 99–123, and Amy Richlin, 'Sulpicia the Satirist', *Classical World*, 86 (1992–3), 125–39. Older studies of Sulpicia II includes I. Cassaniza, 'Il frammento di Sulpicia, Orazio Ep. 12, e Tertulliano, Apol. 46. 10', *Rivista di filologia e di instruzione classica*, 95 (1967), 295–300, and H. Fuchs, 'Das Klagelied der Sulpicia', in *Discordia Concors: Festgabe für Edgar Bonjour*, 2 vols. (Basel: Helbing & Liechenhahn, 1968), i. 32–47.

'if you restore the *cadurcae* for me, it will allow me to lie naked by Calenus': i.e., as Edward Courtney elegantly puts it, the thongs supporting the mattress have broken, and Sulpicia looks forward to their repair.

Courtney further suggests that Martial in 10. 35 and 38 is probably adapting phrases of Sulpicia's own, since we see in these poems some conventional topics of love poetry (e.g. *felix lectulus*, the lovers' 'happy bed'). He also points out that *Sulpiciae Conquestio* lines 4–6 (a poem I will discuss a little later) suggests that its author knew of poems by Sulpicia not only in iambic trimeters, but also in scazons and hendecasyllables.[78] Furthermore, these two lines may also help us to glimpse something of the social context of women's writing in imperial Rome. Male Latin lyric poets write neither about, nor for, marriageable maidens and chaste matrons.[79] But female Latin lyric poets, if we may judge from such a tiny sample, write *as* fiancées or chaste matrons, in the context of a socially sanctioned relationship with one man. Poetry and propriety were compatible phenomena.

Knowledge of Sulpicia's work is attested in Gaul down to the sixth century (on which, see Chapter 3). She is mentioned in the late fourth century, in Ausonius of Bordeaux's *Cento Nuptialis* line 4, 'Sulpicia's little work is wanton, though her appearance is prim': this confirms the impression that she was a poet of married love, perhaps by Christian standards rather explicitly so.[80] The cultivated sixth-century Gallo-Roman bishop Sidonius Apollinaris mentions her in one of his verse epistles, among several other poets now lost: 'you will not read here Gaetulicus, Marus, Pedo . . . nor the elegant words which the playful Muse of Sulpicia wrote about her Calenus'.[81] There is also evidence for knowledge of her work in a long poem emanating from this Gallo-Roman aristocratic milieu, known as *Sulpiciae Conquestio*.[82] The mention of Calenus in this poem makes it clear that it is not a late antique poem by a third Sulpicia, but written in the persona of Sulpicia II. There is nothing in this poem which can be used to test the gender of its author. However, the interest of *Sulpiciae Conquestio* for this study is threefold. First, it demonstrates that Sulpicia's poetry continued to be read with interest in late antique Gaul, some five centuries after it was written. It also suggests that some of her work was on subjects other than love, that she might be supposed the author of a quite long and ambitious poem; and lastly (one of the many ironies which attend the history of women's writing), it was widely circulated in the Renaissance, and believed to be genuine.

The popularity of Martial in the Middle Ages and Renaissance ensured that Sulpicia's name was not forgotten (oddly, the first Sulpicia, daughter of Servius,

---

[78] Courtney, *The Fragmentary Latin Poets*, 361.

[79] Ovid specifically excludes women of his own class from his audience.

[80] Ausonius, *The Works*, ed. Hugh G. Evelyn White (Cambridge, Mass.: Harvard University Press, 1921), i. 390–1. Another Gallo-Roman writer, Fulgentius, in the preface to his *Mythology* (dependent on Ausonius) also mentions her.

[81] Sidonius, *Letters and Poems*, ed. W. B. Anderson (Cambridge, Mass.: Harvard University Press, 1965), 190–1, *Poems* 9. 261–2.

[82] Conte, *Latin Literature*.

was virtually ignored by Renaissance writers).[83] It was believed, of course, after the discovery of the *Conquestio* at Bobbio in 1493, that a long poem by this second Sulpicia had survived: it was printed at Venice in 1498 and, with Ausonius, at Parma in 1499 and Venice in 1501.[84] Juan Luis Vives in his *Instruction of a Christian Woman* quotes Martial's poem, and continues, interpreting it according to his own lights, 'Sulpitia wyf to Caleno, left behynde her holy preceptes of matrimony, that she had usyd in her lyuinge herself...' (6ᵛ⁻ʳ): as he presents it, the result of Sulpicia's action is moral, and thus supports Vives's precept that the only end of learning is moral action.[85] It is merely unfortunate that the two lines of Sulpicia's verse which survive suggest that her work more closely resembled *The Joy of Sex* than anything Vives would have understood as 'holy preceptes'.

Returning to the first century, we may note that other women poets also formed part of Martial's social circle. He mentions 'that Theophila, Canius, who is betrothed to you, and whose mind overflows with Attic learning... The amorous Sappho would have praised her verses: Theophila is more chaste than Sappho and Sappho had not more genius than Theophila' (7. 69). Martial claims (perhaps the first appearance of a motif which will appear repeatedly in this study) that Theophila's work will live because it is not like a woman's writing, and also that it almost equals that of another forgotten woman, Pantaenis, Canius' favourite. It is also interesting that Martial, whose own writing is often obscene, in complimenting women poets of his acquaintance, declares of both Sulpicia and Theophila that the woman is as talented as Sappho, *but chaster*.[86] Another woman whom he would certainly have known, Claudia Rufina, wife of Aulus Rufus Pudens, whom he frequently mentions, was later believed to have been the author of a book of epigrams and an elegy on her husband's death.[87]

The limited amount of surviving evidence suggests that for women under the Roman Empire, a public reputation for verse seems to have been compatible with chaste and respectable marriage. Both Sulpiciae and Cornificia were virtuous *matronae*, and the more shadowy figures of Theophila, Claudia Rufina, and Polla are similarly those of middle-to upper-middle-class wives, not *demi-mondaines*. We have no evidence for poetry by real-life Cynthias—indeed, very little even for the

---

[83] Skoie, *Reading Sulpicia*, 25–110, discusses the two commentaries: those of Bernadinus Cyllenius, 1475, and Joseph Scaliger, 1577.

[84] On all this, see Mirella Ferrari, 'Le scoperte a Bobbio nel 1493: vicende di codici e fortuna di testi', *Italia medievale e umanistica*, 13 (1970), 139–80.

[85] I quote the English translation, by Richard Hyrde. Foster Watson (ed.), *Vives and the Renaissance Education of Women* (London: Edward Arnold, 1912), 29–136 (p. 50). Anne Moss, 'Ovid in Renaissance France: A Survey of the Latin Editions and Commentaries Printed in France before 1600', *Warburg Institute Surveys*, 8 (1982), 8–16 (p. 9), comments, 'it seems a truism of the period that a writer should not or indeed could not describe human behaviour without implying moral judgment on it'.

[86] This trope resurfaces in the Renaissance: the impure Sappho is compared with the pure Catherine des Roches in 1582 (Ann Rosalind Jones, 'Contentious Readings: Urban Humanism and Gender Differences in *La Puce de Madame Des-Roches* (1582)', *Renaissance Quarterly*, 48.1 (1995), 109–28). See also Joan DeJean, *Fictions of Sappho, 1546–1937* (Chicago: University of Chicago Press, 1989), 105.

[87] Phillips, *Theatrum Poetarum*, 238.

existence of a class of refined and educated *hetaerae* in imperial Rome. On this topic, the elegiac poets cannot be, and must not be, treated as social historians.

What male poets have to tell us, in fact, is that in the world of the early Empire, poetic ability, in literary circles at least, was a positively attractive feature in a wife.[88] One interesting figure in this context is the nameless wife of Varus the tragedian: they worked on the text of Virgil together, and also on tragedies, which he presented as his own in public, though much of the work was hers.[89] Women poets, apparently, tended to marry poets; and Martial posits an ideal of companionate marriage in which a woman who writes herself works together with her husband on his verses, or acts as first critic. He represents the marriage of his friend Lucan with Polla Argentaria as a union of this kind: Martial's 10. 64 shows that she read and criticized work: he asks her not to be critical of his epigrams, since her husband writes them too. Apart from being mentioned by Martial, Polla is mentioned by another contemporary, Statius, in his *Sylvae* (2): this ensured that her name was not forgotten, and gave her a permanent status as a literary footnote. In late antiquity, the sixth-century bishop Sidonius Apollinaris is very explicit about the literary aspect of this marriage, which he upholds as a model to a young contemporary: 'why speak of the poets whom Argentaria Polla, twice yoked in wedlock, presents to us?', and letter 2. 10. 6: 'if you lament that . . . your poetical capacity . . . [is] blunted by the society of ladies, Corinna often helped her Naso complete a verse, and so it was with Lesbia and Catullus, Caesennia and Gaetulicus, Argentaria and Lucan . . . '[90] Polla is thus another 'lost woman poet of antiquity' whose name found its way into the Renaissance litany of heroines. Her name was still known in the early modern period: she is mentioned by Phillips in his *Theatrum Poetarum* of 1675, and the seventeenth-century Dutch poet Constantijn Huygens speaks of his wife (who was not in fact particularly literary) as 'the Polla of my pen'.[91] Thus, the picture which is drawn by male writers of classical and late antiquity, from Ovid to Sidonius Apollinaris, and which is picked up by a number of later commentators, is one of elite women's active participation in literary culture. Hemelrijk observes, 'The poetic ideal of a beautiful and sophisticated woman writing poetry may have contributed to the actual participation of women in the fashion of writing amateur poetry during the empire.'[92] This is true as far as it goes, though the introduction of the word 'amateur', with its implication that women's verse is not to be, and never was, taken seriously, may be importing an anachronistic set of assumptions: it is not immediately obvious why the fact that the first Sulpicia was, or became, a married woman makes her 'amateur' in a way that her coeval Tibullus was not.

---

[88] Pliny records that not the least of the joys of marriage to his third wife Calpurnia was her genuine interest in his literary work (*Epistolae* 4. 19, 2–4).

[89] Servius, *In Vergili Eclogis* 3. 5. 20.

[90] Poem 23, line 166 (ed. Anderson, 194–5), and letter 2. 10. 6 (ed. Anderson, 466–9).

[91] *Theatrum Poetarum*, 240, and Peter Davidson and Adriaan van der Weel, *A Selection of the Poems of Constantijn Huygens* (Amsterdam: Amsterdam University Press 1996), 108.

[92] *Matrona Docta*, 177.

2. Epigraphy as a Source for Early Imperial Women's Verse[1]

Most of what we think of as 'classical Latin literature' was written between 100 BC and AD 100, but the second and third centuries after Christ, though they contribute little to the canon of Latin authors which is studied as literature, saw the consolidation of Roman culture in Western Europe and therefore produced a considerable quantity of surviving writing. Since this study is more concerned with the social history of writing than with literature as conventionally defined, it must accordingly be considered. The value of epigraphy as a source for women's writing in Latin is not confined to this period of time, but it is considered here because it is the only source for women's writing in post-classical Rome. Epigraphy continues, however, to be a significant source of Latin verse by women throughout late antiquity and indeed right down to the seventeenth century. Later epigraphic verse attributable to women will be considered in its chronological context.

Classical epigraphic verse attracted considerable interest in later generations. The earliest collections date from the Carolingian Renaissance (for example, the manuscript which is now Paris, Bibliothèque Nationale de France, Lat. 2832),[2] and the Renaissance proper shows a strong revival of interest in collecting this material, particularly in and after the sixteenth century, as many editions bear witness (some are detailed in the Appendix). It is therefore significant to the history of women writers in Latin that women's Latin verse writing was, in this context, taken completely for granted. Some editors, notably Petrus Burmann and Pithoeus, organize their collections thematically, which has the incidental effect of highlighting the attribution of verses to women: Burmann prints, for example, no less than fifteen sets of verses under the heading 'From wives to husbands',[3] as well as a variety of other verse unhesitatingly attributed to mothers, daughters, sisters, or freedwomen.

Literacy was surprisingly widespread in the cities of the early Roman Empire (though far commoner among men than women).[4] However, it is worth observing that in the Pompeiian brothel in which it was evidently customary to write on the

---

[1] There is an earlier version of this chapter in Laurie Churchill et al. (eds.), *Women Writing Latin*, 3 vols. (London: Routledge, 2002), i. 25–44. I am grateful to the editors for helpful criticism.

[2] Described by Ernst Dümmler, in *Neues Archiv*, 4 (1879), 97–199, and discussed by Mark Handley, 'Epitaphs, Models, and Texts: A Carolingian Collection of Late Antique Inscriptions from Burgundy', in Alison Cooley (ed.), *The Afterlife of Inscriptions* (London: Institute of Classical Studies, 2000), 47–56.

[3] Petrus Burmann, *Anthologia Veterum Latinorum Epigrammatum et Poematum, sive Catalecta Poetarum Latinorum in VI Libros Digesta*, 6 vols. in 2 (Amsterdam: Schouten, 1759), ii. 151–62.

[4] On which see W. V. Harris, *Ancient Literacy* (Cambridge, Mass.: Harvard University Press, 1979), 260–1.

walls, some of the more than 120 graffiti which have been recovered were by the whores and not just by the clients.[5] But this still confined literacy to a small subsection of the population, since even at the height of Rome's power, the population was overwhelmingly rural and almost entirely disenfranchised from the benefits of Roman civilization. 'Roman culture', even in its heyday, was the privilege of a tiny minority, perhaps the richest 2–3 per cent of Roman citizens at any one time.

We may be certain that, though it is beyond the reach of historians, women of classes other than the educated elite had a popular culture of their own which included orally transmitted lyrics of various kinds. John Chrysostom, who was patriarch of Constantinople in the late fourth century, is witness to this for the Greek East.[6]

by nature we take such delight in song that even infants clinging at the breast, if they are crying and perturbed, can be put to sleep by singing. This is how the nurses who carry them in their arms, walking them up and down many times and singing them childish ditties, make their eyelids close... Again, women who are weaving, or disentangling the threads on their spindles, often sing: sometimes each of them sings for herself, at other times they all harmonise a melody together.

The same must surely have been the case in the Latin-speaking West, but in antiquity such things were written down only by the purest chance, if they happened to attract the interest of a learned man. The only possible evidence we have for writings which form part of popular culture is preserved epigraphically: incised words preserved as graffiti, curse-tablets, and funerary inscriptions. Whether scratched on tiles or bits of lead, carved on stones, or painted on walls (Pompeii is the principal site where painted material survives), they turn up as part of the archaeological record, and give us random insights into less formal kinds of literacy, including a respectable number of poems attributed to women which were composed in the second and third centuries.

Relatively few Latin graffiti are in verse, and even less of what there is can be assigned to a woman. But a very attractive fragmentary graffito from Pompeii (dating, therefore, to before AD 79) may be of female authorship:[7]

> Amoris ignes si sentires mulio,
> Magi properares, ut videres Venerem
> Diligo iuvenem venustum, rogo, punge, iamus
> Bibisti; iamus, prende lora et excute,
> Pompeios defer, ubi dulcis est amor.
> Meus es...

> If you ever felt the fires of love, mule-driver,
> you would be in more of a hurry to see Venus.

---

[5] James J. Franklin, 'Literacy and the Parietal Inscriptions of Pompeii', in Mary Beard (ed.), *Literacy in the Roman World* (Ann Arbor: University of Michigan Press, 1991), 77–98 (p. 97). See also Elizabeth Woeckner, 'Women's Graffiti from Pompeii', in Churchill et al. (eds.), *Women Writing Latin*, i. 67–84.

[6] John Chrysostom, *Sermon on the Psalms*, PG lv, cols. 156–7.

[7] *CLE*, no. 44, i. 22–3.

I'm fond of a lovely young man; Please, lay it on, let's go
—you've been drinking! Let's go—take the reins and shake them.
—Drive to Pompeii, where love is sweet! You are mine...

Male objects of male lust were usually *pueri*: the object of affection here is an *iuvenis*, a bit too far towards adulthood for conventional Roman patterns of homoerotic desire (though of course people do not always constrain their desire within conventional patterns).[8] The writer originally wrote *puerum* in line 3, deleted it, and wrote *iuvenem* above: one possible reading of this is that the author was sensitive to the homoerotic implications of *puer*, and wished to avoid them, another is simply that it makes a better metrical line.

A particularly problematic category of epigraphic evidence for women's writing in antiquity is the curse-tablet: curses written on sheet lead, and devoted to some appropriate deity. Here, since aggrieved individuals seeking redress in this fashion were mostly uneducated folk of modest means, authorship is impossible to establish: such people might either write a curse themselves if they felt able, or go to a magician and describe what they wanted. Curiously, curse-tablets preponderantly reveal men in pursuit of women, though the literary sources imply that it is women who formed the bulk of the sorcerers' clientele.[9] One possibility is worth including here, since it was at the least instigated by a woman, and although not metrical, it is powerfully patterned. It is a tiny glimpse into the world of the submerged 95 per cent of the Empire's inhabitants:[10]

side A	*side B*
Nomina data	Silonia
mandata	Surum Caenum
ligata	Secundum
ad inferos	ille te
ad illos	sponsus pro[vo]cat
per vim conruant.	eum amo.

This *defixio* is from Kreuznach in Germany (Roman Crucinacum). It is one of a number of surviving Latin curses set by women, unusual because of its strongly rhythmical character.[11] Since the first half sets the spell on those whose names are given, we should probably read 'Silonia' as the object (with the 'm' that marks the

---

[8] A relationship between a man and a *iuvenis* was socially acceptable only if the latter was of non-free status. See Paul Veyne, 'Homosexuality in Ancient Rome', in Philippe Ariès and André Béjin, *Western Sexuality: Practice and Precept in Past and Present Times*, trans. A. Forster (Oxford: Basil Blackwell, 1982), 26–35 (p. 30).

[9] John D. Gager, *Curse Tablets and Binding Spells from the Ancient World* (Oxford: Oxford University Press, 1992), 244. See also Lindsay Watson, *Arae: The Curse Poetry of Antiquity* (Leeds: Francis Cairns, 1991).

[10] Augustus Audollent (ed.), *Defixionum Tabellae Quotquot Innotuerunt tam in Graecis Orienti quam in Totius Occidentalis Partibus Praeter Atticas in Corpore Inscriptionum Atticas Editas* (Paris: Albert Fontemoing, 1904), no. 100, p. 153.

[11] Others may be found ibid. no. 131, p. 187, no. 220, p. 294.

accusative case accidentally omitted), though it may be the name of the setter. We may conjecturally translate: 'The names given, consigned, bound: to the infernal gods. May they go crashing down violently to them. Silonia [*nominative or vocative*]; Surus Caenus Secundus [*accusative*]: That man, though he is married, is propositioning you. I love him.' Syntax is disintegrated into a series of fragmentary ejaculations.

The archaeological record has also produced a fair number of inscribed verses from tombs or memorial inscriptions, which claim to be the work of the wife, daughter, mother, or sister of the deceased person who is being commemorated.[12] Female authorship of epigraphic poetry of course has to be argued, since it is widely assumed that the fact that fewer women were literate means that they *never* wrote inscriptions, but this is an assumption in need of examination. The argument for women's participation in epigraphic poetry must ultimately be based on probability. But we have no need to dismiss the possibility that at least some of the inscriptions attributed to women are what they appear to be. A bereaved individual who wished to memorialize his or her loved ones must surely have gone to a workshop, as many people still do, to commission a stone from a monumental mason, constrained by considerations such as budget, fashion, propriety, personal taste, and availability. No literary sources shed light on the question of whether such a person gave the workman a wax tablet or a piece of papyrus on which she had written the words she wished to have carved, or whether these were necessarily always commissioned from penny-a-line poets or chosen from a set of samples kept by the mason. Lattimore notes,

it seems, on the face of it, highly likely that the client who wanted a poem or phrase could dictate one which he had seen somewhere, or one which he had composed himself, or else fall back on the stonecutter for suggestions.[13]

But it should perhaps be observed that there is only a small number of epitaphs in which a woman speaks either for the deceased, or for herself. I have collected epitaphs purporting to be by women from a variety of sources.[14] The actual proportion of epitaphs in a woman's voice among the total corpus that survives can be judged from the fact that, in the convenient collection of Bücheler, *Carmina Latina Epigraphica*, only about 2 per cent of the poems are cast in the form of a woman commemorating her dead. Most epigraphic poems, for obvious reasons, are

[12] See Brent D. Shaw, 'Latin Funerary Epigraphy and Family Life in the Later Roman Empire', *Historia*, 33 (1984), 457–97.

[13] Richmond Lattimore, *Themes in Greek and Latin Epitaphs* (Urbana: University of Illinois Press, 1962), 19.

[14] In addition to the ones I discuss here, others include Aurelia Eusebia (*CLE*, ii, no. 1180, p. 550), Clodia Africana (*CLE*, i, no. 502, pp. 240–1), Cornelia Galla (*CLE*, i, no. 480, p. 228), Fuficia Agra (*CLE*, ii, no. 1204, p. 564), Iventa Hilara (*CLE*, i, no. 73, p. 38), Julia Parthenope (*CLE*, i, no. 565, pp. 272–3), Maria Malchis (*CLE*, i, no. 101, p. 56), Phile (*CLE*, ii, no. 1089, p. 499), Plotia Capitolina (*CLE*, ii, no. 1150, p. 533), Quarta (*CLE*, ii, no. 1156, p. 535), Servilia (*CLE*, ii, no. 1230, p. 576), Valeria Ursilla (*CLE*, ii, no. 1253, p. 589), Vettia Prima (*CLE*, ii, no. 1213, pp. 568–9). Most of these are for children, some for husbands.

created for (if not necessarily by) people who can afford to commission tomb-stones. Clearly, these people also form the subsection of the community which is prosperous enough for literacy to be a possibility. Harris is certainly correct in suggesting that a much smaller proportion of women were literate in antiquity than men, but that does not in itself necessarily cast doubt on the inscriptions which we have, since they represent such a minute proportion of the total surviving.[15]

The epitaphs which survive from antiquity vary enormously in quality. A stone in North Africa has an inscription clearly from a model-book, which simply says: 'Hic iacet corpus pueri nominandi' ('Here lies the body of a boy named'), suggest-ing that, pathetically, the client who commissioned it was illiterate, and did not realize the name needed to be supplied.[16] Edward Courtney prints a clear case of the use of a professionally composed epitaph on a stone erected by grieving women—clear, because the same poem is also used on another stone.[17] But even without the evidence of the second copy, it would have been a fair deduction, firstly on the basis of probability, because the dedicatee was only an infantryman, so his mother and sister were probably not very high up the Roman social pyramid, but secondly because the verse is wholly impersonal: we learn nothing of this 20-year-old, except that his mother and his sister cared about him: the poem is to, and about, generic Man. Another poem, on another monument raised by a mother for her son, may be by Raielia Secundina herself or by someone else, but in either case it is composed of commonplaces:

Respice praeteriens, oro, titulumque dolebis,
Quam praemature nimium sim mortis adeptus.
Triginta annorum rapta est mihi lux gratissima vitae
Et de gente mea solus sine parvolo vixi.
Quem mater miserum flevit, quod pietatis honore relicta est.
Q. Luccunio Vero Raielia Secundina mater filio piissime fecit

Look at this inscription, wayfarer, I pray, and you will lament,
How very prematurely I was seized by death.
The most lovely light of a life of thirty years was snatched from me
And alone of my family, I lived out my life childless,
My mother bewails poor me, because she has been left destitute of the honour of [filial] devotion.
Raielia Secundina, a mother, most devotedly made this for her son Q. Luccunius Verus

However sincerely she mourned, the unfortunate Raielia did so with an uninspired collection of funerary clichés: enlisting the sympathy of the passing reader for a son 'snatched by premature death' and the pathos of childlessness. These are standard

---

[15] Some additional, perhaps supporting, light is cast on this by Janet Huskinson, 'Women and Learning', in Richard Miles (ed.), *Constructing Identities in Late Antiquity* (London: Routledge, 1999), 190–213. She points out that scrolls or scroll-boxes appeared on sarcophagi intended for both men and women.

[16] Handley, 'Epitaphs, Models, and Texts', 48.

[17] Edward Courtney, *Musa Lapidaria* (Atlanta: Scholars Press, 1995), no. 199, pp. 186–7.

motifs, though even so, there are more details about the individual (his age, his childlessness) than are to be found in the poem cited by Courtney.[18]

What is interesting, however, about the epitaphs raised by women is that a surprising number of them are highly idiosyncratic. One which is of special interest for the level of concentrated emotion which it expresses runs as follows:[19]

> V. Salvidiena Q. L. Hilara
> Salvidienae Faustillae
> Deliciae suae
> eruditate omnibus artibus
> reliquisti mammam tuam
> gementem plangentem plorantem.
> > vixit an. xv
> mensib. iii, dieb. xi, hor. vii
> Virginem eripuit Fatus malus
> Destituisti Vitilla mea
> miseram mammam tuam.

> V. Salvidiena Hilara,[20] freed slavegirl of Quintus
> > to Salvidiena Faustilla,
> > her darling,
> educated in all the arts.
> You have left your mamma
> groaning, wailing, weeping.
> > She lived for fifteen years, three months,
> > eleven days, and seven hours.
> An evil Fate tore her away, a virgin.
> My Vitilla, you have left your mamma miserable.

Formulaic expressions such as 'may the earth lie light on you', 'in eternal sleep', 'farewell', are notably absent in this inscription. The sad specificity of years, months, days, and even hours bespeaks a culture in which horoscopes were made, so the hour of birth was precisely recorded:[21] but here it adds to the obsessive quality of the inscription. Latin epitaphs commonly give the age of the deceased in years, and quite frequently give months and days,[22] but hours are unusual. Many Latin epitaphs see a special pathos in the virgin stolen by death;[23] but few lay such stress on the emotional state of the bereaved: consider the emphatic line, 'gementem plangentem plorantem'. The upbraiding of the dead

---

[18] Lattimore, *Themes*.

[19] *CIL* notes, 'found outside the Collatine gate (in Rome), in a vineyard', thus metropolitan in origin.

[20] Initial 'v' in a funerary inscription may stand for *viva*: 'in life' (compare *CLE*, nos. 959, 1030, ii. 441, 474): my thanks to Dr Janet Fairweather for this observation. However, the fact that the daughter is later addressed as 'Vitilla' suggests this is a first name.

[21] Lattimore, *Themes*, 16: 'In Latin inscriptions, the number of hours in the unfinished day is frequently stated, a practice which Cumont...attributes to belief in astrology.'

[22] For example, Julia Parthenope states that her daughter Lucina lived for 27 years, 10 months, and 13 days.

[23] See Lattimore, *Themes*, 192–94, and also *Aeneid* 6. 305–7.

by the living is a theme which has its parallels, particularly in the case of spouses. Dronke quotes two: Seppia Justina calls her husband 'amanti mendax', false to the woman who loves him, because he has left her, while an anonymous Christian calls her husband 'improbus', villain;[24] but the emphatic use of the word *mamma* (twice) is remarkable. *Mamma* is a baby's word, and appears in only a handful of inscriptions (*mater* is far more usual): all the other examples given in the *Thesaurus Linguae Latinae* are inscribed by affectionate offspring—including the psychologically revealing 'patri et mammae'.[25] This is the only epitaph in which a speaker refers to *herself* as 'mamma'. The epitaph is normally very much a public genre, but this particular example locates itself insistently in the private world of inconsolable personal grief. Another highly idiosyncratic poem is the work of a mother, Clodia Africana, whose 12-year-old son died during the January festivities, when he had gone to the temple with his mother and sister; like Salvidiena Hilara's inscription, its strangeness authenticates it: both women are insistent on details, hopelessly trying to ensure that it is their own beloved child who is remembered. Another bitter poem of maternal bereavement, from a woman, Papiria Tertia of Ferrara, who had outlived the immediate agony of loss, runs:

> Cernis, ut orba meis, hospes, monumenta locavi
> et tristis senior natos miseranda requiro.
> Exemplis referenda mea est deserta senectus
> ut steriles vere possint gaudere maritae.

> Stranger, you see how, a woman bereft of my own [dear ones],
>   I had monuments erected
> and sad, elderly, pitiable, I miss my children.
> My isolated old age should be added to the exemplary proofs
> that barren wives may count themselves truly happy!

In general, it is noticeable that many of the epitaphs which speak in a woman's voice are more immediate, more personal, and more directly concerned with the relationship between the living and the dead than those which speak with the voices of men (though of course, this raises in an acute form the question of whether the Romans were already conscious of a style of writing proper to a female voice, an *écriture féminine*).[26] An example of this is the poem on the monument of Varius Frontonianus, with its strong focus not on the dead man, but on the quality of his wife's tender recollection of him.

> Hic situs est Varius cognomine Frontonianus,
> quem coniunx lepida posuit Cornelia Galla
> Dulcia restituens veteris solacia vitae

---

[24] *WWMA*, 24, H. Geist and G. Pföhl (eds.), *Römische Grabinschriften*, 2nd edn. (Munich: Ernsk Heimeran Verlag, 1976), 35. Lattimore, *Themes*, 181, and see ibid. 198–9. Julia Marulla is addressed on her stone as 'virgo deceptrix' by her anguished parents (Geist and Pföhl (eds.), *Römische Grabinschriften*, 44).

[25] *Thesaurus Linguae Latinae*, s.v. 'mamma': *CIL*, vi. 10016; ix. 5228; vi. 38891, vi. 15585 (quoted).

[26] Courtney, *Musa Lapidaria*, is a good recent collection with translations.

marmoreos voltus statuit, oculos animumque
longius ut kara posset saturare figura.
Hoc solamen erit visus. Nam pignus amoris
pectore contegitur memori dulcedine mentis
nec poterit facili labsum oblivione perire
set dum vita manet, toto est in corde maritus.

Here lies Varius, surnamed Frontonianus
whom his charming wife, Cornelia Galla, laid to rest.
In restitution of the sweet consolations of her former life,
she set up marble effigies, so that she could sate
her eyes and her mind a while longer with his beloved appearance.
This is the consolation of seeing. For the pledge of love
is concealed in the breast by the sweetness of a remembering mind,
nor will it be possible for it to perish, let slip by fickle forgetfulness;
but while life remains, her husband is in her whole heart.

These ten lines survive entire, but due to the state of the stone, we have only the first word at the beginning of subsequent lines: the complete poem would have been twenty lines long. The first words suggest a wistful trajectory for the second half of the poem; 'in sweet ...', 'happy', 'but fate ...', 'snatched ...' 'it was not permitted ...'

Archaeology can also give some insight into the activities of named high-ranking women: in the previous chapter, I suggested that the oeuvre of Sulpicia could be supplemented by an inscribed poem. Julia Balbilla, for example, was a poetess flourishing in the reign of Hadrian. She visited Egypt in AD 130 as part of the entourage accompanying the Emperor Hadrian and his wife Sabina. She was of aristocratic birth. Her grandfather on her father's side had been a king (Antiochus IV of Commagene), while her maternal grandfather may have been Tiberius Claudius Balbillus, a notable astrologer who served as prefect of Egypt from AD 55 to 59 AD. Five poems of hers were carved on the legs of the Colossus of Memnon—they are in Greek, a reminder of the fact that many cultivated Roman writers of the first and second centuries preferred to use that language.[27] There is a single line of Latin prose appended: 'Ego Julia Balbilla Memnonem audivi': 'I, Julia Balbilla, heard Memnon', referring to the mysterious noise the statue was famous for emitting at dawn. A Latin iambic trimeter written on a wall in Rome may possibly represent an otherwise lost Latin oeuvre: 'Balbilla votum debitum reddo tibi': 'Balbilla pays you what she vowed.'[28]

Another epigraphic poem forms an obvious link with the poetry of Julia Balbilla, already mentioned, since it was preserved by being carved on an Egyptian monument and was the work of an aristocratic Roman visitor.

Vidi pyramidas sine te, dulcissime frater,
et tibi quod potui, lacrimas hic maesta profudi

---

[27] A. and E. Bernand, (eds.), *Inscriptions Grecques et Latines de Colosse de Memnon*, (Paris: Le Caire, 1960), 28–31. One of the poems is translated by Emily A. Hemelrijk, *Matrona Docta* (London: Routledge, 1999), 167: see her discussion of Julia Balbilla, pp. 164–70.

[28] *CLE*, i, no. 847, p. 393.

> et nostri memorem luctus hanc sculpo querelam:
> sic nomen Decimi Gentiani pyramida alta
> pontificis comitis tuis, Traiane, triumphis
> lustraque sex intra censoris consulis exstet.

> I have seen the pyramids without you, most sweet brother,
> and I have done what I could for you.
> Grieving, I have poured out my tears here,
> and I am carving this lament, in commemoration of our grief.
> Thus let the name of Decimus Gentianus,
> pontiff, sharer in your triumph, O Trajan,
> censor and consul within the space of six lustra [thirty years],
> stand out on the high pyramid.

As the poem itself proclaims, the grieving sister of Decimus [Terentius] Gentianus wrote a poem in his memory, and had it carved on the pyramid at Memphis in Egypt in AD 106. Its author, who can be conveniently referred to as Terentia since this will certainly have formed part of her name, seems to have been familiar with Horace: her third line evokes *Odes* 3. 2. 50, 'i secundo | Omine et nostri memorem sepulcro | Scalpe querellam.' The original carving has succumbed to the ravages of time, but fortunately it was copied twice in the late Middle Ages, once by a Lüneburg nobleman, Otto von Neuhaus, who in 1336 undertook a pilgrimage to the Holy Land (this is the version printed by Mommsen in *Corpus Inscriptionum Latinorum*) and a second time by Felix Fabri, the preacher-monk of Ulm, who twice made the same pilgrimage, in 1480 and 1483, by which time the monument had suffered considerable attrition. The sister's own name was probably originally given, but was not recorded by either Otto von Neuhaus or Fabri.

There seems no obvious reason to doubt that this poem in hexameters is by the sister of Decimus Gentianus. It should by now be clear that many upper-class girls were capable of such a composition, and this was a very aristocratic family. We are probably in a position to identify its subject. One Terentius Gentianus, who had campaigned with Trajan in the Dacian wars, appears in a stone at Sarmizegetusa with a whole list of honours, including being *censitor* of Macedonia, consul, and pontiff.[29] Degrassi lists [D.] Terentius Gentianus as suffect consul in 116.[30] Our Decimus Gentianus, whose honours are given as including campaigning with Trajan, consulship, the pontificate, and censorship, is most probably the same man: Decimus must then be his first name. The fact that Terentia was visiting Egypt is a testimony to her extremely high status: an expedition which involved ladies was by definition complicated and costly.[31] Tacitus, a writer almost

---

[29] *CIL*, iii. 1463, 'Terentio Gentiano, trib. militum, quaestori trib. pl. pr. leg. Aug. consuli pontif. cens. provinc. Maced. colonia Ulpia Traian. Aug. Dac. Sarmazegetusa patrono.'

[30] Attilio Degrassi, *I fasti consolari dell' impero Romano*, Sussidi eruditi 3, (Rome: Edizioni di storia e letteratura, 1952), 34: L. Fundanius and Lamia Aelianus are given as principal consuls for the year, but three other sets are listed for 116.

[31] A. J. Marshall, 'Roman Women and the Provinces', *Ancient Society*, 6 (1975), 109–27 (p. 121): in the 1st century AD, 'proconsuls, legates, procurators and even quaestors now took their wives and

contemporary with Gentiana, shows that there was considerable hostility towards travel by the womenfolk of Roman officials for this reason.[32]

This poem by Terentius Gentianus' sister is very much public verse. It marks personal loss, and speaks to the common experience of finding a longed-for adventure meaningless without the appropriate person by one's side, yet it seems primarily concerned to inscribe Terentius Gentianus, his status, his relationship with Trajan; an assertion of family, not merely of private emotion within that family. Expressions of status and family pride are frequent, though not inevitable, aspects of epigraphic poetry.

daughters with them as a regular practice'. Tourism becomes increasingly part of the Christian Roman world from the 4th century: see E. D. Hunt, *Holy Land Pilgrimage* (Oxford: Clarendon Press, 1982).

[32] Tacitus, *Annales* 3. 33.

3. Women and Latin Poetry in Late Antiquity

One of the crucial differences between the culture of late antiquity and that of classical Rome is the introduction of Christianity to the Roman world. The effects on the opportunities open to cultivated women were not straightforward. Women had had a public part in some pagan cult observances, and some cults were for women only: the personal and social satisfaction which could be got from this is evidenced by Paulina, the probable author of a poem on her husband Praetextatus which will be discussed later in this chapter. Some of the women writers of this period were pagans, some Christians. But it is notable that in both groups religion had assumed a new importance: there is an otherworldly turn in late antique culture of which the rise of Christianity seems to be a symptom rather than a cause.[1] Another factor which is relevant to the activities of elite women is that their greatly increased involvement in public benefaction allowed the daughters of wealthy families to participate much more fully in the public life of their cities than their ancestresses had done, which gave them more public visibility and personal status. Scholarship has focused on the Eastern Empire (which is much better evidenced), but the same is probably true in the West.[2]

Though paganism evidently had its satisfactions for some late Roman women, Christianity also had a great deal to offer them, which is evidenced by the often-remarked fact that women were conspicuous among the ranks of early converts, even during the period when conversion carried a risk of martyrdom.[3] But, although they played a prominent role in the first three centuries of Christianity, once Christianity became the official religion of the Roman Empire under Constantine the Great, women were gradually marginalized by an increasingly

---

[1] See Ramsay MacMullen, *Paganism in the Roman Empire* (New Haven: Yale University Press, 1981), esp. 116–17, and *Christianising the Roman Empire, AD 100–400* (New Haven: Yale University Press, 1984), 39.

[2] Riet van Bremen, *The Limits of Participation: Women and Civic Life in the Greek East in the Hellenistic and Roman Periods* (Amsterdam: Gieben, 1996); Onno van Nijf, 'Inscriptions and Civic Memory in the Roman East', in Alison Cooley (ed.), *The Afterlife of Inscriptions* (London: Institute of Classical Studies, 2000), 21–36 (p. 21).

[3] A. Harnack, *The Mission and Expansion of Christianity in the First Three Centuries*, trans. James Moffatt, Theological Translation Library 19–20, 2 vols. (London: Williams & Norgate, 1904–5), ii. 139. In Eusebius' horrific account of the martyrs of Lyon, it is a woman, Blandina, who is at the centre of his narrative. Eusebius, *Ecclesiastical History* 5. 1. 41 (trans. G. A. Williamson (Harmondsworth: Penguin, 1989), 145). A very important work which at least redacts a Christian woman's words is C. van Beek (ed.), *Passio SS. Perpetuae et Felicitatis* (Nijmegen: Dekker & van de Vegt, 1936) (also in *PL* iii, cols. 13–176, and Judith Lynn Sebesta, 'Vibia Perpetua: Mystic and Martyr', in Laurie Churchill et al. (eds.), *Women Writing Latin* (New York: Routledge, 2002), i. 103–30). There is an important reassessment of women in the early Church by Averil Cameron, 'Virginity as Metaphor: Women and the Rhetoric of Early Christianity', in Cameron (ed.), *History as Text* (London: Duckworth, 1989), 184–205.

elaborate official hierarchy of priests and bishops, while the actual ministry of women was defined as heretical.[4] Perhaps as a result, we have very little Christian women's writing from the early centuries.[5] One of the earliest Christian women's poems is an epigraphic verse of the kind discussed in the previous chapter, beautifully translated by Dronke:[6]

> Ah, dearest husband, who leave me, wretched, alone!
> Without you, what shall I hold sweet, what shall I believe lovable?
> For whom do I cling on to life and not follow you, villain, into death?
> Let me go with you, hand in hand,
> United to you in the grave that I too much desire!
> Your courtesy, respect and loyalty,
> And being gentle, did not help you—you were doomed to die.
> Only this—if any awareness outlives our bodies—
> I'll let you have my pledge of love forever:
> Husband, I'll keep your bed inviolate.

What is notably absent in this poem is any sense that she expects to 'await the resurrection of the body and the life everlasting', to quote words from the Creed which she must have said every time she went to church. Another very early Christian poem, that of Constantia, wife of Anastasius, whose epitaph she composed in the year 355, is similar in this respect.

> A   X   Ω
> Tristis Anastasio Constantia carmina scribit
> coniunx, qui lucem tenebris mutavit amaris.
> Vita quater denis et quinque annis fuit, eheu
> quam cito praereptus dilectae uxoris amori,
> fletus duodecumum cum Janus sumeret ortum,
> conditus Arbitio consul cum duceret annum.
>   in nomine Dei

> Christ: Alpha and Omega
> Constantia, his sad wedded wife, is writing verses for Anastasius,
> Who has exchanged the light for the bitter shades.
> His life was confined to forty-five years.
> Alas! How swiftly he was snatched from the love of his beloved wife,
> Lamented, while Janus was taking hold of the twelfth rising,
> Buried when Arbieto was leading the year as consul.

---

[4] See Ben Witherington III, *Women in the Earliest Churches* (Cambridge: Cambridge University Press, 1988), for a historically sensitive account of women's gradual exclusion from the developing hierarchy. St Paul himself had women co-workers (pp. 102–27). Ruth Hopkins makes a still greater claim in her *Priscilla, Author of the Epistle to the Hebrews* (New York: Exposition Press, 1969), but such argument can only be based on supposition.

[5] Patricia Wilson-Kastner, *A Lost Tradition* (Washington: University Press of America, 1981), surveys much of the evidence, though she does not explore epigraphic verse. She notes, p. xii, that Tertullian praised 'the holy prophetess Prisca'.

[6] *WWMA*, 24. It is also commented on by Richmond Lattimore, *Themes in Greek and Latin Epitaphs* (Urbana: University of Illinois Press, 1962), 61.

They were a Christian couple, as their names tell us, confirmed by the fact that the inscription was decorated with the Christian symbols of a Chi, for Christ, with alpha and omega, though the content of the epitaph appears entirely pagan. The *amarae tenebrae*, bitter shades, belong to the classical underworld, not to Christian paradise. The poem makes no mention either of Christian consolation or the hope of resurrection which its subject's name ('resurrection' in Greek is *anastasis*) holds forth. In both these cases, the verses may reflect a conversion that was skin-deep, unable to survive the impact of personal trauma, or on the other hand, they may simply reflect the extraordinary conservatism of classical poetic tropes, which remained pagan even after society had been completely Christianized (hence the gods, nymphs, and shepherds of Renaissance and neoclassical verse). It may be that their religion had no comfort to offer these grieving women, or it may be that both are reaching for 'appropriate' words and ideas, and there is simply no room for their Christianity within the well-established conventions of funerary poetry as a genre. On the other hand, the poem for the grave of Pope Damasus which may be the work of his sister Martha, though it is not far removed in time from Constantia's poem, is triumphant in its assurance of resurrection and reunion.[7]

In the declining years of the Empire, literacy continued to flourish in the milieux which had traditionally cultivated such skills. By the fourth century learning was seen as appropriate for elite women, perhaps to a greater extent than in classical Rome, which may be connected with their more public position.[8] Many of the women of the great aristocratic families of Rome were noted for their learning, notably a number of Christian aristocrats, friends of St Jerome (*c*.342–420), who went so far in their enthusiasm for Christian scholarship as to learn Hebrew.[9] We might also bear in mind that one of Jerome's friends, Marcella (325–410), whom he called the foremost student of Scripture in Rome after himself, is said to have credited her writings to male authorities so as not to *appear* to be preaching, which raises the interesting possibility that some women's writing from late antiquity survives in a concealed form.[10]

---

[7] Either this poem is by Damasus, displaying a profound emotional commmitment towards being reunited with his sister, or by Martha, about her brother. The family was Spanish: Damasus (born *c*.304) was pope 366–384. He was himself a noted poet. The *Liber Pontificalis*, begun in the 6th century, notes that he was buried 'close to his mother and sister'. Since the *Liber Pontificalis* was composed at a distance of 200 years from the death of Damasus, the implication that his sister predeceased him is not necessarily based on knowledge. That the arrangement bespeaks sibling closeness is beyond doubt; and Damasus' own poetic ability renders it more, not less, likely that his sister was sufficiently educated to compose verses. See *The Book of Pontiffs (Liber Pontificalis)*, trans. Raymond Davis (Liverpool: Liverpool University Press, 1989), 29–30.

[8] Janet Huskinson, 'Women and Learning', in Richard Miles (ed.), *Constructing Identities in Late Antiquity* (London: Routledge, 1999), has identified clearly Christian sarcophagi showing women reading, or with literary accessories such as scrolls or scroll-boxes.

[9] Elizabeth A. Clark, *Jerome, Chrysostom and Friends* (New York: Edwin Mellen Press, 1979). One letter from Paula and Eustochium to Marcella survives among his letters: *Epistolae*, ed. I. Hilberg, CSEL 54–6 (Vienna: F. Tempsky; Leipzig: G. Freytag, 1910, 1912, 1918), i, no. 46. See also Christa Krumeich, *Hieronymus und die christlichen Feminae Clarissimae* (Bonn: Habelt, 1993).

[10] Jerome, *Epistolae* 127. 9–10, *PL* xxii, cols. 1091–2.

The context for such learning is entirely upper-class, but, within its very restricted social range, not confined to the boys of the family, since by the fourth century the upper classes seem to have developed a positive preference for educated wives and daughters. Even Augustine, who was sceptical of the possibility of friendship with women, thought that the ideal bride should be 'literary, or at least, easily teachable by her husband',[11] and decreed that his mother Monica 'should not be kept from discussing philosophy because of her gender'.[12] In the Christian Greek world, Clement of Alexandria argued that the angels gave learning as a dowry to women—rather than men—because of their natural curiosity and their love of adornment which led them to want to ornament their minds as well as their bodies,[13] and the alchemist Zosimus of Panopolis dedicated his twenty-eight-book treatise to his sister Theosebeia.[14]

Jerome himself has left some detailed advice for an aristocratic young mother, Laeta, on educating her baby daughter: Laeta is to get wooden or ivory letters made for the child to play with, and gradually encourage her to learn to write. She should have a proper tutor from early youth, a learned man, and not some silly woman, so that she will not have to unlearn anything later; she should learn Greek and cultivated Latin. He offers an extensive reading list of Christian literature for the girl to work on in due course.[15] Jerome's circle was particularly serious-minded, but not unique in its stress on learning: educated women continued to flourish in other fifth-century milieux. Ennodius, Bishop of Pavia (*c*.473–521), speaks of a certain 'domna Barbara, Romani flos genii' (lady Barbara, the flower of Roman genius), and of Stephania, 'the most splendid light of the Catholic church'—a phrase which suggests that, whether by example or otherwise, she was thought of as a teacher.[16] Another woman, Eunomia, is highly praised in two poems in a Paris manuscript.[17]

At the very top of society, we find that the imperial women of late antiquity were highly cultivated. A Latin poem is attributed to Constantina, daughter of the Emperor Constantine and wife of first Hannibalinus, then Gallus. She was the founder of a church dedicated to the Roman martyr St Agnes on the Via Nomentana, in Rome, the decorations of which include a fourteen-line poem in her voice: it begins 'I, Constantina, dedicated to Christ, venerating God ... have

---

[11] Augustine, *Soliloquiae* 1. 10 (17), *PL* xxxii, col. 878.

[12] Augustine, *De Ordine* 1. 11, *PL* xxxii, col. 992.

[13] This was picked up by a 17th-century French writer, Pierre Le Moyne, *Les Peintures morales, où les passions sont représentées par tableaux*, 2 vols. (Paris: S. Cramoisy, 1640–3), i. 202–3.

[14] *PLRE* i. 908, 994.

[15] *Ad Laetam de Institutione Filiae, Epistolae* 107, ed. Hilberg, ii. 290–305.

[16] Ennodius, 'Ambrosio et Beato', in *Ennodii Opera*, CSEL VI (Vienna: C. Gerold, 1882), 401–10 (p. 409). S. A. H. Kessell, *Magnus Felix Ennodius: A Gentleman of the Church* (Ann Arbor: University of Michigan Press, 2000), 142–4: she was the sister of Faustus Niger, and Ennodius chides her gently for writing about religious matters in too sophisticated a style (he seems to share Augustine's views on matching style to subject—see Erich Auerbach, *Literary Language and its Public in Late Latin Antiquity and in the Middle Ages*, trans. Ralph Mannheim (Princeton: Princeton University Press, 1965), 48–52).

[17] 'The Praise of Lady Eunomia, a Holy Virgin', and 'Another Laudation of Eunomia', in Alexander Reise (ed.), *Anthologia Latina* (Leipzig: Teubner, 1868), 233–4.

dedicated this church to the victorious virgin Agnes.' Constantine was not of very exalted origins; his father was a self-made general, his mother apparently a barmaid,[18] but that is no reason to suppose that once he had risen in the world, he would have failed to educate his daughter.[19] His half-brother's wife, mother of the future Emperor Julian, had been thoroughly instructed in Homer and Hesiod (which may suggest that Constantina would probably have been more fluent in Greek than in Latin).[20] There is no way of judging whether the poem was written by Constantina, or on her behalf; either seems equally possible. Some subsequent empresses were highly cultivated, though the only certain poet, the Augusta Eudocia (*c*.400–460, wife of Theodosius II), wrote in Greek.[21] The Augusta Pulcheria was praised for her unusual skill in writing and speaking both the Empire's languages.[22] There is a number of letters from the Theodosian Augustae Galla Placidia, Eudoxia, and Eucheria among the letters of Pope Leo I (pope 440–61),[23] a letter from the Augusta Anastasia to the sixth-century Pope Hormisdas, and another from the Visigothic Queen Brunhild to the wife of the Emperor Maurice (suggesting that sixth-century Byzantine Augustae continued to be taught Latin for the purpose of diplomatic correspondence).[24]

The same is true of Roman Gaul as of Italy. Poetry—or at least verse—was cultivated among the aristocracy.[25] The aristocratic Gallic writer Ausonius writes in encouragement to soothe the childish fears of a grandson embarking on his education, 'your father *and mother* went through all this in their day, and have lived to soothe my peaceful and serene old age'.[26] Women in Roman Gaul seem to have had a positive connection with education: Ausonius himself was brought up by his maternal grandmother and aunts (who included the interesting figure of his aunt

[18] See Ramsay MacMullen, *Constantine* (London: Croom Helm, 1969), 21.

[19] MacMullen, ibid. 216, notes that Constantine took great pains with the education of his sons, so he may have done the same for Constantina, who was also an instrument of his dynastic ambitions.

[20] Ammianus Marcellinus, *Histories* 22. 9, confirmed by Julian, 'Misopogon', *The Works of Julian*, trans. Wilmer Cave Wright (Cambridge, Mass.: Harvard University Press, 1921–3), ii. 461.

[21] For a translation of some of her work see Josephine Balmer (trans.), *Classical Women Poets* (Newcastle upon Tyne: Bloodaxe Books, 1996), 115–17. See further Alan Cameron, *Literature and Society in the Early Byzantine World* (Aldershot: Variorum, 1985), which contains both his articles dealing with Eudocia, 'Wandering Poets: A Literary Movement in Byzantine Egypt' (no. I) and 'The Empress and the Poet: Paganism and Politics at the Court of Theodosius II' (no. III), M. D. Usher, *Homeric Stitchings* (Lanham, Md.: Rowman & Littlefield, 1998), Peter van Deun, 'The Poetical Writings of the Empress Eudocia: An Evaluation', in J. Den Boeft and A. Hilhorst (eds.), *Early Christian Poetry* (Leiden: Brill, 1993), 273–82, and Kenneth Holum, *Theodosian Empresses* (Berkeley and Los Angeles: University of California Press, 1982), 112–23.

[22] Holum, *Theodosian Empresses*, 82.

[23] See Friedrich Maassen, *Geschichte der Quellen und der Literatur des canonischen Rechts in Abendlande bis zum Ausgange des Mittelalters* (Gratz: Leuschner & Lubensky, 1870), nos. 420–2, p. 369.

[24] Translated by Dronke, *WWMA*, 27.

[25] John Matthews, *Western Aristocracies and Imperial Court, AD 364–425* (Oxford: Clarendon Press, 1975), 192, points out that some of the *Epigrammata Bobiensia* (which were discovered along with the *Satire* of 'Sulpicia') are attributed to 4th-century aristocrats (Wolfgang Speyer (ed.), *Epigrammata Bobiensia* (Leipzig: Teubner, 1963)).

[26] Ausonius, *Works*, ed. and trans. Hugh G. Evelyn White (Cambridge, Mass.: Harvard University Press, 1921), ii. 74. See also Theodore Haarhoff, *The Schools of Gaul: A Study of Pagan and Christian Education in the Last Century of the Westen Empire* (London: Oxford University Press, 1920), 206–9.

Aemila Hilaria, so 'boyish' she was known by the masculine name 'Hilarus', vowed to perpetual virginity, and entirely occupied with medicine, 'like a man').[27] Nearly two centuries later, Sidonius Apollinaris, Bishop of Clermont-Ferrand, trusted his children's education to his mother and sisters.[28] All these writers imply that in the days of the late Empire, as in earlier centuries, education was a function of class rather than gender.

There is evidence for women poets of the fourth century within the ranks of the senatorial aristocracy: Ausonius' wife Sabina, by his own account, wrote verses which she then embroidered, or perhaps worked into tapestry: in a poem written in his wife's voice, he says, apparently with pride,[29]

> Some weave yarn and some weave verse:
> These make tribute to the Muses of their verse,
> Those of their yarn, O chaste Minerva, [make tribute] to you.
> But I, Sabina, will not divorce conjoined arts,
> Who on my own webs have inscribed my verses.

Proba

The most significant woman Latin poet of late antiquity in terms of her impact on both contemporaries and posterity is without doubt the Roman aristocrat Faltonia Betitia Proba.[30] Her work is particularly hard to assess, because it is a cento, i.e. apart from the introduction, it is composed entirely from lines and half-lines of Virgil's *Aeneid*. The cento is a form popular in the fourth century,[31] and is associated with women, though not peculiar to them; in the Eastern, Greek-speaking half of the Empire, the Augusta Eudocia, already mentioned, wrote Christian centos based on Homer's *Iliad*.[32] Centos were written on many subjects in late antiquity, serious, frivolous, religious, and obscene.[33]

Proba belonged to one of the most aristocratic families in the late Empire, the *gens Anicia*, which also produced the philosopher-poet Boethius. It was also one of the most Christian, as we can tell from her contemporary Jerome. Some doubt has

[27] Ausonius, *Parentalia* 6, in *The Works of Ausonius*, ed. R. P. H. Green, (Oxford: Clarendon Press, 1991), 29–30.

[28] Nora K. Chadwick, *Poetry and Letters in Early Christian Gaul* (London: Bowes & Bowes, 1955) 299.

[29] There are three epigrams on Sabina's work, Ausonius, *Epigrammata* 27–9, ed. Green, 74. This was noticed in the 16th century: she is named as a writer in Anon. [J. Ravisius], *De Memorabilibus et Claris Mulieribus* (Paris: Simon Colinaeus, 1521), 183ʳ.

[30] Wilson-Kastner et al., *A Lost Tradition*, 33–69.

[31] Filippo Ermini, *Il centone di Proba e la poesia centonaria Latina* (Rome: Ermanno Loescher & Co., 1909), F. E. Casolino, 'From Hosidius Geta to Ausonius and Proba: The Many Possibilities of the Cento', *Atene e Roma*, ser. 5 28 (1984), 133–51, and Elizabeth A. Clark and Diane F. Hatch (trans.), *The Golden Bough, the Oaken Cross: The Vergilian Cento of Faltonia Betitia Proba*, American Academy of Religion, Texts and Translation Series 5 (Chico, Calif.: Scholars Press, 1981).

[32] See n. 21. Ermini, *Il centone*, 27 notes that there were ten editions of Eudocia's *Homerocentones* in Western Europe, beginning with Aldus Manutius in 1501.

[33] Ermini, *Il centone*, 52–5, Joseph Octave Delepierre, *Centoniana, ou encyclopédie des centos* (London: Miscellanea of the Philobiblion Society IX–X, 1866–8).

recently been cast on the identity of the poet, though no one denies she was a daughter of the Anicii—the problem is that Proba was a family name, and there were several in successive generations. Danuta Shanzer has argued for a date of composition around the 390s, with the author probably Anicia Faltonia Proba, the granddaughter of the Proba to whom it is usually assigned,[34] while John Matthews counter-argues that 'whatever the plausibility of linguistic parallels between the *Carmen* [*contra Paganos*, written *c*.390] and the *Cento*, the historical evidence for placing the centonist Proba in the middle years of the fourth century . . . is simply too strong'.[35] Two important witnesses to the *Cento*, the lost Codex Mutensis and the eighth-century Vatican City, Biblioteca apostolica, Pal. 1753, name her as the wife of Adelphius, hence, Faltonia Betitia Proba.[36] But her granddaughter Anicia Faltonia Proba may also have been a poet, since it seems quite possible that the lengthy epigraphic poems written to memorialize her husband Petronius Probus are hers: at any rate, they focus strongly on Proba herself and her conjugal grief.[37] Anicia Faltonia's son Anicius Hermogenianus Olybrius was the father of Jerome's beloved, and well-educated, young friend Demetrias.[38] Still later, at the beginning of the sixth century, a letter written to yet another Proba suggests that the women of the family continued to be both well educated and pious.[39]

Proba the centonist prepared herself for the wholly serious venture of writing her *Cento*, an epic of Christian history, by another ambitious composition: but for once, it is possible that the loss of this work is to be attributed not to the attrition of time but to deliberate suppression on her own part. The *Aeneid* opens with the words 'arms and the man I sing', and the narrative unfolds as one of military triumph. Proba's *Cento* opens with a direct repudiation of this.

> Iam dudum temerasse duces pia foedera pacis,
> regnandi miseros tenuit quos dira cupido,
> diversasque neces, regum crudelia bella
> cognatasque acies, pollutos caede parentu
> insignis clipeos nulloque ex hoste tropaea,
> sanguine conspersos tulerat quos fama triumphos,
> innumeris totiens viduatas civibus urbes,
> confiteor, scripsi: satis est meminisse malorum.

---

[34] 'The Anonymous *Carmen contra Paganos* and the Date and Identity of the Centonist Proba', *Revue des études augustiniennes*, 32 (1986), 232–48.

[35] *Western Aristocracies*, 402. Most authorities date the *Cento* between 354 and 370. Robert Markus, 'Paganism, Christianity and the Latin Classics in the Fourth Century', in J. W. Binns (ed.), *Latin Literature in the Fourth Century* (London: Routledge & Kegan Paul, 1974), 1–21 (p. 3), argues for a date in the 350s.

[36] *PLRE* i. 732.

[37] Petronius Probus was also a poet: he dedicated a collection of his own, his father's, and his grandfather's verses to the Emperor Theodosius (*PLRE* i. 740). It might be argued therefore that the epigraphic poems are his own; alternatively, this may be a case of the literary man choosing a literary wife

[38] *PLRE* i. 732.

[39] *Epistola ad Probam [Virginem]*, by Eugippius of Noricum, (fl. *c*.509), CSEL IX.1 (Vienna: 1885), 1–4, *PL* lxii, col. 559.

> I have for a long time now, I confess,
> been writing about how warlords broke pious peace-treaties
> wretched men whom a dire lust for dominion held in its grip;
> and of battle-lines of kinsmen, shields polluted by the slaughter of parents
> and trophies from no [external] enemy,
> bloodstained triumphs which Fame had reported,
> cities bereft so many times of innumerable citizens.
> That is enough of remembering evils![40]

As she implies, her previous work had been a poem about warfare: according to an early manuscript of her work, the Codex Mutensis, she wrote an account of the battle between Constantius and Magnentius before turning to the composition of her *Cento* on sacred history.[41] According to a contemporary source, the *Chronicle of 354*, Adelphius, who was probably our Proba's husband, was accused in 351 of conspiracy (i.e. under Magnentius): this might explain why Proba was interested in him. Such facts as we have about this lost composition have something to tell us about Proba as a poet. It refers to the events of AD 350–3: Constans, the brother of the legitimate emperor Constantius, ruled as Augustus (co-emperor) in the West, until he was murdered by Magnentius, a general of Germanic extraction, who declared himself Augustus. Civil war followed, mostly fought out in Italy, and Magnentius was bloodily defeated. This poem must therefore have been highly political in content, since it dealt with an unsuccessful challenge to the authority of the house of Constantine (who was of course the first Christian emperor, a fact which is bound to have concerned this very Christian writer). Proba had a possible precedent for writing a poem of civil war, Lucan's *Pharsalia*, which is about the war between Caesar and Pompey in the first century BC, but by no stretch of the imagination can this be regarded as a 'feminine' subject. It is more relevant to remember that she was the daughter of a great aristocratic family, and that her own province of Italy suffered particularly heavily from the conflict.

In the *Cento* itself, Proba transcends her apparently self-imposed training as an epic poet by moving to a Christian subject, and she transcends her own poetic gift by making use of the words of Virgil. However, she refers to herself in line 12 as *vatis Proba*, an indication of confidence in herself and her abilities. The Augustan poets distinguish *vatis* from *poeta*: a *vatis* is a serious poet, whose works are instructive, while a *poeta* is a maker of verses.[42] The *Cento* is, in fact, appropriating and subverting a text central to the Latin tradition, which is hardly an act of humility:

---

[40] Three of these lines are adapted from Virgil: *Georgics* 1. 37 and 3. 32, and *Aeneid* 8. 571.

[41] The subscription to Proba's *Cento* in an early codex now lost, *Liber Saec. x, qui Fuit Bybliothecae Monasterii S. Benedictini Padolirensis non procul a Mutina Site*, reported by Montfaucon, states, 'Proba, the wife of Adelphius and the mother of Olybrius and Alypius, after she had written about Constantine's [Constantius'] battle against Magnentius, wrote this book also' (Karl Schenkl, in *Poetae Christiani Minores*, CSEL XVI (Vienna: F. Tempsky, 1888), 513).

[42] J. K. Newman, *Augustus and the New Poetry* (Brussels: Collections Latomus 88, 1967), 'The Concept of *Vates*', 99–206, esp. p. 160–1, discussing Horace, *Ars Poetica* 391–407. See also George Luck, *The Latin Love-Elegy* (New York: Barnes & Noble; London: Faber, 1959), 'Sacra Facit Vates' (chapter on Propertius), 124–40.

her work incorporates and even transcends Virgil for Christian use, making her a true 'thief of language'.[43] Proba keeps Virgil's lines, but overwrites the imperial message in favour of an emperor whose kingdom is not of this world.[44] As Witke observes, the effects are sometimes unexpected: for example, she is the only writer of late antiquity to present the first confrontation of Adam and Eve as romantic.[45]

Perhaps part of the reason for her tackling this apparently perverse task lies in the brief career of the Emperor Julian, later known as 'the Apostate', who ruled 360–3. The *Cento* was probably written within a decade of his death. Julian attempted to return the Empire to paganism, and forbade Christians to teach the pagan classics.[46] This was a deliberate attempt to keep Christians out of positions of power by ensuring that they would become an under-educated group who did not share the tropes and expressions of ruling-class discourse. The panic this caused in the Greek-speaking East was met by the Apollinarii (father and son), who attempted to create a Christian curriculum. They paraphrased the Psalms in pseudo-Homeric hexameters, and rewrote the historical books of the Bible in iambic verse, like that of the classical Greek tragedies.[47] Proba's *Cento* can be seen as an alternative, but even more ingenious, attempt for the Latin-speaking West to counter the core of awkward truth in Julian's taunt that Christians were hypocrites in their use of pagan, classical wisdom: the Christian poet Paulinus of Nola wrote, 'hearts vowed to Christ are closed to the Muses and cannot receive Apollo', but he did so in the beautiful Latin of a man reared on the pagan classics.[48] Virgil had been enthroned as the central curriculum author by the end of the first century BC, and never dislodged. The grammarians, such as Donatus and Servius, took Virgil as a sort of gold standard of Latin verse.[49] But readers of the *Cento* could do so as well. When Vergil was used as a school text, much of the discussion was line by line, relatively independent of context: it would be quite possible to use Proba's *Cento* in much the same way as the *Aeneid* itself.[50] The *Cento* could thus be used for style formation in an orthodox way.[51] The dedication to Arcadius

[43] Though her concern is with religious rather than feminist politics, she has clearly engaged in an act of appropriation, seizing and subverting a canonical male-authored text: on the concept of 'stealing language', see Claudine Herrmann, *Les Voleuses de langue* (Paris: Des Femmes, 1976).

[44] E. Clark and D. Hatch, 'Jesus as Hero in the Vergilian Cento of Faltonia Betitia Proba', *Vergilius*, 27 (1981), 31–9.

[45] Charles Witke, *Numen Litterarum: The Old and the New in Latin Poetry from Constantine to Gregory the Great* (Leiden: Brill, 1971), 195–8.

[46] G. W. Bowersock, *Julian the Apostate* (London: Duckworth, 1978), 83–5.

[47] N. G. Wilson, *Scholars of Byzantium* (London: Duckworth, 1983), 10.

[48] Paulinus, *Epistolae* 31, 29–33 (Vienna: F. Tempsky, 1894), 267–75.

[49] The enthroning of Virgil in the Roman classroom took place at the end of the 1st century BC. H. I. Marrou, *A History of Education in Antiquity*, trans. George Lamb (London: Sheed and Ward, 1936), 278.

[50] Marrou, ibid. 279–80 describes Servius' commentary on Virgil: 'after a rapid introduction that was clearly made as short as possible, came, line by line and word by word, a long and meticulous *explanatio*.' The focus is on a kind of close reading so microscopic that overall sense seems to have been neither here nor there.

[51] A. G. Amatucci, *Storia della letteratura latina* (Bari: Laterza, 1929), 147, suggested Proba's poem was composed on the occasion of Julian's edict of 362, and that l. 23, 'Vergilium cecinisse loquar pia munera Christi', is a direct reply to the words of the imperial edict.

stresses that even within a generation of being written, the *Cento* was a school text.[52]

Jerome was splenetic on the subject of centos: 'they are childish, and like the games of quack philosophers.'[53] This reaction has to do with his extreme sensitivity to, and about, the Latin classics. In 384, he made public a dream which dramatized his sense of guilt about his love of pagan literature, in which he was accused at the bar of heaven of being a Ciceronian rather than a Christian. His accuser then posed the questions, 'What does Horace have to do with the psalter? What does Virgil have to do with the Gospels? What does Cicero have to do with Paul?'[54] The answer, of course, is nothing, which is precisely the problem addressed by Proba's work. However, Jerome could not keep away from the classics: his resolution to confine himself to the Bible did not last long. Since he had many enemies, they naturally cast the letter to Eustochium in his teeth. His riposte was adroit, if disingenuous, and based on an obsure provision of the book of Deuteronomy, 21: 11–13: 'If you see a beautiful woman in the number of captives and wish to have her as wife, you may introduce her into your home if she shaves her hair and cuts her nails and puts off the clothes in which she was captured.' Thus, he claimed, the Bible gave him licence to disport himself with alien literature: he metaphorically 'shaved the hair and pared the nails' of the classics by ignoring what was unsuitable in them.[55] But Proba might very reasonably have replied, if she was still alive to know of this, that her *Cento* went much further, and performed radical surgery on the body of the text. As a matter of taste, one's sympathies are naturally with Jerome, but there is no doubt that Proba has logical consistency on her side.

It is also the case that other responses to Proba's work were far more positive. The aesthetic of the cento was widely appreciated in her own time, and for long after. Usher says of Eudocia,[56]

her Centos are an act of Homeric and biblical interpretation in which surface and symbol possess equal validity. Her art 'is at once Surface and Symbol', the product, we might say, of an 'anagogical' reading of Homer, in the sense defined by Dante ... whose validation of both surface and symbolic meanings stands in a tradition of poetic theory stretching back at least as far as the philosopher Proclus.

What is said here of Eudocia and Homer could equally well have been said of Proba and Virgil. The Emperor Arcadius requested a copy of the work (a fact recorded in the dedicatory poem prefaced to the *Cento* as we now have it, which is not by Proba). The Emperor Valentinian himself composed an epithalamion entirely from lines and half-lines of Virgil and sent it to Ausonius with the suggestion that he should write a piece of his own in rivalry, the genesis of the latter's *Cento*

---

[52] ' ... haec tua semper | accipiunt doceatque suas augusta propago' (ll. 14–15).

[53] Ad Paulinam, *Epistolae* 53. 7, ed. Hilberg, i. 442–65 (p. 454).

[54] Ibid 22. 29–30.

[55] Ibid. 21. 13, pp. 122, 123, and 70. 2, p. 702. Similarly, Augustine sanctions the reading of non-Christian texts by comparing it to the despoiling of the Egyptians (*De Doctrina Christiana*, 2. 40. 60–1, in *Augustini Opera*, CCSL 32, ed. J. Martin (Turnhout: Brepols, 1962), 73—5).

[56] Usher, *Homeric Stitchings*, 145.

Nuptialis.[57] Three hundred years later, Isidore of Seville in his *On Famous Men* suggests not only that Proba's *Cento* was still read, but that it had assumed the status of an almost canonical text.[58]

Proba, the wife of Adelphius the proconsul is the only woman to be ranked among the doctors of the church, because she turned herself to the praise of Christ, composing a cento on Christ taking verses from Virgil. It is not the knowledge which should be admired, but the ingenuity. Nevertheless, this little work is placed among the apocryphal scriptures.

In fact, Proba's *Cento* seems to have become a popular schooltext almost immediately, and retained this role through the fall of the Roman Empire, the rise of the successor states, and the Middle Ages. There are at least four manuscripts from before the ninth century, and it often appears in medieval catalogues of monastic libraries together with Aldhelm and Symphosius' riddles, Cyprian, Gregory, and Fortunatus (as it does in an eighth-century Corbie manuscript now in St Petersburg),[59] or with Adelard and Seneca—either way, with works used in the instruction of children.[60] There are more manuscripts and editions of the *Cento* than of any other single work by a pre-modern woman.

Even in the Renaissance, the usefulness of Proba's work as a school text was very far from being forgotten. She reappears as a curriculum author in Colet's 1518 statues of St Paul's:[61] he prescribes Juvencus, Lactantius, Proba, Prudentius, and Sedulius, 'that wrote theyre wysdom with clene and chast Latin', and two moderns, Baptista Mantuanus and his own friend Erasmus. Other educators of the Renaissance were equally concerned that schoolchildren should be protected from authors who were pagan or obscene, so no doubt Proba had her uses in other classrooms also.[62] The popularity of her work even in the Renaissance is eloquently illustrated by its print history. The *editio princeps* is by Michael Wensler (Basel, *c.*1475), and Ermini lists no less than seven incunables and fourteen sixteenth-century editions. There are many testimonies to the interest which her work excited among humanists, some of which are also listed by Ermini.[63] She was also admired by Maffeo Vegio.[64] In fact, early modern Europe saw a renewed appetite for centos, which were composed on a variety of topics ranging from

[57] Matthews, *Western Aristocracy*.

[58] *De Viris Illustribus, Isidori Opera*, ed. F. Arévalo, 7 vols. (Rome: Antonius Fulgonius, 1797–1803), vii. 149.

[59] St Petersburg, Public Library, F.xiiii. In another early manuscript from Lorsch, Vatican City, Biblioteca apostolica, Pal. 1753, s. viii^{ex}, it appears with the *Ars* of Marius Victorinus, and the *regulae metrum* and *Aenigmata* of Aldhelm: all teaching texts. Ermini, *Il centone*, 65.

[60] Wilson-Kastner et al., *A Lost Tradition*, 33–69.

[61] Printed in Joseph Hirst Lupton, *A Life of Dean Colet* (London: George Bell, 1887), 279.

[62] Françoise Waquet, *Latin: Or the Empire of a Sign*, trans. John Howe (London: Edward Arnold, 1912) 38. See for example the doubts raised by John Owen in his *Theologoumena Pantodapa* I. VIII. xlii (first published 1661), ed. W. Goold in John Owen, *Complete Works*, xvii (Edinburgh: Tu. T. Clark, 1862), 107.

[63] Ermini, *Il centone*, 67.

[64] 'De Proba', in Maffeo Vegio, *Elenco delle opere scritti inediti*, ed. Luigi Raffaele (Bologna: Nicola Zanichelli, 1909), 131.

David and Goliath to the bull 'Unigenitus' and the death of Mary, Queen of Scots.[65] Women continued to be drawn to the form: there is a Latin cento by Angela Nogarola addressed to Pandulfo Malatesta, and another by Helena da Sylva, a nun of Coimbra, while both Vittoria Colonna and Chiara Matraini wrote Italian centos.[66]

Jerome's view that the classics could simply be sanitized for Christian use by carefully nuanced reading and selective blindness is the one which held the field, fortunately for the Renaissance, since it ensured that classical texts continued to be copied through the Middle Ages. But it was by no means certain in late antiquity that his was the view which would prevail. As late as the sixth century, Sidonius Apollinaris reveals that in a properly organized library, such as that of his friend Ferreolus, Christian and pagan literature was segregated. Christian writings were placed by the ladies' seats.[67] This suggests an unease about Christian matrons and maidens perusing possibly obscene classical texts—though it also confirms that the wives and daughters of the elite could do so with ease.

It also suggests that since monks, like women, should avert their eyes from sexually explicit writing, there may have been Christian milieux in which Proba did supersede Vergil. In fact, there is direct evidence that this is the case. Theodore of Tarsus, a learned Greek who was sent from Rome to govern the English Church in the seventh century, seems to have read Proba's *Cento* in preference to the *Aeneid*. Describing Eve in the exegetical work known as *Laterculus Malalianus*, he quotes a description of Eve, made up of half-lines which are widely separated in Vergil's *Aeneid*, but are linked in the *Cento*. Theodore's school at Canterbury may have read no pagan poetry at all: no pagan authors are lemmatized in any of the glossaries which originate there.[68] Aldhelm, a Canterbury alumnus of remarkable learning who died in 703, also read Proba. Interestingly, his letter to a pupil Wihtfrith objects fiercely to the young man's declared intention of going to study in Ireland, on the grounds that he would be studying pagan literature there:[69]

---

[65] Heinrich Meibom, *Cento Vergilianus de Monomachia Davididis Israelitae et Goliathae Philistaei* (Helmsted: Iacobus Lucius, 1589) (note that Meibom had edited Proba in 1597). The cento against 'Unigenitus' by 'Oxonii' was published in Amsterdam in 1726, and Leonhard van Ryssen (Rysennius) published a cento on Mary Stuart at The Hague in 1695. For an exhaustive list, see Delepierre, *Centoniana*.

[66] Jeffrey Schnapp, 'Reading Lessons: Augustine, Proba, and the Christian Detournement of Antiquity', *Stanford Literature Review*, 9.2 (1992), 99–123, and on Colonna and Matraini, see Luciana Borsetto, 'Narciso ed Eco: figura e scrittura nelle lirica femminile del Cinquecento', in Marina Zancau (ed.), *Nel cherchio della luna: figura di donne in alcuni testi del xvi secolo* (Venice: Marsilio, 1983), 192–4.

[67] *Epistola* 2. 9. 4, ed. W. B. Anderson (Cambridge, Mass.: Harvard University Press, 1965), i. 452–5. This idea is supported by Claudius Marius Victor (see below, n. 93) though he confirms that Gallo-Roman women were not content to censor their reading in this way.

[68] Edited and discussed in Michael Lapidge and Bernhard Bischoff (eds.), *Biblical Commentaries from the School of Theodore and Hadrian* (Cambridge: Cambridge University Press, 1994).

[69] *Aldhelmi Opera*, ed. R. Ewald (Berlin: Weidmann, 1919), 479. Aldhelm did also read Virgil, but seems to have maintained a very austere attitude towards pre-Christian literature.

What, I pray you, is the benefit to the sanctity of the orthodox faith in expending energy by reading and studying the foul pollution of base Proserpina . . . or to revere . . . Hermione, the wanton offspring of Menelaus and Helen?

Proba may genuinely have thought that she was saving Virgil for a Christian world, and if the classics had had a less resourceful apologist than St Jerome, she might have done so. In the generations immediately following that of Sidonius Apollinaris, most of the great secular libraries, such as that of Ferreolus, were destroyed. The texts which slipped through the bottleneck of the seventh century did so because they were read and preserved by monks, and monks, fortunately, had been given an argument for reading Virgil and other pre-Christian poets. Aldhelm is the last Anglo-Saxon to take an unqualifiedly negative view of the reading of pagan texts. Anglo-Saxon scholars such as Bede, Egbert, and Alcuin soothed their tender consciences with Jerome's somewhat specious argument about Hebrew hand-maidens,[70] and Charlemagne's advisers recommended that the emperor invest heavily in the copying of every Latin text, pagan or Christian, that they could lay hands on.[71] And thus it is Proba and not Virgil who is now a byway and curiosity of literature, though it might not have been so.

The last pagan poets

Another interesting writer, though of far less posthumous significance, a near-contemporary of Proba's, and like her the object of Jerome's scorn, also resembled her in her extremely aristocratic background and strong religious convictions, though unlike Proba, she was pagan. Fabia Aconia Paulina was the daughter of Fabius Aconius Catullinus Philomathius, city prefect of Rome 324–344 and consul in 349, an indication of her family's high status.[72] She became the wife of Vettius Agorius Praetextatus, who died in 384, after forty years of what seems to have been a true marriage of minds. Praetextatus was a translator of Greek philosophical texts, a pagan, and consul-designate at the time of his death.[73] He was also, according to the elaborate tombstone on which Paulina's poem is preserved, 'augur, priest of Vesta, priest of the Sun, quindecemvir, curialis of Hercules, initiate of Liber and the Eleusinian Mysteries, hierophant, *neocorus*, *tauroboliatus*, and father of fathers'. He followed a classic pattern of Roman paganism in thus following a whole variety of cults: it was this willingness to multiply cult membership which

---

[70] Alcuin justified the reading of the classical poets with the help of Jerome (Philip Jaffé (ed.), *Monumenta Alcuiniana* (Berlin: Weidmann, 1873), letter 147), though later, he came to take a very ascetic view of Virgil, e.g. letter 216, *Monumenta*, 712–14).

[71] L. D. Reynolds et al., *Texts and Transmission* (Oxford: Clarendon Press, 1983), pp. xvi–xvii, sets out the evidence for the extreme tenuity of the classical tradition.

[72] *PLRE* i. 187–8, 675.

[73] Ibid. 722–4. There is an account of the funerary inscription by P. Lambrechts, *Op de grens van Heidendom en Christendom: het grafschrift von Vettius Agorius Praetextatus en Fabia Aconia Paulina* (Brussels: Mededelingen Kon. Vlaamse Akademie 17.3, 1955), and a biography, T. W. J. Nicolaas, *Praetextatus* (Nijmegen: Dekker & Van de Vegt, 1940).

left pagans unable to understand Christian insistence on rejecting all cults but their own.[74] In a contemporary work, Macrobius' *Saturnalia*, Praetextatus is represented as an acknowledged expert on pagan divinities.[75] His wife Paulina shared his interests: she was 'initiate of Ceres and the Eleusinian Mysteries, initiate of Hecate at Aegina, *tauroboliata*, and hierophant'. Though the Roman Empire became officially Christian at about the time Praetextatus was born, pagans, particularly wealthy and important ones such as this couple, were left in peace to follow their own ways: actual persecution of pagans did not begin until the fifth century. St Jerome, who knew many members of the Roman aristocracy, is venomous about both Praetextatus and Paulina in a letter in which he records that the widow gave Praetextatus' funeral oration: one of very few occasions on which a late Roman woman is known to have performed such a public function.[76] The view that Paulina was the author of the long verse inscription on Praetextatus' tomb—which of course cannot be certain, though it is accepted by Dronke—is corroborated by this fact. Interestingly, there is similarly a pair of long poems on the tomb of Petronius Probus, possibly the work of his wife Anicia Faltonia Proba, which are similar in honouring both the dead man and the conjugal relationship. The evidence for devoted, companionate marriage and sharing of interests in the Paulina inscription is found elsewhere in late antiquity: apart from the verses on Probus already mentioned, there are other examples:[77] for instance, Paulinus of Nola and his wife Therasia sent letters in their joint names, while there are other witnesses to their mutual devotion.[78] Others will be mentioned later in this chapter.

It has been suggested by Catlow, its latest editor, that another particularly interesting late pagan long poem, the *Pervigilium Veneris*, was written by a woman (it may be familiar to some readers since T. S. Eliot quotes it in *The Waste Land*). No author's name is associated with it, so the attribution is based on its literary qualities.[79] The poem celebrates an important spring festival, the *trinoctium* (three nights' celebration) of Venus, roughly coincident with the Christian feast of Easter. This was a popular festival which was legitimized as part of the official worship of the Roman Empire in the second century, and survived into the fourth, or perhaps the fifth despite Christianization. In the fourth century, when the *Pervigilium* was written, it was entirely possible to be a pagan without fear of Christian reprisals, particularly for an individual who was not living very close to the centres of power, which were Rome and Constantinople.[80] The *Pervigilium*

---

[74] MacMullen, *Paganism in the Roman Empire*, 2.

[75] Macrobius, *Saturnalia*, ed. J. Willis (Leipzig: Teubner, 1963; 2nd edn. 1970). Praetextatus is a principal speaker throughout.

[76] *Epistolae* 23. 3 (see Matthews, *Western Aristocracies*, 4–6).

[77] Chadwick, *Poetry and Letters*, 152.

[78] Escorial, Real Biblioteca, a. 1. 1, fo. 148, 'Paulinus et Therasia, epistola ad Sebastianum'. See *PLRE* i. 909.

[79] L. Catlow (ed.), *Pervigilium Veneris* (Brussels: Collections Latomus 172, 1980).

[80] See Arnaldo Momigliano, *The Conflict between Paganism and Christianity in the Fourth Century* (Oxford: Clarendon Press, 1963).

is a poem about sexuality and generation: its perspective could be seen as feminine rather than masculine. It speaks of bands of girls roaming in the woods in a way which seems participatory rather than voyeuristic. The awesome yet lovely Dione of the *Pervigilium* is closely akin to Chaucer's Nature, as she appears in the *Parlement of Foules*; so is the idea that there is a specific season, the pagan *trinoctium*, or the Christian St Valentine's day, which is 'the wedding of the world', a natural welling-up of creative sexuality, to which human lovers are also invited.

The language of the *Pervigilium* is extremely interesting. The metre is trochaic tetrameter, a form of verse which was used by the less educated poets of the Roman Empire (cultivated writers employed the hexameter), and strongly associated with popular poetry: it is the Roman equivalent of ballad metre.[81] The poem survives in two manuscripts, both of which are somewhat garbled, but it appears to be irregular in language, metre, and structure: the Victorian edition of J. D. Mackail, the form in which the poem is best known, imposes order and regularity upon it, probably wrongly. The refrain line, 'Cras amet qui nunquam amavit quique amavit cras amet' (tomorrow he will love who has never loved, he who has loved will love tomorrow), is probably a cultic cry associated with the festival, which the poet uses as the structural core of the work. A graffito which survives from Pompeii in the first century,

> May they flourish who love, may they perish who do not know love,
> May they twice perish, who forbid love,

may also be a version of this cry, associable with the *trinoctium*, and thus help to context the later poem.[82]

Cultivated women continue to be a feature of the Roman senatorial aristocracy as long as there was any such thing. There is a poem, apparently the work of a husband and wife, which was found by the shore in Roman Dalmatia (Croatia), near modern Zivogostje, at a point where a spring of sweet water emerges and makes its way down to the sea. It was inscribed on the rock near the source, and appears to date from the fifth century.[83] The husband speaks first:

Licinianus
Litorea praegnas scruposae margine rupis
   inriguus gelido defluit amne latex,
cuius perspicuo per levia saxa meatu
   praedulcis salsam perluit unda Tethyn,
indigenis gratus, aeque labentibus almus:
   incola delicias aduena laudat opes.

[81] William Beare, *Latin Verse and European Song: A Study in Accent and Rhythm* (London: Methuen, 1957), 15.

[82] *CLE*, ii, no. 945, p. 435.

[83] *CIL*, iii. 1894: 'inter Macarscam et Narentae ostia ad vicum Zivogostje sub monasterio S. Crucis ad ipsum maris litus in ima rupe non laevigata leguntur carmina haec scripta pravis litteris... olim miniatis.'

> Salve Nymfa meos dignata invisere finis
> et celebrem cunctis conciliare locum:
> nostra salutifero tu mactas predia fonte,
> Licinianus ego carmine te dominus.

Pelagia

> Diversum sortita capis finemque caputque
> Nymfa, caput cautes, terminus unda tibi est.
> quis queat arcanum sapiens pernoscere fontis?
> nasceris e scopulis, fons, moriture fretis.
> Hoc Pelagia suos fontes epigrammate donat,
> magne, tui pignus, Liciniane, tori.

Licinianus

> Pregnant water, compressed out of a rocky shore-edge, flows down in an ice-cold torrent,
> whose perfectly sweet wave with its pellucid flow over smoothed rocks drenches salty Tethys.
> It is pleasing to the local inhabitants, equally to passers-by,
> the resident praises its delights; the stranger praises its generosity.
> Hail, Nymph! who have deigned to visit my territories,
> and to recommend a famous place to all.
> You bless our estates with a health-giving spring,
> so I, your master Licinianus, [bless] you with a song.

Pelagia

> Nymph, you who have been allotted a discrepant end and beginning:
> your beginning is a rock, your destination is a wave.
> What wise man may be able entirely to fathom the mystery of a spring?
> You are born from the rocks, O spring, to die in sea-straits.
> Pelagia, in this epigram, makes a gift of her own fountains,
> the pledge of your marriage-bed, great Licinianus.

A Licinianus was *quaestor sacri palatii* (West) under Julius Nepos in 474. He was sent on a special mission to Euric, King of the Visigoths, and is described by Sidonius as able and trustworthy.[84] The poem comes out of the same world of elegant accomplishment as Sidonius Apollinaris, and strongly features the copious, 'jewelled style' fashionable at that time,[85] but its address to a *genius loci* is a testimony to the lingering paganism of Roman upper-class discourse—though not necessarily to pagan practice among them. Though it is certainly true that some members of the senatorial aristocracy were still pagan in the fifth century, there were plenty of others who merely used the tropes of classical paganism for literary purposes.[86] In the pagan period, of course, the devotion to springs had been a serious matter: 'The resident spirit of rivers and springs is more than mere metaphor: it is a crucial fact of local cult. A region is characterized—indeed it is

---

[84] *Epistolae* 3. 7. 2.

[85] On which see Michael Roberts, *The Jeweled Style: Poetry and Poetics in Late Antiquity* (Ithaca, NY: Cornell University Press, 1989).

[86] Louise A. Holland, *Janus and the Bridge*, Papers and Monographs of the American Academy in Rome 21 (Rome: American Academy, 1961), 8–20.

personified—in the river flowing through it, or rising in it.'[87] Similarly, Servius comments, 'there is no stream that is not holy'.[88] But by the fifth century, the culting of springs was romantic or antiquarian, rather than a matter of serious religious feeling.

Another Gallo-Roman aristocrat, Eucheria, who flourished in sixth-century Provence, writes with considerable brio. Her only known poem, dismissing proffered love with devastating scorn, ends,

Jungatur nunc cerva asino, nunc tigris onagro,
Jungato fesso concita damna bovi.
Nectareum vitient nunc lasera tetra rosatum
Mellaque cum fessis sint modo mixta malis.
Gemmantem sociemus aquam luteumque barathrum,
Stercoribus mixtis fons eat inriguus.
Praepes funereo cum vulture ludat hirundo,
Cum bubone gravi nunc philomela sonet.
Tristis perspicua sit cum perdice cavannus,
Iunctaque cum corvo pulcra columba cubet.
Haec monstra incertis mutent sibi tempora fatis:
Rusticus et servus sic petat Eucheriam!

Now may the hind be coupled with the ass, now the tiger with a donkey,
Let the fast-moving doe couple with the weary ox.
May nasty resin spoil nectar-like rosé,
Let honey now be mixed with bad pomace
Let us ally sparkling water with a muddy morass,
Let spring-water flow permeated with dung.
May the swift swallow play with the dismal vulture,
Now let the nightingale sound forth along with the grave horned owl:
Let the sad screech-owl be seen in company with the wise partridge,
Let the lovely dove bed down in unison with a crow.
Let these portents change the times for themselves, the Fates be inconstant meanwhile—
And on these terms let a clod and a slave woo Eucheria!

Her parentage is unknown, though she may be related to an earlier Eucherius, Bishop of Lyon, who was known as a writer,[89] or to another noble Eucherius who was a candidate for the bishopric of Bourges and a friend of Sidonius Apollinaris.[90] More certainly, she married Dynamius of Marseille, an important figure in sixth-century Provençal society, the recipient of a number of letters and poems from Venantius Fortunatus. Another of his correspondents was Gregory the Great, and he was himself a poet—so like Cornificia, Polla Argentaria, the wife of Varus, Pelagia, and a number of other Roman women, she evidently shared literary interests with her husband.

[87] David F. Bright, *Haec Mihi Fingebam: Tibullus in his World* (Leiden: Brill, 1978), 56.
[88] Servius, *Ad Aeneadem* 7. 84.
[89] Chadwick, *Poetry and Letters*, 151–2.
[90] Evidence for various late antique Eucherii is in *PLRE* ii. 404–5.

Provence in the sixth century was the most cultivated and Romanized part of the territory controlled by the Merovingian kings of Frankia.[91] The tone of its literature was elegant to the point of frivolity: some unknown poet from this milieu even 'civilized' the service of the Eucharist by rewriting it in hexameters.[92] In the fifth century, Claudius Marius Victor, a rhetorician of Marseille, complained that the Gallo-Roman women he knew were far too interested in the classics; they preferred pagan to Christian authors, and 'they want to know all sorts of recondite things'.[93] Eucheria's name (Romanized Greek), and the hauteur of her poem both suggest that she was a proud daughter of this educated Gallo-Roman aristocracy rather than a Frank or Visigoth. The circles in which she moved were distinctly intellectual. Domnolus, Bishop of nearby Le Mans, refused to move to Avignon on the grounds that he would be bored to death due to lack of civilized conversation.[94] There is an epitaph for Dynamius and Eucheria by their grandson, composed with pride due to their association with Fortunatus, whose patron Dynamius was: the epitaph carefully echoes Fortunatus' style, though its substance is associable rather with an earlier Gallo-Roman poem, Ausonius' *Parentalia*.[95] Sidonius Apollinaris, Bishop of Clermont-Ferrand, also enjoyed a variety of associations with educated women. He noted that his friend Eulalia was fond of reading his (notably involved and abstruse) writings,[96] and wrote to his nephew that marriage was no excuse to stop writing: the pleasures of his marriage might include working at verse together.[97]

The first nuns

One of the most salient aspects of the appeal of Christianity for women was its negative attitude towards human sexuality, since it thus came to offer a socially sanctioned escape route from marriage, sex, and motherhood, which for many seem to have held no charms.[98]

[91] On the culture generally, see Ralph Whitney Mathisen, *Roman Aristocrats in Barbarian Gaul: Strategies for Survival in an Age of Transition* (Austin: University of Texas Press, 1993), and Matthews, *Western Aristocracies*.

[92] *Missale Gallicanum Uetus (Cod. Vat. Palat. Lat. 491)*, ed. L. C. Mohlberg (Rome: Rerum Ecclesiasticarum Documenta, Series Maior 3, 1958), 61–91, verse Mass pp. 74–6. See also A. Wilmart, 'L'Âge et l'ordre des messes de Mone', *Revue bénédictine*, 28 (1911), 371–90 (pp. 23–5).

[93] *De Perversis Aetatis Moribus ad Salmonem Epistola*, PL lvi, col. 970. Compare Sidonius Apollinaris's account of the library of Ferreolus, already discussed.

[94] Gregory of Tours, *Historia Francorum* 6. 9, George, *Venatius Fortunatus*, 16.

[95] See Avitus of Vienne, *Carmen* 31, in *Opera*, ed. R. Peiper (Berlin: Weidmann, 1883), 194, and for comment, Pierre Riché, *Education and Culture in the Barbarian West*, trans. J. J. Contreni (Columbia: University of South Carolina Press, 1976), 186–7. M. Thiébaux, *The Writings of Medieval Women* (New York: Garland, 1987), has suggested that an anonymous letter bound in with a fragment of Baudonivia's life of Radegund was also written by Eucheria (pp. 125–33). MGH *Epistolae* III (Berlin: Weidmann, 1892), 716–18.

[96] Sidonius Apollinaris, *Carmina* 24. 95, ed. and trans. Anderson, i. 326–7.

[97] *Epistolae* 2. 10. 6, ed. and trans. Anderson, i. 466–9.

[98] *Vita Theclae* 15, in *Vie et miracles de S. Thècle*, ed. G. Dagron, Subsidia Hagiographia 62 (Brussels: Société des Bollandistes, 1978), 190–2, trans. Peter Brown, *The Body and Society: Men, Women, and Sexual Renunciation in Early Christianity* (London: Faber and Faber, 1988), 5.

This man [St Paul] has introduced a new teaching, bizarre and disruptive of the human race. He denigrates marriage: yes, marriage, which you might say is the beginning, root and fountainhead of our nature. From it spring fathers, mothers, children and families. Cities, villages and cultivations have appeared because of it. Agriculture, the sailing of the seas, and all the skills of this state—courts, the army, the High Command, philosophy, rhetoric, the whole humming swarm of rhetors—depend on it.

The corollary of this, as Peter Brown points out, was that 'the pressure on the young women was inexorable... [Roman society] could hardly allow private choice since it must mobilise maximum fertility if it [was] to survive at all... for the population of the Roman Empire to remain even stationary, it appears that each woman would have had to produce an *average* of five children.'[99] However, despite the evidence for companionate marriage presented earlier, there is also considerable evidence that many late antique women approached marriage and motherhood with intense reluctance, which Plutarch put down to their being made to marry too young.[100] As Rousselle notes,[101]

The Roman women described by Soranus [a gynaecologist] and later by Galen agreed reluctantly to have intercourse and felt sick during their pregnancies. Some refused to admit they were going to be mothers right up to the birth of their children, and Soranus offered advice to midwives who had to deliver women who would not cooperate.

The last sentence suggests an appalling level of alienation from female biological imperatives, but Soranus gives the impression it was a problem any professional birth attendant might come across. Such matter-of-fact evidence for women's fear and loathing of their manifest destiny offers a grim context for the abundant evidence for upper-class women who refused to marry, refused to remarry if widowed early, or refused to maintain a sexual relationship within marriage (lower-class women are unlikely to have been any more enthusiastic, but their preferences were not consulted, so we have no direct evidence). Once the Roman Empire had become Christian, would-be continent women were able to turn to the Church for protection from their families, and the result was unprecedented: an alliance of men whose theoretic position denigrated women in general with specific women whose agendas they were happy to further since the benefit to themselves was obvious.[102]

It is in the Christian Roman Empire that, for the first time in the history of the Roman world, we find women rulers. The Christian thinking referred to in the last

[99] Peter Brown, *Society and the Holy* (London: Faber and Faber, 1982), 6 and n. 5.

[100] *Comparison of Lycurgus and Numa* 4. 1–3, in *Lives*, ed. B. Perrin, Loeb Classical Library (Cambridge, Mass.: Harvard University Press; London: Heinemann, 1914), 382–401 (p. 395).

[101] Aline Rousselle, *Porneia: On Desire and the Body in Antiquity*, trans. F. Pheasant (Oxford: Basil Blackwell, 1988), 44.

[102] Elizabeth A. Clark, 'Early Christian Women: Sources and Interpretation', in Lynda L. Coon, Katherine J. Haldane, and Elizabeth W. Sommer (eds.), *That Gentle Strength: Historical Perspectives on Women in Christianity* (Charlottesville: University Press of Virginia, 1990), 19–35 (pp. 27–9). See also Margaret R. Miles, 'Becoming Male: Women Martyrs and Ascetics', in *Carnal Knowing: Female Nakedness and Religious Meaning in the Christian West* (Boston: Beacon Press, 1989), 53–62.

paragraph, which distinguishes the suffering, breeding, ignorant mass of woman-kind from elite female individuals—members of a spiritual, intellectual, and/or social elite—who are deemed to 'transcend femininity', interacted with the pro-foundly dynastic impulses of the Roman army to produce the first ruling emp-resses.[103] Such are the ironies of historical process that the anti-elitist idea that women could be spiritual leaders, and that 'in Christ there is neither male nor female', combined with the secular principle of dynasticism to give certain indi-vidual women a chance of immense personal power. As Cloke comments,[104]

a great and constant double-think is in evidence in our sources. All, even the sternest of the Fathers, while embracing apostolic teaching on women as sinful in nature so subject in worship, nonetheless know and approve as 'superior' certain female exemplars to their sex. Every single writer knows of some female paragon or paragons (though each must of course be 'unique' in their virtue).

A significant part of the context for this is economic: as Peter Brown observes, 'the impact of upper-class ascetic women on the Latin church was far out of proportion to their numbers. This was a church that desperately needed lay patrons . . . treatises on virginity no longer circulated as exhortations to a sheltered piety. They were written . . . to persuade emperors, prefects, and provincial governors to allow wealthy widows and virgins to remain dedicated to the church, and to tolerate the redirection of part of the wealth of great families, through such women, to pious causes.'[105] Given the uses to which these tracts, with their fiercely expressed disgust for human sexuality and the lives of ordinary women, were put in later centuries, it is worth stressing the ironic fact that at the time they were produced, many of them were written to theorize and validate the personal goals of specific late antique heiresses; women such as Melania and Olympias, who were the objects of keen competition between potential beneficiaries of their immense wealth.[106] It is also interesting to observe that the same phenomenon of self-interested clerical support for women reappeared in the early sixteenth century, when the prominent Catholic preacher Geiler of Kayserberg put his moral weight behind widows' right to autonomous control over their property, in a context where, as Strasbourg city

---

[103]   This has been studied by Holum, *Theodosian Empresses*.

[104]   Gillian Cloke, *'This Female Man of God'* (London: Routledge, 1995), 23–4.

[105]   Brown, *The Body and Society*, 344–5, and Dyan Elliott, *Spiritual Marriage: Sexual Abstinence in Medieval Wedlock* (Princeton: Princeton University Press, 1993), 55. R. Howard Bloch, *Medieval Misogyny and the Invention of Western Romantic Love* (Chicago: Chicago University Press, 1991), 83–8, addresses the ways in which the Church both fostered the creation of heiresses and defended such women's right to dispose of their property.

[106]   Clark, 'Early Christian Women', 28–9: she observes that a recent (i.e. 1990s) reckoning of the value of Olympias's donations to the Church put the sum (not including real estate) at 900 million dollars—wealth on a scale which might be held to justify a fair amount of casuistry. See also Cloke, *'This Female Man of God'*, 82–99, Elliott, *Spiritual Marriage*, 56, Holum, *Theodosian Empresses*, 71–2, 143–4. Shelly Matthews, *First Converts: Rich Roman Women and the Rhetoric of Mission in Early Judaism and Christianity* (Stanford, Calif.: Stanford University Press, 2001), makes the point that the Jews also both rewarded and exploited the devotion of rich Roman women.

council explicitly stated, guardians were being imposed upon them to prevent them from deeding it all to convents.[107]

One poem which offers an insight into the genuine rewards which ascetic Christianity offered women is that of Taurina, a nun, and the author of an acrostic poem on her four sainted aunts, Licinia, Leontia, Ampelia, and Flavia: the poem was originally epigraphic, but survives in a copy made in 1603.[108]

Lumine virgineo hic splendida membra quiescunt.
Insigneis animo, castae velamine sancto
Crinibus imposito caelum petiere sorores
Innocuae vitae meritis operumque bonorum.
Noxia vincentes Christo medicante venena
Invisi anguis palmam tenuere perennem,
Aspide calcato sponsi virtute triumphant

Letanturque simul pacata in secula missae
Evictis carnis vitiis, saevoque dracone
Obluctante diu subegunt durissima bella.
Nam cunctis exuta malis hic corpora condunt:
Tantus amor tenuit semper sub luce sacratas,
Iungeret ut tumulo sanctarum membra sororum
Alvus quas matris mundo emiserat una,

Ad caelum pariter mittet domus una sepulcri,
Mirifico genetrix fetu, quae quattuor agnas
Protulit electas, claris quae quattuor astris
Emicuit; castosque choro comitante Maria
Letatur gradiens germanis septa puellis.
Ingressae templum Domini venerabile munus
Accipiet, duras quoniam vicere labores,

Floribus et variis operum gemmisque nitentes
Lucis perpetuae magno potientur honore.
Adventum sponsi nunc praestolantur ovantes
Veste sacra comptae, oleo durante beatae
Immortale decus numerosa prole parentes
Aeterno regi fidei pietate sacrarunt.

Nomine sanctarum lector si forte requiris,
ex omni versu te littera prima docebit.
Hunc posuit neptes titulum Taurina sacrata.

Limbs shining with virginal light rest here:
Illustrious for courage, the chaste sisters
Covering their hair with veils, have sought heaven

[107] Merry Wiesner, 'Women's Defense of their Public Role', in Mary Beth Rose (ed.), *Women in the Middle Ages and the Renaissance* (Syracuse, NY: Syracuse University Press, 1986), 1–28 (p. 5).

[108] Acrostics on the subject's name are fairly common in Roman epitaphs. There are examples in H. Geist and G. Pföhl (eds.), *Römische Grabinschriften*, 2nd edn. (Munich: Ernst Heimeran Verlag, 1976), 50, 71, 147, 162. This translation is constrained at various points by the exigencies of preserving the acrostic form.

In the merits of their blameless lives and good works.
Noxious poisons overcome, with Christ as healer,
In spite of the hated Serpent, they have attained to the everlasting palm
Asp trodden down, they triumph by virtue of their Spouse.

Linked they rejoice, sent as they have been into aeons of peace, now that the
Evils of the flesh have been totally conquered,
Only with the savage dragon who is long keeping up the struggle,
Now they are waging most intransigent battles.
They are storing up here bodies divested of all evils, such a great love kept them always
   consecrated, so that
In the tomb it joined the limbs of holy sisters
All given to earth by the womb of one mother.

A single home — that of the tomb — will send them to heaven, a
Mother with wondrous offspring, who brought forth four
Pure lambs, who has flashed forth with four stars;
Environed by a chaste chorus: Mary rejoices
Linked with the girl sisters, as she goes on her way.
In entering the temple of the Lord they will
Attain an honourable reward, since they have overcome harsh struggles.

Flashing with the flowers and jewels of their world,
Light perpetual is the great honour they will gain.
Awaiting the arrival of their Spouse, now, in exultation
Vested with sacred garments, blessed with the oil that endures, parents of an
Innumerable progeny, they have consecrated an undying thing of beauty
All in piety and faith, to the eternal King.

If, reader, you perhaps ask the names of the lady saints,
the first letter from every line will instruct you.
The nun Taurina, their niece, set up this inscription.

Another woman of the next century, also of obviously aristocratic origin, is similarly the product of this otherwordly turn in the mentality of late antiquity. Marcella, who was probably, like Taurina, a nun, was the sister of Hesychius, Bishop of Vienne,[109] and author of verses on his death. There is nothing very surprising about this. An inscription for the fourth-century Pope Damasus, discussed earlier, seems to be by his sister Martha, and at the least registers a strong relationship between them.[110] The sister of another notable Gallo-Roman bishop, Caesarius of Arles (Caesaria), was highly literate, and left letters to prove it;[111] nearer to home, Hesychius' predecessor as bishop, Avitus of Vienne, dedicated a 666-line poem in praise of virginity to his sister Fuscina, suggesting that

---

[109] Not Vienna: there was a number of Roman towns called Vindobona.

[110] Damasus was noted for his friendly relationships with women: Raymond Van Dam, *Leadership and Community in Late Antique Gaul* (Berkeley and Los Angeles: University of California Press, 1985), 76.

[111] Caesaria, 'epistola ad Richildam et Radegundim', written before 587, *Epistolae*, iii ed. W. Gundlach, MGH (Berlin: Weidmann, 1892), 450–3.

she was a woman of cultivation.[112] It seems probable that Marcella was a nun: in this period, brothers and sisters seem often to have gone into religion simultaneously; and in such cases, the sibling tie was often strengthened, since it was unaffected by the requirements of clerical celibacy, and neither had the interests of wife and children to overlay memories of childhood affection.

Hesychius was a signatory of the fifth council of Orléans in 549 and the second council of Paris in 553, suggesting that he was born in the environs of 500 and died in perhaps 570. The poem is unusual in a number of respects; the use of the word *funus*, for corpse, and of course the Sapphic metre, used by pagan Latin poets such as Horace, but uncommon in Christian Latin: both these features suggest that Marcella had received an old-fashioned literary education. Like the writings of earlier Roman women, it expresses a strong sense of family pride. Terentia poem on her brother, given in the previous chapter, lists his public honours: Marcella's poem on hers begins by doing the same, but goes on to focus on achievement of a Christian kind, effective peacemaking, teaching, scholarship. Like Taurina's poem on her aunts, it seems the product of a milieu in which old instincts and loyalties have not been suppressed, but have been effectively redirected to new ends.

> Praesulis iunctum tumuloque Aviti,
> Funus Hesici tegitur sepulchro,
> Qui cluens olim micuit honore
>   Pontificali.
>
> Quique mundanis titulis peractis,
> Quaestor et regum habilis, benignus
> Ambiit demum habitare sacris
>   Incola tectis.
>
> Cultibus Christi sapienter haerens
> Fautor et pacis studuit furentes
> Reddere cives speciali voto
>   Mentis amicae.
>
> Temporum mensor numeros modosve
> Calculo cernens strenuusque doctor
> Unde fraterna docuit libenter
>   Agmina tempus.
>
> Septenum necdum peragens bilustrum
> Corpus huic sedit posuit beatae
> Mente cum iustis habitans refulget
>   Luce perenni.
>
> Quem soror Marcella gemens obisse
> Ultimum praebens lacrimis levamen
> Nomen hic scalpsit titulumque fixit
>   Carmine parvo.

---

[112] *De Consolatoria Castitatis Laude ad Fuscinam Sororem* and *Liber ad Fuscinam* are two of its MS titles), Avitus, *Opera*, 275–94.

And, linked with the tomb of Bishop Avitus,
Enclosed in a sepulchre, is the funeral casket
of Hesychius, a famous man who formerly shone forth
    with pontifical honour,

And a benign man, who, after his worldly posts of honour were completed,
A *quaestor* and a right-hand-man of kings,
Eventually made it his ambition to live as an inhabitant
    of the holy dwelling places.

Adhering with wisdom to the rites of Christ,
And a supporter of peace too, he made it his endeavour
By his special prayer, to render the citizens,
    of friendly disposition.

A measurer of the times, determining numbers and measures by calculation,
And an energetic teacher:
Hence he taught the ranks of brothers
    [the study of] time.

Without yet completing his seventh decade,
He laid down his body for this blessed house,
Residing in the company of the righteous,
    he is refulgent in eternal light.

His sister Marcella, groaning at his departure,
Providing for her tears a final solace,
Carved his name here and fixed in place a plaque
    with a little epigram on it.

PART II

The Middle Ages

4. Women Latin Poets in Early Medieval Europe

The transformation of the political map which substituted a series of successor states for the Western Roman Empire is a highly complex affair. It is very easy mentally to oppose, on the one hand, decadent, toga-wearing Romans, and on the other, unwashed, axe-wielding barbarians, which is a mistake on all kinds of levels. On the most literal, Romans no longer wore the toga, and many barbarians were strangely civilized. More seriously, the Empire's relationship with important barbarian leaders was complex and not necessarily adversarial. For example, in Italy, Theodoric the Ostrogoth destroyed Odoacer, also an Ostrogoth, on behalf of the Emperor Zeno, then ruled as the latter's chosen vice-regent. His authority was absolute, but coins and laws were issued in Zeno's name. In northern France, Chlodovech (Clovis) the Frank was similarly the emperors' chosen deputy, whose duties included crushing the independent, illegitimate authority of one Syragius, whose name shows that he was of ancient senatorial lineage, but who referred to himself as the 'king of the Romans'. Romans, famously, did not have kings, so who is 'the barbarian warlord' here, and who 'the Roman'? In short, viewed from the perspective of the literate elite, the Roman loss of power in the West was not a 'fall', but a complex set of adjustments to a gradually changing political reality.[1]

In the fifth century, the poet Claudian portrays the young Maria, affianced bride of the Emperor Honorius, peacefully reading Greek poets—Homer, 'Orpheus' (i.e. the 'Orphic hymns'), and Sappho—with her mother Serena: a picture of tranquil feminine enjoyment of classical literature, represented as eminently suitable as an occupation for women of senatorial rank.[2] Her mother is 'ipsa genetri[x] magistra', that is, both mother and tutor to Maria. As a panegyrist, Claudian is concerned to present his subject in the most favourable light possible, so it is interesting that the ladies are portrayed as reading verse together rather than sewing or weaving, which were the traditional default activities of aristocratic women. Maria's father was Stilicho, the Vandal commander in chief.[3] A poem preserved among the works of Claudian, 'On a Belt Sent from the Same [Serena] to Arcadius Augustus', was probably written by him, but may just be by Serena herself: it is more likely that she asked her court poet to

---

[1] Patrick Geary, *Before France and Germany: The Creation and Transformation of the Merovingian World* (New York: Oxford University Press, 1988).

[2] Gillian Clark, *Women in Late Antiquity* (Oxford: Clarendon Press, 1993), 134–5.

[3] The body of Maria was disinterred in Rome, in the year 1544, and the grave-goods confirm this impression of sophistication. Lady Frances Norton, *The Applause of Virtue: Memento Mori* (London: John Graves, 1703), 31.

write it on her behalf, but since it is clear that she was an educated woman, we cannot be certain of this.[4]

As the marriage of Stilicho's daughter suggests, the imperial family intermarried freely with barbarians: a daughter of the Theodosian dynasty, Justa Grata Honoria, who considered that she had been improperly excluded from power, voluntarily offered herself to Attila the Hun.[5] Nor were aristocrats with 500-year pedigrees more squeamish than the relatively parvenu emperors. The Anicii, one of the greatest of all Roman families, who produced both the philosopher Boethius and the poetess Proba, intermarried with barbarians on numerous occasions. Anicia Juliana, a major *gens Anicii* heiress of the sixth century, married the highly civilized Goth Areobindus,[6] while the marriage of another Anicius with the last survivor of the lineage of Theodoric the Ostrogoth, his granddaughter Matasuntha, was considered a diplomatic and social coup by *both* families.[7]

The daughters of the great barbarian generals who were thus accepted into the Roman ruling classes were brought up on the *Aeneid* and the *Iliad*, not on Gothic, Vandal, or Frankish heroic saga. Claudian's account of Maria is upheld by Cassiodorus' admiring account of Amalasuntha, daughter of Theodosius the Great, and ruling queen of Italy: he stresses her ability to speak with equal eloquence in Latin, Greek, and her native Gothic.[8] The Italian poet Venantius Fortunatus, who gives us one of the clearest pictures of literary life under barbarian rule, speaks of a young Parisian Frank called by the barbarian name of Vilithuta, stressing that 'she was Roman by education, barbarian by race'.[9] This epitaph could have served for many. The Visigothic (Spanish) princess Brunhild was celebrated for her learning as well as for her forceful personality, beauty, and political ability: Latin letters survive, notably one to the Empress of Byzantium.[10]

One barbarian princess whom we know to have written Latin verse is principally known to us from Fortunatus. Radegund (518–87), who ended her life in the convent of the Holy Cross in Poitiers, which she had founded, began it as a Thuringian princess. She was captured by the Merovingian king Chlotar in 530, and educated as his future wife, an education which seems to have been extensive. Radegund finally succeeding in breaking with Chlotar and taking the veil after his

---

[4] Alexander Reise (ed.), *Anthologia Latina* (Leipzig: Teubner, 1868), 219. I give another poem just possibly by Serena in the Appendix.

[5] Kenneth Holum, *Theodosian Empresses* (Berkeley and Los Angeles: University of California Press, 1982), 1–2.

[6] Martin Harrison, *A Temple for Byzantium* (Austin: University of Texas Press, 1989), 36. There is a Latin letter from Anicia Juliana to Pope Hormisdas in Escorial, Real Biblioteca, ç II 20, fo. 301.

[7] See Walter Goffart, *Narrators of Barbarian History, A.D. 550–800* (Princeton: Princeton University Press, 1988), 69–70.

[8] Cassiodorus, *Variae* 10. 1. 6, trans. S. Barnish (Liverpool: Liverpool University Press, 1992), 146. Four of her letters are in *Variae*, 10. 1, 3, 8, 10.

[9] Venantius Fortunatus, *Opera*, ed. F. Leo, MGH Auctores Antiquissimi 4 (Berlin: Weidmann, 1901). 4. 26. 7. Pierre Riché, *Education and Culture in the Barbarian West*, trans. J. J. Contreni (Columbia: University of South Carolina Press, 1976), 221–22.

[10] *WWMA*, 25, *Epistulae Austrasicae*, ed. W. Gundlach, Corpus Christianorum 117 (Turnhout: Brepols, 1957), 403–70. Riché, *Education and Culture*, 223, notes that Brunhild educated her son herself.

murder of her brother, in about 544. The convent at Poitiers, as befitted a royal foundation, was a place of some sophistication: in a quarrel which broke out shortly after Radegund's death, the nuns complained bitterly about having temporarily to share a bathroom.[11] More importantly, they were highly literate: Caesaria, sister of Bishop Caesarius of Arles, wrote a letter of advice on the foundation, accompanied by a copy of Caesarius' *Rule*, which warns, 'Let there be no woman from among those entering who does not study letters.'[12] We have a letter from Radegund herself,[13] and somewhat later, a nun with the non-Roman name of Baudonivia is a surviving witness to the convent culture, since she wrote a Life of Radegund (in Latin) between 605 and 610, protesting her inadequacy as a writer with considerable rhetorical dexterity.[14]

After her move to Poitiers, a talented and sensitive Italian bishop, Venantius Fortunatus, settled in the same town. He was not, of course, a member of Radegund's community, but he became a close friend both of Radegund herself and of her adopted daughter Agnes. A large quantity of Venantius' poetry survives, including a number of occasional poems accompanying small gifts to Radegund and Agnes, or thanking them for their presents to him. One such poems attests directly to Radegund's own poetry, 'Ad Radegundam': 'On small tablets you have given me great poems, you who are able to return honey out of empty wax.'[15] Neither this poem nor any other short poems by Radegund are known to survive.

The status of two long poems, written in the first person in the voice of Radegund, *De Excidio Thoringiae* and *Ad Artachin*, is problematic. One extreme view is that they are both written by Venantius Fortunatus, the other is that they are both written by Radegund. A number of intermediate positions can also be maintained. Dronke takes the view that Radegund wrote both poems, 'though ... it is hard to rule out some collaboration by Fortunatus in the writing'.[16] George, on the other hand, argues for Venantius' authorship, on grounds of parallels with his technique in other poems.[17] What is certain is that *De Excidio* and the follow-up poem *Ad Artachin* are both very carefully crafted pieces of public writing, expressing things which Radegund wished to have said. As a princess of a defunct royal house, and a divorced ex-queen without surviving male relatives in the West, Radegund could have cut a pitiful figure. The fact that she did not was due entirely

[11] Gregory of Tours, *Historiae Francorum*, 10. 16, trans. Lewis Thorpe (Harmondsworth: Penguin, 1974), 572.

[12] Translated in Marcelle Thiébaux, *The Writings of Medieval Women* (New York: Garland, 1987), 101–6. E. Dümmler et al. (eds.), *Epistolae Merowingici et Karolini Aevi*, I (Berlin: Weidmann, 1892), 450–3.

[13] Jane E. Jeffrey, 'Radegund and the Letter of Foundation', in Laurie Churchill et al. (eds.), *Women Writing Latin* (New York: Routledge, 2002), ii. 11–23.

[14] For a translation see Thiébaux, *The Writings of Medieval Women*, 106–20. Prefatory protestations of incapacity were entirely normal in the early Middle Ages, and do not necessarily indicate uncertainty or diffidence. See Tore Janson, *Latin Prose Prefaces* (Stockholm: Almquist and Wiksell, 1964).

[15] The poem is translated by Judith George, *Venantius Fortunatus* (Oxford: Clarendon Press, 1992), 198–9. The poem was evidently written on a wooden tablet covered with a thin layer of beeswax.

[16] *WWMA*, 28.

[17] George, *Venantius*, 164.

to her intelligence and political ability, which is demonstrated by these poems. As George has made clear, *De Excidio* was written to establish her in Byzantine eyes as an independent agent in international politics, a successful venture, since Justin II responded with the munificent present of a relic of the True Cross.[18] We may take it, therefore, that the content of this interesting pair of long poems is Radegund's, and the final product to some extent collaborative.

De Excidio is addressed to her cousin Amalfrid at Constantinople, her closest surviving male kinsman. It recalls the friendship of their youth, and hopes that the cousin will renew it with a message to show that he is alive and remembers her: [19]

> vel memor esto, tuis primaevis qualis ab annis,
>   Hamalfrede, tibi tunc Radegundis eram,
> quantum me quondam dulcis dilexeris infans
>   et de fratre patris nate, benigne parens.

> Be mindful Amalfrid, my kindly relative, how in your earliest years I
> was then your Radegund; how much you, then a sweet infant, loved
> me, born of your father's brother.

He was, it turned out, dead; so another poem was written, to Artachis, probably the son of Radegund's murdered brother, which again is insistent on familial relations.[20] The information comes from Radegund; it is her ends which are served by pulling the remains of her family together. Whether her relationship with these poems is as author or patron, it is clear that Fortunatus' involvement is as an expression of her agenda.

Some of the literate, and literary, nuns of the sixth and seventh centuries have been discussed in the last pages of Chapter 3, as 'late Romans', but there were also women of Germanic origin who cultivated Latin: for example, Baudonivia has been mentioned as part of the culture of Poitiers, and another Frankish nun, Burginda, made a précis of part of Apponius' tract on the Song of Solomon.[21] An abbess called Boba, which again is a Germanic name, was exchanging Latin letters with Chrodebert, Bishop of Tours, in the later seventh century, as he bears witness.[22]

Towards the end of the eighth century, the balance of power was gradually transferred from the Merovingians to the most important of their aristocratic families, a dynasty later known as the Carolingians. The first great Carolingian monarch, Charles the Great (Charlemagne), was to prove a mighty king, and a dedicated patron of the arts (this has already been discussed with respect to the transmission of classical texts). Women also participated in the so-called 'Carolingian Renaissance'. Charlemagne's sisters Ada and Gisela were educated women,[23]

[18] Ibid. 163–5.

[19] Venatius Fortunatus, *Opera*, ed. Leo, app. I (p. 272).

[20] Ibid. app. III, pp. 278–9. She addresses him as 'care nepos' ('dear nephew').

[21] *Apponii in Canticum Canticorum Expositiones*, ed. B. de Vregille and L. Neyrand (Turnhout: Brepols, 1986), 391–463.

[22] Dümmler et al. (eds.), *Epistolae Merowingici et Karolini Aevi* i. 461–4.

[23] Ada commissioned a spectacular Gospel book written in gold (Trier, Staatsbibliothek, Cod. 22), which contains an inscription which is possibly hers. See now Carl Lamprecht, *Die Trierer*

and so were his daughters. One of them, the Princess Ruothild, became the Abbess of Faremoutiers *c*.840–52. Faremoutiers (Seine et Marne) had been founded in the early seventh century by a distinguished and strong-minded Frankish noblewoman, Fara, or Burgundofara.[24] In the time of Ruothild, a *translatio* (the moving of a saint's relics to a place of greater honour) took place; probably of the relics of St Fara. The saint's body was wrapped in red damask silk of Byzantine origin, with a design depicting the hunt of the Amazons: bare-breasted equestriennes wearing Scythian-style trousers, and wielding Scythian short, composite bows, while snarling, leopard-like beasts curl under their horses' hooves. As Janet Nelson has pointed out, Ruothild and her contemporaries would certainly have recognized these fierce women for who they were, since Orosius' *Seven Books of Histories against the Pagans*, which includes an excursus on the Amazons, was a basic textbook for Carolingian readers.[25] Orosius describes a group of warrior queens who had once conquered the whole of Europe before being subdued by Hercules. When Ruothild chose this silk, she may have attached significance to its design, and not just to its value and beauty—if so, then it might suggest that she perceived monastic life for women as dynamic.

Other early medieval royal women were also literate. Janet Nelson has suggested that Judith, second wife of Louis the Pious, was more literary than her husband: 'it was she, rather than her husband, whom scholars praised for such discernment.'[26] She ensured her son, the future Charles the Bald, had a literary education at the hands of Walahfrid Strabo. Adalperga, the daughter of the last Lombard king, was clearly Latin-literate on the evidence of Paul the Deacon's admiration, as was Irmintrude, wife of Charles the Bald.[27] There is also some evidence that women's education may have been extended beyond royal circles in the eighth and ninth centuries. Charlemagne is known to have been anxious to extend literacy within his kingdom, and a saint called Liutberga of Halberstadt is said to have taught girls the (Latin) Psalms, and then permitted them to go home after their lessons—which indicates that they were not young nuns, but girls in the secular world.[28]

Ada-Handschrift, (Cologne: Gesellschaft für rheinische Geschichtskunde Publikationen, 1984). J. L. Nelson suggests that Gisela, Abbess of Chelles, besides writing in Latin to Alcuin to ask for a Bible commentary, was responsible for *Annales Mettenses Priores*, written at Chelles: 'Gender and Genre in Women Historians of the Early Middle Ages', in J.-P. Genet (ed.), *L'Historiographie médiévale en Europe* (Paris: CNRS, 1991), 149–63 (pp. 157–69).

[24] Burgundofara is described by Jonas, *Vita S. Columbani*, 2. 16, ed. B. Krusch, (Hanover: Hahn, 1905), 266–7. See also J. O'Carroll, *Sainte Fare et Faremoutiers* (Faremoutiers: Abbaye de Faremoutiers, 1956).

[25] J. L. Nelson, 'Women at the Court of Charlemagne: A Case of Monstrous Regiment?', in John Carmi Parsons (ed.), *Medieval Queenship* (Stroud: Alan Sutton, 1993), 43–62.

[26] Janet Nelson, *Charles the Bald* (London: Longman, 1992), 82.

[27] Joan M. Ferrante, 'The Education of Women in the Middle Ages in Theory, Fact, and Fantasy', in Patricia H. Labalme, *Beyond their Sex* (New York: New York University Press, 1980), 9–42 (p. 10). Judith was buried in the church of St Peter in Ghent, with Latin verses written above her tomb, which are probably not her own. They are printed in Francisco Agostino della Chiesa, *Theatro delle donne letterate* (Mondovì: Giovanni Gislandi & Gioranni Tomaso Rossi, 1620), 163.

[28] Rosamond McKitterick, *The Carolingians and the Written Word* (Cambridge: Cambridge University Press, 1989), 219.

Women in the Carolingian world (like Gallo-Roman women of a couple of centuries earlier, and some of their Merovingian predecessors) are strongly associated with the education of the young. A number of learned men are on record as having been educated by their mothers or grandmothers, which sheds light on Dhuoda's forlorn attempt to educate her son at long distance, to be discussed in a moment.[29] This was also true in Anglo-Saxon England, where Alfred the Great's lifelong love of literature was kindled by his mother, who read to her sons from a book of English poetry, and promised the book to whichever of them learned the poems first.[30] McKitterick has concluded that 'a general level of basic literacy and instruction prevailed among the nobility, that educated noblewomen were not unusual in the Carolingian period, and that they may well have customarily played a part in the instruction of their children'.[31]

The culture of Carolingian nunneries was also highly literate, in both Latin and the vernacular.[32] Saint's lives are most often anonymous, but the A *vita* of Balthild is by one of her nuns (as the B *vita* may also be), and there is a *vita* of Adalheid by a nun who actually identifies herself, Bertrada.[33] Rosamond McKitterick has argued that many anonymously authored lives of female saints were written by women in the convents with which the saints were associated.[34] Women also owned, and copied, books. The convent of Chelles wrote many books for the Bishop of Cologne, and was particularly associated with the creation of a distinctive script: it is possible to discern that there was a nun master-scribe, and an atelier where some fourteen nuns worked under her.[35] The nearby convent of Jouarre also maintained an active scriptorium,[36] and at Maaseyck in the eighth century, the

[29] Ibid. 223–4. For example, some Latin letters from Herchenefreda to her son Desiderius survive in his biography, *Vita S. Desiderii*, ed. B. Krusch, MGH Scriptores Rerum Merowingicarum IV (Hanover: Hahn, 1902), 569–70.

[30] Henrietta Leyser, *Medieval Women* (London: Weidenfeld and Nicolson, 1995), 138. Asser, *De Rebus Gestis Ælfredi* 23, ed. W. H. Stevenson (Oxford: Clarendon Press, 1959), 20.

[31] McKitterick, *The Carolingians*, 226.

[32] See Steven A. Stofferahn, 'A Schoolgirl and Mistress Felhin: A Devout Petition from Ninth-Century Saxony', in Churchill et al. (eds.), *Women Writing Latin*, ii. 25–35, and his 'Changing Views of Carolingian Women's Literary Culture: The Evidence from Essen', *Early Medieval Europe*, 8 (1999), 69–97.

[33] The 'A' *Vita* of Balthild is ed. Bruno Krusch, Scriptores Rerum Merowingicarum ii (Hanover: Hahn, 1888), 475–508. See Susan Fonay Wemple, *Women in Frankish Society: Marriage and the Cloister, 500–900* (Philadelphia: University Pennsylvania Press, 1985), 182. Joannes Bollandus *et al.*, *Acta Sanctorum* (Antwerp: Joannes Meursius; Brussels, Société des Bollandistes, in progress), Feb., i. 714–21.

[34] 'Frauen und Schriftlichkeit im Frühmittelalter', H. W. Goetz (ed.), *Weibliche Lebensgestaltung im frühen Mittelalter* (Cologne: Böhlau, 1991), 65–118 (pp. 95–111).

[35] See B. Bischoff, 'Die Kölner Nonnenhandschriften und das Skriptorium von Chelles', *Mittelalterliche Studien*, 3 vols. (Stuttgart: A. Hiersemann, 1966–7), i, 16–34, and Rosamund McKitterick, 'Script and Book Production', in McKitterick (ed.), *Carolingian Culture: Emulation and Innovation* (Cambridge: Cambridge University Press, 1994), 221–47 (pp. 237–8).

[36] R. McKitterick, 'The Diffusion of Insular Culture in Neustria between 650 and 850: The Implications of the Manuscript Evidence', in Hartmut Atsma (ed.), *La Neustrie: les pays au nord de la Loire, 650 à 850*, Beihefte der Francia 16/1 and 16/2, 2 vols. (Sigmaringen: Jan Thorbecke, 1988), 16/2, 395–432 (406–12).

sisters Harlind and Reinhild, who had been educated at Valenciennes, were scribes as well as painters and embroiderers.[37]

Dhuoda

The outstanding woman poet of the Carolingian era was, however, not a nun, but a noblewoman, Dhuoda (*c*.803–after 843).[38] Amost everything we know about her is derived from a Latin poem she wrote as a manual of advice for her 16-year-old son William, which was rediscovered in the seventeenth century by Mabillon. On 29 June 824 she was married to the powerful and politically ambitious Bernard of Septimania, Count of the Spanish Marches, in the imperial palace at Aachen. On 29 November 826, she gave birth to William. Some time thereafter, Bernard sent her to live in Uzès, for reasons which are unknown: his contemporaries alleged that he had become the lover of the Empress Judith, an accusation made with sufficient force for him to challenge his enemies to single combat (none dared take him up on this). Bernard's involvement with Judith had dire consequences for another woman of his family, his sister Gerberga, a nun. She has the unhappy distinction of being the first woman in Europe known to have been executed as a witch, almost certainly an indirect move against Bernard by his and Judith's political enemies.[39]

Bernard visited his wife in 840, made her pregnant again, and left for Aquitaine. Her second son was born on 22 March 841. Three months later, Bernard participated in a civil war, on the losing side. To make peace with the winner, the Emperor Charles the Bald, Bernard sent him his son William (then 14) as a pledge of good faith. Before his second son was six months old, he had him brought to Aquitaine, probably in order to ensure that even if he lost William, he would still have an heir. Dhuoda, abandoned in Uzès, did not even know the name of her baby: he was taken away before he was christened, and Bernard did not trouble to tell her (he was in fact called Bernard after his father). She began to write to William as a substitute for offering him the maternal care which circumstances denied her, very shortly after her second son was taken away. Her book (which is now available in English, French, and Italian translations, so I will not quote from it here) first of all discusses her reasons for writing, then covers topics she considered important: God, the social order, and how to achieve success while remaining personally virtuous. The oldest complete manuscript, now in Barcelona, associates it with school texts, such as Isidore's *Chronicle* and *Differentiae*, and Cato's *Distichs*.[40] The *Manual* is also metrically interesting: while she models her

---

[37] *SS. Herlindis et Renild*, ch. 5, *Acta Sanctorum*, 22 March, iii. 383–92.

[38] See Y. Bessmertny, 'Le Monde vu par une femme noble au ixe siècle: la perception du monde dans l'aristocratie carolingienne', *Le Moyen Âge*, 93 (1987), 162–84, M. A. Claussen, 'Fathers of Power and Mother of Authority: Dhuoda and the *Liber Manualis*', *French Historical Studies*, 19 (1996), 785–809. Marie Anne Majeski, *Dhuoda: Ninth Century Mother and Theologian* (Scranton, Pa.: University of Scranton Press, 1995).

[39] Wemple, *Women*, 95.

[40] *Manuel pour mon fils*, ed. Pierre Riché (Paris: Cerf, 1975), 49.

verse on Latin rhythmic adonics, her prosody is strongly influenced by the Germanic two-stressed alliterative half-line.[41] The *Handbook*, which lays great stress on William's duty of loyalty and obedience to the emperor, his father, and God, was completed on 2 February 843. The following year, Bernard was executed for treason by Charles the Bald, and in 848, William, who had joined the Aquitanian rebels, was captured and executed. It is not known whether Dhuoda was alive to see this. Her second son grew up to acquire the nickname of Bernard Hairypaws: a ruthless and effective politician, who was deprived of his kingdom after an alleged attempt to assassinate Charles the Bald.[42]

Anglo-Saxon England

There is a case for suggesting that the first woman Latin poet of Britain was active in the first century AD. Claudia Rufina, the wife of Aulus Rufus Pudens, frequently mentioned by the poet Martial, was remembered as the author of a book of epigrams, and an elegy on her husband's death is also attributed to her.[43] Since her husband was a Bononian philosopher and member of the equestrian order stationed in Britain, she presumably wrote there. Otherwise, the centuries of the Roman occupation of Britain produce no women Latin poets apart from a woman called Viola who may be the author of a single reversed hexameter in perhaps the fifth century.[44]

However, the Anglo-Saxons, when they embraced literate, Christian culture in the course of the seventh century, took a remarkably liberal attitude towards women's participation in the new learning. Aldhelm is the first Anglo-Saxon Latin poet (and also, the first person demonstrably to have written Latin poetry having learned Latin as a foreign language).[45] *De Virginitate*, his masterpiece, was written for a house of aristocratic nuns at Barking, near London, *c*.600. In the preface, he addresses the ladies Hildelith, Justina, Cuthburg, Osburg, Aldgith, Scholastica, Hidburg, Berngith, Eulalia, and Thecla, who, he says, had sent him a whole budget of letters, characterized by 'extremely rich verbal eloquence'.[46] A little later in the letter, he refers to their study of Latin metrics, which suggests that they attempted verse, though it has disappeared, if so.[47] By the eighth century,

[41] *WWML*, 43, and see Paul von Winterfeld, 'Zur Geschichte der rhythmischen Dichtung', *Neues Archiv*, 25 (1900), 402–404, W. Meyer, 'Ein Merowinger Rhythmus über Fortunatus und altdeutsche Rhythmik in lateinischen Versen', in his *Gesammelte Abhandlungen zur mittelateinischen Rhythmik*, 3 vols. (Berlin: Weidmann, 1936), iii. 72–85.

[42] Nelson, *Charles the Bald* 211–12.

[43] Edward Phillips, *Theatrum Poetarum* (London: for Charles Smith, 1675), 238. See Martial, books 11 and 14.

[44] See Charles Thomas, *Christian Latin, Messages and Images* (Stroud: Tempus, 1998), 142–9.

[45] Michael Lapidge, 'Aldhelm's Latin Poetry and Old English Verse', *Comparative Literature*, 31 (1979), 209–31.

[46] *Aldhelm: The Prose Works*, trans. Michael Lapidge and Michael Herren (Ipswich: D. S. Brewer, 1979), 59–62.

[47] See ibid. See further P. Sims-Williams, 'Cuthswith, Seventh-Century Abbess of Inkberrow, near Worcester, and the Würzburg Manuscript of Jerome on Ecclesiastes', *Anglo-Saxon England*, 5 (1976),

Latin verse composition was certainly taught in some Anglo-Saxon convents south of the Humber—by, as well as to, nuns.[48] Leofgyth, or Leoba, who died in 779, was one of the group of Anglo-Saxons who were gripped by the vision of the conversion of the heathen Saxons. She was related to St Boniface, the leader of this enterprise, and wrote a letter to him, introducing herself, and asking for a reply. It ends with a brief, colourless poem in hexameters, strongly dependent on Aldhelm:

> Arbiter omnipotens, solus qui cuncta creavit,
> in regno patris semper qui lumine fulget,
> qua iugiter flagrans sic regnet gloria Christi,
> inlesum servet semper te iure perenni.

> Omnipotent judge, who alone created all things,
> Who always shines with light in the kingdom of the Father,
> Inasmuch as the burning glory of Christ will reign for ever,
> May he always keep you unharmed as your just due for evermore.

Like some later learned women of the Renaissance, Leofgyth is seeking to introduce herself to a great man by means of a letter which will display her character and abilities to advantage. She ends it thus: 'would you also, if you please, correct the homely style of this my letter and send me as a model a few words of your own, for I deeply long to hear them. The little verses written below have been composed according to the rules of prosody. I made them, not because I imagine myself to have great ability, but because I wished to exercise my budding talents. I hope you will help me with them. I learned how to do it from my mistress Eadburga, who continues with increasing perseverance in her study of the Scriptures.' The letter therefore also tells us that instruction in Latin metrics was part of her convent curriculum. Her overture was met with warm approval, and she went out to Saxony to help Boniface in his work.

An astonishing number of Anglo-Saxon women participated in the German mission; several of whom have left Latin writings of one kind or another—letters mostly, but also a long prose narrative, Hugeburc's *Hodoeporicon*, and three poems.[49] The correspondence between those in various parts of the mission field and their supporters at home and in Frankia is rich and complex; as Christine Fell notes, it bears testimony to the 'friendly co-operation between men and women in

1–21, and 'An Unpublished Seventh- or Eighth-Century Anglo-Latin Letter in Boulougne-sur-Mer MS 74 (82)', *Medium Ævum*, 48 (1979), 1–22. Literacy in early Anglo-Saxon England is discussed by S. Kelly, 'Anglo-Saxon Lay Society and the Written Word', in Rosamond McKitterick (ed.), *The Uses of Literacy in Early Medieval Europe* (Cambridge: Cambridge University Press, 1990), 36–62.

[48] See Mary Pia Heinrich, *The Canonesses and Education in the Early Middle Ages* (Washington: Catholic University of America Press, 1924), 71–4.

[49] See Leyser, *Medieval Women*, 30–1, and Jane Stevenson, 'Brothers and Sisters: Women and Monastic Life in Eighth-Century England and Frankia', *Nederlands archief voor kerkgeschiedenis*, 82.1 (2002), 1–34. The *Hodoeporicon* is ed. O. Holder-Egger, MGH Scriptores XV.1 (Hanover: Hahn, 1887), 80–117, and trans. C. H. Talbot, *The Anglo-Saxon Missionaries in Germany* (London: Sheed and Ward, 1954), 153–77.

religious communities'.[50] Women bore serious responsibilities in this enterprise: both in England and on the Continent, nuns produced many volumes of vitally necessary books for the missionaries, a serious commitment of both time and money,[51] and Cynehild and her daughter Berhtgyth, 'very learned in the liberal arts, were appointed as teachers in the region of Thuringia'.[52] Berhtgyth, who was active *c.*770, has left a little Latin verse. Her surviving writings consist of two letters and two poems, all addressed to her brother Balthard. They were the first cousins of Boniface's coadjutor Lul.[53] The letters are written to her brother (who remained in England) after her mother's death, when she was left alone. There is a possible connection with Hartlepool, where there is a stone monument to one BERCHGYD.[54] This probably does not commemorate our Berhtgyth, since she is likely to have died in Thuringia, but, since names ran in families, may be a relative.[55]

Berhtgyth's letters to her brother are couched in terms of passionate intensity: she is not afraid to use the vocabulary of the Song of Solomon as an expression of the depth of her feeling. Her verse is relatively staid.

> Vale vivens feliciter
> tibi salus per saecula
> vivamus soli Domino
> ut sis sanctus simpliciter,
> tribuatur per culmina
> vita semper in saeculo.
>
> Profecto ipsum precibus
> peto, profusis fletibus
> solo tenus, saepissime
> subrogare auxilia
> ut simus digni gloria
> ubi resonant carmina
> angelorum laetissima
> aethalis laetitia
> clara Christi clementia
> celsae laudes in saecula.

Valeamus, angelicis victrices iuncte millibus, paradisi perpetuis perdurantes in gaudiis, † elonque el †et Michael, Acaddai, Adonai, Alleuatia, Alleluia.

---

[50] Christine Fell, 'Some Implications of the Boniface Correspondence', in Helen Damico and A. Hennessey Olsen (eds.), *New Readings on Women in Old English Literature* (Bloomington: Indiana University Press, 1990), 29–43 (p. 31).

[51] *Vita Bertilae*, ch. 6, cited in Patrick Sims-Williams, *Religion and Literature in Western England, 600–800* (Cambridge: Cambridge University Press, 1990), 110.

[52] Otloh, *Vita S. Bonifacii*, in W. Levison (ed.), *Vitae S. Bonifacii* (Hanover: Hahn, 1905), 222.

[53] Ibid. 138.

[54] F. S. Scott, 'The Hildithryth Stone and Other Hartlepool Name-Stones', *Archaeologia Aeliana*, 4th ser. 34 (1956), 196–212 (pp. 201, 209).

[55] Her work is discussed by Dronke in *WWMA*, 30–3.

Farewell, living happily;
Health to you, for evermore,
Let us live for God alone,
So that you may be holy in simplicity,
And life always for evermore
May be granted by the heights [of heaven].

Indeed, I seek this very thing in my prayers
With tears poured forth right to the ground:
To petition for His support very frequently
So that we may be worthy of glory,
Where the most joyous songs
Of the angels resonate—
The joy of heaven—
By the renowned clemency of Christ
Of high praise for evermore.

May we flourish, victresses joined with the angelic thousands, living forever in the perpetual joys of paradise, ?Elonqueel and Michael, Acaddai, Adonai, Alleuatia, Alleluia.

This poem is in octosyllables, with a regular stress on the last syllable but two in each line (proparoxytone). The use of alliteration is very noticeable: alliteration is a central structural principle in Old English poetry, and is, understandably, often used by Anglo-Saxon authors writing in Latin.[56] Berhtgyth underlines the vehemence of her plea for her and her brother's safety and salvation with a string of magical names (mostly names for God in garbled Hebrew) which she may have thought of as ensuring that her prayer would be heeded. This is not a usual aspect of Anglo-Saxon Christian writing, and is not paralleled elsewhere in the mission's letter collection.[57] St Boniface himself, discussing the case of a half-educated wandering 'holy man' at the Roman synod of 745, makes it clear that he was very opposed to the talismanic use of strange names: 'we, instructed by Your Apostolic Holiness and by divine authority, know the names of but three angels, Michael, Gabriel, and Raphael, whereas he [Aldebert] brought in demons under the disguise of angels.'[58] Another odd feature of the poem is a grammatical solecism: if 'we' is to be taken as Berhtgyth and Balthard, then the rule in Latin is that the male takes precedence (as in French), but Berhtgyth uses 'victrices', the plural of the feminine form 'victrix' rather than the male 'victor'.

Latin learning in Anglo-Saxon England was disrupted by the Viking invasions, but by the tenth century, there are some indications that a few convents—those

---

[56] Lapidge, 'Aldhelm's Latin Poetry'.

[57] Though there is a parallel in an early Italian massbook, the Bobbio Missal, Paris, Bibliothèque Nationale, Lat. 13246, fo. 253ᵛ, a prayer with incantation formula listing angels: E. A. Lowe (ed.), *The Bobbio Missal: A Gallican Mass-Book* (London: For the Henry Bradshaw Society, 1920), 153. Still more relevant, the 8th- or 9th-century London, British Library, Harley 7653, written by a woman with Worcester connections, lists 'Rafael et Uriel gabriel et raguel heremiel et azael' (fo. 4ʳ), ed. F. E. Warren, *The Antiphonary of Bangor*, (London: Harrison and Sons, 1895), ii. 85.

[58] *Acts of the Roman Synod* of 25 Oct. 745. See also Valerie Flint, *The Rise of Magic in Early Medieval Europe* (Oxford: Clarendon Press, 1991), 168–9, 189.

under royal patronage—were cultivating Latin. Nunnaminster, at Winchester, is the convent of which this is most obviously true. A Latin note in the so-called Book of Nunnaminster (another private prayer book) was added there in the tenth century, and another inmate of Nunnaminster was the author of at least some of the material in a compendium of the early eleventh century, London, British Library, Cotton Galba A xiv, including a hymn to St Machutus.[59]

Hrotsvitha and the Ottonian Renaissance

In the tenth century, the Carolingian Empire weakened, and the balance of power in Europe shifted northwards. The dukes of Saxony proclaimed themselves emperors, creating a new dynasty, the Ottonians, who ruled the most opulent court in Western Europe, capable of aspiring to intermarriage with the royal house of Byzantium. Both Rosamond McKitterick and Elisabeth van Houts have argued that it was the women of the Ottonian dynasty, rather than the men, who made themselves responsible for cultural patronage generally, and the fosterage of history writing in particular.[60] There is even women's history from Ottonian Germany: two Lives of Queen Matilda (wife of Henry the Fowler, founder of the Ottonian dynasty) written by two different nuns at Nordhausen *c*.975,[61] and a set of annals was produced at the royal abbey of Quedlinburg.[62] Another result of Ottonian women's patronage of culture is the oeuvre of Hrotsvitha of Gandersheim, poet, playwright, and propagandist (*c*.935–*c*.1000); as with Dhuoda, since her works are readily available in translation, they will not be quoted here for reasons of space.

Hrotsvitha is unique in this study in having spent her adult life in what was effectively a small female monarchy. The resemblances in style between Hrotsvitha's writing and that of the brilliant and quarrelsome Rather of Verona, who came to the Ottonian court in 952 and spent some time there as a guest of the emperor's brother Bruno, suggest that she passed her youth at court rather than being brought up at Gandersheim,[63] but in any case, she became a canoness of

[59] W. de Gray Birch (ed.), *An Ancient Manuscript of the Eighth or Ninth Century, Formerly Belonging to St Mary's Abbey, or Nunnaminster, Winchester* (London: Simpkin & Marshall; Winchester: Warren & Son, 1889), 97, Bernard James Muir (ed.), *A Pre-Conquest English Prayer-Book* (London: For the Henry Bradshaw Society, 1988), 160.

[60] Elisabeth van Houts, 'Women and the Writing of History in the Early Middle Ages: The Case of Abbess Matilda of Essen and Aethelweard', *Early Medieval Europe*, 1.1 (1992), 53–68, and Rosamond McKitterick, 'Ottonian Intellectual Culture and the Role of Theophanu', *Early Medieval Europe*, 2.1 (1993), 53–74 (esp. p. 68).

[61] P. Corbet, *Les Saints ottoniens: sainteté dynastique, sainteté royale et sainteté féminine autour de l'an mil* (Sigmaringen: Jan Thorbecke, 1986), 120–234. See van Houts, 'Women and the Writing of History', 59. Janet Nelson has argued that two important anonymous early medieval chronicle texts, the *Annales Mettenses Priores* and the *Liber Historiae Francorum*, were authored by women, in her 'Perceptions de pouvoir chez les historiennes du Haut Moyen Âge', in M. Rouche (ed.), *Les Femmes au Moyen Âge* (Paris: J. Touzot, 1990), 77–85.

[62] G. H. Pertz (ed.), *Annales Quedlinburgenses*, MGH Scriptores III (Hanover: Hahn, 1834), 22–90.

[63] Peter L. D. Reid, *Tenth-Century Latinity: Rather of Verona* (Los Angeles: Humana Civilitas 6, 1981), Benny R. Reece, *Learning in the Tenth Century* (Greenville, Conn.: Furman University Press, 1968).

Gandersheim, a highly aristocratic convent founded in 852 by the great-grandfather of Otto I, Emperor of Germany. Its abbesses were all members of the ruling family, and held Gandersheim as an autonomous principality, which had its own courts, its own army, minted its own coinage,[64] had its own representative at the imperial Assembly, and was protected directly by the papal see without interference from bishops.[65] It also maintained strong connections with the royal court. Gandersheim was a highly intellectual, cultivated community of women. It contained both nuns, living under strict monastic vows, and canonesses, who were allowed to retain their private fortunes, have their own servants, buy their own books, entertain guests, and come and go. They could also, if they chose, leave Gandersheim permanently in order to marry. Hrotsvitha emerges from her context as a principal witness to a sophisticated tenth-century world of learned aristocrats, both male and female, who studied Classical Latin, Christian Latin, and Greek.

Gerberga II, Hrotsvitha's abbess and friend, was a niece of Otto the Great. She was born *c.*940, and educated at another royal convent, St Emmeram in Regensburg. She was barely 20 when she became the ruler of Gandersheim in 959 (about five years older than Hrotsvitha). She and her sister Hadwig were taught Greek—Gerberga was the beneficiary of Hadwig's education rather than vice versa, since the latter was intended to marry Prince Constantine of Byzantium.[66] Gerberga maintained close relations with the imperial court, particularly with the emperor's learned and literary younger brother Bruno, chancellor, chaplain, and Prince-Bishop of Mainz. In addition to teaching Hrotsvitha, she also instructed Sophia, daughter of Otto II, so thoroughly that, according to the Hildesheim 'Reimchronik', she was able to overcome learned men in disputation.[67] The tomb-verse of Abbess Hadwig of Essen (not Gerberga's sister but another Hadwig, *c.*947–971), of unknown authorship, contains words of Greek, suggesting that Greek was also studied at Essen.[68]

Hrotsvitha's surviving writing includes letters and seven plays, *Gallicanus, Agape, Chionia and Hirena, Drusiana and Callimachus, Mary the Niece of Abraham, The Conversion of Thais, The Passion of the Holy Maidens*, and *The Apocalypse*. She also wrote a series of poetic legends, which are paralleled with the plays in a double cycle, *Maria/Ascension, Gongolf, Pelagius, Theophilus, Basilius, Dionysius*, and *Agnes*.[69] Other, separate, works are her *Gesta Ottonis*, a heroic poem on the

---

[64] Alan M. Stahl, 'Monastic Minting in the Middle Ages', in Andrew MacLeish (ed.), *The Medieval Monastery* (St Cloud: North Star Press, 1985), 65–7.

[65] Heinrich, *The Canonesses*, 75, Edith Ennen, *The Medieval Woman*, trans. Edmund Jephcott (Oxford: Basil Blackwell, 1989), 80–3.

[66] Ekkehard IV, *Casus sancti Galli* 90, ed. H. Haefele (Darmstadt: Wissenschaftliche Buchgesellschaft, 1980), 184.

[67] Lina Eckenstein, *Women under Monasticisim* (Cambridge: Cambridge University Press, 1896), 151. Sophia 'vehemently upheld the role of her family, and played a certain role in imperial politics'. She appears in royal charters, and accompanied her brother Otto III on his first visit to Rome (Ennen, *The Medieval Woman*, 82–3).

[68] Karl Strecker and Gabriel Silagi (eds.), *Die lateinischen Dichten des deutschen Mittelalters*, v: *Die Ottonenzeit* (Munich: Verlag des Monumenta Germaniae Historica, 1979), 303.

[69] On Hrotsvitha, see Barbara K. Gold, 'Hrotswitha Writes Herself: Clamor Validus Gandeshemensis', in Barbara K. Gold, Par Allen Miller, and Charles Platter (eds.), *Sex and Gender in Medieval*

deeds of Otto I, composed *c*.965 and completed before 968 (this commission was given her by Gerberga and Otto II),[70] and *Primordia*, her poem on the origins of Gandersheim, her last work, composed *c*.973.

Hrotsvitha's work was rediscovered by the German humanist Conrad Celtis: his magnificent edition of all her works except *Primordia* was printed in Nuremberg in 1501, with woodcuts by a number of hands, including two by Albrecht Dürer,[71] and evidently generated considerable interest: since from the sixteenth century onward, the existence of learned women was taken as a symptom of cultural sophistication,[72] Hrotsvitha and her work were the focus of legitimate national pride. German humanists were aware of her work even before Celtis had brought out his great edition: Johannes Tritheim mentions her in his *De Scriptoribus Ecclesiasticis* printed in Basel in 1494, and Sebastian Brant has an epigram in her praise in his *Varia Carmina* printed in Basel in 1498. Other German humanists who responded to Celtis's rediscovery include Johan Zeller, who wrote a letter on the rediscovery of her writings to Thomas Pirckheimer,[73] the 'Sodalitatis literariae' which composed 'epigrammata in opera Hroswithae',[74] and Theodor Gresemundus and Valerius Meyensis, who made manuscript copies as late as the sixteenth century.[75] There is also a German translation by Adam Wernher von Themar (b. 1452), and a Hungarian translation of the fifteenth century.[76] She is frequently mentioned in Italian, French, and English catalogues of learned women from the sixteenth and seventeenth centuries.[77]

and Renaissance Texts (New York: State University of New York Press, 1997), 41–70, Katharina M. Wilson (ed.), *Hrotsvit of Gandersheim: Rara Avis in Saxonia?* (Ann Arbor: MARC Publishing, 1987), Katharina M. Wilson, *Hrotsvit of Gandersheim: The Ethics of Authorial Stance* (Leiden: E. J. Brill, 1988), Anne Lyon Haight (ed.), *Hroswitha of Gandersheim: Her Life, Times and Works* (New York: The Hroswitha Club, 1965).

[70] *WWMA*, 75–6.

[71] *Hrosvite Illustris Virginis et Monialis Germano Gente Saxonica Orte Opera Nuper à Conrado Celte Inventa* (Nuremberg: Hieronymus Holtzel, 1501).

[72] The 17th-century Leipzig scholar Johannes Sauerbrei ends his *Diatribe on Learned Women* with the proud boast: 'Since there is no lack of educated women among us, just as there are in Italy, people cannot accuse our Germany of being a barbarian land' ('Cum ergo ne foeminae quidem tot eruditae nobis desint, quid est quod Itali quidam Germaniam nostrum, ut barbaram terram accusant.' Sauerbrei, *Diatriben* (Leipzig: Johann Erich Hahn, 1671), pt. I, sig. E 2^v).

[73] Johann Zeller, 'de Rotwila', letter to Thomas Pirckheimer, London, British Library, Arundel 138, fo. 15^{r-v}.

[74] Berlin, Staatsbibliothek, Stiftung Preussisches Kulturbesitz, Lat. fol. 265.

[75] Pommersfelden, Gräflich Schönbornsche Bibliothek, 308 (2888). s. xvi^{in}, 'Rosvida opera', copied by Theodorius Gresemundus junior of Mainz from Munich 14485, and Berlin, Preussische Staatsbibliothek, Theol. lat. fol. 265. fos. 2–38 (now deposited in Tübingen, Universitätsbibliothek), copied from Celtis's edition by Valerius Meyensis.

[76] Heidelberg, Universitätsbibliothek, Pal. germ 831, and Budapest, Egyetemi Könyvtár (University Library), 6: this manuscript seems to have been made for the Dominican nuns of St Margaret's Island near Budapest. Haight (ed.), *Hrotswitha*, 50.

[77] For example, Luigi Contarini, *Il vago e dilettevole giardino historico, poetico, e geografico* (Vincenza: Francesco Grossi, 1597), 365: 'Rossudia di Sassonia al tempo di Giovanna Papa, dottissima in tutte le scienze, scrive molte cose latine e greche, fece sei comedie, e compose un libro in versi heroici, che tratta de gli Ottoni Imperatori, e un'altro in lode di Maria Vergine.'

The uniqueness of Hrotsvitha's dramas, the first classicizing comedies to be written for hundreds of years, has absorbed a disproportionate share of critical interest in her work. Her political poetry is also of great interest, and is clearly in a continuum with the abundant evidence for Ottonian royal nuns' interest in preserving (and shaping) family history. *Gesta Ottonis* is an epic poem, commissioned by a new ruling dynasty. As such, it must be directly compared with Virgil's *Aeneid*, composed at the behest of Augustus to explain and validate the Roman imperial project. We must conclude from this commission that Hrotsvitha, of all the women poets considered in this book, was the one to enjoy the highest status as a writer in her own milieu.

The opening of *Gesta Ottonis* suggests Hrotsvitha's acquaintance with Einhard's prose life of the great Carolingian Charlemagne, which begins by explaining how and why God saw fit to transfer power away from the Merovingians to the new dynasty. The epic gives a great deal of space to the royal ladies, about whom it offers a considerable amount of information which is not recorded by other historians. The *medias res* into which (following the rules of rhetoric) she plunges is not Otto's triumphant wars of conquest, but royal marriages and dynastic politics. Just as in the case of Proba, who turned explicitly away from the male priorities of war, she does not seek to imitate male ways of writing about politics: she substitutes as her principal subject the unobtrusive diplomacy which was, in the early Middle Ages, considered very much a woman's business,[78] and which she could access very directly through the memories of Gerberga and their common friend, Archbishop Bruno. Hrotsvitha has a strong sense of woman's appropriate sphere, but she worked in a context in which elite women's sphere included active, public life.

The structure of Hrotsvitha's poem is as follows: she begins with the transfer of power from the Franks to the Saxons, the reign of Henry ('the Fowler') with his wife Matilda, and the birth of their three sons: Otto, a born ruler, Henry, a great warrior, and Bruno, a prince of the Church. Then the new emperor Otto marries an Anglo-Saxon princess, Edith, and they have a son, Liudulf. Henry the Fowler dies, Otto takes his throne. His brother Henry then marries Judith, a noblewoman, and there is a rebellion. He is captured by Duke Eberhard, and rescued by his brother Otto. Henry himself rebels, makes penance, and is forgiven. Matilda dies. The story then switches to Otto and Edith's children, Liudolf and Liutgard, and the tribulations of the Italian queen Adelheid. Otto marries Adelheid, and defeats Berengar at Pavia. Liudolf then leads a civil war—here there is a lacuna in the one surviving manuscript—and subsequently father and son are reconciled, an event which is followed by the coronation of Otto and Adelheid.[79]

---

[78] See J. L. Nelson, 'Queens as Jezebels', in Derek Baker (ed.), *Medieval Women. Essays Presented to R. M. T. Hill* (Oxford: Basil Blackwell, for the Ecclesiastical History Society, 1978), 31–77, Pauline Stafford, *Queens, Concubines and Dowagers* (London: Batsford, 1983), and Michael J. Enright, *The Lady with the Mead-Cup* (Dublin: Four Courts, 1996).

[79] Wilson, *Hrotsvit: The Ethics* 111–44, Dennis M. Kratz, 'The Nun's Epic: Hroswitha on Christian Heroism', in Donald E. Reichel (ed.), *Wege der Worte: Festschrift für Wolfgang Fleischhauer* (Cologne: Böhlau, 1978).

This structure minimizes concentration on wars, civil or external, and focuses attention on family politics. She downplays dissension within the royal family: dealing as she unavoidably must with two serious rebellions, she shifts blame away from the Ottonians themselves. The instigators of the feud involving Henry, Otto's brother (and the father of her much-loved abbess, Gerberga), are presented as the counts Evurhard and Gislberht rather than Henry himself, and his attempt to murder Otto (320–35) is an act of madness directly caused by Satan. Similarly, Liudolf's rebellion against his father is mitigated by emphasis on his inner conflicts.

This is not a simple whitewashing job. Hrotsvitha was writing from within, not without, the royal dynasty she describes. Its interests were her interests; her patrons and probably her closest friends were among the dramatis personae of the story. There is no reason to believe her insincere in presenting the thesis that dissension and rebellion among Ottonians is essentially trivial, and what really matters is the greater harmony, the Ottonian mandate to rule given them by God, the essential rightness of their rule. Otto is compared to David (l. 139), the Old Testament model of a righteous king, but peculiarly appropriate to a parvenu dynasty, since David took the kingdom from Saul, which is alluded to in lines 252–4. God looks after his chosen ones, just as he looked after the kings of Israel (Otto was anointed as king, l. 131). As Wilson points out, the range of attributes Hrotsvitha associates with regality are not based on classical values, but on the Old Testament: *sapientia, pietas, iudicia, clementia, fortitudo*, family loyalty, and love of peace.[80] One might add to this list of Hrotsvitha's favourite virtues generosity: both Henry and his wife Judith are described as *generosus* (ll. 157, 183, 357). Generosity was a barbarian virtue; and this is the point where Hrotsvitha's view of royalty coincides with that of the anonymous Anglo-Saxon author of *Beowulf* (perhaps not far distant in time from her).

It is possible to context Hrotsvitha's remarkable achievement. Gandersheim was not the only Ottonian milieu to cultivate the arts. All the communities ruled over by Ottonian royal abbesses contained learned women. As is the case in the ninth century, tenth-century convents contained notable scribes: a prayer book survives written in gold ink on purple parchment *c*.990 by the female master scribe Duriswint.[81] The women of the Ottonian dynasty itself were highly educated, as an aspect of their overall competence. The status of the wives of rulers rose notably from that enjoyed by Carolingian queens, and Ottonian queens were officially described as co-partners in rule: when Theophanu was admitted to the *consortium imperii* in 972, she was described as 'coimperatrix augusta necnon imperii regnorum consors' (Augusta, co-emperor, and partner in rule over the kingdoms).[82] Matilda,

---

[80] Wilson, *Hrotsvit: The Ethics*, 115.

[81] Pommersfelden, Schlossbibliothek, MS 347, originally presented to Otto III. Similarly the Anglo-Saxon nun Eadburg was commissioned to produce a gold-letter Gospels by St Boniface (*Die Briefe des heiligen Bonifatius und Lullus*, ed. M. Tangl, MGH Epistolae Selectae I (Berlin: Wiedmann, 1916), no. 35): writing in gold ink required great skill.

[82] Ennen, *The Medieval Woman*, 61–72, discusses the active political interventions of Ottonian empresses and princesses.

the only daughter of Otto I, was appointed future abbess of Quedlinburg from her cradle, and hence educated as a future nun. As an adult, she was even called *metropolitana*—overseer of bishops—by her biographer.[83] When Otto III went to Italy for a prolonged period at the end of the tenth century, the management of affairs at home was given to Abbess Matilda, who ruled with success as *matricia* (governess) of Germany. She was so interested in the history of her own time that Widukind forwarded his *History of the Saxons* to her book by book for her approval, and there is much other evidence for her concern with history.[84] The three great royal abbeys, Quedlinburg, Gandersheim, and Essen, were normally headed by Ottonian women. During Matilda's minority, the sister of Burchard of Worms protested that she was unsuitable as a temporary abbess because the only book she knew was the Psalter, suggesting that Ottonian abbesses were expected to be well read. The point is reinforced by Cunegunde, wife of the last Saxon emperor, Henry II, who was a great reader, and later gave lessons to her niece Uta.[85]

Uta, who became Abbess of Niedermünster in the tenth century, evidently put her lessons to good use. Her principal monument is an illuminated Gospel book, in which the picture-pages are further decorated with verse inscriptions.[86] Her authorship is suggested by the following verse:

> Virgo dei genetrix, divina pignore felix
> Suscipe vota tue promti serviminis Ute
>
> Virgin mother of God, happy in your Divine Child,
> accept the prayer of your Uta, a woman of willing service.

Towards the end of the Ottonian era, a poem survives from the Ottonian convent of Essen, on a reliquary of Marsus (a confessor) and Lugtrudis (a virgin), made in the reign of Abbess Theophanu (d. 1056).

> Hoc opus eximium gemmis auroque decorum
> Mathildis vovit, Theophanu quod bene solvit
> Regi dans regum Mathildt haec crysea dona
> Abbatissa bona; quae rex deposcit in aevum
> Spiritus Ottonis pauset caelestibus oris.
>
> Matilda made a votive offering of this excellent work,
> Beautiful in its jewels and gold, which Theophanu disposed of;
> Good abbess Matilda, giving to the King of Kings these golden gifts,
> Which the king everlastingly keeps asking for,
> May the spirit of Otto tarry on the celestial shores.

---

[83] Suzanne Wemple, 'Sanctity and Power: The Dual Pursuit of Early Medieval Women', in Renate Bridenthal, Claudia Koonz, and Susan M. Stuard (eds.), *Becoming Visible: Women in European History* (Boston: Houghton Mifflin, 1977), 148.

[84] Eckenstein, *Women*, 153. On Widukind, see Ad. Ebert, *Allgemeine Geschichte der Litteratur des Mittelalters im Abendland*, 3 vols. (Leipzig., 1874–77), iii. 429 n., and on Matilda and history, refs in n. 61 above.

[85] Thiébaux, *The Writings of Medieval Women*, pp. xxi–xiii.

[86] Adam S. Cohen, *The Uta Codex: Art, Philosophy and Religion in Eleventh-Century Germany* (University Park: Pennsylvania State University Press, 2000).

(The reliquary has since been damaged: the version given here includes lines supplied from a copy taken in 1662.) It seems probable that this verse was made by a member of the Essen community, perhaps Theophanu, who is stated here to have fulfilled the vow first made by her predecessor Matilda.

There is evidence Hadwig, the sister of Hrotsvitha's beloved Abbess Gerberga, continued to take an interest in the classical languages as the widowed ex-duchess of Swabia. The historian Ekkehard IV from the monastery of St Gallen (in Switzerland) brought a boy called Purchart to her, because he longed to learn Greek: he pleased her by addressing her in impromptu Latin hexameters, so she gave him a hug and a kiss and agreed to teach him. When he left, she presented him with a copy of Horace and several other books which, says Ekkehard, 'our library contains today'.[87] As Robert Farrel remarks, 'Hadwig is a remarkable and imposing figure, one in whom power, position and classical learning are linked to one another—and more importantly, to a frank female sexuality that is not incompatible with conventional piety.'[88] It is also interesting that an anonymous Ottonian poet, possibly Ekkehard, composed a lengthy poem 'On Powerful Women' (*De Muliere Forti*), based on Bede's allegorization of Proverbs, which proffers a vision of powerful, serene, triumphant nuns, like holy valkyries.[89]

There were many other outstanding and politically significant women among the Ottonians and their immediate connections. Bertha, wife of Adalbert of Tuscany, ruled 'imperially' for ten years after her husband's death, and her daughter-in-law, Marozia *senatrix* ('female senator', a title which would have shocked earlier generations), made herself ruler of Rome 928–32.[90] Gisela, wife of Conrad II, was formally described as the emperor's *necessaria comes* (necessary companion), and *consors imperii* (sharer in royal power).[91] Her sister Matilda wrote the same type of formal Latin prose with rhyming *clausulae* which was used by Hrotsvitha, evidenced in a letter which accompanied her gift of a splendid liturgical manuscript to Misegonus II, King of Poland.[92] Matilda's still more formidable granddaughter, Matilda, Margrave of Tuscany (1046–1115), was an important supporter of Pope Gregory VII in his struggle with the German emperor, Henry IV: she actively engaged in warfare, and intervened with her own troops on behalf of the pope.[93] In her *vita*, Henry is depicted grovelling at her feet

---

[87] Ekkehard IV, *Casus* 94, ed. Haefele, 194.

[88] Joseph Farrell, *The Latin Language and Latin Culture from Ancient to Modern Times* (Cambridge: Cambridge University Press, 2001), 79–81.

[89] Strecker and Silagi (eds.), *Die lateinischen Dichten des deutschen Mittelalters*, v: *Die Ottonenzeit*, 601–10.

[90] K. J. Leyser, *Medieval Germany and its Neighbours, 900–1250* (London: Hambledon Press, 1982), 110, 111.

[91] Ennen, *The Medieval Woman*, 69. Their daughter Beatrix was noted for her devotion to learning, and educated by Adelheid, Abbess of Quedlinburg. Heinrich, *The Canonesses*, 101.

[92] Phil. Ant. Dethier, *Epistola Inedita Mathildis Soror Gislae Imperatricis et Aviae Mathildis Toscanae, Data Anno 1027 aut 1028 ad Misegonum II* (Berlin: Behr, 1842), 4.

[93] See her Life, by Dionigio of Canossa, *Vita Mathildis Celeberrimae Principis Italiae* (written 1114) (Vatican City: Biblioteca apostolica, Lat. 4922) which shows Henry IV kneeling before Matilda on fo. 49ᵛ. Mary Huddy, *Matilda, Countess of Tuscany* (London: John Long, 1906), Paolo Golinelli, *Matilde*

begging her, 'O valiant cousin, go, and intercede for me!'⁹⁴ The intervening dynastic link, Beatrice of Lorraine, was a connection of the French royal family who composed her own Latin epitaph, and introduced her daughter to the rather difficult poetry of Prudentius at an early age.⁹⁵

Anonymous verse from the early Middle Ages

One area of surviving Latin writing which is obviously highly problematic for a study of this kind is the isolated, anonymous lyric in a woman's voice. One can never be certain about the authorship of such poems, preserved more or less by chance in medieval compendia and marginalia. A fairly recent study of medieval woman's song assumes almost without discussion that all songs in a feminine voice are actually male authored. The alternative, that some are actually by women, is dismissed as 'romantic'.⁹⁶ But one of Charlemagne's *Capitularia* for convents famously states, ⁹⁷

No abbess may presume to go out of the convent without our permission, not allow her subordinates to do so: their enclosure should be well maintained, and they should absolutely not presume to write or send *winileodas* from there . . .

A *winileod* is a love song, however that may be defined, or, less suggestively, a poem of friendship (*wine*: friend, *leod*: song). Few kings trouble to legislate against abuses that are not actually taking place, so this is an indirect witness to enclosed women's creative activity. Quite a few Carolingian nuns were certainly Latin-literate, though as early as the ninth century, Frankish was also beginning to be used as a written language, so even the fact that these compositions are (not) to be 'written or sent' does not confirm that they are in Latin. There is a short Latin poem from one Engilbert to his *soror* in a ninth-century manuscript which seems to demand a *winileod* in return.⁹⁸ But no one has ever managed to identify a *winileod* for certain, since it is impossible to be sure that a lyric in a female persona is what it appears to be. One which is worth consideration is the following:⁹⁹

e i Canossa nel cuore del Medioevo (Florence: Camunia, 1996), and Ennen, *The Medieval Woman*, 71. She is remembered by Joanne Sabadino de l'Arienti, *Gynevera* written for Ginevra Sforza [1483], ed. Corrado Ricci and A. Bacchi della Lega (Bologna: Romagnoli-Dall' Acqua, 1888) (p. 25). See also Joan M. Ferrante, 'Women's Role in Latin Letters', in June Hall McCash (ed.), *The Cultural Patronage of Medieval Women* (Athens: University of Georgia Press, 1996), 73–104 (pp. 92–5).

⁹⁴ 'Consobrina valens, fac me benedicere, vade!' See illustration 2 in Ennen, *The Medieval Woman*, between pp. 154 and 155.

⁹⁵ Huddy, *Matilda*, 17.

⁹⁶ Anne Howland Schotter, 'Women's Song in Medieval Latin', in J. F. Plummer, (ed.), *Vox Feminae: Studies in Medieval Woman's Song* (Kalamazoo, Mich.: Studies in Medieval Culture 15, 1981), 19–33 (p. 31 n. 2). But on the other hand, writing in Latin has a better chance of being preserved.

⁹⁷ 'Duplex legationis edictum', AD, 789 in Alfredus Boretius (ed.), *Capitularia Regum Francorum*, 2 vols. (Hanover: Hahn, 1883), i. 63, cap. 19.

⁹⁸ Karl Strecker (ed.), *Die lateinische Dichter des deutschen Mittelalters*, vii: *Nachträge zu den Poetae Aevi Carolini* (Weimar: Hermann Böhlaus, 1951), 174, from Vienna, Staatsbibliothek, 808.

⁹⁹ The eight-syllable lines of this fragmentary poem break down in the last three lines: the version given here is amended to give the octosyllabic structure it seems meant to have. Where I give 'fortasse' the MS has 'forte' , with the same meaning. I hesitate to emend further, and offer 'alba' only with hesitation.

Nam languens amore tuo
consurrexi diluculo
perrexique pedes nuda
per niues et <per> frigora
atque maria rimabar mesta,
si fortasse uentiuola
uela <alba> cernerem
aut frontem nauis conspicerem

For, languishing from love for you,
I rose at crack of dawn,
And went forth barefoot
Through the snow and the cold,
And scanned the sad seas, (or, 'sad, scanned the seas')
In case I might catch sight
Of wind-blown sails,
Or sight the prow of a boat.

This exquisite fragment, obviously indebted to the hypnotic rhythms of the Song of Solomon, is strangely preserved in the middle of a fabliau (a type of folk narrative, sometimes but not inevitably in verse), telling the highly misogynistic story of the 'Snow Child', to which it clearly does not belong. 'Nam languens' portrays a situation often represented in later women's song; the woman waiting longingly for her lover's return.[100] We may compare a poem perhaps similar in date, the Old English *Wife's Lament*: 'ever since my lord departed from this people over the sea, I have had care each dawn, wondering where in the world my lord may be'.[101] But the emotional tone of this short piece is perhaps more like that of Anne Elliot's words in *Persuasion*, 'we certainly do not forget you so soon as you forget us. It is, perhaps, our fate rather than our merit. We cannot help ourselves. We live at home, quiet, confined, and our feelings prey on us.'[102] It survives from one of the earliest collections of medieval lyric poetry, the 'Cambridge Songs': the manuscript is of the mid-eleventh century, and forms part of a classbook for the school at Canterbury.[103] Some poems are probably tenth century, of which 'Nam languens' is one, others even older, so verses from this manuscript can usefully be considered at the end of this chapter rather than at the beginning of the next.

Another important poem from this manuscript, 'O admirabile Veneris idolum', which has long been interpreted as a lyric of male homosexuality (and as such, often quoted), has been recently argued by Benedikt Vollman to be the work of a

---

[100] See Lawrence Lipking, *Abandoned Women and Poetic Tradition* (Chicago: University of Chicago Press, 1988), and Roland Barthes, *A Lover's Discourse* (New York: Hill and Wang, 1978), 15: 'it is Woman who gives shape to absence, elaborates its fiction, for she has time to do so, she weaves, she sings.'

[101] 'Ærest min hlaford gewat heonan of leodum ofer ytha gelac; hæfde ic uhtceare hwær min leodfruma londes wære' (lines 6–8).

[102] *Persuasion*, ch. 23.

[103] A. G. Rigg and G. R. Wieland, 'A Canterbury Classbook of the Mid-Eleventh Century', *Anglo-Saxon England*, 4 (1975), 113–30.

woman, or an exchange of verses between a man and a woman.[104] Such a reading requires a robust acceptance that by the tenth century there were women capable of writing verse of great sophistication: the evidence for the literary life of convents, particularly in the Ottonian world, renders this by no means incredible, and it is worth noting that a substantial amount of the material in the 'Cambridge Songs' collection originated in Ottonian Germany.[105]

Two other very subtle poems from this collection involve a female voice. One which presents a good case for female authorship is 'Levis exsurgit Zephirus', not least because the female voice of this delicate and moving lyric is established only by a single word in the fifth stanza: 'Cum mihi *sola* sedeo' (not 'solus'), and the state of mind it describes, that of a person sitting alone in spring paralysed by depression (implicitly caused by lost love), is one which any young person might experience.[106] It could certainly be the work of a nun, since it makes no reference to any sort of physical relationship, but only to the pain of rejection, which could be, and was, experienced by cloistered women. The delicate eroticism of the first stanza, in which the personified earth, warmed by the sun, seems to spread herself open and proffer the gift of her own pleasure, is of a kind which could be read as feminine:

> Levis exsurgit Zephirus
> et sol procedit tepidus
> iam terra sinus aperit
> dulcore suo affluit.
>
> Ver purpuratum exiit
> ornatos suos induit
> aspergit terram floribus
> ligna silvarum frondibus.
>
> Struunt lustra quadrupedes
> et dulces nidos volucres
> inter ligna florentia
> sua decantant gaudia.
>
> Quod oculis dum video
> et auribus tam audio
> heu, pro tantis gaudiis
> tantis inflor suspiriis.
>
> Cum mihi sola sedeo
> et hec revolvens palleo
> sic forte caput sublevo
> nec audio nec video.

[104] Benedikt K. Vollmann, ' "O admirabile Veneris idolum" (Carmina Cantabrigiensia 48)—ein Mädchenlied?', in. Udo Kindermann et al. (eds.), *Festschrift für Paul Klopsch* (Göttingen: Kümmerle, 1988), 532–43. See also Joseph Szövérffy, *Secular Latin Lyrics and Minor Poetic Forms of the Middle Ages* (Concord, NH: Classical Folia Editions, 1992), 77–9.

[105] Szövérffy, *Secular Latin Lyrics*, 238–42.

[106] Translated in Helen Waddell, *Medieval Latin Lyrics* (Harmondsworth: Penguin, 1929), 168–9 (and frequently elsewhere in anthologies of medieval poetry). See Szövérffy, *Secular Latin Lyrics*, 74.

Tu saltim, Veris gratia
exaudi et considera
frondes, flores et gramina;
nam me languet anima.

The light West wind is arising,
The sun is coming forth warm;
Now the earth is opening her lap,
And flowing with her sweetness.

Spring has come out arrayed in shining silk,
Is putting on its finery,
Is sprinkling the ground with flowers,
And the trees of the woodlands with leaves.

Fourfooted beasts are making their dens,
And the sweet birds their nests;
Between the flowering trees,
They carol forth their joy.

All the time I see this with my eyes,
And hear as much with my ears,
Alas, for such great joys,
I am filled with sighs just as great.

When I [*fem.*] am sitting all by myself
And pondering these things, I grow pale,
If perchance I raise my head,
I neither hear nor see.

You at least, grace of Spring,
Listen and consider
The leaves, the flowers, and grasses,
For my soul is languishing.

The last line is 'nam mea *languet* anima': recall the first line of the last poem discussed, 'nam *languens* amore tuo'. It is a word which inevitably recalls the Song of Songs, 'fulcite me floribus, stipate me malis, quia amore *langueo*': 'stay me with flowers and comfort me with apples, for I am sick with love.' (Cant. 2: 5); to choose this particular word to describe malaise (rather than, say, *taedet*) means that the alert reader adds 'with love' almost unconsciously.

Another poem, 'Iam, dulcis amica, venito' ('Come now, my sweet mistress'), is more problematic and, like both of the other poems discussed here, associable with the Song of Songs. On the surface, it invites the beloved to a tryst in an elegant room, but it could also be read as an allegorization of spiritual experience—the use of phrases from the Song of Solomon, such as 'soror electa' (chosen sister: see Cant. 5: 2), point in this direction.[107] The beloved's mysterious reply (stanza 7, or stanzas 7–8) may be the response of an educated and refined young nun engaged in

[107] This poem has been much discussed. See F. J. E. Raby, *A History of Secular Latin Poetry in the Middle Ages*, (Oxford: Clarendon Press, 1934), i. 303–4, Szövérffy, *Secular Latin Lyrics*, 79–83 and 243 for a bibliography of different readings (and different reconstructions).

the game of spiritual *amicitia* (to be discussed more fully in the next chapter), or it could record the way that mystical experience is more effectively sought during solitary retreats than in the bustle of daily life:[108]

> ...Ego fui sola in silva
> et dilexi loca secreta
> frequenter effugi tumultum
> et vitavi populum multum.
>
> Iam nix glaciesque liquescit,
> Folium et herba virescit,
> Philomena iam cantat in alto,
> Ardet amor cordis in antro.

> I have been alone in the wood (or, 'I have been in a lonely wood')
> And I have loved secluded places,
> Often I have fled from tumult
> And avoided crowds of people.
>
> Now snow and ice are melting,
> Leaf and grass grows green,
> Now the nightingale is singing on high,
> And love is burning in the heart's cavern.

The fact that it was used as a paraliturgical song in St Martial of Limoges suggests that this lyric was, even in its own time, perceived as profoundly ambiguous.[109]

---

[108] Waddell, *Medieval Latin Lyrics*, 156–9. Szövérffy, *Secular Latin Lyrics*, 243.

[109] Peter Dronke, 'The Song of Songs and Medieval Love-Lyric', in *The Medieval Poet and his World* (Rome: Edizioni di storia e letteratura, 1984), 216–25.

5. *Women and Latin Verse in the High Middle Ages*

As this study moves forwards in time, it becomes necessary to engage with European culture's changing relationship with the Latin language. From the tenth century, the identification of Latin with written culture began to dissolve, since in many European languages such as Old Saxon, Old English, and Old French, it is this century which sees the first surviving vernacular literature.[1] And as the second millennium went on, the idea of writing in the vernacular, whichever the local language might be, takes hold, grows, and flourishes in all parts of Europe, so, therefore, second-millennium writers of Latin poetry, whether men or women, are an elite within an elite. Literates in the high Middle Ages were still a small sub-group within the population as a whole, but not every literate was now 'litteratus', which, in contemporary parlance, usually meant literate in Latin. There is an additional problem with this basic question of literacy, which is highlighted by Jan Ziolkowski:[2]

So strong was the oral and oratorical component in medieval education that a person could be educated and proficient in speaking Latin without being able to write it comfortably. In other words, literacy and schooling were not identical.

This is particularly relevant to nuns, most of whom needed to be able to read far more than they needed to be able to write.[3]

Another aspect of medieval culture which needs to be brought in at the outset is that the problem of women's creative writing cannot be separated from that of creative writing in general. In general, creativity and originality in the Middle Ages were not central values.[4] Bernard of Clairvaux's well-known remark that the men of his time were dwarfs standing on the shoulders of giants is a characteristically medieval attitude to the relative status of his contemporaries and the much-admired works of the past. Almost all medieval authors, male and female, however well established, engaged in a ritual display of modesty and incapacity before launching into their subject, though this did not necessarily prevent them from

---

[1] See Roger Wright, *Late Latin and Early Romance in Spain and Carolingian France* (Liverpool: Francis Cairns, 1982).

[2] Jan Ziolkowski, 'Cultural Diglossia and the Nature of Medieval Latin Literature', in Joseph Harris (ed.), *The Ballad and Oral Literature*, Harvard English Studies 17 (Cambridge, Mass.: Harvard University Press, 1991), 193–213.

[3] See for example the chapter on 'Literacy and Learning' in David Bell, *What Nuns Read: Books and Libraries in Medieval English Nunneries* (Kalamazoo, Mich.: Cistercian Publications, 1995), 57–96.

[4] Sabina Flanagan, *Hildegard of Bingen, 1098–1179: A Visionary Life* (London: Routledge, 1989), 41–56.

writing in an effective and original manner.[5] One consequence of this is that much of the surviving Latin writing from the Middle Ages is anonymous, and therefore, unless the writer refers to him- or herself directly, ungendered.[6]

The chance that any one piece of anonymous Latin verse writing is of female authorship is reduced by the barriers which were erected against women's participation in high culture. Most verse writing emanated from *clerici*, trained in the universities which began to arise in the high Middle Ages, institutions which did not admit women as students. Legend, if not life, has more to say about medieval women professors than medieval women students (some of the 'professors' will be discussed in the next chapter).[7] The first story of a female university student is that of a woman called Nawojka who is said to have attended the University of Kraków *c*.1400, having disguised herself as a man.[8] However, it should not be forgotten that there were some convents which both cultivated learning and accepted lay pupils: Wilton, for example, where the poet Muriel flourished, and both Edith, wife of Edward the Confessor, and Matilda, wife of Henry I, were educated;[9] or Argenteuil, where Heloïse became a prodigy of learning. But the only anonymous Latin writing which can really be considered as at all likely to be of female authorship is that which clearly originates from among a group of Latin-literate women, therefore from a nun or a canoness.

Almost all the identifiable Latin women poets of the eleventh to fourteenth centuries appear to have been in religious orders of one kind or another. There were very few Latin-literate laywomen: the minuscule amount of Latin verse by laywomen comes from a tiny handful of nobles, such as Beatrice of Lorraine, possibly the author of a brief inscription on her tomb in the Campo Santo in Pisa, and the Ottonian princess Matilda of Saxony.[10] Nearly all laywomen who had the education and the will to write did so in their vernacular, for example the Anglo-Norman writer

[5] On creativity and innovation in the Middle Ages, see Peter Dronke, *Poetic Individuality in the Middle Ages* (Oxford: Clarendon Press, 1970), on formulae of incapacity, E. R. Curtius, *European Literature and the Latin Middle Ages*, trans. W. R. Trask (London: Routledge & Kegan Paul, 1953), 83–5, 407–13, and Tore Janson, *Latin Prose Prefaces* (Stockholm: Almquist and Wiksell, 1964). With respect to women, see also Joan Ferrante, 'Public Postures, Private Maneuvers', in Mary Erler and Maryanne Kowaleski (eds.), *Women and Power in the Middle Ages* (Athens: University of Georgia Press, 1988), 213–29 (p. 222).

[6] For example, in a self-referential passage, a writer might speak of him- or herself, for example, as *peccator/peccatrix* (a sinner; m/f), or state 'indignus/a sum' (I am unworthy), thus revealing his or her gender. However, in the case of writings copied in convents, only the *scribe*'s gender is revealed, since nuns sometimes adapted prayers for their own use (e.g. London, British Library, Harley 7653, in F. E. Warren, (ed.), *The Antiphonary of Bangor* (London: Harrison and Sons, 1895), ii. 83–6 (p. 86) (masculine *peccator*, feminine *famula* in the same prayer suggests rather superficial adaptation).

[7] There are several such accounts: see discussion in Ch 6.

[8] Michael H. Shank, 'A Female University Student in Late Medieval Kraków', in J. Bennett et al. (eds.), *Sisters and Workers in the Middle Ages* (Chicago: Chicago University Press, 1989), 190–7.

[9] Frank Barlow (ed.), *Life of Edward the Confessor* (Edinburgh: Nelson, 1962), 47, 14, Eadmer, *Historia Novorum in Anglia*, ed. M. Rule (London: Eyre and Spottiswode for HMSO, 1884), 123. Matilda read and wrote Latin; so probably did Edith, who is described as learned.

[10] See Joan M. Ferrante, *To the Glory of her Sex* (Bloomington: Indiana University Press, 1997), 47, J. W. Thompson, *The Literacy of the Laity in the Middle Ages* (Berkeley and Los Angeles: University of California Press, 1939). Latin-literate laywomen include Constance of Brittany, who wrote a letter wooing Louis VII, printed by Léopold Delisle in *Recueil des historiens de Gaules et de la France*, 19 vols.

Marie de France, the Italo-French Christine de Pizan, who wrote in French,[11] and the Provençal *trobairitz* (female troubadours).[12] Marie seems to have known Latin (as did Christine), since in her prologue she states that she considered translating some *bone estoire* from Latin into French before deciding to write the *Lais* themselves, but it obviously did not occur to her to write in that language.[13]

A manual written between 1307 and 1315 in rhymed Provençal by Francesco da Barberino (1264–1348) suggests some context for women's limited access to Latin, since it directly associates literacy for women with the exercise of authority.[14] Daughters of kings and emperors are advised to write and read well because they will later have to govern many lands (he does not specifically say they should read Latin but this may well be what he means). Daughters of marquises, dukes, counts, and barons should learn to read. About the daughters of squires, judges, 'solemn doctors', and gentlemen of similar rank, he says, opinions differ, but he personally thinks they should not.[15] Similarly, Vincent de Beauvais in *De Eruditione Filiorum Nobilium* (on the education of noble children) suggests that young noblewomen should learn to read and write Latin and French, and also learn philosophy, self-knowledge, and self-government.[16]

Though the coming of the Normans may have narrowed possibilities for upper-class women in England in general,[17] the role of royal women actually expanded.[18]

(Paris: Palmé, 1867–80), xvi. 23, and Eleanor of Aquitaine: there are four of her Latin letters in Thomas Rymer, *Foedera, Conventiones, Litera, et Cujuscunque Generis Acta Publica inter Reges Angliae et Alios*, 20 vols. (London: A. & J. Churchill, 1702), i. 72–8, 122. Anselm (1033–1109) wrote in Latin to thirteen laywomen, the *comitissae* and *dominae* Frodelina, Adela [of Blois], Rohaida [daughter of Walter Giffard], Ida [mother of Godefroi de Bouillon], Ermengard, Richeza [his sister], Matilda [queen of Henry I], Clementia, Basilia, 'quaedam domina', another Matilda, Ada, Adelida (*PL* clviii–clix: Anselm's *epistolarium*, nos. I. 37, I. 77, I. 53, II. 24, II. 37, III. 18, III. 56, III. 58, II. 40, III. 43, III. 63, III. 66, III. 67, III. 57, III. 81, III. 97, III. 107, III. 120, III. 128, IV. 12, IV. 30, IV. 43, IV. 54, III. 59, III. 133, III. 138, III. 157, IV. 37, IV. 61).

11 Her *Book of the City of Ladies* is trans. Earl Jeffrey Richards (London: Picador, 1983), *The Treasure of the City of Ladies* is trans. Sarah Lawson (Harmondsworth: Penguin, 1985). Recent scholarship is discussed in Earl Jeffrey Richards (ed.), *Reinterpreting Christine de Pizan* (Athens: University of Georgia Press, 1992).

12 Meg Bogin (ed.), *The Women Troubadours* (London: Paddington Press, 1979).

13 Angela M. Lucas, *Women in the Middle Ages: Religion, Marriage and Letters* (Brighton: Harvester, 1983), 159.

14 Alice A. Hentsch, *De la littérature didactique du Moyen Âge s'addressant spécialement aux femmes* (Cahors: A. Coeslant, 1903), 133, 84, 106–7, and see Margaret Deanesley, *The Lollard Bible* (Cambridge: Cambridge University Press, 1920), 22.

15 See Helen Solterer, *The Master and Minerva* (Berkeley and Los Angeles: University of California Press, 1995), 127, and Charles Stallaert and Philippe van der Haegen, 'De l'instruction publique au moyen âge du viiie au xvie siècle', in *Mémoires couronnés et mémoires des savants étrangers publiés par L'Académie Royale des Sciences, des Lettres et des Beaux-arts de Belgique*, 23 (Brussels: Académie Royale, 1850), 101.

16 Prudence Allen, *The Concept of Woman II* (Grand Rapids, Mich.: William B. Eerdman, 2002), 756.

17 Judith Weiss, 'The Power and Weakness of Women in Anglo-Norman Romance', in Carol M. Meale (ed.), *Women and Literature in Britain, 1150–1500* (Cambridge: Cambridge University Press, 1993), 7–23 (pp. 7–8), but contra, see Anne Klinck, 'Anglo-Saxon Women and the Law', *Journal of Medieval History*, 8 (1982), 107–21.

18 Pauline Stafford documents Anglo-Saxon queens' rise in status and power in the 10th and 11th centuries in *Queen Emma and Queen Edith: Queenship and Women's Power in Eleventh-Century England* (Oxford: Blackwell, 1997).

William the Conqueror's well-educated queen, Mathilde, sat as president of an English court, in the capacity of regent, on at least two occasions, which is more than any Anglo-Saxon queen is ever known to have done.[19] Their daughters and granddaughters were also conspicuously well educated, and some of them, most notably Adela of Blois, who twice acted as William's regent, followed the learned princesses of Ottonian Germany and foreshadowed the learned princesses of Renaissance Italy in that they received a Latin education in order to perform the normally masculine functions of rule, judgement, and patronage.[20] An anonymous poet of the Loire school said of one Norman lady (probably Adela):[21]

> Your reading of Ovid does not lie hidden, your worship,
> Nor the perception of [C]ato which tests for truths.
> You also learned how to speak publicly in the vernacular:
> You have learned to versify in an amazing arrangement.

Her Latin studies are linked with training in public speaking, and with verse writing—presumably in Latin.

The realization that medieval women might write in Latin requires the same kind of change in perception which has recently allowed historians to see that a woman such as Adela of Blois was exercising 'lordship', and that there were twelfth-century writers prepared to argue for the acceptability of female rule.[22] Much has been said about medieval misogyny, and with reason.[23] Conversely, Alcuin Blamires has recently studied the evidence for the case *for* women in medieval culture, and points out that the making of lists of noble and virtuous women, a growth industry of the Renaissance, had roots back into late antiquity, and continued through the Middle Ages.[24] Joan M. Ferrante's perception that, for

---

[19] Pauline Stafford, *Unification and Conquest: A Political and Social History of England in the Tenth and Eleventh Centuries* (London: Edward Arnold, 1989), 173.

[20] The personal power of Adela of Blois is explored by Kimberley A. LoPrete, 'Adela of Blois: Familial Alliances and Female Lordship', in Theodore Evergates (ed.), *Aristocratic Women in Medieval France* (Philadelphia: University of Pennsylvania Press, 1999), 7–43: see also Karen S. Nicholas, 'Countesses as Rulers in Flanders', and Fredric L. Cheyette, 'Women, Poets and Politics in Occitania', in the same volume, pp. 111–37 and 138–78, and Erler and Kowaleski (eds.), *Women and Power in the Middle Ages*. Latin poets' efforts to court Adela and her mother Mathilde are listed by Joseph Szövérffy, *Secular Latin Lyrics and Minor Poetic Forms of the Middle Ages* (Concord, NH: Classical Folia Editions, 1992), 360–4 and by Gerald A. Bond, *The Loving Subject* (Philadelphia: University of Pennsylvania Press, 1995), 129–57.

[21] Bond, *The Loving Subject*, 147–8: I follow his correction of Plato to Cato.

> Lectio Nasonis non te latet, O veneranda,
> Sed neque Catonis sententia vera probanda.
> Tu quoque barbarico nosti sermone profari:
> Ordine mirifico didicisti versificari.

[22] In his life of Edith of Wilton, Goscelin asserts that Edith, a nun, daughter of King Edgar, was offered the throne in the 970s (highly unlikely), but supports his case by contending that many nations had been successfully ruled by women. André Wilmart (ed.), 'La Légende de Ste Edith en prose et vers par le moine Goscelin', *Analecta Bollandiana*, 56 (1938), 5–101, 265–307 (pp. 82–3, 84).

[23] For an overview, see R. Howard Bloch, *Medieval Misogyny and the Invention of Western Romantic Love* (Chicago: Chicago University Press, 1991).

[24] Alcuin Blamires, *The Case for Women in Medieval Culture* (Oxford: Clarendon Press, 1997), 171.

medieval churchmen, theory and practice might inhabit different mental spheres is also worth considering: [25]

> I suggest that when medieval men write theoretically about the female sex, they may condemn it or relegate it to subordinate roles, but when they—even the same men—deal with individual women, they treat them as colleagues or even as superiors. Whatever they may think of the idea of women in such a position, they accept the fact.

This view would help to explain the stance taken towards women by men such as Baudri de Bourgeuil. Lois Huneycutt has addressed the same issue, commenting that 'twelfth-century polemicists could justify placing women in positions of public authority while at the same time denying the abilities of the female sex as a whole'.[26] Ferrante lists some of the many women in authority and women writers who were referred to as 'the glory of their sex' in the Middle Ages.[27] Both she and Huneycutt seem to be suggesting that medieval churchman had a robust tolerance for logical contradictions as long as the result of the contradiction was pragmatically acceptable. They could also, if it seemed necessary to do so, point to the same contradiction in the works of the Fathers of the Church, customarily regarded as authorities on all matters, as Chapter 3 endeavoured to demonstrate.

Medieval convent culture remained Latinate to some extent, since all liturgical services and the Bible itself continued to be in Latin. But it is necessary to consider what is meant by 'convent culture'. Medieval women in religious orders cannot all be assumed to have led the same kind of life. Apart from the basic fact that the ethos of the various religious orders differs considerably, and always has done, the concept of a religious life for women covered a wide field in the Middle Ages. There were three principal divisions. Nuns, who were theoretically enclosed, under the authority of (usually) the local bishop, and who lived under vows of poverty, chastity, and obedience; canonesses such as Hrotsvitha, who also lived under vow, in communities, but who were not required to surrender their personal possessions (some of them also had the right to marry if they chose);[28] and beguines, members of self-ordering female sodalities, who lived in the middle of towns (chiefly in the Low Countries), worked for their collective livings, and moved freely among the townsfolk.[29] Nuns and canonesses tended to be aristocratic, or at least wealthy, since a substantial dowry was needed for entry into a convent (though not as much as for an advantageous marriage), so it is not surprising to find that some of them were well

---

[25] Ferrante, *To the Glory of her Sex*, 6–7.

[26] Lois L. Huneycutt, 'Female Succession and the Language of Power in the Writings of Twelfth-century Churchmen', in John Carmi Parsons (ed.), *Medieval Queenship* (Stroud: Alan Sutton, 1993), 189–201 (p. 191) (and see n. 22 above).

[27] *To the Glory of her Sex*, 6: this specific form of the phrase was applied to Adela of Blois.

[28] See Mary Pia Heinrich, *The Canonesses and Education in the Early Middle Ages* (Washington: Catholic University of America Press, 1924).

[29] Caroline Walker Bynum, *Jesus as Mother* (Berkeley and Los Angeles: University of California Press, 1982), 170–262, esp. pp. 182–3, and Carol Neel, 'The Origins of the Beguines', in Bennett et al. (eds.), *Sisters and Workers in the Middle Ages*, 240–60. See also, for a very nuanced account of varieties of religious life for women, Sarah Foot, *Veiled Women: Female Religious Communities in England, 871–1066*, 2 vols. (Aldershot: Ashgate, 2000).

educated. The beguines, on the other hand, did not recruit from the wealthy and educated, so they are not directly relevant to this enquiry. Those beguines who wrote (such as Hadewijch of Antwerp, Mechthild of Magdeburg, and Marguerite Porete) did so in the language they spoke.[30]

To take a few of the women treated in this book as examples, Radegund, Berhtgyth, Hildegard of Bingen, and Laurentia Strozzi were nuns in the sixth, eighth, twelfth, and sixteenth centuries respectively, and a consideration of their lives suggests that the authority of male ecclesiastical hierarchies weighed ever more heavily on women religious. Lina Eckenstein proposed that the underlying reason for this was economic.[31] Speaking of England (though the same would be true elsewhere in Europe) she comments:

it is worthy of attention that while all nunneries founded during Anglo-Saxon times were abbacies, those founded after the Conquest were generally priories...the Benedictine prioress was in many cases subject to an abbot, her authority varied with the condition of her appointment, but in all cases she was below the abbot in rank. The explanation is to be sought in the system of feudal tenure. Women no longer held property, nunneries were funded and endowed by local barons or by abbots. Where power from the preceding period devolved on the woman in authority, she retained it; but where new appointments were made, the current teaching was in favour of curtailing her power.

An example of continuity which seems to have left a particular group of women in an unusually strong position is the convent at Barking (near London), founded in the seventh century, which continued to attract powerful protectors down to the Dissolution of the Monasteries.[32] It also seems to have had an extensive library.[33] The literacy of Barking nuns *c.*600 has been noted in the previous chapter, and the continued power, wealth, and independence of Barking seems to have allowed their successors to produce a variety of writing in subsequent centuries, much of it translated from Latin. Between 1163 and 1169, an anonymous Barking nun translated Ælred of Rievaulx's *Life of St Edward the Confessor* from Latin to Anglo-Norman verse.[34] Marie of Barking translated a life of St Æthelthryth, and Clemence of Barking wrote a life of St Catherine (whose legend is that of a learned lady, who defeated fifty philosophers in debate) in Anglo-Norman.[35] In the

---

[30] Dronke, *WWML*, 217–28. See also Solterer, *The Master and Minerva*, 128.

[31] *Women under Monasticism* (Cambridge: Cambridge University Press, 1896), 365–405. See also Jane Schulenberg. 'Women's Monastic Communities, 500–1100: Patterns of Expansion and Decline', *Signs*, 14.2 (1989), 261–92, and Eileen Power, *Medieval English Nunneries, c. 1275 to 1535* (Cambridge: Cambridge University Press, 1922), 2.

[32] Power, *Medieval English Nunneries*, 42, 60: Barking had a long line of well-born abbesses, including three queens and two princesses.

[33] Bell, *What Nuns Read*, 41–2.

[34] Östen Södergård (ed.), *La Vie d'Édouard le Confesseur: poème anglo-normand du xiᵉ siècle* (Uppsala: Lundeqvistska bokhandeln, 1948), and also Marie, *Vie de seinte Audrée* (Uppsala: Almqvist & Wiksell, 1955). *The Life of St Catherine by Clemence of Barking* is ed. W. McBain (Oxford: Anglo-Norman Text Society, 1964). See now Jocelyn Wogan-Browne, *Saints' Lives and Women's Literary Culture: Virginity and its Authorizations* (Oxford: Oxford University Press, 2001), on Anglo-Norman hagiography, esp. chs. 2 and 6.

[35] Margaret P. Hannay (ed.), *Silent but for the Word* (Kent, Oh.: Kent State University Press, 1985), 7.

fourteenth century, Barking was under the control of a formidable lady, Dame Katherine of Sutton, who was the author of original liturgical drama in Latin of which, unfortunately, only a description survives.[36]

The survival of any personal writing from the high Middle Ages is an extremely uncertain matter. One aspect of transmission which may have affected the survival of women's writing even more than that of men is that almost everything we do have is in some kind of collection: medieval loose papers are almost never preserved. Light verse and ephemeral poetic exchanges such as the perhaps double-authored 'Iam dulcis amica' discussed in the previous chapter were normally filtered out by time and attrition: copying was expensive, in terms both of material costs and of working hours. Convents were generally poorer than monasteries, and only the very richest scriptoria copied texts for which no immediate use could be seen, therefore such lyrical poems as have come down to us tend to have survived literally in margins, on flyleaves, or on blank half-pages at the end of long documents. It is thus true to say that as far as women's writing in Latin is concerned, absence of evidence is not the same as evidence of absence. Others of the poems that survive are in letter-books—collections of letters which seem to have been used as models—or in other types of miscellany volumes. Since these compendia were almost all made by men, there is a built-in bias against the preservation of women's writing.

Survival rates vary widely. Spain, for example, will not be discussed here, not because it did not enjoy a literary culture in the Middle Ages, but because so little personal or verse writing of any kind from medieval Spain has been preserved. There is some verse from the Catalan monastery of Ripoll,[37] but none from convents, and we cannot have the same insight into the convent culture of medieval Spain as we have into that of France.[38] A nun *c.*975, Ende 'pintrix et dei aiutrix' (painter and servant of God), illustrated an important copy of the Apocalypse of Beatus of Liebana, but no medieval Spanish woman writer in Latin has left any equivalent self-testimony.[39] It is also true that fashions in writing varied from country to country. It may seem surprising, given the burgeoning of women's Latin culture in the Italian Renaissance, that there are no names of women poets surviving from the convents of medieval Italy,[40] but as Tiraboschi has shown,

[36] J. B. L. Tolhurst (ed.), *The Barking Ordinale*, 2 vols. (London: For the Henry Bradshaw Society, 1927–8), i. 107.

[37] Barcelona, Arxiu de la Corona d'Aragó, Ripoll 74, fos. 96ᵛ–101ʳ (12th-century poems added to a 10th-century manuscript). *MREL*, i. 253–9.

[38] What there is is listed in M. C. Díaz y Díaz, *Index Scriptorum Latinorum Medii Aevi Hispanorum*, 2 vols., Acta Salmanticensia Filosofia y Letras XIII.1–2 (Salamanca: Universidad de Salamanca, 1958–9).

[39] Jaime Marqués Casanovas et al. (eds.), *Sancti Beati a Liebana in Apocalypsin Codex Gerundensis*, 2 vols. (Oltun: Urs Graf Verlag, 1962) (facsimile). They mention a Spanish Benedictine nun-scribe called Londegondo who copied a compilation of monastic rules for the monastery of Samos in 912, but no actual women writers (ii. 71).

[40] In the 13th century, Angelica di Bologna (fl. 1225–40), a nun of St Agnes, Bologna, wrote at least one Latin *vita*, but it is unusual to find an identifiable woman writer in Italy before the Renaissance (Jacobus Quetif and Jacobus Echard, *Scriptores Ordinis Praedicatorum* (Paris: Christophe Baillard and Nicolas Simart, 1721), ii. 831). Sarah Josepha Hale, *Woman's Record* (New York: Harper & Brothers, 1860), 95, claims that a Latin letter was written by the 13th-century Galeona Saviola, wife of Brancaleone d'Andalo, to her husband, but gives no location.

Latin verse was little cultivated in medieval Italy, even by men.[41] Subsequent sections of this chapter therefore focus first on France and England (which in the period following the Norman Conquest were closely related cultures) and second, on the German-speaking world.

Anonymous lyrics

The earliest anonymous medieval verse which may be of female authorship has been introduced in the previous chapter, but there is a number of other poems from the high Middle Ages which can also be considered in this context. It is possible to discriminate to some extent between anonymous poems, and to identify some which are almost certainly not by women.[42] Poems in which a female speaking voice presents herself as a dramatic spectacle are unlikely to be of female authorship, especially if the speaker's expressed views coincide to a marked extent with misogynist cliché: as, for instance, in 'Plangit nonna, fletibus' which represents a woeful nun bewailing her dreary life, her horrible clothes and her sordid underwear, her lack of jewellery, and her lack of a man—any man will do.[43] Although the attitude expressed in this poem can be paralleled to some extent by that of a genuine nun, Arcangela Tarabotti, writing in the very different milieu of baroque Venice,[44] it seems worlds away from the self-confident, discriminating, cloistered young women of Le Ronceray or Regensburg who will be discussed later in this chapter, and very much a (naive) man's view of a woman's desires. In such a poem, medieval misogyny, the assumption of women's constant, uncontrollable lust and vanity, lurks just beneath the surface, and seems to relate it not to woman's experience, but to the tropes of comic literature about nuns.[45]

Another criterion which can usefully be brought to bear is historical probability, which helps to exclude a subtler and therefore more difficult poem in a woman's voice, 'Tempus instat floridum', from the famous collection of lyrics known as the *Carmina Burana*, which survives from the thirteenth century.[46] The element of

---

[41] Girolamo Tiraboschi, *Storia della Letteratura italiana* (Modena: Società Tipografica, 1787), iii. 378–94.

[42] An important recent book on vernacular women's verse, Elgal Doss-Quinby, Joan Tasker Grimbert, Wendy Pfeffer, and Elizabeth Aubrey (eds. and trans.), *Songs of the Women Trouvères* (New Haven: Yale University Press, 2001), argues the case for women's participation in the poetic and musical traditions of the Middle Ages.

[43] *MLREL*, ii. 357–9. However, it might also be noted that some medieval nuns *were* aesthetes and/or dandies: see *Aldhelm: The Prose Works*, trans. Michael Lapidge and Michael Herren (Ipswich: D. S. Brewer, 1979), 127–8.

[44] See Daniela De Bellis, 'Attacking Sumptuary Laws in Seicento Venice: Arcangela Tarabotti', in Letizia Panizza (ed.), *Women in Italian Renaissance Culture and Society* (Oxford: European Humanities Research Centre, 2000), 227–42.

[45] See Graciela S. Daichman, *Wayward Nuns in Medieval Literature* (Syracuse, NY: Syracuse University Press, 1986), particularly the chapter on 'chansons de nonne' and fabliau, pp. 65–114.

[46] There is some controversy over dating: see Peter Dronke, 'A Critical Note on Schumann's Dating of the Codex Buranus', *Beiträge zur Geschichte der deutschen Sprache und Literatur*, 84 (1962), 173–83. The *Carmina Burana* is ed. A. Hilka and O. Schumann, i.1: *Die moralisch-satirischen Dichtungen* (1930), i.2: *Die Liebeslieder* (1941), and ii.1, *Einleitung* (Heidelberg, 1930).

prurience in this representation of an unmarried pregnant girl whose lover has apparently fled the country militates against its acceptance as a woman's poem. It is also very hard to envisage a context in which an aristocratic young woman of the twelfth century who found herself in such a position would write in Latin rather than German or French, and conversely, a pregnant nun's position would be far too serious to allow for the relative levity of the poem's treatment (the savage story of the 'Nun of Watton', forced by her fellow nuns to castrate her lover with her own hands, is a reminder of how seriously such a lapse might be regarded).[47] It seems, again, relatively unlikely that the bold and bitter twelfth-century lament in the voice of a married woman whose husband has become a leper (so she has been condemned to share his living death) can actually be exactly what it seems, since there were so few Latin-literate laywomen, though it is not absolutely impossible.[48] But the extraordinary 'Foebus abierat', which Dronke has described as 'one of the most remarkable poems in Medieval Latin', is, on the other hand, wholly ambiguous: in it, a woman is visited by the spirit of her dead (or absent) lover. This may be the dramatization of a pre-existing fiction (though the referent is not obvious, if so) or what it seems to be, a highly original poem by a woman, since its writer could perfectly well be a nun.[49]

One poem which almost certainly is by a nun (possibly by Heloïse) is the highly sophisticated 'Laudis honor, probitatis amor, gentilis honestas', a long poem which proclaims itself as the work of a highly educated woman who resents the criticism she has suffered on account of her *littera* and *studium*, and of her versifying: as she ironically says[50]

> Carminibus recitare novis bene vel male gesta:
>   Iste fuit noster, si tamen error erat . . .
> Non est sanctarum mulierum frangere [fingere?] versus,
>   Quaerere nec nostrum quis sit Aristotiles.

> To recite in new verses good and bad deeds—
>   That was my mistake, if such it was . . .
> It is not for religious women to compose verses
>   Nor ours to ask who Aristotle might be.

Assessment of medieval Latin love poetry in a woman's voice is further complicated by two enormously significant influences, Ovid and the Song of Solomon. Ovid was greatly loved in medieval schools, and half-quotations from Ovid are

---

[47] Giles Constable, 'Ælred of Rievaulx and the Nun of Watton: An Episode in the Early History of the Gilbertine Order', in Derek Baker (ed.), *Medieval Women* (Oxford: Basil Blackwell, 1978), 205–26.

[48] 'In me, dei crudeles nimium', ed. and trans. Peter Dronke, 'Profane Elements in Literature', in Robert L. Benson and Giles Constable (eds.), *Renaissance and Renewal in the Twelfth Century* (Cambridge, Mass.: Harvard University Press, 1982), 569–92 (p. 571). Dronke points to a close parallel in the Renaissance *Emblematum Liber* of Andrea Alciato (Lyon, 1548 and many other editions), emblem 197, which strengthens the probability that the poem is a rhetorical exercise.

[49] *MLREL*, ii. 334–41.

[50] Ed. André Boutemy, 'Recueil poétique du manuscrit Additional British Museum 24,199', *Latomus*, 2 (1938), 31–52 (pp. 42–4) trans. Bond, *The Loving Subject*, 166–9.

found in many medieval women poets, such as 'Mulier' and Constantia, particularly strongly in those writers who are in direct communication with Baudri of Bourgeuil and his literary associates.[51] Ovid's *Heroides*, a series of verse epistles put in the mouths of a series of classical heroines, offered a model of the 'writing woman' to writers of *both* sexes, a model of significance to, among others, Heloïse, Constantia, the author (probably Boncompagno), of a prose letter to a lover in his *Epistolarium*,[52] and the more probably female author of a love letter preserved in Zurich.[53]

The Song of Solomon received a great deal of attention in the high Middle Ages. St Bernard of Clairvaux, for instance, devoted an entire cycle of sermons to the Song of Songs, but another symptom of this widespread interest was a burgeoning of supercharged erotico-religious poetry which may be defined collectively as 'Sapiential'.[54] The intensely powerful erotic vision of the Hebrew poem (superbly translated by St Jerome) was spiritualized without losing any of its essential force, and understood as the search of the soul for God.[55] The soul (or the individual human being), seen in the light of the Song of Songs, takes the part of the female half of the dialogue, the Shunamite who rushes desperately about Jerusalem searching for her absent lover. Thus poetry of love, loss, and longing in a woman's voice might be (and sometimes, was certainly) written by celibate men whose personal experience of women was extremely limited. However, we can hardly be certain that it was not also written by celibate women: in particular, those who read Jerome might have heeded his specific recommendation to his friend Eustochium to devote private time to erotico-mystical meditation on the Song of Songs.[56] Perhaps the most beautiful of these ambiguous poems is the superb eleventh-century 'Quis est hic qui pulsat ad ostium?', a poem which, because of this religious/mystical context, can reveal nothing about the gender of its author from the mere fact of its feminine voicing.[57] Migne places it among the *Carmina*

---

[51] The importance of Ovid in the culture of the Loire school in the 12th century is emphasized by Gerald A. Bond, '*Iocus amoris*: The Poetry of Baudri of Bourgeuil and the Formation of an Ovidian Subculture', *Traditio*, 42 (1986), 143–93. See also Jean-Yves Tilliette, 'Culture classique et humanisme monastique: les poèmes de Baudri de Bourgeuil', in *La Littérature angevine médiévale: actes du colloque du samedi 22 mars 1980* (Paris: H. Champion, 1981), 77–88.

[52] Edited by Dronke, *MLREL*, ii. 483, translated and discussed i. 251–3, from Paris, Bibliothèque Nationale de France, Lat. 8654, fo. 22ʳ.

[53] Zurich, Zentralbibliothek, C 58/275, s. xii, probably written at Schaffhausen, discussed and partially translated by Dronke, *MLREL*, i. 253. See also Gerald Bond, 'Composing Yourself: Ovid's *Heroides*, Baudri of Bourgeuil and the Problem of Persona', in Marilynn R. Desmond (ed.), *Ovid in Medieval Culture*, *Medievalia*, 13 (1989, for 1987), 83–117.

[54] Illuminatingly discussed by Dronke, *MLREL*, i. 164–271, and in 'The Song of Songs and Medieval Love-Lyric', in *The Medieval Poet and his World* (Rome: Edizioni di Storia e Letteratura, 1984), and also by Ann W. Astell, *The Song of Songs in the Middle Ages* (Ithaca, NY: Cornell University Press, 1990).

[55] Jean Leclerq, *Monks and Love in the Twelfth Century: Psycho-Historical Essays* (Oxford: Clarendon Press, 1979).

[56] Jerome, *Epistolae* 22. 25, ed. I. Hilberg (Vienna: F. Tempsky, 1910, 1912, 1918), i, 181–2.

[57] The earliest MS is of the 11th century, Monte Cassino, Biblioteca della Badia, Casinensis 111, p. 409. Printed with translation in *MLREL*, i. 269 and in Astell, *The Song of Songs*, 58–9.

et Preces of St Peter Damian (d. 1072), on grounds, perhaps, of its literary merit.[58]
Another rather simpler poem which may be a woman's is 'Quia sub umbraculum':[59]

> Quia sub umbraculum
> sedi, quem desidero
> amoris signaculo
> dilectissimus, quem video
>   cor meum sic consignat
>   ut generosa dignat.
>
> Surgat, ad me veniat,
> preelectus milium,
> amplexu me leniat,
> pudoris sumens lylium
>   quod illi soli servo,
>   sub castitatis modo.
>
> Because I sat beneath the shade,
> He whom I desire
> With the seal of love,
> My dearest one, whom I see,
> So signs my heart
> As he generously sees fit:[60]
>
> Let him arise, let him come to me
> The chosen of thousands.
> May he soothe me with an embrace,
> Taking the lily of modesty
> Which I am keeping for him alone
> By means of chastity.

Whether this poem relates to mystical experience of the love of Christ—by a devotee of either gender—or, less probably, to a human affair is impossible to determine.

Most of the anonymous lyrics which can most plausibly be attributed to women have now been discussed, but it is also worth examining the possibility that Latin verses in which the gender of the speaker is uncertain but the gender of the love-object female may include homoerotic verse.[61] The Latin rhythmic prose love

---

[58] *PL* cxlv, col. 939.

[59] *MLREL*, ii. 364.

[60] Dronke suggests 'That it admits (dignat) noble things': this version reads *generose* for *generosa*, on the suggestion of Dr Janet Fairweather.

[61] More has been written about male homosexuality in the Middle Ages than about love between women, e.g. John Boswell, *Christianity, Social Tolerance, and Homosexuality* (Chicago: Chicago University Press, 1980). Bernadette J. Brooten, *Love between Women: Early Christian Responses to Female Homoeroticism* (Chicago: University of Chicago Press, 1996), sets out the patristic context. See Helen Rodnite Lemay, 'Some Thirteenth- and Fourteenth-Century Lectures on Female Sexuality', *International Journal of Women's Studies*, 1 (1978), 391–400, Judith C. Brown, *Immodest Acts: The Life of a Lesbian Nun in Renaissance Italy* (Oxford: Oxford University Press, 1986), 128.

letters from Tegernsee include two which are unequivocally composed by one woman who is in love with another, and others where the gender of the love-object is ambiguous, suggesting that passionate friendships were far from unknown in medieval convents: the most explicit of these, 'A', declares, 'when I remember the kisses you gave, and with what words of joy you caressed my little breasts, I want to die, since I am not allowed to see you.'[62] One poem which I would like to put forward in this context is poorly preserved, but interesting, written in the eleventh century on a blank page of a theological manuscript at Sankt-Florian.[63] Following the editorial suggestions of Peter Dronke, the first verse seems to read, [64]

> Cantant omnes volucres
> iam lucescit dies,
> Amica cara, surge sine me
> per portas exire
>
> All the birds are singing;
> The day has almost dawned.
> Darling friend, rise 'sine' me,
> Slip out through the gates.

This beautiful little poem has caused some puzzlement. Dronke observes that later medieval *albae* ('dawn-songs') normally show a man trying to leave his mistress at dawn without being seen: it is strange to have a lover dismissing his mistress, as appears to be the case here, since the songs normally imply that it is the man who takes the risk of moving to and from an assignation.[65] There are two ways of approaching the problem. If 'sine' is the adverb 'without', then if both partners were female (perhaps nuns defying the prohibition against sharing a bed), that would explain the fact that a woman departs: 'darling friend, rise without me...'. Alternatively, 'sine' is the imperative of 'sino', allow, and the speaker, gender unknown, is saying 'rise, [and] *permit* me to slip out through the gates'.[66]

Women Latinists in England and France

One important class of evidence for nuns' Latin literacy in the high Middle Ages is the poems preserved in *rotuli* ('scrolls').[67] These developed out of the confraternity

---

[62] *MLREL*, ii. 476–82. See, as a comparison, a love poem from Bieiris de Romans to Maria (first half 13th century), Bogin (ed.), *The Women Troubadours*, 132–3.

[63] Sankt Florian, Stiftsbibliothek, XI.58, fo. 83ᵛ (s. xi), *MLREL*, ii. 352–3.

[64] Dronke, *MLREL*, ii. 352–3.

[65] Peter Dronke, *The Medieval Lyric*, 2nd edn. (London: Oxford University Press, 1978), 173.

[66] Further difficulty is caused by the structural dynamics of the *alba*: as Jonathan Saville points out, 'the relationship between the man and the woman in the *alba* is one of equality'. *The Medieval Erotic Alba: Structure as Meaning* (New York: Columbia University Press, 1972), 216.

[67] On *rotuli*, see Léopold Delisle, 'Les Monuments paléographiques concernant l'usage de prier pour les morts', *Bibliothèque de l'École des Chartes*, 3 (1846), 361–411, and Daniel Sheerin, 'Sisters in the Literary Agon', in Laurie Churchill, Phyllis R. Brown, and Jane E. Jeffrey (eds.), *Women Writing Latin from Roman Antiquity to Early Modern Europe*, 3 vols. (New York: Routledge, 2002), ii. 93–131.

books (or *libri vitae*), which go back to the ninth century: monasteries linked in confraternities prayed for one another's dead.[68] Therefore, at the death of a more than usually significant individual, the information was taken to other, linked monasteries. From the eleventh century, when the messenger arrived, it was considered polite for one or more of the community to write a poem on the occasion: the resulting poem, or poems, was added to the *rotulus* which he carried. A *rotulus* is thus an anthology of miscellaneous *tituli* (inscription poems) on a common occasion.[69] Relatively few of the many *rotuli* which were made have survived.[70] An early example, composed on the occasion of the death of St Bruno (d. 1101), the founder of the Carthusian order, is lost in its original form, but was printed by Frobenius in Basel some time after 1515. It includes a number of poems from convents, including St Radegund's convent at Poitiers, the convent of St Leger in Normandy, a *coenobium puellarum* dedicated to St Peter, and an *ordo monialium* dedicated to St John. These poems are mostly of no very great intrinsic interest, but they do show that the women's houses expected to speak for themselves in such a formal public context. This is also the message of one of the most important *rotuli* to survive in its original form, that of Mathilde, first abbess of La Trinité at Caen (d. 1113). This roll is over twenty metres in length, and includes many poems by women. It is theoretically possible to believe that all the women's houses to contribute verse to this *rotulus* 'bought in' the requisite expertise, or asked their chaplains to write, but the only two poems from women's houses which have an indication of authorship—'a verse by her niece', from Winchester (Nunnaminster), and 'a poem by the abbess' (Sibille), from Saintes, strongly suggest otherwise, since both are attributed to women.[71] It is interesting that of those women's houses who contributed to *rotuli*, several, including Nunnaminster, wrote them on more than one occasion, suggesting that these convents maintained a tradition of literacy (as is demonstrably the case with a number of convents under royal patronage, such as Caen, Le Ronceray, Wilton, and Nunnaminster).[72]

The convent of Argenteuil, now chiefly famous for Heloïse, who was brought up there, was one of the many women's houses to contribute to the *rotulus* for Mathilde,[73] and they also contributed to the *rotulus* for Vitalis.[74] Léopold Delisle

[68] Gerd Althoff, *Amicitiae und Pacta: Bündnis, Einung, Politik und Gebetsdenken im Beginnenden 10. Jahrhundert* (Hanover: Hahn, 1992).

[69] Günter Bernt, *Das lateinische Epigramm im Übergang von der Spätantike zum frühen Mittelalter*, Münchener Beiträge zur Mediävistik und Renaissance-Forschung 2 (Munich: Arbeo-Gesellschaft, 1968).

[70] 320 mortuary rolls and related documents survive to some extent: Jean Dufour, 'Les Rouleaux des morts', in A. Gruys and J. P. Gumbert (eds.), *Codicologica 3: essais typologiques* (Leiden: E. J. Brill, 1980), 96–100.

[71] The Saintes poem by Abbess Sibille has been discussed by Hugh Feiss, OSB, 'A Poet Abbess from Notre Dame de Saintes', *Magistra: A Journal of Women's Spirituality in History*, 1.1 (1995), 39–53.

[72] See Appendix entries under 'Nun of . . .'

[73] Léopold Delisle (ed.), *Rouleaux des morts du ixᵉ au xvᵉ siècle* (Paris: Veuve Jules Renouard, 1866), no. 184, p. 262.

[74] Léopold Delisle (ed.), *Rouleau mortuaire du B. Vital, abbé de Savigny* (Paris: H. Champion, 1909), p. 22, title 41.

tentatively suggested Heloïse was the author of the verses for Vitalis, since she was in the house at the time when the *rotulus* was presented,[75] but this is not demonstrable: there are cases in *rotuli* of 'pupils' or 'scholars' contributing verses, but when they do, it is only *after* some senior person has had his or her say. There were already women in Argentuil capable of such verse, since one was there in 1113, and, of course, Heloïse could not have been taught there if this had not been the case.

Heloïse, according to Rousselot, was considered the best poet of her generation,[76] but we have no securely attested verse which could be brought into comparison. Constant Mews has argued strongly for the authenticity of the so-called 'Letters of Two Lovers' as correspondence between Abelard and Heloïse at the height of their affair, making Heloïse a considerable poet, a view which is also supported by Stephen Jaeger, though Dronke dissents from it.[77] Certainly, the considerable difference in tone and approach between the two voices in the 'Epistolae' suggests strongly that it is the work of two individuals, one of whom is probably a woman. If this 'mulier' is not Heloïse, then she is another highly sophisticated, classically educated woman who combines passionate love for a man with an equally passionate interest in philosophy.

Mews also suggests that Heloïse, as well as being the author of the *rotulus* poem for Vitalis, wrote 'Laudis honor', mentioned above. The extent of Heloïse's oeuvre has been subject to much sensitive critical discussion recently, so despite its great intrinsic interest, it will not be discussed here, in order to allow space for introducing poems and poets which have not received such attention.

While the 'Epistolae' and 'Laudis honor' bear witness to sophisticated, deeply learned, talented, and passionate women—even more so if they are not all the work of the same person—the comparatively dull *rotuli* poems demonstrate something which is also important: that in twelfth-century convents with pretensions to culture, Latin verse composition was considered highly appropriate. Every time a messenger came by with a *rotulus*, it was desirable for someone to sit down and write a few lines on mortality and eternal reward. Such an ability might have other uses: it might be employed in the context of the internal life of the house, for instance in the poem on Abbess Maud of Wherwell, which may be by her successor Abbess Euphemia,[78] or directed towards external relations. Beatrix of Kent, Abbess of Lacock, who died in 1280, wrote a Latin encomium on Ela, Countess of

---

[75] Delisle (ed.), *Rouleaux*, 299.

[76] Paul Rousselot, *Histoire de l'éducation des femmes* (Paris: Didier et Cie., 1883), i. 30.

[77] Ewald Könsgen was the first to raise the possibility that she is the female voice in *Epistolae Duorum Amantium* in his edition (Leiden: Brill, 1974). This attribution has been explored in depth by Constant Mews, *The Lost Love Letters of Heloise and Abelard* (New York: St Martin's Press, 1999), and by C. Stephen Jaeger, *Ennobling Love* (Philadelphia: University of Pennsylvania Press, 1999), 157–73. Dronke, *WWMA*, 93–7, demurs.

[78] Bell, *What Nuns Read*, 212–13. In later centuries, there is a considerable amount of historical and archival writing by nuns, discussed in subsequent chapters. See in particular Elissa Weaver, 'Le muse in convento: la scrittura profana delle monache italiane (1450–1650)', in Lucetta Scaraffa and Gabriella Zarri (eds.), *Donne e fede: santità e vita religiosa in Italia* (Bari: Laterza, 1994), 253–76.

Warwick, who was the founder of the convent (the unique manuscript of the poem, unfortunately, was destroyed in the Ashburnham House fire of 1731 before anyone thought to transcribe it): the ability to flatter a noble patron is obviously a useful skill. This suggests in turn that the cultivation of Latin verse in wealthy and established convents boasting aristocratic inmates and diplomatic connections with kings, counts, and bishops was perhaps not unusual, and therefore that the attribution of Latin verse to nuns of prestigious convents such as Wilton and Le Ronceray is far from unreasonable.

The *rotuli* represent the public face of convent Latin, but there is also another set of relevant material: the extraordinary verse letters from Regensburg and Tegernsee (discussed below in the 'Germany' section), the poems from Le Ronceray, and remarks by such writers as Serlo of Wilton and Baudri of Bourgeuil, all of which suggest that there was a number of convents in which women culti-vated not only Latin poetry, but also romantic relationships, either with men, or with one another. Since the writers discussed in this chapter were active in the heyday of 'courtly love': an internationally successful revolution in taste which represented an intense, spiritualized relationship between a man and a woman who is normally his senior in age, experience, and/or social position as the ultimate pinnacle of human emotional life, it is not surprising that some nuns' verse reflects this theme.[79] The second half of the unique Regensburg manuscript, which was written early in the twelfth century, is extremely suggestive in this context.[80]

A similar picture is created by the verse correspondence of Baudri of Bourgeuil. He wrote ten verse letters to women, one of which is to his god-daughter Constantia, a nun of Le Ronceray in Angers.[81] She wrote a verse epistle in reply, of eighty-nine elegiac couplets, precisely answering, in length and form, Baudri's letter,[82] in which she addresses the complexities of her subject-position as noblewoman, nun, and passionate friend. This might become an immediate object of suspicion, given Baudri's interest in Ovid's *Heroides*,[83] were it not for the other evidence he produces for literary culture at Le Ronceray. For example, he writes

---

[79] There are many discussions of courtly love (famously that of C. S. Lewis, *The Allegory of Love* (Oxford: Oxford University Press, 1936)): a more recent treatment is that of Jaeger, *Ennobling Love*. See also John Baldwin, *The Language of Sex: Five Voices from Northern France around 1200* (Chicago: University of Chicago Press, 1994).

[80] Munich, Bayerische Staatsbibliothek, Clm lat. 17142.

[81] Constantia's affiliation with Le Ronceray is asserted by Walther Bulst, 'Die liebesbriefgedichte Marbods', in Bernhard Bischoff and Suso Brechter (eds.), *Liber Floridus: Mitellateinische Studien Paul Lehmann Gewidmet* (St Ottilien: Eos, 1950), 287–301. All the names mentioned in Baudri's poems appear in the same period in the Le Ronceray cartulary (see next note). On Le Ronceray itself, see Joseph Avril, 'Les Fondations, l'organisation, et l'évolution des établissements de moniales dans le diocèse d'Angers (du ix\ au xiii\ siècles)', in Michel Parisse (ed.), *Les Religieuses en France, au xiii\ siècle* (Nancy: Presses Universitaires de Nancy, 1983), 27–67 (pp. 30–3). It was a wealthy house, because it was a pilgrimage centre attracting visitors to a celebrated statue of the Virgin (p. 31).

[82] Discussed in detail in *WWMA*, 84–91, and also by Bond, *The Loving Subject*, 42–69, 142–3.

[83] Bond, '*Iocus amoris*', 160: he imitated the *Heroides* with 'Paris Helene/Helena Paridis', and adapted the genre with his 'Florus Ovidio/Ovidius Floro suo'. Dronke, in *WWMA*, offers a persuasive reading of Constantia as author rather than subject: she was also, of course, familiar with Ovid.

'To Emma, that she read his work carefully', while an 'Emma grammatica' appears in the Le Ronceray cartulary.[84] He praises her poems, and speaks of swarms of female disciples who rush to her to be revived by the honey of the parent bee. In a longer poem accompanying a book of his verse, he asks for critical editing and appraisal, for her to censure rather than flatter, to extol, correct, or add.[85] Baudri's associate, Marbod of Rennes, was another notable poet with a number of women friends. Dronke points out that three of his poems to women are called 'rescripta' (replies), suggesting exchanges: most notably, there is a poem which begins 'Darling, I read what you sent me, rejoicing',[86] which seems to be a reply to a poem in a woman's voice which begins 'You promise the joys of nymphs, violets, and rose-flowers', which Dronke has suggested may perhaps have been written by one of the nuns of Le Ronceray.[87]

Similarly Muriel, a nun of Wilton, was a famous poet: she was described as 'inclyta versificatrix', and her grave was pointed out to tourists, along with that of Bede, whose bones were at Wilton for a time. Baudri of Bourgeuil (1046–1130) wrote to Muriel, attracted by her fame, to ask her for an exchange of verses, while Hildebert of Le Mans praised her poetry, and so did Serlo of Wilton.[88] None of her work is known to survive, but someone from Wilton wrote a Latin poem in the *rotulus* of Vitalis of Savigny nine years after her death, suggesting that she was not the only Latin poet to flourish there. One Wiltrudis, an abbess of Wilton, is named in this *rotulus* (therefore recently dead). This is also the name of the author of a long and interesting Latin poem on Susanna, which is therefore possibly localizable in Wilton (however, it is discussed in the next section, since both the manuscript and the author's name are German). There is other evidence that eleventh-century Wilton was a place of considerable cultivation: apart from the laywomen who were educated there, so was a young woman called Eve who maintained a close friendship with both the hagiologist and scholar Goscelin of Canterbury, and Hilary, canon-chaplain of Le Ronceray.[89] Queen Matilda, first

---

[84] Paul Marchegay, *Chronique des églises d'Anjou* (Paris, 1869), iii. 282.

[85] *Les Œuvres poétiques de Baudri de Bourgeuil (1046–1130): édition critique publiée d'après le Ms du Vatican*, ed. Phyllis Abrahams (Paris: H.Champion, 1926), 259, 270–3.

[86] *WWMA*, 85. 'A te missa mihi gaudens carissima legi.' See Bulst, 'Liebesbriefgedichte Marbods', 290.

[87] W. Bulst (ed.), *Carmina Leodensia*, vi, Sitzungsberichte der Heidelberger Akademie der Wissenschaften, Abh. 1 (1975), 16, *WWMA*, 298, and see Mews, *The Lost Love Letters*, 94–5.

[88] J. F. P. Tatlock, 'Muriel: The Earliest English Poetess', *Proceedings of the Modern Language Association of America*, 48 (1933), 317–21 collects together the evidence and makes the gratuitous assumption that she must have been a terrible poet because she was female. See also A. Boutemy, 'Muriel: note sur deux poèmes de Baudri de Bourgeuil et de Serlon de Bayeux', *Le Moyen Âge*, 3rd ser. 6 (1935), 241–51; A. Wilmart, 'L'Élégie d'Hildebert pour Muriel', *Revue bénédictine*, 49 (1937), 376–80; *WWMA*, 85, Baudri, *Carmina*, ed. Karlheinz Hilbert (Heidelberg: C. Winter, 1979), 137, 189–90.

[89] C. H. Talbot (ed.), 'The *Liber Confortatorius* of Goscelin of St Bertin', *Studia Anselmiana*, 37 (1955), 1–117, André Wilmart, 'Eve et Goscelin I', *Revue bénédictine*, 46 (1934), 414–38. Her relationship with Hilary has not been previously noticed, but he gives her parents' names as Apis and Oliva, which confirms her identity beyond doubt. Her monastery, called 'clintonia' in the sole manuscript, is therefore 'Wiltonia'. Hilarius, *Versus et ludi*, ed. John Bernard Fuller (New York: Henry Holt, 1929), 46–53.

wife of Henry I and daughter of King Malcolm of Scotland, was educated at
Romsey and Wilton, and became highly learned, as is evidenced by her Latin
correspondence.[90] (Incidentally, although the convents of medieval Scotland are
not otherwise known as centres of learning, a shadowy Latin poetess, a Benedictine
nun called Elizabeth, or Isabel (fl. 1284), is said to have flourished at Haddington in
the Lothians, known to Louis Jacob, and apparently forgotten in her native land.[91])

Some light is shed on the poems from Regensburg and Le Ronceray by a
twelfth-century poem called *The Council of Remiremont*.[92] It presents a debate on
love amongst the nuns of Remiremont, written as a parody church council, and like
the Regensburg poems, it suggests nuns might have a taste for fairly sophisticated
intellectual games (the attribution to Remiremont may be connected with the
persistent accusations of immorality levelled against that convent and, in particular, the bull of Pope Eugenius III (17 March 1151) which accuses the nuns of
Remiremont of engaging in 'carnal exchanges', reminiscent of Charlemagne's
earlier legislation against 'winileodas').[93] The action takes place in spring, on the
Ides of April. All men except some *honeste clerici* from the diocese of Toul are
excluded, as are older women. The teachings of Ovid are read like a gospel in the
midst of them all. Individual (historically attested) nuns are named: Eva de
Danubrio, Elizabet de Granges, Elizabet de Falcon.[94] The context for such a
writing seems very similar to that of the exchanges between the Regensburg
women and their *magister*, discussed below, though it remains wholly uncertain
who composed this work. It may help in contexting it to observe that there is a
variety of evidence for nuns making their own entertainment in medieval convents,[95] some of which skirted the limits of the legitimate: when Eudes attempted
to reform a small rural Benedictine priory in 1249, he declared,[96]

---

[90] Bell, *What Nuns Read*, 63. In letters to Anselm, she quotes Cicero's *De Senectute*, and mentions
Pythagoras and Socrates. (*PL* clix, ii. 55, 119). She is claimed as the author of a work called *De Mundi
Catastropho* by Thomas Tanner: *Bibliotheca Britanno-Hibernica, sive de Scriptoribus qui in Anglia, Scotia
et Hibernia ad Saeculi XVII Initium Floruerunt* (London: William Bowyer, 1748), 520.

[91] Bibliothèque Nationale de France, Ancien fonds français 22,865, fo 69ʳ: 'Eliza Hadintonia, natione
scota, sanctimonialis ordinis Sancti Benedicti, admirando virtutis et non vulgaris doctrinae haec cum
esset poetrix cultissima scripsit rhythmorum vaticinalium librum quem Saeverici ingenti piaculo
patrum memoria, excusserent.'

[92] Georg Waitz (ed.), 'Das Liebesconcil', *Zeitschrift für deutsches Altertum* (1849), 160–7, F. M.
Warren, 'The Council of Remiremont', *Modern Language Notes*, 22 (1907), 137–40. There is a new
edition, Reuben R. Lee, 'A New Edition of the Council of Remiremont', Ph.D. diss. (University of
Connecticut, 1981).

[93] It may also be relevant that there is evidence for a close relationship between the nuns of
Remiremont and male supporters.

[94] Daichman, *Wayward Nuns*, 58–62.

[95] In England, both Barking and Godstow elected an Abbess of Fools on Holy Innocents Day, to
amuse the novices. Nancy Cotton, *Women Playwrights in England, c.1363–1750* (Lewisburg, Pa.:
Bucknell University Press, 1980), 213, Power, *Medieval English Nunneries*, 312.

[96] Penelope D. Johnson, *Equal in Monastic Profession: Religious Women in Medieval France* (Chicago:
University of Chicago Press, 1991), 116. Power, *Medieval English Nunneries*, 310, notes that in 1549 a
council at Cologne directed a canon against comedians who were in the habit of visiting the German
nunneries and who by their profane plays and amatory acting excited virgins dedicated to God to unholy
desires.

We forbid you to continue the farcical performances which have been your practice at the Feast of the Innocents and of the Blessed Mary Magdalene, to dress up in wordly costume, to dance with each other or with lay folk . . .

A parody church council is something rather different from a dramatization of the life of Mary Magdalene, but both enterprises suggest a rather risky fantasization or acting-out of possibilities which were necessarily denied to the women in question.

Women Latinists in northern Europe

The account of women Latinists in what would become Germany must surely begin with Hildegard of Bingen. Hildegard, unlike many of the writers considered here, was a major literary figure in her own time, and is now probably the best-known woman writer of the Middle Ages, mostly on account of her remarkable music.[97] She wrote a great deal, most of it profoundly original. Dronke comments, 'she remains not just a captivating but an indelibly attractive person . . . she writes a Latin that is as forceful and colourful, and at times as subtle and brilliant, as any in the twelfth century; and her learning is often so astounding that (as she gives no source-references) it still sets countless problems to determine all she had read . . . she was daunting and eccentric; stupendous in her powers of thought and expression; lovable in her warmth and never-wearying freshness'.[98]

Hildegard's biography is presented in detail by Barbara Newman,[99] based on a contemporary biography and autobiographical notes written by Hildegard herself.

---

[97] There is an extensive literature on Hildegard. Important works include Werner Lauter, *Hildegard-Bibliographie* (Alzey: Rheinhessische Druckwerkstätte 1970, 1983, 1998), Anton Brück (ed.), *Hildegard von Bingen, 1179–1979. Festschrift zum 800. Todestag der Heiligen* (Mainz: Gesellschaft für Mittelrheinische Kirchengeschichte, 1979), Peter Dronke and Charles Burnett (eds.), *Hildegard of Bingen: The Context of her Thought and Art* (London: Warburg Institute, 1998), Flanagan, *Hildegard*, and Barbara Newman, *Sister of Wisdom: St Hildegard's Theology of the Feminine* (Aldershot: Scolar, 1987). Her work was widely circulated in manuscript, and there is an early edition of some of her work in *Liber Trium Virorum et Trium Spiritalium Virginum* (Paris: Estienne, 1513). There is a basic modern edition of her works in *PL* cxcvii and J.-B. Pitra, *Analecta S. Hildegardis, Analecta Sacra*, 8 (1882). Most of Hildegard's oeuvre has received modern critical editions: apart from Barbara Newman's edition and translation of the hymns and sequences, Corpus Christianorum Continuatio Medievalis has brought out *Scivias*, ed. Adelgundis Führkötter and Angela Carlevaris (Turnhout: Brepols, 1978), *Liber Vite Meritorum*, ed. Angela Carlevaris (Turnhout: Brepols, 1995), *Liber Divinorum Operum*, ed. Albert Derolez and Peter Dronke (Turnhout: Brepols, 1996), *Hildegardis Bingensis Epistolarium*, 3 vols., ed. Lieven van Acker and Monika Claes (Turnhout: Brepols, 1991–). Other editions: *Causa et Curae*, ed. Paul Kaiser (Leipzig: Trubner, 1903), *Symphonia: A Critical Edition of the Symphoni Armonie Celestium Revelationum*, ed. and trans. Barbara Newman (Ithaca, NY: Cornell University Press, 1988), *Ordo Virtutum*, ed. and trans. Peter Dronke in his *Nine Medieval Latin Plays* (Cambridge: Cambridge University Press, 1994), 147–84. *Vita Hildegardis* is ed. Monika Claes (Turnhout: Brepols, 1993). Translations include *Scivias*, trans. Columba Hart and Jane Bishop (New York: Paulist Press, 1990), *The Letters*, trans. Joseph Baird and Radd Ehrman (New York: Oxford University Press, 1995) (further volumes planned), and Sequentia (an Early Music ensemble) are in the process of recording her complete musical works on eight CDs for Deutsche Harmonia Mundi.

[98] *WWMA*, 200–1.

[99] *Sister of Wisdom*, 4–41.

She was the child of a noble family, the last of ten, and was dedicated as a future nun soon after her birth. It was normal in the twelfth century for parents to decide their children's future in this way, and particularly likely that a tenth child would be thus 'given to God', on the principle, encouraged by the Church, of offering a tithe (one-tenth) of one's possessions for holy purposes.[100] In Hildegard's case, at least, the decision was a singularly happy one. She later recalled that she had begun to see visions at the age of 3, and continued to receive apparently supernatural visions for the rest of her life. Children destined for the cloister normally stayed with their parents during early childhood, and were handed over at 7 or so. Hildegard was offered to God in her eighth year, and entrusted to Jutta, Abbess of Sponheim, whom she came to love dearly, for her education.[101]

Hildegard began to write in her forties, and produced a prodigious oeuvre in cosmology, ethics, medicine, and mystical poetry. She was also a distinguished composer. In 1136, she was elected as abbess of the convent of St Disibod, which may have helped give her the confidence to begin circulating her work. Her visionary writing was condoned and ratified by the pope, which removed the fear that she would find herself persecuted as a heretic. Thereafter, she corresponded freely with the secular and religious leaders of her time, including three successive popes, the German emperors Conrad III and Frederic Barbarossa, King Henry II of England and Eleanor of Aquitaine, and Empress Irene of Byzantium. She undertook preaching journeys, and addressed sermons to monks, bishops, and the laity. Hildegard was accepted as exceptional, a woman who was treated with great seriousness due to her prophetic gifts. She also had an empowering effect on at least one younger woman, Elizabeth of Schönau, a protégée who modelled herself on Hildegard, and also became a visionary. Elizabeth published her *Book of the Ways of God* in 1156: this was in Latin prose.[102]

An important turning point in Hildegard's life occurred in 1150. She moved her community, after a long, hard fight, from the Disibodenberg to another mountain, the Rupertsberg, on the Rhine, giving her greater independence and autonomy: she achieved this by an ingenious form of blackmail, asserting that she had been forbidden by God 'to utter or write anything more in that place'.[103] Pressure was then put on the abbot of the male community on the Disibodenberg (to which the women's convent was subordinate) by her extensive and distinguished international following until he released her. The other event of the 1150s was more personal. She became deeply emotionally involved with a young nun, Richardis,

---

[100] John Boswell, *The Kindness of Strangers* (New York: Pantheon, 1988), 302.

[101] For a convenient assemblage of the evidence, see *Jutta and Hildegard: The Biographical Sources*, trans. Anna Silvas (University Park, Pennsylvania State University Press, 1998).

[102] For information on Elizabeth of Schönau, see Josef Loos, 'Hildegard von Bingen und Elizabeth von Schönau', in Brück (ed.), *Hildegard von Bingen, 1179–1979*, 263–72, Anne Clark, *Elisabeth of Schönau: A Twelfth-Century Visionary* (Philadelphia: University of Pennsylvania Press, 1992), and Kathryn Kerby-Fulton and D. Elliott, 'Self-Image and the Visionary Role in Two Letters from the Correspondence of Elizabeth of Schönau and Hildegard of Bingen', *Vox Benedictina*, 2 (1985), 204–23.

[103] *WWMA*, 150.

who had worked closely with her on Hildegard's book of mystical visions, *Scivias*. According to Hildegard, 'because of her family's distinction, [Richardis] hankered after an appointment of more repute: she wanted to be named abbess of some splendid Church. She pursued this not for the sake of God but for worldly honour.' Hildegard fought to keep Richardis at her side: when the younger nun was given an appointment as abbess, Hildegard refused to release her and wrote a series of wild letters to everyone whom she might possibly enlist on her side, even Pope Eugenius.[104] In the end, she was forced to give in, and was finally able to reconcile herself to Richardis's independence from her.

Hildegard's control of the Latin language presents some interesting issues. Her native language was German, and her education was not extensive, though it is likely that she downplayed both her training and her reading to her biographers, in the interest of stressing the miraculousness of her visionary gift. As a visionary, a prophet, she was faced with the problem of finding words for the inexpressible; and this was compounded by her limited grasp of Latin syntax and vocabulary. The result is that she uses Latin in a uniquely expressive way, packing a highly individual set of values and resonances into certain words (for example *pigmentarii*, classically 'perfume-dealer', which she uses in an extended, metaphoric sense to mean 'priest'). Part of her successive secretaries' job was to tidy up her Latin and make it more comprehensible.[105] Hildegard's attitude to language, and perhaps her difficulties in expressing herself in Latin, is indicated by her invention of an 'Unknown Language': a vocabulary of about 900 words of this language survive, glossed in German.[106] It is a unique creation of her own, mainly a hotchpotch of Greek, Latin, and Hebrew elements, and it seems to be an extreme instance of seizing a language, though of course it shifts, rather than removes, the problem of making herself understood.

Beyond the towering figure of Hildegard, we have clear evidence of German nuns' Latinity associable with specific convents. For example, in the eleventh and early twelfth centuries, the abbey of Hohenburg seems to have been remarkable for learned women.[107] The abbess, Herrad, who took office in 1167, is remembered for her *Hortus Deliciarum*, a large and beautiful book which well deserved the name of 'The Garden of Delights'.[108] This was intended as a sort of basic encyclopedia for her nuns at Hohenburg, and has interesting implications for women's education,

---

[104] *WWMA*, 154–9. Sabina Flanagan, '*Spiritualis Amicitia* in a Twelfth-Century Convent? Hildegard of Bingen and Richardis of Stade', *Parergon*, 29 (1981), 15–21, and Ulrike Wiethaus, 'In Search of Medieval Women's Friendships: Hildegard of Bingen's Letters to her Female Contemporaries', in U. Wiethaus (ed.), *Maps of Flesh and Light: The Religious Experience of Medieval Women Mystics* (Syracuse, NY: Syracuse University Press, 1993), 93–111.

[105] Ildefons Herwegen, 'Les Collaborateurs de Ste Hildegarde', *Revue bénédictine*, 21 (1904), 192–203, 302–15, 381–403.

[106] In Pitra (ed.), *Analecta S. Hildegardis*, 496–502.

[107] It was already ancient: the life of the founder (d. 720) is ed. Bruno Krusch, *Vita Odiliae Abbatissae Hohenburgensis*, MGH SSRM VI (Hanover: Hahn, 1903), 24–50, and there is a 10th-century poem in the Cambridge Songs manuscript which pokes gentle fun at the nuns of Hohenburg: Walther Bulst (ed.), *Carmina Cantabrigiensia* (Heidelberg: Carl Winter Universitätsverlag, 1950), 46–7.

[108] Herrad, *Hortus Deliciarum*, ed. Rosalie Green et al., 2 vols. (London: Brill, 1979).

since it assumes that novices will come in able to read German, but will need to be taught Latin. However, I also want to draw attention to her predecessor as abbess, Richlindis, to whom a couple of short poems in a version of Leonine hexameters are attributed in the *Hortus Deliciarum*. Several more or less contemporary nuns, notably Willetrudis, Beatrix die Küsterin, and the author of a poem 'Ad Fugitivum', wrote in Leonines. Richlindis was the seventh abbess of the convent of the Holy Cross at Pergensee, in the diocese of the Bishop of Eichstatt. She made such a success of it, being particularly known for her learning, that the Emperor Frederic Barbarossa asked her in 1154 to go to the monastery of St Otilia at Hohenburg, which had become lax, and to reform it. She expelled the unsatisfactory inhabitants and, in a few years, gathered together a group of thirty-three nuns, whom she educated so effectively that the reinstituted establishment became the admiration of all. After a time, Richlindis returned to her original house in Pergensee, handing over the reins to Herrad, and died there in a fire.[109]

Another German nun who left a reputation as a Latin poet is Anastasia, a Benedictine nun of Lamspring, an Ottonian foundation in the diocese of Hildesheim, who is said to have rewritten the Gospels into Latin verse.[110] The surviving manuscripts from the nuns' library are now in Wolfenbüttel, but there is no trace of Anastasia's work among them: the most interesting manuscript to survive is Wolfenbüttel, Bibliotheca Augusta, 204 Helmst., a collection of works by Augustine which includes a note stating that the scribe was a nun, Ermengard, writing during the time of Prioress Judtte (Jutta) and the praepositus Gerhard (i.e. 1178–91). Another Lamspring manuscript, Biblioteca Augusta, 558 Helmst. includes the 'Poeta Saxo's' long poem on Charlemagne, and Juvencus' versification of the Gospels, which does suggest that the nuns of Lamspring were interested in poetry: the last may have been the model for Anastasia's lost work.

The Regensburg manuscript, a unique witness to intimate friendships between a group of Latinate nuns and a variety of men, has already been mentioned in the context of a discussion of courtly love. The manuscript is a rag-bag of notes on this and that, including many poems. Occasional historical references place the collection no earlier than 1056, and probably no later than 1098. Dronke suggests that the collection as a whole represents the miscellaneous papers of some scholar sufficiently notable that, on his death, a copy was made of what was in his desk. It would seem that this *magister* had, in his younger days, been a correspondent of the circle of learned young women whose poetry is thus preserved.[111]

Wattenbach, who was the first to write about this collection, suggests that the location of this group was Regensburg, but this is far from certain. The little we

---

[109] Kaspar Brusch, *Monasteriorum Germaniae Praecipuorum ac Maxime Illustrium Centuria Prima* (Ingolstadt: Alexander and Samuel Weissenhorn, 1551), 97ᵛ. 'Rilindis seu Reglindis et Herradis Hohenburgensis Abbatissae, Notitia et Fragmenta', *PL* cxciv, cols. 1537–8.

[110] Christian Franz Paullini, *Das Hoch- und Wohl-gelahrte Teutsche Frauen-Zimmer (Frankfurt: Johann Christoph Stössel, 1705)*, 20.

[111] The Regensburg songs are discussed at length by Dronke in *MLREL*, i. 221–32 and ed. and trans. ii. 422–47.

know about these women, we know from the poems themselves. They are aristo-cratic: they receive visits from noblemen (a Count Hugo is mentioned), clerics, and courtiers. One poem speaks of oppression by 'Ymber' (*imber* is the Latin for 'rain'), apparently a woman in authority (the nickname perhaps hides one of the Germanic women's names beginning with 'rain', such as *Regen*hild), so it seems that discip-line could be irksome to such self-willed and confident young women as these. Dronke observes: 'in at least two of the poems we see women who no longer feel the need to stress (like Dhuoda or Hrotsvitha) that they are merely women—frail, lesser creatures compared with men. Instead, they see themselves as "makers of manners".'[112] It is worth stressing that these verses survive completely by chance. The collection reveals a level of conventual education considerably greater than one would have predicted; and offers the possibility that there were many learned and sophisticated women flourishing in twelfth-century convents. The nuns who wrote these letters are expert players of the game of courtly love: the fluctuations of their relationships with their correspondents do not imply clandestine assignations and illicit sex, but strong intellectual, emotional, and spiritual ties which were perceived, at least by the nuns themselves, as compatible with vows of celibacy.[113]

Other German convents in the same period were noted for women scribes, notable Wessobrunn, where the female master scribe Diemud was active between 1057 and 1130.[114] Her contemporary Leukardis of Mallersdorf was similarly famed for her scribal work, and the convents of Admunt and Wittewierum produced many books.[115] The former also produced a writer, Gertrude of Admunt.[116] Transcription does not necessarily cause composition, but a focus on the production of books rather than embroidery helps to create an atmosphere in which composition may be possible, not least because it ensures that writing materials are readily available. Elsewhere in Germany, Peter of Dacia corre-sponded in Latin with Christine of Stommeln, called 'die Kölsche', from her place of birth, Cologne.[117]

Another German convent which is noted for learned and able women is Helfta, which came to its florescence somewhat later than the houses already discussed. It is said of Gertrude the Great that 'she was occupied from morning to night translating from Latin into German',[118] 'of a passionate and ambitious nature, she devoted all her energies to mastering the liberal arts, but in consequence of a vision that came to her at twenty-five, she cast them aside and plunged into

[112] *WWMA*, 92.

[113] See, for a more detailed discussion of the type of emotional relationship briefly outlined here, Jaeger, *Ennobling Love*. He discusses the Regensburg material pp. 74–8.

[114] Jean Mabillon, *Acta Sanctorum Ordinis Benedicti* (Paris: Louis Billaine, 1668–1701), iii. 494–6.

[115] Eckenstein, *Women under Monasticism*, 236–7.

[116] Anon. (ed.), 'Vita, ut Videtur, cuiusdam Magistrae Monialium Admuntensium in Styria, Saeculo xii' [by Gertrude of Admunt], *Analecta Bollandiana*, 12 (1893), 356–66.

[117] Margot Schmidt, 'An Example of Spiritual Friendship: The Correspondence between Heinrich of Nördlingen and Margaretha Ebner', in Wiethaus (ed.), *Maps of Flesh and Light*, 74–92 (p. 74).

[118] *Revelationes Gertrudianae ac Mechtildianae*, ed. Monks of Solesmes, 2 vols. (Poitiers: Henri Oudin, 1875), i. 23.

religious study'.[119] She was one of a number of interesting women active at Helfta in the thirteenth century. Gertrude's *Exercitia Spiritualia* are written in rhyme, but with varying rhythm, perhaps best designated as rhymed prose,[120] and she also composed some quatrains. Other members of the community also wrote in Latin, notably Mechthild von Hackeborn.[121]

It is possible to demonstrate, therefore, that from the eleventh to the thirteenth centuries, there were German nuns who wrote Latin verse. In addition to the various learned and able women already discussed, there are two of very high achievement who remain regrettably obscure. One is Beatrix 'die Küsterin' ('the sacristan), who wrote a long poem in Leonine hexameters on the Miracles of the Virgin (a popular subject in the twelfth century).[122] It seems to have achieved some popularity, perhaps on account of its subject, since it survives in three manuscripts.[123]

The second, whom I wish to discuss at length, is a woman called Willetrudis who was the author of a long poem on Susanna and the Elders, preserved in a single manuscript now in Munich. She was highly educated, and was almost certainly a nun; the tone in which she addresses the sisters suggests that she may have been an abbess: that and her name is all that can be said about her for certain. The Munich catalogue gives no information about provenance, and the manuscript context is simply of a collection of narrative poems. There is a Willetrudis who was first abbess of Hohenvart and flourished *c.*1090, though the house has no literary associations that I know of.[124] Alternatively, it may be that the Frankish name is misleading, and this poem should in fact be assigned to the Anglo-Norman world; in 1122, Wilton, a house strongly associated with literary women, named 'abbess Wiltrudis' among the recently dead for whom they invited reciprocal prayers, and the poem which Wilton produced in that year on the death of Vitalis was in Leonine hexameters similar to those in which this poem is composed.

The story Willetrudis tells can be summarized as follows. Joachim, a rich citizen of Babylon, married the beautiful Susanna. Two elders among the Jews who spent time at Joachim's house took to spying on her as she walked in the garden. One hot afternoon, she decided to wash herself, and sent her two maids to bring oil and

[119] Eckenstein, *Women under Monasticism*, 347. See also Caroline Walker Bynum, 'Women Mystics in the Thirteenth Century: The Case of the Nuns of Helfta', in her *Jesus as Mother*, 170–262.

[120] *Revelationes*, i. 617–720. For the form, see also E. Norden, *Die antike Kunstprosa* (Leipzig: B. G. Teubner, 1923), and K. Polheim, *Die lateinische Reimprosa* (Berlin: Weidmann, 1925).

[121] Eckenstein, *Women under Monasticism*, 328. Note that Mechthild's *De Veritate et Falsitate Virtutum et Vitiorum* (*Revelationes*, ii. 613–14) is, like many of Gertrude's compositions, in rhymed prose.

[122] Discussed by Richard Southern, in his *Medieval Humanism* (Oxford: Basil Blackwell, 1970), 172–3.

[123] H. Waterphul, *Die Geschichte der Maria Legende von Beatrix die Küsterin*, diss. (Universität Göttingen, 1904), A. Mussafia, 'Studien zu den mittelalterlichen Marienlegenden III', *Sitzungsberichte der phil.-hist. Klasse der kaiserliche Akademie der Wissenschaften*, 119 (9) (Vienna: F. Tempsky, 1889), 7–13.

[124] Brusch, *Monasteriorum Germaniae ... Centuria Prima*, 150^v.

soap, and to shut the garden doors, unaware that the elders were concealed inside. They accosted her, and threatened that if she did not submit to them, they would say she had been entertaining a young lover. However, she screamed for help, and they duly calumniated her: naturally, as elders and judges, they were believed. But Daniel, who was then a mere youth, spoke up in the assembly, and asserted her innocence. He separated the two elders, and interrogated the first, asking what tree Susanna and her alleged lover had been misbehaving under. 'A mastic tree', he said. The second, similarly questioned, said it had been a holm oak. At which point, the assembled Jews realized that they had both been lying, and Susanna's name was cleared.

It is an interesting story for a medieval woman to choose to tell, since medieval narratives of womanhood so often represent them as temptresses, seducers, or snares for the male eye.[125] In this tale, on the other hand, the woman is entirely innocent, and since she prefers the potential loss of honour and life to actual, but concealed, sin, her behaviour is both saintly, and a model for secular good conduct. The relevance of Susanna as a model for chaste wifehood is obvious, but she might also be held up for admiration to virgins, because of the story's stress on the way she prioritizes God's knowledge of her over other people's. There are several stories about virginal women saints who meekly suffer unjust accusations.[126] It may also be worth observing that two prose pieces connect Susanna with nuns: one of Peter Abelard's sermons for Heloïse and the nuns of the Paraclete is on Susanna: Ferrante observes that it is unusual for a married woman to be held up as an example of virtue to virgins,—but of course, Heloïse was not a virgin, which may be why Abelard uses her in this context.[127] The second is a letter in which Hildegard of Bingen compares *herself* with the calumniated Susanna.[128] In addition, the Barking *Life of Edward the Confessor* appeals to Susanna as one of those saved by God, comparing her with Joseph—a comparison also made by Willetrudis.[129]

The story attracted a number of medieval writers. Apart from that of Willetrudis, I know of four other poems on this theme dating from the high Middle Ages.[130] The most important and widely circulated version was written in the twelfth century, and is attributed to Petrus de Riga,[131] though it was printed in the *Patrologia Latina* among the works of Hildebert of Lanvardin, and as Faral points out, if the poem were in fact his, then it would have to have been a juvenile

---

[125] See, for an account of this, Bloch, *Medieval Misogyny.*

[126] For example, Palladius, *Lausiac History* 34, trans. W. K. Lowther Clark (London: SPCK, 1918), 118.

[127] Abelard, *Opera*, ed. V. Cousin, 2 vols. (Paris: A. Durand, 1849–69), i. 537–46, no. 29. Ferrante, *To the Glory of her Sex*, 66.

[128] *Vita*, ii. 3.

[129] Ferrante, *To the Glory of her Sex*, 185.

[130] J. H. Mozley, 'Susanna and the Elders: Three Medieval Poems', *Studi Medievali*, NS 3 (1930), 27–52.

[131] *Notices et extraits des MSS de la Bibliothèque Nationale*, 29.2 (1891), 352–8. This edition was taken from a 13th-century MS formerly in the library of Queen Christina of Sweden.

work.[132] In some manuscripts it forms part of a long series of versified incidents from the Bible called *Aurora*; but it may originally have been written separately, since a number of manuscripts survive in which it is free-standing.[133]

Petrus de Riga's poem is roughly contemporary, and comparable to Willeitrudis's work in its length and scope. Some of the details he chooses to emphasize form a very interesting contrast to Willetrudis's poem and show something of the way that Willetrudis's version is unusual, in a way that suggests something of the unconscious biases of a medieval man tackling this story. We are told that it was intensely hot (l. 135), and the water played temptingly in Joachim's garden.

> There the baths invited Susanna. She rose,
> Hurried there, she did not know there was any trickery in the place.
> She tested (*temptat*) the water, she praised what she had tested, naked
> She went into what she had praised, and the two old men saw her naked.

Note the repetition of *nuda*—and of *temptare*. Susanna is actively a 'temptress'—of course, what Petrus primarily means is that she 'tests' the water and finds its temperature attractive, but in doing so, she also unconsciously 'tempts' the elders. The meanings elide, one into the other. She goes into the garden, takes all her clothes off to bathe: the verses linger on her beauty, her milky neck and golden hair. So far, so mildly pornographic. The section is summed up thus:

> What more? Her shape captivates the old men,
> they are drawn by illicit desire

It is the verbs of agency which are worth dwelling on. Susanna 'fraudam nescit', she does not expect trickery, yet somehow she seems to be being held responsible. Her beauty *captivates* the old men; her desirability *draws* them. It is as if we are being told that they, not she, are innocent victims. Other aspects to observe: Susanna is by herself. She goes, apparently all alone, to the garden, takes her clothes off to bathe properly, as in a Roman bath.

Let us now turn to Willetrudis. Susanna decides to go to her husband's orchard

> Ut fuerat sueta famulabus tunc comitata
> Pomeriumque viri voluit quia fonte lavari
> Nam fervens estus fuerat tum valde molestus
> Intrat ... (59–62)

> As was her custom, accompanied by her serving-women,
> she entered her husband's orchard, because she wanted to wash in the spring,
> For the burning heat was then extremely tiresome.

This Susanna habitually moves about in a group of women. She decides to wash but the word used here is *lavare*, which does not have quite the comprehensive

---

132 *PL* clxxi, cols. 1287–92, Matthew de Vendôme, *Opera*, in Edmond Faral (ed.), *Les Arts poétiques du xiie et du xiiie siècle* (Paris: H. Champion, 1924), 169.
133 London, British Library, Harley 747, fos. 92ᵛ–95ʳ.

implications of *balneare*.[134] We are perhaps to assume that she removes some of her garments, but we are not actually told that she does so: the idea of her sensual indulgence in the pleasure of cool water on a boiling hot day, and also the idea of her physical exposure, is played down—for all that we are told, she may just be dabbling her hands and face. Note also that Willetrudis puts some emphasis on the point that the evil conspiracy of the judges preceded Susanna's inadvertent self-exposure, and therefore that their behaviour can in no sense be said to be caused by it.

Though Willetrudis's text is extremely faithful to the story in the Vulgate outlined above, all the points where she diverges from it seem to me interesting. She begins her narrative with a prologue. Susanna is presented to the reader as a model of female virtue (ll. 17-20): This passage suggests to me that the *versus* is addressed primarily by a nun to other nuns:

> Sicque pudicicia quondam studet alma SUSANNA
> Cum qua luctatur donec magis inde probatur
> Hinc monit[a]e mores libeat munire sorores
> Tramite uirtutum teneamus...(ll. 16-19)

> Thus the blessed Susanna took care with her chastity, once upon a time,
> with which she strove, until from that she was proved the greater.
> Hence [we] sisters are warned, one ought to fortify one's morals.
> Let us hold to the path of virtue...

The blessed Susanna's example fortifies *sorores*: sisters, probably in the sense of nuns. The prologue moves into the first person plural: *teneamus*, later *spectemus*: it is therefore we *sorores* who are edified and strengthened by the example of Susanna. This suggests that Willetrudis was writing for her community, as, for example, both Richlindis and Herrad wrote for their nuns at Hohenburg.

Moving onto the main text; Willetrudis begins by locating Babylon, not geographically, but spiritually: this ancient city produced many holy prophets and athletes of God (ll. 1-6). We then have Joachim's position as a leading citizen, and his marriage to the beautiful and virtuous Susanna, and an account of the way that his house is a meeting place for the worthies of the Babylonian Jewish community and is therefore used as a sort of courtroom. This is all straight from the Vulgate, but Susanna's visit to the orchard is significantly nuanced. When the citizenry come to the house for justice, Susanna retreats to the privacy and seclusion of the orchard. Her action therefore implies a chaste and prudent retreat from undue exposure to all and sundry; this Susanna is trying to avoid trouble, not cause it.

> Et domus hec Ioachim populorum dat iura diatim
> Cumque revertisset populus qui iura petisset
> Susannae moris hac certis mansit in horis
> Intrat pomerium domui quod forte propinquum
> Imminet ac fontis placidis se balneat undis (ll. 41-5)

---

[134] She uses *balneare* once, but *lavare* several times.

And this house of Joachim's house gave justice to the people daily:
When the people returned who were seeking judgment,
This customarily remained within fixed hours: as for Susanna,
She enters the orchard, which was near the house,
And washes herself in the calm waters of the spring.

The elders are overcome by the beauty of Susanna's *face* (ll. 46–7)—which of course, they see because they are honoured guests of her husband—rather than by catching glimpses of her nudity: it is on that basis that they plot to seduce her. This, together with her own exemplary behaviour, puts the onus of guilt firmly onto them.

When she is attacked, there is a torrent of metaphors: she is like a dove, or perhaps a swan, or a tender lamb in the mouth of a wolf, or in the grip of a kite. The drama takes its course: the elders make their offer and are indignantly refused, Susanna puts her trust in God. The next significant moment is when she comes to be judged on the following day.

Que bene firmata domini spe nilque morata
Orans cum psalmis comitata parentibus almis
Ac sibi cognatis cum cunctis vel sibi notis
Promptius accelerat: simul huc perveniet et intrat
Omnis deflet eam quisquis cognoverat illam (ll. 161–5)

She, well fortified by the hope of the Lord and making no delay,
Hastens quite promptly, praying with psalms, accompanied by her kind parents,
And her relatives, and indeed, all those known to her,
When she gets there and enters,
Everyone weeps who has known her.

The impulse of other medieval tellers of this tale is to reduce the cast to Susanna, the elders, and Daniel. The impulse of Willetrudis seems to be precisely opposite. She surrounds her heroine with a large and sympathetic crowd of parents, relations, and friends. Other treatments of the story take the view that if a very beautiful woman is accused of adultery, this accusation will be immediately believed, however virtuous she may have seemed: Willetrudis, conversely, creates an anguished support group, reluctant to believe ill of her unless the case against her is proved. This is a highly original twist in a story which otherwise sticks closer to the Vulgate than any other version. The next step is also unexpected: the balance of sympathy is already tilted towards Susanna, when Willetrudis makes one of her few interventions in the narrative:

Iusserunt tolli vestes de corpore molli
Ac visu dignae violant pudibunda Susannae
Quo mens pravata conspectu sit saciata
O male perversi peius post pessima versi (ll. 169–72)

They have ordered the clothes stripped from her soft body,
And they violate with their gaze the secret parts of Susanna,
So that thereby a depraved mentality may be satiated by the sight:
O how wickedly perverse men become worse after the worst!

Willetrudis does not offer a vision of Susanna naked in her orchard; but she does at this point, in causing the elders further to abuse their position. The passage focuses on the violence which is done to Susanna by being looked at, and the depravity of the minds which choose to satisfy themselves in this way: having been prevented from literal rape in private, the elders are so shameless, or so self-indulgent, that they take the opportunity to commit a metaphoric rape in public. This passage completely reverses the assumptions which medieval (male) writers normally make about women and the gaze: Petrus de Riga by contrast, chose to imply that even though Susanna is virtuous, her beauty exerts a compelling, magnetic force to which men respond, apparently helplessly: in other words, the problem of male lust lies with women.[135] What Willetrudis expresses here is an absolute conviction that the problem lies with male lack of self-control.

The other thing which Willetrudis does here, by moving the stripping of Susanna from her undressing herself in a context of pleasure (however innocent), to being forcibly stripped before her entire community, is to evoke the virgin martyrs. Susanna is referred to at various points in the text as *sancta*; but more conclusively, the model for a chaste, God-fearing woman stripped and mistreated by unjust judges, in the midst of a community some of which, at least, is on her side, is found in the Acts of the Martyrs. In the story of St Anastasia and her three lovely servant maids (told by Hrotsvitha in her play *Dulcitius*, and later by Jacobus de Voragine in the *Golden Legend*), the wicked prefect demands that the maids be stripped so that, having been thwarted in his attempt actually to have sex with them, he can at least enjoy the sight of their beauty.[136] This appears to be a direct parallel to the behaviour of the elders in this version of the story. St Agnes, similarly, is stripped, prior to being thrown in a brothel.[137] Most versions of the story of Susanna leave the reader (or viewer) to some extent complicit with the elders: by mapping the elders' behaviour onto that of the monstrous tyrants of the saints' lives, Willetrudis short-circuits this response, and is made able to present Susanna as an extraordinarily strong and positive figure.

This impression of Susanna is strengthened after the elders have made their accusation against her. Petrus de Riga's Susanna is silent. Alan of Melsa's Susanna apostrophizes God at the moment when the elders put their proposition to her; but she goes all to pieces in public: she falters out four lines, then *pudor* and *timor* silence her—just as if she were actually guilty.[138] Willetrudis's Susanna, on the other hand, is buoyed up by her faith in God and her knowledge of her own righteousness: she makes a long, moving speech, placing herself in the hands of God, and declaring her trust in divine wisdom (ll. 210–28). Her steadfastness is, again, reminiscent of the martyrs, and it is perhaps this literary model which allows

[135] See Bloch, *Medieval Misogyny*, 31.

[136] Hippolyte Delehaye, *Étude sur le légendier romain: les saints de novembre et de décembre* (Brussels: Société des Bollandistes, 1956), 227–35, Jacobus de Voragine, *The Golden Legend*, trans. William Granger Ryan, 2 vols. (Princeton: Princeton University Press, 1993), i. 43–4.

[137] *Golden Legend*, i. 103.

[138] Mozley, 'Susanna', 48–9.

Willetrudis to present her heroine as a *femina fortis*, as strong-minded as she is beautiful. Susanna goes unflinchingly towards a martyr's death:

> Ducitur ad mortem totam comitata cohortem
> Martyrium mente complens vitaque manente (ll. 233–4)

> She is led towards death, surrounded by the whole crowd,
> Completing her martyrdom in her mind, while life remained

—apart from the strength of mind thus exhibited, it is once more worth observing that again, she is not isolated, but surrounded by an apparently sympathetic crowd.

In the nick of time, of course, the boy Daniel arises from the crowd, and intervenes. One interesting aspect of Willetrudis's treatment is that he does not in any real sense become the hero of the narrative. It is his *inspiration*—which is given him by God—not his own qualities which is stressed. Daniel is God's answer to Susanna's prayer, essentially, a bit-player in her drama, no more the hero than Balaam's ass. Conversely, since the basic structure of Petrus de Riga's version is one of forensic speeches for and against Susanna, it is hardly surprising that it is Daniel's brilliance which is to the fore in his text.

Willetrudis continues to tell the tale of Daniel's simple but elegant solution to the problem, and the evil elders are hustled out to suffer the fate they designed for their victim. From line 301, Susanna returns to the centre of the picture. It is not Daniel's genius but her virtue which is the key, just as it is in the Vulgate, which at this point says, 'therefore Chelcias and his wife praised God for their daughter Susanna, with Joachim her husband, and all the kindred, because there was no dishonesty found in her'. The Book of Susanna more or less stops here, but Willetrudis does not. In her text, the entire Jewish population of Babylon, rich and poor together, unite in a canticle-like utterance praising God and the great virtue of Susanna, whom they compare to Joseph, falsely accused by Potiphar's wife.

Willetrudis ends by pointing the moral. Susanna's triumphant chastity is a model not merely for virtuous wives, but for virgins who are married to the Lamb—that is, nuns, a further confirmation that she is writing from a convent. What we have here is therefore something very unusual. A poem from the Latin Middle Ages, by a woman, which unflinchingly takes on medieval misogyny (in particular, the idea that women are somehow entirely to blame for human sexual impulses), and presents an ideal of active and heroic womanhood. Humour is always an index to cultural assumptions, and it is therefore significant that the itchy, unsatisfied wives and nuns of medieval Europe's folk songs and fabliaux represent a set of vulgar assumptions about women and their needs: in particular, the belief that it is not so much unnatural as virtually impossible for women to get along without men. But not all our evidence from late antiquity and the Middle Ages is of this kind. In their own writings, many women from the fourth century onwards made it absolutely clear that they could get along very well indeed without men, and indeed, preferred to do so. Susanna is a married woman (though her husband Joachim is barely in evidence in this version; it is Susanna's parents and kin who seem to hover about her in her ordeal), but the context in which we see her is not one of fulfilling marital duties, but of repelling an attack on her integrity.

If we look at medieval women's own writings, we see a variety of positive images of women, particularly celibate women.[139] These include saints' lives, such as the Life of Radegund by Baudonivia, and more unusual compositions, such as Hrotsvitha of Gandersheim's poem on the foundation of her own community, *De Situ Gandesheimensis*. Saints' lives tend to show the individual—the saint—starkly outlined against the background of their social context. But it is clear that, as well as finding a sense of individual identity and personal dignity in a life of virginity, some women were positively empowered by living in a community with other celibate women. Caroline Walker Bynum has noted, with respect to the nuns of Helfta in the thirteenth century,

the contrast between the more anxious quality of the writing of Mechtild of Magdeburg, who lived most of her life as a quasi religous, or beguine, and became one only as a young adult, and the positive sense of self found in Gertrude and Mechtild of Hackeborn who entered the convent as children, suggests that women who grew up in monasteries were less likely to be influenced by the contemporary stereotype of women as morally and intellectually inferior. Such women were more likely to see themselves as functioning with a full range of male and female, governing and comforting roles, paralleling the full range of the operations of God.[140]

The implication here is of an emotionally autonomous and sustaining world of women, which does not look outside itself for something which it senses to be missing. Similarly, the female mystics described by Bynum have a quality of self-esteem and self-respect which runs counter to the way in which they are perceived by men:

In contrast to twelfth-century Cistercian monks who used much inverted imagery for themselves and included references to weak women as a way of speaking of their abasement and renunciation as monks, these nuns do not refer to the inferiority of women. In contrast to twelfth- and thirteenth-century exegetical convention, they do not use women as a symbol of flesh, or lust, or of the irrational.[141]

Similarly, Hildegard of Bingen, another woman brought up within a convent, evolved her own, highly original ideas about the nature of womanhood, and diverged from orthodox assumptions in a variety of ways, including holding that women are less concupiscent than men, not more so.[142] Willetrudis is another of

---

[139] Katharina M. Wilson, '*Figmenta* versus *Veritas*: Dame Alice and the Medieval Literary Depiction of Women by Women', *Tulsa Studies in Women's Literature*, 4.1 (1985), 17–32.

[140] Bynum, *Jesus as Mother*, 185.

[141] Ibid. 226, and see M.-T. d'Alverny, 'Comment les théologiens... voient la femme?', *Cahiers de civilisation médiévale*, 20 (1977), 105–29 and E. McLaughlin, 'Equality of Souls, Inequality of Sexes: Women in Medieval Theology', in R. R. Reuther (ed.), *Religion and Sexism* (New York: Simon & Schuster, 1974), 213–66.

[142] Bynum, *Jesus as Mother*, 92; *Scivias*, ed. Führkötter and Carlevaris, pt. 2, vision 3, § 22 (i. 147–8), pt. 1, vision 2, §§ 11–12 (i. 19–21), and pt. 2, vision 6, §§ 76 and 77 (i. 290–1)

these voices from the convent, speaking out of a nuns' culture which is very far from abjectly conceding the view of 'women as the source of all evil' about which they must have heard so very much.[143]

[143] Penelope D. Johnson, 'Mulier et Monialis: The Medieval Nun's Self-Image', *Thought*, 64 (1989), 242–53.

PART III

The Renaissance

6. *Italy: Renaissance Women Scholars*

By the sixteenth century, Italy had become famous for its learned women even as far afield as England: Richard Mulcaster observed in 1581, 'nay do we not see in our countrey, some of that sex so excellently well trained, and so rarely qualified, either for the tounges themselves or for the matter in the tounges: as they may be opposed by any of comparison . . . to the *Italian* ladies who dare write themselves, and deserve fame for so doing? whose excellencie is so geason [rare], as they be rather wonders to gaze at, then presidents to follow.'[1] From the fourteenth to the seventeenth centuries, Italy produced more women who wrote Latin, both in verse and prose, than any other country in Europe, as well as more women who wrote verse and prose in their own language. Their work has understandably attracted more discussion than that of women Latinists from any other country: notably, Margaret L. King has published on Maddalena Scrovegni and Isotta Nogarola; Albert Rabil and Diana Robin on Laura Cereta, and Holt Parker on the Nogarolas and Costanza Varano.[2] It was possible for an Italian woman to be celebrated for her linguistic skill as early as 1354: in that year, the contemporary *Cronaca italiana di Bologna* reports apparently with pride that the Emperor Charles IV and his wife were accompanied on their solemn entry into Bologna by the widow of a local lawyer, Giovanna Buonsignori, née Bianchetti, who was fluent in German, Bohemian (Czech), and Italian.[3]

The first influential catalogue of women, that of Boccaccio (claimed by him to be the first collection of women's biographies ever written), was first circulated in 1355, and revised by him until at least 1359.[4] The last and longest version contains 104 biographies, of which only three are concerned with women famous for

---

[1] Richard Mulcaster (1530–1611), quoted in Shirley Nelson Kersey, *Classics in the Education of Girls and Women* (Metuchen, NJ: Scarecrow Press, Inc., 1981), 52–67 (p. 54).

[2] See Margaret L, King, 'The Religious Retreat of Isotta Nogarola (1418–1466)', *Signs*, 3 (1978), 807–22; 'Book-Lined Cells: Women and Humanism in the Early Italian Renaissance', in Patricia H. Labalme (ed.), *Beyond their Sex* (New York: New York University Press, 1980), 66–90; 'Goddess and Captive: Antonio Loschi's Epistolatory Tribute to Maddalena Scrovegni (1389)' *Medievalia et Humanistica* (1988), 103–27; Albert Rabil, Jr., *Laura Cereta: Quattrocento Humanist* (Binghamton, NY: Medieval and Renaissance Texts and Studies, 1981), Diana Robin, 'Women, Space and Renaissance Discourse', in Barbara K. Gold et al. (eds.), *Sex and Gender in Medieval and Renaissance Texts* (New York: State University of New York Press, 1997), 165–87, Holt Parker, 'Latin and Greek Poetry by Five Renaissance Italian Women Humanists', in Gold et al. (eds.), *Sex and Gender*, 247–86.

[3] Girolamo Tiraboschi, *Storia della letteratura italiana* (Modena: Società tipografica, 1787), iv. 506.

[4] Alcuin Blamires, *The Case for Women in Medieval Culture* (Oxford: Clarendon Press, 1997), 66–8, 172, demonstrates that his work in fact emerges from a tradition of writing about exemplary women going back as far as late antiquity. Note also that Plutarch's work on the virtues of women, *De Claris Mulieribus*, appeared in a Latin translation by Alamanno Rinuccini (1419–99) at some point in the late 15th century (no place, date, or publisher is given).

writing: Sappho, Cornificia, and Proba, together with one, Hortensia, who was famous for her public speaking. He concludes with the remark, 'I have reached the women of our time, in which the number of illustrious ones is so small that I think it more suitable to come to an end here [with Joanna, Queen of Sicily] rather than proceed further.'[5] But Jacopo Foresti da Bergamo's *On Famous Women* (*De Claris Mulieribus*), published in Ferrara in 1497 and much plundered by later writers, lists hundreds of women, good and bad, including a noble gallery of contemporaries made famous either by the writing they circulated or by their public performance as orators, often in Latin, which includes Battista Malatesta, Costanza Varano, the three Nogarolas, and Domitilla Trivulzi Torelli. In the intervening 150 years, something had clearly changed for Italian women. Gabriella Zarri has drawn attention to the rise in the numbers of humanist tracts praising illustrious women from the fifteenth to the sixteenth centuries, and their increasing tendency over time to list contemporaries, which means that despite the overwhelming impression of sameness which they give, many such works contain genuine information about women in the immediate milieu of the writer.[6] It also indicates that women deemed worth mentioning were flourishing in increasing numbers.

It is hardly possible to identify a single position taken by Italian humanist men towards women's intellectual aspirations. Those who troubled to write on the subject were on the whole encouraging, though concerned that learning must not lead to inappropriate forms of behaviour and the assumption of masculine privileges, while a number of those who were parents went out of their way to educate promising daughters.[7] Vespasiano da Bisticci, in praising Andrea Accaiuoli (the dedicatee of Boccaccio's *De Claris Mulieribus*) goes so far as to adapt the central humanist concept of the 'homo universalis' (the 'Renaissance man'): he describes her almost untranslatably with the words 'fu donna universale'.[8]

Furthermore, from the point of view of the intellectual balance sheet of the city as a whole, women scholars and writers were very definitely valued: by the sixteenth century, for a city to harbour a handful of women poets and scholars was perceived by literati as an index of civilization, a view which can be seen establishing itself during the previous century.[9] Hailing a young woman as 'O

[5] *Concerning Famous Women*, trans. Guido Guarino (New Brunswick, NJ: Rutgers University Press, 1963), conclusion, 251. Now ed. and trans. Virginia Brown (Cambridge, Mass.: Harvard University Press, 2001).

[6] Gabriella Zarri, *Le sante vive: profesie di corte e devozione femminile tra '400 e '500* (Turin: Rosenberg and Sellier, 1990), 32–9. See also Pamela Joseph Benson, *The Invention of the Renaissance Woman* (University Park: Pennsylvania State University Press, 1992), 31. It is notable that when Boccaccio's work was translated into Italian by Betussi (*Libro di M. Giovanni Boccaccio delle donne illustri* (Florence: Filippo Giunta, 1596)), it was extensively supplemented with accounts of recent Italian women.

[7] On the education of women in Renaissance Italy generally, see Gabriella Zarri, 'Le istituzione dell'educazione femminile', in her *Recinti* (Bologna: Il Mulino, 2000), 145–200, and the bibliography she gives on p. 147.

[8] Vespasiano da Bisticci, *Vite di uomini illustri del secolo xv*, ed. Ludovico Frati (Bologna: Romagnoli-Dall'Acqua, 1892), 294.

[9] This is directly stated by Johannes Sauerbrei, in his *Diatriben Academicam de Foeminarum Eruditione* (Leipzig: Johann Erich Hahn, 1671), pt. I, sig. E 2ᵛ). See also Francine Daeneus, 'Superiore perché

virgin ornament of Italy' ('O decus Italiae virgo'), as Poliziano does in addressing Cassandra Fedele, echoing Turnus' address to Camilla in *Aeneid* 11. 508, tells us something, if not anything very straightforward, about the way in which that particular woman was perceived by her contemporaries, but it also tells us something more general: that by the fifteenth century, a woman not actually a sovereign who was speaking in public had at least in some contexts come to be perceived as a glory rather than as a discredit to her community.[10]

One important fact to bear in mind, however, is that Italy was not itself a nation. While 'Italy' in the mouth of Poliziano obviously meant something, it was more of a geographical or linguistic than a political term (as it also was for Virgil, from whom the phrase is taken). There was a considerable difference between one part of Italy and another, and one way in which this is expressed is in attitudes towards learned women: the republic of Venice and its dependencies produced substantial numbers; the republic of Florence very few, apart from the famous Greek scholar Alessandra Scala;[11] the republic of Genoa, apparently none until the seventeenth century.[12] There were social levels and regions where the range of possibilities for daughters of the elite included a sophisticated Latin-based education, and others where it did not. Among the various courts of Renaissance Italy, highly educated women flourished in some, notably those of Pesaro, Urbino, Correggio, Milan, Ferrara, and Mantua, but not in all: when Eleonora, daughter of King Ferrante of Naples, came to Ferrara in 1473 as the wife of Ercole d'Este, she was an accomplished musician, but not a poet or a scholar.[13]

The continued strength of Latin in Italy at a time when other Romance-speaking nations such as France and Spain were turning to the vernacular is an interesting phenomenon in itself. It may derive from the similarity of Italian to Latin, but may also, perhaps, be linked with the absence of a generally agreed

inferiore: il paradosso della superiorità della donna in alcuni trattati italiani del Cinquecento', in Vanna Gentili (ed.), *Transgressione tragica e norma domestica: esemplari di tipologie femminili alla letteratura europaea* (Rome: Bulzoni, 1983), 11–50.

[10] M. L. King and Albert Rabil (trans.), *Her Immaculate Hand* (Asheville, NC: Pegasus Press, 1997), 126–7.

[11] 1475–1506: she was the daughter of Bartolomeo Scala, secretary of the Florentine republic. She was learned in Latin and Greek, and wrote poetry in Greek.

[12] The first Genoese woman of letters I know of is St Catherine [Adorno] of Genoa (1447–1510), whose *Libro della vita e dottrina* was first published Genova: Belloni, 1551. She wrote nothing herself, but her words were recorded by her spiritual advisers Cattaneo Marabotto and Ettore Vernazza. The first Genoese secular woman writer seems to be Maria Spinola, who flourished in the mid-16th century, and was praised by Pietro Aretino (Bandini Buti, ii. 276–77). Two learned women of the 17th century, Maria Elena Lusignani and Clelia Grillo Borromeo, are mentioned by Tiraboschi, *Storia*, viii. 466 and in Cosenza, respectively. Bizarrely, one of the few Renaissance Italian girls to study Latin at a school was Genoese: Catharinetta, the daughter of a barber, began studying elementary Latin grammar with her brother on 4 June 1500. Paul F. Grendler, *Schooling in Renaissance Italy* (Baltimore: Johns Hopkins University Press, 1989), 96. Steven A. Epstein, *Genoa and the Genoese, 958–1528* (Chapel Hill: University of North Carolina Press, 1996), identifies no Genoese tradition of learned women.

[13] Mary Agnes Cannon, *The Education of Women during the Renaissance* (Washington: Catholic Education Press, 1916), 42. However, she became a competent ruler, as the funeral orations on her death bear witness: John M. McManaman, *Funeral Oratory and the Cultural Ideals of Italian Humanism* (Chapel Hill: University of North Carolina Press, 1989), 113.

standard Italian and the consequent continued vigour of Italy's dialects.[14] Fourteenth-century Italy led the world in the revival of classical Latin which is the essential tool of Renaissance discourse.[15] The uses of Latin in the Renaissance were various: Latin was the language of the clerisy, the universities, and also of lawyers, diplomats, scientists, and doctors—people whose professional lives made it necessary, or at least useful, to maintain a community of culture which crossed the boundaries imposed by national languages.[16] It is often assumed that none of these uses would apply to women, since they could not become clerics or lawyers, and did not normally become official diplomats (though we may note that Catherine of Aragon was invested with the formal credentials of ambassador to Henry VII by her father Fernando of Aragon for two years, from 1506 to 1508,[17] and women's action as unofficial diplomats is visible in a number of different contexts from as early as the fifteenth century).[18] There is also some evidence that women became doctors, discussed below.

However, only in very exceptional and contingent circumstances did women become university professors, and they did not become professional humanists: they did not attend universities, and no fifteenth-century patron retained a woman scholar as secretary, tutor, or court poet (with the possible exception of Charles V of France, patron of Christine de Pizan). Most Italian women humanists were aristocrats: the participation of other women of less exalted rank in the public arena of humanist discussion and debate was complicated by the social values attached to verbal challenge and combat, an activity central to humanism and incompatible with norms of feminine behaviour.[19] The discourse of inter-humanist exchange comprehended vicious invective as well as high-souled *amicitia*.[20] Clough notes that 'the second half of the fifteenth century witnessed excessive acrimony and

---

[14] Epstein, *Genoa and the Genoese*, 161–2, points to the continued importance of Latin specifically in Genoa. See also Cecil Grayson, *A Renaissance Controversy: Latin or Italian?* (Oxford: Clarendon Press, 1960), and Lori J. Walters, 'The Royal Vernacular: Poet and Patron in Christine de Pizan's Charles V and the Sept Psaumes Allegorisées', in Renate Blumenfeld-Kosinski et al. (eds.), *The Vernacular Spirit* (New York: Palgrave, 2002), 145–82 (pp. 147–8), where she discusses Dante's defence of the vulgar tongue together with his argument that the absence of an Italian monarch prevented the development of a linguistic as well as political unity.

[15] The difference between medieval and Renaissance Latin is well explored in Ann Moss, *Renaissance Thought and the Latin Language Turn*.

[16] Note that Peter Burke, *The Art of Conversation* (Ithaca, NY: Cornell University Press, 1993), 34–65, suggests the continued utility of Latin as a means of communication down to the 19th century in many contexts *beyond* those of the academy: his argument is not addressed to the issue of gender, but is clearly relevant to it.

[17] Garrett Mattingly, *Catherine of Aragon* (London: Jonathan Cape, 1942; repr. 1963) 75–8. This was during her 'widowhood': her marriage to Arthur was from November 1501 to April 1502, that to Henry took place in 1509. Philippe-Joseph Caffiaux, *Défenses du beau sexe* (Amsterdam: Aux dépens de la Compagnie, 1757), i. 169, discusses other Renaissance women diplomats.

[18] As unofficial diplomats, women are of course very important: the overlap between the purposes of diplomacy and those of elite marriage ensured that this was the case long before the Renaissance. For a long view, see Michael J. Enright, *The Lady with the Mead-Cup* (Dublin: Four Courts, 1996).

[19] Mario Biagioli, *Galileo, Courtier* (Chicago: Chicago University Press, 1993), 55.

[20] Both these are discussed by Lauro Martines, *Strong Words: Writing and Social Strain in the Italian Renaissance* (Baltimore: Johns Hopkins University Press, 2001), esp. 14–15, 24–36.

vituperation among scholars'.[21] Furthermore, other conventions of humanist discourse also created serious problems for would-be humanist women: the language of patronage and the language of love poetry overlapped substantially, which effectively debarred women from seeking patronage unless they were prepared to be understood as making a pass.

Lisa Jardine perceives an absence of productive purpose in women's writing, noting that women were not involved in retrieving the residue of antiquity (a central preoccupation of humanist scholarship).[22] Certainly, this is not an important feature of many women's intellectual life in fifteenth-century Italy, though we may note in passing that some German and Low Countries women humanists were active in this field, and that the Nogarolas were enthusiastic collectors and redactors of rare texts: the fragmentary MS of the *Satyricon* which is now Vatican City, Barberini lat. 4 was owned by Isotta, while her sister Ginevra can be found transcribing exotica: a manuscript of Justinus survives from her hand.[23]

The issue of the transcription of manuscripts is related to more general issues of the circulation of texts, including those written by women themselves. A general aspect of culture which needs now to be considered, since it will be relevant to all subsequent chapters, is the question of dissemination—the rise of printing and its implications. Printing was invented in the 1450s, and spread out from its first home in Germany with surprising speed: the first Italian press was in Venice in 1469.[24] Works by women were printed from very early on in the century: Proba's *Cento* appeared a mere three years later, printed by Bartolomeo Girardini.[25] However, the rise of print, important though it is, conceals something important about text transmission and reception in the fifteenth century and even later. Manuscripts continued to be made, and some writers preferred manuscript, for aesthetic, social, or practical reasons.[26] Some patrons preferred manuscripts, or would only buy print copies if the text was very special, e.g. printed on vellum (Isabella d'Este was a book-buyer of this type).[27] Within coterie circles, textual transmission as manuscript continued to be very important as late as the eighteenth

---

[21] Cecil H. Clough, 'The Cult of Antiquity: Letters and Letter Collections', in Clough (ed.), *Cultural Aspects of the Italian Renaissance: Essays in Honour of Paul Oskar Kristeller* (Manchester: Manchester University Press; New York: Alfred F. Zambelli, 1976), 33–67 (p. 46).

[22] Lisa Jardine, ' "O Decus Italiae Virgo", or the Myth of the Learned Lady in the Renaissance', *Historical Journal*, 28 (1985), 799–819 (pp. 812–17), and 'Isotta Nogarola: Women Humanists— Education for What?' *History of Education*, 12 (1983), 231–44.

[23] Yale, University Library, Marston 279.

[24] Brian Richardson, *Printing, Writers and Readers in Renaissance Italy* (Cambridge: Cambridge University Press, 1999), 4. See also the classic account of Elisabeth Eisenstein, *The Printing Press as an Agent of Change* (Cambridge: Cambridge University Press, 1979).

[25] Cassandra Fedele's *oratio* for Bertuccio Lamberto was twice printed in the 15th century (Mutine, 1482; Venice: Hieronymus de Sanctis, 1488), and there is verse by Isabella Sforza in *Rime dell'arguto e faceto poeta Bernardo Bellinioni fiorentino* (Milan: Filippo de Montegazzi, 1493) (see Pietro Leopoldo Ferri, *Biblioteca femminile italiana* (Padua: Crescini, 1842), 160, 18) and see Introduction, above p. 24.

[26] Richardson, *Printing, Writers and Readers*, 77–104.

[27] Susan Groag Bell, 'Medieval Women Book Owners', in J. Bennett et al. (eds.), *Sisters and Workers in the Middle Ages* (Chicago: Chicago University Press, 1989), 135–61 (p. 144).

century, something which is relevant to many women writers, particularly those of the elite.[28]

The roots of scribal publication go back to the ancient world: a classic example which can be quoted is an exchange between Sulpicius Severus, an important Gallo-Roman writer of the fourth century, and his mother-in-law Bassula, who had constituted herself his publisher in this special sense: 'you have not left in my house one scrap of paper, one small book, or one letter; for you steal them all and publish the lot. If I write a personal letter to a friend; if I happen, in a lighter moment, to dictate something which I would like, nevertheless, to keep secret, everything reaches you almost before it is written or dictated...Now to say nothing of the rest, I wonder how the letter which I wrote a little while to the deacon Aurelius reached you so quickly? For I am at Toulouse, and you are in Trier.'[29] The same situation obtained in Renaissance Italy. Letters were circulated, with or without the author's permission, and sometimes, as Bassula seems to have done, a specific individual constituted him- or herself the 'publisher'. Often, though not invariably, the work was formally issued once complete in an archetype prepared under the author's direct supervision.[30] It is important to realize that, as Cecil Clough has warned, a letter collection might or might not consist of letters actually sent: Petrarch filled out a series with fictive correspondence, and Bembo created a dramatic narrative out of his letter collection which effectively reversed the truth.[31]

One major humanist woman writer, Laura Cereta, prepared such a collection. A finished manuscript of her *epistolae familiares* circulated among prominent scholars in Brescia, Verona, and Venice by 1488/92, which she had consciously published herself in this sense: she refers in a letter to 'this grand volume of epistles, for which the final draft is now being copied out'.[32] Albert Rabil points out not only that she intended her letters from the beginning as public documents, but also that many of the letters are more or less formal orations—prompting the question of whether they ever had an existence as actual letters.[33] This is not unimportant, since if we can take her work at face value, she was communicating in complex humanist Latin with no fewer than thirteen other women, including her mother and sisters, most of whom are unattested outside her correspondence, with the exception of Cassandra Fedele. Names such as 'Nazaria Olympica', the abbess 'Veneranda', 'Europa solitaria', and 'Lucilia Vernacula' (to whom an invective is addressed suggesting that, like Isotta Nogarola, Cereta was capable of expressing as much venom as any male humanist) do not inspire confidence in the historicity of

---

[28] For later centuries, this phenomenon is discussed by Harold Love, *Scribal Publication in Seventeenth-Century England* (Oxford: Clarendon Press, 1993), and Margaret J. M. Ezell, *Social Authorship and the Advent of Print* (Baltimore: Johns Hopkins University Press, 1999).

[29] N. K. Chadwick, *Poetry and Letters in Early Christian Gaul* (London: Bowes & Bowes, 1955), 93–4.

[30] Richardson, *Printing, Writers and Readers*, 49–50.

[31] Clough, 'The Cult of Antiquity', 35.

[32] *Laura Cereta: Collected Letters of a Renaissance Feminist*, trans. Diana Robin (Chicago: University of Chicago Press, 1997), 34, letter to Sigismondo de Bucci.

[33] Rabil, *Laura Cereta*, 24–5.

her correspondence.[34] Similarly, her attack on a man who does not believe in learned women is addressed to one Bibolo Semproni,[35] suggesting that she has chosen the safer path of creating a fictional detractor to argue against rather than writing an actual letter to someone capable of giving as good as he got.

Cereta aside, the experience of a number of women humanists in fifteenth-century Italy was that their work was circulated as soon as written: letters addressed to one individual were in fact copied and passed on, by the recipient or others. Some fifteenth-century women give a clear impression that their work was circulated without permission, notably Isotta Nogarola, whose correspondence with Guarino is discussed below. It is evident from this exchange that for her to send a letter to Guarino was a public act (and that before she wrote to him, other people had already showed him letters by her): like Sulpicius Severus a thousand years before, she found her correspondence was passing from hand to hand whether she wished it or not.

There is other evidence for the circulation of women's letters in Latin. In 1493, Poliziano took Cassandra Fedele's letters to Alessandra Scala, and had Scala read them out to the Florentine academy, an assembly which included her father Bartolommeo Scala, Marsilio Ficino, and Pico della Mirandola.[36] A Bolognese lady, Niccolosa Castellani Sanuti (b. 1453), achieved some celebrity when she addressed a Latin speech to Cardinal Bessarion, then papal legate in Bologna, asking him to repeal a decree in which he had prohibited the wearing of sumptuous dresses by the ladies of her city.[37] This speech, which is extremely long, makes direct reference to the Roman oratrix Hortensia, the classical precedent of the Roman sumptuary law (the Lex Oppia), and the classical precedent of opposition to it, from Hortensia and also from Cato.[38] She goes on to discuss notable women of antiquity, and also of the present day: of the latter, she says that their letters circulate in manuscript. 'There are many letters and speeches and most elegant

---

[34] The first name suggests the Christian humanist, at once Nazarene and Olympian, the second simply means 'venerable', 'Europa solitaria' is the solitary wanderer, 'vernacula' suggests an ignorant person who knows no Latin.

[35] 'Bibolo' meaning 'the drunken man'. Sempronia in Sallust's *Bellum Catilinae* is presented by him as both educated and vicious (see Ch. 1).

[36] A. Grafton and L. Jardine, *From Humanism to the Humanities* (London: Duckworth, 1986), 53.

[37] She herself was known to Laura Cereta, who includes her in a list of learned women in a polemic letter on women's education to the possibly fictitious Bibolo Semproni (trans. Robin, 78).

[38] Livy, *Ab Urbe Condita* 34. 1–8 discusses the repeal of the Lex Oppia in 195 BC, at which, he says, respectable women rioted for the right to wear expensive clothes and a woman (Hortensia) put their case in court (34. 1. 5–6 and 8.1–3). See also S. Dixon, 'Polybius and Roman Women and Property', *American Journal of Philology*, 106 (1985), 147–70. Sanuti's work is also contexted by a contemporary *Declamatione delle gentildonne di Cesena intorno alle Pompe* (Cesena: Bartolomeo Raverio, 1575), in which the gentlewomen of Cesena similarly defend themselves against the recent sumptuary law issued by the president of Romagna, in Italian. We might note that Sanuti's own work was scribally published: at least eight manuscripts survive (detailed in *Iter Italicum*). See also Diane Owen Hughes, 'Sumptuary Law and Social Relations in Renaissance Italy', in John Bossy (ed.), *Disputes and Settlements* (Cambridge: Cambridge University Press, 1983), 69–100, and Jane Bridgeman, ' "Pagare le pompe": Why Quattrocento Sumptuary Laws did not Work', in Letizia Panizza (ed.), *Women in Italian Renaissance Culture and Society* (Oxford: European Humanities Research Centre, 2000), 209–26.

verses from Costanza, wife of Alessandro Sforza [Costanza Varano] and others, which are in people's hands now.'[39] Both Costanza Varano and Isotta Nogarola were in fact 'scribally published' writers, since in both cases there is a number of manuscripts containing roughly the same material: the manuscripts of Varano's poems in the Appendix tell their own story,[40] since they show that the poems often travelled as a group, and the same is true of Nogarola's letters.[41] If it were possible to believe Arturo Pomello, 564 manuscripts of Isotta Nogarola's letters could be found in the second half of the seventeenth century in one Parisian library alone: the number provokes instant scepticism, but even if it is a typographic error and 56, 64, or even 5 or 6 was meant, it suggests a diffusion so wide that 'publication' is the only appropriate term.[42]

For good or ill (and both Isotta Nogarola and Laura Cereta declare that it sometimes earned them the scorn and anger of other women, as well as of some men) fifteenth-century humanist women had a high public profile. In many cases, their writing was made public, even if it was not published in the sense of being committed to print; and the question which it posed was essentially whether the writers were to be admired or execrated. Received opinion, as both male and female contemporaries attest, was strongly against, but among other humanists, admiration is very much easier to demonstrate. It is also important to observe that the number of surviving manuscripts of women's writing tells its own story. It is relatively unusual outside Italy for women's writings in Latin to be preserved in multiple copies, but common within it, as the Appendix bears witness. The circulation of manuscript copies is direct evidence that a work attracted interest.

[39] Lodovico Frati, *La vita privata in Bologna dal secolo xiii al xvii*, 2nd edn. (Bologna: Nicola Zanichelli, 1928), 251–62 (p. 256).

[40] Six of her letters and her orations travel together, e.g. Florence, Biblioteca nazionale, II X 31, fos. 43^r–45, Florence, Biblioteca Riccardiana, 924 (N III 15), fos. 263^v–264^r, Venice, Biblioteca Marciana, Lat. XIV.7 (4319), fos. 27^r–29^r, Verona, Biblioteca Comunale, 68 (1393), fos. 43^v–46^v. Another three letters are preserved, two in Milan, Biblioteca Ambrosiana, S. 222 inf. (4) (the replies are also in this MS), one in Venice, Biblioteca Marciana, Lat. XIV.7 (4319), fo. 28^r.

[41] Collections of her letters survive in Naples, Biblioteca Nazionale, V F 17, s. xv, Paris, Bibliothèque Nationale de France, 8580, Parma, Biblioteca Palatina, Pal. 262, fos. 91–130 (a collection of Nogarola's letters within a larger collection), Verona, Biblioteca Capitolare, CCLVI (228), Vatican City, Biblioteca apostolica, Vat. lat. 5127, Vienna, Nationalsbibliothek, 3481, Wolfenbüttel, Herzog August Bibliothek, 83.25, Aug. fol. s. xv 2859, fos. 79–84, Florence, Biblioteca Riccardiana, 924 (N III 15), Munich, Bayerische Staatsbibliothek, Clm lat. 5639, s. xv, and Cambridge, University Library, Add. 6188, s. xv. There are also letters in Munich, Bayerische Staatsbibliothek, Clm lat. 418 and 522.

[42] Arturo Pomello, *Le Nogarola* (Verona, 1908), quoted in *ECWW*, ii. 922. According to Sarah Josepha Hale, *Woman's Record* (New York: Harper & Brothers, 1860), 133–4, the library was that of Jacques Auguste de Thou (Thuanus). De Thou's library passed to one of his sons, and was sold off later when the family got into financial difficulties: much, though not all, of the collection ended up in the Bibliothèque Royale, so one should now expect to find at least some of these manuscripts in the Bibliothèque Nationale in Paris. One known Nogarola MS, Paris, Bibliothèque Nationale de France, 8580, did come from de Thou's collection (*Isotae Nogarolae... opera*, ed. Abel, i, p. clvi). My thanks to Dr Ingrid de Smet for information on de Thou.

The fourteenth century: women and the universities

In the late Middle Ages in Italy, some aspects of the university world which had previously the province of churchmen moved into the secular sphere; most notably, law and medicine. In both these areas, therefore, there came to be professors who became the fathers of legitimate families; which therefore opened up for the first time the possibility of a professional class which might produce educated daughters. There is evidence that women benefited from this.

The medical school of Salerno, with roots back deep into the Middle Ages, seems to have had a number of women associated with it in the late Middle Ages, quite apart from the legendary (though not mythical) gynaecologist Trotula, whose name is now thought to conceal that of a genuine practitioner, Trota, active in the eleventh or twelfth century, the author of *Practica Secundum Trotam*.[43] There are obvious reasons why doctors should pay more attention to women's knowledge than mathematicians or grammarians, but it is worth noting that a number of fourteenth-century women are noted in the Salernitan records as the authors of medical texts on subjects unconnected with specifically female ailments. Perhaps the best attested is the fourteenth-century Costanza Calenda, doctor of Salerno,[44] but other names mentioned include Mercuriadis, and Rebecca Guarna.[45] Christine de Pizan, author of the *Book of the City of Ladies*, may be an indirect beneficiary of this Italian medical humanism, since she was the daughter of an erudite Italian doctor who became physician and court astrologer of Charles V (she is discussed in Chapter 7). In the fifteenth century, Dorotea Bocchi, another doctor, is said not only to have continued her father's lectures in medicine and moral philosophy at the University of Bologna, but to have been awarded a salary of her own, of 100 lire.[46] There was also apparently a Latin poet, Abella, connected with the school of Salerno in the fourteenth century: she was the author of two

---

[43] John F. Benton, 'Trotula, Women's Problems, and the Professionalization of Medicine in the Middle Ages', *Bulletin of the History of Medicine*, 1 (1985), 30–53 (pp. 41–6). Benson demonstrates that Trota's work fell into obscurity, though three other spurious works circulated under the name of Trotula. On Salerno, see P. O. Kristeller, 'The School of Salerno', in his *Studies in Renaissance Thought and Letters* (Rome: Edizioni di storia e letteratura, 1956), 495–551. Women seriously practising as doctors is a long story: Ausonius' medical aunt Hilara, in the 4th century, was mentioned in Ch. 3; and in the Middle Ages, apart from the Salernitan school, there is a variety of evidence for women as doctors: for example, Katherine 'la surgiene' in London *c.*1286 (Henrietta Leyser, *Medieval Women* (London: Weidenfeld and Nicolson, 1995), 138). A number of later English women such as Judith Squire, Charlotte Charke, and Jane Barker (see Index) learned Latin in order to practise medicine, and the same may be true elsewhere in Europe.

[44] Salvatore de Renzi (ed.), *Storia documentata della Scuola Medica di Salerno* (Naples: Tipografia del Filatre Sebezio, 1852–9; 1857–9), i. 569. She became a lecturer at Naples and is mentioned in documents there in 1422 and 1423. Calenda was the daughter of the dean of the faculty of medicine: the documents testifying to her career as perhaps the first female university-trained professional in Western history were destroyed during the Second World War but survive in modern copies. Margaret L. King, 'Isotta Nogarola, umanista e devota', in Ottavia Niccoli (ed.), *Rinascimento al femminile* (Bari: Laterza, 1991), 45. See also P. O. Kristeller, 'Learned Women of Early Modern Italy: Humanists and University Scholars', in Labalme (ed.), *Beyond their Sex*, 91–116 (p. 115 n. 2).

[45] de Renzi (ed.), *Storia documentata*, i. 569.

[46] Bandini Buti, i. 99

verse treatises mentioned in Salerno records, *De Atrabile* ('on black bile', considered to be the cause of melancholia), *De Natura Seminis Homini* ('on the nature of human seed', which was perhaps a contribution to the long-running debate on the process of human conception before the discovery of the female ovum). These texts (or unattributed poems on these subjects) do not survive in the Salernitan corpus as we now have it.[47] However, one thought-provoking item which does survive among Salernitan records is an anonymous late medieval Latin poem on female disorders, ostensibly written for the information of women wanting to avoid embarrassing interviews with male doctors. This is conceivably of female authorship.[48] It is comparable with the longest of the three works attributed to Trotula, *Trotula Major*, in which the writer explains (in Latin) that she or he is writing because 'women dare not reveal their distress to a male physician'. As Monica Green observes, it is hardly logical to conclude that this Latin treatise was written for the use of male doctors alone, since it claims to address the needs of women who are embarrassed to talk to men about their intimate problems. It seems therefore possible that it was either intended for use by women doctors, or by Latinate women anxious about their own physical state.[49]

There are also persistent stories that lawyers began to include women among their number in the very early Renaissance. In the thirteenth century, Accursia, daughter of Andreas Accursius, is said not only to have taught law, but to have written a tract, 'whether a wife should be taken by a educated man, and if so, what sort?', which according to Juncker was published in Leiden by Elzevir in 1629 with other *opuscula*.[50] Bologna, the oldest and most prestigious of Italian law schools, is, perhaps unsurprisingly, the one which has the most persistent record of female professional involvement with the law. The most elaborately attested of the Bolognese women lawyers is Bitisia Gozzadini (1209–61). A number of books state that the oldest calendar of Bologna University records her doctorate, awarded on 3 June 1236, and that three years later, Bishop Enrico della Fratta assigned her a chair in the public study hall, thus making her a professor, a level of professional recognition for a woman which was not to be equalled for more than 600 years.[51] Unfortunately, the documents thus confidently referred to were almost certainly

[47] de Renzi (ed.), *Storia documentata*, i. 569.

[48] Ibid., iv. 1–176.

[49] Monica Green, 'Women's Medical Practice and Health Care in Medieval Europe', in Bennett et al. (eds.), *Sisters and Workers in the Middle Ages*, 39–78 (p. 66).

[50] M. Christianus Juncker, *Schediasma Historicum* (Leipzig: Joh. Friedrich Gleditsch, 1692), 16. Unfortunately I have not managed to locate this work: it is not the anonymous 'Dissertatio de Literati Matrimonio' in Petrus Scriverius (ed.), *Dominico Baudii Amores* (Amsterdam: Ludovicus Elzevir, 1638), 349–84. Bandini Buti, i. 16, notes that the earliest reference to Accursia is 14th century, and states that Alberico da Rosciate records that her *acta* are preserved at Bologna.

[51] Piero Addeo, *Eva Togata* (Naples: Editrice Rispoli anonima, 1939), 25–30 (p. 26), states that she wrote works on law, *De Negotiis Gestis*, and *De Justitia et Jure*, and also recited the funeral oration for Bishop della Fratta and, in 1244, gave a famous oration to Pope Innocent IV. Addeo's source is the wholly unreliable Macchiavelli's *Bitisia Gozzadina*, a book which was written in support of his dedicatee Maria Vittoria Delfini Dossi's unsuccessful effort to gain a doctorate (Bruno Neveau, 'Doctrix et Magistra', in Colette Nativel (ed.), *Femmes savantes, savoir des femmes* (Geneva: Droz, 1999), 27–37 (p. 30)).

invented by the Bolognese antiquarian Carlo Antonio Machiavelli in the eighteenth century, and the basis for his assertions seems not to be recoverable.[52]

Apart from Bitisia Gozzadini, women as teachers and legal specialists are also persistently associated with the d'Andrea/Calderini dynasty. Giovanni d'Andrea was apparently the son of a Florentine priest called Boniconti and his concubine Novella. He was adopted by the Bolognese nobleman Giovanni Calderini, a great patron of learned men, and became a famous exponent of canon law. He was elected professor at Bologna, though he later taught at Pisa and Padua before returning to Bologna where he died of the plague. His wife Milanzia, daughter of the famous jurisconsult Buonincontro dall'Ospedale, was also very learned, and was thought as early as the sixteenth century to have taught at Bologna.[53] Both his daughters, Bettina and Novella, born in the early fourteenth century, left a reputation as legal specialists, and perhaps as lecturers. Novella d'Andrea is said to have substituted for her father as lecturer, and is mentioned in this capacity in Christine de Pizan's *Book of the City of Ladies* I. 36: Christine attaches to her the story that she lectured from behind a veil, a story which is told of a number of medieval women *cathedraticae*, both in Europe and in the Islamic world. However, it may be relevant that Christine's father Tommaso da Pizzano was Bolognese, and was in Bologna at the time when Giovanni d'Andrea was active there. Another witness to Novella, Jean le Fèvre, tells a different story about her: that she demonstrated woman's intellectual equality with man in a public, all-day lecture with more than seventy propositions.[54] He was writing in the late fourteenth century, so again, this testimony to Novella's having some kind of public profile is near enough in time to her to have some degree of credibility. Photographs of the remains of her tomb are printed by Addeo, who claims they survive in the Museo civico of Bologna (where they are not now displayed): interestingly, one of the two long sides shows a group of scholars listening to a lecture.[55]

---

[52] Bologna, Biblioteca communale dell'Archiginnasio, Gozzadini I, which is almost certainly Macchiavelli's 'calendar' since it is arranged like a martyrology by saints' days, fails to mention her in the entries on 3 June, anywhere else in June, or, apparently, anywhere else at all. There is no actual calendar for the law school from so early in its history. Bitisia probably existed and was buried in the church of St Vittore, Bologna, but the evidence for this strangely circumstantial career seems to evaporate on close examination. I should like to thank the Rare Books Librarian in Bologna for the entire afternoon which she spent with me patiently searching for any kind of support for Macchiavelli's assertions. In addition to *Bitisia Gozzadina*, Macchiavelli (and his brother Alessandro) published a variety of learned works in Latin under the name of their sister Maria Elisabeth Macchiavelli (according to Giancalro Roversi (ed.), *Donne celebre della Emilia-Romagna e del Montefeltro* (Bologna: Edizione Grafis, 1993), 128–9), and they seem to have been completely unscrupulous about inventing 'evidence'.

[53] 'Refert etiam Joannes Andreae literatissimam habuisse uxorem, quae sibi et Cyno legum doctori compatri multoties de difficillibus Juris respondebat' (Bartolomeo Cassaneo (Burgundius), *Catalogus Gloriae Mundi* (Venice: Haeredes Vincentii Valgrissi, 1576), 46): see also Addeo, *Eva Togata*, 33–5.

[54] Blamires, *The Case for Women*, 37. The notion that Andrea dedicated a commentary to his daughter when he called it *Novella in Decretales* (mentioned by Blamires) is problematic, since the use of the term 'novella' for a book of law goes back to the 6th-century Emperor Justinian.

[55] Addeo, *Eva Togata*, 47–9. This may be associable with the series of funeral monuments to teachers offering a visual depiction of teaching which were made in 13th- and 14th-century Bologna: see R. Grandi, *I monumenti dei dottori e la scultura a Bologna, 1267–1368* (Bologna: Istituto per la storia di Bologna, 1982).

Outside the law faculty, other women's names are also associated with Bologna in the fifteenth century: Bettina Sangiorgi and Teodora Crisolora (wife of Francesco Filelfo) as teachers of Greek, and Giovanna Bianchetti as a teacher of Latin, while Niccolosa Sanuti (whose own writings show that she had obviously achieved a thorough Latin education by some means or other) attended lectures.[56] Allen cites 'University records' for these facts, but given the known activities of the feminist forger Carlo Antonio Machiavelli, in the absence of actual confirmation from Bolognese archives (which I have not been in a position to make), all this information must be treated as highly dubious for the time being. However, while all these women are insufficiently well evidenced for the stories told about them to be treated as historical, their stories went unchallenged in the fifteenth and sixteenth centuries when the defenders of learned women were arguing on their behalf. They were therefore very useful, since they gave two or three hundred years' worth of precedent to level against doubters who treated women's education as a dangerous innovation.

The fifteenth century: women and the humanists

The question of what use Latin was to women deserves further consideration. There were reasons why some specific women were educated as humanists: one is that in some but not all aristocratic families during the course of the fifteenth century, it came to be perceived as redounding to the glory of the family. The aristocratic families who educated their daughters did so not with the intention that they should become professional humanists, but that they should write letters, compose verses, or deliver public speeches expressing the family's stance on political developments. They were, in fact, a useful adjunct to more official forms of diplomatic activity.[57]

A serious reason for noblewomen to demonstrate humanistic competence in Latin is that they thereby demonstrated fitness for rule. The case of the fifteenth-century noblewoman Isabella d'Este is instructive in this context: as the daughter of Ercole I, Duke of Ferrara, she received a classic humanist education, and studied Latin with Battista Guarino, Sebastiano de Lugo, and Jacopo Gallino, but she had no natural gift in this direction. As she grew older, she became increasingly anxious to acquire a skill she perceived as intellectually and socially prestigious, and over a period of years, with a series of tutors, she determinedly struggled to master the humanist curriculum. Her efforts reveal 'her determination to conform to the traditional humanist image of an educated ruler', and her failure casts an interesting light on the need for a Renaissance daughter of the nobility to

---

[56] Prudence Allen, *The Concept of Woman II* (Grand Rapids, Mich.: William B. Eerdman, 2002), 935.

[57] Lisa Jardine, *Worldly Goods* (London: Macmillan, 1996), 252–3. For a daughter such as Costanza Varano to fulfil this role was further to authenticate the humanist credentials of the household.

be a humanist. She evidently felt that a person of her cultural pretensions and family background could not use gender as an excuse. Though it cost her a good deal of frustration and was ultimately futile, she kept pushing herself in this direction—evidently feeling that, despite the fact that she was an enlightened patron of art, a discriminating book-buyer,[58] and a more than capable executant musician, her difficulty with Latin was a serious gap in her credibility.[59] In various times and places, some Renaissance Italian courts were ruled by women for months or years at a time, either as subalterns during husbands' prolonged absences, or as regents for minor sons. Since they were exercising masculine functions, they were required to use the masculine discourse acquired by humanist education. For all her difficulties with Latin, Isabella d'Este ruled Mantua as regent for both her husband and her son, and is praised for her political ability by Marius Equicola.[60] The literary production of noble oratrices or poets in Latin was valued for reasons extrinsic to its merits or demerits as literature, since eloquence was an art essential to public life.[61]

Another reason for teaching aristocratic women Latin was that they, in turn, could teach their children, as the famous Battista da Montefeltro taught her equally famous granddaughter Costanza Varano (and probably her daughter, who was also Latin-literate):[62] a variety of contemporary Italian commentators stress that overseeing the education of children is an important part of a mother's duties.[63] It may also have been the case (though this is more clearly true by the sixteenth century) that intellectual companionship was in some advanced circles coming to be seen as a desirable aspect of the marital relationship.[64] The family was more important than the individual in Renaissance Italy: the lives and work of the

---

[58] Bell, 'Medieval Women Book Owners', 144: she commissioned the printing of many books, and was a determined collector of rarities.

[59] Iain Fenlon, 'Gender and Generation: Patterns of Music Patronage among the Este, 1471–1539', in Marianne Pade, Lene Waage Petersen, and Daniele Quarta (eds.), *La corte di Ferrara e il suo mecanatismo 1441–1598*, Renaessance Studier 4 (Copenhagen: Museum Tusculanum Forlag; Modena: Edizioni Panini 1990), 213–34.

[60] *Marii Equicoli Olivetani de Mulieribus, ad D. Margaritam Cantelmam* (Ferrara: Lorenzo Rossi, 1501), sig. Bii^v.

[61] McManaman, *Funeral Oratory*, 113–14, comments that funeral orations for women such as Eleonora of Aragon and Battista Malatesta stressed their possession of practical wisdom and learning alongside traditional feminine virtues such as modesty and chastity. They are praised for acting as effective regents.

[62] Polissena Grimaldi demonstrates this by writing to her in Latin: London, British Library, Add. 19061, 'Epistola d[ominae] Polixene Grimaldae ad illustrissimam dominam Elizabethan Varaneam Camerini Dominam' (fos. 20^r–22^r)

[63] For example, Domitilla Trivulzi (1481–c.1530), the daughter of a Milanese aristocrat, who is said to have composed Greek and Latin poetry. She married Francesco Torelli, Conte di Montechiarugulo, and had a son, Paolo, whose education she supervised: this is mentioned in Foresti's *De Claris Mulieribus* and Ariosto's *Orlando furioso* 46, st. 4. The controversialist Peter Martyr (Pietro Martire Vermigli) was taught Latin by his mother, Maria Fumantina, and they translated the comedies of Terence together. Vespasiano da Bisticci, *Vite di uomini illustri*, 296–7, praises the Duchess of Mantua, Paola Gonzaga, for her care in getting the best possible humanist education for her children, both boys and girls.

[64] Allen, *The Concept of Woman II*, 756, points out that Leon Battista Alberti (1404–72) tentatively suggests this in his *Della famiglia*, but in a chain of 'if' clauses suggesting that this was an ideal seldom realized.

women whom we see in this study were subordinated to family needs and concerns, but so (though generally less restrictively) were those of their brothers.

On a lower social level, some daughters of educationalists may have contributed to their families' reputations, as walking illustrations of their fathers' pedagogic talents: the humanist Battista Guarino educated his daughter, though it is not clear to what intended end, since she died young.[65] The sixteenth-century Olimpia Morata (who will be discussed in Chapter 11) is a clearer example, though she also had a position of her own as tutor to the daughters of the Duke and Duchess of Ferrara.[66]

One of the numerous Renaissance outlines for the education of girls was made by Leonardo Bruni for Battista da Montefeltro early in the fifteenth century: as King comments, it recommends that:[67]

> she should read ... the whole spectrum of the *studia humanitatis* that men of this generation had formed for themselves, with the striking exception of rhetoric: 'for why should the subtleties of ... rhetorical conundrums consume the powers of a woman, who never sees the forum? The art of delivery ... [is] so far from being the concern of a woman that if she should gesture energetically with her arms as she spoke and shout with violent emphasis, she would probably be thought mad and put under restraint.'

This is often taken to mean that Italian humanists decreed that women should not speak in public; but the *asperitas fori*, the rough-and-tumble of the forum, though an essential aspect of the world of the professional humanist, was not the only sort of public rhetoric to be important in Renaissance life.

There is no evidence that Renaissance Italian women ever hurled aggressive accusations at men in courtrooms in the manner Bruni describes.[68] But on the other hand, the public delivery of orations and poems was also of great cultural significance, and women were quite frequently called upon to perform in this way. They were also praised for so doing: for example, Giannantonio Campano in his eulogy on Battista Sforza supported his praise of Sforza as a speaker by emphasizing that Pius II had not only admired her personally, but expressed a general

---

[65] Cambridge, University Library, Add. 6188.

[66] Olimpia Morata, *Opere*, ed. Lanfranco Coretti, 2 vols., *Deputazione provinciale ferrarese di storia patria*, Atti e memorie NS XI.1–2 (1954). Her works were edited immediately after her death by her old friend Coelio Secundo Curio, and published at Basel in 1552. She achieved international fame, particularly in Protestant Europe. There are at least four 19th-century biographies of her.

[67] Margaret L. King, *Women of the Renaissance* (Chicago: Chicago University Press, 1991), 194. See now Craig Kallendorf (ed. and trans.), *Humanist Educational Treatises* (Cambridge, Mass.: Harvard University Press, 2002), 92–125.

[68] See Addeo, *Eva Togata*, for some early evidence of women in the legal profession in Italy, though not all of his alleged sources are reliable, especially when he is drawing on Macchiavelli. Though a number of late medieval women's names are mentioned, particularly in Bologna, as professors of law, they are not named as practising lawyers. One 16th-century woman from Bergamo, the poetess Isotta Grumella, née Brembati (d. 1586), is said to have pleaded several lawsuits by herself. Jean Buyze, *The Tenth Muse* (Berkeley: Shameless Hussy Press, 1980), 18: there are certainly a couple of legal documents to which she is a party in Bergamo, Biblioteca civica Angelo Mai, AB 92, 'Isotta Brembati cede a Giovanni Battista de Vacis parte dell'acqua della coda di serio passate per Sforziaca e Dalmine', and ibid., Gabinetto 2 sopra 11 (7), 'atto di donazione di beni in Dalmine'.

endorsement of women acting in this fashion.[69] In the fifteenth century, court occasions were marked by formal orations which were not in any sense adversarial, and were therefore far more accessible to women participants.[70] Undeterred by Bruni's strictures against shouting and gesticulating, which were of course irrelevant to the nature of the performance, Battista da Montefeltro herself spoke in public, delivering a Latin oration before the Emperor Sigismund,[71] and educated her granddaughter Costanza Varano to do likewise—Varano did so on a number of occasions, discussed below.[72] Bruni also saw the possession of high abilities in verse, prose, elocution (and penmanship) as positively feminine, linking them with the other resources of the noblewoman:[73]

I would have our writer possess a rhetorical *garniture de toilette*, a fine wardrobe, an abundant stock of domestic furniture, if I may call it that, which she can produce and disply as the need arises for every type of writing.

This abstract description is confirmed in its relevance by the nature of the oeuvre which has been preserved as the work of Battista and her granddaughter. Bruni stressed that an educated woman needed to be able to read aloud extremely well, with a proper understanding of Latin vowel quantity (thus, as it seems, opening up some kind of undefined space in which a woman's voice might be expected to be heard), and declared that she should be able to compose and write in both verse and prose.[74]

Other fifteenth-century women certainly performed in public as orators: Ippolita Sforza, daughter of Francesco Sforza, Duke of Milan, made public speeches on at least three occasions, to Tristano Visconti and Beatrice d'Este in 1455, to Pope Pius II in 1459, and to her mother Bianca Maria Sforza before 1465.[75] Other fifteenth-century oratrices include Battista Montefeltro's great-granddaughter Battista Sforza, Cassandra Fedele,[76] Isotta Nogarola, Domitilla Trivulzi, a forgotten daughter of the Pazzi of Florence, Paola Malatesta of Rimini, Batista Berti of

---

[69] *Oratio Funebris pro Baptista Sphortia Urbini Comitissa ac Principe Illustrissima* (Cagli: Roberto di Fano and Bernadino di Bergamo, 1476).

[70] Clough, 'The Cult of Antiquity', 39.

[71] Kristeller, 'Learned Women', 93–4. See now also Marinella Bonvini Mazzanti, *Battista Sforza Montefeltro: una 'principessa' nel rinascimento italiano* (Urbino: Quattroventi, 1993).

[72] Cecil H. Clough, 'Daughters and Wives of the Montefeltro', *Renaissance Studies*, 10.1 (Mar. 1996), 31–55.

[73] Kallendorf (ed.), *Humanist Educational Treatises*, 102–3: 'sitque illi ad omne genus scribendi mundus quidam et ornatus ac (ut ita dixerim) abundantissima domi supellex, quam promat, cum opus it, et in lucem educat.'

[74] Ibid. 98–101.

[75] Her speech before Tristano Visconti and Beatrice d'Este is in Ferrara, Biblioteca Comunale Ariostea, I 240, fos. 100ᵛ–102ʳ, the speech to Pope Pius II (and his reply) survives as Munich, Clm 14610, fo. 192–4. The text of her speech for Bianca Maria Sforza was published by G. G. Meersseman, 'La raccolta dell'umanita fiammingo Giovanni de Veris, "De Arte Epistolandi" ', *Italia mediovali e umanistica*, 15 (1972), 250–1, and translated in King and Rabil, *Her Immaculate Hand*, 44–6.

[76] Carl C. Schlam, 'Cassandra Fidelis as a Latin Orator', *Acta Conventus Neo-Latini Sanctandreani*, Proceedings of the Fifth International Congress of Neo-Latin Studies, ed. I. D Macfarlane (Binghamton, NY: Medieval and Renaissance Texts and Studies, 1986), 185–91.

Siena, and even a woman of less exalted rank, Polissena Messalto.[77] By contrast to these performances, which were far more often praised than criticized, Laura Cereta's burlesque 'Dialogue on the Death of an Ass' mimics the form of the formal consolatory oration, and thus approaches the masculine world of the 'forum': it is not surprising to find that it generated some censure.[78] In any case, the existence of these oratrices and the public space which they occupied did not prompt any kind of rethinking of the position of women more generally. It is noteworthy that Italian humanists who worked on Plato distorted passages on the potential equality of (some) women with men either by mistranslating, or by rendering them obscurely.[79]

Isotta Nogarola

The patrician Venetian family of the Nogarolas is a good starting point for this study, since it produced women scholars over several generations, including Isotta, whose life is often considered to typify the problems faced by a fifteenth-century Italian woman scholar. But before discussing Isotta herself, it may be desirable to go back at least a generation and widen the focus a little.[80] The Nogarolas, a patrician family of Verona, were notably learned, with a strong tradition of educating daughters even before Isotta. A fourteenth-century female Nogarola, Antonia, left a shadowy literary reputation,[81] but the first to leave actual writing is Angela/Agnola (born perhaps *c.* 1360, d. 1420/30).[82] Angela Nogarola has a variety of connections with an important early Renaissance woman scholar,

[77] For Sforza, see Marinella Bonvini Mazzanti, *Battista Sforza Montefeltro* (Urbino: Quattroventi, 1993), 96–101, Fedele, see King and Rabil (trans.), *Her Immaculate Hand*, 48–50, Nogarola, see 'Ven. in Christo P.D. Victori de Rosatis Oratio Imperfecta', Modena, Biblioteca Estense, α.Q.7.36 (olim XII.F.18), Pazzi, see Francisco Agostino della Chiesa, *Theatro delle donne letterate* (Mondovi: Giovanni Gisland, & Giovanni Tomaso Rossi, 1620), 270, for Trivulzi, see Lodovico Domenichi, *La nobiltà delle donne* (Venice: Gabriel Giolito, 1549), 240, who claims that she delivered Ciceronian orations on a number of occasions, and also spoke in Greek. Malatesta is noticed in Louis Jacob, 'Bibliothèque des femmes illustres par leurs écrits', Paris, Bibliothèque Nationale du France, Ancien fonds français 22865, fo. 158ʳ⁻ᵛ (and also by Maria Ludovica Lenzi, *Donne e madonne* (Turin: Loescher, 1982), 206). Berti is noticed in Ginerra Canonici Fachini, *Prospetto biografico delle donne italiane rinomate in letteratura* (Venice: Tipografia di Alvisopoli, 1824), 74. Four copies of Messalto's oration on Thomas Mocenigus are listed in *Iter Italicum*: Kraków, Biblioteka Jagellonska, 126, fo. 35ʳ⁻ᵛ and 173, fo. 200ʳ⁻ᵛ, Kraków, Biblioteka Muzeum Narodowego w Krakowie, Oddzial Zbiory Czartoryskich (the former Czartoryski museum, now part of the National Museum) 1242, fos. 348–9, and Wrocław, Biblioteka Zakladu Narodowego in Ossolinskich, 601/1.

[78] *Collected Letters*, trans. Robin, 180–202.

[79] Allen, *The Concept of Woman II*, 728.

[80] For a general background see S. Chojnacki, 'Patrician Women in Early Renaissance Venice', *Studies in the Renaissance*, 21 (1974), 176–203.

[81] The daughter of Zanfredo Nogarola and Paola Boncarri, she was born in 1308, learned Greek and Latin, and married in 1328. She allegedly wrote in prose and verse, and acquired fame as a writer, though nothing seems to survive. Bandini Buti, ii. 82.

[82] Her poem to Gian Galeazzo Visconti is datable to 1387: it is therefore reasonable to suggest that she was born in the 1360s.

Maddalena Scrovegni of Padua (1356–1429), who has also been much discussed because she was the subject of a poem called *The Temple of Chastity*, written by Antonio Loschi (Lusco) in 1389. This has sometimes been treated as paradigmatic of contemporary attitudes towards women scholars, so we should perhaps pause over it before returning to the Nogarolas.[83]

Maddalena's study, the site of her intellectual activity, is identified by the author with the Temple that houses the personification of Chastity. That same Temple is later identified with Memory, a major function of mind, and the images engraved on its walls are identified with thoughts stored in memory ... by these strange links, Maddalena's learning is bound to the chastity by which she wins the regard of the poet ... he erects for Scrovegni a temple in her honour, and binds her captive within it.

It has been argued from this poem, which portrays Scrovegni's study as a temple to Chastity in frozen Scythia, the land of the Amazons, and from the life story of Isotta Nogarola, discussed below, that the basic paradigm for the humanist woman was the virgin-scholar.

The situation may in fact be rather more complex. Scrovegni at the time this poem was written was a widow. Her family, the Scrovegni, were exiled in the early days of the Carrara regime in her native city of Padua, but later, they were the richest and most powerful native family to support the Carrara regime under Francesco il Vecchio. Her father Ugolino da Scrovegni worked hard at recovering land and tithes, and performed a variety of state services for the Carrara. He made an advantageous marriage for Maddalena, his only daughter, uniting her with the noble knight Francesco Manfredi, son of a former podestà of Padua, in 1376 when she was 20. She was widowed early and returned to Padua by 1381.[84] There is no evidence for the attitude she took either to this marriage or to its end after a mere five years, but no one would assume on the basis of these facts that she was a virgin. Her own correspondence implies a considerable involvement in contemporary politics: Loschi's boreal, white-marble 'Temple' was no ivory tower.[85] Her 1388 letter to Jacopo dal Verme translated by King and Rabil excused a family volte-face; their abandonment of the Carrara and their new support for the Visconti.[86] It is a type of diplomatic letter which could usefully be entrusted to a woman, since the posture of 'naïveté', or 'simplicity' available to women could be used to create a personal contact which might, with luck, offset the hard, sharp realities of political

---

[83] King and Rabil (trans.), *Her Immaculate Hand*, 13. See also King, 'Goddess and Captive'. MSS are Bologna, Biblioteca universitaria, 3977 (Antonio Loschi's letter-book), fos. 3ᵛ–6ʳ, and Leiden, Universiteitsbibliotheek, Vulc. 20, fos. 6–8ᵛ (s. xvi).

[84] Benjamin G. Kohl, *Padua under the Carrara 1318–1405* (Baltimore: Johns Hopkins University Press, 1998), 175–7.

[85] King's focus on Loschi's response to Scrovegni has sidelined Scrovegni's own activity. In addition to the letter to Jacopo dal Verme, the enemy of the Carrara, which is printed in King and Rabil (trans.), *Her Immaculate Hand*, 34–5, I know of two more letters written by Maddalena Scrovegni herself, now in Milan, Biblioteca Ambrosiana, C. 141 inf. One is to the Queen of Sicily, fo: 151ʳ⁻ᵛ, the other to Galeazzo Visconti, Duke of Milan. fos. 167ᵛ–168.

[86] A. Medin, 'Maddalena degli Scrovegni e le discordie tra i Carraresi e gli Scrovegni, *Atti e memorie dell'Accademia di Padova*, NS 12 (1895–6), 243–72.

bargaining between men. A woman's letter could also, if necessary, be subsequently disowned as 'foolish'; a useful convention, since it allowed negotiations to be opened with a minimum of mutual commitment. Similarly, Scrovegni's acquaintance, Isotta Nogarola's aunt Angela, welcomed conquerors to her city with Latin verses which implictly tested the parameters for new political relationships.

Loschi's poem on Scrovegni was commissioned by the Visconti as a friendly response to the letter she wrote to Jacopo dal Verme, and was evidently a diplomatic gesture directed not simply to Maddalena, but through her to the Scrovegni. To present Maddalena as an embodiment of the tougher female virtues is also indirectly to commend the Scrovegni, since such a woman was necessarily the product of a virtuous and well-conducted family. *The Temple of Chastity* links fierceness, intellect, strength, and chastity: it thus explores a set of tropes about aggressive female virtue which have as one of their starting points Prudentius' fourth-century *Psychomachia*, or 'Battle of the Virtues and Vices' (who are all presented as female personifications, slugging it out in ways which express their intrinsic nature) and, as another, Orosius' account of the Amazons. Thus it is written out of a particular political situation to which the presentation of Scrovegni as chaste virago is particularly relevant, since a change of political position, such as the Scrovegni family had just made, could be, and sometimes was, symbolically represented as whoredom.[87] It endorses Scrovegni's own decision not to remarry. There seems every reason to think, therefore, that it is intended as a poem about Scrovegni, chaste widow, *femme forte*, and *femme politique*, rather than as a statement about women in general.

Humanist education stressed the ability to argue any position;[88] and perhaps we should be chary of assuming that a work which associates the learned woman with frozen chastity represents the permanent conviction of that author himself, let alone of humanist men in general. For Angela Nogarola, who was also an acquaintance of Antonio Loschi, perhaps his pupil,[89] married Antonio, Conde d'Arco, in 1396, and continued to write Latin poetry for public occasions after her marriage as well as before. The same Loschi who is so apparently committed to chastity for humanist women when he writes on Scrovegni refrains from making an issue of this in his long Latin poem to Angela Nogarola, then unmarried; in fact, his poem places her not in a frozen wasteland but in a *locus amoenus* of streams, woods, and fertile fields.[90] The other humanist men who write to her, whether before or after her marriage, do not concern themselves with this issue.[91] We might also note that Angela Nogarola sent a letter to Scrovegni—who was evidently part of the same cultural milieu—so the latter was not as isolated as Loschi makes her appear.[92]

---

[87] This has biblical precedent: see for example Ezekiel 23: 4.

[88] Rosalie L. Colie, *Paradoxia Epidemica* (Princeton: Princeton University Press, 1966), 102.

[89] Parker, 'Latin and Greek Poetry', 250–1.

[90] Antonio Lusus ad Angelam Nogarolam, Bologna, Biblioteca Universitaria, 3977 (A), fos. 16ʳ–17ʳ.

[91] We can see from two poems to her, by Antonio de Romagno (Vatican City, Biblioteca Apostolica, Lat. 5223. fo. 25ʳ⁻ᵛ), and Giovanni Nicola Salernus (Perugia, Biblioteca Comunale Augusta, D 53, fo. 65ᵛ), as well as a letter to her from Matheus de Aurelianis, Florence, Biblioteca Riccardiana, 784 (M IV 32), that Angela was on friendly terms with a number of male humanists besides Loschi.

[92] Florence, Biblioteca Riccardiana, 784.

Angela Nogarola's poem to the lord of Rimini, Pandulfo Malatesta, asking for the return of a book, is particularly interesting: alternate lines are taken from other poets (Virgil, Ovid, Horace, Lucan, Petrarch), thus demonstrating the depth and width of her reading, and paired with rhyming lines of her own. The admiration in which Proba's *Cento* was held in the Renaissance made it one of the literary forms most easily associable with women: while, as Holt Parker says, 'this is not a polished product', as a way of inoffensively jogging the memory of a *condottiere*, it is highly ingenious: his reply suggests that he was delighted by her wit. Several other of her poems clearly belong in the public rather than the private sphere: in an address to Gian Galeazzo Visconti when he seized Verona in 1387, and another, written seventeen years later, hailing another new master, Jacopo de Carrara: 'we see Angela Nogarola, in her role as countess of Arco, as a visible presence in the highest level of political games-playing.'[93] It is worth noting, also, that Angela Nogarola's writing was not confined to brief verses in connection with contemporary politics: she was also the author of an ambitious Latin work of considerable length, her *Liber de Virtutibus*. Another poem responds to Niccolò de Facino's accusation that she was not the author of the poem she sent him, which opens:

> Non aliena meis imponere vellere membris
> me iuvat et levibus circumdare brachia pennis
> alterius: picti nota est mihi fabula corvi.
> nec mihi virtutum laudes conscendere cura est,
> nec veterum lauros nobis ascribere vatum.

> It does not help me to put alien garments on my limbs
> and to surround my arms with the light feathers of another:
> the story of the painted crow is known to me.
> Nor is it my concern to rise to the praises of the virtuous,
> nor that the laurels of the ancient poets should be ascribed to me...

Women poets, particularly those who wrote in Latin, were often accused of plagiarism, an accusation which was particularly galling when it came from another woman scholar (as Laura Cereta found when she was put down by Cassandra Fedele),[94] but was always annoying: Elizabeth Weston met the same response when she sent a poem to James I, and expressed equal irritation.[95]

Following in what is evidently an established family tradition, several of the many children of Leonardo Nogarola (brother of Angela) and Bianca Borromeo were demonstrably highly educated.[96] Isotta and her sisters Ginevra and Laura learned Greek and Latin at an early age, first under Matteo Bosso, then under

[93] Parker, 'Latin and Greek Poetry', 257. See also Kohl, *Padua under the Carrara*, 329–34.

[94] Laura Cereta was furious to get a reply to a letter sent to Cassandra Fedele which suggested that her father had written it for her. *Laura Cereta*, trans. Robin, 141–4, 145–8.

[95] Elizabeth Jane Weston, *Collected Writings*, ed. Donald Cheney and Brenda Hosington (Toronto: Toronto University Press, 2000) 176–9.

[96] Note also that Angela Nogarola is said to have fostered the intellectual aspirations of a niece by marriage, Alda Torelli Lonata, daughter of Luigi Torelli. L.-P., *repertoire universel, historique, biographique des femmes célèbres*, 4 vols. in 2 (Paris: Achille Désauges, 1826), iv. 338.

Martino Rizzoni, a distinguished humanist and pupil of Guarino of Verona. Isotta notes that it was her mother (the sister of the humanist Cardinal Borromeo), rather than her father, who had provided her with her humanist education.[97] Their brother Ludovico was also a scholar.[98] Verona in the fifteenth century was a highly cultivated place. It harboured famous women poets, Medea degli Aleardi and Polissena Grimaldi, the latter also a poet in Latin,[99] and it was the place of origin of the famous humanist Guarino Guarini, often referred to as Guarino Veronese,[100] and, once upon a time, of the poet Catullus, as the Veronese were even more proud to remember.[101] It is therefore significant that Costanza Varano, praising Isotta Nogarola; declares:[102]

> O Verona, tuis urbs foecundissima poetis,
> Plus trahet haec laudis iam vate puella Catullo!

> O Verona, city most fertile in your poets,
> This girl already attracts more praise than the bard Catullus!

Isotta herself moved to Venice in 1438 to escape the plague, and did not return to Verona until 1441, although she continued to correspond with a number of Veronese, including Guarino, to whom she first wrote in 1436. She began the correspondence writing as pupil to master: 'O Guarino, I previously feared to write to you, a great man.' The letter, however, reveals that several of her letters written to others had already been seen by him, so he certainly knew who she was. Just to be on the safe side, moreover, her letter mentions a selection of the virtuous literary ladies of antiquity, Cornificia, Nicaulis, Faunia, Cornelia, and Portia. Unfortunately, she did not receive an immediate reply, and wrote again, very sharply, to say that his failure to respond had put her in a ridiculous position and the entire city was laughing at her—in effect, demanding a reply, which she promptly received. He wrote, he implies, on the same

[97] Margaret L. King, *The Death of the Child Valerio Marcello* (Chicago: University of Chicago Press, 1994), 36–7.

[98] He was the author of a variety of works including a Latin translation of John of Damascus' *De His qui in Fide Dormiunt*, published in Verona: Stephanus et Fratres Sabios, 1532, and a study of Italian students of Greek, *De Viris Illustribus Genere Italis qui Graece Scripserunt*.

[99] Orazio d'Uva, *Un'erudita del secolo xv* (Trani: V. Vecchi, 1904), 4. Medea Aleardi was a friend of a Giovanni Nogarola: Guglielmo Pacchini (ed.), *Un codice inedito de la Biblioteca Estense: un poeta ed una poetessa petrarchisti nel secolo xv* (Modena, Cooperativa tipografia, 1907) (he does not seem to be a sibling of Isotta's, if Abel's Nogarola genealogy may be relied upon). Polissena Grimaldi wrote a number of Latin works, including poems and a letter 'on why so few learned women are found in our times'. See below, n. 141.

[100] See Scipione Maffei, *Verona Illustrata* (Milan: Società tipografica de' classici italiani, 1825), for an overview of Veronese culture. A number of learned women from Verona are referred to by later writers as 'x' Veronese rather than by surname: for example, Lucrezia Marinella writes of Ginevra Nogarola as 'Ginevra Veronese', *The Nobility and Excellence of Women*, ed. and trans. Anne Dunhill (Chicago: Chicago University Press, 1999), 91, and Laura Brenzona as 'Laura Veronese', ibid. 86, as do Petrus Lotichius, *Gynaicologia* (Rinteln: Petrus Lucius, 1630), 127, and Joannes Broscius, *Apologia pro Sexu Fæmineo*, (Frankfurt: Petrus Brubachius, 1544), 61.

[101] Julia Haig Gaisser, *Catullus and his Renaissance Readers* (Oxford: Clarendon Press, 1993). Catullus' poems were rediscovered in the 13th century. A statue of the poet was put up in the Loggia del Consiglio in Verona in 1492, and he was a focus of intense local patriotism (p. 57).

[102] In *Isotae Nogarolae... Opera*, ed. Abel, ii. 7–8.

day that her letter reached him ('I got your letter full of complaints and accusations this evening...'), telling her not to worry so much about public opinion, which suggests a certain insensitivity to the additional problem which her gender posed for her.[103] But there is more than just gender politics governing the discourse of these letters. A similar letter of self-introduction to Francesco Barbaro had caused Isotta no difficulties,[104] and shortly after this exchange, Hieronymo Guarino, the young son of Guarino Guarini, wrote to open a correspondence with Isotta and Genevra, and just as Isotta had done when she first wrote to his father, he writes in terms of abject respect, as from tyro to master.[105] There were authority relationships within humanist structures of discourse which had to be observed, even when they reversed ordinary rules of authority based on gender.

Isotta became friendly with Ludovico Foscarini, the son of the Doge of Venice, who presided over a literary salon, and this gave her an additional entrée into learned society. It was with Foscarini that she wrote her best-known work, a prose dialogue on the relative sinfulness of Adam and Eve, written in 1451 and published more than a hundred years later by a family member, Francesco Nogarola.[106] She was a notable book collector, whose tastes included some decidedly rare authors.[107] She wrote very little Latin verse, but she is the author of a long poem (ninety-two lines) on the family summer retreat, Castel d'Azzano, a place she evidently loved. This is cast in the form of an elegy on its tutelary deity, the nymph Cyane, and gives a further insight into the happier side of her life, not immured in a book-lined cell, but composing in the grounds of an elegant villa, and enjoying the friendship of Ludovico Gonzaga and the poet Pontano:

> Salvete, O Cyani fontes dulcesque recessus
> in medioque alnis consita silva lacu.
> Aonidum salvete choris loca grata sororum
> et quae cum Bromio Phoebus adire solet.
> docta mihi quoties quaerenti carmina Musas
> profuit in vestro comperiisse sinu...
> haec quoties Gonsaga et amore et sanguine iunctus
> Mantua quo gaudet praeside, tecta subit.
> huc quoque Pontanus Musis comitatus amoeni
> non semel accessit captus amore loci.

> Hail, O springs of Cyane, and sweet retreats,
> and wood thick with alders, in the middle of the lake.
> Hail, places loved by the choir of Aonian sisters [the Muses],
> where Phoebus is accustomed to come with Bromius [Bacchus].
> How often, seeking learned songs, it has profited me
> to find the muses in your lap...

---

[103] *Ibid.* i. 64–78, 79–82, 83–92.   [104] *Ibid.* 6–11.   [105] *Ibid.* 93–102.

[106] King and Rabil (trans.), *Her Immaculate Hand*, 57–69.

[107] D. M. Robathon, 'A Fifteenth-Century Bluestocking', *Medievalia et Humanistica*, 2 (1944), 106–11, and see also N. A. Oldfather, 'Quotation from Hesiod and Euripides by Isotta Nogarola', *Medievalia et Humanistica*, 3 (1945), 132.

How often has Gonzaga, linked with me both in blood and in friendship,
at whose leadership Mantua rejoices, come under this roof.
Here also Pontano, companion of the Muses, has come more than once,
captured by this pleasant spot...

Isotta lived as a celibate, despite offers of marriage, but did not enter holy
orders; a 'third way' also followed by a number of later Italian women scholars,
notably Elena Piscopia and Martha Marchina. This liminal mode of life left her
open to a vicious attack by an anonymous pamphleteer in 1438 who accused her of
incest with her brother Ludovico. The libel was not well received, and generated
no debate.[108] However, after this episode, she retreated from her relatively public
position as a scholar and intellectual into a more private mode of life, shared with
her mother, in the house of her brother Antonio. The libel is clearly intended for
the entire family (Ludovico, her brother, apart from being incestuous, is also
accused of sodomy, then a capital crime), and is an example of the humanist
'war of words' peculiar only in that a woman is one of its targets.[109] The unpleasant
shock of this attack was clearly a turning point in her life, but Segarizzi suggests
that little attention was paid to it by contemporaries,[110] since, as he points out, it
was not followed up, and furthermore, against this solitary attack we must set a
chorus of praise from male fellow humanists,[111] who include Giovanni Mario
Filelfo, Panfilo Sasso, Zavarise nella Pantea, Antonio Lazise, and Laura Brenzona's
friend Antonio Panteo.[112] Two humanist women also wrote in her support: Clara
Lanzavegia, who enlisted Filelfo on her behalf, and Costanza Varano. Her most
famous work, the dialogue with Foscarini, post-dates the libel episode by thirteen
years, suggesting a less than total eclipse of her humanist activity. She is also seen
occupying a public position at the Council of Mantua in 1459, where she sent a
letter to be read, urging war against the Turks.[113]

[108] The pamphlet and its author is discussed by A. Segarizzi, 'Niccolò Barbo, patrizio veneziano del
sec. xv e le accuse contro Isotta Nogarola', *Giornale storico della letteratura italiana*, 43 (1904), 39–54. For
her way of life, see King, 'Isotta Nogarola, umanista e devota', 13.

[109] Sharon T. Stroccia, 'Gender and the Rites of Honour in Italian Renaissance Cities', in Judith C.
Brown and Robert C. Davis (eds.), *Gender and Society in Renaissance Italy* (Harlow: Longman, 1988),
39–60 (pp. 54–5), establishes that the vocabulary of sexual insult was female centred, either assailing a
woman for failing to adhere to sexual mores, or indicting a man as product or victim of her illicit sexual
relations.

[110] 'Alle cui sfuriate però non dovettero dal importanza i contemporanei, se giudichiamo dallo scorso
numero degli essemplari dell'invettiva giunti a noi e dal silenzio co con guaccolta.'

[111] 'D'altra parte s'unisce al coro degli altri scrittori per lodare la virtù e la sapienza della vergine
Isotta e conseguentemente i meriti della famiglia Nogarola.'

[112] Maffei, *Verona Illustrata* iii. 186–90 (p. 187). Isotta is also discussed in Joanne Sabadino de
l'Arienti, *Gynevera*, ed. Corrado Ricci and A. Bacchi della Rega (Bologna: Ronagnoli-Dall'Acqua,
1888), 173–80, who compares her to the Vestal Virgin Marcia. As Segarizzi observes, polite mentions
of her abound in discussions of learned women. Poems on her include Joannes Antonius (Pantheus),
Venice, Biblioteca Marciana, Lat. XII 161 (4456), fo. 18, Eusebio Borgo, in *Isotta Nogarolae...Opera*,
ed. Abel, i. 221 and 247–8, anon., ibid. 220, and anon., 'Eia Age Musa Novas in Carmine Concipe
Vires', Leipzig, Stadtbibliothek, Rep. 1. 8° 85b fo. 47ᵛ and Treviso, Communale 170, fos. 127ᵛ–128;
with another anon., 'Flumine Cive Loco Nutritur Pulchra Verona', in the same two manuscripts.

[113] *Isotae Nogarolae...Opera*, ed. Abel, ii. 143–56. Admiringly discussed in *Libro di M. Giovanni
Boccaccio...tradotto...per M. Giuseppe Betussi*, ch. xiii, pp. 348–50 (p. 347)).

Her sister Ginevra, after a promising start, gave up writing when she married at 23. It is she who boasted of, in the phrase now made famous by King and Rabil, 'her immaculate hand'.[114] The sisters' old friend Damiano dal Borgo notes sadly that she was greatly changed by two years of marriage, and constantly ill: his account may suggest that it was difficult pregnancies and too much to do rather than prejudice against married women scholars which accounts for her retreat from the world of learning, since neither her mother Bianca nor her aunt Angela seem to have been considered barred from humanist intercourse by their respective marriages: Bianca is lavishly praised by the humanist Giorgio Bevilacqua as a modern image of Cornelia (i.e. the educated mother of educated children).[115] Another sister, Laura, married twice (first Cristoforo Pellegrini, and second, the Doge of Venice, Nicolò Trono), and left a reputation for writing in Latin and Greek in theological subjects.[116] There is also evidence for a continuing family tradition of educating women. Ludovico's daughter Giulia (b. *c*.1420) was educated by her aunt Isotta in the classical languages. Her father wanted her to marry, but she preferred to become a nun and took the habit of St Clare in Verona.[117] She acquired particular notice as a mathematician, and received two long Latin letters in support of her monastic vocation from Petrus Donatus.[118] Another of Ludovico's daughters, Isotta, has not left a reputation as a learned woman, but she married Lucas Brembati of Bergamo and became the mother of a daughter, Isotta Brembati Grumella, who was also famed for her learning, and thus represents at least a fourth generation of educated Nogarola women.[119]

Isotta Nogarola's mode of life is not as characteristic of women humanists as is sometimes suggested. Her choice of virginity was certainly a matter for public debate: there is, for example, a letter from Paolo Maffei urging her to remain a virgin.[120] Her second letter to Guarino enlarges on the difficulties of a woman student; and she thus appears both to be extremely self-conscious about her position, and to attract a similar consciousness in her male correspondents.[121] Damiano dal Borgo describes her sister Ginevra as silenced by marriage. But it is worth remembering that the Renaissance letter is a highly literary construct, and

---

[114] de l'Arienti, *Gynevera*, 167–73. A manuscript of Justinus, written in her hand; survives as Yale University Library, Marston 279, is signed with the words, 'Genevra anogarolis scripsi manu mea immaculata'. Stephanie Jed, 'Chastity on the Page', in M. Miciel and J. Schiesari (eds.), *Refiguring Woman* (Ithaca, NY: Cornell University Press, 1991), 119–21, notes that humanists spoke of handwriting as 'chaste' when it was clear and classical, and also that a codex was 'emaculatus', unstained, when it was flawlessly correct. Ginevra may therefore be making a boast of her competence rather than her purity.

[115] *Isotae Nogarolae... Opera*, ed. Abel, i. 20–1.

[116] Bandini Buti, ii. 85.

[117] Ibid. 83.

[118] Milan, Biblioteca Ambrosiana, I 160 P sup., fos. 1–15ᵛ.

[119] Two works attest her position in the literary life of Bergamo, Marco Publio Fontana, *Ad Isottam Brembatam Grumellam Ode* (Brescia: Gio. Britannico, 1573), and *Rime funerali di diversi illustri ingegni, composte nella volgare e latina favella in morte della Sig. Isotta Brembata Grumella* (Bergamo: Camino Ventura & Co. 1587). A poem in this last by Achille Muti (p. 96) states that she wrote in Italian, Spanish, and Latin. She is said to have acted as her own lawyer (see n. 68 above).

[120] Maffei, *Verona Illustrata*, pt. 2, iii. 170.

[121] *Isotae Nogarolae... Opera*, ed. Abel, i. 65–78, 79–81.

that the inescapable models for Latin letters sent from scholarly men to virginal women are those of St Jerome, which praise celibacy, exalt the virginal life, and speak eloquently of the pains and indignity of marriage and motherhood. On the other hand, the fact that Ginevra's writing pre-dated her marriage was not even noticed by those of her contemporaries who did not know the two women personally, so they therefore give the impression that learning and marriage are entirely compatible. De l'Arienti's *Gynevera*, written for Ginevra Sforza di Benti-voglio in 1482, praises Ginevra Nogarola at length for her crystal-clear (*luculente*) letters and orations, and compares her to a series of highly educated Roman matrons, Portia, Emilia Tertia, the wife of Scipio Africanus, and Claudia Quinta.[122] Isotta is also praised at length in this work and compared to the Vestal Virgin Marcia, but her sister is not thereby denigrated.[123]

The possibility that Isotta and Ginevra Nogarola's stories show us a first generation of humanist women whose life choices were understood, for want of any other appropriate paradigm, as quasi-monastic is militated against by the fact that Latinate women from the same milieu in the previous generation—Angela Nogarola and Maddalena Scrovegni—had married. Twenty-seven Italian women Latinists flourishing between 1400 and 1500 are identified in the Appendix. The marital status of ten is unknown; of the other seventeen, fourteen became wives (one unwillingly so), two sought the cloister and gave up humanism, while only one was an uncloistered virgin, Isotta herself. It is therefore seriously to be asked whether the male humanist response to Isotta was actually reinforcing and valid-ating a choice she was already known to have made: it cannot have been an attempt to force her into a pre-existing mould, since no such mould existed.

Furthermore, there is better evidence that in the fifteenth century becoming a nun meant an end to humanist activity than there is that women were silenced by marriage. Other contemporary women poets of a comparable social rank to the Nogarola (such as their fellow Veronese Laura Schioppa, née Brenzona, discussed below) did marry and continue to write. The same is true of the generation immediately following that of Isotta. The Milanese lady Domitilla Trivulzi (1481–*c*.1530), wife of Francesco Torelli, was much celebrated;[124] the Florentine prodigy Alessandra Scala (1475–1506) married a fellow Greek scholar, Michael Marullo. Veronica Gàmbara (1485–1550), Isotta's great-niece, began writing to Pietro Bembo as a maiden of 17, and married the lord of Correggio at 24 without attracting Bembo's reproaches.[125] Her extensive oeuvre, some of which she pub-

---

[122] de l'Arienti, *Gynevera*, 167–73. Ginevra Sforza was the half-sister of Battista Sforza, so almost certainly highly educated: she was first married at the age of 12 in 1454.

[123] Ibid. 173–80. Jacopo Foresti also discussed both sisters (see below p. 419).

[124] She is mentioned in Foresti's *De Claris Mulieribus*, Ludovico Domenichi, *La nobiltà delle donne*, 240, and in *Orlando furioso* 46, st. 4. There are also two poems 'De Trivultia' by Ariosto, in Jo. Matthaeus Toscanus (ed.), *Carmina Illustrium Poetarum Italorum* (Paris: Gilles Gorbin, 1576–7), 269ʳ, 272ʳ.

[125] Richard Poss, 'A Renaissance Gentildonna: Veronica Gàmbara', in *WWRR*, 47–66. See also Rinaldo Corso, *Vita di Giberto III di Correggio, detto il difensore* (Ancona: Astolfo de Grandi, 1566), which includes 'Vita di Veronica Gàmbara per Rinaldo Corso', sig. E4ʳ–F3ʳ.

lished, and much of which she circulated, was mostly written as wife or widow, and the same is true of the great Vittoria Colonna. The problem with the intellectual life of married women in the Italian Renaissance may in fact reside less in an automatic male equation of learning with virginity, for which the evidence is concentrated in the letters to and from Isotta Nogarola, than in the amount of work expected of the mistress of the household. An unlucky woman such as Ginevra Nogarola who found herself debilitated by difficult pregnancies had neither the time nor the energy for private study: rearing five successful sons evidently took all her personal resources, as well it might.[126] By contrast, Veronica Gàmbara, a mother of two who was widowed early, was able to divide her time between ruling Correggio and pursuing her intellectual interests. It seems empirically to be the case that the Renaissance Italian women who circulated their writing were either unmarried or the mothers of two or fewer children: this suggests that the problem for intellectually aspirant married women was at least as much practical as ideological.

Apart from the Nogarola family itself, in which the three generations of classically educated women must have been mutually supportive (certainly, Isotta writes eloquently of her intellectual communion with her mother),[127] we can also see connections between the Nogarola and other humanist women which were relatively free of the problems which potentially attended interactions with humanist men, or with non-humanist women. It is curious, and interesting, that a number of Italian women humanists write to, or in praise of, their mothers (rather than of their fathers or of both parents together).[128] There were also extra-familial contacts between women humanists. A woman, perhaps of Verona, called Clara Lanzavegia (again, she mentions that she was married) boldly solicited the support of Giovanni Mario Filelfo for Isotta in a Latin poem: whereas it was apparently risky for Isotta herself to solicit the attention of Guarino, to appeal on another woman's behalf was perhaps more within the remit of the womanly as the fifteenth century understood it.[129] Isotta also received a poem of praise from the noblewoman Costanza Varano, which has already been quoted.

---

[126] Laura Cereta observes in a letter to Sigismondo de Bucci, her father's attorney, 'I still don't have any time that is unoccupied, not even to catch my breath... I have no free time at all to spend on my books unless I work productively during the nights and sleep very little...' Diana Robin, 'Women, Space and Renaissance Discourse', in Gold, Miller, and Platter (eds.), *Sex and Gender*, 176–7 gives a full translation of the letter, no. II in *Epistolae Laurae Ceretae*, ed. Iacopo Filippo Tomasini (Padua: Sebastiano Sardi, 1640). Ginevra's family is discussed by Jacopo Foresti, *Opus de Claris Selectisque Plurimis Mulieribus* (Serrara: L. de Rubeis, 1497), 150.

[127] King, *The Death of... Valerio Marcello*, 36–7.

[128] Apart from Nogarola's comments, evidence for Italian humanist women's concern to honour their mothers includes an oration in honour of Bianca Maria Sforza by her daughter Ippolita, trans. King and Rabil, *Her Immaculate Hand*, 44–6, Ginevra Rangone's Latin poem to her mother, and Antonia Rusca's elaborate tomb and epigraphic verse for her mother, illustrated and discussed in Catherine E. King, *Renaissance Women Patrons* (Manchester: Manchester University Press, 1998), 225.

[129] Printed in *Isotae Nogarolae... Opera*, ed. Abel, ii. 361–2. Filelfo's response is also printed by Abel.

The Costanza Varano who made the surprising claim that Nogarola's fame surpassed that of Catullus was a noblewoman, the daughter of Elisabetta Malatesta and Piergentile Varano, lord of Camerino, where she was born probably on 23 October 1428. Her mother fled with the children to Pesaro in 1434 after their father was killed by his brothers, so she was educated in Pesaro, partly at the hands of her learned grandmother Battista da Montefeltro, the recipient of the important letter from Leonardo Bruni on women's education which has already been mentioned, and herself the author of several Latin works in prose, as well as poetry in Italian.[130] Another tutor named by Ratti is Guidantonio, Count of Urbino, her great-uncle.[131] Though, as the daughter of a minor ruling family, her social status is different from that of Isotta Nogarola, her family story is comparable in that it demonstrates a commitment to the education of daughters extending over many generations—six, in this case, from Battista da Montefeltro, Varano's grandmother, to Vittoria Colonna, poet and friend of Michelangelo, who was Varano's great-granddaughter.[132] It is worth noting that her father's family was also distinguished for learned women.[133]

Varano's education is quite visibly put to use by her family as part of their diplomatic resources, just as her grandmother's had been. She composed and delivered at 15 a Latin address to Francesco Sforza, Duke of Milan, on behalf of her brother Rodolfo, which was part of a family campaign to restore him to his rights in Camerino, and which also made her famous. A congratulatory letter to her by Guiniforte Barzizza begins: 'O honour and splendour of Latin-speaking girls, what [connection] should there be between me and you, or between me and the magnanimous princes your parents, that I do not hesitate to send you letters?'[134] Such a beginning is eloquent of the social distance between a member of a princely family, even a teenage girl, and a professional humanist. Others of Varano's surviving Latin works are connected with the same campaign on behalf of Rodolfo.

---

130 Mazzanti, *Battista Sforza*.

131 In Niccolò Ratti, *Della famiglia Sforza*, 2 vols. (Rome: Il Salomoni, 1794–5), ii. 96.

132 Costanza's daughter Battista Sforza married Federico da Montefeltro. Their daughter Agnesina married Fabrizio Colonna, by whom she had Vittoria. Although Vittoria Colonna was chiefly famous for her poetry and prose in Italian (notably *Litere della divina Vettoria Colonna, Marchesana di Pescara alla Duchessa de Amalfi, sopra la vita contemplativa di santa Catharina* (Venice: Giov. Anto. and Pietro de Nicolini, 1545), published in her lifetime), she wrote at least one surviving Latin poem. Her authorship is demonstrated by Silvio Pasquazi, 'La poesia in latino', in Walter Moretti (ed.), *Il Rinascimento: la letteratura (Storia di Ferrara*, vii) (Ferrara: Edizione Librit, 1995), 100–56 (p. 132). By contrast, a poem in her name, headed 'Marchionissa de Pescharia' in Venice, Biblioteca Marciana, Lat. XII 248 (10625), fo. 131ʳ, 'Non viviam sine te mi Brute haud territa dixit' is *in persona*.

133 Camilla da Varano, who became a Poor Clare, produced twenty-two works between 1479 and her death in 1524, letters, prayers, and treatises in a fine Latin style, and also a spiritual autobiography: see Giacomo Boccanera, *Biografa e scritti della B. Camilla Battista da Varana, clarissa di Camerino (1458–1524)*, (esi: Scuola tipografica Francescana, 1958). The manuscript of her *vita spirituale* is in Fabriano, Biblioteca comunale, 131.

134 'Quid mihi aut tecum latinarum virginum decus ac splendor, aut cum Principibus magnanimis parentibus tuis, ut litteras ad te dare non dubitem?' Milan, Biblioteca Ambrosiana, S 222 inf. (4), fo. 1ʳ⁻ᵛ. This collection also includes Varano's exchange of letters with a later Duke of Milan, Filippo Maria Sforza. Barzizza was the tutor of Galeazzo Maria Sforza: Cesare Cantu, 'Guiniforte Barzizza: maestro di Galeazzo Maria Sforza', *Archivio storico lombardo* (1894), 399–442.

She wrote a poem to Alfonso I, King of Naples, begging his help for her brother, and recited a Latin oration in his presence when he came to Marca. In 1444, when her brother Rodolfo's right as lord of Camerino was restored, she made another Latin address before the people of that town. Her poem to Giovanni Gonzaga, interestingly, begins 'often my father and my lord commands me to write': there could hardly be a clearer statement that her Latin verse was not merely sanctioned, but was part of the work she was expected to do.

Costanza Varano married Alessandro Sforza, Count of Pesaro, in 1444, as the heir of her parents. Alessandro ceded the seigneury of Pesaro to Galeozzo Malatesta, Costanza's maternal uncle. She was married by proxy, the proxy being Federico di Montefeltro, Count of Urbino, and joined her husband at Pesaro in April 1445. Her marriage was brief: she became the mother of two children (Costanzo and Battista) in two years, and died of the second, eight days after giving birth, in 1447. She clearly did not give up humanist activity on her marriage, since her last verses were made for her husband while on her deathbed.

Her daughter Battista was also brought up not only to be educated (her teacher was Martinus Phileticus), but to display her learning in public, delivering her first Latin speech at the unprecedentedly tender age of 4.[135] As time went on, she was regularly expected to greet distinguished visitors with an appropriate Latin speech.[136] Battista Sforza continued studying Greek after her marriage. By the time she was 15, she was mandated full powers by her husband to rule his vicariates during his frequent absences as a *condottiere*: her education was not an elegant accomplishment, but an aspect of her fitness for rule, as Cecil Clough has demonstrated. Like her sister-in-law Ippolita Sforza, she gave an oration in front of Pius II. But although the speech by her sister-in-law Ippolita was famous, and there is no manuscript record of this speech by Battista, there is a variety of contemporary evidence that it is not merely a doublet of Ippolita's. Battista visited Pius II in Rome, arriving in October 1461, and, according to an eyewitness account, he listened to her with great attention.[137] As had been the case with Battista herself, her daughter Giovanna was given full power by her husband's will to rule his vicariates until their son came of age, and exercised it.[138]

Costanza Varano's death is celebrated by a number of humanists, notably Giovanni Mario Filelfo, who wrote a whole cycle of poems on the deaths of her and her husband.[139] This brings us back to the circle of Isotta Nogarola (also praised by Filelfo, on the instigation of Clara Lanzavegia), since both Costanza Varano and

---

[135] de l'Arienti, *Gynevera*, 288–312. She married Federico da Montefeltro, Duke of Urbino. Costanza's son Costanzo similarly married Camilla d'Aragona, who had been taught Latin, Spanish, and French: della Chiesa, *Theatro delle donne letterate*, 116.

[136] Pietro Paolo de Ribera Valentianus, *Le glorie immortali de . . . donne illustri* (Venice: Evangelista Benchino, 1609), 281.

[137] The visit and the testimonies to it are discussed by Mazzanti, *Battista Sforza*, 96–101.

[138] Clough, 'Daughters and Wives', 48–9.

[139] Also *Epitaphium Constantiae Sforzae*, Florence, Biblioteca Riccardiana, 924, fos. 199ᵛ, 200, 208. See Augusto Marinoni, 'Documenta per la storia del rinascimento Italiano: poesie in morte di Costanza Varano Sforza', *Convivium* (1956), 579–89.

her mother, Elisabetta Malatesta, received Latin letters praising their learning from
a Veronese noblewoman who was very probably known to Isotta, Polissena Grimaldi.[140] Grimaldi's two surviving Latin poems are in praise of Francesco Sforza
and Bianca Visconti (Varano's brother-and sister-in-law), so despite her relative
obscurity, she is evidently another woman whose poetry must be seen as public and
political in intention. There are also Latin letters from Grimaldi to Alfonso of
Aragon (who was a correspondent of Costanza Varano's), and to another woman,
Santia, Duchess of Andria and Countess of Canossa.[141]

Still another Veronese woman Latin poet flourishing in the mid-fifteenth
century, Laura Brenzona, must have had some connection with the Nogarola
family, since one of her surviving poems is on the death of Isotta's equally scholarly
brother Ludovico Nogarola.[142] She may have been married to Giacomo Schioppi,
a friend of the poet-bishop Niccolò Perotti, or to Aurelio Schioppi, a playwright.[143] There is a substantial amount of poetry addressed to Laura Schioppa
under that name, and the idea that it is transgressive for her to write while being a
wife seems never to be raised. Paolo Giovio mentions her in a work written in 1530,
describing her as still charming and beautiful despite the ravages of age (suggesting, furthermore, that it was not invariably the case that women dropped into
oblivion once they left their teens, since she was still apparently encountering men
of letters in her very mature years).[144] She is also represented in Bartolomeo
Pagello's *epistolae familiares* along with a Leonardo Nogarola, and Antonio Panteo.[145] Other writers associable with her include Antonio Venier, Paolo Ramusio,
and Niccolò Perotti. Brenzona is a poet of substantial achievement: she wrote a
Latin *epyllion* of nearly a thousand lines to the Admiral of Venice, Roberto
Sanseverinato, on his victory against the Turks (1497), as well as a collection of
Latin verses now in Verona which demonstrate that she was intimately part of a
circle of poets, and a collection of verse in Italian.[146] Domenichi states that she was
particularly known for her use of Sapphics and also composed orations in Greek

---

[140] Letter to Elisabetta Malatesta, London, British Library, Add. 19061, fos. 20ʳ–22ʳ. Letter to
Costanza Varano, Florence, Biblioteca Laurentiana, Cod. lat. 56 Plut. 90, sup. 56, fos. 59ᵛ–60ʳ.

[141] Florence, Biblioteca Laurentiana, Cod. lat. 56 Plut. 90, sup. 56, fos. 58ᵛ–59ᵛ, 60ᵛ–61ʳ. There are
other Latin letters by her in London, British Library, Add. 19061, fos. 22ʳ–26ᵛ, Gotha, Landesbibliothek (Forschungsbibliothek), Chart. B. 239, fos. 76ᵛ–79, Bern, Bürgerbibliothek, 527, fos. 210–211ᵛ,
and perhaps also Basel, Universitätsbibliothek, F viii.18, fo. 54–54ᵛ (not seen).

[142] Maffei, *Verona Illustrata*, iii. 214–17. Verona, Biblioteca comunale, 280 (1336), fo. 14ʳ.

[143] Giovanni Mercati, *Per la cronologia della vita e degli scritti di Niccolò Perotti, archivescovo di
Siponto*, Studi e testi 44 (Rome: Biblioteca apostolica Vaticana, 1925), 28.

[144] Giovio, *Dialogus de Viris et Foeminis Aetate nostra Florentibus*, in Ernesto Travi and Marigrazia
Penco (eds.), *Pauli Iovii Opera*, ix: *Dialogi et Descriptiones* (Rome: Istituto poligrafica e zecca dello stato,
1984), 147–323 (p. 288).

[145] Barbara Marx, *Bartolomeo Pagello: Epistolae Familares (1464–1523): Materiale zur Vicentiner
Kulturgeschichte des 15. Jahrhunderts und kritisch Edition des Briefwechsels* (Padua: Antenore, 1978).

[146] Her Italian verse has recently been published: Massimo Castoldi (ed.), *Rime per Laura Brenzoni
Schioppo dal codice Marciana It. cl. ix. 163* (Bologna: Commissione per i testi di lingua, 1994).

and Latin, suggesting that other writings of hers circulated which are not now to be found.[147] She became widely known and celebrated, even beyond Italy.[148]

Another important woman poet who also has a Nogarola connection is Veronica Gàmbara (1485–1550), Ginevra Nogarola's great-niece.[149] She was the daughter of Count Gianfrancesco da Gàmbara and Alda Pia, so her father was the brother of Ginevra Nogarola's husband Brunoro da Gàmbara. Like the Nogarola, the Gàmbara family seems to have had a policy of educating daughters. There is some trace of a Dorothea Gàmbara earlier in the century,[150] and Veronica's sister Violante also had a reputation as a poet.[151] It is interesting to note that her husband Giberto was the third lord of Correggio in sequence to choose a wife who was capable of writing Latin verse: Niccolò Postumo da Correggio had married Cassandra Colleoni, and their son Giangaleazzo had married Ginevra Rangone, both of whom are represented in the Appendix: this is probably not a mere coincidence, but an indication that the lords of Correggio expected their wives to carry responsibility, and therefore selected them for learning, intelligence, and eloquence as well as more traditional virtues such as beauty, fecundity, and good family.

Veronica Gàmbara is remembered for her extensive writings in Italian, but she also made some use of Latin. The Italian poetry falls into four categories, love poems to her husband, poems on political issues, devotional poems, and Virgilian pastoral. Very little was printed in her lifetime, though she was known throughout Italy as a poet by 1530 (suggesting that she chose to circulate her writing in manuscript), but one of the few things she did choose to publish was a Latin dedicatory verse on behalf of Annibale Camilli, an expression of kindly patronage for a young writer.

> Hannibalis primos quisquis duce Pallade fructus
> Inspicie. Invidie stet procul ignis edax.
> Equior autorie nam si respexeris annos
> Ista coles annis nobiliora dabit.

> See here the first fruits of Annibale, guided by Pallas,
> May the gnawing fire of envy remain far distant.
> For if you consider the years of the author more fairly,
> He will give his quills more noble things in years to come.

---

[147] Domenichi, *La nobiltà delle donne*, 238ᵛ.

[148] There is a poem on Laura Brenzona under her married name (Schioppa) by Julius Caesar Scaliger in his *Poemata*, published in 1574 (p. 374): Italian humanists who write to or about her include Paolo Ramusio, Giovanni Battista Possevino, Dante Alighieri III, and Marcellus Philoxenus. See Maffei, *Verona Illustrata*, iii. 214–17, and for Philoxenus' verse, Venice, Biblioteca Marciana, Lat. xiv. 243 (4070).

[149] On whom see Cesare Bozzetti et al. (eds.), *Veronica Gàmbara e la poesia del suo tempo nell'Italia settentrionale* (Florence: Leo Olschki, 1989) and Rinaldina Russell, 'Veronica Gàmbara', in her *Italian Women Writers: A Bio-bibliographical Sourcebook* (Westport, Conn.: Greenwood Press, 1994), 145–53.

[150] The recipient of a eulogy by Petrus Candidus Decembrius: there is also a *Responsio Dorotheae de Gàmbara per S. Cribellium* (Cosenza, *Supp.* 129), suggesting that she corresponded in Latin.

[151] Bandini Buti, i. 289.

She also wrote Italian verses in praise of Vittoria Colonna,[152] an expression of deep and serious interest in a contemporary woman. Rinaldo Corso, author of a study of Colonna which is the only sixteenth-century Italian commentary on a living poet, wrote this up from notes which he had made on Gàmbara's copy of Colonna, which they had studied together.[153]

As a young woman, Veronica Gàmbara studied Greek and Latin, philosophy, Scripture, and theology, especially patristics. She first wrote to Pietro Bembo at the age of 17, and began sending him her work two years later; he became her poetic mentor. In 1509, she married Giberto, lord of Correggio (as his second wife), and her small court became something of a salon.[154] She was publicly visible as a learned woman during her wifehood: notably, she was in Bologna in 1515 at the time of the meeting between François I and Pope Leo X, since the former was charmed by her.[155] Giberto died in 1518, and Veronica took power as regent of Correggio, which she ruled effectively for most of the rest of her life.[156] The painter Correggio's 1518 *Portrait of a Lady* in black and white, holding a cup engraved with an inscription from the *Odyssey*, apparently intended to depict Circe with a cup of nepenthe, may also represent the recently widowed Veronica; now, like Circe, mistress of her own territory.[157] In 1530, she was again in Bologna, for the coronation of Charles V. She had the considerable advantage of a brother who was not only a cardinal but vicelegate of Bologna: with his countenance, she held court as a woman of letters, visited by Bembo, Molza, Trissino, Flaminio, Tolomei, and others: her brother's official position perhaps meant that her activity as a salon hostess was seen as an aspect of the city's reception of distinguished guests: her brother was, being a churchman, unmarried, so it is possible that she was acting for, or with, him.[158] On 23 March 1530 she received Charles V herself at Correggio, a visit which was repeated two years later (another painting by Correggio commemorates the occasion), and hailed him in Latin verse. Gàmbara spent

152 Cannon, *The Education of Women*, 14, gives text and translation.

153 See Corso, *Dichiaratione sopra le seconda parte delle rime della divina Vittoria Colonna* (Bologna: G.-B. Faelli, 1543; 2nd edn. 1558). Thanks to Abigail Brundin, author of a forthcoming edition and study of Colonna's gift manuscript made for Michelangelo, for this information. Corso also wrote an account of his patroness in his *Vita di Giberto terzo di Correggio, detto il difensore* (Ancona: A de Grandi, 1566), which includes a 'Vita di Veronica Gàmbara', sig. E4ʳ–F3ʳ.

154 Alberto Ghidini, 'La contea di Corregio ai tempi di Veronica Gàmbara', in Cesare Bozzetti et al. (eds.), *Veronica Gàmbara e la poesia del suo tempo nell' Italia settentrionale* (Florence: Leo Olschki, 1989) 79–98 (pp. 90–8).

155 Gaetano Giordani (ed.), *Della venuta e dimora in Bologna del sommo pontefice Clemente VII per la coronazione di Carlo V Imperatore, celebrato l'anno mdxxx, cronaca*, 2 vols. in 1 (Bologna: Fonderia e tip. gov., 1842), ii. 55 n. 216.

156 Of her two sons, Ippolito pursued a military career, serving first the Venetian republic, later Charles V and Felipe II of Spain, while Girolamo entered the Church and became Archbishop of Taranto.

157 Lucia Fornari Schianchi, *Correggio* (Florence: Scala, 1994), 16 and 21 (now in St Petersburg, Hermitage).

158 Giordani (ed.), *Della venuta e dimora in Bologna*, 77–8, C. H. Clough, 'Pietro Bembo, Madonna G., Berenice and Veronica Gàmbara', *Commentari dell'Ateneo di Brescia per l'anno 1963*, 162 (1965), 209–17.

her last years in quiet study and meditation, rarely travelling. She corresponded with a number of humanists, notably with Pietro Bembo and Pietro Aretino—the latter later turned against her and described her as 'a laureated harlot', an attack she seems to have shrugged off, perhaps because Aretino's reputation for venomousness was such that she could afford to ignore him.[159] It is significant that Gàmbara turned to Latin for her ode on Charles V. As a sovereign, albeit on a small scale, greeting another sovereign, it was appropriate to make use of the language of maximum dignity.

Veronica Gàmbara seems to have educated her stepdaughter conscientiously,[160] and her sister Violante's daughter Camilla is said to have written Latin epigrams of outstanding elegance.[161] A Latin poem to her, by Niccolò d'Arco, links her learning with that of her mother: 'Since your mother is [a] Minerva, learned Camilla, why should I wonder that you make skilful verses?'[162]

A number of ducal families beside the da Montefeltri educated their daughters, notably the Gonzaga of Mantua.[163] Paola Malatesta, wife of Gianfrancesco Gonzaga, is praised by Vespasiano da Bisticci for imitating her sister-in-law, the learned Battista Malatesta, and hiring Vittorino da Feltre to teach her children. It is claimed by some later writers that she wrote Latin prose and verse herself.[164] Her daughter Cecilia Gonzaga (b. 1425) was a woman educated to the highest humanist standards.[165] She was an acquaintance of Costanza Varano, who wrote her a letter,[166] and she is also the recipient of a letter on virginity from Gregorio Correr, which is modelled on Jerome's letter on the same subject to his learned young friend Demetrias, and will be discussed later. Elisabetta Gonzaga (1471–1526), Duchess of Urbino, was the centre of the court immortalized in Castiglione's *Courtier*. She was also a learned woman noted as a political figure, 'whose education contributed to her political and social competence, and who encouraged high culture through her patronage'.[167]

Another north Italian ruling family, the Sforza of Milan, similarly had a commitment to the education of daughters. When Francesco Sforza married the daughter of the last Visconti, Bianca Maria, and became Duke of Milan in 1450, he

---

[159] A. Luzio and R. Renier, 'La cultura e le relazione letterarie d'Isabella d'Este Gonzaga 3: Gruppo Lombardo', *Giornale storico della letteratura italiana*, 36 (1900), 325–49 (p. 347).

[160] Her stepdaughter Costanza studied alongside her, according to the dedication of H. C. Corrigiani's *Artium et Medicinae Doctoris de Subjecto Totius Logicae Quaestio*: quoted in Girolamo Tiraboschi, *Bibliotheca Modenense* (Modena: Società tipografica, 1783), i. 374–5.

[161] Her father was the Cavaliere Valente Valenti, and she married Conte Giacomo Michele dal Verme in 1543. See Betussi, *Libro di M. Giovanni Boccaccio*, ch. xlix, pp. 470–2.

[162] Quoted by Bandini Buti, ii. 325.

[163] Cecilia Gonzaga was educated in the Mantua school of Vittorino da Feltre with her brothers, and entered a convent on her father's death. William Harrison Woodward, *Vittorino da Feltre and Other Humanist Educators* (Cambridge: Cambridge University Press, 1905), 50, 76–7.

[164] della Chiesa, *Theatro delle donne Letterate*, 269.

[165] da Bisticci, *Vite di uomini illustri*, 297. According to Frati's footnote, 'she wrote in Latin verse with great ease and elegance'.

[166] Translated in King and Rabil, *Her Immaculate Hand*, 53–4.

[167] Ibid. 21.

established a school for the education of his children, so, like Cecilia Gonzaga, Ippolita Sforza received her humanist education in a palace school with her brothers and sisters. She was taught Greek by Constantine Lascaris and was also taught by Baldo Martorelli, a pupil of Vittorino da Feltre.[168] Her marriage to Alfonso, Duke of Calabria, son of the King of Sicily, took place in 1465 when she was 20. The trousseau she took south included twelve books, including Cicero's *De Senectute* which she had copied herself, and she stopped to buy manuscripts on the way.[169] Her father died in 1466, and her mother took the reins of government for two years until Galeazzo Maria, the heir, returned from France in 1468. Ippolita Sforza was famous as an orator: the Latin address she made to the humanist Pope Pius II at Mantua in 1459, when she was only 14, circulated widely in manuscript.[170] Her two other orations, which also date to her girlhood, were less well known: one was addressed to her mother, the other to Tristano Visconti and Beatrice d'Este.[171]

As Duchess of Calabria, Ippolita emulated her mother in patronizing men of letters and displaying great competence in her role as duchess.[172] It has been said that she ceased to write after she married, but this is not the case: her Latin poem on the death of her father the Duke of Milan is self-dating to 1466.[173] Welch has demonstrated Ippolita Sforza's continued involvement with her birth family throughout her life, and the fact that her one surviving literary effort as Duchess of Calabria shows her as first and foremost a Sforza only goes to confirm this impression. It is a lament for the death of her father, and an expression of family pride and identity: it begins with an invocation to her mother and then to her brothers, and it ends,

> Est socer ille meus Siculum rex gloria regum
> Est meus hic coniux altera spes Latii

168 Cannon, *The Education of Women*, 39. It is also worth observing that Polissena Grimaldi of Verona addressed verses to Francesco Sforza and Bianca Visconti, suggesting they were thought of as well disposed to educated women.

169 Elisabeth Pellegrin, *La Bibliothèque des Visconti et des Sforza, ducs de Milan, au XVe siècle* (Paris: Institut de Recherche et d'Histoire des Textes, 1955), 67. Her *De Senectute* is now London, British Library, Add. 2984.

170 Munich, Clm 14610, fos. 192–4; Venice, Biblioteca Marciana, XIV 128 (4333), fos. 154ᵛ, 155ʳ; XIV 228 (4498), fos. 268ʳ–269ʳ, reply 270ʳ, Lat. XII 206 (4133), Bologna, Biblioteca Universitaria, 1434 (2720), fos. 116ᵛ–117, Berlin, Staatsbibliothek, Lat. oct. 200, and Prague, Strahovsna Knihovna, D F IV 2. It is translated in *Her Immaculate Hand*, 46–8, from the edition of C. Corvisieri, *Notabilita temporum di Angelo de Tummulillis da Sant'Elia* (Livorno: Fonti per la storia d'Italia, VII, 1890), 231–3.

171 The first is translated in *Her Immaculate Hand*, 44–6 from the edition of G. G. Meersseman, 'La raccolta dell'umanista fiammingo Giovanni de Veris, "De arte epistolandi" ', *Italia medioevale e umanistica*, 15 (1972), 250–1, the second is edited by Anna Maria Cesari, 'Un'orazione inedita di Ippolita Sforza e alcune lettere di Galeazzo Maria Sforza', *Archivo storico lombardo*, ser. 9.4 (1964–5), 50–65, while the third may be found in Ferrara, Biblioteca Comunale Ariostea, I 240, fo. 100ᵛ.

172 E. S. Welch, 'Between Milan and Naples: Ippolita Maria Sforza, Duchess of Calabria', in D. Abulafia (ed.), *The French Descent into Renaissance Italy: Antecedents and Effects*, (Aldershot, NH: Variorum, 1995), 123–36. On her mother, see E. W. Swain, 'Il potere d'un amicizia: iniziative e competenze di due nobile donne Rinascimentali', *Memoria*, 21 (1987), 7–23.

173 King and Rabil (trans.), *Her Immaculate Hand*, 21.

Nil socer ipse magis nec conjux deligit eque
    Fratribus Ipolite nil genitrice magis
Hiis igitur sevum phar est lenire dolorem
    Hiis propria sunt magno vota ferenda deo.

My father-in-law is king and glory of the kingdom of Sicily,
    My husband is another hope for Latium,
But neither my father-in-law himself, or my husband, please me more
    Than Ippolita's brothers, or her mother.
Therefore for these, there is a light to relieve severe grief
    For these are proper prayers to be uttered to almighty God.

Elena Coppoli (1425–1500) is another Latin poet whose story is instructive and well documented.[174] She was the daughter of Francesco Coppoli, a jurist, and a man with strongly humanist interests and contacts.[175] His marriage to a Perugian noblewoman, which took place in 1415, remained childless for ten years. Eventually, following a visit of the great preacher St Bernadino of Siena to Perugia in 1424, his wife Leonarda conceived, and their daughter was born in the following year. Elena's Life preserved in the monastery of St Lucia in Foligno states specifically that despairing of a legitimate son, Francesco decided to educate his only child as if she had been a boy. She was extremely well educated in Latin, Greek, and the liberal arts (her teachers included a master called Luca, since she writes a distich to him, expressing her gratitude for her education):

Praemia digna, precor, domino Dii reddite Lucae:
    Non ego pro tali munere dona feram

I pray that a worthy reward may be given by God to master Luca;
    I cannot offer a return for such a gift.

She evidently possessed a literary reputation in her teens, since there is an epigram by the humanist Porcellius in her honour, which describes her as a 'Perugian virgin and poet'.[176] The four surviving poems were almost certainly written while she was still living in her father's house, on grounds of tone and content. It seems evident from the shape of this narrative that in her father's mind, in the absence of a son, an educated daughter represented a positive advantage over an uneducated one, and that the study of *litterae humaniores* was apparently perceived by him as raising her position in the marriage market—though Elena's own intentions were otherwise.

Her family arranged a marriage for her with a nobleman, Rodolfo di Fabrizio Signorelli da Perugia, in 1441, but in 1446 she left him and eloped to the Poor Clare convent of St Lucia at Foligno, where she took the veil (assuming the name of Cecilia, presumably because the late antique St Cecilia had similarly been forced

[174] P. Antonio Fantezzi, OFM, 'Documenti intorno alla Beata Cecilia Coppoli clarissa (1426–1500)', *Archivum Franciscanum Historicum*, 19 (1926), 194–225, 334–84.

[175] He corresponded with Ambrogio Traversari: see Cosenza, i. 1094.

[176] 'Porcelli ad Helenam de Coppolis Virginem Perusinam ac Vatem', in Giovanni Battista Vermiglioli, *Bibliografia degli scrittori perugini* (Perugia: Francesco Badexel, 1828), i. 343–6 (p. 344).

into marriage). She was an outstandingly successful nun, rose to be abbess of her convent, and is recognized by the Church as *beata*.[177] Her will suggests her bitterness against her own family for trying to deflect her from her vocation: the only member of her birth family she left anything to was a bastard son of her father's (everything else went to St Lucia's). If humanism meant anything to her, it was perhaps that being educated like a boy left her with an 'unfeminine' sense of having a right to determine her own course of life (the same might be said of the later Catalan scholar-nun Juliana Morell).

There is no Latin verse production from fifteenth-century Italian convents that has as yet come to light. The convents did not lay stress on Latin literacy for their inmates, but the voluntary monachization of such women as Giulia Nogarola, Cecilia Gonzaga, Alessandra Scala, and Elena Coppoli ensured that there were Latin-literate women to be found there. Laura Cereta mentions that she was taught Latin by a nun.[178] Nuns produced a wider variety of writing than has sometimes been recognized: this is truer of the sixteenth century than the fifteenth, but even fifteenth-century nuns were active as authors.[179] A number of fifteenth-century nuns were noted for their writing in Italian, such as Camilla Battista Varano (1458–1524), bastard daughter of Giulio Cesare Varano, lord of Camerino (hence, great-niece of Costanza Varano), and recipient of an aristocratic education,[180] and, most famously, Caterina Vegri (1413–63), canonized as St Catherine of Bologna, daughter of a Bolognese court servant of the d'Este, who also wrote in Latin (prose).[181] Maia Isotta, the signatory of a fifteenth-century group of Latin love letters in the library at Siena addressed to Andrea Contrario, appears on internal evidence within the letters to have been a nun: the letters are dubiously ascribed to Isotta Nogarola, but 'Maia' is not a name associated with her in any genuine correspondence, the references in the letters to the wearing of a nun's habit do not fit her, and, of course, there is no evidence to support the idea that she was in love with Contrario or anybody else. If, conversely, the letters are malicious fabrications, one would expect them to conform more accurately to Nogarola's life; it is

---

177 'Il testamento del b. Cecilia Coppoli da Perugia', *Archivium Franciscanum Historicum*, 69 (1976), 219–26.

178 Laura Cereta, *Collected Letters*, 5.

179 Kate Lowe, 'History Writing from within the Convent in Cinquecento Italy: The Nuns' Version', in Panizza (ed.) *Women*, 104–21. See also Elissa Weaver, 'Le muse in convento: la scrittura profana della monache italiane (1450–1650)', in Lucetta Scaraffia and Gabriella Zarri (eds.), *Donne e fede: santità e vita religiosa in Italia* (Bari: Laterza, 1994), 253–76.

180 All her known works are edited as *Le opere spirituali: nuova edizione del quinto centenario del nascita secondo I più antichi codici e stampe e con aggiunta di alcuni inediti*, ed. G. Boccanera (Jesi, Scuda tipografica francescana 1958).

181 Her *Le sette armi spirituali* was first published in Bologna by Baldassare Azzoguidi, *c*.1475: there were four subsequent editions, and also a Latin translation by G. A. Flaminio, published in 1522. See Mary Martin McLoughlin, 'Creating and Recreating Communities of Women: The Case of Corpus Domini, Ferrara, 1406–1432', *Signs*, 14.2 (1989), 293–20, and Joseph R. Berrigan, 'Saint Catherine of Bologna', *WWRR*, 81–95. Vegri grew up at the d'Este court as playmate and then lady-in-waiting to Margarita d'Este, was trained as a calligrapher and miniaturist, and was also taught Latin (Berrigan, 'Saint Catherine', 81, 83)

therefore legitimate to argue that these letters are in fact by a highly educated and unhappy nun.[182]

However, it may be significant that Battista Malatesta, who wrote in Latin as well as Italian during her secular life, seems to have written only Italian verse once she had taken the veil.[183] Even women known to have been competent in Latin in fifteenth-century Italy, such as Elena Coppoli, seem to have left this humanistic accomplishment outside the convent walls. Two letters may help to illuminate the range of contemporary attitudes. Francesco Barbaro in writing to his daughter Costanza, a nun, in 1447 clearly expected her to be responsive to humanist modes of writing, and did not suggest that she turn her mind entirely away from pagan authors.[184] By contrast, Gregorio Correr's letter to the learned Cecilia Gonzaga notes that in her secular life he had heard her 'make some verses not without elegance', and warns her that now she is a nun, these talents might be put to use only in the service of the Church: he cites the examples of Pope Damasus and St Hilary of Poitiers to demonstrate that it is possible to write in a humanist way on Christian themes. While he does not positively desire her to imitate Proba, he suggests that if she finds the secular verse in which she is so well instructed recurring to her mind, she should, like Proba, turn it to Christian purposes by making sacred parodies: ideally, 'the bride of Christ should read nothing but the Sacred Scriptures', but he recognizes that someone as profoundly cultivated as she will find much of her secular reading is fixed in her memory.[185] He is not unsympathetic to her intellectual life; in fact he lovingly details his own neoclassical verse, which he gave up on entering the Church, in order to demonstrate to her that this is a sacrifice to be made by men as well as women.

It is worth noticing that Correr does not ban Cecilia from writing Latin poetry using a humanist discourse (Damasus and Hilary, writers of the fourth century, were both the masters of an elegant classical style),[186] he seeks only to control her subject matter. But in practice, she seems not to have made the attempt, though

---

[182] Discussed by d'Uva, *Un'erudita del secolo xv*.

[183] Pesaro, Biblioteca Oliveriana, 454 gives a 'lauda fatta per madonna Battista Donna del Signor Ghaleazzo de Malatesti da Pesaro, dipoi vochata suora Geronima dell'ordine di Santa Chiara, doctissima in poesia e di vita perfettissime' (fos. 39–46), three other *laude*, and a 'moralis cantilena'—all in Italian.

[184] Allan, *The Concept of Woman II*, 724.

[185] Ambrogio Traversari, *Epistulae et Orationes* (Florence: Typ. Caesareas, 1757), 1073–5. He quotes examples of Christianized lines from Virgil and Horace. The letter is translated in King and Rabil, *Her Immaculate Hand*, 91–105, but from G. B. Contarini, *Anecdota Veneta* (Venice, 1757), 33–44, which seems to vary from the text in Traversari (there are several MSS, Modena, Biblioteca Estense, Est. lat. 772 (α R 8,13), fos. 44–49ᵛ, Venice, Biblioteca Marciana, Lat. XII 155 (3953), fos. 8oᵛ–89ᵛ, and also Prague, Lobkovitz Collection, 522, nov. xxiii G 44 (from *Iter Italicum*), so there may be significant textual variations).

[186] The verse of Damasus, pope and poet, was immensely influential in the Renaissance: the most recent critical edition is that of Antonio Ferrua (Vatican City: Tipografia poliglotta, 1942). The hymns attributed to Hilary in Correr's time are now recognized as spurious, though three do survive which Correr could not have known (*Hymni Latini Antiquissimi LXXV, Psalmi III* (Heidelberg: F. H. Kerle, 1956), 31–5). Hilary's style is complex and bespeaks an excellent education. He is probably cited here (rather than, e.g., Sedulius or Juvencus) because Correr believed that he had addressed verse to his daughter.

the later Laurentia Strozzi, discussed in Chapter 11, is a good example of a nun who actually did succeed in integrating humanism with monasticism. More generally, with the exception of a fifteenth-century Ferrarese Poor Clare—possibly Caterina Vegri—who produced 5,610 unmetrical Latin verses on Jesus (a prodigious accomplishment but not a humanist one), no Latin verse seems to have been written in Renaissance Italian convents.[187] The present state of the evidence for Renaissance nuns therefore suggests that fifteenth-century convents, though possibly tolerant of humanist reading, were not hospitable to independent humanist activity on the part of their inmates.

---

[187] Antonio Libanori, *Ferrara d'Oro*, 2 vols. (Ferrara: Alfonso and Giambattista Maresti, 1665–74), ii. 3, 73. See also Pellegrino Antonio Orlandi, *Notizie degli scrittori bolognesi* (Bologna: Constantino Pisarri, 1714), 56–7. This is a very unusual case of 'automatic' composition in Latin, analogous to the vernacular productions of Protestant prophetesses such as Anna Trapnel, since the nun herself held them to be dictated to her by Christ (on Trapnel, see Jane Stevenson and Peter Davidson (eds.), *Early Modern Women Poets, 1520–1700* (Oxford: Oxford University Press, 2001), 295–301; on Vegri more generally, see references in n. 181).

7. Women and Latin in Renaissance France

The story of women and Latin in France is necessarily a sub-plot of the trajectory of Latin itself in French-speaking territories. The Latinate Frenchwomen of the high Middle Ages probably outnumber those of the rest of Europe, especially if Anglo-Normans are included, but this distinguished record is not maintained past the twelfth century. However, this is not so much because Frenchwomen were debarred from participation in culture, as on account of the precocious strength of French vernacular literature in the late Middle Ages, which was being promoted by Louis IX as early as the thirteenth century.[1]

Women played a positive role in this French turn towards the vernacular. In the twelfth century, Matilda, first wife of Henry I of England (mentioned in Chapter 5), commissioned a version of *The Voyage of Saint Brendan* for herself in Latin, but then arranged for a translation into Norman French 'for her ladies and maidens'.[2] By the thirteenth century, Latin was increasingly a language for technical discussion among churchmen rather than the primary vehicle for literature, and translation was therefore a growth industry.[3] King Louis IX commissioned Vincent de Beauvais's *Speculum Historiale* in 1238, but almost as soon as the ink was dry, his wife, Marguerite de Provence, commissioned a French translation from John de Vignai.[4] In 1298, Raymond Lull presented King Philippe IV with his *Arbor Philosophiae Amoris*, and at the same time gave Queen Jeanne the same work in French.[5] Some non-royal late medieval women were also conspicuous as patronesses of translations, notably Yolande of Saint Pol. A variety of early

---

[1] Lori J. Walters, 'The Royal Vernacular: Poet and Patron in Christine de Pizan's Charles V and the Sept Psaumes Allegorisées', in Renate Blumenfeld-Kosinski et al. (eds.), *The Vernacular Spirit* (New York: Palgrave, 2002), 145–82 (p. 147).

[2] Dominica Legge, *Anglo-Norman Literature and its Background* (Oxford: Clarendon Press, 1963), 10.

[3] Stephen G. Nichols, 'Foreword', in June Hall McCash (ed.), *The Cultural Patronage of Medieval Women* (Athens: University of Georgia Press, 1996), pp. xvi–xvii.

[4] Susan Groag Bell, 'Medieval Women Book Owners', In J. Bennett et al. (eds.), *Sisters and Workers in the Middle Ages* (Chicago: Chicago University Press, 1989), 153: Bell also has other stories about the commissioning of vernacular translations. See also Anne-Marie Legaré, 'Reassessing Women's Librar-ies in Late Medieval France', *Renaissance Studies*, 10.2 (1996), 209–36 (p. 221). Queen Marguerite also commissioned a work directly from Vincent of Beauvais, *De Eruditione Filiorum Nobilium* (1247/9), which, at her request, contained chapters on noble daughters (based on Jerome's advice to Laeta). June Hall McCash, 'Cultural Patronage: An Overview', in McCash (ed.), *The Cultural Patronage of Medieval Women*, 1–49 (p. 22).

[5] James W. Thompson, *The Literacy of the Laity in the Middle Ages* (Berkeley and Los Angeles: University of California Press, 1939), 132. See also M. Jones, 'Les Manuscrits d'Anne de Bretagne, reine de France', *Mémoires de la Société Historique et Archéologique de Bretagne* (1978), 43–81 and Thomas Tolley, 'States of Independence: Women Regents as Patrons of the Visual Arts in Renaissance France', *Renaissance Studies*, 10.2 (1996), 237–58.

thirteenth-century translations of Latin historical and hagiographic texts have been associated with Yolande's patronage,[6] but most conspicuously, she sponsored a vernacular translation of the history of Pseudo-Turpin. The prologue to the translation states, 'when he knew he was going to die, he sent the book to his sister, the good Yolande, countess of St Pol. And he begged her to keep the book for love of him, for as long as she lived. And the worthy countess has kept the book up to now. And now she asks me to translate it from Latin into vernacular prose because not everyone can read it in Latin, and it will be better preserved in the vernacular.'[7] The perception that any work would be better preserved in the vernacular than in Latin bespeaks in itself a major cultural shift from the assumptions of the twelfth century.

However, even in the thirteenth century, there were still aristocratic laywomen who read Latin. Blanche of Navarre was apparently one such, since Adam of Perseigne sent sermons to her in Latin, saying they would lose in translation, assuming, therefore, that she could read them.[8] Alix, Countess of Chartres (daughter of the Latin-literate Eleanor of Aquitaine), was another lay correspondent of Adam of Perseigne to whom he wrote in Latin, knowing she understood the language at least up to a point—he adds that if she had any difficulty with his prose, she should ask her chaplain to explain it.[9] For the most part, however, late medieval educated Frenchwomen—even queens—read French, and accounts of Latinate women are even harder to find in the fourteenth century than in the thirteenth.

Christine de Pizan (Italian by origin, but French by formation) is perhaps the most important woman seriously to study and argue about the position of women in this period, and also one of the most learned. Though she wrote in Middle French, her education was Latin based: she read extensively in Latin, and translated part of Thomas Aquinas's *Commentary on Aristotle's Metaphysics*.[10] It has been strongly argued by Lori J. Walters that she was capable of writing a Latin distich, though probably not of extended prose composition in Latin, but that, in any case, she had chosen to 'situate herself as "translator" '.[11] Further, some Latin was being taught to women in Paris in 1380: the Cantor of Notre-Dame summoned a meeting of teachers who included women specifically said to be teaching the *ars grammatica*: obviously, they were educated women themselves, but they were also more likely to have been teaching girls than boys.[12] Yolande of France, Duchess of

---

[6] C. Meredith-Jones, 'The Chronicle of Turpin in Saintonge', *Speculum*, 13.2 (1938), 160–70, Gabrielle Spiegel, *Romancing the Past: The Rise of Vernacular Prose Historiography in the Thirteenth Century* (Berkeley and Los Angeles: University of California Press, 1993), 12, 70–1, 93, 344.

[7] Paris, Bibliothèque Nationale de France, Fr. 124. See also Bell, 'Medieval Women Book Owners'.

[8] Adam de Perseigne, *Lettres*, ed. Jean Bouvet, 2 vols. (Paris: Éditions du Cerf, 1960), ep. 30.

[9] Ibid. ep. 27.

[10] Liliane Dulac and Christine Reno, 'L'Humanisme vers 1400: essai d'exploration à partir d'un cas marginal: Christine de Pizan traductrice de Thomas d'Aquin', in Monique Ornato and Nicole Pons (eds.), *Pratiques de la culture écrite en France au XVe siècle* (Louvain-la-Neuve: Fédération Internationale des Instituts d'Études Médiévales, 1995), 160–78, Susan Groag Bell, 'Christine de Pizan (1364–1430): Humanism and the Problem of the Studious Woman', *Feminist Studies*, 3 (1975), 173–84, assumes that her Latin was scant, but recent work is revising this position.

[11] 'The Royal Vernacular', 163–6, quotation, p. 172.

[12] John William Adamson, *The Illiterate Anglo-Saxon, and Other Essays on Education* (Cambridge: Cambridge University Press, 1966), 59.

Savoy, was writing in Latin to Lorenzo de' Medici in 1474,[13] and at least one French abbess, Maria de Alberta, was able to write a Latin letter in 1441, but she was probably quite unusual by that date.[14]

The queens and the court

The Renaissance brought about a change in this as in other respects. The 'New Learning' was strongly focused on Latin, and sixteenth-century France boasted both Latin-literate royal women and Latinate humanist households. The French royal family itself became remarkable for highly educated women from as early as the fifteenth century. Anne de Beaujeu, daughter of Louis XI and Charlotte of Savoy, acted as regent for her brother Charles VIII and also educated a whole group of important little girls, who included her brother's subsequently repudiated fiancée Marguerite of Austria (later Regent of the Netherlands for her father the Emperor Maximilian), Louise of Savoy, later mother of François I, and her own daughter, Suzanne de Bourbon (it is worth noting in this context that the practice of educating princesses in a group by definition produced a cohort of female peers who had a princess's education).[15] The curriculum was a humanist one and included the study of Plato, with the assistance of Boethius' commentary.[16]

Anne de Bretagne (b. 1476) arrived in France as queen (first of Charles VIII, then of Louis XII) in 1496, already a woman of culture and refinement. She became a patron of letters, and pursued her own intellectual interests.[17] Tolley observes that 'it is possible to detect in Anne's choice of reading a particular preoccupation with women in positions of power'.[18] She was educated as a future reigning duchess from the age of 3, and was consequently taught French, Breton, Latin, Greek, and some Hebrew. She was crowned as duchess at 10, two years before her father's death,[19] and pressured into marrying Charles by his sister Anne

---

[13] Florence, Archivio di Stato, Archivio della Reppublica, Lettere varie 15, fo. 108.

[14] Printed in Léopold Delisle (ed.), *Rouleaux des morts du ixᵉ au xvᵉ siècle recueillis et publiés par la Société de l'Histoire de France* (Paris: Veuve J. Renouard, 1866), 483–4.

[15] Other examples include the group around the Infanta Maria of Portugal (see Américo da Costa Ramalho, *Para a história do humanismo em Portugal* (Coimbra: Instituto Nacional de la Investigação Cientifica, 1988), 90), and the group around Mary Tudor, which included Katherine Parr and Katherine Willoughby, the future Duchess of Suffolk.

[16] Anne de Beaujeu has left a useful insight into the education and conduct of French royal women in this period, a set of instructions for her daughter Suzanne de Bourbon. Leningrad, Publicnaja Biblioteka, Franc. Q VIII 2, printed as Anne de Beaujeu, *A la requeste de treshaulte et puissante princesse ma dame Susanne de Bourbon* (Lyon: Le Prince [?1534]). See also Christopher Hare, *The High and Puissant Princess Marguerite of Austria* (London: Harper & Brothers, 1907), 34.

[17] L. Clark Keating, *Studies on the Literary Salon in France, 1550–1615* (Cambridge, Mass.: Harvard University Press, 1941), 8. It is worth noting that these included commissioning a work on famous women, Antoine Dufour, *Les Vies des femmes illustres* (*c.*1505), now ed. G. Jeanneau, *Antoine Dufour, O.P.: Les Vies des femmes célèbres* (Geneva: Droz, 1970).

[18] Tolley, 'States of Independence'. See also Jones, 'Les Manuscrits d'Anne de Bretagne, reine de France'.

[19] Lisa Hopkins, *Women Who Would be Kings* (London: Vision Press, 1991), 28–30.

de Beaujeu (she herself had wished to marry the Emperor Maximilian of Austria). During her widowhood, after her marriage to Charles and before her remarriage to his brother Louis, she returned to Brittany and began striking coins with her image as duchess. She created an order of ladies, which she called 'la Cordelière', a sort of equivalent to the male orders of chivalry. She was the mother of Claude, later wife of François I, and Renée, later duchess of Ferrara, both of whom were thoroughly and humanistically educated.[20] Louise of Savoy, mother of François I, who had been taught by Anne de Beaujeu, was able to follow her son's education closely, choose books for him, and commission new works.[21]

In the next generation, Louise's daughter, the sister of François I, Marguerite de Navarre (also called Marguerite d'Angoulême, Duchess of Alençon and later Queen of Navarre), was not only a poet in French, but one of the most enthusiastic of French disciples of the Neoplatonic philosopher Marsilio Ficino.[22] She was taught Latin, Spanish, and Italian in childhood, and in later years taught herself Greek and studied Hebrew with Paul Paradis.[23] She had a strong affection for Latin: the humanist Nicolas Bourbon, whom she had entrusted with the education of her daughter Jeanne d'Albret, once apologized to her in Latin for having dedicated another work to her in their native tongue.[24] In 1517, François gave his sister the duchy of Berry, including the University of Bourges, which she thereafter patronized to its advantage—she invited Andrea Alciato to the school of jurisprudence (he was the tutor of the important Reformation leaders Jean Calvin and Théodore de Bèze), and gave the chair of Greek and Latin to Jacques Amyot.[25] As this patronage suggests, she was also the undisputed patroness of reform thinking in France.[26] Brantôme mentions that before her brother came to the throne, the learned men of Louis XII's circle referred to her as their Maecenas, and 'foreign ambassadors reported her impressive learning when they had occasion to converse with her'.[27] Charmarie Blaisdell concludes, '[she] was reared as a princess and educated to serve the crown. In accordance with the ideals of humanism and the "new learning" which had become fashionable at court, aristocratic women often received educations comparable or superior to those of their brothers and husbands.'[28]

---

20 See Émile Gabory, *Anne de Bretagne* (Paris: Plon, 1941).

21 Legaré, 'Reassessing Women's Libraries', 109.

22 Frances Yates, *The French Academies of the Sixteenth Century* (London: Warburg Institute, 1947; repr. 1988), 3. C. J. Blaisdell, 'Marguerite de Navarre and her Circle (1492–1549)', in Jean R. Brink (ed.), *Privileging Gender in Early Modern England* (Kirksville, Mo.: Sixteenth Century Journal Publishers, 1993), 36–53.

23 Winifred Stephens, *Margaret of France, Duchess of Savoy, 1523–74* (London: John Lane, Booley Head, 1912), 36.

24 Nancy L. Roelker, *Queen of Navarre: Jeanne d'Albret, 1528–1572* (Cambridge: Mass.: Belknap Press, 1968), 33.

25 Stephens, *Margaret of France*, 138.

26 See Pierre Jourda, *Marguerite d'Angoulême* (Paris: H. Champion, 1930).

27 Pierre de Bourdeille, Seigneur de Brantôme, *Œuvres complètes*, II vols., ed. C. J. N. Monmerqué, (Paris: Veuve Jules Renouard, 1864–82), viii. 115, 118.

28 Blaisdell, 'Marguerite de Navarre and her Circle (1492–1549)', 38.

Marguerite's daughter Jeanne d'Albret was competently educated in French and Latin: though she wrote exclusively in French, she translated one of Erasmus' Latin *Dialogues* into that language, probably as an exercise.[29] Marguerite's niece Marguerite de France, Duchess of Savoy, the daughter of François I, was not only an acknowledged scholar, but patroness of the early literary efforts of the Pléiade poets, particularly Ronsard.[30] She learned Latin, Italian, and Greek, and the Venetian ambassador Cavalli wrote that she attained to complete mastery over all three tongues. As an adult, she took pleasure in reading Plutarch in the original with Amyot and discussing the *Ethics* of Aristotle with the Florentine poet Baccio del Bene. She was probably taught together with her brothers, whose tutor was Benedictus Tagliacarnus, once secretary to the republic of Genoa. Her Greek teacher was Pontronius.[31] As Duchess of Berry (in succession to her aunt Marguerite de Navarre) she gathered literary friends around her to form a salon of Pléiade poets and university professors between 1550 and 1559.[32] She was also much concerned with the University of Bourges, founded in 1463, which already owed much to both Anne de Bretagne and Marguerite de Navarre, and appointed Jacques de Cujas to succeed her aunt's appointment, Alciato, in the chair of jurisprudence.

Catherine de Médicis, the Italian queen of Henri II, was less literary in her interests than the family she married into (though, like many Italian women of her social class, she was well educated, and her tastes included Greek and mathematics, as well as hunting, as can be seen from the remains of her large library),[33] but she was nevertheless of considerable cultural importance. She came to France in 1533, when she was only 14, and was educated by her husband's aunt Marguerite de Navarre. Charmarie Blaisdell has observed that 'A direct line of female influence on French political and cultural life can be traced from Anne de Beaujeu through these women [Anne de Bretagne, Louise of Savoy] to Catherine de Medici... educated and influenced by Marguerite de Navarre, Catherine continued the tradition of female influence and dominated the French court and politics in the second half of the sixteenth century.'[34] Interestingly, despite the Salic law which barred women from the French throne, she was the dedicatee of a treatise on

[29] London, British Library, Add. 22782. Her education is outlined by Roelker, *Queen of Navarre*, 32–3.

[30] Roger Peyre, *Une princesse de la Renaissance: Marguerite de France, duchesse de Berry, duchesse de Savoie* (Paris: E. Paul, 1902), Paule H. Bordeaux, *Louise de Savoie* (Paris: Plon, 1954). Blaisdell, 'Marguerite de Navarre and her Circle (1492–1549)'.

[31] See Michel de L'Hospital, *Œuvres complètes*, ed. P.-J.-S. Dufey, 3 vols. (Paris: A. Boulland, 1824–5), i. 24, 96: de L'Hospital asks Pontronius whether amid her many cares the princess still delights in the society of Cicero, Virgil, and Horace. Stephens, *Margaret of France*, 37–8.

[32] This may account for an Italian collection of poems dedicated to her: *Rime de gli Academici Eterei dedicate alla serenissima Madama Margherita di Vallois duchesse da Savoia* (n.p., n.d.).

[33] Her collection included a large number of Greek and Latin books on all subjects, and also books in Hebrew. A 776-article inventory made in 1589 estimated her library at 16,200 volumes. See Ernest Quentin Bauchart, *Les Femmes bibliophiles de France* (Paris: Damascène Morgand, 1886), i. 93.

[34] Brink (ed.), *Privileging Gender*, 37. See Irene Mahoney, *Madame Catherine* (New York: McCann and Geogheghan, 1975).

women as rulers by Estienne Forcadel.[35] Catherine, in turn, presided over a royal nursery which included not just her own daughters, but her daughter-in-law Mary Stuart, Queen of Scots.

As a potential ruling Queen of Scotland and Queen of France, Mary Stuart was taught Latin. She is on record as having given a Latin oration in her early teens on women's capacity for knowledge before Henri II.[36]

She was extremely learned in Latin. When she was thirteen or fourteen, she declaimed before King Henri, the Queen and the whole court, publically in the Salle du Louvre, an oration in Latin which she had made, ... defending against general opinion that it was appropriate to women to know letters and the liberal arts.

This oral defence must have some relationship with the 'defence of learned women' which appears in Mary's surviving Latin exercise book, which is not the fruit of deep and wide research.[37] Poliziano's letter 13 in book III of his *Epistolae* is on the subject of learned women, prompted by his acquaintance with the scholarly prodigy Cassandra Fedele,[38] and Poliziano's letter together with the commentary of Franciscus Silvius in the edition of Poliziano printed in Paris in 1523 contains almost all the names used in this exercise. The interest of Mary's book of themes is not exhausted by this episode. One of their most salient features is that some of them are couched in the form of letters to her cousin Elizabeth, a disconcerting reminder of the way that the English throne was kept before her eyes even in her early youth. Soon after she returned to Scotland, Mary was reported to be reading Livy every evening after dinner with George Buchanan.[39] She also owned a copy of Sallust, now at Trinity College, Dublin, which contains her autograph signature and many manuscript notes, suggesting close study.[40] Both Livy and Sallust were standard fare for Renaissance rulers.

Mary's sisters-in-law, the three daughters of Henri II, were equally well educated: Elisabeth, afterwards Queen of Spain, Claude, Duchess of Lorraine, and yet another Marguerite, Marguerite de Valois, who married the future Henri IV, then King of Navarre. All three were taught by Jean Dorat, the greatest Hellenist in Paris.[41] Dorat was himself a member of the group of humanist poets referred to as the Pléiade, though considerably older than the other poets, who looked on him as their great teacher and classical expert. This influence was diffused largely through his lectures: he was teaching in the decade before 1550 at the Collège de Coqueret,

[35] *Foeminae Illustres Regnis Gubernandis*, p. II (pp. 35–49) of his *Henrico III Francorum et Poloniae Regi, Relata* (Paris: Guillaume Chaudiere, 1579).

[36] Pierre de Bourdeille, Seigneur de Brantôme, *Œuvres complètes*, ed. Lalanne, vii. 405.

[37] *Latin Themes of Mary Queen of Scots*, ed. Anatole de Montaiglon (London: Wharton Club, 1855), letter xxv.

[38] M. L. King and A. Rabil (trans.), *Her Immaculate Hand* (Asheville, NC: Pegasus Press, 1997), 69–73, and see Ch. 6.

[39] I. D. Macfarlane, *Buchanan* (London: Duckworth, 1981), 208. Randolph to Cecil, St Andrews, 7 Apr. 1562 (*CSP Foreign* (1561–2), ed. Joseph Stevenson (London: Longmans, Green, Reader & Dyer, 1865), 584).

[40] *Notes & Queries*, 1st ser. 4 (1851), 316, 385–6.

[41] Robert J. Sealy, *The Palace Academy of Henry III* (Geneva: Droz, 1981), 14.

of which he was principal. There he was joined by his young pupil Jean-Antoine de Baïf, Ronsard, and others.[42]

In 1554, Dorat combined his tuition of the princesses with that of their bastard half-brother Henri d'Angoulême in the house of Jean de Morel, who then carried on with Henri's education: Henri d'Angoulême grew up conspicuously learned and stayed with Morel until 1567. This will certainly have allowed the Valois princesses to meet three of the most learned young women of Paris, Morel's own daughters, Camille, Diane, and Lucrèce (on whom more later); but it is also worth noting that Dorat was strongly supportive of learned women. His own daughter Madeleine is said to have been learned, and was the recipient of elegant Latin eclogues,[43] though she has not left a reputation as a writer. He exchanged verses and letters with learned women: he supported Anne de Marquets' publication of her *Sonets* with a poem,[44] contributed to the Seymour sisters' *Hecatodistichon* (discussed in Chapter 10),[45] and wrote verses for Camille de Morel, who also wrote verses to him.[46]

Among the princesses, Marguerite de Valois ('la reine Margot') most conspicuously took full advantage of her education. Seventy-two volumes of Greek and Latin classics from her extensive library survive, including Seneca, Aristotle, Cicero, Apthonius, Justinian, Ausonius, Homer, Lucan, Virgil, Callimachus, Pindar, and Pausanias.[47] She was a highly sophisticated woman, and her marriage to the somewhat rustic Henri de Bourbon in 1572 was not a meeting of affinities. Furthermore, it precipitated the St Bartholomew's Day Massacre, during which she defended her Huguenot bridegroom with courage, and refused to consider a divorce. It may have struck her that the debt her husband thus owed her was one which potentially gave her an unusual amount of leverage in her marriage. Like her great-aunt, the first Queen Marguerite of Navarre, she not only read a great deal but also wrote poetry—and as her library suggests, she was also fond of studying the classics, the Scriptures, and philosophy. The verse which is securely attributed to her is in French, but she may also have written Latin verse: a poem now in the Marciana in Venice is attributed to her, and her level of education certainly makes this possible.[48] She owned more than a thousand manuscripts and printed books.[49] When Polish ambassadors arrived in Paris in August 1573 to invite her brother to the throne, Marguerite made a dazzling appearance, and dazzled them no less,

---

[42] H. Chamard, *Histoire de la Pléiade*, 4 vols. (Paris: H. Didier, 1939–63), i. 81–5.

[43] Paris, Bibliothèque Nationale de France, Dupuy 951, fos. 185ʳ–186ʳ, 186ᵛ–190ᵛ.

[44] *Sonets, prieres et devises en forme de pasquins, pour l'assemblée de Messieurs les prelats et docteurs, tenue à Poissy* (Paris: Guillaume Morel, 1566): includes Jean Dorat, 'In Annae Marquetae Virginis Sacra Poemata', sig. b 1ᵛ.

[45] *Hecadodistichon* (1550 edn.), sig. c 2ʳ and ᵛ, 7ʳ. There are further verses in the 2nd edn. of 1551.

[46] 'Nam Carolus te qui doceat, is mihi Praeses docetur', printed by Pierre de Nolhac, *Ronsard et l'humanisme* (Paris: E. Champion, 1921), 176.

[47] Bauchard, *Les Femmes bibliophiles*, i. 146–59.

[48] Éliane Viennot, 'Écriture et culture chez Marguerite de Valois', in Nativel (ed.), *Femmes savantes*, 167–70. And see also É. Viennot, 'Les Poésies de Marguerite de Valois', *XVIIe siècle*, 183 (1994), 349–75. She left little poetry, though in a variety of metres.

[49] Simonne Ratel, 'La Cour de la reine Marguerite', *Revue du seizième siècle*, 11 (1924), 194.

according to Brantôme, by responding to the Bishop of Poznań's Latin address to her with a graceful and pertinent speech in the same language.[50]

Marguerite played an active role in politics on at least one occasion, when she was sent to negotiate with the rebellious Netherlands, and was successful in persuading them to invite her youngest brother the Duc d'Alençon, a moderate Catholic, as governor. However, her life was rendered unproductive by the almost complete mutual indifference between herself and her husband, complicated by her staunch Catholicism and the Protestantism of her husband's kingdom of Navarre; he kept a series of mistresses, and she lived apart from him with a series of lovers, usually in different towns, so she was less part of the political and diplomatic life of Navarre than her abilities and education might have seemed to justify. Furthermore, the mutual dislike between herself and her other brother Henri III ensured that he did not make the kind of use of her that contemporary Hapsburgs were making of their female relatives.

After the death of Henri III and the accession of Henri IV, Marguerite became offically Queen of France, though only in name. Negotiations between herself and Henri, anxious to marry his mistress Gabrielle d'Estrées and legitimate their sons, were prolonged by the simple fact that she required to be bought off and there was no money to spare: it was not until ten years after the death of Henri III that she finally received the funds promised, and duly petitioned the pope to end her marriage. She was allowed to keep the title of Queen of Navarre, but no longer that of Queen of France. Gabrielle died of a stroke shortly before the divorce came through, but Henri married Marie de Médicis, who bore a son, Louis, nine months after the marriage, securing the line. Marguerite and Henri became good friends in their later years, addressing one another as brother and sister. She was allowed to take up residence near the court: she became friendly with Marie de Médicis, and even attended the coronation which installed her as Queen of France: thus the last of the Valois walked symbolically with the first of the Bourbons.

From the early sixteenth century, the new learning of the royal women began to spread out into the aristocracy.[51] Aymée de Lafayette, Baillive of Caen, was Jeanne d'Albret's foster-mother and *gouvernante*: the inscription she placed on her husband's tomb suggests she was also Latin-literate, since it involves verbal play on her own name, Aymée, in Latin *amata* (the beloved): 'Dying while yet alive, Amata built this for her beloved (*amatus*) husband with everflowing tears.'[52] Anne de Parthenay, Mme de Pons (d. 1549), an avowed Protestant and friend of Renée of Ferrara, certainly read Latin.[53] Her niece Catherine de Parthenay, Dame de Rohan-Soubise (1554–1631), read Greek. She translated Isocrates, spent many

[50] Pierre de Bourdeille, Seigneur de Brantôme, *Œuvres complètes*, ed. Lalanne, viii. 40–1.

[51] A new attitude towards women is suggested by works such as Etienne Forcadel, *De Illustribus Foeminis* (Paris: Guill. Chaudière, 1579).

[52] 'Viva moriens amata amatissimo conjugi continuiis cum lachrymis construxit.' Roelker, *Jeanne d'Albret*, 21.

[53] Paul Rousselot, *Histoire de l'éducation des femmes* (Paris: Didier et (ie., 1883), i. 169.

years studying mathematics and astronomy,[54] and also wrote a play, *Holopherne*, performed in 1574. Diane de Poitiers, mistress of François I, was educated as well as sophisticated and beautiful: on the evidence of surviving books from her library, her reading included Latin classics and the Church Fathers.[55]

Despite the evidence that a number of women of the court other than the Valois themselves studed Latin, humanism was not a major aspect of court culture. Hilarion de Coste, writing in 1630, remarked that as early as the 1570s, the French court was, compared to other European courts, notably short of Latinists.[56] Probably the most spectacularly learned noblewomen of the Valois court was Catherine de Clermont, Duchesse de Retz.[57] Nicolas Rapin states that she wrote both classically 'measured' and ordinary verse (suggesting she understood something of classical metrics, and possibly that she wrote Latin verse), and describes her reading Chrysostom, Augustine, Plato, Plutarch, Cato, Cicero, the two Senecas, and Virgil: plainly she read Greek as well as Latin.[58] A poem to the Duchesse de Retz by Marie de Romieu of Viviers stresses, 'Greek is familiar to you ... Latin is ordinary, and the Italian tongue.'[59] The conversation at one of her dinner parties is enthusiastically described by Etienne Pasquier who says that Macrobius could have made a book of it (referring to Macrobius' *Saturnalia*, a late antique book of table-talk which amongst other subjects discusses the wit of Augustus' daughter Julia).[60] She was a woman of grave and religious character, who exerted some influence on public affairs. Yates suggests that she is the most significant French woman academician in the sixteenth century.[61] Her *album amicorum* survives, containing more than 150 poems in French, Latin, and Italian—all unfortunately anonymous.[62] When a group of Eastern European notables came to Paris in 1573 to offer the crown of Poland to Henri III, it was the Duchesse de Retz who played the extremely responsible role of official interpreter, and also made a Latin oration.[63] Her achievement was striking, but the group from Poland, Lithuania, and the

[54] Margaret Alic, *Hypatia's Heritage* (London: The Women's Press, 1986), 134.

[55] Sarah Sider, 'Dianne de Poitiers' [*sic*], in *WWRR*, 158–76. See also Quentin Bauchart, *Les Femmes bibliophiles*, i.

[56] Hilarion de Coste, *Les Eloges et vies des reynes, princesses, dames et demoiselles illustres en pieté, courage et doctrine* (Paris: Sébastien Cramoisy, 1630).

[57] Her contemporary reputation is confirmed by the obscure poet Du Souhait, who lists her as one of the nine French Muses in his *Les Neuf muses françoises* ... (Paris: J. Rezé, 1599) (the others are Mme and Mlle de Guise, Mmes de Marmoutiers, de Menelay, d'Urfé, de Revel, de Saincthoussany, and de Perot: a list of the forgotten, none of whom seem to have published anything at the time).

[58] Nicolas Rapin, *Œuvres latines et françoises* (Paris: P. Chevalier, 1610).

[59] *Les Premiers œuvres poétiques de Ma Damoiselle Marie de Romieu, Vivaroise* (Paris: Lucas Breyer, 1581), fo. 11.

[60] Etienne Pasquier, *Œuvres complètes*, 2 vols. (Geneva: Slatkine, 1971), ii. 898. See Amy Richlin, 'Julia's Jokes, Galla Placidia, and the Roman Use of Women as Political Icons', in Barbara Garlick et al. (eds.), *Stereotypes of Women in Power* (Westport, Conn.: Greenwood Press, 1992), 65–91.

[61] Yates, *French Academies*, 105, and Sealy, *The Palace Academy of Henry III*.

[62] Paris, Bibliothèque Nationale de France, Fr. 25455.

[63] Jacques Lavand, *Un poète de cour au temps des derniers Valois* (Paris: E. Droz, 1936), 77, de Coste, *Les Eloges et vies des reynes*, 332–3: '[elle] servit plus souvent d'Interprete à leurs Maiestez.'

Palatinate were also struck by how few other French courtiers, of either gender, could meet them on equal terms:[64]

They were astonished that the greater part of our French nobility neither spoke nor understood the Latin language. Certainly, the nobility of Germany, Poland, Hungary, Flanders, Scotland and England and the other countries which we consider semi-barbarian excel above ours, in that they study literature, for the most part, as far as the knowledge of Latin, which serves them for conversing and negotiating with other nations.

Another woman associated with court circles is one of the few Renaissance French nuns to make any sort of impact on the literary world. She was, of course, highly aristocratic. Her name was Claudine de Bectoz, daughter of Jacques, Vibailly de Graisivaudan, and she took the veil at Saint Honorat-de-Tarascon under the name Scholastica (after the sister of St Benedict).[65] She is described as having acquired a perfect knowledge of Latin authors: Domenichi claimed, a year after her death, that she equalled the writers of the Middle Ages, a somewhat backhanded compliment from a Renaissance humanist.[66] François I and Marguerite de Navarre visited her on their joint progress through Provence, and she exchanged letters with French and Italian humanists.[67] She was nominated as abbess of her convent on 1 January 1542, and died there on 17 March 1547. She is said by contemporaries to have written Latin verse, but nothing seems to have been kept.[68]

Although the nuns of Sainte-Claire in Grenoble were found to be translating works by Luther from Latin to French in the first quarter of the sixteenth century,[69] the only other high-profile literary nun in sixteenth-century France flourished in the second half of the century: Anne de Marquets, celebrated by Jean Dorat, and also admired by Karel Utenhove.[70] She was a Dominican nun, professed at Poissy, who read Greek and Latin with facility: Claude d'Espence asked

---

[64] '[ils] furent estonnez la pluspart de ce que nostre Noblesse Française ne parloit n'y n'entendoit la langue Latine. Certes la Noblesse d'Allemagne, de Pologne, de Hongrie, de Flandres, d'Ecosse, et d'Angleterre, et les autres pays que nous estimons demy-barbares, excelle pourtant sur la nostre, en ce qu'elle estudie aux bonnes lettres, pour le moins iusques à la cognoissance de la langue Latine, qui leur sert pour converser et traiter avec les nations estrangeres.' De Coste, *Les Eloges et vies des reynes*, 334.

[65] St Scholastica (6th century) had a reputation as the writer of a rule for nuns and many letters, which may have influenced her choice. Prospero Mondosio, *Bibliotheca Romana, seu Romanorum Scriptorum Centuria*, 2 vols. (Rome: Francisco de Lazaris, 1692), ii. 124.

[66] *La nobiltà delle donne* (Venice: Gabriel Giolito, 1549), 271–2.

[67] Evelyne Berriot-Salvadore, *Les Femmes dans la société française de la Renaissance* (Geneva: Droz, 1990), 423, has found Latin letters in Aix, Bibliothèque Méjanes, 761: see U. L. Saulnier, *Études Rabelaisiennes* (Geneva), 5 (1964), 65, 119, 132.

[68] Apart from the three letters in Aix already mentioned, the only other surviving work found by the author of the article in *Dictionnaire de biographie française* (Paris: Librairie Letouzey & Ané 1933–   ), v, cols. 1254–5, is her *Response* to the *Chanson* of Bonaventure des Périers.

[69] Berriot-Salvadore, *Les Femmes*, 343.

[70] Dorat wrote a Latin poem of congratulation to her, printed in Anne de Marquets, *Sonets, prieres et devises, en forme de pasquins*, sig. A 6ᵛ, and also in Paris, Bibliothèque Nationale de France, Dupuy 951. Utenhove sent a Latin letter to Antoinette de Loynes, Munich, Staatsbibliothek, 10383, fo. 264 (May 1562), with two odes by 'Anna Marquesia', which Paul de Foix (then French ambassador to England) considered very beautiful.

her assistance with translating a Latin elegy in 1563.[71] Most of her poetry is in French, but she wrote a few Latin distichs, and published a translation from the Latin of Flaminio.[72] Curiously (considering the latter's attraction towards Calvinism), she was an admirer of Jeanne d'Albret.[73]

The academies, so strongly a feature of Italian intellectual life, also sprang up in sixteenth-century France, initially under royal patronage. Women were certainly involved with the French Palace Academy. The Duchesse de Retz, already mentioned as one of the most learned women at court,[74] is known to have debated the excellence of the moral and intellectual virtues there with Mme de Lignerolles.[75] Dale, writing intelligence reports to Sir Francis Walsingham in 1576, mentions the Academy's weekly meeting in the king's chamber: 'the auditors are none but the King, the Queen of Navarre, the Duke of Nevers, the Countess of Retz, and another lady or two.'[76] The involvement of women in such a context was both practically and psychologically straightforward, since the meetings took place in private space (the king's closet), not in any kind of public arena. Marguerite de Valois also founded an academy in her Paris residence on her return from Usson, which was perhaps more like a forerunner of the later salons.[77] The friends who met here included the very learned Mlle de Beaulieu.[78] The Duchesse de Retz hosted similar meetings,[79] and another venture of the same kind took place in Lyon, at the home of the Duchesse's 'bas-bleu' mother-in-law, Marie de Pierre-Vire (mother of her second husband, Albert de Gondi), particularly between 1532 and 1536.[80] This group was called the *Sodalitium*, and its habitués were *sodales*: a Latin word for 'companion' which is without gender overtones.[81] Another

---

[71] Claude d'Espence and Anne de Marquets, *Urbanum Meditationum in hoc Sacro et Civili Bello Elegia* (Paris: Morel, 1563). Berriot-Salvadore, *Les Femmes*, 425, and see Mary Hilarine Seiler, *Anne de Marquets, poétesse religieuse du xvie siècle* (Washington: Catholic University of America, 1931), 45–50.

[72] Anne de Marquets, *Les Divines Poésies de Marc Antoine Flaminius, mises en français avec le latin respondant* (Paris: Nicolas Chesneau, 1568).

[73] *Catalogue des livres composant la bibliothèque du Baron J. de Rothschild*, 5 vols. (Paris, 1884–1920), ii. 2918.

[74] Marguerite de Navarre speaks of her in her letters. Rousseloet, *Histoire de l'éducation des femmes*, i. 139. A list of women who took hieroglyphic *imprese* (an indication that they were probably associates of the French Academy, since most of the men who do so also are almost certainly Academicians) can be derived from Pierre L'Anglois, *Discours des hieroglyphes aegyptiens, emblemes, devises et armoiries* (Paris: A. L'Angelier, 1584), 58[v]–107[r]. It runs as follows: les dames des Roches (poets, mother and daughter), Mme de Richelieu, Camille de Morel (poet, in Greek, Latin, and French), Mme Isabeau Martin, Mme de Surgères (Ronsard's 'Hélène'), Mme la Mareschale de Retz (named as an Academician by Dale).

[75] Frances Yates outlines court ladies' involvement with the Palace Academy in her *French Academies*, 32–3. See for a contemporary account Théodore Agrippa d'Aubigné: 'À mes filles touchant les femmes doctes de nostre siècle', i. 445–50 (pp. 447–8).

[76] *CSP Foreign* (1576), ed. A. J. Crosby (London: Longman, 1880), 242.

[77] Sealy, *The Palace Academy of Henry III*, 173.

[78] Ratel, 'La Cour de la reine Marguerite', 11 (1924), 16.

[79] Lavand, *Un poète de cour*, 72–107.

[80] Berriot-Salvadore, *Les Femmes*, 453, Albert Baur, *Maurice Scève et la Renaissance lyonnaise* (Paris: H. Champion, 1906), 18–19.

[81] Paul Ardouin, *Maurice Scève, Pernette du Guillet, Louise Labé* (Paris: A.-G. Nizet, 1981), 21: 'Le cercle mondain de Marie-Catherine de Pierre Vire (Dame du Perron) réunissait à la fois les gens du monde et les poètes.'

informal Lyon academy of the sixteenth century, 'La Société Angélique', met at la Montagne Fourvière.[82]

Camille de Morel

Among the humanists strongly connected with the court, the household of Jean de Morel (1511–81), in which two highly educated parents produced a trio of learned daughters, is of particular importance to this narrative.[83] Morel was a minor aristocrat, the Sieur de Grigny, and a native of Embrun. He travelled in Italy and Switzerland as informer to François I, and settled down in Paris, where he held important positions in the household of Henri II and Catherine de Médicis.[84] He was successively *maréchal de logis* to Catherine de Médicis, *maître d'hôtel* to Henri II, and *gouverneur* of Henri's illegitimate son Henri d'Angoulême. This enabled him to broker relationships between poets and scholars and his royal patrons, and he became noted for his support and protection of young poets. He married Antoinette de Loynes, widow of Lubin Dallier, advocate in the Parliament of Paris. She came of a cultivated family, with humanist connections in Orléans,[85] was herself a poet, and could read and write Latin: some of her French verses were printed in her lifetime, and a number of lively letters in French and Latin also survive.[86] The Morels' home in Paris was a meeting point for most of the significant intellectual figures of mid-sixteenth-century France. Ronsard, Du Bellay, Dorat, Salmon Macrin, Lancelot de Carles, Michel de L'Hospital, Jean Mercier, Guillaume Aubert, and others were frequent visitors, prompting Scévole de Sainte-Marthe to describe the house as a veritable temple of the Muses. The comments of the mistress of the household, in a letter which she wrote to Nicolas Bourbon, show that like many welcoming and gracious homes, it was all somewhat more trouble than it appeared to her delighted guests. She writes to thank him for kindness shown to her children, and regrets her own studies are little more advanced than theirs. By way of excuse, she enumerates the duties which claim her attention in order of precedence: her religious obligations, her care for her husband, who must be freed to serve letters by her efforts, her children, for whose

[82] Edith Sichel, *Women and Men of the French Renaissance* (London: A. Constable & Co.; Philadelphia: J. B. Lippincott Co., 1901), 231.

[83] M. Gerard Davis, 'A Humanist Family in the Sixteenth Century', in W. Moore et al. (eds.), *The French Mind: Studies in Honour of Gustave Rudler* (Oxford: Clarendon Press, 1952), 1–16.

[84] Willem Janssen, *Charles Utenhove* (Maastricht: Van Aelst, 1939), 20,

[85] MacFarlane, *Buchanan*, 180

[86] For example, there is a sonnet in Charles de Sainte-Marthe et al., *Oraison funebre de l'incomparable Marguerite royne de Navarre, duchesse d'Alençon... plus, epitaphes de ladicte dame, par aulcuns poetes français* (Paris: K. and C. Chaulvière, 1550), 142–3. See also Pierre Nolhac, *Lettres de Joachim Du Bellay* (Paris: H. Champion, 1883), 24 n. 1. There are several Latin letters in Camerarius' collection of humanist letters and poetry: two to Alamanus, Munich, Bayerische Staatsbibliothek, Clm lat. 10383, fo. 239^r, one to Nicolas Bourbon, ibid., fo. 233^r, and one to Henri d'Angoulême on fo. 235^r. There are also letters of hers in Paris, Bibliothèque Nationale de France, Ancien fonds français 4673, fos. 44, 46, 49, and Lat. 10327, fo. 141.

education she is personally responsible, and finally, household cares, domestic matters, and business.

The three daughters of Jean de Morel and Antoinette de Loynes, Camille, Lucrèce, and Diane (their very names bespeak their parents' humanist pretensions), were tutored by Karel Utenhove (b. 1536), an amiable polymath and highly proficient linguist who has left verses in French, German, English, Italian, Spanish, Latin, Greek, Hebrew, and Syriac.[87] Utenhove was their teacher from 1556, when he arrived in Paris, until 1562, when he left for England with the French embassy led by Paul de Foix. Utenhove was a Protestant, and there were rumours that he was attempting to seduce his pupils from Catholicism.[88] He was certainly reading Buchanan's Latin verse drama with the de Morel girls, which, given that Buchanan was a Calvinist, was open to misinterpretation, and may be the basis of the accusation.[89] The parting was in no sense acrimonious, and there is evidence both for continued good relations and for Utenhove's own lack of bigotry in a courteous letter he wrote to Antoinette de Loynes the year he left her employment, which accompanied a copy of two odes by the nun Anne des Marquets, which, he says, he thinks she might enjoy, since Paul de Foix considered them very beautiful.[90]

Camille de Morel, the oldest of the three, seems to have been the only one of the sisters to write Latin verse, but all three were highly visible as learned damsels from an extremely early age.[91] When Du Bellay published his *Epithalame sur le mariage de... Philibert Emanuel, duc de Savoye et... Marguerite de France* (1559), his address to the reader records that Mme de Morel and her three daughters had actually sung the epithalamion: the youngest of the girls, Diane, was only 8 at the time.[92] Camille had taken the part of an Amazon warrior. The previous year, in 1558, Diane, at 7, had composed a Latin address for Marguerite de France.[93] Though the only surviving writing from Lucrèce is in French,[94] Camille published Latin verses on the death of Henri II, written when she was 12, and continued to publish throughout her life.[95] All three daughters received pretty compliments

---

[87] See Colletet, *Vie de Charles Uytenhove*, BN, Nouv. acq. fr. 3073, fo. 489.

[88] Both Jean de Morel and his father-in-law François de Loynes had been friends of Erasmus (S. F. Will, 'Camille de Morel', *PMLA* 51 (1936), 83–4): they remained Catholic humanists rather than becoming disciples of reform.

[89] *Georgii Buchanani Scoti Poetae Eximii, Franciscanus et Fratres* (Basel: Thomas Guarinus, 1568) includes Utenhove's 'Argumentum in Jephthen Buchanani, ad Lucretiam Morellam', 307.

[90] Munich, Bayerische Staatsbibliothek, Clm lat. 10383, fo. 264, May 1562. Des Marquets herself was a highly visible and productive poet. She published four collections of her *Sonets* and *Divines poesies* in 1562, 1566, 1568, 1605, and an edition accompanied by a translation from the Latin verse of Marc Antoine Flaminius in 1568. She includes short Latin verses in her *Sonets, prieres et devises* of 1562.

[91] For example, in *Joachimi Bellaii Audini Poematum Libri Quatuor* (Paris: F. Morel, 1558), 32ᵛ: 'De Camilla, Lucretia et Anna [Diana].'

[92] Will, 'Camille de Morel', 95, Jan van Dorsten, *The Anglo-Dutch Renaissance* (Leiden: University Press, 1988), 64.

[93] Munich, Bayerische Staatsbibliothek, Clm lat. 10383, fo. 239ʳ.

[94] Ibid., fo. 240ʳ.

[95] D. J. Hartley, 'La Mort du roi Henri II (1559) et sa commémoration poétique: document bibliographique', *Bibliothèque d'humanisme et Renaissance*, 47 (1985), 379–88.

from contemporary poets,[96] and Joachim Du Bellay notes that Camille was composing in French and Latin from the age of 10.[97] She also knew Greek, Spanish, and Italian, and performed publicly as an oratrix, earning the praise of Erycius Puteanus.[98] Poems of hers are scattered through the works of contemporary writers, and she was also in contact with at least one other woman Latin poet, since a letter and poem to her from Johanna Otho survive, discussed in Chapter 9.[99] Utenhove was a friend of both young women, and it is he who suggested that Otho should write.

Utenhove seems to have made a determined and persistent attempt to publicize his erstwhile pupil. He includes in his own *Xenia*, a collection which is addressed to Elizabeth I, a poem to the queen by Camille.[100] It is interesting also to find Utenhove supporting Camille's public career in another context: having lectured publicly in London on Thucydides, with Mildred Cecil as guest of honour, he made acquaintance with her, and then, in a letter to Jean de Morel, suggested that Camille write to the great lady and start an elegant literary correspondence: if this ever happened, it has left no trace.[101] A variant version of the first of Camille's poems in *Xenia* is preserved in a collection of polyglot verses on Queen Elizabeth which Utenhove presented to William Cecil in manuscript in February 1561, with versions of the same poem in Hebrew, Latin, Greek, French, and English. The text includes his own Latin version as well as the one by Camille: there is no possibility that he is leaning on her ability, rather, he is seeking to include her.[102] We might note that while Elizabeth was normally served by English noblewomen, her entourage at various times included Helena Snakenborg, a Swede, and Mary Yetswiert, a Belgian, who was serving in 1557/8.[103] It was not unrealistic or impossible that she might have employed Camille either as a foreign language tutor/secretary, or at some future point, had she married (as everybody, of course, expected her to do at that stage of the reign), as a tutor to a daughter: Utenhove

[96] Jan Dousa's playful parody of Catullus III addressed to three learned sisters, *Lusus in Echini sive Erinacei Mortem*, is probably also addressed to the de Morels (*Iani Dousae à Noortwiik Odarum Britannicarum Liber* (Leiden, 1586)).

[97] Extreme precocity was also a feature of Italian Renaissance women poets. It is clear that there was a similar audience for well-trained little girls in France. Louise Sarrasin was already famous for her learning by the age of 8. Sir Thomas Browne, *Musæum Clausum, or Bibliotheca Abscondita* (*The Works of Sir Thomas Browne*, ed. Charles Sayle (Edinburgh: John Grant, 1907), iii. 350–5 (p. 355)).

[98] *Erycii Puteani Epistolarum Promulsis Centuria (1–5)* (Louvain, 1612), Centuria II, ep. 94.

[99] R. L. Hawkins, 'A Letter from One Maiden of the Renaissance to Another', *Modern Language Notes*, 22.8 (1907), 245.

[100] *Caroli Utenhovii F. Patricii Gandavensis* XENIA *seu ad Illustrium Aliquot Europae Hominum Nomina, Allusionum (Intertextis Alicubi Ioach. Bellaii eiusdem Argumenti Versibus), Liber Primus* (Basel: Thomas Guarinus, 1568). Dedication: 'Ad Elizabetham Sereniss. Angl. Franc. Hib. &c. Reginam', 15–16: 'Cum meus extremos iret praeceptor ad Anglos.'

[101] Munich, Bayerische Staatsbibliothek, Clm lat. 10383.

[102] London, Public Record Office, SP 70/48, fos. 4ᵛ–9ʳ (fo. 6ᵛ).

[103] See Charlotte Merton, 'The Women who Served Queen Mary and Queen Elizabeth', Ph.D. diss. (Cambridge University, 1992), 247 ff., Cambridge, University Library, PhD LC 2/4/3, fo. 63ᵛ. Two other women 'being . . . servants of the Queen and strangers born' are listed in the 1580s, Jane Brusselles and Barbara Hakes, London, British Library, Add. 24492, fo. 36ʳ.

seems to be exerting himself to try and find his ex-student actual employment of a kind commensurate with her social status.

Perhaps as a result of Utenhove's efforts, Camille's name and achievements were known all over Europe. Elizabeth Jane Weston, in Prague, knew of her,[104] and so did Conrad Bachmann, professor in Giessen, who wrote a poem on Helena Maria à Wackenfels, a child prodigy who died at almost 10,[105]

> Now [Philippa] Lazea, now [Olimpia] Morata count for nothing
> You will also surpass learned Camille [de Morel]

This absurd encomium (absurd, since the poor child's only surviving work is one little German poem) reveals clearly the international profile enjoyed by women Latinists: Philippa Lazea's life was spent between Pola, Padua, and Trieste, Olimpia Morata was a Ferrarese who died in Heidelberg, while Camille spent her life in Paris, yet all three names were known in Giessen, and assumed to be recognizable in Prague, all of which suggests that any new contender for the title of *docta puella* was automatically mapped against an international frame of reference.

This poem and the other witnesses to her fame also suggest that the Morel women were part of the cultural capital of the French court. Their performances as actors, singers, poets, and oratrices made them living witnesses that the court possessed a sophisticated humanist culture, and therefore Camille de Morel was a species of professional humanist, even if not in the sense in which the phrase is usually employed. She wrote nothing that was not occasional: most of her published work dates from the 1560s, when she was in her teens, though she continued to write and publish through the 1570s.

Camille's later life has been read by Will as parallel to that of some of the early humanist women of Italy, such as Cassandra Fedele, in that her admiring audience dwindled as she aged. But this is by no means wholly true: it would be interesting to know how Gabriel Harvey, would-be courtier and native of Saffron Walden, contrived to solicit verse from her when she was past 30 for his *Gratulationes Valdinenses*, presented to Queen Elizabeth in 1578: this contains epigrams by both Utenhove and Buchanan, either of whom could have made the introduction. It must also be noted that Paul Melissus made the most assiduous efforts to persuade the 36-year-old Camille into an exchange of verses after he met her in Paris in 1584. He had known of her since at least 1574, on the evidence of an excited response to Utenhove's having sent him her verses which was printed in the first edition of *Schediasmata*.[106] The second edition of *Schediasmata*, published in 1586,

---

[104] She compares herself with the sisters, in a poem addressed to Erich Lymburch: 'O, if my Muse were comparable with the skilful Morellae, a praise which was worthy of me would arise from my Muses.'

[105] Lehms, *Teutchlands galante Poetinnen* (Frankfurt am Main: Samuel Tobias Hocter, 1745), 272–6 (p. 275). She was the daughter of Johann Matthias Wacker, one of Elizabeth Weston's patrons at the court of Rudolf II. R. J. W. Evans, *Rudolf II and his World* (Oxford: Oxford University Press, 1973), 154–5.

[106] *Melissi Schediasmata Poetica* (Frankfurt: Corvinus, 1574), 75. Discussed by Pierre de Nolhac, *Un poète rhenan ami de la Pléiade* (Paris: H. Champion, 1923), 71–2.

includes no less than seven poems to Camille de Morel, but she made no response—it may be relevant that her father had died in 1583, the last of her family, and she was perhaps no longer interested in such games. Her last major work was a *tumulus* in her father's memory.[107] This is rendered interesting by the fact that it is padded by all the correspondence which lay behind its production. In addition to long poems of her own on her father, mother, and sister, there is a series of poems addressed to humanists of her father's generation, calling them sharply to account: the poem to Jean de la Gessée, an old friend for whom she had written on previous occasions, opens, 'Do even you despise the ashes of so dear a friend?', and she is equally uncompromising with Scévole de Sainte-Marthe: in the interests of her father's memory, she could be exigent and peremptory. Interestingly, a letter from de la Gessée to Jean Marquis which is also included acknowledges the righteousness of her stance. The book is in many respects saddening; it gives the impression of being the work of a woman who had outlived the people she most cared about, her father, mother, and sister Lucrèce, coming reluctantly to terms with the idea that her father was a forgotten man. The poem on her sister speaks for the general tone of the collection:

AD LUCRETIÆ MORELLÆ MANES CAMILLA MORELLA SOROR

Cur terrestre solum, Lucretia, linquere, cælos
    Scandere cur sine me fata dedêre tibi?
Dulcia te quondam moestæ solatia mentis,
    Delicias, animæ dimidiúmque meæ:
Te nostræ dudum fortuna inimica quietis
    Te rapiens, ipsam me mihi surripuit.
Cùm subit effigies eius tristissima lucis
    (Si lux in tantis ulla fuit tenebris)
Ultima qua veterem verè testantia amorem,
    Et tristi summum diximus ore vale,
Qua tibi, semianimis, suspiria summa trahenti
    Amplexus summos, oscula summa dedi:
Pectora lethiferi videor traiecta sagittis
    Disrumpi, & planè sensibus orba meis.
Quid memorem ingenii raras, Lucretia, dotes?
    Quid referam linguæ gratia quanta tuæ?
Vtque tui dignè gravitatem nominis implens,
    Intactæ exemplar virginitatis eras?
Vt superûm in primis, Musarum hinc sacra colebas,
    (Chara soror) meus est hæc meminisse dolor.
Est meminisse dolor, quia te, mea cura, caremus,
    Quódque es virtuti tam citò rapta tuæ.
At meminisse iuvat, quia qui sine crimine vixit,
    Ille diu vixit, nescius estque mori.

---

[107] The Renaissance French *tumulus* is discussed by J. Ijsewijn, G. Tournoy, and M. de Schepper, 'Jean Dorat and his *Tumulus Iani Brynonis*', in Grahame Castor and Terence Cave (eds.), *Neo-Latin and the Vernacular in Renaissance France* (Oxford: Clarendon Press, 1984), 129–55.

Camille de Morel, her sister, to the spirit of Lucrèce de Morel

Lucrèce, why did you leave the earth alone,
    To ascend into heaven, why did the fates give this to you without me?
You who were once the sweet solace of my sad mind,
    My darling, and half of my soul:
Not long ago, a fortune inimical to our peace,
    In snatching you, stole me from myself.
When that most sad image of its light went underground
    (If there can be any light in such darkness)
Which was, truly, the last witnesses to ancient love,
    And we said the last farewell with sad mouths.
Half-dead, fetching the last sighs,
    The last embraces, and the final kisses which I gave to you,
I broke my heart, which seemed pierced with lethal arrows,
    And clearly lost the sphere of my senses.
What can I recall of your rare gifts of wit, Lucrèce?
    What can I bring back of your great talent for languages
Or that you worthily lived up to the dignity of your name
    And were the exemplar of chaste virginity?
Above all, dear sister, it is my grief to remember
    You used to cultivate the sacred gifts of the divine Muses,
It is grief to remember, since I lack you, my dear,
    And what you are in your excellence, so swiftly snatched.
But it helps to remember, since a person who lived without sin
    Lived long, and does not know how to die.

Utenhove was still in touch with her in 1598 (he died in 1600), and he seems to have been the last person to tempt her to composition. She continued to be mentioned by French men of letters in the early seventeenth century, and it seems she spent her last years living quietly on her mother's estate at Grigny, corresponding regularly with Pierre de l'Estoile, and with at least one educated woman friend, Mlle d'Aurigny.[108] L'Estoile reveals that she had become an ardent Protestant, so it is also possible that her apparent eclipse was due not to the indifference of the learned world, or to depression, but to a refocusing of her interests away from humanism.

French women humanists

On less exalted social levels, the sixteenth century also saw the rise of professional humanists: professors, poets, and printers. One of the most famous French humanist households is that of the scholar-printer Robert Estienne in Paris, whose printing works in the Rue Saint-Jean-de-Beauvais acted as a kind of salon for scholars. Estienne married the daughter of a scholar, and the whole family spoke Latin at

---

[108] Will, 'Camille de Morel', 116.

table in their house in Paris 'so that the very maidservants came to understand what was said and even to speak it a little'.[109] Similarly, in Montaigne's childhood home, everyone in the household was expected to use or acquire a few Latin phrases, including housemaids and valets: thus Montaigne grew up with Latin as his mother tongue.[110] As Waquet has stressed, this facility with Latin as a spoken language was unusual; but in houses where it was a language of daily use, the women of the household were Latinate. Jacques Auguste de Thou, a noted French humanist, seems to have taken a Latin-literate woman, Maria Barbansona, as his first wife, on the evidence of a Latin poem attributed to her and included in a manuscript anthology of his works.[111] The depth of women's participation in Renaissance Latin cultures (which in itself affected only a narrow band of the population) is suggested by the fact that France, most unusually, produced two female scholar-printers, printing Latin and Greek: Charlotte Guillard[112] and Edmonda Tusana, who was briefly King's Printer in Greek in 1540 in succession to her first husband, Conrad Neobar. Tusana published Greek texts in 1540 and 1541 before marrying another printer, J. Bogard, and probably continuing to work as part of the family firm.[113] To understand the full implication of this, it is necessary to remember that the work of a Renaissance printer was not confined to physically getting print onto paper, but was more like that of a modern academic editor.[114]

A number of important woman poets of the French Renaissance read Latin and depended to some extent on Latin literature. Louise Labé, the famous poetess of Lyon, is the most distinguished of these. She studied music, letters, the practice of arms, needlework, Latin, Italian, and perhaps Spanish and Greek. Latin literature (particularly the poems of Catullus) was very important to her French poetics, and a collection of her Latin verse apparently survived until the early eighteenth century, when it was tragically lost.[115] Other literary women of Lyon, later of Poitiers, are connected with Labé, the mother and daughter poets Madeleine and Catherine des Roches (Madeleine Neveau and Catherine Fradonnet). They entered on a

---

[109] Elizabeth Armstrong, *Robert Estienne, Royal Printer* (Cambridge: Cambridge University Press, 1954), 15–16. See also Anthony Grafton, *Bring out your Dead: The Past as Revelation* (2001), 142–3, which discusses women's use of Latin as a spoken, rather than written language.

[110] Dorothy Gabe Coleman, *The Gallo-Roman Muse: Aspects of Roman Literary Tradition in Sixteenth-Century France* (Cambridge: Cambridge University Press, 1979), 110.

[111] Paris, Bibliothèque Nationale de France, Dupuy 460 is a manuscript consisting mostly of poems by Jacques Auguste de Thou, dating between the 1580s and 1605. It also contains some poems by friends.

[112] Armstrong, *Robert Estienne*, 135. See further Beatrice Beech, 'Charlotte Guillard: A Sixteenth Century Business Woman', *Renaissance Quarterly*, 36 (1983), 345–67.

[113] She was perhaps a relative of Tusanus, the professor of Greek of whom Bogard published several posthumous editions. Armstrong, *Robert Estienne*, 124.

[114] Astonishing numbers of women are involved with printing in 16th-century Europe, but relatively few are identifiable as scholar-printers. See 'Women in the Printing Business', in Erdmann, 227–80 for a list of 16th-century books printed by women.

[115] See Jeanne Prine, in WWRR, 132–57, Gertrude Hamish, *Love Elegies in the Renaissance: Marot, Louise Labé and Ronsard* (Saratoga, Calif.: Stanford French and Italian Studies, 1979), and the Appendix.

co-publication with her of a translation of Longus' *Daphnis and Chloe* in 1578.[116] The dames des Roches have been studied by Ann Rosalind Jones, who points to 'recent research into early modern social groups in which women gained access to literary language [which] has focused on the coteries in which they learned to perform alongside men, improvising poems later printed in books'.[117] They were also interplicated with literary society more generally, in the case of Catherine, in a slightly startling and comic way: it was the sight of a flea walking on her bosom which was the starting point of the strange and often obscene Renaissance French genre of 'puce' poems.[118] It is easy to get the impression from the 'puce' poems that Catherine was nothing more than an articulate and witty *salonnière*. In fact, though she wrote in French, she read Greek and Latin, studied Ficino on Plato, and wrote feminist dialogues supporting women's education.[119] She also published translations from Pythagoras' *Symbola*,[120] and Claudian's *De Raptu Proserpinae*.[121] Mesdames des Roches were the first women in France to publish their private correspondence: the genre of informal letters was not, at that time, popular in France, though it was to become so.[122] Both of them were friends of both Julius Caesar Scaliger and Scévole de Sainte-Marthe (already mentioned as an acquaintance of Camille de Morel): the latter had the highest opinion of them both.

As these women's works suggest, Lyon was a very important centre of regional culture.[123] The pattern of French culture was unlike that of contemporary England, in that the capital did not necessarily drain talent towards itself, and publishers in major provincial cities were eager to sell local writers to local readers. Probably the earliest woman's work to be published in Lyon is Anne de Beaujeu's conduct book for her daughter, which appeared *c.*1534.[124] As early as the 1540s, Antoine du Moulin of Lyon adduced the *Rymnes* of Pernette du Guillet as proof that the city's spirit invigorated 'tous les sexes'.[125] Du Guillet, a Lyonnaise Neoplatonist and poet

---

[116] Longus, *Histoire des amours pastoralles de Daphnis et de Chloé* (Paris: Parent (or L'Angelier), 1578).

[117] Ann Rosalind Jones, 'Contentious Readings: Urban Humanism and Gender Difference in *La Puce de Madame des-Roches* (1582)', *Renaissance Quarterly*, 48.1 (1995), 109–28 (p. 109). See also C. H. Winn, 'Mère, fille, femme, muse: maternité et créativité dans les œuvres des dames des Roches', *Travaux de littérature*, 4 (1991), 101–18, George E. Diller, *Les Dames des Roches: étude sur la vie littéraire à Poitiers dans la deuxième moitié du seizième siècle* (Geneva: Droz, 1936): this last points to a marked tendency towards collaborative compositions of all kinds in the last third of the century.

[118] *La Puce de Madame Des-Roches, qui est un recueil de divers poëmes grecs, latins, et françois, composez par plusieurs doctes personnages aux grans iours tenus à Poitiers* (Paris: L'Angelier, 1583), Keating, *Studies* 49–69. Diller, *Les Dames des Roches.*

[119] Keating, *Studies*, 62–3.

[120] *Les Enigmes de Pythagore*, in *Les Œuvres* (Paris: Abel L'Angelier, 1582), fos. 14ᵛ–18ᵛ.

[121] *Les Missives de Mesdames des Roches de Poitiers mere et fille: avec le ravissement de Proserpine prins du latin de Clodian* (Paris: Abel L'Angelier, 1586), fos. 41–66.

[122] Ibid.

[123] See Anon., *Biographie lyonnaise, ou catalogue des Lyonnais digne de mémoire* (Paris: Techener; Lyon: Giberton & Brun, 1839), for an overview of the Lyonnais, and on the 16th century, A. Baur, *Maurice Scève et la Renaissance lyonnnaise* (Paris: Champion, 1906), *Actes du colloque sur l'humanisme lyonnais au xviᵉ siècle* (Grenoble: Presses Universitaires de Grenoble, 1974), and n. 126 below.

[124] Anne de Beaujeu, *A la requeste de treshaulte et puissante princesse ma dame Susanne de Bourbon*

[125] Anne Rosalind Jones, 'The Lyonnais Neoplatonist, Pernette Du Guillet', in WWRR, 219–31. See also Ardouin, *Maurice Scève, Pernette du Guillet, Louise Labé.*

(*c.*1520–1545), was one of the first middle-class women to study the classical languages. At the time of her early death, she read Italian and Spanish, had mastered Latin, and was studying Greek. Similarly in the 1550s, Labé's publisher, Jean de Tournes, made a great point of presenting Louise Labé as a Lyonnaise. Another woman of Lyon with a great reputation for learning was Louise Sarrasin, noticed by a number of admiring contemporaries, including Paul Melissus:[126] unfortunately, nothing of hers seems to have survived in print or manuscript.

A number of other names of sixteenth-century learned Frenchwomen are recoverable. Jeanne de la Fontaine of Berry wrote an epic poem on Theseus (in French) in the first half of the sixteenth century which attracted the admiration of Joannes Secundus, expressed in a Latin poem addressed to her.[127] Hélisenne de Crenne, whose real name was Marguerite Briet, Demoiselle de Picardie, a member of the minor aristocracy, is another Latin-literate woman writer of the period who ventured into print. Though she wrote entirely in French, she translated the first four books of the *Aeneid* and dedicated them to François I.[128] She is better known as the author-heroine of *Les Angoysses douloureuses qui procedent d'amours*, though she also published a collection of letters and an allegorical treatise in Paris from 1538 to 1542.[129] Anne Tullonne, of Macon, was known punningly as 'Tulliana' on account of her highly Ciceronian style.[130] We might also note here an otherwise unknown woman, Delphina Tornatoria, who wrote a Latin letter to M. Montpellier from Tarascon.[131] Louise Barclay, née Debonnaire, wife of John Barclay, the author of *Argenis*, is the possible author of a Latin poem on Peirsec, and credited as such by a number of writers on women, though the poem was more probably written by Barclay in his wife's name.[132]

One of the more interesting women Latinists of the sixteenth century is the long-lived Marie de Jars de Gournay:[133] unlike most educated women, she

126 Sir Thomas Browne (*Musæum Clausum*, 355) speaks of her, and Melissus includes a poem to her in *Schediasmatum Reliquiae* (n. pl., 1575), 107–8. She had a reputation as a child prodigy, but lived to marry three times, and in old age read Greek and Latin medical works to her third husband, Marco Offrendi of Cremona, who had gone blind (Jacques Pernetti, *Recherches pour servir à l'histoire de Lyon ou les Lyonnois dignes de mémoire*, 2 vols. (Lyon: Chez les Freres Duplain, Libraires, 1757), i. 235–6).

127 *Ioannis Secundus Hagiensis Opera, nunc Primum in Lucem Edita* (Utrecht: Harmannus Borculous, 1561), sig. F.1. François Grudé de la Croix du Maine, *Premier volume de la bibliothèque du sieur de la Croix-du-Maine* (Paris: Abel L'Angelier, 1584), 494 identifies her.

128 Rousselot, *Histoire de l'éducation des femmes*, i. 186.

129 Kittye delle Robbins-Herring, 'Hélisenne de Crenne: Champion of Women's Rights', *WWRR*, 177–218. *Les Angoysses*... is translated as *The Torments of Love*, by Lisa Neal and Steven Rendall (Minneapolis: University of Minnesota Press, 1996).

130 Françons Billon, *Le Fort inexpugnable de l'honneur du sexe femenin* (Paris: Jan D'Allyer, 1555), 35ᵛ.

131 Munich, Bayerische Staatsbibliothek, 1084 (Collectio Camerariana 33), fos. 241–2.

132 Pierre Gassendi, *Viris Illustris Nicolaie Claudii Fabricii de Peirsec, Senatoris Aquisextiensis Vita, per Petrum Gassendum Praepositum Ecclesiae Diniensis* (Paris: S. Cramoisy, 1641), 167–8. She was certainly literate: there is a letter of hers to her son, 'Lettere scritte à suo Figliolo avanti la sua partenza per l'Inghilterra', in Vatican City, Biblioteca Apostolica, Ottobonensis 12445, p. 138.

133 Marie's surname was Le Jars, while de Gournay was her father's title: in her autobiography of 1641, she called herself Marie Le Jars, la dame de Gournay, and signed herself as Marie de Gournay le Jars in a letter to Justus Lipsius in 1593 (Marjorie H. Ilsley, *A Daughter of the Renaissance* (The Hague: Mouton & Co., 1963), 11). Posterity, however, seems to be agreed that she is Marie de Gournay.

educated herself, with no support from either of her parents. Her father was, at the time of her birth, a minor nobleman on the way up, holding a number of reasonably important posts. She was the eldest of six children. Guillaume de Jars, Marie's father, died in 1577: the long series of religious wars, with concomitant inflation, property damage, and mounting taxes, left his widow in a difficult position: with her debts mounting, she found herself unable to sustain life in Paris, and fled to their provincial castle of Gournay-sur-Aronde in 1580. Marie withdrew into herself, and spent as much time as possible reading. Finding some parallel French–Latin texts, she realized that she could teach herself Latin:[134]

She stayed with her mother until she was nearly twenty-five, under whom, in the hours when she was not [formally] dressed, she learned letters by herself, and also Latin, without a grammar and without assistance, apposing books in that language translated into French with the originals.

Later, she learned some Greek with the assistance of an unnamed tutor. Louis de Jars, certainly a relative and probably her uncle, was a friend of Ronsard and Dorat, and author of a play called *Lucelle* published in 1576: it is possible that he to some extent supported her aspirations.

In 1584, Marie came across the *Essais* of Michel de Montaigne, and fell in love not merely with the essays, but with their author. This was to be the passion of her life; which might be read as a relatively benign version of the story of Heloïse. Her concentrated hero-worship found a due response, and she became Montaigne's 'fille d'alliance', later his editor. Marie de Gournay's writing is basically in French, but her ability to write, as well as read, Latin is shown by the distich at the conclusion of the 'Épître' with which she opens her first published work, *Le Proumenoir de Monsieur de Montaigne par sa fille d'alliance*.

> Nec metus, in celebres ne nostrum nomen amicos
> Invideant inferre, finant modo fatu, nepos.
>
> Anxieties do not prevent [me from] inflicting my name as a descendant
> on famous friends, but nor do they fix this as my fate.

She also translated the *Life of Socrates* by Diogenes Laertius, at the request of an unnamed nobleman, but was less successful when she imitated a *Greek Anthology* epigram with one of her own: she was accused of lacking wit and point.[135] Her works also include a considerable volume of translation from Latin authors, including Virgil, Tacitus, Sallust, Ovid, and Cicero.[136] She is interesting as one of the first women in Europe to seek to live on her own as an independent woman

---

134 Ilsley, *A Daughter of the Renaissance*, 19: 'elle garda sa mère jusqu'à près de 25 ans sous laquelle à des heures pour la plus part desrobées, elle apprit les lettres seule, et mesme le Latin sans grammaire et sans ayde, confrontant les Livres de cette Langue Traduicts en François, contre les originaux...'

135 James Hutton, *The Greek Anthology in France* (Ithaca, NY: Cornell University Press, 1946), 452–3.

136 For the most part published, as *Versions de quelques pièces de Virgile, Tacite, et Saluste, avec l'institution de Monseigneur frère unique du roy* (Paris: Fleury-Bourriquant, 1619).

of letters.[137] When she visited the Netherlands in 1597, she was received in Brussels in some state; a reception which she owed to her admirer Justus Lipsius. She was met by a group of distinguished citizens headed by the Councillor of Brabant and the Quartermaster General, and entertained and fêted for several days.[138]

Marie de Gournay is principally remembered for her stance on women's education in her widely read work *L'Egalité des hommes et des femmes*, published in 1622, and reprinted in all editions of her collected works. This is not the first feminist tract to be published in France, an honour which perhaps goes to Charlotte de Bracchart, who published an *Harengue* addressed to men who prohibit learning to women at Chalon-sur-Saône in 1604,[139] but it is probably the most famous in its day. Her long life makes her a transitional figure; a woman intellectually formed by the French Renaissance, contemporary with Johanna van Pallandt, who survived into the world of the *précieuses*, of Mlle de Scudéry and Mme de Sévigné.

[137] A letter from de Gournay to van Schurman survives, 20 Oct. 1639, in The Hague, Koniglijke Bibliotheek (mentioned by Joyce Irwin, 'Anna Maria van Schurman: The Star of Utrecht', in J. R. Brink (ed.), *Female Scholars* (Montreal: Eden Press Women's Publications, 1980), 68–85 (p. 85 n. 21)).

[138] Ilsley, *A Daughter of the Renaissance*, 82. Henri Carton, *Histoire des femmes écrivains de la France* (Paris: A. Dupret, 1886), 75, quotes two poems written to Marie de Gournay by Justus Lipsius and Daniel Heinsius.

[139] Marie de Romieu published a defence of women, *Les Premières œuvres poétiques de Mademoiselle Marie de Romieu, vivaroise, contenant un bref discours que l'excellence de la femme surpasse celle d'homme* (Paris: L. Breyer, 1581). I have not seen the still earlier Nicole Estienne, *L'Apologie pour les femmes contre ceux qui les méprisent*, mentioned by Rousselot, *Histoire de l'éducation des femmes*, i. 186–7 (presumably a version of 'Les Misères de la femme mariée' attributed to the same author and listed by Ruth Kelso, *Doctrine for the Lady of the Renaissance* (Urbana: University of Illinois Press, 1956; repr. 1978), 363).

8. *Women Latin Poets in Spain and Portugal*

We know of very few medieval Spanish women who wrote in Latin. The sixth-century Spanish princess Brunhild (discussed in an earlier chapter) was highly literate, as was, apparently, a Visigothic woman called Caesaria who wrote a verse epitaph for her husband. A twelfth- and a thirteenth-century queen, Teresia and Berengaria, wrote Latin letters, and the *liber anniversorum* of St Catherine's monastery in Barcelona was kept in Latin in the thirteenth century.[1] A number of inmates of another thirteenth-century Catalan convent, Sant Pere de les Puelles (also in Barcelona), used Latin.[2]

Late medieval Spain produced a number of interesting women writers, some of whom have been studied by Ronald Surtz.[3] At the same time, there is an extensive literature of misogyny and the denial of an active role to women in Spain, epitomized by the suspicion expressed by the Castilian poet Carvajal, active 1457–60: 'Amad, amadores, muger que non sabe': 'love, lovers, an ignorant woman.'[4] Similarly, in the seventeenth century, Brantôme quotes 'the Spanish saying, "De una mula que haza hin, y de una hija que habla latin, libera nos Domine" ': 'from a whinnying mule and a daughter that knows Latin, Lord deliver us.'[5] But despite the preference expressed by Carvajal (which it is probably fair to assume reflects popular literature generally), there were women contemporaries of his, such as Leonor López de Córdoba,[6] who were very far from ignorant, and also writers of various kinds, such as Florencia Pinar and Teresa de Cartagena.[7] It is also worth

---

[1] M. C. Díaz y Díaz, *Index Scriptorum Latinorum Medii Aevi Hispanorum*, 2 vols. (Salamanca: Universidad de Salamanca, Acta Salmanticensia Filosofia y Letras XIII.1–2, 1958–9), no. 937, p. 213, nos. 1229 (a letter from one queen to another, Berengaria of León to Blanche of France) and 1230, p. 264, no. 1355, p. 286.

[2] Linda McMillin, 'Anonymous Lives: Documents from the Benedictine Convent of Sant Pere de les Puelles', in Laurie Churchill et al. (eds.), *Women Writing Latin from Antiquity to Early Modern Europe* (New York: Routledge, 2002), ii. 265–80.

[3] Ronald E. Surtz, *Writing Women in Late Medieval and Early Modern Spain* (Philadelphia: University of Pennsylvania Press, 1995).

[4] Ibid. 2. Jacob Ormstein, 'Misogyny and Pro-feminism in Early Castilian Literature', *Modern Language Quarterly*, 3 (1942), 221–34, Michael Solomon, *The Literature of Misogyny in Medieval Spain* (Cambridge: Cambridge University Press, 1997). Issues relating to clerical control over women are also addressed by Ronald Surtz in 'Female Patronage of Vernacular Religious Works in Fifteenth-Century Castile: Aristocratic Women and their Confessors', in Renate Blumenfeld-Kosinski et al. (eds.), *The Vernacular Spirit* (New York: Palgrave, 2002), 263–82.

[5] Pierre de Bourdeille, Seigneur de Brantôme, *The Lives of Gallant Ladies*, trans. H.M. (London: Pushkin Press, 1943), discourse 7, ch. 2, anecdote 22.

[6] Clara Estow, 'Leonor López de Córdoba: Portrait of a Medieval Courtier', *Fifteenth Century Studies*, 5 (1982), 23–46.

[7] On Florencia Pinar, see K. M. Wilson, *Medieval Women Writers* (Athens: University of Georgia Press, 1984), 320–32. Teresa de Cartagena was the author of *Arboleda*.

noting that María, queen of Juan II, attempted to counteract this literature of misogyny by commissioning works on virtuous and illustrious women.[8] Even before the accession of the 'reyes católicos', Fernando and Isabel (known in English as Ferdinand and Isabella), with their strong commitment to religion above all else, almost all the writing by women which survives is religious. The dominance of the vernacular is also very noticeable in the late Middle Ages: before the humanist revival of the late fifteenth century, men as well as women tended to write in Spanish.[9] In Aragon, Castile, and Portugal alike, the vernaculars had become the official languages even of the administration and the judiciary as early as the thirteenth century. Latin was therefore not needed for the conduct of the secular affairs of the kingdom, and was consequently not part of secular culture.[10]

The only fifteenth-century Spanish woman to write Latin verse seems to have been the royal nun Costanza de Castilla (*c.*1400–1478). She and her brother had a good claim to be seen as the legitimate heirs of Pedro I ('the Cruel'), their grandfather. He had entered into a questionably legal relationship with a Spanish noblewoman, perhaps Juana de Castro, and had by her a son called Juan de Castilla who was imprisoned for most of his life as a potential threat to the Trastamara dynasty of northern Castile, which had usurped the throne of Castile on Pedro's death. Juan married his jailer's daughter, Elvira de Falces, and had two children. Their fate was determined by their cousin, the then Queen of Castile, Catalina, who had legitimized the Trastamara usurpation of the throne by marrying the heir of the usurper Enrique II, Enrique III.[11] He died the year their heir was born, in 1406, and against his wishes, she assumed co-regency with her brother-in-law Fernando de Antequera, and held it till 1418. In the interests of her Trastamara offspring, she arranged the neutralization of Costanza and her brother as potential threats to the succession by making them, respectively, a Dominican nun and a priest. However, Costanza de Castilla remained close to royal circles, and was evidently well educated. She left a manuscript book of prayers and religious compositions of various kinds, written or copied in the reign of Enrique IV (1454–74).[12] This has in it a private liturgical office, the Hours of the Nails, composed in commemoration of the nails of Christ's Passion. This work includes four apparently original Latin hymns: the fact that they all have the same, very specific doxology relating to the Nails suggests strongly that they are her own

[8] Mosen Diego de Valera, *Tratado en deffension de virtuosas mugeres*, and Alonso de Cartagena, *Libro de las mugeres ilustres*: see Barbara Matulka, *The Novels of Juan de Flores and their European Diffusion* (New York: New York University Press, 1931), 14–15. She also mentions other defence texts not instigated by Queen María but written in her time, Alvaro de Luna, *Libro de las virtuosas y claras mugeres* (1446), Juan Rodríguez del Padrón, *Triunfo de las donas* (1443), and Martín de Córdoba, *Jardín de las nobles doncellas*.

[9] See for example Peter Linehan, *Ladies of Zamorra* (Manchester: Manchester University Press, 1997), a study of a convent of nuns in 13th-century Spain.

[10] Helen Nader, *The Mendoza Family in the Spanish Renaissance, 1350 to 1550* (New Brunswick, NJ: Rutgers University Press, 1979), 80–1.

[11] She was another descendant of Pedro the Cruel through his wife Blanche of Bourbon.

[12] Madrid, Biblioteca Nacional, 7495, edited as Constanza de Castilla, *Libro de devociones y oficios*, ed. Constance L. Wilkins, Exeter Hispanic Texts (Exeter: University of Exeter Press, 1998).

work, written in imitation of medieval liturgical hymns in the metre associated with St Ambrose, iambic dimeter. The first of these sets out the basic premiss of her office,

> Eterne Rex Altissime,
> Pater superne glorie,
> qui redemptorem hominis
> tuum dedisti Filium . . .
>
> Ihesu vere pelicane
> qui mortuos quos [quum] vidisti
> filios ut ipsi viverent.
> tua viscera rupisti.
>
> Vivificatos sanguine
> vultu benigno respice,
> ne pereant in prelio
> tuo defende clipeo
>
> Gloria tibi, Domine
> qui per clavorum vulnera
> tuum dedisti sanguinem
> redenptionis precium.

> Eternal, highest King
> Father of supernal glory,
> who gave as a redeemer
> for mankind, your own son . . .
>
> Jesus, true Pelican,
> who, when you saw the dead
> tore your own vitals
> that they might live as your sons.
>
> Look down with favouring countenance
> on those brought alive by your blood,
> lest they perish in battle
> defend them with your shield
>
> Glory to you, O Lord
> who through the wounds of the nails
> gave your own blood
> as the price of redemption.

From the reign of Fernando and Isabel onwards, the history of women's cultural production in Spain and Portugal is powerfully influenced by the confessional politics of the Spanish monarchy, which in turn, were clearly influenced by the fact that Spain was a frontier state between the Christian and the Muslim worlds. If what now remains in manuscript and early printed sources accurately reflects what there once was, women's creative energies were for the most part channelled into religious activity not only in the Middle Ages, as is the case throughout Europe, but in subsequent centuries, a cultural bias which resulted in such remarkable and influential nuns as St Teresa of Jesus (or of Avila, 1515–82), mystic, visionary, and founder of the Carmelites,[13] and the mystic, visionary, and adviser to Felipe IV, Sor María de Ágreda (1602–55). The works of St Teresa were published from shortly after her death,[14] those of María de Ágreda from shortly after they were first written.[15] Despite the extensive literature of misogyny and contempt for women in general which continued to be written,[16] some individual nuns in early modern Spain (notably the two already mentioned) enjoyed a degree of political and social influence which is hardly to be paralleled in any other European country;[17] and women mystics and visionaries of other kinds were also highly significant in more local communities.[18] The great Cardinal Cisneros was an active promoter of translation of religious writings of interest to women, including material on the mystics Angela of Foligno and Catherine of Siena, and a powerful supporter of two Spanish women visionaries, Sor María de Santo Domingo and Madre Juana de la Cruz, whose spirituality was certainly influenced by these translations.[19]

Some of the religious contexts in which Spanish women were prominent were unorthodox. Isabel de la Cruz, a sister of the Franciscan order, founded an important sect called the Alumbrados, or Illuminists, based on a Netherlandic

[13] For a brief account with bibliography, see Ciriaco Morón-Arroyo, 'The Human Value of the Divine: Saint Teresa of Jesus', in *WWRR*, 401–31.

[14] *Los libros de la Madre*, 3 vols. (Salamanca: Foquel, 1588, 1589; Barcelona: Cendrat, 1588; Madrid: Flamenco, 1597), *Libro primero* . . . , (Saragossa: Tabano, 1592), and Italian translation (Rome: Faccinotti, 1599), *Camino de perfection* (Evora: Viuda Burgos, 1583; Salamanca: Foquel, 1585; Valencia: Huete, 1586), *Practica y exercicio spiritual* (Córdoba: Cea, 1598).

[15] T. D. Kendrick, *Mary of Ágreda* (London: Routledge & Kegan Paul, 1967), 94–154. Her writings are listed pp. 159–65. There are at least eighty-nine editions and sixty-eight summaries and anthologies, together with translations into many languages (including Latin, Greek, and Arabic) of her best-known work, *The Mystical City of God*, giving her oeuvre a real claim to being one of the most widely circulated by any woman anywhere in early modern Europe.

[16] Stephanie Merrim, *Early Modern Women's Writing and Sor Juana Inés de la Cruz* (Nashville: Vanderbilt University Press, 1999), 40–50.

[17] Though there were some politically important women visionaries in early modern Italy. Among others, Luca da Narni advised Ercole I d'Este of Ferrara and Osanna Andreasi and Stefane Quinzana were attached to the court of Mantua. Adriano Prosperi, 'Dalle "divini madri" ai "padri spirituali" ', in Elisja Schulte von Kessel (ed.), *Women and Men in Spiritual Culture* (The Hague: Staatsuitgeverij, 1986), 71–91, and Gabriella Zarri, 'Living Saints: A Typology of Female Sanctity in the Early Sixteenth Century', in Daniel E. Bornstein and Roberto Rusconi (eds.), *Women and Religion in Medieval and Renaissance Italy*, trans. Margery J. Schneider (Chicago: University of Chicago Press, 1996), 219–303. In 16th-century England, Elizabeth Barton, the 'Nun of Kent', became a figurehead for opposition to Henry VIII's divorce. See Alan Neame, *The Holy Maid of Kent: The Life of Elizabeth Barton, 1506–1534* (London: Hodder & Stoughton, 1971).

[18] See for example Richard L. Kagan, *Lucrecia's Dreams: Politics and Prophecy in Sixteenth-Century Spain* (Berkeley and Los Angeles: University of California Press, 1990): Lucrezia de León's 'dreams' amounted to explicit political criticism of the government of Felipe II.

[19] Elizabeth Teresa Howe, 'Cisneros and the Translation of Women's Spirituality', in Blumenfeld-Kosinski et al. (eds.), *The Vernacular Spirit*, 283–96. Philippe-Joseph Caffiaux, *Defenses du beau sexe* (Amsterdam: Aux dépens de la compagnie, 1757), ii. 256 claims that the Spanish translation of the Latin Life of the Blessed Angela of Foligno (published 1518) was made by a woman, Francesca de Lorios—however it is not listed in Erdmann and I have not seen a copy. A much later work drawing on Cisneros's initative certainly was by a woman, Isabel de Lianò, *Historia de la vida muerte y milagros de s. Catalina de Siena* (Valladolid: Margarita Sanchez, 1604), dedicated to Margaret of Austria.

style of pietism which stressed mental prayer at the expense of form and ceremony, and was severely repressed by the authorities because it was thought to tend towards Protestantism. She organized devotional centres in such towns as Alcalá and Toledo. Another leading *alumbrada*, the director of the Alumbrados of Valladolid, was also a woman, Francisca Hernández. She turned informer after her arrest and denounced one after another the leading Erasmians of Spain.[20] María de Cazalla, on the other hand, followed her inner guiding with heroic persistence: 'the attraction she had for scholars and members of the Mendoza family [who will be discussed later] testifies to a personality of exceptional force.'[21] In looking at women humanists, this chapter is not directly addressing the women thought most interesting and important by even highly educated contemporaries: the small number of women Latinists in the Peninsula compared to those in Italy or France in the same period must surely be related not to backwardness or barbarism, but to the fact that real opportunities for the exercise of self-expression or political and social power were to be found in an entirely different context.[22]

Perhaps the most widely read works by a pre-modern Spanish woman which were not religious are two internationally popular chivalric romances, *Palmerin de Oliva* and *Primaleon*, by an anonymous woman from Burgos, the sort of romances immortally satirized in Miguel de Cervantes' *Don Quixote*.[23] Another sixteenth-century Spanish woman, Beatriz Bernal, published a work of history.[24] Otherwise, aside from quotidian manuscript records relating to such matters as disputes over property, almost all of the women who published or left records in manuscript were nuns, and a substantial proportion were visionaries, though there was also a flourishing genre of religious autobiography, often elicited by confessors as part of a process of self-examination.[25] While a number of women writers in Italy and France can be shown to have published their work in manuscript ('scribal publication'), perhaps the only Spanish woman to have done so was María de Ágreda, whose works are the only writing by any woman to be extensively represented in the record of Spanish manuscripts.

After the unification of Aragon and Castile under Fernando and Isabel in 1474, the 'reyes católicos' encouraged the reception of the Renaissance in Spain. The first book to be printed in Spain had appeared only two years before, in 1472:

---

[20] Alastair Hamilton, *Heresy and Mysticism in Sixteenth-Century Spain: The Alumbrados* (Cambridge: James Clarke, 1992), Marcel Bataillon, *Érasme et l'Espagne*, 3 vols. (Geneva: Droz, 1991), i. 74, 190.

[21] Hamilton, *Heresy and Mysticism*, 27.

[22] Nader, *The Mendoza Family*, additionally argues that the Spanish reception of the Renaissance was to a great extent through translations (pp. 132–8).

[23] Henry Thomas, 'The Palmerin Romances', *Transactions of the Bibliographical Society*, 13 (1913–15), 17–144. Latin verses by Juan Angor de Transmiera in the first edition of *Palmerin de Oliva* declare 'As the sun outshines the moon and Antonio de Lebrixia the scholars, so this learned lady outshines the men of Spain.'

[24] Beatriz Bernal, *Comiença la hystoria de los invictos y magnanimos cavalleros don Cristalin de España* (first printed Valladolid: Villaquran, 1545; repr. Alcalá de Henares: Iniguez de Lequerica, 1587), and translated into Italian (Venice: Tramezzino, 1557–8).

[25] Darcy Donahue, 'Writing Lives: Nuns and Confessors as Auto/biographers in Early Modern Spain', *Journal of Hispanic Philology*, 13 (1989), 231–9. See also Electa Arenal and Stacey Schlau, *Untold Sisters: Hispanic Nuns in their Own Words* (Albuquerque: University of New Mexico Press, 1989).

under the 'reyes católicos', printing expanded, and several presses were estab-lished.[26] They also sponsored university chairs, and encouraged the study of Latin.[27] Fernando's kingdom of Aragon did not permit women to wield power in their own right, but as early as 1473, we see him dealing with a French invasion in Aragon when he was needed in Castile by leaving his sister, Juana of Aragon, as lieutenant in his stead.[28] Queen Isabel, on the other hand, exercised complete royal authority in her own right. Fernando was a little startled to find that when she was raised to the throne of Castile in Segovia in 1574, the procession which formed as she left the church was headed by a horseman holding a naked sword point up, to indicate the presence of a bearer of royal authority. It was then made clear to him that she had deliberately adopted this 'kingly' attribute, and that, in Castile, he was king-consort only.[29] However, once he had got over the shock, the royal couple ruled with rare unanimity, though without amalgamating their kingdoms. They dealt with the enormous issue of Isabel's marital subordination combined with political superiority (Castile being considerably the more important kingdom) by writing to, and addressing, one another in the terms created by courtly love, as lady and knight, a set of conventions which created a useful space in which power relations were reversed.[30] As a mistress of the contradictions of her position, Isabel was, in her very different way, as successful a female monarch as Elizabeth I.

Though the universities were open only to men, as was the case throughout Europe, Queen Isabel herself was a learned woman: her confessor, Hernando de Talavera, enjoined study upon her as part of her royal duty.[31] She inherited an extensive library of 101 manuscripts from her father, Juan II of Castile, and took it upon herself to learn Latin as an adult.[32] Her preferred reading continued to be vernacular romances, but she did read in Latin: her favourite Latin author was the historian Livy, who was often recommended to Renaissance monarchs (Mary, Queen of Scots, similarly, read Livy with George Buchanan).[33] Isabel's tutor was Doña Beatriz Galindez, known as 'La Latina'. This woman, greatly admired for her learning by contemporaries,[34] had initially been destined for the convent, but chose royal service instead. She married Francisco Ramíres de Madrid, known as 'el Artillero' for his valour in the wars of Granada, and after his death, she retired from the court and dedicated herself to charity. The works attributed to her include *Notas y comentarios sobre Aristóteles* (a commentary on the Greek

---

[26] Carlos Romero de Lecea, *El V centenario de la introducción de la imprenta en España* (Madrid: Joyas Bibliográficas, 1972).

[27] Pietro Verrua, *Cultori della poesia latina in Ispagna durante il regno di Ferdinando il Cattolico* (Adria: Vidalle, 1906).

[28] Peggy K. Liss, *Isabel the Queen* (New York: Oxford University Press, 1992), 91, 104–5.

[29] Ibid. 97, 104–5.

[30] Ibid. 211.

[31] Ibid. 125. Both Iñigo López de Mendoza, second Conde de Tendilla, and Juan Pacheco were tutors of her predecessor, the Infanta Juana, which suggests that she was also carefully educated. Nader, *The Mendoza Family*, 151.

[32] Lucio Marineo, *Opus de Rebus Hispaniae Memorabilibus* (Madrid: M. de Eguia, 1533), fo. clxxxiiv.

[33] Liss, *Isabel*, 254. See also I. D. Macfarlane, *Buchanan* (London: Duckworth, 1981), 208.

[34] e.g. Francisco Ximénez, *Carro de las donas* (Valladolid: Juan de Villaquiran, 1542), bk. II, ch. 63.

philosopher), and a number of Latin poems.[35] Though a variety of surviving documents attest to her existence, her writings, and her relationship with the royal household, none of her own writings seem to have been preserved.

Queen Isabel was also a promoter of learning in other women. Having found that Latin was useful to her, she ensured that her daughters were adequately equipped for the lives they would lead as future queens: they were instructed initially by Franciscan tutors, and she also engaged leading humanists, Antonio Geraldini and his brother Alessandro, for more advanced instruction. The princesses read the Christian poets Prudentius and Juvencus, the Church Fathers Ambrose, Augustine, Gregory, and Jerome, the classical moralist Seneca, some Latin history, civil and canon law. Interestingly, this rather medieval curriculum, strong on Christian Latin, and notably devoid of pagan poets such as Virgil and Ovid, is also a highly patriotic one: Prudentius, Juvencus, and Seneca were all Spaniards.[36] The Princess Juana is said to have been able to improvise harangues in Latin; since Italian humanist educational techniques stressed verbal fluency, this may well be the case.[37] Her sister Catherine, later wife of Henry VIII, was very well educated. As an adult, she was recognized as a skilful diplomat versed in languages and knowledgeable in affairs of state (she even led an army in the field),[38] and her education for rule is tacitly recognized by the conspiracy organized by Eustache Chapuys, ambassador of Emperor Charles V, which sought to depose Henry and place Catherine on the throne as regent for Mary.[39]

Throughout the sixteenth century, Hapsburg princesses were well educated, because they were expected to be able to handle authority. Mary of Hungary was Regent of the Netherlands, as her aunt Marguerite had been before her, and was a correspondent of Erasmus.[40] Joanna of Austria, a little later, left a number of minor works in Latin.[41] Her brother Felipe II of Spain was in the habit of employing his female relatives in viceregal capacities, since he trusted them: Margaret of Parma was Regent of the Netherlands for a considerable time, and towards the end of his life, he intended his daughter Isabella to rule the Netherlands after him.[42] Outside her own family, Queen Isabel promoted the study of Latin for nuns: for example,

[35] Dolores Gomez Molleda, 'La cultura femenina en la época de Isabel la Católica', *Revista de archivos, bibliotecas y museos*, 61 (1955), 148, 176–9.

[36] Garrett Mattingly, *Catherine of Aragon* (London: Jonathan Cape, 1942; repr. 1963), 17–18. Nader, *The Mendoza Family*, 83: 15th-century 'caballero humanism' was highly conscious of the 'Spanish' Romans, and Spain's claim to be heir of Rome.

[37] Rousselot, *Histoire de l'éducation des femmes*, i. 164.

[38] Mattingly, *Catherine of Aragon*, 120–1. Catherine's martial exploits are given a heroic treatment in a French poem, 'Borbonidos', Paris, Bibliothèque Nationale de France, Lat. 14162. fos. 27ᵛ–29ʳ.

[39] Constance Jordan, 'Feminism and the Humanists', *Renaissance Quarterly*, 36.2 (1983), 198–201.

[40] Letter 2820, in *Opus Epistolarum Des. Erasmi*, ed. P. S. Allen and H. M. Allen (Oxford: Clarendon Press, 1906–58), from Brussels, 13 June 1533: see Anne M. O'Donnell, 'Contemporary Women in the Letters of Erasmus', *Grasmus of Rotterdam Society Yearbook*, 9 (1989), 34–72.

[41] A 'Vita S. Didaci a Joanna Austriae latine reddita' is mentioned in *Antigua lista de manoscritos latinos y griegos inéditos de Escorial, publícala con prólogo, notas y dos apéndices* (Madrid: P. B. Fernández, 1902): there are also manuscripts of other exercises in Naples, Biblioteca Nazionale, V H 345 and Madrid, Biblioteca Nacional, 17582. Both of the latter are dedicated to her brother Felipe.

[42] Geoffrey Parker, *Philip II* (London: Hutchinson, 1979), 68, 195–6.

when she founded a convent at Granada in 1500 she looked for a Latin-literate woman to teach Latin to the other nuns.[43] A number of sixteenth-century nuns evidently benefited from this concern. Sor María Tellez, a Franciscan of the convent of Tordesillas, published a translation of a Latin tract by Dionysius (Denys) the Carthusian in 1539.[44] Later, Doña María Vela y Cueta entered the Benedictine convent of St Ana in Avila having already learned from her mother embroidery, music, Latin, and the Scriptures. She became teacher of the novices in 1601 due to her Latin learning.[45]

Following Queen Isabel's lead, from early in the sixteenth century, a number of humanist men, though naturally concerned primarily with promoting Latin studies for men and boys, gave some attention to the education of Spanish women who remained in the world. The humanist education of the royal family may have affected the education of their immediate entourage: it is said, for example, that Gregoria and Luisa Perez, the daughters of Antonio Perez, chief minister of Felipe II, were educated in Latin. A slightly later young woman with an academic father at court, Caterina Stella, daughter of Felipe II's royal historian, is claimed as a Latin and Spanish poet by della Chiesa.[46] Humanist, rather than court, circles also began to include women. John Vergara, one of a pair of scholarly brothers, for example, writing to Erasmus, boasted to him that their sister was also educated enough to have read Erasmus' work first in Spanish, then in Latin—this was in 1528.[47] It is notable that two of the leading humanist professors in Spain, the grammarian Antonio de Lebrija of Alcalà, known as 'the phoenix of scholars',[48] and Juan Sobrarias, professor of liberal arts at the University of Saragossa, educated their respective daughters, Francisca de Lebrija and Juana Sobrarias. Both young women are said to have lectured as occasional substitutes for their fathers.[49] Juana Sobrarias, additionally, is said to have composed the Latin verse inscription on her father's tomb. Bomli also claims that, most unusually, a woman student matriculated at Salamanca in 1546, Clara Chitera, a student of medicine and mathematics.[50]

---

[43] Vincente Belrán de Heredia, *Cartularia de la Universidad de Salamanca*, 6 vols. (Salamanca: Universidad de Salamanca, 1970–2), iii. 307.

[44] María Tellez, *Pasion de nuestro Señor Jesucriso* (Valladolid: Nicolas Tremy, 1539).

[45] Milagros Ortega Costa, 'Spanish Women in the Reformation', in Sherrin Marshall (ed.), *Women in Reformation and Counter-Reformation Europe* (Bloomington: Indiana University Press, 1989), 89–119 (p. 103).

[46] Francisco Agostino della Chiesa, *Theatro delle donne letterate* (Mondovi: Giovanni Gislandi & Giovanni Tomaso Rossi, 1620), 122–3. Diego Ignacio Parada, *Escritoras y eruditas españolas* (Madrid: Librerias de A. de San Martín, 1881), 190, describes her as a historian herself.

[47] *Erasmi Epistolae*, letter 2004, Madrid, 29 June 1528, ed. Allen and Allen, vii. 411/52–6. In this letter, Isabella Vergara sends greetings together with her brother.

[48] Author of *Introductiones Latinae*, an immensely successful Latin grammar, see Caro Lynn, *A College Professor of the Renaissance* (Chicago: University of Chicago Press, 1937), 96.

[49] P. W. Bomli, *La Femme dans l'Espagne du siècle d'or* (The Hague: Martin Nijhoff, 1950), 157. See also Molleda, 'La cultura femenina en la época de Isabel la Católica'.

[50] Bomli, *La Femme*, 159–60. I found no mention of this woman anywhere during the admittedly brief time I spent in Salamanca.

As we have seen, the Italian Geraldini brothers were co-opted into the education of the royal princesses. Another Italian, the Sicilian Lucio Marineo, who was strongly encouraged in his work by Fernando and Isabel,[51] was associated in a variety of ways with educated women.[52] In his various writings, he notes the achievements of Ángel Carlet, daughter of Barón de Carlet, a pupil of Andrés Estanco, who was versed in Greek and Latin and is credited with various epistles and orations. He also wrote to Lucia de Medrano, who is said to have lectured in classics at Salamanca,[53] and to Ana Cervatón, a lady distinguished for birth, beauty, and erudition, who was maid of honour to Queen Germaine (Germaine de Foix, niece of Louis XII, second wife of Fernando of Aragon). Her commitment to learning was such that when the Duke of Alva sought to marry her, he took up classical studies so he could correspond with her in Latin.[54] Her Latin reply to Marineo waves off his flattery with some elegance.

Some insight into Marineo's attitude to learned women can be found in a letter which he wrote to Joanna Contrera of Segovia, the niece of López de Baena, who had sent him one of her Latin letters, in which, interestingly, she applied the word *herois* to herself. *Herois* is properly speaking the female form of 'hero', but following the immense success of Ovid's *Heroides*, there was a case for understanding the word to signify 'a woman who writes': a number of European writers of the late Renaissance seem to use it in this way.[55] Marineo sent corrections, mostly on uncontroversial matters of style. She replied at once, and questioned his comment on her *herois*. He went into it again, and rebuked her: 'though it can justly be granted to the nobility of your family or the quality of your learning, yet it is not suitable for a girl of your years.'[56] Nonetheless, he is said to have supported her work, perhaps out of compliment to López de Baena, since he allegedly published a collection of her writings entitled *Joanna Contrerae, Puellae Doctae, Epistolarum Carminum et Orationes Aliquod* (to which I can find no recent bibliographic reference).[57]

---

[51] Lynn, *A College Professor*; see also his letters. *Lucio Marinei Siculi Epistolarum Familiarum Libri Decem et Septem* (Valladolid: A. G. Brocar, 1514), 7, 32^v, 109^v–110, 110^v, 115, 115^v, 117, 118 (there is a letter from Queen Isabel to Marineo, sig. Aii), and Pietro Verrua, *Nel mondo umanistico spagnuolo spighendo dall 'Epistolario' di Lucio Marineo Siculo* (Rovigo: Tip. Cond. Servadei, 1906).

[52] Marineo, *Epistolae Familiares*, sig. C 5^v–6^r introduces his work on notable and excellent ladies of Spain.

[53] Ibid., xii, ep. xxxiii, p. 114. Nicolás Antonio, *Biblioteca Hispana* (Rome: Nicolaus Angelus Tinussius, 1672), ii. 351–2.

[54] Marineo, *Epistolae Familiares*, sig. n 8^r. Her letter in reply was written at Burgos, 14 Oct. 1512 (sig. n 8^v). Antonio, *Biblioteca Hispana*, prints the letter and reply, ii. 339–40.

[55] Many of the French humanists who honoured the Seymours used *herois* to describe them (see Ch. 10).

[56] *Epistolarum Familiarum Libri Decem & Septem* (Valladolid: Arnaldo Guilielmo Brocario, 1514). See further Pietro Verrua, *Una lezione epistolare di latino a una donzella spagnuola 1504* (Bobbio: A. Cella, 1912).

[57] It is mentioned by Serrano y Sanz, *Apuntes*, i.1, p. 278, and by Gil González Dávila, *Teatro eclesiástico de las iglesias metropolitanas y catedrales de los reynos de las dos Castillas*, 4 vols. (Madrid, 1645–1700), i. 525. It is not, however, in Erdmann.

Marineo was also on close terms with a number of women of the Enríquez family (connections of the Mendozas).[58] Countess Anna Enríquez replied to a panegyric by Lucio Marineo on the Enríquez family, evoked by the fact that grandfather, father, and son, Alfonso, Fadrique, and Alfonso, were successively admirals of Spain. He wrote the tomb-verse for a sculpture group in their memory at the church in Palencia, and sent it to Countess Anna, who sent a poem approving his work.[59] He was also friendly with María de Velasco, mother of the Admiral Don Fadrique Henríquez, and wife of Juan Velázquez de Cuéllar, contador mayor of Castile, a member of the royal council; husband and wife were patrons of Marineo. María de Velasco corresponded with Marineo in Latin.[60] He tutored their five sons in the year 1511, and remained friendly with the family thereafter.

Renaissance Spain also gives us a clear-cut example of the 'intellectual family': the Mendozas, children of the second Conde de Tendilla, who was 'equally distinguished by his successes in arms, letters, and love', according to Prescott.[61] His children were exceptionally scholarly in their interests. They included Diego Hurtado de Mendoza, who became a historian, and was the friend of the poet Doña Magdalena Bobadilla,[62] the poet Juan Hurtado de Mendoza, who was friendly with the Latin woman poet Catalina Paz, and their sisters, Doña María Pacheco and Doña María de Mendoza, who were widely celebrated for their learning, and corresponded with Spanish humanists.[63] An Escorial manuscript credits María de Mendoza with learning in Latin, Greek, mathematics, and poetry. Paulo Manucio commented, 'when we read what she writes, we adjudge it absolutely equal in wit to ancient writers';[64] while Alvar Gómez de Castro of Toledo wrote a number of Latin letters and verses to her.[65] María Pacheco's reputation among contemporary Spanish humanists is witnessed by the existence of a *tumulus* in her honour.[66]

---

[58] Nader, *The Mendoza Family*, 43.

[59] Lynn, *A College Professor*, 62. Benedetto Croce, *La Spagna nella vita italiana* (Bari: Laterza, 1917), 66.

[60] Lynn, *A College Professor*, 229.

[61] William H. Prescott, *History of the Reign of Ferdinand and Isabella the Catholic*, last edn. ed. J. F. Kirk (London: Sonnenschein, 1895), 347. Nader, *The Mendoza Family*, points out, p. xii, 'it was common for one or more children of a marriage to carry the mother's family name': hence María Pacheco (her mother was Francisca Pacheco, daughter of her father's successor as tutor to the Infanta Juana, Juan Pacheco).

[62] R. Foulché-Delbosc (ed.), 'Correspondencia de doña Magdalena de Bobadilla', *Revue hispanique*, 8 (1901), 1–59. These letters are in Spanish; she was, however, 'doctissima in Latina', according to Antonio, *Biblioteca Hispana*, ii. 346. A María de Bobadilla printed a poem in Guardia de Resende, *Canconiero general* (Lisbon: Hernan de Campos, 1516): this may be the same woman.

[63] Juana de Mendoza, who published a vernacular poem in Guardia de Resende, *Canconiero general* mentioned by Erdmann (p. 224), may also be a relative.

[64] 'cum autem ea quae scripsit legimus, vel antiquis scriptoribus ingenii praestantia simillimam judicamus'. *Apuntes*, ii.1, p. 54.

[65] One is printed, 'ad illustrissimam D. Mariam Mendociam', inc. 'nunc tandem moriar', in Fernando Mena, *Commentaria in libros de sanguinis [e]missione et purgatione* (Alcalá: Officina Brocarii, 1558). Others are in *Apuntes*, ii. 2, pp. 658–61. See also Molleda, 'La cultura femenina en la época de Isabel la Católica', 181–4.

[66] Escorial, Biblioteca Real, V ii 3, fos. 12–276, *Ad Illustrissimae D.Mariae Pacciechae Tumulum*: 'Principibus genita et Padillae coniugis ultrix.' The first line refers to her heroic defence of Toledo for nine months after the execution of her husband (see Ortega Costa, 'Spanish Women in the Reformation', 93–4).

Another Spanish family with strong humanist tendencies is that of the Dantiscos. Early in the sixteenth century, Isabel del Gada, a young widow in Valladolid, had an affair with the Polish humanist Jan Dantyszek (1485–1543), resident Polish ambassador at the court of Charles V, which produced two children, a boy who died young, and a girl, Juana (b. 1526). Dantyszek left his mistress and their daughter and returned to Poland *c*.1532, and Isabel was literate enough to pursue him by letter.[67] Juana married her father's friend, the respected Spanish humanist and Erasmian Jacobo Gracián de Alderek in 1546, and became the mother of thirteen children. One was a well-known writer, Lucas Gracián Dantisco (1543–87), a second, Thomas Gracián Dantisco, became Secretary of Languages under Felipe III and married a woman with a contemporary reputation as a Latin poet, Lorenza Méndez de Zurita,[68] and a third, Jerónimo Gracián, became a conspicuously learned priest, and was the intimate friend of St Teresa of Jesus.[69] This series of connections suggest a family pattern of learning and friendly association with highly educated women.

It is also clear that a number of humanist men active in Spain took a friendly and fostering attitude towards humanist women. Alvar Gómez de Castro, already mentioned in connection with María de Mendoza, also wrote a short poem to the most famous of all Peninsular women Latinists, Luisa Sigea.[70] Further, he was one of the tutors of Leonor Méndez de Zurita, wife of Tomás Gracián Dantisco. He can also be found sending a Latin poem by a woman to a male friend; in a letter to Pedro de la Rua he says 'I am sending you a recently written poem by Maria Magdalena' (the author is María Magdalena de Padilla).[71] Doña Padilla, attested by that name in a number of different places, may in fact be the woman also identified as María Pacheco, since the latter became the wife of Juan de Padilla; if this is indeed so, then she was the sister of Diego Hurtato de Mendoza mentioned above; and a substantial amount of the women's Latin production of Renaissance Spain was concentrated in a single family.

The account of women Latin poets in the Peninsula has thus far been somewhat depressingly based on second-hand sources, many of them contemporary, or near-contemporary, but nonetheless, no real substitute for surviving work.

---

[67] Harold B. Segel, *Renaissance Culture in Poland* (Ithaca, NY: Cornell University Press, 1989), 178–9. Her letters are in Zbigniew Nowak, *Jan Dantyszek* (Wrocław: Zaklad Narodwy im Ossolinskich, 1982), 200–2 (not seen: I do not know if they are in Spanish or Latin).

[68] She was taught by Alvar Gómez de Castro and Maestro Serna, and spent her life in Valladolid. Her daughter Margarita was baptized there in 1601, and she was certainly dead by 1605. Lope de Vega wrote a poem in her praise mentioning her poems in Latin, hymns, and letters. Juan Perez de Moya, *Varia historia de sanctos e illustres mugeres en todo genero de virtudes* (Madrid: Francisco Sanchez, 1583), 310, also refers to 'sus Epistolas y versos latinos, compuestos con muy elegante estilo . . .' (*Apuntes*, ii. 1, p. 48).

[69] Otger Steggink, 'Spiritual Friendship in Teresa of Avila', in Elisja Schulte van Kessel (ed.), *Women and Men in Spiritual Culture* (The Hague: Staatsuitgeverij, 1986), 213–23, 218–21.

[70] A. Schott, *Hispanioe Bibliothecae seu de Academiis et Bibliothecis* (Frankfurt: Claudius Marnius & Haeredes Ioan. Aubrii, 1608), 342. There are also two Latin letters from her to him in Madrid, Biblioteca Naçional, 18673.

[71] Madrid, Biblioteca Naçional, 8424, fo. 135. Unfortunately the poem has not been preserved with the letter.

Catalina Paz, on the other hand, has left some actual verse. She was a native either of Badajoz or of Alcalá de Henares, and was buried in Guadalajara at the age of only 27. She contributed introductory verses to Juan Hurtado de Mendoza's book of verse, *El buen placer trobado en trece discantes de cuarte rima castellana*: printed in Alcalá in 1550. All her surviving verse is connected with Hurtado de Mendoza: two poems are preserved because they are printed in *El buen placer*, and another two, in an eighteenth-century manuscript copy, probably owe their survival to their association with the poet. The most personal of them is a long poem on the death of her mother, of which this is the first half:[72]

Ad clarissimum virum Dominum Joannem Hurtadum Mendoçam, de obitu matris

Maxima curarum requies cum sola mearum
Solamenque meo nec non comes una labori
Inclyte Ioannes, mihi sit pia mater adempta,
Nulla fuit toto natae quae charior orbe
Cuique magis dilecta fuit non filia matri,
Quod mihi solamen tanto vis ferre dolori
Ponere naufragii, quod me tua musa timorem
Admonet, an portus potero sperare secundos?
Infelix ullos aegre nun gaudia menti
Ulla meae tandem veniant sperare licebit?
Naufragio hoc facto nobis dum vita supersit,
Quid faustum felixque putas jam posse videri?
Hei mihi quod tecum comitem mea mater abire,
Non licuit tantumque meum finire dolorem;
Illa quidem spero fato meliore potitur
Optatis fruitur dempto secura timore
Et felix curas liquit liquitque labores
Ad superos migrans requies ubi summa videtur;
At mihi nulla meis subeunt solatia curis
Nec levat hoc nostrum tantum finitve dolorem,
Nam mea tam chara cum sit domus orba parente
Amisso fluitat ceu navis in equore clavo

To the noble man, Don Joannes Hurtado de Mendoza, on the death of her mother

O noble Juan, since my blessed mother has been taken from me,
The greatest and only reliever and solace of my cares
And the sole companion of my labours:
There was never in the whole world a woman dearer to her daughter
Or a daughter who was more a delight to this mother.
Because you wish to bring me consolation in such a great grief,
Because your Muse advises me to set aside fear of shipwreck,
Should I be able to hope, unhappy though I am, for any favourable havens?
Shall it now be permitted, with a struggle,
To hope that any joys may come in the end to my mind?

[72] Janet Fairweather suggested the following emendations: 'quod', line 7 (for 'quid'), 'Ad', line 18 (for 'at')

What do you think can now seem auspicious and happy?
Alas, that it was not permitted for me to depart with you, my mother,
As your companion, and bring to an end such great grief as is mine.
She, I hope, is in possession of a better fate,
Is enjoying the objects of her desire, free from fear,
And blessed as she is, has left behind cares and left behind troubles,
By going to join those above, where there seems to be the greatest peace.
But no consolations come to the rescue of my troubles,
Nor does this relieve this grief of ours—so great is it.
For since my house is bereft of so dear a parent,
It tosses about, like a ship at sea which has lost its anchor.

Like a number of poems and other writings by fifteenth- and sixteenth-century Italians, this poem testifies to a close companionate relationship between humanist daughters and their mothers. Paz is highly praised by Matamoros, who laments her death thus:[73]

For here died that Catalina Paz, who having barely completed her twenty-seventh year, in the flower of her life, was snatched by a cruel and immature death from her contemporaries, in Caracas, now called Guadalajara, attracting the inconsolable grief of the muse. Alas, what verses of wit, flourishing at the highest peak of eloquence, did Fate lay low on that day? Who is more polished in letters than she who died and was buried?

Another sixteenth-century woman who may be a relative of Catalina Paz, a Franciscan nun called Doña Elena de Paz, of Salamanca, is mentioned by Serrano y Santz as the author of a 'Soneto á D. Francisco de Borja y Aragón' (on Francisco de Borgia, one of the first Jesuits). She is also said to have written in Latin.[74]

Luisa Sigea

By far the most famous woman Latinist of the Peninsula is Luisa Sigea (1522–60).[75] She is the only one whose reputation has survived to the end of the twentieth

---

[73] Alfonso Garcia Matamoros, *De Asserenda Hispanorum Eruditione* (Madrid: Juan Brocar, 1553), fo. 59ʳ. 'Nam haec fuit illa Catharina Pacensis, quae nondum expleto aetatis anno vicesimo septimo, in ipso vitae flore Caracae, quae nunc Guadalajara, acerba et inmatura morte è vivis proxima aetate erepta, insanibilem attulit musis dolorem. Heu, quae ingenii versa illa die ad summam gloriam eloquentiae florescens fortuna prostravit? Quae non literae politiores cum illa mortuae, et sepultae fuerunt?'

[74] In *Aplauso gratulatorio de la insigne escuela de Salamanca, al ilustrísimo Señor Don Franciso la restauración de los votos de los estudientes*, (Barcelona: Sebastián de Carmellas, n.d.). Serrano y Sanz, *Apuntes*, ii. 1, cites Juan Bautista Cubié, *Las mujeres vindicadas* (Madrid: A. Perez de Soto, 1768), 'who says that she wrote many works in Latin and Spanish which would make up a bulky volume'.

[75] Luisa Sigea's works are in Paul Allut, *Aloysia Sygea et Nicolas Chorier* (Lyon: N. Scheuring, 1862), and *Luisa Sigea: dialogue des deux jeunes filles sur la vie de cour et la vie de retraite (1552)*, ed. Odette Sauvage (Paris: Presses Universitaires de France, 1970). The most recent study is Edward V. George, 'Luisa Sigea (1522–1560): Iberian Scholar-Poet', in Churchill et al. (eds.), *Women Writing Latin*, iii. 167–87, but see also Odette Sauvage, 'Recherches sur Luisa Sigea', *Bulletin des études portugaises*, NS 31 (1970), 36–60, Inès Rada, 'Profil et trajectoire d'une femme humaniste: Luisa Sigea', in Augustin Redondo (ed.), *Images de la femme en Espagne au xviᵉ et xviiᵉ siècles* (Paris: Publications de la Sorbonne, 1994), 339–49.

century, though to some extent for a most unfortunate reason: the name of this learned, devout, and serious lady was attached to a famous work of pornography as an impertinent jest by its true author, Nicholas Chorier.[76] Her own version of her biography, briefly outlined in a letter she wrote to Felipe II in 1559, is, 'though my place of origin is Tarançon, I was brought up in Portugal, and am of French stock, and I was educated in the Latin, Greek, Hebrew, Syriac, and, to some extent, Arabic, languages by my father and other tutors'.[77] Her father was perhaps from Nîmes (where the name Sygée is found). He attended the University of Alcalá, where he learned Latin, Greek, and Hebrew, married a Spanish noblewoman, and had four children by her, two sons and two daughters. He tutored all four of his children in all the languages at his command, and hired a tutor to teach Arabic and Syriac also to his brilliant daughter Luisa: his elder son, also very talented, went first to the Complutensian University of Madrid and later to Coimbra. The second sister, Angela, was known as a Greek and Latin scholar, but her great forte, all commentators assert, was music. She married Antonio de Mellomogo.[78]

The family moved to Lisbon in 1542, where Sigea was invited to court, and became tutor to the Infanta Doña Maria of Portugal (1521–77), daughter of King Manoel by his third wife, Eleanor (Leonor) of Austria, who was herself the daughter of the Hapsburg Philip the Fair and Juana (daughter of Isabel) of Spain.[79] She taught her to some purpose: Allut quotes a Latin letter written by Maria to her mother Eleanor after the latter had made a second marriage to François I of France, which is both fluent and elegant.[80] Furthermore, the fact that the Infanta Maria sought to create a correspondence with her cousin Mary Tudor in 1546, three years into Sigea's career as her tutor, can possibly be attributed to the latter's influence: the Infanta's letter speaks of 'having heard of the fame of her virtuous learning'.[81] A long Latin poem to the infanta, quoted by Antonio, describes her as another Zenobia or Eudocia;[82] Resendius, more pertinently, describes her as 'another Sigea'.[83]

After thirteen years at court, Luisa Sigea and her family retired to the little village of Torres-Novas in 1555, and she married Francisco de Cuevas, an impoverished nobleman from Burgos, in 1557. Her experience of life at court was bitter: writing

[76] *Aloisiae Sigeae Toletanae Satyra Sotadica de Arcanis Amoris et Veneris*, first printed in 1659/60: see Roger Thompson, *Unfit for Modest Ears* (Totowa, NJ: Rowman and Littlefield, 1979), 28–33.

[77] London, British Library, Add. 9939, fos. 145ʳ–146ʳ (fo. 145ʳ).

[78] Allut, *Aloysia Sygea*, 8.

[79] António Moro and Sánchez Coello, 'A princesa esquecida: D. Maria de Portugal (1521–1578)', in Annemarie Jordan (ed.), *Retrato de corte em Portugal: o legado de António Moro (1552–1572)* (Lisbon: Quetzal Editores, 1994), 63–72.

[80] Allut, *Aloysia Sygea*, 11.

[81] David Loades, *The Reign of Mary Tudor* (London: Ernest Benn, 1979), 132, *Letters and Papers*, 5 Nov. 1546, 21, 355. Another Latin letter from the infanta to Eusebius of Coimbra is mentioned by Antonio, *Biblioteca Hispana*, ii. 346.

[82] Antonio, *Biblioteca Hispana*, ii. 346.

[83] L. Andreas Resendius, *Antiquitatum Lusitanae, et de Municipio Eborem, Libri V* (Cologne: Arnoldus Mylius, 1600), ii. 78–82 (p. 80). Resendius also praises her erudition in a prose *oratio*, ii. 266–84 (p. 281).

(in Latin) to her brother-in-law Alfonso de Cuevas, she explains that she had spent thirteen years of 'onerous servitude' with the infanta, only to find that, at the end, she was refused her due salary.[84] It is unsurprising to find that one of her major works, a Latin dialogue between two young women about the relative desirability of court and private life, comes down firmly against courts.[85] The rest of her short life was spent in chronic money worries, as she and her husband sought for patronage. She met María, Queen of Hungary, in Burgos,[86] and three surviving letters tell a sad story: the first, written from Burgos in 1557, reminds the queen of her promise to remunerate her services and those of her husband, the second excuses herself from attending on the queen at Valladolid, the third, in March 1558, apologizes for her tardiness in fulfilling the queen's orders due to the inconveniences of advanced pregnancy.[87] The queen did finally make a commitment to the de Cuevas: she brought them to Valladolid, numbered Sigea among her *dames de maison*, and gave de Cuevas the post of secretary. It briefly seemed as if they were established at last, but this was illusory. After a few months, the queen died, leaving them with nothing but a small pension. A letter to Felipe II survives asking for a court position for de Cuevas, but nothing came of it.[88] Luisa Sigea died in poverty in 1560, leaving a daughter. As Allut sadly comments, her contemporaries Camões and Cervantes fared no better, so the limited achievement of Spanish humanism (not just of women humanists) may be partly explained by absence of serious royal sponsorship or interest in the generations which followed Fernando and Isabel.[89]

Sigea's greatest monument as a Latin poet is the long poem *Sintra*, published in 1566.[90] This describes the site of the royal palace at Sintra, together with a visionary projection of the political future of her patron, Doña Maria, which looks forward unambiguously to a future, never in fact realized, in which Maria will become the wife of her cousin Felipe II, emperor over the Spanish territories in both Europe and the New World (the death of Edward VI in 1553 and accession of Mary Tudor, another cousin, made the English queen a more tempting prize, so the Portuguese negotiations were dropped in favour of the English marriage which actually occurred). This negotiation was a matter of common knowledge.[91] The

---

[84] Allut, *Aloysia Sygea*, 11–12.

[85] *Luisa Sigea*, ed. Sauvage.

[86] Another daughter of Juana of Castile: she married Lewis II of Hungary and Bohemia. She was Governor of the Low Countries for Felipe II. There she was admired by many scholars, Erasmus among them, while her entourage provided a direct line of contact between the Southern Netherlands and the Austrian lands. R. J. W. Evans, *Rudolf II and his World* (Oxford: Oxford University Press, 1973), 117. She was sympathetic to the reformist idea of Erasmus, and wrote to him: letter 2820, *Erasmi Epistolae*, Brussels, 13 June, 1533. O'Donnell, 'Contemporary Women in the Letters of Erasmus'.

[87] Translated by George, 'Luisa Sigea', 179–80.

[88] Allut, *Aloysia Sygea*, 14, trans. George, 'Luisa Sigea', 180–1.

[89] Ibid., 15.

[90] There are two variant texts of *Sintra*. The text and translation given here are of the version published in 1556 and by Allut, since it was probably the best known. The variant text survives in a manuscript, Toledo, Biblioteca Pública, 338 and is published by both Serrano y Sanz and George (who translates it).

[91] Loades, *Mary Tudor*, 110.

poem therefore implicitly suggests something of the pressures, and humiliations, of the lives of princesses, since it is apparently written in response to depression and anxiety on the infanta's part: the reassurances offered by the Nymph suggest that she felt life was passing her by, and despaired of her future. Felipe's negotiations would naturally date to the early 1550s, which is to say, after the Infanta Maria had hit the dangerous age of 30 in 1551, and so the poem must come from these years, and possibly from 1553, after the negotiations with the Hapsburgs had ground to a halt.[92] Maria, courted in her youth by many European princes, in the event was never married.[93]

Another interesting feature of *Sintra* is its structural similarity with earlier women's poems: with Sappho's *Hymn to Aphrodite*, and (still more closely) with a work firmly believed to be by a woman, the late antique 'Sulpicia's' *Satire*: a long invocation containing description, followed by an answer, which in both the *Satire* and *Sintra* is cast in the form of a prophecy.

'Nympha loci custos, vitreo quæ gurgite lymphas
    Concipis, & divum pandere fata potes:
Tu mihi fatorum seriem, "quæ regia virgo
    Regna manet?", resera, "quosve manet thalamos?" '
Illa libens roseo (dum sic loquor) intonat ore:
    'Quod, virgo, rogitas, accipe, nec dubita.
Neptunus genitor nuper me ad summa tonantis
    Atria perduxit concelebrata deis.
Consititerant cuncti vescentes nectare, nec non
    Ambrosia: at postquam mensa remota fuit,
Digna petunt divi regali in principe dona,
    Imperio ut superet, quas superat meritis.
Docta Minerva aderat, cantusque inventor Apollo,
    Nec non Calliope, pignora cara Iovis,
Quos coluit virgo, quorumque exercuit artes,
    Illi gratantes munera pulchra petunt.
Iuppiter adridens vultu, quo sidera lustrat,
    Respondet divis, quo petiere simul:
'Gaudete, O superi: perstare immota potentis
    Principis augustae maxima fata volo.
Nec, licet adspiciat quasdam nunc carpere regna,

---

[92] Loades, ibid. 112, notes that Felipe, responding to his father's letter suggesting that they pursue Mary Tudor rather than the infanta, states that he had decided to break off discussions because he deemed the dowry offered insufficient. *CSP (Spanish)*, ed. Martin A. S. Hume (London: Eyre and Spottiswoode for HMSO, 1892–4), xi. 177–8. He was, however, intimating to the Portuguese that he would accept their terms, so it is hard to know how much of his changing state of mind would have been visible in Portugal.

[93] She is sometimes said to have been married to Alessandro Farnese, Prince of Parma, but that is due to a confusion of this Infanta Maria with another Portuguese Infanta Maria (1538–77), also learned, the daughter of one of her elder half-brothers, Dom Duarte. Apart from, inevitably, occupying herself with religion, she was also interested in food on the evidence of her *Livro de cozinha da Infanta D. Maria: Codice Portugues I.E. 3 da Biblioteca Nacional de Napoles*, ed. Giacinto Manuppella, Biblioteca de Autores Portugueses (Lisbon: Impr. Nacional, Casa da Moeda, 1987).

Desperet: capient mox sua fata locum.
Non nisi per magnos vincuntur magna labores:
  Nec tulit ignavos regia celsa deos.
Quosque aliæ sponsos captent, visuntur ubique:
  Quem sibi fata parant, non nisi summa tenet.
Hæc reget imperium felix, quum nupserit, orbis:
  Pacatus dominæ cedet uterque polus.
Vade ergo, & timidæ referas, quæ diximus, ore
  Fatidico, ut lætos exigat illa dies.
Nec sis sollicita, aut metuas prædicere fata:
  Succedent votis ordine cuncta tuis.

'O nymph, guardian of this place, you who bring forth the waters from the glassy fountain,
And are able to show forth the decrees of the gods,
Unlock to me the sequence of the fates, whether the royal virgin
Will dwell in her kingdoms, or will dwell in which marriage-chambers?'
While I was still saying this, she willingly prophesied with her rosy lips:
'What you have requested, O virgin, receive now, and do not doubt it.
Neptune my father recently took me up to the courts of the thunderer,
Where the gods celebrate together.
They all sat around feeding on nectar and ambrosia,
And after the table was removed, on behalf of the royal princess,
The gods sought worthy gifts,
That she might rise in ruling power above those whom she surpasses in merit.
Learned Minerva was there, and Apollo, inventor of song, and Calliope, graceful pleaders
  for her to Jove.
Those whom the virgin had cultivated, those whose arts she practised,
Now reciprocating, ask for splendid gifts for her.
Jupiter, who illumines the stars, with smiling face,
Responded to the gods, who made their petitions at the same time,
'Rejoice, O heavenly ones: I intend that the mighty fate
Of the powerful and august princess will stand immovable.
Nor should she despair, even though it may be that now she perceives others taking
  kingdoms:
Soon her fates will take their rightful place.
Only by great efforts are great things achieved:
A heavenly kingdom will not tolerate unworthy gods.
Other [princesses] take various spouses, they may be found everywhere,
He whom the fates have set aside for her lives only at the very summit.
Happy woman, she will rule an empire of the world, when she marries,
And both poles, pacified, will submit to a mistress.
Go therefore, and take back to that timid one with prophetic lips,
What we have said so that she may pass happy days.
Nor should you be troubled, or fear to predict fate:
All things will happen in sequence according to your prayers.'

Sigea's other surviving poems are short epigrams, two of them on Hieronymus de Brito, a Portuguese poet and theologian, and the long work in Latin prose already mentioned. Luisa Sigea corresponded with another woman Latin poet of the time,

María Magdalena de Padilla, mentioned above: a letter survives.[94] Two letters which she wrote to the humanist Alvar Gomez de Castro are also preserved.[95]

Portugal

The life history of Luisa Sigea serves as a reminder that the culture of Portugal is not identical with that of Spain. Despite the political unification of Spain and Portugal during the sixteenth century, the Portuguese remained strongly conscious of their separate cultural tradition and their separate royal line (much intermarried though it was with Spain). A number of Portuguese women were distinguished for their culture. A number of aristocratic and royal women are associated with the humanist Cataldo Parísio Siculo, who arrived in Portugal in 1485, notably the Infanta Dona Juana, the Queen Dona Leonor, wife of João II, the Marquesa de Vila Real and her sister Dona Leonor de Noronha, and others, and are mentioned in his letters.[96] An oration of his on the adventus of Elizabeth, daughter of Fernando and Isabel and wife of the Infante Afonso, son of João and Leonor, stresses her learning.[97] In the sixteenth century, the Princess Maria, tutored by Luisa Sigea, has already been briefly discussed, but mention should also be made of a later sixteenth-century princess, Maria, Princess of Parma, eldest daughter of Duarte, Infante of Portugal, the sixth son of King Manoel. She spoke Castilian, Italian, and Latin, wrote in Latin 'extremely elegantly', and knew some Greek. According to Hilarion de Coste, a manual for life, or *pratique spirituelle*, was found on her death in 1577, edited and printed in Italy by 'une dame de son cour', and translated into various languages.[98] Another Portuguese princess, Caterina, daughter of Duarte, Infante of Portugal, according to della Chiesa, studied Latin and Greek and wrote with elegance in both languages.[99] A marginally royal woman, Soror Berengaria de Villa de Conde, daughter of two Portuguese royal bastards, who became a nun in the convent of Clares of Villa de Conde, wrote a Latin rule for her house.[100]

---

[94] *Apuntes*, ii. 2, p. 663.

[95] Allut, *Aloysia Sygea*, 19–21.

[96] Américo da Costa Ramalho, *Para a história do humanismo em Portugal* (Coimbra: Instituto Nacional de la Investigação Científica, 1988), 101, Carolina Michaëlis de Vasconcelas, *A Infanta D. Maria de Portugal (1521–1577), e as suas damas* (Lisbon: Biblioteca Nacional, 1983) (facsimile of 1st edn. (Oporto, 1902), with introduction by da Costa Ramalho).

[97] Cataldo Parísio Siculo, *Duas orações*, ed. Maria Margarida Brandão Gomes da Silva (Coimbra: Centro de Estudos Clássicos e Humanísticos, 1974), 58.

[98] Hilarion de Coste, *Les Eloges et vies des reynes* (Paris: Sebastien Cramoisy, 1630), 556–61. The work he refers to is almost certainly *Pratica spirituale di una serva di Dio, al cui essempio può qualsivoglia monaca o persona spirituale essercitarsi* (Macerata: Martellini, 1577).

[99] Della Chiesa, *Theatro delle donne letterate*, 122. She was the wife of Giovanni, duke of Aragon. Damião de Froes Perym, *Theatro heroino* (Lisbon: Oficina da Musica de Theotonio Artunes Lima, 1736–40), i. 231, also states that she translated S. Lourenço Justiniano's *Disciplina Monastica* out of Latin, and that this was printed in the convent of Santa Cruz in Coimbra.

[100] Frey Juis dos Anjos, *Iardim de Portugal* (Coimbra, 1626), 243–5. He quotes extracts.

In actual court circles, we find a series of highly educated women, notably a maid of honour to Queen Catherine of Portugal, Joanna Vaz, who is said to have written extensively in Latin,[101] and is described as director of the 'aula regia'.[102] Her contemporary, Publia Hortensia de Castro, studied Latin, rhetoric, logic, philosophy, metaphysics, and theology: the fact that her parents named her after Publia Hortensia, the famous classical Roman oratrix, suggests that they had intended from her birth that she should become an educated woman.[103] Carolina de Vasconcelos attributes Latin verse to her.[104] She engaged in public disputations on Aristotle at the age of 17.[105] Nicolàs Antonio, drawing on the *Biblioteca lusitana* of Jorge Cardoso, states that Hortensia composed in Latin in imitation of the Psalms of David, and also composed other psalm-like verses praying for the safe return of Dom Duarte of Portugal from his expedition to Africa. All these works seem to be lost, but the fact that Felipe II gave her a life pension suggests that she was taken seriously in her own time.[106] Another Portuguese woman shared her interest in the Psalms: the learned Agueda Lopez of Lisbon wrote 150 poems in imitation of the Psalter, probably in the vernacular.[107]

Other women who were remembered for their learning include Dona Leanor de Noronha of Vila Real (1488–1567) who translated into Portuguese from Latin,[108] Margarita de Noronha, a Dominican nun, who published a translation of the Latin rules and constitution of her order,[109] a woman from Lisbon who published a very early work on women,[110] and Suor Violante da Ceo (1601–93).[111] However, very few

[101] 'Pello bom estilo com que escrevia quaesquer materias un lingua latina, & pella grão pró fidão, com que declarara qualquer Poeta, on autor que lhe metião nar mãos.' Ibid. 401. Antonio, *Biblioteca hispana*, ii. 340, 'in aula Mariae Infantis Portugalliae cum Luisa Sigea literis et eloquentia Latina floruit'. Andreas Resendius wrote verses on her, 'Porro autem comitum, quae jam maturior aevi' (printed by Antonio), and a Latin letter addressed to her by Rodrigo Sanches is printed in Américo da Costa Ramalho (ed.), *Latim Renascentista em Portugal* (Coimbra: Instituto Nacional de Investigação Científica, 1985), 154–5, addressing her as 'Lusitanae decus', and inviting her to correct his Latin style. See also da Costa Ramalho, *Para a história do humanismo em Portugal*, 96.

[102] Michaëlis de Vasconcelas, *A Infanta D. Maria de Portugal (1521–1577), e as suas damas*, 36–7.

[103] Dos Anjos, *Iardim de Portugal*, 402. Mentioned Antonio, *Biblioteca Hispana*, ii. 347.

[104] p. 110.

[105] Jacobo Menoetius (ed.), *Lucio Andrea Resendius, Libri Quatuor de Antiquitatibus Lusitanae* (Ebora, 1593), 'puella septendecim annorum, Publia Hortensia a Castro, studiis Aristotelicis non vulgariter instructa, publice disputans multis doctis viris, quae preposuerat convellentibus, cum summa dexteritate nec minori lepori argumentationum cavillationes eluderet.' Quoted by Serrano y Sanz, *Apuntes*, i. 247–8.

[106] Antonio, *Biblioteca Hispana*, ii. 347.

[107] Dos Anjos, *Iardim de Portugal*, 308–14.

[108] Ibid. 406–8. Two translations were published, *Coronica geral de Marco Antonio Cocio Sabeico... tresladada do latim em lingoagē portugues*, 2 vols. (Coimbra: Ioam de Barrier and Joam Alvarez, 1550–3), *Este liuro he do começo da historea de nossa redēnçam, que se fez pera consolaçam dos que nam sabē latin*, 2 vols. (Lisbon: German Galharde, 1552; and later editions).

[109] Froes Perym, *Theatro heroino*, ii. 123–4. She is listed as a learned lady in Charles Gerbier, *Eulogium Heroinum* (London: T. M. & A. C., 1650), and mentioned in Antonio, *Biblioteca Hispana*, ii. 347, who adds that she became a nun in Lisbon.

[110] Cristina [no surname], *Espelho o qual falla de tres estados de molheres* (Lisbon: Campos, 1518).

[111] Jacobus Quetif and Jacobus Echard, *Scriptores Ordinis Praedicatorum* (Paris: Christophe Baillard and Nicolas Simart, 1721), ii. 844–5 declare that she 'cultivated the sacred Latin muses', however, her two published volumes of verse are in Portuguese. Aubrey Bell, *Portuguese Literature* (Oxford: Clarendon Press, 1922), 107.

Portuguese women are credited with an actual writing in Latin, other than Joanna Vaz and Publia Hortensia de Castro: one such is Felipa Núñez of Ébora, who, according to Froes Perym, wrote *A Life of the Three Holy Kings* in Latin.[112] However, no surviving Latin verse can be securely attributed to any Portuguese woman of the Renaissance other than Luisa Sigea. There is some evidence for the continuation of a tradition of educating Portuguese noblewomen into the seventeenth century. The philosopher Duquesa, María Alencastria, Duquesa de Aveiro,[113] though she published nothing, is, however, written up at considerable length by Damião de Froes Perym in the eighteenth century, who quotes one of her Latin letters.[114]

Other evidence for Latin woman poets in the Peninsula is of a more indirect kind. Poetic *justas* or *certamina* were a feature of Peninsular life from the sixteenth century, sometimes confined to a particular institution, such as a seminary, sometimes open.[115] One of Catalina Paz's surviving Latin poems congratulates Juan Hurtado de Mendoza for his success in such a competition. Some women evidently felt free to participate: for example, Doña Antonia de Alarcón published a winning Spanish poem in the *Exequias* for Felipe III.[116] She also contributed to another on the death of Margaret of Austria, and to a Jesuit collection on the canonization of St Ignatius Loyola.[117]

Alcina lists Latin *justas* in which contributions were mostly anonymous: hence it is impossible to discover whether women participated, let alone were victorious.[118] The *certamen poeticum* in Madrid in 1542 seems to have attracted women, since Alfonso Garcia Matamoros of Madrid, writing in 1553, speaks of 'the very many learned women I have personally known', and refers to a particular woman who distinguished herself even above the 'crowd' of Latinate women, and was a prizewinner in poetic *certamina* for her Latin verse: annoyingly, he adds, 'no one who is not from Madrid will know the woman I want to allude to'.[119] Similarly,

---

[112] Froes Perym, *Theatro heroino*, i. 388, *Apuntes*, ii.1, p. 86.

[113] She learned Latin and Greek and was interested in peripatetic philosophy and theology: see *Emmanuelis Martini, ecclesiae Alonensis decani, epistolarum libri . . . accedunt auctoris vitae a Gregorio Majansio* (Amsterdam: J. Wetstenius and G. Smith, 1738), 37: The duquesa was well known enough in her own time to be celebrated in an Italian work on contemporary learned women, G. N. Bandiera, *Trattato degli studi delle donne, in due parte diviso, opera d'un accademico Intronato* (Venice: F. Pitteri, 1740), 148–9. She is the dedicatee of a Life of the Virgin by the nun Sor Catalina de Jesús y San Francisco, printed in 1693 (*Apuntes*, i. 609), and was admired by Sor Juana de la Cruz, who addressed a long poem to her.

[114] *Teatro heroino*, ii. 226–41 (pp. 239–40). The letter is dated 1684.

[115] Juan F. Alcina, *Repertorio de la poesia latina del Renascimento en España* (Salamanca: Ediciones Universidad de Salamanca, 1995), 104–20 lists Latin *justas* in which contributions were anonymous. The *certamen poeticum* in Madrid in 1542 (ibid. 105) may have attracted women.

[116] *Exequias. Tumulo y pompa funeral, que la Universidad de Salamance hizo en las honras del rey nuestra señor don Felipe III* (Salamanca: Antonio Vasquez, 1621). It is interesting and perhaps significant that a work in praise of women was printed in Italy for the Spanish market in the 16th century, Juan Spinola, *Dialogo in laude de las mugeres, intitulado Ginaece paenes* (Milan: Michele Tini, 1580).

[117] *Apuntes*, i. 18.

[118] Alcina, *Repertorio*, 104–20, esp. p. 105.

[119] Matamoros, *De Asserenda Hispanorum Eruditione*, fo. 59ʳ. Comparison with Juan Costa, *Govierno del Ciudadano* (Saragossa: Juan de Altarach, 1584), 377, suggests that he may be referring to Ángel Carlet, who is described in the latter work as 'celebrated by Matamoros'. Ángel Carlet, daughter of

Anna de Osorio is also said to have won competitions for Latin verse at both Alcalá and Seville, but there is no way of establishing whether any of her compositions are among those that survive.[120]

The cultural turn of seventeenth-century Spain was away from even the limited humanism of the sixteenth century towards a highly distinctive form of intense pietism marked by complex ritual observances. Politics and piety were inextricably mutually involved, in ways which gave royal women, and some others, a great deal of practical power: as Sánchez notes, 'the [Convent of the] Descalzas was actually one of the political centres in Madrid'.[121] An extraordinarily high proportion of all surviving Spanish manuscripts containing women's writings seem to be of works by María de Ágreda, a woman of immense significance in the Spain of her day, and the regular adviser of Felipe IV, with whom she exchanged more than 600 letters: there are thirty-seven manuscripts of works by Sor María in the published parts of the catalogue of the Biblioteca Nacional alone.[122] Not all nuns turned towards mysticism or politics: it is interesting to find that a Córdoban nun, Doña Catalina Alfonso Fernández, published two poems in praise of the Mexican 'phoenix' Sor Juana Inés de la Cruz in the Spanish editions of the latter's work (in *Fama y obras*, she is one of no less than six women who do so)[123] and also seconded her in writing in praise of the contemporary Swedish poet Sophia Elisabeth Brenner,[124] suggesting that this most brilliant of baroque women writers in the Hispanic languages was admired by other nuns as well as by women in the world.

A few early modern Catalan women left a name for scholarship. Doña Isabel de Josa y Cardona, who was remembered as very learned, wrote a work called *Tristis Isabella*, described in a 1902 handlist to the Escorial manuscripts, and since apparently lost.[125] Another Catalan woman scholar, Angela of Barcelona, is yet more shadowy.[126] But the only Catalan who became internationally famous was

Barón de Carlet, pupil of Andrés Estanco, was versed in Greek and Latin, and various epistles and orations are attributed to her. She lived in Valencia, and is also mentioned by Marineo.

[120] Matamoros, *De Asserenda Hispanorum Eruditione*, fo. 59ʳ. She is thought to have been the daughter of Don Diego de Osorio, lord of Aborca and Governor of Burgos (*Apuntes*, ii.1, p. 90). Serrano y Santz also listes a Doña Costanza Osorio of Seville (1565–1637), who learned Latin and was a nun in the 'convento de Dueñas', so this may have been a family with a tendency to educate daughters.

[121] Discussed in Magdalena S. Sánchez, *The Empress, the Queen, and the Nun* (Baltimore: Johns Hopkins University Press, 1998).

[122] Kendrick, *Mary of Ágreda*, 94–154. He notes, p. 5, that she acquired 'a small knowledge of Latin', but she always wrote in Spanish. Her writings are listed pp. 159–65.

[123] *Apuntes*, i. 22: the editions are *Poesias de la unica poetisa americana, musa dezima, Soror Juana Inés de la Cruz* (Madrid: Juan Garcia Infançon, 1690), and *Fama y obras posthumas del fenix de Mexico, decima Musa, poetisa americana, Sor Juana Inés de la Cruz* (Madrid: Manuel Ruiz de Muya, 1700), in which sig. ¶¶¶¶¶¶¶¶2ᵛ–sig. ¶¶¶¶¶¶¶¶2ᵛ consists of poems by women, all of which speak of the deceased Sor Juana as heroic and marvellous, wearing 'the invisible crown of fame'.

[124] See p. 357–8.

[125] *Apuntes* refers it to *Antigua lista de manoscritos latinos y griegos inéditos de Escorial, publícala con prólogo, notas y dos apéndices* (Madrid: P. B. Fernández, 1902). On Isabel de Josa, see Matamoros, *De Asserenda Hispanorum Eruditione*, 58ᵛ. She is frequently mentioned in 17th-century works on women, e.g. Valentinus Gottfried Herckliss, *De Cultu Heroinarum Sago vel Toga Illustrium* (Leipzig: Joh. Andreas Schaners, 1620), sig. C4ʳ.

[126] Antonio, *Biblioteca Hispana*, ii. 340, della Chiesa, *Theatro delle donne letterate*, 77.

Juliana/Julienne Morell, a Dominican nun (1593–1653), who certainly read Latin, Greek, Hebrew, and, allegedly, eleven other languages,[127] and published translations from Latin.[128] A brief biographical account of this woman by her contemporary and associate Mère Marie de Merle de Beauchamps, contains many points of interest. Like many learned women, Juliana became so because that was what her father wanted for her: there is a surviving Latin letter which she wrote to him when she was only 7.[129] He must also have taught her to write Latin verse, since, according to Mère Marie, she composed some 300 lines of verse during her eight-month final illness, which were written down by her fellow nuns because she was too weak to hold a pen.[130] The Morells left Barcelona after her father committed a murder and fled to Lyon (a city which was proud to acknowledge a number of learned women in the sixteenth and seventeenth centuries), where they lived for some time. She defended a Latin philosophical thesis publicly in Lyon before Margaret of Austria in 1606 (another example of the woman scholar performing in public in extreme youth): the title, though not the thesis itself, survives in the Biblioteca Nacional.[131]

According to Mère Marie, in the same year, her father decided that her studies had advanced to the point where he wanted her to start working for the degree of doctor of law, and accordingly removed to Avignon, where he had some reason to think the university authorities would welcome this (the move was necessary since studying for a doctorate normally required, as it does today, a stated period of residence in the relevant university town). However, Juliana, now 14, was determined to enter religion, against the wishes of her father, who intended a brilliant academic future for her, and beat her repeatedly in an effort to force her compliance. She compromised with him so far as to make another Latin public defence in Avignon, and as a result of the publicity thus attracted, attached the interest and support of local notables, the vicelegate and the Princesse de Condé. She was then able to use their influence and protection to detach herself from her father's power and enter the Dominican convent of St Praxedes in Avignon. Her father made repeated attempts to get her out again and refused to pay her convent dowry, a sum which was eventually met by the pope, Cardinal de Joyeuse, and his lordship the

---

[127] Fortunée B. Briquet, *Dictionnaire historique, littéraire, et bibliographique* (Paris: De Gillé, 1804), 247.

[128] She translated St Vincent Ferrer, *Traité de la vie spirituelle*, from Latin into French (this was published in Lyon, 1617), his spiritual exercises in 1637, a translation of the rule of St Augustine, and a history of the monastery of St Praxedes. *Apuntes*, ii. 1, pp. 63–6.

[129] This is translated into English as an introduction to *A Treatise on the Spiritual Life, by St Vincent Ferrer*, trans. Dominican Nuns of Corpus Christi (London: Blackfriars Publications, 1957), 9, which also includes Morell's commentary on this work. The nuns give no indication of the whereabouts of the original text which they translate.

[130] Quetif and Echart, *Scriptores Ordinis Praedicatorum*, ii. 845–6, support the testimony of Mère Marie by noting that 'rhythmos et alia plura pia scripsit aut e Latinis gallice vertit, partim edita, partim MS a suis sanctimonialibus servata'. There may thus still be manuscript material relating to Sr. Juliana in Dominican hands, though Napoleon's suppression of the monasteries was notoriously destructive of French monastic records.

[131] *Apuntes*, ii.1, pp. 63–6.

referendary. She was received on 8 June 1509, at the age of 15. Her father's last attempt to salvage his original intentions was to offer her/the convent a valuable library worth 2,000 crowns if she would only make another defence (in the convent parlour), and thereby obtain a doctorate, which she refused to do.

This story is instructive in a number of ways. If Morell had got his way, then his daughter Juliana, not Elena Piscopia, would have received the first formal doctorate awarded to a woman, circa 1610, a good two generations earlier than the Venetian. Her father (whose actions are of course visible only through the filter of Mère Marie's perceptions, heavily partisan of Sr. Juliana and her vocation) seems to have seen some very positive gain in having a learned daughter: he strongly desired her to become famous, and therefore he presumably hoped to capitalize on this fame (Mère Marie, naturally, is not interested in, and therefore not explicit about, his motives, or his relationship with the law faculty). Though Juliana's sights were set on the convent, she was able to use the leverage given her by her public fame in order to achieve this end: it was the fact that she had favourably impressed notables such as the Princesse de Condé which got her away from her father's control and into St Praxedes, and subsequently persuaded the pope and others to pay her dowry.

Like the later Piscopia, she also performed as a learned woman: Mère Marie records a man 'of high and illustrious lineage' coming to the convent because he wanted to hear her speak various languages, in the same way that Piscopia performed for interested, high-status visitors.[132] Also, if Mère Marie can be relied on, we are forced to conclude that the law faculty of University of Avignon thought that sufficiently favourable publicity would accrue to them if they laureated this young woman that they were prepared not only to do so, but to stretch a quite important point and hold the public examination not in the university aula, but in the convent parlour, with the candidate answering from behind the grille. Piscopia received her doctorate at least in part because her father was an immensely wealthy and influential local intellectual whom the University of Padua was reluctant to offend. Morell was merely the daughter of an émigré, a learned man with an unpleasant reputation for violence, and, moreover, an enclosed nun. Her story is therefore the more astonishing.

The family of Mendoza is of particular interest as an illustration of the cultural trend of baroque Spain. As we have seen, in the sixteenth century, the children of the Conde de Tendilla, male and female alike, had been known for their humanist attainments. The daughter of the accomplished humanist and friend of Catalina Paz, Juan Hurtado de Mendoza, was María de Mendoza y Pacheco. She married Francisco de Carvajal, and their daughter, Luisa de Carvajal y Mendoza (1566–1614), turned out to be at least as remarkable a woman as her learned great-aunts. However, despite the strong humanist heritage of the family, the fact that she had an impulse to write, and even the fact that she was orphaned at an early age and brought up largely by Juan Hurtado de Mendoza, who might have been expected

---

[132] *A Treatise*, 16.

to educate her in the mode of his youth, Luisa's considerable energies were channelled not into humanism, but into fervent religiosity. All her writings are in Spanish, religious poetry and some spiritual prose. She neither married nor entered a convent, but opposed her family's wishes and went to England, with immense courage, as a Catholic missionary. She was effective at converting non-Catholics, bolstering the faith of her co-religionists, and rescuing the bodies of executed Catholics for later veneration: subsequently, she commented that being a woman had helped her because the English never suspected a woman could be a missionary.[133]

It is similarly typical of the cultural turn of early modern Spain that in the eighteenth century, the profoundly learned Doña María Isidra Quintina de Guzmán y la Cerda of Madrid, though she read Latin, Greek, French, and Italian, and took a doctorate in philosophy and *litterae humaniores* in 1785 defending the thesis 'anima hominis est spiritualis',[134] published nothing but an enormous, six-volume work of pious meditations in Spanish, *Año Christiana, ó meditaciones para todos los dies sobre les misterios de nuestra Redencia*, published in Madrid in 1754. One of the Spanish ladies-in-waiting of the future Empress Maria Theresa was highly learned, Doña Catalina Rizo: unfortunately her work, *Anathemasotericon pro Vita Patris Servata*, which looks from the title as if it was in Latin and was once listed among the manuscripts of the Biblioteca Nacional, seems to have vanished.[135] Though Doña Mariana Alderete, Marquesa de la Rosa del Monte, who flourished in Madrid in the mid-eighteenth century, studied Latin and Greek, she seems to have left only poetry in Spanish.[136]

Thus, by the eighteenth century, the triumph of the vernacular was almost, but not quite, total. Doña Francisca Irene de Navia y Osorio (1726–42), the daughter of Don Alvaro de Navia y Osorio, Viscount del Puerto and Marquess de Santa Cruz de Macerado, who was distinguished as writer, politician, and soldier, was born in Turin while her father was ambassador to Italy. He died in 1732, and his widow returned to Madrid as matron of honour to Queen Isabel de Farnese. Their children, including Francisca, were educated by the erudite Franciscan Bernard Ward, who taught them Latin, English, French, Italian, and German. In 1750, Doña Francisca married the Marquess de Grimalda, and had three children by him, all of whom died before reaching adulthood. Her intellectual interests continued throughout her life: she translated from French and Latin, though she

---

[133] Her biography was published shortly after her death: *Vida y virtudes de la venerable virgen Doña Luisa de Carvajal y Mendoza* (Madrid: Imprenta Real, 1632). Some of her Spanish poems are printed on pp. 208–20 of the *Vida*, and there is a later collection, *Poesías espirituales de la Venerable Doña Luisa de Carvajal y Mendoza, muestras de su ingenio y de su espíritu* (Seville: A. Izquierdo y Sob., 1885). See also Ortega Costa, 'Spanish Women in the Reformation', 89–119 (p. 108), and Michael E. Williams, *St Alban's College, Valladolid: Four Centuries of English Catholic Presence in Spain* (London: C. Hurst & Co.; New York, St Martin's Press, 1986), 64–6.

[134] Joseph Antonio Álvarez y Baena, *Hijos de Madrid, illustres en santidad, dignidades, armas, ciencias y artes, diccionario histórico*, 4 vols. (Madrid: Benito Cano, 1789), iv. 67. See *Memorial literario*, June 1785.

[135] *Apuntes*, ii. 1, p. 149.

[136] Ibid., i. 22.

did not necessarily seek to publish her work, and wrote poetry in Latin and Spanish. The only original work of hers to survive is a poem in Latin hexameters written when she was 16. Given the family's long sojourn in Turin, the education given to Doña Francisca may reflect Italian influence on her parents' ideas about what was suitable for their daughter, though it is also worth observing the context in which her poem was preserved, the *Memorial literario instructivo y curioso de la corte de Madrid*. From the mid-seventeenth through to the eighteenth century, periodicals of general literary interest such as as the French *Mercure galant*, the English *Athenian Mercury* and *Gentleman's Magazine*, and the Swedish *Stockholms Magazin* took notice of female prodigies of learning. This notice in the *Memorial literario* suggests that by the late eighteenth century, such a woman was thought interesting to polite society even in Spain.

9. Women Latinists of the Renaissance in Northern and Central Europe

For the purposes of this chapter, I am grouping together women who fall some-where within the following set of definitions: humanists whose mother tongue is a Germanic language other than English (thus including the Low Countries), particularly continental Protestant humanists, and also north-eastern Europeans from Slavic-speaking countries of the Holy Roman Empire, since the numbers of the latter are so small that the exigencies of bookmaking require them to be grouped in some way, however artificially, within a chapter. It will therefore consider women who lived in regions as mutually distant (and distinct) as Poland, Bohemia, and the Netherlands, with a principal focus on the territories which we would now define as Germany.

The Renaissance and the Reformation in Germany are mutually interlinked to an inextricable extent; but in order to assess the effects on elite women's educa-tional opportunities, it is necessary to begin with a brief assessment of German convent culture at the end of the Middle Ages, since for late medieval women, Latin education was hardly a possibility in any other context.[1] Late medieval Danish queens and noblewomen at least put their names to Latin documents, but these are not certainly the work of the woman in question.[2] The political and intellectual high point of convent culture was the eleventh and twelfth centuries, before the Gregorian reform ordered strict claustration, and the universities emerged to provide advanced education for men only. However, the convents of Greater Germany were remarkable for their educated women in the twelfth century (the century of Hildegard of Bingen, Elizabeth of Schönau, and Herrad of Hohenburg), and even the thirteenth (the century of Gertrude of Helfta). While this legacy may not seem directly relevant to the sixteenth century, there were specific German convents which gave women unusual opportunities from the Ottonian period through to the Reformation and even beyond: Gandersheim, Quedlinburg, and Gernrode were free imperial abbeys whose abbesses were among the most powerful women in the Empire. Free imperial abbeys had only the emperor as their overlord: the abbess had jurisdiction over the abbey, but was

---

[1] That does not imply that they were illiterate in German. Heide Wunder, *He is the Sun, She is the Moon*, trans. Thomas Dunlap (Cambridge, Mass,: Harvard University Press, 1988) 88–9. See also Edith Ennen, *The Medieval Woman*, trans. Edmund Jephcott (Oxford: Basil Blackwell, 1989) 20, 221–2.

[2] C. A. Christensen (gen. ed.), *Diplomatarium Danicum* (Copenhagen: Ejnar Munksgaards Forlag, series in progress), volume for 1250–65, e.g. documents printed pp. 25–6, 113, 133–4, 177–8, 269–70, 288–90, 247–8, 272–3, 370–1.

also *Landesherr* of the land and villages belonging to it. Residents did not take formal vows and were not strictly cloistered: they could leave if they chose, belonged to no order, and were only loosely under the jurisdiction of a bishop.[3] Gandersheim and Quedlinburg were not disbanded at the Reformation. They both boasted aristocratic, learned inhabitants as late as the seventeenth century, several of whom are discussed later in the chapter on the German baroque.

Germany

In the century which led up to the Reformation, the opportunities available to religious women underwent a sad decline, though it needs to be said that some of the women's houses were far from moribund in the latter Middle Ages, as we can see from their involvement in pre-Reformation reform movements designed to return convent life to its pristine standards. Particularly after the Council of Konstanz, many convents passed stricter rules, and nuns travelled from reformed convents to convents with ambitions of improvement, in order to help them restore discipline.[4] The reformer Johann Busch gives an account of the reform of the Marienberg convent at Helmstedt in the late fifteenth century by two nuns and a lay sister from Bronopia, near Kampen: Tecla, one of the nuns, taught the novices to read Latin and 'to write letters and missives in a masterly manner, in good Latin'.[5] The teaching of Latin seems here to be perceived as part of the process of reform. Nonetheless, the convents were less and less concerned to teach Latin to nuns—the Dominicans were probably the order which held out most strongly against vernacularization.[6] Marie-Luise Ehrenschwendtner points to the convent of Unterlinden in particular as one which continued to have 'a comparatively large number of nuns who were able to read, write and translate Latin' down to the fifteenth century. Some of the *Schwesternbücher* produced in German convents were in Latin, notably that of Katharina of Gebersweiler, a nun of Unterlinden. Since these books were made by nuns to be read by other nuns, the use of Latin tells us that the author was not only Latinate, but also regarded Latin as a suitable medium of communication towards her fellows.[7] The Dominican bibliography also mentions Gertrude of Reinfelden, writing in Latin as well as German *c.*1266, and a Swiss nun who wrote in Latin, Elsbeth Stagel (d. 1360), the 'spiritual daughter' of Heinrich Seuse (Henry Suso).[8]

---

[3] Merry Wiesner, *Gender, Church and State in Early Modern Germany* (London: Longman, 1998), 48–50.

[4] Lina Eckenstein, *Women under Monasticism* (Cambridge: Cambridge University Press, 1896), 418.

[5] Eileen Power, *Medieval English Nunneries, c.1275 to 1535* (Cambridge: Cambridge University Press, 1922), 682–4. She quotes, p. 684, a Latin letter from the novices to Tecla.

[6] Marie-Luise Ehrenschwendtner, 'Puellae Literatae: The Use of the Vernacular in the Dominican Convents of Southern Germany', in Diane Watt (ed.), *Medieval Women in their Communities* (Cardiff: University of Wales Press, 1997), 49–71 (p. 56).

[7] Gertrud Jaron Lewis, *By Women, for Women, about Women: The Sister-Books of Fourteenth Century Germany* (Toronto: Pontifical Institute of Medieval Studies, 1996).

[8] Jacobus Quetif and Jacobus Echard, *Scriptores Ordinis Praedicatorum* (Paris: Christophe Baillard and Nicolas Simart, 1721), ii. 831. Stagel is further discussed in Ulrike Wiethaus, 'Thieves and

Following the account of Johann Butzbach (d. 1526), author of an unpublished history of German literature written in 1505, Janssen makes mention of a number of German nuns distinguished for their erudition from a variety of orders: Gertrude von Koblenz, Augustinian canoness of Vallendar, mistress of the novices, and Christine von der Leyne, Augustinian canoness of Marienthal, both of whom are praised for their literary abilities, Barbara von Dahlberg, the niece of Bishop von Dahlberg of Worms, who was a learned Benedictine of Marienberg, Aleydis Raiskop, a Benedictine nun who composed seven Latin homilies on St Paul,[9] and Richmondis von der Horst, Abbess of Seebach, who was a Latin correspondent of Trithemius.[10] Furthermore, a number of nuns published works in the vernacular, such as Ursula von Mönsterberg, and Barbara and Katharina Rem.[11] A Latin life of the venerable Juliane de Cornelian survives from the hand of the nun Katharina Mast, a nun of Valle-ducis, written in 1485,[12] and della Chiesa mentions a Bavarian abbess, Anna von Pferingerim (d. 1451), who translated the *Vita Hilarii* into German from Latin.[13] The evidence is very mixed. On the one hand, convent repressiveness is suggested by the fact that when the humanist Charitas Pirckheimer (1467–1532) was appointed Abbess of St Clara in Nuremberg in 1503, her acceptance was made conditional on her giving up Latin correspondence: her brother Willibald comments on this fact with indignation.[14] On the other, there were still noble nuns who used Latin with ease, such as Pirckheimer's friend Apollonia van der Lann,[15] and Marta von Druppach, a noblewoman of French descent who became the twelfth prioress of Frauenarach. Some while before 1549, she wrote an epitaph for her sister Walburga, also a nun, which was preserved at the convent and recorded by Kaspar Brusch.

Carnivals: Gender in Dominican Literature of the Fourteenth Century', in Renate Blumenfeld-Kosinski et al. (eds.), *The Vernacular Spirit* (New York: Palgrave, 2002), 209–38, who argues that a number of Dominican nuns appropriated Latin both for liturgical use and as a trigger for ecstatic experiences.

[9] I have seen a reference to a biography, K. Kossert, *Aleydis Raiscop. Die Humanisten von Nonnenwerk* (1985), but have not located a copy. A Latin letter which may be hers is in Bonn, Universitätsbibliothek, S 247, s. xvi, 'Soror Alcydis sanctimonialis in insula Rolandi, letter to Joh. de Largo Monte et Jac. Siberti de Monasterio Eyfflie dat. 1506', fos. 3–7ᵛ (not seen).

[10] Johannes Janssen, *History of the German People at the Close of the Middle Ages*, trans. M. S. Mitchell and A. M. Christie, 2 vols. (London: Kegan Paul, Trench, Trübner & Co., 1896), 26.

[11] *Christlich Ursach des verlassen Klosters zu Fryberg* (Wittenberg: H. Lufft, 1528), and *Antwurt zwayer Closter Frauwen im Kathariner Closter zu Augspurg, an Bernhart Remen* (Augsburg: Philipp Ulhart, 1523).

[12] Munich, Bayerische Staatsbibliothek, Lat. 10899 (Pal. 899). I have not had an opportunity to examine this, so am unable to state whether Katharina Mast was scribe, author, or both.

[13] Francisco Agostino della Chiesa, *Theatro delle donne letterate* (Mondovi: Giovanni Gislandi & Giovanni Tomaso Rossi, 1620), 69. She was the daughter of one of the principal families of Bavaria and Abbess of Neuburg.

[14] Eckenstein, *Women*, 463. Yet Willibald Pirckheimer's daughter became abbess there as well, after Charitas and her sister Clare, and was also known for her learning (Kaspar Brusch, *Monasteriorum Germaniae . . . Centuria Prima* (Ingolstadt: Alexander and Samuel Weyssenhorn, 1551), 108ᵛ).

[15] Christian Franz Paullini, *Das Hoch- und Wohl-gelahrte Teutsche Frauen-Zimmer* (Frankfurt: Johann Christoph Stössel, 1705), 21. 'studieren wegen nach Cölln geschickt, wo sie auch so wohl im Latein / als Mathematischen Wissenschaften.' She became an abbess in the Benedictine order and died in 1474.

Even where convents had abandoned Latin education, they were not necessarily dens of ignorance.[16] They were strongly involved in the propagation of vernacular learning, as we learn from Johann Busch: 'in the district of Utrecht alone, there are more than one hundred free associations of nuns and sisters possessing large collections of German books, which are used daily for private and communal reading. The men and women all round this neighbourhood from the highest to the lowest, have numbers of German books which they read and study.'[17] At least one German convent was seriously studying music.[18] This cut little ice with the German humanists. Conrad Celtis, one of the earliest of them, writes contemptuously of convents where they sang the Latin liturgy without comprehending it:[19]

> They sing, and they do not understand what they ask in the sacred song,
> Like a cow mooing in the middle of the marketplace.

The Reformation itself came out of a reform movement within German Catholicism, and the effects on women were mixed. Celtis's sweeping, humanist dismissal of convent culture is neither fair nor accurate. Charitas Pirckheimer was not in fact silenced by St Clara's, she continued to be something of a public figure, and a doughty fighter for the Counter-Reformation.[20] Several of her Latin letters were published during her lifetime, in 1515, by which time she had been a nun for thirty-five years, so the 'ban' on her Latin writing was evidently less than total.[21] She was far from being the only nun to defend Catholicism, a reminder that for some women, the convent was a positive choice.[22] She also wrote Latin verses, which are essentially medieval in form: their heavy use of alliteration suggests a strong influence from German models. Celtis, in a poem in which he addresses her in his favourite Sapphic metre, says:

> O virgin with a well-educated Roman tongue,
> Bright light and crown of virgins,
> I beg, take this my little gift,
>   With a smiling face....
>
> ... You are the glory of the German mouth for rarity
> O virgin, like the Roman girls

---

[16] There is some very interesting evidence for late medieval German convent culture in Jeffrey F. Hamburger, *Nuns as Artists: The Visual Culture of a Medieval Convent* (Berkeley and Los Angeles: University of California Press, 1997).

[17] Quoted in Janssen, *History of the German People*, 26.

[18] Brusch, *Monasteriorum Germaniae... Centuria Prima*, 174ʳ: In Urspringen, under the Abbess Magdalene à Monte (who flourished 1540–50), the nuns studied 'musica figuralis' (counterpoint) with the master Blasius Hippolytus.

[19] Conrad Celtis, *Fünf Bücher Epigramme*, ed. Karl Hartfelder (Berlin: S. Calvary, 1881), IV. 85.

[20] On Pirckheimer as controversialist, see Paula S. Datsko Barker, 'Charitas Pirckheimer: A Female Humanist Confronts the Reformation', *Sixteenth Century Journal*, 26 (1995), 259–72. Another German nun, Katharina Rem, also published a defence of monasticism in 1523: see n. 11.

[21] *Epistola Doctoris Scheuerli ad Charitatem Abbatissam... Epistolae Reverende Matris Charitatis Pirckheymerin Abbatissae Sanctae Clarae* (Nuremberg: Friedrich Peypus, 1515).

[22] See Merry Wiesner-Hanks and Joan Skocir (trans.), *Convents Confront the Reformation: Writings by Catholic and Protestant Nuns in Germany* (Milwaukee: Marquette University Press, 1996).

> Or those of Spain, or those which long ago
> France held in her cloisters

It is interesting that Celtis looks back as well as sideways, setting Pirckheimer on the one hand in a context of the learned women of the Italian and Spanish Renaissance, and on the other, demonstrating that the educated nuns of the high Middle Ages had not been entirely forgotten.[23]

Humanism also opened up new possibilities for educated laywomen. One of the first German laywomen to write in Latin verse since the Ottonian period was, apparently, Marguerite von Staffel, an aristocratic woman of the Rheingau who was the wife of the deputy Adam von Allendorf, and died in 1471. She allegedly wrote poetry in both Latin and German, including metrical lives of St Bernard and St Hildegard, though none of these works seems to have been preserved.[24] In the sixteenth century, we begin to hear of other humanist wives. Celtis speaks of the wife of one 'Telicornus', who learned Latin and then Greek from her husband and became proficient enough to make a public oration;[25] showing that as early as the sixteenth century, there were German men prepared to allow their own womenfolk to imitate the example set by Italian learned women and speak in Latin in public. As the story of Telicornus and his wife suggests, examples of the new-style humanist family in which husband and wife shared intellectual interests as well as family concerns, lauded by Erasmus, had begun to appear in fifteenth-century Western Europe. Another example is that of the family of the learned Johannes Canter, who came from Groningen in Friesland to Cologne in 1489: according to the *Koelhoffsche Chronik*, his wife was also very learned, and they taught their sons and daughters Latin as soon as they could speak. Their daughter Ursula 'because of her great learning in all the arts...must be counted among the most learned women who has ever lived, of whom the city of Groningen and all Friesland can be proud'. It is noteworthy that before the fifteenth century was out, the idea that a spectacularly learned woman was a proper object of national pride had been successfully imported from Italy to the North.[26] Fifteenth-century Germany also produced educating mothers: Albrecht von Eybe (1420–75), author of *Margarita Poetica* (which included a Latin poem by a woman, Angela/Angelina), dedicated it to his mother, whom he gratefully remembered as his first educator—he subsequently went to Italy where he studied Latin and Greek. Van Eyb maintained a lifelong interest in the position of women, and kept a notebook of citations from Greek philosophers and Latin poets on the subject. He also wrote a defence of the dignity of women in marriage, his *Ehebüchlein*,[27] and an unpub-

---

[23] Josef Pfanner (ed.), *Briefe von, an und über Caritas Pirckheimer (aus dem Jahren 1498–1530)* (Landshut: Solanus-Druck, 1966), 103–6.

[24] Frantz Joseph Bodmann, *Rheingauische Alterthümer oder Landes- und Regiment-Verfassung des westlichen oder Niederherrheingaues im mittlern Zeitalter* (Mainz, 1819), 552.

[25] Celtis, *Fünf Bücher Epigramme*, IV. 39.

[26] Quoted from Ennen, *The Medieval Woman*, 200.

[27] Published Augsburg: Gunther Zainer, 1472.

lished *Clarissimarum Feminarum Laudacio* (1459) praising 'the art, wisdom and virtue of women in our time'.[28]

Another Latinate woman, Margarethe Welser, is better known than Marguerite von Staffel or Ursula Canter. She was the daughter of the great merchant Anton Welser in Augsburg, and she married Conrad Peutinger, the Augsburg town clerk, who was also a notable scholar, when she was 18. She brought a humanist Latin education to her marriage: her husband, however, made it his task to continue and promote his wife's further study. She corresponded with Erasmus, and compiled a book on the Latin inscriptions of Augsburg, an enterprise enthusiastically endorsed by her husband.[29] In the introduction, she quotes Sidonius Apollinaris; using him to make the point that marriage was an opportunity for, not an escape from, the life of the mind, which was to be shared between husband and wife.[30] The Peutinger daughters were prepared for a future as learned women from a very early age. Peutinger was influenced by Italian thinking: German scholars of the early Renaissance by preference received their education in Italy, and the prominence of Italian learned women seemed to him a model to imitate.[31] Accordingly, their daughter Juliane made a Latin speech before the Emperor Maximilian on his visit to Augsburg when she was a little less than 4 years old, following the example of Battista Sforza, who gave a Latin speech in public at the same age.[32] Unusually, for such a 'dog walking on its hind legs' (i.e. interesting only for the fact that it was done at all rather than for how well it was done), the speech is preserved.[33]

---

[28] *Margarita Poetica* (Strasbourg: G. Husner, 1473). Prudence Allen, *The Concept of Woman II* (Grand Rapids Mich.: William B. Eerdman, 2002), 735–8.

[29] Munich, Bayerische Staatsbibliothek, Clm lat. 4018 (1511), fos. 1–19, with a letter from Conrad Peutinger sending his wife's work to Michael Hummelberg, fo. 19ʳ. This collection was later printed as *Margarita Velseria, Conrad Peutingerari Coniunx, ad Christophorum Fratrem Epistola Multa Rerum Antiquarum Cognitione Insignis*, ed. H. A. Mertens (Augsburg: Klett & Franck, 1778). See also Anne M. O'Donnell, 'Contemporary Women in the Letters of Erasmus'. *Erasmus of Rotterdam Society Yearbook*, 9 (1989), 34–72.

[30] Welser, *Epistola*, ed. Mertens, 16, quoting Sidonius Apollinaris, *Epistola* 2. 10. 6. She also gives a whole list of learned and intellectually active Roman women: Theophila, Sulpicia, Violantilla (see Statius), Claudia Rufina (see Martial), etc. Her collection of inscriptions is scholarly and well organized. J. W. Binns, *Intellectual Culture in Elizabethan and Jacobean England* (Leeds: Francis Cairns, 1990), 53, makes the point that Sidonius Apollinaris was influential on the writing of virtuoso Latin in the Renaissance.

[31] Wunder, *He is the Sun*, 43.

[32] Joanne Sabadino de l'Arienti, *Gynevera*, ed. Carrado Ricci and A. Bacchi della Lega (Bologna: Ronagnoli-Dall'Acqua, 1888), 288–312.

[33] Johann Georg Lotter, *Historiae Vitae atque Memoriae Conradi Peutingeri, Jurisconsulti Augustani*, ed. Franciscus Antonius Veith (Augsburg: Conr. Henr. Stage, 1783): 'Acclamatio publica ad Invictum Caesarem Maximilianum P. F. Augustum Iulianae Peutingerin puellae Augustensis natae tunc anno III m X dies XXIV.' The speech runs: 'Urbs Augusta Vindelicorum. Sacratissimi Caesar. unde michi origo est. Divo Augusto olim dedicata, atque ab eius privigno Decimo Druso Tib. Neronis et Liviae Drusillae Fil. restituta. a te nunc Optimo Sacri Ro[manae] Imperii Moderatore mirum in modum aveta atque amplificata est. Bonum faustum que Maiestati Domuique Tuae. Sic enim nos perpetuam felicitatem et laeta huic rei publicae praecari aestimamus. Senatus ergo Maiestatem tuam consenciens cum Populo Augustensi consalutat Patrem Patriae'. M[aiestatis] T[uae] observandissima Juliana dixi.' It is of course not her own composition: its concern to establish the ancient dignity and imperial status of Augsburg reflects her parents' political agenda. According to Erdmann, the speech was printed in Augsburg by Radolt, 1505, and in Mainz, by Schöffer, 1520 (p. 205).

A somewhat grim light is shed on this glorious moment for Augsburg humanism by a letter from Peutinger to his wife in 1503, which makes it clear that little Juliane was drilled for this feat, with iron determination, for the best part of a year.[34] It is good to know that she was canny enough to get something out of it: whatever her parents may have primed her to ask for, 'when the child had given her speech and the emperor asked her what she would like as a gift, she replied [in German], "Give me a lovely dolly" '.[35] Juliane Peutinger, like a Communist-bloc girl gymnast of the 1980s, lost her childhood in order to aggrandize her place of origin; but the difference is that in 1603, it was humanism and not athletics which carried status. Paradoxically, the power and might of Augsburg was well represented by the tiny voice of a very little girl, because of all that it implied about the sophistication and internationalism of its merchant princes.

When Juliane died in childhood, her sister Konstanze (a name used in Germany, but also one which recalls the famous Costanza Varano, perhaps intentionally so) succeeded her as the family's 'puella docta', which suggests their parents' continuing aspiration towards matching the achievements of Italian women in their own daughters. Konstanze grew up to marry a humanist nobleman, the Ritter Melchior Soiter von Windach, Chancellor of the Pfalzgraf Friedrich II, and exchanged Latin verses with the poet Ulrich von Hutten.[36]

Maximilian himself took his daughter Margaret of Austria seriously (as outlined in Chapter 7, she in fact received a careful humanist education at the French court), and was equally concerned that his granddaughters should be well read and Latinate. Margaret served for much of her adult life as her father's regent in the Netherlands, so her education served a severely practical purpose, as was the case with many later Hapsburg princesses. The catalogue of Margaret's private library at Malines survives, about 150 manuscripts in Latin and French. Though she wrote verse only in French, she was entirely at ease with Latin, and sometimes wrote in it.[37]

The merchant princes of Augsburg and Nuremberg, such as the Welsers, Peutingers, and Pirckheimers,[38] were perhaps pioneers in educating daughters not intended for the service of the Church, but theirs was an example which was followed elsewhere in Germany, especially after the arrival of the distinguished Italian Protestant refugee Olimpia Morata (discussed in Chapter 11), which can only have raised the public profile of learned women. The persistent legend that Morata held the chair of Greek at Heidelberg seems to be no more than myth,[39]

[34] Johann Georg Lotter, *Historiae Vitae atque Meritorum Conradi Peutingeri Augustani* (Leipzig: Bernard Cristoph Breitkopff, 1728), 27.

[35] 'Quum haec orasset puella, et Imperator, quodnam munus peteret, interrogaret, respondit: "Schenke mir eine hübsche Tocken" ' (ibid. 24).

[36] *Historia Vitae atque Meritorum Conradi Peutingeri . . . post Iohann Georg Lotterum*, ed. Veith, 25.

[37] Christopher Hare, *The High and Puissant Princess Marguerite of Austria* (London: Harper & Brothers, 1907), 323–4, 107–8.

[38] For a general account, see Lisa Jardine, *Worldly Goods* (London: Macmillan, 1996), 346–7.

[39] Niklas Holzberg, 'Olympia Morata und die Anfänge des Griechischen an der Universität Heidelberg', *Heidelberger Jahrbücher*, 31 (1987), 77–83.

but when she was in Germany, she did teach the young daughter of her own one-time preceptor, Theodora Senf, daughter of Johann Senf (Sinapius), along with her own young brother.[40] Another Ferrara connection of hers, Coelius Secundus Curio, who also fled to the Protestant north, brought his family with him when he took the chair of Latin literature at Basel. He was the father of four daughters, all well educated, who died of the plague in their early twenties.[41] Violante (b. 1541) was said to have been the most talented. Angela, the third daughter (b. 1543), read Latin, French, Italian, and German. Three of her Latin letters were preserved, and later printed; one to her father, one to her brother, and, interestingly, a third to an aristocratic Polish woman, Sophia Sbasia (probably Zbanski).[42] Curio himself declared that she acted as his editorial assistant.[43] What is more, Curio's was a powerful voice arguing for the education of girls, on the basis of his own experience: 'We do not debar . . . girls from letters and study, since there are many who are more able to pursue them than boys are.'[44] Curio had connections with the community of English Protestant exiles in the time of Mary Tudor, and was a friend of Sir Anthony Cooke, father of the learned Cooke sisters.[45]

The model for imitation supplied by the Welsers, Peutingers, and Italian émigrés was in fact used notably by the still more famous merchant princes, the Fuggers of Augsburg. 'The Fugger daughters . . . adorned with every gift of virtue and learning, distinguished for knowledge of various languages and arts, were imitators of the Peutingerian Graces (i.e. Juliane and Konstanze) in the curriculum of their studies.'[46] The aspect of deliberate emulation is interesting—it is not so much that Juliane Peutinger was a role model for individual girls themselves, as far as we know, but that she supplied a social model for parents who wished to see themselves as belonging to a group distinguished for culture as well as wealth. Similarly, Anna Maria Cramer of Magdeburg (1603–27), who studied Latin and

---

[40] Christopher Hare, *Men and Women of the Italian Reformation* (London: Stanley Paul & Co., 1914), 174.

[41] Their lives are sketched in a memorial volume, *De Quatuor Caelii Secundi Curioni Filiarum Vita* (Basel: Petrus Perna, 1565).

[42] J. G. Schelhorn, *Amoenitates Literariae* (Frankfurt: Daniel Bartholomaeus, 1725–30), xiii. 363–8. Sbasia is perhaps a connection of Abraham Sbaski (*sic*), to whom Curio wrote a letter published in vol. ii of his 1580 edition of Olimpia Morata, p. 339. See Markus Kutter, *Celio Secondo Curione: Sein Leben und sein Werk* (Basel: Helbing and Lichtenhahn, 1955), where he is named as Abraham Zbanski (p. 218).

[43] Schelhorn, *Amoenitates*, 364: 'Parenti saepe magno et collatione Codicem corrigendos Authores Latinos, erat auxilio, et si quando molestum esset legere, ipsa anagnostae vicem supplebat.'

[44] 'Puellas . . . a literis et doctrinis non arcemus, quippe quae plerumque magis habiles ad eas sequendas quam mares sint.' Coelius Secundus Curio, *De Liberis Pie Christianeque Educandis*, in his *Araneus seu de Providentia Dei, Libellus Vere Aureus, cum Aliis Nonnullis eisdem Opusculis Lectu Dignissimis* (Basel: Oporinus, 1544), 129 (see also p. 153).

[45] John Cheke, *Iohannis Cheki Angli de Pronuntiatione Graecae* (Basel: Nicolas Episcopius [Bischoff] Junior, 1555), sig. A 4ʳ, gives a letter written by Curio to Cooke from Basel in 1555.

[46] 'Fuggeriae . . . filiae, omnigene virtutum et literatum dote ornatissimae, variarum linguarum et artium rerumque peritia cultissimae, Peutingerianas Gratias in studiorum cursu imitatae.' Andreas Planer, *Tactatus [sic] de Gyneceo Docto* (Wittenberg: Johann Godfrid Meyer, 1715), 39. See also Johannis Paschius, *Gynaeceum Doctum* (Wittenberg: Christian Finkel, 1701), 35, on Isabella Fugger, a good Latinist, and Martha Schad, *Die Frauen des Hauses Fugger von der Lilie, (15.–17. Jahrhundert) Augsburg-Ortenberg-Trient* (Tübingen: Mohr, 1989).

Hebrew, is specifically said to have been 'another Olimpia Morata'.[47] She is very frequently mentioned in accounts of learned women for a girl who was only 14 when she died, so evidently she was brought up to be a prodigy and advertised as such. A later Welser daughter, Philippine (1527–80), was also a woman of remarkable achievements, and clearly of some learning. She married the emperor's son Archduke Ferdinand to the fury of many, some of whom accused her of employing magical means to entrap him, and she had an interest in science, since she has left five German-language manuscripts of remedies, recipes, and experiments.[48]

Of course, the Reformation was necessarily as much a factor in the experience of sixteenth-century learned German women as the Renaissance. One aspect of the Reformation which is particularly relevant that it is the first great movement in Western culture to be supported by printing, and that the atmosphere of polemic which it produced prompted women to begin to write in support of their beliefs to a greater extent than ever before and to publish what they wrote, increasing its chance of survival.[49] In this context of a new urgency in articulating personal belief, some sixteenth-century women began to see religious instruction as part of their God-given duty. Despite the formulation of a new theory of patriarchal marriage in which the Protestant *paterfamilias* became the priestly head of his household,[50] the reformers drew on women for support, and many women found the new movement profoundly exciting and spiritually liberating. The redoubtable aristocrat Argula von Grumbach challenged the Catholic establishment to public debate in 1523, and her first publication in support of Luther, despite her freely admitted lack of Latin, went through fourteen editions.[51] Katharina Zell is another woman reformer, from Strasbourg, who published her work.[52] Calvin's Geneva similarly saw active women polemicists, notably Marie Dentière for the reform, and the Poor Clare Jeanne de Jussie against it.[53]

---

[47] Paullini, *Das Hoch- und Wohl-gelahrte Teutsche Frauen-Zimmer* (1705), 33: see also Johannes Sauerbrei, *Diatriben Academicam de Foeminam Eruditione* (Leipzig: Johann Erich Hahn, 1671), and Georg Christian Lehms, *Teutchlands galante Poetinnen* (Frankfurt am Main: Samuel Tibias Hocter, 1715), 23–4.

[48] Franciscus Antonius Veith, *Bibliotheca Augustana, Complectus Notitias Varias de Vita et Scriptis Eruditorum quos Augusta Vindelica Orbi Litterato vel Dedit vel Aluit*, 4 vols. (Augsburg: Self-published, 1785), i. 131–8. See also Munich, Bayerische Staatsbibliothek, Clm lat. 11454 and entry in Dorothea Waley Singer, *Catalogue of Latin and Vernacular Alchemical Manuscripts in Great Britain and Ireland*, 3 vols. (Brussels: M. Lamertin, 1928–31).

[49] Charmarie Jenkins Blaisdell, 'Calvin's Letters to Women: The Courting of Ladies in High Places', *Sixteenth Century Journal*, 13.3 (1982), 67–84 (p. 68).

[50] Steven Ozment, *When Fathers Ruled* (Cambridge, Mass.: Harvard University Press, 1983), and Lyndal Roper, *The Holy Household* (Oxford: Clarendon Press, 1989).

[51] Peter Matheson (ed.), *Argula von Grumbach: A Woman's Voice in the Reformation* (Edinburgh: T. & T. Clark, 1995), 54.

[52] Elsie Anne McKee (ed.), *Katherine Schütz Zell*, 2 vols. (Leiden: Brill, 1999). See also her *Reforming Popular Piety in Sixteenth Century Strasbourg: Katharine Schütz Zell and her Hymnbook*, Studies in Reformed Theology and History (Princeton: Princeton Theological Seminary 2/4, Fall 1994).

[53] Thomas Head, 'Marie Dentière, a Propagandist for the Reformation', *WWRR*, 260–86 (p. 262). See also John Lee Thompson, *John Calvin and the Daughters of Sarah: Women in Regular and Exceptional Roles in the Exegesis of Calvin, his Predecessors and his Contemporaries* (Geneva: Droz, 1992), 44.

Several of the German reformers are associated with the advancement of learning for women. Erasmus is in some respects an ambiguous ally for women, but he did recommend that girls of the upper bourgeoisie should be educated:[54]

Families who will not let their daughters learn a trade because of their status and position in society... are nonetheless quite right to instruct them in tapestry work, silk weaving, or playing an instrument, to enable them to cheat boredom; they would do even better to have them instructed in the humanities. Weaving, for example, is an occupation that leaves the mind free to listen to young men's chatter and reply to their banter, but a girl intent on her books has no thought for anything else... Finally, reading good books not only forestalls idleness, but also fills girls' minds with the best of good principles, and inculcates virtue.

He corresponded with few women (though he exchanged letters with Sir Thomas More's daughter Margaret, with Margarethe Welser, and with the Hapsburg princess Mary of Hungary).[55] However, he handsomely acknowledged the impression which the Englishwoman Margaret More (Roper) made on him, in his dialogue 'The Abbot and the Learned Lady', in which opposition to women's learning is associated with all that is most bigoted, complacent, and stupid in the established Church.[56] Erasmus himself remained unmarried, but the ideal presented by his friend Sir Thomas More, that only an educated wife is a true companion, is one he seems to share in principle.[57] Elsewhere in reformist circles, Anna, the daughter of Philip Melanchthon, was humanistically educated (she was born in 1420), and is often referred to by later writers as a good Latinist.[58]

Towards the end of the sixteenth century, the ideal of companionate marriage erected by Sir Thomas More seems, in some circles at least, to have spilled over into actual life.[59] The marriage of Paul Schede (who preferred to be known by his mother's maiden name, Melissus) is a case in point. Melissus was librarian of the Palatine Library, and a man with friends all over Europe. He studied at Jena under Strigel, then at Vienna, where the Emperor Ferdinand gave him the title of poet laureate. He fought in the Hungarian war and spent time at Wittenberg and

---

[54] 'The Institution of Marriage', in *Erasmus on Women*, trans. Erika Rummel (Toronto: University of Toronto Press, 1996), 79–130 (p. 85). See also J. Kelley Sowards, 'Erasmus and the Education of Women', *Sixteenth Century Journal*, 13 (1982), 77–90.

[55] O'Donnell, 'Contemporary Women in the Letters of Erasmus' (he was also in contact with one of the earliest Spanish women humanists, Isabella Vergara: see discussion in Ch. 8).

[56] Translated in *Erasmus on Women*, 174–9.

[57] Quoted in Pamela Joseph Benson, *The Invention of the Renaissance Woman* (University Park: Pennsylvania State University Press, 1992), 158–9.

[58] 'Virgo non solum forma sed et latina lingua peritia insignis.' See Melchior Adam, *In Vitis Philosophorum Germanorum* (Heidelberg: J. Rosa, 1615), 227. Her epitaph is printed in Nathan Chytraeus, *Variorum in Europa Itinerum Deliciae, seu, ex Variis Manuscriptis Selectiora Tantum Inscriptionum Maxime Recentium Monumenta* (Herborn: C. Corvinus, 1594). Sauerbrei, *Diatriben*, sig. D.i. Melanchthon had an unusually close relationship with his children for a man of his time: Vigneul-Marville reports with contemptuous amazement that he was to be found reading one-handedly while rocking the cradle with the other (quoted in Wendy Gibson, *Women in Seventeenth-Century France* (London: Routledge, 1989), 14).

[59] Ozment, *When Fathers Ruled*, discusses this point.

Würzburg, but settled at the Pfalzgraf's court in Heidelberg.[60] He married Aemilia Jordan, daughter of Ludovic Jordan, a councillor in the Palatinate.[61] Melissus' collection of poems, *Schediasmata*, includes thirteen poems addressed to 'Rosina':[62] one such leaves the addressee's identity beyond doubt, since it is rather charmingly titled 'to Rosina, even though she is already married to me'.[63] It would therefore seem that 'Rosina' (little rose) was a nickname: this is corroborated by the names of their two children, both, in a sense, named after their mother, Aemilius and Rosina. The tone of Melissus' numerous poems to Rosina is profoundly affectionate. In addition, two poems in the *Schediasmata*, one in French, one in Latin, are addressed by Rosina to Melissus, and, like his own verses, are very warm in tone, suggesting a genuinely companionate relationship.[64]

> *Rosina ad Melissum*
>
> Desine Paule tuam spinas urgere Rosinam;
>   Desine tot sentes fingere totque rubos.
> Nescis, ne circum florentia lilia nasci?
>   Nescis, in mediis te residere rosis?
> Non ego jure tibi potera dilecte, negas:
>   Nec mihi te quisquam jure negare potest.
> Fata repugnabunt, trutina pensata Iehovae.
>   Ceu meus es, tua sum, ceu tua sum, meus es.
> Ergo gigne (licet) mihi lilia mille, Melisse.
>   Mox tibi parturiam mille Rosina rosas
> Quam mihi jucundum est assuesse Melissa vocare
>   Quam dulce et suave est nomen, amice tuum!
> Si nihil in te esset, mihi quo redamabilis esses:
>   Digna favore tui nominis umbra foret.

> Paul, cease to provoke your Rosina's thorns
>   Cease to bring out as many briars as brambles.
> Do you not know, that all around flourishing lilies are springing?
>   Do you not know, that you live in the midst of roses?
> Darling, you deny I am not able to do as you ask:
>   Neither am I able to deny anything you ask of me.
> The fates reject it, weighed in the scales of God.
>   Just as you are mine, I yours, so I am yours, you mine.
> Therefore, since it is possible, make me a thousand lilies, Melissus,
>   Soon Rosina will bring forth a thousand roses for you.
> What a joy it is for me to get used to calling 'Melissus',
>   My friend: how sweet and delightful your name is!

---

[60] Pierre de Nolhac, *Un poète rhénan ami de la Pléiade* (Paris: H. Champion, 1923), 5, 13. See also Possidius Zitter, *Vita Pauli Melissi Schedii* (Würzburg: Carol Philipp Boiton, 1834), or Otto Taubert, *Paul Schede (Melissus), Leben und Schrift* (Bonn: Carthausius, 1859).

[61] Jean-Jacques Boissard, *Icones Quinquaginta Virorum Illustrium Doctrina et Eruditione Praestantium*, 4 vols. (Frankfurt: T. de Bry, 1597–9), ii. 93.

[62] *Melissi Schediasmata Poetica* (Frankfurt: Corvinus, 1574), 19, 392, 393, 394, 394, 394, 397, 398, 399, 646, 654, 654–5, 656.

[63] Ibid. 392.   [64] Ibid. 631–2, 672.

If there were nothing in you, which might be loved in return by me;
Then the shadow of your name alone would win affection.

Other examples of the devoted, Latinate, Protestant wife include Elizabeth
Herder, credited on her husband Laurens Herder's funeral inscription in Heidelberg as its author, and of course Olimpia Morata, discussed in Chapter 11. An
interesting tract, 'A Dissertation on the Marriage of Literary People', published
with a variety of other works on marriage including Sir Thomas More's 'How to
Choose a Wife' and the Dutch humanist Daniel Heinsius' 'Letter on Whether, or
What Sort of Wife should be Taken by a Man of Letters', argues strongly that
learned men should marry women of the same kind, on the grounds that they will
add intellectual companionship to the other rewards of marriage.[65] There seems to
be evidence that this occurred in a number of cases.

Beyond the ranks of professional humanists and their immediate associates, we
also find that some German noblewomen, apart from the Hapsburgs, began to be
educated in Latin in the course of the sixteenth century. The Electress Elizabeth of
Brandenburg, mother of Joachim II, must have been one of the first, since she
became proficient in the classics in the early sixteenth century,[66] this may be due to
the family's Italian connections. The earlier Barbara of Brandenburg (1422–81),
having come to Mantua as the child-bride of Ludovico Gonzaga, was classically
educated by Vittorino da Feltre, and may have kept in contact with her family,
since her eldest son also married a German, Margherita of Bavaria, a Wittelsbach.
Her reputation was known to Albrecht von Eyb.[67] Some German noblewomen
sought knowledge with the encouragement of their husbands as well as their
fathers: Juliane von Nassau-Siegen (1587–1643) spoke several languages and was
encouraged by her learned husband, the Landgraf Moritz of Hesse, to study
mathematics. In return, she encouraged him to convert to the reformed confession,
which he did. Her stepdaughter Elisabeth (1596–1625) joined her brothers at the
court school for classes in Latin, Italian, music, painting, and geometry.[68]

It is well known that Anne of Cleves, the German fourth wife of Henry VIII,
was uneducated to an extent which was embarrassing in England:[69]

---

[65] Petrus Scriverius (ed.), *Dominico Baudii Amores* (Amsterdam: Ludovicus Elzevir, 1638), Thomas
Morus, Anglus, 'Qualis Uxor Deligenda, ad Candidum', 281–8, Danielis Heinsius, 'Epistola an et Qualis
Viro Literato Fit Ducenda Uxor', 291–345, Anon. 'Dissertatio de Literati Matrimonio', 349–84. M.
Christianus Juncker, *Schediasma Historicum* (Leipzig: Joh. Friedrich Gleditsch, 1692), 16, states that a
tract by Accursia (daughter of Francesco Accursio (1182–1268) of Bologna, 'an viro literato ducendo sit
uxor, et qualis?', was published in a collection of *opuscula* by Elzevir, but it is not this anonymous
'Dissertatio'.

[66] Georg Schuster and Friedrich Wagner, *Die Jugend und Erziehung des Kürfürsten von Brandenburg und
Könige von Preussen* (Berlin: A. Hofmann & Co., 1906), Kürfürstin Elizabeth, who learned Latin, p. 330.

[67] William Harrison Woodward, *Vittorino da Feltre and Other Humanist Educators* (Cambridge:
Cambridge University Press, 1905), 78 n., Allen, *The Concept of Woman II*, 738.

[68] Felicitas Bachmann et al., *Weibsbildung: Wie Frauen trotz allem zu Wissen kame* (Berlin: Elefanten,
1990), 24. Wunder, *He is the Sun*, 157.

[69] Nicholas Wotton to Henry VIII, on Anne of Cleves, Henry Ellis, *Original Letters Illustrative of
English History*, 3 vols. (London: Harding, Triphook and Lepard, 1824), ii. 121–2. From Cotton
Vitellius B xxi, fo. 186 (much burnt).

She canne reede and wryte her . . . [burnt] but Frenche, Latyn, or other langiage she . . . one
nor yet canne not synge nor pleye upon onye instrument; for they take it here yn Germanye
for a rebuke and an occasion of lightenesse that great Ladyes shuld be lernyd or have enye
knowledge of musike.

However, it is not clear if this was as universally true as Wotton claims (Anne must
have been contemporary with the Electress Elizabeth), or if he was putting the best
possible face on Anne's ignorance, but if it was, within two generations, it had
ceased to be true: German elites, like those of Italy in the previous century, had
come to take a wide spectrum of attitudes towards the education of their daughters.

By the late sixteenth century, a number of German women humanists became
known outside their immediate circles, and even outside Germany: Paul Melissus
praised Euphrosine Hainzel in his verse, implying that she was writing in Latin: as
so often in this account, her poetry which he claimed would 'outlast iron and steel'
has vanished without trace.[70] Paulus Rutingius of Rostock was friendly with a
woman called Cordula, whom he describes as an *anagrammatista* (in the sixteenth
century, this meant someone who composed poems which opened with a name, an
anagram of it, and then explored the significance of the anagram in a poem):[71] his
work is also interesting in that it demonstrates that a writer from the Baltic area was
aware of a whole series of what he calls 'puellae Phoebicolae', that is, women
followers of Apollo (and hence of the Muses); 'Urania', that is, Tycho Brahe's
sister Sophia (why she should be 'Urania' is explained below), Elizabeth Jane
Weston, an Englishwoman living in Prague, and Anna Utenhovia and Anna van
Pallandt, two learned nieces of Karel Utenhove, who will also be discussed later in
this chapter.[72] All of these women were known for their Latin verse, suggesting
that Cordula's lost anagrams may also have been in Latin.

The Low Countries

There is early evidence for the education of girls in the Low Countries: in both
northern France and Brabant in the late Middle Ages, a primary school for girls
was commonly established at the same time as one for boys. In Brussels, there was

---

[70] Johann Carl Conrad Oelrichs, *Historisch-diplomatische Beyträge zur Geschichte der Gelahrheit*
(Berlin: Buchhandlung der Realschule, 1768), 17.

[71] Compare the entire book of anagrams published by Mary Fage, which illustrates the general shape
of an anagram as it is then understood, *Fame's Roule* (London: Richard Oulton, 1637): a sample is
published in Jane Stevenson and Peter Davidson (eds.), *Early Modern Women Poets, 1520–1700*
(Oxford: Oxford University Press, 2001), 262–3.

[72]   . . . Satagunt certare puellæ
                    Vobiscum metris! plaudire Phœbicolæ.
          Cui non VRANIA? & cui non VTENHOVIA
                    Doctæ virgineâ fundere mente melos
          Cui non VVESTONIA Angla? atque Anna Pallantia nota?
                    Doctæ virgineâ fundere mente melos.

Anagrammatum Pauli Rutingii Rostochiensis Centuria (Rostock: Stephanus Myliander, 1606), 59.

even an unusual girls' school which made provision for upper-level instruction, so laywomen were able to pursue studies beyond the rudiments to the *ars dictaminis*.[73] Furthermore, as Solterer has observed, 'béguines created a milieu in which the exegesis of canonical Latin texts was pursued together with the reading of contemporary literature', an intellectual environment which fostered some degree of Latin competence among women in the context of serious religious enquiry among women studying together.[74] Katharine van Naaldwyck, daughter of the Count of Holland and Hainault in the fifteenth century, had apparently been taught Latin in her father's house, though she was not intended for the cloister.[75] Generally, however, Latin was not taught to women.[76]

Probably the first known woman Latin poet of the Low Countries was Isabella Everaerts, sister of several famous brothers, Johannes Secundus (Jan Everaerts/Nicolai) (b. 1511), an internationally known neo-Latin poet, author of the highly erotic *Basiae*, Everard Nicolai, president of Mechelin, and Nicolaes Nicolai, called Grudius.[77] They were the children of the jurist Nicolaes Everaerts, a distinguished citizen of Middelburg in Zeeland. As an adult, Isabella Everaerts took the veil and became mother superior of the convent of St Agnes in Delft. A Latin verse epistle from Secundus to his sister printed in his posthumous collection of verse describes her as 'Isabella, inferior to no man', and praises her Latin poetry, comparing her with Ovid's protégée Perilla, Cicero's daughter Tullia, and Cornelia, the mother of the Gracchi.[78] Again, none of the verse which prompted this brotherly admiration has been kept.

Isabella was not the only nun of the early sixteenth-century Netherlands to write verse. Grudius, another of the Everaerts brothers, engaged in a literary joust with a nun called Anna Suys who was, he says, renowned for her Latin verse on religious subjects: he declares that due to her gifts, she should be known not as Anna, but as Calliope. Anna replied,[79]

> Ruga genis, et muta chelys, nec munera formae
> si mihi, qui dicar Calliopaea tibi?
> Laedere parce deam: sit fas ut, nomine iusto
> aut Cijbele, aut Beroe Virgiliana vocer.

[73] Charles Stallaert and Paul van der Haegen, 'De l'instruction publique au Moyen Âge du viiiᵉ au xviᵉ siècle', in *Mémoires couronnés et mémoires des savants étrangers* (Brussels: Académie Royale, 1850), 101.

[74] Helen Solterer, *The Master and Minerva* (Berkeley and Los Angeles: University of California Press, 1995), 128.

[75] C. S. Durrant, *A Link between Flemish Mystics and English Martyrs* (London: Burns and Oates, 1925), 141–4.

[76] M. A. Nauwelarts, 'Opvoeding van meisjes in de 16ᵉ eeuw', *Spiegel Historiael*, 10 (1975), 130–7.

[77] Surnames were only just coming in in 16th-century Holland: the Everaerts were an important family, but most contemporaries would have referred to these men as sons of Nicolas—Nicolai (Latin) or Nicolaeszoon (Dutch).

[78] *Ioannis Secundus Hagiensis Opera nunc Primum in Lucem Edita* (Utrecht: Harmannus Borculous [*sic*], 1561), Epistolarum lib. I, sig. M 5ᵛ–M[6]ʳ.

[79] Anna Suys (latinized as 'Susia') was born in Utrecht, but lived in Dordrecht. She is described in Matthys Balen, *Beschryvinge der Stad Dordrecht* (Dordrecht: S. onder de Linde, 1677), 203.

> Since I have wrinkled cheeks, my lyre is mute, and I have no gift of beauty,
> By whom might I have been called Calliope to you?
> Do not offend the goddess: I ought to be called by an appropriate name,
> Either Cybele, or Virgil's Beroë.

Her response is genial and sophisticated: she is evidently unperturbed by her loss, or lack, of physical beauty. Cybele was the 'mother of the gods', and therefore might be envisaged as an elderly woman, while Beroë, an old woman, is an extremely minor character in Virgil's *Aeneid*. Put together in this way, they suggest an amiable ability to take, and make, a joke, and a thorough knowledge of classical literature.

While it is clear from Isabella Everaerts and Anna Suys that some convents in the Catholic Netherlands promoted or permitted humanist learning, secular women Latinists also throve in reformed circles. One such, Anne de Tserclaes, known as a Latin scholar, married the English Protestant bishop John Hooper at Basel towards the end of 1546. She was the sister-in-law of Valérand Poullain, the successor to Calvin at Strasbourg, so she originated within the central elite of Calvinist reform.[80] Similarly, a Protestant religious refugee who settled in Norwich in the 1560s, Catherine Tishem, or Thysmans, the mother of the antiquarian and scholar Jan Gruter, knew Latin, French, Italian, and English, and could read Galen in the original Greek, according to Venator's Latin panegyric on Gruter. Venator also states that it was she who taught her son Latin and Greek; the mention of Galen suggests that her own particular interest was medicine.[81]

The most significant Low Countries woman Latinist of the late sixteenth century, since she published two books of verse under her own name, is Johanna Otho. She was born, probably in Ghent, *c.*1545/50, and her father, Johann Otho, a native of Bruges, was a teacher, grammarian, translator, and cosmographer. Circa 1545, he opened a school of ancient languages in Ghent. One of his most distinguished pupils at this school became an internationally famous polyglot poet, scholar and diplomat, Karel Utenhove, who retained the most affectionate memories of his old master. It is not surprising to find that a woman with this thorough an education was the daughter of a professional educator. Protestant humanist education was acquired by continuous and daily contact with a master (*contubernium*): normally only women who had access to a master within the family circle could have this experience.[82]

The context of the family's move away from Ghent, which occurred in the 1560s, seems to have been their clandestine conversion to Protestantism. Duisburg

---

[80] There is an implication that her family was one concerned to educate women: F.-V. Goethals, *Dictionnaire... des familles nobles de Belgique* (Brussels: Polack-Duvivier, 1849–52) does not mention her, but observes that the family of T'Serclaes de Tilly included a 'femme politique' at the end of the 16th century.

[81] Leonard Forster, *Janus Gruter's English Years* (Leiden: Leiden University Press, 1967), 36. She is mentioned in Ballard.

[82] Mark Morford, *Stoics and Neostoics: Rubens and the Circle of Justus Lipsius* (Princeton: Princeton University Press, 1991), 16, 28.

was an important Protestant centre at this time; and it seems that Otho was a secret convert, though he held a certificate claiming that he was a good Catholic. An important source for Johanna Otho's early life is a letter she wrote to her contemporary, the Parisian Latin poet Camille de Morel (an erstwhile pupil of Utenhove's), on Utenhove's suggestion.[83] It was written in 1566, in Duisburg, when Camille was 19, and Johanna probably about the same age. It mentions a brother, then in Paris, but says nothing else about her family: the reference to domestic cares may suggest that her mother is dead.[84]

When Sir Karel Utenhove came to us from England (a man among those my father once instructed in letters for whom he feels a unique affection), he gave me your poem. When I read it, I cannot describe how pleased I was. For in this country, I have heard of no maiden particularly skilled in humane letters; for which reason, it is appropriate that I should congratulate you equally on your good fortune, wit and education, since you do not blush to conjoin Latin and Greek letters with maidenly conduct within such a renowned family, and you do not deem the mysteries of Phoebus and the nine Muses unworthy of your studies. For me, indeed, if I am to admit the truth, no pleasure can come my way which is so great that, through concern for it, I would be able to give second place to Latin and Greek letters. It is by them that I measure not only my enjoyment, but indeed my happiness. If only I were able to spurn domestic cares (something which, in us, most people regard as a crime) for their sake! I would not at all mind dedicating myself to the Muses alone. Forgive my audacity, illustrious virgin, in daring to burden your most erudite ears with this unsophisticated letter. Sir Karel Utenhove asked my father that I should send you some piece of writing, albeit in prose, and slide myself into your acquaintance through the medium of letters; so if this is an error, your kindness will attribute it entirely to Sir Karel Utenhove. Farewell, most learned Camilla, and deign to inscribe me in the list of your servants. I have a brother in Paris. I wish that, through your recommendation, he could live in your pious family or somewhere else, rather than looking after himself. Again, farewell. From Duisburg [in the duchy of Cleves], the day before the calends of October [30 September].

The letter is an interesting one in a number of respects. For one thing, she underestimates her countrywomen—or perhaps one should say that the rhetoric of uniqueness is the appropriate one for her to adopt in this very formal letter. Utenhove's father (also called Karel) moved in the circle of Erasmus, and so had probably heard of Margarethe Welser and Charitas Pirckheimer; Utenhove himself numbered three, or possibly four, women Latin poets in his immediate *family*, let alone his wider circle of acquaintances; and another woman Latinist friend of his, who, like Johanna Otho herself, was from Ghent, was in print by 1568 (Petronia Lansenberg). Otho's claim to isolation may therefore be strategic rather than literally true. Other points to notice in the letter include her sense of the burden of domesticity and her concern for her brother: she is a product of the level of society which needed rather than dispensed patronage, unlike most Italian

---

[83] Utenhove also sent a poem commending Johanna Otho to Jean de Morel, printed in his *Xenia* (Basel: T. Guarinus Nervius, 1568), 68–9.

[84] R. L. Hawkins, 'A Letter from One Maiden of the Renaissance to Another', *Modern Language Notes*, 22–8 (1907), 245.

woman humanists and, indeed, unlike Camille de Morel. She is not writing 'to make contact', she is using a contact made by Karel Utenhove, who owed a debt of gratitude to Johann Otho, to put some pressure on Camille's family of educated minor nobility to take her brother under their wing. It does not represent the beginning of a friendship between learned young women, but an attempt to pull strings on her brother's behalf. The long poem which she sent with the letter was unfortunate in its choice of subject: it expatiates at some length on the standard humanist trope of comparing the solid joys and lasting pleasures of religion and scholarship with the ephemeral delights of royal courts (a subject also addressed by their contemporary Luisa Sigea); it thus appears to have been written in ignorance of the fact that Camille de Morel was not a professor's daughter much like herself but a courtier, and there is no evidence that the contact came to anything.

Through Utenhove, a genial man, with a gift for friendship nearly as remarkable as his gift for languages, whose acquaintance included scholars in England, France, the Low Countries, and the Holy Roman Empire, Otho had a link with the wider world of Protestant humanism and, since Utenhove had links with at least ten women Latin poets,[85] she also potentially had connections with other learned women. In addition to putting her in touch with Camille de Morel, Utenhove must also have introduced her to at least one other of his French friends, since she made a Latin version of the Pléiade poet Jean Dorat's Greek poem on Utenhove's own edition of Callimachus. She also came to the notice of Utenhove's friend Paul Melissus, who was, again, a man of very wide acquaintance, female as well as male, as we can see from a little poem he sent to Utenhove which was published in 1575:[86]

> Having returned safe from the shores of Italy,
> I lovingly greet both Pallantia and learned Othonia:
> If neither the one nor the other receives it,
> Then, Karel, have this greeting for yourself.

'Pallantia' is Utenhove's niece, Johanna van Pallandt, a brilliant young woman, also a Latin poet, about whom Melissus felt strongly (he published no less than seven poems to her in his *Schediasmata*). This little verse is of some importance since it provides evidence that Utenhove was in friendly contact with Johanna Otho as much as a decade later than the Otho/Morel exchange, and therefore suggests that they remained friends for life. She was also friendly with the Belgian humanist

---

[85] Apart from Otho, they are Anna and Johanna von Pallandt, Anna Utenhovia, Margaretha Bock van Gutmansdorf, Petronia Lansenberg, Camille de Morel, Elizabeth I, Mildred Cecil, and friends' wives Rosina Schede and Maria Thou.

[86]   Sospes reversus Italis ab oris,
    Pallantiamque Otoniamque doctam
    Saluto amanter. Ni illa et haec recepsit,
    Tibi salutem Carole hanc habeto.

See, for further information on this relationship, F. Vyncke, 'Melissus, Charles Utenhove fils et les humanistes rhénans', *Slavica Gandensia*, 12 (1985), 249–57.

Jacques Yetzweirt, who wrote a poem on her in 1577 when she and her father paid a short visit to Ghent on their way back to Duisburg in that year.[87]

Some time after 1566, the year in which she wrote her letter to Camille de Morel, Johanna Otho married Willem Mayart, an advocate of the Council of Flanders. Her husband died before 1616, since her published poems declare her to be *vidua*. Like many other learned women, she had something of a public life, as we learn from Sweertius' survey of the intellectual life of the country, *Athena Belgica*:[88]

We have heard Johanna Otho, daughter of Johann [Otho] of Ghent, the poetess, and the widow of Willem Mayart, who used to be the advocate to the provincial council of Flanders, discoursing most elegantly in Latin in my own house, to great wonder and admiration, in the presence of Mr. Laurens Beyerlinckx and Dr. Lodowijk Nonius.

Her poetry is of interest for a variety of reasons, not the least of which is that it is essentially public verse. This is not a poetess shyly scribbling in her closet, but a person who is prepared to make a public claim for attention. The first book makes a clear bid for patronage by apostrophizing practically every Protestant monarch in Europe, as well as a number of now-forgotten luminaries of Strasbourg and Antwerp. The second half of the volume, which is more introspective, is for that reason intrinsically more interesting. It contains a variety of poems on virginity, true widowhood, and learning, which seem to constitute a relatively private meditation on her own status as a learned woman who was not a learned virgin. The volume is a quarto, quite handsomely produced. Her second book, which came out in the following year (and, in fact, largely reproduces poems printed in her first volume), is a testimony to a public persona, since it represents her verse production as composed in the context of public performance: it is called 'Poems, or Extempore Entertainments', which is precisely what Sweertius represents her as doing in the passage quoted above. In the sixteenth and seventeenth centuries, poetry was often a public performance art, as well as a private pleasure, and the extemporary composition was greatly admired and sometimes printed.

In one of the poems from the relatively personal second book of the *Carmina*, though it is basically a poem written to flatter her friends and patrons, Charles Boisot and Karel Utenhove, Johanna Otho gives some serious thought to the intrinsic difficulties of being a woman Latin poet. In lines 7–8 she refers to the existence of a general view that if women mix in literary circles, it is in order to 'be seen', to flirt, rather than to take part. Her muse is 'inhibited', *impedita*, and inelegant, which brings us to the whole question of the muse and what Otho can

---

[87] Frank Leys, 'Deux documents sur l'amitié entre Jacques Yetzweirt et Jeanne Otho', *Latomus*, 48 (1989), 424–34.

[88] 'Ioanna Othonia, Ioanni filia Gandensis, Poetria, vidua Guilielmi Mayarti, in provinciali concilio Flandriae quondam Advocati, quam latine loquiendi opulentem in aedibus meis cum stupore et admiratione audivimus, praesentibus D. Laur. Beyerlincx et Lud. Nonio medico.' *Athenae Belgicae* (Antwerp: Gulielmus à Tongres, 1628), 468–9. She also receives honourable mention in Antonius Sanderus, *Flandria Illustrata* (Cologne: Cornelius Egmondt & Co., 1641), i. 162, and in Valerius Andreas, *Biblioteca Belgica* (Louvain: ap. Henricus Hasternius, 1623), 519.

do with her. The relationship between poet and muse is a significant one in the sixteenth century; however seriously or playfully, it is an almost inescapable poetic trope, and a very difficult one for women: her friend Yetzwiert refers to Otho *as* a muse, and this is very common as a response to Latin women poets (its history goes back to Plato's epigram on Sappho in the *Greek Anthology*.[89]

The essential problem is that many writers understood the relationship between poet and muse as sexual. Some women writers wave away the problem, by interpreting the writer/muse relationship as sisterly: the Englishwoman Martha Moulsworth claimed cheerfully in 1632, 'the muses ffemalls are, and therefore of Us ffemales take some care', but this is unusual. In Otho's poem, she accepts the sexualized relation of poets and muses; a muse, as she presents it, has a basic attraction towards handsome young men; if she bothers to assist a girl at all, her assistance is grudging and perfunctory. As Otho presents it, the muse will drop her flat the moment some attractive fellow appears: she presents herself as a sort of literary 'gooseberry'. The mood is comic self-pity, self-deprecation, but there is an undersong of seriousness. Though Otho, as the daughter of a learned man, living in a context where her learning was appreciated, was in a very advantageous position for a woman of her generation, she very well knew that it is not the same thing to be writing as a woman. Her poem begins,

> O quam macra genas mea es Thalia
> Permultis metuo parum placebit,
> Quod neglecto habitu, decore nullo
> Ausa es doctiloquos adire vates,
> Spectatumque venire sacra Phoebi
> Docti mystica: non puto latere
> Te, quod vulgus habet frequens in ore
> Ut spectentur adesse si puellae
> Spectatum veniant, subis quid ergo
> Absque ullo meliore grata cultu
> Phoebi tecta oculosque celsa vestri,
> O quam macra genas mea Thalia
> Vultum tetrica et impedita vocem
> Nostros versiculos canis legisque
> Cur es tristior et parum venusta
> Cur me destituis tu favore?
> Morosa et nimium coacta, fundo
> Duros illepido labore versus,
> Sacro numine destituta vestro,
> Aspectu juvenes, virosque longe
> Te amplecti video venustiore.
> Nam quod præcipue colas, amesque

---

[89] The number of women hailed as the Tenth Muse, from Sappho herself to Anne Bradstreet ('The Tenth Muse Lately Sprung up in America'), is legion. A number of 'tenth muse' poems, not all addressed to Sappho, are found in the *Greek Anthology*, and the title is bandied about again in the 16th and 17th centuries.

Non me docta latet Thalia, nec non
Quos in deliciis habere pergas.
Quos vatum numero dices sacrorum,
Quos inter celebres semel Poëtas
Scribent sæcula dedicata Musis,
Illis oscula mille, mille suaves
Amplexus dare non vereris: At nos
Et nostri similes, honore nullo
Dignas Castalio putas: Jacemus
Neglectæ studiis sine arte vanis,
Absque ullo penitus decore vestri.
Ingens virginei caterva cœtus.
Sic tantum juvenes amas, colisque
Sic tantum pueros tibi puellis
Ornas post habitis, facisque, parvi
Nostras cum gemitu gravi querelas.

O how lean-cheeked you are, my Thalia!
The fact that you have dared to approach bards of learned utterance,
And to come to view the mystic rites of learned Phoebus,
Will, I fear, not be very pleasing to many people.
I do not think you are unaware,
Of the saying which the general public has on its lips,
That if girls come to view,
They are there to be viewed: why then do you enter
Beneath the pleasant roofs of Phoebus
Without any better adornment?
O how lean-cheeked you are, my Thalia!
It is with a repulsive expression and with impairment of voice
That you are singing and reading our little verses.
Why are you somewhat gloomy and not particularly charming?
Why are you depriving me of your favour?
Morose and under too much constraint, I am pouring forth
Painful verses, with unpleasant laboriousness,
Destitute of your sacred divine power,
I see you embrace men, and youths,
With more loving gaze.
For it does not escape me, learned Thalia,
What you particularly care for and love,
Nor who they are whom you are going to have as your favourites,
Whom you are going to assign to the number of holy bards,
Whom, once they are among the famous poets,
Centuries dedicated to the Muses will commit to writing.
You do not fear to give a thousand kisses,
A thousand sweet embraces: But as for us,
And those like us: you think us females worthy of no Castalian honour.
We lie neglected, our endeavours fruitless,
Without artistry, utterly and completely without the beauty of you —

The huge host of the community of virgin girls.
To such an extent do you only love and cherish young men;
To such an extent do you only adorn boys, in preference to girls,
And do not take seriously our deeply sighed complaints!

Karel Utenhove, as has already been mentioned, came of a family with an extra-ordinary tradition of educating daughters.[90] His father had been a friend of Erasmus for a time (though the latter came to consider him a disappointment who did not fulfil his promise),[91] and perhaps imbibed Erasmus' admiration for the relatively new concept of the 'learned household', exemplified by the family of Sir Thomas More and more locally by the Welsers and Pirckheimers in Germany. Utenhove's own marriage to Ursula Flodrop was childless, but he adopted his brother's daughter Anna Utenhovia, who was taught Latin, Greek, and the writing of Latin verse. He was also close to his other nieces, Anna and Johanna van Pallandt (Latinized as Pallantia) as a number of loving letters bear witness. Ursula Flodrop's great-niece, Margaretha Bock von Gutmansdorf, was also part of this interacting circle, since she married Utenhove's close friend Marquard Freher.[92] All four of these women may have been educated by Utenhove; certainly, all four wrote Latin verse, and maintained contacts with a variety of Protestant humanists who formed part of Utenhove's circle of acquaintance: Anna van Pallandt wrote verses for Jacob Monau and Jan Gruter (a younger scholar, also a relative, who had been virtually adopted by Utenhove),[93] and engaged in a contest of extempore verse with Johann Posthius, which she won. Johanna exchanged verses with Paul Melissus, and was also friendly with the philologist Franciscus Modius,[94] Anna Utenhovia wrote to, or on, Posthius, Monau, and Gruter, and additionally to Nikolas Klopfer and Marquard Freher.[95] Margaretha Bock von Gutmansdorf wrote Latin verses to Joseph Scaliger, a great admirer of learned women,[96] and

[90] The nearest thing to a biography is Willem Janssen, *Charles Utenhove* (Maastricht: van Aelst, 1939). See also Leonard Forster, 'Charles Utenhove and Germany', in P. K. King and P. F Vincent, *European Context: Studies in the History and Literature of the Netherlands Presented to Theodoor Weevers* (Cambridge: Publications of the Modern Humanities Research Association 4, 1971), 60–80.

[91] Petr G. Bietenholz (ed.), *Contemporaries of Erasmus: A Biographical Register of the Renaissance and Reformation*, 3 vols. (Toronto: University of Toronto Press, 1985), iii. 362–3.

[92] Her intimacy with Utenhove's household is suggested by the fact that he was using her as an amanuensis late in life: Vatican City, Bibliotheca Apostolica, Pal. lat. 1906, fo. 195 contains a poem written in the hand of Margaretha Bock von Gutmansdorf at Utenhove's dictation. Another poem in the same manuscript, fo. 187ʳ, addressed to Jan Gruter, was written out for him by Anna Utenhovia.

[93] Karel Utenhove Sr. married Anna de Grutere, so Jan Gruter was related to Utenhove Jr.

[94] He encountered her when she was still a child at Eberfeld and Neuss, and sent her his comments on the text of the epistles of Pliny the Younger when she was at Comburg in 1583 (Franciscus Modius, *Francisci Modii Brugi Novantiquae Lectiones* (Frankfurt: Andreas Wechel, 1584), 49–54). Modius had a certain abstract interest in women, witnessed by his compilation of a *Gynaeceum sive Theatrum Mulierum* (a work on contemporary costume) published in Frankfurt in 1586.

[95] Another of her friends was Karol Antoniades, who wrote her a Latin letter copied in Paris, Bibliothèque Nationale de France, Lat. 18592, fo. 67ᵛ.

[96] See *Julii Caesaris Scaligeri Viri Clarissimi Poemata*, dedicated to Costanza Rangone (Heidelberg, 1574), which contains a number of laudatory poems on learned women. Rangone's sister Ginevra wrote Latin verse.

additionally, she allowed a German poem in praise of Utenhove to reach print: this last was printed in his necrology.[97]

This group of women show something of the mobility we associate with male humanists. Johanna van Pallandt seems to have been in Paris in 1669: Melissus recalls meeting her there in a letter he wrote to Hieronymus Baumgarten on 29 June 1590, from Heidelberg. He saw her at the house of the scholar-printer Henri Estienne,[98] playing and singing the lyrics of Orlando de Lassus to the accompaniment of a lute. He thought her extraordinarily beautiful, and was so smitten that the experience cast him into a fever.[99] The episode indicates that Johanna van Pallandt was welcome in the most advanced and cultivated circles of Paris, since Estienne's house was a sort of intellectuals' salon, and de Lassus' music was distinctly avant-garde. Karel Utenhove had known de Lassus during his time in France,[100] but he had left for England in 1562: while her uncle may have recommended her to his associates, she therefore cannot have been visiting under his direct auspices. Some twenty years later, Anna Utenhovia was actually offered a job, one of relatively few women humanists of whom this can be said: she was invited by a Wittelsbach princess, Eleanor of Prussia, to come and teach French to her daughters in 1591. For reasons which the surviving correspondence does not state, she refused to do so: the story has to be reconstructed from Utenhove's letter of apology and a letter he wrote to Galien Wier, his close friend, asking him to smooth matters over as far as possible. The final solution to this diplomatic impasse was that Utenhove proposed himself as alternative tutor to the young princesses, though in the end, nothing came of it.[101]

Another woman from the same social milieu (like Otho, a native of Ghent), who signs herself Petronia Lansenberg, became part of the Dutch community in London, and lived there for some time, possibly all her life. Since she was a member of the Dutch Calvinist Church in London, it is probable that her departure from Ghent, like that of Otho, was religiously motivated. She was perhaps the sister of the Gantois astronomer Philipp van Lansberge, since the latter's father, Daniel van Lansberge, Seigneur de Meulebeke, embraced the reform and went to France and from thence to England.[102] In any case, it seems likely that she gained her knowledge of Latin and Greek in the family circle. Her friendship with Karel Utenhove is illustrated by a number of Latin poems published in his *Xenia*, so it may be that it was this that led the van Lansberges to choose London for their exile (his brother Jan Utenhove was pastor of the Dutch

[97] In Wilhelm Fabricius' *De Combustionibus* (Basel: Sumptibus Ludovici Regis, 1607), which includes a *tumulus* for Utenhove.

[98] The Estienne establishment in the Rue Saint-Jean-de-Beauvais acted as a kind of salon for scholars. Robert Estienne married a scholar's daughter, and the household used Latin as the language of daily life, children and all. Elizabeth Armstrong, *Robert Estienne, Royal Printer* (Cambridge: Cambridge University Press, 1954), 15–16.

[99] Ernest Weber (ed.), *Virorum Clarorum Saec. xvi et xvii Epistolae Selectae* (Leipzig: B. G. Teubner, 1894), 29–30.

[100] Paris, Bibliothèque Nationale, Nouv. acq. fr. 3073, fo. 491 (a life of Utenhove).

[101] Munich, Bayerische Statsbibliothek, Clm Lat. 10369, fos. 161, 169.

[102] E. de Seyn, *Dictionnaire des écrivains belges*, 2 vols. (Bruges: Éditions Exelsior, 1931), ii. 1921–2.

church at Austin Friars). Another learned female Lansenberg is attested (most probably either a sister or Petronia herself, using a different first name), Maria Lansenberg, mother of Johann Leurinus of Leiden: Jakob Smalcius states that he saw a volume of her Latin epigrams, dedicated to Queen Elizabeth of England, which was shown him in 1660 by her son, who was his fellow student.[103]

Petronia Lansenberg taught calligraphy, like her better-known and slightly younger contemporary the Huguenot Esther Inglis (also an exile in England and Scotland for religion's sake), as we know from the history of the future theologian Petrus Bertius, who was sent to England at three months of age. He received his education in Latin, Greek, and French in suburban London, under Christian Rychius and his stepdaughter (*privigna*) Petronia Lansenberg, from whom he learned calligraphy and music.[104] Elegant examples of Lansenberg's calligraphic script are to be found in the *alba amicorum* of the doyen of the London Dutch community, Emanuel van Meteren, and of Jan Dousa of Noortwijk, who lived in Leiden. There is further confirmation of her professional activity as a writing mistress in a booklet now in the Newberry Library, Chicago, dated 1576: 'Petronia Lancenberga gives this little book, written with her own hand, as a gift to Willem Rychius.' He may have been her half-brother (in the affectionate dedicatory poem, she describes him as *cognata*). Each following page has a line or two of Latin in her exquisite italic, with another few lines in one or another variant on court-hand, with text in French. A less expert hand, probably that of Willem, since his name is repeated several times on fo. 2ʳ, copies some of these lines (room is left for this): it is clear overall from these additions that she successfully taught him her italic but that he did not master the vernacular hands. The book ends with further verses in French and Flemish, which may well be hers.

The mention of *alba amicorum* perhaps justifies an explanatory digression. From the sixteenth century onwards, substantial numbers of well-connected and educated people in many parts of northern Europe kept a friendship album, that is, a book of blank pages in which their friends could write: these are often embellished with drawings, particularly coats of arms: in run-of-the-mill *alba*, friends and acquaintances wrote signatures and perhaps mottoes, and in more literary circles, they often wrote verse. Such *alba* survive in great numbers in the Low Countries, Germany, and Scandinavia from the sixteenth to eighteenth centuries.[105]

A slightly more elaborate type of album also existed, in which the owner chose a motto, or *symbolum*, and expected his or her acquaintances to respond to it, ideally

103 Sauerbrei, *Diatriben*, pt. II (Smalcius), sigs. F. 1ᵛ, F2ʳ⁻ᵛ (F2ᵛ).

104 Johannes Meursius, *Athenae Batavae, sive de Urbe Leidensi et Academia Virique Clavis, Libri II* (Leiden, 1625), ii. 233.

105 See C. L. Heesakkers and K. Thomassen, *Voorlopige Lijst van Alba Amicorum uit de Nederlanden voor 1800* (The Hague: Koniglijke Bibliotheek, 1986), K. Thomassen, *Alba Amicorum: Vijf eeuwen vriendschap op papier gezet: het Album Amicorum en het poëziealbum in de Nederlanden* (The Hague: Koniglijke Bibliotheek, 1990). There is extensive German work on *Stammbücher*, see in particular Wolfgang Klose, *Corpus Album Amicorum: Beschreibendes Verzeichnis der Stammbücher des 16. Jahrhunderts* (Stuttgart: Anton Hiersemann Verlag, 1988). The good collection of *alba* in Stockholm is catalogued in Lotte Kurras and Eva Dillman, *Die Stammbücher der königlichen Bibliothek Stockholm* (Stockholm: Kungliga Biblioteket, 1988).

with verses or epigrams. The poet Kaspar Brusch and other members of his circle had chosen *symbola* by the 1540s:[106] he published a Latin poem which he had written for Elisabeth, Duchess of Saxony and daughter of the Landgrave of Hesse, on her *symbolum*, 'Deus Omnia Potest' (God can do all things), in 1543.[107] As a fashionable form, the symbolum album is more characteristic of the later sixteenth century. Jacob Monau, doyen of Wrocław humanism in the last years of the sixteenth century, kept a particularly well-known album, which was printed and published, and included verses from Anna Utenhovia. A slightly later Silesian *symbolum*, that of Balthasar Exner, was also printed, and is graced with contributions from Elizabeth Jane Weston, who also wrote on the *symbolum* of Jiří (George) Carolides. Women also took mottoes and created *symbolum* albums: as we have seen, Elisabeth of Saxony is one of the earliest to do so, and Elizabeth Jane Weston had one herself (her motto was 'Spes Mea Christus': 'Christ is my hope').[108]

Alba amicorum are a important source for northern European women's participation in a wide range of coteries and intellectual circles. Even if they only wrote a signature and a motto, as is often the case, each album, by definition, gives a glimpse of a particular individual's social circle, and therefore bears witness to the participation of women in domestic and intimate contexts of poetic exchange. Women also often owned such albums, so in such cases we can get a picture of a woman's own group of friends and associates; for example, a Low Countries noblewoman, Catherine van Eck, kept an album now in the Bodleian Library, which has a frontispiece poem of her own composition, and contains a variety of other verse, much of it by women (in French and Dutch).[109] Apart from Petronia Lansenberg and Elisabeth Jane Weston, already mentioned, other Latinate women contributed to *alba*: one of the few such from Scotland, that of George Craigie, has a mild Latin joke on the front pastedown attributed to one Elisa Abuja:

> qui difert puer, cui rei similis est?
>   atramento scripto in carta bona:
> qui difert senex, cui similis est?
>   atramento scripto in carta bibula.

> A distracting[110] boy: what thing does he resemble?
>   Ink written on good paper.
> A distracting old man, what thing does he resemble:
>   Ink written on blotting paper.

---

[106] There are several in Kaspar Brusch, *Encomia Hubae Slaccenuualdensis, ac Thermarum Carolinarum apud Boemas* (Wittenberg: Josef Sophon, 1642), sig. F1r–F2r.

[107] Kaspar Brusch, *Sylvarum... Liber* (Leipzig: Michaelis Blum, 1543), 75.

[108] *Collected Writings*, ed. Donald Cheney and Brenda Hosington (Toronto: Toronto University Press, 2000), 152–3.

[109] Oxford, Bodleian Library, Rawlinson B 4. See generally Marie-Ange Delen, 'Frauenalben als Quelle', in Wolfgang Klose (ed.), *Frauen und Adelskultur im 16. Jahrhundert* (Wiesbaden: Otto Harrassowitz, 1989), 75–93.

[110] The intended meaning of *differe* is hard to determine. *Differe* = 'delay', or 'report on'; 'gossip about' might also be considered: thanks to Dr Janet Fairweather for her thoughts on this.

Central Europe

The court of Rudolf II at Prague was one of the most remarkable in sixteenth-century Europe. The emperor was an aesthete, a collector, and a man of restless intelligence. His court was a magnet for scientists, such as Tycho Brahe and Johann Keppler, alchemists, such as John Dee and Edward Kelley, charlatans, artists, craftsmen, and spies. It also featured learned women, the most remarkable of whom is the English-born Elizabeth Jane Weston (1582–1612). Her life story is still far from certain, though some of her early history can be reconstructed from her long poem on the death of her mother. As a result, her mother's identity is clearer than her father's: she was Joanna Kelley (born 1563, as Joanna, or Jane, Cooper). She knew Latin well, according to her daughter. Joanna was married to someone called Weston by 1579, since her elder child, John Francis Weston, was born in 1580. Elizabeth Jane was born in 1582, and when she was six months old, their father died. The children were looked after for some time by their grandparents, but the grandmothers both died, and the children's fates were then reconsidered. Meanwhile, Joanna remarried swiftly. She was Edward Kelley's wife by 1583 (the children may, however, have continued to be fostered by their grandparents for some time).

Edward Kelley was a distinctly suspicious character, a con-man, magician, and alchemist closely associated with John Dee. His early history is completely unknown. Dee tells us that the Kelley marriage was strained from early on. He records Kelley saying in 1583: 'I cannot abide my wife; I love her not, nay, I abhor her, and there in the house I am misliked, because I favour her no better.'[111] Another reference to Joanna in the Dee papers is a prayer for her to be granted children, in 1587. It appears that her marriage with Kelley was infertile, and the problems between them related (at least in part) to his longing for children. At some unknown point in their early lives, Joanna brought her own children into Kelley's household, and he seems to have treated them as his own. After some continental wanderings, Kelley moved back to Prague in 1589, and impressed Rudolf II so greatly that he received a knighthood. He also claimed he was an Irish nobleman, descended from the ancient Irish lords of Huí Máine, in Connacht, Weston's 'de Imany', as is recorded in the Prague state papers for 1589.[112] In this period of his prosperity, he was conscientious about educating his stepchildren: John Francis was sent to study at Ingolstadt (an indication that the children were reared as Catholics). But in 1591, relations with the emperor soured. Kelley's household was arrested and tortured, while Joanna was put under house arrest. Kelley was imprisoned, and in 1597 he died. Elizabeth Weston was 15 in 1597, and she seems to have loved her stepfather without reservation, a relationship which was clearly reciprocated. Kelley was without doubt a cheat, fraudster, and liar, but

---

[111] Susan Bassnett, 'Elizabeth Jane Weston: The Hidden Roots of Poetry', in S. Fučíková (ed.), *Prag im 1600* (Luca: Freren, 1988) 9–15 (p. 12).

[112] R. J. W. Evans, *Rudolf II and his World* (Oxford: Oxford University Press, 1973), 226–7.

Weston was perhaps the only intelligent person in Europe who believed in him absolutely. She saw him as an unjustly mistreated man, and campaigned vigorously for the restitution of his property.

Kelley's death left her (and her mother) on their own financial resources, since John Francis died soon after his stepfather. Astonishingly, she responded to this by becoming a writer. Her literary activity seems to have been conducted with complete professionalism. A very large proportion of her total oeuvre consists of poems in praise of various grandees, mostly in Prague: this is exactly what one would expect from a writer in the public arena, dependent on patronage. In 1603, she married Johannes Leo of Eisenach, a lawyer, and an agent of Christian van Anhalt.[113] He was also interested in alchemy. Anhalt was an enthusiastic Calvinist, but deeply involved in mystical and Paracelsist movements. He was the patron of Oswald Croll, cabbalist, Paracelsist, and alchemist, and close friend of Peter Wok of Rosenberg/Rozmberk.[114] Croll's *Basilica Chymica* constantly cites Hermes Trismegistus and Hermetic texts with reverence, and respects Renaissance Neoplatonists such as Pico della Mirandola: Weston contributed a prefatory poem, for which we have Croll's soliciting letter.[115] She continued to write after her marriage, while giving birth to and caring for seven children (four sons and three daughters) before her early death.

Martin von Baldhoven, Weston's principal patron and editor, mentions two other Bohemian women remarkable for their learning, Helena Maria Wackeriana à Wackenfels,[116] and Catharina, daughter of Nicolas Albertus.[117] As an indication of the pitfalls which bestrew this investigation, the allegedly brilliant daughter of J. M. Wacker von Wackenfels is known to have died before she was 10. It is perhaps reasonable to surmise that it was the success of Elizabeth Jane Weston which prompted Wacker to educate his young daughter in this fashion. Unsurprisingly, given her age at death, she seems to have left nothing but a little hymn in German.[118]

'Catharina, daughter of Nicolas Albertus' is a more interesting case. She was actually Alzbeta, or Elisabetha, Albertina von Kammeneck, daughter of Mikulás

[113] On whom see Frances Yates, *The Rosicrucian Enlightenment* (London: Routledge and Kegan Paul, 1972).

[114] Claus-Peter Clasen, *The Palatinate in European History 1555–1618* (Oxford: Basil Blackwell, 1966), 23.

[115] *Collected Writings*, ed. Cheney and Hosington, 166–7.

[116] Wacker was born *c.*1550 at Konstanz, and was very much of inner court circles. He converted to Catholicism in 1592, and was a man of wide talents, with a gift for languages, and a Latin poet in the classicizing style.

[117] His catalogue of learned women is not original work, but is a reworking of an earlier catalogue by Jean Tixier, Seigneur de Ravisy (d. 1524), *De Memorabilibus et Claris Mulieribus Aliquot Diversorum Scriptorum Opera* (Paris: Simon Colinaeus, 1521), to which he has added the names of eight later women.

[118] Lehms, *Teutschlands galante Poetinnen* (Frankfurt: Samuel Tobias Hocter, 1745), 272–6, (p. 275)).

Albert z Kaménka, and her father, like Wacker, was an important figure in Rudolfine court circles. She and her sister Anna were contemporaries of Weston's, and known to her. A number of German writers mention her, and state that she studied Hebrew, Greek, and Latin.[119] Her Latin letter to Balthasar Exner suggests that only a very tiny proportion of Czechs believed in educating women.[120]

My sister Anne and I spend more time on needle, distaff, hearth, loom, and broom than on the letters which—you may be amazed to hear—are not much praised by most Bohemians, nay, are considered not only useless for a virgin's concern but actually shameful. It grieves and shames our father that he taught us letters.

However, her reputation is substantiated by a single surviving Latin poem, a set of commendatory verses addressed to the poet Gregor Kleppisch, and printed in his *Himlischer Jordan/ Christi Jesu Tauffe* in 1630, when she must have been well into her middle years, so despite the discouragement she voices in this letter, she evidently kept up her Latin studies in later life.

Two other very learned women who spent time in Prague are not mentioned either by Baldhoven or by Weston (though the latter was noticed by Paulus Rutingius): the Latin poet Elisabet Winkler, and Sophia Brahe, sister of the great astronomer, Tycho.[121] The Brahes were Danish nobles: their father, Otto, served as Royal Counsel to King Christian III, and their mother was also a noblewoman. Sophia was very closely associated with her brother in his work at the royal observatory, Uranienborg, on Hven Island. The attachment between them was powerful, and Tycho probably cared more for her than for any other woman.[122] She married twice. Her first marriage to the nobleman Otto Thott of Eriksholm ended with his early death in 1688. They had one son, Tage. Sophia dedicated herself conscientiously to the administration of Eriksholm until Tage reached maturity, then returned to Uranienborg to continue her scientific work. While in Uranienborg, she met with a young nobleman called Erik Lange of Engelsholm, who, after a career as an astrologer and magician, had turned to Tycho Brahe for further education. The couple fell deeply in love, to the dismay of all the Brahe family except Tycho, and became engaged in 1590. Lange fled Denmark to escape his creditors, and the couple did not marry until 1602. He died in 1613, in Prague, and Sophia then returned to Denmark, where she continued to work on astronomy, astrology, and genealogy for the remainder of her long life. The long *heroides* poem attributed to her, *Urania Titani* (written 1594), is actually

119 Paullini, *Das Hoch- und Wohl-gelahrte Teutsche Frauen-Zimmer* (2nd edn. 1712), 17.

120 Balthasar Exner, *Anchora Utriusque Vitae, hoc est, Symbolum Spero Meliora* (Hanau: Wechel, 1619), 227.

121 Johann Caspar Eberti, *Schlesiens Hoch- und Wohlgelehrte Frauenzimmer* (Wrocław: Michael Rorlach, 1727), 79. F. R. Friis, *Sofie Brahe Ottesdatter: En Biografisk Skildring* (Copenhagen: G. E. C. Gad's Universiteitsboghandel, 1905).

122 Victor Thoren, *The Lord of Uraniborg: A Biography of Tycho Brahe* (Cambridge: Cambridge University Press, 1990), 424.

the work of Tycho Brahe,[123] but a brief verse attributed to their joint authorship suggests that she could and did write Latin. However, Paulus Rutingius' poem to Cordula cited above seems to suggest that *Urania Titani* circulated in manuscript in Central Europe, and was attributed to her at the time.

Apart from the women active in the milieu of Rudolf II, there seem to be almost no other Renaissance women Latinists, either poets or prose writers, anywhere in Bohemia, Hungary, or any other part of Central Europe. Milada, daughter of Boleslaus, who founded the convent of St George in Prague c.1417 was a very early Latin-literate woman, as were the nuns of her community, but nothing is known to have been produced there.[124] Despite the intense cultivation of humanist Latin in Central Europe, which produced poets of European stature such as Janus Pannonius (János Csezmicei) and Jiři Carolides, no women writers are mentioned in Birnbaum,[125] nor have I found any in Truhlár and Hrdina's valuable checklist of neo-Latin writers apart from Weston herself.[126] Micesula, Queen of Bosnia, is respectfully addressed in Latin in or before 1543 by Kaspar Brusch in a way that suggests he expected her to be able to read what he says.[127]

A number of women who married into the Hungarian royal family were humanistically educated, notably Beatrice of Aragon (1457–1508), Queen of Hungary—this is not surprising, since she was the fourth daughter of Ferrante I of Naples, and therefore brought up at an Italian court.[128] Her daughter Mary of Hungary was also taught Latin, and has left letters in that language.[129] There is also a Latin letter (written in 1519) from Anne of Hungary, betrothed to the Archduke Ferdinand, and Ferdinand's sister Mary, aged 14, affianced wife of Louis of Hungary, to Margaret of Austria on the death of her father.[130] A woman

---

[123] Peter Zeeberg, *Tycho Brahe's 'Urania Titani', et digt om Sophie Brahe*, Renæssencestudier 7 (Copenhagen Museum Tusculanums Forlag, 1994) (text, pp. 136–68). There are two texts: a manuscript in Vienna, Nationalbibliothek, Cod. lat. 10686 12, a fair copy, not in Tycho's hand but with corrections in his hand, and a printed version in Peder Hansen Resen, *Inscriptiones Hafnienses* (Copenhagen: Henricus Gödianus, 1668).

[124] Jean Mabillon, *Acta Sanctorum Ordinis Benedicti* (Paris: Louis Billaine, 1668–1701), iii. 490.

[125] Marianne D. Birnbaum, *Humanists in a Shattered World: Croatian and Hungarian Latinity in the Sixteenth Century* (Columbus, Oh., Slavica Publishers, 1986).

[126] Z. A. Truhlár and Karel Hrdina, *Enchiridion Renatae Poesis Latinae in Bohemia et Moravia Cultae*, 5 vols. (Prague: Academia, 1966–82). See Shayne Mitchell, ' "Altera Italia": Recent Research on Humanism in Renaissance Hungary', *Bulletin of the Society for Renaissance Studies*, 14.2 (1977), 1–6, for an overview of the currrent work on Hungarian humanism.

[127] Brusch, *Sylvarum . . . Liber*, 'Ad Serenissimam Dominam D. Micesulam Reginam Bosniae', 24–5.

[128] A MS of Cicero's *De Senectute* was made for her when she was 10: Cicero and Virgil played an important part in her education. In 1474 she was betrothed to Matthias Corvinus, and two years later was crowned Queen of Hungary. *Books by and about Women* (London: Bernard Quaritch, 1994), 25. Her humanist credentials are further suggested by Aurelio Lippi Brandolini, *Symposium de Virginitate et Pudicitia Conjugali*, ed. J. Ábel, in *Isodalomtörténet Kösleményck* 2 (1889/90), in which she is given a speaking role. There is an old biography by A. Berceviczy, *Beatrix kisályné*, trans. into French c.1914. Her letters are also edited by Berceviczy. (I owe this information to Dr Shayne Mitchell.)

[129] After her husband's death at Mohács in 1526, she retired to Brussels taking with her the court of Buda and the remains of the Hungarian humanist tradition which dated from Matthias Corvinus. See Ch. 8 n. 86.

[130] Hare, *Marguerite of Austria*, 254: the letter is printed in full.

called Anna, wife of a royal counsellor called Valentini (d. 1597), claims in the first line of his Latin verse epitaph that she is its author, but the nun Lea Ráskai, the first certain Hungarian woman writer outside the royal family, wrote in the vernacular.[131] It is, however, interesting that her convent owned a Hungarian translation of the works of Hrotsvitha.[132]

Poland

Humanism took root in Poland in the fifteenth century, with the assistance of visitors from Germany and Italy, such as Conrad Celtis and Filippo Buonaccorsi, to say nothing of Bona Sforza, daughter of Gian Galeazzo Sforza, who came to Poland as the second wife of King Zygmunt/Sigismund I in 1518.[133] Celtis dubbed Poland 'an Amazon society' due to what he saw as the atypically prominent position of women in public life; and it even produced what may have been the first woman to attend university (disguised as a man), Nawojka.[134] The Jagiellon university at Kraków, one of the principal centres of humanism in the country by the mid-fifteenth century, was founded by the Piast Kazimierz the Great, and lavishly endowed by Jadwiga/Hedvig, Queen of Wladyslaw/Ladislas Jagiellon, who bequeathed her entire fortune to it on her death, while another woman endowed a chair of classical poetry there in 1449. However, there appears to be no evidence that women actually became humanists in the fifteenth century (indeed, it has recently been stated that Polish women did not take up the pen until the seventeenth century, though this is not the case).[135] A number of fifteenth-century Polish women interacted with foreign humanists, but apparently not on equal terms. Filippo Buonaccorsi wrote Latin verses to his Polish mistress Fannia Swentocha, but described her (perhaps jokingly) as a 'tavern maid'. (His poems to her were collected under the title *Fannietum* in 1471).[136] Hasilina, the young wife of an old nobleman in Kraków who became the mistress of Conrad

---

[131] She wrote the Legend of blessed Margaret in 1510. She was a Dominican nun at *Margit sziget* (Margaret's island), named for her heroine. Suzanne Wemple, 'Lea Ráskai, a Dominican Author', *WWRR*, 435–45.

[132] The manuscript which is now Budapest, Egyetemi Könyvtár (University Library), 6 seems to have been made for the nuns of *Margit sziget*. Anne Lyon Haight (ed.), *Hroswitha of Gandersheim* (New York: The Hroswitha Club, 1965), 50.

[133] Joseph Kallenbach, *Les Humanistes polonais* (Fribourg: Consociatio Sancti Pauli, 1891), 6, Harold B. Segel, *Renaissance Culture in Poland* (Ithaca, NY: Cornell University Press, 1989), Jerzy Starnawski, 'La Reine Catherine de la dynastie Jagellon, auteur d'épitres', in Michel Bastiaensen, *La Femme lettrée à la Renaissance* (Brussels: Peeters, 1997), 15–23 (p. 15): see also *Acta Conventus Neo-Lat. Hafniensis*, 917–23. Polish queens continued to use Latin for diplomatic correspondence into the 17th century (see Ch. 13).

[134] Michael H. Shank, 'A Female University Student in Late Medieval Kraków', in J. Bennett et al. (eds.), *Sisters and Workers in the Middle Ages* (Chicago: Chicago University Press, 1989), 190–7.

[135] Starnawski, 'La Reine Catherine', 15: 'Quant à la littérature polonaise, les premiers auteurs femmes d'œuvres en poésie et en prose apparaissent au xviie siècle, et c'est seulement au xviiie siècle qu'on rencontre Elisabeth Druzbecka et Constance Benislawska, deux poétesses de talent.'

[136] Segel, *Renaissance Culture in Poland*, 51.

Celtis, was the subject of book I of his *Quattuor Libri Amorum Secundum Quattuor Latera Germaniae* (*Four Books of Love Affairs, in the Four Parts of Germany*, 1502), but is most unlikely to have read Latin, since Celtis records that an intermediary, Wilczek z Boczowa, acted as go-between and translator until he managed to learn some Polish.[137]

However, the climate of new learning in sixteenth-century Poland included women. Marcin Kromer (*c.*1512–1589), Bishop of Ermeland, described the new Poland of the late sixteenth century in the following optimistic terms:[138]

There is eagerness, in fact, for people—the poor alongside the rich, the nobility and the bourgeois, especially—to send male children to schools and to masters, and for their tender childhood to be steeped in Latin letters. Many people provide keep for tutors in their homes. And so, not even in the middle of Latium would one find so many people in the ordinary population with whom one might nevertheless speak in Latin. Noble and bourgeois girls learn, at home and in convents, to read and write in the vernacular, indeed also in the Latin language.

Probably the first Polish woman to publish a book is Zofia Oleśnika, a descendant of an aristocratic family, the Szafarańców of Pieskowa Skala. She and her husband Mikołaj Oleśnicki (who was a classical scholar) were Calvinists: he founded a Calvinist church in Pińczow, for which she wrote a Polish Protestant hymnal in 1556 which was printed in Kraków by Łazar Andrysowicz Piseñnowa.[139] Both words and music are credited to her.

The evidence for Latinity among sixteenth-century Polish women is, as so often, clearest for the royal family. Katarzyna/Catherine Jagelonska (1526–83), daughter of Zygmunt I and Bona Sforza, left a variety of letters, some of which are in Latin.[140] A Polish princess of the next generation, Anna Wasa, daughter of Katarzyna Jagelonska and Jan III Wasa, or Vasa, King of Sweden, read Polish, Swedish, French, and Latin. She became a Protestant, which estranged her from the court of her fiercely Catholic brother Zygmunt III, King of Poland, so she lived in semi-retirement studying, and promoting the study of botany, zoology, and other sciences.[141] The learning of her brother's second wife, Queen Constantia, is suggested by the facts that she was patron of the alchemist Michael Sendivogius, and author of a Latin letter to Margaret of Austria, queen of Felipe III of Spain.[142]

---

[137] Ibid. 103.

[138] Marcin Kromer, *Polonia, sive de Situ, Populis, Moribus, Magistratibus et Republica Regni Polonici* (Cologne: Maternus Cholinus, 1577; 2nd edn. 1578; Kraków: Nakl. Akademii Umiejetnosci, 1901), quoted in Kallenbach, *Les Humanistes*, 10–11.

[139] *Pieśñ nowa, w której jest dziękowanie Panu Bogu.* See *Nowy Korbut* (Warsaw: Instylist Badari Literarkich Polskiej Academii Nauk, 1963–), iii. 31–2. My thanks to Lenka Vytlacilova and Piotr Urbanski for help with Polish-language sources. Kallenbach, *Les Humanistes*, 6–7, sketches the Reformation in Poland.

[140] Starnawski, 'La Reine Catherine', 19.

[141] Information from Lenka Vytlacilova, Charles University.

[142] Madrid, Biblioteca Naçional, 1462, fo. 264ʳ. Both Constantia and her sister Anna (Zygmunt's first wife) were daughters of the Hapsburg Duke Charles of Styria. Margaret of Austria, another Hapsburg from the Styrian branch of the family, was certainly taught Latin: her elder sister Anna began to study it

Another piece of evidence for women's education among the elite is the Latin letter written by Angela Curio to the 'nobilissima puella polona' Sophia Sbasia (probably Zbanski) in 1563, though the context in which it is preserved, unfortunately, does not include anything from Sbasia in reply. But there is other indirect evidence for cultivated Polish women in the sixteenth century. Several wealthy urban women were enrolled as honorary students at the University of Kraków in the sixteenth century, as a reward for their patronage of the institution: these included Queen Anna Jagelonska, Zofia Gołowa, widow of a tavern-keeper, who seems to have been an honorary student 1580–1, Zofia Zweiergania, Barbara, the wife of a shoemaker, and others.[143] There was also a Polish woman printer of both Polish and Latin books in Kraków active 1536–51, Helena Unglerowna, the widow of Florian Ungler, who published as 'vidua Ungleri' or 'vidua Floriani'.[144] Since to be an early modern printer required editorial as well as mechanical skills, it is fair to assume that this woman was competent in Latin.

at the age of 6. Magdalena S. Sánchez, *The Empress, the Queen and the Nun* (Baltimore: Johns Hopkins University Press, 1998), 71. She was a bibliophile, and owned nearly 400 books (Anne-Marie Legaré, 'Reassessing Women's Libraries in Late Medieval France', *Renaissance Studies*, 10.2 (1996), 109).

[143] Unfortunately, I am dependent on Ms Vytlacilova for this information, and I do not know whether this honorary status gave these women access either to books or to lectures.

[144] Stefan Krol, *101 Kobiet Polskich* (Warsaw: Książka i Wiedza, 1988), 21–2, and see Alodius Kaweckiej-Grycczowej, *Drukarze Dawnej Polski od xv do xviii wieku* (Wrocław: Ossolinskich Wydwnictwo Polskiej Akademii Nauk, 1983), i. 313–25 (my thanks to Piotr Urbanski for sending me a Xerox of this). She is not noticed in Erdmann.

The English were making political capital of their countrywomen's reputation for learning by as early as 1550, as we can see from John Coke's *Debate betweene the Heraldes of Englande and France*. In this context of international one-upmanship between old enemies, he smugly claims, 'Also we haue dyvers gentylwomen in Englande, which be not onely well estudied in holy Scrypture, but also in the Greke and Latyn tonges as maystres More, maystres Anne Coke, Maystres Clement, and others beynge an estraunge thing to you and other nations.'[1] His chauvinism was misplaced, of course: had Coke not written both sides of the so-called 'Debate', the French herald could have produced just as impressive a collection of learned gentlewomen by 1550, and the women of both countries together would have made a poor showing beside their Italian contemporaries, but it is interesting to see that the reputation of Englishwomen for learning had become a matter for national pride.

This reputation owes so much to the family of Henry VIII's chancellor Sir Thomas More (two of the women mentioned by Coke were members of the More household, 'maystres More' and 'Maystres Clement'),[2] that it is worth asking whether, as Mattingly has suggested, it was Henry VIII's queen, the humanistic-ally educated Catherine of Aragon (daughter of Fernando and Isabel), who provided the model for the new style of educated woman.[3] Certainly, access to the new learning for Englishwomen seems to have begun in court circles, and in Henry's reign. Before the Mores, there is very little evidence for learned women in late medieval England, even in the royal family. Margaret Beaufort, mother of Henry VII, though she was one of the most learned women in England and translated the *Speculum Aureum* of Dionysius (Denys) the Carthusian, confessed to Bishop John Fisher that 'in her youthe she had not gyven her to the understandynge of Latyn wherein she had a lytell percevynge', something she came to regret.[4] It is worth stopping to ask when Margaret Beaufort thought her 'youthe' was, given that she was married at 7 or 8, married for a second time, widowed, and a mother by 13, and therefore functionally adult by 12. Henry VIII's sisters were not given humanist

---

[1] (London: Richarde Wyer, 1550), sig. K 1.

[2] 'Maystres Clement' is More's foster-daughter Margaret Gigs, wife of John Clement. The third woman named, 'Anne Coke', is the humanist Anne Cooke, later the wife of Sir Nicholas Bacon.

[3] Garrett Mattingly, *Catherine of Aragon* (London: Jonathan Cape, 1942; repr. 1963), 142–3.

[4] Michael K. Jones and Malcolm S. Underwood, *The King's Mother: Lady Margaret Beaufort, Countess of Richmond and Derby* (Cambridge: Cambridge University Press, 1992), 184. But there are indications she had not given up on Latin even in old age: Cambridge, St John's College Archives, D 91.21, p. 9 'to Sir Christopher clerk of the closet for a book bought for my lady grace called Vergil, 6s 8d.'

educations (though it is interesting to note that in response to the change coming over court culture, his sister Mary apparently started to learn Latin in the 1520s).[5] Another aristocrat, Eleanor Percy, Duchess of Buckingham, makes some use of Latin in her prayer to the Virgin.[6] The most prestigious convents may have kept up their Latin. Katherine of Sutton, Abbess of Barking, wrote a liturgical play in Latin between 1363 and 1376,[7] and the nuns of Chester may, on the basis of a charming lullaby, 'Qui creavit celum, lully lully lu', preserved in their Processional, still have studied Latin in the fifteenth century.[8]

The international fame of the women of the More household is due to More's friendship with Desiderius Erasmus, the colossus of early sixteenth-century scholarship. Erasmus met More's daughter Margaret More, later Roper, in the 1520s. She wrote him a Latin letter which still survives in autograph,[9] and he broadcast her fame in his published writings. She is almost certainly the model for the 'Learned Lady' in his colloquy of the Abbot and the Learned Lady.[10] Margaret More's reputation is also substantiable by a variety of solid achievements, not all of which have survived. Thomas Stapleton notes that he saw Greek and Latin prose and verse by Margaret More, and she is known to have written a treatise on the Four Last Things in friendly competition with her father, though only his unfinished treatment was published.[11] A letter of More's to Margaret is about a letter of hers which he showed to John Veysey: he had read one of her Latin letters and some of her Latin verses, and expressed himself charmed.[12] Another member of the household, More's foster-daughter Margaret Gigs, was particularly interested in algebra, and married John Clements, a distinguished Grecian, who helped

[5] Foster Watson (ed.), *Vives and the Renaissance Education of Women* (London: Edward Arnold, 1912), 159–73 (pp. 172–3): since Richard Hyrde, who makes this claim, is writing to Mary's own daughter, he is unlikely to have been misinformed.

[6] London, British Library, Arundel 318, fo. 152^{r-v}. The poem, a translation of a well-known Latin hymn 'Gaude virgo, mater Christi', with refrain lines left in Latin, is edited by the Countess of Arundel, wife of her great-great-grandson, who contributes a final verse. Alexandra Barratt (ed.), *Women's Writing in Middle English* (Harlow: Longman, 1992), 279–81.

[7] J. B. L. Tolhurst (ed.), *The Barking Ordinale*, 2 vols. (London: For the Henry Bradshaw Society, 1927–8), i. 107.

[8] J. Wickham Legge (ed.), *The Processional of the Nuns of Chester* (London: For the Henry Bradshaw Society, 1899), 26–7. The manuscript is dated *c*.1425.

[9] Epistola 2233, in *Opus Epistolarum Des. Erasmi*, ed. P. S. Allen and H. M. Allen (Oxford: Clarendon Press, 1906–58), Chelsea, 4 Nov. 1529. E. E. Reynolds, *Margaret Roper, Eldest Daughter of St Thomas More* (London: Burns & Oates, 1960), prints a photograph of the holograph letter between pp. 54 and 55. See also Anne M. O'Donnell, 'Contemporary Women in the Letters of Erasmus', *Erasmus of Rotterdam Society Year Book*, 9 (1989), 34–72; Elizabeth McCutcheon, 'Life and Letters: Editing the Writings of Margaret Roper', in W. Speed Hill (ed.), *New Ways of Looking at Old Texts* (Binghamton, NY: Medieval and Renaissance Texts and Studies, 1993), 111–17; and Lee Cullen Khanna (ed.), *Early Tudor Translators: Margaret Beaufort, Margaret More Roper and Mary Basset*, The Early Modern Englishwoman: The Printed Writings (Aldershot: Ashgate, 1998).

[10] Translated in *Erasmus on Women*, trans. Erika Rummel (Toronto: University of Toronto Press, 1996), 174–9.

[11] *The Life and Illustrious Martyrdom of Sir Thomas More*, trans. Philip E. Hallett, ed. E. E. Reynolds (London, Burns and Oates 1966), 103–4, 106–17.

[12] E. M. G. Routh, *Sir Thomas More and his Friends* (London: Oxford University Press, 1934), 133–4.

with the Aldine edition of Galen. 'As the only Englishman who could wear the mantle of Linacre, his prestige in the humanist community was probably unsurpassed, and both he and his wife received the tribute of one of Leland's *Epithalamia*.'[13] Later in her life, as an exile in Madrid for the sake of religion with four grown daughters to worry about, Margaret Gigs gave a well-received Latin oration before Felipe II of Spain, according to Perez de Moya, probably an indirect request for royal help. Since he was generous to English and Irish exiles, she may well have received it: if she did, then her Latin learning will have been of direct use to her.[14]

As Coke's little treatise indicates, More's daughters and protégées were admired in England. Still earlier, in 1524, Margaret Roper's translation from Erasmus, *A Devout Treatise upon the Paternoster*, was published with an introduction by Richard Hyrde which makes a strong argument that the Mores should be seen as a vanguard of change. 'And the Latin and the Greek tongue I see not but there is as little hurt in them [for women], as in books of English and French.'[15] They were also held up internationally, notably by Erasmus, as examples of the new idea of companionate marriage in which husbands and wives shared common intellectual interests, also found in contemporary Germany and the Low Countries. Thomas More's Latin epigram on choosing a wife, published 1516, argues that only an educated woman is a true friend and companion: 'it will be difficult to choose between her perfect power of expression and her thoughtful understanding of all kinds of affairs.'[16] More's letter to Gonell makes clear his commitment to the ideal of virtue acquired through education, especially for women.[17] In his *Epigram*, More endows women with *virtus*—involving intellectual, moral, and rhetorical strength—not merely with *castitas*. He repeatedly connects *virtus* and learning, and considers both desirable for women.[18]

Though he had not married an educated woman himself (he would have found it hard to locate one in his own generation, at least in England), More reared his daughters and protégées to be women capable of undertaking this kind of relationship. Margaret, in turn, conscientiously educated her own daughter. Roger Ascham revealed in a letter of 15 January 1554 to Mary Clarke, née Roper, that

---

[13] J. K. McConica, *English Humanists and Reformation Politics* (Oxford: Clarendon Press, 1965), 270.

[14] Pietro Paolo de Ribera Valentianus, *Le glorie immortali de'... donne illustre*: (Venice: Evangelista Benchino, 1609), 306, an account taken from Juan Perez de Moya, *Varia historia de sanctos e illustres mugeres en todo genero de virtudes* (Madrid: Francisco Sanchez, 1583), iii. 311ᵛ. Felipe II displayed some sympathy for learned women as such: he gave a life pension to the Portuguese Latinist Publia Hortensia de Castro, and Luisa Sigea sought his patronage: see Ch. 8.

[15] Watson (ed.), *Vives*, 165.

[16] Petrus Scriverius (ed.), *Dominico Baudii Amores* (Amsterdam: Ludovicus Elzevir, 1638), Thomas Morus, Anglus, 'Qualis uxor deligenda, ad Candidum', 281–8. Trans. from Pamela Joseph Benson, *The Invention of the Renaissance Woman* (University Park: Pennsylvania State University Press, 1992), 158–9.

[17] E. F. Rogers (ed.), *Correspondence of Sir Thomas More* (Princeton: Princeton University Press, 1947), no 63. Judith P. Jones and Sherianne Sellers Seibel, 'Thomas More's Feminism: to Reform or Re-form', in Michael J. Moore (ed.), *Quincentennial Essays on St Thomas More* (Boone, NC: Appalachian State University Press, 1978), 67–77 (p. 71).

[18] Lee Cullen Khanna, 'Images of Women in Thomas More's Poetry', in Moore (ed.), *Quincentennial Essays*, 78–88 (pp. 82–3).

Margaret about twenty years earlier had tried to persuade him to become a tutor in Greek and Latin to herself and Margaret's other children (and that, having failed to do so, she had found them an alternative teacher).[19] Her daughter Mary Clarke, later Mary Basset, translated her grandfather Sir Thomas More's *of the Sorowe, Werinesse, Feare, and Prayer of Christ before hys Taking* from Latin to English as well as making a Latin version of the first book of Eusebius' *Ecclesiastical History* with an English version of the first five books,[20] and was considered one of the learned lights of the court of Queen Mary Tudor.[21] Though the More family was strongly Catholic, and thus not directly influenced by Protestant ideas of marriage as the necessary goal of women, it is clear that education was perceived in successive generations of this family as associated with an ideal of companionate marriage rather than as a preparation for the convent.

With the fall of Sir Thomas More, his family scattered into recusancy and exile. They continued to educate their daughters for generations, but they were no longer in the mainstream of England's cultural life.[22] Perhaps the next genuinely high-profile women Latinists in England were Protestants: the Seymour sisters, the first Englishwomen to publish a printed volume of their verse.[23] They were the daughters of Edward Seymour, Duke of Somerset, and Lord Protector, who ended his life disgraced and executed. Their aunt Jane Seymour (1509–37) had been the third wife of Henry VIII. Their uncle Thomas Seymour was the last husband of Henry's sixth wife, Katherine Parr; and appears also to have made advances to the young Princess Elizabeth.[24] They were three of the ten children (six daughters, four sons) whom Seymour had by his second wife Anne Stanhope. Jane, the youngest (1541–61), was directly involved with her father's political life: he was accused of plotting to marry her to the sickly young prince Edward VI, whose early death brought Mary Tudor and then Elizabeth I to the throne.[25] This seems very far from unlikely: there was a potential bar had they been Catholics, in that Jane and Edward were first cousins (he was the son of Queen Jane Seymour), but the Seymour family had come out firmly as Protestants.

The education of the Seymour girls has to be understood in this highly political context. The girls with a direct claim on the throne such as Mary Tudor, Elizabeth, Lady Jane and Lady Katherine Grey, were all highly educated (as

[19] Roger Ascham, *The Whole Works*, ed. J. A. Giles, 3 vols. (London: Library of Old Authors, 1865), i, ep. 166.

[20] This is preserved in manuscript, London, British Library, Harley 1860, dedicated during the reign of Edward VI to the future Queen Mary. This seems to be the actual MS presented to Mary, though it has lost its original binding of purple velvet. McConica, *English Humanists*, 266.

[21] Maria Dowling, *Humanism in the Age of Henry VIII* (Beckenham: Croom Helm, 1986), 222.

[22] For a fuller account, see my 'Women Catholics and Latin Culture', in a forthcoming volume on *Catholic Culture in Early Modern England*, to be edited by Arthur Marotti, Frances Dolan, and Ron Corthell.

[23] Brenda M. Hosington, 'England's First Female-Authored Encomium: The Seymour Sisters' *Hecatodistichon* (1550), to Marguerite de Navarre. Text, Translation, Notes, and Commentary', *Studies in Philology*, 93 (1996), 117–63.

[24] William Seymour, *Ordeal by Ambition* (London: Sidgwick and Jackson, 1972), 225–7.

[25] Ibid. 344, 353.

were the girls who kept them company in the schoolroom, such as Katherine Brandon, née Willoughby, Duchess of Suffolk, and Katherine Parr, both of whom benefited from the teaching of the humanist Jean Luis Vives alongside their contemporary Mary Tudor).[26] Seymour was in effect identifying his children as potential future princesses by lavishing the resources on them that he did: his sister's brief but glorious career had perhaps suggested to him that a family's advancement could be furthered by its daughters as well as its sons.

The Seymour sisters are sometimes said to have had Thomas Cranmer, later the Archbishop of Canterbury, as one of their tutors for three years. This was not the case: they had a man called John Crane, mentioned in Denisot's *Epistle* to the girls as 'Joannes Crannus, vester preceptor', possibly a relative of the William Crane who was a member of Somerset's household and testified against him in his trial in 1551. More importantly, the French *littérateur* Nicholas Denisot (later the editor of their distichs for Marguerite de Navarre) was another;[27] while Thomas Norton was the preceptor of the Seymour boys. Anne was married twice, as her funeral sermon indicates,[28] while Margaret and Jane died unwed.[29]

The sisters' book of distichs on the death of Marguerite de Navarre, published in Paris, is probably a witness to the ambitiousness of their family.[30] As 'learned maids', there was a social propriety which they could invoke in writing on the death of another notably learned lady; but to produce something so very long, under the auspices of a man with strong connections to both the French court and the Pléiade, can only be seen as a bid to raise their profile abroad. It is also interesting that they are informed (presumably by Denisot) of Marguerite's actual behaviour on her deathbed: she is known to have pronounced the name of Jesus three times as she died, which is directly reflected in distich 89 (Margaret's).[31]

Margaret Seymour, the least historically visible of the three since she neither married, like her sister Anne, nor became a maid of honour, like her sister Jane, was perceived as the most talented by Denisot. One rather complex piece of evidence for this is that Denisot is the probable author of a novel called *L'Amant resuscité de la mort d'amour*,[32] which is prefaced by an eulogy on the name 'Margaret', and lists seven famous Margarets, including Margaret Seymour and her grandmother of the same name. Harris argues that the name of the principal character in the novel, Marguerite, Contesse de Meyssor, is an anagram of

---

[26] George Ballard, *Memoirs of Several Ladies of Great Britain*, ed. Ruth Perry (Detroit: Wayne State University Press, 1985), 122–3, gives a Latin letter from Katherine Parr to Mary Tudor.

[27] Clement Jugé, *Nicolas Denisot du Mans (1515–1559): essai sur sa vie et ses œuvres* (Mans, 1907; repr. Geneva: Slatkine, 1969).

[28] Seymour, *Ordeal by Ambition*, 338.

[29] Ibid. 367.

[30] Guy Bedouelle, 'L'Image de Marguerite de Navarre dans l'Angleterre du xvie siècle', in Michel Bastiaensen (ed.), *La Femme lettrée à la Renaissance* (Brussels: Peeters, 1997), 95–106.

[31] Jugé, *Nicolas Denisot*, 62.

[32] His authorship was argued by Margaret Harris, *A Study of Théodose Valentinian's 'Amant resuscité de la mort d'amour': A Religious Novel of Sentiment, and its Possible Connexions with Nicolas Denisot du Mans* (Geneva: Droz, 1966): see Hosington, 'England's First Female-Authored Encomium'.

Margaret Seymour. The younger Margaret is singled out for special commendation, and it is suggested that her verse is so perfect that no man could better it. She is described as one of France's three graces together with two members of the French royal family, Marguerite, Duchesse de Berry, and Marguerite de Navarre. Pierre de Mireurs singles out Margaret for special praise in his Latin epistle in the 1550 edition of the *Hecatodistichon*,[33] and in the 1551 edition, her work is also particularly noticed by Salomon Macrin in 'De Tribus Heroinis Sororibus Anglicis' as 'elegant'.

During the reign of Elizabeth, a number of Englishwomen became known for their learning, starting with the queen herself. Mary Tudor, her elder sister, was very carefully educated, but she does not seem to have had any personal taste for humanism.[34] Elizabeth, on the other hand, made it an important part of her public persona. Her court culture was insular, capricious in its adoption of continental models, and not strongly intellectual; however, in the first half of the reign, Elizabeth's court was anxious to appear civilized in the eyes of sophisticated foreigners such as Paul Melissus and his Flemish friend the amiable polymath Karel Utenhove.

Gabriel Harvey (who was not a courtier) suggested that court ladies should read extensively: the authors he suggests for their perusal are Boccaccio, Cavicaeus, Castiglione, Ovid, Virgil, Aeneas Sylvius, Dante, Baptista Mantuanus, Petrarch, Callimachus and his imitators, the 'Callimachi novi', Hoedus, Bembo, Lucian, and Monophilus (most of whom would have to be read in either Latin or Italian), together with three English writers, Chaucer, Surrey, and Gascoigne.[35] As a picture of the actual Elizabethan court, this was a pious hope, but it does suggest that a new, Italian-influenced standard of what constituted civilized knowledge was beginning to be established in England.[36] The coterie of Elizabethan humanists was a small one, and the only poet of international stature that the British Isles produced was a Scot (George Buchanan): it is significant that in 1563, near the beginning of Elizabeth's reign, the well-connected Petrus Ramus confessed that he could not name a single English scholar.[37] Few English names appear in Latin poems of compliment written on the Continent during Elizabeth's reign, and those

[33] sig. biiiiv.

[34] Her translation of the Prayer of St Thomas Aquinas, done when she was 12, survives: Dowling, *Humanism*, 228. She spoke Latin, Italian, and French, and could read her mother's letters in Spanish. She later undertook the translation of Erasmus' paraphrase of the Gospel of John at the urging of Katherine Parr, and communicated with Katherine in Latin (see David Loades, *The Reign of Mary Tudor* (London: Ernest Benn, 1979)). Juan Luis Vives wrote *De Instructione Feminae* (printed Basel: Robert Winter, 1538, and translated into English by Richard Hyrde, London: Thomas Berthelet, 1540) as a syllabus for her, though her first tutor was Thomas Linacre. From 1525, when she was nominally Princess of Wales with a court at Ludlow, she was taught by John Featherstone.

[35] *Gabrielis Harveii Gratulationum Valdinensium, Libri Quatuor, ad Illustrissimam Augustissimam Principem Elizabetam* (London: Henry Binneman, 1578), written for the queen's visit to Saffron Walden.

[36] J. W. Binns, *Intellectual Culture in Elizabethan and Jacobean England* (Leeds: Francis Cairns, 1990), 19.

[37] J. A. van Dorsten, *The Radical Arts* (Leiden: Thomas Brown Institute, 1970), 12.

that do fall into two categories: in the first half of the reign, some of the diehard English Protestants who had sought exile during the reign of Queen Mary (such as John Cheke and Sir Anthony Cooke) maintained links which they had made with continental Protestants, and in the second half of the reign, those individuals connected with the Anglo-Dutch Protestant alliance of 1585, most notably Leicester and his nephew Sir Philip Sidney, were honoured by Protestant humanists, particularly those directly connected with the Low Countries.[38] It is particularly interesting to find that Cooke, father of famously learned daughters, was in friendly contact with Coelius Secundus Curio, who educated his own daughters, spoke strongly in favour of women's education, and edited the works of his close friend Olimpia Morata.[39]

The queen herself was one of the most scholarly members of her court. She was given a full humanist education in Latin, Greek, and modern languages: her principal tutor was Roger Ascham, who spoke admiringly of her abilities.[40] Several of her early letters are in Latin, and she used Latin for diplomatic purposes throughout her life.[41] Her fluency in foreign languages, ancient and modern, was frequently remarked on by contemporaries.[42] William Cecil, her chancellor, comments after she lost her temper with a Polish ambassador; 'to this, I swear by the Living God, that her majesty made one of the best answers extempore in Latin that ever I heard.'[43] Her reply to the Polish embassy in 1597 is preserved, authenticated by Cecil and others,[44] and she spoke extempore in Latin on a number of other occasions, particularly when she was visiting Oxford or Cambridge. Her own cultural production is heavily weighted towards translations—she produced a surprisingly large number of rough, swiftly composed, and extremely careless

---

[38] R. C. Strong and J. A. van Dorsten, *Leicester's Triumph* (Leiden: University Press; London: Oxford University Press, 1964), 27–30.

[39] John Cheke, *Iohannis Cheki Angli de Pronuntiatione Graecae* (Basel: Nicolas Episcopius [Bischoff] Junior, 1555), sig. A 4ʳ, gives a letter written by Curio to Cooke from Basel in 1555.

[40] T. W. Baldwin, *William Shakespere's Small Latine and Lesse Greeke*, 2 vols. (Urbana: University of Illinois Press, 1944), 176–84, is enlightening on the way she was trained, and ultimately dismissive of her learning: though this must be contexted by his manifest dislike of the whole concept of women scholars.

[41] See, for example, Victor von Klarwill (ed.), *Queen Elizabeth and Some Foreigners, Being an Series of Hitherto Unpublished Letters from the Archive of the Hapsburg Family* (London: John Lane, Bodley Head Ltd., 1928), 25–6, Latin letter from Elizabeth to Ferdinand I in her own hand, 28 Nov. 1558, and a letter from the ambassador George von Helffenstein to Ferdinand, 16 Mar. 1559, p. 48, in which he notes, 'the queen during our walk [in the garden] further told me that if I had any further commission of your Imperial Majesty's to communicate, I might do it freely then, as the maid of honour on duty did not understand Latin'. See Dana F. Sutton, 'The Queen's Latin', *Neulateinische Jahrbuch/Journal of Neo-Latin Language and Literature*, 2 (2000), 233–40.

[42] Paul Henzner, *Travels in England during the Reign of Queen Elizabeth* (London: Cassell & Co., 1889), 48. 'besides being well skilled in Greek, Latin, and the languages I have mentioned, she is skilled in Spanish, Scotch, and Dutch.' Her skill with languages is also evidenced by her polyglot manuscript prayer book, written *c.*1579–82, London, British Library, Facsimile 218.

[43] London, Public Record Office, CSP Dom. Eliz. 264/51(i).

[44] Wolfenbüttel, Augustischen Hss II 317–8, 2309 30.11 Aug. fol. s. xvii, fos. 307–15: 'Responsiones Elizabethae reginae Angliae oratori regis Poloniae Sigismundi tum verbo tum scripto datae per nos consiliaros regios, dd. in palatio Grevicensi [Greenwich] 1597, Aug. 13, subscripserunt W. Burghley, Ch. Howard, R. Cecyll, Jo. Forteschewe.'

translations from Latin and Greek which seem to have doubled as exercises in keeping her languages fluent,[45] and some kind of relief from the tensions of her life: William Camden, for example, asserted that her translation of Boethius' *Consolation of Philosophy*—a classic work on reversal of fortune—was undertaken as a result of her grief over Henri IV's conversion to Catholicism, and completed between 10 October and 5 November 1593.[46] She also translated parts of Horace's *Ars Poetica*, and Plutarch's *Moralia* (from Greek).[47] Few of her courtiers, with the possible exception of the Cecils, were as diligent in keeping their school Latin and Greek in repair. Her Latin verse consists only of a few short pieces, which include responses to continental humanists.[48] The only Latin poem of any length which is attributed to her is a response to a poem of compliment by Paul Melissus, librarian of the Palatine Library in Heidelberg.

> Grata Camena tua est, gratissima dona, Melisse:
>   Gratior est animi dulcis imago tui.
> At quae tanta movet te causa, quis impetus urget,
>   Ex homine ingenuo servus ut esse velis?
> Haud nostrum est arctis vates includere septis,
>   Aut vel tantillum deminuisse caput.
> Tu potius liber fieres, laxante patrona
>   Vincula, si famula conditione fores.
> Sed vatum es princeps; ego vati subdita, dum me
>   Materiam celsi carminis ipse legis,
> Quem regum pudeat tantum coluisse poetam,
>   Nos ex semideis qui facit esse deos?

> Your Muse is pleasant, Melissus, your gifts most pleasant:
> Pleasanter still is the image of your sweet disposition.
> But what is the reason so great as to move you, the impulse that urges you,
> That you should want to turn from a free man into a slave?
> It is hardly our custom to keep poets in narrow confines
> Or to lessen your standing to the slightest degree.
> Rather, you would become free, with your patroness
> Loosening your chains, if you had been in a servile condition.
> But you are a prince of poets; I, a poet's subject, as long as
> You choose me as the matter of exalted song.

---

[45] At various points in her life, she apologized more than once to foreign ambassadors for her inadequate command of one language or another, on grounds of being out of practice: see Klarwill (ed.), *Queen Elizabeth and Some Foreigners*, 59, 187, 194. She was evidently highly conscious of the need to work at a language in order to maintain fluency.

[46] William Camden, *The Historie of the most Renowned and Victorious Princesse Elizabeth* (London: Benjamin Fisher, 1630), bk 43, p. 51. London, British Library, Lansdowne 253, fo. 200.

[47] Caroline Pemberton (ed.), *Queen Elizabeth's Englishings*, Early English Text Society os 113 (London, Kegan Paul, Trench, Trubner & Co., 1899), considers the translations very poor: Leicester Bradner, *The Poems of Queen Elizabeth* (Providence, RI: Brown University Press, 1960), 82, points out that Pemberton has failed to take into account the difference between Elizabethan and modern texts of the Latin originals.

[48] Johann Caspar Eberti, *Eröffnetes Cabinet dess Gelehrten Frauen-zimmer* (Frankfurt: Michael Rohrlachs sel. Wittib und Erben, 1700), 139.

What ruling monarch would be ashamed to have reverenced such a great poet
Who makes us, out of demigods, into gods?

The poem is interesting for its nuanced reading of power relations between poet and patron (a perception to which the early modern period was generally strangely obtuse):[49] Melissus speaks as a suppliant, but Elizabeth points out that by the very act of writing, he has made her a 'subject'.

Some of the women of Elizabeth's court bore a substantial part of the burden of presenting it as culturally sophisticated. Among the most significant, in the first decade or so of the reign, are Mildred, the wife of William Cecil, Lord Burghley,[50] and her three sisters, Anne, Lady Bacon, Elizabeth, Lady Russell, and Katherine Killigrew. Mildred's husband William Cecil, one of Elizabeth's chief advisers, was one of the most obviously humanist figures at Elizabeth's court, as Jan van Dorsten has pointed out, in a formulation which also underscores the importance of Mildred herself.[51]

Unlike Dudley, [Cecil] was a scholar, a lover of books, and a man of great intellectual curiosity. He and his wife Mildred . . . had their children tutored to a high degree of erudition, and in their house Classical studies, philosophy and science, and at least certain kinds of poetry and music could seek refuge. Indeed, Cecil House was England's nearest equivalent of a humanist salon since the days of More.

This is confirmed by Utenhove, who described Cecil in a poem as 'another Maecenas for our age'.[52] But Mildred had an independent status and importance. Roger Ascham couples her with Lady Jane Grey as one of the two most learned ladies in England, in a generation where there was considerable competition for that title.[53] She has left very little writing which survives, though there is clear evidence that more was written. The hard evidence for Mildred as a poet comes down to one surviving verse (in Greek),[54] with some evidence that others existed. She may have contributed to the unsigned verses on Sir Anthony Cooke's epitaph at Romford Church, Essex: when he died at Gidea Hall in 1576, an alabaster monument was erected to his memory in the church, embellished with epitaphs in Greek, Latin, and English. These may well have been written by his daughters, in

---

[49] I consider this point, with examples, in my 'Women, Writing and Scribal Publication in the Sixteenth Century', *English Manuscript Studies*, 9 (2000), 1–31 (pp. 15–18).

[50] I have treated Mildred Cecil at greater length in an article, 'Mildred Cecil, Lady Burleigh: Poet, Patron, Politician', in *Early Modern Women's Manuscript Writing: Selected Papers of the Trinity/ Trent Colloquium*, ed. Victoria Burke and Jonathan Gibson, The Early Modern Englishwoman (Aldershot: Ashgate Publishing), 51–73.

[51] Jan van Dorsten, 'Mr Secretary Cecil: Patron of Letters', in his *The Anglo-Dutch Renaissance: Seven Essays* (Leiden: Leiden University Press; London: Oxford University Press, 1988), 28–37 (p. 31). Both William and Mildred Cecil clearly acted as the patrons of a variety of humanist poets and intellectuals, such as Utenhove, Franciscus Junius, and Daniel Rogers, as well as of Anglo-Latin poets such as John Herd, Giles and Phineas Fletcher, and Christopher Ockland.

[52] Paris, Bibliothèque Nationale de France, Lat. 18592 (a collection of Utenhove's letters), fo. 40: 'nostrique Moecenas es alter seculi.'

[53] David Cecil, *The Cecils of Hatfield House* (London: Cardinal, 1975), 80.

[54] Cambridge, University Library, Ii.5.37 ('the Bartholo Sylva MS'), p. vʳ.

tribute to his teaching, and while Elizabeth, Lady Russell, was the family specialist in funerary poetry, so we might reasonably guess that hers was the chief hand at work, the other sisters may have wanted to make their own contributions.[55]

Much of what is recorded about her literary life suggests that Mildred's primary interest was in classical and patristic Greek. She must have begun learning the language from her father, but Giles Lawrence, of Christ Church, Oxford, was her Greek tutor in her youth, and claimed later that she 'egalled if not overmatched' contemporary Grecians.[56] She also had at some point a Greek teacher referred to as John Ακανθινος (which means 'spiny': the most probable English names this could represent are Thorney or perhaps Sharpe).[57]

The evidence for her activities as a patron are various. Specific dedications to Mildred, rather than to Cecil, indicate her involvement with the Anglo-Latin poets of the period. Phineas Fletcher presented her with his 'Querela Collegii Regali', an allegorical account of the troubles of King's College, Cambridge, with provost Philip Baker, in which Telethusa (the college) laments the harsh treatment received from her husband Daphnis (Baker). This was the first Latin pastoral to be written in England, and is an indication that she was thought receptive to innovative and groundbreaking humanist writing.[58] Giles Fletcher also dedicated a set of five Latin eclogues to her: since the second celebrates the marriage of Anne Cecil with Edward Vere, they can be dated to 1571.[59] A decade later, Christopher Ockland's Latin heroic poem *Elizabetha* is dedicated to 'The very noble and above all learned woman, most skilled in both Greek and Latin letters, Lady Mildred, the most praiseworthy wife of Lord Burghley, the great Treasurer of England'.[60] This suggests that she continued to be seen as a desirable patron, even ten years after she had retired from court life and to some extent lost the queen's favour.[61]

The earliest set of poems to be addressed to her from abroad are by a Low Countries humanist, Franciscus Junius, dated July 1565.[62] Junius, who had spent the previous four months editing Eunapius, was discreetly looking for support; but

---

[55] Stephen J. Barns, 'The Cookes of Gidea Hall', *Essex Review*, 21 [81] (1912). 1–9 (p. 3). The verses are printed in John Strype, *Annals of the Reformation*, 4th edn., 3 vols. (Oxford: Clarendon Press, 1824), ii. 604–7, and see appendix II.

[56] Retha M. Warnicke, *Women of the English Renaissance and Reformation* (Westport, Conn.: Greenwood Press, 1983), 105.

[57] *CSP (Domestic) of the Reign of Edward VI, 1547–1553*, ed C. S. Knighton, (London: HMSO, 1992), 195, letter from Dr William Turner, Dean of Wells, to William Cecil.

[58] *Historical Manuscripts Commission Report on the Manuscripts of the Marquis of Salisbury Preserved at Hatfield House*, 17 vols. (London: for HMSO, 1892–1904), xiii. 103.

[59] London, Hatfield House, Cecil Papers 248.1–5, *Hatfield Calendar*, xiii. 109.

[60] ειρηναρχια *sive Elizabetha* (London: C. Barkerus, 1582).

[61] Other dedications in printed books are listed in Franklin B. Williams, *Index of Dedications and Commendatory Verses* (London: The Bibliographical Society, 1962), 35: Ulpian Fulwell, *Ars Adulandi* (1576), and Thomas Drant's translation of Horace's *Satires* (1566).

[62] London, Public Record Office, SP 12/47, fos. 14–20. Three poems to Cecil complain that the queen is refusing to listen to him, and stress the urgency of his suit, which Cecil is asked to expedite. But there are also two poems to Mildred herself (fos. 17–18), the first of which begs her to soften her husband's heart, while the second lauds her as a second Sappho.

it is interesting that he looked to Mildred as well as to William: while most of the sheaf of poems are to William Cecil, two (fos. 17–18), are addressed directly to Mildred, and flatter her as both scholar and writer. Notably, in the longer of the two, which describes her as 'distinguished for her birth and her learning', the Muses declare that now Lady Burleigh has come along, 'Lesbian Sappho may not eternally merit our praise'. Another set of verses from a grateful client also offers some evidence for Mildred Cecil's Latin verse composition. The four poems 'To Mildred, wife of William Cecil, a matron outstanding for her virtue and learning' written by George Buchanan (who was also friendly with Sir Anthony Cooke, William Cecil, Mildred's sister Katherine Killigrew, and her husband Sir Henry) imply that she sent him poetry, probably in Latin. This material is difficult to date. Buchanan was friendly with the Cookes as a family from the 1560s, and particularly friendly with Katherine Killigrew towards the end of the 1570s,[63] so it probably dates from early in the reign of Elizabeth: MacFarlane suggests 1568/9.[64] His first poem is a new-year *xenium* (gift), sent, apparently, speculatively, and hinting that the author might benefit from her taking an interest in him. The second opens,[65]

> Mildred, since you have sent me a poem more precious than gold,
> I am forever delighted by your wit.

From his reply, her poem seems to have said that she considered wealth a disease, which she might rid herself of by sending it to Buchanan: it is clear, therefore, that she did not content herself with sending verses only, but was mindful of her proper duty as a patron. The third of Buchanan's poems implies her generosity, and suggests that it might spur his muse to greater efforts,[66] while a fourth says specifically, 'you have given good gold in return for a bad poem'.[67] In writing this lost poem to Buchanan, Mildred was displaying a skill which was not purely literary in its implications. The ability to produce a well-turned poem in one or other of the learned languages was one of the ways in which sixteenth-century politicians sorted out the players from the pawns: to exchange verse, and to respond intelligently to the reception of verse, was in itself a tool of diplomatic life.

Mildred Cecil's relationship with the international Protestant humanist community was not confined to Junius and Buchanan. She and her husband were also

---

[63] I. D. MacFarlane, *Buchanan* (London: Duckworth, 1981), 236, 303.

[64] Ibid. 329. The textual tradition is little help. The poems to Mildred are in Buchanan's third book of *Epigrammata*, which first saw print in 1584 (ibid. 303–5), though the fourth poem is in one of the most important MSS of Buchanan's poems, Paris, Bibliothèque Nationale de France Nouv. acq. lat. 106 fo. 29ʳ⁻ᵛ, which was written in the late 1570s and owned by Katherine Killigrew (it may be in her hand).

[65] George Buchanan, *Georgii Buchanani Scoti Poemata* (Amsterdam: Henricius Wetstenius, 1687), 395–6.

[66]

> Quod Mildreda mihi carmen pretiosus auro
> Miseris, ingenio gratulor usque tuo.

[67] It is worth observing that, having discussed this set of poems, and thus demonstrated the seriousness with which Buchanan took Mildred Cecil, MacFarlane gratuitously adds, 'some have thought she confused scholarship and tedium' (*Buchanan*, 329).

connected with one of Buchanan's closest friends, Karel (Charles) Utenhove of Ghent, a Protestant who spent time in England, and was a person of good standing at the English court, which he visited in 1562. Utenhove was one of the most learned men of his age, the son of a personal friend of Erasmus, with acquaintances all over Europe, and was internationally famous for his gift for languages: he wrote poetry in at least ten (Latin, Greek, Hebrew, Syriac, French, German, Flemish, Italian, French, and English).[68] Cecil himself was Utenhove's chief patron in England;[69] but an important piece of evidence for Mildred's *independent* relations with Utenhove is a letter which he wrote to Jean de Morel in 1564, from London, reporting that he had given a public lecture on Thucydides, well attended by English scholars, with Mildred Cecil as guest of honour. He then expatiates on Mildred, praising her writing in both Latin and Greek.[70]

I am making great advances with Greek. Recently, I was lecturing on Thucydides to the noble lady Mildred Cecil (wife of the great Sir William Cecil), whose father was the illustrious Sir Anthony Cooke, in the presence of the other English people who have a reputation for learning, and I think she showed me more than sufficient [favour]. How much progress she has made in Greek (as to her Latin, in which she excels all, I am silent) I would prefer you to learn from me by the Atticisms in the letters she wrote me.

Evidently, he copied her letters and sent them to Paris, an example of the way humanists tended to circulate letters in manuscript rather than treating them as private communications.[71]

It is clear from these interchanges with both Buchanan and Utenhove, highly international and very well-known humanist poets, that during the reign of Elizabeth it was well worth courting Mildred Cecil separately from her husband. It is also clear that in a familiar humanist fashion, her letter was circulated in manuscript. A further implication of this report is that on this occasion, one of the none-too-frequent moments when Elizabethan court culture rose to the kind of classical, humanist occasion that interested the French court or the more intellectual Italian dukedoms, a woman sat in the chair of honour: it is a picture worth dwelling on, since it is often implied that any kind of prestige which might attach to classical culture was entirely engrossed by church and university men. What we glimpse in the writings of Utenhove and Buchanan are traces of Mildred Cecil's high-profile participation in a literary world which is not merely public, but international, even though we now have so little of her actual writing.

---

[68] For a sketch of Utenhove's career, see Willem Janssen, *Charles Utenhove* (Maastricht: van Aelst, 1939). He made a number of friends in England, such as Daniel Rogers and Sir Philip Sidney, and he was a very close friend of Buchanan. He had London connections: his uncle Jan was the pastor of the Dutch church in London, and he had a number of friends in the London Dutch community (Leonard Forster, *Janus Gruter's English Years* (Leiden: Leiden University Press, 1967), 44–8).

[69] Which may also account for the link between the Cecils and Buchanan: see MacFarlane, *Buchanan*, 226–7.

[70] Munich, Bayerische Staatsbibliothek, Clm lat. 10383, fo. 260ʳ.

[71] The longer of the two poems in London, Public Record Office, SP 12/47, fos. 14–20, 'Dialogue on the Learned Wife of Cecil', is copied in the hand of Jan Dousa, in Paris, Bibliothèque Nationale de France, Dupuy 951, fo. 291ʳ, which suggests that it was circulating among Protestant humanists on the Continent.

Her sister Anne Bacon was known particularly as a translator, though she has also left a single Latin poem. She published a book of fourteen sermons translated from the Italian of Bernadino Ochino in 1550, when she was 22, which presumably accounts for Coke's mention of her, quoted above.[72] Early in the reign of Elizabeth, on the insistence of her brother-in-law William Cecil,[73] she also published an English translation of John Jewell's *An Apology for the Church of England*. This was a highly responsible and significant undertaking. The *Apologia* was the official document defining the precise theological position of the Church of England, which the Convocation of 1563 had ordered to be placed 'in all cathedral and collegiate churches, and also in private houses'. It attempted to draw an intellectually coherent line between extreme Protestant positions and Roman Catholicism, and the precise meaning of each word was therefore of the highest importance.[74] M.C., the editor of the second edition of Anne's *Apologie* (the first, of 1562, contains no introductory material), who may be her sister Mildred, stresses that the translation was published without her consent or knowledge.[75]

Elizabeth, Lady Russell, was by far the most significant poet of the sisters, in terms of both quantity and quality. She also translated *A Way of Reconciliation... touching the True Nature and Substance of the Body and Blood of Christ* from Latin to English, published in 1605, and dedicated to her daughter Anne Herbert, with a short Latin poem.[76] Most of her surviving Latin verse is funerary, and some of it is remarkable for its emotional vividness, as can be seen from this lament for her first husband, Thomas Hoby (the translator of Castiglione's *Il cortegiano*):

ELIZABETH HOBAEA conjux, ad THOMAN HOBAEUM, Equitem Maritum

O dulcis conjux, animae pars maxima nostrae,
    Cujus erat vitae vita medulla meae,
Cur ita conjunctos divellunt invida fata?
    Cur ego sum viduo sola relicta thoro?
Anglia faelices, faelices *Gallia* vidit,
    Per mare, per terras noster abivit amor,
Par fortunatum fuimus dum viximus una,
    Corpus erat duplex, spiritus unus erat.
Sed nihil in terris durat charissime conjux,

[72] Mary Ellen Lamb, 'The Cooke Sisters: Attitudes towards Learned Women', in Margaret P. Hannay (ed.), *Silent but for the Word* (Kent, Oh.: Kent State University Press, 1985), 108.

[73] Letter of 8 May 1561, when Throgmorton was ambassador to France. Conyers Read, *Mr Secretary Cecil and Queen Elizabeth* (London: Jonathan Cape, 1955), 262.

[74] C. S. Lewis comments on her translation in his *English Literature in the Sixteenth Century, Excluding Drama* (Oxford: Clarendon Press, 1954), 307: 'if quality without bulk were enough, Lady Bacon might be put forward as the best of all sixteenth-century translators.'

[75] Lamb, 'Cooke Sisters', 117, suggests that the editor is male, but Richard Verstegan, a Catholic contemporary, identified M.C. as Mildred Cecil, adding: 'which twaine were sisters, and wives unto Cecill and Bacon; and gave their assistance and helping hands, in the plot of this newe erected synagog' (*A Declaration of the True Causes of the Great Troubles* ([Antwerp?], 1592), 12). It is perhaps a pointer in this direction that Anne's learned industry is held up as a model for imitation by other gentlewomen, who 'shall (I trust) hereby be alured from vain delights to doinges of more perfect glory' (sig. A2v).

[76] Elaine V. Beilin (ed.), *Protestant Translators: Anne Lock Prowse and Elizabeth Russell*, The Early Modern Englishwoman: The Printed Writings (Aldershot: Ashgate, 1998).

Tu mihi, tu testis flebilis esse potes.
Dum patriae servis, dum publica commoda tractas,
    Occidis, ignota triste cadaver humo.
Et miseri nati flammis febrilibus ardent.
    Quid facerem tantis, heu mihi mersa malis!
Infælix conjux, infælix mater oberro,
    Te vir adempte fleo, vos mea membra fleo
Exeo funestis terris, hinc rapta cadaver
    Conjugis, hinc prolis languida membra traho.
Sic uterum gestans, redeo terraque Marique
    In patriam luctu perdita, mortis amans.
Chare mihi conjux, et praestantissime Thoma,
    Cujus erat rectum, et nobile quicquid erat.
Elizabetha, tibi quondam gratissima sponsa,
    Haec lacrymis refert verba referta piis.
Non potui prohibere mori, sed mortua membra,
    Quo potero, faciam semper honore coli.
Te Deus, aut similem Thomae mihi redde maritum,
    Aut reddant Thomae me mea fata viro.

Beloved husband, greatest part of our soul,
whose life used to be the marrow of my life,
why are the malignant fates tearing apart people who were united in this way?
Why am I left alone in a widowed bed?
England saw us happy, France saw us happy,
our loves travelled away by sea and by land,
we were a fortunate pair so long as we lived together.
Our bodies were twofold: our spirit was one.
But, darling husband, nothing endures in this world,
you, O you, can be to me a witness fit to provoke tears.
While you were serving your country, while you were dealing with the public good,
you died, a miserable corpse, on unfamiliar soil;
and my poor children were aflame with burning fevers!
What was I to do, immersed as I was, alas, in such great afflictions?
Unhappy wife, unhappy mother, I wander about,
I weep for you, husband taken from me, I weep for the bodily members which are my own;
I am leaving lands which have brought death; having been torn away <from> here,
I am dragging home the corpse of my husband,
and the feeble limbs of my children.
Thus, carrying an unborn child in my womb, I am returning, by sea and land,
to my native place, lost in grief, and in love with death.
My dearest husband, and my most excellent Thomas,
to whom belonged rectitude and whatever was noble,
Elizabeth your wife, once most pleasing to you,
offers these words replete with affectionate tears.
I could not prevent them from dying, but now that they are dead,
I will always, as far as I am able, undertake to have these limbs reverenced with honour.
O God, either give me back a husband like Thomas,
or may my fate return me to Thomas my husband!

Other women of the high aristocracy had a reputation for great learning, but few of them put it to much use. Henry Fitzalan, twelfth Earl of Arundel, took great care with the education of his daughters, Jane and Mary Fitzalan (1536–76 and 1540–57).[77] Both women left a number of formal exercises, instigated by their father: Mary died at only 17, but she left four small quarto volumes of exercises, presented to her father as successive new-year gifts in the last four years of her life, a book of *sententiae* attributed to Plato, Aristotle, Seneca, and others, translated from Latin to English, a volume on Alexander Severus, *sententiae* translated from Greek to English, and *sententiae* translated from Greek to Latin.[78] Jane translated Isocrates' oration *Archidamus* and the second and third orations of Isocrates to Nicocles from Greek to Latin, and Euripides' *Iphigeneia* into English, which, she says, she loved doing.[79] Jane, as Lady Lumley, continued to buy books and to be concerned with literature,[80] but once she had acquired a perfect reading knowledge of Greek and Latin, she seems to have had no desire to write in either language.

Outside court circles, there were other milieux in England by the mid-sixteenth century which promoted the study of classical languages for girls. We should also remember that the Elizabethan era saw extensive translation from classical languages, which put classical and humanist literature increasingly within women's grasp even if they only read English.[81] Bishop Hooper (whose wife Anne de Tserclaes was the daughter of a humanist family in Belgium, and very well educated)[82] was evidently ambitious for his daughter to become a Protestant Margaret More: he wrote to her godfather Henry Bullinger, 'Our little Rachel is making progress in both body and mind. She understands the English, German, French and Latin languages very tolerably, and especially the Latin.' She was, at the time of writing, 2 years old.[83] Another Elizabethan bishop's daughter, luckier in that she lived to grow up (Rachel Hooper died at 6), Judith Aylmer, was later

---

[77] William Bercher, *A Dyssputacion off the Nobylyte off Wymen*, ed. R. Warwick Bond (London: Roxburgh Club, 1904), i. 155.

[78] Now London, British Library, Royal 12 A i–iv. On new-year gifts, see Binns, *Intellectual Culture*, 75 and Edwin Haviland Miller, 'New Years Day Gift Books in the Sixteenth Century', *Studies in Bibliography*, 15 (1962), 233–41.

[79] London, British Library, Royal 15 A ix. See Dorothy Gardiner, *English Girlhood at School* (Oxford: Clarendon Press, 1929), 180. Now printed in Diane Purkiss (ed.), *Three Tragedies by Renaissance Women*, (Harmondsworth: Penguin, 1998), 1–35.

[80] See Sears Jayne and Francis R. Johnson, *The Lumley Library: The Catalogue of 1609* (London: Trustees of the British Museum, 1956).

[81] Julia G. Ebel, 'A Numerical Survey of Elizabethan Translations', *Library*, 5th ser. 22.2 (1967), 104–27. Louis B. Wright, *Middle-Class Culture in Elizabethan England* (Chapel Hill: University of North Carolina Press, 1935), 339–72. J. W. Saunders, 'From Manuscript to Print', *Transactions of the Leeds Philological Society*, 6 (1951), 507–28, (p. 513), notes that as early as the 16th century, 'John Croke's wife and Edmund Becke's cousin who knew no Latin secured the poems they wanted'—that is, by getting some Latinate individual in their circle to translate them.

[82] Anne de Tserclaes was the sister-in-law of Valérand Poullain, the successor to Calvin at Strasbourg. F.-V. Goethals, *Dictionnaire... des familles nobles de Belgique* (Brussels: Polack-Duvivier, 1849–52) does not mention her specifically, but notes that the family of T'Serclaes de Tilly included a 'femme politique' at the end of the 16th century, suggesting a degree of commitment to educated women.

[83] Mary Prior, 'Reviled and Crucified Marriages: The Position of Tudor Bishops' Wives', in Mary Prior (ed.), *Women in English Society, 1500–1800* (London: Routledge, 1985), 118–48.

described as 'a rare scholler of that sex, furnished with the Greeke and Latine tongue and withall a very good physicion, not an empiricke, but grounded in theory, as well as expert in the practise, being able to deale with Galen as he wrot in his owne language.'[84] Her father had been the tutor of Lady Jane Grey before becoming Bishop of London: it is interesting that he chose to give his own daughter an education similar to that of his royal charge. Clearly, Judith Aylmer's main interest was medicine, since Ley's account highlights the reading of Galen: many sixteenth-century women studied medicine,[85] though few other than Judith Aylmer, Margaret Gigs, and a Flemish woman resident in England, Catherine Tishem or Thysmans, [86] can have done so by going back to Greek texts.

One of the very few women from outside court or ecclesiastical circles to leave any Latin verse is Anne Lok (b. *c*.1534).[87] Anne Lok, or Lock, was the elder daughter of Stephen Vaughan, a member of the Merchant Adventurers' Company in the time of Henry VIII. From 1538, he was governor of the Merchant Adventurers' factory at Antwerp. He converted to Protestantism early in the 1530s and married Margaret Gwynnethe, a silkwoman at the Tudor court, with whom he had three children, Anne, Jane, and Stephen. The tutor whom he chose for them was a Mr Cob, apparently a Fleming, who was proficient in Latin, Greek, and French, possibly because the household also included a son of George Brooke, the sixth Lord Cobham, who was living with them. It seems clear from Anne's surviving Latin poem that the children were educated together.[88] Margaret Vaughan died in 1545, and he remarried on his return to London, choosing Margery Brinklow, the widow of a London mercer, of uncompromisingly Protestant outlook, and in 1549 he died. Anne married Henry Lok, probably around 1552, another mercer with interests in Antwerp who also happened to be her father's neighbour in Cheapside; her husband's family was similar to her own, though considerably richer. The Loks were cultivated and rather literary in their tastes: they also read Protestant books illicitly smuggled into England in the 1530s.[89] Henry Lok could write Latin, in the italic hand which was then becoming fashionable. It was as a result of their religious enthusiasm that Anne Lok made probably the most important friendship of her life, with John Knox, who first met her in London in the winter of 1552/3,

---

[84] William Andrews Clarke Memorial Library, L6815 M3 C734, fo. 181. From an encomium on John Squire, son of Adam Squire (Aylmer's personal chaplain), and Judith Aylmer, by John Squire's curate, Roger Ley.

[85] F. G. Emmison, *Elizabethan Life: Essex Gentry's Wills* (Chelmsford: Essex County Council, 1978), 36–7: Dame Frances Paulett divides her physic and medicine books between her two daughters-in-law, Jeronima and Katherine Waldegrave.

[86] Catherine Tishem was a member of the exiled Dutch community in Norwich. She knew Latin, French, Italian, and English, and could read Galen in the original Greek, according to Venator's Latin panegyric on Gruter. Forster, *Janus Gruter's English Years*, 36.

[87] *The Collected Works of Anne Vaughan Lock*, ed. Susan M. Felch, Medieval and Renaissance Texts and Studies 185 (Tempe: Arizona Center for Medieval and Renaissance Studies, 1999); Elaine V. Beilin (ed.), *Protestant Translators: Anne Lock Prowse and Elizabeth Russell*, The Early Modern Englishwoman: The Printed Writings (Aldershot: Ashgate, 1998).

[88] *Collected Works*, ed. Felch, p. xxi.

[89] Ibid., p. xxiii.

and lived with the young couple for a time before leaving England. Knox and his hostess entered into a passionate spiritual friendship, of great importance to both, which is witnessed by thirteen surviving letters from Knox to Anne Lok.[90] Once settled in Geneva, Knox bent his iron will to persuading his friend to leave her husband and family and join him in exile. Six months later, Anne Lok arrived in Geneva accompanied by two small children, Henry and Anne, and a maid, but without her husband. She buried Anne within four days of their arrival; probably a grim witness to the difficulties of the journey.

One witness to how she spent her time in Geneva is her translation of John Calvin's sermons on the song of Hezekiah, which she dedicated to her fellow religious exile Katherine Brandon, née Willoughby (by now Katherine Bertie), dowager Duchess of Suffolk, together with *A Meditation of a Penitent Sinner*, a metrical paraphrase of the fifty-first Psalm, which she published in 1560, though it is probably not her own work. Queen Mary died in 1558, and the Marian exiles began flooding homewards, including Anne Lok, who was back in her husband's house in Cheapside by June 1559. Nothing further is heard of her until 1571, when her husband died: she was presumably a leading light among the London 'godly', but published nothing and had no public profile. Henry Lok bequeathed her all his worldly goods and appointed her sole executrix of his will, a testimony that no breath of scandal can ever have touched her association with Knox.

She very promptly married again: not another businessman, but one of the most outstanding extreme Protestant preachers of the day, Edward Dering, five years her junior, whose zeal, throughout his short career, was matched only by his lack of tact. In May 1571 the Cooke sisters involved the Derings in the creation of a beautiful presentation manuscript of the *Sylvae* of the Italian Protestant Bartolo Silva for the Earl of Leicester (the principal supporter of radical Protestantism among those closest to the queen), with dedicatory poems from all four sisters, Anne, and Edward Dering himself. However much good this may have done, it could not counteract Dering's continued rashness. He lectured on the Epistle to the Hebrews at St Paul's in 1573, which had two effects: he was thought by some to be the most notable preacher of his day, but he was also brought before the Star Chamber in May of that year, and silenced at the queen's personal command in December, despite the best efforts of Katherine Killigrew. Dering, meanwhile had other troubles. He was tubercular, and by the summer of 1575, he had begun to spit blood. He died in 1576. Anne's last marriage was a much calmer affair: she married a draper, Richard Prowse, three times Mayor of Exeter, some time before 1583, and spent the last decade or so of her life in Devon. In 1590, she sent another work of her own to the press, a translation from Jean Taffin's French text, *Of the Markes of the Children of God and of their Comfort in Afflictions*, which she dedicated to Ann, countess of Warwick. She died between 1590 and 1603.

[90] A. Daniel Frankforter, 'Correspondence with Women: The Case of John Knox', *Journal of the Rocky Mountain Medieval and Renaissance Association*, 6 (1985), 159–72.

There were other London citizen women who were highly literate. Elizabeth Lucar, née Withypoll (1510–37), daughter of Paul Withypoll, citizen of London, read Latin, Spanish, and Italian, and allegedly wrote in these languages.[91] Jocosa, the wife of William Hone, wrote an epitaph in Latin hexameters for her husband which is still *in situ* in the church of St Bartholomew the Less,[92] and a Mrs Allington left a similar monument for hers.[93] There were also Latin-literate country gentlefolk. Martha Moulsworth, née Dorsett, born in 1577, writes in her autobiographic poem,[94]

> My ffather was a Man of spottles ffame
> of gentle Birth, & Dorsett was his name . . .
> By him I was brought upp in godlie pietie
> In modest chearefullness, & sad sobrietie
> Nor onlie so, Beyond my sex & kind
> He did with learning Lattin decke [my] mind
> And whie nott so? the muses ffemalls are
> and therefore of Us ffemales take some care
> Two Universities we have of men
> o thatt we had but one of women then . . .

She found no use for her Latin in later life, as she confesses, but she was very well read: her acquaintance with the Byzantine historian Nicephorus, whom she most probably accessed in Latin,[95] suggests that she, one of her husbands, or just perhaps her father, had an extensive library. She was not in a modern sense 'brought upp' by her father, who died when she was only $2\frac{1}{2}$, but he may well have given instructions that she should be educated.

Beyond London, another possible Latinate wife is a shadowy figure, but of considerable interest. In St Mary's Church, Sebergham, Cumbria, there is a monument to Thomas Denton of Warnell, a local magnate,[96] entirely in Latin, which includes two sets of verses: a rather elegant distich from a person self-described as Denton's 'soboles' ('companion'), signing as 'B.E.',[97] and identifiable from an English inscription on another slab, now destroyed, as Bernard Ellis.[98] and

[91] Ballard, *Memoirs*, ed. Perry, 36–7.

[92] In Edward Hatton, *A New View of London* (London: R. Chiswell etc., 1708), i. 148.

[93] Ibid., ii. 536.

[94] *'My Name was Martha': A Renaissance Woman's Autobiographical Poem by Martha Moulsworth*, ed. Robert C. Evans and Barbara Wiedemann (West Cornwall, Conn.: Locust Hill Press, 1993), ll. 21–2, 27–34, p. 5.

[95] She refers in her poem to Nicephorus Xanthopolus (Callistos), *Ecclesiastica Historia* 2, ch. 40: there were two Latin editions of this Greek text in the 16th century (Basel, 1561, and Paris, 1562), and one in 1630.

[96] Warnell was a local estate, which had originated as an abbatial hunting preserve: see T. H. B. Graham, 'Sebergham', *Transactions of the Cumberland and Westmorland Antiquarian and Archaeological Society*, NS 23 (1923), 49–55.

[97] Printed in Nikolaus Pevsner, *The Buildings of England: Cumberland and Westmorland* (Harmondsworth: Penguin, 1967), 188.

[98] William Nicolson, *Miscellany of the Diocese of Carlisle*, ed. R. S. Ferguson (London: George Bell & Sons; Carlisle: E. Thomson & Sons, 1877), 10–11. The Denton monument also once included an

a somewhat less polished pair of elegiac couplets which seem to be introduced by the words 'Per me, A.D. uxor'. This suggests first that Mrs Denton is the author of the couplets, and furthermore, the shape of the inscription seems to imply that she was part of a milieu in which Latin was used; that is, she and Ellis have used this inscription as a sort of miniature *tumulus*. The second Mrs Denton, who is responsible for this monument, was Anne Aislabie, from a Yorkshire family. All that is otherwise known about her is that she was presented as a recusant on 26 December 1599. It is noteworthy, therefore, that the English poem which also once formed part of this monument hints, in coded language, that Denton was a church papist.[99] This all serves as a reminder that, in the second half of the century, Protestantism did not have a monopoly on literacy or educated women.

In conclusion, it is not inadvertently or without due consideration that the title of this chapter refers to 'England' rather than to the British Isles. At least two sixteenth-century Irishwomen seem to have had some command of Latin prose. Gráinne O'Malley (*c.*1530–1603), demonstrated her ability to converse with Elizabeth I in Latin when summoned to answer charges of piracy. Her command of Latin and her nautical skills as a sea captain and leader of a fleet down the west coast of Ireland raise tantalizing questions about her education, as Margaret MacCurtain observes.[100] At about the same time, a Hebridean noblewoman, Katherine daughter of Hector Mór Maclean of Duart, the widowed Countess of Argyll, was noted for her linguistic accomplishments: 'beyng not unlernyd in the Latyn tong, speckyth good French, and as is sayd, som lyttel Italyone.'[101] She married the Calbhach O'Donnell as her second husband (he died in 1566), and betrayed him to the English: she was therefore subsequently raped and imprisoned for more than two years by Shane O'Neill.[102] Elizabeth Legge (b. 1580) is described by George Ballard as educated in Latin, English, French, Spanish, and Irish, but he frankly admits, 'what use she made of this learning . . . I know not'. She lived to an enormous age (Ballard says 105) and did not marry.[103] Beyond these few names, there seems to be nothing.[104]

English poem by John Ellis, also recorded by Nicolson: the complex as a whole is reminiscent of Lady Elizabeth Russell's monument for her husband and brother-in-law at Bisham, with inscriptions by both herself and others.

[99] This is no longer *in situ*, but is printed by Nicolson.

[100] Margaret MacCurtain, 'Women, Education and Learning in Early Modern Ireland', in Margaret MacCurtain and Mary O'Dowd (eds.), *Women in Early Modern Ireland* (Edinburgh: Edinburgh University Press, 1991), 160–78 (p. 164). Anne Chambers, *Granuaile: The Life and Times of Grace O'Malley, c.1530–1603* (Dublin: Wolfhound Press, 1979), includes a facsimile of O'Malley's Latin petition to Queen Elizabeth in 1593, pp. 136–7. See also pp. 25, 55, 62.

[101] John Bannerman, 'Literacy in the Highlands', in Ian B. Cowan and Duncan Shaw (eds.), *The Renaissance and Reformation in Scotland: Essays in Honour of Gordon Donaldson* (Edinburgh: Scottish Academic Press, 1983), 214–35, quoting *CSP Ireland* (1509–73), ed H. C. Hamilton (London: Longman, Green, Longman & Roberts, 1860), 172.

[102] R. Bagwell, *Ireland under the Tudors*, 3 vols. (London: Longmans & Co., 1885–90), ii. 21.

[103] Ballard, *Memoirs*, ed. Perry, 320. She is also remembered in L.-P., *Répertoire universel, historique, biographique des femmes célèbres* (Paris: Achille Désauges, 1826), ii. 169.

[104] Thanks to Dr Anthony Harvey of the *Dictionary of Medieval Latin from Celtic Sources* for checking his records for me.

There is no trace of any Welsh women's writing in Latin,[105] and the evidence for Scotland is both scanty and peculiar. Mary, Queen of Scots was highly educated, but does not belong in this context: her Latinity is discussed in the context of French court culture. A highly educated woman called Angela is described in an Italian letter of the fifteenth century as 'a virgin from a/the noble family of the Scots' ('ex egregio Scottorum stirpe virgo'),[106] but this more probably means that she was a daughter of the Scotti, a noble family of Piacenza, who had a reputation for humanism, than that she was from a Scottish noble family.[107] Marie Maitland, daughter of Maitland of Lethington, and almost certainly the author of a Scots poem of considerable learning and sophistication, was the recipient of verses which make great claims for her, comparing her work to that of Sappho and Olimpia Morata, but the only writing which is probably hers is in Scots.[108] Compared to England, it is a very thin showing, and particularly surprising given that neo-Latin verse was assiduously cultivated in sixteenth- and seventeenth-century Scotland, and indeed that one of the very few poets of this island anyone on the Continent had heard of (George Buchanan) was a Scot.

The only woman brought up in Scotland who is known to have written any Latin verse at all was the daughter of French Protestant exiles, Esther Inglis/ Langlois, later Kello (1569/71–1624).[109] She became the most famous of early modern woman calligraphers, patronized by Elizabeth I and James I. Surviving specimens of her work range in date from 1586 to 1624. Early modern women generally had poor handwriting because they were not properly taught, a fact which often attracted adverse comment from men,[110] but there are notable exceptions: apart from Esther Inglis and her mother, we might note Ginevra Nogarola, mistress of a humanist copy-hand,[111] and Petronia Lansenberg, a possibly profes-

---

[105] Dr Ceri Davies assures me of this (pers. comm.). Jane Cartwright, 'The Desire to Corrupt: Convent and Community in Medieval Wales', in Diane Watt (ed.), *Medieval Women in their Communities* (Cadiff: University of Wales Press, 1997), 20–47, (p. 27), states, 'it is not known whether nuns in Wales were Latin-literate, or indeed literate at all'.

[106] Milan, Biblioteca Ambrosiana, Sussidio B 226 (GS VI 15), fos. 8–9.

[107] A poem by Joannes Petrus Feretrius (fl. 1500) refers to poetry (context suggests Latin), by 'Francisca Scotta'. James Hutton, *The Greek Anthology in Italy to the Year 1802* (Ithaca, NY: Cornell University Press, 1935), 165, from *Sena Vetus, per Io. Petrum Feretrium... Carmine Illustrata* (Siena: Simeone Rubeo, 1513), vs. 378–81. An Artemisia Scotti also had a reputation as a poet; nothing survives (Bandini Buti, ii. 242).

[108] Cambridge, Magdalen College, Pepys Library 2251, fo. 126ʳ, W. A. Craigie (ed.), *The Maitland Quarto Manuscript*, Scottish Text Society, NS 9, Blackwood (Edinburgh: Blackwood, 1920), 257. See also Jane Stevenson and Peter Davidson (eds.), *Early Modern Women Poets, 1520–1700* (Oxford: Oxford University Press, 2001), 97–8, 543.

[109] David Laing, 'Notes Relating to Mrs Esther Langlois (Inglis), the Celebrated Calligraphist', *Proceedings of the Society of Antiquaries of Scotland*, 5 (1854–66), 6, p. 283, David Agnew, *Protestant Exiles from France, Chiefly in the Reign of Louis XIV, or, The Hugenot Refugees and their Descendants in Great Britain and Ireland*, 2 vols. (Edinburgh: Privately printed, 1886), i. 102–3.

[110] Danielle Clarke, *The Politics of Early Modern Women's Writing* (Harlow: Pearson Education Ltd., 2001), 39.

[111] Yale University Library, Marston 279 is in her hand.

sional calligrapher and writing teacher.[112] Many of the women discussed in these pages from whom we have autograph writing wrote good hands, an aspect of their generally superior educations, for example, Mildred, Lady Burleigh, Elizabeth Jane Weston, and Johanna Otho.[113] Inglis was the daughter of Huguenot refugees who came initially to London but subsequently settled in Scotland. Her date of birth can be established by the 1571 register of aliens, which notes that in the parish of Blackfriars in London in that year were Nicholas Inglishe, Frenchman, schoolmaster, and householder, Mary his wife, David his son, and 'Yester' his daughter, and that they '[came] into this realm about two years past for religion'.[114] A book which she wrote in 1624 gives her age as 53; which would make her born in 1571, but it is possible that deliberately or otherwise, she knocked two years off her age. Her father was schoolmaster in Edinburgh from 1574, and taught calligraphy, 'forming of his pupils hands to a perfyte schap of lettir'. Her mother was Marie Prestot, also a calligrapher, who is known to have written two small books for the library of James VI: a sheet of her work survives in the Newberry Library, Chicago (highly similar to her daughter's work), which suggests that both parents may have taught Esther.[115] She married Bartholomew Kello, who was also a calligrapher (though his contribution to Craigie's *album amicorum* is not polished),[116] as well as being a Calvinist pastor. She and Kello lived in Edinburgh for a number of years before accompanying James VI to London. Kello was collated to the rectory of Willingdale Spain, near Chelmsford, in 1607, and in 1615 they returned to Edinburgh. They had one son, Samuel, who graduated from Edinburgh University and became minister of Spixall in Suffolk. Some of the manuscripts she produced contain her own verses in Scots or French, or sometimes Latin.

---

[112] There is a specimen page of her calligraphy in Chicago, Newberry Library, ZW 546 L. 222. She taught calligraphy professionally: see Johannes Meursius, *Athenae Batavae, sive de Urbe Leidensi et Academia Virique Clavis, Libri II* (Leiden: 1625), ii. 233.

[113] Lady Burleigh's hand is witnessed in London, British Library, Royal 17 B xviii, fos. 1–23, Weston's in a dedicatory poem on the second flysheet of a British Library copy of her *Parthenicon*, London, British Library, C 61 d 2, and Johanna Otho's in a dedicatory letter to the *senati* of Heidelberg on the back flyleaf of the copy of her 1616 *Carmina* in The Hague, Konincklijke Bibliotheek, 123 C 3. Elizabeth Isham, one of the Ishams of Lamport, a family given to educating daughters, wrote a fine, highly trained italic (see a letter of 1645, Northamptonshire Record Office, IL 251, printed (with photograph) in Linda Pollock, *A Lasting Relationship: Parents and Children over Three Centuries* (London: Fourth Estate, 1987), 226).

[114] R. E. G. and E. F. Kirk, *Returns of Aliens Dwelling in the City and Suburbs of London, Henry VII–James I* (London: Publications of the Huguenot Society of London, 1887), ii. 15.

[115] Chicago, Newberry Library, ZW 543.P.922. Like her daughter's work, it is closely imitative of a printed page, and displays a wide range of hands. See *Miscellany of the Scottish History Society* (Edinburgh: Scottish History Society, 1893), i. p. li.

[116] Edinburgh, Edinburgh University Library, Laing III, 525.

PART IV

The Early Modern Period

11. *Italian Women Poets of the Sixteenth Century and After*

It is perhaps unsurprising that it seems to be a general impression that learned women, who are so astonishing a feature of Renaissance Italy, ceased to be a feature of Italian culture after the first impetus of the Renaissance had passed. In and after the sixteenth century, a flood of publications in the vernacular by women of many kinds obscures a continuing steady trickle of publication (together with other forms of dissemination) of works by women in the learned languages. However, one of the most famous of all women Latinists, the Venetian Elena Piscopia, the first woman to be unequivocally awarded a doctorate, flourished in the seventeenth century, and there were others as prodigiously learned: when Gioerida Sitti Maani, the Persian wife of the traveller Piero della Valla, died, her elaborate funeral, in 1627, included a catafalque with, on its pedestals, epitaphs in the languages she knew: Italian, French, Spanish, Portuguese, Persian, Turkish, Armenian, Latin, ancient Greek, modern Greek, Syriac, and Arabic.[1]

In many ways, the opportunities available to women writers actually increased after the Renaissance. Italy in the sixteenth century saw a flowering of women writers in both poetry and prose on a scale which has no equal anywhere else in Europe, and considerably outperforms their predecessors, the women of the Quattrocento; their cultural production includes poetry by writers such as the noblewomen Vittoria Colonna and Irene di Spilimbergo,[2] the actress Isabella Andreini,[3] and the courtesan Tullia d'Aragona, as well as the first prose fiction by women, such as Tullia d'

---

[1] The catafalque is described by Girolamo Rocchi, *Funerale della signora Sitti Maani Gioerida della Valle, celebrato in Roma, l'anno 1627* (Rome: Erede di Bartolomeo Zannetti, 1627). See also Maurizio Fagiolo dell'Arco, *Corpus delle feste a Roma*, i: *La festa barocca* (Rome: Edizioni de Luca, 1997) 268–9.

[2] Vittoria Colonna published nine editions of her *Rime* during her lifetime (Erdmann, 211). Her collected poems, *Tutte le rime* (Venice: G. B. e Mel. Stessa, 1588), includes a vast commentary, and she is the subject of the only 16th-century Italian critical study of a living poet, Rinaldo Corso, *Dichiaratione sopra la seconda parte delle rime della divina Vittoria Colonna* (Bologna: G.-B. Faelli, 1543). The *Libellus de Triumphali Martyrio Virginis Theodosiae* by the Pescara writer Francesco Nero, addressed to her (Madrid, Biblioteca Naçional, 1352), suggests that she read Latin with pleasure, and she occasionally wrote in the language (see Joseph Gibaldi in *WWRR*, 22–46, and the Appendix). On Spilimbergo, see Anne Jacobson Schutte, 'Irene di Spilimbergo: The Image of a Creative Woman in Late Renaissance Italy', *Renaissance Quarterly*, 44 (1991), 42–61. Her death was marked by a commemorative volume in which many of the verses are by women, *Rime di diversi nobilissimi et excellentissimi autori in morte della Signora Irene delle signiore di Spilimbergo* (Venice: Domenico, Gio. Battista Guerra, 1561).

[3] See Penny Morris et al., 'Bibliographical Guide to Women Writers and their Work', in Letizia Panizza and Sharon Wood (eds), *A History of Women's Writing in Italy* (Cambridge: Cambridge University Press, 2000), 283.

Aragona's romance *Il meschino*, published in 1560.[4] Moderata Fonte, better known for her pro-women polemic, also published a book-length verse romance modelled on Ariosto in 1581.[5] It is also worth observing that women begin to write and publish on scientific subjects, both in the vernacular and in Latin.[6] Galileo Galilei's longest and most detailed work on the relationship of religion and science was written for Grand Duchess Cristina of Tuscany, who was genuinely interested in the issue.[7]

Another feature of women's writing in this period is the publication of letters: in the fifteenth century, as we have seen, women often circulated letters in manuscript, but few were printed.[8] As Eisenstein has pointed out, the development of printing catered to a great interest in letters in the Renaissance, resulting in a proliferation of manuals of epistolography and anthologies of letters of all kinds.[9] As in other European countries, a number of women became famous as letter writers.[10] Collections specifically of women's writing begin to be made, notably Ludovico Domenichi's *Rime diverse d'alcune nobilissime e virtuosissime donne*, published in Lucca in 1559,[11] as well as a continued production of writing about noble, learned, or virtuous women, some of it protesting Acidalus' misogynist *jeu d'esprit* which enquired whether women were to be considered human.[12]

[4] See ibid. 296. The attribution of *Il meschino* to d'Aragona has been questioned (Erdmann, 110). There is also a prose novel called *Urania* by the 16th-century Paduan Julia Bigolina, not to my knowledge published, in Vatican City, Biblioteca Apostolica Vaticana, Fondo Patetta 358.

[5] Moderata Fonte, *Tredici canti del Floridoro* (Venice: Rampazzetti, 1581).

[6] Giustina Vegeri, wife of Giorgio, Marchese del Caretto, published *De anni cursi equinoctio et de Caesaris calendario reformando ac phase legitimo celebrando commentariolo* (Savona, 1579). Isabella Cortese's *I secreti* was first published Venice: Iacomo Cornetti, 1584, and translated into other languages.

[7] *Discoveries and Opinions of Galileo*, trans. Stillman Drake, (New York: Doubleday Anchor, 1957), 151–2, 173–215.

[8] The letters of Isotta Nogarola, Costanza Varano, and Laura Cereta certainly circulated in manuscript: see discussion in Ch. 6.

[9] Elisabeth Eisenstein, *The Printing Press as an Agent of Change* (Cambridge: Cambridge University Press, 1979), 190. See also A. Gerlo, 'The *Opus de Conscribendis Epistolis* of Erasmus and the Tradition of the *Ars Epistolica*', in R. R. Bolgar (ed.), *Classical Influences on European Culture, AD 500–1500* (Cambridge: Cambridge University Press, 1971), 103–14.

[10] For example, *Litere della divina Vettoria Colonna, Marchesa di Pescara alla Duchessa de Amalfi, sopra la vita contemplativa di santa Catharina* (Venice: Giov. Anto. and Pietro de Nicolini, 1545), Veronica Franco, *Lettere familiari e diversi* (Venice, 1580) (both these collections came out while the author was still alive). There were five editions of the letters of Isabella Andreini, the earliest published in 1607, and a collection of women's letters was made by Ortensio Lando, *Lettere di molte valorose donne* (Venice: Giolito, 1548). The 15th-century Laura Cereta and Cassandra Fedele's letters were edited, both by Iacopo Filippo Tomasini, the former in 1640, as *Epistolae* (Padua: Sebastiano Sardi), the latter as *Epistolae et Orationes Posthumae* (Padua: Sebastiano Sardi, 1636). Italian women's letters have been studied by M. L. Doglio, *Lettera e donna: scrittura epistolare al femmile tra Quattro e Cinquecento* (Rome: Bulzoni, 1993).

[11] Domenichi took an interest in learned women: he edited Laura Terracina's *Rime*, published in Venice in 1566, and also wrote two studies, *La nobiltà delle donne* (Venice: Gabriel Giolito, 1549) and *La donna di corte, discorso di Ludovico Domenichi* (Lucca, 1564) B.- Fagiani (Lucca: Busdrago, 1964)). Another early collection of women's verse is *Per donne romane rime di diversi raccolte da Muzio Manfredi* (Bologna: Benacci, 1575).

[12] Manfred Fleischer, 'Are Women Human? The Debate of 1595 between Valens Acidalius and Simon Gediccus', *Sixteenth Century Journal*, 12.2 (1981), 105–20. Erdmann lists 16th-century 'Books on and for Women', 155–98. See Theresa M. Kenney (trans.), *'Women are not Human': An Anonymous Treatise and Responses* (New York: Crossroad Publications, 1998), or Clive Hart (ed. and trans.), *Disputatio Nova contra Mulieres (1595)* (Lewiston, NY: Edwin Mellen Press, 1998).

While specialists in Italian women's history are, for good reason, anxious to stress that Italian women were very far from being on an equal footing with men, their participation in the more public aspects of culture was on a scale vastly surpassing that of the women of any other country. All in all, Erdmann lists no fewer than 210 Italian women who ventured into print in the sixteenth century alone,[13] and this figure can be supplemented, and possibly doubled, with the very large numbers who left writings in manuscript, since scribal publication continued to be an important mode of circulating texts. For example, a manuscript was made of seventy-five Latin letters from Parthenia Gallerana (d. 1572) to a variety of addressees who include her husband (Gianbattista Magnoldo) and no less than eleven women, amongst whom are Anna d'Este, Marguerite de Valois, and Camilla Valenti (niece of Veronica Gàmbara), in some cases, together with their replies. This manuscript, described by Francisco Arisio, was evidently a fair copy which was made accessible to interested persons.[14]

The whole question of print in early modern Italy is a highly complex one. It was almost certainly easier to get into print than it was in most other parts of Europe, since presses proliferated, fostering the publication of ephemeral items with extremely local distribution, such as orations and verses on the deaths of local notables (this seems also to have been the case in Germany). It is a serious question whether a work such as Girolamo Colleoni's *Notizia degli scrittori piu celebri che anno illustrato la patria loro di Correggio*, undated, and printed in Correggio some time in the late seventeenth century, ever circulated outside the town, and one also wonders whether the original edition was numbered in dozens rather than hundreds.[15]

By the sixteenth century, the position of the learned woman was an established one in Italy. Cities were proud to harbour them; and local historians were delighted to be able to point to a number of learned women among their distinguished citizenry.[16] One of the most distinct features of Italian civic life in the Renaissance and subsequently is local patriotism. There is an all but uncountable number of Italian publications from at least the sixteenth century onwards on local worthies and heroes: the examination of almost any one of these will produce one or more women remembered for their poetry and/or learning (sometimes on all but

---

[13] France comes nearest, with a mere thirty. Erdmann, 206–23.

[14] Francisco Arisio, *Cremona Literata* (Pama: Alberto Pazzoni & Paolo Monte, 1702–41), ii. 256–7 (Arisio gives the index to the volume but does not reproduce it).

[15] The same is surprisingly true of Italy today: items such as death notices are published as printed posters, and books of real academic interest are financed by local savings banks and, in effect, available only locally.

[16] There is also a number of 16th- and 17th-century works specifically concerned with the praise of notable women and focused on women writers, such as Antonio di Paolo Masini, *Cataloge delle donne in lettere praeclare* (1612), Giuseppe Betussi, *Libro di M. Giovanni Boccaccio delle donne illustri* (Florence: Filippo Giunta, 1596), Julio Cesare Capacio, *Illustrium Mulierem . . . Elogio* (Naples: Io. Iacobus Carlinus and Constantinus Vitale, 1608), Francisco Agostino della Chiesa, *Theatro delle donne letterate*, (Mondovi, Giovanni, Gislandi & Giovanni Tomaso Rossi, 1620), Lorenzo Legati, *Musei Poetriarum . . . Primitiae* (Bologna: Heredes Vittore Benaccio, 1668).

imperceptible grounds).[17] That astonishing survival of an older world, Cassandra Fedele, orating before the Queen of Poland in 1556 at the age of 91, is in the mid-sixteenth century able to imply a substantial body of 'many distinguished and renowned women', for whom she declares herself empowered to speak—a note she was certainly not striking in her earlier orations in the long-ago 1480s.[18]

By the late sixteenth century, it was even possible for Torquato Tasso to distinguish between two female modes of existence, 'femminile' and 'donnesca' (appropriate to a great lady), and argue that the 'feminine' moral virtues, however suitable to a member of the bourgeoisie or lesser nobility, were not relevant to a princess, who is enjoined by her royal status to practise heroic 'masculine' virtues such as eloquence, liberality, and magnificence—as Tasso sees it, it is therefore forgivable, though regrettable, if she neglects 'feminine' virtues such as chastity in pursuit of royal virtues, as in the cases of Semiramis and Cleopatra.[19] The princess is, as it were, functionally a man by virtue of her birth, and hence the masculine standard of morality applies to her—although this point of view was indignantly disputed by women, who considered it potentially double-edged.[20] It was, however, perhaps the first formal restatement of Plato's argument that some women could occupy roles normally assigned to men since the Golden Age of Athens. This generalized support for an expanded role for elite women in some quarters coexisted, of course, with prejudice and obstruction in others. Against the pride in local heroines evidenced by works such as Tomai's *Historia di Ravenna*, we may contrast the negative remarks about learned women quoted by contemporary feminists such as Modesta da Pozzo.[21]

All the same, it is clear that much had changed in Italy by the sixteenth century. Among other considerations, the sixteenth century is the century of the Reformation, with its enormous consequences for both those who remained Catholic and those who did not: while it is well known that Protestantism provided a major stimulus to the education of girls, at least as far as elementary literacy was concerned, the fact that the backlash of the Counter-Reformation in Catholic

---

[17] For example, Tomaso Tomai, *Historia di Ravenna* (Ravenna: Francesco Tebaldini da Osimo, 1580), pt. iv, p. 211, discusses Aura Ghezzi, daughter of a family important in Ravenna since the 12th century: he had seen some of her Latin verse, and judged it excellent. Similarly, della Chiesa's *Catalogo de' scrittori piemontesi, savoiardi, e nizzardi* gives the impression of a positive desire to find women writers of these regions (of whom there were few).

[18] *Cassandra Fedele: Letters and Orations*, trans. Diana Robin (Chicago: Chicago University Press, 2000), 163. Constance Jordan comments in *Renaissance Quarterly*, 55.1 (2002), 263, 'who these women are is unclear'.

[19] Similarly the advice given to Queen Isabel of Castile focused on her practice of public virtues such as courage, justice, and liberality, though in Spain it was assumed that ideal feminine qualities were compatible with this (Liss, *Isabel*, 123–5).

[20] *Discorso della virtù feminile e donnesca* (Venice: Bernardo Giunta, 1582), dedicated to Eleanora Gonzaga, Duchess of Mantua. At one time or another, Tasso wrote verses for Tarquinia Molza, Margherita Sarocchi, Marguerite de Valois, and Isotta Brembati. See further Ian MacLean, *Woman Triumphant* (Oxford: Clarendon Press, 1977), 19–20 and Constance Jordan, *Renaissance Feminism: Literary Text and Political Models* (Ithaca, NY: Cornell University Press, 1990), 147–8.

[21] Ginevra Conti Oderisio, *Donne e società nel Seicento: Lucrezia Marinelli e Arcangela Tarabotti*, Biblioteca di cultura, 167 (Rome: Bulzoni, 1979).

countries also stimulated literacy has received less attention.[22] For women of a scholarly bent, it is far from impossible to argue that society on the whole had changed for the better, surprising though this may seem. Important sixteenth-century women Latinists include Olimpia Morata, Laurentia Strozzi, Tarquinia Molza, and Margherita Sarocchi, women of extensive achievement who were applauded by contemporaries. This can be usefully contexted by the statement of Virginia Cox:[23]

From the 1580s ... the range of women's published production broadened significantly, quickly coming to encompass practically every polite literary genre of the day ... the most obvious [reason] is simply precedent: writing over a century after women humanists had first caught the eye of the Italian literary public, and with a substantial tradition of published women writers behind them, writers of Fonte's and Campiglia's generation were better poised than their mothers or grandmothers to venture an incursion into traditionally 'masculine' genres.

She also notes that another significant reason for the expansion of women's writing is 'a significant moral reorientation of Italian literature, prompted by the social and spiritual concerns of the Counter-Reformation': since literature in general became more decorous, less adversarial, less sexually explicit, and more pious, it became both more attractive and more accessible to women writers.[24] But the writing of romances, pastoral dialogues, and other forms newly popular in the sixteenth century went on side by side with a continued presence of women in more erudite, Latin-based literary genres: for example, Margherita Sarocchi's heroic poem *La Scanderbeide* was published in Rome in 1606, and a variety of other women wrote, and in some cases published, translations from Latin and works of scholarship.[25] This is particularly significant in that Latin was not as much of a minority interest in Italy as it was becoming elsewhere in Europe: just over half (51.8 per cent) of all sixteenth-century Italian publications were still in Latin, an unusually high figure

---

[22] Harvey J. Graff, 'On Literacy in the Renaissance: Review and Reflections', *History of Education*, 12 (1983), 69–85.

[23] Virginia Cox, 'Fiction, 1560–1650', in Panizza and Wood (eds.), *A History of Women's Writing in Italy*, 52–64(53).

[24] See Ugo Rozzo, 'Italian Literature on the Index', in Gigliola Fragnito (ed.), *Church, Censorship and Culture in Early Modern Italy*, trans. Adrian Belton (Cambridge: Cambridge University Press, 2001), 194–222. Carlo Dionisotti has pointed out that in the first half of the 16th century, half of Italian intellectuals were in one way or another dependent on the Church ('Chierici e laici', *Geografia e storia della letteratura italiana* (Turin: Einaudi, 1967), 47–71).

[25] For example, Fiametta Ubaldina, who flourished *c*.1585, translated the comedies of Terence, according to Louis Jacob, 'Bibliothèque des femmes illustres par leurs écrits', Paris, Bibliothèque Nationale de France, Ancien fonds français 22865, fo. 86ᵛ; Diana Corradini translated the *Aeneid*, and her autograph was preserved in the library of Aloysius Corradini (Jacobus Philippus Tomasini, *Bibliothecae Patavinae Manuscriptae Publicae et Privatae* (Udine: Nicola Schiratti, 1639), 95: since lost, though Giuseppe Vedova, *Biografica degli scrittori padovani*, 2 vols. (Padua: Tipi della Minerva, 1832), says he saw it), and so did the Mantuan Emilia Gonzaga Arrivabene: Bandini Buti, i. 45. The well-known poet Laura Battiferri Ammanati made a verse translation of the Epistle of Lentulus (an apocryphal letter claiming to give a physical description of Christ), which Bandini Buti, i. 33 states is in Florence, Biblioteca Riccordiana, II. v. 463 (this is not a normal form for a Riccordiana call-number, and the library disclaims all knowledge of it).

compared to elsewhere in contemporary Western Europe. The seventeenth century shows wide regional variation; from 21 per cent of output in Venice, to 56 per cent in Padua, the university town of the Veneto, dropping below 30 per cent for the country as a whole, which is still a very high percentage compared with France or England.[26]

Seventeenth-century Italy is relatively little discussed compared to the flood of publications on the Italian Renaissance, which is hardly surprising. The flow of internationally significant writers of genius which we associate with the Renaissance in Italy had dried to a trickle by the end of the sixteenth century, but the critical and historiographic assessment of Italian writing in the seventeenth century is perhaps even more negative than the facts warrant. Literary historians generally perceive it as a century of intellectual and artistic decadence, characterized by hollow exercises in virtuoso artifice.[27] Cox states that 'no Italian woman writer successfully mastered the showy, brilliant and erudite poetic language of the Italian Baroque', but while it may be true that this language turn 'remarginalized' women writers in the vernacular, some Latin poets, notably Martha Marchina, were able to meet the challenge more effectively.[28]

The widely held view that 'the tradition of female humanism ... had died everywhere in Europe by the seventeenth century' is, as this and subsequent chapters will endeavour to show, true neither of Italy, nor of the rest of Europe.[29] Humanism itself had changed character;[30] and the rising tide of complaint by seventeenth-century women about their educational and other opportunities may actually result not from the slamming of previously open doors in their faces, but from the fact that there was an increasing number of women who expected and demanded more from their lives. There is a surprising number of highly educated seventeenth-century women writers in Italy, and a wide variety of women's writing, which includes a series of articulate protests against the position and education of women, notably those of Lucrezia Marinella and Moderata Fonte, as well as a considerable number of Latin poets.[31]

---

[26] Françoise Waquet, *Latin: Or the Empire of a Sign*, trans. John Howe (London: Verso, 2000), 82.

[27] Domenico Sella, *Italy in the Seventeenth Century* (London: Longman, 1997), 188. See also Carlo Ossola, *Autunno del Rinascimento* (Florence: Olschki, 1971), and, of course, numerous writings by Benedetto Croce, notably 'Appunti di letteratura secentesca inedita o rara', *La Critica*, 3rd ser. 28 (1929), 468–80.

[28] Cox, 'Fiction', 63.

[29] Margaret L. King, *Women of the Renaissance* (Chicago: Chicago University Press, 1991), 211.

[30] 'Christian humanism', might even be said potentially to foster women's participation, since frivolity and obscenity were discarded. See Dionisotti, 'Chierici e laici', and also Margo Todd, *Christian Humanism and the Puritan Social Order* (Cambridge: Cambridge University Press, 1987), 22–95. It is a feature of both Reformation and Counter-Reformation education: in the Catholic world, most specifically associated with the Jesuits. See John W. O'Malley, *The First Jesuits* (Cambridge, Mass.: Harvard University Press, 1993), 253–64.

[31] In the year 1600, both these women published book-length works arguing the case for women's moral and intellectual equality with men. Virginia Cox, 'The Single Self: Feminist Thought and the Marriage Market in Early Modern Venice', *Renaissance Quarterly*, 48.3 (1995), 513–81. Arcangela Tarabotti, discussed below, also wrote on this subject: her *Che le donne siano della spezie degli uomini*, first published in 1651, is ed. Letizia Panizza (London: Institute of Romance Studies, 1994).

Olimpia Morata

The first woman I want to discuss in some detail exemplifies both the continuities and the changes of the mid-sixteenth century insofar as they affected learned women. Olimpia Morata (1526–51) was born in Ferrara in 1526, the daughter of a man of letters and professional grammarian called Fulvio Pellegrino Morato, a native of Mantua who had taught in several universities.[32] Her formative years were spent in Ferrara, where her father had been appointed tutor to the younger sons of Duke Alfonso d'Este (Ippolito and Alfonso, brothers of the next duke, Ercole II). In educating his daughter, Morato was following the example of earlier humanists such as Battista Guarino and Giovanni Caldiera.[33] As his friend Coelio Secundo Curio later recalled, he took pains to educate his daughter and instil a love of classical learning in her. However, the lives of both father and daughter were disrupted by one of the most significant events of the century, the Reformation. Morato had to leave Ferrara in 1533, perhaps because he had written in favour of Reformation doctrines. He went into exile in Vincenza, taking his daughter, though in 1538 he was recalled by Duke Ercole II and resumed his lectures at the university. Morata was then 12. She began to learn Greek with the German Protestant Chilian Senf (Sinopius), and her fame began to spread among her father's humanist acquaintances: Lilio Giraldi and Bartolomeo Riccio both remark on her. Other friends of her father's who admired the young prodigy included Johann Senf, brother of her Greek tutor, the poet Leon Jamet, and Alberto Lollio.[34] Celio Calcagnini, mathematician, poet, and archaeologist, an old friend of Morato's, took particular notice of her, and asked his friend in a letter 'to drop a kiss on the forehead of that infant Delia [Grace]'.[35]

When Morata was 14, Renée/Renata, daughter of Louis XII and Duchess of Ferrara, invited her to court as somewhere between tutor and companion to her

---

[32] The first attempt at a biography is Georg Ludwig Nolten, *Commentaria Historico-critica de Olympiae Moratae Vita, Scriptis, Fatis, et Laudibus* (Frankfurt ad Viadrum: Carol. Theophil. Strauss, 1775). She attracted a number of 19th-century biographies, which include anon. [Amelia Gillespie Smyth], *Olympia Morata: Her Times, Life and Writings* (London: Smith, Elder & Co., 1836); R. Turnbull, *Olympia Morata: Her Life and Times* (Boston: Sabbaty, 1846), and J. Bonnet, *Vie d'Olympia Morata: épisode de la renaissance et de la reforme en Italie*, 2nd edn. (Paris: Marc Ducloux, 1854). Her work has been collected and edited on a number of occasions: *Olympiae Fulviae Moratae Foeminae Doctissimae ac Plane Diuinae Orationes, Dialogi, Epistolae, Carmina, tam Latina quam Graeca*, ed. Coelio Secundo Curio (Basel: Petrus Perna, 1562), L. Carotti, 'Notizie sugli scritti minori di Olimpia Morata', *Annali di Scuola normale di Pisa*, 11 (1942), 48–60, *Olimpia Morata Opere*, ed. Lanfranco Coretti (Ferrara: Deputazione provinciale ferrarese di storia patria, *Atti e memorie*, NS 11.1, 2 (1954), and trans. Holt N. Parker, *Olympia Morata: The Complete Writings of an Italian Heretic* (Chicago: University of Chicago Press, 2003).

[33] The former educated his daughter Paola, on the evidence of a memorial poem he wrote for her, in Cambridge, University Library, Add. 6188. The latter was a Venetian humanist and physician, who composed a commentary on Cato for his daughter Caterina. In the second edition he notes that she composed a work 'de laudibus sanctorum'. In 1451 she married Andrea Contrarini, after which she gave birth to several children and ran a patrician household. M. L. King and Albert Rabil (trans.), *Her Immaculate Hand* (Asheville, NC: Pegasus Press, 1997), 18–19.

[34] See Nolten, *Commentaria Historico-critica*.

[35] Caelio Calcagnini, *Opera* (Basel: H. Frobenius and Nicholas Episcopius (Bischoff), 1644), 182.

daughter Anna, who was five years younger.[36] It is perhaps worth posing the unanswerable question of whether it was in fact the birth of Anna d'Este which led Morato to educate his own daughter so intensively: the practicality of entrusting the education of princesses to well-trained humanist women seems to have struck a number of European courts at about this time.[37] Both young women were given further education at the hands of Chilian Senf. During her years at court, Olimpia gave a variety of public exhibitions of her learning: she wrote poems and dialogues, and delivered three Latin essays on Cicero's *Paradoxes* from memory as lectures in Renée's private academy when she was barely 16.[38]

In the 1540s, Morata turned away from the classics and towards religion. One of her few Latin verses (she preferred to write verse in Greek)[39] stresses the need for inward intention to conform with outward action in a way which seems characteristic of her thought:[40]

> Quae virgo est, nisi mente quoque est et corpore virgo
>   Haec laudem nullam virginitatis habet.
> Quae virgo est, uni Christo ni tota dicata est
>   Haec Veneris virgo est, totaque mancipium.
>
> A virgin, unless she is virgin in mind as well as in body,
>   Has none of the glory of virginity.
> A virgin, unless she is dedicated totally to Christ alone,
>   Is a virgin of Venus, and totally a slave.

As a product of a culture which preferred to avert its eyes from the enforced monachization of a far greater number of aristocratic girls than felt any vocation for the convent, this is a more provocative statement than it might seem. Morata, as this poem indirectly suggests, became a Calvinist, under the influence of several of the people most significant in her life, her father, the brothers Senf, her patron Renée, who had strong leanings towards the reformed religion,[41] and the preacher Coelio Secundo Curio, a native of Piedmont protected by Renée, who became very close to both Morato and his daughter. Morato was taken ill in 1548, and she left court to look after him. He probably died in the same year, and Renée seems to

---

[36] Daughter of Anne de Bretagne and Louis XII, sister of Queen Claude. She was brought up with her cousin Marguerite d'Angoulême, later the Queen of Navarre, and known as one of the most learned women in France. She was very concerned with her children's education, and they were well trained enough to act in Terence's *Adelphoi* before Pope Paul III at the ages of 13 (Anna), 12 (Alfonso), 8 (Lucrezia), and 4: Christopher Hare, *Men and Women of the Italian Reformation* (London: Stanley Paul & Co., 1914). See also E. Rodocanachi, *Renée de France, duchesse de Ferrare* (Paris; Paul Ollendorff, 1896).

[37] The most outstanding example is that of Luisa Sigea, tutor of the Infanta Maria of Portugal.

[38] A manuscript witness to at least part of this survives: 'Ciceronis paradoxa prolegomena', Basel, Öffentliche Bibliothek der Universität, II. 76 (E VI 24), also in the 1580 edition of her *Opera*, 1–8.

[39] A number of these are published in *Opera*: there is also an autograph Greek poem in Sapphic metre in Munich, Bayerische Staatsbibliothek, Clm lat. 10363, fo. 220.

[40] It also suggests that she was familiar with Jerome's *Adversus Jovinianum*, 357 (*PL* xxiii, col. 231): 'there are virgins in the flesh, not in the spirit, whose body is intact, their soul corrupt; but that virgin is a sacrifice to Christ, whose mind has not been defiled by thought, nor her flesh by lust.'

[41] C. J. Blaisdell, 'Renée de France between Reform and Counter-reform', *Archiv für Reformationsgeschichte*, 63 (1972), 196–225.

have dropped Morata about this time, for reasons which are now obscure, though they may perhaps relate to the religious tensions between Renée and her husband, which focused on the upbringing of their children: it is not improper to surmise that the duke would have objected to a devout Calvinist being his daughter's companion and friend.[42]

In any case, with her father dead, Morata became the effective head of the family, with three younger sisters and a young brother to care for, but she was no longer welcome at court. In 1549, a doctor and philosopher, Andreas Grunthler from Schweinfurt in Bavaria, joined the University of Ferrara and lived in the house of Johann and Chilian Senf, where he was treated as a son. He and Morata married, by the reformed rite, towards the end of 1550: characteristically, she wrote a Greek ode on the occasion. Grunthler then returned to Germany, hoping to find a chair in Bavaria, while Morata remained in Ferrara writing letters, some of which survive to suggest that the relationship was a closely companionate one. This first venture of Grunthler's was unsuccessful. He returned to Ferrara to fetch his wife, and taking her young brother Emilius with them, they went together to Augsburg, where George Hermann, chancellor to the Holy Roman Emperor, was eager to offer them hospitality while they looked around for a chair of medicine for Grunthler. The princely merchant house of the Fuggers of Augsburg, strongly committed to culture (and also to the education of daughters), took an interest in both young scholars.[43] Hermann obtained for Grunthler the position of chief physician to the Emperor Ferdinand, which he felt obliged to refuse since they would have had to become Catholics. The decision is explained in an apologetic letter from Morata to Hermann's son, which also indicates that it was mutually arrived at: the principle of patriarchal obedience associated with Protestant marriage does not seem to have characterized this relationship.[44]

During this period, Morata renewed her correspondence with her father's old friend Curio, now professor of Latin at Basel: it was Curio who, at her express invitation, produced a posthumous edition of her work.[45] Grunthler then received an urgent request to return to his native town, Schweinfurt, since the emperor had sent a Spanish army to winter there, and they needed a medical officer. While Grunthler busied himself with the Spaniards, Morata wrote a series of works, including imitations of the Psalms in classical Greek, and Latin dialogues, some of which she sent to Curio. Her 'interlocutor' in the dialogues is a highly educated woman friend, Lavinia della Rovere: one of the latter's own letters is also printed in

---

[42] Renée, having converted to Protestantism, resisted the pressure of inquisitors to return to orthodoxy until her children were taken from her, upon which she agreed to conform at least outwardly. King, *Women of the Renaissance*, 20.

[43] Andreas Planer, *Tactatus [sic] de Gyneceo Docto* (Wittenberg: Johann Godfrid Meyer, 1715), 39.

[44] The theorization of Protestant marriage is discussed by Steven Ozment, *When Fathers Ruled* (Cambridge, Mass.: Harvard University Press, 1983), and Lyndal Roper, *The Holy Household* (Oxford: Clarendon Press, 1989). The experience of Morata seems less like this model than it is like the companionate ideal proposed by Thomas More.

[45] Gertrud Weiss-Hählin, 'Olympia Fulvia Morata in Schweinfurt', *Zeitschrift für bayerische Kirchengeschichte*, 30 (1961), 175–83.

the 1580 edition.[46] Unhappily, in 1551 Schweinfurt fell victim to local politics, and became the theatre of an attempt by a coalition of the bishops of Bamburg and Würzburg, the Elector of Saxony, and the Duke of Braunschweig to eradicate Albrecht of Brandenburg, who had taken refuge there. The siege lasted for fourteen months of continuous bombardment, plague, and famine, and the city was eventually fired: Morata's books and writings were destroyed along with all their other possessions, and the couple fled the city as refugees. They were hospitably received at Fürstenburg by the Count of Rhineck, and, subsequently, the elector palatine, brother-in-law of the count, offered Grunthler the chair of medicine at Heidelberg, where they settled. Her friends among the German humanists, hearing that she had lost her library, were generous in sending her books (a gesture of supportiveness towards a woman scholar which would be hard to parallel in the fifteenth century), but her health had been ruined by the dreadful conditions they had endured during the siege of Schweinfurt: in her last letter to Curio she mentions both fever and a suffocating cough, so it seems possible that she had contracted tuberculosis. Aware that she was dying, she sent him as much of her verse as she could write out from memory, with the request that he be 'her Aristarchus', that is, her editor—she was evidently eager that her writings be published, which is, again, more characteristic of sixteenth-century humanism than of the century before.

Tarquinia Molza

A slightly later woman Latinist, Tarquinia Molza of Modena (1542–1617), is, like Morata, also associated with the Este of Ferrara, though in a later generation. Though she has been little studied, she is one of the most interesting learned women of the late sixteenth century. Unlike some of her sisters of the early Renaissance, she seems to have been regarded with universal admiration, and to have continued to write and associate with learned men throughout her life. Her father Camillo, the son of a distinguished humanist (Francesco Maria Molza, a friend of Veronica Gàmbara) by a wife he had deserted, recognized her rare talent, as did Giovanni Poliziano, who was teaching her brothers, but began teaching her as well.[47] Her father then found her a whole series of teachers, who included Francesco Patrizi, with whom she studied Plato and Aristotle.[48] It is clear from her

[46] Morata, *Opera* (1580), 89–90. The letter is dated 1549: on p. 130, Morata declares that no one in Italy is more learned than her friend. On della Rovere, see Louis Ponnelle and Louis Bourdet, *St Philip Neri and the Roman Society of his Times (1515–1595)*, trans. R. F. Kerr (London: Sheed and Ward, 1932), 508, Augusto Vernarecci, *Lavinia Feltria della Rovere* (Fossombrone: Monacelli, 1896).

[47] Francesco Patrizi, *L'amorosa filosofia*, ed. John Charles Nelson (Florence: Felice le Monnier, 1963), 19.

[48] See the summary in Cosenza, iii, no. 2335 and Girolamo Tiraboschi, *Biblioteca Modenense* (Modena: Societa tipografia, 1783), iii. 244–53. Patrizi was a man of considerable importance both as a scholar and as an original thinker. See Luigi Firpo, 'The Flowering and Withering of Speculative Philosophy—Italian Philosophy and the Counter Reformation: The Condemnation of Francesco Patrizi', in Eric Cochrane (ed.), *The Late Italian Renaissance, 1525–1630* (London: Macmillan, 1970), 266–84.

work, both printed and manuscript, that she was a serious student of Plato for most of her life.

Her father Camillo died in 1558, and two years later she married Paolo Porrino. The marriage was by all accounts happy but childless. She became renowned as a singer from very early in the 1570s, and her poems were set to music from 1571 by Luzzasco Luzzaschi and G. L. Primavera.[49] Porrino died either in 1569 or 1579,[50] and Patrizi, who remained in touch with her, subsequently refers to her as 'Artemisia', after the famously devoted widow of Mausolus. As a childless widow, she became her husband's sole heir, and was able to lead a quiet, independent life on what he left her. She nevertheless chose to take a public position some years later, when Duke Alfonso II d'Este came to hear of her and invited her to the court of Ferrara in 1582. Here, her position was a very interesting one. Duke Alfonso had married for the third time in 1579, and his young wife shared his passion for music. Under her influence, a group of court ladies was assembled who owed their position to their musical ability rather than their families, known as the *concerto di donne*. Their role was professional, but their status was that of ladies-in-waiting: rather than receiving a servant's wages, they were fed, housed, clothed, paid a salary, lent the prestige of the court, and, where appropriate, provided with dowries and found husbands.[51] In fact, they were a vocal chamber-music group of highly professional musicians whose members were part of the inner circle of the court, while at the same time their sophisticated vocal abilities gave an immense impetus to the development of the madrigal, a key early modern musical form. Molza finally joined this group in 1583, as a soprano and skilled player of the viola and the lute: her fellow musicians included a woman of a similarly humanist background, Anna, the daughter of Giovanni Battista Guarini, together with Laura Peverara, the daughter of a wealthy Mantuan merchant, and Livia d'Arco, a member of a minor Mantuan noble house (just possibly a descendant of Angela Nogarola).

Molza was a highly visible member of the court: Torquato Tasso (1554–95) wrote several poems to her, one of them a madrigal on the theme of *Anthologia Palatina* VII. 669, and Duke Alfonso himself fought a joust in her honour in 1585.[52] Towards the end of the 1580s, she began a love affair with the madrigalist Giaches Wert, which came to light in October 1589, and led to her banishment from Ferrara. She retired to Modena, and gathered a sophisticated group of friends around herself. Evidence for attitudes to her and her work includes an entire volume of verses in her praise, by Pincetta and others, in Modenese dialect, dated 1570, hailing her as a local heroine.[53] Torquato Tasso's admiration for her has already been

---

[49] Anthony Newcomb, *The Madrigal at Ferrara* (Princeton: Princeton University Press, 1980), i. 187.

[50] In *Opuscoli*, in *Delle poesie volgari e latini di: Francesco Maria Molza*, ed. Pierantonio Serassi, 3 vols. (Bergamo: Pietro Lancelotti, 1767), ii. 10, Serassi gives the date 1569, Tiraboschi gives 1579. Alternatively, Nelson in his edition of Patrizi, *L'amorosa filosofia*, p. xv, puts the date of Porrino's death at 1578 since he has a speaking part in the first dialogue, composed in 1577.

[51] Newcomb, *The Madrigal*, i. 7.

[52] Ibid. 187.

[53] This survives in two manuscripts, Modena, Biblioteca Estense, a T. 7.1 (ital. 224), with another copy in British Library, Add. 22336 (dated 1570).

mentioned, and Patrizi dedicates vol. iii of his *Discussiones Peripateticae* to her (printed, and probably written, in 1581). She was made an honorary citizen of Rome on 8 December 1600,[54] and she was also made Cittadinaza of Modena,[55] in both case, honours which reflect the honourable and public position which she enjoyed as the result of her literary and musical fame, despite the personal scandal which had ended her career in Ferrara. These awards of citizenship suggest that her experience was unlike that of her Renaissance predecessors in that public interest in her did not disappear with her youthful glamour: in 1600, she was 58. She also became a member of the Accademia degli Innominati in Parma, with the name 'l'Unica'.[56]

Much of the information redacted here comes from the biography of her written by Francesco Patrizi, her teacher and friend. He also made use of her for his own literary purposes, and presents her as a 'new Diotima' (the woman philosopher quoted by Socrates in Plato's *Symposium*) and philosopher of love in his set of dialogues *L'amorosa filisofia*, written in the late 1570s, which use her as a central speaking character—as in his model, the *Symposium*, she is the only woman to speak.[57] An indication of her own interest in Platonizing theories of love is in Modena, Biblioteca Estense, g. H. 7. 2, a 'Discourse of love made by Tarquinia Molza to the Grand Duke', a fine, professionally written small presentation book in Italian, presumably dedicated to Alfonso d'Este and thus probably written in the 1580s. Her approach is very abstract, and similar to that of Patrizi (and, of course, to that of their common sources, Plato's *Symposium* together with Marsilio Ficino's commentary thereon):[58] for example, on fo. 5ʳ, she quotes Empedocles, to the effect that love is the first cause. The discussion centres on the five grades of love, the lowest of which is desire of continuation of the species (i.e. sexual love), while the fifth and highest grade is love of God. Poems by, and to, her are printed in a number of contemporary collections, and a collection of her works was edited in the eighteenth century by Serassi. However, her commonplace book, now in Modena, was not known to Serassi, though it was known to Vendelli: it includes Hebrew exercises, a collection of her grandfather's Latin verse, and an Italian translation of Plato's *Crito*.[59] Her published Latin poems are not a central part of her oeuvre, which was mostly concerned with Greek philosophy, but are graceful demonstrations of facility; occasional productions, such as verses on Cardinal Cintio Aldobrandini for a volume in his honour, on the image of the Virgin attributed to St Luke

---

[54] There is a full Latin text of the decree in Domenico Vendelli (ed.), *Opusculi Inediti di Tarquinia Molza Modenense* (Bergamo: Pietro Lancellotti, 1750), 21.

[55] Tiraboschi, *Biblioteca Modenense*, iii. 244–53 (p. 250).

[56] Ibid. 245–6.

[57] *L'amorosa filosofia*, ed. Nelson. The autograph of this work is Parma, Biblioteca Palatina, Cod. Pal. 418. The date of the first dialogue is given as 1577.

[58] Ficino's very influential commentary, which argues that all desire is in reality a desire for God, was published with his edition of Plato, first published in Florence in 1484 and reprinted on a number of occasions.

[59] Modena, Archivio Storico Comunale, RAS V 4. Vendelli prints material from it, including *Crito*, 70–80.

which was, again, the subject of a collection of verses by contemporaries,[60] and prefatory verses in Marcus Condoratus' *De Bono Universi Liber*.[61]

Philippa Lazea, Jean-Jacques Boissard, and evidence for the lives of learned women

There is an interesting instance of the way that all knowledge of a woman's life and work can sometimes depend on her association with a single man in the various works of the French poet and antiquarian Jean-Jacques Boissard. His works provide our only evidence for Philippa Lazea (1546–76), whom he describes as 'Polona Illyria'—not Polish, but from Pola in Illyria, now Bosnia. Boissard addressed a number of poems to Philippa Lazea, with whom he appears to have been in love for some time before his marriage to another woman.[62] At least three of her poems are preserved by him, but there were clearly more: one of his poems is titled 'To Philippa Lazea, the Polan Illyrian, on her book of poems', implying that at some stage she sent him a body of work.[63] Another poem criticizes her prosody; and is followed by three fulsome apologies, which suggests that she was in the habit of sending him verses, and had ceased to do so following criticism she considered insulting.[64] In a brief account of her life, which he published in 1591, he mentions a series of other poems, 'Flora et Zephyrus' and 'Polyxenae Immolatio', both of which drew their subjects from classical mythology, 'De Laudibus Bombicum' ('In Praise of Silk'), and lyrics and hymns in praise of St Catherine. All that has actually survived is poems in praise of, or in answer to, Jean-Jacques Boissard himself. The answer-poem is the most interesting: he wrote to her, saying [65]

> Rightly you have deserved the additional names of
> 'The Illyrian Sappho' for your work:
> No girl has ever been more worthy of them.

She replied, warily refusing this praise which separated her from other women (in the metre associated with Sappho):[66]

---

[60] She was one of three women to contribute verse to the St Luke volume, and one of two to do so in Latin, a fact which is celebrated by Ascanius Persius in a poem of compliment to all three published in Lorenzo Legati, *Musei Poetriarum Primitiae* (Bologna: Heredes Victorii Benatii, 1668) 22.

[61] I have not managed to locate a copy of this work, which Cosenza (iii. 2335), states was published in Padua in 1593.

[62] Some of his poems suggest strong attachment, notably one (pp. 164–5) which begins, 'I love you, I tell you, Philippa, I love you: I am practically dying of frustrated love' ('Amo te, fateor, Philippa, amo te: Immo depereo impotente amore'). The possibility that this represents a measure of genuine feeling is supported by a poem to his wife Maria Aubria, which begins with a farewell to all previous attachments, whom he names as Fulvia, Philippa, and Melantho (the other two women are the Romans Fulvia and Melantho Laeta).

[63] Jean-Jacques Boissard, *Poemata* (Metz: Abrahamus Faber, 1589), 317.

[64] Ibid. 173, with three 'palinodes', pp. 173–6.

[65] Ibid. 317. 'Iusta operi Illyricae merita es cognomina Sapphus Dignior his umquam nulla puella fuit.'

[66] This may be a deliberate allusion to the poetry of Sappho herself. Her other surviving poems do not use this metre.

Sufficit, si me relegant puellae,
Que colunt dulci studio Minervam,
Sufficit. Si me relegat suo cum
   Ianus Alardo.

It is enough, if the girls who cultivate Minerva in sweet study count me in;
It is enough, if Jean-Jacques counts me in with his Alardus.

He returns to the attack in a subsequent poem, suggesting that if he is blinded by partiality, she on her side is deceived by her modesty.[67] Lazea's use of the figure of Minerva, not Sappho, is also interesting in that she rejects the potentially isolating strategy of Boissard, who wants her to claim primacy over other women poets. Her preference is to see herself as part of a group, a strategy also employed by other women Latinists, such as Weston.

It would be easy to assume on the basis of this exchange that Boissard was concerned to isolate and marginalize Lazea; so it is interesting to find that this rhetoric of Lazea's singularity must be contexted by the fact that, by his own declaration, Boissard knew at least three other women poets writing in Latin,[68] the Roman Fulvia Laeta, whom he described as a poor poet in Latin, though a very good one in Italian, Octavia Cleopassa of Otranto in Calabria, whose hymns were published by her brother at the end of his own Latin verse, and Timandra Raphais, whose Latin verse he describes as 'not inelegant'.[69] The same collection of engravings and brief biographies of notable people (mostly contemporaries) which yields these descriptions also mentions other women Latinists, Marica Castelsammarina of Ravenna (d. 1576), and Melantho (Nigella) Laeta, who was, he says, much more deeply learned than her sister Fulvia, though she did not write verse.[70] Other women friends of his (whom he also celebrates as poets) were a mother and daughter called Aelia and Silvia Zaborella.[71] There is a humanist family of Zabarelli, some of whom lived in Padua, on the evidence of a poem by Paul Melissus, *In Iac. Zabarellam Patavinum*, so they, like Lazea, Cleopassa and Castelsammarina, may have been among his Paduan acquaintances.[72]

Read in isolation, the poem to Lazea suggests not only that she was the sole woman Latin poet Boissard knew, but that he held the opinion that there should only be one such at a time. However, most unusually, the nature of his oeuvre allows one to get behind this poem, and to see, in fact, a man who seems at ease with numbering a variety of learned women among his acquaintance, and even with making critical judgement on which wrote well and which badly, which is also most unusual, since works which list learned women tend to an uncritical enthu-

[67] Boissard, *Poemata*, 318–19, l. 7.

[68] James Hutton, *The Greek Anthology in France* (Ithaca, NY: Cornell University Press, 1946), 125.

[69] Jean-Jacques Boissard, *Icones Diversorum Hominum Fama et Rebus Gestis Illustrium* (Metz: Abraham Faber, 1591), 104, 98, 88.

[70] Boissard, *Icones*, 96, 106.

[71] Boissard, *Poemata*, 292.

[72] Paulus Melissus, *Mele sive Odae ad Noribergam et Septemviros Reipub. Norib.* (Nuremberg: Haeredes Montani, 1575), 68.

siasm for any evidence of learning in their subjects whatsoever: a dog walking on its hind legs is not usually criticized for its deportment. It is also worth noting that Lazea, the Laetas, Cleopassa, Raphais, Castelsammarina, and the Zaborelle—eight highly educated women poets—are known only from Boissard, and, in the case of Lazea, also from sources dependent on him. They function as a salutary reminder of how dependent we are on sources that actually interest themselves in women, and also hint that women's writing, even in Latin, may in Italy be ignored not because it is anomalous or censured, but because it is too much part of the ordinary texture of things to be worth remarking.

Learned women and the convent in post-Tridentine Italy

The careers of Morata and Molza, both the daughters of humanist families, suggest a degree of continuity with the experience of their fifteenth-century predecessors, though aspects of both, particularly Molza's ability to find honourable and lucrative employment, perhaps bespeak a changing world, increasingly relaxed about women's public exercise of their intellectual and other abilities. Other aspects of the changes affecting women in the sixteenth century were more ominous. Cecilia Coppoli, discussed in the chapter on women in the Italian Renaissance, fled marriage for the convent,[73] and her contemporary Cecilia Gonzaga similarly fought her father for the privilege of becoming a nun.[74] Though there were still great ladies who longed for the protection of convent walls,[75] by the sixteenth century, a far greater number of women were trying, or would have wished, to flee in the opposite direction. In early modern Italy, despite a respectable amount of evidence for contented and passionately devout nuns, a substantial proportion of the upper-class women who entered convents were enclosed unwillingly, due to the spiralling cost of dowering them as brides.[76] In Florentine patrician families, for example, 28 per cent of daughters entered a convent in the sixteenth century, and 50 per cent in the seventeenth: similarly, half the daughters of the Venetian patriciate in the seventeenth century were nuns. Such numbers can bear no realistic relationship to actual vocations for the cloistered life.[77] Moreover,

---

[73] Her behaviour is more characteristic of late medieval Italy: Carol Lansing notes that 'women who chose the church over marriage against the wishes of their families are much in evidence' in 13th-century Italy, in *The Florentine Magnates: Lineage and Faction in a Medieval Community* (Princeton: Princeton University Press, 1991), 132.

[74] See the contemporary letter by Gregorio Correr, in Ambrogio Traversari, *Epistulae et Orationes* (Florence: Typ. Caesareas, 1757), 1073–5, and della Chiesa, *Theatro delle donne letterate*, 110.

[75] Carolyn Valone, 'Roman Matrons as Patrons: Various Views of the Cloister Wall', in Craig Manson (ed.), *The Crannied Wall* (Ann Arbor: University of Michigan Press, 1991), 49–72 (pp. 68–9).

[76] Domenico Sella, *Italy in the Seventeenth Century* (London: Longman, 1997), 119–20, looks at women's religious lives in Italy, and the problem of forced vocations. See also Gabriella Zarri, *Recinti* (Bologna: Il Mulino, 2000), 43–143.

[77] R. Burr Litchfield, 'Demographic Characteristics of Florentine Patrician Families, Sixteenth to Nineteenth Centuries', *Journal of Economic History*, 29 (1969), 197, 203, Jutta Gisela Sperling, *Convents and the Body Politic in Late Renaissance Venice* (Chicago: Chicago University Press, 1999). See also

by 1600, even the social dignity represented by a convent was not always attainable. Virginia Cox points out that this generation of women saw the creation of the patrician spinster: since even dowries for convents were getting out of control in lockstep with the rise in marriage dowries, patrician women were being left statusless, as their brothers' servants.[78] Perhaps it is not surprising that it is at this time that the first two full-length works by Italian woman writers arguing the case for women's moral and intellectual equality with men appeared, those of Lucrezia Marinella and Moderata Fonte. Both women were Venetians.[79]

A further difficulty for 'surplus' women was caused by the redefinition of convent life reached at the Council of Trent in 1563, which ruled that all female convents must be in strict *clausura*: that is, there were no orders of religious women free to move about in the world, as so many medieval nuns had done.[80] It is revealing that after the suppression of Florence's largest convent, Santissima Annunziata, the building served (and continued to do so until recently) as the city's high-security prison.[81] From the late sixteenth century, a nun was imprisoned for life, and, says Weaver, the period during which this battle was most fiercely fought was the late sixteenth and early seventeenth centuries,[82] a timeframe which coincides with an all-time high in enforced monachization. A seventeenth-century Venetian nun, Arcangela Tarabotti, denounced convents as a 'monastic hell',[83] and a variety of writers, both male and female, attest to the despair and bitterness felt by women forced into the cloister.

However, convents were not simply prisons. For some women, temperamentally suited to the conventual life, it offered them excellent opportunities for quiet study and contemplation, and the cultivation and exercise of taste, or even of

Francesca Medioli, 'To Take or Not to Take the Veil: Selected Italian Case Histories, the Renaissance and After', in Letizia Panizza (ed.), *Women in Italian Renaissance Culture and Society* (Oxford: European Humanities Research Centre, 2000), 122–37. Patterns varied considerably from one city-state to another: Samuel J. Cohen, Jr., *Women in the Streets: Essays on Sex and Power in Renaissance Italy* (Baltimore: Johns Hopkins University Press, 1996), 84–5.

[78] Cox, 'The Single Self'.

[79] Lucrezia Marinella, *The Nobility and Excellence of Women and the Defects and Vices of Men*, first published as *La nobiltà e eccelenze delle donne* (Venice: Gio. Battista Ciotti, 1600), is trans. Anne Dunhill (Chicago: Chicago University Press, 1999). Moderata Fonte, *The Worth of Women*, first published as *Il merito delle donne* (Venice: Imberti, 1600), is trans. Virginia Cox (Chicago: Chicago University Press, 1997). There is a critical edition by Adriana Chemello, *Il merito delle donne* (Venice: Eidos, 1988). Fonte's treatise, which came out after the author's death in 1592, was published with a prefatory letter by her daughter Caecilia de Zorzi.

[80] Katherine Gill, 'Open Monasteries for Women in Late Medieval and Early Modern Italy: Two Roman Examples', in Monson (ed.), *The Crannied Wall*, 15–47.

[81] Elissa Weaver, 'The Convent Wall in Tuscan Convent Drama', ibid. 73–86 (p. 75).

[82] Ibid. 73.

[83] Arcangela Tarabotti wrote a number of texts: her *Paradiso monacale libri tre con un 'Soliloquio a Dio'* was pub. Venice, 1643. The other side, her *Inferno Monacale*, went unpublished until 1991, ed. Francesca Medioli, *L'Inferno monacale di Arcangela Tarabotti* (Turin: Rosenberg and Sellier, 1991). Other works: *Semplicita ingennata* (1654), *Antisatira in riposta al 'Lusso donnesco'* (1644), *Che le donne siano della spetie degli huomini* (1651). All but *L'Inferno* were published at Venice. Ginevra Conti Odorisio, *Donna e società nel Seicento: Lucrezia Marinelli e Arcangela Tarabotti* (Rome: Bulzoni, 1979), 194–214.

power.[84] Much recent work, notably that of Elissa Weaver, suggests that convent culture of the sixteenth and seventeenth centuries could be livelier than is generally imagined.[85] It seems probable, for example, that the Abbess Giovanna da Piacenza, who commissioned a roomful of mythological paintings from Correggio for her convent in Parma between 1518 and 1519, was a cultivated woman, and shared her interests with others in her community.[86] The evidence for convent culture is particularly good in the area of music, and more and more evidence is coming to light not only of nuns distinguished both as musicians and composers, but of music as an important part of convent life.[87] A famous singer of the late sixteenth century, Laura Bovia, after a sojourn in the *concerto di donne* at the court of Francesco de' Medici in Florence (which was modelled on that of Ferrara), retired to a convent, 'where, in the Offices of this Holy Week, many people have come to hear her sing and play'. With her family's permission, she was asked to leave the convent and take another professional position, at the court of Mantua.[88]

There is also abundant evidence for nuns as dramatists: nuns' plays were often published, in both the sixteenth and seventeenth centuries.[89] For example, Raffaella de' Sernigi's *La rappresantatione di Moise quando idio ogli dette le lettie in sul monte Synoi*, was published twice in *c*.1550 and 1578; *Rapprezentazione di Santa Cecelia, vergine e martire* by Cherubina Venturelli, a nun at Santa Caterina in Avella, went into several editions. Clemenza Ninci, a Benedictine playwright at the convent of San Michele in Prato, wrote a play, *Lo sposalito d'Ipparchia Filosofa*,

[84] Kate Lowe, 'Elections of Abbesses and Notions of Identity in Fifteenth- and Sixteenth-Century Italy, with Special Reference to Venice', *Renaissance Quarterly*, 54 (2001), 389–429, and Garry M. Radke, 'Nuns and their Art: The Case of San Zaccaria in Renaissance Venice', ibid. 430–59.

[85] Elissa Weaver, 'Spiritual Fun: A Study of Sixteenth-Century Tuscan Convent Theater', in Mary Beth Rose (ed.), *Women in the Middle Ages and the Renaissance: Literary and Historical Perspective* (Syracuse, NY: Syracuse University Press, 1986), 173–205, and 'Suor Maria Clemente Ruoti, Playwright and Academician', in E. Ann Matter and John Coakley (ed.), *Creative Women in Medieval and Early Modern Italy: A Religious and Artistic Renaissance*, 281–96 and see also Monson (ed.), *The Crannied Wall*. The convent plays of Antonia Pulci have been published, as *Florentine Drama for Convent and Festival*, ed. and trans. James Wyatt Cook and Barbara Collier Cook (Chicago: Chicago University Press, 1996).

[86] Jean Seznec, *The Survival of the Pagan Gods: The Mythological Tradition and its Place in Renaissance Humanism and Art*, Bollingen Series 38 (Princeton: Princeton University Press, 1953), 117–18, and Lucia Fornari Schianchi, *Correggio* (Florence: Scala, 1994), 22–9. More generally, see M.-A. Winkelmes, 'Taking Part: Benedictine Nuns as Patrons of Art and Architecture', in G. Johnson and S. Matthews Grieco (eds.), *Picturing Women in Renaissance and Baroque Italy* (Cambridge: Cambridge University Press, 1997), 91–110.

[87] For example, Craig A. Monson, *Disembodied Voices: Music and Culture in an Early Modern Italian Convent* (Berkeley and Los Angeles: University of California Press, 1995), Robert L. Kendrick, *Celestial Sirens: Nuns and their Music in Early Modern Milan* (Oxford: Clarendon, 1996), and Colleen Reardon, *Holy Concord within Sacred Walls: Nuns and Music in Siena, 1575–1700* (Oxford: Oxford University Press, 2001). See also Slim, Monson, Macey, and Kendrick in Monson (ed.), *The Crannied Wall*.

[88] Newcomb, *The Madrigal*, i. 99. However, she returned to the convent, where she continued to delight lay audiences, on the evidence of Camillo Cortellini's first book of madrigals, dated December 1582.

[89] Elissa B. Weaver, 'Le muse in convento: la scrittura profana delle monache italiane (1450–1650)', in Lucetta Scaraffia and Gabriella Zarri (eds.), *Donne e fede: santità e vita religiosa in Italia* (Bari: Laterza, 1994), 253–76.

whose central issue is whether a woman should marry or study. The protagonist, a noblewoman, prefers study to marriage, and when pressed by her family, resolves the dilemma by agreeing to marry her teacher so she will have both options.[90] The fantasy figure of Hipparchia represents a goal more nearly attainable than might first seem to be the case. The great majority of the sixteenth- and seventeenth-century learned women of Italy married, and in a number of instances, their marriages were demonstrably to men who shared their intellectual interests, for instance, those of Morata and Molza, already discussed, and that of the Greek-language poet Ippolita Paleotti, married to fellow humanist Paride Grassi.[91]

A number of sixteenth- and seventeenth-century nuns studied Latin (though the generality did not), and put it to a variety of uses. Some nuns were orally competent in Latin, for example, Cornelia Baglioni, a Servite nun of Perugia, who was capable of addressing Pope Paul III in that language.[92] At Santa Maria delle Vergine, a prestigious Venetian convent founded in the twelfth century, the election of the abbess was customarily accompanied by a Latin oration given by one of the nuns: at least four were subsequently published. The oration of Aurelia Quirino, given before the doge in 1598 and mentioned by Jacob, was particularly well known,[93] others which survive include those of Maria Electa Faletra, delivered on 8 June 1615 before the doge, Elena Dolfin, delivered in 1694, and Maria Aurora Bragadin, delivered in 1717.[94] There is also Latin writing of various kinds by nuns: Suor Francisca à Gesù Maria (d. 1651), a nun of Rome, composed two Latin offices, as well as writing an autobiography.[95] Jacob also mentions Barbara da Correggio (fl. 1556, daughter of the Latin poet Cassandra Colleoni and nun of San Antonio in Lombardy), and Battista Vernaccia (d. 1583) as nuns who wrote and

---

[90] Weaver, 'Suor Maria', 290. Florence, Cod. Ricc. 2974 III, published in abridged form by Cesare Guasti, in *Calendario pratese del 1850*, 5 (Prato, 1849), 53–101.

[91] Cosenza, iii. 2549: see Carlo Malagola, *Conferenze intorno ad Antonio Urceo*, 2 vols. (n. p.: Tipi Fava e Garagnani, 1875–6), i. 125, and *Ad Hippolytam Palaeottam Crassam Iulii Iacobonii Panegyricus* (Bologna: Ioannes Rossius, 1581). All I have located of her writing are two letters, one Greek, one Latin, Bologna, Archivio Isolani, F. 30. 99. 18 (CN 58), not seen, and possibly not still extant, and Vatican City, Biblioteca Apostolica, Vat. Lat. 6410, fo. 119 (also not seen). Her participation in the intellectual life of her time is suggested by the fact that she was among the visitors to Ulisse Aldrovandi's museum: he describes her as 'studiosa' (Paula Findlen, *Possessing Nature: Museums, Collecting and Scientific Culture in Early Modern Italy* (Berkeley and Los Angeles: University of California Press, 1994), 141).

[92] Giovanni Battista Vermiglioli, *Bibliografia degi: scrittori perugini* (Perugia: Francesco Baduel, 1828), i. 82–3.

[93] Jacob, 'Bibliothèque', fo. 17ᵛ: he had seen a printed copy (Venice: Giovanni Antonio Ranparetti, 1598). This oration was particularly famous, and was printed in F. Sansovino, *Venetia città nobilissima e singolare*, 2nd edn, (Venice: 1604), 126ᵛ–128ʳ. See Mary Laven, *Virgins of Venice* (London: Viking, 2002), 76.

[94] The first is noticed in Jacob, 'Bibliothèque fo. 143ʳ, who states that it was published in Venice by Robertus Megettus and Evangelistus de Chirico, 1615, in quarto; the second is *Gratulatio Coram Serenissimo Principe et Excellentissimo Collegio, in Solemni Inauguratione Mariae Dianae Grimanae Sacri Asceterii, Sanctae Mariae de Virginibus Antistitae, Habita ab Helena Delphina, Anno Domini 1694* (Venice: Andreas Poletti, 1694), the third is *Virtutis Optio Laudatio Coram Serenissimo Principe Joanne Cornelio et Excelentissimo Collegio in Solemni Inauguratione Blanchae Delphinae Sacri Asceterii Sanctae Mariae de Virginibus* (Venice: Jacobus Thomasinus, 1717). See Lowe, 'Elections of Abbesses', 406.

[95] Prospero Mondosio, *Bibliotheca Romana* (Rome: Francisco de Legaris, 1692), ii. 81–2. Her sister Isabella Farnese was also a writer, but in Italian (ibid.).

published in Latin.[96] The mystic Domitilla Graziani (nun by 1551, d. 1580), a Poor Clare of Perugia, left both Italian poems and Latin letters.[97] Other nuns were historians: Marta dalla Rosa, a Dominican nun of St Agnes in Bologna, self-described as 'of advanced age' in 1562, left a Latin text, conserved at the convent of St Agnes, an account of the foundation of the convent in 1219 by Suor Diana Andalò of Bologna.[98] Angelica Baitelli of Brescia wrote in Italian but translated from Latin in order to give other less learned nuns access to the history of their convent.[99] Baitelli's convent, Sts Salvatore and Giulia, like that of Santa Maria delle Vergine, was old (founded in the eighth century) and wealthy, which is obviously relevant to its ability to allow nuns to pursue their intellectual interests.[100] There were nuns who translated from Latin, such as Maria Stella Scutellari of Parma (1648–1702), who published a substantial collection of contemplative texts, with an apologia for women's scholarship in the preface.[101] Quite a number of names of early modern nuns who studied Latin or even Greek but wrote in Italian are preserved: Felice Rasponi of Ravenna, for example, had a particular interest in philosophy: she read Latin, and studied Aristotle and Plato, though she wrote entirely in Italian.[102]

With these facts in mind, the career of the Dominican nun and Latin poet Laurentia Strozzi (1514–91) becomes less anomalous. She was the daughter of Zacharias Strozzi, from one of the leading families in Florence, and the sister of the learned Cyriacus Strozzi, an architect and philosopher who taught at the University of Bologna.[103] She was brought up in the Dominican convent of San Niccolò

---

[96] Jacob, 'Bibliothèque', fos. 20ᵛ and 17ᵛ–19ᵛ. Domenichi, *La nobiltà delle donne*, 272, adds Scholastica Bettona.

[97] Vermiglioli refers to 'liber epistolarum, libro di sonetti' (the change of language suggests the latter is in Italian) and 'epistolae suor Domitillae Gratianae in domo paterna scriptae', all in MSS of 'il monistero dello Povere' (Poor Clares), in the diocese of Perugia (*Bibliografia degli scrittori perugini*, ii. 32–3).

[98] Published in part by Giovanni Michele Pio in *Delle vite gli huomini illustri di S. Domenico* (Bologna: Sebastiano Bonomi, 1620), cols. 100–1. See also M. G. Cambria, *Il monastero domenicano di Sant'Agnese in Bologna, storia e documenti* (Bologna, 1973).

[99] Silvia Evangelisti, 'Angelica Baitelli: A Woman Writing in a Convent in Seventeenth-Century Italy', in Els Kloek et al (eds.), *Women of the Golden Age* (Hilversum: Verloren, 1994), 157–65 (p. 159).

[100] Suzanne F. Wemple, 'S. Salvatore/S. Giulia: A Case Study in the Endowment and Patronage of a Major Female Monastery in Northern Italy', in J. Kirschner and S. F. Wemple (eds.), *Women of the Medieval World* (Oxford: Oxford University Press, 1985), 85–102.

[101] *Le meditazione e soliloquii e manuale di S. Augustino Vescovo e dottore, le meditazione di S. Anselmo vescovo Cantuariense, le mediatazion di S. Bernado abbate, le contemplazioni del'amor divino del'idiota sapiente* (Modena: Capponi, 1694). I have not seen this (it is listed in Magnoald Ziegelbauer, *Historia rei leterarie ordinis sancti Benedictis in IV partes distributa* (Augsburg: M. Veith, 1754), iii. 538): if any reader locates a copy, it is perhaps worth looking to see if the last of the works listed is in fact translated from the English of Dame Gertrude More, *The Holy Practises of a Devine Lover or the Saintly Ideots Devotions* (Paris: Lewis de la Fosse, 1657).

[102] Pietro Paolo Ginanni, *Memorie storico-critiche degli scrittori ravennati* (Faenza: Giosettantonio Archi, 1769), ii. 258. Ginanni also notes that one of her fellow nuns wrote her *vita* (i. 37), and claims there was at the time of writing a copy in the library of St Vitale in Ravenna.

[103] Giovanna Pierattini, 'Suor Lorenza Strozzi: poetessa domenicana (1514–1591)', *Memorie domenicane*, 59 (1942), 113–15, 142–5, 177–83; 60 (1943), 19–25. There is a published biography of her brother, [Matthaeus Strozzi], *Vita Kyriaci Strozae* (Paris: Plantin, 1604).

in Prato, and at 13 decided to remain there and make her profession as a nun,
changing her name to Lorenza (Laurentia) from her birth-name of Francesca. She
took her vows in 1529. San Niccolò was very much a family concern of the
Strozzi.[104] There were five Strozzi women there in 1529, including Laurentia's
aunt Antonia, so she was not isolated from her family, but very much within it. Her
education cannot be taken as characteristic of Italian convent life (though the
Dominicans were one of the most learned orders), since a special tutor was sent
in to teach her Latin and Greek. The principal result of this was a volume of Latin
hymns in classical metres, some consciously modelled on Horace, published at the
Giunta Press in Florence in 1588, and dedicated to the Bishop of Pistoia, who was
in overall authority over the convents of Prato. This, for example, is her ode on the
Eucharist.

> Plaudat æther orbis, atque uos fideles psallite:
>   Nam superno patre natus: matre casta in tempore,
>   Pascha condit, seque tradit in salutem gentium
> Mortis hora iam propinqua, uescitur cum filiis:
>   Perficitque dogma primum: quod dedit iam patribus:
>   Ordinat nouumque, pascit filiorum Pectora.
> Manna præbet dulce Mundo, sub figura tritici,
>   Angelorum panis, unde, sit cibus credentium,
>   Vertitur merumque verbis in Tonantis sanguinem.
> Dona turbæ dans Iesus; verba dixit talia,
>   Corpus est meum, quod ore sumitis chrissimi:
>   Mente casta gustet omnis in magistri pignore.
> Inde poculum dat illis, dicta sacra proferens,
>   Pro reatu datur sanguis meus viuentium,
>   Hunc bibentes passionem conditoris innouent.
> Hunc sacerdos uerba complens hostiam purissimam,
>   Singulis diebus offert ante Patrem maximum,
>   Et vocatur omnis insons ad sacrum convivium.
> Corda quærit pura Christus, atque munda crimine:
>   Innocentiumque menteis, replet alto flumine,
>   Qui reatus seruat intus, non fruetur nectare.
> Nam bonos fouetque, alitque, sacra cœli victima,
>   Impiosque morte perdit, ducit ac ad inferos
>   Concupiscens regna summa pellat ad se noxia.
> Esca salue porta vitæ, lacte melle dulcior,
>   Christe Iesv, Sol refulgens, gaudium potissimum,
>   Fac colentes te beatis collocari sedibus.   Amen.

The uppermost air of the round universe applauds: sing psalms, too, you faithful people!
    For the Son of the eternal Father, born of a chaste mother within time,
        is instituting a Passover and surrendering himself for the salvation of the peoples.
Now the hour of death is near, he is taking food with his sons;

104 Silvestro Bardazzi and Eugenio Castellani, *S. Niccolò a Prato* (Prato: Edizioni del Palazzo, 1984).

and he is bringing to completion the first religion[105] which he has before this
    given to the Patriarchs,
and is ordaining a new one: he is feeding the hearts of his sons.
He is offering sweet manna for the World, under the guise of wheat:
    the bread of angels, to the end that there should be from it the nourishment of
        believers; by his words, too,
    wine is turned into the blood of the Thunderer.
JESUS, bestowing gifts to the crowd, spoke words of this sort:
    'What you are taking in your mouth, most beloved people, is my body:
    let everyone taste it with a chaste mind, in token of the Master.'
Hence he gives the cup to them, pronouncing the holy utterances,
    'My blood is given for the guilt of the living.
    Those who drink it will renew the passion of the Institutor.'[106]
A priest, acting in fulfilment of these[107] words,
    offers every day a most pure sacrifice before the greatest Father,
    and every innocent person is called to the sacred banquet.
Christ seeks pure hearts, and hearts clean of sin
    and fills the minds of innocent people from a deep river.
    The person who holds on to guilt inwardly will not gain advantage from the
        nectar.
For the sacred victim of heaven cherishes and nourishes the good,
    and destroys the wicked by death, and leads them to the powers below.
    The person desirous of the realms on high drives from[108] him noxious things.
Hail, food, the gate of life, sweeter than milk or honey,
    Christ JESUS, refulgent sun, most potent joy:
    cause those who worship you to be settled in the blessed abodes. Amen.

This is heavily typological in an almost medieval fashion, alluding to several Old
Testament stories held to prefigure the Passion, and written in trochaic tetrameter,
an important metre for late antique hymns (used, for example, by Venantius
Fortunatus). The two hymns opening with 'Pange, lingua' by Fortunatus and St
Thomas Aquinas are important models for this particular poem, yet the diction is
classicizing: note, for example, that for God, she uses 'the Thunderer', one of the
titles of Jupiter. The work is very much in the spirit of the recommendations which
Gregorio Correr made to the considerably earlier Cecilia Gonzaga.[109] Laurentia
Strozzi was not the only Latinist, or the only writer, at her convent. Arcangela
Alamanni (born in Florence *c*.1550), wrote several Latin letters on the life and
death of Laurentia Strozzi, including one to her nephew, preserved with the title
'Letter to Zacharias Montius, on the holy life and happy death of his maternal

---

[105] For the use of *dogma* = 'religion', 'belief-system', see G. W. H. Lampe, *A Patristic Greek Lexicon*
(Oxford: Clarendon Press, 1961). It does not seem ever to be used as equivalent to 'Law' or 'Covenant'.
My thanks to Dr Janet Fairweather for this note.

[106] *Conditor*, cf. 'Pascha condit' in line 3.

[107] Reading conjecturally: *haec* for *hunc* (l. 15).

[108] Reading conjecturally *ab* for *ad* (l. 24).

[109] Ambrogio Traversari, *Epistulae et Orationes* (Florence: Typ. Caesareas, 1757), 1073–5. The letter
is translated in King and Rabil, *Her Immaculate Hand*, 91–105.

aunt, called Sister Strozzi'.[110] There was also a playwright at the convent at the same time, Beatrice de Sera (1515–86), author of *Amor de virtu*, a protest against the conventual imprisonment of women in the guise of a devotional drama, which has been discussed by Margaret King and Elissa Weaver.[111]

Unlike Beatrice de Sera, Suor Lorenza seems to have been happy in her profession. The convent was by no means intellectually isolated. She was in touch with her family; her bishop approved of her work; and she specifically mentions the encouragement and interest of her fellow nuns in her writing—it is evident from their own writings that some of them were interesting and well-educated women. In addition, we might note that she also came to know two important religious reformers, Bernardino Ochino (also a confidant of the poet Vittoria Colonna) and Pietro Martire Vermigli, both of whom later became Protestants, though her own faith evidently remained securely Catholic. These friendships, however potentially dangerous to her peace of mind, suggest that contact with lively and questioning intellects was not lacking in her life. She was admired and respected in her own time: only one year after Filippo Giunta published her *Hymni*, she was noticed in Michael Poccantius' catalogue of Florentine authors.[112] Her reputation also travelled abroad: the hymns were translated into French by Simon Georges Pavillon, and republished in Paris in 1601. There is a variety of notices of her life and death in contemporary writers, including a biography by Sébastian Rouillard.[113] Her death is celebrated by a poem from the Wittenberg scholar Sebastian Hornmold, dated 1608, in which he has done her the honour of an elaborate double acrostic,[114] as well as by one from Aurelius Laurentius Albrisius and another by Philip of Parma.[115] Quetif and Echard list five other contemporary poems on Strozzi, as well as other forms of acknowledgement of her life and work.[116]

A number of other Italian nuns wrote Latin verse, though no others were as distinguished. Febronia Pannolini, the daughter of an old noble family of Bologna, became a Dominican nun in the monastery of St Agnes in Bologna, which had

---

[110] 'Epistolae ad Zacharium Montium, De piis moribus et felici morte eius materterae dictae Sororis Stroziae et aliae ad alios', noticed by Bandini Buti, i. 23. The Alamanni were another humanist family: a number of Latin works by male Alamanni are listed in Kristeller's *Iter Italicum*.

[111] Margaret L. King, *Women of the Renaissance* (Chicago: Chicago University Press, 1991), 88, Weaver, 'Spiritual Fun', 192.

[112] Michael Poccantius, *Catalogus Scriptorum Florentinorum* (Florence: F. Giunta, 1589), 106.

[113] Sébastian Rouillard, *Vita Laurentiae Stroziae* (Paris: Plantin, 1610). Anon. [Cesare Guasti], *Bibliographia Pratense* (Prato: Giuseppe Pontecchi, 1844), 160, attributes this to Zaccaria Monti, on whose work it is based, and also mentions a Latin eulogy by the Jesuit Masson published in Paris in the same year.

[114] Bibliothèque Nationale de France, Dupuy 348: 'Clarorum virorum elegia', fo. 170ʳ–ᵛ. Notice of her life (in Italian), and epitaph, 171ᵛ (the latter is also in Jacob, 'Bibliothèque', fos. 125–6, and Rouillard, *Vita*). Hornmold seems to have been interested in learned women, since he solicited Latin verse from Elizabeth Jane Weston for his anthology on intoxication: see *Elizabeth Jane Weston: Collected Writings*, ed. Donald Cheney and Brenda Hosington (Toronto: Toronto University Press, 2000), 362–5.

[115] In Madrid, Biblioteca Naçional, 6028 and Milan, Biblioteca Ambrosiana, O 23 sup. fo. 110.

[116] Jacobus Quetif and Jacobus Echard, *Scriptores Ordinis Praedicatorum* (Paris: Christophe Baillard and Nicolas Simart, 1721), ii. 841–3.

earlier harboured both a thirteenth-century Latinate nun, Angelica,[117] and the sixteenth-century Marta dalla Rosa.[118] She published slight, pleasant verses in occasional volumes, in both Latin and Italian: several of her poems appear in volumes to which Tarquinia Molza also contributed, so they may have been known to one another. A rather later Bolognese nun, Suor Maria Raimonda Constanza Berlingero, is also said to have written Latin and Italian verse.[119] The only known Latin poem of Gironda Cerrini of Perugia (1626–1703), who later became Suor Anna Maria Cristina de Gesù, was published when she was 17: it is a contribution to the necrology of a local notable: the editor, Verduccioli, notes that he asked her father whether 'our Sappho' might oblige with a poem, and was delighted to print the rather lame result, an interesting insight into the way that, at that time, public fame could combine with blameless propriety. After becoming a nun, she wrote quite extensively in Italian: her works included *Il trionfo di s. Filippo Neri, dramma per musica*, of which the manuscript is or was in the Oratorio of Perugia.[120] She was a member of the Perugian Accademia dei Virtuosi.[121]

The lives of Laurentia Strozzi and the other Latinate nuns discussed here, as well as those of the various cloistered musicians and playwrights who have recently been studied, suggests that convent culture, despite the enclosure forced on post-Tridentine nuns, could be something more rewarding than critics such as Arcangela Tarabotti suggest. In particular, the Dominican order seems to have been conspicuous in maintaining a commitment to learning at a time when the Franciscans and Benedictines were letting this go by the board, which is also the case in late medieval Germany.[122] Obviously, *clausura* meant that a convent could be stifling, and the life was an endless frustration for women who longed for romantic love, the dignity and social status of wifehood and motherhood, or even for elegant clothes, a subject on which Tarabotti speaks with feeling.[123] But for many, it was simply the only life they knew, and for some, it held positive attractions. It was only rare spirits in early modern Europe who challenged the view that their individual destinies were subordinate to the needs of their kin-group.[124] For others

---

[117] Ibid. 831.

[118] Giovanni Fantuzzi, *Notizie degli scrittori bolognesi* (Bologna: Stamperia di San Tommaso d'Aquino, 1784–8), vi. 271–2.

[119] Giancalvo Roversi (ed.), *Donne celebre della Emilia-Romagna e del Montefeltro* (Bologna: Edizione Grafis, 1993) 140.

[120] She also wrote 'Sopra le girate che si fanno per la Cappelle di Santa Maria degli Angeli, Canzone', in Fra Stefano da Bettona, *Trattato dell'indulgentia plenaria*, (Venice, 1652), 19–22; other occasional Italian verses are said by Vermiglioli to have been printed.

[121] Vermiglioli, *Bibliografia degli scrittori perugini*, i. 321–2.

[122] William A. Hinnebusch, *The History of the Dominican Order, i: Origins and Growth to 1500* (Staten Island, NY: Alba House, 1966), 384.

[123] Daniela de Bellis, 'Attacking Sumptuary Laws in Seicento Venice: Arcangela Tarabotti', in Panizza (ed.), *Women*, 226–42 (pp. 231–2).

[124] In passing, we may note that convent life could be emotionally, and, for some, even sexually, satisfying. The case of Benedetta Carlini has been made famous by Judith C. Brown, *Immodest Acts: The Life of a Lesbian Nun in Renaissance Italy* (New York: Oxford University Press, 1986), but note also the lives discussed by Mary Martin McLoughlin, 'Creating and Recreating Communities of Women: The Case of Corpus Domini, Ferrara 1406–1432', *Signs*, 14.2 (1989), 293–320.

who were temperamentally suited to community life, it represented a variety of opportunities to exercise personal talents.

Elena Lucrezia Piscopia

The famous Elena Lucretia Cornaro Piscopia (1646–84) was neither nun nor wife: her status was one of triumphant liminality. If she had been born earlier, she might have become a nun, but she quite clearly did not wish to be cloistered any more than she wished to marry. Such a life had once been feasible in one of the 'open monasteries' which were part of the Italian scene before the Council of Trent,[125] but in a world where the convent meant claustration, she evolved a highly personal solution to her dilemma. She resembles Isotta Nogarola, her equally famous predecessor, in that she made a voluntary choice of celibacy without entering a convent; but the contrasts between her life and that of Nogarola are also instructive, as are the resemblances between her story and that of the Catalan Juliana Morell, discussed above in Chapter 8.

Piscopia was the daughter of a wealthy Venetian aristocrat, Gian Battista Cornaro, an educated man and a patron of scholars and the arts: for example, he was one of the first patrons of the Venetian academy of the Delfici, founded in 1647, and he also supported a variety of other learned individuals and endeavours.[126] Her mother was a lower-class woman, Zanetta Boni, so Piscopia was technically illegitimate, since her father was not legally permitted to marry outside his class. However, he had no other wife, and went to great lengths to try and legitimate his family (though in the event, he succeeded only with his sons).[127] This seems to have had no effect on the marriageability of Piscopia or her sister.[128] At the age of 7, she was recognized as unusually intelligent by her confessor, Giovanni Battista Fabris, parish priest of St Luca, who therefore spoke seriously to her father about the advisability of teaching her Greek. Cornaro in fact hired both tutors in Greek and Latin. On her eleventh birthday, Piscopia made a vow of virginity, perhaps in imitation of St Aloysius Gonzaga, who vowed chastity at the age of 9: she had a particular devotion to St Aloysius which prompted her, on the death of Fabris, to seek a Jesuit as her next confessor. When she entered her teens, and her capacity for absorbing education appeared inexhaustible, she was given a whole series of further tutors in Hebrew, Spanish, French, Arabic, and modern Greek.

---

[125] Gill, 'Open Monasteries for Women in Late Medieval and Early Modern Italy'.

[126] Francesco Ludovico Maschietto, *Elena Lucrezia Cornaro Piscopia (1646–1684)* (Padua: Editrice Antenore, 1978) 70.

[127] Sperling, *Convents and the Body Politic in Late Renaissance Venice*, 20, has light to shed on the social context of this relationship and Piscopia's legitimacy.

[128] Piscopia was sought in marriage by an unnamed Austrian prince; and her sister married a Venetian with the notably patrician name of Vendramin. Antonio Lupis, *L'eroina veneta, overo la vita di Elena Lucretia Cornara Piscopia* (Venice: Per il Curti, 1689), is dedicated to the sister, Caterina Vendramina. There was a third sister who became a nun: her name is not preserved.

As an adult, her day began with prayer and four hours of study, then Mass.[129] After lunch, she entered on public business: correspondence took much of her time, which is in itself direct evidence that she was well known to contemporaries. Most of these letters she destroyed in her last illness, fearing that her father would use them to enhance her consequence, though thirty in Italian and Latin have been found by Maschietto,[130] to which we may add one in Latin which, interestingly, is written to another learned woman, the Danish Helena Margarethe Friis, which must be connected with Piscopia's known exchange with Friis's uncle Otto Sperling.[131] She thought of becoming a nun, but was persuaded against this by her friend the Ven. Mary Felix, founder of the female Capuchin community at Santa Maria della Grazia in Venice. In 1665, as she approached her twentieth year, her father became insistent that she should marry. She was already internationally famous: in this same year, Johann Heinrich Hottinger dedicated the sixth volume of his *Historia Ecclesiastica* to Cornaro as 'the father of a very great daughter'.[132] The fame of her learning ensured no shortage of eligible suitors according to both of her contemporary biographers, who appear to assume that her scholarship positively raised her saleability in the marriage market. Her father had a portrait made of her (now in the Museo civico at Padua), and asked Pope Alexander VII to write dispensing her from her vow of virginity, on the grounds that she had made it without his permission and was in any case too young to understand what she was doing, which the latter did. Elena, dismayed, promptly asked Abbot Cornelio Codanini of the monastery of St Giorgio Maggiore to give her the Benedictine habit as an oblate, and to let her renew her vow of chastity at his hands.

The self-invented status of oblate gave her a remarkable degree of personal freedom. In the early Middle Ages, an oblate was a child, such as Hildegard of Bingen, who was given to the Church by his or her parents, normally at the age of 7. On reaching adulthood, the oblate was expected to make his or her profession. Benedictine nuns were strictly enclosed, but by successfully reinventing the status of oblate as an open-ended one entered into as an adult under terms devised by herself, Elena was able to go on living the life of a Venetian patrician's daughter with an entourage of personal servants and a private study and library in her father's house, while wearing a Benedictine habit (since she detested the time-consuming business of dressing up, this doubtless simplified her life considerably). Deza comments on her essentially paradoxical and liminal status, 'To sum up, the

---

[129] Massimiliano Deza, *Vita di Helena Lucretia Cornara Piscopia* (dedicated to Eleanora, Princess of Monferrato) (Venice: Antonio Bosio, 1686), notes (pp. 37–8), 'Terminate queste Orationi, applicarsi allo studio per quattr'hore continue nel principio, e proseguimento del quali inalzava la mente à Dio, ed implorara l'aiuto della Santissima Vergine, come Madre della Divina Sapienza': it is interesting that she should have evolved a special devotion to the Virgin as Divine Wisdom.

[130] Maschietto, *Elena Lucrezia*, 153–5, 159–60.

[131] 'Helenae Lucretiae Corneliae Episcopiae epistola ad Lenoram Margaretham Sperlings, Patavii 1679', Munich, Bayerische Staatsbibliothek, Clm lat. 1085 (Collectio Camerariana 34), fo. 247ʳ–ᵛ. See Marianne Alenius, 'Love at First (W)ink', in Graham de Caie and Holger Nørgaard (eds.), *A Literary Miscellany Presented to Eric Jacobsen* (Copenhagen: University of Copenhagen Press, 1988), 169.

[132] Johann Heinrich Hottinger, *Historiae Ecclesiasticae Novi Testamenti...Saeculi XVI, Pars II* (Zurich: J. H. Hamberger, 1664).

Lord wanted her to live as a hermit in the city, a nun in her father's house, and an Idea of virtue for women in the world.'[133]

Her status as a public intellectual is suggested by the fact that at 24, she became a member of the Academy of the Pacifici in Venice, for whom she wrote three Latin discourses, the second of which was delivered when she became president.[134] She also became a member of the Infecondi of Rome two years later, in 1672, and gave them a *discorso* on the 'Madonna delle Neve' (a famous Roman miracle story).[135] Perhaps unsurprisingly, given her lifelong admiration for the Society of Jesus, her most visible activity in the 1670s is her involvement with the campaign to canonize a Venetian Jesuit, Giacomo Lubrani. In a context chosen by herself, she was evidently happy to make use of her name, prestige, and curiosity value on Lubrani's behalf by editing and publishing a book in his praise, which also includes verse of her own in seven languages.[136] She also corresponded with the academies which had made her a member and sent contributions to their various publications, whether or not she appeared in person. She wrote this elegant poem for the Infecondi, whose motto was 'germinabit': 'it will sprout', which also makes allusion to the Madonna of the Snow.

> Infoecunda nives inter, gelidasque pruinas,
> 　　Germen ubi nullum, nulla nec herba viret,
> Non sine spe fructus Academia dicitur; illam
> 　　Venturi inscriptum Germinis, omen alit.
> Sume animos foelix Academia; surget ab Astris
> 　　Edita proventu nobiliora seges.
> Non opus hoc Cereris, niveae sed Virginis, Ergo
> 　　Quae foecunda cupis Germina, Virgo dabit.

To the famous Academy of the Infertile at Rome with the superscription, 'Germinabit' (it will sprout)

> The Academy, infertile though it is among snows and icy frosts,
> 　　Where no shoot, where no plant grows green,
> Is said to be not without hope of fruit;
> 　　The written prognostication of the coming shoot fosters it.
> Happy Academy, take courage, there shall arise—
> 　　Brought forth from the Stars—a harvest of nobler provenance.
> This is not the work of Ceres, but of the snow-white Virgin,
> 　　Therefore, it is the Virgin who will give the fecund shoots which you desire.

---

[133] 'Mà in fine il Signor le voleva Romita nella Città, Religiosa nella Casa Paterna, et Idea di Virtù alle Donne del Secolo'. Deza, *Vita di Helena Lucretia Cornara Piscopia*, 43.

[134] These are printed in *Helenae Lucretiae (quae et Scholastica) Corneliae Piscopiae Virginis Pietate, et Eruditione Admirabilis, Ordine S. Benedicti Privatis Votis Adscriptae, Opera*, ed. Benedetto Bacchini (Parma: Ippolito Rusati, 1688), 51–106. Lupis, *L'eroina veneta*, 59–60, outlines her relationship with academies.

[135] Vatican City, Biblioteca apostolica, Barb. Lat. 4502, dd. 98ᵛ–103ᵛ.

[136] *Seconda corona intrecciata da varii letterati co' fiori de' loro ingegni, per coronar di novo il molto reverendo padre Iacomo Lubrani, della Compagnia di Giesù, predicatore nella chiesa del venerando monistero di San Lorenzo, e Coriseo trà gli Oratori sacri di Venezia nell'anno 1675* (Venice: Antonio Bosio, 1675).

Later in the 1670s, her father, unable to persuade her into marriage, suggested that she take a doctor's degree at Padua. She is possibly not the first woman to take a doctorate—apart from the late medieval Italians discussed in Chapter 5, there is the interesting case of the painter Lavinia Fontana, who is said to have received a doctorate from Bologna in 1580.[137] However, Piscopia is certainly the first woman to do so in such a glare of publicity that the whole process can be examined. She had no particular wish to do so—at least, according to the somewhat hagiographic *vitae* which offer our sole witnesses to her state of mind—but felt that, having gone against her father's wishes in refusing to marry, she owed it to him to gratify at least some of his intentions for her. Accordingly, she moved to a subsidiary Cornaro family palazzo in Padua,[138] since the university required intending doctoral students to undergo a number of years of study in Padua itself, and set about a gruelling course of study. She also undertook a public dispute in her own palace against a young Greek, with an audience which included twenty-six procurators of St Mark and most of the Venetian senate: she discoursed in Latin, ancient, and modern Greek, and justified her increasing fame: this, again, was set up by her father. More importantly, she worked for her doctorate under Carlo Rinaldini, a philosopher, and Ippolito Marchetti, a theologian, and successfully took her degree on 25 June 1678.

The public 'viva' occurred in front of enormous crowds, especially from Venice. So many people wanted to come to the ceremony that it had to be held in the Basilica of St Anthony rather than the university aula. She may have been aware that the Basilica held, near the east door, the tomb of a medieval woman remembered for her learning, Bettina d'Andrea (*c.*1327–1355),[139] but in any case, a pulpit was placed for her near the altar of the Virgin. The procedure was for the student to choose a book, from which any passage could then be selected at random for him, or in this case her, to discourse on. She chose Aristotle, whom she had studied with Rinaldini. Her defence was completely successful, and she was laureated by Rinaldini, her promoter. While a few medieval women, mostly lawyers, are described as 'laureati', and there are earlier accounts of women defending theses publically, notably Novella d'Andrea and Juliana Morell,[140] Elena Piscopia is the first woman unequivocally to be awarded a degree after a public examination.

---

[137] Caroline Murphy, 'Lavinia Fontana: The Making of a Woman Artist', in Kloek et al. (eds.), *Women of the Golden Age*, 171–81 (p. 176). It may be relevant that her mother Antonia was a de Bonardis, from a prolific printing house with close ties to the university. A small self-portrait, dated 1580, now in the Uffizi, shows her in the kind of studio used by serious artists and scholars, with a book, and small fragments of antiquities, little bronzes, etc. (p. 179).

[138] Palazzo Giustiniani, near the Basilica of St Anthony.

[139] Piero Addeo, *Eva Togata* (Naples: Editrice Rispoli anonima, 1939), 39–43, with a picture of her tomb. Addeo notes that Bettina d'Andrea was mentioned by a 16th-century poet, Giulio Cesare Croce, so her name may not have been entirely forgotten in Piscopia's time.

[140] Furthermore, Arisio gives an account of the learned Lucretia Vidalenga Campana (d. 1630) defending theological theses publically before Cardinal Paul Sfondrato and a more general audience, to applause, but this event did not have the status of an examination. Arisio, *Cremona Literata*, iii. 218. D'Andrea is disussed in Ch. 6, Morell in Ch. 8.

Her doctorate was an international sensation, reported, for instance, by the *Mercure galant* only three months later, and also reported in Leipzig, Lyon, Amsterdam, Altenberg, and Utrecht.[141] Within Italy, several academies hastened to elect her: the Academy of the Ricovrati at Padua was the first to hold a meeting in her honour at which she was present, a few days after she received her doctorate.[142] She repaid this compliment by writing graceful formal verse in their honour.[143] The Intronati of Siena and the Dodonei of Rome also elected her a member: she was already a member of the Infecondi.[144] In the years after her doctorate, she was found on more than one occasion publically performing as a woman scholar. Cardinal César d'Estrées paid her a formal visit at the family palazzo in Padua in 1680 accompanied by a group of learned men of various kinds including two doctors from the Sorbonne. She read to him in Greek from Isocrates and commented on the passage, spoke Hebrew, French, Spanish, and Latin to him, and gave a recital on the organ and clavicymbal. That evening, they met at the Ricovrati, where she delivered an elegant discourse in his praise, to his great pleasure.[145] She used her prestige in various ways; for example, to promote the work of her erstwhile professor Rinaldini with a series of formal letters to Cardinal Bouillon in 1681.[146] She put on a similar performance for a group of learned visitors from Germany.[147] One of the public occasions which called forth a response from her was the liberation of Vienna from the Turks in 1683, on which she wrote at length in Latin.[148]

Piscopia died in 1684 of some painful wasting disease: the recorded symptoms might suggest cancer or tuberculosis. She was clearly unwell for years before her death, since there is a pathetic contrast between the engravings of her when she was 22, which show a bouncing, round-faced girl, and those of ten years later, which show a too-thin, fragile woman with hollow eyes. Apart from her lack of physical stamina, she must be seen as extraordinarily successful: in a world which offered two distinctly unattractive possibilities, enclosure in the cloister or the risks of marriage, she evolved a highly personal solution which seems to have suited her temperament well.

Piscopia's early death was celebrated on an unprecedented scale. The University of Padua struck a medal, with her portrait on one side and, on the other, the dew of heaven falling into an open oyster (which we are to imagine transforming it into

---

[141] *Le Mercure galant*, (Sept. 1678), 150–9: for the others, see Maschietto, *Elena Lucrezia*, 129.

[142] The laudation was printed: Ottone Bronckhorst, *La dama di lettere, applausi ad Elena Cornaro Piscopia academica Ricovrata, dedicata alle donne di Padua* (Padua: Stamperia dell'Università de' Legisti, 15 July 1678). The Infecondi similarly produced *Applausi accademici alla laurea filosofica di Elena Lucrezia Cornaro Piscopia, accademica Infeconda composti e raccolti dall'accademica stessa* (Rome: Giacomo Dragondelli, 1679).

[143] *Poesie de' signori accademici Infecondi di Roma* (Venice: Nicolò Pezzana, 1678), 341.

[144] Lupis, *L'eroina veneta*, 59–60.

[145] Maschietto, *Elena Lucrezia*, 143–4.

[146] Ibid. 148–9.

[147] J. Fabricius (a theologian at Altdorf), in J. G. Schelhorn, *Amoenitates Literariae* (Frankfort: Daniel Bartholomaeus, 1725–30), v (1726), 218.

[148] *Opera*, ed. Bacchini, 113–31, 139–41, and *Poesie de' signori accademici Infecondi*, 31–47, 49–53.

pearls), an emblem of the relationship of divine inspiration to the workings of genius.[149] The Ricovrati published a special memorial volume of verse, which included Latin poetry by at least three other women,[150] and so did the Infecondi of Rome.[151] News of her death, and reactions to it, travelled abroad: John Evelyn, in a eulogy of Piscopia in a letter written in 1689, says '[she] had her obsequies celebrated at Rome by a solemn procession, & elogie of all the witts of that renowned citty'.[152] Though she insisted on being buried in St Justina, the Benedictine abbey in Padua, since she regarded herself as a member of the Benedictine order,[153] her father put pressure on the Conventual Friars in charge of the Basilica of St Anthony in Padua—the most prestigious church in the city—to let him erect a gigantic marble cenotaph by a distinguished baroque sculptor, Bernardo Tabacco of Bassano. It extended from a side pilaster to almost the middle of the nave (though the basilica is one of the biggest churches in Italy), and was decorated with sculptured figures representing Faith, Charity, Purity, Death, Time, Aristotle, Plato, Democritus, and Seneca, topped with a life-sized statue of Elena Lucrezia.[154] It was dismantled forty-three years later, once her father was dead, since it occupied a huge amount of space and obstructed the view of the main altar: it was replaced by a bust in a niche in one of the central pillars and a lengthy inscription (which are still *in situ*). Her obsequies were thus celebrated on a scale which implies that the academicians and leading citizens of Rome, Venice, and Padua shared her father's view that her life had been a phenomenal one, worthy of the greatest respect.

Her life was also celebrated almost immediately with biographies, all of a tone which borders on the hagiographic, which show her as a perfect daughter of the Church.[155] She is a woman who has persistently attracted hagiography, though the view given of her life differs in interesting ways at different times: the Life by a nineteenth-century Benedictine abbess, Matilda Pynsent, stresses the opposition between a saintly Elena Lucrezia, determined to divide her time between prayer and study in true Benedictine fashion, and a tyrannical father determined to get value from her one way or another; in contrast, the Nicola Fusco study published

---

[149] Illustrated in Maschietto, *Elena Lucrezia*, facing p. 231.

[150] *Compositione degli academici Ricovrati per la morte della nob. D. Signora Elena Lucretia Cornaro Piscopia, dedicate al'excelenza del signior Gio. Battista, suo padre* (Padua: Pietro Maria Frambolto, 1684), which went into a second edition in 1686

[151] *Le pompe funebre celebrate da' signori accademici Infecondi di Roma per la morte dell'illustrissima Signora Elena Lucrezia Cornara Piscopia, accademica detta 'L'Inalterabile'* (Padua: Cadarino, 1686).

[152] *Memoirs of John Evelyn*, ed. William Bray (London: Henry Colburn, 1827), iv. 298–9.

[153] Her grave was rediscovered in the 19th century, and has since been the focus of a variety of hagiographic activity: see anon. [Matilda Pynsent], *Life of Helen Lucretia Cornaro Piscopia* (Rome: St Benedict's, 1896), and Nicola Fusco, *Elena Lucrezia Cornaro Piscopia (1646–1684)* (Pittsburgh: United States Committee for the Elena Lucrezia Cornaro Piscopia Tercentenary, 1975). She is also the subject of the Great Window of the Thompson Memorial Library of Vassar College (1906), in which she could be easily mistaken for St Catherine of Alexandria disputing with pagan philosophers.

[154] There is a sketch made from Deza's description in Maschietto, *Elena Lucrezia*, 231.

[155] Deza, *Vita di Helena Lucretia Cornara Piscopia*, Lupis, *L'eroina veneta*, and another Life by Benedetto Bacchini in his edition of her *Opera*.

in America in 1975 presents the father as a great man married to a mean-minded, avaricious peasant, seeking consolation in an ideal meeting of minds with his daughter, in which the daughter is happy to concur.[156]

Piscopia's story illustrates the new respectability of the learned woman. Her father's great wealth is obviously highly relevant to the way she was treated, but so is the willingness of Italian and foreign savants to honour and admire her. However, two other lives of contemporaries shed some light on the qualified extent to which her success can be seen as opening doors for other less high-profile women. Piscopia corresponded with the Contessa Veronica Malaguzzi Valeri of Reggio Emilia (1631–90), also an aristocrat, though of a less exalted variety. She was one of eleven children, a number which left their father rather at a loss how to provide for them all. However, when, at only 4, Veronica became fascinated by her elder brothers' Latin lessons, he let this daughter study various disciplines privately, and observing her rapid progress, it struck him that profit might be made from her. She wrote a thesis, *Conclusiones Theologicae*, which was dedicated to the Empress Maria Theresa,[157] and her father instituted a vigorous attempt to find her a patron in the courts of France, Austria, and Tuscany, in which he failed entirely: laudatory letters came back, as they had for Piscopia, but nothing in the way of practical sponsorship, so Veronica Malaguzzi took refuge in the convent of the Visitation in Modena, where she died in 1690, and disappeared from history.[158] What is interesting about this story is not her failure, but the fact that her father had conceived the notion that there could be purely economic return on investment in a cultivated daughter.[159]

Another woman's history is illuminating in a different way: that of Gabriella Patin/Patino. Her Parisian father, after a chequered career, had ended up as professor of medicine at Padua, and was president of the Ricovrati at the time of Piscopia's degree. Both his daughters were highly educated, and wrote in Latin as well as French and Italian. Only a few months after Piscopia was awarded her doctorate, Patin tried to institute proceedings to laureate his own elder daughter, Gabriella. This was firmly blocked, on two counts. On the one hand, Cardinal Gregorio Barbarigo was horrified to think that Piscopia's cathedration might be the thin end of a wedge: he set his face firmly against any further laureation of women, and was firm that Piscopia should not be treated as a precedent. On the other, Piscopia's own father, Giovanni Battista Cornaro, was furious. Patin was to some extent a client of his, since Cornaro had spoken for him when he was given the chair of medicine at Padua, and he saw the initiative partly in terms of a client getting ideas above his station, and partly as a mean attempt to steal his own daughter's thunder.[160]

---

[156] The account of Maschietto, *Elena Lucrezia*, puts the entire narrative on a more scholarly footing.
[157] Bandini Buti, i. 361.
[158] She published a drama, *L'innocente riconosciuta*, based on the life of St Genovefa (Bologna, 1660, not seen), and a variety of other works. Ginevra Canonici Fachini, *Prospetto biografico delle donne italiane rinomate in letteratura* (Venice: Tipografia di Alvisopoli, 1824), 155. Tiraboschi, *Biblioteca Modenense*, iii. 128–37, lists all her works, and also a collection of verse in her honour, Tommaso Martinelli et al., *Ghirlanda de Pinda* (Bologna: Giacomo Monti, 1664).
[159] Maschietto, *Elena Lucrezia*, 127–8.
[160] Ibid. 136.

However, what these stories have in common is fathers who perceive very definite benefits in encouraging a daughter's academic bent, whether in terms of fame or of fortune; a consensus that a famous daughter conferred prestige, and was an instrument of family glory. Piscopia's extraordinary achievement did little to expand possibilities for other women, at least in her own time; yet it is depressing to think that if Patin had managed to negotiate his way through the local politics, the principle that Padua awarded degrees to women would have been established by 1680.

Piscopia was long remembered. Her name became proverbial in Venice: if a woman did something unusually clever, someone might exclaim 'La xe na Piscopia!' (she's another Piscopia!).[161] A later Venetian woman aristocrat, poet, and Ricovrata, Caterina Dolfin Tron (1736–93), arranged for the portrait statue from Piscopia's cenotaph in the basilica to be given to the Ateneo of Padua in 1773, suggesting that her memory lingered on among the educated women of Venice.[162]

Martha Marchina

Another of the most extraordinary women Latinists of her own or any other age is Martha Marchina (1600–42), whose life suggests some interesting comparisons with that of Elena Piscopia. Though she was neither wealthy nor a noblewoman, she became a noted Latin poet, and her work was published in book form. Almost all the information we have about her comes from the biographical essay in the volume in question, which is called *Musa Posthuma*. She was the daughter of a Neapolitan soap-boiler living in Rome, a poor man, though one who seems to have cherished hopes of upward mobility. On the early death of his wife, he put his sons in charge of his young daughter Martha, and got the boys places at the free school of the Oratorian Fathers (who had been founded in the mid-sixteenth century by St Philip Neri), St Maria in Vallicella. After a while the headmaster, Ludovico Santolino, was struck by the boys' progress and went to see their father, who disclaimed any knowledge of it, and declared that it was all due to their sister. Further investigation showed that Martha was hearing her brothers' lessons at home, and thus educating herself at second hand as well as securing their own grasp on what they learned.[163] Santolino took an interest in this remarkable girl, and mentioned her to Antonio Quaerengo and Iacopo Volpone of the Oratorian Fathers. She was put through her paces, judged genuine, and brought to the notice of Cardinal Spada, who became her patron. She neither married nor became a nun, but continued to work for her father and live quietly at home, though her literary connections place her firmly in one of the most active intellectual circles of baroque

[161] Ibid. 168.
[162] Ibid. 227.
[163] Another remarkable woman, the Venetian feminist Modesta da Pozzo, author of *Il merito del donne*, acquired a Latin education the same way. Grendler, *Schooling*, 94–5.

Rome. The published collection *Musa Posthuma* contains letters and poems, mostly religious, though a substantial number are to or about members of the Spada family and other patron figures. It was edited by Francisco Macedo, and dedicated to Christina, ex-queen of Sweden, from a collection of her verses which had belonged to Cardinal Spada: Macedo had extracted them from Virgilio Spada, his heir. Macedo gives a hint as to why her work was admired by contemporaries. He describes it as graceful and distinguished, with a strong sense of the appropriate, neither over-ornamented, nor lax.[164] Her verses still make that impression today. They are elegant, often a little melancholy. She has a baroque taste for paradox and contrast: for example a poem on the Visitation of the Virgin ends: 'So go, Virgin Mother, climb the mountains, but alas—the child that you carry in your belly will soon himself carry the Cross.'[165]

She also enjoyed witty structures, such as this virtually untranslatable epigram in *versus rapportati*,[166] the cleverness of which lies in the way that the appositional structure sets up complex resonances between the triads (for example, Christ instructs and conquers, as well as kindles, human love): it is also, of course, as three-in-one, a representation of the Trinity. A *fax* is often a wedding torch, a meaning which the use of 'Venus' as a word for love seems to support, but it is also the light of the sun. The third term of the epigram is therefore a twist, evoking in four words the highly affective, quasi-erotic pietism of the baroque.

> Iesus, Christus, Amor docuit, superavit, adussit
> Terram, Erebum, Venerem: lege, cruore, face.
>
> Jesus teaches the world with his law;
> as Christ, he conquers Hell with his blood,
> as Love, he kindles Desire with his light.[167]

She writes to one of her brothers in the following terms when he criticized her verse, pointing out tartly that criticism is easier than composition:[168]

> Esse videris homo rigidus, nimiumque severus,
>   dum, germane, tibi carmina nulla placent.
> Desipit hoc, inquis, dura isthaec, illa redundant,
>   hoc iacet, ista tument, hoc hiat, illa cadunt.
> Innumeras notas in nostro carmine mendas:
>   atqui ego non bona, tu carmina nulla facis.
>
> You appear to be a straitlaced fellow, and too severe,
>   My brother, since none of my verses ever please you.
> This one is silly, you say, this is harsh, the other is wordy,
>   This is flat, these are tumid, this one has a hole in it, those others collapse—

---

[164] 'nitidus et facilis, non fucatus, non neglectus'.　　[165] *Musa Posthuma*, 20.

[166] This verse-form is common in medieval Latin, and not infrequent in Renaissance neo-Latin. J. W. Binns, *Intellectual Culture in Elizabethan and Jacobean England* (Leeds: Francis Cairns, 1990), 55–6.

[167] More literally, 'Jesus, Christ, Love, has taught, has overcome, has kindled, the Earth, Hell, Desire: by his law, by his blood, by his torch.'

[168] *Musa Posthuma*, 67.

> You criticize innumerable faults in my verses—
> And yet it is I who compose the no-good poems, you compose none.

Despite her modest and retired way of life, Martha's fame travelled abroad: she is discussed in Rossi's *Pinacotheca Imaginum Illustrium, Doctrinae vel Ingenii Laude, Virorum* published in Cologne in 1645, a year before her death, and seventeen years before the publication of her book.[169] Rossi's account of her life is mostly accurate (though he assigns the brothers' education to the Jesuits, not the Oratorians, perhaps the result of a misunderstanding), and since he notes Antonio Quaerengo as a source of information, it seems that the Oratorians were proud of her.[170] So, it seems, were the Spada: Carlo di S. Antonio in his book on the modern epigram, *De Arte Epigrammatica sive de Ratione Epigrammatis Rite Conficendi, Libellus*, published in Cologne in 1650 (twelve years before *Musa Posthuma*), quotes excerpts from several of her poems as models of style.[171] Again, this suggests that somebody, probably Cardinal Spada or his brother Virgilio Spada, was showing her poems around to interested parties long before they were eventually published. Rossi quotes a splendid monumental inscription, which he claims is in Santa Maria in Vallicella (it seems to be there no longer),[172] suggesting that this girl of humble origins was buried with great ceremony by the Oratorian Fathers, almost as if she were one of themselves.[173]

Gabriela Zarri has recently explored the concept of a 'third state' for early modern Italian women, neither marriage nor the cloister, but a condition of voluntary celibacy within dedicated but uncloistered institutions, allowing both religious dedication and secular participation: a state rendered necessary by, on the one hand, the extreme difficulty of marriage for elite women, and the recent redefinition of the cloister as strictly enclosed.[174] Though a hugely wealthy Venetian

---

[169] Ianus Nicias Erythraeus [Rossi], *Pinacotheca Imaginum Illustrium* (Cologne: Judocus Kalcovius, 1645), 234–41.

[170] 'Erant ea epigrammata adeo eleganti stylo confecta, adeo venustis argutisque conclusa sententiis, ut Antonio Quaerengo, qui ea legerat, fides fieri non posset, fuisse ab ipsa elaborata atque perfecta.'

[171] Carlo di S. Antonio, *De Arte Epigrammatica sive de Ratione Epigrammatis Rite Conficendi, Libellus* (Cologne: E. Egmond et Socios, 1650), 80–1, 87–8.

[172] The Chiesa Nuova underwent extensive rebuilding in its first hundred years, particularly in the side chapels, and there was also a fire in the early 17th century, so it may at some point have been destroyed. *Santa Maria in Vallicella, chiesa nuova* (Rome: Tipi Centenari, 1974), and see further Antonella Pampalone, *La cappella della famiglia Spada nella chiesa nuova: testimonianze documentarie* (Rome: Ministero per i beni culturali e ambientali, 1993). The fire destroyed St Philip Neri's original quarters, so since Marchina's tomb is said to have been by his chapel, it may also have fallen victim. My thanks to Fr. Rupert for showing me parts of Santa Maria not normally accessible to visitors.

[173] Printed in *Musa Posthuma*, sig. §§ 6ʳ and in Erythraeus [Rossi], *Pinacotheca Imaginum Illustrium*, iii. 234–41. 'DOM. Martae Marchinae, ortu Neapolitanae, virgini educatione Romanae, cui, ad insignae pietatis ac pudicitiae studium, mirus sapientiae amor, vel septenni accessit. Eòque deinceps, pari morum atque ingenii cultu Humaniores artes, ac Latinam, in primis poësim ad veterum normam, atque aemulationem. Suo ipsa instructo, eximiè calluit exercitucel; Hebraicis Graecisque literis docta, Severiores disciplinas, fastu procul, religiose attigit Animi quaesito magis ornatu, quàm nominis, cuius gloriam sponte latius in Urbis luce, dum planè abiecit. In finum transmisit immortalitatis, ob. v. id. Apr. Ad MDCXLVI, aetatis XLVI. Patres congregationis Oratorii, quos illa vitae probae accurandae habuerat monitores, Curatores post funeris, monumentum benè merenti, pos[uit].'

[174] In *Recinti*, 459–477, and in Silvana Seidel Mechi, Anne Jacobson Schutte, and Thomas Kuehn (eds.), *Tempi e spazi di vita femminile tra medioevo ad età moderna* (Bologna: Società editrice il Mulino,

patrician and a soap-boiler's daughter occupied very different places in the stratified societies of early modern Italy, both were women of high intelligence and religious inclinations who seem to have reached for very similar solutions: living under their respective fathers' protection, but in the context of a close relationship with the Church, or rather, with a specific group of clerical sympathizers.

Learned women in seventeenth-century society

For educated women who did not become nuns (and even for some who did), sixteenth- and seventeenth-century Italy offered an important new kind of public space. The academies, which sprang up in most towns of any size in Italy from the second half of the sixteenth century onwards, were an obvious place where women could occupy a public position: in the records both of the academies themselves, and of educated women, many women are named as academy members.[175] Conor Fahy has warned against reading too much into this, suggesting that women were 'no more than an ornament, simply adding to the glory of parents, teachers and public institutions'.[176] However, the concept of 'shedding lustre on public institutions' requires interrogation. For early modern Italian women, it did not merely imply forming an agreeable and elegantly dressed audience, as one might easily assume, it might also involve their rising to their feet before an educated audience of local dignitaries to harangue them in Latin, which is by no means without interest. Some academies, though by no means all, conducted their ordinary meetings in Latin, but given that some women were trained to speak as well as write in that language, it would be a mistake to conclude from this that they were necessarily all excluded.[177]

Perhaps the earliest women to have been members of an academy were the poets Veronica Gàmbara and Diamante Dolfin, both members of the Sonnachiosi of Bologna in the 1540s.[178] The house of Veronica Gàmbara was itself an academy,

---

1999), 311–34. Zarri cites a contemporary treatise on the subject, Gabrielle Suchon, *Du celibat volontaire ou la vie sans engagement*, published in 1700: 'the "third way" is the only one which gives women an authentic liberty.'

[175] For an overview of the academies, see Michele Maylender, *Storia delle accademie d'Italia*, 5 vols. (Bologna: Licino Capelli, 1926–30). See also David S. Chambers, *Italian Academies of the Sixteenth Century* (London: Warburg, 1995), and William J. Bouwsma, *The Waning of the Renaissance, 1550–1640* (New Haven: Yale University Press, 2000), 11–12. 2,200 academies were formed in Italy between the 16th and 19th centuries.

[176] 'Women and Literary Academies', in Panizza (ed.), *Women* 438–52: the formulation quoted here is that of Elisabetta Graziosi, in her 'Arcadia Femminile: presenze e modelli', *Filologia e critica*, 17 (1992), 321–58.

[177] Fahy, 'Women', 445.

[178] 'Accademici Sonnacchiosi nel 1542 e 1543', in 'Miscellanea di notizie storiche bolognesi raccolte dal co. Baldassare Carrati' (19th century), Bologna, Biblioteca comunale dell'Archiginnasio, B961, pp. 353–4. Ippolita Clara (d. 1552), who translated Virgil and is named as a member of the Immobili of Alessandria, cannot be much later (Simone Albonico, 'Ippolita Clara', in Cesare Bozzetti et al. (eds.), *Veronica Gàmbara e la poesia del suo tempo nell'Italia settentrionale* (Florence: Leo Olschki, 1989), 323–53.

according to her protégé Rinaldo Corso.[179] The Italian-language poet Laura Battiferri Ammanati (1523–89) was a high-profile recruit to both the Intronati of Siena and the Assorditi of Urbino.[180] It is interesting to find that another woman poet of Siena, Virginia Salvi, was elected unopposed to a smaller Sienese academy, the Travagliati, which she had petitioned for admission, on the grounds that 'they had at last found a means of getting even with the Intronati, who had managed to secure the great Battiferri'.[181] This was in 1560, and it suggests strongly that even this early in the history of the academies, distinguished women were perceived as trophies, which is neither equality nor grudging toleration, but the creation of a special category for them to inhabit. It is also notable that the existence of 'the great Battiferri' did not close, but created, an opening for her fellow townswoman.

Several other of the women writers of the sixteenth century boasted membership of an academy, including a Paduan, Isabella Andreini (d. 1604), which may have helped to encourage the Ricovrati in their later interest in learned women (it has already been noted that a variety of learned women friends of Jean-Jacques Boissard spent part of their lives in Padua in the late sixteenth century).[182] Other sixteenth-century women contribute to academy collections, so were presumably members.[183] The academy of Piacenza admitted Ippolita Borromeo and Camilla Valente,[184] while the Apatisti of Florence admitted a nun, the playwright Maria Clemente Ruoti, in 1649,[185] and subsequently, four more women.[186] The Ricovrati of Padua admitted Elena Piscopia in 1669, and were so convinced that the experiment had been a success that they admitted at least twenty-eight women during the century that followed.[187] The Arcadi of Rome also admitted many women.[188] There were two academies specifically for women, the Accademia delle Assicurate, Siena, under the

---

[179] Rinaldo Corso, *Vita di Giberto III di Correggio* (Ancona: Astolfo de Grandi, 1566), sig. F 1ᵛ, 'la casa di Veronica era una Academia, ove ogni giorni si riducevano à discorrer di nobili quistion con lei il Bembo sopranominato, il Capello, il Molza, il Mauro, et quanti huomini famosi di tutte Europa.'

[180] Her work was published during her lifetime, Laura Battiferri Ammannati, *Il primo libro dell'opere toscane* (Florence: Giunti, 1560).

[181] Fahy, 'Women', 444. Virginia Salvi was not a nonentity: she published *Lettera e sonetti della Sig. Virginia Salvi, et della Sig. Beatrice sua Figliuola, a M. Celio Magno* (Venice: Domenico & Giovanni Battista Guerra, 1571). Many of her verses were published in 16th-century anthologies (M.-F. Piéjus, 'Les Poétesses siennoises entre le jeu et l'écriture', in *Les Femmes écrivains en Italie au Moyen Âge et à la Renaissance* (Aix-en-Provence: Centre Aixois de Recherches Italiennes, 1994), 322–7).

[182] For example, Laura Terracina was a member of the Incogniti, with the name 'Phoebea', Isabella Andreini belonged to the Intenti, with the name 'l'Acesso', and Tarquinia Molza was a member of the Innominati, as 'l'Unica'.

[183] Dafne di Piazza contributes to *Accademia di enigmi in sonetti agli accademici fiorentini, suoi amanti* (Venice: Alessi, 1552), Laura, Marta, and Onofria Bonanni contribute poems to *Rime degli accademici Accessi*, ed. Antonio Alfano (Palermo: Maida, 1571).

[184] E. Cochrane, *Italy, 1530–1630* (London: Longmans, 1988), 219.

[185] Author of *Giacob patriarca* (Pisa: Francesco delle Dote, 1637). See Weaver, 'Suor Maria', 283.

[186] These included Maria Selvaggia Borghini of Pisa, listed among those members who in the years following 1695 had often addressed the society.

[187] Attilio Maggiolo, *I soci dell'Accademia Patavina, dalla sua fondazione (1599)* (Padua: Accademia Patavina di science lettere ed arti, 1983).

[188] Five that I know of for certain: Maria Selvaggia Borghini, Anna Maria Ardoini, Diamante Medaglia Faini, Teresa Bandettini, and Cristina Roccati. The first four certainly knew Latin (Ardoini wrote in it, Borghini, Faini, and Bandettini translated from it) and were published writers, while Roccati

protection of Vittoria della Rovere, Grand Duchess of Tuscany, and the Accademia Cortesiana, Naples, named after a Marchesa Cortese. The Accademia dei Rinvigoriti also had illustrious women members in the seventeenth century.[189]

Academies varied in character. Some, notably the Accademia della Crusca of Florence, were concerned almost entirely with purifying and improving the Italian language.[190] Many were concerned to encourage verse production, both Italian and Latin.[191] Others were more essentially meeting places for philosophical debate and, as Fahy has shown, many of the activities of academies of this kind excluded or marginalized women. The Invaghiti of Mantua, who admitted no women, mounted formal lectures on subjects such as Aristotle's *Poetics*, though in carnival time they organized public lectures on subjects chosen to appeal to women: in 1658, Giulio Cesare Gonzaga set forth fifteen conclusions on love, for public debate: men who wished to speak had to declare their identity, but women were allowed to speak *incognito*—thus despite the general policy of the academy, he was prepared for this formal debate to attract women speakers.[192] Academies which admitted women regularly tended to have a different character. Burke comments on the atmosphere of the meetings of the Incogniti of Venice:[193]

Women were allowed to attend the meetings, which had an erotic, frivolous, yet learned atmosphere, not unlike that of a Paris salon of the period. The academy discussed such topics as the value of ugliness, why A is the first letter of the alphabet, and why Pythagoras objected to beans.

This suggests a space for women, but in the context of a sort of smattering, semi-intellectualism which ensured that an academy of this sort was no kind of forum for serious scholarly activity. However, another of Venice's academies, the Accademia Veneziana or Accademia della Fama, which also admitted women, was a forum for 'advanced' thought of various kinds, with strong libertine associations.[194] Another important Venetian forum for intellectual life was the private salon of Domenico Venier, a place where writers, artists, musicians, and patrician scholars met to discuss questions such as Greek, Latin, and Provençal poetic forms.[195] Venier

was awarded a Ph.D., so there is a case to be made that they were admitted as intellectuals rather than as ornaments.

[189] Maylender, *Storie delle accademie*, v, 1.

[190] Cortesio Marconcini, *L'Academia della Crusca dalle origini alla prima edizione del vocabulario* (Pisa: Valenti, 1910): no women are listed as members before 1610.

[191] Eric W. Cochrane, *Tradition and Enlightenment in the Tuscan Academies, 1690–1800* (Rome, Edizione di storia e letteratura, 1961), 19.

[192] Fahy, 'Women', 445.

[193] Peter Burke, *Venice and Amsterdam: A Study of Seventeenth-Century Elites* (Cambridge: Polity Press, 1994), 81.

[194] Lina Bolzoni, 'Rendere visibile il sapere: l'Accademia Veneziana fra modernità e utopia', and Iain Fenlon, 'Zarlino and the Accademia Venetiana', both in D. S. Chambers and F. Quiviger (eds.), *Italian Academies of the Sixteenth Century* (London: Warburg Institute, 1995), 61–75, 79–89. The Venetian academy, though its first programme was concerned with editing and translating classical texts, was sidetracked by members' interests which included religious ecumenism and the Hermetic tradition.

[195] Margaret F. Rosenthal, *The Honest Courtesan: Veronica Franco, Citizen and Writer in Sixteenth-Century Venice* (Chicago: University of Chicago Press, 1992, 177–8).

offered his protection and advice to a number of women poets and intellectuals, who included Moderata Fonte, Irene di Spilimbergo, Veronica Gàmbara, and Veronica Franco.[196]

At the very least, the widespread presence of women in academies, forums for the intellectual and cultural life of the locality, demonstrates that learned Italian women had a place in public, at a local level, from the sixteenth century onwards. Public speaking in certain contexts is quite obviously seen as appropriate at least to noblewomen from the mid-fifteenth century, as the number of surviving fifteenth-century orations bear witness; but the laudatory oration in Latin continued to be an arena for public performances by learned women for centuries afterwards, not all of them aristocrats. In the sixteenth century, Issicratea del Monte of Rovigo was called on for public laudations,[197] and so were the famous Olimpia Morata and the obscure Diana Corradini of Padua, Suor Cornelia Baglioni, and Isabella Sansever-ino Villanovia, Principessa of Salmo.[198] As we have already seen, the nuns of Santa Maria delle Vergine regularly produced an oratrix each time they elected a new abbess. Their fellow Venetian, the famous Elena Piscopia, of course performed in this way.[199] Carlotta Patino gave a public oration on the liberation of Vienna before the Ricovrati of Padua in 1683,[200] and her sister Gabriella similarly addressed them in 1680 on philosophy.[201] Even in the eighteenth century, women were still orating in Latin: for example, Maria Gaetana Agnesi (1718–99), who later became an internationally respected mathematician and scientist, gave a Latin oration (a translation of Gemelli's Italian original) before a local academy at the age of

[196] Ibid. 89.

[197] Issicratea del Monte, *Oratione nella congratulatione del principe Seb. Veniero*, (Venice: Dom, e G. B. Guerra, 1577), and *Seconda oratione nella congratulatione etc.* (Venice: Dom. et G. B. Guerra, 1578), 'Alla Imperatrice Maria' (widow of Maximilian II), in *Delle orationi volgarmente scritte da diversi huomini illustri de tempi nostri* (Venice: Altobello Salicato, 1584), 277ᵛ–284ᵛ. Iacobus Philippus Tomasini, *Elogia Virorum Literis et Sapientia Illustrium* (Padua: Sebastiano Sardi, 1644), 364–7 speaks of other prose essays in Latin, *De Paupertatis Laudibus* and *De Contemptu Mundanae Vanitatis*, and claims also to have seen Latin verse. She also published in Italian: two Italian poems are printed in *Corone et altre rime in tutte le lingue principali del Mondo in lode dell' illustre Sr. Luigi Ancarano di Spoleto* (Padua: Livio Ferro, 1681), 121–2, and also a 'riposta' to a poem addressed to her, p. 201. See also Vincenzo de Vit, *Dell'illustre donzella Issicratea Monti Rodigina* (Padua: Tipografio del Seminario, 1845).

[198] Morata's are printed in *Olympiae Fulviae Moratae Foeminae Doctissimae ac Plane Diuinae Orationes, Dialogi, Epistolae, Carmina, tam Latina quam Graeca* (Basel: Petrus Perna, 1562). Corradini gave a Latin oration before Cardinal Cornaro in 1586, Iacobus Philippus Tomasini, *Bibliothecae Patavinae Manuscriptae* (Udine: Nicola Schiratti, 1639), 95, Baglioni spoke before Pope Paul III, Vermiglioli, *Bibliografia degli scrittori perugini*, i. 82–3, and Villanovia recited a Latin oration in Avellino: Bandini Buti, ii. 353.

[199] 'Discorso accademico sopra la Madonna del Neve recitato nell'Accademia degli Infecondi in S. Carlo de' Catinari a die 4 agosto 1667 dall'illustrissima signora Elena Lucrezia Cornaro Piscopia', Vatican City, Biblioteca apostolica vaticana, Barberini lat. 4502, fos. 98–103.

[200] *Oratio de Liberata Civitate Vienna Habita Patavii, Prid. Kal. Nov. MDCLXXXIII, a Carola Catharina Patina, Parisina, Academica* (the page-numbers of the copy in the British Library [BL 1054 e 31] are 175–82, with no indication of what work it has been detached from: the *Biographie universelle*, 83 vols. (Paris: Michand Frères, 1811–53) xxxii. 254, states that the *Oratio* was published in Padua in 1683).

[201] *Conclusiones Philosophicae, quas Deo Dante, Tueri Conabitur Gabrielis Carola Patina, Die viii Febr. MDCLXXX Praeside Carolo Patino* (Padua: Gian-battista Pasquati, 1680).

10,[202] *Oration in which is Demonstrated that the Study of the Liberal Arts by Women is in no way Abhorrent*, which was immediately published.[203] The fact of her extreme youth at the time of this performance suggests that she was being treated as a curiosity, but she was undoubtedly taken seriously in later life: in 1749 she was offered the chair of mathematics at Bologna, an honour she refused.[204]

One academy which was particularly inclusive towards women was that of the Ricovrati of Padua, already mentioned as having welcomed Piscopia. This is probably due to one man, their president in the later seventeenth century, Charles Patin, Italianized as Patino, professor of medicine in Paris and later lecturer in medicine at the university of Padua. His enthusiasm for learned women began in the family: his wife (Madeleine, the daughter of a distinguished doctor, Pierre Hommetz) was an educated woman and taught her two daughters, the Carlotta and Gabriella Patino mentioned in the previous paragraph, as Latin orators: the family in some ways resembles that of the Morels, a century earlier.[205] Both daughters (and their mother) became members of the Ricovrati, and both daughters published extensively in Latin and Italian.[206] Many notable women were invited to join the Ricovrati, preponderantly French, which suggests the direct influence of Patin. In 1679, the year after the admission of their first woman member, Piscopia, the Ricovrati admitted Patin's elder daughter Gabriella Patino, Anne Dacier, the famous French classicist,[207] Mme Rousserau, and Marie-Jeanne Heritier de Villadon, who was known as 'le nouveau Telesille'. By the end of the century, women

---

[202] There were at least two academies in Bologna, the Ardenti and the Diffetosi.

[203] Published Milan: Joseph Richinus Malatesta, 1727, with another edition in a published debate on women's education, Giovanni Antonio Volpi, *Discorsi accademici di vari autori viventi, intorno agli studii delle donne, la maggior parte recitati nell'accademia dei Ricovrati di Padova* (Padua: Stamperia del Seminario, 1729), 93–105.

[204] Bruno Neveu, 'Doctrix et Magistra', in Colette Nativel (ed.), *Femmes savantes, savoir des femmes* (Geneva: Droz, 1999), 27–37 (p. 35). Agnesi also published *Propositiones Philosophiae, quas Crebris Disputationibus Domi Habitis Coram Clarissimis Viris Explicabat Extempore* (Milan: Joseph Richinus Malatesta, 1738) a collection of Latin essays, originally given as orations in her father's home to the groups of learned men he entertained there, and a serious mathematical work, *Instituzioni analitiche* (Milan: Regia ducal corte, 1748), which was recognized across Europe and translated into English (by John Colson, 1801) and French (by Pierre Thomas Antelmy, 1775). There are Latin and Italian letters in *Elogio storico di Donna Maria Gaetana Agnesi* (Milan: Giuseppe Galeazzi, 1799).

[205] Madeleine Patin was the author of *Riflessioni moral e cristiane ricavate dalle Epistole di S. Paolo*, published in 1680, and dedicated to Empress Eleonora of Austria (from Maggiolo, *I soci dell'Accademia Patavina*).

[206] Gabriella Patino is the author of *De Phoenice in Numismate Imper. Antonini Caracallae, Espressa Epistola*, (Venice, 1683). The *Biographie universelle*, xxxii. 254, also mentions a panegyric on Louis XIV, delivered to the Ricovrati, and *Conclusiones Philosophicae*. There is German verse quoted in Johannis Paschius, *Gynaeceum Doctum* (Wittenberg: Christian Finkel, 1701), 51, besides the Latin verse given in the Appendix. Carlotta Patino published *Relatio de Literis Apologeticis, etc.* (according to the *Biographie universelle*, xxxii. 254), *Oratio de Liberata Civitate Vienna Habita Patavii* (see n. 200 above), *Tabellae Selectae et Explicatae* (Padua: Typographia Seminarii, 1691), *Epistola ad L. Schroeckium, de Patris sui Morbo et Morte*, in Schelhorn, *Amoenitates*, xiii. 39–47, and *Qu'il faut tenir sa parole. Nouvelle hebraïque* (Amsterdam: Pierre Brunel, 1688).

[207] The daughter of Tanneguy Le Fèvre, the most influential 17th-century French Hellenist, she translated a number of classical authors, including Anacreon and Sappho. Emmanuel Bury, 'Madame Dacier', in Nativel (ed.), *Femmes savantes*, 209–20.

members included Elisabeth-Sophie de Chéron[208] and Madeleine de Scudéry,[209] as well as some Italians, including the distinguished scholar Maria Selvaggia Borghini (1654–1731): almost all the Italians listed, as well as the Frenchwomen, had a reputation as writers or poets.[210] Few of the Frenchwomen can ever have set foot in Padua, but they were recognized there, and in one case at least, a woman member actually present stood in for one who was not. Madeleine Patin notes in a letter to Charles Guyonnet du Vertron, author of *La Nouvelle Pandore*, 'Carlotta has translated into Latin verse one of the poems of the illustrious Mademoiselle de Scudéry. She has publicly read everything which you have been kind enough to send us from our Sappho.'[211] Thus, Carlotta was translating the French poems of Mlle de Scudéry (who became a Ricovrata in 1685) into Latin, always a gesture of honour towards the work thus translated. She was also acting, as it were, as a *performer* of Scudéry: though Mlle de Scudéry rarely left Paris, and never France, this learned young woman was giving readings from her work to the Ricovrati, as Scudéry would have done herself had she ever gone to Padua. This comment also suggests that de Scudéry took her position as a Ricovrata seriously, and sent contributions to be read in the Academy.

Beyond the ranks of those, like the Patino sisters, who were taught by their parents, women's access to education probably broadened in the seventeenth century. One clue to this is an edict issued by the Archbishop of Turin in 1625: 'let no priest work as physician or surgeon, or as attorney in a secular court or as notary in private transactions. Let them abstain from trade... and from *teaching women how to read, write, sing or play an instrument*...' The reality reflected by this edict is that many clerics lived in utter poverty, and did what they could to supplement their income.[212] If the wife or daughter of some noble or professional man decided she wanted to read Virgil, as did Anna Maria Ardoini, to be discussed below, she was unlikely to experience difficulty in finding a teacher. Moreover, the respectability of the hours she would necessarily spend closeted with him would be supported by his clerical status.

Some early modern noblewomen were still educated in the classical languages, as some, though not all, women of their class had been for generations, depending on local fashion, personal inclination, and parental theory. The evidence for their

---

[208] Author of a variety of works: see Ch. 12, n. 23. Her knowledge of Latin is demonstrated by her translation of a Latin poem on the Trianon by Boutard: M. de Vertron, *La Nouvelle Pandore*, 2nd edn. (Paris: Nicolas le Clerc, 1703), i. 381.

[209] The author of a series of long romances, such as *Artamenes*, a woman of 'encyclopedic culture' (Wendy Gibson, *Women in Seventeenth-Century France* (London: Routledge, 1989), 24). Dorothy McDougall, *Madeleine de Scudéry: Her Romantic Life and Death* (London: Methuen, 1938).

[210] Borghini studied Latin literature, and translated Tertullian (*Opere cattoliche morali di Tertulliano* (Rome: Fratelli Pagliarini, 1756)), and was a member of a number of academies, including the Apatisti. Ambrogio Levati, *Dizionario biografico cronologico* (Milan: Nicolò Bettoni, 1821–2), i. 111–12. M. Christianus Juncker adds that she was interested in mathematics and philosophy and composed Latin verse (*Schediasma Historicum* (Leipzig: Joh. Friedrich Gleditsch, 1692), 70). Maggiolo, *I soci dell'Accademia Patavina*, lists women members, with brief notes on their works.

[211] De Vertron, *La Nouvelle Pandore*, 408.

[212] Domenico Sella, *Italy in the Seventeenth Century* (London: Longman, 1997), 109–10.

learning is not easy to find, since their manuscripts seem seldom, if ever, to have made it into local archives, and few ventured into print, but a number are mentioned by regional historians of the late seventeenth and eighteenth centuries: Lucrezia Bebbi, for example, daughter of Conte Antonio Bebbi of Reggio Emilia, and wife of Niccolò Sassatelli. Giovanni Guasco notes that she was educated in literature by Antonio Caraffa, and very well taught in Hebrew, Greek, and Latin. He also says that she read widely in rhetoric, history, and poetry, and wrote Latin with the same facility as Italian. A long Latin poem of hers on the horrors of war addressed to the people of Reggio is printed (in part) by Guasco.[213] Her poem is interesting for its studious classicism: like one of the scholars of Byzantium, Contessa Lucrezia looks for elegant, antique periphrasis for post-classical concepts such as 'nun', 'church', 'priest', 'mass':

> Tigna ruunt, lapidesque pluunt, laquearia fumant,
>   Strata jacet fornix, rupta columna cadit.
> Hinc moesti Cives, manibus post terga revinctis,
>   Sordida limosi carceris antra colunt.
> Hic foricas quaerit: tumulis latet ille parentum,
>   Vipereis dapibus languida membra cibans.
> Hic se fluminibus subterlabentibus offert,
>   Nescio quis tutum jussit abire Deus.
> Scinduntur tabulae, quibus extant jura priorum
>   Scripta patrum, et cunctis lex metuenda reis.
> Pupilli pereunt, violantur tectaque Divum,
>   Et rapitur Vestae Virgo dicata Deae.
> Grata viro nimiùm luctanti carpitur Uxor,
>   Heu dolor, heu pietas, unguibus ora secans.
> Barbarus en gravidae crudeli pectora matris
>   Proh scelus infandum, transfigit ense ferox.
> Et dulcem spectans nutrix deplorat Alumnum,
>   Illisum tetricis tempora marmoribus.
> Occidit et mediis Flamen velut ostia Templis,
>   Dum peragit superis Orgia sacra Deis.
> Haec vobis, miseri mortales, funera Martis
>   Tristia belligeri noxia stella parit.

> Masonry falls to ruin, the stones rain down, the roofs smoke,
>   An arch lies flattened, a broken column collapses.
> And then the lamenting citizens, with their hands shackled behind their backs,
>   Go to dwell in the squalid caverns of a muddy prison.
> One man makes for the privies: another hides in the tombs of his ancestors,
>   Feeding languid limbs on feasts that are poisonous.
> One man makes an offering of himself to river-currents flowing by:
>   Some God—I know not which—has given the order for him to escape in safety.

---

[213] Guasco, *Storia letteraria del principio e progresso dell'Accademia di belle lettere in Reggio* (Reggio: Ippolito Vetrotti, 1711), 32–6, poem pp. 34–6. He mentions another local woman poet evidently of some ambition, and possibly writing in Latin, Contessa Lucia Bojarda, p. 25.

The tablets are broken, on which the judicial enactments of their forebears survived,
    And a law to be feared by all guilty parties,
Wards of court perish, and the temple-roofs of the Gods are outraged,
    The Vestal Virgin, dedicated to the Goddess, is raped.
A wife pleasing to her husband, who is struggling mightily, is snatched away,
    Tearing her cheeks with her nails—alas the sorrow, alas the devotion!.
See, a barbarian in his ferocity pierces through with his sword
    The breast of a pregnant mother—abominable atrocity!
And the nurse, looking on, bewails her sweet foster-child,
    His brains dashed out on the unyielding marble slab.
The Flamen falls like a sacrificial victim in the midst of the temples
    While he is engaged in the sacred Feast for the Gods above.
These, wretched mortals, are the grievous death-rites
    Which the noxious star of war-bringing Mars brings to you.

The whole poem is both graphic and highly formal, reminiscent of nothing so much as one of the numerous Renaissance paintings of classical battles, with a strong focus on the horrors of war as they affect women and children. Similarly, the existence, and learning, of Falamisca di Monte, from Canzano in the Abruzzi, who studied Latin and Greek and wrote a long poem in praise of the city of Altri, is dependent on Niccolò Toppi, who records the first ten lines of her work,[214] and the Latinity of Gironda Cerrini of Perugia is witnessed only by the fact that she was invited to contribute to a necrology on the death of a local notable.[215]

The Sicilian Anna Maria Ardoini (1672–1700) is a baroque woman Latinist with an unusually high public profile—like Bebbi, a noblewoman. She was born in Messina, a member of the ruling family, and was scholarly in her interests from youth. She originally decided she wanted to learn Latin in order to read the *Aeneid* in the original, but in fact became so familiar with the language as actually to imitate Virgil. She married the lord of Piombino, Giovanni Battista Ludovisi, in 1697 but was widowed within the year, after which she governed independently. She was a member of the Roman Academic of the Arcadi, which, by the late seventeenth century, admitted a number of women writers. She used Latin (like some Renaissance women poets) for public, political verse (her *Rosa Parnassi* was published in Naples in 1687, and consists mostly of verse in Latin addressed to figures in the circle of Joseph, Grand Duke of Austria[216]), while she used Italian for an opera written for performance at her home in Piombino and published in Rome.[217] It is worth observing that, while the learned women of the fifteenth

---

[214] Niccolo Toppi, *Biblioteca Napoletana* (Naples: Antonio Bulifon, 1688), i. 80.

[215] *In Funere Iosephi A Giaceto Castelvillani Comitis &c. Oratio Felicis Verduccioli* (Perugia: Typographia Episcopali, 1643), 30–1. A number of Italian writings survive: she wrote a sacred opera, *Il trionfo di s. Filippo Neri, dramma per musica*, of which the MS is or was in the Oratorio of Perugia, and a poem, 'Sopra le girate che si fanno per la Cappelle di Santa Maria degli Angeli, canzone', in da Bettona, *Trattato dell'indulgentia plenaria*, 19–22.

[216] My thanks to Michael Wyatt for looking at the only known copy for me in Naples.

[217] *Li rivali generosi, dramma per musica da recitarsi nel giardino Ludovisio, composta da donne Anna Maria Ardoini Ludovisi, Principessa di Piombino, fra gl'Arcadi, Getilde Faresia* (Rome: Campana, 1697).

century cluster in north Italy and the Veneto, by the seventeenth century, the fashion for women's education was pan-Italian: it had even spread to regions of the extreme south often represented as wild and uncivilized, such as Sicily and the Abruzzi.

In the eighteenth century, in Italy as elsewhere in Europe, the salon offered women a new kind of public space. As Adriana Chemello has shown, eighteenth-century Venice had its *salonnières* as well as Paris, elegant and cultivated upper-class women such as Isabella Teotochi Albrizzi and Giustina Renier Michel: one of the earliest such salons, which had a man as president (Domenico Venier), has already been mentioned.[218] There were also still women intellectuals in Venice, notably Luisa Gozzi, née Bergalli, who was taught Latin by Antonio Sforza. Bergalli published a series of translations of the plays of Terence in Venice from 1727 to 1731, and also collected and edited *Componimenti poetici delle più illustri rimatrici d'ogni secolo*, published in two volumes in Venice in 1726, an anthology of poems and miscellaneous compositions by about 250 female poets from the thirteenth to the eighteenth century, making her one of the first women concerned to recover women's writing from previous eras. She was facilitated in doing so by her close intellectual ties with the outstanding Venetian scholars of her day, Apostolo Zeno, Alvise Mocenigo, and Antonio Sforza, who allowed her access to the vast Marciana and Soranzo libraries, and Zeno's own substantial collections.[219]

As Ricuperati has observed, the intellectual life of eighteenth-century Italy was less negligible than is sometimes thought.[220] An anonymous member of the Intronati insisted in 1740 that Italy was just as well stocked with learned women as ever, and there is a surprising amount of evidence to support his view.[221] Women poets, writers, and intellectuals continued to be found in all parts of Italy; such as Diamante Faini Medaglia of Brescia,[222] Vittoria Galeotti of Naples, Oliva Cocchi of Livorno, and Francesca Manzoni Giusto of Milan,[223] all published poets, who all had some acquaintance with Latin. A Roman woman whose name suggests French origins, Susanna le Maitre (1718–98), left seventy Latin letters, besides translations from Latin and Greek, and made two academy orations in

[218] Chemello, 'Literary Critics and Scholars, 1700–1850', in Panizza and Wood (eds.), *A History*, 135–48 (pp. 139–41).

[219] Ibid, 135–7.

[220] Giuseppe Ricuperati, 'The Renewal of the Dialogue between Italy and Europe: Intellectuals and Cultural Institutions from the End of the Seventeenth Century to the First Decades of the Eighteenth Century', in Dino Carpenetto and Giuseppe Ricuperati, *Italy in the Age of Reason* (London: Longman, 1987), 78–95 (pp. 80, 123).

[221] *Trattato degli studi delle donne, in due parti diviso, opera d'un'accademico intronato* (Venice: Francesco Pitteri, 1740), ii. 34.

[222] She published *Versi e prose di Diamante Faini Medaglia* (Salò: Bartolomeo Righetti, 1774), which includes Latin translations (pp. 98–101), she was a member of several academies, the Unanimi of Salò, the Ordini of Padua, and the Agiati of Roveredo, and was accepted as a member of the local literati: see Antonio Brognoli, *Elogi di Bresciani per dottrina excelenti del secolo xviii* (Brescia: Pietro Vescovi, 1735), 257–74. Her concerns also extended to mathematics: see Margaret Alic, *Hypatia's Heritage* (London: Women's Press, 1986), 135.

[223] On these three, see Bandini Buti, i. 284, 160, and Sarah Josepha Hale, *Woman's Record* (New York: Harper & Brothers, 1860), 401.

Latin.[224] Other eighteenth-century Italian women who translated from Latin or
Greek include Maria Selvaggia Borghini (1654–1731),[225] who also wrote Latin
verse, according to Ménage,[226] Francesca Manzoni Giusto (d. 1743), who trans-
lated Ovid's *Tristiae*,[227] Luisa Gozzi Bergalli (1703–79), translator of Terence, and
Fortunate Sulge Fantastici (1755–1817), who translated Anacreon. It is also interesting to find an Italian woman, Eleonora Barbapiccola of Salerno, translating
Descartes.[228] Two eighteenth-century women members of the Arcadi, Caterina
Borghini ('Erato Dionea') and Caterina Imperiale ('Arsinda Poliades'), published
Latin poems in the two-volume *Arcadum Carmina* of 1756–7. Borghini was the
niece of Maria Selvaggia Borghini, who had been educated and brought up by her;
she wrote considerable quantities of Latin verse in the manner of Tibullus.[229] The
last known Arcadian woman Latin poet, Enrica Dionigi ('Aurilla Gnidio'), flourished as late as 1808.[230] Learned women continued to be admired in some circles
within Italy: it is interesting to find that a Bolognese nobleman, Senatore Conte
Gioseffo Filippo Calderini, maintained a collection of portraits of the learned
ladies of Bologna in the early eighteenth century.[231] Maria Petronilla Caboni (b.
1749), a nun of the Congregation of the Immaculate Conception in Ascoli,
published a Latin dissertation on a legal topic, *De Jure Christi Domini ad Regnum
Temporale Judaeorum* ('The Right of the Lord Jesus over the Temporal Kingdom
of the Jews'), in 1774, but the contemporary notice of this suggests that the
dissertation was written as an exercise rather than to earn her a doctorate.[232]
Like other early modern learned women, she disputed formally against men.[233]

While it might seem that the intellectual opportunities open to outstanding Italian
women declined towards the level set by other European countries in the course of the

[224] Anon. (ed.), *Bibliografia Romana I* (Rome: Eredi Botta, 1880), 149.

[225] Levati, *Dizionario*, i. 111–12. She translated Tertullian, *Opere cattoliche morali di Tertulliano*
(Rome: Fratelli Paglianini, 1756), and was a member of a number of academies, including the Apatisti.

[226] Gilles de Ménage's 'Lezzione d'Egidio Menagio sopra'l sonetto VII di Messer Francesco
Petrarca' first printed in his *Mescolanze* of 1678, is also in Ménage, *Historia Mulierum Philosopharum*
(Lyon: Anisson, J. Posnel and C. Rigaud, 1690), where 'Lezzione' is printed (separately paginated), after
the main work: pp. 58–74 comprises a study of learned women. My thanks to Richard Maber for
clarifying this (NB, the Amsterdam edition of *Historia Mulierum Philosopharum* (Henricus Wetstenius,
1692) does not include this appendix).

[227] *I cinque libri delle tristezze di Publio Ovidio Nasone, tradotti da una pastorella arcade* (Milan: Regio
Ducae Palazzo, 1745).

[228] Fachini, *Prospetto biografico delle donne italiane*, 172.

[229] Francesco Clodoveo Maria Pentolini, *Le donne illustre* (Livorno: Gio. Vincenzo Falorni, 1776),
i. 232.

[230] Like earlier women Latinists, she was evidently an object of interest from very early in her life:
Pesaro, Biblioteca Oliveriana, 1908.III.6 preserves 'primi versi di Enrichietta Dionigi Romana nell'età di
circo anni dieci' (in Italian).

[231] Pellegrino Antonio Orlandi, *Notizie degli scrittori bolognesi* (Bologna: Constantino Pisarri, 1714),
94. The set of engraved playing cards by Giovanni Palazzi (1681) depicting famous aristocratic and
citizen women writers and patrons of Venice, now in Venice, Biblioteca Civico Correr, seems to be
similarly an expression of local pride and interest in women worthies.

[232] *Efemeridi letterarie di Roma*, iii (Rome: Libreria all'Insegna d'Omero al Corso, 1774), 196–8. Her
dissertation was published by Joannes Leonardi de Monte Alto, 1774. Interestingly, she was one of four
sisters all of whom were educated in Latin, rhetoric, and dialectic as well as sacred studies.

[233] *Efemeridi*, 197.

eighteenth century, there is one Italian institution which stands out as exceptional. The receptivity of the University of Bologna in the eighteenth century towards outstandingly able and educated women is noteworthy, especially given that the contemporary Venetian Luisa Bergalli laments 'that almost universal preconception that we women have no ability to make our mark in the arts'.[234] It would occur to few to enquire whether this precluded women making a mark in the sciences;[235] but while the University of Padua was not persuaded to renew the experiment after laureating Piscopia in the seventeenth century, the University of Bologna took a more progressive attitude.[236] Laura Bassi (1711–78) became a doctor of philosophy of Bologna, and published two Latin dissertations on mechanics and hydraulics.[237] Cristina Roccati (b. 1732) also took a Ph.D. at Bologna,[238] while Maddalena Canedi Noè was admitted as a doctor of law of Bologna in 1807.[239]

Maria Gaetana Agnesi (1718–99) was invited to join the faculty of mathematics at Bologna but refused,[240] but Anna Morandi Mazolini (1716–74) held the chair of anatomy from 1760 as successor to her husband, and was famous for her wax models, many of which survive. She made original discoveries in anatomy, and was also offered the chair of anatomy at Milan.[241] Still another woman, Zaffira Fenetti Bagnocavallo (1785–1817), learned Greek and Latin, studied surgery at Bologna, was laureated by the medical faculty, and became a surgeon.[242] Even more

[234] Quoted by Chemello, 'Literary Critics', 135. The later Pietro Rosati's *In Mulieres Litteratas, Carmen Interamnatis in Certamine Poetico Hoefftiano* (Amsterdam: Joh. Muller, 1897), jocularly paranoid, suggests by contrast that women are making all too much of an impact in the world of letters: it opens, 'Alas, watch out, men! take care, look to what is yours, concealed fire lurks in the ashes!' ('Heus vigilate, viri, heus, agitur res vestra, cavete suppositus cineri latet ignis'), and makes the point that 19th-century women continued to write in Greek and Latin (though he thinks they should not), p. 9.

[235] In addition to the women associable with Bologna, it is also interesting to recall Diamante Faini Medaglia, mentioned above, n. 222, and the much earlier Theodora Danti of Perugia (1498–1573), who studied astronomy, and is said to have written both poetry and a commentary on Euclid: Vermiglioli, *Bibliografia degli scrittori perugini*, i. 366 (he had not seen copies; but her astronomer nephew Egnatio Danti acknowledges her handsomely as his teacher in mathematics and astronomy in his translation *La Sfera di Messer Giovanni Sacrobosco* (Florence: Giunti, 1571), suggesting that her reputation for learning was soundly based), and Maria Marcina Columna, who printed a *Discorso astrosofico delle mutatione de' tempi* in 1672 according to Mondosio, *Bibliotheca Romana*, ii. 236–7.

[236] Recently studied: *Alma Mater Studiorum: la presenza femminile dal xviii al xx secolo. richerche sul rapporta donna e cultura universitaria nell'Ateneo Bolognese* (Bologna: CLUEB, 1989).

[237] E. Melli, 'Laura Bassi Veratti: ridiscussioni e nuovi spunti', ibid. 71–9. Bassi was given the right to teach as professor, but not in public (an awkward compromise), and was offered the chair of experimental physics in 1776.

[238] de Vit, *Dell'illustre donzella Issicratea Monti Rodigina* 22. Roccati took a doctorate in Bologna, studied in Padua, and was a member of six academies. Pietro Leopoldo Ferri, *Biblioteca femminile italiana* (Padua: Crescini, 1842), 311, saw twelve of her Latin letters and two in Italian. She also wrote Latin verse. There is an oration in her praise by Giuseppe Grotto, *Delle lode della dottoressa Cristina Roccati* (Venice: Fracasso, 1815). She taught physics at the Scientific Institute of Rovigo (Alic, *Hypatia's Heritage*, 135).

[239] Hale, *Woman's Record*, 761.

[240] Neveu, 'Doctrix et Magistra', 35. See note 204 above. Alic, *Hypatia's Heritage*, 136–7, quotes a French traveller whose account of Agnesi indicates that she performed the woman scholar just as Piscopia had once done, speaking formally in Latin.

[241] Alic, *Hypatia's Heritage*, 104.

[242] Fachini, *Prospetto biografica*, 216–17. Pentolini, *Le donne illustre*, i. 114–15, gives a reference to *Efemeridi letterarie*, xxv. 1774.

unusually, Clotilde Tambroni became professor of Greek, and delivered an oration in Latin at the inauguration of a female colleague, Maria Dalle-Donne (1776–1842), professor of obstetrics. Like a number of contemporary Englishwomen versed in classical languages, Tambroni tended to produce parallel versions of her compositions: those she published were in Greek and Italian.[243] She was certainly a member of an academy, since she had an Arcadian name, Doriclea Sicionia.[244] Dalle-Donne herself is also credited with Latin verse: 'she excelled in writing both Latin and Italian verses, but of this accomplishment she thought so lightly that she never kept any copies of her production.'[245] It is worth posing the question whether the hospitability of eighteenth-century Bologna towards women scholars was influenced by the fantasies of the Bolognese lawyer Carlo Antonio Macchiavelli, who marked a contemporary attempt to gain a doctorate by another would-be woman lawyer, Maria Vittoria Dolfin Dosia, with an almost wholly fictitious account of the medieval women *cathedratica* of Bologna, lavishly referenced to non-existent documents, which was widely circulated and accepted as factual, and therefore led the eighteenth-century Bolognese themselves to believe that they already had a 500-year-long history of women faculty members.[246]

Perhaps the last Italian woman Latin poet before the universities began opening to women is Luisa Angoletti (1863–1925). She learned Greek and Latin from her uncle Emmanuele Bazzanello, and composed Latin distichs on the death of Giovanni Battista Zanella in 1884. In the following year, she wrote a Latin poem in 561 hexameters. Her career was, however, as a pianist, accompanying her violinist brother.[247] Thus even in the nineteenth century, a few Italian woman were still taught Latin, either as a result of their own inclination, or because a classical education was the tradition of their family.

---

[243] Her published works include *Ode pindarica greco-italiana* (Bologna, 1793), *Ode saffica greca e italiana* (Parma: Bodoniani, 1794), *Elegia greca* (Parma: Reale tipografia, 1795) (Ferri, *Biblioteca femminile*, 357–8).

[244] Levati, *Dizionario*, iii. 173–4, and see also the printed memorial sermon by Filippo Schiassi, *Sermo habitus in Archiginnasio Bononiensi xii Kal. Iulii, a. mdcccvii* (Bologna, 1817).

[245] Hale, *Woman's Record*, 876: she was born in Roncastaldo, near Bologna, and was taught Latin on the instigation of her uncle, a priest. She took a medical degree at Bologna on 1 Aug. 1799, and subsequently became professor of obstetrics.

[246] Carlo Antonio Macchiavelli, *Bitisia Gozzadina* (Bologna: G. B. Blanco, 1722). Roversi, *Donne celebre della Emilia-Romagna*, 128–9, warns that Macchiavelli and his brother Alessandro (who were both lawyers), in addition to the work already cited, published a variety of learned works in Latin under the name of their sister Maria Elisabetta Macchiavelli.

[247] Bandini Buti, i. 41.

12. *French Women Latinists in the 'Grand Siècle'*

In France, it is not the case that Latin poets went unadmired by an élite of learned women: Madame de Sévigné, Madame de la Fayette, la duchesse de Bouillon, la Grande Dauphine, Elisabeth de Rochechouart, abbess of Fontevrault, mademoiselle du Pré, mademoiselle de Serment, mademoiselle Chéron, etc. Many of them composed Latin verses themselves, which would be not uninteresting to study; but they ought to be the subject of a special work.[1]

If I may be forgiven for starting a chapter on a personal note, of all the trying moments in the history of a project which has had its fair share of setbacks, reading this sentence in the Abbé Vissac's *De la poésie latine* was perhaps the most purely tantalizing.

French culture in the seventeenth century took place almost entirely in French, to an extent which was unusual within Europe. By 1600, French was a language increasingly deemed sufficient for any requirements: the establishment of the Académie Française, like some of the Italian academies, was an enterprise aimed at raising the vernacular to classic status by refining, purifying, and regulating it (a similar enterprise was undertaken in Germany in the eighteenth century). At the end of the sixteenth century in France, less than 25 per cent of all books printed were in Latin, and this figure continued to decline until by 1764, ancient and foreign languages together accounted for only 4.5 per cent of literary production.[2] The 'time of translations', a phrase of Henri-Jean Martin's, and applied by him to the mid-seventeenth century, is less a time than an era, which began then, but has not yet come to an end, nor is now likely to.[3] There is an astonishing amount of translation from Latin into French in the seventeenth century, some of it by women, so much so that, by the mid-century, access to all classical texts of importance could be achieved without the trouble of learning Latin or Greek.[4]

The cultural dominance of French, not merely in France but in Europe more generally, is witnessed by a letter sent from John Norris, a philosopher sympathetic to women's learning, to the bluestocking poet Elizabeth Thomas (1675–1731) with a sort of curriculum, in which he says: 'for some of them [the authors mentioned] there will be a Necessity of a Language or two, Latin is more difficult, and French will now answer all, which therefore I would have you learn out of Hand. It is the most commanding, and therefore most useful Language at present.'[5] In fact, Elizabeth

---

[1] J.-A. Vissac, *De la poésie latine en France au siècle de Louis XIV* (Paris: A. Durand, 1862), 224–5.
[2] Françoise Waquet, *Latin: Or the Empire of a Sign*, trans. John Howe (London: Verso, 2000) 81.
[3] H.-J. Martin, *Livre, pouvoir et société à Paris au xviie siècle (1598–1701)* (Geneva: Droz, 1969), 607.
[4] Waquet, *Latin*, 176.
[5] Ruth Perry, *The Celebrated Mary Astell* (Chicago: University of Chicago Press, 1986), 484–5 n. 60.

Thomas decided to learn both,[6] but most women did not. The only place where French was resisted was in the field of professional diplomacy, where the political neutrality of Latin had its own kind of value: a tract setting out the rules of diplomatic engagement between England and France in the early seventeenth century states that 'English monarchs have the power to treat with our Kings in Latin, and to send their instructions in the same language', according to a statute passed in 1413 and still considered relevant, and notes that many other nations do the same, 'since Latin is the common language of most of the Princes and Christian States of Europe'.[7] It was only in the nineteenth century that French took over as the essential language of diplomacy.[8]

It is easy to conclude from these facts that Latin was entirely abandoned as a literary language in seventeenth-century France. Vissac's learned book, with which this chapter began, is a study aimed at demonstrating that this was not the case: as he is able to show, scores of French writers, preponderantly church-men, wrote Latin verse. It also seems evident from what he says in the sentence quoted at the head of the chapter that he had seen Latin verse by a variety of Frenchwomen, that he considers it sufficient at least in quantity to justify an 'ouvrage spécial': it is particularly regrettable, therefore, that such a work was never written, either by himself or anyone else.

Another important feature of French society in the seventeenth century is the cultural and political significance of women, which contrived to coexist with institutionalized misogyny. Female literacy was more widespread in France even than in Italy (despite the fact that elite Italian women wrote so much more).[9] The prominence of women at the highest level of early modern French politics begins with Anne de Beaujeu, regent for her brother Charles VIII, and Catherine de Médicis, regent for several of her sons, in the sixteenth century, and continues down to Marie de Médicis, regent for Louis XIII, and Anne of Austria, regent for Louis XIV, in the seventeenth.[10] For a country proud to maintain the Salic law which debarred women from the succession, France was actually ruled by women for a surprising proportion of the time between 1500 and the Revolution. Other women, mostly noble, played a significant role in statecraft and diplomacy, and, during the Fronde, even in civil revolt.[11] The seventeenth century is also the age of the salons, and of the *précieuses*: other women, some noble, some from the professional classes, played an equally important part in the history of literature and criticism.[12] A substantial number of the most significant arbiters of taste—such

---

[6] Roger Lonsdale (ed.), *Eighteenth-Century Women Poets* (Oxford: Oxford University Press, 1990), 32.

[7] Paris, Bibliothèque Nationale de France, Dupuy 33, fos. 313^r–335^v, (fo. 332^{r-v}).

[8] Waquet, *Latin*, 97.

[9] Charmarie J. Blaisdell, 'Angela Merici and the Ursulines', in R. L. de Molen (ed.), *Religious Orders of the Catholic Reformation* (New York: Fordham University Press, 1994), 98–136.

[10] Wendy Gibson, *Women in Seventeenth-Century France* (London: Routledge, 1989), 1–2.

[11] Wendy Gibson, *A Tragic Farce: The Fronde* (Exeter: Elm Bank Publications, 1998).

[12] On elite women in 17th-century France, see Ian MacLean, *Woman Triumphant* (Oxford: Clarendon Press, 1977), Caroline Lougee, *Le Paradis du femmes: Women, Salons and Social Stratification in Seventeenth-Century France* (Princeton: Princeton University Press, 1976), Linda Timmermans, *L'Accès*

as the Marquise de Rambouillet and Mme de Sévigné—were women. The fact that, as we shall see, Latin writing by Frenchwomen in the baroque period is a phenomenon of little cultural significance, except for the formal respect which continues to be accorded to Latinity, is perhaps more a testimony to the declining fortunes of Latin than to the cultural insignificance of elite women.

The list of names given by Vissac forms a possible starting point. Mme de Sévigné is well known as a hostess, *salonnière*, and writer of letters, but it is not directly obvious from what she wrote that she read Spanish, Italian, and Latin.[13] She was devoted to her daughter, and her family tradition was clearly one in which women learned Latin, since her brilliant granddaughter, Mme de Simiane, published imitations both of poems from the *Greek Anthology*, and of the Latin verse of Joannes Secundus.[14] Mme de Sévigné's friend Mme de Lafayette, author of perhaps the first important French novel, *La Princesse de Clèves*, was a vastly cultivated woman known to have a good understanding of Latin. She received Latin letters from Gilles Ménage and may have replied in kind: 'one of his Latin letters [to her] is entirely taken up with pedantic details of editions of Ovid' (which he presumably believes she is capable of taking an interest in), while another Latin note of 1661 includes the words 'Tu ad me rescribe, Gallicè saltem, si Latinè non potes' ('write back to me, in French at least, if you cannot do it in Latin'), which implies that he believed her capable of writing a Latin letter but not fluently or quickly.[15] The Grande Dauphine was the melancholy, delicate, and religious Marie-Anne-Christine-Victoire de Bavière, sister of the Elector of Bavaria and therefore a Wittelsbach, which is to say, a member of a highly cultivated family which, in the seventeenth century, gave a number of its daughters a literary education.[16] Elisabeth de Rochechouart (born Marie-Madeleine-Gabrielle de Rochechouart-Mortemart) was the sister of Louis XIV's witty mistress Mme de Montespan, and became a highly academic abbess, with a thorough knowledge of Latin, Italian, and Spanish, who learned enough Greek to produce a good translation of Plato's *Symposium* using Ficino's Latin version as an aid.[17] Mlle Du Pré was taught Latin by her uncle Desmarets de Saint-Sorlin, a member of the Académie Française, was devoted to Cartesian philosophy,[18] and corresponded

des femmes à la culture (1598–1715): un débat d'idées de saint François de Sales à la marquise de Lambert, Bibliothèque Littéraire de la Renaissance, série 3, 26 (Paris: Champion, 1993).

13 Fortunée B. Briquet, *Dictionnaire historique, littéraire, et bibliographique* (Paris: de Gille, 1804), 311.

14 Pauline de Grignan, Mme de Simiane (1674–1737), a lady-in-waiting to the Duchess of Orléans. She was held brilliant in her early years, and published imitations of poems from the *Greek Anthology*, 9. 440, 455; 16. 160. See James Hutton, *The Greek Anthology in France* (Ithaca, NY: Cornell University Press, 1946), 309–10. She published a volume called *Porte-feuille de Madame* ***, *contenant diverses odes, idyles, et sonnets, des imitations de Jean Second, l'histoire du cœur de Loulou et autres opuscules* (Paris, 1715).

15 Richard Maber, 'Scholars and Friends: Gilles Ménage and his Correspondents', *Seventeenth Century*, 10.2 (1992), 255–76 (p. 266).

16 See Friedrich Schmidt, *Geschichte der Erziehung der Pfältzischen Wittelsbacher*, Monumenta Germaniae Paedagogica XIX (Berlin: A. Hofmann, 1899), 286, and Cornelia Niekus Moore, *The Maiden's Mirror* (Wiesbaden: Otto Harrassowitz, 1987), 47–9.

17 *Nouvelle Biographie générale*, 46 vols., (Paris: Firmin-Didot, 1852–66), xlii.

18 This is significant, since Descartes's thesis that mind, as a single immaterial substance, was necessarily identical in both genders was understandably attractive to women: he was supported in

with the writers Madeleine de Scudéry and Mlle de La Vigne.[19] Louise Anastasie de Serment (1642–92) certainly wrote poetry in French, and is said to have collaborated with Quinault on his operas.[20] Elisabeth-Sophie Chéron (1648–1711) was primarily a professional painter, daughter of the miniaturist Henri Chéron, but was also known as a musician and poet: her Latinity is demonstrated by her translation of a Latin poem by the Abbé Boutard called *Trianaeum* (i.e, on the Trianon at Versailles).[21]

It is worth pausing a little over Elisabeth-Sophie Chéron. She was highly educated, and the product of a mixed marriage; her mother was Catholic, her father Protestant. Her father abandoned his family when she was only 16, and she became a professional painter in order to support her mother, her younger siblings, and herself.[22] She was also known as a musician, wrote poetry and essays, and was a member of the Académie Royale and the Ricovrati of Padua, in both institutions as a poet rather than a painter.[23] While she did not make a living directly from her Latinity, her high personal culture was, so to say, part of her stock-in-trade, or of her mystique as a *femme d'esprit*, part of what earned her royal patronage. She was not merely selling her pictures, but the fact that she was herself an interesting person and worth meeting, and the 500l. pension she was awarded by Louis XIV was a reward for her social standing, not simply for her ability as a painter. In later life, she learned Hebrew in order to translate Old Testament poetry, and married Jacques Le Hay, the King's Engineer, when she was 44.[24] To sum up, the available evidence for these women, who were, with the exception of de Chéron, both aristocratic and wealthy, suggests that they were people of the highest cultivation. While that does not prove that they wrote Latin verse, or were capable of so doing, it makes Vissac's claim on their behalf at the least a plausible one.

Some voices in seventeenth-century France still spoke up for the education of women, notably Poullain de la Barre, a Cartesian who took the radical view that women would be perfectly capable of holding posts in institutions such as the

---

his own time by Elizabeth von der Pfalz and Queen Christina of Sweden, and subsequently influenced a wide variety of women with philosophical interests.

[19] *Nouvelle Biographie générale*, xv, cols. 362–3. She is the author of *Réponses d'Iris à Climène*, published by Dominique Bonhours in *Recueil de vers choisis* (Paris: George & Louis Josse, 1693).

[20] Sarah Josepha Hale, *Woman's Record* (New York: Harper & Brothers, 1860), 500; source unstated, Frances Yates, *The French Academies of the Sixteenth Century* (London: Warburg Institute, 1947), 301, notes that Quinault was very much part of the world of the French academies, and if he was collaborating with Serment, also an academician, this is of interest.

[21] M. de Vertron, *La Nouvelle Pandore* (Paris: Nicolas le Clerc, 1703), i. 381.

[22] *Nouvelle Biographie générale*. x, cols. 223–4.

[23] She published *Essay des psaumes et cantiques mis en vers et enrichis de figures par Mlle *** (Paris, 1694), in 8º, with 25 plates engraved by her brother Louis Chéron, and *Livre à dessins* (Paris, 1796) (model drawings from the Old Masters). Two other books were published after her death, *Cantique d'Habacuc et le Pseaume 103, en vers français* (1714) and *Les Cerises renversées*, published in 1717 with Boivin's translation of *Batrychomachia*. It is interesting that she seems also to have translated part of one of the early German pro-women tracts, that of Johannes Frawenlob (Paris, Bibliothèque de l'Arsenal, 6591, fos 59ʳ–60ᵛ). There is also a life of Chéron in this MS, fos. 61ʳ–63ᵛ.

[24] Briquet, *Dictionnaire*, 199–202, Germaine Greer, *The Obstacle Race* (London: Secker and Warburg, 1979), 72–4.

Church, the army, and the judicature, since the difference of gender was a purely physical matter.[25] The arguments which he raised were still alive in the mid-eighteenth century: in 1753, Philippe Joseph Caffiaux attempted to revive Poullain's work, which he declared to have had too little effect in altering opinion.[26] The cultural trend, however, was in quite another direction: it was Fénelon rather than de la Barre who was the quoted authority on girls' education to subsequent generations in France, and though he suggested a wide reading syllabus for girls, his focus was on religious and moral education.[27]

However, there is also evidence for continued cultivation of Latin among seventeenth-century Frenchwomen beyond the pages of Vissac. One French woman classicist became internationally famous, Anne Dacier, daughter of Tanneguy Le Fèvre, the most influential French Hellenist of the early seventeenth century. She read and translated Latin, Greek, and Italian, and was particularly noted for her translations of Homer, Anacreon, and Sappho.[28] She was born *c*.1647, the eldest of her parents' five children and the only girl—perhaps reason enough for her to be educated with her brothers without evoking the legend that her father began to teach her when she piped up to correct one of her brothers while engaged in the feminine occupation of sewing in a corner of the schoolroom.[29] Tanneguy Le Fèvre had pioneered a distinctive and successful pedagogic method, which aimed at interesting the child by approaching the subject playfully, and perhaps wished to see how it worked with a girl. Her early works are signed 'Tanaquilli Fabri Filia', suggesting a strong identity as the daughter of her father, which is also found in a number of more or less contemporary learned women whose fathers were educators, such as Johanna Otho and Bathsua Rainolds.

Though she met Dacier, the man by whose name she is generally known, at an early age since he was a pupil of her father's, her first marriage was to Jean Lesnier, a printer-bookseller from a line of printer-booksellers in Saumur, who printed some of her father's works. This marriage occurred by 1664, and Sainte-Beuve notes that it was not a happy one. There was a son, who was born and died in 1669, and the marriage seems to have ended around 1670. When Tanneguy Le Fèvre died in 1672, his daughter joined Dacier in Paris. Of her three children, the eldest, Marie, was born in Saumur in 1670 or 1671, and seems therefore most likely to be

[25] François Poullain de La Barre, *De l'égalité des deux sexes* (Paris, 1673). He does not, however, argue that the status quo should be altered to allow this to occur. Gibson, *Women*, 18–19. See also François Poullain de La Barre, *Three Cartesian Feminist Treatises*, trans. Vivien Bosley (Chicago: Chicago University Press, 2002).

[26] Philippe-Joseph Caffiaux, *Défenses du beau sexe* (Amsterdam: Aux dépens de la compagnie, 1757).

[27] François de Salignac de La Mothe Fénelon, *Education des filles* (Paris: Pierre Abouin, 1687). See further Jean H. Bloch, 'Women and the Reform of the Nation', in Eva Jacobs et al. (eds.), *Women and Society in Eighteenth-Century France: Essays in Honour of John Stephenson Spink* (London: Athlone Press, 1979), 3–18 (p. 3).

[28] Emmanuel Bury, 'Madame Dacier', in Colette Nativel (ed.), *Femmes savantes, savoir des femmes* (Geneva: Droz, 1999), 209–20, and Susanna van Dijk, 'Madame Dacier jugée par les journalistes: femme ou savante?', in *Traces des femmes: présence féminine dans le journalisme français du xviiie siècle* (Amsterdam-Maarsen: APA Holland UP 1988), 191–225.

[29] Bury, 'Madame Dacier', 211.

the child of Lesnier. A son was born in 1684, and a second daughter in 1693. She seems to have married Dacier on 4 November 1683, perhaps in consequence of the eventual death of her husband, her conversion to Catholicism (her earlier Protestantism would have put difficulties in the way of a legal marriage), the incipient birth of her son, or all three.[30]

Apart from Anne Dacier, there were other Frenchwomen who translated from Latin. Françoise-Marguerite de Joncoux translated the Latin notes of Pascal's *Lettres provinciales*,[31] a Mlle Ramies translated some *Odes* of Horace into French verse,[32] as did both Mlle de Castille,[33] and the better-known Antoinette de Ligier de La Garde, Mme Deshoulières.[34] Further evidence that Mme Deshoulières read Latin is found in a Latin poem addressed to her by Gilles Ménage in 1687 (Ménage has already been encountered, above, encouraging Mme de Lafayette to write Latin prose), titled 'Mademoiselle Deshoulières, victor in a contest of poets'.[35] His verses reflect her victory in a poetic *certamen* set by the Académie Française on the unpromising subject of 'the interest which the king takes in the education of his nobility, at home and at Saint-Cyr'. This was evidently a notable victory, since apart from being hailed by Ménage, it is noted as far afield as Germany.[36] Saint-Cyr, incidentally, was a school for young noblewomen, founded by Louis XIV and his morganatic wife Mme de Maintenon, who had herself been taught Latin, Spanish, and Italian by the husband of her youth, the poet Paul Scarron.

Jean-Louis Guez de Balzac, generally no admirer of learned women, wrote a poem to a contemporary, Mme Desloges, which directly implies she studied, and perhaps wrote in, Italian, Latin, and Greek.[37] He congratulates her for 'hiding her knowledge like a theft', a compliment which goes some way towards explaining why it is so hard to find out about highly educated women in early modern France.[38] A slightly earlier woman, Barbe Porquini, Dame Rolly (d. 1620), who was Italian by ancestry, but born in Liège, is credited with a Latin work called *Hortus Animae*, and another work, also in Latin, on the influence of women on the

[30] Ibid. 214.

[31] F. Ellen Weaver, 'Erudition, Spirituality and Women: the Jansenist contribution', in Sherrin Marshall (ed.), *Women in Reformation and Counter-Reformation Europe* (Bloomington: Indiana University Press, 1989) 189–206 (p. 200).

[32] 'Voïes son eloge dans le Mercure de mais 1681'. de Vertron, *La Nouvelle Pandore*.

[33] L.-P., *Répertoire universel, historique, biographique des femmes célèbres* (Paris: Achille Désauges, 1826), ii. 29.

[34] See *Œuvres de Mme et de Mlle Deshoulieres*, new edn., 2 vols. (Paris: Prault Fils, 1753), 'De la premiere ode d'Horace, à M. Colbert', i. 26–9.

[35] 'Hulleria Virgo in Certamine Poëtarum Victrix, 1687', ibid., ii. 204–5.

[36] M. Christianus Juncker, *Schediasma Historicum* (Leipzig: Joh. Griedrich Gleditsch, 1692), 48, Valentinus Gottfried Herckliss, *De Cultu Heroinarum Sago vel Toga Illustrium* (Leipzig: Joh. Andreas Schaners, 1620), sig. C 3ᵛ.

[37] Paris, Bibliothèque Mazarine, 4398, fo. 2ᵛ. For his views more generally, see MacLean, *Woman Triumphant*, 138, where he quotes a letter from de Balzac (*Lettres... seconde partie*, 2 vols. (Paris: Pierre Resolet, 1636), ii. 869–79) in which he describes two types he considers unseemly, the 'femme cavalier', and the 'femme docteur'. Both descriptions owe much to Juvenal's sixth satire.

[38] Quoted by Dorothy Anne Liot Backer, *Precious Women* (New York: Basil Books, 1974), 112.

characters of men: a consideration often advanced as a reason for educating women more thoroughly. I have found no copy of either to date.[39]

Despite the absence of evidence for Latin verse from the pens of the well-known heroines of French culture in the Grand Siècle, there is some surviving verse from French women Latinists—though not much. Notably, there is the interesting if obscure figure of Mme de Roquemontrousse of Carpentras, celebrated by Devizé in the *Mercure galant*, and subsequently mentioned by a number of writers on learned women, all of whom draw their information from this article.[40] She was the only child of her father, one of the richest gentlemen in the province, who chose to educate her as if she had been a boy. Like Mlle Du Pré, she was interested in Cartesian philosophy, but she also studied geometry and astronomy, and she had a reputation as a versifier in Latin: 'when she was minded to divert herself in making Latin verses, hardly anyone could undertake to surpass her.'[41] Like Mlle Ramies and Mme Deshoulières, she translated from Horace's *Odes*; more unusually for a woman of her generation, she translated *into* Latin verse: she translated Guyonnet de Vertron's verses on the death of Mlle Deshoulières from French, and also a dialogue-poem in which the speakers were France and Germany: a few original verses also survive, notably a little poem addressed to her husband:

> Es mihi per somnum visus diademate cinctus
> > Regales leges proiciens populo
> Ast ubi contigerat cum somno visa perire,
> > O utinam, dixi, somnia vera forent
>
> You were shown to me in a dream, crowned with a diadem
> > Laying down royal laws, for the people
> Yet when the visions seemed to perish with the dream,
> > I said, O would that dreams were true!

This seems to be a case of a provincial gentlewoman of markedly scholarly interests writing verse for her own entertainment, far removed from considerations of intellectual fashion in the metropolis.

The marked centralization of French culture marginalizes such figures: another woman, perhaps similarly learned, was encountered by the romance writer and essayist Madeleine de Scudéry during a visit she made with her brother to Marseille in 1644. She is referred to by Mlle de Scudéry under the soubriquet 'Diodée'. She complained that 'Diodée' 'frequently quotes Trismegistus, Zoroaster (if I remember rightly) and such gentlemen with whom I have no acquaintance'.[42] 'Diodée's' crime is having the temerity to be a provincial intellectual who

[39] Briquet, *Dictionnaire*, 295.

[40] *Le Mercure galant* (Feb. 1682), 192–7. The *Mercure galant* article is picked up by Juncker's *Schediasma*, 57–8 and Johann Caspar Eberti; *Eröffnetes Cabinet dess Gelehrten Frauen-zimmers* (Frankfurt: Michael Rohrlachs sel. Wittib und Erben, 1700, 2nd edn. 1706), 255. Neither of these writers has any additional source of information. See also Henri Bardon, *En lisant le Mercure galant* (Rome: Edizioni dell'Ateneo, 1962), 12.

[41] Juncker, *Schediasma*, 57–8.

[42] Chantal Morlet Chantalat, 'Parler du savoir, savoir pour parler: Madeleine de Scudéry et la vulgarisation galante', in Nativel (ed.), *Femmes savantes*, 177–95 (p. 181).

is not taking her cue from the centre: Hermeticism was no longer in fashion in the salon circles in which Mlle de Scudéry moved, so the lady from Paris is neither interested nor admiring.

Another learned but highly liminal figure is Marie de Moulin, described by Sir Thomas Browne as one of the 'two learned Women of our age'.[43] She was the niece of André Rivet, a French Huguenot professor at Leiden, and was a native of Sedan in the Ardennes, from whence she removed to the Low Countries because of her commitment to Protestantism. Her learning did not result in much work of her own (though Browne claims she corresponded with Anna Maria van Schurman in Hebrew, which is possible, since van Schurman replied to Dorothy Moore in that language).[44] She emerges into brief visibility in the context of a debate between van Schurman and Mlle de Scudéry on the subject of the chastity of Joan of Arc, which she mediated—at the outset, she was a friend of van Schurman's (who was a correspondent of Rivet, hence the epistolary acquaintance of these women), and by the end of the exchange, she was a friend of Mlle de Scudéry also.[45]

One of the few places in which Latin poetry by seventeenth-century French-women becomes at all visible is in a volume of tributes to one of the most famous women intellectuals of the age, Elena Piscopia, *Compositione degli academici Ricovrati per la morte della nob. D. Signora Elena Lucretia Cornaro Piscopia*, discussed in the previous chapter. By the time of Piscopia's death in 1684, the records of the Ricovrati (which are very well preserved, and have been recently edited)[46] included at least four women members, all French: Carlotta Patino (daughter of the president of the Ricovrati), Anne Dacier, Mme Rousserau, and Louise Serment. Charles Patin, or Patino, president of the Ricovrati when Piscopia was elected, seems to have instituted a policy of inviting learned women to join the Ricovrati, a policy which was maintained in later generations. Many distinguished French-women of the later seventeenth and eighteenth centuries, including Madeleine de Scudéry and Mme Deshoulières, became Ricovratae. According to du Vertron (whose account is not entirely compatible with the records maintained in Padua itself), no less than twenty Frenchwomen were, or had been, members between 1678 and the time of writing, 1698.[47]

The female contributions to the *Compositione* are various, and include poems in French and Italian as well as Latin. The Patino contribution, discussed in Chapter 11, is far from exhausting the interest of the *Compositione*. No less than five poems, four in French and one in Latin, are the work of a Frenchwoman who chooses to refer to herself as 'la Musette de Paris' or 'La Petite Musette' (a *musette* is a

[43] Sir Thomas Browne, *Musæum Clausum, or Bibliotheca Abscondita* (*The Works of Sir Thomas Browne*, ed. Charles Sayle (Edinburgh: John Grant, 1907), iii. 350–5), 355.

[44] *Nobilissimae Virginis Annae Mariae à Schurman Opuscula* (Leiden: Elzevier, 1643), 195–9.

[45] Dorothy McDougall, *Madeleine de Scudéry: Her Romantic Life and Death* (London: Methuen, 1938), 62. In van Schurman's *Opuscula*, there are French letters to Mademoiselle Du Moulin, pp. 274–6.

[46] Attilio Maggiolo, *I soci dell'Accademia Patavina* (Padua: Accademia Patavina di scienze lettere ed arti, 1983).

[47] Vertron, *La Nouvelle Pandore*, i. 425–6.

relatively simple species of bagpipe; the associations are pastoral). Perhaps the most likely woman to be sheltering behind this *nom de plume* is the spectacularly learned but extremely modest Anne Dacier (mentioned above), who became a Ricovrata in 1679. A testimony both to the internationalism of the Ricovrati and to international interest in the astonishing Piscopia is found in the little Latin verse contributed by 'Helena Sibylla Vagenseila Germania, Altorfina', who was 17 at the time. She was not herself a member of the Ricovrati, but both her husband, Daniel Wilhelm Moller, philologist, professor of metaphysics, and librarian of the University of Altdorf, and her father, the professor of classics Johann Christoph Wagenseil, were members and they presumably encouraged her to do so. There was clearly some contact between the Wagenseils and the Patins, since a Latin poem to Helena Wagenseil by Charles Patin is printed by Haendel,[48] and in 1688, Carlotta Patino published *Il faut tenir sa parole*, a short fiction translated from Hebrew to Latin by Helena Wagenseil's father Johann Christoph Wagenseil, then from Latin to French by herself.

Another of the few thoroughly educated Frenchwomen of the seventeenth century was Gabrielle Émilie Le Tonnelier de Breteuil, Marquise de Châtelet-Laumont, the mistress of Voltaire. She was tutored in Latin, Italian—by her father—English, mathematics, and the sciences, and in later life put almost all of her areas of study to the test by translating and commenting on Isaac Newton's *Principia Mathematica*.[49] She was still working on the commentary on the day she died. She was a member of one of the academies of Bologna: her friend Cideville wrote,[50]

> When Bologna proudly displays, in Italy
> Its register adorned with the fair name of Émilie,
> Why is the fair sex, so greatly loved by us,
> Excluded, in France, from the Academy?

In fact, she had tested the defences of the French Académie des Sciences by entering anonymously for their prize essay in 1736, on the subject *La Nature du feu et sa propagation*. She did not win, and nor did Voltaire, who had also entered, but both their essays were printed.[51] She published another scientific work, intended to explain the work of Newton, in 1738, *Institutions physiques*, under her own name.

One of the few places in France which continued to support Latin learning for women through the seventeenth century is the *Mercure galant*, a journal which has already been mentioned as the sole source of information on the life and work of Mme de Roquemontrousse. The *Mercure* was aimed at the nobility and the Parisian bourgeoisie, and since it was successful and long-lived, must have pleased its audience. It devoted considerable space to Greek and Roman antiquity, pub-

---

[48] Christoph Christian Haendel, *Dissertatio de Eruditis Gemaniae Mulieribus* (Altdorf: Heinrich Meyer, 1688), 22–3.

[49] Esther Ehrman, *Mme Du Châtelet* (Leamington Spa: Berg, 1986).

[50] From René Vaillot, *Madame Du Châtelet* (Paris: Albin Michel, 1978), 263.

[51] Ehrman, *Mme Du Châtelet*, 30–1.

lished Latin verse, medallions and inscriptions in Latin, kept readers abreast of current scholarship, and made extensive reference to classical culture.[52] The editors of the *Mercure* aimed their work at an audience definitely conceptualized as including women, and they encouraged their women readers to study: they reported, for example, the award of a doctorate to Elena Piscopia.[53] It is also interesting that the same issue which discussed Piscopia's doctorate advertised as among the contents of its next 'some lines of Latin, in favour of those of the fair sex who study that language'.[54] The *Mercure* and the work of Claude Charles Guyonnet, M. du Vertron, are principal sources for the activities of educated women in the France of the Grand Siècle.

As the seventeenth century fades into the eighteenth, evidence for women Latinists is less and less easy to find. Mme de Genlis (1746–1830), however, offers the following thought-provoking dialogue, represented as between contemporaries, in her 'The Two Reputations', an exchange between Luzincourt and Aurelia:[55]

'You must own that ladies do not now understand Greek.'
'And I must likewise own that men do not either. We learn the Greek alphabet, after which we read translations! Then we say we understand Greek and this is the whole mystery. As to other languages, we meet with many ladies who understand English, Italian, Spanish, and even Latin.'
'Latin!'
'Yes, you yourself are acquainted with three.'
'What! Three women who understand Latin!'
'Yes, madam, who understand Latin. There are Madame N—, Mademoiselle N—, her daughter, and Madame the Marchioness N—, who all understand it as perfectly as the most studious men.'
'Understand Latin! and I who have been acquainted with them these three years, never to suspect it! Women may then be modest as well as learned, and scholars without being pedants; nay, without wishing to have their abilities known...'

As Mme de Genlis hints, there probably continued to be some remarkably learned women in France, but, like their sisters of the seventeenth century in other countries, they were anxious to conceal it. Quentin Bauchart's study of major collections of books made by women includes a section on Louise-Françoise de Harlay de Cèly, Marquise de Vieuxbourg (1680–1736), the owner of a very important library which included a number of Latin works: owning a book is not necessarily the same as reading it, but it is at least possible that this scholarly woman was mistress of Latin.[56] Still more unusual was Anne Girard who, according to Fortunée Briquet, wrote Latin verses for the entry of the queen (Marie

[52] Henri Bardon in his *En lisant le Mercure galant*, 6.
[53] *Le Mercure galant* (Sept. 1678), 150–9.
[54] Ibid. 334.
[55] Trans. Hale, *Woman's Record*, 324.
[56] *Catalogus Librorum Illustriss. Lud. Franciscae de Harlay, Ludovico-Renati March. de Vielbourg Viduae* (Paris: Gabriel Martin, 1735). Ernest Quentin Bauchart, *Les Femmes bibliophiles de France* (Paris: Damascène Morgand, 1886), ii. 422–3.

Antoinette) into Paris in the eighteenth century.[57] Apart from Girard, Fortunée Briquet mentions only three eighteenth-century Frenchwomen who studied Latin: Eulalie Guillois, decapitated in year two of the Republic in her late teens, the Abbess of Sainte-Perrine-de-la-Villette, who translated the *Vita Spiritualis* of St Vincent Ferrer into French, and a much-married lady, born as Marie-Anne-Henriette Payon de l'Estang in 1746, later Mme d'Autremont, Mme de Bourdic, and finally Mme Viot, who studied German, Latin, Italian, and English, but appears to have written entirely in French.[58] Given the large numbers of French-women who were writing and publishing in the age of the Enlightenment, it is a dismally short list. We might also notice in passing the interesting figure of Marie Anne Boccage of Rouen, née Du Fiquet (1710–1802), described as 'Venus in beauty, Minerva in talent', who seems like a figure from an earlier age: there is no evidence that she read or wrote Latin, but her work evidently depended on classical models. She was the author of an epic poem, the *Columbiad*, and a tragedy, *Les Amazones*, a member of academies in Rome, Bologna, Padua, Lyon, and Rouen, and her work was translated into English, Spanish, German, and Italian.[59] Another interesting woman who used Latin in a purely practical context is Marie Lavoisier, née Paulze (1758–1836), who learned Latin and English as an aspect of a life spent helping her husband, Antoine Lavoisier, with his work on chemistry.[60]

Mercier's *Tableau de Paris*, published between 1781 and 1788, paints on the whole a dismal picture of women's educational attainments. However, in his chapter on 'Ton du grand mond' he notes the existence of highly educated women in sophisticated circles: he also takes issue with Molière for his satire on bluestockings, *Les Femmes savantes*, on the grounds that 'intending to rap ped-antry, he rapped the desire for instruction', and therefore retarded the progress of society.[61]

The education of girls took a sharp downwards turn in the eighteenth century, under the influence of Rousseau; the depressant effect of Molière is probably not significant. Mme de Lambert's Rousseauist *Réflexions nouvelles sur les femmes* proposed an education for girls which was to consist of a smattering of history, philosophy, and ethics.[62] She did, on the other hand, recommend Latin, because it is the language of the Church—the implication is of a reading knowledge only—while she considered Italian dangerous. She stressed that scholarship is a vice against which the daughter must be on guard.[63] Her views are contexted by Madelyn Gutwirth, who observed that by the 1770s, the Rousseauist camp had come distinctly to dominate French cultural discourse, and women's right to

---

[57] Briquet, *Dictionnaire* 157. These seem not to survive in any form.

[58] Ibid. 166, 339, 340.

[59] Jean Buyze, *The Tenth Muse* (Berkeley: Shameless Hussy Press, 1980), 15.

[60] Margaret Alic, *Hypatia's Heritage* (London: Women's Press, 1986), 96–7.

[61] John Lough, 'Women in Mercier's *Le Tableau de Paris*', in Jacobs et al. (eds.), *Women and Society in Eighteenth-Century France*, 116–7.

[62] *Œuvres*, ed. Robert Granderoute (Paris: H. Champion, 1990), 213–37.

[63] Liselotte Steinbrügge, *The Moral Sex: Women's Nature in the French Enlightenment*, trans. Pamela E. Selwyn (New York: Oxford University Press, 1995), 18.

education was thus seen almost entirely in terms of their duty to educate their children—potentially, if the children were sons, a reason to learn Latin, but the focus of maternal education was essentially moral rather than intellectual.[64] Preparation for maternity is a note repeatedly struck by French writers on women's education, though by the late nineteenth century, some are actually advocating the introduction of basic Latin into female education, albeit for Rousseauist reasons: 'future housewives and mothers would be happy later on to find themselves able to supervise their sons' first steps in the subject.'[65]

Charles Rollin, in the *Supplement* to his *Traité de la manière d'enseigner et d'étudier les belles-lettres*, takes a somewhat different tack. He wholly accepts that girls and women might have the intellectual ability to master Latin; and points to Mme Dacier as an indication that talent was not gender specific. Having conceded this point, he simply denies that women have anything to do with Latin, since their sole function is as home-makers. He follows the tradition of Aristotle's *Politics* in claiming that there is an absolute division of function between men and women: Latin, obviously, belongs to the world of men. The obvious exceptions, such as women rulers, the poet Sappho, and so forth, do not disturb this general proposition, since such cases are to be treated individually—a classic example of the 'doublethink' that had permitted the public activity of politically or socially significant women together with the maintenance of the status quo since the Middle Ages. His argument moves onto even more problematic grounds when in addition to women rulers, he permits two class exceptions: nuns, who would have to recite or sing in Latin, and a curious group of learned spinsters—'Christian virgins and widows living in the world but separated from it in heart and mind, having wholly renounced its dangerous pleasures'.[66] He was thinking, perhaps, of women such as Isotta Nogarola, Elena Piscopia, or the French Marie de Gournay, who died in 1645, or he may have been reading Gabrielle Suchon.[67] He takes no account of the realities of his times, in which such Frenchwomen as were learned and used Latin were almost all educated aristocrats, and married. But his exceptions are interesting ones. They allow so many loopholes to the principle that women are intellectually as well as physically confined to the home that, in fact, it would be hard for anyone trying to prevent a particular woman from educating herself to bring Rollin to his (or her) assistance, since he has conceded the argument based on incapacity. Furthermore, aristocrats who enjoyed both the life of the mind and the 'dangerous pleasures' of the world, such as the Marquise de Châtelet, the Marquise de Vieuxbourg, or Mme de Genlis's Marchioness N—, were not likely to be dissuaded by such an argument.

[64] Madelyn Gutwirth, *The Twilight of the Goddesses: Women and Representation in the French Revolutionary Era* (New Brunswick, NJ: Rutgers University Press, 1992).

[65] Waquet, *Latin*, 225.

[66] Rollin, *Supplément au Traité de la manière d'enseigner et d'étudier les belles-lettres* (Paris: Veuve Estienne, 1734), 53–60. Waquet, *Latin*, 223–4.

[67] Gabrielle Suchon, *Du celibat volontaire ou la vie sans engagement* (Paris: Jean & Michel Guignard, 1700), argued in favour of a 'third way' for women, a retired, celibate life dedicated to study and the life of the mind.

13. *Anna Maria van Schurman and Other Women Scholars of Northern and Central Europe*

The women's work considered in this chapter (which is divided into sections on 'Germany', anachronistically thus identified, the Netherlands, Scandinavia, and Poland) must be looked at within the context of the extremely patchy survival even of printed books in these regions. Curt von Faber du Faur points out that German baroque books are rarer than those of the Reformation or even of German incunables.[1] Both the latter classes had value, religious or antiquarian, in the eighteenth century. By contrast, the writing of the baroque was seen as primitive in the light of the new German classicism, and the books themselves were not lovely objects, since the poverty of Germany in and after the Thirty Years War ensured that the vast majority were poorly printed on cheap paper. Only a proportion escaped destruction; and in consequence, quite a number of women's works known to have existed cannot now be found, though it is very much to be hoped that more may yet come to light.

Germany

Despite the proud record of German women humanists detailed in an earlier chapter, the entry of German women into the professions was slow and hesitant. Perhaps the first German woman to practise medicine with academic approval graduated in 1754, having successfully defended her Latin dissertation.[2] Therefore, since the defenders of elite women's right to read Virgil and pen Latin epithalamia were in no way compelled to think of their protégées as potential competitors, they were many.[3] The tone of rational encouragement struck by Christoph Christian Haendel is not unusual: 'But my own opinion is that women who are clever, of good birth, wealthy, and those to whom the favour of Fortune has given legitimate leisure, can praiseworthily spend their leisure on

---

[1] Curt von Faber du Faur, *German Baroque Literature* (New Haven: Yale University Press, 1958), pp. vii–viii.

[2] Dorothea Christiane Erxleben was accepted as a student at the University of Halle with a special dispensation from Frederick the Great. *SKGF*, p. x.

[3] Barbara Becker-Cantarino, 'Die "gelehrte Frau" und die Institutionen und Organisasionsformen der Gelehrsamkeit am Beispiel der Anna Maria von Schurman (1608–1678)', in Sebastian Neumeister and Conrad Wiedemann (eds.), *Res Publica Litteraria* (Wièsbaden: Otto Harrassowitz, 1987), ii. 559–76 (p. 561), and Jean M. Woods, 'Das Gelarhte Frauenzimmer und die deutschen Frauenlexicon, 1631–1763', ibid. 577–87.

letters, better than on other things.'[4] Western European women Latinists did not present themselves as striking a blow for womankind, or demand to enter the professions. Anna Maria van Schurman, author of the most explicit pro-woman argument produced in this region, merely argued that exceptions such as herself should be allowed to exercise their talent, a view which the defenders of learned women had no trouble in endorsing. There is a surprising number of academic works on women written in seventeenth-century Germany.[5] Some of them are dissertations,[6] others disputations presenting a case for and against, which examine subjects ranging from whether women should be learned to whether they could fight duels.[7]

Latin was the language for any poetry which had pretensions towards cultivation in Germany in the early seventeenth century,[8] in fact, German commitment to the classics was such that even as late as 1765, almost a fifth of the books published in Germany were in a classical tongue.[9] And, as Heide Wunder has pointed out, it was difficult for women to make up for the formal mastery taught at school.[10] In the early modern German-speaking world which she describes, with rare exceptions, learned women were mostly gifted amateurs, and treated as such. Standards of education of women in general were not high, and while daughters of the nobility and the bourgeois middle class often enjoyed a good literary education, it was not a professional one.[11] For writing on themes such as religion and members of the family for local consumption, it was not necessary to learn all the rules of art.

---

[4] *Dissertatio de Eruditis Germaniae Mulieribus* (Altdorf: Heinrich Meyer, 1688).

[5] Many are listed in *SKGF* and discussed in the texts mentioned in n. 3. Apart from van Schurman, a German woman entered the lists on her own account, Anna Catharina Zurburg (or Thorberg) (1695–1721), author of 'De Feminis Eruditione Conspicuis', and 'De Iure Sexu Feminei ad Perdiscendos Artes Liberales' (witnessed by Johann Martin Müller, *Das gelehrte Hadeln oder historische Nachricht von gelehrten Hadelern, ihrem Leben und Schriften* (Ottendorf: Self-published, 1754), 199–204: I have not located a copy of either work).

[6] For example, Haendel, *Dissertatio*, Johann Friedrich Hekel, *Dissertatiuncula de Foeminis Litteratis* (Rudolstadt: Schulzianus, 1686), Sebastian Korthold, *Disquisitio de Poetriis Puellis* (Keil: Barthold Reuther, 1700).

[7] Johannes Sauerbrei's *Diatriben Academicam de Foeminarum Eruditione* (Leipzig: Johann Erich Hahn, 1671) is an important example of the former; on the latter topic, see Johann Jacobus Hassler, *De Foeminis Fortitudine Sagatae Claris* (Leipzig: Johann Coler, 1695), and Johann Riemer, *Duella Mulierum, Disputabat Praeses Joannes Riemer et Respondens Samuel Capzovius* (Weissenfelsae: Johannis Brühl, 1680).

[8] Robert M. Browning, *German Baroque Poetry, 1618–1723* (University Park: Pennsylvania State University Press, 1971).

[9] Ruth P. Dawson, *The Contested Quill* (Newark: University of Delaware Press, 2002), 52.

[10] Heide Wunder, *He is the Sun, She is the Moon* (Cambridge, Mass.: Harvard University Press, 1988) 110. The same point was made by Jonathan Swift, *Letter to a Very Young Lady on her Marriage*, quoted by Josephine Kamm, *Hope Deferred* (London: Methuen, 1965), 117.

[11] See Cornelia Niekus Moore, *The Maiden's Mirror* (Wiesbaden: Otto Harrassowitz, 1987), for an account of women's education generally, and for women and the classics, Sarah Colvin, ' "Die Zung is dieses Schwert": Classical Tongues and Gendered Curricula in German Schooling to 1908', in Yun Lee Too and Niall Livingstone (eds.), *Pedagogy and Power* (Cambridge: Cambridge University Press, 1998), 47–67, who makes it clear that the knowledge of Latin acquired by the women discussed here was not gained in school. See also Erich Kleinschmidt, 'Gelehrte Frauenbildung und frühneuzeitgeistliche Mentalität', in Neumeister and Wiedemann (eds.), *Res Publica Litteraria*, ii. 549–57.

Writing was a very professional business up until the end of the eighteenth century: it was the replacement of highly formalized education by 'genius' as a principal criterion of excellence which opened up a path for such women as Sidonia Zäuneman and Magdalena Sibylle Rieger, both of whom were crowned poet laureate by the University of Göttingen in the eighteenth century.[12] However, the impression of genteel insufficiency which this broad description creates is one which needs to be nuanced. While they might have failed to meet the standards of the German professoriate, had these ever been considered appropriate to apply to them, there were German women who were very well educated indeed.

Pietism, a distinctive religious movement of seventeenth-century Germany, was significant for contemporary women, and attracted a number of notable scholars. The Pietist movement, which formed around the charismatic Frankfurt preacher Philipp Jakob Spener, sought a renewal of Lutheran religious feeling within the existing religious structure. One of its consequences was the creation of small groups of like-minded Christians who engaged in biblical study, charity, and mystical fellowship, a form of coterie activity in a context of mutual support among serious Christians which held an obvious potential attraction for women.[13] One such, Juliana Patientia Schult (1680–1701), taught the daughters of the Pietist community in Halle.[14] She was herself a student of Hebrew, Greek, Latin (Lehms quotes a Latin letter she wrote to her father in 1696),[15] French, arithmetic, geography, genealogy, and poetry, but her principal interest during her short life was religion.

Another Pietist woman whose achievement was not, as Schult's was, cut short by early death was the aristocratic Henrietta Catharina von Gersdorff. Born von Friesin, she married Nicolaus Bauer, Baron von Gersdorff, and in later life turned to Pietism. Jakob Smalcius in Sauerbrei's *Diatriben Academicam* claims her as the author of a Latin epithalamion, *In Auspicatissimum Conjugium Serenissimorum Principum Haereditariorum Electoris Saxoniae ac Regnorum Daniae Norvegiaeque* (1667), printed anonymously,[16] and also implies that there is a gratulatory or dedicatory Latin poem by her in Heinrich and Karl von Friesin's *Poemata*, a work I have not managed to locate. Von Gersdorff is praised by Otto Praetorius in a pamphlet, *Secessus Roethaviensis*, quoted by Sauerbrei: 'with what delight do you yourself write poems, not only in the vernacular, but even in the Latin language, and freely read over the poems composed by others?'[17] She was certainly the author of another Latin epithalamion:

[12] *SKGF*, p. x.

[13] Natalie Zemon Davis, *Women on the Margins* (Cambridge, Mass.: Harvard University Press, 1995), 158. See also F. Stoeffler, *German Pietism during the Eighteenth Century*, Studies in the History of Religions (Leiden: E. J. Brill, 1973).

[14] Ulrike Witt, *Bekehrung, Bildung und Biographie: Frauen in Umkreis des Hallesche Pietismus* (Tübingen: Max Niemeyer Verlag, 1996), 194–9.

[15] Georg Christian Lehms, *Teutschlands galante Poetinnen* (Frankfort am Main: Anton Heinscheidt, 1715), 182–90—a letter of birthday greetings, 28 Feb. 1696. See also Moore, *The Maiden's Mirror*, 52.

[16] *Diatriben*, pt. II (Smalcius), sig. E3ᵛ.

[17] 'quâ felicitate et ipsa pangis carmina, non vernacula tantum sed latina etiam lingua, et composita ab aliis quam libenter lectitas?'

Purpureas Matuta genas, ac plena rosarum
    Ora, & odoratas exere pulchra comas:
Tuque, fores aperi nascentis, & alma diei
    Atria felici sidere pande, Venus.
Aut si nostra sequi, Divae, consulta velitis,
    Sub mare formarum condite grande decus
Pulchrius exoritur sidus

O Musa, at numero quae praestas una noveno,
    O Charis, at priscis gratior una tribus!
Quis digne celebret sublimia pectora, & illa
    Ingenii atque artis culmina summa Tuae?
Tum formae vultusque satis quis cantet honores,
    Quis speciem dignam Principe laude vehat?
Divinae feriunt jam dudum sidera dotes
    Virtutesque ejus blandus Olympus habet.

Lovely Matuta, show forth your blushing cheeks,
    Your lips full of roses, and your scented tresses:
And you, kind Venus, unbar the thresholds of the nascent day
    And open up its forecourts, under a fortunate star.
Or else, Goddesses, if you should wish to follow our advice,
    Hide the great glories of your beauty under the sea—
A more beautiful star is emerging.

O Muse—but you alone excel the band of nine,
    O Grace—but you alone are more lovely than the three ancient ones!
Who may worthily celebrate your goodheartedness,
    And the lofty achievements of your intellect and art?
Then, who may sufficiently sing the glories of your body and face,
    Who will exalt in praise a beauty worthy of a princess?
Her divine endowments have already, for a long time, been striking the stars
    And a well-disposed Olympus keeps hold of her virtues.

This poem was printed twice in her lifetime. She also published many poems in German. Probably her earliest published work is *Heilsame Betrachtung, von dem Leiden und Sterben unsers Heilands Jesus Christus* (Wittenberg, 1665), and after her death, her *Geistreiche Lieder* were published in Halle in 1749. She lived mostly in Dresden, and lived up to her principles by opening her mansion in Groszhennesdorf to those who were in need.[18] Her daughter Charlotte Juliana Gersdorff also had a reputation as a Latin poet.[19]

The most extensive surviving Latin poem to be written by a Pietist woman is also one of the most problematic. Curt von Faber du Faur in his *German Baroque Literature* notes that *Cosilia und Responsa Theologica: oder gottsgelehrte Rathschläge und Antworten, über denen wichtigsten strücken und zuständen eches göttlichen*

[18] Faber du Faur, *German Baroque Literature*, 372.

[19] Johann Caspar Eberti, *Eröffnetes Cabinet dess Gelehrten Frauen-zimmers* (Frankfurt: Michael Rohrlachs sel. Wittib und Erben, 1700; 2nd edn. 1706), 161.

Wandels, nebenst neuen geistlichen Gedichten, der Weiszheit Garten, Gewächs genannt, gemein gemacht och Gottfried Arnold, published under the auspices of Gottfried Arnold in 1705, was not by him, but was thought to be by a woman from its first publication.[20] The British Library catalogue suggests that the author was Margareta Susanna Sprögel, wife of the court dean Sprögel and mother-in-law of Gottfried Arnold (who was, like Henrietta Catharina von Gersdorff, a learned Pietist). Other possible names are Johanna Eleonora Peterson and Anna Katharina Schafsmid, both of whom were also active within this milieu. The *Cosilia* is an enormous book of 910 pages. Parts I and II are prose, Part III, 'Der Weiszheit Garten-Gewächts', consists of 100 letters, followed by a collection of verses, mostly German, with one in Dutch, and the long Latin 'canticle', which is in quatrains divided into thirty-nine sections averaging five quatrains in length. Were it not for the content which is subtly of its time, it would be easy to take this canticle for a medieval composition. Its form certainly endorses the idea of a woman's authorship, since it is hard to imagine any product of a seventeenth-century *Gymnasium* writing Latin like this.

Some German professors, like members of the learned professions in other countries, educated their daughters, a few of whom became famous for their learning. Maria Barbara Lehmann, the daughter of a Leipzig professor of theology, read Latin, Italian, and French,[21] Anna Weisbruck, the wife of Johann Forster, the professor of Hebrew at Wittenberg, was herself skilled in Hebrew and Syriac, and wrote a dialogue-work with her husband on the group of Old Testament texts which were read as prophecies of Christ (such as Isaiah 7: 14).[22] The learned doctor Ulrich Ellenbog educated his four sons and five daughters himself, 'not only in real Christian virtue but also in the sciences and in Latin and Greek'. The daughter of Heinrich Stromer, chief doctor of Mainz, was another such.[23] Gertrud Möller, née Eyssler (1641–1705), another professor's daughter, was educated by her father and became an excellent scholar. She was accepted in the Nuremberg literary society called the 'Pegnesischer Blumenorden' (discussed below), and was crowned poet laureate in 1671.[24]

Some of these professors' daughters also wrote Latin verse. Lehms records the literary reputation of Maria Elisabeth Rings, daughter of Professor Rings of Frankfurt, well known for her talents in painting, mathematics, Latin, French, and music, and prints an affectionate Latin verse written to her brother.

[20] Faber du Faur, *German Baroque Literature,* 375

[21] Andreas Planer, *Tactatus [sic] de Gyneceo Docto* (Wittenberg: Johann Godfrid Meyer, 1715), 49.

[22] Briefly described in J. G. Schelhorn, *Amoenitates Literariae* (Frankfort: Daniel Bartholomaeus, 1725–30), xiv. 210.

[23] 'Henrici Stromeri Aurbacensis Medici, Archiatri Moguntini filia, quam eleganter latine loquentem se audivisse testatur Muslerus, *In Oratione* p. 157', Johannis Paschius, *Gynaeceum Doctum* (Wittenberg: Christian Finkel, 1701), 57.

[24] Moore, *The Maiden's Mirror,* 51, 54, daughter of Michael Eyssler, professor of logic and metaphysics. Professor Titius' eulogium of her compares her to Weston and van Schurman. Lehms, *Teutschlands galante Poetinnen* (1715), 138–40.

Nam tibi mellifluos antiquum est volvere versus,
Auribus altisonos et resonare modos,
Sic legis, O felix, calamo que scripsit amoeno,
Affinis, frater, vera Camoenae soror.

Since it is an old practice of yours to compose mellifluous verses,
And to make deep-sounded rhythms resonate in the ears, likewise,
O happy brother, you are reading what your sister has written with a pleasant pen,
A true kinswoman to the Latin muse.

Helena Sibylla, the daughter of Johann Christoph Wagenseil, jurist and professor of classics in Altdorf, was also exceptionally well educated. At her father's instigation, she was taught Latin and Hebrew in order to participate in advanced Bible study.[25] She continued to move in intellectual circles as an adult, since she married another professor at Altdorf, the philologist Daniel Wilhelm Moller (1642–1712). One Latin epigram, on the death of her father, was published by Lehms, and so was a youthful tribute to Elena Piscopia in *Composizioni degli academici Ricovrati per la morte della nobilissima donna Signora Elena Lucrezia Cornara Piscopia*, published when she was 17. Her father and later her husband were members of the Ricovrati, suggesting that they were part of the world of international scholarly connections.[26] That she herself also maintained international contacts is indicated by a poem to her by Charles Patin, president of the Ricovrati, which is printed by Christoph Christian Haendel,[27] and the fact that she herself seems to have corresponded in Latin with, and sent verse to, the Dutch antiquarian and poet Theodoor Jansson of Almeloveen.[28]

Helena Wagenseil's Latin verse on her father is in line with the general run of women's vernacular literary production at this time. As Merry Wiesner notes, women often wrote poems to commemorate the deaths of their fathers and mothers, sometimes published along with the pastoral funeral sermon—the large Stolberg collection of funeral sermons at the Herzog August Bibliothek in Wolfenbüttel has many examples—but did not write poetry commemorating their husbands. 'At least in terms of sentiments they were willing to express publicly, early modern German women saw their family vocation as primarily maternal and filial, rather than spousal.'[29] Poems from a daughter to a father are a strong feature of German humanist cultural production, hard to parallel elsewhere: contemporary women in Italy, England, or France were far more likely to write on their husbands (and Italians sometimes also on their mothers). Perhaps the earliest such is Margaret of Austria's lament (in French) on the death of her father, the Emperor Maximilian, in 1519.[30] The fact that many educated German women had been

25 M. Christianus Juncker, *Schediasma Historicum* (Leipzig: Joh. Friedrich Gleditsch, 1692), 84.
26 Some further evidence for this was discussed in the previous chapter, p.332.
27 *Dissertatio*, 22–3.
28 Schelhorn, *Amoenitates* v. 200–1.
29 Merry Wiesner, *Gender, Church and State in Early Modern Germany* (London: Longman, 1998), 42.
30 Christopher Hare, *The High and Puissant Princess Marguerite of Austria* (London: Harper & Brothers, 1907), 256–8.

taught by their fathers perhaps reinforced this bond. One sixteenth-century German woman, Elizabeth Herder, wrote a Latin poem commemorating her husband, discussed in an earlier chapter, but the later Latin women poets discussed here wrote primarily for various members of the family they had been born into, and often show a particularly close relationship with their fathers.

Latin was also alive in court and aristocratic circles, even among women. As Moore notes, 'Education for noble girls resembled in many ways that offered in the cloister. In both cases, a carefully regulated environment prepared the young woman for a lifelong vocation to which, in addition to its other skills, literacy and the reading of "good books" contributed.' Between the ages of 6 and 9, girls of the noble or landed gentry class were generally taught by a governess, sometimes by a family member, and some of them learned Latin, particularly sentences and proverbs. The aim of reading Latin was comprehension and memorization, and grammar was normally deemed superfluous.[31] However, some families were more ambitious than others, particularly in the context of those courts which aspired to become intellectual and literary centres. Though noble parents did not necessarily consider literacy a springboard to further academic study, J. J. Müller speaks of a 'literarization and scientification' of princely education in the seventeenth century, which had an effect on the education of noblewomen.[32] Moore points to several courts in which the educational tradition was particularly strong: the Catholic Wittelsbach courts in Munich and Düsseldorf, the Lutheran courts in Wolfenbüttel and Rudolstadt, and the reformed Anhalt court. The mother of Maria and Maximiliana von Wittelsbach had them educated in German and Latin, reading, writing, and rhetoric, as well as in all kinds of womanly crafts such as sewing, embroidery, and knitting.[33] Ernesta Augusta von Anhalt-Bernburg (1636–59) read Hebrew, Greek, Latin, and French.[34] Noblewomen also sometimes caught up their education in later life: the Duchess Dorothea Maria of Saxony-Weimar ordered the school reformer Ratichius (Ratke) to her court in 1612 to instruct her and her ladies in Latin using his new and highly controversial method.[35] A much later German noblewoman who also took education very seriously, Caroline, Countess of Wied-Neuwied (1720–95), formed a sort of academy to discuss important questions, with the aim of educating the heir of Wied-Neuwied. One of the questions they asked was 'whether it is good for women to learn Latin'.[36]

Catharina Ursula, Landgräfin von Hessen-Kassel (1593–1615), is an early example of the educated princess. She was born at Karlsburg, the daughter of

---

[31] Moore, *The Maiden's Mirror*, 48.

[32] 'Fürstenziehung im 17. Jahrhundert, am Beispiel Herzog Anton Ulrichs von Braunschweig und Lüneburg', Albrecht Schöne (ed.), *Stadt-Schule-Universität Buchwesen im 17. Jahrhundert*, (Munich: Beck, 1970), 243–60, 295–300, esp. 249.

[33] Moore, *The Maiden's Mirror*, 44; Friedrich Schmidt, *Geschichte der Erziehung der Pfälsichen Wittelsbacher* (Berlin: A. Hofman & Co., 1899), 286.

[34] *SKGF*, p. 1.

[35] H. Stoerl, 'Wolfgang Ratke (Ratichius)', *Neue Jahrbücher für Philologie und Pädagogik*, 46 (1876), 121–71 (p. 128).

[36] Wunder, *He is the Sun*, 158–9.

Georg Friedrich, Margrave of Baden-Durlach. They were a cultivated family: two of her sisters, Anna and Elizabeth von Baden-Durlach, published poetry in German, attested by Lehms.[37] One Latin distich of hers survives, and according to Eberti she was the author of a work called *Festium Veritatis*, preserved (presumably in manuscript) in the library at Durlach.[38] Her sister Anna von Baden-Durlach (1617–72) was also theologically inclined.[39] Johann Valentin Andreae in his exchange of Latin letters with Sibylla Ursula von Braunschweig-Lüneburg, discussed below, explicitly measures her learnedness against that of the sisters of Baden-Durlach.[40] Similarly, Antonia von Württemberg (1613–79),[41] a member of the ducal family of Württemberg, studied Latin, Hebrew, and the cabbala, and is one of the few early modern women to have turned her hand to architecture.[42] Haendel states that 'an ingenious hieroglyphic structure stands in the Church of the Holy Trinity in the town of Deynach, called the Antonia Tower'. He also notes that she was assisted in working out the design by Balthasar Rathius of Tübingen.

The royal family of the Palatinate was also known for educated women: this goes back at least as far as Louisa Juliana, mother of the Elector Frederick, briefly King of Bohemia.[43] Elizabeth von der Pfalz (1618–80), eldest daughter of Frederick and Elizabeth of Bohemia, the sister of Elector Karl Ludwig, was brought up by Louisa Juliana, her grandmother, and was internationally known for her learning (her family nickname was 'la Grecque') and, above all, for her friendship with Descartes.[44] She corresponded with Anna Maria van Schurman.[45] Her youngest sister Sophia of Hanover (1630–1714) was also Latinate, also interested in Descartes, and a patron of Gottfried Wilhelm Leibniz.[46] Sophia transmitted her intellectual interests to her daughter Sophie Charlotte, who instigated her husband, Frederick I of Prussia, to found the Berlin Academy of Sciences.

---

[37] Lehms, *Teutschlands galante Poetinnen* (1715), 20: see also *SKGF*, 51.

[38] Ebert; *Eröffnetes Cabinet*, 82–3. Lehms mentions a book on the Margräfin and her work in the same library (*Teutschlands galante Poetinnen*, 19).

[39] Moore, *The Maiden's Mirror*, 47.

[40] The intellectual tone of the Baden-Durlachs was perpetuated in subsequent generations. Margräfin Caroline Luise von Baden-Durlach (1723–83) had an education which covered literature, art, and languages but she was a polymath who also developed a keen interest in experimentatation. Wunder, *He is the Sun*, 155.

[41] Her father was Herzog Johann Friedrich of Württemberg. She learned Hebrew from Johann Jacob Strelin, pastor in Münster near Stuttgart. Her sisters Anna Johanna and Sibylla also had intellectual interests: Anna Johanna in measurement and the liberal arts, Sibylla in history and genealogy. Wunder, *He is the Sun*, 157.

[42] Haendel, *Dissertatio*, 5.

[43] Munich, Bayerische Staatsbibliothek, Clm lat. 1102 (Collectio Camerariana 51), no. 52, 'Loysae Julianae, comitissae de Sain et Witgenstein memoriale contra primum punctum memorialis Trevirensis', 7 Aug. 1633.

[44] Elizabeth Godfrey, *A Sister of Prince Rupert* (London: John Lane, 1909).

[45] Van Schurman, *Opuscula*, 281–7 (p. 285). She was also in correspondence with Joachim Camerarius: there is a letter of hers in Munich, Bayerische Staatsbibliothek, Camerarius Collection 13, no. 290.

[46] See Jonathan Israel, *Radical Enlightenment: Philosophy and the Making of Modernity, 1650–1700* (Oxford: Oxford University Press, 2001), 86. Walpole claims that she was Latin-literate: H. Walpole, *Reminiscences*, ed. P. Toynbee (Oxford: Clarendon Press, 1924), 121.

The Braunschweig-Lüneburgs of Wolfenbüttel were another notably learned ducal family in baroque Germany. The first Herzog August's library is the core of the famous collection still preserved in the town. His granddaughter Sibylla Ursula von Braunschweig-Lüneburg, mentioned above, the daughter of Herzog August the Younger, was educated with her brothers and sisters by Justus Georg Schottelius. She published five poems in German, three of them public, declamatory verses addressed to her father—note that, again, that it is the father–daughter relationship which provoked published writing.[47] She also took some part in the writing of her brother's long romance *Aramena*,[48] but though most of her published work is in German, she was Latinate. Johann Valentin Andreae, a Braunschweig-Lüneburg protégé, includes a long series of Latin letters from Sibylla Ursula to himself in a work on education dedicated to her father.[49] By 1652, she was writing to Andreae about her increasing interest in purifying and expanding the German language—making it more classical—rather than in writing in Latin *per se*: it is this, rather than lack of capacity, which probably accounts for the fact that her surviving verse is in the vernacular. Sibylla Ursula's stepmother, Fürstin Sophie Elisabeth, née von Mecklenburg, attained prominence for both her musical and her literary interests.[50] She read French and translated Honoré d'Urfé's romance *Astrée*, but she also wrote music, German poems, and meditations, and designed court masques, in which most of the family, their friends, courtiers, and a few professionals took part. Her *Minerva's Banquet* of 1655 includes a long ode in Latin. She is given as sole deviser of this piece, though the fact that the various seventeenth- and early eighteenth-century critics interested in learned women do not describe her as a Latinist calls her authorship of this ode into question (they were not, however, omniscient). It is worth noting also that she was a member of a species of literary academy on something like the Italian model, the Pegnesischer Blumenorden, which admitted many women, and has already been mentioned.[51]

[47] Poems in *Gebortstagglückwunch an den Vater* (Wolfenbüttel: Stern, 1639), *Applausus Quibus... Domini Augusti Natalem Septuagensimum Octavum Princips [sic] Clientes et Ministri Avide Mactarunt et Coronarunt* (Wolfenbüttel: Stern, 1656), *Serenissimo et Illustrisimo Principi ac Domino, Domino Augusto, Duc Brunovicensi et Lunaeburgensi* (Wolfenbüttel: Stern, 1656), *Janus Christianus* (Wolfenbüttel: Stern, 1657), *Obeliscus Genialis* (Wolfenbüttel: Stern, 1657).

[48] Blake Lee Spahr, *Anton Ulrich and Aramena: The Genesis and Development of a Baroque Novel*, University of California Publications in Modern Philology 76 (Berkeley and Los Angeles: University of California Press, 1966), 178–80.

[49] *Sereniss. Domus Augustae Selenianae Principis Juventutis utriusque Sexus Pietatis, Eruditionis, Comitatisque Exemplum sine Pari* (Ulm: Balthasar Kühn, 1659).

[50] Wunder, *He is the Sun*, 157.

[51] The Blumenorden was a bourgeois association, playfully pastoral, and concerned with German-language poetry. Blake Lee Spahr, *The Archives of the Pegnesischer Blumenorden: A Survey and Reference Guide*, University of California Publications in Modern Philology 57 (Berkeley and Los Angeles: University of California Press, 1960). Other women members are mentioned by Haendel, *Dissertatio* (1688): Barbara Helena Langia, known as *Erone* (p. 13), Regina Magdalena Limburgeria, *Magdalis* (p. 14), Gertrudis Mölleria, *Mornille* (p. 15), Barbara Juliana Mülleria, *Daphnes* (p. 15), Anna Maria Nützelia, *Amarillis* (p. 16), Elisabetha de Senis, *Celinde* (p. 21). The Herzogin Sophie Elisabeth von Braunschweig-Lüneburg (1613–76) was also a member. A number of members were women of learning and achievement. Langia and Mölleria were both Latinists, and the scholarly, Latinate Margaretha Sibylla von Einsiedel was also associated with the Blumenorden (thanks to Anna Carrdus for this

The importance of such coterie groups in fostering women's writing has been recently emphasized by Ute Brandes.[52] It should perhaps also be noted that Pietist meeting groups, and indeed courts, have a coterie aspect which in some cases clearly operated in favour of learned women.

Latinate court ladies (at least, those who have left evidence for their learning) were a rarer breed in Germany than highly educated princesses. One such is Maria Loysa von Degenfeld, morganatic second wife of Karl Ludwig von der Pfalz, elector palatine, the brother of Elizabeth and Sophia. His wife, Charlotte von der Pfalz (1627–86), was mortally offended when Karl Ludwig rejected her new-year present and gave it to a nobleman: she discussed this with her lady in waiting, Maria Loysa, who suggested that she should refuse to sleep with him. This was the beginning of a process which led eventually to his divorce from Charlotte, and a morganatic marriage with Maria Loysa.[53] The Latin correspondence between the lovers seems to have become famous (or notorious), and was circulated.[54] It was a highly literary one: their private mutual reference point was *Eurylaeus and Lucretia*, the Latin novella of the humanist future pope Aeneas Sylvius Piccolomini.[55]

Though it is clear that the intellectual lives of women at some of the German courts are well worth attention, as are the activities of women immediately related to professional educators, it is one of the interesting features of German women's writing in Latin in the baroque that a number of those who do so are neither aristocrats nor professors' daughters, but merely educated gentlewomen. Though bourgeois daughters were educated at home (Protestant parents were particularly reluctant to trust their girls outside the family circle), their education sometimes achieved a high standard. Elisabeth Katharina Störteroggen (b. 1679) demanded to learn Latin. Her mother found her a tutor, a teacher at the local Latin school who was willing to give her private lessons: she went on to learn Greek, Hebrew, and French.[56] Margarethe Susanna von Kuntsch (b. 1651) is another interesting case: she notes that, 'from an early age, I was more inclined towards learning Latin, French and science, but my parents [she was the daughter of a court official] were more farsighted than I, and judged sensibly that such was more an exercise for

---

information). The taking of academy names of a vaguely classicizing kind is a feature borrowed from Italian academies such as the Arcadi.

[52] Ute Brandes, 'Studiestrube, Dichterklub, Hofgesellschaft, Kreativität und Kulturaler Rahmen weiblischer Erzlkust in Barock', in Gisela Brinker-Gabler (ed.), *Deutsche Literatur von Frauen*, 2 vols. (Munich: C. H. Beck, 1988), 222–47.

[53] Wunder, *He is the Sun*, 160.

[54] One of her Latin letters is quoted by Eberti, who found it in Paschius, *Gynaeceum*: Eberti, *Eröffnetes Cabinet*, 125–7: he picks up on the literary quality of the letter by associating it with *heroides*. The correspondence is discussed in Schelhorn, *Amoenitates*, i. 262–8, 'observationes de epistolis Caroli Ludovici Electoris Palatini et Degenfeldiae Baronissae amatoris.'

[55] Aeneas Sylvius and Niklas von Wyle, *The Tale of Two Lovers: Eurialius and Lucretia*, ed. E. J. Morrall (Amsterdam: Rodopi, 1988), gives Latin text with Niklas von Wyle's 15th-century German translation. There is an anonymous 16th-century English translation: *The Two Lovers: The Goodly History of Lady Lucrece and her Lover Eurialius*, ed. Emily O'Brien and Kenneth R. Bartlett (Ottawa: Dovehouse Editions, 1999).

[56] Moore, *The Maiden's Mirror*, 51.

noblewomen than for women of the middle class'. However, she did learn Latin, French, and other 'scientific subjects', and became a poet.[57] An interesting pair who surface in a number of accounts, a deeply pious widow called Catharina Junckerin who lived with Margarethe Guerit, known as a Latinist, seem to represent an unusual case of an intellectual life shared between unrelated women.[58] Another internationally attested form of cultural participation by women, the public Latin oration, is also occasionally found in the German-speaking world; in the eighteenth century Anna Christina Ehrenfried von Balthasar gave one such, and also acquired a doctorate in philosophy.[59] There were also early modern German women who translated from Latin[60] and, in one case known to me, into that language.[61]

Euphrosine Aue (1677–1715), an educated gentlewoman, published quite extensively in Latin. She was born, lived, and died at Colberg in Pomerania, and though her father Johann Aue was an educated man, he was not an educationalist, but a doctor and privy counsellor. She married twice: her first husband was Carl Cristoph Fritz, Hauptmann, and her second husband was G. Martin Henneken, a merchant. The Latin poems seen by Oelrichs (of which only one seems still to be extant) were published as pamphlets, and seem all to have been of a very public character: obituary poems, marriage poems, and panegyrics. It is noteworthy that the first were written when she was only 9, implying the active involvement of her family in creating her as a published poet. At least two are for a family occasion—the death of the wife of Johann Aue, who must be a relative, and the marriage of a Gottfried Aue—while several others reflect politically important events. Her death was marked by a composition very similar to her own writings, three poems by Christian Trotz, put in the mouths of the Three Graces, in Latin, Italian, and French.[62]

The relationship between Margaretha Sibylla von Einsiedel (1642–90) and her milieu seems to have been similar. She married twice (Rudolph von Bünau in 1658, and Curt Löser in 1664), and attracted public commendation and praise from contemporaries: for example, she was one of the dedicatees, with Henrietta Catharina von Gersdorff, of Smalcius' reply to Sauerbrei.[63] She was known as 'the Misnian Minerva' (Misnia being Dresden) and—like many other learned

---

57 Moore, *The Maiden's Mirror*, 31. A posthumous collection of her poetry was published, *Sämmtliche geist- und weltliche Gedichte* (Halle: Neue Buchhandlung, 1720). See Gisela Brinker-Gabler, *Deutsche Dichterinnen vom 16. Jahrhundert bis zum Gegenwort* (Frankfurt am Main: Fischer, 1978), 101–6.

58 'Caspar Bruschius Redivivus', *Gründliche Beschreibung des Fichtel-Berges* (Nuremberg: Georg Schewen, 1683), 7.

59 Johann Carl Conrad Oelrichs, *Historisch-diplomatisch Beyträge zur Geschichte der Gelahrheit* (Berlin: Buchhardlung der Realschule, 1768), 8.

60 Sibylla von Schwarzin (1621–50) translated the first book of Ovid's *Metamorphoses*, Oelrichs, *Historisch-diplomatisch Beyträge*, 20–1, as did Anna Ovena Hoyer (1584–1655) discussed below.

61 Haendel, *Dissertatio*, 13, notes that Barbara Helena Langia of Nuremberg, a member of the Pegnesischer Blumenorden, translated from French into Latin.

62 Christian Trotz, *Monumentum quod Nobilissimae et Omnium Virtutum, Quibus hic Sexus Commendari Meruit, Corona Ornatissimae nec non Doctissimae Matronae Dominae Euphrosynae Aveniae*...(Stargard: Ernst, 1715).

63 Praised by Smalcius, sig. F1v. See also Paschius, *Gynaeceum*, 44–5.

women—as 'the tenth Muse'. She brought up seven children, two from her first and two from her second marriage, together with three Löser stepchildren. Despite these responsibilities, she continued to study Hebrew, Greek, Latin, Italian, French, mathematics, church history, and theology, and is also described as 'a Saxon Cornelia': that is, a woman who combined deep learning with family commitments.[64] Haendel notes that she was the author of a prose work, *Politicae Christianae*, of which no copy has yet come to light. Her only certain work in Latin is a poem on the death of Anna Sibilla Löser, her second husband's first wife. The pamphlet which contains it also includes Latin and Greek poems by Curt von Einsiedel and Heinrich von Einsiedel, most probably her brothers, suggesting a long-standing friendship between the two families. Another possible Latin poem of Margaretha Sibylla's is a version of a German poem which is certainly hers. It is accompanied by a Latin translation said to have been done by an admirer; while there are other examples of women's writing translated *into* Latin in the seventeenth century (for example, Otto Sperling translated the poems of the Danish princess Eleanora Christina, daughter of Christian IV,[65] poems by the Norwegian Dorothe Engelbredsdatter are translated by Jacob Oersted and Joacim Jacobus Kaae,[66] the Duchess of Newcastle's *The World's Olio* survives in a Latin translation,[67] and Joseph Scaliger translated a French poem by Catherine des Roches into Greek),[68] she may be modestly concealing her own work.[69]

It is thus clear that a number of women from the professional classes were taught Latin in seventeenth-century Germany, and also that there is a substantial overlap between girls' Latin literacy and an unusual degree of religious commitment. There is also a surprisingly high correlation between women's learning Latin and their publishing poetry or prose in German, suggesting that the acquisition of the learned language strengthened women's confidence in their own abilities even if they did not use it directly. But as Ruth P. Dawson has recently shown, though in the eighteenth century intellectually ambitious German women felt their lack of Latin, very few—even fewer than in the seventeenth century—were able to acquire it. Charlotte Amalia Henrici, the wife of a professor and mother of ten who wrote Latin verse, was a very unusual figure in her own time.[70]

---

[64] Haendel, *Dissertatio*, 8.

[65] Albert Thrura, *Gynaeceum Daniae Litterarum* (Altona: Jonas Korte, 1732), 43–7. Sperling is the author of 'De Foeminis Doctis', Copenhagen, Kongelige Bibliothek, GK S 2110.

[66] Thrura, *Gynaeceum*, 47–53.

[67] *Olio seu Mundum*, London, British Library, Harley 7538 (this is a draft, and no author is given).

[68] Paris, Bibliothèque Nationale, Dupuy 395, 'recueil des lettres et d'opuscules latin de Joseph Scaliger' (autograph). 'Protrepticum ad christianissimum Henricum III, Francisce et Poloniae regem, expressum ex versibus Gallicis Catharinae des Roches, Pictaviensis, puellae... en vers grecs', fo. 172.

[69] Christopher Nicolai, *Die überaus grosse und reiche Barmherzigheit Gottes, Wie Sie und an den Neuerbaueten Clödnischen Altar Sinn-reich erwiesen und dargestellt ist* (Wittenberg, 1886). I owe this reference to Anna Carrdus.

[70] Dawson, *The Contested Quill*, 51–2. Other Latinate women of the late 18th century mentioned by Dawson include Luise Adelgunde Culmus Gottschad (1713–62), whose husband, Johann Christoph Gottschad, a professor of Göttingen, went strongly against the cultural current of his time by arguing for and encouraging higher learning in women, and the novelist Wilhelmine von Gersdorf, whose name suggests a connection with the learned von Gersdorffs of the 17th century.

The Low Countries

The education of women in the Low Countries was generally not of a very high standard: middle- and upper-class girls in the seventeenth century learned a little French and music, but the principal focus of their education was practical and related to housewifely skills.[71] There were exceptions to the rule, however. The woman who above all acted as the touchstone for the Protestant defenders (and detractors) of learned women in the seventeenth century is Anna Maria van Schurman (1607–78).[72] She was born in Cologne, but became the most outstanding woman scholar of early modern Holland, whither her family moved when she was a child, and one of the most celebrated in the whole of the Protestant world. By 1675, Edward Phillips could describe her as 'an Hollandish lady, of the most celebrated Fame of any of her Sex that I have heard of in Europe at this day';[73] and she is the only woman whose writings are included in Edward Reynolds's 1658 list of inspirational reading for Christian women.[74] Her education began on conventional lines, with French and music, but when her father became aware of how much Anna was, unprompted, picking up from her brother's Latin lessons (he was tutoring his sons at home, so Anna was in a position to eavesdrop), he encouraged her to take part, and then, as her promise revealed itself, he got private tutors for her.

This is a paradigmatic story for early modern women Latinists in families where brothers were educated both in Latin and at home: the early history of Anne Dacier, née Le Fèvre, is very similar, and another reported case is that of Mme de Brassac, later governess of the young Louis XIV.[75] Anna Maria van Schurman learned Latin, and went on to learn Greek, Hebrew, Syriac, and Coptic. She was also a notable artist, who practised the very Dutch craft of engraving on glass. One of her several self-portrait copper engravings shows a sure and delicate feeling for surface textures such as crisply curled hair and elaborate lace; a less certain grasp of volume.[76] She was not a vain woman: what the self-portraits indicate is the extent to which her milieu demanded that she make her subject herself.

Van Schurman acquired a very public position as a woman scholar, exchanging letters and poems with a wide variety of learned correspondents including Salmasius and Descartes and a number of women who will be discussed below. She was

[71] J. A. Worp (ed.), *Een onwaerdeelycke vrouw. Brieven en verzen van een aan Maria Tesselschade* (Utrecht: HES, 1976 [1918]), p. xvi.

[72] Mirjam de Baar et al. (eds.), *Choosing the Better Part: Anna Maria van Schurman (1607–1678)* (Dordrecht: Kluwer Academic Press, 1996): see also Becker-Cantarino, 'Die "gelehrte Frau" '. There is a new edition of her complete works promised by Dr Pieta van Beek of the University of Stellenbosch.

[73] Edward Phillips, *Theatrum Poetarum*, (London: for Charles Smith, 1675), 254.

[74] Edward Reynolds, *Imitation and Caution for Christian Women* (London: E. M. for George Calvert, 1658), 2.

[75] Claude Dulong, 'From Conversation to Creation', in Natalie Zemon Davis and Arlette Farge (eds.), *A History of Women in the West III: Renaissance and Enlightenment Paradoxes* (Cambridge, Mass.: Belknap Press, 1993), 395–419 (p. 399).

[76] Amsterdam, Rijksprentenkabinet, reproduced in L. Strengholt, *Constanter: het leven von Constantijn Huygens* (Amsterdam: Querido, 1987), 112.

also very much part of the literary circle which assembled round the Dutch poet Pieter Corneliszoon Hooft at Muiden Castle (the so-called *Muidenkring*, i.e Muiden circle). This included other learned women, notably the Roemers sisters, who were artists and poets and also read Latin, Greek, and Italian,[77] and the singer Francisca Duarte, the cultivated daughter of a family of Sephardic Jews in Antwerp. At least one other of these women, Tesselschade Roemers, wrote Latin verse, since two poems survive, discussed below. The Muidenkring also included the most notable men in Dutch literary life, such as Constantijn Huygens and Jacob Cats. The close friendship between Huygens and van Schurman is evidenced by the many Latin poems they exchanged. Cats, himself a popular poet, was irresistibly drawn to brilliant women. His book *Maagdewapen* ('The Maiden's Coat of Arms') was, in effect, a public love letter to Anna Roemers. The principal features of the *wapen* he drew up for the ideal girl featured bees, for industry, and a tulip, for beauty, supported by a lamb for simplicity and a puppy for aptitude.[78] Rejected by Anna Roemers, he subsequently paid his addresses to Anna van Schurman, whom he offered to marry, consoling himself for the second rejection which followed with the thought that she had dedicated herself to a life of celibate scholarship.

It is interesting that when the new University of Utrecht was founded in 1636, its rector, Gisbert Voet, asked Anna van Schurman, the town's most illustrious woman, to write the customary Latin ode for the inaugural ceremony: a very public honour of a kind more frequently offered to Italian women than those of other nations.[79] She makes a pointed comment in this address about the exclusion of women from the student body, and in fact, Voet also arranged for her to attend lectures there, though unseen by the male students, which implies a special arrangement rather than the establishment of a precedent for co-education. She was greatly honoured, and her opinion was sought on a variety of issues of the day, notably the debate, initiated by a professor of medicine from Dordrecht, Jan van Beverwyck, as to whether it was interfering with divine providence to try and prolong the lives of sick people.[80]

Van Beverwyck also embarrassed her considerably by his publication *Van de Wtnementheyt des Vrouwelyken Geslachts* ('On the Excellence of the Female Sex', 1643), which was written at her request, and dedicated to her. This work reveals an

---

[77] Katharina M. Wilson and Frank J. Warnke (eds.), *Women Writers of the Seventeenth Century* (Athens: University of Georgia Press, 1989), 141–88.

[78] Simon Schama, *The Embarrassment of Riches: An Interpretation of Dutch Culture in the Golden Age* (London: Collins, 1987), 408.

[79] A number of instances are discussed in Ch. 6 and 11. Schurman's oration is *Inclytae et Antiquae Urbi Trajectinae Nova Academia Nuperrime Donatae Gratulatur*. She also wrote a Dutch version, printed in *Sermoen van de Nutticheydt der Academien ende Schoelen mitsgaders der Wetenschappen ende Consten die in de selve gheleert werden . . .* door Gisbertus Voetius (Utrecht, 1636). See Pieta van Beek, 'Sol Iustitiae Illustra nos: de "femme savante" Anna Maria van Schurman (1607–1678) en de Universiteit van Utrecht', *Akroterion*, 40 (1995), 145–62.

[80] 'De Vitae Humanae Terminis Responsum', in Jan van Beverwyck, *Epistolica Quaestio de Vitae Termino Fatali an Mobili?* (Leiden, 1639).

unqualified enthusiasm for women (though its tone is difficult to judge, and it may be to some extent tongue in cheek):[81] in addition to the usual parade of examples of learning and virtue, it includes instances of female martial heroism in the defence of various Dutch towns during the long wars with Spain, such as Kenau von Hassellaar, also praised by Paul Melissus.[82] Her response was cautious:[83]

truly I admired your overflowing kindness whereby you have been pleased not only by your elegant style to assert that which alone I lately requested of you, the glory of learning and wisdom to our sex, but to so favour our cause as to equal us everywhere to men, that I may not say, to prefer us.

Van Beverwyck was not a negligible figure. Besides being a professor of medicine, he was also a regent of Dordrecht. His first wife, Anna van Duverden, was well educated, and he announced in *Van de Wtnementheyt* that he wanted to educate his own daughters to van Schurman's level.[84] He also provides evidence that a number of women contemporaries besides van Schurman were educated in several languages, including Latin, such as Franske van Doyem, 'la muse Frisonne'. [85] It is interesting to see such a man making an argument for women's aptitude and ability. It is also significant that this work was published in a cheap octavo format adorned with simple woodcuts as well as in a large, expensive quarto decorated with engravings: this is the early modern equivalent of bringing out a paperback as well as a hardback edition, and thus an indication that the work in question is expected to sell.

Anna van Schurman was particularly interested in women's educational opportunities. Later in the 1630s, she wrote a treatise on the education of women, *De Ingenii Muliebris ad Doctrinam, et Meliores Litteras Aptitudine*, which was translated into English in 1659 as *The Learned Maid, or Whether a Maid may be a Scholar* (and also into French).[86] She corresponded with the English woman scholar Bathsua Rainolds (Makin).[87] Another English feminist friend and correspondent was Dorothy Moore, who wrote a proposal for women's education in England which went unpublished. Despite these contacts, she seems to have known little of the tradition of learned women in England. In a letter to the learned

[81] Cornelia Niekus Moore, ' "Niet de geboorte maar de gewoonte": Johan van Beverwyck's *Van de Wtnemenheyt des vrouwelicken geslachts* in een Europese context', in Arie-Jan Geldenblom and Harald Hendrix (eds.), *De vrouw in de Renaissance* (Amsterdam: Amsterdam University Press, 1994), 28–41 (p. 41).

[82] Paul Melissus, *Melissi Schediasmata Poetica* (Paris: Arnold Sittart, 1586), 640, *In Picturam Kenniae Harlemiae, Viraginis Bellicosissimae*: see Gerda H. Kurz, *Kenu Symonsdochter van Haerlem* (Assen: van Gorcum, 1956).

[83] This letter is translated with her own *De Ingenii Muliebris...Aptitudine* in *The Learned Maid*, 37–40.

[84] Lia van Gemert, 'The Power of the Weaker Vessels: Simon Schama and Johan van Beverwijk on Women', in Els Kloek et al. (eds.), *Women of the Golden Age* (Hilversum: Verloren, 1994), 39–50.

[85] Thus known for her study of music, Latin, French, and Italian. *Van de Wtnementheyt des vrouwelicken geslachts* (Dordrecht: Hendrick van Esch, 1643), 77.

[86] *Question celebre. S'il est necessaire, ou non, que les filles soient sçavantes*, trans. Sr. Colletet (Paris: Rolet le Duc, 1646).

[87] *Opuscula*, 162–4.

princess Elizabeth von der Pfalz, daughter of Elizabeth Stuart, she juxtaposes only Elizabeth I and Lady Jane Grey with 'the many illustrious women of Greece and Rome'.[88] Her correspondence is remarkably polyglot, and much of it is exchanged with other learned women. Makin wrote to her in Greek, and she wrote to Dorothy Moore in Hebrew. She wrote in French to Elizabeth von der Pfalz, Madame Contel, Anne de Rohan (a French poet), and Mlle du Moulin.[89] She also exchanged correspondence with the aged Marie de Gournay (forty years her senior), whom she hails as a heroine for her defence of women:[90]

> Palladis arma geris, bellis animosa virago;
>   utque geras lauros, Palladis arma geris.
> Sic decet innocui causam te dicere sexus,
>   et propria insontes vertere tela viros.
> I prae Gornacense decus, tua signa sequemur:
>   quippe tibi potior, robore, causa praeit.
>
> You bear the arms of Pallas, virago courageous in war;
> That you may wear the laurels, you bear the arms of Pallas.
> So, it is fitting that you should plead the cause of the harmless sex,
> And that men should, without doing harm, reverse their own weapons.
> Go ahead, glory of Gournay, we will follow your standards,
> Seeing that a cause superior in strength to yourself is leading the way!

As well as acknowledging the work of older women, she was kindly and fostering to younger scholars. She wrote a Latin panegyric poem in support of a young Danish noblewoman, Birgitta Thott (1610–62), who went on to translate the works of Seneca into Danish.[91]

Van Schurman's later life took an unhappier turn. Deeply religious all her life, even by the standards of the times, she was attracted to an unorthodox religious teacher, Jean de La Badie, with whom she joined forces to found a small Quaker-like sect, which was vigorously persecuted, and she spent the last ten years of her life with him. She thus ended her life moving from place to place with her co-religionists (who later attracted another of early modern Germany's most remarkable women, the painter and entomologist Maria Sibylla Merian).[92] Schurman composed a spiritual autobiography, *Eukleria, seu Melioris Partis Electio* ('The Choice of the Better Part', with reference to Mary Magdalene) a sort of

---

[88] Ibid. 281–7, letter to 'madame la princesse de Boheme', p. 285: 'J'oferois opposer une seule Elizabeth en sa vie Reyne d'Angleterre, et une Jeanne Graye à toutes les illustres femmes de la Grèce et de la Rome ancienne.' See Wilson and Warnke (eds.), *Women Writers*, 171–4.

[89] *Opuscula*, 149–76.

[90] *Magni ac Generosi Animi Heroinae Gornacensi, Causam Sexus Nostri Fortiter Defendenti Gratulatur*, ibid. 303 (this is with reference to Marie de Gournay's *L'Egalité des hommes et des femmes* (Paris, 1622)). There is a letter from de Gournay to van Schurman in The Hague, Koninklijke Bibliotheek, 133 B 8, letter number 76, dated 20 Oct. 1639.

[91] Marianne Alenius, 'Learned Scandinavian Women in the Seventeenth and Eighteenth Centuries', in Alexander Dalzell et al. (eds.), *Acta Conventus Neo-Latini Torontoniensis* (Binghamton, NY: Medieval and Renaissance Text Society, 1991), 181.

[92] Davis, *Women on the Margins*, 157–60.

'apologia pro vita sua' to try and explain herself to her old friends, whose opinion she still valued. She died at Wieuwerd in Friesland, completely alienated from her previous associates.

The fame of Anna Maria van Schurman has tended to give the impression that she was not merely the cynosure, but the phoenix of Netherlandic women's culture. This is not entirely the case: she was probably the only woman to study Syriac in her immediate milieu,[93] but she was not the only Latinist. One of her personal friends, Maria Roemers, known as Tesselschade (this odd name, Texel–damage, arose because her birth coincided with a disaster to her merchant father's ships at Texel in Friesland), was able to write Latin verse. She wrote a number of occasional poems on the visit of Marie de Médicis, exiled Queen Dowager of France, to the Low Countries in 1638 (she was en route to stay with her daughter, Queen Henrietta Maria of England), and one in Italian, two in Latin, were collected, probably by an Italian since the biographic note on author and context are in that language, and copied in François-Nicolas Baudot's *Women Distinguished for Virtue and Knowledge*, now in the Bibliothèque Mazarine in Paris.[94]

> Arnus habet flores vestrae Regina iuventae
> > fructibus aestivis Sequana dignus erat.
> Jure suo primos retinet sibi Gallia; sorte
> > cum Tamesi reliquos dividis ante Iber.
> Unica in Autumno Batavis instaret oliva
> > Namque hac non Tamesis non superaret Iber.

> O Queen, the Arno enjoyed the flowers of your youth,
> The Seine was worthy of your summer fruits,
> France keeps for itself, rightfully, the first fruits;
> The rest, you divide by lot with the Thames, O Ebro.
> Would that the unparalleled olive tree would come to the Dutch in the autumn,
> For this way, neither the Thames nor the Ebro would have superiority.

Curiously, the Latin verses were not collected within Holland, though the Italian poem was printed at the time along with her friend Jacob Vondel's *Welcome for Marie de Medici*.[95] Tesselschade's collected poems reveal her secure position within a literary coterie composed of some of the most intelligent and powerful people in Holland.[96] At least two, Caspar Barlaeus and Constantijn Huygens, wrote to her in Latin, which helps to confirm her understanding of the language and hence her authorship of the Paris poems.[97]

---

[93] Though note that this language was also studied by Anna Weisbruck, wife of Johann Forster, the professor of Hebrew at Wittenberg, mentioned above.

[94] Paris, Bibliothèque Mazarine, 4398, fo. 217ᵛ. Discussed in Ian Maclean, *Woman Triumphant* (Oxford: Clarendon Press, 1977), 27–8.

[95] Worp (ed.), *Een onwaerdeelycke vrouw 179, and note p. xxxi.*

[96] Apart from the poems and letters printed by Worp, see also Mieke Smits-Velt, *Maria Tesselschade en haar literaire vrienden* (Amsterdam: Universiteitsbibliotheek van Amsterdam, 1994).

[97] Worp (ed.), *Een onwaerdeelycke vrouw,* 142–3, 144, 165.

Another woman Latin poet who, like Johanna Otho earlier in the century, published her work, was also clearly part of the literary world of her time despite her bourgeois background and milieu. Elisabeth Hoofman (1664–1736) was born in Haarlem, the daughter of Joost Hoofman, a leading merchant of the town. As early as her sixth year, she began to make little verses, and she learned Latin by the age of 16. On 22 August 1693 she married Pieter Koolaart, also a merchant of Haarlem, though not a successful one, as his third wife. They were forced to leave Haarlem, and went first to Lisse, then in 1721 to Kassel, where he was director of commerce. She brought up a stepdaughter Hester, who was deaf, and had a daughter of her own, Petronella Elizabeth. She died at Kassel, in Hesse: her last few years were spent in poverty after her husband's death in 1732.[98] Most of her surviving work is political, and celebrates the battles and triumphs of the landgraves of Hessen-Kassel (Karl I, on whom she wrote, was a highly enlightened and cultivated person, patron of the scientist Johann Bessler). An exception is her *Messias, of heylige herdes-zang op de geboorte van den Heyland* ('Messiah, or Holy Shepherds' Song on the Birth of the Saviour') an eclogue in parallel versions, Latin and Dutch, published in 1729. Most of her work is collected in the posthumous edition by Willem Kops, and she is mentioned in *La Biographie universelle*.[99] An interesting piece of evidence for her relations with other writers is provided by a friendly poem she wrote to Theodoor Jansson van Almeloveen on his recovery from illness in 1696, when she was a young married woman still living in Haarlem (Jansson was a distinguished classical scholar, antiquary, and editor of Latin texts).[100] Rather interestingly, this poem survives because Jansson received it shortly before a letter from a German woman Latinist, Helena Sibylla Wagenseil (1669–1735), discussed above, who had also sent him verses—he enclosed it in his Latin reply to the latter, because he thought it would interest her, thus making the two young women aware of one another.

There is a Dutch example of the internationally familiar paradigm of the 'pedagogue's learned daughter', Margaretha Godewijk (1627–77), the daughter of Pieter van Godewijk, Corrector of the Latin school in Dordrecht. According to Matthias Balen, she studied Greek, Latin, Italian, French, and English,[101] and she wrote in Latin and Dutch. A manuscript volume of poetry is preserved in The Hague,[102] not autograph, but copied from apparently lost manuscripts of Margaretha and her father probably *c*.1900 (almost certainly the manuscript book mentioned by van der Aa as having been made by the Tilburg predikant Gillis Dionysius Jacobus Schotel, who also wrote a book on van Schurman). The

---

[98] J. H. Hoeufft (ed.), *Parnasus Latino-Belgicus, sive Plerique e Poetis Belgii Latinis, Epigrammata atque Adnotationi Illustrati* (Amsterdam: Peter den Kengst en fil., 1819), 201.

[99] *Biographie universelle* 83 vols, (Paris: Michaud Frères, 1811–53) xx. 532.

[100] Another poem to Jansson is in her published poems, *De Naaglaatene Gedichten von Elizabeth Koolaart geb. Hoofman*, ed Willem Kops (Haarlem: Jan Bosch, 1774), 179. Jansson was a person of some consequence in the *respublica litterarum*: there is a collection of letters addressed to him in the Camerarius collection, Munich, Staatsbibliothek, Clm lat. 18085 (no. 34).

[101] Matthys Balen, *Beschryvinge der Stad Dordrecht* (Dordrecht: S. onder de Linde, 1677), 203.

[102] The Hague, Koniglijke Bibliotheek 128 F 10.

manuscript contains a quantity of poetry in Dutch and English, including what seem to be the *disjecta membra* of an emblem book (Latin distichs, Dutch verses of normally four lines, and a brief description of an accompanying image, not given), a variety of Latin verse of poor quality, and a self-portrait tipped in from an unnamed book (p. 203), an engraving described as a copy of a painting. She also published at least one Latin poem, a Restoration ode contributed to a volume of congratulation to the new Charles II. Like Anna Maria van Schurman, she was a friend of Jan van Beverwyck, and wrote a Latin poem in his honour. She is the last certain woman Latin poet of the Netherlands, though a number of subsequent women writers were highly educated.

A similar, slightly later figure, Sara Maria van der Wilp (1716–1803), daughter of the Conrector of the Latin school in Amsterdam, wrote only in Dutch (though she translated Alexander Pope's *Messiah*, itself based on Virgil's Fourth Eclogue).[103] A still later poet, Joanna-Catharina van Goethem (1720–76), from the East Flemish town of Vrasene, had a great reputation for learning, having been taught Latin by her father: she certainly translated from Latin, and may also have written in that language.[104] Juliana Cornelia, Baronesse de Lannoy (1738–82), learned Latin and wrote on classical themes, but did not write in Latin.[105] A very interesting person, a noblewoman called F. C. Roscam who must have flourished in the 1730s, is gratefully remembered by the black theologian and controversialist Jacobus Elisa Johannes Capitein (1717–47). She seems not to have written anything, but she was obviously a person of influence as well as learning: Capitein records, 'she greatly helped me in learning Latin, and then taught me the rudiments of Greek, Hebrew and Syriac. She is dedicated to unblemished piety and to the study of languages, and she makes her house available to young students without charge.'[106] The shadowy Roscam serves as an indication that even in the eighteenth century, the tradition most visibly represented by van Schurman quietly continued.

Scandinavia

Another remarkable aspect of northern baroque culture is a late efflorescence of women Latinists in Scandinavia.[107] Neo-Latin culture in Sweden, Denmark,

[103] Riet Schenkeveld-van der Dussen et al., *Met en zonder lauwerkranz* (Amsterdam: Amsterdam University Press, 1997), 561–4.

[104] Ibid. 565–71.

[105] Ibid. 632–8. De Lannoy also wrote in defence of women: W. B. de Vries, ' "De wonderbaare daad" en andere gedichten van Juliana Cornelia de Lannoy over de capaciteiten van vrouwen', in H. Duits, A. J. Gelderblom, and M. B. Smits-Veldt (eds.), *Klinkend Boeket. Studies over renaissancesonnetten voor Marijke Spies* (Hilversum: Verloren, 1994), 173–8.

[106] Jacobus Elisa Johannes Capitein, *Dissertatio Politico-theologica de Servitute Libertti Christianae non Contraria* (Leiden: Samuel Luchmans, 1742), p. xv, translated as *The Agony of Asar*, by Grant Parker (Princeton: Markus Wiener, 2001), 92.

[107] Alenius, 'Learned Scandinavian Women'.

Norway, and Iceland was essentially a by-product of the Lutheran reformation: by the late sixteenth century, there was a Latin boys' school in every provincial town in Denmark, the primary purpose of which was to produce Latin-literate pastors.[108] The situation in Sweden was similar, though Swedish culture flowered into something of a neo-Latin golden age in the seventeenth century, in which Latin was the natural language of literary expression.[109] In Norway, the educated intelligentsia was smaller: books were very scarce and expensive, and only about 200 Norwegian young men attended university in the second half of the sixteenth century.[110] Finland is more linguistically complex; in the eighteenth century, the people spoke Finnish, while the aristocracy, clergy, and urban middle class spoke Swedish, neither of which was perceived as a language of culture, and therefore learning was expressed in Latin.[111] Latin education for women in all the Nordic countries was therefore a by-product; the result of the new class of educated men bringing their knowledge home. Lutheran pastors were permitted to marry, and the phrase 'pastor's daughter' frequently figures in accounts of Scandinavian learned women.

Latin figured in the lives of Scandinavian princesses, as it did in the lives of many early modern royal women. By the late sixteenth century, both the Danish and the Swedish royal families were studying Latin. When Erik, Prince of Sweden, offered marriage to Elizabeth I, he was able to write to her personally in Latin. But the most famous baroque Scandinavian princess is of course Christina of Sweden (1626–86).[112] She was the daughter of the great warrior king Gustavus Adolphus, and was reared as a future ruler, so therefore thoroughly educated. It is worth noting that she (and her cousin Eleonora, who shared her studies)[113] was taught the art of declamation: clearly, her status as queen overrode any possible cavils that public speaking was not a womanly art, as it did for Elizabeth I, but it is interesting that her cousin took part in these lessons also.[114] Christina grew up to have markedly scholarly tastes, reading freely in Latin and modern languages. Her library was famous; much of it is now in the Vatican, while other books form the core of the University Library in Leiden, brought there by her erstwhile librarian,

---

[108] Minne Skafte Jensen (ed.), *A History of Nordic Neo-Latin Literature* (Odense: Odense University Press, 1995), 20. See also Ruth Nilsson, 'Lärda Kvinnor i Sverige', in Marianne Alenius and Peter Zeeberg (eds.), *Litteratur og Laerdom* (Copenhagen: Museum Tusculanum Forl., 1987), 57–64.

[109] Hans Aili, 'Sweden', in Jensen (ed.), *History of Nordic Neo-Latin*, 139.

[110] Anders Anton von Stiernman, 'Gynæceum Sveciæ litterarum eler Anmärkningat om Lärde och Namnkunniga Swenska Fruentimmer', *Stockholms Magazin for 1780* (Stockholm: Magnus Swederus, 1780), 207–54, prints a Latin letter from Skytte to her father, written in 1628, pp. 252–4. See also Inger Ekerem, 'Norway', in Jensen (ed.), *History of Nordic Neo-Latin*, 69.

[111] Iiro Kajanto, in Jensen (ed.), *History of Nordic Neo-Latin*, 159–200.

[112] Susanna Åkerman, *Queen Christina of Sweden and her Circle: The Transformation of a Seventeenth-Century Philosophical Libertine* (Leiden: E. J. Brill, 1991). See for a more biographic account Georgina Masson, *Queen Christina* (London: Martin Secker & Warburg, 1968).

[113] She was the daughter of John Casimir of Pfalz-Zweibrücken-Kleeburg, a Wittelsbach, that is, a member of a family at least some branches of which took the education of its daughters seriously.

[114] Masson, *Queen Christina*, 56. However, she notes that Eleonora stops being mentioned as a schoolroom companion by 1641.

Isaac Vossius.[115] After her father's death at the Battle of Lützen in 1632, she came to the throne at the age of 6, and Sweden was ruled by a regency while she remained a minor. Once she began ruling in her own right, she soon found herself in disagreement with the nobility who had acted as regents. Although she played a significant role in the ending of the Thirty Years War, her works of educational reform, improvement, and philanthropy were beyond what the resources of the country could sustain. Apart from the frustration caused by this, she was repelled by the notion of marriage, and as early as 1651 began to consider abdicating in favour of her younger cousin, the future Charles X: she did so in 1654. Queen Christina certainly used Latin fluently, since Latin letters survive in some number, but she preferred French for her personal writing. Ulrica Eleonora, Queen of Charles XI, read Latin, French, Italian, Danish, German, and Swedish, as her library at Drottningholm bears witness.[116] Her daughter, another Ulrica Eleonora (1688–1741), governed the kingdom during the absence of her brother Charles XII, and was proclaimed queen after his death in 1719. It seems probable therefore that she was educated for rule.

Royal ladies aside, perhaps the first highly educated woman to appear in Sweden was in fact a German, Anna Ovena Hoyer.[117] She was born at Eyderstadt in Holstein in 1584, and died at Westerwick in Sweden in 1655. Her father Hans Owen/Oven was an astronomer, and her husband, Hermann Hoyer van Hoyerswört, was related to the Danish royal house. Though she is not known to have written in Latin, she read Latin, Greek, and Hebrew, and translated one of the most popular of neo-Latin prose works, the novella *Euryali et Lucretiae*, from the Latin of Aeneas Silvius Piccolomini, a translation which was published in Schleswig in 1617.[118] She was supported by the then Herzogin of Wolfenbüttel (who was a Danish princess, the sister of Anne of Denmark), and, when she fled to Sweden on account of opposition to her protection of Anabaptists and other sectarians, also by Queen Maria Eleonora, Queen Christina's mother.

The first native-born women Latinists appear in Sweden around the turn of the seventeenth century. Catharina Bure (1601–78) is one of the earliest. She was the daughter of Gustavus Adophus' tutor, the first 'riksantikvarie', or royal historian, of Sweden, Johannes Tomas Buræus (Johann Bure), and of Margareta Bang.[119] She

---

[115] One useful guide to what was actually in her library is the catalogue made by Vossius in 1650, reprinted in facsimile, *Katalog över handskriften I kungl. Biblioteket I Stockholm skriven omkr. 1650, under ledig av Isaac Vossius*, ed. Christian Callmer (Stockholm: Kungl. Boktryckeriet, 1971). See also C. Callmer, 'Königin Christina, ihre Bibliothekare und ihre Handschriften. Beiträge zur Europäischen Bibliotheksgeschichte', *Acta Bibliothecae Regiae Stockholmiensis*, 30 (1977), 43–93.

[116] There are at least twelve printed Latin panegyrics on her death in 1693, an unusual number; she also received a Latin panegyric ode on her formal entry into Stockholm from the pen of Josua Arnd, *Carmen Panegyricum* (Guestrow: Typis Schieppelianis, 1680).

[117] She published a book of poems, *Annae Ovenae Hoijers Geistliche und Weltliche Poemata* (Amsterdam: Ludwig Elzevier, 1650). See Brigitte Edith Archibald, 'A View of Practical Living: Anna Owena Hoyers', in *WWRR*, 304–26.

[118] *SKGF*, 55. See n. 55 on *Eurialius and Lucretia*.

[119] Von Stiernman, 'Gynæceum Sveciæ', 210–11. Some of her Latin letters, including letters to her father, are in von Stiernman, *Bibliotheca SuioGothica*, 7 vols (Stockholm: Gercken, 1731), ii. 805.

exchanged Latin letters with a slightly younger Swedish noblewoman, Wendela Skytte (1609–28).[120] Von Stiernman records that Skytte composed Latin orations as well as Latin letters,[121] and also that the daughter of the Bishop of Gotheborg, Hedvig Eleonora Klingenstierna (who flourished in the second half of the seventeenth century), pronounced a Latin oration at the Gymnasium of Lynköping, probably the most northerly instances of this Europe-wide phenomenon.[122]

The first actual woman Latin poet of Sweden, as far as anyone knows, is Sophia Elisabeth Brenner, née Weber (1659–1730). Sophia Weber was the daughter of a merchant of German ancestry, born in Stockholm, who believed in women's education, and had her taught as if she were a boy, an education which included Latin. She married Elias Brenner, a Finno-Swedish miniature painter and numismatist, in 1680. The couple took their place among Swedish artists and writers, and Sophia presided over a salon which was visited by many leading figures of the day. She is an amazing exception to the rule of thumb that pre-modern women writers had few or no children. In a letter to Otto Sperling, she explains why she did not write more: 'I have fifteen living children, the first five of whom I nursed myself.'[123]

Despite this staggering record of maternity, she is considered the first notable Swedish-language woman poet. She proclaimed her linguistic patriotism and preference for writing in Swedish, while maintaining her presence in the international *respublica litterarum* through verse in Latin. As a Latinist, her oeuvre may be compared with that of German Latin poets such as Euphrosine Aue, since it consists mainly of occasional poetry for weddings and funerals. Her considerable contemporary success is attributable both to her own determined professionalism, and also to the desire of learned Swedes to promote her as an object of legitimate national pride.

The Swedish scholar Urbanus Hiärne was introduced to the principle of publishing by subscription during a visit to England: Brenner's *Poetiske Dikter* (1713), an elaborate and expensive production, is the first Swedish book to have been published in this way. Other significant evidence for her position within Swedish culture is provided by the appendix to *Poetiska Dikter*, a collection of 'testimonia' *On the Famous Poetess of the Swedes*. It opens with a letter to Brenner by Hiärne, which places her on a level with Anna Maria van Schurman, Anne Dacier, Olimpia Morata, and Elena Cornaro Piscopia, recent and very high-profile learned women. This is followed by two women's poems of compliment, both in Spanish: a sonnet by a nun, Doña Catalina de Alfaro Fernández de Córdoba, and a

---

[120] Marianne Alenius, 'Om alle slags berömdvärda kvinnnoperoner Gynæceum—en kvinnalitteraturhistoria', in Elisabeth Møller Jensen (ed.), *I Guds Namm* (Höganas: A. B. Wiken, 1993), 217–32 (p. 232). Wendela Skytte was daughter of Johann Skytte, 'de riksrådet friherre', and Maria Jacobsdatter. In 1626, she married Hans Kyle. Von Stiernman, 'Gynæceum Sveciæ', 247–9, gives an account of her, and prints a Latin letter from Skytte to her father, pp. 254–6.

[121] *Bibliotheca SuioGothica*, i. 597.

[122] Von Stiernman, 'Gynæceum Sveciæ', 215.

[123] Marianne Alenius, 'Love at First (W)ink', in Graham de Caie and Holger Nørgaard (eds.), *A Literary Miscellany Presented to Eric Jacobsen* (Copenhagen: University of Copenhagen Press, 1988), 178.

long poem in thirty-seven quatrains by the Mexican poet and mystic, Sor Juana
Inés de la Cruz, on sig. A2ᵛ–A3ᵛ. which addresses her as 'the great Minerva of the
Goths' (because the Swedes were believed to be descended from the Goths of the
ancient world). Both these poems are variants on ones published in Sor Juana's
own first collection, *Inundacion castalida de la unica poetisa, musa dezima*, published
in Madrid by Juan Garcia Infanzon, in 1689: Sor Catalina's addressed to Sor Juana
herself, and Sor Juana's to the learned Duquesa de Aveiro, raising the question of
whether the adaptations were made by the authors or by another hand.[124] In any
case, these poems were the result of active solicitation by her supporters within
Sweden, as Elisabet Göransson has demonstrated.[125] Johan Gabriel Sparenfeldt
(or Sparfvenfeldt) peregrinated through Europe, and wherever he went, he asked
learned men and women to write on Sophia Brenner. By 1696, she was assisting his
publicity campaign by putting together 'packages of recommendation' consisting
of both her own poems and poems about her. These often generated replies. Otto
Sperling, who was writing on learned women at the time, was delighted to be in
touch with her.[126] Sebastian Korthold dedicated his *Essay on Women Poets*, which
focused on women writing in the classical languages, to her.[127] She corresponded
voluminously in Latin as well as Swedish: more than thirty letters to and from her
survive, many exchanged with Otto Sperling, though there are also two women
correspondents, Katarina Bååth and Catherina Gyllengrip.[128] As Göransson has
shown, she became very much a literary businesswoman: when a poem was
commissioned from her in memory of Tsar Peter the Great of Russia, she
demurred because she had had no reply to a poem of the previous year on the
Tsarina Catherine I. Once paid—and sent a medal for good measure—she announced her willingness to write.[129] Brenner championed an ideal of freedom

---

[124] The complexities of this are considerable and there is no space to discuss them here: I have
treated the issue at length in a paper, 'Sor Juana and the Position of the Woman Intellectual in Spanish
America', which will I hope be forthcoming in a collection of essays on Mexico City in the 1680s edited
by Jean Andrews.

[125] In a paper read at the Eleventh International Congress of the Societas Internationalis Studii
Neolatinis Provehendis, Cambridge, 30 July–5 August 2000, based on material which forms part of her
Ph.D. thesis on Sophia Elisabeth Brenner's correspondence. She has also written a paper on women's
correspondence with Otto Sperling, to be published in the next volume of *Supplementa Humanistica
Lovaniensia*.

[126] His *De Foeminis Doctis* survives in manuscript, Copenhagen, Kungliga Bibliotek, GK S 2110, but
was never published. He seems to have contributed material to Thrura's *Gynaeceum Daniae Litterarum*.
See also Alenius, 'Love at First (W)ink'. There is a surviving letter from Elena Piscopia to Leonora
Margaretha Sperling, Munich, Bayerische Staatsbibliothek, Clm lat. 1085 (Collectio Camerariana 34),
fo. 247ʳ⁻ᵛ: this is almost certainly Helena Margarethe Rosenbielke, née Friis, who was the niece of Otto
Sperling and was educated by him, introduced in *litterae humaniores* in earliest youth, and taught Latin.
Thrura, *Gynaeceum*, 58.

[127] *Disquisitio de Poetriis Puellis, Missis ab Adriano Bailleto* (Keil: Barthold Reuther, 1700).

[128] Karin Westman Berg, Valborg Lindgärde, and Marianne Alenius, 'Wår Swenska Minerva: om
Sophia Elisabeth Brenner', in Lensen (ed.), *I Guds Namm*, 325–40 (p. 336).

[129] J. Küttner, 'V. N Tatiščevs mission i Sverige, 1724–1726', *Lychnos* (1990), 109–64 (pp. 151–2).
Interestingly, at about the same time the Dutch poet (resident in Germany) Elisabeth Koolaart was
writing in praise of Peter the Great: see her *De Naaglaatene Gedichten von Elizabeth Koolaart geb.
Hoofman*, ed Willem Kops (Haarlem: Jan Bosch, 1774).

within, rather than outwith, marriage: she exhorted other women to marry, but what she envisaged of marriage was a sharing of intellectual pursuits on equal terms with men. She also demanded women's right to study, but as amateurs: she did not ask for access to the professions.[130] It is understandable that a mother of fifteen should perceive marriage as constituting a job in itself.

Like those of Anna Maria van Schurman, to whom she was compared, Sophia Elisabeth Brenner's outstanding achievements can be contexted against a background of other learned women in her milieu. While Queen Ulrica Eleonora seems not to have written in Latin herself, she gathered around her a coterie of highly educated court ladies, and though Brenner was not a courtier, she had connections with those who were.[131] Maria Gustava Gyllenstierna (1672–1739) translated Josephus' *Jewish History*, so she may have known Latin or even Greek (though it is more likely she translated from an existing modern-language version). She also wrote Swedish verse in praise of Sophia Brenner, 'Wår dyra Skalde Fru', and translated from German.[132] Another of the Queen's ladies, Ebba Maria de la Gardie, wrote verses in Ulrica Eleonora's praise,[133] and the queen also attracted a variety of other verse collected in the same manuscript (the contents of which are mostly anonymous) and a Latin panegyric of unknown authorship.[134]

The most remarkable of Ulrica Eleonora's ladies is also one of the most glamorous and surprising of women Latinists in Sweden and, indeed, northern Europe generally: Maria Aurora, Gräfin von Königsmarck (1662–1728), the dedicatee of Lehms's *Deutschlands galante Poetinnen*, an extremely important collection of early modern German women's writing.[135] She was a highly cultivated woman, who also wrote in French, Italian, Swedish, and English, and was brought up in Stockholm, though part of her early life was also spent in Paris. She was a prolific poet in German and French, and her participation in the cultural life of the Swedish court is evidenced in various ways: for example, she instigated a performance of Racine's *Iphigénie* at the court in Stockholm in 1684, in which she acted the part of Clytemnestra. She was a patron of Sophia Elisabeth Brenner, who directed poems both to her and to her brothers Karl Johann and Otto Wilhelm Königsmarck. Her own surviving Latin verse, as so often with aristocratic women, is devoted to family necrology.

---

[130] Alenius, 'Love at First (W)ink', 175.

[131] Valborg Lindgärde, 'Om kungadotter som offras i männenskrig, Hovkretsan kring drottning Ulrika Eleonora', in Jensen (ed.), *I Guds Namm*, 311–16.

[132] Valborg Lindgärde, 'Grevinnan på Tyresö Slott, Om Maria Gustava Gyllenstierna', in Jensen (ed.), *I Guds Namm*, 317–24. There is a manuscript of poems which she translated from German in Stockholm, Kungl. Biblioteket, A 591, 'Om Herrans Jesu Christi heliga lefwerne, oversatt från tysken, 260 sonetten.'

[133] Uppsala, Universitetsbiblioteket, Psalmsk. 389 (unpaginated). See von Stiernman, 'Gynæceum Sveciæ', 208–9.

[134] Uppsala, Universitetsbiblioteket, Ihre 125 (6).

[135] Lehms, *Teutschlands galante Poetinnen* (1715), sig. A5ᵛ–7ᵛ. On Lehms's work, see Winfried von Borell, 'Georg Christian Lehms: Ein vergessener Barockdichter und Vorkämpfer des Frauenstudiums', *Jahrbuch der Schlesischen Friedrich-Wilhelm Universität zu Breslau*, 9 (1964), 50–105. There is a biography of von Königsmarck, by Birger Mörner.

In August 1694, she went to Dresden, initially with the hopes of persuading its new ruler, Churprinz Augustus II , 'the Strong', to interest himself in the fate of her younger brother Philipp Christoph (or, as the English emissary George Stepney cynically commented, to persuade him to disgorge the 30,000 dollars he owed Philipp Christoph in gambling debts).[136] Philipp Christoph had been murdered a couple of months previously by four courtiers in the service of Ernst Augustus of Hanover, to avenge the insult to the family represented by his open affair with Sophia Dorothea, the wife of George Louis, Elector of Hanover (the future King George I of England). Augustus was duly persuaded to make an official inquiry into the assassination, but more significantly, by the end of the month, his acquaintance with Aurora had ripened to the extent that she was recognized as one of the king's principal mistresses. She publicly partnered the elector at the Carnival of 1695, and played the goddess Aurora in a masque, the *Götteraufzug* ('cavalcade of the gods'), on 7 February.[137] A year later, in February 1696, she produced an opera-ballet, *Das Musenfest*, at court. The previous October, she had borne the elector a child, Moritz Hermann, later one of Louis XV's most famous commanders, known as Mauritz von Sachsen, or 'le maréchal de Saxe' (through whom she was the great-great-great-grandmother of George Sand, whose real Christian name was Aurore). She left the court after producing her opera, and bought a house in Silesia where she lived in retirement for a couple of years, though she often visited Saxony.[138] She seems to have continued to perform some diplomatic functions: she and her sister helped to entertain Tsar Peter the Great when he passed through Dresden in June 1698 on his way to meet Augustus at Rawa Ruska, and she is known on one occasion to have acted as a confidential messenger on her ex-lover's behalf. At some time before 1704, she carried 'several letters of dangerous consequence to the liberty of Poland' between Augustus (who had become King of Poland) and the King of Sweden.[139] She was also involved as a go-between in negotiating peace with Sweden in 1705.[140]

Late in the 1690s, she transferred her principal residence to the royal convent of Quedlinburg. An Ottonian foundation in Saxony-Anhalt, it had been established in the tenth century by Matilda, widow of Henry the Fowler, as a collegiate foundation for aristocratic women (and is discussed in Chapter 4). In the 1540s, Anna von Stelberg, as abbess, accepted the Reformation for Quedlinburg, making it a Lutheran sodality which survived until the Napoleonic suppression.[141] Its abbesses effectively controlled the town: when it attempted to assert municipal independence in the fifteenth century by joining the Hanseatic League, the

[136] Tony Sharp, *Pleasure and Ambition* (London: I. B. Tauris, 2001), 87.

[137] Ibid. 112.

[138] Ibid. 217.

[139] Ibid. 205–6.

[140] Ibid. 221.

[141] Merry Wiesner, 'The Holy Roman Empire: Women and Politics', in Hilda L. Smith (ed.), *Women Writers and the Early Modern British Political Tradition* (Cambridge: Cambridge University Press, 1998), 305–23 (p. 311).

abbesses succeeded in re-establishing ecclesiastical dominance, which is one reason why Quedlinburg never developed into a major city. The abbesses of free imperial convents, as Merry Wiesner has pointed out, functioned like the city council of a free imperial city, as the penultimate legal authority, answering only to the emperor. A contemporary of von Königsmarck's, Friedrich Ernst Kettner, used the example of Quedlinburg to defend the principle of women's rule.[142]

It was a highly cultivated as well as aristocratic institution. One of von Königs-marck's immediate predecessors as abbess was also a poet, Anna Sophia von Hessen-Darmstadt (1638–83), who entered the Quedlinburg Stift at 17 and later became its abbess. She was very learned, and defended her publication of devotional poems and songs, *Der Treue Seelenfreund* (Jena: Georg Segenwald, 1658), with Augustine's dictum 'Praise ye, all virgins', and van Schurman's defence of learned women.[143] Von Königsmarck was signing as 'Pröbstin der Abtei zu Quedlinburg' by 1707.[144] She was not, of course, enclosed, since Quedlinburg was Lutheran rather than Catholic, so she may have been there for some time before 1707, alternating diplomatic with religious duties.[145]

The number of Latinate people in Norway was considerably smaller than in Sweden, reflecting the size of the population more generally, but it produced at least one Latin woman poet. Cille Gad (*c.*1675–1711), daughter of Canutus Gad, 'auditor militae' in Bergen, is one of the very few Norwegian women Latinists. She perhaps owed her education to her status as an only child. According to Thrura, she had the reputation of being able to compose Latin verse extempore,[146] and she was greatly admired by Copenhagen scholars. Her translations into Greek and Latin of 'The Treasure of the God-Loving Soul' (*Den Gud-Elskende Sjælens Skat*)

---

[142] Friedrich Ernst Kettner, *Kirchen und Reformations Historie du Kaysel. Freezen weltlichen Stifts Quedlinburgs* (Quedlinburg: Theodore Schwan, 1710), contains a convoluted argument in support of the idea that women's authority need not be a curse, and in support of his position includes a long list of ancient and contemporary female rulers. Wiesner, *Gender, Church and State*, 48–50. This seems to be another case of distinguishing between (despicable) women and (admirable) educated noblewomen.

[143] Her work was suspect in the eyes of some Lutheran theologians who thought she overstressed the ubiquity of Christ's presence too strongly in her comment that women could feel this presence equally with men. Yet the book was reprinted several times. Wiesner, *Gender, Church and State*, 61.

[144] These details about her life are taken from Birger Mörner, *Maria Aurora Königsmarck* (Stockholm: P. A. Norstedt & Söners Förlag, 1914).

[145] Sarah Josepha Hale, *Woman's Record* (New York: Harper & Brothers, 1860), 515–16, claims that in the 1710s she spent some time in Russia, where she was instrumental in the rescue of the Tsarevich Alexei's unloved wife, Carolina Christina Sophia of Braunschweig-Lüneburg, whom he had left for dead, successfully smuggling her to Paris, from whence she ended up living quietly in Louisiana. While this seems consistent with von Königsmarck's general character, and she was certainly good friends with the Braunschweig-Lüneburg family, it seems probable that Hale has been misled by some kind of narrative in support of the claims of the Louisiana 'ex-Tsarina', who was probably one of the variety of enterprising individuals in America who claimed a status as quondam European royals (a phenomenon familiar enough to be mocked by Mark Twain: the personnel on Huckleberry Finn's raft included both 'the rightful Duke of Bridgewater' and 'the poor disappointed Dauphin, Looey the Seventeenth'). Thomas Mann mentions the story in ch. 3 of *Doctor Faustus*, so it was evidently widely believed.

[146] 'Carmina Latina fudit promtissime, quod fatentur, qui scribenti testis oculati assederunt. Varia Poëseos suae specimina typis publicis Hafniae submississe fertur, in quibus mihi solum innotescit.' Thrura, *Gynaeceum*, 63–4.

were lost in the fire of Bergen in 1702. She did not marry, but had an affair with a Dutch seaman, Matthias Boudaan, which ended tragically: she gave birth to a child with no assistance, and it was subsequently found dead. She was accused of infanticide and condemned to death in 1707. She was eventually given a royal pardon, but the experience left her a broken woman and she died not long after her release.[147] She wrote to Otto Sperling to thank him for including her in his collection of learned women: her first communication with him was a verse epistle in Latin in which she apologizes for the crudity of her performance since she had no books with her in prison. He, as well as writing back, wrote to the king on her behalf, though his well-intentioned argument that 'one cannot execute a woman who knows Latin and Greek' is unlikely to have been persuasive.[148] The only poem of hers which is printed was a commendatory verse for Thomas Jacobaeus, printed in his Ph.D. thesis on the eyes of insects; which is to say, acknowledging the cultural production of a family member: a classic type of location in which early modern women's verse is preserved. It was printed in 1708, when she was in prison, so it must have been thought even at that time that her name would bring lustre rather than tarnish upon her associates.

Women of the Danish royal family, like those of Sweden, were sometimes Latin-literate, though they tended towards the sciences rather than the arts. Queen Sophia, daughter of Ulrich III, Duke of Mecklenburg and wife of Frederick II, supervised the education of her daughters, who included Anne of Denmark.[149] In her widowhood, having been prevented from ruling as regent for her son (Christian IV), who came to the throne at 11, she instead pursued interests in astronomy, chemistry, and other sciences at her own separate court on the island of Falster. Her granddaughter Eleanora Christina (1621–98), daughter of Christian IV of Denmark and Kirstine Munk, became the wife of Corfits Ulfeldt, prime minister of Denmark until the death of Christian IV in 1648. She was imprisoned in the Blue Tower in 1663 for twenty-two years in a room without a window, where she wrote *Jammersminde* (memories of woe), a Danish classic. She was Latinate, read Danish, French, and German, and was learned in theology, astronomy, and mathematics.[150] Her *Hæltinners Pryd*, a pro-women work modelled on Madeleine de Scudéry's *Femmes illustres* and written 1671–85, is the first work in defence of women written by a woman in Scandinavia, and formed the basis for

147 Ekerem, 'Norway' 77. Some biographical details are from Elisabeth Møller Jensen (ed.), *Liv och verk* (Malmö: Bra Böcker, 2000), 99.

148 Alenius, 'Love at First (W)ink', 173, and 'Kan man henrette en kvinde, der kan græsk og latin? Om Otto Sperling og Cille Gad', in M. S. Christensen (ed.), *Hvad tales her om? Festschrift til Johnny Christensen* (Copenhagen: Museum Tusculanum, 1996).

149 There is an undated Latin letter by Anne of Denmark to the Doge of Venice, Marino Grimani, in the Leicestershire County Record Office, DG7, Lit. 2, fo. 41. On Queen Sophia as well as her daughter, see Leeds Barroll, *Anna of Denmark, Queen of England* (Philadelphia: University of Pennsylvania Press, 2001), 16.

150 *Memoirs of Leonora Christina, Daughter of Christian IV of Denmark, Written during her Imprisonment in the Blue Tower at Copenhagen, 1663–1685*, trans. F. E. Bunnett (London: Henry S. King & Co., 1872); Jensen (ed.), *Liv och verk*, 177.

Otto Sperling's *De Feminis Doctis*.[151] Her contemporary Anna Sophie, daughter of King Frederick III of Denmark (ruled 1648–70), was an educated woman who knew German, Latin, French, Spanish, and Italian beside her native Danish.[152]

Beyond the royal family, the primary listing of learned women for Denmark is that of Albert Thrura, *Gynaeceum Daniae Litterarum: Feminis Danorum Eruditione vel Scriptis Claris Conspicuum*.[153] He discusses a wide variety of educated women considering the small population of Denmark at the time. Birgitta Thott, wife of Otto Giøe, has already been mentioned as a protégée of Anna Maria van Schurman. After being widowed in 1642 she acquired a knowledge of Latin, Greek, and Hebrew: it is important to notice that her studies did not begin until after her husband's death.[154] Probably with the intention of writing for other women, since most of them did not have the opportunity to acquire Latin, she wrote an ambitious work of *c*.200 folio pages, 'on a blessed life', in Danish, which Alenius dates to 1650.[155] Besides traditional moral and philosophical topics, the author devotes a special chapter to the benefits women can derive from study. Thott also translated into Danish from French, Latin, English, and probably Greek.

It is interesting to find that Thomas Bartholin, who wrote so warmly about the learned women of his country in *De Scriptis Danorum*, educated his own daughter, Margaretha Bartholina, who married Christian Muller. With her father's encouragement she studied Latin and wrote verse in Danish. Thura quotes two Latin poems to her, by Magnus Scheel and Thomas Bartholin.[156]

One notable feature of the relationship of learned women to society in the seventeenth century in various parts of Europe is that some of them were treated as a significant cultural desideratum. Anna Maria van Schurman had this experience, and so did Sophia Elisabeth Brenner, whose supporters actively canvassed for international response to the woman they presented as the Sappho of Stockholm. There was an equivalent figure in Denmark, Maria Below, who married Christian Holck, gave birth to eight children, and died in 1651.[157] Her status is

---

[151] Alenius, 'Om alle slags berömdvärda kvinnnoperoner Gynæceum—en kvinnalitteraturhistoria', 217–32 (p. 222).

[152] Sharp, *Pleasure and Ambition*, 3.

[153] See also Matthaeus Schecht, 'Schediasma, Exhibens Specimen de Eruditis Mulieribus Daniae', *Novo Literario Maris Balthici et Septentrionis* (Lübeck, 1700), 209–19, and Marianne Alenius, 'Skrifter om laerde danske kvinder', in Alenius and Zeeberg (eds.), *Litteratur og Laerdom*, 35–48.

[154] Marianne Alenius, 'Birgitte Thott, *Om et lyksaligt Liv*', in Marianne Alenius, Birger Bergh, Ivan Boserup, Karsten Friis-Jensen, and Minna Skafte Jensen (eds.), *Latin og Nationalsprog i Norden efter Reformationen*, Renaessancestudier 5 (Copenhagen: Museums Tusculanums Forlag, 1991), 142–55.

[155] This work is mentioned by Thrura, under the title, 'tractatus de via ad felicem vitam' (p. 117). The original MS is lost but a copy survives, Sorø, Akademis Bibliothek, A VI, 19. Albertus Bartholinus, *De Scriptis Danorum, Liber Postumus*, ed. Thomas Bartholinus (Copenhagen: Matthias Godiccheniu, 1666), 16, mentions her translation of Seneca (published in folio), and adds to it a translation of Epictetus, published in Copenhagen in 1661 in duodecimo, and a variety of other translations from French and English, also published in Copenhagen, and all apparently lost, since they do not appear in the Scandinavian neo-Latin database.

[156] Thrura, *Gynaeceum*, 19–20.

[157] 'linguam suam promte & terse loqui latina, Gallica at Italica . . . nec Graecae linguae ignara.' Thrura, *Gynaeceum*, 21. Auth. of 'versifizierte Polemische Schrift', *Honori et Amori Memoriae Comitis Holchii zur Antwort auff die Lahme fratzen eines Diffamenten der sich doch nicht nennen darff*, 1633, *SKGF*, 6.

directly illustrated in a poem by Thomas Bartholin describing her as 'the light of her fatherland', and 'the star of Denmark', comparing her with van Schurman, 'the star of Holland'.[158] Though there is no evidence that she wrote anything but a polemic which in some way defended her husband's reputation, Bartholin promoted her as another van Schurman.[159] Apart from Thrura and Bartholin, she is also noticed by Louis Jacob and by Tomasini, who quotes Bartholin's poem mentioned above.[160] Eulogies on her death include a contribution by her countrywoman Birgitta Thott (in Danish).

It is relatively easy to find Danish women of learning who translated into their own language, and also examples of learned mothers allowing their daughters a literary education. For example, Catharina Bilde, married to Falco Giøe, translated extensively from German to Danish on theological subjects.[161] Their daughter Susanna Giøe (b. 1688), wife of Praebiorn Brahe, translated Vives's *De Educatione Virginum* from French—a work first written for the education of Mary Tudor, at the behest of her mother Catherine of Aragon. Another interesting and even more highly educated mother–daughter pair are Susana Juul and her daughter Ana Margareta Quitsov. Juul studied Latin, Greek, Dutch, English, French, and German, and left translations from Latin and German, including a Danish translation of the first three books of *De Bello Gallico*.[162] She personally taught her daughter Latin and German along with Danish till the age of 9, after which she was passed to a series of tutors to study Latin literature, Greek, French, and Hebrew. Quitsov wrote a number of Latin letters which survive, including an interesting account of her education which she addressed to Otto Sperling in 1673.[163] She was also, according to Thrura, the author of 'varia arguta epigrammata', which unfortunately were never printed. Another learned Dane, Anna Margrethe Bredal, has left a variety of writing in Latin, including a panegyric on Christian V and two letters to Otto Sperling.[164] There also seem to have been Latin poets besides those already mentioned. Elisabetha Rhumann, a native of Copenhagen, is said to have composed Latin verses in her old age—she died in 1707.[165]

Perhaps the last woman Latin poet of Denmark, Lyche Sophia Friis, flourished in the mid-eighteenth century. She was born in Odense in 1699, the daughter of the Borgemester (Burgomeister), and was a student of poetry in Danish, Latin,

Noticed in Louis Jacob, 'Bibliothèque des femmes illustres par leurs écrits', Paris, Bibliothèque Nationale de France, Ancien fonds français 22865, fos. 235ᵛ–236ʳ.

[158] Jacobus Philippus Tomasini, *Elogia Virorum Literis et Sapientia Illustrium* (Padua: Sebanstiano Sardi, 1644), 343.

[159] Thomas Bartholinus, *De Luce Animalium* (Leiden: Franciscus Hackius, 1647), 289.

[160] Paris, Bibliothèque Nationale de France, Ancien fonds français 22865, fos. 235ᵛ–236ʳ. Jacob corresponded with Bartholin, as did Tomasini.

[161] Thrura, *Gynaeceum*, 23.

[162] Ibid. 76–7. Alenius, 'Love at First (W)ink', 172.

[163] Thrura, *Gynaeceum*, 96–105.

[164] Thrura, ibid., prints a Latin letter giving a brief autobiography, pp. 36–9 and another, pp. 39–40. See also Jensen (ed.), *Liv och verk*, 50, Alenius, 'Love at First (W)ink', 170–1.

[165] Thrura, *Gynaeceum*, 107.

German, French, and Greek. As far as Thrura knows, she died unmarried. At least three works were printed, apparently as broadsheets or pamphlets (they do not survive in their original form, though one is reproduced by Thrura, and two by Schönau). The two which were printed are part-Danish, part-Latin; one is on Martin Luther, the other on the accession of Frederick III. Schönau also prints two Latin letters from Friis to Magister Eischow, whom she describes as 'frater', both written from Lund in 1747, and his replies.[166] Her verse oeuvre is comparable to other northern European women's Latin verse of the seventeenth century, such as that of Euphrosine Aue, Elisabeth Koolaart, Anna Memorata, and the English Rachel Jevon: Latin used for a formal, public ode printed as a pamphlet to record some significant event.

Poland

In seventeenth-century Poland, there is some indication that royal brides continued to be Latinate. One such, Luisa Maria Gonzaga, Queen of Poland (1611–67), is credited with letters, *opusculi*, and a Latin dissertation, 'whether women ought to study'.[167] There were also several woman Latinists, of whom the most important are Sophiana Corbiniana and, above all, the woman known as the 'virgo Polona', Anna Memorata. Well known in her own time, she was born in Łożebrica, and was of Czech descent. Her father, Andrzej Jakub, was a highly educated man, a graduate of the Gdańsk gymnasium, and moved to Leszno, where he became pastor. Leszno, then administered by the Leszczyński family, was economically and intellectually vibrant: it was the capital of the immigrant 'Czech Brethren' who settled there after the defeat of Czech Protestants in 1620 at the Battle of the White Mountain, and was the home of many scholars and writers. Apart from Memorata, another notable woman was Krystyna Poniatowska (1610–44), wife of Daniel Vetter, printer to the Czech Brethren (and printer of many of Memorata's own works), who was a well-known visionary.[168]

Memorata studied under Jan Amos Komeñski, better known as Comenius, then master of the grammar school, the Lesneum, and learned Latin and Greek as well as Polish, German, and Czech. Such of her oeuvre as survives resembles that of contemporary German women Latinists such as Euphrosine Aue; it consists of poems on important people, such as the *voivode* of Leszno, and on fellow poets; there are also epithalamia and occasional poems. Most of her known work was collected by Chrystian Teodor Schosser and published by him in 1641 in his *Laurifolium*. Additionally, Johannes Sauerbrei records that she contributed a verse

---

[166] Friedrich Christian Schönau, *Samling af Danske lærde Fruentimer* (Copenhagen: J. W. Bopp, 1753), i. 647–51 (pp. 656–60).

[167] Francesco Clodoveo Maria Pentolini, *Le donne illustre* (Livorno: Gio. Vincenzo Fatorni, 1776), ii. 13. She was married first to Wladyslaw IV and then to his half-brother Jan Casimir.

[168] Information from Dr Piotr Urbanski, to whom my thanks.

to the *album amicorum* of the Leipzig scholar Andreas Brummer.[169] The poems of compliment to her which are preserved with her own verses indicate that the names of the late sixteenth-century women humanists were well remembered in the circles in which she moved: the poem on her by Schosser compares her with Elizabeth Jane Weston (whom he had known),[170] 'Albertina' (most probably Alzbeta Albertina von Kammeneck, who had published Latin verse relatively recently, in 1630), and Olimpia Morata.[171] Similarly, another admirer, Samuel Heerman, cites Morata, Anna Maria van Schurman, 'Melissa' (most probably Paul Melissus' wife Aemilia/Rosina), and, again, Weston.[172]

The late Josef Ijsewijn refers in his *Companion to Neo-Latin Studies* to 'the Polish Sophia Corbiniana' [*sic*] as a known Latin poet, though he gives no further information of any kind;[173] and she is not noticed in Polish encyclopedias.[174] A woman of almost identical name who is noticed in Louis Jacob's 'Bibliothèque des femmes illustres par leurs écrits',[175] Anna Sophia Corbiniana, is probably the same person, and is there described as German by race, a native of Leipzig, and a very distinguished Latinist and scholar. Jacob implies that some of her work was printed, though I have yet to find copies of the works referred to.[176] However, some verse has come to light to substantiate this reputation: two poems to Fabio Chigi of Siena, on his election to the papacy as Pope Alexander VII on 7 April 1655. They survive in a Vatican manuscript, a carefully written-out presentation bifolium preserved in the extensive Chigi *classis*, quite probably in Corbiniana's own hand, and are both graceful poems of compliment. They are signed 'Sophiana Bernharda, nata Corbiniana', and thus indicate that by 1655, she was married to a man named Bernhard.[177]

It should have become clear in the course of Chapter 9 that Kraków was probably the best place to be a woman with intellectual interests in the whole of Poland during the Renaissance, and this also seems to have been true in the

---

169 Sauerbrei, *Diatriben*, § 50, sig. C2.

170 There are two poems by Schosser addressed to Weston in his *Laurifolium sive Schediasmatum Poeticorum Libri*, iv (Fribourg: Georg Hoffman, 1622), 3ᵛ–4.

171 Teodor Wierszbowski (ed.), *Anny Memoraty, 'Dziewicy Polskiéj', Łacinskie Wiersze, z lat 1640– 1644* (Warsaw: K. Kowalewskiego, 1895), 17–18.

172 Ibid. 13–14.

173 Jozef Ijsewijn, *Companion to Neo-Latin Studies* (Louvain: Louvain University Press, 1990, 1998), i. 31.

174 Here I must thank Dr Z. Jagodzinski at the Polish Library, Hammersmith, who spent an afternoon going through Polish-language reference material with me.

175 Paris, Bibliothèque Nationale de France, Ancien fonds français 22865, fo. 22ᵛ.

176 'Natione Germana, patria Lipsichis, et divina undequaque doctissima exquisiti ingenii et non vulgaris literaturae, philosophis ab oratrix eximia, nec nam in lingua latina compendium observationibus dialecticis et philologicis illustratum, urati flaviae apud Gasparum Losemannum in 120 ut Gabeo ex segedis et U. Claudii doresmieulx ad nos transmissis qui haec desunt sumpsit ex quodam catalogo autumnali francofurtensi in classe philosophorum caetera me latent sicuti et tempore quo vixit.'

177 Chigi, a highly cultivated man, travelled outside Italy: he was papal nuncio during the negotiations for the Peace of Westphalia (1648) which took place in Münster and Osnabrück (Friedrich Heer, *The Holy Roman Empire*, trans. Janet Sondheimer (London: Phoenix, 1968), 211). It is therefore impossible to draw any conclusions about where Corbiniana may have encountered him.

seventeenth century. The Piotrkowczyk family, important in seventeenth-century Kraków, seem to have developed a commitment to educated women. In 1620, J. Piotrkowczyk, a doctor of philosophy, took up his father's trade of printing, aided by his wife Jadwiga. She was literate in Polish and Latin, and wrote religious poetry in first Latin, then Polish. In 1663, a book of her poems was published. After her husband's death she continued to run their printing house 1645–66 until their son Stanislas Teodor, also a poet, came of age. He married another highly educated woman, Anna Teresa z Pernussów, who also wrote in Latin and Polish. She is said to have published a book, *On the Virtues and Vices of Polish Women* (*De Virtutibus et Vitiis Mulierum Polanarum*), described as the first book by a Polish woman which is not about religion, which was apparently in Latin.[178]

A number of other Polish women of the seventeenth century were highly educated and used Latin fluently in pursuit of scientific ends. There were two notable Polish women astronomers, the 'Silesian Pallas', Maria Kunicka (*c*.1600–1664), whose book of astronomical tables, *Urania Propitia sive Tabulae Astronomicae*, was printed in Oels by Johan Seyffert in 1650,[179] and Ell'bieta Koopmanówna Heweliusszowa, who was the author of *On Comets* (*Cometographia, sive Totam Naturam Cometarum*), printed in 1687.[180] Both women received royal patronage, Kunicka from the Piast princes in Brzeg, who supported her, Heweliusszowa from King Jan Sobiesky.

Perhaps the last work to be considered here is that of Maria Josepha of Austria (1699–1757), Queen of Poland. She was the daughter of Joseph I of Austria, and is given as the author of a verse epistle to her husband Augustus III, Churprinz of Saxony and King of Poland (the son of Augustus the Strong), written in 1757 and surviving in manuscript. She was an educated and cultivated woman (for example, she directed the opera with which the new Dresden opera house was inagurated in 1719, *Giove in Argo*), and there is no a priori reason to assume that she was necessarily incapable of this composition.

---

[178] Stefan Krol, *101 Kobiet Polskien* (Warsaw: Ksiązkai Wiedza, 1988), 39–40. I have been unable to find a copy of this work or a proper bibliographic reference to it.

[179] This work is noticed in a letter from Cyprian Kinner to Samuel Hartlib, 19 June, 1647 (University of Sheffield, Hartlib Papers, 1/33/8B). I would like to thank Professor Howard Hotson for this reference. See also Zbigniew Kadlubek, *Pallas Silesia: Neulateinisches Jahrbuch/Journal of Neo-Latin Language and Culture*, 2 (2000).

[180] Information from Ms Lenka Vytlacilova, to whom much thanks.

14. *Women and Latin in Early Modern England*

Samuel Pepys, in his famous diary, refers casually to encountering a woman Latinist: 'among other strangers that come, there was Mr Hempson and his wife, a pretty woman, and speaks Latin.'[1] Evidently worthy of note in 1661, but not astonishing. Some twenty years earlier, Dr Denton, physician to the king, wrote in the uncertainties of the Civil War of his 7-year-old daughter Anne,[2]

> my highest ambition of all is to have her so much Latin as to understand a Latin testament, which is enough to understand a Drs bill and to write one, and then I could (if God bless me with life and health) leave her a portion without money . . . I would faine have her of as many trades as I could to get her living by, for I am in no great likelihood to provide her a portion.

It seems from this that he saw a positive utility in his daughter's acquisition of practical Latin: 'a portion without money'.[3] Anne was an enthusiastic scholar: she wrote cheerfully to her disapproving godfather Sir Ralph Verney, 'i know you and my coussenes will outrech me in French, but i am a-goeing whaar i hop i shal outrech you in ebri, grek and laten'.[4] The *Essay to Revive the Ancient Attainments of Gentlewomen* attributed to Bathsua Makin (though, as Noel Malcolm has shown, more probably the work of Mark Lewis[5]) also suggests that positive benefit might accrue to Latinate women, on the grounds that it might give them a position in an aristocratic household, just as Makin herself became tutor to Charles I's daughter Elizabeth. The *Essay* makes this argument for the utility of women's learning directly, and in words similar to those of Dr Denton: 'Here is a sure Portion . . . How many born to good Fortunes, when their Wealth hath been wasted, have supported themselves and Families too by their Wisdom?'[6] It also points out the utility of this for society as a whole: 'Had we a sufficient number of Females thus instructed to furnish the Nurseries of Noble Families, their Children might be

---

[1] *The Diary of Samuel Pepys*, ed. Henry Wheatley, 3 vols. (1659–67) (London: G. Bell & Sons, 1952), 9 Apr. 1661. A longer treatment of much of the material covered by this chapter is in Jane Stevenson, 'Anglo-Latin Women Poets of the Seventeenth and Eighteenth Centuries', *Seventeenth Century*, 16.1 (2001), 1–36.

[2] Miriam Slater, *Family Life in the Seventeenth Century: The Verneys of Claydon House* (London: Routledge & Kegan Paul, 1984), 135.

[3] The fact that Latin was needed 'to understand a Drs bill and to write one' explains why a number of women with medical interests learned Latin, such as Charlotte Charke, Jane Barker (b. 1652), and Judith Aylmer.

[4] Frances Parthenope Verney and Margaret M. Verney (eds.), *Memoirs of the Verney Family during the Seventeenth Century* (London: Longmans & Co., 1925), i. 501.

[5] Noel Malcolm, 'The Lady Vanishes', *TLS* (5 Nov. 1999), 28. My thanks to Dr Malcolm for letting me see a more detailed presentation of his evidence.

[6] Anon., *An Essay to Revive the Ancient Education of Gentlewomen* (London: J.D., 1673), 41.

improved in the Knowledge of the Learned Tongues before they were aware.'[7] In a household blessed with more brains than money, there might be good reason to think carefully about the possibility of educating a daughter, for her own sake, as Dr Denton suggests, or for the sake of the family more generally.

Although royal women were often Latin-literate as late as the eighteenth century,[8] the great ladies of the Stuart and Hanoverian courts, unlike their Tudor predecessors, found that there was no social cachet in being able to discuss Latin poets or the Greek Fathers. Latin itself continued to be very important in seventeenth-century England,[9] but court culture varied with the tastes and character of the queen. Mary of Modena's court was rather intellectual: her Italian attendants brought translations of Greek and Latin poems to court, and they encouraged English women to translate romances from French and other languages.[10] There were three English-language poets in her immediate entourage, Jane Barker, Anne Finch, and Anne Killigrew.[11] The Hanoverian queens were less literary, though Queen Caroline (1683–1737), wife of George II, was highly intelligent and scientifically minded: a friend, pupil, and patron of Gottfried Wilhelm Leibniz, she intervened in the dispute between Newton and Leibniz over the discovery of calculus.[12] She also supported the Anglo-Saxon scholar Elizabeth Elstob, suggesting that she felt some degree of interest in educated women.[13] The next queen of England, Charlotte von Mecklenburg-Strelitz, was a duller, more domestic figure, who drove the lively Frances Burney nearly mad with boredom.[14]

When Lawrence Stone states that 'the period when a learned education was given to aristocratic women did not last much longer than forty years, from about 1520 to 1560', he is in fact referring only to high-profile women at court.[15] Members of the upper gentry and relatively minor aristocracy and educated citizens continued to behave much as their grandfathers had done, and educate, or fail to educate, their daughters according to the traditional practice of their own specific family. Leaving the royal family and its satellites to one side, the kinds of men who had their daughters taught Latin (or taught them themselves) in the

[7] Ibid. 28. It is obvious that the situation here envisaged would also benefit the women themselves.

[8] Princess Elizabeth, sister of Charles I, was educated by Bathsua Makin. Princess Sophia of Hanover, mother of George I, was interested in science and philosophy, and read Latin (H. Walpole, *Reminiscences*, ed. P. Toynbee (Oxford: Clarendon Press, 1924), 121). The Duke of Cumberland, son of George II, wrote Latin letters to his sister. It is reasonable to assume that she could read them (my thanks to Dr James Binns for this information).

[9] W. T. Myers, *The Relation of Latin and English as Living Languages in England during the Age of Milton* (Dayton, Va: Ruebush-Elkins Co., 1913). See also Leicester Bradner, *Musae Anglicanae* (New York: Modern Language Association of America, 1940), on English neo-Latin verse.

[10] Carol Barash, *English Women's Poetry, 1649–1714: Politics, Community and Linguistic Authority* (Oxford: Clarendon Press, 1996), 149.

[11] Ibid. 150. Other members of her circle who had poetic connections include Catherine Sedley and the Countess of Roscommon, wife of the poet Wentworth Dillon.

[12] Onno Klapp (ed.), *Correspondez von Leibnitz mit Caroline* (New York: Georg Olms, 1973).

[13] Elizabeth Elstob, *The Rudiments of Grammar for the English-Saxon Tongue, First Given in English: With an Apology for the Study of Northern Antiquities* (London: W. Bowyer, 1715), sig. A2–4.

[14] Margaret Ann Doody, *Frances Burney* (Cambridge: Cambridge University Press, 1988), 174–5.

[15] Lawrence Stone, *The Family, Sex and Marriage in England, 1500–1800*, abridged edn. (Harmondsworth: Penguin, 1979), 143.

1550s did so in the 1650s, and may well have done so in the 1750s.[16] The sixteenth century has been considered in an earlier chapter. In the seventeenth century, some country gentry and educated professionals—such as the earls of Huntingdon, the Apsleys, Dr Baynard (physician, surgeon, and bibliophile), and Henry Rainolds (schoolmaster)—taught their daughters Latin, or had them taught, and in the eighteenth century, so did a number of men of similar status: Samuel Wesley taught his daughter Mehetabel both Latin and Greek alongside his famous sons John and Charles,[17] and similarly, Jacob More, a schoolmaster in Bristol, and Thomas Seward, canon of Lichfield, taught Latin to their respective daughters, the writers Hannah More and Anna Seward.[18]

As Lawrence Stone also points out, by the 1630s, many of the upper squirearchy and aristocracy educated their sons at home. Though he does not say so, the presence of a tutor in the home would obviously open up the possibility of education for daughters.[19] Furthermore, the Civil War left a number of educated men under house arrest, or unemployed, and thus with time on their hands, and thrown into the company of their own children. This may have spurred some of them to educate their girls: one such possible beneficiary of paternal leisure is Rachel Jevon, the daughter of a Worcestershire clergyman, Daniel Jevon, and his wife Elizabeth, who was christened at Broom in Worcestershire in 1627. Her family may have been connected with a gentry family of Jevons in Staffordshire, but were impoverished by the Civil War. Her father, a loyal clergyman of the diocese of Worcester, though threatened and imprisoned, contrived to preserve his flock, so that not one took arms against His Majesty, but became impoverished, and could only give his children 'education, without maintenance'. This is to say, he was deprived of his living during the Civil War, which may explain why he made use of his enforced idleness to teach his daughter Latin, perhaps to give her 'a portion without money'. Rachel Jevon wrote a long and ambitious Restoration ode, as a parallel text in English and Latin: *Carmen* θριαμβευτικον *Regiae Maiestatis Caroli II Principum et Christianorum Optimi in Exoptatissimums eius Restaurationem*, in Latin, and *Exultationis Carmen*, in English.[20] She followed this up with specific requests for a position: in 1662 she petitioned Charles II 'for the place of one of the meanest servants about the Queen', and subsequently, sent another petition described simply as 'For the place of Rocker to the Queen' (something of a sinecure, since the unfortunate Catherine of Braganza was childless): both these requests survive in the State Papers. It seems entirely possible that

[16] Margaret Ezell, *The Patriarch's Wife* (Chapel Hill: University of North Carolina Press, 1987), concludes: 'it does not appear that women's education came to "a sudden end" in 1603, or, indeed, that it declined significantly from previous generations either in quality or extent' (p. 16).

[17] Roger Lonsdale (ed.), *Eighteenth-Century Women Poets* (Oxford: Oxford University Press, 1990), 110.

[18] For more examples, see R. Fowler, 'On Not Knowing Greek', *Classical Journal*, 78 (1983), 337–49.

[19] Lawrence Stone, 'The Educational Revolution in England, 1560–1640', *Past and Present*, 28 (1964), 41–80 (p. 45).

[20] Printed in Jane Stevenson and Peter Davidson (eds.), *Early Modern Women Poets, 1520–1700* (Oxford: Oxford University Press, 2001), 317–25.

her father educated her with the intention of allowing her to attract attention and capitalize on the interest thus gained by finding a patron, as the fathers of some sixteenth-century women Latinists such as Olimpia Morata and Luisa Sigea had done. Unfortunately, the continued heirlessness of Charles II—even assuming that he would have wished to see a princess classically educated—meant there was no context in which Jevon's learning could be put to effective use, and she dropped back into the obscurity from which she had briefly emerged.

It is easy enough to find negative contemporary reactions to women Latinists, such as this remark by Sir Ralph Verney: 'let not your girle learne Latin, nor Short hand; the difficulty of the first may keep her from that Vice, for so I must esteem it in a woeman.'[21] However, as we have seen, his correspondent (William Denton) was of a different opinion, and moreover, such negativity is sometimes clearly evoked by the attainments or interests of actual women, as in this case, or by a perceptible trend *towards* allowing women more education, which is made visible partly by the outcry of those who disapproved. It is worth observing that so normative and middle-class a text as *The Gentlewoman's Companion or, a Guide to the Female Sex* (attributed to Hannah Woolley and to some extent based on her work, but disowned by her) recommends some study of Latin to gentlewomen of the 1670s, on the grounds that it would improve their speaking, writing, spelling, and comprehension of English:[22]

Now since it may hence appear, Ladies, that you have no Pygmaean Souls, but as capable of Gygantick growth as of your Male opponents; apply yourself to your Grammar by time, and let your endeavours be indefatigable, and not to be tired in apprehending the first principles of the Latin tongue.

Seventeenth-century women whose interests were scholarly, or theological, were therefore not necessarily debarred by linguistic ignorance from pursuing their researches. The gentlewoman Elizabeth Warren published a volume called *Spiritual Thrift* in 1646 which is a meditation on passages from the works of Plato, Aristotle, Cicero, Plutarch, and Augustine, written in English, but copiously adorned with marginal notes in Latin, which may suggest that she had hopes of a readership outside England.[23] Rather similarly, Diana Primrose, the author of *A Chaine of Pearle*, published in 1630, took material from part I of William Camden's *Annals of Queen Elizabeth*, published in London in Latin in 1615, in French in 1624, and in an English translation from the French in 1625.[24] Her book is

[21] Verney and Verney (eds.), *Memoirs of the Verney Family*, 72.

[22] From the second edition (London: Edward Thomas, 1675), reprinted with introduction by Caterina Albano (Totnes: Prospect Books, 2001), 87. On the authorship, see Elaine Hobby, *Virtue of Necessity: English Women's Writing, 1646–1688* (London: Virago, 1988), 172–4.

[23] *Spiritual Thrift, or, Meditations Wherein Humble Christians (as in a Mirror) May View the Verity of their Saving Graces* (London: R.L. for Henry Shepherd, 1646).

[24] *A Chaine of Pearle, Or a Memoriall of the Peerles Graces, and Heroick Vertues of Queene Elizabeth of Glorious Memory. Dat Rosa Mel Apibus, qua Sugit Aranea Virus* ('The rose, from which the Spider sucks poison, gives honey to the Bees') (London: Printed for Thomas Paine, to be sold by Philip Watchouse, 1630).

sprinkled with Latin tags and mottoes, suggesting that, even if she primarily drew on the English or French version, she was also able to make use of the Latin text.

There is a substantial amount of evidence that seventeenth- and eighteenth-century England was well stocked with educated, more or less Latinate gentlewomen. As Isaac Watts observes, there were many Stuart gentlewomen 'rich in Learning, yet averse to Show'.[25] Martha, Lady Giffard, read Latin with ease, made an accomplished English translation of Horace's 'O fons Bandusiae',[26] and advised her niece Lady Berkeley in 1698, 'I would faine advise about yʳ reading what I practice myself not to read anything very serious before you goe to bed; that would be a good time to read Virgil in, and let yʳ Turkish history only goe a dayes.'[27] John Evelyn's great friend Margaret Godolphin included Tertullian in Latin among the writers she chose to study.[28] Similarly, Anna Hume, daughter of the Scots historian, poet, and essayist David Hume of Godscroft, is usually given credit for the English translation of the Latin verses in her father's *History of the Houses of Douglas and Angus*,[29] thus making her one of the very few Scotswomen who was educated in Latin.[30]

Other daughters of the gentry in the seventeenth century who studied the classical languages include Dudleya North, Lady Frances Norton, and Dorothy Pakington. Citizen women might also be well read: Dame Sarah Cowper (1644–1720), the daughter of a London merchant, made a memorandum of her library in London (the phrasing seems to imply that she had other collections of books elsewhere). The 133 volumes listed include 'L'Strang's Seneca, Montaigns Essays in three parts, Memoirs of China, Plutarchs Lives in five parts, Plutarchs Morals in five parts, Philip l'Comines, Bacons Essays, Erasmus in English, Epictetus, Puffendorf, Turkish Spy, Cicero of yᵉ Gods, Tully's Offices, Grotius of Religion, Erasmus Praise of Folly, Ruler of Health, the Countess of Warwick, Erasmus Christian Souldier'.[31] Her library consisted mainly of English translations (though Epictetus was at this time only available in Greek or French), but it is clear that her reading included a great deal which had been originally published in Latin or Greek.

There is also clear evidence that some gentry-level men were still supportive of intellectual activity among their women friends and relations and, indeed, some

[25] *An Account of the Life & Death of Elizabeth Bury*, ed. Samuel Bury (Bristol: J. Penn, 1720), sig. R3ᵛ.

[26] Stevenson and Davidson (eds.), *Early Modern Women Poets*, 345.

[27] Julia C. Longe, *Martha, Lady Giffard* (London: George Allen, 1911), 213.

[28] BL Evelyn MS, Bound F. 38, in Evelyn's hand, 'Devotions of Mrs Blagge which I copied out at the request of my Lady Sylvia', includes two selections from Tertullian, *Ad Uxorem* (p. 20). The inclusion of the Tertullian passages (without translation) would seem to imply that Lady Sylvia also understood Latin.

[29] She may also be the 'Gentlewoman' responsible for the editing and publication of this work, referred to in a letter of William Drummond of Hawthornden (Edinburgh, National Library of Scotland, MS 2061, no. 30).

[30] Though it is interesting that of the 18th-century Edinburgh inscriptions printed by Andrew Duncan, *Elogiorum Sepulchralium Edinensium Dilectus* (Edinburgh: Neill & Co., 1815), three in Latin, on pp. 10, 15, and 65, are attributed to, or claimed by, women, two widows and a mother.

[31] Hertfordshire County Record Office, D/EP F 36.

evidence that learned women might still be considered a national ornament. Lord Cornbury decided to furnish Clarendon House with pictures of famous or learned Englishmen, and when John Evelyn advised him on this project in March 1666/7, he suggested the inclusion of both Lady Jane Grey and Elizabeth Jane Weston in his selection of 'The Learned'.[32] Charles Hatton wrote in 1678, 'I am very pleased to hear that not only my nephews but my nieces are so good Latin scholars',[33] while Sir James Langham, an unusually good Latinist himself, was delighted to find Mary Isham as erudite as she proved, as her brother proudly reports:[34] 'having entered the dining-room, as he speaks Latin well, he [Sir James Langham] discoursed with Sister Mary [then 18], and praised her very much. He said Richardson spoke of her knowing Tully, Virgil and Buchanan well.' Sir James Langham did not merely admire erudite girls from a safe distance: he chose a classically educated woman as his (second) wife, Lady Elizabeth Hastings, daughter of the Countess of Huntingdon.[35] She and her mother had both been taught Latin by Bathsua Makin.[36]

At a lower level of society, we may consider the interesting figure of Anne Ley, born *c*.1600, the wife of Roger Ley, curate of St Leonard's Church, Shoreditch. The Leys spent their lives in deep poverty, despite having a loyal patron in John Squire, vicar of St Leonards, and kept a school in Shoreditch to eke out their income. Anne was highly literate in English and Latin: her surviving commonplace book (containing material written from the 1620s to 1641) includes her English poems and her letters in both languages, written to her husband, her father, friends, to a stranger to suggest that he preach in a less offensive style, and to young university men, probably erstwhile pupils.[37]

A group who need a moment's special consideration in this context, since they had a particular stake in Latin learning, were Catholic nuns. The constitutions of the English Benedictine convents at Cambrai and Paris specifically state that the divine office and profession ceremonies were sung in Latin by the quire nuns.[38]

---

[32] *Memoirs of John Evelyn*, ed. William Bray (London: Henry Colburn, 1827), ii. 307 (diary entry for 20 Dec. 1688).

[33] Ezell, *The Patriarch's Wife*, 15.

[34] *The Diary of Thomas Isham of Lamport (1658–81) Kept by him in Latin from 1671 to 1673 at his Father's Command*, trans. Robert Isham (Norwich: Miller & Leavins, 1875). Mary was born in 1654, Vere 1655, Thomas (the heir) 1656: this close succession of children may help to explain why the elder girls were educated with their brother.

[35] Her grandmother, the prophetess Lady Eleanor Davies, seems also to have had some Latin: she probably composed the Latin text of her tract *Prophetia* – there is no a priori reason to say that she did not, since she includes Latin passages in other tracts and wrote Latin words in the margin in her own hand. See Esther S. Cope, *Handmaid of the Holy Spirit: Dame Eleanor Davies, Never soe Mad a Ladie* (Ann Arbor: University of Michigan Press, 1992), 121.

[36] *An Essay*, 10. The former translated the Latin poetry of Peter Du Moulin (San Marino, Huntingdon Library, MS CH HA 9465, letter from Du Moulin to the countess thanking her for her translations). In her elegy on Lady Elizabeth's death, Makin notes, 'she | in Latin, French, Italian, happily | advanced with pleasure.' The only direct evidence for Lady Elizabeth's Latinity is the inscription on the monument she raised for her brother, in St James, Liberty of Westminster (Edward Hatton, *A New View of London* (London: R. Chiswell etc., 1708), ii. 819).

[37] Los Angeles, William Andrews Clarke Memorial Library, L6815 M3 C734.

[38] Lille, Archives du Département du Nord, 20H1.

Thus Latin was a part of everyday life for them, and the post-Reformation temper makes it unlikely that they were content to parrot what they sang.[39] In particular, the More family and its connections continued to educate their daughters for generations after the death of the illustrious and martyred ancestor who had set the family pattern in this respect.[40] Some Catholic girls learned Latin in the family— Mary Ward had been taught by her grandmother Ursula Wright by the time she was 10.[41] In the 1580s, in the manor house of Braddocks, between Thaxted and Saffron Walden (Essex), Thomas and Jane Wiseman educated all eight of their children in Latin: 'the daughters as well as the sons were brought up to learning of the Latin tongue and Mr Wiseman, every Friday, would make an exhortation in Latin thereby to exercise them in that language as also to give them good instruction.'[42] The various seventeenth-century convent annals, such as those published by the Catholic Record Society, make it absolutely clear that many, though not all, nuns learned Latin. For example: 'In this year (1633) upon the 8th day of July died most blessedly our worthy Mother Prioress (Mary Wiseman). She had her Latin tongue perfect, and hath left us many homilies and sermons of the holy fathers translated into English, which she did with great facility, whilst some small respite of health permitted her.'[43] It is worth observing that the surviving library catalogue of the Benedictine nuns of Cambrai, Cambrai, BN 901, contains two copies of Alvares' *Introduction to the Latin Tongue for Young Students*, 1684 and 1686, suggesting that some of the women who came to the convent without Latin proceeded to learn it. A letter by Dom Augustine Baker on the nuns of Cambrai written in 1629 notes, 'I wish I had Hilton's *Scala Perfectionis* in Latin. It would help the understanding of the English (and some of them understand Latin).'[44] The only Latin verse emanating from the English convents of the Low Countries, however, is the following:[45] 'the lady Lucy, in the world called Mrs Elizabeth

[39] Adam Hamilton (ed.), *Chronicle of the English . . . Canonesses . . . in Louvain, 1625–1644* (Edinburgh: Sands & Co., 1906), ii. 47, says revealingly of Dame Paula Hubert: 'finding herself very weak, and not apt to learn Latin, she would not undertake any more than to be a white sister' (i.e. not a quire nun).

[40] Mary Bassett, the daughter of Margaret Roper, née More, was 'well experted in the latine and greeke tonges'. John Harpsfield, quoted by J. K. McConica, *English Humanists and Reformation Politics* (Oxford: Clarendon Press, 1965), 266. Two generations later, Dame Bridget More (b. 1609) could write Latin: there is a letter of hers in Vatican City, Biblioteca Apostolica, Lat. Barberini 8624, no. 35. Lady Mary Roper, abbess of the English convent at Ghent, 'had no means to impart her thoughts to any Stranger, but by an Interpreter's tongue' (Sir Tobie Matthew, *The Life of Lady Lucy Knatchbull, now First Printed from the Original Manuscript* (London: Sheed and Ward, 1931), 216), but this may mean that she spoke no French, Spanish, or Dutch.

[41] Margaret Mary Littlehales, *Mary Ward: Pilgrim and Mystic* (Tunbridge Wells: Burns and Oates, 1998), 20.

[42] C. S. Durrant, *A Link between Flemish Mystics and English Martyrs* (London: Burns and Oates, 1925), 422.

[43] Hamilton (ed.), *Chronicle of the English . . . Canonesses in Louvain, 1625–1644*, ii. 104 (she was one of the Wisemans of Braddocks).

[44] Dorothy L. Latz (ed.), '*Glow-Worm Light*' (Salzburg: Institut für Anglistik und Amerikanistik, 1989), 27.

[45] The Lady Abbess of St Scholastica's Abbey, Teignmouth (ed.), *Abbess Neville's Annal of Five Communities of English Benedictine Nuns in Flanders, 1598–1687*, Catholic Record Society 6, Miscellanea 5 (London: Burns and Oates, 1909), 1–72. Mary Neville (Dame Anne) (b. 1605), daughter of Henry,

Knatchbull, dyed at Gaunt [Ghent in Flanders] 1629 on the 5th of August the 45 yeare of her age the 19th of her profession, the 6th of her prelature and Superiority in the monastery of the Immaculate Conception of the ever glorious virgin Mary Mother of God, and of the holy order of St Benedict, of the English Nation. Then followeth 6 verses in Latin'—which Dame Anne Neville, unfortunately, records only in English translation, probably her own.

> Domina Lucie Knatchbull
> Anagramate
> Which in English are as followeth

> The name of Mother clayms tears by right
> in this sad and shadowed monument:
> She Lucy was and by her light
> The world receavde all tru content
> but whilst on earth her rays were cast
> The heavens grew envious of our bliss
> And drew her to yourselves in hast
> We to the[ir] wills must be submiss
> Ther lik the moone [at] full, she shines in glory
> And will on earth assist and ayd us in our story.

We have here by implication Latin verse writing by an English Benedictine nun. This house certainly used Latin, and some members read it fluently. Elsewhere in the same narrative Dame Anne records the resolution of a dispute over authority (p. 28): 'Wee immediatly gave them the latin statutes to peruse, and poyntd out the place where it gives the community the choyce of tow Religious men to be present with the Bishope...' There could be no clearer demonstration of the way that knowledge of Latin could be power: it made a great difference to enclosed nuns if they could choose their own supervisors.

Thus, while the *court* culture of Stuart England no longer favoured classically educated women, who consequently do not have as high a public profile as they did in the sixteenth century, it is clear from these and other examples that there were still country gentry families in the seventeenth century who continued to educate their daughters comparably with their sons, and also that a few women of lower status continued to be taught in this way, such as Anne Ley, and also Mary Mollineux, whom I will discuss a little later. It should be stating the obvious to observe that decisions relating to the education of any one girl were based on the individual family's attitude to education, but it seems not to be as obvious as it should be.[46] Margaret Spufford, with respect to basic literacy among the poor, demonstrated that in some early modern families, a 'tradition of literacy' existed independent of economic factors.[47] On the basis of the evidence offered in this

Baron Abergavenny, was the abbess of a community which was founded from that of Ghent and settled at Pontoise (p. 22). On Lady Lucy, see Matthew, *The Life of Lady Lucy Knatchbull.*

[46] Ezell, *The Patriarch's Wife*, 13.

[47] *Contrasting Communities: English Villagers in the Sixteenth and Seventeenth Centuries* (Cambridge: Cambridge University Press, 1974), 203–4.

chapter, there seems also a case to be made that at an elite level, a 'tradition of learning' was maintained in some families and not others. Despite the conduct books and other forms of prescriptive text dealing with the formation of the ideal girl,[48] narratives of individual lives suggest that early modern English society was very far from unanimous about the degree of education appropriate to the daughters of the gentry.

Only a few seventeenth- and eighteenth-century Englishwomen can be shown to have written Latin verse. Of these, only three, Bathsua Makin, Rachel Jevon, and Elizabeth Tollet, published substantial quantities. Rachel Jevon has already been discussed, and Elizabeth Tollet will be treated together with other women of the eighteenth century, but Bathsua Rainolds, later Makin (1600–after 1673), requires examination here. She is a person long known to students of early modern women, though it is only recently that her life and work has been successfully pieced together.[49] Her grandfather was Henry Reginald/Reginaldus/Rainold, who lived in Ipswich until the 1580s or 1590s, and is known to have translated two books of Latin sermons by the German humanist Christopher Hegendorff.[50] Her father, another Henry, moved to Stepney by 1600, and became a schoolmaster.[51] According to Simonds d'Ewes, who was taught in the school, his daughter was a great deal more able and better educated than he was. However, this is the kind of family paradigm which is repeatedly found for women Latin poets in various centuries and countries: behind the learned maiden stands a family of men, and sometimes women, with a strong commitment to learning, often demonstrably educators or scholars.[52] She is best known, ironically, for a work which is probably not hers, *An Essay to Revive the Ancient Attainments of Gentlewomen*, printed in London in 1973.[53] But much earlier, as a young girl of 16, Bathsua Rainolds collected together evidence for her precocious multilinguality in a published book, *Musa Virginea Graeco-latino-gallica*, published in 1616, containing rather awkward poems in Latin, Greek, French, Hebrew, and Italian.[54] Since this is dedicated to James I

---

[48] See for example Suzanne W. Hull, *Chaste, Silent and Obedient: English Books for Women, 1475–1640* (San Marino, Calif.: Huntington Library, 1982).

[49] The evidence for her life is most fully presented in Frances Teague, *Bathsua Makin, Woman of Learning* (Lewisburg, Pa.: Bucknell University Press, 1989).

[50] Christopher Hegendorff, *Domestycal or Householde Sermons . . . nowe Fyrst Translated out of Laten by H. Reginalde* (Ipswich: J. Oswen, 1548), and *The Second Parte . . .* (Worcester: J. Oswen, 1549).

[51] J. R. Brink, 'Bathsua Makin: Educator and Linguist (1608–1675?)', in Brink (ed.), *Female Scholars* (Montreal: Eden Press Women's Publications, 1980), 86–100, Frances Teague, 'The Identity of Bathsua Makin', *Biography*, 16 (1993), 1–17, J. R. Brink, 'Bathsua Rainolds Makin: "Most Learned Matron" ', *Harvard Language Quarterly*, 54 (1991), 313–26.

[52] The households of Sir Thomas More and Sir Anthony Cooke are well-known examples, others include the Pirckheimers in Nuremberg, and the families of Olimpia Morata and Luisa Sigea in Ferrara and Lisbon respectively.

[53] See n. 5 above.

[54] *Musa Virginea Graeco-latino-gallica* (London: Edward Griffin for John Hodgets, 1616), facsimile edn. *Neo-Latin Women Writers: Elizabeth Jane Weston and Bathsua Reginald [Makin]*, ed. Donald Cheney, The Early Modern Englishwoman: The Printed Writings (Aldershot: Ashgate, 2001). See Anne Leslie Saunders, 'Bathsua Reginald Makin', in Laurie Churchill et al. (eds.), *Women Writing Latin from Roman Antiquity to Early Modern Europe* (New York: Routledge, 2002), iii, 247–80.

and consists almost entirely of poems on members of the royal family, it seems virtually certain that she was doing so in order to attract patronage.[55] This is a reasonable sample of her oeuvre:[56]

> Fingitur Antiquis Pandora habuisse Minervæ
> Ingenium, os Veneris, donaque, Phæbe, tua:
> At si Pythagoræ sunt dogmata vera putarem
> Hanc animam pectus, Diva, petisse tuum.
> Haec namque, & longè his in Te majora refulgent,
> Relligio, & verae Nobilitatis honos.

> Pandora was portrayed by the ancients
> With the wit of Minerva, the face of Venus, and, Apollo, your gifts:
> If I were to imagine that the ideas of Pythagoras are true,
> I would think, O goddess, that her soul had sought your breast.
> May these qualities long shine out yet more greatly in you:
> Religion, and the honour of true Nobility.

The sentiments are entirely conventional. Anne of Denmark could read and write Latin;[57] but evidence for her possession of 'Apollo's gifts' is not easily found, and that she possessed 'the face of Venus' is distinctly overstating the case. Furthermore, she was a Catholic, and Rainolds was vehemently Protestant: all in all, the verse bespeaks almost complete ignorance of its subject. Like the slightly older Elizabeth Weston and Aemilia Lanyer, Rainolds was apparently attempting to use poetry as a stepping stone to social or financial advancement: it is worth observing that the full title is in effect an advertisement for her father. Success in such an endeavour, however, was a matter of luck, since finding a patron was a highly problematic business, especially for a woman. Her father wrote something very similar a few years later, a broadside of Latin poems praising James I, Charles I, and Henrietta Maria, printed in 1625, the year of James's death and Charles's accession and marriage.[58] It seems probable that in 1616, Bathsua Rainolds had no court connections which would enable her to target one Stuart in particular. Print was thus an appropriate strategy; one book could be, and probably was, sent to each of her addressees: the British Library copy is the one given to King James, the Cambridge copy is the one given to Prince Charles. Both are personalized: in James's copy, the word 'finis' at the end is given a manuscript modification, and is prefixed with 'Regis Laus nescia': 'The praise of the king knows no—END.' The Cambridge copy, similarly, has a tiny handwritten poem: 'Principis Caroli laus NESCIA [finis] / Et absit omnia fraus' ('The praise of Charles knows no—END—and

---

[55] Bathsua's book is addressed to James I, and also includes poems to his queen, Anne of Denmark, his son Charles (later Charles I), and the Elector Palatine, his son in law. See Saunders, 'Bathsua Reginald'.

[56] *Ad Annam Dei Gratiae Magnae Britanniae, Franciae et Hyberniae Reginam Longe Augustissimam, Serenissimam et Prudentissimam,* in *Musa Virginea,* sig. A3.

[57] There is an undated Latin letter by Anne of Denmark to the Doge of Venice, Marino Grimani, in Leicester Record Office, DG7, Lit. 2, fo. 41.

[58] *Magnae Britanniae Chronographa Imperialia, seu Trophea Trina* (London, 1625).

all deceit is absent'). Both also have a handwritten macaronic inscription on the title page, 'Musam, μη μαχαιραν' ('The Muse, not a sword').[59]

In the short term, the project earned her presentation at court and, probably, an often-quoted put-down from King James: 'when a learned maid was presented to King James for an English rarity, because she could speake and rite pure Latine, Greeke and Hebrew, the King ask'd "But can shee spin?" '[60] In the longer term, though, it perhaps earned her the position of tutor to the Princess Elizabeth. Her husband Richard Makin, whom she married in 1621, was a minor court servant in the 1620s and 1630s, but then lost his place, which may explain why Bathsua herself was seeking court preferment in the 1640s.[61] The publication of *Musa Virginea* was no more transgressive or self-assertive than writing it in the first place; both were evidently done with the active assistance and co-operation of her father.

She continued to write Latin verse in later life, though her writing in Latin is laborious and not very successful. A Latin poem on the Parliamentarian Sir Henry Vane is preserved in Oxford, Bodleian Library, Rawl. Poet. 116, a manuscript belonging to the Elyot nephews of her admirer Sir Simonds d'Ewes. Many of her friends were Parliamentarian, even though she herself was directly dependent on the court and, in the early *Musa Virginea* at least, a stout defender of royal authority: it was Simonds d'Ewes who put her in touch with Anna Maria van Schurman, suggesting that he continued to have some concern for her. Another surviving late Latin poem is an elegy for the Countess of Huntingdon's son now in the Huntington Library. Both poems are verse written for a patron, of a standard humanist kind. Her last known Latin poem, on Robert Boyle, must have been composed when she was 81.

Other seventeenth-century women Latin poets include Jane Owen (?c.1600–after 1628), a connection, perhaps the niece, of one of the most famous Latin poets ever produced by the British Isles, the epigrammatist John Owen (so probably there is, again, at least one highly educated man in the previous generation of the family).[62] Her existence is revealed in an epigram by John Owen, which runs (quoted in a contemporary translation),[63]

> *To Mistris Iane Owen, a very learned Woman*
> Of thy five sisters, *Iane*, I know but thee,
> I onely have heard what their number bee:
> I cannot one of them by their names call;
> Yet if they be like thee, I know them all.
> Addition
> Faire, modest, learned, wise, beyond my prayse:
> Happy is he shall marry one of these.

[59] This may possibly be related to James VI's well-known dislike of edged weapons.

[60] *The Commonplace Book of John Collet 1633*, 129, in William J. Thoms (ed.), *Anecdotes and Traditions Illustrative of Early English History and Literature* (London: Camden Society, 1839), 125.

[61] Biographical details are from Teague, 'The Identity', and Brink, 'Bathsua Rainolds'. See also Teague, *Bathsua Makin*.

[62] On Owen, see Bradner, *Musae Anglicanae*, 87–90.

[63] J. R. C. Martyn, *Joannis Audonei Epigrammata*, 2 vols. (Leiden, 1876), appendix I, 146 (1st pub. London: Simon Waterson, 1622), ii. 68. The translation is from *Quodlibets* (see next note), 11.

There is more direct evidence for her capacity in her epigram on Owen, published on a prefatory page in the earliest editions.

> Quod fuit, est et semper erit sollemne poetis
> Carpimur in libris foemina, virque tuis,
> Iudice me tamen haec epigrammata salsa merentur
> Laudet ut ingenium vir, mulierque tuum.

This is translated in Robert Hayman's translation of Owen's epigrams, which is dedicated to women: the preface declares that the epigrams are being translated for the sake of the Beauties, 'because they cannot understand Latin'.[64] But on p. 40, as a coda to the epigrams, he gives the verses in praise of John Owen from the early editions, including the following:

Praise-worthy verses of Learned Mistris Iane Owen of Oxford, in praise of my Iohn Owen, translated out of her Latine

> It was, and is Poets quaint property,
> To carpe at men, and womens vanity:
> Yet this I iudge, thy salt lines merit it
> Both men and women will commend thy wit.

Hayman then adds: '*To the same learned Woman, whose vertues I reverence, I dedicate this Encomiastick.*'

> I'd rather have thy praises on my side
> Then any Womans I doe know beside:
> Thy wit and iudgment is more iust and able,
> Then many miriads of the unlearned rabble.

Hayman refers to Owen as 'my Friend'. The epigrams of Owen are translated by another friend, John Vicars. Hayman is plainly a member of Owen's personal circle; but all the same it is interesting that this woman's literary reputation and her work circulates outside the immediate family.[65] There is little to be gleaned from this verse, beyond the fact that she participated in the economy of mutual praise which is central to humanist poetic activity, but we might also observe that Owen's epigram specifically associates her virtue, her learning, and marriageability.

Retha Warnicke suggests this Jane Owen may be the identical with the Jane Owen who wrote *An Antidote against Purgatory*, published posthumously, probably

---

[64] *Quodlibets, Lately Come over from New Britaniola, or Newfound-Land. Epigrams and Other Small Parcells Both Morall and Divine, the first four bookes being the Authors owne: the rest translated out of that Excellent Epigrammatist, Mr. Iohn Owen, and other rare Authors: with two Epistles of that excellently wittie Doctor, Francis Rablais: Translated out of his French at Large. All of them Composed and done at Harbor-Grace in Britaniola, anciently called Newfound-Land*, by R.H., Sometimes Governor of the Plantation there (London: Printed by Elizabeth Allde, for Roger Michell, Pauls Church-yard, at the Signe of the Bulls-head, 1628).

[65] Professor David Norbrook has suggested to me (pers. comm.) that she is also the author of an epigraphic poem on two male Owens, perhaps her brothers.

on the Continent, in 1634.[66] This is problematic. The facts in favour of the suggestion are that the Catholic Jane Owen, who translated from Latin with facility, is described on her title page both as 'the honour of her sex for learning in England' and as 'late of God-Stow in Oxfordshire'. But John Owen was so actively hostile to Catholicism as to cause a rich Catholic uncle to disinherit him, and his works were placed on the *Index*.[67] Hayman himself was notably anti-Catholic. For such men, had the learned Jane Owen they knew belonged to the Catholic branch of the family, it is hard to see how her learning could have attracted such epithets as 'learned' and 'wise', or verbs such as 'reverence'. It might be possible to resolve the problem by suggesting that she converted late in life, but there is not the slightest indication in *An Antidote* that this might be the case.

One of the more surprising women Latin poets of the seventeenth century is a Quaker, Mary Mollineux (1651–95). Though Quakerism was largely a working-class movement at its outset, there was a number of educated gentlewomen among the early converts, women such as Anne Whitehead, Anne Docwra, and Margaret Fell.[68] Mollineux's cousin, who provides a brief biography in the posthumous collection *Fruits of Retirement*, notes that she was an only child, and that her weak eyesight led her father to educate her in Latin, Greek, arithmetic, 'Physick and Chyrurgy' rather than conventional feminine skills: as in a number of other cases, such as that of Judith Squire, mentioned above, classical languages and medicine are bracketed together. Curiously, she preferred to communicate with her husband in Latin, even on her deathbed: one of her last utterances, which he records in his memoir of her, was 'ne nimis solicitus esto': 'don't worry about me too much.'[69] Mary Mollineux's devotion to Latin is particularly remarkable, not to say strange, since to Quakers, Latin was 'the language of the Beast', a clear reference to the Church of Rome and a possible reference to the monopolies of the learned which Latin helped to defend.[70] However, her father may have been a Catholic who became a Quaker: the poem on pp. 102–6 (written in 1682) hints as much, so her Latin education may derive from a rather different milieu from the one she chose as an adult. Her husband records and translates three of her Latin poems, of which this poem in Sapphics is the longest:[71]

[66] Jane Owen, *An Antidote against Purgatory or Discourse, Wherein it is Shewed that Good-Workes, and Almes-Deeds, Performed in the Name of Christ, are a Chiefe Meanes for the Preventing, or Mitigating the Torments of Purgatory* (Saint-Omer: English College Press, 1634), reprinted as English Recusant Literature 166 (Menston: Scolar Press, 1973). This Jane Owen was also certainly Latin-literate: she translates extensively from Cardinal Bellarmine's *Liber de Aeterna Felicitate* and *De Gemitu Columbae*.

[67] Bradner, *Musae Anglicanae*, 89.

[68] See Stevenson and Davidson (eds.), *Early Modern Women Poets*, 346–7, 310–11, Phyllis Mack, *Visionary Women: Ecstatic Prophecy in Seventeenth-Century England* (Berkeley and Los Angeles: University of California Press, 1992), 139–40.

[69] Mary Mollineux, *Fruits of Retirement, or, Miscellaneous Poems, Moral and Divine, Being Contemplative, Letters &c, Written on Variety of Subjects and Occasions* (London: Printed and Sold by Mary Hinde, at no. 2 in George-Yard, Lombard Street, 1772; first published 1702).

[70] Richard Foster Jones, *The Triumph of the English Language* (London: Oxford University Press, 1953), 314.

[71] *Fruits of Retirement* sig. B8ᵛ.

In a Letter dated the 9th of the Twelfth Month, 1691, she sent to me in Prison these lines, viz.

I

Qui nocent Sanctis, Dominus locutus,
Hi fui tangunt Oculi Pupillam,
Sentient iram, quoque reddet istis
Praemia dira.

II

Si Deo credis, filioque Christo
Quisquis es Vir desipiensque rudis!
Cautus es ne tu Domino repugnas
Cordeque pugnis

III

Stultus at dixit sibi Corde, nullus
Est Deus: spernens igitur doceri
Saepe protervus ruit in ruinam
Absque timore

M.M.

I

The Lord, of them that hurt his Saints, doth say
They touch the Apple of his Eye, and they
Shall feel his Anger; he will them requite
With dreadful Plagues, in Death's eternal Night.

II

If then thou believest God, and Christ his son,
Whoe'er thou art, thou rude and foolish Man,
Beware, lest thou the Lord of Heaven resist
And Fight against him both with Heart and Fist.

III

But in his heart the foolish Man hath said
There is no God; and therefore not dismay'd,
To slight his Teachings: he, in Froward Wrath
Runs fearless on in Ruin's dreadful path.

Englished by H.M. [her husband]

She signified her Haste in the writing of these, because the Bearer staid for the Letter, and that she had not made any of such Quantities for above twenty years.

There is some further evidence for the existence of other early modern women Latin poets. Apparently one of the most ambitious was Anne Baynard, if we may judge by contemporary responses to her, but her work has sadly been lost. She was the daughter of Edward Baynard, a physician and surgeon practising in the City of London by profession, and a scholarly bibliophile by inclination,[72] so he may also

---

[72] A catalogue of his collection, which was sold after his death in 1721, lists some 300 works in Greek, Latin, French, and Italian. Dorothy Gardiner, *English Girlhood at School* (Cambridge: Cambridge University Press, 1929), 383.

be presumed to have supported and encouraged his daughter's education. According to John Prude in her funeral sermon, 'she set her self to the Composing of many things in the Latine Tongue, which were rare and useful in their kind'.[73] Jeremy Collier's *Great Historical Dictionary*, quoted by Ballard, adds that Anne Baynard disputed with Socinians (early Unitarians, who doubted the doctrine of the Trinity) in 'severe satyrs written in the Latin tongue'.[74] No trace of these is preserved, though her work was known beyond her family circle: she is mentioned, for example, by 'Eugenia' in *The Female Advocate* (1700) who declares, 'Learning becomes us as well as the Men. Several of the French Ladies, and with us the late incomparable Mrs. Baynard, and the Lady that is Mr. Norris's Correspondent [Mary Astell], and many more, are Witnesses of this.' Thomas Browne wrote two sets of verses on her death, one of which, like 'Eugenia's' remark, implies that she was known as a poet beyond her family circle.[75] 'Eugenia' herself was far from ignorant: she notes, 'I shall not brag that I understand a little Greek and Latin . . . having made some attempt to look into the more solid parts of Learning.' Later in her work, she argues, with respect to 1 Corinthians 7: 34, that the same Greek word is used of men pleasing their wives and wives pleasing their husbands, and therefore a wife's duty is not intrinsically different from that of a husband, which suggests not merely that she knew some Greek, but that she was capable of using the knowledge effectively.[76] A number of the defenders of women's right to education who sprang up in the Stuart period were well educated besides Mary Astell and 'Eugenia'; Marey More, for example, also challenges the existing translation of the New Testament as biased against women.[77] So were some of

---

[73] *A Sermon at the Funeral of the Learned and Ingenious Mrs Ann Baynard . . . Preached at the Parish Church of Barnes in the County of Surrey the 16 June 1697* (London: For Daniel Brown, 1697), 24.

[74] George Ballard, *Memoirs of Several Ladies of Great Britain*, ed. Ruth Perry (Detroit: Wayne State University Press, 1985), 317. The reference is to Jeremy Collier, *The Great Historical, Geographical and Poetical Dictionary: Being a Curious Miscellany of Sacred and Profane History*, 2 vols. (London: Henry Rhodes, 1701). My thanks to Maisie Brown of the Barnes & Mortlake History Society, who investigated the possible survival of her work in Barnes on my behalf.

[75] Thomas Browne, *Works*, 5 vols. (London, 1720), iii. 288–90. This is part of the long poem in alcaics:

> Hence Cornata receives you with chaste kisses
> as you shine in the chorus of virgins
> Schurmanna, amazed by the sight of you,
> desires the vision, and rejoices in it.

The other ladies in the virginal chorus are Elena Cornaro Piscopia (1646–84) and Anna Maria van Schurman (1607–78), both of whom were Greek and Latin scholars and poets, and unmarried.

[76] *The Female Advocate, or a Plea for the Just Liberty of the Tender Sex, and Particularly of Married Women, Being Reflections on a Late Rude and Disingenuous Discourse Delivered by Mr John Sprint*, By a Lady of Quality (London: Andrew Bell, 1700), pp. vi, 10. It is dedicated by Eugenia to Lady W——ley (probably not Lady Mary Wortley [Montagu] who, though already intellectually ambitious, was only 11).

[77] Ezell, *The Patriarch's Wife*, prints More's 'The Woman's Right', 191–203, from London, British Library, Harley 3198.

the women dramatists: Mary Pix was a Latin scholar,[78] and so was Catherine Trotter.[79]

Another potential source of Latin verse by women is inscription on tombstones—inevitably problematic, since there is no way of being certain whether such a poem was instigated by, or written by, the woman in question.[80] I have found a number of such poems in seventeenth-century England: two which are of interest are by Sarah Staples and Martha Norton. The first wrote on her husband, the second, more unusually, on her aunt: no manuscript material is preserved from either woman, that I have been able to find. Sarah Staples's brief poem runs as follows:

> Quod cum coelicolis habitas, pars altera nostra,
> Non dolet, hic tantum me superasse dolet.
> Hoc posuit moestissima uxor SARA.
>
> That you live with the inhabitants of heaven,
> one part of us does not mourn: But he mourns,
> that he is so far above me.
> This was placed by the griefstricken wife, Sarah.

Though very short, the thought is distinctly complex. It insists on the abiding unity of husband and wife, who are each 'pars altera' of a single whole, 'nostra'. The expected pattern of thought is reversed: the wife is the one who does *not* grieve, because the husband is in heaven; he, on the other hand, must regret that he has overleaped her. Implicit in this idea that he finds something regrettable in being in a superior position to his still-living wife is the equality of the relationship they had enjoyed until his death.

The seventeenth century also produces Ireland's first and apparently last woman Latin poet. There is little evidence for women's learning in Ireland: Katherine Philips's friend 'Philo-philippa' was Irish, strongly feminist, and had an extensive classical education, revealed in the poem she published in 1667, which had given her an acquaintance with some of the learned and/or heroic women of the past, such as Cornelia, mother of the Gracchi, but we do not know her name, let alone whether she accessed classical literature in Latin or in translation. The rather later Constantia Grierson, née Crawley (1705–32), wrote the Latin

---

[78] Her father, a graduate of both English universities, was rector of the Buckingham parish of Padbury and master of the Royal Latin (Free) School in Buckingham. In the anonymous satirical play *The Female Wits* (London: For William Turner, 1704), she tries to engage her rivals, Delariviere Manley and Catherine Trotter, in a 'Latin dispute'.

[79] She was taught some Latin and logic, and learned French on her own.

[80] A number of Latin inscriptions in Oxford College chapels are attributed to women: Maria Hutchenson claims to be the author of a poem celebrating her late husband, erstwhile president of St John's (1605), as does the mother of Arthur Tomkyns: non-verse Latin inscriptions claimed by women include Mrs Man, mother of the subject (1973), Bridget Broughton, the subject's sister (1710), Maria Pocock, wife of the Hebrew scholar Edward Pocock (1691), Maria Smalridge (1719), another widow, and Anna Littleton (1683) writing as heir of the deceased (Antony à Wood, *The History and Antiquities of the Colleges and Halls in the University of Oxford*, ed. John Gutch, 3 vols. (Oxford: Clarendon Press, 1786), iii. 295, 296. 477, 492, 497.

dedication of her husband's edition of Terence. She issued three editions of Latin classics with her husband, of Virgil, Terence, and Tacitus, and was perceived by contemporaries as playing a major part in the work. But the poet Eleanor Burnell is an unique figure, the only woman from an 'Old English' (i.e. Hiberno-Norman) family who is known to have written anything.[81] Robert Burnell was appointed Baron of the Exchequer in Ireland in 1402, and the family acquired the manor and lands of Balgriffin in the country of Dublin in the early fifteenth century. In 1535, John Burnell was attainted and executed at Tyburn for having been one of the principal supporters of Thomas Fitzgerald in his war against the Pale. Henry Burnell was thought able by Sir Henry Sidney in 1577, but 'he thirsteth earnestly to see the English government withdrawn from hence'. He was nonetheless appointed Justice of the Queen's Bench in 1589. During the persecution of recusants in 1605, although very aged, he was put under house arrest for having participated in a deputation formed by the principal Roman Catholics of the Pale to petition for a remission of the religious disabilities imposed on them.[82] Her family background was thus both aristocratic and strongly Catholic.[83]

Her father, also a Henry Burnell, is the author of *Landgartha. A Tragie-Comedy, as it was Presented in the New Theater in Dublin, with Good Applause, Being an Ancient Story*. The two surviving poems, one in hexameters, one in elegiac couplets, are among the prefatory verses in her father's play, which was performed in the Werburgh Street Theatre in Dublin on St Patrick's Day 1640, the last play performed in Ireland before the Civil War broke out.[84] The prologue of *Landgartha* is spoken by an Amazon with a battle-axe in her hand; and the prefatory epistle comments, 'Bodily force too in a woman (were it but to defend its own Fort) is a perfection, though it cannot be expected but from a few of you.' It suggests an attitude in Henry Burnell which might also account for his daughter's sophisticated education.[85] Nothing is known of how Eleanor Burnell fared in the tragedy which was 1640s Ireland. Her father became a member of the Irish confederation set up in 1642,[86] and Gilbert claims that he wrote other plays 'which haveing never

---

[81]   Richard Stanihurst, who was also Old English, celebrated the learning of a good number of his compatriots, but all of them were male. 'A Plain and Perfect Description of Ireland', in R. Holinshed (ed.), *Chronicles of England, Scotland and Ireland* (London: J. Harrison, 1577).

[82]   John T. Gilbert, *A History of the City of Dublin* (1st edn. Dublin, 1854–9), 3 vols., facsimile edn. (Shannon: Irish University Press, 1972), i. 296.

[83]   Her mother was Lady Frances Dillon, daughter of Sir James Dillon, the first Earl of Roscommon. My thanks to Professor Jane Ohlmeyer for help with Irish prosopography.

[84]   Henry Burnell, *Landgartha. A Tragie-Comedy, as it was Presented in the New Theater in Dublin, with Good Applause, Being an Ancient Story*, written by H.B. (Dublin, 1641). Other writers of gratulatory verse are John Bermingham, Henry Burnell's cousin, and Philippus Patricius, in Latin. Alan J. Fletcher, *Drama and the Performing Arts in Pre-Cromwellian Ireland* (Cambridge: D. S. Brewer, 2001), 450. It was not usual to perform plays during Lent, but the opening session of the Dublin Parliament had taken place the day before, and apparently court needs had been allowed to supersede both precedence and principle.

[85]   The choice of metaphor also suggests that he might perhaps have known François Billon, *Le Fort inexpugnable de l'honneur du sexe femenin* (Paris: Jan D'Allyer, 1555).

[86]   Peter Kavanagh, *The Irish Theatre, Being a History of the Drama in Ireland from the Earliest Period up to the Present Day* (Tralee: Kerryman Ltd., 1946), 40–5.

been published, are not now accessible';[87] but the family disappears from historical record. The first of her poems reads as follows:

Patri suo Charissimo operis Encomium
Melpomene tua tela (parens) contexta Thalia est,[88]
   judicio quamvis non trutinanda meo est:[89]
Me tua sed certam solers facundia verax
   expertorum hominum & fama diurna facit,
Te nullis potuisse tuis errare, decorum
   omnimodo Scænis, sed tenuisse triplex;
Nempe modum retinendo (docent ut scripta sagacis
   Flacci) personæ, temporis, atque loci.
Ad te à Iuvernis flexit victoria vatem
   partibus his cedunt Brutiginæque tibi.
Fama quidam tendet, quacunque auratus Apollo
   se tua [sedet ?]: tu vivis dum vehet amnis aquas.
Tu pater Aonio deducens vertice musas,
   gloria (non fallor) posteritatis eris.
Terra tuas certum est exhauriet extera laudes;
   clarescet scriptis insula nostra tuis

Melpomene—your loom, Father—when woven together, is also Thalia—
Though she ought not to be weighed in my scale!
However, your skilled, truthful eloquence,
And the daily report of competent men,
Makes me certain that you cannot have erred in any of your undertakings,
But have in all ways maintained threefold propriety on the stage:
Namely, by exercising restraint
(As the writings of the sagacious Horace instruct)
With regard to person, time and place.
Victory has turned away from the Irish towards you [in your capacity as] a poet,
And the [English] descended from Brutus in these regions yield to you.
Your fame indeed will spread wherever golden Apollo [abides][90];
You will live so long as the river [Liffey?] conveys its waters.
You, Father, bringing the Muses down from the Aonian mountain-top,
Are to be, unless I am mistaken, the glory of posterity.
It is certain that a foreign land will drink its fill of your praises;
Our island shall become famous thanks to your writings.

---

[87] i. 41. One piece which may possibly be ascribed to him is *The Worlds Idol: Plutus, a Comedy, Written in Greek by Aristophanes*, translated by H.H.B., together with his notes (London: Printed by W.G., 1659). The notes make no reference to Ireland, but are learned and odd: authors cited include the Bible, Montaigne, Herodotus, Diodorus Siculus, Antiphanes, Xenophon, Dio Cassius, and Menander. It would be usual to find that the father of a Latinate daughter was more than usually learned.

[88] Reading conjecturally *est* for *et*: my thanks to Dr Janet Fairweather for advice.

[89] The interpretation of lines 1–2 with their mixed metaphors is difficult. Burnell compares her father's literary work with a loom. *Tua tela* has to be nominative, not ablative, because of the scansion, and it is improbable that *tela* should be construed as neuter pl. 'weapons', in view of the 'weaving' connotations of *contexta*.

[90] *se tua* cannot possibly be right, but what the correct reading might be is unclear. A verb is required: I tentatively suggest 'sedet'.

The survival rate of the works of these seventeenth-century women is infuriatingly small. Rachel Jevon bobs up into a brief, if glorious, visibility, then vanishes. The work of Anne Baynard is lost completely, that of Jane Owen and the Benedictine nun is suggested only by a single poem. Sarah Staples and Martha Norton have left one poem each, with no papers, no context. But they provide at least a glimpse into an early modern England in which a number of educated gentlewomen periodically assayed writing in the language of power.

It is worth noting that the eighteenth century also saw an abstract interest in learned women. George Ballard's *Memoirs of Several Ladies of Great Britain Who Have Been Celebrated for their Writings or Skill in the Learned Languages, Arts and Sciences*, privately printed in 1572, is a serious, if not very successful, attempt by an amateur scholar to retrieve information about learned Englishwomen, particularly those of the sixteenth century.[91] It is also interesting that a woman friend of Ballard's, Elizabeth Elstob, the famous woman student of Anglo-Saxon, began an encyclopedia of learned women, which was to cover Europe as well as the British Isles. The manuscript of this abortive project is now in the Bodleian, a large quarto, with a new letter of the alphabet every few pages, which is otherwise all but pristine, though such notes and quotations as it does contain show that she was a confident reader of Latin and Greek as well as of Old English.[92] George Hickes said in 1712 of another of her projects, 'it will be the credit of our country, to which Mrs Elstob will be counted abroad, as great an ornament in her way as Madame Dacier is in France': an indication that the idea of the woman scholar as 'national ornament' was not yet dead.[93]

Eighteenth-century Englishwomen also had a new public arena for their writing. The *Gentleman's Magazine* performed for them a role similar to that which the *Mercure galant* had had for seventeenth-century Frenchwomen (and John Dunton's *Athenian Mercury* for seventeenth-century Englishwomen): it encouraged their intellectual and literary aspirations, and provided a forum for publication. Apart from Elizabeth Carter, a regular contributor who published Latin and Greek epigrams as well as translations from the classical languages in their pages, the *Gentleman's Magazine* took notice of, among other contemporaries, Elizabeth Tollet, and recorded notable women of the past such as the sixteenth-century Lady Jane and Lady Mary Fitzalan, daughters of the Duke of Arundel. In fact, the *Gentleman's Magazine* published many articles on women, only a quarter of which supported the traditional idea of women as the weaker sex (many of these reprints from other publications): most of what they published on women was sympathetic

---

[91] The significance of Ballard, and the nature of his agendas, is discussed by Margaret Ezell, *Writing Women's Literary History* (Baltimore: Johns Hopkins University Press, 1993), 79–87.

[92] Oxford, Bodleian Library, Ballard 64. Elstob's mother Jane was an admirer of learning 'especially in her own sex', and had taught Elizabeth some Latin by the age of 8. Ada Wallas, *Before the Bluestockings* (London: George Allen & Unwin, 1929), 133.

[93] Brink (ed.), *Female Scholars*, 2.

to their desire for education and greater economic opportunity, or even suggested concrete measures of reform.[94]

Apart from the *Gentleman's Magazine*, voices generally in favour of classical education for women were still to be heard in the eighteenth century.[95] For example, the master of Tonbridge School, Vicesimus Knox, declares: 'there are many prejudices entertained against the character of the learned lady, and perhaps, if all ladies were profoundly educated, some inconveniences might arise from it, but I must own, it does not appear to me, that a woman will be rendered less acceptable in the world, or less qualified to perform her duty in it, by having employed the time from six to sixteen in the cultivation of her mind.'[96] He also speaks positively in favour of classical studies for gentlewomen: 'Whenever a young lady in opulent circumstances appears to possess a genius, and an inclination, for learned pursuits, I will venture to say, she ought, if her situation and connections permit, to be early instructed in the elements of Latin and Greek. Her mind is certainly as capable of improvement as that of the other sex . . . the method to be pursued must be exactly the same as that which is used in the private tuition of boys, when it is judiciously conducted.'[97] Knox on Liberal Education was a well-received work which went through many editions, not the outpouring of a solitary eccentric; it was evidently read by influential people. Anna Barbauld, perhaps optimistically, thought that learning Latin '[would] not in the present state of things excite either a smile or a stare in fashionable company'.[98] Mrs Chapone, another very influential voice in the education of girls in the eighteenth century (who had taught herself some Latin as well as French and Italian),[99] was inclined to be ambivalent: 'I respect the abilities and application of those ladies who have attained them . . . yet I would by no means advise . . . [any] woman who is not strongly impelled by a particular genius to engage in such studies,' yet on the other hand, her grounds are that 'the real knowledge that they supply is not essential, since the English, French, or Italian tongues afford tolerable translations of all the most valuable productions of antiquity'. She assumes that a graceful and accomplished woman will read seriously in classical literature, and says of Homer and Virgil in translation, 'every body reads [them] that reads at all'—incidentally, she strongly recommends that Virgil be read in Annibale Caro's Italian version.[100]

[94] Jean E. Hunter, 'The Eighteenth-Century Englishwoman: According to the *Gentleman's Magazine*', *Woman in the Eighteenth Century and Other Essays*, ed. Paul Fritz and Richard Morton (Toronto: Samuel Stevens; Sarasota, Fla.: Hakkert, 1976), 73–88.

[95] See A. H. Upham, 'English Femmes Savantes at the End of the Seventeenth Century', *Journal of English and Germanic Philology*, 12 (1913), 262–76.

[96] *Liberal Education: or, a Practical Treatise on the Methods of Acquiring Useful and Polite Learning*, 10th edn. (London: Charles Dilly, 1789), 'On the Literary Education of Women', 324–36 (p. 324).

[97] Ibid. 329.

[98] 'On Female Studies', reprinted in Mary R. Mahl and Helene Koon (eds.), *The Female Spectator: English Women Writers before 1800* (Bloomington: Indiana University Press, 1977), 268.

[99] Sylvia Harcstark Myers, *The Bluestocking Circle* (Oxford: Clarendon Press, 1990), 77–8. Myers notes that Mrs Chapone was an only daughter with three brothers.

[100] *Letters on the Improvement of the Mind*, 3rd edn. (Dublin: For the United Company of Booksellers, 1777), 100–3.

She may not have been a Latinist, but Mrs Chapone's ideal young gentlewoman would have been, by modern English or American standards, quite an accomplished linguist. We also find eighteenth- and early nineteenth-century Englishwomen teaching Latin to their children: for example, an otherwise unknown Mrs Anne Robbins, and the mothers of two famous sons, the great classicist Richard Bentley, and Charles Dickens.[101]

A famous and distinguished eighteenth-century woman writer, the bluestocking Elizabeth Carter, was learned in both Greek and Latin.[102]

It was her most eager desire to be a scholar ... the slowness with which she conquered the impediments, that always oppose the beginning of the study of the dead languages, was such as wearied even the patience of her father ... but she was determined to overcome the difficulty.

A long, reflective poem on her eighteenth birthday is preserved in parallel-text Latin and English versions.[103] There seems no a priori reason to assume that the Latin text is not her own work. The fact that, despite her 'slowness', she had successfully mastered Latin (and Greek) verse is demonstrated by two epigrams, one in a Greek and Latin version written to Dr Johnson, and another on a visit to Alexander Pope's garden, written in answer to another, and published in the *Gentleman's Magazine* for 1738 together with her own English version.[104]

> En! marcet Laurus nec quicquam sinit *Elisam*
>   Furtim sacrilega diripuisse manu:
> Illa petit sedem magis aptam, tempora Popi,
>   Et florere negat pauperiore solo.
>
> Eliza.
>
> In vain Eliza's daring hand
> Usurp'd the laurel-bough
> Remov'd from Pope's the wreath must fade
> On ev'ry meaner brow.
>
> Thus gay exotics, when transferr'd
> To climates not their own,
> Loose all their lively bloom, and droop
> Beneath a paler sun.

Elizabeth Carter is spoken of as the bluest of the bluestockings because she translated Epictetus, but while the depth of her knowledge of Greek is something very out of the ordinary, as a student of Latin, she is a less isolated figure than she

---

101 Amanda Vickery, *The Gentleman's Daughter: Women's Lives in Georgian England* (New Haven: Yale University Press, 1998), 114, Peter Ackroyd, *Dickens* (London: Sinclair-Stevenson, 1996).

102 Montagu Pennington, *Memoirs of the Life of Mrs Elizabeth Carter* (London: F. C. and J. Rivington, 1807), 6.

103 Pennington gives *In Diem Natalem*, ibid. 348–53.

104 A more literal version is, 'See! The laurel is wilting and nothing permits Eliza to have snatched it furtively with a sacrilegious hand. It seeks a more suitable resting place, the temples of Pope, and says it cannot flourish on poorer soil.'

appears: to name only other obvious Queens of the Blues, Hester Thrale read Latin and translated Latin poetry (notably that of her friend Dr Johnson).[105] She says of her parents, 'I was their Joynt Play Thing, and although Education was a Word then unknown, as applied to Females; They had taught me to read and speak and think, and translate from the French, till I was half a Prodigy.' She studied Latin with Arthur Collier, who, despite an early letter saying 'You are enough to make a Parson swear', taught her to write the language with facility.[106] Dr Johnson, when he lived with the Thrales, insisted on teaching Latin to Queeney Thrale and Frances Burney (also a member of the household at the time): the latter's father, Charles Burney, mocked the scheme and eventually resorted to forbidding her to continue, leading Mrs Thrale to comment privately that he was a 'narrow Souled Goose-Cap'.[107] Hannah More was also solidly grounded in Latin.[108] Lady Mary Wortley Montagu taught herself Latin, so effectively that her juvenilia at 16 or so include an imitation of Ovid's *Heroides*, the death of Adonis from his *Metamorphoses*, and an imitation of Virgil's Tenth Eclogue;[109] Sarah Fielding, another friend of Mrs Thrale's, learned first Latin, then Greek:[110]

I have heard Doctor Collier say that Harry Fielding quite doated on his Sister Sally till she had made herself through his—Dr Collier's—Assistance, a competent Scholar, & could construe the 6th Book of Virgil: he then began to joke, & afterwards to taunt her, as a literary Lady &c. till she resolved on Study—and became eminent in her Knowledge of the Greek Language, after which her Brother never more could perswade himself to endure her Company with Civility—

But by the eighteenth century, the *sprezzatura* of polite society was not compatible with too much booklearning; those who had it did not parade it.[111] For all the

---

[105] She was from a landed gentry family, and grew up mainly in London. She was educated at home by her mother and aunt in French, Italian, Latin, and Spanish, and subsequently studied Latin, logic, and rhetoric with Arthur Collier. See A. Hayward (ed.), *Dr Johnson's Mrs Thrale* (Edinburgh: T. N. Foulis, 1910), 12. Her *Retrospection...*, a history of the last 1,800 years (2 vols., London: John Stockdale, 1801) makes it clear that she used Latin sources with ease, and includes translations (e.g. i. 44).

[106] James L. Clifford, *Hester Lynch Piozzi (Mrs Thrale)* (Oxford: Clarendon Press, 1941), 9, 26.

[107] Doody, *Frances Burney*, 241. Burney, however, also indicates that her father was not averse to his daughters acquiring some classical *culture*: writing to her older sister Hester, she said, 'well I recollect your reading with our dear Mother all Pope's Works, and Pitt's Aeneid.' Hester cannot have been more than 10. (ibid. 21.)

[108] She was the fourth daughter of Jacob More, a Tory, high-churchman, and headmaster of the free school at Fishponds, Stapleton, who taught her Latin. Janet Todd, *A Dictionary of British and American Women Writers* (London: Methuen, 1984), 224. Note that the heroine of Hannah More's *Coelebs in Search of a Wife* learns Latin in secret and blushes to have it discovered.

[109] It was her admiration for the *Metamorphoses* which induced her to study Latin. Robert Halsband, *The Life of Lady Mary Wortley Montagu* (Oxford: Clarendon Press, 1956), 5–7. See also Isobel Grundy, 'Books and the Woman: An Eighteenth Century Owner and her Libraries', *English Studies in Canada*, 20.1 (1994), 1–22.

[110] Doody, *Frances Burney* 241. The brother's attitude is interesting, but so is the fact that it did not act as a deterrent.

[111] Lady Mary Wortley Montagu advised her daughter that her granddaughter should not be allowed to 'think herself learned, when she can read Latin and Greek'. *The Works of Lady Mary Wortley Montagu*, ed. I. Dalloway, 5 vols. (London: R. Phillips, 1803), iv. 180–3.

friendly support of individual men which has already been quoted, there was a great deal more mockery and hostility. The literary types of the learned woman, such as Pope's Phoebe Clinket and Smollett's Narcissa's aunt, were dreary pedants or frightful-looking learned hags: faced with such mockery, the great majority of clever, well-educated women went to lengths *not* to be identified as *femmes savantes*. For example, Jemina, Marchioness Grey, an early and close friend of Catherine Talbot, expressed her unease at the idea she might be suspected of being overly learned. The Bishop of Oxford, Thomas Secker (Talbot's 'foster father'), called on Lady Grey and offered to lend her a new translation of Horace, suggesting that their conversation had been highly literary.[112] The four volumes arrived next day while she was making tea, as she explains in a letter to Catherine Talbot. Naturally, they were first presented to her husband, who disowned them, and referred them to his wife, who was forced to own up to them in company: 'An English Translation is always one should think Unexceptionable—but then it had Latin of One Side, and *which* I read you know may be doubtful.' A well-intentioned guest started telling her about 'Electrical Experiments' and suggested a day when she could come and observe them—the mortified Lady Grey made her escape, devoutly hoping she did not leave behind her 'the Character of *Précieuse*, *Femme Sçavante*, Linguist, Poetess, Mathematician, & any other name that any Art can be distinguished by'.[113] She thus followed the advice of John Gregory in his well-known work *A Father's Legacy to his Daughter* (1774) that learned women should 'keep it a profound secret, especially from men'.[114] It would seem that women followed his advice so whole-heartedly that their secret is secret still; despite the obvious fact that this popular book of advice acknowledges, implicitly, that there *were* still learned ladies.[115] Elizabeth Robinson complained that 'there is a Mahometan Error crept even into the Christian Church that Women have no Souls, & it is thought very absurd for us to pretend to read or think like Reasonable Creatures', but her assessment of women's situation must be contexted by the fact that she herself read enough Latin to quote Horace in the original, read widely in translations from the classics, and encouraged her sister to do likewise as a relief from the tedium of provincial life.[116] The fact that in the eighteenth century more women were complaining

[112] Secker, apart from encouraging young women in his immediate circle, subscribed for three copies of Ballard's *Memoirs*, and his private memoranda included notes on Elena Piscopia and Laura Bassi (Myers, *The Bluestocking Circle*, 133, from Secker's notebooks, London, Lambeth Palace Library, 2564, fos. 285, 461).

[113] Myers, *The Bluestocking Circle*, 5, from Bedfordshire County Record Office, Lucas Papers L 30/9a/4, pp. 30–2.

[114] John Gregory, *A Father's Legacy to his Daughter* (London: W. Stratton & T. Cadell, 1774), 31.

[115] This fact is not always acknowledged: see Beth Kowaleski-Wallace, 'Milton's Daughters: The Education of Eighteenth-Century Women Writers', *Feminist Studies*, 12 (1986), 275–94. But there were even ladies who made an affectation of learning and looked down on their 'ignorant' sisters: Myers, *The Bluestocking Circle*, 41. A provincial gentlewoman of Warwickshire, Catherine Maria Throckmorton, was studying Latin, Greek, Italian, and Spanish, on the evidence of an affectionate, unsigned letter from a neighbour who seems neither surprised nor shocked (Warwickshire Record Office, CR 1998/TCD/fol. 3/5).

[116] Myers, *The Bluestocking Circle*, 39, 41. 42.

about their lack of access to education may in fact illustrate rising hopes and expectations rather than falling educational standards.

While bearing in mind that we have plenty of evidence for girls learning Latin from a private tutor (as Mrs Thrale did), or from their fathers, so that schools are only part of the picture, the schools themselves were not as universally useless as they are sometimes believed to be. Even in the eighteenth century, it is possible to demonstrate that there were girls' schools which taught more than elegant accomplishments. As Mrs Chapone makes clear, the study of French was as much taken for granted as the study of dancing.[117] Charlotte Charke (1713–66) attended a fashionable girls' boarding school from the ages of 8 to 10 (1721–3), where she learned Italian, music, geography, and Latin.[118] She described her education as 'not only a genteel, but in fact a liberal one, and such indeed as might have been sufficient for a son instead of a daughter'. Ellis Cornelia Knight (1758–1837) similarly attended a seminary for girls where she learned French, Latin, Greek, mathematics, geography, and history:[119] the similarity of her curriculum to that of Charlotte Charke suggests that this may be the same school, unnamed by either woman. Mary Darby, who in later life became the beautiful actress known as 'Perdita' Robinson (1758–1800), attended a number of schools as a girl, including that of Mrs Meribah Lorrington at Chelsea. She remembered Mrs Lorrington admiringly as 'the most extensively accomplished female that I ever remember to have met with . . . She had a sound knowledge of the Classics . . . ' Unfortunately, by the time she became a schoolmistress, she had also become an alcoholic: Mary was taken away.[120] Towards the end of the century, in 1790, Elizabeth Benger, née Ogilvy, who became a poet and writer, was sent at 12 to a *boys'* school in order to learn Latin,[121] and her contemporary Mary Russell Mitford, later the author of *Our Village*, attended a rather good school at Hans Place, run by M. de Saint-Quintin, a French émigré and inveterate gambler; the sort of place where 'those who chose to learn had full opportunity of learning'. She learned Latin there, despite her father's objection that the subject 'would occupy more of your time than you could conveniently appropriate to it'.[122]

---

[117] 'Dancing and the knowledge of the French tongue are now so universal that they cannot be dispensed with in the education of a gentlewoman.' *Letters*, 99.

[118] From her autobiography, *A Narrative of the Life of Mrs Charlotte Charke . . . Written by Herself* (London: For W. Reeve, A. Dodd, and E. Cook, 1755). She conceived a passionate interest in medicine and set up her own dispensary, in which her knowledge of Latin will have been of direct practical utility to her.

[119] Scholarly historian, novelist, translator, and poet. Her mother Philippina Knight took special care with her daughter's education. Todd, *Dictionary* (she is the subject of an encomiastic poem from an Italian woman contemporary: Maria Maddalena Morelli Fernandes, 'Sonetto alla nobilissima e valorosissima Dama Cornelia Knight', published as a single sheet. Pietro Leopoldo Ferri, *Biblioteca femminile italiana* (Padua: Crescini, 1842), 247).

[120] Josephine Kamm, *Hope Deferred: Girls' Education in English History* (London: Methuen, 1965), 138.

[121] She published poetry anonymously in periodicals, novels, translations, and biographies of Elizabeth Hamilton, Anne Boleyn, and Mary, Queen of Scots. She was friendly with Mary Lamb, Mrs Barbauld, LEL, and Elizabeth Hamilton. Jean Buyze, *The Tenth Muse* (Berkeley: Shameless Hussy Press, 1980), 11.

[122] *The Life of Mary Russell Mitford*, ed. Revd A. G. L'Estrange (London: Richard Bentley, 1870). See Kamm, *Hope Deferred*, 139.

Of the women poets active in the eighteenth century who actually write in Latin (as opposed to translating from it—a rather larger group) perhaps the most interesting is Elizabeth Tollet (1694–1754), the daughter of George Tollet, Commissioner of the Navy under William III and Anne. She was brought up as a child in the Tower of London (as, coincidentally, was a somewhat earlier woman Latinist, Lucy Hutchinson, née Apsley, who translated Lucretius). According to the anonymous biographer who edited her collection of poems, Elizabeth Tollet 'received a handsome fortune from her father, who observing her extraordinary Genius, gave her [an] excellent education'. As a result, she wrote fluent French, Italian, and Latin. She seems to have had one brother, who attended St John's College, Cambridge: relations between the siblings were cordial, on the evidence of a number of affectionate poems to him included in her published collection. Later in her life, she lived at Stratford and West Ham, in Essex, where she died, and was buried.[123] She was a friend of Sir Isaac Newton, who commended some of her first essays. Another close friend, on whom she wrote two Latin poems after his death, was John Woodward (1665–1728), geologist, physician, and antiquarian, a man who often served as president of the Royal Society: this may suggest something of the intellectual circles in which she moved. She amassed an extensive library, never married, and left her estate to her eldest nephew.

Her poetry circulated in manuscript in her lifetime,[124] and she published a collection of verse, *Poems on Several Occasions, with Anne Boleyn to King Henry the Eighth: An Epistle* (anonymous in 1724 while she was still alive; attributed after her death in two later editions, 1755 and 1760). Her poems are in a variety of forms in both English and Latin. She was also one of the few women to attempt a heroisletter on the model of Ovid's *Heroides*,[125] 'Anne Boleyn to King Henry the Eighth'. The collection bears witness to her awareness of earlier women's writing in Latin: she translates the distich said to have been written by Lady Jane Grey in the Tower, and imitates Mary, Queen of Scots' Buxton distich. Both of these are printed in George Ballard's collection, published in 1752, only two years before her death: but since they appear in the 1724 edition of her work, she must have got them from other sources. Lady Jane's distich is in Foxe's *Book of Martyrs*, which was still being read as Protestant hagiography in the eighteenth century: the question of where the Buxton distich may have come from is less easily resolved.

Tollet's Latin verse is highly competent; mostly on Christian subjects, including three poetic versions of psalms, and a paraphrase of part of the Book of Job—such paraphrases were a literary genre of the early eighteenth century, practised by such poets as Elizabeth Rowe (née Singer). In every way, her Latin oeuvre is directly

---

[123] There is an account of Elizabeth Tollet in the *Gentleman's Magazine* (1815), ii, p. 484.

[124] e.g. *A New Ballad, to the Tune of All you Ladies Now at Land &c*, London, British Library, Harley 7316, fos. 68ᵛ–69ᵛ.

[125] Ann Francis (1738–1800), educated in Latin, Greek, and Hebrew, published *Miscellaneous Poems, by a Lady* (Norwich, For the author, 1790), which included heroinic epistles. Anne Finch, Countess of Winchilsea, published an epistle from 'Alexander to Hephaestion', and 'Col. Maddens Lady, late Miss Cooper', wrote an unpublished 'Abelard to Eloisa', Bodley, Eng. poet. e.40, fos. 88ʳ–96ʳ, possibly in the 1740s.

comparable with that of male contemporaries: solemn, musical, and fundamentally serious-minded: the Renaissance enjoyment of jests, word-play, and wit in Latin verse was not part of the eighteenth-century aesthetic, which preferred to keep such moods for vernacular composition.

Sarah Losh of Wreay in Cumberland (1785–1853), though not a Latin poet, is one of the most interesting educated provincial gentlewomen of the early nineteenth century, and though hardly any evidence of her Latin writing survives, her life illustrates the usefulness of a classical education to a well-circumstanced woman. She was the daughter of a family not unlike the mid-seventeenth-century Ishams of Lamport. Her father John Losh was himself an educated man (a graduate of Trinity College, Cambridge) who became a pioneer industrial chemist.[126] He had two daughters, mutually devoted, of whom the elder, Sarah, studied French, Latin, Greek, and mathematics, chiefly with the local parson, William Gaskin. When Katherine, the younger sister, died in 1835, Sarah, who was passionately interested in architecture and had travelled with her sister in Italy, decided to memorialize her by designing a church, 'reminiscent of their travels and beautified by symbolic conceits'. One is reminded of the architectural projects of an earlier educated Cumbrian woman, Lady Anne Clifford.[127] Her church, a profoundly original building far ahead of its time, was consecrated in 1842. The font was partly carved by Sarah herself; the statue of her sister, by David Dunbar, was a working-up of a sketch which Sarah had made of Katherine near Naples in 1817, and the monument in honour of the parents (designed before Katherine's death) gives evidence of her Latinity in its inscriptions.[128] The building, which the architectural historian Nikolaus Pevsner regarded as 'one of the best of all Victorian churches', bespeaks considerable knowledge of the classical tradition, combined with complete confidence in her own judgement: her use of a Roman basilican form with Romanesque and Lombardic detailing and a decorative scheme which prefigures the art nouveau of fifty years later is like nothing which she could have seen anywhere.[129] Sarah Losh seems to have made little direct use of her Latin and Greek, apart from extempore translation from classical texts during family reading-aloud sessions in the evenings,[130] but her confidence in her abilities to fulfil the duties of her position as her father's heir, and consequently as a landowner, patron, and capitalist as well as architect, was surely underpinned by her access to the full range of masculine knowledge.

---

[126] Henry Lonsdale, *The Worthies of Cumberland*, 6 vols. (London: George Routledge & Sons, 1873), iv. 196–7.

[127] See Richard T. Spence, *Lady Ann Clifford* (Stroud: Sutton Publishing, 1997).

[128] These are now difficult to read, but are given by Lonsdale, *Worthies*, 219–21.

[129] Apart from *The Buildings of England: Cumberland and Westmorland* (Harmondsworth: Penguin, 1967), 210–14, Pevsner published an article, 'Sarah Losh's Church', *Architectural Review*, 142 (1067), 65–7.

[130] Lonsdale, who knew Sarah Losh personally, described her doing this 'in so quiet a style as to lead to no suspicion of its being the translation of the moment', p. 204. He also notes, 'Miss Losh was fertile in thought, and found gratification in filling pages of manuscript with both prose and verse. Unfortunately she preserved nothing' (p. 206).

The ambiguous status of both the Latinate woman and Latin itself in the seventeenth and eighteenth centuries is perhaps indicated by the fact that a surprising number of the poems discussed here are parallel texts; published in Latin *and* English versions: Rachel Jevon's very ambitious work, and two longish poems by Mary Monck and Elizabeth Carter have been mentioned; but we find versions of the same poem in two or more languages in Bathsua Rainolds's book as well, while others of this small body of work were translated by contemporaries. The Latin-educated were by this time a relatively small section of the reading public; and rather than accepting that Latin was a mystery best left to the learned, early modern readers, in England as in France, increasingly demanded translations: as Elizabeth Johnson declares, 'we Read Plutarch now 'tis Translated'. By writing parallel texts, a woman such as Rachel Jevon could have her cake and eat it, simultaneously signalling her right to be considered as among the learned, and opening her work to those who were unable to read Latin. The awareness of a potential audience who were not Latin-readers implied by the production of parallel texts is also signalled by the nun's translation of her sister's poem on Dame Lucy Knatchbull, Hayman's translation of both John and Jane Owen, and Henry Mollineux's translation of his wife's verses. They are testimony not to the transgressiveness of women's writing in Latin, but to the dwindling importance of Latin as a literary language, even while classical reference and a Latinate vocabulary remained central to cultivated discourse.

15. *The New World*

Colonial and revolutionary America

Anne Bradstreet (1612–72), the most significant woman writer of seventeenth-century America, did not, as far as we know, read Latin, though she came from a background in England which would have made this a distinct possibility. She was born in Northampton, and her father Thomas Dudley was at that time chief steward in the household of the Earl of Lincoln. It was apparently with his encouragement that she read widely as a girl: she described him as 'a magazine of history'. As the daughter of so senior and trusted a servant, she had free run of the extensive library at Sempringham Castle, and made good use of it: to judge from her own poems, Du Bartas and Sir Philip Sidney were favourites of hers, while Edmund Spenser was particularly influential on her own practice as a poet.[1] As an adult in North Andover, Massachusetts, she and her husband came to own over 800 books, a remarkable figure for a private household which did not have a professional concern with education. However, the considerable learning evidenced in her verse was accumulated through extensive reading in English, and perhaps French, though since her beloved Du Bartas was available in English translation by the time she was writing, even this is uncertain.

North American colonial society became far more settled and secure in the eighteenth century, but though it is possible to point to a number of women who read Latin, none of them is known to have written in it. One such is Susanna Wright (1697–1784), a Quaker, born in Warrington, Lancashire, the daughter of Patience Gibson and John Wright. As she grew up, she was noted for her fluency in French and competence in Italian and Latin, and her background in natural philosophy. The early Quakers generally distrusted Latin because of its Catholic associations, though some used it (notably Mary Mollineux, who is discussed in Chapter 14), but as the Quakers themselves became more integrated into society, this seems less and less the case.[2] Wright's father moved to Chester, Pennsylvania, and established himself as a shopkeeper by 1714. She was a voracious reader, and

---

[1] *The Tenth Muse Lately Sprung up in America, Or Severall Poems, Compiled with Great Variety of Wit and Learning, Full of Delight. Wherein especially is contained a compleat discourse and description of The Four Elements, Constitutions, Ages of Man, Seasons of the Year. Together with an Exact Epitome of the Four Monarchies, viz. the Assyrian, Persian, Grecian and Roman. Also a Dialogue between Old England and New, concerning the late troubles. With divers other pleasant and serious Poems. By a Gentlewoman in those Parts* (London: Stephen Bowtell, 1650).

[2] Richard Foster Jones, *The Triumph of the English Language* (London: Oxford University Press, 1953), 314.

confided to Benjamin Rush that 'the pleasure of reading was to her a most tremendous blessing'. After moving to America, she exchanged English verses with friends, but did not seek publication.[3] Another Pennsylvanian, Sarah Wister (1761–1804), was educated with other daughters of the first families of Philadelphia. Their schoolmaster was a well-known Quaker, Anthony Benezet. She studied French, Latin, and English literature, and occasionally published some of her own poetry. Similarly, an eighteenth-century New Yorker, Anne Eliza Bleeker, née Schuyler (1752–83), read Homer, Virgil, Theocritus, Ariosto, and Tasso, and wrote poetry: this information comes from the posthumous volume of her verse published by her daughter Margaretta Faugeres in 1793.[4] As in contemporary England, some girls educated at home in serious-minded, intellectual households were taught Latin. For example, Theodosia Burr, the daughter of Aaron Burr, who was born in 1783, was taught Latin and Greek, and required by her father to keep a daily journal for his inspection.[5]

However, there is no evidence of any kind that the knowledge thus acquired by Theodosia Burr and other girls whose fathers held similar views resulted in any women's writing in the Latin language, whether poetry or prose.[6] This is to do not merely with the position of women, but with the status of Latin generally. The first transatlantic equivalent of a grammar school, the Boston Latin School, was based on an English model, but the model did not naturalize well.[7] Harvard University still produced Latin poets in the eighteenth century,[8] but compared to the thousands of lines of Latin verse (and prose) written in eighteenth- and nineteenth-century England (to say nothing of the rest of Europe), the neo-Latin verse of the United States forms an exiguously slender sheaf.[9] Explicit doubts were expressed as to the relevance of Latin in the new society which was being created; in particular, Benjamin Rush, who has already been mentioned, was an eloquent spokesman against the use of Latin even by men, as, earlier, was

---

[3] Pattie Cowell, *Women Poets in Pre-Revolutionary America* (Troy, NY: Whitston Publishing Co., 1981), 215–21.

[4] *The Posthumous Works of Anne Eliza Bleeker* (New York: T. & J. Swords, 1793).

[5] *Correspondence of Aaron Burr and his Daughter Theodosia*, ed. Mark van Doren (New York: Covici-Friede Inc., 1929), esp. 12–23.

[6] Leo M. Kaiser, 'A Census of American Latin Verse, 1625–1825', *Proceedings of the American Antiquarian Society*, 91.2 (1981), 197–299, gives nothing at all: the only remote possibilities are two poems credited to 'Sibylla Americana', on Louis XVII of France, 1781 and 1782 (nos 260–1, p. 269), but there is no reason to assume that a person writing in the persona of a sibyl is female. American Latin is further explored by Leo M. Kaiser, *Early American Latin Verse, 1625–1825: An Anthology* (Chicago: Bolchazy-Carducci, 1984) and by Gilbert L. Gigliotti, 'Musae Americanae: The Neo-Latin Poetry of Colonial and Revolutionary America', Ph.D. (Catholic University of America, Washington, 1992). Professor Gigliotti kindly assured me in an email that he has found no women's Latin verse anywhere in the United States.

[7] Francoise Waquet, *Latin: Or the Empire of a Sign*, trans. John Howe (London: Verso 2000), 22, and see Meyer Reinhold, *Classica Americana: The Greek and Roman Heritage in the United States* (Detroit: Wayne State University Press, 1984), 25–8.

[8] Leicester Bradner, *Musae Anglicanae*, (New York: Modern Language Association of America, 1940) 369.

[9] See Kaiser, 'A Census of American Latin Verse'.

Thomas Paine.[10] Some women continued to be instructed in Latin in the family: Sarah Hale says of her contemporary Sarah Margaret Fuller, author of *Women in the Nineteenth Century*, 'most particularly did the father instruct his daughter in the learning he considered of the first importance—the classic tongues'.[11] Similarly, Sarah Hall of Philadelphia 'obtained an extensive knowledge of the ancient classics by hearing her brothers recite their Latin and Greek lessons to their father'.[12] Later on, Latin was introduced into women's school and college education during the nineteenth century (as it was in most European countries), and flourished in women's colleges such as Bryn Mawr and Wellesley.[13] Gaining access to Latin in this context was presented as a feminist victory. Predictably, however, the point at which classics began to be presented as appealing to, and suitable for, women was precisely that at which it had ceased to be a royal road to professional advantage.[14]

The first black woman poet of America, Phyllis Wheatley (1753–84), was also Latin-literate; she is the only woman known to be black whose story forms any part of this book.[15] She was bought in the Boston slave market at the age of 6 or 7, and the Wheatley family, having recognized her obvious intelligence, made considerable efforts to educate her. Within sixteen months she was reading the Bible fluently. She went on to learn Latin, and it is moving to note that it was Latin which offered some sort of interface between her African formation and her co-option into American life. Reading the Roman playwright Terence, she observed that his full name was Publius Terentianus Afer: 'the African', from which she reasonably concluded that one at least of the admired authors of antiquity was of African birth, a thought she found sustaining.[16] Thus for her, this single fact taken from the European classical tradition, frail bridge though it was between her original identity and the culture which she acquired, was the only one made available to her which did not implicitly encourage her to regard herself merely as an empty vessel to be filled with European culture.

[10] Waquet, *Latin*, 38, 180.

[11] *Woman's Record*, (New York: Harper & Brothers, 1860) 665. Sarah Hale also says of herself, 'to my brother I owe what knowledge I possess of the Latin, and the higher branches of mathematics and of mental philosophy' (p. 687).

[12] Ibid. 878.

[13] Waquet, *Latin*, 226.

[14] Caroline Winterer, *The Culture of Classicism: Ancient Greece and Rome in American Intellectual Life, 1780–1910* (Baltimore: Johns Hopkins University Press, 2002), 120.

[15] She was not the only 18th-century black person to study Latin, though the only known black Latin poets are male: see Introduction, n. 50. The only possibly black woman to have any kind of visibility in antiquity is a late antique 'muliercula quaedam ex Africa' (poor little woman from Africa) mentioned by Marcellus Burdigalensis as having introduced a new and excellent medicine for intestinal spasms. *De Medicamentis Liber*, ed. Maximilian Niedermann (Leipzig: B. G. Teubner, 1916), 19. 7, p. 228.

[16] *Critical Review*, 21 (1766), 282. Peter Fryer, *Staying Power* (London: Pluto Press, 1984), 91. Her writings were published as *Poems on Various Subjects, Religious and Moral* (London: Bell, 1773).

Ibero-America

While the preponderantly Protestant society of colonial and revolutionary America had very little actual use for Latinate women, the position was obviously different in the Spanish Americas because of the continued importance of Latin to the Catholic Church. This is reflected in Ibero-American women's cultural production. Spanish colonial society was a complex affair. By 1550, emigrant Spanish women were a substantial presence in Spanish colonial society: 'increasing numbers of Spaniards, believing that their fellow settlers presented good opportunities for an advantageous marriage in America, began to import their unmarried sisters, cousins and nieces...the arrival of Spanish women reached a high point of 28 to 40 percent of all immigrants by the end of the [sixteenth] century.'[17] These immigrants were not the sweepings of the Peninsula (the pattern is wholly unlike that of English women emigrants, who, outside New England, were most commonly working-class women or criminals), but included educated women of good family. It is also worth observing that literary activity in the colony began surprisingly early: for example, the first Latin poem published in Mexico appeared in 1540, and the first published collection of (Spanish) verse in 1546,[18] and in the Biblioteca Naçional in Madrid there is a manuscript anthology of Spanish verse which was made in Mexico in 1557.[19] Printing in Mexico goes back to 1539.[20] The teaching of Latin to indigenes also began very early in Mexico.[21]

At the same time, the *conquistadors* recognized the validity of indigenous claims to nobility; and in many cases consolidated their rule by marrying local princesses. Inés Yupanqui, daughter of the Inca Huayna Capac, was given to Francisco Pizarro by her brother the Inca Atahualpa, and bore him two children. She subsequently married a page in Pizarro's retinue and was rewarded with an *encomienda*. In Mexico, Isabel/Techichopotzin Moctezuma (*c.*1510–1550) had five husbands in her short life, the second of whom was the last Aztec emperor, Cuauhtémoc, as well as having an affair with Hernán Cortés which produced a son. All her children by her various husbands (two Aztecs, three Spaniards), with the

---

[17] Susan Migden Socolow, *The Women of Colonial Latin America* (Cambridge: Cambridge University Press, 2000), 54.

[18] The former, by Christoforo Cabrera, in *Manuel de Adultos*, printed by Jan Cromberger, the latter is Bartolomeo las Casas's *Canciones spiritual*. Joaquín García Icazbalcetta, *Bibliografia mexicana del siglo xvi* (Mexico City: Fondo de Cultura Económica, 1954), 58, 76.

[19] Madrid, Biblioteca Nacional 2973.

[20] See Icazbalcetta, *Bibliografia*, and José Toribio Medina, *La emprunta en México (1559–1821)* (Santiago de Chile: Impresa en Casa del Autor 1912; repr. Mexico City, Universidad Nacional Autónoma de México, 1989) and José Toribio Medina, *Historia de la emprenta en los antiguos dominios españoles de América e Oceanía*, 2 vols. (Santiago de Chile: Fondo Histórico y Bibliográfico José Toribio Medina, 1958).

[21] Waquet, *Latin*, 43. See further Igacio Osorio-Romero, 'La enseñanza del latin a los Indios', in Alexander Dalzell, Charles Fantazzi, and Richard J. Schoeck (eds.), *Acta Conventus Neo-Latini Torontoniensis: Proceedings of the Seventh International Congress of Neo-Latin Studies, Toronto, 8 August to 13 August, 1988* (Binghamton, NY: Medieval and Renaissance Texts and Studies, 1991), 863–4.

exception of two daughters who became nuns, became part of the Mexican colonial nobility, as did her illegitimate son.[22]

Convents were an important aspect of Spanish American life: the first convent in Mexico City, Nuestra Señora de la Concepción, was founded in 1540, only nineteen years after the Spanish conquest, and the first convent in Lima was built within twenty-six years of the foundation of the colony. In all, no less than thirty-eight convents were founded in Mexico before the eighteenth century. They fulfilled a religious and social need; allowing families to maintain their social status by disembarrassing themselves of surplus daughters who would otherwise marry beneath the family's aspirations, and allowing wealthy and prominent women to express their religiosity, enhance their social status, and prepare for their future.[23] Convents were frequently founded by wealthy widows who themselves took religious vows, thus providing for themselves a comfortable, socially prestigious retirement. Convent life varied widely, and not all nuns led lives of fasting and flagellation (though some did, notably those in discalced—literally, shoeless—orders). Nuns in calced orders were allowed to keep their private possessions, such as slaves, silver, cash, books, and pictures: the Poor Clares of Salvador, unlike Poor Clares in other parts of the world, were famous for their costly and extravagant lifestyle. The daughters of the wealthy, forced to sacrifice sexual gratification and the social prestige and private satisfactions deriving from motherhood for the sake of their families, were in some cases compensated with a life of private dandyism spent in a personal suite of rooms adorned with imported furniture, attended by both servants and slaves, while wearing habits decked with ribbons and embroidery.[24] Such nuns obviously had the potential ability to devote themselves to intellectual pursuits. Nuns were far more literate than other groups of women, and hundreds have left writings of various kinds: chronicles, histories, spiritual biographies, mystical writings, poetry, and plays; almost invariably in the vernacular.[25]

An important feature of all colonial life in Ibero-America was the maintenance of racial distinction, though it was done in a way distinctly different from Protestant colonial systems. Spanish society was obsessed with *limpieza de sangre* (the proven absence of Jewish or Moorish blood), from the fifteenth century onwards (despite the fact that many of the Peninsula's most talented citizens, including St Teresa of Avila and St John of the Cross, possessed the despicable stigma of Jewish ancestry). In the colonial situation, absence of African blood came to carry the same significance.[26] However, since the Aztec and Maya aristocracies were

---

[22] Socolow, *Women*, 35–6.

[23] Ibid., 92–3, Edith Couturier, ' "For the Greater Service of God": Opulent Foundations and Women's Philanthropy in Colonial Mexico', in Kathleen D. Macarthy (ed.), *Lady Bountiful Revisited: Women, Philanthropy and Power* (New Brunswick, NJ: Rutgers University Press, 1990), 199–241.

[24] Asunción Lavrin, 'Values and Meaning of Monastic Life for Nuns in Colonial Mexico', *Catholic Historical Review*, 58 (1972), 367–87.

[25] Socolow, *Women*, 102. See also Electa Arenal and Stacey Schlau, *Untold Sisters: Hispanic Nuns in their Own Works* (Albuquerque: University of New Mexico Press, 1989).

[26] There is an interesting unprinted document in which this cultural assumption is challenged: 'Letter of a black woman to a nun who despised her for her colour, in which she defends the colour black, with poetic *razones* and examples from antiquity', Madrid, Biblioteca Nacional, 6149, fos. 236–237ᵛ.

recognized by the Spanish authorities, intermarriage with local nobility was considered legitimate. Convents were, however, segregated, though there were convents for both Indian (*cacique*) and Spanish (*criollo*) elite women.

It was normal for nuns to be taught Latin, even those from indigenous families, provided they were of the nobility. Elisa Tudela quotes the opinion of Antonio Pérez: that 'the ability of certain indigenous women, alienated as they were from the *logos* because of their sex and their race, to learn Latin and to speak it "better than their natural language" was clearly a reason to celebrate the action of divine grace'.[27] At the very least, this is direct evidence that Latin was taught to them. Susan Socolow has similarly pointed to the statutes of the monastery of Corpus Christi, founded in Mexico City in 1724 for Indian women: 'Postulates to the Corpus Christi convent were required to be full-blooded Indian, legitimate, daughters of nobles, never linked to idolatry, at least fifteen years old, able to read Latin, trained in domestic arts (sewing, embroidery), never betrothed or married, and virtuous.'[28] It is worth pausing over the fact that the daughters of the *cacique* nobility were, at least in theory, required to be Latin-literate *before* they were admitted, a stipulation which could not have been made in all parts of Europe: English nuns, for instance, often learned Latin after their profession.[29] From 1724 to 1821, Corpus Christi admitted 147 novices, of whom 105 eventually made their profession as nuns.

Some of the convents of seventeenth-century Mexico were highly cultivated: in particular, music was of great importance in convent life. Many convents conducted schools of music and, as in contemporary Italy, attracted crowds of listeners who came on holy days to hear the nuns singing from behind their curtained grilles. The College of Santa Rosa de Santa María in Valladolid (Morelia) required its postulants to show a certificate of legitimacy and purity of blood; once admitted, they spent much of their time working on music. The archive contains music composed, possibly by the nuns, for performance in church or by pupils: cantatas, arias, motets, carols, and several Masses, including one for a four-part choir, violins, and trumpets. Some individual nuns achieved fame as musicians, including St Rose of Lima.[30] Elsewhere in seventeenth-century Ibero-America, the beautiful Juana de Maldonado, a young nun of La Concepción in Guatemala,

---

[27] Elisa Sampson Vera Tudela, 'Fashioning a *Cacique* Nun', *Gender and History*, 9.2 (Aug. 1997), 171–200, drawing on Mexico, Archivio General de la Nación, Sección Historia, vol. 109. Exp. 2, unfoliated. See now Tudela, *Colonial Angels: Narratives of Gender and Spirituality in Mexico, 1580–1750* (Austin: University of Texas Press, 2000).

[28] Socolow, *Women*, 105. Anne Miriam Gallagher, 'The Indian Nuns of Mexico City's Monasterio of Corpus Christi, 1724–1821', in Asunción Lavrin (ed.), *Latin American Women* (Westport, Conn.: Greenwood Press, 1978), 15–72.

[29] Adam Hamilton (ed.), *The Chronicle of the English Augustine Canonesses Regular of the Lateran at St Monica's in Louvain, 1625–1644*, (Edinburgh: Sands & Co., 1906), ii. 47, Dorothy L. Latz, '*Glow-Worm Light*' (Salzburg: Institut für Anglistik und Amerikanistik, 1989), 27. The Cambrai library catalogue, Cambrai, BN 901, contains two copies of Alvares's *Introduction to the Latin Tongue for Young Students*, 1684 and 1686.

[30] Pál Kelemen, *Baroque and Rococo in Latin America* (New York: Macmillan, 1951), 235.

was in the habit of entertaining her companions with witty improvised verses and music.[31]

Mexican convent culture also produced an outstanding woman intellectual and Latin poet, Sor Juana de la Cruz (1648–95), born Juana Ramírez de Asbaje in San Miguel Nepantla, a village in the foothills of Popocatépetl.[32] She was illegitimate, but was identified as a genius even as a child, and she persuaded her elder sister's teachers to begin educating her when she was 3. She and her mother lived with her grandfather Pedro Ramírez until his death in 1656. He had an excellent library, and Sor Juana later testified that she was free to browse in it. An important piece of evidence for this turned up in the form of a copy of Octaviano della Mirandola's *Illustrium Poetarum Flores*, an anthology of classical Latin poetry published in Lyon in 1590, which had in it the signatures first of Ramírez, then of Juana Inés de la Cruz, suggesting that she took it with her into the convent.[33]

After her grandfather's death, she spent some time in the home of her wealthy aunt Doña María Ramirez and her husband Juan de Mata in Mexico City, and at 15 was admitted to the viceregal court as lady-in-waiting to the Marquise de Mancera, the newly arrived vicereine. At about 17, she undertook a public test of her talent, in which forty scholars from all disciplines questioned her, and she defended herself; a style of public performance which has a number of parallels.[34] At 18 or so, she decided she had no interest in marriage: this decision may have been influenced by the social realities of her situation, that a woman whose personal and intellectual gifts were not backed up by solid wealth and a secure social position might have found a satisfactory marriage rather difficult: as Paz observes, she speaks of the life of a woman courtier merely as one of 'defending her virtue'.[35] Whatever her true feelings may have been, her decision was a highly rational one. She briefly entered the convent of San José de las Carmelitas Descalzas, but found the life far too severe for her temperament. She returned to the world, and a year and a half later entered the convent of San Jerónimo, which was a *criollo* house in which several of her women relatives also became nuns, known for the mildness of its discipline. Her dowry, 3,000 pesos, was paid not by her family, but by Pedro Velásquez de la Cadena, a wealthy man who sponsored would-be nuns as an act of charity.

The cell which Sor Juana bought within San Jerónimo as her permanent home was in effect a small two-storey house, with a bathroom (which boasted braziers for heating water), a kitchen, a sitting room, a bedroom, and room for her companions: she owned a mulatto slave, Juana de San José, and at various times, her half-sisters

---

[31] Thomas Gage, *The English-American: A New Survey of the West Indies, 1648*, ed. A. P. Newton (London: G. Routledge and Sons, 1928), 202–3.

[32] Octavio Paz, *Sor Juana* (London: Faber and Faber, 1988). This draws on a compilation of Sor Juana's autobiographic writings, *A Woman of Genius: The Intellectual Autobiography of Sor Juana Inès de la Cruz*, trans. Margaret Sayers Peden (Salisbury, Colo.: Lime Rock Press, 1982).

[33] Paz, *Sor Juana*, 78.

[34] Pamela Kirk, *Sor Juana Inés de la Cruz: Religion, Art and Feminism* (New York: Continuum, 1999), 21.

[35] Paz, *Sor Juana*, 101, 106–7.

and niece probably lived with her.[36] The portrait of her by Miguel Cabrera shows her seated in a comfortable armchair at a large worktable covered with a table-carpet and littered with books; behind her the wall is literally covered from floor to ceiling with volumes in folio, the only relief to the serried ranks of books being an expensive-looking clock.[37] She enjoyed Virgil, Horace, Ovid, Lucan, Martial, and Statius among the poets, and among classical Latin prose writers she particularly valued Seneca, Cicero, and Macrobius. Her favourite patristic Latinists were St. Jerome and St. Augustine, and she certainly read some of the key works of Renaissance occultism, such as the *Corpus Hermeticum*.[38] Her principal role within the convent was as archivist and bookkeeper. Though the nuns were, like all Counter-Reformation nuns, enclosed, they received visitors. Not only her old patroness the vicereine but also the viceroy were regular callers, and the convent enjoyed a variety of other distinguished visitors, both clerical and secular.

For twenty years, she wrote voluminously, entertained, and did what she pleased: 'she stopped writing letters only when she was in the locutory chatting with visitors.'[39] She wrote *villancicos*, i.e. liturgical poems, songs for *loas*, lyrics for dances, plays, and mystical prose. She was greatly honoured when, on the appointment of the new viceroy in 1680, she was entrusted with working out a scheme of decoration of a triumphal arch by the cathedral, thirty metres high by sixteen wide: this work is described in her *Allegorical Neptune*. The Greek god of the title serves as an allegorical representation of the viceroy, Tomás Antonio de la Cerda, Conde de Paredes. Festivals were an essential aspect of the public life of early modern Europe (and Ibero-America), learned, allusive spectacles intended to express serious truths about the relationship between ruler and ruled.[40] She is the only woman anywhere in the early modern world known to have been commissioned to produce such a work. The text which survives is partly a description of the painted arch erected to welcome the viceroy and his wife, with inscriptions to be painted on it, and partly a text in Spanish verse, read on the occasion. Some of the inscriptions were in Latin, of which this is one.

> Desine, pacifera bellantem, Pallas, oliva
> desine, Neptuni vincere, Pallas, equum,
> Vicisti, donasque tuo de nomine Athenis
> nomen: Neptunus dat tibi et ipse suum.
> Scilicet ingenium melior Sapientia victum
> occupat, et totum complet amore sui.
> Si tamen hic certas: Neptunia Mexicus audit,

---

[36] Paz, *Sor Juana*, 128.

[37] Illustrated by Paz, ibid. 237.

[38] Ibid. 251–7.

[39] Ibid. 130.

[40] The literature of early modern festival culture is extensive. For basic orientation, see Roy Strong, *Art and Power: Renaissance Festivals, 1450–1650* (Woodbridge: Boydell Press, 1984). For Ibero-America, see Agustín González Enciso and Jesús María Usunáriz Garayoa (ed.), *Imagen del rey, imagen de los reinos: las ceremonias públicas en la España moderna (1500–1814)*, (Pamplona: Ediciones Universidad de Navarra, 1999).

Neptuno, et Palmam nostra Lacuna refert.
Gaudeat hinc foelix Sapientum turba virorum:
  praemia sub gemino Numine certa tenet.

Refrain, Pallas [Athene], with your peacebearing olive, from being victorious,
Over the the war-waging horse of Neptune,
You won; and you give to Athens a name from your own name:
Neptune also gives his name to you.
Be it known that a better Wisdom is in possession of a vanquished mind
And is filling it entirely with love of her.
If, however you fight here, the Mexican hears the things of Neptune,
And our Lagoon will give the palm back to Neptune.
Hence let the fortunate crowed of wise men rejoice;
It has in its grasp rewards which are a certainty, under twofold divine sanction.

It is typically learned and allusive. According to Greek myth, Athena and Neptune competed over the city of Athens, but the citizens judged Athena's gift to them, the olive, more significant than Neptune's gift of the horse. Sor Juana is here representing Mexico as a new Athens, but one to which the horse, instrument of the *conquistadors'* triumph, is more important than the olive; she may also imply an identification of the vicereine with Pallas, and the viceroy with Neptune: thus, since the feminine figure yields gracefully to the male, both in fact smile on the new settlement.

Sor Juana's awareness of a tradition of women writers is witnessed by her *Respuesta de la poetisa a la muy ilustre sor Filotea de la Cruz*.[41] She mentions a variety of classical worthies, Polla Argentaria, Arete, Nicostrata, Aspasia, Hypatia, and Corinna, names which will by now be very familiar. She is also interested in the heritage of Christian women: not only Jerome's friends such as Paula and Eustochium, and his contemporary Proba, but the medieval mystics St Bridget of Sweden and Gertrude the Great, whose work was well known in early modern Spain,[42] and nearer her own time, Queen Isabel 'la católica' and Queen Christina of Sweden (both of whom combined learning with being, in one sense or another, Catholic heroines).[43] She links Queen Christina with learned women from the Peninsula, the Portuguese Duquesa de Aveiro (discussed in Chapter 8), to whom she wrote a long poem of praise, and the Spanish Condesa de Villaumbrosa. The only women, however, to whom she explicitly appeals as examples in her work outside the *Respuesta* are St Teresa and Sor María de Ágreda.[44]

Latin verse accounts for only a tiny proportion of the four volumes of Sor Juana's verse, which is mostly in Ibero-American Spanish, but she uses the

---

[41] *Obras completas*, ed. Monterde, 827–48. *Respuesta a Sor Filotea de la Cruz* is ed. and trans. Electa Arenal and Amanda Powell (New York: Feminist Press at the City University of New York, *c*.1994).

[42] José Adriano Moreira de Freitas Carvalho, *Gertrudes de Helfta e Espanha: contribuição para estudo da historia da espiritualidad peninsular nos séculos xvi e xvii* (Oporto: Instituto Nacional de Investigação Científica, 1981).

[43] Stephanie Merrim, *Early Modern Women's Writing and Sor Juana Inés de la Cruz* (Nashville: Vanderbilt University Press, 1999), 202–4.

[44] Ibid., p. xii.

language with facility. The few of her poems to be written in Latin are almost all *villancicos*. This term initially referred to Christmas carols, but around 1630 was redefined as compositions sung at matins on religious holidays. Each one was a set of eight or nine lyrics using eight- or six-syllable lines, with a refrain, a variation, and an *envoi* (*estrebilla*); the cathedrals of Mexico City, Puebla, Oaxaca, and Valladolid (Morelia) celebrated all important holy days with these compositions, which, fortunately, were printed as well as performed. Almost all contemporary Mexican poets composed them, but Sor Juana was a specialist. She composed 232 *villancicos*, mostly for Mexico City, but also for Puebla and Oaxaca.[45]

She was markedly sensitive to the politics of language. In a poem to the Contesa de Paredes, she shows remarkable ingenuity in making Latin work for her, not against her, in order to withdraw herself from the discourses which governed women as such.[46]

I know that in Latin, only married women are called *uxor*, or feminine, and that *virgin* is of common gender, neither masculine nor feminine. So I do not consider it proper to be considered a woman, for I am not a woman to serve as wife to any man, and I only know that my own body, without inclining to one sex or another, is neuter or abstract, solely the dwelling of my soul.

In her sacred poems, she draws attention to and problematizes the use of Latin, but not because it is a language inappropriate to her gender: rather, because it is a barrier to comprehension for the majority of the people.[47] What she writes is not classical but ecclesiastical Latin, and, as with her passages of Nahuatl, she subordinates the language to Spanish prosody and metrics. Her determined inclusiveness is witnessed elsewhere in the *villancicos*, in which she uses Nahuatl alongside Spanish in order that all sections of Mexican society should be drawn into the celebrations: there is a *tocotín*—a term which may derive from an Indian dance—in one of the first *villancicos* she composed, in 1676, using Nahuatl words and Spanish metrics. She also uses passages of what seem to be representations of black creole dance lyrics.

One of her Latin *villancicos* illustrates the allusiveness of her style; it is on St Peter, whose name is not mentioned throughout (these are six of its ten verses, of which the first eight form a single sentence). St Peter, founder of the papacy, therefore first Bishop of Rome, is compared and contrasted with Romulus, founder of Rome and slayer of his brother Remus.

> Ille qui Romulo melior
> Urbem condidit invictam
> et omnium terrarum urbium
> fecit ut esset Regina:

[45] Paz, *Sor Juana*, 307–25.

[46] Translation from Asunción Lavrin, 'Unlike Sor Juana? The Model Nun in the Literature of Colonial Mexico', in Stephanie Merrim (ed.), *Feminist Perspectives on Sor Juana Inés de la Cruz* (Detroit: Wayne State University Press, 1991), 61–85.

[47] For example in Villancicos, *Obras completas*, ed. Monterde, 223–4, 229–36.

per quem, Catholicae fidei
exculta vera doctrina,
discipul est Veritatis
quae erat erroris Magistra

cuius ornata praesidio
multo fortius est munita
humilitate Christiana
quam bellica disciplina:

qui effuso sanguine proprio
maculam detersit illam,
qua surgentis moenia Romae
manus polluit fratricida: . . .

annis meritisque plenus
mortalem deserit vitam
ut, qui Apostolicam habuit
aeternam Sedem accipiat. (from a poem of 10 stanzas)

(Estribillo)
Gaudete, Caeli! Exultate, Sydera,
quia inter vos nova Stella lucet affixa.
cuius caelesti candore
novo fulgent splendore
ampla Caeli domicilia!
Gaudete, Caeli! Exultate, Sydera!

That man, better than Romulus,
Who founded an unconquered city,
And caused it to be Queen
Over all the cities of the earth:

He through whom, thoroughly educated by
The true doctrine of the Catholic faith,
She is the disciple of Truth,
Who used to be the Instructress of error.

Equipped by whose protection,
She is fortified more strongly
By Christian humility
Than by the discipline of war

That man who through the spilling of his own blood
Cleansed that stain
By which a fratricidal hand
Polluted the walls of Rome . . .

. . . full of years and merit
Leaves mortal life
So that he who held the apostolic see
May receive a dwelling place that is for ever.

Chorus
Rejoice, heavens! rejoice, stars,

Since a new star shines, fixed among you,
By whose celestial brightness
The capacious dwelling places of heaven
Are refulgent with new splendour!
Rejoice, heavens! rejoice, stars!

Sor Juana's last years were sad ones: in 1694, she was persuaded to renounce letters, under the influence of the ascetic Núñez de Miranda, her confessor, following a period in which she had been heavily criticized for her worldliness: after twenty-five years as a nun, she was brought to confess that 'for many years, I have lived in religion without religion', and to embark on a new life as a penitent. She gave up her books and musical instruments to be sold to help the poor. The following year, an epidemic infection of some kind broke out in S. Jeronimo, and carried her off, at only 46.[48]

There is an impressive testimony to the internationalism of learned women in the poem which Sor Juana may have written for the Swedish poetess Sophia Brenner, who wrote in Swedish, Latin, German, and French. In an appendix to Brenner's *Poetiska Dikter* of 1713 there is a collection of gratulatory verses which were solicited on her behalf by Urbanus Hiärne and other associates, including one attributed to Sor Juana (discussed above in Chapter 13).

Following on from Sor Juana, there were Mexican women who were taught Latin even in the eighteenth century. Two Latin epigrams survive from the pen of one María Teresa Medrano, in interesting circumstances. As Victor Mínguez has recently made clear, as well as the ceremonial which greeted incoming viceroys, already discussed with regard to Sor Juana, the succession of kings in Spain in itself was greeted in their American possessions with spectacular festivities, which functioned as a reminder of the mutual relation of king and subjects.[49] The ceremonies for the inauguration of Fernando VI were held in 1747; documentation survives for four, in Mexico, Mérida, Guadalajara, and Durango. Those of Mexico were particularly extensive, and two festival books were produced the following year (in both cases, as it happens, by a woman printer).[50] The festivities were further elaborated by one of the city's most distinguished religious institutions, the Jesuit College of St Ildefonso of Mexico, which again resulted in a book. A debating competition with music was held in the college for the coronation-day celebrations, and poems were recited. These were prizewinners resulting from an open

---

[48] Merrim, *Early Modern Women's Writing*, 34–7, acutely discusses Sor Juana's self-creation as a glorious anomaly, and the suddenness and completeness with which her *fama* was turned against her.

[49] Victor Mínguez, 'Los "reyes de las Americas": presencia y propaganda de la monarquía hispánica en el Nuevo Mundo', in Enciso and Usunáriz Garayoa (eds.), *Imagen del rey*, 231–58.

[50] J. Mariano de Abarca, *El sol en léon. Solemnes aplausos conque, el rey Nuestro Señor D. Fernando VI. sol de las Españas. Fuè delebrado el dia II de Febrero del año 1748*... (Mexico City: En la Imprunta del Nuevo Resado de Doña Maria de Ribera, en el Empedradillo, 1748), and Juan Gregorio de Campos y Martínez, *El Iris, diadema immortal. Description de los festivos aplausos con que celebró la feliz elevacion al trono de nostro rey, y Señor D. Fernando Sexto*... (Mexico City: Por la Viuda de D. Joseph Bernardo de Hogal, 1748).

competition, in which local poets had sent in their work anonymously:[51] the Jesuits simply note that two of the Latin epigrams were by Doña María. Teresa Medrano, without elaborating or expressing surprise. A Spanish 'soneto' by her is also published, 'Del Chaôs informe el dedo Soberano', and the winning Spanish 'soneto' (a long poem in couplets, not a Petrarchan sonnet) is also by a woman, Doña Ana María González y Zúñiga.[52] Neither woman is described as a nun, and their writing is not singled out for special comment, and hence, no biographic information is preserved, though both their names suggest *criollo* rather than *cacique* descent. The implication of the *Cifra feliz* therefore seems to be that women had an accepted role in the intellectual life of eighteenth-century Mexico. This is disputed by Asunción Lavrin,[53] but conversely, Serrano y Santz names another eleven Mexican women poets, of, context suggests, the eighteenth century: Ana Anaga, Josefa Campos, Josefa Guzmán, Nicolasa Hurtado, Clementa Mazo, Josefa Navarro, Micaela Neira, Elvira Rojas, Josefa Sórrez, Micaela Velasco, and Mariana Velásquez, all of whom are said to have taken part in poetic 'justas'.[54]

Most of the surviving writing by Latin American women is from Mexico, but colonial Peru was also a society in which monachization created an interface between women and Latin. The convent of Santa Clara in Cuzco dates from 1551: the 6-year-old daughter of an Inca ruler was among the first entrants. The Dominican convent of Santa Catalina, founded 1605, was built on the site of the *acllahuasi*, the home of the virgins dedicated to the service of the ruling Inca.[55] Despite the age and status of these convents, their inhabitants did not become known for their writing in any mode, though they were involved with the education of girls, as well as, of course, with the necessity of educating nuns themselves to perform their duties correctly. There is some trace of women active as writers in seventeenth-century Peru, such as a woman calling herself 'Amarilis', who wrote a verse epistle to Lope de Vega before 1621, and another pseudonymous woman, 'Clarinda', who wrote a 'Discorso en loor de la poesía',[56] and Doña Josefa de Alarcón, 'gloria del Perú', who published a poem on the funeral of Baltasar Carlos in 1648.[57] At least

---

[51] Reference has been made in Ch. 8, p. 218, to the poetic *certamen* as a feature of Spanish literary production, and the occasional participation of women. In Mexico, these *certamina* were highly public events which involved a large proportion of the local intelligentsia, and winning poems were read out by the master of ceremonies before a large audience of local worthies. Irving A. Leonard, *Baroque Times in Old Mexico* (Ann Arbor: University of Michigan Press, 1959), 153.

[52] *Cifra feliz de las dichas imponderables, que se promete la monarchia hespañola baxo el suspirado dominio de su augusto soberano el Señor D. Fernando VI* (Salamanca: Imprenta de la Santa Cruz, 1748), 157, 262.

[53] 'In Search of the Colonial Woman in Mexico: The Seventeenth and Eighteenth Centuries', in Lavrin (ed.), *Latin American Women* 23–59.

[54] *Apuntes*, i. 633, ii. 655. He also mentions Ana María de Zúñiga.

[55] Kathryn Burns, *Colonial Habits: Convents and the Spiritual Economy of Cuzco, Peru* (Durham, NC: Duke University Press, 1999), 2, 88–9.

[56] Georgina Sabat-Rivers, 'Amarilis's Verse Epistle and her Love for Lope: Seeing and Hearing', in Bruno M. Damiani and Ruth El Saffar (eds.), *Studies in Honor of Elian Rivers* (Potomac, Mass.: Scripta Humanistica, 1989), 152–68.

[57] *Apuntes*, i. 19: in *Relacion de las funerales exequias que hizo el Santo y Apostólico Tribunal de la Inquisicion de los Reyes del Peru al Serenissimo Principe de las Asturias* (Lima: Julien Santes de Saldaña for Jorge Lopez de Herrera, 1648).

one of Lima's academies, the Academia Anártida, admitted women, and women appeared in theatrical performances, usually dressed as men.[58]

It is interesting that a work praising Pierre Le Moyne's *Gallerie des femmes fortes*,[59] which had been translated into Spanish, was published in Lima in 1702: Le Moyne's work is essentially hagiographic, and praises paragons of female virtue, but it does include active virtues such as successful rule. The Peruvian commentator, who is *alguacil* of the court of Lima, points proudly to the recent career of such a *femme forte* in Peru itself—St Rose of Lima.[60] This 'aprobación' may be part of the context which produces, later in the eighteenth century, a Peruvian laywoman famous for her learning: Doña Josefa Cruzat y Munive. She was a noblewoman, born in Guamanga *c.*1720, and she married Francisco Félix de la Vega in 1740. Her poetry is said by Mendiburu to have been mostly in Latin, but nothing is known to survive.[61]

[58] Socolow, *Women*, 167.

[59] Pierre le Moyne, *La Gallerie des femmes fortes* (Paris: Antoine de Sommaville, 1647), dedicated to the regent, Anne of Austria.

[60] Pedro Joseph Bermudez de la Torre y Solièr, *Aprobacion* (Lima: D. Blas de Ayessa, 1702).

[61] See Manuel de Mendiburu, *Diccionario histórico-biográfico del Perú*, 8 vols. (Lima: Imprenta Enrique Palacios, 1932), ii. 468: 'sabia perfectamente el Latin y otros idiomas.' Also noticed in Elvira Garcia y García, *La mujer peruana a través de los siglos*, 2 vols. (Lima: Imprenta Americana, 1924), i. 154. My thanks to Dr A. César Castro of the Universidad Nacional Mayor de San Marcos in Lima for checking to see whether any further information about this woman has been preserved in Peru.

Conclusion

In 1967, Walter Ong published an often-cited article, 'Latin Language Study as a Renaissance Puberty Rite'.[1] Its basic thesis was that boys' Latin learning functioned as a *rite de passage*, taking them out of the family, away from the protective care of nurses, mothers, and other women, and recreating them within a homosocial context as men capable of exercising authority. It followed that women and Latin belonged in mutually oppositional worlds. Robert Adams Day, following Ong, used the vocabulary of anthropology to be still more definite:[2]

If clean literature is bounded by the lines laid down in antiquity and if clean literary practitioners are men of position, by definition trained in the classics, clean women cannot of course practice literature for the simple reason that they never did, except for the two ancient Greek monsters, Sappho and Corinna.

There are two important points here: the first is that any reader who has endured this far will realize that 'they *never* did' fails as an argument because it is not true for any time between the first century BC and the eighteenth century AD, let alone thereafter. The huge amount of evidence, both practical and theoretical, for the cultural accommodation of learned women and women in authority in most parts of Europe makes this too simple a model. The second point is that Ong and Day, in focusing on the sociocultural aspects of language acquisition, are tackling a question which is obviously of the highest significance for a language which, from the early Middle Ages onwards, was not acquired as a mother tongue but solely as a badge of identity.

The relationship of Latin to post-medieval women is therefore something which has to be carefully nuanced. The process of turning girls into women has not, historically, hinged on education, since before the twentieth century, the difference between girlhood and womanhood was normally conceptualized as turning on sexual experience, on account of its social *sequelae*: i.e. motherhood, and the exercise of domestic authority. The mere knowledge of Latin, or even of Latin and Greek, did not in itself give women the wherewithal to compete with other women in any meaningful way, and it certainly did not give them the capacity to compete with men for patronage or professional advantage.

---

[1] W. J. Ong, SJ, 'Latin Language Study as a Renaissance Puberty Rite', *Studies in Philology*, 56 (1959), 103–24, and see also Ong, *The Presence of the Word* (New Haven: Yale University Press, 1967), 251.

[2] Robert Adams Day, 'Muses in the Mud: The *Female Wits* Anthropologically Considered', *Women's Studies*, 7 (1980), 61–74 (p. 68).

Almost all women Latinists shared a class and a race with the power elite; they had been brought up with the same values and they were stakeholders in the status quo. Their visible, ineradicable otherness meant that their ability to menace the vested interests of their fathers, brothers, and friends was extremely limited, as long as their desire to learn Latin was not accompanied by a demand to enter the professions. Before the nineteenth century, only a very few did so. The access that Latin gave women to networks of power was a peculiar one, dependent on continued good behaviour.

Edmund Leach once suggested that if the phenomenon of higher education is considered anthropologically in terms of its function, then its purpose is to establish a class of literati to operate the network of power relationships in a bureaucratic system. As he sees it, the ostensible justification of classical learning is no more than pseudo-rationalism, concealing a pragmatic subtext, which is the need to ensure that members of the elite share the same cultural background.[3] The mastery of Latin is not a neutral accomplishment, since, from the days of the Roman empire until this century, control of Latin (or, sometimes, of the right sort of Latin) was a defining feature of the professional classes.[4] Foster Watson may not have been thinking of gender issues when he commented that the general use of Latin led to the 'freemasonry' of learned men, but, like freemasonry, it had the effect of creating an arena from which women were (apparently) excluded.[5] This set of perceptions seems to support Ong's point, but Leach also observes the basic fact which this book has been concerned to demonstrate: 'There have in fact always been a number of learned women, and it hasn't needed an elaborate set of scholarly institutions to create them.'[6] That this statement is the simple truth can be abundantly corroborated.

At the same time, Leach's basic argument is further illuminated by Mario Biagioli's perception that early modern universities were not merely educational in the sense of dispensing knowledge, but were also devices for reproducing social hierarchies; an aspect of their overall function which, even if unacknowledged, militated against the extension of university-based education to women, however often this was argued on intellectual grounds.[7] This helps to explain why the fact that a number of women had proved their intellectual ability outside the universities did not result in the opening-up of universities to the talented of either

[3] Edmund Leach, *Culture and Nature, or La Femme sauvage* (London: Bedford College [The Stevenson Lecture], 1968), 7.

[4] See Christopher Stray, 'Schoolboys and Gentlemen: Classical Pedagogy and Authority in the English Public School', in Yun Lee Too and Niall Livingstone (eds.), *Pedagogy and Power* (Cambridge: Cambridge University Press, 1998), 29–46.

[5] His point is elaborated by Françoise Waquet, *Latin: Or the Empire of a Sign*, trans. John Howe (London: Verso, 2000), 215, with respect to various parts of Europe.

[6] *Culture and Nature*, 12.

[7] Mario Biagioli, *Galileo, Courtier* (Chicago: Chicago University Press, 1993), 84, and see Pierre Bourdieu and Jean-Claude Passeron, *La Reproduction: éléments pour un théâtre du système d'enseignement* (Paris: Minuit, 1970), 82.

gender.[8] What this study brings to light, therefore, is not so much an expansion of the possibilities generally believed to be available to 'women', as the fact that at a wide variety of places and times, men of the ruling elite have been sufficiently relaxed about the class allegiance of their daughters that they have permitted them to acquire one of the essential tools of 'manhood', convinced that this held no revolutionary menace whatsoever.

One aspect of the principle of limitation which was applied to learned women is revealed by the case of Elena Piscopia: she gained her Ph.D. in philosophy, but she had wanted to graduate in theology. Her motives are unknown, but they may perhaps have simply been that she was more interested in God than in Aristotle. But this could not be permitted, because a degree in theology gave her an automatic right to preach, which created an obvious paradox, since women had to 'learn in silence with all subjection' (1 Timothy 1: 11–12). A copy of a rewritten ceremonial for Piscopia's theology degree survives: perhaps the most significant alteration comes where an ordinary candidate was told: 'I present you with a book closed and opened, with the right of interpreting, expounding, glossing, preaching, and opening the divine mysteries to the faithful on suitable occasions. Sit in the chair of Christ to teach publicly, and pursue in word and deed all that will strengthen the Catholic faith.' Piscopia would have been told, 'I present you with a book closed and open, in order to meditate on and describe the divine mysteries; but not to preach or teach publicly, according to the Apostle's warning, that women are not permitted to teach in the church.'[9] But even this was not enough: the relevant authorities concluded that there was no way that a doctorate in theology could be transformed into merely an abstract recognition of knowledge and ability; it was transformative, because it entailed induction into minor orders, so even this modified ceremonial failed to meet the case. All the same, Piscopia did receive a higher degree; a qualified victory, as the journalists of Europe recognized at the time.

If one starts from the a priori position that women are invariably silenced by social constraints, then it is easy to be inattentive to the women's voices that do survive. Furthermore, there are risks in assuming complete consistency and logic in men's treatment of women. There is a variety of contexts in which the boundaries of who could and could not speak were more easily relaxed for a ruling-class woman, however that is locally defined, than for a subordinate-class man. Within specific relationships, individual men (such as Piscopia's father, William Cecil, or Felipe IV) insisted that particular daughters, wives, or women religious were eminently worthy of being listened to regardless of what was said or believed about women in general, sometimes because they considered the women under discussion either as outworks of themselves or as conduits for divine

---

[8] Bologna is the exception that proves the rule, but, as discussed in Ch. 11, this may be the result of a fundamental misapprehension about their own history—a reality erected on a fiction.

[9] Francesco Ludovico Maschietto, *Elena Lucrezia Cornaro Piscopia (1646–1684)* (Padua: Editrice Antenore, 1978), 239–40.

wisdom. 'Men' of the European elite were not only affected by their allegiance to one another as members of the same privileged gender, they were also fathers and heads of families, and these roles might pull in different directions. For example, in sixteenth-century Italy a particularly clear area of doublethink concerned with women related to dowries: the same men, as public figures, inveighed against dowry inflation, and as private citizens contributed to it by getting the best possible deal for their own children.[10] Similarly, a man might perfectly well support the view that women should be silent and invisible as a general proposition, and yet raise his own child to become a spectacular exception. The women thus privileged were of course left in a complex and potentially difficult position, aware that this ascription of 'special status' could be withdrawn at any moment by their male supporters should they stray beyond what was acceptable, and occasionally also faced with hostility from 'mere' women who perceived them as breaking ranks, breaking the rules, or getting away with something.

Another point which has emerged clearly from this study is that after the Renaissance, learned women, like women rulers, successfully won themselves a measure of general acceptance by the end of the fifteenth century. The earliest Italian women scholars record a degree of opposition, from women as well as men,[11] as well as of praise and encouragement, also from women as well as men. Sixteenth-century Italian women Latinists do not record such attacks, and in the seventeenth century, Elena Piscopia, whose social position was not wholly dissimilar to that of Isotta Nogarola, on the margins of the Venetian patriciate,[12] seems to have been treated as a national asset on a scale which would have astounded the earlier woman. It may be that women scholars ceased to attract hostile attention because it gradually became obvious to all but the most paranoid that such women had been visibly part of society for a hundred, then for two hundred, years without effecting any fundamental change in gender relations whatsoever. By the seventeenth century, it is extremely easy to find learned men hailing women of achievement with delight, particularly if they are fellow countrywomen. In many different European countries, a social niche had opened up for the local poetess and learned lady; a fact completely tangential to the educational opportunities extended to women in general, and seldom related to it by anyone.

To understand the 'bluestockings' and *gelehrten Frauen* of early modern Europe some preconceptions must be cast aside. It is easy to imagine that a woman writer was—as the Countess of Winchilsea said she was—necessarily an 'intruder on the rights of men'.[13] How much more so, a woman who usurped Latin, the Father Tongue, the language of authority. We would like to see transgressive, Promethean

---

[10] Virginia Cox, 'The Single Self', *Renaissance Quarterly*, 483 (1995), S13–81.

[11] Both Nogarola and Cereta refer to this.

[12] Isotta Nogarola's sister Laura married a doge, suggesting that the family was the most acceptable type of non-patrician, while Piscopia was the technically illegitimate daughter of a patrician.

[13] Jane Stevenson and Peter Davidson (eds.), *Early Modern Women Poets, 1520–1700* (Oxford: Oxford University Press, 2001), 259.

women, seizing a power which had been denied them, and it is also all too easy for us to imagine that once the intellectual competence of women had been exhaustively demonstrated, the professions should have begun to make a place for them. But neither of these propositions answers the facts. We do not find solitary heroines among the learned women of early modern Europe so much as dutiful daughters. We also find that a number of outstandingly learned women voice the high importance they attach to education, or even the principle that if all women were educated like their brothers (that is to say, with the education appropriate to their rank, whatever that might be) then the general intellectual standard among women would be as high as among their male peers: to give one example among many, María de Zayas y Sotomayor, a writer of verses and novellas in the style of Boccaccio's *Decameron* and Marguerite de Navarre's *Heptameron*, declares, 'if in their education they were given books and preceptors rather than fine linen, working cases and sketches for embroidery frames, then they would be as capable as men of filling official posts and university chairs.'[14] Moreover, they evidently proved their point after a fashion: of the literally hundreds of works dealing with learned women written in the sixteenth and seventeenth centuries, the great majority comment admiringly on the achievement of contemporaries, with a nod at the past; while some are implicitly patronizing, ironic, or tongue in cheek, I cannot think of a single example which is straightforwardly hostile.[15] A *femme savante* such as Anna Maria van Schurman or Sophia Elisabeth Brenner was surrounded by a chorus of approbation. But María de Zayas is exceptional in suggesting that something ought to come of all this: all that most seventeenth-century learned women asked for was the right to learn languages, study the liberal arts, and be left in peace in the library.[16] Their sometimes considerable achievements are very seldom accompanied by any formulation of a demand for even a limited access to professional status. Men were occasionally bolder on their behalf: notably Johann Christian Itter, who published a serious work on the academic profession in 1679, in which he posed the question 'are women capable of holding academic status?', and answered it with a potentially revolutionary, 'why not?'[17] In France, the Cartesian Poullain de La Barre similarly argued that women should be able, and permitted, to discharge any public office.[18] But if women had in fact demanded to do so, they would doubtless have met much the same hostility and

[14] Sandra M. Foa, 'Maria de Zayas y Sotomayor, Sibyl of Madrid (1590?–1661)', in J. R. Brink (ed.), *Female Scholars* (Montreal: Eden Press Women's Publications, 1980), 54–67. Her *Desangaños amorosos* was published in 1647.

[15] There are, of course, works dealing with women in general which are hostile to them.

[16] Stephanie Merrim, *Early Modern Women's Writing and Sor Juana Inés de la Cruz* (Nashville: Vanderbilt University Press, 1999), 73, refers to María de Zayas's 'extreme games'.

[17] Bruno Neveu, 'Doctrix et Magistra', in Colette Nativel (ed.), *Femmes savante, savoir des femmes* (Geneva: Droz, 1999), 27–37 (p. 36). Johan Christian Itter, *Diatriben de Gradibus Academicis* (Frankfurt am Main: Fridericus Knochius, 1878), 200. Interestingly, I could not find this clause in the second edition (Giessen: A. D. Fabri, 1679).

[18] François Poullain de La Barre, *De l'égalité des deux sexes* (Paris, 1673).

anger that many of the pioneering women professionals encountered in the nineteenth century.

Reactions to women rulers show a similar trajectory from the Renaissance to the early modern period to that of reactions to learned women, from unthinking horror to acceptance and in some cases, notably that of Elizabeth I, even praise. Yolanda of Aragon (1384–1443), wife of Louis II, was criticized in the most basic terms in 1440:[19]

> What are modern men shown in such a spectacle,
>   since a hen rules cocks, and a cunt rules penises?

An italic hand has added verses to the same effect, 'When the kingdom is ruled by a cunt, the whole people cries 'Woe!'—it is the destruction of a kingdom to be ruled by a woman' (there is a verbal play on "vulvae' and 'ob veh').[20] Anatomy is all: a female ruler is nothing but a set of sexual organs, and therefore submissive, to the destruction of her people. The first ruling queen of England, Mary Tudor, was greeted less obscenely but no less dismissively in a poem also preserved in the Bibliothèque Nationale, composed when she declared war on France: to this poet, she has no credibility, since she must substitute womanly accoutrements of various kinds for manly weapons: for example, a *hasta* in her hand is not a spear but a distaff.[21] Her successor Elizabeth was treated with far more respect: there were those, particularly Catholics, who considered her Machiavellian, evil, or duplicitous, but nobody dismissed her as negligible.[22] By the seventeenth century (the century of Queen Anne, the Empress Maria Theresa, and the regencies of Marie de Médicis and Anne of Austria), it was possible for a woman ruler—Catherine I, Tsarina of Russia—to be styled 'the great'.

But even by the time of Yolanda of Aragon, women had been rulers, as regents or sometimes even in their own right, for centuries.[23] The competence of the majority of these women, like the competence of outstanding women writers, effected no change in the theorization of women's position, which, to the great majority of writers, was a blanket condemnation of women in general, accompanied by a pragmatic acceptance that certain outstanding individuals were somehow 'beyond their sex'. This basic position, despite its internal contradictions, suffered

---

[19] Paris, Bibliothèque Nationale, Collections Dupuy 736.

> 'Quid nunc monstra viri patuntur tanta moderni?
>   Quod Gallina regit Gallos et vulva priapos?'

[20] 'Regna regunt vulvae, gens tota clamat simul ob veh, interitus regni est a muliere regi.'

[21] Paris, Bibliothèque Nationale, Dupuy 837, fo. 232ᵛ. However, in marked contrast, in the third book of his *Historia ecclesiastica della rivoluzion d'Inghilterra* (Rome: Facciotti, 1594), Girolamo Pollini weaves a parable of 'virile' ladies—Amazons, Cleopatra, Judith, Deborah, etc.—who 'have honoured this most frail and weak sex with their enterprise' and situates Mary in their company.

[22] See Tasso, *Discorso della virtù femminile, e donnesca*, where he speaks admiringly of Elizabeth, despite her Protestantism.

[23] Armin Wolf, 'Reigning Queens in Medieval Europe: When, Where, and Why', in John Carmi Parsons (ed.), *Medieval Queenship* (Stroud: Alan Sutton, 1993). Lisa Hopkins, *Women who Would be Kings* (London: Vision Press, 1991), continues the story down to the 16th century.

a certain amount of attrition, but did not substantially alter until the nineteenth century.

The point where the stately litanies of women rulers, women scholars, and outstanding women of all kinds actually began to make any kind of difference to social perceptions of the abilities of women in general coincides in time with a vastly expanded need for professionals of all kinds which in turn arose from the redeployment of the mass of the population from the countryside to industrial cities, and the subsequent need for a more educated workforce. This may be more than a coincidence, since this cultural turn was combined with social and medical advances which enabled a gradually increasing number of European societies to draft middle-class women out of full-time childbearing in the knowledge that most of the children they did produce would live to grow up. Arguments for women's general intellectual competence developed coterminously with the development of economic niches for women teachers, doctors, secretaries, and civil servants and the developments in contraception which allowed such women to plan their reproductive strategies. Such a determinist analysis is anathema to many, but it seems foolhardy to overlook these aspects of the problem presented by admitting women to the professions, since it is hardly possible to imagine a society in which economic opportunity, minimal infant mortality, and effective contraception were *not* preconditions for permitting large numbers of women to take up white-collar jobs. Women in general, according to Virginia Woolf, should 'let flowers fall on the tomb of Aphra Behn, for it was she who earned them the right to speak their minds'. I hope that I have shown in these pages that women academics might be better employed honouring the grave of Elena Piscopia, but it would show a fitting sense of the complex debts we owe to the past if what was laid there was not, or not only, academics' laurel, but also wreaths of *hevea brasiliensis*—the rubber tree, since the introduction of rubber into Europe marks the practical beginning of effective contraception for the mass market.

Another question which I would like to address in this conclusion is inclusivity, since it is easy to assume that the traditions covered in an avowedly international survey of this kind are a fair representation of what there is, or has been. The representation of women in this volume confirms the a priori assumption that their access to the elite culture of their milieu is highly culture specific. But there is another aspect which needs to be considered before the pattern of survival is identified as a pattern of production: patterns of preservation are also culture specific. For example, in the early Middle Ages, both Celtic Ireland and Anglo-Saxon England experienced a florescence of Christian culture centred in monasteries, with large numbers of women committed to a monastic life, and both cultures showed a strong commitment to missionary work.[24] There is a respectable

---

[24] On Anglo-Saxons, see Jane Stevenson, 'Anglo-Latin Women Poets', in Katherine O'Brien O'Keeffe and Andy Orchard (eds.), *A Festschrift in Honour of Michael Lapidge* (Toronto: University of Toronto Press, forthcoming), on Ireland, Christina Harrington, *Women in a Celtic Church: Ireland c.450–1150* (Oxford: Oxford University Press, 2002), 92.

amount of Latin writing, both prose and verse, by Anglo-Saxon nuns, while from Ireland there is none—the first known Irish woman Latin poet, Eleanor Burnell, flourished only in the seventeenth century—but it is hard to be certain what might be the correct conclusion to draw. Before assuming that Irishwomen wrote absolutely nothing in Latin because nothing is to be found, it is worth observing some crucial facts.[25] Irish women's communities were almost all small, poor, and short-lived, and therefore would have found it hard to build up a library and a scriptorium, but even if they did, they would have been unable to secure the future of what was written in the way that, for example, the group of men's communities in Ireland and Scotland associated with St Columba preserved manuscripts from the saint's own times onwards. Irish women were also apparently excluded from missionary work, which Anglo-Saxon women were not, and no women's names are preserved among the ranks of the famous Irish 'wandering scholars'.[26] This is significant, since a very large proportion of the surviving literature of both the early Irish and early English churches survives due to having been copied on the Continent. It is probably true that fewer Irish than Anglo-Saxon nuns learned how to write Latin, but it is certain that the odds are drastically stacked against anything being preserved.

Another area which seems at the time of writing to have harboured almost no women Latinists is Central Europe—the Czech Republic, Slovakia, Austria, Hungary, and Romania—an enormous, largely Catholic (hence Latin-using) region which produced a vast amount of Latin literature in the Renaissance and subsequent centuries (including some internationally famous writers) without, as far as I can discover, extending its demonstrable commitment to neo-Latin to the daughters and sisters of its many poets, scholars, and educated rulers (thus far, Anna Valentini is the only possible Hungarian neo-Latin poet to have surfaced, and there is only one Czech).[27] But it is hard to believe that this is the case, and the problem may in fact relate to the current state of cataloguing, and the difficulty experienced by a Western European scholar without the relevant languages trying to find out about Slavic cultural history.[28] It is easier to account for the absence of

---

[25] My thanks to Anthony Harvey for checking the database of the *Dictionary of Medieval Latin from Celtic Sources*; he found no women.

[26] For example, a speech put in the mouth of an Irish woman anchorite by the 7th-century Jonas states that she would go abroad 'nisi fragilis sexus obstasset', *Vita Columbani* 1. 3, ed. Bruno Krusch (Hanover: Hahn, 1905), 156–7. However, a sentence in the Life of St Odilia of Hohenburg claims that the saint looked after women pilgrims, whether from 'Scotia' or 'Britannia'. *Vita Odiliae Abbatissae Hohenburgensis*, MGH Scriptores Rerum Merowingicarum VI, ed. Bruno Krusch (Hanover: Hahn, 1903), 24–50 (p. 45).

[27] I exclude the former Yugoslavia, since the eastern Adriatic seaboard produced Latinate women both in late antiquity and in the Renaissance, when it was part of the territories of the Venetian republic.

[28] I am greatly indebted to a variety of Central European scholars, notably Piotr Urbanski, Piotr Kuhiwczak, and Lenka Vrylacilova, for attempting to remedy my ignorance, when, as I am well aware, they were all burdened with much urgent business of their own. Sarah Josepha Hale, *Woman's Record* (New York: Harper & Brothers, 1860), 278, describes a familiar type of 'infant phenomenon' in the unusual milieu of 18th-century St Petersburg, Elizabeth Culman (1816–33), who died possessed of nine languages including Latin and Ancient Greek, and had translated the *Odes* of Anacreon.

women Latinists in North America, since neo-Latin was distinctly a minority interest there.[29] The situation in Spain is different again: after a triumphant humanist début in the sixteenth century, the cultural turn away from humanism towards a highly distinctive form of piety seems genuinely to have diverted women's energies towards other forms of achievement, and also led to an indifference to the monuments of Spanish humanism which has militated against the survival of such texts as were produced.

Another aspect of this study which gradually made itself obvious is that in extending it across the whole of Europe and the New World, I was doing no more nor less than women scholars and their defenders had done in the early modern period. For example, Paul Melissus, in Heidelberg, wrote in Latin to or about the following women: his wife Aemilia, Elizabeth I of England, Johanna van Pallandt, who moved between Paris and Flanders, Elizabeth Jane Weston, living in Prague, Kenau of Haarlem,[30] Euphrosine Hainzel, a German,[31] Louise Sarrasin of Lyon,[32] and Lavinia Cata of Venice.[33] In the following century, Anna Maria van Schurman maintained a correspondence in a variety of languages with women who included Bathsua Makin in England, Elizabeth von der Pfalz (the princess palatine) in Heidelberg,[34] Marie de Gournay and Anne de Rohan in Paris,[35] Birgitta Thott in Copenhagen (who, like de Gournay, merited a poem from her pen),[36] and Marie du Moulin of Sedan.[37] In the same century, the Ricovrati of Padua admitted women from Italy, France, and Germany, and Elena Piscopia was writing in Latin to the Danish Helena Margarethe Friis. Perhaps the most startling illustration of the interconnectedness of the world occupied by early modern learned women is the way that Swedish supporters of Sophia Elisabeth Brenner reached out as far as Mexico to solicit a poem from Sor Juana Inés de la Cruz.

It is clear that in a large number of cases, men sympathetic towards learned women went to lengths to introduce them to one another. For example, when Theodoor Jansson of Almeloveen was sent a Latin poem by his fellow Netherlander Elisabeth

---

[29] Leo M. Kaiser, *Early American Latin Verse, 1625–1825: An Anthology* (Chicago: Bolchazy-Carducci, 1984) includes no women: furthermore, Gilbert G. Gigliotti, author of *'Musae Americanae: The Neo-Latin poetry of Colonial and Revolutionary America'*, Ph.D. diss. (Catholic University of America, Washington, 1992) assures me by email that there is no trace of any American neo-Latin woman poet.

[30] Paul Melissus, *Melissi Schediasmata Poetica*, 2nd edn. (Paris: Arnold Sittart, 1586), 640, *In Picturam Kenniae Harlemiae, Viraginis Bellicosissimae*. Kenau Simons Hasselaar was not a scholar, but was a leader in the defence of Haarlem in 1573: see Gerda H. Kurz, *Kenu Symonsdochter van Haerlem* (Assen: Van Gorcum, 1956).

[31] Johan Carl Conrad Oelrichs, *Historisch-diplomatische Beyträge zur Geschichte der Gelahrheit* (Berlin: Buchhandlung der Realschule, 1768), 17. Melissus affirms that she wrote poetry herself, 'which will outlast iron and steel'.

[32] Johann Heinrich Alsted, *Encyclopaedia Septem Tomis Distincta*, 7 vols. (Herborn, 1630), i. 551 *[Melissi] ad Ludovicam Saracenam Virginem Hebraice, Graece et Latine Doctam*.

[33] *Schediasmata*, 2nd edn., iii. 229.

[34] *Opuscula*, 281–7 (p. 85).

[35] Letters to Anne de Rohan: ibid. 293–300.

[36] Albert Thrura, *Gynaeceum Daniae Litterarum* (Altona: Jonas Korte, 1732), 119.

[37] *Opuscula*, 274–6.

Koolaart in 1696, he sent it on to another friend of his, Helena Sibylla Wagenseil.[38] Karel Utenhove went out of his way to make connections between learned women on a number of occasions,[39] and also in the sixteenth century, Daniel Heinsius wrote to Jan Dousa to introduce Elizabeth Jane Weston to him. Perhaps the most remarkable case is that of Sophia Elisabeth Brenner, launched upon the learned world by a cohort of admiring Swedes. This obviously calls into question the thesis that women scholars were isolated. By the seventeenth century, in the great majority of cases, they were very well integrated into their individual milieux, and the same is true of many women in earlier times. Nor are there often clear grounds for concluding that a woman was fretting for more than her circumstances permitted her: a few of the pioneering Italians of the fifteenth century express considerable bitterness at the way men and, even worse, other women sneer at them, but if they did not achieve peace in their time, they seem to have done so for their successors.

Another important issue to do with the relationship of women scholars to their society is the question of whether or not they were able to marry. The rhetoric which allowed actual learned women to coexist with a theoretic denigration of women in general tended to assign them to a separate category of not-woman: it is often thought, therefore, that learned woman, because they were 'beyond their sex', were de-sexed. Indeed, some women, notably Sor Juana Inés de la Cruz, make this claim on their own behalf. But with respect to the women given in the Appendix as acknowledged Latin poets flourishing after 1400 (the preponderance of nuns in the Middle Ages obviously creates complications for this analysis if it is taken back to earlier centuries), the figures are as follows: thirty-two were single but in the world, eighteen were nuns, forty-four are sufficiently obscure that the point cannot be decided, and 107 were married. While we are considering some 200 women, and hence a very small proportion of elite marriages across Europe, these figures seem to support the view that throughout Renaissance and early modern Europe, the men who did not think of learned women as social hermaphrodites or monsters were sufficient to the number of such women who wished to marry.

In most of the milieux they inhabited, learned maidens seem to have become learned wives without either exciting horror or ceasing to write. In particular, the seventeenth century saw the emergence of learned and virtuous matrons all across both Catholic and Protestant Europe, wives and daughters of country gentry or men of the professional classes, who wrote and sometimes published Latin verse, often about family members and friends, in the context of a blameless, domesticated life of the mind and, in many cases, a companionate marriage based on shared intellectual interests: women such as Gabriella Patino in Padua, Sophia Elisabeth Brenner in Stockholm, Helena Sibylla Wagenseil in Altdorf, Sarah Staples in London, Euphrosine Aue in Colberg, Lucrezia Bebbi in Reggio, and Sophiana Corbiniana somewhere in Poland. It seems fair to conclude that a number of early

---

[38] J. G. Schelhorn, *Amoenitates Literariae* (Frankfurt: Daniel Bartholomaeus, 1725–30), v. 200–1.

[39] Willem Janssen, *Charles Utenhove* (Maastricht: Van Aelst, 1939), 88. Letter to Jean de Morel, London, 26 July 1564, suggesting the introduction of Camille de Morel to Lady Burleigh.

modern people, male and female, were able simultaneously to entertain mutually contradictory ideas—about 'women', and about specific educated and well-behaved female members of their own class—which should not in itself be surprising.

It is also worth observing that the rhetorical strategies of those, male and female, who were moved to comment on learned women seem to have varied with the life choices made by the women themselves to an extent which is not always recognized. Anna Maria van Schurman writes to Marie de Gournay—single by choice—as a virago bearing the arms of Pallas, while nearly two centuries earlier, Antonio Lusco wrote to Maddalena Scrovegni, a young widow who had decided not to remarry, as a chaste, armed Amazon. On the other hand, Margaretha Sibylla von Einsiedel, mother and stepmother of seven, is praised by Paschius and others as 'a Saxon Cornelia', that is, identified with the most apposite classical model for a woman both learned and immersed in maternal duties, the mother of the Gracchi.[40] The same trope was used to praise Bianca Borromeo, humanist mother of many children, among whom were the scholarly Isotta and Genevra Nogarola.[41] Jacopo Foresti's influential work on women published in 1497 devotes chapters to Angela, Genevra, and Isotta Nogarola, in that order. Angela is praised for her public speaking, elegant Latin verse, and erudition, all of which help to make her an admirable and effective wife for the ruler of Arco.[42] She is compared to Cornificia and Proba, married aristocrats who were also Latin poets. Genevra is praised for her virtue, learning, and the excellence and effectiveness of the upbringing she gave her five sons: she is compared with Aemilia Tertia, wife of Scipio, as a devoted wife who was also an intellectual companion, and with Niobe, as a mother of splendid children. Isotta is praised for her commitment to chastity and her erudition (specific works are mentioned), and compared vaguely to 'the women of old': thus, humanist learning is presented as an appropriate and admirable aspect of the life of a wife (childless, it seems, since children are not mentioned), a mother, and a virgin respectively.

A very useful figure for anyone who wished to praise a woman writer who was a wife engaged in a companionate marriage but not remembered as a mother was Polla Argentaria, wife of the poet Lucan, repeatedly called on as a model for the woman who shares her husband's intellectual life, and even writes alongside him (Sulpicia II was also occasionally cited in this context). More originally, Francisco Patrizi refers to his widowed friend Tarquinia Molza as 'Artemisia', in recollection of Queen Artemisia of Caria, whose monument in memory of her husband Mausolus (the original 'mausoleum') was one of the Seven Wonders of the World,[43] and the virginal Martha Marchina is compared not only to the Muses

---

[40] Johannis Paschius, *Gynaeceum Doctum*, (Wittenberg: Christian Fintrel, 1701), 44–5.

[41] Giorgio Bevilacqua praised her in these terms, as Margaret King notes, 'Isotta Nogarola: umanista e devota (1418–1466)', in Ottavia a Niccoli (ed.), *Rinascimento al femminile* (Bari: Laterza, 1991), 4.

[42] *Opus de Claris Selectisque Plurimis Mulieribus* (Ferrara: L. de Rubeis, 1497), 149, 150, 151.

[43] The trope of Artemisia (i.e., 'living only for one's husband's memory') was also used by women themselves: it is exploited by Catherine de Médicis during her widowhood and regency: see Sheila ffolliott, 'Catherine de' Medici as Artemisia: Figuring the Powerful Widow', in Margaret W. Ferguson et al. (eds.), *Rewriting the Renaissance* (Chicago: Chicago University Press, 1986), 227–41.

and Sappho, but also to the Amazon queen Penthesilea.[44] Other women who were sometimes called upon as models and examples for the learned Christian woman are St Jerome's learned friends Paula, Marcella, Blesilla, Eustochium, Demetrias, and others: usefully, some members of this group were virgins, some matrons.[45]

The question of how a woman is represented is never a simple one, but it is assuredly simple-minded to assume that all the women discussed in these many pages were trapped within a straightforward grid definable as 'the learned woman' (virginal, father oriented, marginalized), and forced to conform to it.[46] The majority of the male writers concerned with learned women lauded their particular friends or protégées as perfect models of womanhood in terms which relate to the woman's own self-fashioning. Thus Elena Piscopia, who flatly defied her father's wish that she should marry, is praised for her perfect chastity by her biographers. The somewhat later Maria Aurora von Königsmarck, ex-courtier, quondam royal mistress, and prioress of Quedlinburg, is lauded by Lehms for her wit, knowledge, and poetic ability—obviously, the less said about her chastity the better, so nothing is said of it at all. When Sophia Elisabeth Brenner writes in praise of von Königsmarck in 1687, her chosen *comparanda* are Cleopatra, Cornelia, and Sappho, two out of three of whom were more distinguished for brilliance than for virtue.[47] Apart from von Königsmarck, the libertine canoness, the learned women described in these pages include disobedient daughters (e.g. Piscopia), defiant wives (e.g. Elena Coppoli), an unmarried mother and probable infanticide (Cille Gad), and a woman strongly suspected of having murdered her husband (Mary Stuart). Three of the four women just mentioned were not merely praised by contemporaries: they came within a respectable distance of being canonized.[48] This last point, incidentally, throws up an issue of some importance: it has been stated, or assumed, in a variety of contexts that Protestantism was more fostering to educated women than post-Tridentine Catholicism. It is therefore worth observing that some sixty-six of the poets listed in the Appendix who flourished after 1500 were probably Protestant (i.e. if I do not know for certain, I at least know they were brought up in Protestant countries), while 122 were, by the same criteria, Catholic: a ratio of 1 : 2 in favour of Catholics.

---

[44] *Musa Posthuma*, sig. §§ 7ᵛ.

[45] Mary Agnes Cannon, *The Education of Women during the Renaissance* (Washington: Catholic Education Press, 1916), 79, quotes Lebrija hailing the new learning of Spanish women fostered by Queen Isabel as a revival of the Christian Roman matrons of the 4th century. Doña Isabel de Josa y Cardona was also compared to Paula: Alfonso Garcia Matamoros, *De Asserenda Hispanorum Eruditione* (Madrid: Joan Brocar, 1553), 58ᵛ.

[46] Diana Robin, 'Women, Space and Renaissance Discourse', in Barbara K. Gold et al. (eds.), *Sex and Gender in Medieval and Renaissance Texts* (New York: State University of New York Press, 1997), 165–87 (p. 170), notes that the canonical biographies of Cassandra Fedele provide an example of a priori distortions in women's individual and collective histories.

[47] Brenner, *Poetiske Dikter* (Gedersholm: Julius Georg Matthias, 1713), 196.

[48] The *processus* for Mary, Queen of Scots survives in the Congregation of Rites in the Vatican Archivio Segreto, and she is treated as a martyr in Le Moyne's *Gallerie des femmes fortes* (Paris: Antoine de Sommaville, 1647), 351–6: Coppoli was reckoned a *beata*, and it is clear from the contemporary lives that some initial moves towards the canonization of Piscopia were undertaken, and possibly revived in the time of Matilda Pynsent.

The praise of learned women inevitably partakes of cliché, but the clichés are potentially, and sometimes actually, nuanced. Rhetoricians had at their disposal, at the very least, the Muses, the Graces, Minerva, Sappho, Cornelia mother of the Gracchi, Sulpicia, Polla Argentaria, Diotima (the wise woman who instructed Socrates on love in Plato's *Symposium*), Artemisia, and a whole host of positive images from the Bible such as Holy Wisdom, Susanna, Deborah, Hannah, and the Virgin Mary (it is worth recalling that the Virgin was remembered not only as the mother of God but as the poet of the 'Magnificat', and an authority on the life of Christ).[49] While there is an almost unbelievably large number of humanist poems which imitate the epigrams of the *Greek Anthology* and say of a particular woman either that she is a Tenth Muse, a Fourth Grace, or a Second (but chaster) Sappho, beyond this starting point, it is often the case that the presentation of a particular woman is shaded in significant ways depending on her actual circumstances.[50] It is also worth observing that neither the Muses, the Graces, nor Sappho are strongly associated with virginity: a married woman could be just as much a 'Tenth Muse' as any learned maiden, while the legend of Sappho assigned her a husband, a daughter, and a male lover as well as associating her with other women, whether as lover, friend, or teacher.

Another point worth observing is that of the learned men whose fates entangled them with learned women, a surprising number made acquaintance with more than one. Paul Melissus has already been referred to; his friend Karel Utenhove was involved with learned women all his life, as was Lucio Marineo Siculo in early sixteenth-century Spain. Joseph Scaliger, author of only the second commentary ever made on the poems of Sulpicia I, was in correspondence with Elizabeth Weston, the recipient of a Latin poem by Margarethe Bock van Gutmansdorf, and a close friend of the learned 'Dames des Roches'.[51] In the seventeenth century, Chrystian Teodor Schosser was connected with both Elizabeth Weston and Anna Memorata, Otto Sperling was a correspondent and associate of many learned women in Scandinavia, and based his *De Feminis Doctis* on the work of Eleanora

---

[49] Apart from being the author of the 'Magnificat' Mary also has an important place in Christian literature as a source and, hence, as an authority. It was understood by the exegetes that she subsequently became the teacher of the Evangelists, especially Luke and John, who was her adopted son (John 19: 26). The apocryphal letters purporting to represent an exchange of correspondence between St Ignatius, Mary, and St John, widely circulated in the Middle Ages, suggest that the image of Mary as teacher was of some importance to women. See J. B. Lightfoot (ed.), *The Apostolic Fathers*, 3 vols. (London: Macmillan, 1889), iii. 69–72.

[50] Iiro Kajanto, *Christina Heroina: Mythological and Historical Exemplification in the Latin Panegyrics on Christina Queen of Sweden* (Helsinki: Suomalainen hiedeakatemia, 1993), is a major study of a single, interesting woman (incidentally, he overlooked a panegyric by Anna Maria van Schurman, recently rediscovered by Dr Pieta van Beek, to be published in her forthcoming edition).

[51] See Weston, *Collected Writings*, ed. Donald Cheney and Brenda Hosington (Toronto: Toronto University Press, 2000), 174–5, 330–1, Paris, Bibliothèque Nationale, Dupuy 395 ('Recueil des lettres et d'opuscules latin de Joseph Scaliger'), fo. 172. His father Julius Caesar Scaliger was also an admirer of women Latin poets: he wrote verses on Laura Brenzona, Veronica Gàmbara, and Ginevra Rangone (in *Julii Caesaris Scaligeri Viri Clarissimi Poemata* (dedicated to the latter's sister, Constanza Rangone) (Heidelberg: Commelin, 1574)).

Christina Ulfeldt,[52] while in Italy, Francisco Macedo, who edited the life of Martha Marchina, was one of the several authors of the epigrams which adorn the engraving of Elena Piscopia made when she was 22, and also wrote voluminously in praise of Queen Christina of Sweden.[53] Similarly, Iacobo Filippo Tomasini shows a different kind of *pietas* towards learned women by editing both Laura Cereta and Cassandra Fedele, and showing a notable sensitivity towards women scholars in his encyclopedic writings.[54] It seems as if a number of the learned men who enjoyed the society of learned women made positive efforts to seek out and encourage them. Otto Sperling, for example, assumed (correctly) that Sophia Brenner would want other Swedish learned women to be promoted, and begged her to tell him of any she knew.[55] When such men wrote verses on women, they tended to stress the unique abilities of the woman addressed, but often, their actions suggest rather that they adopt the discourse of uniqueness as appropriate to laudatory verse, while in fact they show themselves well aware of a wider context, and in some cases actively put women in touch with one another: this is the case, for example, with Theodoor Jansson who made a contact between his two Latinate women friends Elisabeth Koolaart and Helena Sibylla Wagenseil, and Simonds d'Ewes, who introduced Bathsua Makin to Anna Maria van Schurman. Even girls who were prepared to launch themselves on a course of study without parental support, such as Marie de Gournay or Martha Marchina, tended to pick up at least one sympathetic male adviser along the way—in the first case, first her uncle, then Michel de Montaigne, in the second, Antonio Quaerengo and Cardinal Spada.

There is also the issue of women's support and encouragement of one another. Costanza Varano and Clara Lanzavegia, for example, wrote in praise and support of Isotta Nogarola; Anna Maria van Schurman praised Birgitta Thott, and there are many other examples of the kind. It is possible to find strongly affectionate relationships between preceptrices and their pupils: Jutta and Hildegard of Bingen, for example, and much later, Luisa Sigea's poem *Sintra* suggests a deeply sympathetic understanding of her mistress/pupil the infanta's anxious position. But there is also evidence for extremely close relationships within the family,

---

[52] Marianne Alenius, 'Om alle slags berömdvärda kvinnnoperoner Gynæceum—en kvinnalitteraturhistoria', in Elisabeth Møller Jensen (ed.), *I Guds Namm* (Höganas: A. B. Wiken, 1993), 217–32, (p. 222).

[53] Nicola Fusco, *Elena Lucrezia Cornaro Piscopia (1646–1684)* (Pittsburgh: United States Committee for the Elena Lucrezia Cornaro Piscopia Tercentenary, 1975), 27 (Francesco Ludovico Maschietto, *Elena Lucrezia Cornaro Piscopia (1646–1684)* (Padua: Editrice Antenore, 1978) 70, also notes that Macedo received the patronage of Elena Piscopia's father), and Iiro Kajanto, 'Queen Christina in Latin Panegyrics', in *Acta Conventus Neo-Latini Hafniensis* (Binghamton, NY: Medieval and Renaissance Text Society, 1992), 43–60 (p. 47).

[54] For example, he discusses the Dane Kirsten Holck and Issicratea Monti of Rovigo in his *Elogiae Literis et Sapientia Illustrium* (Padua: Sebastiani Sardi, 1644), 343, 364–7, and Diana Corradini in his *Bibliothecae Patavinae Manuscriptae Publicae et Privatae* (Udine: Nicola Schiratti, 1639), 95.

[55] Marianne Alenius, 'Love at First (W)ink', in Graham Caie and Holger Nørgaard (eds.), *A Literary Miscellany Presented to Eric Jacobsen* (Copenhagen: University of Copenhagen Press, 1988), 180: in her reply, she suggested Ebba Maria de la Gardie, Ulrica Eleonora, Aurora von Königsmarck, and Queen Christina.

notably between intellectual mothers and daughters: a number of laments written in Latin by bereaved daughters such as Catalina Paz, Elizabeth Jane Weston, and Ginevra Rangone suggest a deep emotional investment in filiality. In various parts of the early modern world, as well as in the convents of the Middle Ages, educated, mutually devoted mothers and daughters lived, worked, and even wrote together as adults; such as the early medieval Cynehild and Berhtgyth, the fifteenth-century Isotta Nogarola and her mother in Verona, and, still later, the Patins and Aelia and Silvia Zaborella in Padua, the Morels in Paris, Madeleine and Catherine des Roches in Lyon. There were also sisters, such as the Cookes and the Morels, who were bound by chains of lifelong love and loyalty which included shared intellectual projects.

It is also worth posing the question of whether learning Latin ever did women any good, aside from the disinterested pursuit of knowledge for its own sake, since so few of those mentioned in this book held anything resembling a professional position. The answer seems, in a surprising number of cases, to be yes. Phyllis Wheatley is a special case: it was Latin, not American English, which gave her, or seemed to, the encouraging exemplar of a highly literate African poet (i.e. Terence). Sophia Elisabeth Brenner was a businesslike and professional poet in both Latin and Swedish, who expected to make money from her writing and did. More generally, Latin gave some women access to work: in seventeenth-century England, we find women such as Anne Denton, Jane Barker, and Charlotte Charke, who all had an interest in medicine, learning Latin so as to be able to make up a doctor's bill. Women who practised medicine have surfaced repeatedly in the course of this account, since all such who aimed to go beyond folk medicine and empiric healing needed access to the learned languages.[56] The status of an apothecary in the seventeenth century was not high, but it was at least better than that of a seamstress.[57] And, as a bizarre exception to general rules, there were women professors in late eighteenth-century Bologna. Some learned women were active as printers or editors, such as Constantia Grierson in Ireland, Helena Ungelerowna in Poland, and Charlotte Guillard and Edmonda Tusana in Paris. Other women from the sixteenth century onwards spent at least part of their adult lives as professional

---

[56] For an overview, see Muriel Joy Hughes, *Women Healers in Medieval Life and Literature* (New York: Morningside Heights, 1947). Ausonius' aunt Hilara was a pre-medieval women doctor, and in the early modern period, a strong interest in medicine, or actual practice as a healer, is also shown by numerous women. Women Galenists include Margaret Gigs (Maria Dowling, *Humanism in the Age of Henry VIII* (Beckenham: Croom Helm, 1986), 222), Judith Squire, née Aylmer, Catherine Tishem, and Jane Barker. Additionally, the Quaker Mary Mollineux was educated in Latin, Greek, 'Physick and Chyrurgy'. Medicine was a normal part of elite women's activities. Dame Frances Paulett's will divides her physic and medicine books between her two daughters-in-law (F. G. Emmison, *Elizabethan Life: Essex Gentry's Wills* (Chelmsford: Essex County Council, 1978), 36–7), while Lady Margaret Hoby and other gentry women doctored the poor, and even performed surgery (Lucinda McCray Beier, *Sufferers and Healers: The Experience of Illness in Seventeenth-Century England* (London: Routledge and Kegan Paul, 1987), 211–41).

[57] There is an eloquent account of the difficulties a 17th-century woman faced in earning a living in a doggerel poem by Elizabeth With, in Jane Stevenson and Peter Davidson (eds.), *Early Modern Women Poets 1520–1700*, (Oxford: Oxford University Press, 2001), 342–3.

educators, whether as tutors or schoolmistresses; for example, Luisa Sigea, Olimpia Morata, and Bathsua Makin, and for these women, their linguistic knowledge served a directly useful purpose. Less directly, the Latinity of the French painter Elisabeth-Sophie de Chéron was part of what helped her to make her way in the world, since it added to her interestingness.

With respect to women's personal lives, the developing concept of the companionate marriage from the sixteenth century on meant that some men actually sought out wives who could share their interests—and some of these relationships seem, on available evidence, to have been characterized by mutual respect and devotion. Similarly, much earlier, the marriage of shared intellectual and/or religious interests seems also to have been a feature of elite society in late antiquity. While their Latinity did not always bear obvious fruit in terms of publications, it is probable that it significantly altered the texture of such women's lives. Sir Nicholas Bacon, Lord Chancellor of England, wrote pedestrian but touchingly sincere verses to his learned wife Anne Cooke in 1558, after his 'greate sicknes':

> Thinkeinge also with howe good will
> The Idle tymes whiche yrkesome be
> You have made shorte throwe your good skill
> In readeinge pleasante thinges to me
> Whereof profitte we bothe did se,
> As wittenes can if they coulde speake
> Bothe your Tullye and my Senecke.

As he indicates, their shared reading of Cicero and Seneca is a central aspect of their partnership, which was intellectual as well as physical and practical.[58]

In another indirect sense, knowledge of Latin seems to have been empowering to women.[59] Germaine Greer's pioneering anthology of seventeenth-century women's verse, *Kissing the Rod*, features the work of fifty poets of whom just over a third could certainly read Latin, a proportion so unexpectedly high that it suggests that knowledge of the learned language may have increased women's confidence in the value of their work as writers even if they did not care, or feel able, to write in it (though I cannot claim the same detailed knowledge of early modern German women writers, the material in Chapter 13 suggests a correlation between women known to have been taught Latin and published poets, and there is a similarly good correlation in Italy). In the next century, not only the bluestockings, but other respected women writers such as Mary Sherwood, Hannah More, and her friend Anna Seward frequently turn out, on close investigation, to have been Latin-literate, a knowledge concealed, or at least not paraded, which again may have helped them to assume a public place with confidence.

---

[58] Quoted in Elizabeth McCutcheon, *Sir Nicholas Bacon's Great House Sententiae*, English Literary Renaissance supplements 3 (1977).

[59] The following pages of brief survey will be confined to the English tradition since it is the most familiar to me: it would be interesting to see whether this is also true for Germany, Italy, or France, but this must be left for other commentators.

This point may be endorsed, backhandedly, by a comment of Swift's: 'those who are commonly called *learned women*, have lost all manner of credit by their impertinent talkativeness, and conceit of themselves.'[60] This suggests both that the caricature 'learned woman' had become a stereotype, and that to be identified as such was socially disastrous: there is a variety of evidence that this was the case in England, France, and Germany.[61] But there is a fair amount of evidence that the myth coexisted with considerable numbers of the discreetly well educated who tried to avoid being seen in this light, just as, in the 1970s, demonized yet risible bra-burning 'women's libbers' coexisted with large numbers of people who were so anxious not to be associated with this image that they regularly prefaced their remarks with 'I'm not a feminist, but ...' though they were nonetheless concerned to better the position of women.[62]

In the nineteenth century, the biographies of a surprising number of distinguished women reveal some knowledge of Latin, which again raises the possibility that the knowledge was empowering: Mary Shelley read Latin and Greek as well as French and Italian.[63] George Eliot spoke, as well as read, French, German, Italian, and Spanish, but in addition, 'Greek and Latin she could read with thorough delight to herself, and Hebrew was a favourite study to the end of her life'.[64] The height from which she was able to patronize 'silly novels by lady novelists' must surely owe much to the fact that she was not, in the terms set by men, ignorant.[65] Moreover, the most interesting fact to be elicited from that essay is that to the imagination of semi-literate women novelists of the 1850s such as the authors of *Compensation* and *Laura Gay*, knowledge of Greek, Latin, and sometimes even Hebrew was an aspect of exotic, aristocratic glamour—suggesting a rather surprising presupposition that a mid-nineteenth-century aristocratic heroine was made more, not less, attractive by a command of the classical tongues.

It also comes as a surprise to find that, as Q. D. Leavis pointed out, the home education of many nineteenth-century women writers included at least some

---

[60] Jonathan Swift, *Letter to a Very Young Lady on her Marriage*, quoted by Josephine Kamm, *Hope Deferred* (London: Methven, 1965), 117.

[61] Ruth P. Dawson, *The Contested Quill* (New York: University of Delaware Press, 2002), astutely observes (p. 359) that in 18th-century German, 'the label "scholarly woman" had more to do with how a woman behaved [i.e. it implied she was neurotic, slovenly, unfashionable, and arrogant] than with what she knew'. Molière, of course, created an equivalently unappealing stereotype 'femme savante' for France.

[62] The media definition of feminists as bra-burners was achieved despite the fact that no known women's group of the 1960s/1970s ever burned their bras; a widely circulated and believed non-fact which helps one to see how writers in earlier centuries got away with defining learned women as either unfeminine or non-existent (Ethel Klein, *Gender Politics* (Cambridge, Mass.: Harvard University Press, 1985), 23–4).

[63] Joanne Shattock, *The Oxford Guide to British Women Writers* (Oxford: Oxford University Press, 1994), 387. See also R. Fowler, 'On Not Knowing Greek', *Classical Journal*, 78 (1983), 337–49.

[64] John Cross, *Life of George Eliot*, quoted by Q. D. Leavis, 'Women Writers of the Nineteenth Century', in her *Collected Essays III: The Novel and Religious Controversy*, ed. G. Singh (Cambridge: Cambridge University Press, 1989), 99–121 (p. 110). She was teaching herself Latin by the time she was 21, Greek by 27: Jenny Uglow, *George Eliot* (London: Virago, 1987), 20, 39.

[65] In a famous essay thus titled, *Westminster Review*, 66 (Oct. 1856), 422–61.

acquaintance with Latin.[66] Eliza Lynn Linton, right-wing scourge of the New Woman, was brought up in a country parsonage, where her free access to her father's library and help from her father and brothers gave her French, together with some Italian, German, Spanish, Latin, Greek, and Hebrew.[67] Charlotte M. Yonge had the same sort of background,[68] and one of the most famous of all daughters of a country parsonage, Emily Brontë, has left fragmentary translations from Virgil and notes on Aeschylus and Euripides as witness to her interest in classical writers.[69] Mrs Humphry Ward educated herself in the same way; and the 'uneducated' Harriet Martineau was translating Tacitus as an exercise in her late teens.[70] Sara Coleridge (1802–52), daughter of the poet Samuel and no mean poet herself, was Latin-literate, since her father was supportive of advanced education for girls.[71] Late in her life, the suffragette, journalist, and translator of Greek plays Augusta Webster sent Coleridge a copy of her own playful Latin verse translation of Samuel Coleridge's comic satire 'The Devil's Walk'.[72] In a completely different context, Mary Kingsley the explorer taught herself Latin as one of her first ventures out of approved feminine behaviour: she took only two books with her to West Africa, and one of them was her battered old copy of Horace.[73] More unexpectedly, Lillie Langtry felt that her position as a *fin-de-siècle* society beauty needed to be consolidated by acquiring the ability to make educated conversation, and sought a crash course in Latin and classical studies from Oscar Wilde.[74]

Even John Ruskin, in his famous (or infamous) essay 'Of Queens' Gardens', published in *Sesame and Lilies*, advocated turning girls 'loose into the old library every wet day'.[75] From the fifteenth century until the nineteenth, 'the run of the library' is crucial to the development of women scholars, and not a few women writers. With only a few exceptions, the women whose lives and works have been discussed here were the products of homes or convents in which there was a library

---

66 In 'Women Writers of the Nineteenth Century'.

67 Yopie Prins, 'Greek Maenads, Victorian Spinsters', in Richard Dellamora (ed.), *Victorian Sexual Dissidence* (Chicago: University of Chicago Press, 1999), 43–81.

68 Shattock, *British Women Writers*, 480–1.

69 Juliet Barker, *The Brontës* (London: Weidenfeld and Nicolson, 1994), 289.

70 Leavis, 'Women Writers of the Nineteenth Century', 104–5, 107, 109. Dr Arnold Hunt pointed out to me a pair of poems by Charles and Mary Lamb, *Works*, ed. Thomas Hutchinson (Oxford: Oxford University Press, 1924), 474–6, 'The Sister's Expostulation on the Brother's Learning Latin' and 'The Brother's Reply', which ends (rather than endorsing their gender-based separation) with, 'If our parents will agree | you shall Latin learn with me.'

71 Sara Coleridge translated Martin Dobrizhöffer's *Historia de Abiponibus*, a book on Paraguay, in 1821. Shattock, *British Women Writers*, 111. See also Dierdre David, *Intellectual Women and Victorian Patriarchy* (London: Macmillan, 1987), 233–4 and Fowler, 'On Not Knowing Greek', 340.

72 Thanks to Professor Yopie Prins for this information on Augusta Webster.

73 Katherine Frank, *A Voyager Out: The Life of Mary Kingsley* (London: Hamish Hamilton, 1987), 65. The other book was Albert Günther's *Study of Fishes*.

74 Richard Ellmann, *Oscar Wilde* (London: Hamish Hamilton, 1988), 109.

75 Deirdre David, *Intellectual Women and Victorian Patriarchy* (London: Macmillan, 1987), 15. Ruskin in fact urges equal education for women, on the theory that they would thus be better companions to their husbands, while simultaneously urging that men and women occupy utterly different spheres (he assumes that women would never think of using this education for their own purposes).

of substantial size, including books in more than one language, which was not barred to them: even in the eighteenth and nineteenth (and twentieth?) centuries, women thus formed are a significant sub-group among women writers. Again and again across the last 400 years, where the circumstances which allowed a woman to acquire an education are recoverable, a daughter was either taught Latin because her father took it as axiomatic that a child of his should be seriously educated, or she was attracted into sharing the interests of her father—sometimes of both parents. Absence of formal education is by no means the same thing as absence of education. Thus, the importance of the classical languages (Greek as well as Latin) in underpinning the work of high-achieving women continued through the nineteenth century: the cultural turn which created a new interest in Greek in that century was, as Yopie Prins has shown,[76] shared by many nineteenth- and early twentieth-century women writers from Elizabeth Barrett Browning to H.D.[77]

Latin is part of the formation even of some more recent women writers. Marguerite Yourcenar (1903–87), one of the greatest of twentieth-century French novelists, was educated by her father and read Latin at 10 and Greek at 12;[78] more unexpectedly, perhaps, Richmal Crompton (1890–1969), author of the 'William' books, was a classics teacher.[79] Mary MacCarthy, author of *The Group*, went so far as to declare that 'I cannot see an ablative absolute or a passage of indirect discourse without happy tears springing to my eyes';[80] and, on a rather different note, Lorna Sage says in her memoir that when she began learning Latin she fell in love with it because of what it symbolically and practically represented, and *because* of its utter lack of relevance to her life: 'Latin, the great dead language that only existed in writing, would compensate for my speechlessness, vindicate my sleepless nights and in general redeem my utter lack of social graces.'[81] In conclusion, there would seem to be grounds for suggesting that the first century since the birth of Christ in which Latin was of little significance to European women writers is the twentieth, and possibly even the twenty-first.

---

[76] See Frank M. Turner, *The Greek Heritage in Victorian Britain* (New Haven: Yale University Press, 1981), David J. DeLaura, *Hebrew and Hellene in Victorian England: Newman, Arnold, and Pater* (Austin: University of Texas Press, 1969), Linda Dowling, *Hellenism and Homosexuality in Victorian Oxford* (Ithaca, NY: Cornell University Press, 1994).

[77] Yopie Prins, *Victorian Sappho* (Princeton: Princeton University Press, 1999). See also her 'Greek Maenads, Victorian Spinsters'. Mary Beard, conversely, points out in *The Invention of Jane Harrison* (Cambridge, Mass.: Harvard University Press, 2000) that there were still women powerfully moved by Latin, notably Harrison's one-time intimate Eugénie Strong, née Sellers, assistant director of the British School at Rome (pp. 12–29, esp. p. 28). It is perhaps worth noting, which Beard does not, that Strong was a Catholic: Anglican and Nonconformist suspicion of 'Rome' clearly had a part to play in the redirection of British classicists towards Greek. See further Joseph Farrell, *The Latin Language and Latin Culture from Ancient to Modern Times* (Cambridge: Cambridge University Press, 2001), 28–9, 32–35.

[78] E. M. Satani and D. W. Zimmerman (eds.), *French Women Writers: A Bio-bibliographical Source Book* (New York: Greenwood Press, 1991), 535.

[79] Shattock, *British Women Writers*, 122–3.

[80] *Memoirs of a Catholic Girlhood* (London: Heinemann, 1963), 130.

[81] Lorna Sage, *Bad Blood* (London: Fourth Estate, 2000), 143 (she also records that her grandfather, a vicar, taught her mother Latin at home, p. 51).

Appendix
Checklist of Women Latin Poets and their Works

Many poems listed here, whether they survive in manuscript or an early printed text, have never been edited: I give here all the bibliographic information which I possess, ordered as follows: title/first line (poems and collections of verse are given as far as possible in chronological order), manuscript(s), early editions(s), modern edition(s), translation(s): in a few cases in which a particular manuscript text is clearly copied from a printed source, I give the edition first. For the sake of inclusiveness, I also include writers and works which I have not been able to find, referenced from the first secondary source to name them, in the hope that they may yet turn up somewhere, as well as works firmly attributed to specific women which seem to me unlikely to be by the woman to whom they are attributed (such entries are set off within angle brackets). To facilitate further work on Renaissance and Early modern printed texts, many of which are very rare indeed, I am noting where I personally have seen, or know of, a copy (which is not necessarily to imply that there are no other copies) of all books mentioned published before 1900, as well as giving the call-numbers of manuscripts. Call-numbers are given in square brackets after the first citation of the book in each entry. In the case of epigraphic poems surviving from late antiquity or earlier, I give the *Corpus Inscriptionum Latinorum* (*CIL*) as the primary reference. It has not been possible to pursue absolutely all early modern editions of epigraphic poems, since the final stages of research for this book had to be concentrated down to books available in Britain, and, for the most part, those in the British Library.

For the poets themselves, I give the maiden name (which is, in most cases, the name under which the poet wrote), with married name in brackets: where the married name is better known, I cross-reference. Applying a parallel principle to nuns, I give the original first name (where known), with name in religion in brackets, and cross-reference where appropriate. This is followed by a date, sometimes very approximate (especially with epigraphic verse), and location, where known: where more than one location is given, the first is the place of origin, the second and subsequent the place or places where the poet spent her adult life, in chronological order. Translations listed are into English unless otherwise specified.

'A'

s. xii   Tegernsee? (Germany)

'G. unice sue rose'

MS: Munich, Bayerische Staatsbibliothek, Clm 19411, fos. 69ʳ–70ʳ
Editions: *MLREL*, ii. 480–2 (with trans.)
Jürgen Kühnel, *Du bist mîn, ih bin dîn. Die lateinischen Leibes-(und Freundschafts-)
  Briefe des Clm 19411* (Göppingen: Kummerle, 1977) (with German trans.),
  64–7

Abuja, Elisa
before 1602   ?
Elisæ Abujæ γνώμη: '*qui difert puer, cui rei similis est?*'

MS: Edinburgh University Library, Laing III, 525, Album Amicorum Georgii
  Craigii Edinburgensis, 1602, on the front paste-down

<Ada (sister of Charlemagne)
s. viii
Inscription in the so-called 'Ada Gospels': 'Hic liber est vitae Paradisi, quatuor
amnes' (possibly but not demonstrably her work)

MS: Trier, Staatsbibliothek, Cod. 22 [not seen]
Edition: Kaspar Brusch, *Monasteriorum Germaniae Praecipuorum ac Maxime
  Illustrium Centuria Prima* (Ingolstadt: Alexander & Samuel Weyssenhorn,
  1551), 126ᵛ. [The Hague, Konincklijke Bibliotheek, 549 B 6]>

Adrichomia, Cornelia
s. xvi   Delft (the Netherlands)
'Carminibus mysticis ac varia oratione illustris virgo'

Referred to Muslerus, *In Orat.* 158, by Johann Sauerbrei, *Diatriben Academicam
  de Foeminarum Eruditione, Priorem, Consensu Inclutae Facultatis Philosophicae
  in Almi Lipsiensi* (Leipzig: Johann Erich Hahn, 1676), sig. C4ᵛ [Munich,
  Bayerische Staatsbibliothek, 4 Diss. 5212]

'Corpus humo, Superis animam, Cornelia, condo'

Quoted as her self-epitaph, Johannis Paschius, *Gynaeceum Doctum, sive Dissertatio Historico-literaria, vom Gelehrten Frauenzimmer* (Wittenberg: Christian
  Finkel, 1701), 24, but more probably by Petrus Opmeer, to whom it is also
  attributed. [Wolfenbüttel, Herzog August Bibliothek, Li 6896]

Aislabie, Anne (Denton)

b. *c.*1540　　　　　　　　　　　　　　　　Sebergham, Cumbria (England)

De me, A.D. Uxor: 'Cumbria Warnellem Thomam Deplorat Ademptum' (1616)

Monument of Thomas Denton, to right of altar, St Mary's, Sebergham, Cumbria

Inscription: *in situ*

> *Photograph*: C. Roy Hudleston and R. S. Boumphrey, *Cumberland Families and Heraldry*, Cumbria and Westmorland Antiquarian and Archaeological Society, ES 23 (1978), facing p. 88

> *Early description* (1702–3): William Nicolson, *Miscellany of the Diocese of Carlisle*, ed. R. S. Ferguson (London: George Bell & Sons; Carlisle: E. Thomson & Sons, 1877), 10–11 [London, British Library, Ac. 5630/2]

> R. S. Ferguson, 'The Relph and Denton Monument in Sebergham Church', *Transactions of the Cumbria and Westmorland Antiquarian and Archaeological Society*, 7 (1884), 253–8 (pp. 257–8) [London, British Library, Ac. 5630]

Alarcón, Christovalina

s. xvi　　　　　　　　　　　　　　　　　　　　　　　　　　Spain

Famous for her ability as a Latin poet favouring hendecasyllables

> Nicolò Antonio, *Biblioteca Hispana, sive Hispanorum qui Usquam sive Latine sive Populari sive Alii Quamvis Lingua Scripto Aliquid Consignaverunt Notitia*, 2 vols. (Rome: Nicolaus Angelus Tinussius, 1672), ii. 343 [Oxford, Bodleian Library, F 1 1, 2 Jur]

Albana, Lucia

s. xv　　　　　　　　　　　　　　　　　　　　　　　　Venice (Italy)

Ad Magnificam et Pudicissimam Marietam Contarena, Lucia Albana: 'Invidias Marietta tuae iam gratia forme'

> *MS*: Venice, Biblioteca Marciana, Lat. XII 225 (4410), p. 37

Alberini, Rodiana

1477–1517　　　　　　　　　　　　　　　　　　　　　Parma (Italy)

Latin verse

> Attributed to her by Ireneo Affò, *Memorie degli scrittori e letterati parmigiani*, 7 vols. (Parma: Stamperia Reale, 1789–1833), iii. 193, drawing on Niccolò Liburnio, *La spada di Dante Alighieri* (Venice: Gio. Antonio di Nicolini da

Sabio, 1534), sig. A4ᵛ–Ciiʳ [Vatican City, Biblioteca apostolica, Bibliografia
II. Italia.Parma.1 (1–6); Capponi V 540 (2)]

Allington, —
?   London (England)
'Hospes qui fuerim quondam, qui quaeris, Amice'

> *Inscription*: a monument on the south side of the Rolls Chapel, Chancery Lane,
> London, of the Corinthian order, with a man, woman, and three children
> kneeling.
> In Edward Hatton, *A New View of London*, 2 vols. (London: R. Chiswell, R &
> J. Churchill, T. Horne, J. Nicholson, and R. Knaplock, 1708), ii. 536
> [London, British Library, E/351. 7–8]

Amarantio
'Amarantio Agathemens soror pro meritis tribuit'

> *Inscription*: *CLE* iii (2135)
> *ICL*, 33 (694)

'Amata'
Rescriptum: 'Non redit in florem, sed munus perdit amantis'

> *MS*: Leiden, UB Voss. Lat. O 16, 'Carmina Latina Varia', fo. 19ʳ

> *Edition*: Alexander Riese (ed.), *Anthologia Latina, sive Poesis Latinae Supplemen-
> tum*, 4 vols. (Leipzig: B. G. Teubner, 1868–97), i. 25 [Vatican City, Biblioteca
> Apostolica, Lett. lat. ant. 1.1.Anthologia.1]

<? 'Ambrosina'
s. xv   Italy
'*Responsio Ambrosinae*': 'Tu audes calamo divas, vir perdite, ninphas'

> *MSS*: Vatican City, Biblioteca Apostolica, Urb. lat. 643, fo. 92ᵛ
> Ravenna, Biblioteca classense, 271, fo. 146

> *Edition*: *Poesie latine inedite di A. Beccadelli detto il Panormita*, ed. Adolfo
> Cinquini and Roberto Valentini (Aosta: Giuseppe Allasia, 1907), 27 (this
> poem is most probably a *jeu d'esprit* of Beccadelli's) [Vatican City, Biblioteca
> Apostolica, Lett. lat. med. V 7 (int. 3)]>

Anastasia, Dame (OSB)
s. xiv/xv?   Lamspring (Germany)
Latin verse (nothing known to survive)

Attested by C. F. Paullini, *Das Hoch- und Wohl-gelahrte Teutsche Frauen-Zimmer* (Frankfurt: Johnn Cristoph Stösseln, 1705) 20; 2nd edn., 1712 [London, British Library, 10705.aa.11; Munich, Bayerische Staatsbibliothek, H.Lit. p. 290]

Angela/Angelina (Piccolomini?)

s. xv   Italy

Angeline Dive ad Marrasium Siciliensem Epistula Responsiva ad eum Epistolam: 'Quid quereris? quid te tanto merore fatigas?'

MSS: Bern, Bürgerbibliothek, 527, fo. 26
Volterra, Biblioteca Comunale Guarnacciana, 5031 Marrasius, fos. 4–5
Florence, Biblioteca Nazionale, Nuovi aquisti 1126, fos. 90ᵛ–92
Paris, Bibliothèque Nationale de France, Nouv. acq. lat. 623, fos. 23–31 (s. xv).

Edition: Albrecht von Eybe, *Margarita Poetica* (Strasbourg: G. Husner, 1473), fo. 148; 2nd edn. (Strasbourg: Joannes Priis, 1503), sig. t 8ᵛ [London, British Library, IC.1033; Vatican City, Biblioteca Apostolica, R.G. Neolat. IV.73]

Verses of Angelina to Maffeo Vegio

MS: Nicosia (Enna), Biblioteca Comunale, 21 (formerly 33) [not seen, reference from *Iter*]

Angoletti, Luisa

1863–1925   Italy
Latin poem on the death of Giovanni Battista Zanella (1885) [not seen]

Latin poem in 561 hexameters (1886) [not seen]

Bandini Buti, i. 41

Apolonia

?   Telesia in Samnium (Greece)
'Apolonia quae vocitabar'

Inscription: Petrus Pithoeus (ed.), *Epigrammata et Poematia Vetera*, 2 vols. (Paris: N. Gillius, 1590), ii. 134 [London, British Library, 1001.e.1]
Io. Matthaeus Toscanus, *Carmina Illustrium Poetarum Italorum* (Paris: Gilles Gorbin, 1576), 92 [London, British Library 238.i.38]
Giovanni Battista Ferretti (ed.), *Musae Lapidariae*, 5 vols. in 1 (Verona: Rubeis, 1672), iv. 271 [London, British Library, 143.e.22]
Philippe Labbé (ed.), *Thesaurus Epitaphium Veterum ac Recentiorum* (Paris, 1666), pt. I, p. 9 [London, British Library, 11405.bb.18]

Francesco Maria Bonada (ed.), *Anthologia, seu Collectio Omnium Veterum Inscriptionum Poeticarum*, 2 vols. (Rome, 1751), ii. 114 (22) [London, British Library, 671.g.1–2]

Petrus Burmann (ed.), *Anthologia Veterum Latinorum Epigrammatum et Poematum, sive Catalecta Poetarum Latinorum in VI Libros Digesta*, 6 vols. in 2 (Amsterdam: Schouten, 1759, 1773), ii. 195 (IV.cclvii) [London, British Library, 54.f.13]

Heinrich Meyer (ed.), *Anthologia Veterum Latinorum Epigrammatum et Poematum*, 2 vols. in 1 (Leipzig: Gerhard Fleischer, 1835), i. 140 (1359) [London, British Library, 011388.b.14]

CIL, ix. 2272

CLE, ii. 719–20 (1523)

<Aquila, Catarina

s. xvi   possibly Verona (Italy)

Catarinae Aquilae in Marito Revocendo Carmen: 'Quod modo nullo salus te disedente relicta est'

MS: London, British Library, Add. 12054, fo. 30ᵛ

This is credited to a mid-sixteenth-century poet, Niccolò Sicco (the volume is one of 'N. Sicci et aliorum poemata': fo. 45ᵛ is incorrectly attributed to Siccus and belongs to F. M. Molza, though since the latter's academy name was 'Padre Sicco' it is an understandable mistake and may not imply that the attributions are generally incorrect>

Aquilana, Catharina

s. xv/xvi   ?

Catharina Aquilana Catherine Aquile: 'Lentus, et ignota coniux regione moratur'

MS: London, British Library, Add. 19907, fos. 156–7

Ardinghelli, Maria Angela

b. 1730   Naples (Italy)

Elegia Latina: 'nella Raccolte per l'apertura della Libreria del Principe Tarsia' [not seen]

Attested by Ginevra Canonici Fachini, *Prospetto biografico delle donne Italiane rinomate in letteratura* (Venice: Tipografia di Alvisopoli, 1824), 167–8 [Vatican City, Biblioteca Apostolica, Z 2350 5.C.2]

Ardoino, Anna Maria (Ludovisi)

1672–1700   Messina/Piombino (Italy)

Rosa Parnassi: Plaudens Triumpho Imperiali S.M.C Invictissimi Leopoldi de Austria Romanorum Imperatoris, eiusque Dignissimae Uxoris Eleanorae Magdalenae

Palavini Rheni (Naples: S. Castaldun, 1687) [Naples, Biblioteca nazionale, B.Branc.55.E23]

Asbaje, Juana Ramirez de (Sor Juana Inés de la Cruz)
s. xvii   Mexico City (Mexico)
Villancico II: 'Illa quae Dominum Caeli'

> *Editions*: *Villancigos quese cantaron en la santa iglesia metropolitana de Mexico, en los maitines de la purissima conception de Nuestra Señora, a devocion de vn afecto al misterio* (Mexico City: La Viuda de Bernardo Calderón, 1676) [not seen]
> A. M. Plancarte (ed.), *Obras completas de Sor Juana Inés de la Cruz*, 4 vols. (Mexico City: Fondo de Cultura Económico, 1951), ii. 4–5
> Francisco Monterde (ed.), *Sor Juana Inés de la Cruz: obras completas* (Mexico City: Editorial Porrúa, 1989), 206

Diálogo: 'Hodie Nolascus divinus' (macaronic, Spanish/Latin)

> *Editions*: *Villancicos . . . San Pedro Nolasco* (1677) [not seen]
> Plancarte, ii. 40–1
> Monterde, 224

Villancico IV: 'Ille qui Romulo melior'

> *Editions*: *Villancicos que se cantaron en la S.I. catedral de Méjico, a los maitines del gloriosisimo príncipe de la Iglesia, el Sr. San Pedro* (1677) [not seen]
> Plancarte, ii. 49–50
> Monterde, 229

Epigramma: 'Desine pacifera bellantem, Pallas, oliva'

> *Editions*: *Neptuno allegorico, oceano de colores, simulacro politico* (Mexico City: Juan Ribera en el Empedradillo, [?1681]), 19 [Santiago de Chile, Biblioteca Nacional, Collectio Medinensis 15 (2)]
> Monterde, 798–9

Villancico V: 'Regina Superum'

> *Editions*: *Villancicos que se cantaron en la santa iglesia metropolitana de Mexico, en honor de Maria Santissima Madre de Dios, en su Assumpcion triumphante* (Mexico City: Herederos de la Viuda de Bernardo Calderon, 1686) [not seen]
> Plancarte, ii. 308
> Monterde, 357

Anagrama que celebra la concepción de María Santísima: 'Sumens illud Ave'
Epigramma: 'Nomine materno, mutata parte, Camilla'

> *Editions*: Plancarte, i. 59
> Monterde, 78

Una décima ajena en dos versiones latinas: 'Iam Anima Verbo adhaeret'; 'Iam coepit Anima exire'

> *Editions*: Plancarte, i. 262–3
> Monterde, 126

Villancico II—latino y castellano: 'Divina Maria'

> *Edition*: Monterde, 235

Villancico V: 'Ista, quam omnibus'

> *Edition*: Monterde, 238

Villancico VIII—ensalada: 'O Domina speciosa'

> *Edition*: Monterde, 253

Tres letras sueltas a la encarnación *Villancico III*: 'O Domina Caeli'

> *Editions*:
> Plancarte, ii. 223–4
> Monterde, 316

'Caelestis Auriga'

> *Edition*: Monterde, 357

'Aspasia'
s. xv   Mantua (Italy)
'Lampridium carum Musis hic Mantua servat'

> Sepulchral inscription in the church of St Andrea, Mantua, credited to the *amica* of Lampridius, a Latin poet of Cremona. Her name (almost certainly a sobriquet) is given as Aspasia: Paolo Giovio, *Elogia Veris Clarorum Virorum Imaginibus Apposito quae in Musaeo Ioviano Comi Spectantur* (Venice: Michael Tramezino, 1546), 62r–v. [London, British Library, 135.c.18]

Atilia Onesima

? Veleia (Italy)

D.M. Atiliae Severillae Filiae Piisimae Atilia Onesime Matre: 'Hunc titulum natae genetrix decepta paravi'

Inscription: Pietro de Lama, *Inscrizione antiche* (Parma: Carmignani, 1818), 118 (xlvi) [London, British Library, 813.h.52]

Heinrich Meyer (ed.), *Anthologia Veterum Latinorum Epigrammatum et Poematum*, 2 vols. in 1 (Leipzig: Gerhard Fleischer, 1835), i. 184 (1534) [London, British Library, 011388. b. 14]

CIL, xi. 1209

CLE, ii. 740–1 (1550)

Atis Maria

? Geneva (Switzerland)

'G[aio] Ars. Marciano optimo iuveni et pientissimo'

Inscription: Johann Caspar von Orelli (ed.), *Inscriptiones in Helvetia Reperta* (Zurich, 1828), 259 [not seen]

CIL, xii. 2611

CLE, ii. 769 (1596)

Attusia Lucana Sabina, wife of Ausonius

s. iv Bordeaux (France)

Verse (lost)

Attested by Ausonius, *Epigrammata* 18, 19. *The Works of Ausonius*, ed. R. P. H. Green (Oxford: Clarendon Press, 1991), 74

Aue, Euphrosine (Fritz, Henneken)

1677–1715 Colberg, Pomerania (Germany)

Carmen Latinum in Obit. Annae Gadesbuschiae, Conjugis Thom. Hopii 2 Mai, 1686, 4°, 1 leaf [not seen]

Described by Johann Carl Conrad Oelrichs, *Historisch-diplomatisch Beyträge zur Geschichte der Gelaharheit besonders im Herzogthum Pommern* (Berlin: Verlag des Buchhandlung der Real-Schule, 1767), 5 [Wolfenbüttel, Herzog August Bibliothek, Ea. 504]

Teutsch und lat. Gedicht auf den Tod Mart. Sylvest. Grabes, den 18 Dec. 1686, folio [not seen]

Oelrichs, 5

Elegia: 'Alcides quantus fuerat Bellator Achilles'

Edition: Cypressus Brandenburgica, in Ultimum Honorem Serenissimi ac Potentissimi Principis et Domini Domini Friderici Wilhelmi Magni, Electori, et Marcionis Brandenburgensis, &c. &c. &c. à Subjectissima Serva Euphrosina Avenia (Brandenburg: Ulrich Liebpert, 1688) [Wolfenbüttel, Herzog August Bibliothek, Gm. gr.-20 3 (12)]

Teutsch und lat. Gedicht als der Churf. Friedrich III mit seiner Gemahlin in Colberg angekommen, 1690, 1 leaf, in the form of a patent [not seen]

Oelrichs, 5

Carmen Lat. in Nuptias Wendio-Hassianas, 7 Oct. 1690. folio, 1 leaf [not seen]

Oelrichs, 6 (quotes four lines)

Carmen Lat. in Obit. Cathar. Elisab. Neandrae, Conjug. John. Avenii 20 Nov. 1694, 4° [not seen]

Oelrichs, 6

Teutsches und lat. Gedicht auf den Tod Georg Wends, 1695, 2 ½ leaves [not seen]

Oelrichs, 6

Teutsches und lat. Gedicht auf die Hochzeit H. Gottfr. Auen mit Jfr Louysa Sophia Heilerin, 1698, folio, 2 leaves [not seen]

Oelrichs, 6

Teutsches und lat. Gedicht auf Joh. Wild. Zierolds Hochzeit den 15 Mai 1699, folio, 1 leaf [not seen]

Oelrichs, 6

Teutsches und lat. Gedicht auf die Vermähkybd /g, / fruedrichs Landgrafens zu Hessen mit der Chur-Printzessin von Brandenb. Louysa Doroth. Sophia, Stargard, 1700, folio, 1 leaf [not seen]

Oelrichs, 6

Carmen Lat. in Magisterium m. Andr. Casp. Rothii, Leipzig, 1702 Celebratum, folio. 1 leaf [not seen]

Oelrichs, 6

Aurelia Eusebia

s. i/ii   Tortona (Italy)

'Quot merui vitam, moriens quot et ipse rogavi'

> *Inscription*: *CIL*, v. 7404
> *CLE*, ii. 550 (1180)

'B'

s. xii   ?Tegernsee (Germany)

'C. super mel et fauum dulciori'

> *MS*: Munich, Bayerische Staatsbibliothek, Clm 19411, fos. 69ʳ–70ʳ

> Editions: *MLREL*, ii. 478–82 (with trans.)
> Jürgen Kühnel, *Du bist mîn, ih bin dîn. Die lateinischen Leibes-(und Freundschafts-) Briefe des Clm 19411* (Göppingen: Kummerle, 1977) (with German trans.), 60–1

Possibly also 'C. cara karissime'

> *MS*: Munich, Bayerische Staatsbibliothek, Clm 19411, fos. 69ʳ–70ʳ

> *Editions*: *MLREL*, ii. 476–7 (with trans.)
> Kühnel, pp. 58–61

Baitelli, Giulia

s. xvii   Brescia (Italy)

> Antonio Brognoli, *Elogi di Bresciani per Dottrina Eccellenti, del Secolo xviii* (Brescia: Pietro Vescovi, 1785), 201, records that she consulted two local notables, il Canonico Gagliardi and l'Abbate Garbelli, about her Latin verse [Vatican City, Biblioteca Apostolica, Bibliografia II.Italia.Brescia.2]

Balbilla

s. ii?   Rome (Italy)

'Balbilla votum debitum reddo tibi' (single line)

> *Inscription*: *CLE*, i. 393 (847)
> Possibly the work of the Julia Balbilla who has left two surviving poems in Greek

Barbansona, Maria (Thou)

s. xvi   Paris (France)

Maria Barbansona, Jo. Barrensis Novi-Benegonii Mariae B. Amitae F. Manibus: 'Vellem, post obitum votis locus esset amicis'

> *MS*: Paris, Bibliothèque Nationale de France, Dupuy 460, fos. 163ʳ–164ᵛ

Barrile, Anna Resta
s. xx   Bologna (Italy)
Poemata (Bologna, 1983) [not seen]

> Mentioned by Josef Ijsewijn, *Companion to Neo-Latin Studies*, 2 vols. (Louvain: Louvain University Press/Peeters, 1990, 1998), i. 31

Baynard, Anne
1674–97   Mortlake (England)
'Severe satyrs written in the Latin tongue'

> Attested by Jeremy Collier, *The Great Historical, Geographical and Poetical Dictionary: Being a Curious Miscellany of Sacred and Profane History*, 2 vols. (London: Henry Rhodes, 1701) [London, British Library, L.R.297.b.2]

Beatrice (nun)
s. xii   Le Ronceray (France)
Verse exchange

> Implied by Baudri de Bourgeuil, *Les Œuvres poétiques de Baudri de Bourgeuil (1046–1130): édition critique publiée d'après le Ms du Vatican*, ed. Phyllis Abrahams (Paris: H. Champion, 1926), 260–1

Beatrice of Lorraine
1140–84   Lucca/Canossa/Pisa (Italy)
'Quamvis peccatrix, sum domna vocata Beatrix' (monostich)

> *Inscription*: Pisa, Campo Santo

> *Editions*: Mary Huddy, *Matilda, Countess of Tuscany* (London: John Long, 1906), 159 (with photograph), trans. p. 157
> F. J. E. Raby, *A History of Christian-Latin Poetry from the Beginnings to the Close of the Middle Ages* (Oxford: Clarendon Press, 1927), 454

Beatrix of Kent
d. *c.*1280   Lacock (England)
Elogium Foeminae Nobilissimae Elae Comitissae de Warwick (lost)

> Formerly in the Cottonian Library, Cotton Tiberius B XIII, fo. 5, destroyed in the fire of 1731

> Witnessed by Thomas Tanner, *Bibliotheca Britanno-Hibernica, sive de Scriptoribus qui in Anglia, Scotia et Hibernia ad Saeculi xvii Initium Floruerunt* (London: William Bowyer, 1748), 82 [London, British Library, 680. g. 16]

Beatrix die Küsterin
Middle Ages   Germany
'Virgo fuit quedam, metrici quam plenius edam'

MSS: Basel, Universitätsbibliothek, A VI 37, fos. 89–97 (s. xv)
Sankt Gallen, Stiftsbibliothek, 587, 176–91 (s. xiv)
Hildesheim, Stadtbibliothek, Cod. 6, fo. 18 (s. xv)

Bebbi, Lucrezia (Sassatelli)
late s. xvii   Reggio Emilia (Italy)
Ad Populum Reggiensem de Futuris Eventibus Belli Elegia: 'Tristia convexi populo
quid sidera coeli'

MS: Bologna, Biblioteca comunale dell'Archiginnasio, B 3557, fos. 6ʳ–7ᵛ

Edition: Giovanni Guasco, *Storia letteraria del principio e progresso dell'Accademia
   di belle lettere in Reggio* (Reggio: Ippolito Vedrotti, 1711), 34–6 [Vatican City,
   Biblioteca apostolica, Bibliografia II. Italia.Reggio Emilia I]

Berhtgyth
fl. *c.*770   England/Thuringia (Germany)
'Pro me quaero oramina'

MS: Vienna, Österreichische Nationalbibliothek, Lat. 751, fo. 34ᵛ

Editions: Epistulae S. Bonifacii, ed. Nicolaus Serarius (Mainz: M. Demen, 1629),
   64 (and other edns. 1618, 1654, 1677) [London, British Library, 1009.b.12]
Sancti Bonifacii Archiepiscopi Epistolae . . . Ordine Chronologico Dispositae, ed.
   Stephan Alexander Würdtwein (Mainz: Crass, 1789), 151 [London, British
   Library, 692. g. 15]
Sancti Bonifacii Opera, ed. J. A. Giles (London: D. Nutt, 1844), i. 139 [London,
   British Library, RB 23.a.2532]
S. Bonifatii et Lulli Epistolae, ed. Philipp Jaffé (Berlin: Weidmann, 1866), 149
   [London, British Library, 2392. f. 4]
S. Bonifatii et Lulli Epistolae, ed. Ernst Dümmler (Berlin: Weidmann, 1892), 148
PL lxxxix, cols. 797–8
Epistolae S. Bonifacii, ed. M. Tangl (Berlin: Weidmann, 1916) 286–7

'Vale vivens feliciter'

MS: Vienna, Österreichische Nationalbibliothek, Lat. 751, fo. 35ʳ

Editions: Serarius, 43
Würdtwein, 150

Giles, i. 140
Jaffé, 148
Dümmler, 147
PL lxxxix, cols. 797–8
Tangl, 285

Berlingero, Suor Maria Raimonda Constanza
s. xvii   Bologna (Italy)
Writings apparently lost: noted for ability as a poet in Italian and Latin

Giancalvo Roversi (ed.), *Donne celebre della Emilia-Romagna e del Montefeltro* (Bologna: Edizione Grafis, 1993), 140

Bianchini, Alessandra (Volta)
s. xvii   Bologna (Italy)
Writings apparently lost

Attested by Pellegrino Antonio Orlandi, *Notizie degli scrittori bolognesi, e dell'opere loro stampate e manoscritte* (Bologna: Constantino Pisarri, 1714), 43 [Vatican City, Biblioteca Apostolica, Bibliografia. II. Italia.Bologna.2 Cons.]

Bocchi, Costanza (Malvezzi)
s. xvi, d. after 1567   Bologna (Italy)
Writings apparently lost

Attested by Pellegrino Antonio Orlandi, *Notizie degli scrittori bolognesi, e dell'opere loro stampate e manoscritte* (Bologna: Constantino Pisarri, 1714), 95: his account implies that he has seen some of her Latin verse [Vatican City, Biblioteca Apostolica, Bibliografia II. Italia.Bologna.2 Cons.]

Bock van Gutmansdorf, Margaretha (Freher)
fl. 1600   Heidelberg (Palatinate)
Josepho Scaligero Margareta Boxias: 'Genus deorum, ornate Scaliger deis' (after 1599)

MS: Munich, Bayerische Staatsbibliothek, Clm lat. 10384, fo. 275 (s. xvii)

Bojarda, Lucia
s. xv   Reggio Emilia (Italy)
Writings apparently lost: surviving description suggests an attempt at a Latin epic

Attested by Giovanni Guasco, *Storia litteraria del principio e progresso dell'Academia di belle lettere in Reggio* (Reggio: Ippolito Vedrotti, 1711), 25–6 [Vatican City, Biblioteca Apostolica, Bibliografia II. Italia.Reggio Emilia I]

Borghini, Caterina
1st half s. xviii   Pisa (Italy)
Ad Fratrum Elegia: 'Cum Patriam, dulcesque lares, carosque Parentes'

   Edition: *Arcadum Carmina, Pars Altera* (Rome: Giuseppe & Filippo de Rossi,
      1756), 96–8 [London, British Library, 78. c. 35]

Elegia: 'Parva, sed apta mihi jucunda grata recessu'

   Edition: ibid. 98–100

Elegie Latine Due (Padua: Tipografia del seminario, 1826) [one a praise of dark
eyes, one a praise of blue eyes] [not seen]

   Mentioned in Pietro Leopoldo Ferri, *Biblioteca femminile italiana* (Padua: Cres-
      cini, 1842), 79 [London, British Library, 11907. cc. 6]

Other Latin elegies on various subjects, modelled on Tibullus, 'la Perla', 'il Caffè',
'le Valle Benedetta', 'la sua propria villa di Capannoli' [not seen]

   Attested by Francesco Clodoveo Maria Pentolini, *Le donne illustre: canti dieci*,
      2 vols. (Livorno: Gio. Vincenzo Falorni, 1776), i. 232 [Vatican City, Biblio-
      teca Apostolica, Barberini JJJ VIII 5–6]

Brahe, Sophia
c.1556–1643   Denmark/Prague (Czech Republic)/Denmark
Tycho Brahe lusit haec cum Sophia sorore sua in praedio Andreae Schelii: 'Juno
quidem gazas amat, ut non spernit Amorem'

   Edition: *Danske Magazin*, 3 (1947), 12–32, 43–52 (p. 18)

   <*Urania Titani: Urania til Titan* (1594), Vienna, Österreichische Nationalsbi-
      bliothek, Lat. 10686, published in Peder Hansen Resen, *Inscriptiones Hafniensis
      Latinae, Danicae et Germanicae, Una cum Inscriptonibus Amagiensibus Uranibur-
      gicis et Stellaeburgicis necnon Duabus Epistolis* (Copenhagen: Henricus Gödianus,
      1668), 410–29, is a poem by her brother Tycho Brahe, written in her name[1]>

Braun, Angela
late Middle Ages
Angela Braun ad Magistrum Joh. Birmust Erford: 'Ut tibi quam multas mittat tua
virgo salutes'

   MS: Prague, Biblioteca Metropolitana, 1347, fo. 110r–v

   [1] I should like to thank Dr Thomsen for a Xerox copy of this: there is a copy in Copenhagen,
Kongelige Bibliotek.

Brenzona, Laura (Schioppa)
fl. 1460   Verona (Italy)
Carmina Antonii Panthei Recitata in Laudem Magnifici Domini Antonii Venerio per Lauram Brenzonam, et in Laudem Francisce Brenzone Sponse eius Sororis: 'Praeter Antoni decus o venere'

> *MS*: Verona, Biblioteca Comunale, 280 (1336), fos. 3–6ʳ

Responsio Laure ad eundem Paulum Ramusium: 'Caelicolas utinam hec servat vox Paule beatos'

> *MS*: Verona, Biblioteca Comunale, 280 (1336), fo. 7ʳ

Epitaphium: 'Hic decus est patriae, quem Stirps Nogarola creavit'

> *MS*: Verona, Biblioteca Comunale, 280 (1336), fo. 14ʳ

Laure Brenzone Veronensis Carmen ad Inclytum D. Robertum Sanseverinatem: 'Virgineo quendam tenues in pectore vires'

> *MS*: Venice, Biblioteca Marciana, Lat. xii. cvi.6 (4460), fos. 2ʳ–23ʳ

<Brosamerus, Rosina (Posthuis)
s. xvi   Gesmersheim (Palatinate)
Blandinae Posthio: 'Quod gemis absentem, quod cantas carmine POSTHI'

> *Edition*: *Johannis Posthii Gesmershemii Parergorum Poeticorum Libri Duo* (Heidelberg: Hieronymus Commelin, 1595), 196 [The Hague, Konincklijke Bibliotheek, 1714. D. 10]

> This verse may be *in persona*>

Burnell, Eleanor
fl. 1639   Dublin (Ireland)
Patri suo Charissimo Operis Encomium: 'Multiplici ratione fateor, mea carmina (quamvis)'

> *Edition*: Henry Burnell, *Landgartha. A Tragie-Comedy, as it was Presented in the New Theater in Dublin, with Good Applause, being an Ancient Story, Written by H.B.* (Dublin, 1641), sig. A3ʳ [London, British Library, 162. c. 27]

Aliud: 'Melpomene tua tela (parens) contexta Thalia et'

> *Edition*: ibid., sig. A3ʳ

Caelia Chloe
late antiquity   Rome (Italy)
'Tu, pia tu mater cineres operire momento'

>   *Inscription*: *CIL*, vi. 15876
>   *CLE*, i. 201 (431)

Caesaria, wife of Carudis
fl. s. vi/vii?   Palafrugell/Tarragona (Spain)
'[Caru]do, coniugi optimo, [in pa]ce quiescenti, Caesaria'

>   *Inscription*: D. José Vives, *Inscripciones cristianas de la España romana y visigoda*,
>   2nd edn. (Barcelona: J. M. Viader, 1969), no. 300, p. 95

Calwerin, Maria
s. xvii
Latin verse

>   *MS*: Ulm, Stadbibliothek, 6727 (a collection of poems mostly by, some to,
>   Sebastian Hornmold, who had a variety of connections with Latinate
>   women) [not seen: reference from *Iter*]

Candidia Quintina and Valeria Maximina (mother and daughter)
                                                                Arles (France)
D.M. Q. Candidi Benigni Fabri Tignarii Corporis Arelatensis: 'Ars cui summa fuit
fabricae, studium doctrina'

>   *Inscription*: Petrus Burmann (ed.), *Anthologia Veterum Latinorum Epigrammatum
>   et Poematum, sive Catalecta Poetarum Latinorum in VI Libros Digesta*, 6 vols. in
>   2 (Amsterdam: Schouten, 1759, 1773), ii. 235 (IV.cccxxi) [London, British
>   Library, 54. f. 13]
>   Heinrich Meyer (ed.), *Anthologia Veterum Latinorum Epigrammatum et Poema-
>   tum*, 2 vols. in 1 (Leipzig: Gerhard Fleischer, 1835), ii. 175 (1496) [London,
>   British Library, 011388. b. 14]
>   *CIL*, xii. 99 (722)
>   *CLE*, i. 229–30 (483)
>   Hermann Dessau (ed.), *Inscriptiones Latinae Selectae*, 3 vols. (Berlin:
>   Weidmann, 1892–1916), ii.2, p. 815 (7715) [London, British Library, 7706.
>   d. 21]
>   Edward Courtney (ed. and trans.), *Musa Lapidaria: A Selection of Latin Verse
>   Inscriptions* (Atlanta: Scholars Press, 1995), 130–1 (132)

Carter, Elizabeth
1717–1806   London (England)
Εις τον επιγραμματιστον, *Latinè*: 'Blanditiae Veneris procul, O procul este dolosae'[Latin and Greek]

> *Edition*: *Gentleman's Magazine*, 8 (May 1738), 272 [London, British Library, RAR. 052]

Epigram: 'En marcet Laurus, nec quicquam juvit *Elizam*'

> *MS*: London, British Library, Add. 4457, fo. 73ᵛ

> *Editions*: *Gentleman's Magazine*, 8 (Aug. 1738), 429 [London, British Library, RAR. 052]
> Montagu Pennington, *Memoirs of the Life of Mrs Elizabeth Carter, with a New Edition of her Poems, Some of Which have Never Appeared Before, to Which are Added, Some Miscellaneous Essays in Prose* (London: F. C. and J. Rivington, 1807), 26 [London, British Library, 1501/85]

In Diem Natalem: 'Tu Deus Omnipotens, quo dante, hoc aethere vescor'

> *Editions*: Pennington (ed.), *Memoirs* 348–53 [Pennington notes, 'there is no name to this Latin translation', so there is nothing to suggest that it is not her own work]

Cecilia of Flanders
c.1060–1197   Caen (France)
Verse and other writings

> Attested by Baudri of Bourgeuil: *Les Œuvres poétiques de Baudri de Bourgeuil (1046–1130): édition critique publiée d'après le Ms du Vatican*, ed. Phyllis Abrahams (Paris: H. Champion, 1926), 255–6

Cerrini, Gironda (Suor Anna Maria Cristina de Gesù)
1626–1703   Perugia/Caldarola (Italy)
'Utraque stylum suum huc asserat Pallas'

> *Edition*: Felice Verduccioli, *In Funebre Josephi a Giaceto Castelvimani Comitis, Oratio Felicis Verduccioli* (Perugia: Typographia Episcopali, 1643), 30–1 [Perugia, Biblioteca Comunale Augusta, I.H.93]

Christine de Pizan
c.1363–*c*.1430   Venice (Italy)/Paris (France)
'Fructibus eloquii prophete in nomine Christi' (1404)

MSS: Brussels, Bibliothèque Royale, 10987 [not seen]

Brussels, Bibliothèque Royale, IV 1093 (Ancien Collection J. Dumont à Palaiseau), ('Sept Psaumes allégorisés' fos. 1–88) [not seen]

Paris, Bibliothèque Nationale de France, Fr. 15216 ('Sept Psaumes allégorisés' fos. 1–48) [not seen]

Edition: *Les Sept Psaumes Allégorisés of Christine de Pisan: A Critical Edition from the Brussels and Paris Manuscripts*, ed. Ruth Ringland Rains (Washington: Catholic University of America Press, 1965) (from Brussels, BR 10987), 158

Translation: Lori J. Walters, 'The Royal Vernacular: Poet and Patron in Christine de Pizan's Charles V and the Sept Psaumes Allegorisées', in Renate Blumenfeld-Kosinski, Duncan Robertson, and Nancy Warren (eds.), *The Vernacular Spirit: Essays on Medieval Religious Literature* (New York: Palgrave, 2002), 145–82 (p. 164)

Cleopassa, Octavia
s. xvi   Otranto (Italy)
'Scripsit aliquot hymnos latinos'

According to Jean-Jacques Boissard, *Icones Diversorum Hominum Fama et Rebus Gestis Illustrium* (Metz: Abraham Faber, 1591), 98, who also notes that her brother Laelius Cleopassus published them at the back of his own *Poemata* (Cleopassus published *Epigrammata*, *Basia*, *Amplexus*, *Silvae*, *Elegiae*, and *Conflictus Navalem in Sinu Corinthiaco*, according to Boissard, 94. Not found) [London, British Library, 683. e. 17]

Clodia Africana
?   Rome (Italy)
'Hospes, ad hoc tumulum dum perlegis acta resiste'

Inscription: *CIL*, vi. 14578, for M. L. Catellus Florus
CLE, i. 240–1 (502)

Colleoni, Cassandra (da Correggio)
d. 1519   Correggio (Italy)
'Conjugis hoc claros cineres Cassandra Sepulcro' (1508)

Inscription: printed in Girolamo Colleoni, *Notizia degli scrittori piu celebri che anno illustrato la patria loro di Correggio* (Correggio: Privately printed, n.d. [late s. xvii?]), p. xvi [Vatican City, Biblioteca Apostolica, Bibliografia. II. Italia.Correggio I]

Colonna, Vittoria (d'Avalos), Marchesa di Pescara

1490–1547   Pescara (Italy)

Divae Victoriae Aterninae Responsio ad Danielem Finum: 'Certe ego nec mundum vici; nec vincere possum'

MS: Ferrara, Biblioteca comunale Ariostea, I. 437, fo. 209^{r-v}

The Latin poem headed *Marchionissa de Pescharia*: 'Non viviam sine te mi Brute haud territa dixit' in Venice, Biblioteca Marciana, Lat. XII 248 (10625), fo. 131^r appears to be *in persona*

Constantia (I)

fl. 355   Rome (Italy)

'Tristis Anastasio Constantia carmina scribit'

Inscription: Giovanni Battista Rossi (ed.), *Inscriptiones Christianae Urbis Romae Septimo Saeculo Antiquiores*, 2 vols. (Rome: Officina libraria Pontifica (Filippo Cuggiani), 1888), i. 76 (127) [London, British Library, 7708. f. 16]

CLE, i. 312–13 (660)

Constantia (II)

*c.*1065–after 1129   Le Ronceray, Angers (France)

'Perlegi vestram studiosa indagine cartam'

MS: Vatican City, Biblioteca Apostolica, Reg. 1351, fos. 143^r–146^r

Editions: *Les Œuvres poétiques de Baudri de Bourgeuil (1046–1130): édition critique publiée d'après le Ms du Vatican*, ed. Phyllis Abrahams (Paris: H. Champion, 1926), 344–9

O. Schumann, 'Baudri von Bourgeuil als Dichter', in *Studien zur lateinischen Dichtung des Mittelalters. Ehrengabe für Karl Strecker* (Dresden: Buchdr. de Unihelm und Bertha v. Baensch Stiftung, 1931), 158–70 (pp. 162–3)

Baldricus Burgualianus Carmina, ed. K. Hilbert (Heidelberg: Carl Winter Universitäts Verlag, 1979), no. 201, pp. 271–6

Gerald A. Bond (with trans.), *The Loving Subject* (Philadelphia: University of Pennsylvania Press, 1995), 182–93

Constantina, daughter of Constantine the Great, wife of Hannibalinus and Gallus

mid-s. iv   Constantinople (Turkey)

'Constantina deum venerans Christoque dicata'

Inscription: Giovanni Battista Rossi (ed.), *Inscriptiones Christianae Urbis Romae Septimo Saeculo Antiquiores*, 2 vols. (Rome: Officina libraria Pontifica (Filippo Cuggiani), 1888), ii.1, p. 44 [London, British Library, 7708. f. 16]
CLE, i. 146 (301)

This poem is from a church dedicated to the Roman martyr St Agnes which Constantina founded on the Via Nomentana, in Rome.

Constanza de Castilla
c.1400–1478   Madrid (Spain)
'Eterne Rex Altissime'

  MS: Madrid, Biblioteca Nacional, 7495, fo. 44ᵛ

  Edition: Constanza de Castilla, *Book of Devotions*, ed. Constance L. Wilkins (Exeter: University of Exeter Press, 1998), 52

'Dulces clavi amabiles'

  MS: ibid., fo. 45ᵛ

  Edition: Wilkins, 53

'Eterni Pater luminis'

  MS: ibid., fo. 45ᵛ

  Edition: Wilkins, 53–4

'Agnus ablator criminum'

  MS: ibid., fo. 53ʳ

  Edition: Wilkins, 60

?Contareni, Marieta
mid-s. xv   Venice (Italy)
Ad Karolum: 'Si tibi me viro coniunctam credis amore'

  MS: Cambridge, University Library, Add. 6188, fo. 71ᵛ

Contreras, Juana
early s. xvi   Segovia (Spain)
Her writings are said to have been printed in the sixteenth century under the
title *Joanna Contrerae, Puellae Doctae, Epistolarum Carminum et Orationes
Aliquod*, ed. Lucio Marineo Siculo (not found): see *Apuntes*, i.i, p. 278
[Cambridge, University Library, 743.01.b.1.268]

Cooke, Anne (Bacon)
1528?–1610   Essex/London (England)
[title erased]: 'Se titulo prodit hic, quantasque recondat'

   MS: Cambridge, University Library, Ii.5.37, p. viiiʳ (MS has original pagination)

   Editions: Louise Schleiner, *Tudor and Stuart Women Writers* (Bloomington:
      Indiana University Press, 1994), 42 (with trans.)
   Jane Stevenson and Peter Davidson (eds.), *Early Modern Women Poets* (Oxford:
      Oxford University Press, 2001), 23 (with trans.)

<She may just possibly have written her husband's epitaph, 'Hic Nicolaum ne
Baconem conditum' (1578)

   Edition: H.H. [Henry Howard], *Ecclesia Sancti Pauli Illustrata* (London: John
      Norton, 1633), sig. D4ᵛ; however, this is attributed to George Buchanan in
      Paris, Bibliothèque Nationale de France, 106, fo. 62ʳ [Oxford, Bodleian
      Library, 40 E 5 (1) Jur]>

Cooke, Elizabeth (Hoby, Russell)
1540–1609   Essex/London (England)
From the tomb of Thomas Noke, Esq., d. 1567: 'O multum dilecte senex, pater
atque vocatus' (1567)

   Inscription: ed. Elias Ashmole, *The Antiquities of Berkshire*, 3 vols. (London:
      E. Curll, 1719), ii. 491 [London, British Library, 10361. d. 6]
   Louise Schleiner, *Tudor and Stuart Women Writers* (Bloomington: Indiana
      University Press, 1994), 210–11 (with trans.)

ELIZABETHA HOBAEA *Conjux, ad* THOMAM HOBAEUM, *Equitem Maritum:* 'O dulcis
conjux, animae pars maxima nostrae' (1566)

   Inscription: *in situ*, Bisham Abbey, Berkshire, not now legible

Editions: Ashmole, ii. 467–8

Schleiner, 206–7 (with trans.)

Paul Hentzner, *Travels in England during the Reign of Queen Elizabeth (1596)*, trans. Sir Robert Naunton (London: Cassell & Co., 1889), 28–9 (and other editions) [London, British Library, 12208. bb. 15/165]

Jane Stevenson and Peter Davidson (eds.), *Early Modern Women Poets* (Oxford: Oxford University Press, 2001), 45–6 (with trans.)

Elisa Cokia M. M. Thomae Hobii Mariti Incomparabilis: 'O chare consors, coniugium ô dulcissime' (1566)

MS: Paris, Bibliothèque Nationale de France, Collections Dupuy 951, fo. 122ᵛ

ELIZABETHA HOBAEA, *Soror ad* PHILIPPUM HOBAEUM, *Equitem Fratrem*: 'Tuque tuae stirpis non gloria parva *Philippe*' (1566)

Inscription: *in situ*, Bisham Abbey, Berkshire, not now legible

Editions: Ashmole, ii. 468–9

Schleiner, 207–9 (with trans.)

ELIZABETHAE HOBEAE, *Matris, in Obitum Duarum Filiarum* ELIZABETHAE, *et* ANNAE, *Epicedium*: 'ELIZABETHA jacet, (eheu mea viscera) fato' (1570)

Inscription: *in situ*, Bisham Abbey, Berkshire, not now legible

Editions: Ashmole, ii. 470–1

Schleiner, 209–10 (with trans.)

Stevenson and Davidson, 47 (with trans.)

Elizabethae in Obitum Katharinae Sororis Epicaedia: 'Chara valeto Soror, in Coelo morte triumphas' (1583)

John Stow, *A Survay of London* (London: John Windet, 1603), 259–60 [London, British Library, 578 b 2]

George Ballard, *Memoirs of Several Ladies of Great Britain Who Have Been Celebrated for their Writings or Skill in the Learned Languages, Arts and Sciences* (Oxford: W. Jackson for the author, 1752), 204 (with trans. p. 206) [Oxford, Bodleian Library, DD.1.Jur]

George Ballard, *Memoirs of Several Ladies of Great Britain Who Have Been Celebrated for their Writings or Skill in the Learned Languages, Arts and Sciences*, ed. Ruth Perry (Detroit: Wayne State University Press, 1985), 206–7, 208

Schleiner, 210 (with trans.)

'Mens mea crudeli laniatur saucia morsu' (1585)

Inscription: *in situ*, Westminster Abbey

Reges, Reginae, Nobiles et Alii in Ecclesia Collegiata B. Petri Westmonasterii sepulti (London: E. Bullifant, 1606), 45 [London, British Library, C. 32. e. 4]

Jodocus Crull, *The Antiquities of St Peter's, or, the Abbey-Church of Westminster*, 2nd edn., 2 vols. (London, 1715), i. 47–9 [London, British Library, 010349. tt. 45]

Paul Henzner, *A Journey into England. By P. Hentzner, in the Year MDXCVIII*, ed. Horace Walpole, trans. Richard Bentley (Strawberry-Hill: Privately printed, 1757), 26 [London, British Library, 1049. f. 2]

John Dart, *Westmonasterium, or, the History and Antiquities of St Peters Westminster*, 2 vols. (London: James Cole, [1723], reissue London: T. Bowles, J. Bowles, 1742), i. 115–16 [London, British Library, 208 i 4; 689 ee 22]

Paul Hentzner, *Travels in England during the Reign of Queen Elizabeth (1596)*, trans. Sir Robert Naunton (London: Cassell & Co., 1889), 28–9 (and other editions) [London, British Library, 12208. bb. 15/165]

Schleiner, 47–8 (with trans.)

Translation: Betty Travitsky, *The Paradise of Women: Writing by Englishwomen of the Renaissance* (Westport, Conn.: Greenwood Press, 1981), 23–4

Carmina Aerumnosae Matris in Superstites Filias: 'plangite nunc natae' (1585)
Reges, Reginae, 45

John Strype, *Annals of the Reformation*, 3rd edn., 4 vols. (London: Edward Symon, 1735), iii.1, p. 277

Dart, i. 115

Crull, 37

Schleiner, 48–9 (with trans.)

Carmina Aerumnosae Matris Dominae Elizabethae Russ [sic.] in Obitum Filii: 'En solamen avi, patris pergrata voluptas'

Reges, Reginae, 45

Dart, i. 115

Crull, 37

Schleiner, 49 (with trans.)

To the R Honorable my Sorowfull Nephew Mr Secretary at his House: 'Chara mihi multos coniunx dilecta per annos' (Feb. 1597)

MS: Hatfield House, Cecil Papers 140, no. 82

To the R Honorable my Very Loving Nephew Sir Robert Cecill Knyght Chauncellor of the Duchy and Secretary to the Queenes Most Excellent Maiesty: 'Quid voveat Dulci Nutricula magis Alumno' (22 Oct. 1597)

MS: Hatfield House, Cecil Papers 175, no. 118

Verses to Lord Keeper Egerton, in Condolence for the Loss of his Son Thomas: 'Hunc Deus Altitonans Caelesti Numine Favon' (1599)

MS: San Marino, Huntington Library, EL. 11738

Edition: Steven W. May, *The Elizabethan Courtier Poets: The Poems and their Contexts* (Asheville, NC: Pegasus Press, 1999), 365

In ANNAM Filiam: 'Ut veniens annus tibi plurima commodet, Anna'
Editions: *A Way of Reconciliation* (London: R. Barker, 1605), sig. A3 [Washington, Folger Shakespeare Library [not seen]/Early English Books no. 974:21]
Strype, ii. 470
Ballard (1752), 199–200
Ballard (1985), 203
Elaine V. Beilin (ed.), *Protestant Translators: Anne Lock Prowse and Elizabeth Russell* (Aldershot: Ashgate, 2000), sig. A3

Cooke, Katherine (Killigrew)
1542?–1583   Essex/London/Cornwall (England)
'Qui Buchanane meo te dicit nomine salvum' (distich)

MS: Paris, Bibliothèque Nationale de France, Nouv. acq. lat. 106, fo. 78^v. Possibly autograph

'Visere quae mallem iubeo te vivere salvum' (distich)

MS: Paris, Bibliothèque Nationale de France, Nouv. acq. lat. 106, fo. 78^v. Possibly autograph

'Si mihi quem cupio cures Mildreda remitti'

MSS: Cambridge, University Library, Ff.5.14, fo. 107 (miscellany book of W. Kytton, with trans.)
Oxford, Corpus Christi College, 316 [not seen]
Dublin, Marsh's Library, 23.5.21, fo. 22^v [not seen]

Editions: Sir John Harington in his notes to book 37 of his *Orlando furioso in English Heroical Verse* (London: Richard Field, 1591), 314 [London, British Library, C. 70. g. 1]

George Ballard, *Memoirs of Several Ladies of Great Britain Who Have Been Celebrated for their Writings or Skill in the Learned Languages, Arts and Sciences* (Oxford: W. Jackson for the author, 1752), 203 (with trans.) [Oxford, Bodleian Library, DD.1.Jur]

There is also a badly garbled version in Anon. [Mark Lewis?], *Essay to Revive the Ancient Attainments of Gentlewomen* (London: J.D., 1673), with trans. pp. 20–1 [London, British Library, 1031. g. 19]

George Ballard, *Memoirs of Several Ladies of Great Britain Who Have Been Celebrated for their Writings or Skill in the Learned Languages, Arts and Sciences*, ed. Ruth Perry (Detroit: Wayne State University Press, 1985), 205–6

Louise Schleiner, *Tudor and Stuart Women Writers* (Bloomington: Indiana University Press, 1994), 45 (with trans.)

Jane Stevenson and Peter Davidson (eds.), *Early Modern Women Poets* (Oxford: Oxford University Press, 2001), 63–4 (with trans.)

Translation: Sarah Josepha Hale, *Woman's Record* (New York: Harper & Brothers, 1860), 374.

Cathelina Chillegrea in D.B. Sylva: 'Qui cupis assiduos coeli cognoscere cursus'

MS: Cambridge, University Library, Ii.5.37, fo. viii^v

Edition: Schleiner, 44 (with trans.)

In Mortem Suam haec Carmina dum Vixerat Scripsit D. Katharina Killigreia

Inscription: London, church of St Thomas the Apostle, Vintry ward (not extant)

Editions: John Stow, *A Survey of London* (London: John Windet, 1603), 259–60 [London, British Library, 578. b. 2]
Ballard (1752), 204, with trans.
Schleiner, 257
Ballard (1985), 206, 208
Stevenson and Davidson, 64 (with trans.)

Coppoli, Elena (Signorelli: later Suor Cecilia)
1426–1500   Perugia/Foligno (Italy)
Ad ventos ut placentur: 'Non ego vos, Venti, laesi, nec numina vestrum'

MS: Florence, Bibliotheca Riccordiana, 606 (L. IV. 28), fo. 156ᵛ

Editions: Giovanni Lami, *Catalogus Codicum Manuscriptorum qui in Bibliotheca Riccordiana Florentiae Adservantur* (Livorno: Antonio Sanctini et Socios, 1761), 230 [Vatican City, Biblioteca Apostolica, Barberini 2 xi 52]

Gio. Battista Vermiglioli, *Bibliografia degli scrittori perugini*, 2 vols. (Perugia: Francesco Baduel, 1828), i. 345 [Vatican City, Biblioteca apostolica, Bibliografia II.Italia.Perugia.2 (1–2).Cons]

Poesie latine di Elena Coppoli, poetessa perugine del secolo xv, recati in versi italiani dal Professore Antoni Mezzanotte (Perugia: Tipografia Baduel, 1832), no pagination (with Italian trans.) [Vatican City, Biblioteca Apostolica, Mai. X.A III.42 (int. g)]

A. Fantozzi, 'Documenti intorno alla Beata Cecilia Coppoli Clarissa (1426-1500)', *Archivum Franciscanum Historicum*, 19 (1926), 194–225, 334–84 (p. 195)

Eadem ad Praeceptorem: 'Praemia digna, precor, domino Dii reddite Lucae'

MS: ibid., fo. 157ʳ

Editions: Lami, 230
Vermiglioli, 345
Mezzanotte, no pagination
Fantozzi, 195

Eadem Epithaphium Magdalenae: 'Perlege: marmoreo sum contumulata sepulchro'

MS: ibid., fo. 157ʳ

Editions: Lami, 230
Vermiglioli, 346
Mezzanotte, no pagination
Fantozzi, 195

Ad Camillam Sociam: 'Oro tuum spiret vultus, Camilla, decorem'

MS: ibid., fo. 157ʳ

Editions: Lami, 230
Vermiglioli, 346
Mezzanotte, no pagination
Fantozzi, 195

Corbiniana, Sophiana (Bernharda)
fl. 1655   Leipzig (Germany)/Poland
ECHO LAUDUM Sanctissimi Domini Nostri ALEXANDRI VII: 'Quem Virum Solis comitata currum'

> *MS*: Vatican City, Biblioteca Apostolica, Chigi D.III.40, fos. 46r–48r

ENCOMIUM Munificentiae Sanctissimi Domini Nostri ALEXANDRI VII: 'Non ergò frustrà credimus aureis'

> *MS*: ibid., fos. 48r–49r

Other writing in Latin

> Implied by Josef Ijsewijn, *Companion to Neo-Latin Studies*, 2 vols. (Louvain: Louvain, University Press Peeters, 1990, 1998), i. 31, no references given

Cordula
s. xvi/xvii   Germany
Anagram verses (not found)

> Attested by Paulus Rutingius of Rostock in his *Anagrammatum Pauli Rutingii Rostochiensis Centuria* (Rostock: Stephanus Myliander, 1606), 59 [The Hague, Koninklijke Bibliotheek, 849. C. 19]

Cornelia Galla
s. ii   Ammaedara (North Africa)
'Hic situs est Varius cognomine Frontonianus'

> *Inscription*: *CLE*, i. 228 (480)
> H. Geist and G. Pfohl (eds. and German trans.), *Römische Grabinschriften* (Munich: Ernst Heimeran Verlag, 1969), 42 (51)

Cornificia, wife of Camerius
fl. 50–40 BC   Rome (Italy)
Nothing known to survive

> Latin epigrams attested by St Jerome, *Chronicon*, s.a. 41 BC

Cruzat y Muinire, Josefa (de la Vega)
b. *c.*1720   Guamanga (Peru)
Latin verse

Attested by Manuel de Mendiburu, *Diccionario histórico-biográfico del Perú*, 8 vols. (Lima: J. Francisco Solis (i–iv), Bolognesi (v–viii), 1874–90), ii. 468 [London, British Library, 010885.e.31]

d'Alsinois, Valentine (Denisot)

s. xvi   Paris (France)

'Musarum decima, & charitum quarta, inclyta Regum'

> *Editions*: *Le Tombeau de Marguerite de Valois, royne de Navarre, faict premiere-ment en disticques latins par les trois sœurs princesses en Angleterre, depuis traduictz en grec, italien & francois par plusieurs des excellentz poétes de la France, avecques plusieurs odes, hymnes, cantiques, epitaphes, sur le mesme subiect* (Paris: De l'Imprimerie de Michel Fezandat & Robert Granlon, 1551), sig. C Iʳ [London, British Library, 1073. e. 11 (1)]
>
> Facsimile edition *Anne, Margaret and Jane Seymour*, ed. Brenda Hosington, The Early Modern Englishwoman: The Printed Writings (Aldershot: Ashgate 2000)
>
> Johannis Paschius, *Gynaeceum Doctum, sive Dissertatio Historico-literaria, vom Gelehrten Frauenzimmer, antea Wittebergae Ano 1686 Publice Exposita* (Wittenberg: Christian Finkel, 1701), 47 [Wolfenbüttel, Herzog August Bibliothek, M: Li. 6896]
>
> Jan van Beverwijk, *Van de Wtnementheyt des vrouwelicken geslachts* (Dordrecht: Hendrick van Esch, 1643), 53 [The Hague, Koniglijke Bibliotheek, 30. G. 28]

Da Sylva, Helena (sor)

s. xvi/xvii?   Coimbra (Portugal)

Virgilian cento on the Virgin

> Attested by Damião de Froes Perym, *Theatro Heroina, ABCedeario historico, e catalogo das Mulheres illustres em Armas letres, Acçoens Heroicas e Artes Liberaes*, 2 vols. (Lisboa Occidental: Officina Sylvania e Academia Real, 1736–40). i. 429 [London, British Library, 10604.i.3]

<Debonnaire, Louise (Barclay) (?)

s. xvii

'Vera loquor, multum, divine Viassiae, iuvit'

> Pierre Gassendi, *Viris Illustris Nicolai Claudii Fabricii de Piersec, Senatoris Aquisextiensis Vita, per Petrum Gassendum Praepositum Ecclesiae Diniensis* (Paris: 1642), 167–7 [NB this work, the source for the editions listed below, credits it to her husband John Barclay writing in her name, on unknown grounds]

Johann Deckherr, *De Scriptis Adespotis, Pseudepigraphis et Suppositiis Conjectura*, 3rd edn. (Antwerp: Isbrand Haring, 1686), 87 [Oxford, Balliol College Library, Special Collections 0905.b.04]

Christian Juncker, *Schediasma Historicum de Ephemeridibus sive Diarii Eruditorum ... in Appendice Exhibetur Centuria Foeminarum Eruditione et Scriptis Illustrium, ab eodem Collecta* (Leipzig: Friedrich Gleditsch, 1692), 21–2 [London, British Library, 610.a.1]

Pierre Bayle, *Dictionnaire historique et critique*, 2nd edn., 3 vols. (Rotterdam: Reimer Leers, 1702), i. 478 [Oxford, Bodleian Library, I.1.12–14 Art.]>

de Castro, Publia Hortensia

s. xvi   Villaviciosa (Portugal)

Latin poems composed in imitation of the Psalms of David [not seen]

In the *Biblioteca Lusitana* of Jorge Cardoso in the eighteenth century according to Nicolò Antonio, *Biblioteca Hispana, sive Hispanorum qui Usquam sive Latine sive Populari sive Alia Quavis Linqua Scripto Aliquid Consignaverunt Notitia*, 2 vols. (Rome: Nicolaus Angelus Tinussius, 1672), ii. 347 [Oxford, Bodleian Library, F.1.1, 2 Jur]

'Varias poesias (en latim e portugues)'

Attested by Carolina Michaëlis de Vasconcelas, *A Infanta D. Maria de Portugal (1521–1577), e as suas damas* (Lisbon: Biblioteca Nacional, 1983) (facsimile of 1st edn. Oporto, 1902, with introduction by Americo da Costa Ramalho), 110

de Gournay, Marie le Jars

1565–1645   Gournay-sur-Aronde/Paris (France)

'Nec metus, in celebres ne nostrum nomen amicos' (26 November 1588)

Edition: Marie de Gournay, *Le Proumenoir de Monsieur de Montaigne par sa fille d'alliance* (Paris: Abel l'Angelier, 1594), sig. B 1ᵛ [London, British Library, C. 175.m.31]

de' Monti, Falamisca

s. xvi/xvii   Canzano, Abruzzi (Italy)

'Diruta Marte jacent, nec bis, nec terque, quaterque'

Edition: Niccolò Toppi, *Biblioteca Napoletana*, 2 vols. (Naples: Antonio Bulifon, 1678), i. 80 [Vatican City, Biblioteca Apostolica, Bibliografia II.Italia.Napoli 2]

d'Ennetières, or Dentière, Marie

1486–1550s?   Tournai/Tornrijk (Belgium)

Latin verse

Fortunée Briquet states, on unknown grounds, 'Elle composa aussi du poésies latines. Ses vers ne manquent point de grâce.' Fortunée B. Briquet, *Diction-naire historique, littéraire, et bibliographique des françaises et des étrangères naturalisées en France* (Paris: De Gillé, 1804), 138 (and facsimile edn. Indigo et Côté-femmes Éditions, 1997) [Paris, Bibliothèque Sainte Geneviève, Passerole M cote 8Y sup. 67353]

de Roquemontrousse, Madame
s. xvii   Carpentras (France)

Traduction du dialogue entre la France et l'Allemagne: 'Victorem subiit capta Hei-deberga, triumphans'

> *Edition*: Claude Charles Guyonnet de Vertron, *La Nouvelle Pandore, ou les femmes illustres du siècle de Louis le Grand*, 2 vols. (Paris: Veuve C. Mazuel, 1698), i. 143–5 (also 2nd edn. Paris: Nicolas le Clerc, 1703, same pagination) [Paris, Bibliothèque de l'Arsenal, 8º BL.15901/1–2, 2nd edn. Oxford, Bodleian Library, Vet. E4.f.329/1–2]

'Inter inhorrentes obscurâ nocte tumultus'

> *Edition*: De Vertron, 150

Sur la mort de Madame Deshoulières: 'Ars fuit Hulleriae LODOICUM et fortia facta'

> *Edition*: De Vertron, 410

'Es mihi per somnum visus diademate cinctus'

> *Editions*: *Le Mercure galant* (Feb. 1682), 194 [Paris, Bibliothèque de l'Arsenal, 8º H.26.484]
>
> Christian Juncker, *Schediasma Historicum de Ephemeridibus sive Diarii Eruditor-um ... in Appendice Exhibetur Centuria Foeminarum Eruditione et Scriptis Illu-strium, ab eodem Collecta* (Leipzig: Friedrich Gleditsch, 1692), 57–8 [London, British Library, 610.a.1]
>
> Henri Bardon, *En lisant le Mercure galant: essai sur la culture latine en France au temps de Louis XIV*, Quaderni della Rivista di cultura classica e medioevale 5 (Rome: Edizioni dell'Ateneo, 1962), 12

de' Santi, Joanna (Conti)
s. xvi   Correggio/Bologna (Italy)
Poet in Latin and Italian

Attested in Paris, Bibliothèque Nationale de France, Ancien fonds français 22865, fo. 111ᵛ and in Francisco Agostino della Chiesa, *Theatro delle donne letterate* (Mondovi: Giovanni Gislandi & Giovanni Tomaso Rossi, 1620), 170–1 [Paris, Bibliothèque Nationale de France, G.21, 404]

Deschamps, Magdalene

fl. 1584   Paris (France)
Latin and Greek verse on the death of François Balduin

Attested by a contemporary, François Grudé de la Croix Dumain, *Premier volume de la bibliothèque du sieur de la Croix-du-Maine* (Paris: Abel l'Angelier, 1584), 498: [Oxford, Bodleian Library, C.2.15 (1) Art.]

de Serment, Louise-Anastasie

1642–92   Grenoble/Paris (France)
'Ses productions consistent dans plusieurs morceaux de Poésies latines et françaises'

Fortunée B. Briquet, *Dictionnaire historique, littéraire, et bibliographique des françaises et des étrangères naturalisées en France* (Paris: De Gillé, 1804), 310 (and facsimile edn. Indigo et Côté-femmes Éditions, 1997) [Paris, Bibliothèque Sainte Geneviève, Passerole M cote 8Y sup. 67353]

d'Este, Aurelia

1683–1719
Latin Verse

According to Tiraboschi, there is Latin verse in the *Poesie degli Accademici di Brà*, of which she was a member: Girolamo Tiraboschi, *Biblioteca Modenense, o notizie delle vita e delle opere degli scrittori natii degli stati del serenissimo signor Duca di Modena*, 6 vols. (Modena: Società tipografia, 1783), ii. 234 [London, British Library, 10632.v.31]

Dhuoda

c.803–after 843   Septimania/Uzès (France)
Epigrama Operis Subsequentis: 'Deus, summe lucis conditor, poli'

From *Liber Manualis*:
MSS: Nîmes, Bibliothèque Municipale, 393, fos. 1–32 (fragments) (s. x)
Barcelona, Biblioteca Central, 569, fos. 57–88 (s. xiv)
Paris, Bibliothèque Nationale de France, Lat. 12293, fos. 1–90 (s. xvii)

Editions: Jean Mabillon, *Acta Sanctorum Ordinis Sancti Benedicti*, 9 vols. (Paris: 1668–1701 [not seen]; 2nd edn. Venice: Sebastiano Coleti & Giuseppe Bettinelli, 1733–8), v.1, pp. 704–10 (p. 709) [Vatican City, Biblioteca Apostolica, Ordini Religiosi III Benedittini 7 (1–9)]

PL cvi, cols 109–118

Édouard Bondurand, *L'Éducation carolingienne: Le Manuel de Dhuoda* (Paris: Alphonse Picard, 1887) 47–9, [Aberdeen, University Library, X.879 Dod]

Karl Strecker, 'Rhythmi ex Libro Manuali Dhuodanae Deprompti', *Poetae Latini Aevi Carolini*, 4.2.1 (Berlin: Weidmann, 1914), 701–17, 701–8

Pierre Riché (with French trans.), *Manuel pour mon fils*, Sources Chrétiennes (Paris: Éditions du Cerf, 1975), 72–9

Marcelle Thiébaux (with English trans.), *Dhuoda: Handbook for her Warrior Son* (Cambridge: Cambridge University Press, 1998), 42–7

Dichterinnen des Altertums und des frühen Mittlalters, ed. and (German) trans. Helène Homeyer (Paderborn: F. Schöningh, 1979), 192–5 (text and German trans.)

Translations: Carol Neel, *Handbook for William* (Lincoln: University of Nebraska Press, 1991; 2nd edn. Washington: Catholic University of America Press, 1999)

(Italian) I. Biffi, *Educare nel Medioevo: per la formazione di mio figlio* (Milan: Jaca Book, 1997)

De Temporibus Tuis: 'Quadrans in quatuor iam habes annos usque perductos'

From *Liber Manualis*:
Editions: Mabillon, 709
PL cvi, cols 109–118
Bondurand, 225–6
Strecker, 701–17 (pp. 708–9)
Riché, 338–41
Thiébaux (with English trans.), 218–19

Translations: Neel, 95–6
(Italian) Biffi [not seen]
Homeyer, 198–9 (text and German trans.)

De Versibus ex Litteris Compostis tuis: 'Vt valeas, vigeas, optime prolis'

From *Liber Manualis*:
Editions: Mabillon, 706
PL cvi, cols 109–118
Bondurand, 228–30
Strecker, 701–17 (pp. 710–12)
Riché, 340–7
Thiébaux (with English trans.), 220–3

Translations: Neel, 96–8
(Italian) Biffi [not seen]
Homeyer, 198–9 (text and German trans.)

Hic Lege, Lector, Versiculos Epitaphii: 'De terra formatum, hoc in tumulo Duodane corpus jacet humanum'

From *Liber Manualis*:
Editions: Mabillon, 710
PL cvi, cols 109–118
Bondurand, 240–1
Strecker, 701–17 (pp. 713–14)
Riché, 356–9
Thiébaux (with English trans.), 228–31

Translations: Neel, 101–2
(Italian) Biffi [not seen]
Homeyer, 200–1 (text and German trans.)

Excerpts: Wilhelm Meyer, *Gesammelte Abhandlungen sur Mittelateinische Rhyth-mik*, 3 vols. (Berlin: Weidmann, 1905–36, iii. 72–85, 242–4

Dionigi, Enrica (Orfei)
fl. 1808　　　　　　　　　　　　　　　　　　　　　　　　　Rome (Italy)
Della signora Enrica Dionigi, Romana, fra le pastorelle d'Arcadia Aurilla Gnidio: 'Ut prope jam saecli DIODORUM vincere metam'

　　Edition: *Poesie e prose in morte del cav. Saviero Bettinelli fra gli Arcadi Diodoro Delfico, recitate dai soci de la R. Accademia di Mantova e dai pastori arcdi della colonia Virgiliana* (Mantua: Francesco Agazzi, 1808), 87 [London, British Library, 1451.e.22]

di Somma, Silvia, Marchesa di Bagno
s. xvi　　　　　　　　　　　　　　　　　　　　　　　　　Bagno (Italy)
Described as a Latin poet: only Italian verse known to survive

　　Bandini Buti, i. 244

Domnica, wife of Hosius
late antiquity　　　　　　　　　　　　　　　　　　　　　Milan (Italy)
'Lux patriae, sublime decus pater Osius urbis'

　　Inscription: Janus Gruter (ed.), *Inscriptiones Antiquae Totius Orbis Romanae*, 2 vols. (Heidelberg: Commelin, 1602–3), plate mlvi.8 (there are also reissues 1603, 1616, 1707) [London, British Library, C. 75. i. 3]

Giovanni Battista Ferretti (ed.), *Musae Lapidariae*, 5 vols. in 1 (Verona: Rubeis, 1672), iii. 203 [London, British Library, 143. e. 22]

William Fleetwood (ed.), *Inscriptionum Antiquorum Sylloge*, 2 vols. in 1 (London: William Graves & T. Childe, 1691), ii. 452 [London, British Library, 604. d. 12]

Petrus Burmann (ed.), *Anthologia Veterum Latinorum Epigrammatum et Poematum, sive Catalecta Poetarum Latinorum in VI Libros Digesta*, 6 vols. in 2 (Amsterdam: Schouten, 1759, 1773), ii. 161 (IV.ccxvi) [London, British Library, 54. f. 13]

Heinrich Meyer (ed.), *Anthologia Veterum Latinorum Epigrammatum et Poematum*, 2 vols. in 1 (Leipzig: Gerhard Fleischer, 1835), ii. 131 (1324) [London, British Library, 011388. b. 14]

CIL, v.2, p. 688 (6253)

CLE, ii. 673 (1413)

Druppach, Martha von

mid-s.xvi   Frauenarach (Germany)

'Huc sua Walburgis posuit demortua membra'

Edition: Kaspar Brusch, *Monasteriorum Germaniae Praecipuorum ac Maxime Illustrium Centuria Prima* (Ingolstadt: Alexander & Samuel Weyssenhorn, 155, 39r–v [The Hague, Konincklijke Bibliotheek, 549. B. 6]

Einsiedel, Margaretha Sibylla von (von Bünau, Löser)

1642–90   Altenberg (Germany)

'Haud stabile est quicquam, sunt cuncta obnoxia letho'

Edition: *Mit=traurender Cypressen=Zwieg über den allzufrühen; doch seligen am 2. April beschehenen Antritt der Hoch=Edelgebohrnen Ehr=und Tugendvolkommenen Frauen Fr. Anna Sibyllen Löserin gebohrner Körbitzin Des Hoch= Edelgebohrnen Gestrengen und Vesten Herrn Curt Lösers auff Sahlitz Haynichen Nenckersdorff Reinhards und Meura sc. Churfürstl. Durchl. zu Sachsen wolbestellen Raths und Cammer=Herrn der Chur=Sachsen Erb=Marschalln Auch Ober=Steuer=Einnehmers und der löblischen Landschafft des Hertzogthums Sachsen-Altenburg Directoris &c. Nunmehr wolseligen Eheliebsten auffgestecket und Als Ihr am 29. benenneten Monats der letzten Ehrendienst in der Kirche zu Kohren bey rühmwürdigen Leichbegängniss erzieget wurde schuldiger massen Aus dem Hause Syhra überschicket Im Jahr 1663* (Altenberg: Joh. Bernhard Bauerfincken, [1663]), sig. A2r [Wolfenbüttel, Herzog August Bibliothek, Xa 1: 18 (2)]

Elizabeth I

1558–1603   London (England)

Reginae Responsum: 'Grata Camena tua est, gratissima dona'

Editions: Paul Melissus, *Mele sive Odae ad Noribergam et Septemviros Reipub. Norib.* (Nuremberg: Haeredes Montani, 1575), 72 [Oxford, Bodleian Library, Antiq. e.G.40 (1)]

Leicester Bradner, *Poems of Queen Elizabeth I* (Providence, RI: Brown University Press, 1964), 10

James E. Phillips, 'Elizabeth I as a Latin Poet: An Epigram on Paul Melissus', *Renaissance News*, 16.4 (1963), 289–98 (with trans.)

Jane Stevenson and Peter Davidson (eds.), *Early Modern Women Poets* (Oxford: Oxford University Press, 2001), 29 (with trans.)

GENUS INFOELIX VITAE: 'Multum vigilavi, laboravi, presto multis fui' (with own trans.)

MS: autograph, flyleaf of Henry Bull, *Christian Prayers and Holy Meditations* (London: Henry Middleton, 1570), copy now in the Pierpont Morgan Library, New York

Editions: Carl F. Bühler, 'Libri Impressi cum Notis Manuscriptis', *Modern Language Notes*, 53 (1938), 245–9

Stevenson and Davidson, 28 (with trans.)

[Distich, attributed to Elizabeth on unknown authority: 'In Thalamis Regina: tuis hac nocte cubarem'

Editions: Johann Caspar Eberti, *Eröffnetes Cabinet dess Gelehrten Frauenzimmers* (Frankfurt: Michael Rohrlachs sel. Wittib und Erben, 1700; 2nd edn. (1706), p. 139 (and facsimile edn. Munich: Iudicium, 1990) [Oxford, Taylorian Library, EN. 807. A. 1; London, British Library, 10603. aaa.2]

Georg Christian Lehms, *Teutschlands galante Poetinnen, mit ihren sinnreichen und netten Proben, nebst einem Anhang ausländischer Dames so sich gleichfalls durch schöne Poesien [ben] der curieusen Welt bekannt gemacht* (Frankfurt am Main: Anton Heinscheidt, 1715), pt. II, p. 71] [London, British Library, 11525. dd. 21]

[Jacobus Smalcius (respondent), *Diatriben Academicam de Foeminarum Eruditione, Posteriorem, Consensu Inclutae Facultatis Philosophicae in Almi Lipsiensi* (Leipzig: Johann Erich Hahn, 1676), sig. E 2ᵛ, is incorrect in attributing a Latin verse recorded by Caspar Laudismann in his *Consiliis de Addiscendis Linguis Exoticis Gallia et Italia* (Leipzig: Tobias Beyer, 1614), 100, *Cui regina respondet*: 'Heu nemo adest mortalium', to Elizabeth] [Munich, Bayerische Staatsbibliothek, 4 Diss. 5212]

Emma

s.xii   Le Ronceray (France)

Nothing known to survive

Latin verses praised by Baudri of Bourgeuil: *Les Œuvres poétiques de Baudri de
Bourgeuil (1046–1130): édition critique publiée d'après le Ms du Vatican*, ed.
Phyllis Abrahams (Paris: H. Champion, 1926), 259, 270–3

Eucheria

fl. 2nd half s.vi   Marseille (France)

'Aurea concordi quae fulgent fila metallo'

MSS: Paris, Bibliothèque Nationale de France, Lat. 8071, fo. 58ʳ
Groningen, Universiteitsbibliotheek, 8, fo. 177ᵛ (s. x) [not seen]
Valenciennes, Bibliothèque Municipale, 387 [not seen]
Vienna, Österreichische Nationalbibliothek, Lat. 277, fo. 55 [not seen]
Paris, Bibliothèque Nationale de France, Lat. 8440 [not seen]

Editions: Petrus Burmannus (ed.), *Poetae Latinae Minores* (Leiden: Conrad
   Wishoff and Daniel Goedval, 1731) (and other editions), i, 11, pp. 407–18
   (v. cxxxiii) [London, British Library, 54 f. 13]
Heinrich Meyer (ed.), *Anthologia Veterum Latinorum Epigrammatum et Poema-
   tum*, 2 vols. in 1 (Leipzig: Gerhard Fleischer, 1835), i. 152 (385) [London,
   British Library, 011388. b. 14]
Johann Christian Wernsdorf (ed.), *Poetae Latini Minores*, 10 vols. (Altenberg:
   Richter, 1780–98), iii. 97–102 [London, British Library, 160. k. 10–19]
J. R. Th. Caboret-Dupaty (ed.), *Poetae Latini Minores* (Paris, 1842), 408–16
Alexander Riese (ed.), *Anthologia Latina, sive Poesis Latinae Supplementum*,
   4 vols. (Leipzig: B. G. Teubner, 1868–97), i. 253–4 [Vatican City, Biblioteca
   apostolica, Lett. lat. ant. 1.1.Anthologia.1]
Paul Heinrich Emil Baehrens (ed.), *Poetae Latinae Minores*, 5 vols. (Leipzig:
   B. G. Teubner, 1879–86), v. 361–3 [Oxford, Bodleian Library, 2972. e. 13]
Helène Homeyer (ed. and German trans.), *Dichterinnen des Altertums und des
   frühen Mittelalters* (Paderborn: F. Schöningh, 1979), 185–7

Translation: *WWMA* (partial), 28

<Euphemia (?)

d. 1257   Wherwell, Hampshire (England)

In Obitum Abatissae Matildae: 'Demulcere nequit cantu Philomena dolore'

MS: St Petersburg, Saltykov-Shchedrin Library Q.v.I, 62, fos. 11ʳ–12ᵛ

Edition: A. Staerk, *Les Manuscrits latins du Vᵉ au XIIIᵉ siècle conservés à la Bibliothèque Impériale de Saint-Pétersbourg*, 2 vols. (St Petersburg: Krois, 1910), i. 275 [Aberdeen, University Library, xf4717 Sta]

Euphemia, who wrote the *epistola consolatoria* which follows these verses, is possibly but not certainly their author>

Fabia Pyrallis

Ligurium (Italy)

A Fabio Daphno Fabia Pyrallis coniugi carissimo posuit: '[digna] viro posuit coniunx memorabilis aevo'

Inscription: Ludovico Antonio Muratori (ed.), *Novus Thesaurus Veterum Inscriptionum*, 4 vols. (Milan: Ex Aedibus Palatinis, 1739–42), iii. 1341.10 [London, British Library, 1705. b. 7]

Petrus Burmann (ed.), *Anthologia Veterum Latinorum Epigrammatum et Poematum, sive Catalecta Poetarum Latinorum in VI Libros Digesta*, 6 vols. in 2 (Amsterdam: Schouten, 1759, 1773), ii. 157–8 (IV.ccviii) [London, British Library, 54. f. 13]

Heinrich Meyer (ed.), *Anthologia Veterum Latinorum Epigrammatum et Poematum*, 2 vols. in 1 (Leipzig: Gerhard Fleischer, 1835), ii. 172 (1482) [London, British Library, 011388. b. 14]

Ariodante Fabretti (ed.), *Corpus Inscriptionum Italicarum Antiquioris Aevi* (Augustus Taurinorum: Officina regia, 1867) (III.190) [London, British Library, 7707. g. 8]

CIL, vi.3, p. 1931 (17518)

CLE, ii. 569–70 (1215)

Facula

s. xii?

Germany?

'Facula fulva viri datur hic reli-nempe-giosa'

MS: Munich, Bayerische Staatsbibliothek, Clm 23592 fo. 3 (s. xiv).

Fausta

?

Kemnaden (Germany)

Distich: 'Si facias, quod Fausta jubet, faustissima quaeque'

Edition: C. F. Paullini, *Die Hoch- und Wohl-gelahrte Deutsche Frauen-Zimmer* (Frankfurt: Johnn Cristoph Stösseln, 1705), 40–1 [London, British Library, aa. II. 10705]

Fedele, Cassandra (Mappelli)
1465–1558   Venice (Italy)
Sanctissimo Christi in Terris Vicario Pape Paulo III Cassandra Fidelis Veneta Genibus Flexis: 'Ecclesie culmen: custos pietatis, et aequi'

> *MS*: Venice, Biblioteca Marciana, Lat. XIV. 235 (4714), fo. 13ʳ

> *Edition*: Maria Petrettini, *Vita di Cassandra Fedele* (Venice: Pinelli, 1814), 34 [not seen], 2nd, edn. (Venice: Giuseppe Grimaldo, 1852), 39 [Venice, Biblioteca Marciana, Misc. 686.8]

Ad Lucinam pro vita Grilli, et Francisca que in puerperio obiit: 'Infantem mirare novum quem Grillus alumnus'

> *MS*: Venice, Biblioteca Marciana, Lat. XIV. 235 (4714), fo. 13ʳ

'Calcavi quae omnes optant meliora secuta'

> *Edition*: Petrettini, *Vita*, 19 [not seen], 2nd edn. 24

'Dant tibi Rhamnusi, Musae de nomine nomen'

> *Edition*: Petrettini, *Vita*, 41 [not seen], 2nd edn., 43 (given to Petrettini by the Abate Moschini, note p. 43)

Fitzalan, Lady Jane (Lumley)
(1956–76)   Cheam (England)
'Vixi dum volui, volui dum, Christi, volebas'

> *Inscription*: *in situ*, St Dunstan's, Cheam, Surrey

> *Editions*: John Aubrey, *The Natural History and Antiquities of Surrey, Begun in the Year 1673*, 5 vols. (London: E. Curll, 1719), ii. 114–15 [London, British Library, 290. b. 27–31]
> George Ballard, *Memoirs of Several Ladies of Great Britain Who Have Been Celebrated for their Writings or Skill in the Learned Languages, Arts and Sciences* (Oxford: W. Jackson for the Author, 1752), p. 122 (with translation) [Oxford: Bodleian Library, DD. 1.Jur]
> George Ballard, *Memoirs of Several Ladies of Great Britain Who Have Been Celebrated for their Writings or Skill in the Learned Languages, Arts and Sciences*, ed. Ruth Perry (Detroit: Wayne State University Press, 1985), 145

Freire, Maria, Marquesa de Vila Real

early s. xvi   Portugal

'Existem nao so cartas mas igualmente poemas latinas'

Attribution in Carolina Michaëlis de Vasconcelas, *A Infanta D. Maria de Portugal (1521–1577), e as suas damas* (Lisbon: Biblioteca Nacional, 1983) (facsimile of 1st edn. Oporto, 1902, with introduction by Americo da Costa Ramalho), p. viii.

Friesin, Henrietta Catharina von (Gersdorff)

1648–1726   Halle (Germany)

In Conjugium Princ. Sax. et Dan.: 'Purpureas Matuta genas, ac plena rosarum' (1666)

> *Editions*: Sebastian Kortholt, *Disquisitio de Poetriis Puellis, Omissis ab Adriano Bailleto* (Keil: Berthold Reuther, 1700), 29 [Wolfenbüttel, Herzog August Bibliothek, Da. 271]
>
> Justus Henricus Langschmidt, *De Feminis Prima Aetate Eruditione ac Scriptis Illustribus* (Wittenberg, 1700), 16 [London, British Library, 8385. df. 2 (17)]
>
> Johann Dietrich Starck, *De Feminis Prima Aetate Eruditione ac Scriptis Illustribus et Nobilibus* (Wittenberg: Gerdesianus, 1703), 16 [Wolfenbüttel, Herzog August Bibliothek, 77.2. QuN (38)]

Carmen Gratulatorium in Auspicatissimum Conjugium Serenissimum Principum (Johann Georg III) (Dresden, 1667)

> *Edition*: quotations (14 lines in all) in Jacobus Smalcius (response), Johannes Sauerbrei, *Diatriben Academicam de Foeminam Eruditione, Posteriorem, Consensu Inclutae Facultatis Philosophicae in Alma Lipsiensi, sub Praesidio…* *M. Jacobi Thomasii* (Leipzig: Johann Erich Hahn, 1671), § 50, sig. E4r [Munich, Bayerische Staatsbibliothek, 4 Diss. 5212]

Carmen Heroicum Imperatori Leopoldi I. Sacrum, 1690 [not seen]

SKGF, 35

Further Latin verse

> Attested by C. F. Paullini, *Das Hoch- und Wohl-gelahrte Teutsche Frauen-Zimmer* (Frankfurt: Johnn Cristoph Stösseln, 1705), 53; 2nd edn. 1712 [London, British Library, 1705.aa.11; Munich, Bayerische Staatsbibliothek, H. Lit. p. 290

Friis, Lyche Sophia
1699–after 1719　　　　　　　　　　　　　　　　Odense/Lund (Denmark)
Dend Salig, Doctor Morten Luther, indføres saaledes takkendes og talendes til Danmarks og Norges, de Venders og Gothers, Hertuger udi Slesvig, Holstein, Stamarn og Ditmersken, Grever udi Oldenborg og Delmenhost, Stoormægtigste Konger, paa Jubel-Fæsten 1717: [opens with 22 lines of Danish, inc. 'Tak, Förste Friderich, for Du toog ind i Norden'] 'Tentarunt portas Erebi subvertere Waldus'

> *Editions*: *In Festum Magnum Jubilaeum, Anno 1717 Editum, et Augustissimo Danorum Monarchae, Friderico Quarto Oblatum, Postea quoque Hilariis Evangelicis Excelentiss. Ernesti Sal. Cypriani* (Copenhagen: John. Bircherod, 1717) [also 2nd edn. Gotha, 1719, not seen], printed in Albert Thrura, *Gynaeceum Daniae Litterarum: Feminis Danorum Eruditione vel Scriptis Claris Conspicuum* (Altona: Jonas Korte, 1732), 61–2 [Wolfenbüttel, Herzog August Bibliothek, M: Da. 517]

> Friedrich Christian Schönau, *Samling af Danske lærde Fruentimer*, 2 vols. (Copenhagen: J. W. Bopp, 1753), 633–6 [London, British Library, 275. c. 14]

Carmen Gratulatorium in Nuptias Celsissimi Danorum Principis Christiani, et Illustr. ac Clementissimae Principis Sophiae Magdalenae, Danice, Germanice, Gallice, Latine et Graece Elaboratum [not seen]

> Described by Thrura, 62

Til kong Friderick den Fierde: 'Ut fugiunt horae, sic non consumimur horis' (Copenhagen, 1 Jan. 1719), issued as broadsheet

> Printed Schönau, 636–41

'*Carmina varia* (sed nondum impressa)'

> Attested by Thrura, 62

Fuficia Agra
?　　　　　　　　　　　　　　　　Spalato (Croatia, former Yugoslavia)
'Crudeles Parcae nimium matercula dicit'

> *Inscription*:
> M. P. Katančić (ed.), *Istri Adcolarum Geographia Vetus e Monumentis Epigraphicis... Illustrata*, 2 parts in 1 vol. (Buda: University of Hungary, 1826–7), ii. 29 (190) [London, British Library, 10205. ee. 1]
> Heinrich Meyer (ed.), *Anthologia Veterum Latinorum Epigrammatum et Poematum*, 2 vols. (Leipzig: Gerhard Fleischer, 1835), i. 183 (1532) [London, British Library, 011388. b. 14]

CIL, iii.1, p. 335 (2341), also suppl. 8623
CLE, ii. 564 (1204)

Gad, Cille

c.1675–1711 Bergen/Copenhagen (Denmark)
Verse letter (80 distichs) addressed to Otto Sperling Jr.

MS: Copenhagen, Kongelige Bibliotek, Ny kgl. saml 596 (4) [not seen]

Avitae, hoc est Nobilissimae, Spei Pereximio Praesidi, Domino Thomae Jacobaeo:
'Invia Virtuti via nulla putatur, & adde:'

Editions: Th. Jacobæus 1708, *Dissertatio de Oculis Insectorum* (Copenhagen: Reg.
Majest. et Universit. Typographeo, 1708), 17–18 [London, British Library,
B. 561 (9)]
Albert Thrura, *Gynaeceum Daniae Litterarum: Feminis Danorum Eruditione vel
Scriptis Claris Conspicuum* (Altona: Jonas Korte, 1732), 64 [Wolfenbüttel,
Herzog August Bibliothek, M: Da. 517]
Friedrich Christian Schönau, *Samling af Danske lærde Fruentimer*, 2 vols.
(Copenhagen: J. W. Bopp, 1753), 666 [London, British Library, 275. c. 14]

Gagis, Sibylla de

s. xii Nivelles/Aywières (Belgium)
Epitaphium Liutgardis

Inscription: attested by Joannes Molanus, *Ad Natales Sanctorum Belgii Auctuar-
ium* (Douai: Petrus Auroy, 1626), 209; it may survive as an inscription at
Aywières [London, British Library, 1371. c. 1]

Galíndez de Carvajal, Beatriz (Ramírez)

1475–1534 Madrid (Spain)
Latin verse [not seen]

Attested by Francisco Ximénez, *Carro de las doñas* (Valladolid, 1542), bk. II, ch. 63,
and said to be edited in M. Menéndez Pelayo, *Antología de poetas líricos castella-
nos III* (Madrid: Viuda de Hernando c.a., 1944), 22, 34, 114–16 [not seen]

Gàmbara, Veronica (da Correggio)

1485–1550 Brescia/Bologna/Correggio (Italy)
Auspiciat. Victoria Caesari: 'Inger ingentes pateras minister'

Edition: Luigi Amaduzzi, *Undici lettere inedite di Veronica Gambara e un'ode
Latine tradotta in volgare* (Guastalla: R. Pecorini, 1889), 17–18 [Vatican City,
Biblioteca Apostolica, Coll. Gen. II 9 (int. 2)]

Eadem Veronica Lectori: 'Hannibalis primos quisquis duce Pallade fructus'

> *Editions*: *Hannibalis Camilli Corrigiensis Artium et Medicinae Doctoris de Subiecto Totius Logicae Questio, de Maximo et Minimo, Quadraginta Asinaria Sophismata* (Bologna: Benedictus Hectoria, 23 Nov. 1520), sig. G 3ᵛ [Florence, Biblioteca nazionale centrale, B. 17 misc. 7. 60. 5]
>
> Girolamo Tiraboschi, *Biblioteca Modenense, o notizie delle vita e delle opere degli scrittori natii degli stati del serenissimo signor Duca di Modena*, 6 vols. (Modena: Società tipografia, 1783), ii. 135 [London, British Library, 10632. v. 31]

<Gerlinda
?   Hohenburg (Germany)
Anagrammata et Carmina Varia [not seen]

> Attested by Louis Jacob, 'Bibliothèque des femmes illustres par leurs écrits', Paris, Bibliothèque Nationale de France, Ancien fonds français 22865, fo. 90ᵛ, who states that she was Abbess of Hohenburg. She is therefore probably a double of Richlindis (q.v.)>

Gersdorff, Charlotta Juliana
s. xvii   Germany
Latin verse [not seen]

> Attested by Johann Caspar Eberti, *Eröffnetes Cabinet dess Gelehrten Frauenzimmers* (Frankfurt: Michael Rohrlachs sel. Wittib und Erben, 1700; 2nd edn. 1706) 161 (facsimile edn. Munich: Iudicium, 1990) [Oxford, Taylorian Library, EN. 807. A. 1; London, British Library, 10603. aaa. 2]

Gertrude the Great/Gertrude of Helfta
s. xiii   Helfta (Germany)
Quatrains in Exercitia Spiritualia VII: Praeparatio ad Mortem: 'Causa tibi sit agnita', 'Externi huc advenimus', 'Dives pauper effectus es', 'Felix, qui sitit, Charitas', 'Grandis est tibi gloria'

> *Editions*: *Revelationes Gertrudianae ac Mechtildianae*, ed. Monks of Solesmes, 2 vols. (Poitiers: Henri Oudin, 1875–7), i. 703, 705, 707, 712, 714 [London, British Library, 3706. f. 1]
>
> Gertrude la Grande, *Œuvres spirituelles*, ed. J. Hourlier and A. Schmitt, Sources Chrétiennes 127 (Paris: Éditions du Cerf, 1967), with (French) trans. pp. 268–9, 272–3, 278–9, 288–9, 294–5
>
> *Translation*: a Benedictine nun of Regina Laudis, *The Exercises of Saint Gertrude* (Westminster, Md.: Newman Press, 1956)

Ghezzi, Aura
fl. before 1574   Ravenna (Italy)
Elegy in Praise of the Virgin (Latin hexameters)

Lost: described but not printed by Tomaso Tomai, *Historia di Ravenna, divisa in quattor parti* (Ravenna: Francesco Tebaldini da Osimo, 1580), pt. iv, p. 211 [London, British Library, 172. c. 22]

Giovio, Cassandra (Magnocavallo)
b. 1538/43   Milan (Italy)
'de duodecim fontibus Comum ambientibus'

Attested by Bandini Buti, i. 303–4, who states that an Italian translation by M. (Maurizio?) Monti was published, but does not say where (it is not in Maurizio Monti, *Storia di Como*, 3 vols. (Como: Co' Torchi di c. Pietro Ostinelli, 1829))

Girard, Annie
s. xviii   Paris (France)
'Vers Latins, à la Reine, sur son entrée à Paris'

Attested by Fortunée B. Briquet, *Dictionnaire historique, littéraire, et bibliographique des françaises et des étrangères naturalisées en France* (Paris: De Gillé, 1804), 157 (and facsimile edn. Indigo et Côté-femmes Éditions, 1997) [Paris, Bibliothèque Sainte Geneviève, Passerole M cote 8Y sup. 67353]

Godewijk, Margaretha van
1627–77   Dordrecht (the Netherlands)
In Historiam Restaurationis Celsissimi et Invictissimi Principis Caroli II, Magnae Britanniae, Franciae, et Hyberniae Regis, a Doctissimo Viro Lamberto Sylvio Descriptam: 'Vir praestans, quondam, nobis funesta dedisti'

Edition: Konincklijke Beeltenis of Waerachtige Historie van Karel de II, trans. Lambert van Bos (Dordrecht: Abraham Andriesz, 1661), sig. *5^{r-v} [London, British Library, G. 96. 1]

In Symbolum meum, Deus nostrum Asylum: 'Seu moror seu vivo, meum sit Christus Asylum'

MS: The Hague, Konincklijke Bibliotheek, 128. F. 10, fo. 51^r

Ad Cives Dordracenos: 'Hos, qui Dordrechti sedetis'

MS: The Hague, Konincklijke Bibliotheek, 128. F. 10, fo. 56^{r-v}

In Furentes et Fanaticos Anglos, Bellum Gerentes Adversus Batavos: 'Angli veniunt destruentes'

MS: The Hague, Konincklijke Bibliotheek, 128. F. 10, fos. 56^v–57^r

Responsio ad Parentum meum Charissimum, D. Petrum Godewyck, quum Nuper ad me Dedisset Versus suos Latinos Rhythmicos: 'Pater chare cum legissem'

MS: The Hague, Konincklijke Bibliotheek, 128. F. 10, fos. 59^r–60^v

In Creatorem Mundi: 'Sancta manu condedisti'

MS: The Hague, Konincklijke Bibliotheek, 128. F. 10, fos. 60^v–61^r

In Laudem Doctissimi Viri, Clarissimique Iohannis Beverovici, Teabini et Doctoris Medicinae Primarie apud Dordracenos: 'Quid jam sento, si vis scire'

MS: The Hague, Konincklijke Bibliotheek, 128. F. 10, fo. 61^r

Gonzaga, Cecilia
d. 1451   Mantua (Italy)
Latin verse

Attested by Gregorio Correr who heard her reciting it, *Gregorii Corrarii Proto-notaris Apostolico ad Caeceliam Gonzagam*, in Ambrogio Traversari, *Epistolae et Orationes* (Florence: Typ. Caesareas, 1759), cols. 1064–76 (col. 1074) [Vatican Library, Biblioteca Apostolica, Lett. Lat. Mod. III Traversari.folio 1 (2)]

Grey, Lady Jane (Dudley)
1537–54   London (England)
'Certaine Verses Written by the Said Lady Iane with a Pin': 'Non aliena putes homini' (1554)

Inscription: originally in Tower of London

Editions: T. Bentley (ed.), *The Monument of Matrones Conteining Seven Severall Lamps of Virginitie, or Distinct Treatises*, 3 vols. (London: H. Denham, 1582) i. 102 [London, British Library, G. 12047–9]

George Ballard, *Memoirs of Several Ladies of Great Britain Who Have Been Celebrated for their Writings or Skill in the Learned Languages, Arts and Sciences* (Oxford: W. Jackson for the Author, 1752), 116–18 [Oxford, Bodleian Library, DD.1.Jur]

[Elizabeth Tollet], *Poems on Several Occasions, with Anne Boleyn to King Henry the Eighth: An Epistle* (London: John Clarke, 1724), 27 (with trans.) [London, British Library, 1490. k. 1]

Elizabeth Tollet, *Poems on Several Occasions, with Anne Boleyn to King Henry VIII, an Epistle* (London: John Clarke, 1755), 33 (with trans.) [London, British Library, 11631. aa. 37]

George Ballard, *Memoirs of Several Ladies of Great Britain Who Have Been Celebrated for their Writings or Skill in the Learned Languages, Arts and Sciences*, ed. Ruth Perry (Detroit: Wayne State University Press, 1985), 140

Jane Stevenson and Peter Davidson (eds.), *Early Modern Women Poets* (Oxford: Oxford University Press, 2001), 43–4 (with trans.)

Grimaldi, Polissena

s. xv/xvi   Verona (Italy)

Oratio Continens Laudes Excelentissimi Domini Domini Francesci Sfortie Comitis Illustrissimi Edita per Polisenam de Grimaldis de Verona: 'Flammiger eois totam surgebat ab oris'

MSS: Florence, Biblioteca Laurentiana, Cod. lat. 56, plut. 90 sup. 56, fos. 57^v–58^r
London, British Library, Add. 19061, 26^r–28^r

Ad Serenissimam et Excelentissimam Dominam Dominam Blancham de Vicecomitibus Comitissae Gloriosissimam: 'Vellem posse tibi calamo illustrissimo princeps'

MS: Florence, Biblioteca Laurentiana, Cod. lat. Laurent. 56, plut. 90 sup. 56, 58^{r-v}

'H'

fl. s. xii   Tegernsee (Germany)
'S. suo dilecto'

MS: Munich, Bayerische Staatsbibliothek, Clm 19411, fos. 69^r–70^r

Editions: MLREL, ii. 472–3 (with trans.)
Jürgen Kühnel, *Du bist mîn, ih bin dîn. Die lateinischen Leibes-(und Freundschafts-) Briefe des Clm 19411* (Göppingen: Kummerle, 1977) (with German trans.), 50–1

Hadwig

c.947–971   Essen (Germany)
'Hic supplex Hadauuih Pinnosae virginis almum'

Edition: Karl Strecker and Gabriel Silagi (eds.), *Die lateinischen Dichten des deutschen Mittelalters*, v: *Die Ottonenzeit* (Leipzig: Karl W. Hiersemann; Munich: Verlag des Monumenta Germaniae Historica, 1937–79), 675

Hantschel, Anna (Lauban)

1574–1626   Sprottau/Brieg (Germany)

Ad Aemiliam Melissam [Aemilia Jordan, q.r., wife of Paul Schede/Melissus]: 'Parne tuo nostrum sit munus, ô æmula cantu'

> *Edition*: Johann Caspar Eberti, *Schlesiens Hoch- und Wohlgelehrtes Frauenzimmer nebst unterschiedenen Poetinnen so sich durch schöne und artige Poesien ben der curieusen Welt bestandt gemacht* (Wrocław: Michael Rohrlach, 1727), 39–40 (facsimile edn. Munich: Iudicium, 1990) [London, British Library, 10707.bb.35 (1)]

<?Heloïse

*c.*1095–1164

> Léopold Delisle tentatively suggested she was the anonymous nun of Argenteuil who contributed to the mortuary roll of Bishop Vitalis, since she was in the house at the time when it was presented (Léopold Delisle (ed.), *Rouleaux des morts du ixe au xve siècle recueillis et publiés par la Société de l'Histoire de France* (Paris: Veuve J. Renouard, 1866), 299, see below under 'Nuns of Argenteuil'), a suggestion supported by Constant Mews (*The Lost Love Letters of Heloise and Abelard: Perceptions of Dialogue in Twelfth-Century France* (New York: St Martins Press, 1999), 162–3)

> Mews, drawing on the pioneering work of Ewald Könsgen, has also made a strong case that she is author of the poems in a female voice in *Epistolae Duorum Amantium*, which are therefore presented here:

'Oculo suo'

> *MS*: Troyes, Bibliothèque Municipale, 1452 (*c.*1471), fos. 159^r–167^v [not seen]

> *Editions*: Ewald Könsgen (ed.), *Epistolae Duorum Amantium* (Leiden: Brill, 1974), no. 27, p. 17
> Mews, 212–13 (with trans.)

'Nolis atque velis, tibi corde manebo fidelis'

> *Editions*: Könsgen, no. 38b, pp. 20–1
> Mews, no. 38b. pp. 218–21

'Sicut in axe poli nil est equabile soli'

Editions: Könsgen, no. 49, p. 26
Mews, 230–1

'Omine felici ceptis assis, Clio, nostri.'

Editions: Könsgen, no. 66, p. 37
Mews, 246–7

'Littera, vade meas et amico ferte querelas'

Editions: Könsgen, no. 69, pp. 38–9
Mews, 248–9

'Flos juvenis ave, lux et decus imperiale'

Editions: Könsgen, no. 73, p. 41
Mews, 252–3

'Quam michimet vellem mitti, tibi mitto salutem'

Editions: Könsgen, no. 82, pp. 46–7
Mews, 260–3

'Laudis honor, probitatis amor, gentilis honestas'
MS: London, British Library, Add. 24199

> *Editions*: André Boutemy, 'Recueil poétique du manuscrit Additional British
> Museum 24199', *Latomus*, 2 (1938), 31–52 (pp. 42–4)
> Gerald A. Bond, *The Loving Subject: Desire, Eloquence and Power in Romanesque
> France* (Philadelphia: University of Pennsylvania Press, 1995), 166–9 (with
> trans.)
> Mews, 164–6 (with trans.): he suggests, pp. 167–8, that Heloïse may be the
> author>

Helpis
s. vi?   Sicily/Rome (Italy)
<Two hymns, both in honour of SS Peter and Paul

> Repeatedly attributed to 'Helpis', described as the wife of Boethius (whose wife
> was in fact called Rusticiana). Dag Norberg has demonstrated that one is by
> Paulinus of Aquileia, the other by a Carolingian imitator (*L'Œuvre poétique de
> Paulin d'Aquilée* (Stockholm: Almqvist & Wiksell, 1979), 76 n. 12)>

'Helpis dicta fui, Siculae regionis alumna'

Inscription: probably no longer surviving as such: it was in Rome in the portico of St Peter's

MS: Paris, Bibliothèque Nationale de France, Lat. 2832, fo. 120ᵛ (s. viii)

Editions: Lilius Gregorius Giraldus, *Historiae Poetarum qua Graecam tam Latinam Dialogi Decem*, (Basel, 1545), 651 (partial) [Vatican City, Biblioteca apostolica, R.G. Classici 1726]

Petrus Pithoeus (ed.), *Epigrammata et Poematia Vetera*, 2 vols. (Paris: N. Gillius, 1590), ii. 115 [London, British Library, 1001.e.1]

Franciscus Sweertius (ed.), *Epitaphia Joco-seria* (Cologne; B. Gualther, 1623), 41 [London, British Library, 1213. d. 32]

Philippe Labbé (ed.), *Thesaurus Epitaphium Veterum ac Recentiorum* (Paris, 1666), 103 [London, British Library, 11405. bb. 18]

Georg Christian Lehms, *Teutschlands galante Poetinnen mit ihren sinnreichen und netten Proben, nebst einem Anhang ausländlischer Dames so sich gleichfalls durch schone Poesien bey der curieusen Welt bekannt gemacht, und eine Vorrede: Dass das Weibliche Geschlecht so geschickt zum Studieren, als das männliche* (Frankfurt am Main: Anton Heinscheidt for Samuel Tobias Hocter, 1745), repr. Zentralantiquariat der DDR (Leipzig, 1973), 78 [Cambridge, University Library, 746.17.d.95.33]

Io. Christianus Wolf, *Mulierum Graecum quae Oratione Prosa Usae sunt Fragmenta et Elogia Graece et Latinae* (Hamburg: Abraham Vandenhoeck, 1735), 329–30 [Vatican City, Biblioteca Apostolica, Ferraioli III. 931]

CLE, ii. 683 (1432)

H. Geist and G. Pfohl (eds. and German trans.), *Römische Grabinschriften* (Munich: Ernst Heimeran Verlag, 1969), 193 (530)

Translations: anon. [Mark Lewis?], *Essay to Revive the Antient Education of Gentlewomen* (London: J.D., 1673), 19 [London, British Library, 1031. g. 19]

WWMA, 25–6

Henrici, Charlotte Amalia

d. 1779   Altona (Germany)

A memoir by her husband, a professor of Altona, states that she wrote Latin, among other languages, and composed verse: 'Auszug eines Schreibens, den Todt der Frau Professorinn Henrici, zu Altona, betreffend, for ihrem Wittber, an einen Prediger im Herzogthum Gotha', in Charlotte Henriette Hezel, *Wochenblatt für's schöne Geschlecht* ([Ilmenau, 1779]; repr. Hanau: Müller & Kiepenheuer, 1967), 250–1 [Wolfenbüttel, Herzog August Bibliothek, 24.693]

Herder, Elizabeth

2nd half s. xvi   Heidelberg (Germany)

Memoriae et Honori M. Laurentii Herderinus Lochensis &c., Elisabetha Uxor: 'Vitae curriculo gravi et molesto'

Inscription: not known to be extant

Edition: Melchior Adam (ed.), *Apographum Monumentorum Haidelbergensium, Accesit Mantissa Neoburgicorum ad Nicrum, et Aliorum* (Heidelberg: Andreas Cambierius, 1612), 50 [The Hague, Konincklijke Bibliotheek, 3107. B. 3]

Herrad of Hohenburg

1125/30–95   Hohenburg (Germany)

Rithmus de eo quod Adam de uetito pomo comedit: 'Die quadam'

Edition: *Hortus Deliciarum*, ed. Rosalie Green et al., Studies of the Warburg Institute 36, 2 vols. (London: Warburg Institute, 1979), fo. 18ʳ, no. 69 (MS now destroyed)

De Primo Homine. Rithmus: 'Primus parens hominum'

Editions: Green et al., no. 374

Fiona Griffiths: 'Herrad of Hohenbourg and the Poetry of the Hortus Deliciarum', in Laurie Churchill, Phyllis R. Brown, and Jane E. Jeffrey (eds.), *Women Writing Latin from Roman Antiquity to Early Modern Europe*, 3 vols. (New York: Routledge, 2002) ii. 231–63 (pp. 246–50, 256–60) (with trans.)

Rithmus de Domini nostro Jhesu Christo: 'O Rex pie'

Editions: Green et al., no. 595
Griffiths, 250–2, 260–2

Rithmus Herradis Abbatisse per quem Hohenburgenses Virgunculas Amabiliter Salutat et ad Veri Sponsi Fidem Dilectionemque Salubriter Invitat: 'salve cohors virginum'

Editions: Kaspar Brusch, *Monasteriorum Germaniae Praecipuorum ac Maxime Illusrium Centuria Prima* (Ingolstadt: Alexander & Samuel Weyssenhorn, 1551), 155ʳ–156ʳ [The Hague, Konincklijke Bibliotheek, 549. B. 6]
Magnoald Ziegelbauer, *Historia Rei Leterariae Ordinis S. Benedicti*, 4 vols. (Augsburg: M. Veith, 1754), iii. 509–10 [Vatican City, Biblioteca Apostolica, Bibliografia Folio.Benedettini I (1–4)]

PL cxciv, cols. 1539–42
Green et al., no. 1
Griffiths, 141–6, 153–6 (with trans.)

Ejusdem Herradis ad easdem Sorores Tetrastichon: 'O nivei flores dantes virtutis odores'

   Editions: Brusch, 156ʳ
   Ziegelbauer, 510
   PL cxciv, col. 1541
   Green et al., fo. 323ʳ, cat. no. 346
   Griffiths, 252, 262 (with trans.)

Ejusdem ad Christum Distichon: 'Esto nostrorum pia meres Christi laborum'

   Brusch, 156ʳ
   Ziegelbaur, 510
   PL cxciv, col. 1541
   Green et al., fo. 323ʳ, cat. no. 346
   Griffiths, 252, 262 (with trans.)

Hessen-Kassel, Catharina Ursula, Landgräfin von
1593–1615   Karlsburg / Marburg (Germany)
'Christe, tuum verbum da credere, daque fateri'

   Editions: Georg Christian Lehms, *Teutschlands galante Poetinnen mit ihren sinn-reichen und netten Proben, nebst einem Anhang ausländlischer Dames so sich gleichfalls durch schöne Poesien bey der curieusen Welt bekannt gemacht, und eine Vorrede: Dass das weibliche Geschlecht so geschickt zum Studieren, als das männliche* (Frankfurt am Main: Anton Heinscheidt for Samuel Tobias Hocter, 1745; repr. Leipzig: Zentralantiquariat der DDR, 1973), 20 [Cambridge, University Library, 746.17.d.95.33]
   Johann Caspar Eberti, *Eröffnetes Cabinet dess Gelehrten Frauen-zimmers*, (Frankfurt: Michael Rohrlachs sel. Wittib und Erben, 1700; 2nd edn. 1706), 82–3 (facsimile edn. Munich: Iudicium, 1990) [Oxford, Taylorian Library, EN. 807. A. 1; London, British Library, 10603. aaa. 2]

<Heugelis
high Middle Ages   Hungary
Prophetia S. Heugelide, Filie Regis Ungariae: 'O insigne lilium roratum principibus'

   MS: Munich, Bayerische Staatsbibliothek, Clm 14134, fo. 26ᵛ (s. xv)>

Hildegard of Bingen[2]

1098–1179 Disibodenberg, Rupertsberg (Germany)

Symphonia armonie celestium revelationum

MSS: Dendermonde, St Pieters-&-Paulus abdij cod. 9, fos. 153ʳ–170ᵛ (Ruperts-berg, *c*.1175)

Wiesbaden, Hessischen Landesbibliothek Hs. 2, fos. 466ʳᵃ–481ᵛᵇ (Rupertsberg, 1180–90)

Stuttgart, Würrtembergischen Landesbibliothek Cod. Theol. Phil. 4° 253 (s. xii), fo. 40ᵛ

Vienna, Österreichischen Nationalbibliothek 881, fos. 205ʳᵇ and 405ᵛᵃ (s. xii)

Vienna, Österreichischen Nationalbibliothek 1016, fo. 118ᵛ (s. xiii)

Vienna, Österreichischen Nationalbibliothek 963 (s. xiii)

Editions: *Die Lieder der hl. Hildegard*, ed. Ludwig Bronarski (Leipzig: Breitkopf & Härtel, 1992) [edition of music only incidentally concerned with words]

Lieder, ed. and (German) trans. Pudentiana Barth OSB, M. Immaculata Ritscher, OSB, and Joseph Schmidt-Görg (Salzburg: Otto Kuller, 1969)

Symphonia, ed. and trans. Barbara Newman (Ithaca, NY: Cornell University Press, 1988; 2nd edn. 1998)

Louanges, ed. and (French) trans. Laurence Moulinier (Paris: E.L.A. La Dif-férence, 1990)

Hildegundis

Carmina in Honorem Joannis Baptistae (not preserved)

Attested by Caesarius of Heisterbach, *Illustrium Miraculorum et Historiarum Memorabilium, Libri XII* (Cologne: Arnoldus Mylius, 1591), viii, ch. 50, pp. 164–5 [Wolfenbüttel, Herzog August Bibliothek, Alvensleben Ac. 456]

Hone, Jocosa

late s. xvi London (England)

'Ecce sub hoc tumulo Gulielmus conditur Honus'

Inscription: survives *in situ* on the north wall of the nave in St Bartholomew the Less, Faringdon ward, London

Edition: Edward Hatton, *A New View of London*, 2 vols. (London: R. Chiswell, R & J. Churchill, T. Horne, J. Nicholson, and R. Knaplock, 1708), i. 148 (a very inaccurate text) [London, British Library, E/351. 7–8]

---

[2] Listing of manuscripts is based on the work of Barth, Ritscher, Schmidt-Görg and Newman, to whom the reader is referred.

Hoofman, Elisabeth (Koolaart)
1664–1736   Haarlem/Lisse (the Netherlands) / Kassel (Germany)
Ad Clarissimum Virum Theodorum Janssonium ab Almeloveen, De Recuperata eius Sanitate, Ode Gratulatoria: 'Nunc juvat laetis resonare chordis' (1696)

> *Edition*: J. G. Schelhorn, *Amoenitates Literariae, Quibus Variae Observationes, Scripta item Quaedam Anecdota et Rariora Opuscula Exhibentur*, 14 vols. (Frankfurt: Daniel Bartholomaeus, 1726), v. 200–1 [Harold Jantz collection of German Baroque Literature, no. 2216, reel 457]

Messias, of heylige herdes-zang op de geboorte van den Heyland ... bij ... den Kersdag toegezangen, in Latyns en Nederduyts gedigt an Karel I, Landgraaf van Hessen: 'Pastorum cantus Zerebiae et agrestis Iasis' (1729) (n.p., 1729) [The Hague, Konincklijke Bibliotheek, 852. B. 294]

Caroliportus Conditori suo Caroli Hassiæ Landgravio, Dedicatus ipso eius Natali xix Kal. Sept. 1724: 'Magne, quem votis hodie secundis'

> *Edition*: *De Naaglaatene Gedichten von Elizabeth Koolaart geb. Hoofman*, ed Willem Kops (Haarlem: Jan Bosch, 1774), 161–72 [The Hague, Konincklijke Bibliotheek, 1350. B. 105]

Ode in Expeditionem Guillielmi III contra Gallos: 'Quis fabulosas semideum manus'

> *Edition*: Kops, 173–8

Ad Clarissimum Virum Theodorum Janssonium ab Almeloveen cum I Academia Harderovicena Professionem Historiarum et Eloquentiae Auspicaretur, viii Kal. Maii, 1697: 'Magnum Thespiadum decus sororum'

> *Edition*: Kops, 179–80

Ad Maritum Petrum Colartium, Pro Thesauro Antiquitatum Graevi sibi in Strenam Ablato: 'Quantum cum caput efferens decorum'

> *Edition*: Kops, 179–82

In Funere Blandissimi Pueri Justi Abraham Hoofmanni, e Fratre Nepotis, Defuncti VI non. Mart. 1725

> *Edition*: Kops, 183–6

Carolus Ecloga in Natalem Septuagesimum Tertium Caroli I Hassiæ Landgravis, celebratum xix Kal. Sept. 1726: 'Thyrsis, ne teneros malesanum laederet agnos'

Edition: Kops, 187–92

Carmina in Nuptias Petri Colasii et Elisae Hofmannae, Celebratur Harlemi X Kal Aug. 1693

Edition: Kops, 193–5

Hrotsvitha of Gandersheim[3]

c. 935–*c.*1000   Gandersheim (Germany)
Dedicatio: 'Salve, regalis proles clarissima stirpis'
MSS: Munich, Bayerische Staatsbibliothek, Clm 14485 (Em. E 108) (s. xi)
Pommersfelden, Gräflich Schönbornsche Bibliothek, 308 (2888) (s. xvi^in) (copy
   of above made by Theodorius Gresemundus)
<lost: 'opera Hrosvite illustris monialis', Altzelle, Cistercian Monastery, 03,
   mentioned in MS catalogue of the library, 'Monasterii Veteris Cellae
   Abbates' (1514) in Leipzig, Universitätsbibliothek, 678)>

Editions: *Hrosvite Illustris Virginis et Monialis Germano Gente Saxonica Orte
   Opera Nuper à Conrado Celte Inventa* (Nuremberg: Hieronymus Holtzel,
   sub Privilegio Sodalitis [*sic*] Celticae, 1501) (based on Munich, Clm 14485,
   which contains everything except *Primordia* and the lost *Vitae Paparum*)
   [Wolfenbüttel, Herzog August Bibliothek, A:113 Quod. 2º]
Hroswithae Opera, ed. H. L. Schurtzfleisch (Wittenberg: Schroedter, 1707)
   [Wolfenbüttel, Herzog August Bibliothek, M: QuN 245 (1)]
Opera, PL cxxxvii, cols. 939–1208
Die Werke der Hrotsvitha ed. K. A. Barack (Nuremberg, Bauer & Raspe, 1858)
   [Paris, Bibliothèque Nationale de France, YC-10969]
Opera, ed. Paul von Winterfeld, Scriptores Rerum Germanicarum (Berlin:
   Weidmann, 1902; 2nd edn. 1912)
Hrotsvithae Opera, ed. Karl Strecker (Leipzig: Teubner, 1906; 2nd edn. 1930)
I poemetti di Hrotsvit, ed. F. Ermini, Poeti epici Latini del secolo X (Rome:
   Istituto Angelo Calogera, 1920)
'*The Non-dramatic Works of Hrotswitha*', ed. and trans. Sr. M. Gonsalva Wie-
   gand (Ph. D. diss., St Louis University, 1936)
Hrotsvithae Opera, ed. Helène Homeyer (Munich: F. Schöningh, 1970), 40
Œuvres poétiques, ed. and trans. Monique Goullet (Grenoble: J. Millon, 2000)
Hrotsvit: Opera Omnia, ed. Walter Berschin (Munich: W. G. Saur Verlag, 2001)
Translations: (German) Helène Homeyer (trans.), *Hrotsvithas Werke* (Pader-
   born: F. Schöningh, 1936)

---

[3] This list is based on the work of Anne Lyon Haight, *Hroswitha of Gandersheim: Her Life, Times and Works* (New York: Hroswitha Club, 1965), with additions. All the poems listed, down to 'Gesta Ottonis', are in the MSS and editions mentioned above unless otherwise stated. While I have sourced copies of older editions for the convenience of others, I have not seen them, so I am not giving page references to them.

(German) O. Baumhauer, J. Bendixen and T. G. Pfund (trans.), *Sämtliche Dichtungen* (Munich: Winkler, 1966)

Maria: 'Unica spes mundi dominatrix inclita caeli'

    Additional MS: Klagenfurt, Studienbibliothek, Perg. 44

    Edition: *Opera*, ed. Homeyer, 48–80

Ascensio: 'Postquam corporeo Christus velamine tecturi'

    Edition: *Opera*, ed. Homeyer, 85–150

Invocatio: 'O pie lucisator, mundi rerumque parator'

    Edition: *Opera*, ed. Homeyer, 99

Gongulfus: 'Tempore quo regni gessit Pippinus eoi'

    Edition: *Opera*, ed. Homeyer, 99–122

Invocatio: 'Inclite Pelagi, martir fortissime Christi'

    Edition: *Opera*, ed. Homeyer, 131–46

Pelagius: 'Pontibus occiduis fulsit clarum decus orbis'

    Edition: *Opera*, ed. Homeyer, 130

Theophilus: 'Postquam lux fidei crescens per climata mundi'

    Edition: *Opera*, ed. Homeyer, 154–70

Dedicatio: 'En tibi versiculos, Gerberg, fero, domna, novellos'

    Edition: *Opera*, ed. Homeyer, 176

Basilius: 'Qui velit exemplum veniae comprendere certum'

    Edition: *Opera*, ed. Homeyer, 177–86

Dionysius: 'Dum factor summae, mediae rationis et imae'

    Edition: *Opera*, ed. Homeyer, 177–86

Agnes: 'Virgo, quae, vanas mundi pompas ruituri'

Edition: *Opera*, ed. Homeyer, 210–26

Poem on the Vision of St John: Iohannes caelum virgo vidit patefactum'
MS: Munich, Bayerische Staatsbibliothek, Clm 14485 (Em. E. 108) (s. xi)

    Editions: Not in *Opera*, ed. Celtes, or works based thereon.
    Comoediae sex, ed. J. Bendixen (Lübeck: Libraria Dittmeriana, 1857, repr. 1862)
       (not seen)
    Barack, *Werke* 361–2
    Opera, ed. von Winterfeld, 200

Gesta Ottonis: 'Pollens imperii regnator caesariani'

    Additional MS: Berlin, Preussische Staatsbibliothek, Theol. lat. fol. 265. fos.,
    2–38 (now deposited in Tübingen, Universitätsbibliothek), copied from
    Celtes's edition by Valerius Meyensis.

    Editions: *Opera*, ed. Celtes
Justus Reuber (ed.), *Veterum Scriptorum, qui Caesarum et Imperatorum Germa-
    nicorum Res per Aliquot Saecula Gestas Literis Mandarunt* (Frankfurt: Haer-
    edes Andreas Wechel, 1584), 162–80 (also later edns. Hanover, 1619,
    Frankfurt am Main, 1726) [London, British Library, 10604. i. 5]
Heinrich Meibom (ed.), *Primi et Antiquissimi Historiae Saxonicae Scriptoris Witi-
    chindi Monachis . . . Annalium Libri Tres* (Frankfurt: Aubrius & Schleich, 1621),
    79–107 [Wolfenbüttel, Herzog August Bibliothek, H: T. 828. a 2° Helmst.]
Heinrich Meibom (ed.), *Rerum Germanicarum Tomi Tres*, 3 vols. (Helmstadt:
    Georg Wolfgang Hamm, 1688), i. 709–26 [London, British Library, 170. k. 8, 9]
Georg Christian Johann (ed.), *Veterum Scriptorum . . . Tomus Unus, a Justo
    Reubero Olim Editus* (Frankfurt, 1726), 221–50
G. H. Pertz (ed.), *Scriptores Rerum Germanicarum IV*, Monumenta Germaniae
    Historica, (Hanover, 1841), 302–35
Hrotsvitha's Otto-Lied, ed. and trans. (German) Wilhelm Gundlach, vol. i. of
    Heldenlieder der deutschen Kaiserzeit, aus dem Lateinischen überzetszt (Inns-
    brück: Wagner, 1894) [Wolfenbüttel, Herzog August Bibliothek, M: Gl.
    2072]
Opera, ed. Winterfeld, pp. 201–28

    Translations: (German) K. F. A. Nobbe, (trans.), *Geschichte Odos des Grossen*
    (Leipzig: Nikolaischule, 1851; 2nd edn. 1852)
    (German) T. G. M. Pfund (trans.), *Der Hrotsuitha Gedicht über Gandersheims
    Gründung und die Thaten Kaiser Oddo I* (Berlin, 1860) (also Leipzig, 1888)
    [London, British Library, 9325. cc. 31]

(English) Sr. Mary Bernadine Bergman (trans.), 'Hrotsvithae Liber Tertius', Ph. D. diss. (St Louis University, 1943)

Primordia: 'Ecce meae supplex humilis devotio mentis'

MSS: Gandersheim Abbey [lost]: lent to Heinrich Bodo (1470–1553), mentioned in his *Syntagma de Constructione Coenobii Gandesiani*, Wolfenbüttel, Herzog August Bibliothek, 19.13. Aug. 4°
Hildesheim, Behrens Collection [lost], discovered in 1706
Fragments: Ludinghausen, Gräfliche Plettenbergschen Bibliothek zu Nordkirchen [lost], MS compiled by J. Rosenthal, *Catalogus Abbatissarum Gandershemensium*, 1725
Coburg, library of the former Ducal Castle [lost, seen by Georg Waitz, 1841]
Hanover, former Royal Library case VI (Bibl. Meibom. 64) [lost, seen by Georg Waitz, 1843]

Editions: Nicolaus Schaten, *Annalium Paderbornensium II Partes* (Neuhus: Christoph Nagel, 1693), i. 128 [Wolfenbüttel, Herzog August Bibliothek, M: Gm. 4° 768]
Johann Georg Leuckfeld, *Antiquitates Gandersheimenses* (Wolfenbüttel: Freytag, 1709), 409–26 [Wolfenbüttel, Herzog August Bibliothek, M: Gn Sammelbet. 89 (1)]
Gottfried Wilhem von Leibnitz, *Scriptores Rerum Brunsvicensium Illustrationi Inservientes*, 3 vols. (Hanover: Förster, 1707–11), ii. 319–30 [Wolfenbüttel, Herzog August Bibliothek, M: Gn. 4° 1572]
Johann Christoph Harenberg, *Historia Ecclesiae Ganderhemensis . . . in Supplementum . . . Scriptorum Rerum Brunsvicensium Leibnitzianae Adornatum* (Hanover: Förster, 1734), 469–76 [Wolfenbüttel, Herzog August Bibliothek, M: Gn. 4° 838]
Pertz, 302–35
Translations: (German) T. G. M. Pfund (trans.), *Der Hrotsuitha Gedicht über Gandersheims Gründung und die Thaten Kaiser Oddo I* (Berlin, 1860) (also Leipzig, 1888)
(English) Sr. Mary Bernadine Bergman (trans.), 'Hrotsvithae Liber Tertius', Ph. D. diss. (St Louis University, 1943)

<Lost, hexameter *Vitae Paparum SS. Anastasii et Innocentii*

Gandersheim Abbey [lost]: lent to Heinrich Bodo (1470–1553), mentioned in his *Syntagma de Constructione Coenobii Gandesiani*, Wolfenbüttel, Herzog August Bibliothek, 19.13. Aug. 4°.>

Hutchenson, Maria
fl. 1605   Oxford (England)
'Qui musas studiis, qui muris auxit et aedes'

Inscription: Oxford, St John's College Chapel

Edition: Antony à Wood, *The History and Antiquities of the Colleges and Halls in the University of Oxford*, ed. John Gutch, 3 vols. (Oxford: Clarendon, 1786), iii. 560 [London. British Library, HLR. 378.42574]

Imperiale, Caterina (Pallavicini, Marchesa Mombaruti)

mid-s. xviii   Italy

De Aranea in Lauro Elegia: 'Pensilis argutâ defundat aranea lauro'

Edition: *Arcadum Carmina, Pars Prior* (Rome: Giuseppe & Filippo de Rossi, 1757), 69–70 [London, British Library, 78. c. 34]

Epigramma: 'Quid nam sit tempus? se scire, aut dicere posse'

Edition: ibid. 70

Epigramma: 'Non re, sed famâ vivunt plerique, colorem'

Edition: ibid. 70–1

Epigramma: 'Foemina, quae formae studeat, studeatque placere'

Edition: ibid. 71

<Inglis, Esther (Kello)

1571–1624   London; Edinburgh; London; Willingdale Spain (Essex); Edinburgh

Les C.L. Pseaumes de David escrites en diverses sortes de lettres par Esther Anglois Françoise. A Lislebourg en Escosse, 1599: 'Non omnis vivit, vita qui spirat in ista' (quatrain, may be hers)

MS: Washington, Folger Shakespeare Library, V.a.93, fo. 1ᵛ]

Argumenta Singulorum Capitum Ecclesiastici per Tetrasticha Manu Estherae Inglis Exarata: 'A solo coeli domino sapientia manat'

MS: New York, Pierpont Morgan Library, MA. 2149 (autograph, not seen)

Argumenta Singulorum Capitum Geneseos Tetrasticha: 'Condidit e nihilo Dominus mare, sydera, terram'

MS: private collection, Northamptonshire, described A. H. Scott-Elliott and Elspeth Yeo, 'Calligraphic Manuscripts of Esther Inglis (1571–1624): A Catalogue', *Papers of the Bibliographical Society of America*, 84.1 (1990), 55–6 (the tetrastichs on Genesis in Cambridge, Mass., Houghton Library, MS Sumner 75 (autograph, unfoliated) and Cambridge, Mass., Houghton Library, MS Typ 428 (autograph, unfoliated) are a version by Guillaume Paradin (Scott-Elliott and Yeo, 64)

Argumenta Psalmorum Davidis per Tetrasticha Manu Estherae Inglis Exarata: 'Ille beatus erit vivetque per omnia foelix'

   MSS: Cambridge, Mass., Houghton Library, Typ. 212 (autograph)
      Washington, Folger Shakespeare Library, V. a. 94 (autograph, not seen)

Argumenta Singulorum Capitum Evangelii Matthaei Apostoli, per Tetrasticha: 'Maiores numerant sancti et primordia Christi'

   MS: private collection, Scotland, described Scott-Elliott and Yeo, 61–2

These four sets of tetrastichs on Ecclesiasticus, Genesis, Matthew, and the Psalms are not certainly her own work: they may be hers, written in collaboration with her husband, or by some other hand entirely>

Irpinia Avia
?   Diani/Lucania (Italy)
'D.M. C. Puculeio C.f. Pontoro qui vixit annis xiii'

   Inscription: CLE, ii. 758 (1569)

Isabella, Principessa di Villamarina
s. xvi   Salerno (Italy)
Paulo Manutio heard her reciting Latin verse and prose in Avellano

   Attested in Ginevra Canonici Fachini, *Prospetto biografico delle donne Italiane rinomate in letteratura* (Venice: Tipografia di Alvisopoli, 1824), 141 [Vatican City, Biblioteca apostolica, Z. 2350. 5.C.2]

Iventa Hilara
?   Benevento (Italy)
'Hospes resiste et quae sum in monumento lege'

   Inscription: CIL, ix. 1527
   CLE, i. 38 (no. 73)

Jeanne Françoise d'Orléans

s. xvi   Paris/Talleburg (France)

Verse

Attested by Juan Perez de Moya, *Varia historia de sanctos e illustres mugeres en todo género de virtudes. Recopilado de varias autores* (Madrid: Francisco San-chez, 1583), 313ᵛ [London, British Library, 613. d. 31]

Jevon, Rachel

*c.*1627–after 1662   Broom (England)

Carmen θριαμβευτικον *regiae maiestatis Caroli II principum et Christianorum optimi in exoptatissimums eius restaurationem*: 'Alme PATER Patriae, Celeberrime CAROLE REGUM!' (London: John Macock 1660), [Oxford, Bodleian Library, Gough Lond. 2 (6)]

> *Edition and translation*: Jane Stevenson and Peter Davidson (eds.), *Early Modern Women Poets* (Oxford: Oxford University Press, 2001), 317–25 (the English version is her own)

Jordan, Aemilia, 'Rosina' (Schede)

s. xvi   Palatinate/Heidelberg (Germany)

Rosina ad Melissum: 'Desine Paule tuam spinas urgere Rosinam'

> *Editions*: Paul Melissus, *Schediasmatum Reliquiae* (Frankfurt: Georgius Corvi-nus, 1575), 442 [Oxford, Bodleian Library, Douce M. 221]
>
> Second edition: *Schediasmata Poetica* (Paris: Arnold Sittart, 1586), 672 [Oxford, Bodleian Library, 88 M. 9. Art.]
>
> Jane Stevenson, 'Johanna Otho (Othonia) and Women's Latin Poetry in Reformed Europe', in Laurie Churchill, Phyllis R. Brown, and Jane E. Jeffrey (eds.), *Women Writing Latin from Roman Antiquity to Early Modern Europe*, 3 vols. (New York: Routledge, 2002), iii. 189–215 (pp. 206, 213–14) (with trans.)

Rosina Melisso: 'Nunc animi pendes nunc anxia pectorem firmas'
Editions: Paul Melissus, *Schediasmatum Reliquiae*, 440–1
Schediasmata Poetica, 631–2

Juana Inés de la Cruz, Sor *see* Asbaje, Juana Ramírez de

Julia Marcella

                                                                Capenato, near Soracte (Italy)

Julia Marcella Clodio Fabato marito: 'Terrenum corpus, coelestis spiritus in me'

Inscription: Petrus Pithoeus (ed.), *Epigrammata et Poematia Vetera*, 2 vols. (Paris: N. Gillius, 1590), ii. 125–6 [London, British Library, 1001.e.1]

Petrus Burmann (ed.), *Anthologia Veterum Latinorum Epigrammatum et Poematum, sive Catalecta Poetarum Latinorum in VI Libros Digesta*, 6 vols. in 2 (Amsterdam: Schouten, 1759, 1773), ii. 151 (IV.ccii) [London, British Library, 54. f. 13]

Heinrich Meyer (ed.), *Anthologia Veterum Latinorum Epigrammatum et Poematum*, 2 vols. in 1 (Leipzig: Gerhard Fleischer, 1835), ii. 130 (1319) [London, British Library, 011388. b. 14]

CIL, xi.1, p. 584 (3963)

CLE, i. 283 (591)

Julia Parthenope
s. iii   Arles (France)
'O dolor, quantae lacrimae fecere sepulchrum'

Inscription: *CIL*, xii. 825, 827

CLE, i. 272–3 (565)

Kammeneck, Elisabetha [Alzbeta] Albertina von
fl. 1600/1630   Prague? (Bohemia, now Czech Republic)
Ad Insigniter Nobilitatum Poëtam Caesarium Gregorium Kleppisium von Dippoldswald: 'Kleppisi, decus atque insignis gloria Vatum'

Edition: Gregorius Kleppisius, *Himlischer Jordan/ Christi Jesu Tauffe: Un Selighachtendes Wasserbad aller mit sünd behafften Christgläubigen Seden* (Nuremberg: Wolfgang Endter, 1630) [Janz, German Baroque Literature (microfilm coll.), no. 1495, reel 301]

Königsmarck, Maria Aurora, Gräfin von
1662–1728   Stade/Stockholm/Quedlinburg (Germany)
In Memoriam Celsissimi Domini Dn Otthonis Wilhelmi Konigsmarcki Comitis in Westerwijk et Stegholm etc. S.L.M.tis Suedica Caroli XI Quondam in Pomerania, Rugis Wismaria Generalis Gubernatoris Potentissimaeque Reipublicae Venetae Generalis Campi—Marschalli Excelentissimi, cum Generosi Corporis Exuviae Anno 1691 19 die Januarii Omnium Matri Redderentur Stadae: 'Dum Veneto Adriacii sua jura rogabit in undis'

MS: Uppsala, Universitetsbiblioteket, Palmsk. 389 [unpaginated]

In eius tumulum: 'Hic situs Arctoi Legis Dux, primaque belli'

MS: Uppsala, Universitetsbiblioteket, Palmsk. 389 [unpaginated]

In Illustrissimum Carolum Iohannem Konigsmarkium: 'Hic Konigsmarkum properate Carolus umbra'

MS: Uppsala, Universitetsbiblioteket, Palmsk. 389 [unpaginated]

Editions: Birger Mörner, *Maria Aurora Königsmarck, en Kronika* (Stockholm:
   P. A. Norstedt & Söners Forlag, 1914), 84 [private copy]
Maria Aurora Königsmarck, eine Chronik (Munich: Georg Müller, 1922) (German translation of above) [Wolfenbüttel, Herzog August Bibliothek, M: Db.
   2481]

Labé, Louise (Perrin)
1522–66   Lyon (France)
'Beaucoup de vers latins de la composition de Louise Labbé'

   Attested by Jacques Pernetti, seen by him in the possession of Claude-François
      Menestrier (1631–1705), *Recherches pour servir à l'histoire de Lyon ou les
      Lyonnois dignes de mémoire*, 2 vols. (Lyon: Chez les Freres Duplain, Libraires,
      1757), i. 352–3 [London, British Library, 10171.bb.35]

Laeta, Fulvia
s. xvi   Rome (Italy)
'mediocriter exercitata in carmine Latino'

   According to a personal acquaintance, Jean-Jacques Boissard, *Icones Diversorum
      Hominum Fama et Rebus Gestis Illustrium* (Metz: Abraham Faber, 1591), 104
      [London, British Library, 683. e. 17]

<Lansenberg, Maria (Leurinus)
late s. xvi   Ghent ?Leiden (Belgium)
Epigrammata ad Serenissimam Angliae Reginam Elizabetham et Varia Epigrammata
(lost)

   Attested by Jacobus Smalcius (respondent), *Academicam de Foeminarum Erudi-
      tione, Posteriorem, Consensu Inclutae Facultatis Philosophicae in Almi Lipsiensi*
      (Leipzig: Johann Erich Hahn, 1676), sig. F1ᵛ and F2ʳ⁻ᵛ, who saw a book of
      her Latin verse in the possession of her son, Johann Leurinus, in Leiden.
      Sister of Petronia Lansenberg, or the same woman using a different Christian
      name? [Munich, Bayerische Staatsbiliothek, 4 Diss. 5212]>

Lansenberg, Petronia
late s. xvi   Ghent (Belgium)/London (England)
Carolo Utenhovio Petronia Lansenbergia: 'Quod si prima viros laudarum tempora
doctos'

Edition: *Caroli Utenhovii F. Patricii Gandavensis* XENIA *seu ad Illustrium Aliquot Europae Hominum Nomina, Allusionum (Intertextis Alicubi Ioach. Bellaii Eiusdem Argumenti Versibus), Liber Primus* (Basel: Thomas Guarinus, 1568), 111–12 [Oxford, Bodleian Library, 8º B. 47 Art. Seld.]

MS: Munich, Bayerische Staatsbibliothek, Clm 10384, fo. 274 (copy from the printed text)

Petroniae Lans. *CU*: 'Inter Apollinei celeberrima nomina coetus'

Edition: *Xenia*, 112
MS: Munich, Bayerische Staatsbibliothek, Clm 10384, fo. 274 (copy from printed text)

Εις Παλλαδα δεκασ[τ]ιχον: 'Virgineo vultu quam cernis (lector amice)'

MS: Oxford, Bodleian Library, Douce 68, fo. 37 (autograph, *album amicorum* of Emanuel Meteren)

Et Nobilitate et Literis Ornatissimo D. Iano Douzae, Gratulatorium Carmen: 'Cum tua perlego suavissima carmina, Jane'

MSS: Leiden, Universiteitsbibliotheek, BPL. 1406, fo. 32ʳ (autograph, *album amicorum* of Jan Dousa)
Munich, Bayerische Staatsbibliothek, Clm 10384, fo. 274ʳ (copy of above)

Edition: facsimile edn. Chris Heesakkers, *Een network aan de basis van de Leidse universitet. Het album amicorum van Janus Dousa* (Leiden: Universiteitsbibliotheek Leiden/Uitgeverij Jongbloed, 2000)

'Hunc mittit librum Petronia nunc tibi chara'

MS: (autograph), Chicago, Newberry Library, ZW. 546. L. 222, fo. 3ʳ

Lanzavegia, Clara
s. xv   Verona? (Italy)
Clara Lanzavegia Mario Philelpho Poetae Sal[utavit]: 'Clara rogo Marium, precibus si flectere possim'

MSS: Verona, Biblioteca capitolare, cclxxi (243), fos. 2ʳ⁻ᵛ
Berlin, Deutsche Staatsbibliothek, Hamilton 510, fos. 1ʳ⁻ᵛ
Camaldoli, Archivio del sacro eremo, 1130, fos. 648–9
Venice, Bibliotheca monasterii S. Michaelis, 1130 [not seen]

Editions: J.-B. Mitterelli, *Bibliotheca Codicum Manuscriptorum Monasterii S. Michaelis Venetiarum* (Venice: Typographia Fentiana, 1779), cols. 648–9 [London, British Library, 122. k. 10]

J.-B. Mitterelli, in *Memorie per servire all'istoria letteraria*, 12 vols. (Venice, 1753–8), vi. 41–57 [not seen]

Memorie scientifiche della Accademia Valdarnese del Poggio, 6, pt. 5 (1841), 40 [Vatican City, Biblioteca apostolica, R.G. Scienze IV.112]

Isotae Nogarolae Veronensis Opera quae Supersunt Omnia, ed. Eugenius Abel, 2 vols. (Viènna: Gerold & Cie., 1886), ii. 361–2 [London, British Library, 12227. e. 5]

Lazea, Philippa
1546–76   Pula (Bosnia)/Padua (Italy)

Ad I.I. Boissardum Philippa Lazea: 'Magnum opus tentat, variaeque plenum'

Edition: Jean-Jacques Boissard, *Iani Iacobi Boissardi Vesuntini Poemata* (Metz: Abrahamus Faber, 1589), 317–19 [Oxford, Bodleian Library, 8º B. 34. Art.]

Philippa Lazea, Polona Illyrica: 'Hem: quid aspicio? labella cuja haec?'

Editions: Boissard, *Poemata*, 4
Jean-Jacques Boissard, *Iani Iacobi Boissardi Vesuntini Emblematum Liber* (Frankfurt: T. de Bry, 1593), sig. A 4ʳ [London, British Library, 89. k. 25]

Diversorum Auctorum Epigrammata in Effigiem Jani Jacobi Boissardi: Philippa Lazea Polona [not seen; may be either the previous, or the next poem]

MS: Berlin, Deutsche Staatsbibliothek, Hamilton 103, fos. 5ʳ–6 [not seen]

In Icones Virorum Doctrina Illustrium Iani Iacobi Boissardi Vesuntini, Carmen sapphicum: 'Dum viros, claræ quibus aura lucis'

Edition: Jean-Jacques Boissard, *Icones Quinquaginta Virorum Illustrium Doctrina et Eruditione Praestantium cum Eorum Vitis Descriptio a J. J. Boissardo*, 4 vols. (Frankfurt am Main: Matthias Becker for Haeredes Theodori de Bry, 1597–9), 27–8 [London, British Library, 611. e. 6]

Other poems Jean-Jacques Boissard, in his brief *vita* of Lazea, in *Icones Diversorum Hominum Fama et Rebus Gestis Illustrium* (Metz: Abraham Faber, 1591), 92, lists a number of poems: 'Flora et Zephyrus', 'Polyxenae immolatio', 'de laudibus bombicum' (in praise of silk), and lyrics and hymns in praise of St Catherine [London, British Library, 683. e. 17]

Johann Caspar Eberi, *Eröffnetes Cabinet dess Gelehrten Frauen-zimmers*, (Frankfurt: Michael Rohrlachs sel. Wittib und Erben, 1700; 2nd edn. 1706), 211 (Facsimile edn. Munich: Iudicium, 1990) attributes to Philippa 'Lacaea' a life of St Catherine in sapphic metre [Oxford, Taylorian Library, EN. 807. A. 1; London, British Library, 10603. aaa. 2]

? Le Fèvre, Anne (Lesnier, Dacier)
1651–1720
See 'Musette de Paris'

Leofgyth (Leoba, Thrutgeba)
d. 779   Wimborne (England)/Bischofsheim (Germany)
'Arbiter omnipotens, solus qui cuncta creavit'

MSS: Munich, Bayerische Staatsbibliothek, 8112, fo. 106ʳ
Karlsruhe, Badische Landesbibliothek, Rastatt 22 (olim Darmstadt 94), fo. 85ᵛ
Vienna, Österreichische Nationalbibliothek, Lat. 751 (olim Theol. 259), fo. 21ʳ

Editions: *Epistulae S. Bonifacii*, ed. Nicolaus Serarius (Mainz: M. Demen, 1629), 36 (and other edns. 1618, 1654, 1677) [London, British Library, 1009.b.12]
Sancti Bonifacii Archiepiscopi Epistolae... Ordine Chronologico Dispositae, ed. Stephan Alexander Würdtwein (Mainz, 1789), 21 [London, British Library, 692. g. 15]
Sancti Bonifacii Opera, ed. J. A. Giles (London: D. Nutt, 1844), i. 21 [London, British Library, RB 23.a.2532]
S. Bonifatii et Lulli Epistolae, ed. Philipp Jaffé (Berlin, 1866), 23 [London, British Library, 2392. f. 4]
S. Bonifatii et Lulli Epistolae, ed. Ernst Dümmler (Berlin: Weidmann, 1892), 281 *PL* lxxxix, cols. 797–8
Epistolae S. Bonifacii, ed. M. Tangl (Berlin: Weidmann, 1916), no. 29, pp. 102–4 (p. 104)
C. H. Talbot (ed. and trans.), *The Anglo-Saxon Missionaries in Germany* (London: Sheed and Ward, 1954), 88

Translations: (German) Reinhold Rau (ed. and trans.), *Briefe des Bonifatius, Willibalds Leben des Bonifatius* (Darmstadt: Wissenschaftliche Buchgesellschaft, 1968), 104–5
The Letters of Saint Boniface, trans. Ephraim Emerton (New York: Columbia University Press, 1960), 60

<?Lippa
*c.*1580   northern Italy
Reply to Publius Franciscus Spinula: 'O utinam faciant oculos me numina totum' (both sides of the exchange may be his)
James Hutton, *The Greek Anthology in Italy* (Ithaca, NY: Cornell University Press, 1935), 248–9>

Lok, Anne (Prowse, Dering, Vaughan)
*c.*1534–after 1590   London (England)/Antwerp (Belgium)/London/Geneva
(Switzerland)/Exeter

Anna Dering in Barth[olomeum] Sylva[m] Medicu[m] Tauriniensiu[m]: 'Ut iuvat
umbriferum levibus nemus omne susuris'

    MS: Cambridge, University Library, Ii.5.37, p. v^v (MS has original pagination)

      Editions: *The Collected Works of Anne Vaughan Lock*, ed. Susan M. Felch,
        Medieval and Renaissance Texts and Studies 185 (Tempe: Arizona Center
        for Medieval and Renaissance Studies, 1999), 72 (with photograph of MS,
        p. 71)
      Jane Stevenson and Peter Davidson (eds.), *Early Modern Women Poets* (Oxford:
        Oxford University Press, 2001), 32 (with trans.)

Ludula
late antiquity   Trier (Germany)
'Ursiniano subdiacono sub hoc tumulo ossa quiescunt'

    Inscription: St Paul's, Trier

    Editions: *CLE*, i. 367 (773)
    H. Geist and G. Pfohl (ed. and German trans.), *Römische Grabinschriften*
      (Munich: Ernst Heimeran Verlag, 1969), 181 (490)

Makin, Bathsua *see* Rainolds, Bathsua

Malatesta, Paola (Gonzaga)
fl. 1430   Pesaro/Mantua (Italy)
Latin verse and prose

    Claimed by Francisco Agostino della Chiesa, *Theatro delle donne letterate* (Mon-
      dovi: Giovanni Gislandi & Giovanni Tomaso Rossi, 1620), 269. [Paris,
      Bibliothèque Nationale de France, G. 21, 404]

Marcella
s.v/vi   Vienne (France)
EPITAPHIUM SANCTI HESICII [EPISCOPI]: 'Praesulis iunctum tumulo-
que Aviti'

    Inscription: in Paris, Bibliothèque Nationale de France, Lat. 2832, fo. 114^r (s.
      viii)

Editions: Jean du Bois Olivio (ed.), in *Viennae Antiquitates*, appendix to *Bibliotheca Floriacensis Vetus Bibliotheca, Benedictina, Sancta, Apostolica*, 3 vols. (Lyon: Horatio Cardon, 1605), iii. 35–6 [London, British Library, 861.f.2]

Edmond Le Blant (ed.), *Inscriptions chrétiennes du Gaule antérieures au xiiie siècle*, 2 vols. (Paris: Imprimerie Impériale, 1856–65), ii. 7, no. 413 [London, British Library, 4632.f.17]

Jean Le Lièvre, *Histoire de l'antiquité et saincteté de la cité de Vienne en la Gaule Celtique* (Vienne: Jean Poyet, 1623) [Vatican City, Biblioteca apostolica, Barberini R. VII. 34]

Rudolf Peiper (ed.), *Alcimi Ecdicii Aviti Viennensis Episcopi Opera*, MGH AA 6.2 (Berlin: Weidmann, 1883), 187 [London, British Library, HLL.943 (MG-S1)]

Marchina, Martha

1600–42   Rome (Italy)
Marthae Marchinae Virginis Neapolitane Musa Posthuma (Rome: Philippus Maria Mancini, 1662) [Rome, Biblioteca Nazionale Vittorio Emanuele, 6.20.C.44]

Ad lectorem: 'Praecipis ex isto demi mala carmina libro'

Editions: *Musa Posthuma*, 91

Juan Bautista Aguilar, *Varias, hermosas flores del Parnaso, que in quatro floridos, visitos quadros, plantaron iunto a su cristilina fuente D. Antonio Hurtado de Mendoza; D. Antonio de Sólis... y otros illustres poetas de España* (Valencia: Francisco Mestre, 1680), sig. ¶¶ 4ᵛ [London, British Library, 11451.e.1]

De S. Laurentio Martyre: 'Subtectos latere spernit Laurentius ignes'

Editions: *Musa Posthuma*, 38
Aguilar, 39, with (Spanish) trans. by Aguilar

De Pastore et Justo Fratribus Projectis Tabellis ad Mortem Properantibus: 'Cernis, ut impavidus densos concurrit in hostes'

Editions: *Musa Posthuma*, 36
Sebastian Kortholt, *Disquisitio de Poetriis Puellis* (Keil: Barthold Reuther, 1700), 26 [Wolfenbüttel, Herzog August Bibliothek, M: Da. 271]

De Iisdem Genuum Vestigia Lapidi Impressa Reliquentibus: 'Digna Deo soboles, coeli duo sidera fratres'

Editions: *Musa Posthuma*, 35–6
Kortholt, 27

De Puero Jesu Vagiente: 'Ad Pueri cunas properans e sedibus altis'

Editions: *Musa Posthuma*, 2–3
Benedetto Croce, 'Appunti di letteratura secentesca inedita o rara', *La Critica*,
3rd ser 28 (1929), 468–80 (p. 471)

In Fratrem suum: 'Esse videris homo rigidus, nimiumque severus'

Editions: *Musa Posthuma*, 67
Croce, 471

Carlo di S. Antonio, *De Arte Epigrammatica sive de Ratione Epigrammatis Rite
Conficendi, Libellus* (Coloniae Ubiorum: E. Egmond et Socios, 1650), 80–1,
87–8, quotes excerpts from several poems as models of style [London, British
Library, 1089.e.12]

Marcien, Anna Maria (Pflaum)
fl. 1689 Leipzig (Germany)
Latin poetry

Attested by Georg Christian Lehms, *Teutschlands galante Poetinnen, mit ihren
sinnreichen und netten Proben, nebst einem Anhang ausländischer Dames so sich
gleichfalls durch schöne Poesien [bey] der curieusen Welt bekannt gemacht*
(Frankfurt am Main: Anton Heinscheidt, 1715), 156 [London, British Library, 11525.dd.21]

Marguerite de Valois, wife of Henri IV
s. xvi Paris/Navarre/Usson (France)
'O quae coelicoli edita, sis mihi'

MS: Venice, Biblioteca Marciana, Lat. XII 232 (3985), viii, 10ʳ

Georg Christian Lehms, *Teutschlands galante Poetinnen, mit ihren sinnreichen und
netten Proben, nebst einem Anhang ausländischer Dames so sich gleichfalls durch
schöne Poesien [bey] der curieusen Welt bekannt gemacht* (Frankfurt am Main:
Anton Heinscheidt, 1715), warns that Barclay wrote a poem in her person:
this is in John Barclay, *Euphormionis Lusinini Satyricon*, 4 parts (n.p.; 1613):
pt. II, p. 109, 'O patria, O arces, O dulcia tecta parentum' [London, British
Library, 11525.dd.21]

Maria de Guadalupe Alencastre y Cardenas, Duquesa de Aveiro, Arcos y Maqueda
2nd half s. xvii Portugal
'Haec requies mea in saeculum saeculi'

One of a series of epitaphs in Portuguese and Latin for her parents and herself
Damião de Froes Perym (pseudonym of Frei João de S. Pedro), *Theatro Heroino*,
2 vols. (Lisbon: Oficina da Musica de Theotonio Antunes Lima (I), Regia
Officina Sylvania e Academia Real (II) 1736–40), [London, British Library,
10604, i.3]), ii. 41

Maria Josepha, Queen of Poland

fl. 1757   Dresden (Germany)/Pirn (Poland)
*Epistola Reginae Poloniae, ad Regem in Castris Pirnensibus a Borussis Cinctum, Regi
Regina*: 'Scilicet haec nobis vix nomina sola supersunt' (1757)

> *MS*: Vatican City, Biblioteca Apostolica Cod. vat. lat. 11697, fos. 278–279ᵛ
> (s. xviii)

Maria Malchis

late s. i   Rome (Italy)
'... consummatus litteris'

> *Inscription*: *CIL*, vi. 8991
> *CLE*, i. 56 (101)

Marieta: *see* Contarini, Marieta

Marquets, Anne de, Sœur

s. xvi   Poissy (France)
Carolus Lotaringus: 'Praeclarus princeps hinc usque ad sydera notus'

> *Edition*: Anne de Marquets, *Sonets, prieres et devises, en forme de pasquins, par
> l'assemblée de messieurs les prelats et docteurs, tenue à Poissy* (Paris: Guillaume
> Morel, 1563), sig. A 5ᵛ [Paris, Bibliothèque de l'Arsenal, 8º B.11614 Rés.]

*Icy finissent les meditations et prieres à Dieu, lesquel les pour le bien de la religion, Sœur
Anne de Marquets treshumble religieuse de Poissy, faisoit*: 'Si qua videbuntur non tam
exculta atque polita'

> *Edition*: *Sonets*, sig. C 4ʳ

Martha, sister of Pope Damasus

s. iv   Rome (Italy)
'Qui gradiens pelagi fluctus compressit amaros'

> *Inscription*: E. Diehl (ed.), *Inscriptiones Latinae Christianae Veteres*, 3 vols.
> (Berlin: Weidmann, 1925–31), i. no. 969
> H. Geist and G. Pfohl (eds. and German trans.), *Römische Grabinschriften*
> (Munich: Ernst Heimeran Verlag, 1969), 179 (485)

Mathild of Saxony

*c.*1000–after 1033 Saxony/Franconia/Lotharingia (Germany)

'Hunc librum Regi Mahthilt donat Misegoni' (distich)

> *Edition*: Phil. Ant. Dethier, *Epistola Inedita Mathildis Soror Gislae Imperatricis et Aviae Mathildis Toscanae, Data Anno 1027 aut 1028 ad Misegonum II* (Berlin: Behr, 1842), 3 [London, British Library, 9475.cc.12]

<Mecklenburg, Sophie Elisabeth von (Braunschweig-Lüneburg)

s. xvii Wolfenbüttel (Germany)

'Dux Auguste, pii Moderator Guelphice Sceptri'

> *Edition*: *Der Minervae Banquet, welches zu . . . ehren auff den LXXVII Geburts-Tag des . . . Herrn Augusti, Herzogs zu Brunswyg und Lunäburg, nemlich den 10 Aprilis dess 1655* (Wolfenbüttel: Johann and Heinrich den Sternen, 1655), sig. A3ᵛ–4ʳ (no other name is given for this Latin ode, and *Minervae Banquet* as a whole is attributed to her) [German Baroque Literature Microfilm Collection (von Faber du Faur), no. 422d reel 82]>

Medrano, María Teresa

s. xviii Mexico City (Mexico)

'O! Pigeat meminisse tuos Hispania Reges'

> *Edition*: *Cifra feliz de las dichas imponderables que se promete la monarchía hespañola baxo el suspirado domina de su augusto soberano el Señor Fernando VI (que Dios prospere) . . . Justa literaria, certamen poético, con que la humilde lealtad, y reconocida gratitud del Real, y más antiqui Colegio de S. Ildefonso de México celebro el dia 23 de enero del año de 1748 la exaltación al solio de su augusto protector* (Salamanca: Imprenta de la Santa Cruz, n.d. [1748?]), 147 [Salamanca, Bibliotheca Universitaria, 34.425]

'Quid refert numeres Ferdinandum ordine Sextum'

> *Edition*: ibid. 147

Memorata, Anna⁴

1615–after 1644 Łożebrica/Leszno (Poland)

Epithalamion (Latin)

> *Edition*: *Sacris Hymenois . . . Michaelis Henrici Beles . . . et Mariannae . . . Jacobi Wolfhagii Filiae* (Leszno: D. Funk, 1635) [not seen]

---

⁴ I am most grateful to Dr Piotr Urbanski and Dr Ursula Philips for sending me Xerox copies of the Wierszbowski and Rott editions; but I am therefore unfortunately unable to give call-numbers.

Magnifico, Nobilissimo ac Excellentissimo Viro D. Christian-Theodoro Schossero, Aemiliano, Comiti Palatino Caesareo, Philosophiae et Medicinae Doctori, Poetae Laureato, etc.: 'Sol, oculus mundi, dum illustrat lampada terras' (28 July 1640)

> *Editions*: Chrystian Teodor Schosser, *Laurifolium sive Schediasmatum Poeticorum Libri* (Leszno: Daniel Vetter, 1641), viii, sig. F 8 [not seen]
> Teodor Wierszbowski (ed.), *Anny Memoraty, 'Dzwiewicy Polskiéj', Łacinskie Wiersze, z lat 1640–1644* (Warsaw: K. Kowalewskiego, 1895), 24

Magnifico, Nobilissime ac Experientissimo Viro, Domino Christian-Theodoro Schossero, Aemiliano, Comiti Palatino Caesareo, Phil. et Medic. Doctori. Poet. Laur. etc. Domino meo Gratioso; 'Admiror doctos elogos, clarissime vates' (3 Mar. 1641)

> *Edition*: Zbigniew Kadlubek and Dariusz Rott (eds.), *Anna Memorata: Niech Daruje Apollo te Wiersze, Wybór Poezji* (Katowice-Pszczyna: Biblioteka Fundacji 'Pallas Silesia', Druga Pozycja Wydawnicza, 1998), 16–17 (with Polish trans.)

D. Christian-Theodoro Schossero, Aemiliano, Comiti Palatino Caesareo, Phil. et Medic. Doctori. Poet. Laur. etc. etc. etc.: 'Magne vir, ah quo me ian non dignaris honore'

> *Editions*: *Laurifolium*, viii, sig. G 3
> Wierszbowski, 26

D. Christian-Theodoro Schossero, Aemiliano, Comiti Palatino Caesareo, Phil. et Medic. Doctori. Poet. Laur. etc. etc. etc. Salutem: 'Quid sibi tanta volunt, quaeso, praeconia laudum' (24 Jan. 1641)

> *Editions*: *Laurifolium*, viii, sig. G 4
> Wierszbowski, 26–7

Nobili Insignique Eruditione et Pietate Praedito Domino Constantino Schaumio, Poetae Laureato, Generosorum de Bal Inspectori Fidelissimo, Salutem: 'Ach! quorsum tant haec spectant praeconia laudum'

> *Editions*: *Laurifolium*, viii, sig. G 6
> Wierszbowski, 27

Clarissimo Viro Domino M. Davidi Attinentio-Zugehor, Poetae Laureatae Caesareo: 'Semper adest merces virtuti gloria praestans'

> *Editions*: *Laurifolium*, ix, sig. M 8
> Wierszbowski, 29
> Kadlubek and Rott, 18–19

Clarissimo, Eruditissimoque Domino Andreae Tscherningio, Boleslaviensi Silesio, Poetae Laureato Cesareo: 'Quam primum vidi doctissima carmina vatis'

> *Editions*: *Laurofolium*, ix, sig. O 8
> Wierszbowski, 29–30
> Kadlubek and Rott, 20–1

Honori Nuptiarum Nobilissimi ac Praestantissimi Juvenis Domini Mauritii Rudolphi, Glogowiensis, Sponsi, ac Pudicissimae Virginis Magdlenae Schulleriae, Sponsae Dantisci Borussorum, ad Diem 24 Novemb. Anno Christi Celebrandarum: 'Quid, nove Sponse, Tibi, Tibi quid, nova Sponsa precabor?'

> *Edition*: Kadlubek and Rott, 22–3

Amplissimo Consultissimoque Viro Domino Samueli Spechtio Iurisconsulto, Illustrissimi Comitis in Leschno Secretario et Civitatis Leschnensis Consular: 'Si mihi felices essent in carmina vires' (8 Aug. 1640)

> *Editions*: *Laurifolium*, viii, sig. F 8 [not seen]
> Wierszbowski, 25
> Kadlubek and Rott, 24–5

Clarissimo atque Doctissimo Viro D. Samueli Spechtio Iurisconsulti: 'Nescio, quid faciam, quo spes et vota rependam'

> *Editions*: *Laurifolium*, viii, sig. G 1 [not seen]
> Wierszbowski, 25–6

Illustrissimo, Magnifico ac Vere Generoso Domino Adamo Grodziecki de te in Wyszyno et Castellano Miedzierzicensi, Domino meo Clarissimo, Strenae Loco Humillime Offert: 'Mos vetus, illustris fautor, nunc obtinet, olim' (1642)

> *MS*: Poznań, Biblioteca Raczyñskich, II.H.c.19 (autograph: not seen, cf. Wierszbowski)

> *Editions*: Leszno, Daniel Vetter, 1642 [not seen]
> Wierszbowski, 33
> Kadlubek and Rott, 26–7

Illustrissimo, Magnifico, ac Vere Generoso Domino Domino Adamo Grodziecki de et in Wyszyno etc. Castellano Miedzirecensi, Domino meo Clementissimo, Humillime Offert et Dicat: 'Illustris certe es genio, generose dynasta' (21 Mar. 1641)

> *MS*: Poznań, Biblioteca Raczyñskich, II.H.c.19 (autograph: not seen, cf. Wierszbowski)

Edition: Wierszbowski, 30–1

Illustrissimo, Magnifico, ac Vere Generoso Domino Domino Adamo Grodziecki de et in Wyszyno etc. Castellano Miedzirecensi, Domino meo Clementissimo, et Summo Musarum Patrono, Plurimum Observando: 'Ut solet auricomus post turbida numina Titan' (25 Mar. 1641)

> *MS*: Poznań, Biblioteca Raczyñskich, II.H.c.19 (autograph: not seen, cf. Wierszbowski)
> *Edition*: Wierszbowski, 31–2

Propempticon, in Felicem Cracoviam Discessum Illustrissimi, Magnifici et Generosissimi Domini Dni Adami Grodziecki de et in Wyszyn etc. etc. et. Castellani Miedzerzicensis, Musarum Patroni Colendissimi: 'Inclyte Sarmaticos inter Grodziecki dynastas' (2 Mar. 1644)

> *MS*: Poznań, Biblioteca Raczyñskich, II.H.c.19 (autograph: not seen, cf. Wierszbowski)
> *Editions: Kwartaluiku naukowym* (Kraków, 1835), i. 172 [not seen: cf. Wierszbowski]
> Wierszbowski, 34

Carmen Gratulatorium de Felici et Auspicato Lesnam IV Calend. Octobr. Anni Currentis 1644 Ingressu Illustrissimi Herois et Magnifici ac Generosiss. Domini Dn. Caspari Comitis a Döhnhof Palatini Siradiensis, etc.: 'Inter Sarmaticos, age, palatine, dynastas'

> *Editions*: (Leszno: Wigand Funk, 1644) [not seen: cf. Wierszbowski]
> Wierszbowski, 35–6

Ad Comitem de Leszno Lesczczynsky

> Seen by Johannis Paschius, *Gynaeceum Doctum, sive Dissertatio Historico-literaria, vom Gelehrten Frauenzimmer, antea Wittebergae Ano 1686 Publice Exposita* (Wittenberg: Christian Finkel, 1701), 48 [Wolfenbüttel, Herzog August Bibliothek, M: Li 6896]

Ad Andream Brummer

> Seen by Johannes Sauerbrei, *Diatriben Academicam de Foeminam Eruditione, Priorem Consensu Inclutae Facultatis Philosophicae in Alma Lipsiensi, sub Praesidio . . . M. Jacobi Thomasii* (Leipzig: Johann Erich Hahn, 1671), § 50, sig. C 4ʳ [Munich, Bayerische Staatsbibliothek, 4 Diss. 5212]

Méndez de Zurita, Lorenza (Dantisco)
d. before 1605   Madrid/Valladolid (Spain)
Latin verses

Attested by a contemporary, Juan Perez de Moya, *Varia historia de sanctos e illustres mugeres en todo género de virtudes. Recopilado de varias autores* (Madrid: Francisco Sanchez, 1583), fo. 310 [London, British Library, 613.d.31]

Messalto, Polissena (da Andria)
s. xv   Muggia (Croatia, former Yugoslavia)
Polissena Mesilta Muglensis Nicolai Peregrini Affinis, pro Ipso Nicolao Respondet Io. La. Re. f.: 'Gratulor et letor te surexisse poetam'

MS: Venice, Biblioteca Marciana, Marc. Lat.XII. 44 (4375), fo. 43ᵛ

Edition: Arnaldo Seganizzi, 'Un poeta feltrino dal secolo xv', *Atti dell'Academia scientifica Veneto-Trentino-Istriana*, Classe di scienze storiche, filologiche e filosofiche (Padova) 1, (1904), 16–33 (p. 32) [Vatican City, Biblioteca Apostolica, Ferraioli IV. 9252]

Molesworth, Mary (Monck)
1677?–1715   London (England)/Dublin (Ireland)/Bath
'Elegie on a favourite DOG, to her Father': 'Lugubrem scissis Musam plorare capillis'

Edition: *Marinda: Poems and Translations upon Several Occasions* (London: J. Tonson, 1716), 2 vols. i. 66–71 [London, British Library, 994.c.18]

Mollineux, Mary *see* Southworth, Mary

Molza, Tarquinia (Porrino)
1542–1617   Modena (Italy)
De Fonte: 'Hoc fonte proprium est blandos inducere somnos'

Editions: *Delle poesie volgari e latine di Francesco Maria Molza*, ed. Pierantonio Serassi, 3 vols. (Bergamo: Pietro Lancellotti, 1747) (includes *Opuscoli di Tarquinia Molza, nipote dell'autore*, separately paginated), ii. 85 [London, British Library, 240.11.28]
Opuscula Inediti di Tarquinia Molza Modenese, ed. Domenico Vandelli (Bergamo: Pietro Lancellotti, 1750), 85 [Vatican City, Biblioteca Apostolica, Ferraioli IV. 9252 (int. 2)]

De Cynthio Card. Aldobrandino: 'Te celebrat, Cynthi, virtute insigne et ostro'
Editions: Serassi, ii. 85
Vandelli, 85

De Eodem: 'Tu solus, Cynthi, te ipsum velut alter Apollo'

Editions: Giulio Segni (ed.), *Tempio all'Illustrissimo et Reverendissimo Signor Cinthio Aldobrandini Cardinale S. Giorgio, Nipote del Sommo Pontefice Clemente Ottavo* (Bologna: Heredi di Giovanni Rossi, 1600). Latin verse (separately paginated), p. 21 [London, British Library, 11427.ee.2]
Serassi, ii. 85
Vandelli, 85

Latin verses

MS: Copenhagen, Kongelige Bibliothek, Gl kgl samling 2040 [not seen]

Latin poem in praise of Camillo Paleotti

MS: Bologna, Archivio Isolani, F.4.73.7.8 [not seen: this is a private archive, currently in the possession of Gualtiero Conti and Francesco Cavazza-Isolani, Via S Stefano 16, Bologna. The document may have been destroyed in the Second World War since it has not acquired a CN (cartoni nuova) number]

Latin tetrastich

Edition: *Marci Condorati Cretensis de Bono Universi Liber* (Padua, 1593) [not seen], mentioned in Girolamo Tiraboschi, *Biblioteca Modenense, o notizie della vita e delle opere degli scrittori nati degli stati del serenissimo signor Duca di Modena*, 6 vols. (Modena: Società tipografica, 1783), iii. 244–53 [London, British Library, 10632.v.31]

'Felsina clara Virum ingeniis, at clarior almae'

Edition: [Giulio Segni *et al.*] *Componimenti poetici volgari, latini e Greci di diversi sopra la s. Imagine della Beata Virgine dipinta a s. Luca* (Bologna: Vittorio Benacci, 1601), 61 [Bologna, Biblioteca Comunale dell'Archiginnasio, 16.A.vi.27]
second edition, in *Historia della santa Imagine della gloriosa Vergine ...* (Bologna: Vittorio Benacci, 1603), 61 [Bologna, Biblioteca comunale dell'Archiginnasio, A.v.H.vii.33]
Serassi, ii. 86
Vandelli, 86

Monck, Mary *see* Molesworth, Mary

Monti, Issicratea
1564–84   Rovigo (Italy)
Latin poems

Attested by Iacobi Philippi Tomasini, *Elogia Virorum Literis et Sapientia Illustrium ad Vivum Expressis Imaginibus Exornata* (Padua: Sebastiano Sardi,
1644), 364–7 [London, British Library, 611.f.3]

Morata, Olimpia Fulvia (Grundler)
1526/7–1555   Ferrara (Italy)/Schweinfurt (Germany)
In Eutychum Pontanum Gallum: 'Nunquam eadem cunctos monit traxitve voluptas'

> *Editions*: *Olympia Fulvia Moratae Foeminae Doctissimae ac Pane Divinae Ora-
> tiones, Dialogi, Epistolae, Carmina, tam Latina quam Graeca* (Basel: Petrus
> Perna, 1562), 248 [Oxford, Balliol College, Special Collections 0650.a.13]
> Holt N. Parker, *Olympia Morata: The Complete Writings of an Italian Heretic*
> (Chicago: University of Chicago Press, 2003), 179 (with trans.)

Olympiae de Vera Virginitate: 'Quae virgo est, nisi mente quoque est, et corpore
virgo' (1549)

> *Editions*: 1562, 249
> *Olympiae Fulviae Moratae Mulieris Omnium Eruditissimae Latine et Graeca, quae
> Haberi Potuerunt, Monumento, eaque Plane Divino, cum Eruditorum de Ipsa
> Iudiciis et Laudibus; cum Hippolytae Taurellae Elegia Elegantissima* (Basel:
> Petrus Perna, 1558), 87 [Oxford, Bodleian Library, Seld. 88 C.12.Art. (2)]
> Olimpia Morata, *Opere*, ed. Lanfranco Coretti, 2 vols. Deputazione Provinciale
> Ferrarese di storia patria, Atti e memorie, NS XI.1–2 (1954)
> Olimpia Morata, *Opera*, ed. A. Wendehorst and G. Pfeiffer, Fränkische Lebens-
> bilder 10 (Neustadt: Aisch, 1982)
> Holt N. Parker, 'Olimpia Fulvia Morata (1526/7–1555): Humanist, Heretic,
> Heroine', in Laurie Churchill, Phyllis R. Brown, and Jane E. Jeffrey (eds.),
> *Women Writing Latin from Roman Antiquity to Early Modern Europe*, 3 vols.
> (New York: Routledge, 2002), iii. 133–65 (pp. 148, 163) (with trans.)
> Parker, *Olympia Morata*, 179–80

Olympiae Fides: 'Sic Deus humanum gentem vel semper amavit' (1549–55)

> *Editions*: 1562, 249
> 1558, 87
> Parker, 'Olimpia Fulvia Morata', 148, 163 (with trans.)
> Parker, *Olympia Morata*, 183 (with trans.)

Olympiae Votum: 'Dissolvi cupio, tanta est fiducia menti' (1555)

> *Editions*: 1562, 249
> 1558, 87

Georg Ludwig Nolten, *Commentaria Historico-critica de Olympiae Moratae Vita, Scriptis, Fatis et Laudibus* (Frankfurt: Carl. Theophil. Strauss, 1775), 157 [Vatican City, Biblioteca Apostolica, R.G. Storia V 1007]

Parker, 'Olimpia Fulvia Morata', 148, 163 (with trans.)

Parker, *Olympia Morata*, 183 (with trans.)

Latin verses

    MS: Salzburg, Öffentliche Universitätsbibliothek, M.135, fo. 198 [not seen]

Epigramma de Davide: 'Non erat in patria me quisquam junior aula'

    MS: Florence, Biblioteca Riccardiana, 3997, fo. 184ʳ

Distichon: 'Quam miserum est, tanto sejungi tempore amantes'

    Editions: Cyriacus Spangenberg, *Adels Spiegel: Historischer ausfürlichen Bericht* (Schmalkalden: Michel Schmueck, 1591), 425 [Wolfenbüttel, Herzog August Bibliothek, H: T.958 2° Helmst.]

Georg Christian Lehms, *Teutschlands galante Poetinnen, mit ihren sinnreichen und netten Proben, nebst einem Anhang ausländischer Dames so sich gleichfalls durch schöne Poesien [bey] der curieusen Welt bekannt gemacht* (Frankfurt am Main: Anton Heinscheidt, 1715), pt. II, p. 176 [London, British Library, 11525.dd.21]

Parker, *Olympia Morata*, 181 (with trans.)

More, Margaret (Roper)

1504–44   London (England)

Latin verse

    Attested by Thomas More, quoted in Thomas Stapleton, *Tres Thomae, seu de S. Thomae Apostoli Rebus Gestis, de S. Thoma Archiepiscopo Cantuariensis et Martyris, D. Thomae Mori Angliae quondam Cancellario, Vita*, 2 vols. (Douai: J. Bogard, 1588), 237, 242–3 [London, British Library, 1125.a.6]

Translation: *The Life and Illustrious Martyrdom of Sir Thomas More*, trans. Philip E. Hallett, ed. E. E. Reynolds (New York: Fordham University Press, 1966), 103–4, 106–17. Verse is also mentioned in a letter from Sir Thomas More to Margaret herself (trans. in E. M. G. Routh, *Sir Thomas More and his Friends* (London: Oxford University Press, 1934), 133–4)

Morel, Camille de

1547–after 1611   Paris (France)

Camillae, Iani Morelli Ebredunei Filia, Elegia, 'Herricus antiquis Gallorum Regibus ortus'

Editions: Carolus (Karel) Utenhove, *Epitaphium in Mortem Henrici Gallorum Regis Christianissimi* (Paris: Robert Estienne, 1560), sig. B 4ʳ–C 1ʳ [The Hague, Koniglijke Bibliotheek, 3146.F.15]

S. F. Will, 'Camille de Morel: A Prodigy of the Renaissance', *PMLA* 51 (1936), 83–119 (p. 94)

Ioach. Bellaii in sui Ipsius Mortem. Idem Latine, Camilla Morella Interprete: 'Contegor hoc tumulo generosa stirpe parentum'

Editions: *Epitaphium*, sig. E 4
Will, 96–7

Camillae Morellae Jani Morelli Ebredunei F. Dialogus J. Morellus et A. Deloina: 'Dic mihi quis lapidum iacet hac sub mole sepultus?'

Editions: *Epitaphium*, sig. F 3–4
Will, 97–8

Ad Serenissimam Angliae Reginam: 'Cum meus extremos iret praeceptor ad Anglos'

Edition: *Caroli Utenhovii F. Patricii Gandavensis* XENIA *seu ad Illustrium Aliquot Europae Hominum Nomina, Allusionum (Intertextis Alicubi Ioach. Bellaii eiusdem Argumenti Versibus), Liber Primus* (Basel: Thomas Guarinus, 1568), 15–16 [Oxford, Bodleian Library, 88 B 47 Art. Seld.];

MS: Munich, Bayerische Staatsbibliothek, Clm lat. 10384, fo. 272 [copy from printed text]

Antonia Deloina ex Graeco C.U. Camilla Morella Interprete: 'Credita quae Phoebi Delus fuit insula nutrix'

Editions: *Epitaphium*, sig. D 4
Utenhove, *Xenia*, 67

MS: Munich, Bayerische Staatsbibliothek, Clm lat. 10384, fo. 273 [copy from printed text]
Will, 111

Ad eundem Galliae Regem Carolum Nonum Christianissimum in Europam Ger. Mercatoris. Europa Loquitur: 'En ego totius quae sum pars tertia mundi'

Edition: Utenhove, *Xenia*, 29
MS: Munich, Bayerische Staatsbibliothek, Clm lat. 10384, fo. 273 [copy from printed text]

Ioach. Bellaii & Camillae Morellae Dialogismus Extemporalis: 'At tu Musarum princeps, tu solus Apollo'

> *Editions*: Utenhove, *Xenia*, 81
> Will, 93

Camilla Morella Car. Utenhovio f[ilio]: 'Carole tum nostro laberis pectore primum'

> *Edition*: Utenhove, *Xenia*, 112

In Typographiam Musarum Matrem Camilla Morella J. Morelli Ebredunei filia ex Graeco J. Aurati: 'Carmine Musarúmque Patrem, Musasque puellas'

> *Editions*: undated folio printed (?) in Paris by Robert Estienne [Paris, Bibliothè-
> que Nationale de France, Rés m.Yc.335]
> Will, 104

A Camilla Morella Virgine Annorum Vix Sedecim ex Ebraeo: 'Vellem equidem de more anni redeuntis in orbem' (1563)

> *MS*: London, Public Record Office, SP 70/48, fos. 4^v–9^r (fo. 6^v)

> *Edition*: *Xenia*, 12–13 (variant, inc. 'Fert animus de more anni redeuntis in orbem)

Carolo Utenhovio Camilla Morella: 'Dico vale, nec dico vale tibi Carole, namque' (1562)

> *MS*: Munich, Bayerische Staatsbibliothek, Clm lat. 10384, fo. 262

In Obitum Giliberti Dagoltii Elegantissimi Juvenis, 'Dum Gilibertus'

> *MS*: Munich, Bayerische Staatsbibliothek, Clm lat. 10384, fos. 269, 321^v [draft
> and fair copy]

Ad Auratum (Dorat)

> *MS*: Munich, Bayerische Staatsbibliothek, Clm 10383, fo. 249

Camilla Morella ad Michaelem Hospitalium, Galliae Nomophiliacem.: 'Legibus usa tuis, quae Gallia floruit olim'

> *MS*: Munich, Bayerische Staatsbibliothek, Clm 10384, fos. 247–8

Camillae Morellae Versus: 'Hoc ego si feci, vel si fecisse quid unquam'

MS: Munich, Bayerische Staatsbibliothek, Clm 10384, fos. 245–6

Ad I. Gessaeum, Camillae Morellae Carmen: 'Haec auctura tuum, non ornatura Libellum'

> *Edition*: Jean de la Gessée, *Epigrammaton ad Principes et Magnates Galliae* (Paris: D. du Pré, 1574), fo. 2ʳ [Paris, Bibliothèque Mazarine, 21470]

D. Vegetio Camilla Morella: 'O quoties memini iugiter dixissis nonulla'

> *MS*: Paris, Bibliothèque Nationale de France, Collections Dupuy 837, fo. 26ʳ

Camillae Morellae, Virginis Francae, Epigramma: 'Qua merui culpa, ne sit, Regina, videndi'

> *Edition*: *Gabrielis Harveii Gratulationum Valdinensium, Libri Quatuor, ad Illustrissimam Augustissimam Principem Elizabetam* (London: Henry Binneman, 1578), 1 [Cambridge, University Library, Syn 7.60.154¹⁰]

Camillae Morellae in Ioan. Morelli Patris sui Charissimi Obitum: 'Si virtus potuit mori, Morelle'

> *Editions*: *V.C. Ioann. Morelli Ebredun. Consiliarii Oeconomique Regii, Moderatoris Illustrissimi Principis Henrici Engolismaei, Magni Franciae Prioris, Tumulus* (Paris: Federicus Morellus, 1583), 3–5 [London, British Library, 837.h.8]
> Will (partial transcript), 109

Ad Ioannem Iesseum, Camilla Morella: 'Tu quoque tam chari cineres contemneris amici?'

> *MS*: London, British Library, Sloane 2764, fo. 12

> *Edition*: *Tumulus*, 12–13

Camilla Morella ad P. Bulengerum: 'Ut credam memorem te, Bulengere, Morelli'

> *Edition*: ibid., 25

In Antoniae Deloinae Matris Chariss. Tumulum, Camillae Morellae Epitaphium: 'Nos igitur miseras, nos (heu) tua viscera, natus'

> *Editions*: ibid., 43–4
> Will (partial transcript), 112

Alius eiusdem: 'Docta suo condigno viro Deloïna Morello'

  Edition: *Tumulus*, 44

Ad Lucretiae Morellae Manes Camilla Morella Soror: 'Cur terrestre solum, Lucretia, linquere, caelos'

  Edition: *Tumulus*, 44–5

Camilla Morella ad Ronsardum: 'Clare nepos clari vera probitate Morelli'

  Editions: *Tumulus*, 45–6
  Will (partial transcript), 106

Ad Scaev. Sammarthanum: 'Tu ne etiam veteris dicere oblitus amici?'

  Edition: *Tumulus*, 46–7

Ad Carolum Utenhovium, Camilla Morella: 'Nunc, docte Utenhovi, canas triumphum'

  Editions: *Tumulus*, 47–8
  Will (partial transcript), 106

Ad eandem [Camillam] in Frontispicium Theatri Urbium Francisci Hogenbergi Dialogismus (Camilla's is the second voice) *Camilla Morella*: 'Diva tenens summum tabulati in culmine sedem' (1598)

  MS: Paris, Bibliothèque Nationale de France, Lat. 18592, fos. 86ʳ–87ᵛ

Morell, Juliana
1593–1653   Barcelona (Spain), Lyon (France), Avignon
C.300 lines of Latin verse on the mysteries of the Rosary, the miraculous image of
St Dominic, and similar subjects

  Attested by contemporary biographer, Mère Marie de Merle de Beauchamps,
    and possibly preserved by the nuns of St Praxedes at Avignon. Mère Marie's
    account is translated (no details of original given) in *A Treatise on the Spiritual
    Life, by St Vincent Ferrer*, OP, trans. Dominican Nuns of Corpus Christi
    (London: Blackfriars Publications, 1957), 21

'Mulier'
s. xii   France
See under 'Heloïse' for a persuasive attribution of *Epistola Duorum Amantium*.

Muriel
d. before 1113   Wilton (England)
Nothing known to survive

Poems are attested by Hildebert of Le Mans, 'Versus ad Quandam Virginem Scilicet Muriel', in A. Wilmart, 'L'Élégie d'Hildibert pour Muriel', *Revue bénédictine*, 49 (1937), 376–84 (pp. 379–80) and by Baudri de Bourgeuil, *Les Œuvres
poétiques de Baudri de Bourgeuil (1046–1130): édition critique publiée d'après le
Ms du Vatican*, ed. Phyllis Abrahams (Paris: H. Champion, 1926), 256–7

'La Musette de Paris' (Anne le Fèvre (Dacier)?)
fl. 1684   Paris (France)
Epitaphium Helenae Lucretiae Cornarae Piscopiae Nob. Venetae, Laureatae: 'Hic
CORNARA jacet duplici radiosa corona'

> *Edition: Composizione per la morte di Elena Lucrezia Cornaro Piscopia, dedicate a
> Gianbattisto suo padre, Procuratore di S. Marco dal Co. Alessandro ab. de
> Lazaro, Principe dell'Accademia* (Padua: P. M. Frambotto, 1684), 55 [Padua,
> Biblioteca Museo Civico di Padova, BP.473.VIII]

'N'
fl. s.xii   Tegernsee? (Germany)
'H. quondam carissimo'

> *MS*: Munich, Bayerische Staatsbibliothek, Clm 19411, fos. 69ʳ–70ʳ

> *Editions*: *MLREL*, ii. 472–3
> Jürgen Kühnel, *Du bist mîn, ih bin dîn. Die lateinischen Leibes-(und Freundschafts-)
> Briefe des Clm 19411* (Göppingen: Kummerle, 1977) (with German trans.),
> 68–71

**Navia y Osorio, Doña Francisca Irene de (de Navia y Bellet, Marquesa de
Grimaldo)**
1726–42   Turin (Italy)/Madrid (Spain)
*Italia sibi Gratulator de Adventu Serenissimi Philippi Borbonii, eumque ut Properet
Invitat*: 'Ergo venit nostras dudum expectatus ad oras'

> *Editions*: 'Memorias de la exceletisima Señora Doña Maria Francesca Irene de
> Navia y Bellet, Marquesa de Grimaldo', *Memorial literario instructivo y curioso
> de la corte de Madrid*, 8 (1786), 67–73 (pp. 71–3) [London, British Library,
> P.P.4055]
> Diego Ignacio Parada, *Escritoras y eruditas españolas* (Madrid: Librerías de A. de
> San Martin, 1881), 149–50 [London, British Library, 11825.p.7]

Nicolai, Isabella
early s. xvi   Middelburg/Delft (the Netherlands)
Verse lost

> Attested by her brother, *Ioannis Secundus Hagiensis Opera nunc Primum in Lucem Edita* (Utrecht: Harmannus Borculous [*sic*], 1541), *Epistolarum* lib. I, sig M 5ᵛ–M 6ʳ (also 2nd edn. Paris, 1561) [The Hague, Koninglijke Bibliotheek, 1702.D.40; 1713.F.32]

Nogarola, Angela (D'Arco)
fl. *c.*1400–1430   Verona (Italy)
'O Comes Aonidum radiis decorate Minervae'

> *MS*: Modena, Biblioteca Estense, α G.5.15. (old classmark Est. Ital. 427), fos. 90ᵛ–91

Per Angelam de Nogarolis D[omino] V[isconti] Devotissimam ex Abundanti Gaudio Tamquam Corvum Crocitantem: 'Magne parens qui cuncta regis per principis aulam' (1387)

> *MS*: Florence, Biblioteca Riccardiana, 784 (M. IV. 32), fo. 145

> *Editions*: *Isotae Nogarolae Veronensis Opera quae Supersunt Omnia*, ed. Eugenius Abel, 2 vols. (Vienna: Gerold & Cie., 1886), ii. 300 [London, British Library, 12227.e.5]
>
> Holt N. Parker, 'Latin and Greek Poetry by Five Renaissance Italian Women Humanists', in Barbara K. Gold, Paul Allen Miller, and Charles Platter (eds.), *Sex and Gender in Medieval and Renaissance Texts: The Latin Tradition* (Albany: State University of New York Press, 1997), 247–86 (p. 255) (with trans.)
>
> Holt N. Parker, 'Angela Nogarola (ca. 1400) and Isotta Nogarola (1418–1466): Thieves of Language', in Laurie Churchill, Phyllis R. Brown, and Jane E. Jeffrey (eds.), *Women Writing Latin from Roman Antiquity to Early Modern Europe*, 3 vols. (New York: Routledge, 2002), iii. 11–30 (pp. 20, 25) (with trans.)

Dominae A. de N ad Antonium Luschum: 'Si modo me veniens studiis iuvenilibus actam'

> *MSS*: London, British Library, Harley 3716, fo. 75
> Mantua, Biblioteca Comunale, A. 1.8
> Munich, Universitätsbibliothek, 4. 768
> Trento, Biblioteca Comunale, 4973
> Venice, Biblioteca Marciana, Lat. XII. cvii.5 (4689), fos. 98ʳ and 104ʳ (two copies)

Editions: Abel, ii. 304
Parker, 'Latin and Greek Poetry', 251 (with trans.)
Parker, 'Angela Nogarola', 18, 23 (with trans.)

Ad Magnificum Dominum Dominum Pandulfum de Malatestis: 'Nate dea, quae nunc animo sententia surgit?'

MSS: Florence, Biblioteca Riccardiana, 784 (M.IV.32)
Savignano sul Rubicone, Biblioteca dell'Accademia Rubiconia dei Filopatri no. 71

Editions: Abel, ii. 291–326
Parker, 'Latin and Greek Poetry', 252–3 (with trans.)
Parker, 'Angela Nogarola', 18–19, 23–4 (with trans.)

Incluto et Glorioso Principi Domino Jacobo de Carraria: 'Summe parens rerum, summe regnator Olimpi'

MSS: Florence, Biblioteca Riccardiana, 784, 144^v–145
Kremsmünster, Stiftsbibliothek, 4, fo. 186
Pommersfelden, Gräflich Schönbarnsche Bibliothek, 168, fo. 183^v

Editions: Abel, ii. 291–326
Parker, 'Latin and Greek Poetry', 256–7 (with trans.)
Parker, 'Angela Nogarola', 20, 25–6 (with trans.)

Ad Nicolaum de Facino: 'Ac veterum laudes nobis adscribere vatum'

MS: Florence, Biblioteca Riccardiana, 784, fo. 162^v

Edition: Abel, ii. 302–3

Ad Nicolaum de Facino Vicentinum: 'Non aliena meis imponere vellera membris'

MSS: Florence, Biblioteca Riccardiana, 784, fo. 163
Modena, Biblioteca Estense, α G.5.15 (old classmark Est. Ital. 427), fo. 89

Editions: Abel, ii. 301
Parker, 'Latin and Greek Poetry', 257–8 (with trans.)
Parker, 'Angela Nogarola', 19, 25 (with trans.)

*Liber de Virtutibu*s: 'Ardua virtutum faciles cape, lector, ad usus'

MS: Modena, Biblioteca Estense, α G.5.15 (old classmark Est. Ital. 427), fos. 91–6

Editions: Abel, ii. 312–26

Parker (part only), 'Latin and Greek Poetry', 259–60 (with trans.)

Nogarola, Isotta

c.1416–1466   Verona (Italy)

Elegia de Laudibus Cyanei Ruris: 'Salvete, O Cyani fontes dulcesque recessus'

    MSS: Milan, Biblioteca Ambrosiana, J. 54 inf. (s. xvi)

    Milan, Biblioteca Ambrosiana, Q. 68 sup. (s. xvi)

    Venice, Bibliotheca Monasterii S. Michaelis, 721

    Editions: *Isotae Nogarolae . . . Dialogus quo Utrum Adam vel Eve Magis Peccaverit,*
       Quaestio Satis Nota sed non Adeo Explicata, Continetur (Venice: Aldus, 1563),
       31–4 [Paris, Bibliothèque Nationale de France, A. 3584 (4)]

    Isotae Nogarolae Veronensis Opera quae Supersunt Omnia, ed. Eugenius Abel, 2
       vols. (Vienna: Gerold & Cie., 1886), ii. 261–4 [London, British Library,
       12227. e. 5]

    Holt Parker, 'Latin and Greek Poetry by Five Renaissance Italian Women
       Humanists', in Barbara K. Gold, Paul Allen Miller, and Charles Platter
       (eds.), *Sex and Gender in Medieval and Renaissance Texts: The Latin Tradition*
       (Albany: State University of New York Press, 1997), 247–86 (pp. 263–6)
       (with trans.)

    Holt Parker, 'Angela Nogarola (ca. 1400) and Isotta Nogarola (1418–1466):
       Thieves of Language', in Laurie Churchill, Phyllis R. Brown, and Jane E.
       Jeffrey (eds.), *Women Writing Latin from Roman Antiquity to Early Modern*
       Europe, 3 vols. (New York: Routledge, 2002), iii. 11–30 (pp. 21–3, 26–9) (with
       trans.)

Isota ad Guarinum

    MS: Parma, Biblioteca Palatina, Parm. 259, fos. 92ᵛ–93ᵛ (s. xv) [not seen]

    Margaret L. King is planning a complete edition of the works of Isotta Nogarola

Norton, Martha

fl. 1620   Canterbury? (England)

'Si laudata Venus Juno si sacra Minerva'

    Inscription: Canterbury Cathedral, possibly still *in situ*

    MS: London, British Library, Egerton 3310. A, fo. 26ʳ

Nun of Admont

s. xiii   Admont (Germany)

Prologus Scribae: 'Fulgida vita Dei famulae seu forma trophaei'

Anon. (ed.), 'Vita, ut Videtur, Cuiusdam Magistrae Monialium Admuntensium in Styria, Saeculo xii' [by Gertrude of Admont], *Analecta Bollandiana*, 12 (1893), 356–66 (pp. 359–60) [London, British Library, HLR. 270.0922]

Nun of Amesbury
s. xii   Amesbury (England)
Titulus Sancti Mariae et Sancti Melorii Ambesbiensis Ecclesiae: 'nulli vitae datur qui mortis lege fruatur' (1113)

> *Editions*: Léopold Delisle (ed.), *Rouleaux des morts du ixe au xve siècle recueillis et publiés par la Société de l'Histoire de France* (Paris: Veuve J. Renouard, 1866), titulus 13, pp. 188–9 [Oxford, Bodleian Library, 2372.d.84]
>
> Daniel Sheerin, 'Sisters in the Literary Agon', in Laurie Churchill, Phyllis R. Brown, and Jane E. Jeffrey (eds.), *Women Writing Latin from Roman Antiquity to Early Modern Europe*, 3 vols. (New York: Routledge, 2002), ii. 93–131 (pp. 111, 122)

Nuns of Argenteuil
s. xii   Argenteuil (France)
Titulus S. Mariae Argentoilensis Ecclesiae: 'Sit tibi, Mathildis, requies super ardua coeli' (1113)

> *Edition*: Léopold Delisle (ed.), *Rouleaux des morts du ixe au xve siècle recueillis et publiés par la Société de l'Histoire de France* (Paris: Veuve J. Renouard, 1866), titulus 184, p. 262 [Oxford, Bodleian Library, 2372.d.84]

'Mors, gladius vibrans, animam cum corpore vastans' (1113)

> *Edition*: ibid., titulus 184, p. 262

Titulus: 'Flet pastore pio grex desolatus adempto' (1122) (also see above, under **Heloïse**)

> *Editions*: Léopold Delisle (ed.), *Rouleaux des morts du ixe au xve siècle recueillis et publiés par la Société de l'Histoire de France* (Paris: Veuve J. Renouard, 1866), titulus 41, p. 299 [Oxford, Bodleian Library, 2372.d.84]
>
> *Rouleau mortuaire du B. Vital, abbé de Savigny*, facsimile ed. Léopold Delisle (Paris: H. Champion, 1909), titulus 41 [Cambridge, University Library, 899.bb.53]
>
> Constant Mews, *The Lost Love Letters of Heloise and Abelard: Perceptions of Dialogue in Twelfth-Century France* (New York: St Martin's Press, 1999), 162–3 (with trans.)

<Nun of Auxerre?>[5]

s. xii   Auxerre (France)

Titulus Sancti Juliani Monacharum: 'Abbatissae debent mori' (1113)

> *Editions*: Léopold Delisle (ed.), *Rouleaux des morts du ixe au xve siècle recueillis et publiés par la Société de l'Histoire de France* (Paris: Veuve J. Renouard, 1866), titulus 217, pp. 276–7 [Oxford, Bodleian Library, 2372.d.84]
>
> Heresvitha Hengstl, *Totenklage und Nachruf in der mitellateinische Literatur seit die Ausgang der Antike*, diss. (Munich, 1935), 60
>
> Daniel Sheerin, 'Sisters in the Literary Agon', in Laurie Churchill, Phyllis R. Brown, and Jane E. Jeffrey (eds.), *Women Writing Latin from Roman Antiquity to Early Modern Europe*, 3 vols. (New York: Routledge, 2002), ii. 93–131 (pp. 117, 129–30) (with trans.)>

Nun of Avenay

s. xii   Avenay (France)

'Qui regis orbem dasque salutem, rex bone regum' (1113)

> *Editions*: Léopold Delisle (ed.), *Rouleaux des morts du ixe au xve siècle recueillis et publiés par la Société de l'Histoire de France* (Paris: Veuve J. Renouard, 1866), titulus 180, p. 257 [Oxford, Bodleian Library, 2372.d.84]
>
> Daniel Sheerin, 'Sisters in the Literary Agon', in Laurie Churchill, Phyllis R. Brown, and Jane E. Jeffrey (eds.), *Women Writing Latin from Roman Antiquity to Early Modern Europe*, 3 vols. (New York: Routledge, 2002), ii. 93–131 (pp. 116, 128) (with trans.)

Nun of Beaumont

s. xii   Beaumont (France)

Titulus s. Mariae Bellimontis: 'Legibus inferni careant et gaudia coeli' (1113)

> *Editions*: Léopold Delisle (ed.), *Rouleaux des morts du ixe au xve siècle recueillis et publiés par la Société de l'Histoire de France* (Paris: Veuve J. Renouard, 1866), titulus 121, p. 229 [Oxford, Bodleian Library, 2372.d.84]
>
> Daniel Sheerin, 'Sisters in the Literary Agon', in Laurie Churchill, Phyllis R. Brown, and Jane E. Jeffrey (eds.), *Women Writing Latin from Roman Antiquity to Early Modern Europe*, 3 vols. (New York: Routledge, 2002), ii. 93–131 (pp. 113, 124) (with trans.)

---

[5] This verse expresses a standard trope of medieval amatory poetry in representing the abbess as the jailer of sexually frustrated nuns (cf. *MLREL*, ii. 357–9): it is probably the work of a *clericus*. Though a verse which probably is by a woman, the Regensburg 'Gaude quod primam', is also comparable, the motif's inappropriateness in this context suggests its author saw women's lives as one-dimensional.

Nun of Caen

s. xii   Caen (France)

Titulus Sanctae Trinitatis Cadomi: 'Dum vixit, mundo quem sprevit cessit ab isto' (1122)

> *Editions*: Léopold Delisle (ed.), *Rouleaux des morts du ixᵉ au xvᵉ siècle recueillis et publiés par la Société de l'Histoire de France* (Paris: Veuve J. Renouard, 1866), titulus 3, p. 285 [Oxford, Bodleian Library, 2372.d.84]
>
> *Rouleau mortuaire du B. Vital, Abbé de Savigny*, facsimile ed. Léopold Delisle (Paris: H. Champion, 1909), titulus 3 [Cambridge, University Library, 899.bb.53]

<Nun of Canonsleigh (?)

s. xiii   Canonsleigh (England)

In Solemnitate Sancta Etheldredae, ad Vesperas: 'Ave gemma preciosa'

> *MS*: London, British Library, Cotton Cleopatra C.vi, fo. 198ʳ>

Nuns of Chelles

s. xii   Chelles (France)

Titulus Ecclesiae Baltildis atque Mariae: 'Virginibus suis aliarum lax [*sic*: lex, laus?] monacarum' (1113)

> *Editions*: Léopold Delisle (ed.), *Rouleaux des morts du ixᵉ au xvᵉ siècle recueillis et publiés par la Société de l'Histoire de France* (Paris: Veuve J. Renouard, 1866), titulus 187, pp. 262–3 [Oxford, Bodleian Library, 2372.d.84]
>
> Daniel Sheerin, 'Sisters in the Literary Agon', in Laurie Churchill, Phyllis R. Brown, and Jane E. Jeffrey (eds.), *Women Writing Latin from Roman Antiquity to Early Modern Europe*, 3 vols. (New York: Routledge, 2002), ii. 93–131 (pp. 116, 128) (with trans.)

s. xiii

Titulus: 'Extitit hic parma protectis fortis ad arma' (1233)

> *Edition*: Léopold Delisle (ed.), *Rouleaux des morts du ixᵉ au xvᵉ siècle recueillis et publiés par la Société de l'Histoire de France* (Paris: Veuve J. Renouard, 1866), titulus 14, p. 410 [Oxford, Bodleian Library, 2372.d.84]

Nun of Corpus Christi, Ferrara *see* Vegri, Caterina

Nun of Ghent

fl. 1629   England/Ghent (Belgium)

Epitaph for Dame Lucy Knatchbull

Inscription: English translation survives. The Lady Abbess of St Scholastica's Abbey, Teignmouth (ed.), *Abbess Neville's Annal of Five Communities of English Benedictine Nuns in Flanders, 1598–1687*, Catholic Record Society 6, Miscellanea 5 (London: Burns and Oates, 1909), 1–72 (p. 22)

<Nun of Saint-Ausone?[6]

s. xii   Angoulême (France)

Titulus Sancti Ausonii Martyris eiusdem Urbis: 'Si moriatur anus, non est plangenda puellis'

> *Editions*: Léopold Delisle (ed.), *Rouleaux des morts du ixe au xve siècle recueillis et publiés par la Société de l'Histoire de France* (Paris: Veuve J. Renouard, 1866), titulus 147, p. 245 [Oxford, Bodleian Library, 2372.d.84]
>
> Daniel Sheerin, 'Sisters in the Literary Agon', in Laurie Churchill, Phyllis R. Brown, and Jane E. Jeffrey (eds.), *Women Writing Latin from Roman Antiquity to Early Modern Europe*, 3 vols. (New York: Routledge, 2002), ii. 93–131 (pp. 115, 127) (with trans.)>

Nun of St George, Rennes

s. xii   Rennes (France)

Titulus Sancti Georgii Redonensis: 'Carne tegi nostra non respuit omnicreator' (1113)

> *Editions*: Léopold Delisle (ed.), *Rouleaux des morts du ixe au xve siècle recueillis et publiés par la Société de l'Histoire de France* (Paris: Veuve J. Renouard, 1866), titulus 98, p. 221 [Oxford, Bodleian Library, 2372.d.84]
>
> Daniel Sheerin, 'Sisters in the Literary Agon', in Laurie Churchill, Phyllis R. Brown, and Jane E. Jeffrey (eds.), *Women Writing Latin from Roman Antiquity to Early Modern Europe*, 3 vols. (New York: Routledge, 2002), ii. 93–131 (pp. 112, 123–4) (with trans.)

Nun of Saint-Julien-du-Pré

s. xii   Saint-Julien-du-Pré (France)

Titulus Santi Juliani de Prato: 'Plurima Mathildis te laudat turba virorum' (1113)

> *Editions*: Léopold Delisle (ed.), *Rouleaux des morts du ixe au xve siècle recueillis et publiés par la Société de l'Histoire de France* (Paris: Veuve J. Renouard, 1866), titulus 141, pp. 238–9 [Oxford, Bodleian Library, 2372.d.84]

---

[6] While the only persons named in this section of the *rotulus* are female, the casual misogyny and lack of respect towards senior women evidenced by these verses 'composed after a cup of wine' suggest both that they were written by a *clericus*, and that none of the women at Saint-Ausone was able to read them—an easier hypothesis than that they are the work of an alcoholic and cynical nun.

Daniel Sheerin, 'Sisters in the Literary Agon', in Laurie Churchill, Phyllis R. Brown, and Jane E. Jeffrey (eds.), *Women Writing Latin from Roman Antiquity to Early Modern Europe*, 3 vols. (New York: Routledge, 2002), ii. 93–131 (pp. 113, 124–5) (with trans.)

Nun of St Marie, Jouarre

s. xii   Jouarre (France)

Titulus Sanctae Mariae Jotrensis Ecclesiae: 'Haec sunt nostrorum solatia summa laborum'(1113)

> *Editions*: Léopold Delisle (ed.), *Rouleaux des morts du ixe au xve siècle recueillis et publiés par la Société de l'Histoire de France* (Paris: Veuve J. Renouard, 1866), titulus 198, p. 262 [Oxford, Bodleian Library, 2372.d.84]
>
> Daniel Sheerin, 'Sisters in the Literary Agon', in Laurie Churchill, Phyllis R. Brown, and Jane E. Jeffrey (eds.), *Women Writing Latin from Roman Antiquity to Early Modern Europe*, 3 vols. (New York: Routledge, 2002), ii. 93–131 (pp. 116, 128–9) (with trans.)

Nun of St Marie, Lisieux

s. xii   Lisieux (France)

Titulus Sanctae Mariae Lexoviensis: 'Cuncta petunt lapsum quaecunque vocantur ad ortum' (1113)

> *Editions*: Léopold Delisle (ed.), *Rouleaux des morts du ixe au xve siècle recueillis et publiés par la Société de l'Histoire de France* (Paris: Veuve J. Renouard, 1866), titulus 62, p. 205 [Oxford, Bodleian Library, 2372.d.84]
>
> Daniel Sheerin, 'Sisters in the Literary Agon', in Laurie Churchill, Phyllis R. Brown, and Jane E. Jeffrey (eds.), *Women Writing Latin from Roman Antiquity to Early Modern Europe*, 3 vols. (New York: Routledge, 2002), 93–131 (pp. 112, 122–3) (with trans.)

Nun of St Marie, Montvilliers

s. xii   Montvilliers (France)

Titulus Sancti Mariae Vilarensis: 'Sedibus aetheriis maneat sociata Mathildis' (1113)

> *Editions*: Léopold Delisle (ed.), *Rouleaux des morts du ixe au xve siècle recueillis et publiés par la Société de l'Histoire de France* (Paris: Veuve J. Renouard, 1866), titulus 72, p. 210 [Oxford, Bodleian Library, 2372.d.84]
>
> Daniel Sheerin, 'Sisters in the Literary Agon', in Laurie Churchill, Phyllis R. Brown, and Jane E. Jeffrey (eds.), *Women Writing Latin from Roman Antiquity to Early Modern Europe*, 3 vols. (New York: Routledge, 2002), ii. 93–131 (pp. 112, 123) (with trans.)

Nuns of St Marie, Saintes (*see also* Sibille)

s. xii   Saintes (France)
Titulus Sanctae Mariae Sanctoniensis: 'O mortalis homo, casus reminiscere mortis'
(1113)

> *Editions*: Léopold Delisle (ed.), *Rouleaux des morts du ixe au xve siècle recueillis et
> publiés par la Société de l'Histoire de France* (Paris: Veuve J. Renouard, 1866),
> titulus 144, p. 242 [Oxford, Bodleian Library, 2372.d.84]
> Hugh Feiss, OSB, 'A Poet Abbess from Notre Dame de Saintes', *Magistra: A
> Journal of Women's Spirituality in History*, 1.1 (1995), 39–53 (p. 48), trans. p. 51
> Daniel Sheerin, 'Sisters in the Literary Agon', in Laurie Churchill, Phyllis R.
> Brown, and Jane E. Jeffrey (eds.), *Women Writing Latin from Roman Antiquity
> to Early Modern Europe*, 3 vols. (New York: Routledge, 2002), ii. 93–131
> (pp. 113–14, 125) (with trans.)

'Est manifesta satis humanae debilitatis' (this may also be by Sibille, q.v.) (1113)

> *Editions*:

> Delisle, 243–4
> Feiss, 50, trans. pp. 53–4
> Sheerin, 115, trans. pp. 126–7

Nun of St Marie, Soissons
s. xii   Soissons (France)
Titulus Coenobii Beate Mariae Suessonis ad Sanctimoniales: 'Versibus abbatis si
posset vota novari' (1157)

> *Editions*: Léopold Delisle (ed.), *Rouleaux des morts du ixe au xve siècle recueillis et
> publiés par la Société de l'Histoire de France* (Paris: Veuve J. Renouard, 1866),
> titulus 1, p. 371 [Oxford, Bodleian Library, 2372.d.84]
> Daniel Sheerin, 'Sisters in the Literary Agon', in Laurie Churchill, Phyllis R.
> Brown, and Jane E. Jeffrey (eds.), *Women Writing Latin from Roman Antiquity
> to Early Modern Europe*, 3 vols. (New York: Routledge, 2002), ii. 93–131
> (pp. 116, 127–8) (with trans.)

Nun of St Marie, Troyes
s. xii   Troyes (France)
Titulus Sanctae Mariae Trecorum Sanctarum Monialium: 'Haec genitrix mundo
filiarum mansit in Christo' (1113)

> *Editions*: Léopold Delisle (ed.), *Rouleaux des morts du ixe au xve siècle recueillis et
> publiés par la Société de l'Histoire de France* (Paris: Veuve J. Renouard, 1866),
> titulus 207, pp. 270–1 [Oxford, Bodleian Library, 2372.d.84]

Daniel Sheerin, 'Sisters in the Literary Agon', in Laurie Churchill, Phyllis R. Brown, and Jane E. Jeffrey (eds.), *Women Writing Latin from Roman Antiquity to Early Modern Europe*, 3 vols. (New York: Routledge, 2002), ii. 93–131 (pp. 117, 129) (with trans.)

Nun of St Mary and St Edith, Wilton

fl. 1122   Wilton (England)
Titulus Sanctæ Mariæ Sanctæque Eadithæ Wiltoniensis Æcclesiæ: 'Gloria quid rerum, vel quid mora longa dierum' (1122)

> *Editions*: Léopold Delisle (ed.), *Rouleaux des morts du ixᵉ au xvᵉ siècle recueillis et publiés par la Société de l'Histoire de France* (Paris: Veuve J. Renouard, 1866), titulus 153, p. 328 [Oxford, Bodleian Library, 2372.d.84]
>
> *Rouleau mortuaire du B. Vital, Abbé de Savigny*, facsimile ed. Léopold Delisle (Paris: H. Champion, 1909), titulus 153 [Cambridge, University Library, 899.bb.53]

Nun of St Mary and St Edward, Shaftesbury

s. xii   Shaftesbury (England)
Titulus Sancte Mariæ et Sancti Edguardi Scephtoniensis Eclesiæ: 'O mors crudelis, nullique probata fidelis' (1113)

> *Editions*: Léopold Delisle (ed.), *Rouleaux des morts du ixᵉ au xvᵉ siècle recueillis et publiés par la Société de l'Histoire de France* (Paris: Veuve J. Renouard, 1866), titulus 18, pp. 188–90 [Oxford, Bodleian Library, 2372.d.84]
>
> Daniel Sheerin, 'Sisters in the Literary Agon', in Laurie Churchill, Phyllis R. Brown, and Jane E. Jeffrey (eds.), *Women Writing Latin from Roman Antiquity to Early Modern Europe*, 3 vols. (New York: Routledge, 2002), ii. 93–131 (pp. 111, 122) (with trans.)

Nuns of St Paul, Rouen

s. xii   Rouen (France)
Titulus Sancti Pauli Rothomagi, 'non hanc condempnet sententia judicalis' (1113)

> *Editions*: Léopold Delisle (ed.), *Rouleaux des morts du ixᵉ au xvᵉ siècle recueillis et publiés par la Société de l'Histoire de France* (Paris: Veuve J. Renouard, 1866), titulus 80, p. 213 [Oxford, Bodleian Library, 2372.d.84]
>
> Daniel Sheerin, 'Sisters in the Literary Agon', in Laurie Churchill, Phyllis R. Brown, and Jane E. Jeffrey (eds.), *Women Writing Latin from Roman Antiquity to Early Modern Europe*, 3 vols. (New York: Routledge, 2002), ii. 93–131 (pp. 112, 123)

Titulus S. Pauli Rothomagi: 'Quisquis coelesti vult esse beatus in aula' (1122)

> *Editions*: Delisle, titulus 20, p. 293

Rouleau mortuaire du B. Vital, Abbé de Savigny, facsimile ed. Léopold Delisle (Paris: H. Champion, 1909), titulus 3 [Cambridge, University Library, 899.bb.53]

Nuns of St Peter, Reims

s. xi/xii   Reims (France)
'Te, Guifrede Pater, patris qui nomine semper' (1051)

Edition: Léopold Delisle (ed.), *Rouleaux des morts du ix⁹ au xv⁹ siècle recueillis et publiés par la Société de l'Histoire de France* (Paris: Veuve J. Renouard, 1866), titulus 62, p. 85 [Oxford, Bodleian Library, 2372.d.84]

Titulus Sancti Petri Remensis Coenobii: 'Pro bono mortali quod sprevit mente sagaci' (1113)

Editions: ibid., titulus 202, p. 269

Daniel Sheerin, 'Sisters in the Literary Agon', in Laurie Churchill, Phyllis R. Brown, and Jane E. Jeffrey (eds.), *Women Writing Latin from Roman Antiquity to Early Modern Europe*, 3 vols. (New York: Routledge, 2002), ii. 93–131 (pp. 117, 128) (with trans.)

Nuns of St Mary and St Eadburg, Winchester ('Nunnaminster')

early s. xi–s. xii   Winchester (England)
'Sancte Machute...' (hymn: incipit is damaged, parts survive intact, rhymed octosyllables)

MS: London, British Library, Cotton Galba A. xiv, fos. 125ᵛ–126ᵛ

Edition: Bernard James Muir (ed.), *A Pre-Conquest English Prayer-Book* (London, For the Henry Bradshaw Society, 1988), 160

Titulus Gloriosae Dei Genitricis Mariae et Sanctae Eadburgae Virginis Wintoniensis Ecclesiae: 'Proh dolor! Argentum, vestis, nec gemma, nec aurum' (1113)

Editions: Léopold Delisle (ed.), *Rouleaux des morts du ix⁹ au xv⁹ siècle recueillis et publiés par la Société de l'Histoire de France* (Paris: Veuve J. Renouard, 1866), titulus 11, p. 187 [Oxford, Bodleian Library, 2372.d.84]

Daniel Sheerin, 'Sisters in the Literary Agon', in Laurie Churchill, Phyllis R. Brown, and Jane E. Jeffrey (eds.), *Women Writing Latin from Roman Antiquity to Early Modern Europe*, 3 vols. (New York: Routledge, 2002), ii. 93–131 (pp. 110, 121) (with trans.)

'Nos matris laudem melius reticendo colemus' (1113)

Editions: Delisle, 187
Sheerin, 110–11, 121 (with trans.)

Versus Cuiusdam Neptis suae: 'Post obitum matri prope sis, reverenda Maria' (1113)

Editions: Delisle, 187–8
Sheerin, 111, 121–2 (with trans.)

Titulus S. Mariae et Sanctae Eadburgae Virginis Wintoniensis: 'Sit semper Christi requies aeterna Vitali' (1122), single line

> *Editions*: Léopold Delisle (ed.), *Rouleaux des morts du ixe au xve siècle recueillis et publiés par la Société de l'Histoire de France* (Paris: Veuve J. Renouard, 1866), titulus 184, p. 339 [Oxford, Bodleian Library, 2372.d.84]
> *Rouleau mortuaire du B. Vital, Abbé de Savigny*, facsimile ed. Léopold Delisle (Paris: H. Champion, 1909), titulus 3 [Cambridge, University Library, 899.bb.53]

'Salva et incolomis maneat per secula scriptrix' (single hexameter, colophon)

> *MS*: Oxford: Bodleian Library, Bodl. 451

Nun of St John (?)
1102
Ordo Monialium Titulus Sci Johannis Baptisti in Memoriam Beati Brunonis: 'Bruno laudavis: tua vita decens renovatur'

> *Edition*: *Vita Beati Brunonis Confessoris Primi Institutionis Ordinis Carthusiensis* (Basel: J. Frobenius, *c.* 1515) [Oxford, Bodleian Library, Douce 257]

Nun of Saint-Léger-de-Préaux
s. xii   Lisieux (France)
Titulus S. Leodegarii: 'Dum sic polleret super hoc, dum fama volaret' (1113)
> *Editions*: Léopold Delisle (ed.), *Rouleaux des morts du ixe au xve siècle recueillis et publiés par la Société de l'Histoire de France* (Paris: Veuve J. Renouard, 1866), titulus 66, p. 207 [Oxford, Bodleian Library, 2372.d.84]
> Daniel Sheerin, 'Sisters in the Literary Agon', in Laurie Churchill, Phyllis R. Brown, and Jane E. Jeffrey (eds.), *Women Writing Latin from Roman Antiquity to Early Modern Europe*, 3 vols. (New York: Routledge, 2002), ii. 93–131 (pp. 112, 122–3) (with trans.)

Nun of St Peter (?)
1102
Titulus Sancti Petri Coenobii Puellarum: 'Vite forma pie totius acerva sophie'

Edition: *Vita Beati Brunonis Confessoris Primi Institutionis Ordinis Carthusiensis* (Basel: J. Frobenius, *c*.1515) [Oxford, Bodleian Library, Douce 257]

Nun of St Radegund (Holy Cross), Poitiers
1102   Poitiers (France)
Titulus Sancte Radegundis Regine Pictavis: 'Rex immense deus qui verbo cuncta creasti'

Editions: *Vita Beati Brunonis Confessoris Primi Institutionis Ordinis Carthusiensis* (Basel: J. Frobenius, *c*. 1515) [Oxford Bodleian Library, Douce 257]

Oldenburg, Anna Sophia (Redslob)
s. xvii   Vismar (Germany)
Extempore Latin verse

Attested by Christoph Christian Haendel, *Dissertatio de Eruditis Germaniae Mulieribus* (Altdorf: Heinrich Meyer, 1688), 18, and Johannis Paschius, *Gynaeceum Doctum, sive Dissertatio Historico-literaria, vom Gelehrten Frauenzimmer, antea Wittebergae Ano 1686 Publice Exposita* (Wittenberg: Christian Finkel, 1701), 53 [Wolfenbüttel, Herzog August Bibliothek, Bb.5; Wolfenbüttel, Herzog August Bibliothek, Li. 6896]

Orge
classical period?   Noricum [Austria]

'. . . nunc matris pietatem abet per dominica rura'
  Inscription: *CIL*, iii. 5695, suppl. 11827
    CLE, i. 274 (568)

Osorio, Ana
s. xvi   Burgos (Spain)
Not seen

She is said to have been awarded prizes for her Latin poetry at Alcalà and Seville. Alfonso Garcia Matamoros, *De Asserenda Hispanorum Eruditione, sive de Viris Hispaniae Doctis Narratio Apologetica* (Madrid: Juan Brocar, 1553), 59 [Salamanca, Biblioteca Universitaria, 1a/33749]

Otho, Johanna (Mayart)
c.1545–after 1617   Ghent (Belgium)/Duisburg (Germany)/Antwerp
Poematia sive Lusus Extemporanei Ioannae Othoniae (Antwerp, 1617) [The Hague, Konincklijke Bibliotheek, 761. H. 4]

Carminum Diversorum Libri Duo (Antwerp, 1616) [The Hague, Konincklijke Bibliotheek, 123. C. 3]

Ad Camillam Morellam Gerere, Pietate et Literis Latinis et Graecis Nobilem Virginem, Jana Jani Othonis Filia: 'Ore mihi vultuque licet nota Camilla'

> *MS*: Munich, Bayerische Staatsbibliothek, Clm 10384, fos. 250–1 (autograph presentation fair copy)

'Callimachum qui omnes scribendis praevenit hymnis'

> *MS*: Paris, Bibliothèque Nationale de France, Collections Dupuy 951, fo. 151ʳ

Ad suam Thaliam: 'O quam macra genas meas es Thalia'

> *Edition*:
> *Carminum . . . libri*, pt. II, sig. L3ʳ–4ʳ Jane Stevenson, 'Johanna Otho (Othonia) and Women's Latin Poetry in Reformed Europe', in Laurie Churchill, Phyllis R. Brown, and Jane E. Jeffrey (eds.), *Women Writing Latin from Roman Antiquity to Early Modern Europe*, 3 vols. (New York: Routledge, 2002), iii. 189–215 (pp. 199–201, 207–9) (with trans.)

Potentissimi Principis Friderici Comitis Palatini Rheni, . . . et Elizabethae, Jacobi Regis Magnae Britanniae Filiae Epithalamion: 'καιρετε δεσποτιδες, θεαι'

> *Edition*:
> *Carminum . . . libri*, pt. I, sig. B3ʳ–C2ᵛ Stevenson, 201–6, 209–13 (with trans.)

Owen, Jane
c.1580–after 1628   Oxford (England)
In Laudem Autoris: 'Quod fuit, est et semper erit sollemne poetis'

> *Edition*: John Owen, *Epigrammatum Libri Tres Autore Joanne Owen Cambro-Britanno, Novi Collegii Oxonienses Nuper Socio* (London: John Windet for Simon Waterson, 1606), sig. A 2ᵛ (in first three editions); 3rd edn. (Humfrey Lownes for Simon Waterson, 1607) [London, British Library, 1489. f. 68 (3rd edn.)]

> *Translation*: Robert Hayman's *Quodlibets, Lately Come over from New Britaniola, or Newfound-Land. Epigrams and Other Small Parcells Both Morall and Divine, the first four bookes being the Authors owne: the rest translated out of that Excellent Epigrammatist, Mr. Iohn Owen, and other rare Authors: with two Epistles of that excellently wittie Doctor, Francis Rablais: Translated out of his French at Large. All of them Composed and done at Harbor-Grace in Britaniola, anciently called*

Newfound-Land, by R.H, Sometimes Governor of the Plantation there (London: Printed by Elizabeth Allde, for Roger Michell, Pauls Church-yard, at the Signe of the Bulls-head, 1628), p. II, p. 40 [Oxford, Bodleian Library, Mal. 716 (4 & 5)]

In Mortem Charissimorum Fratrum Ludovici Owen Gener. et Griffini Owen: 'Carmina cogit amor, sed amor disjungere fratres' (1607)

> *Inscription*: St Aldate's Church, Oxford, north aisle, *in situ*.
> *Editions*: Anthony à Wood, *Survey of the Antiquities of the City of Oxford, Composed in 1661–6 by Anthony Wood*, ed. Andrew Clark, 3 vols. (Oxford: Clarendon Press for the Oxford Historical Society, 1889–99), iii. 135 [London, British Library, Ac. 8126/99]

Padilla, Maria Magdalena

s. xvi   Spain
Nothing is known to survive, but she wrote at least one Latin poem

> Mentioned by her contemporary Alvar Gómez de Castro in a letter to Pedro de la Rua: 'mitto ad te Mariae Magdalenae poema quod nuper excussatum est'

> *MS*: Madrid, Biblioteca Naçional, 8424, fo. 135

Paleotti, Ippolita (Grassi)

d. 1581   Bologna (Italy)
Her verse in Latin and Greek seems to be lost but is attested by contemporaries

> Giovanni Fantuzzi, *Notizie degli scrittori bolognesi*, 8 vols. (Bologna: Stamperìa di San Tommaso d'Aquino, 1781–94) vi. 259 [Vatican City, Biblioteca apostolica, Bibliografia.II. Italia. Bologna.a.1]

Pallantia/van Pallandt, Anna (Rulanda)

later s. xvi   Eberfeld/Neuss/Comburg (Germany)
Anna Palanda Iohan. Posthio S.: 'Quod Cerebrum Persis Joviale, suavique, quod ursis'

> *Edition*: Johannes Posthius, *Parergorum Poeticorum Libri Duo* (Heidelberg: Hieronymus Commelin, 1595), 204 [The Hague, Konincklijke Bibliotheek, 1714. D. 10]

Annæ Palandæ Rulandidos ad Ioann. Posthium Iatropoëtam Incomparabilem Adonii: 'Speque Fideque'

> *Edition*: Jacob Monavius, *Symbolum* (Gorlitz: Johannes Rhamba, 1595), 221–2 [The Hague, Konincklijke Bibliotheek, 1714 F 9]

Variant text (addressed to Monau) Düsseldorf MS [not seen, referred to in margin p. 222]

Aliud in illud τοῦ *Ipse* ἀναγραμματισμον *Sepi ANNÆ PAL. RUL. Distichon*: 'Certa Iacobe Fide, nutantia pectora Sepi'

Edition: Monavius, 222–3 [The Hague, Konincklijke Bibliotheek, 1714. F. 9]

Annae Pallantiae et Annae Utenhoviae Acrostichon: 'IA-ne pater cedat cui matutinus Horati'

MS: London, British Library, Burney 370, fo. 41ᵛ

Pallantia/van Pallandt, Johanna
b. *c.*1560   Ghent (Belgium)/Paris (France)
JOHANNA PALLANTIA P. MELISSO, Viro Clariss[imo]: 'Scandere quae condis tantummodo carmina novi'

> *Editions*: Paul Melissus, *Melica* (Frankfurt: Corvinus, 1574), 88–91 [Munich, Bayerische Staatsbibliothek, P.o.lat. 922]
> Georg Christian Lehms, *Teutschlands galante Poetinnen, mit ihren sinnreichen und netten Proben, nebst einem Anhang ausländischer Dames so sich gleichfalls durch schöne Poesien [ben] der curieusen Welt bekannt gemacht* (Frankfurt am Main: Anton Heinscheidt, 1715), pt. II, p. 186 [London, British Library, 11525. dd. 21]

Pannolini, Febronia, Suor
fl. 1590/1610   Bologna (Italy)
'Quos, Dea coelipotens, divina retulit olim'

> *Editions*: [Giulio Segni et al.] *Componimenti poetici volgari, latini e greci di diversi sopra la s. Imagine della Beata Virgine dipinta a s. Luca* (Bologna: Vittorio Benacci, 1601), 61 [Bologna, Biblioteca Comunale dell'Archiginnasio, 16.A.vi.27]
> Lorenzo Legati, *Musei Poetriarum Primitiae* (Bologna: Heredes Victorio Benacci, 1668), 22 [Vatican City, Biblioteca Apostolica Cicognara IV.M.45 (int. 3)]
> Giovanni Fantuzzi, *Notizie degli scrittori bolognesi*, 8 vols. (Bologna: Stamperia di San Tommaso d'Aquino, 1784–8), vi. 270–2 [Vatican City, Biblioteca apostolica, Bibliografia II.Italia. Bologna.a.1]

'Cynthius aetherea non tam mortalibus arce'

> *Edition*: *Tempio all'illustrissimo et reverendissimo Signor Cinthio Aldobrandini Cardinale S. Giorgio, nipote del Sommo Pontefice Clemente Ottavo*, ed. Giulio Segni (Bologna: Heredi di Giovanni Rossi, 1600) [Latin section], p. 98 [London, British Library, 11427. ee. 2]

Latin verse

> *Editions*: *Corona di varie composizioni ecc. nella morte del Cardinal Cintio Aldo-brandini*, ed. Don Bernadino Guidoni (Padua: Pasquali, 1610) [not seen: Guidoni's *Corona di varie compositioni poetiche fatte nella morte dell'illustrissimo e reverendissimo Cardinale Cintio Aldobrandini* (Padua: Pasquali, n.d.), in Venice, Biblioteca Marciana, Misc. 2476.6, contains no women's writing, but there may be a second edition, revised and augmented under the title given above]

Papiria Tertia

Ferrara (Italy)

'Cernis, ut orba meis, hospes, monumenta locavi'

> *Inscription*: *CLE*, i. 173 (369)
> H. Geist and G. Pfohl (eds. and German trans.), *Römische Grabinschriften* (Munich: Ernst Heimeran Verlag, 1969), 52 (82)
> *Translation*: *WWMA*, 25

Patino, Carlotta Caterina (Rosa)
b. 2nd half s. xvii   Paris (France) Padua (Italy)
'Lucretia extinctâ, quis digne carmina condat?'

> *Edition*: *Composizione per la morte di Elena Lucrezia Cornaro Piscopia, dedicate a Gianbattisto suo padre, procuratore di S. Marco dal Co. Alessandro ab. de Lazaro, principe dell'Accademia* (Padua: P. M. Frambotto, 1684), 55 [Padua, Biblioteca museo civico di Padova, BP. 473. VIII]

Latin translations of verses by Madeleine de Scudéry

> Referred to by her mother Madeleine Patin, in Claude Charles Guyonnet de Vertron, *La Nouvelle Pandore, ou les femmes illustres du siècle de Louis le Grand* (Paris: Veuve C. Mazuel, 1698), 408; 2nd edn. (Paris: Nicolas le Clerc, 1703) [Paris, Bibliothèque de l'Arsenal, 8° B. 2. 21471; Oxford, Bodleian Library, Vet.E4. f. 329/1–2]

Patino, Gabriella Carlotta
b. 2nd half s. xvii   Paris (France)/Padua (Italy)
In Urbem Venetam: 'Quo sit ingenio VENETI, Gens aspera bello'

> *Edition*: Johann Friderich Hekel, *Dissertatiuncula de Foeminis Litteratis, qua Actum Aretalogicum Alterum* (Rudolstadt: Schulzianus, 1686), 2–3 [London, British Library, 12301. m. 15 (12)]

E Terris ad Coelos Transitus, Illustriss. et Excellentiss. D.D. Helenæ Lucretiæ Corneliæ Piscopiæ, Nobilis Venetæ, Academicæ, Laureatæ: 'Lucretia et morum candore et lumine mentis'

> *Edition*: *Composizione per la morte di Elena Lucrezia Cornaro Piscopia, dedicate a Gianbattisto suo padre, procuratore di S. Marco dal Co. Alessandro ab. de Lazaro, principe dell'Accademia* (Padua: P. M. Frambotto, 1684), 42 [Padua, Biblioteca museo civico di Padova, BP. 473. VIII]

Paulina, Fabia Aconia
late s. iv   Rome (Italy)
'Splendor parentum nil mihi maius dedit'

Inscription: now in the Capitoline Museum

Editions: *CLE*, i. 62–4 (111)
Petrus Burmann (ed.), *Anthologia Veterum Latinorum Epigrammatum et Poematum, sive Catalecta Poetarum Latinorum in VI Libros Digesta*, 6 vols. in 2 (Amsterdam: Schouten, 1759, 1773), ii. 149–50 (IV.cci) [London, British Library, 54. f. 13]
Heinrich Meyer (ed.), *Anthologia Veterum Latinorum Epigrammatum et Poematum*, 2 vols. in 1 (Leipzig: Gerhard Fleischer, 1835), ii. 145 (1315) [London, British Library, 011388. b. 14]
Edward Courtney, *Musa Lapidaria: A Selection of Latin Verse Inscriptions* (Atlanta: Scholars Press, 1995), no. 32, pp. 56–61

Translation: *WWMA*, 20–22

Paz, Catalina de
Mid-s. xvi   Badajoz/Alcalá de Henares/Guadalajara (Spain)
Liber Loquitur ad Malevolos, per Facundum os Catherinae de Pace: 'Invide ne linguae tuae me contagia laedant'

> *Editions*: Juan Hurtado de Mendoza, *Buen plazer trobado en treze discantes de cuarta rima castellana según imitación de trobas francesces* (Alcalá de Henares: Joan Brocar, 1550), sig. + 8ᵛ [London, British Library, C.63.a.24]
> *Apuntes*, ii.2, pp. 663–4 [Cambridge, University Library, 743.01.b.1.268]

Eiusdem Dominae Catherinae de Pace Intercalare Carmen, quo Invitat ad Honestam Animi Voluptatem quam Liber Docet: 'Huc iuvenes properate, gradus huc flectite vestros'

> *Editions*: de Mendoza, sig. + 8ᵛ–A1ʳ
> *Apuntes*, ii.2, pp. 663–4

In Laudem Doctissimi Viri Joannis Hurtadi Mendoçae, de Parto Triumpho in Musarum Certamine, Dominae Catharinae de Paz. Epigramma: 'Inter mille viros quod sit tibi reddita palma'

Edition: Apuntes, ii.2, pp. 663–4

Ad Clarissimum Virum Dominum Joannem Hurtadum Mendoçam, de Obitu Matris: 'Maxima curarum requies cum sola mearum'

Edition: Apuntes, ii.2, pp. 663–4

Paz, Helena
s. xvi/xvii
Latin verse

> Attested by Damião de Froes Perym, *Theatro Heroino ABCedario historico, e catalogo das mulheres illustres em Armas, letres, Acçoens Heroicas e artes Liberaes,* 2 vols. (Lisbon occidental: Oficina da Musica da Theotonio Atunes Lima / Regia officina Sylvania e Academia Real, 1736–40) I 430 [London, British Library, 10604. i. 3]

Pazzi, ——
*c.*1470   Florence (Italy)
Latin verse

> Attested by Francesco Agostino della Chiesa, *Theatro delle donne letterate* (Mondovi: Giovanni Gislandi & Giovanni Tomaso Rossi, 1620), 270 [Paris, Bibliothèque Nationale de France, G. 21, 404]

Pelagia
mid-s. v   Zigovosje (Croatia, former Yugoslavia)
'Diversum sortita capis finemque caputque'

> *Inscription: CIL,* iii.1, p. 300 (1894)
> *CLE,* i. 728–9 (1531)
> V. Hoffiller and Baldwin Saria (eds.), *Antike Inschriften aus Jugoslavien* (Zagreb: Druck der Fondsdruckerei der 'Narodne novine', 1938), ii. 7

Perilla
s. i AD   Rome (Italy)
Nothing known to survive

> Attested by Ovid in *Tristia* 3. 7.

Pernussów, Anna Teresa (Piotrowczykowa)
s. xvii   Kraków (Poland)
Latin verse

> Attested by Stefan Krol, *101 Kobiet Polskien: slad w historii* (Warsaw: Książka
> Wiedza, 1988), 39–40

Phile

Rome (Italy)

'Hic Clytius carus cunctis iustusq[ue] piusq[ue]'
Inscription: *CIL*, vi, no. 7243
CLE, ii. 499 (1089)

Piotrowczykowa, Anna Teresa, *see* Pernussów, Anna Teresa

Piotrowczykowa, Jadwiga
s. xvii   Kraków (Poland)
Latin verse

> Attested by Stefan Krol, *101 Kobiet Polskien: slad w historii* (Warsaw: Książka i
> Wiedza, 1988), 39–40

Pirckheimer, Charitas
1467–1532   Nuremberg (Germany)
Van dem heiligen hochwirdigen Sacrament schon gruβ: 'Ave vivens hostia, veritas et
vita'

> *MS*: Munich, Bayerische Staatsbibliothek, Cod. germ. 7380, fos. 205–11

> *Edition*: *Caritas Pirckheimer—Quellensammlung*, ed. Josef Pfanner, 4 vols. i: *Das
> Gebetbuch der Caritas Pirckheimer* (Landshut: Solanus Druck für Caritas-
> Pirckheimer-Forschung, 1961), 64–6

Aber schon gruβ van dem Sacrament: 'Salve saluberrima salus infirmorum'

> *MS*: Munich, Bayerische Staatsbibliothek, Cod. germ. 7380, fos. 205–11

> *Editions*: F. J. Mone, *Lateinische Hymnen des Mittelalters* (Freiburg in Breisgau:
> 1853), 296–7.
> Pfanner, 66–7

Piscopia, Elena Lucrezia Cornaro
1646–84   Venice/Padua (Italy)
Epigramma Greco-Latino

> *Edition*: *Epantismalogia overo Raccogliamento poetico dei più fioriti ingegni nella*
> *solenne coronatioe in filosofia e medicina del signor Angelo Sumachi nob. Di Zante*
> (Padua: Cadorino, 1668), 7 [not seen: attested in Francesco Ludovico
> Maschietto, *Elena Lucrezia Cornaro Piscopia (1646–1684)* (Padua: Editrice
> Antenore, 1978), 161]

Epigramma Graecum Interpretatione Latina ad Cunas Augustissimi Infantis Ioseph
Ignati, nunc Hungariae Regis: 'Aspicis, ut cingunt natalia Sydera Cunas'

> *Editions*: *Compositioni delli signori academici Ricovrati per la nascita del serenissimo*
> *principe Gioseppe, Giacomo, Ignatio, Antonio, Giovanni, Eustachio, Archiduca*
> *d'Austria*, ed. Carlo Patino (Padua: Frambotti, 1678), 57 [London, British
> Library, 1054. e. 29]
> Johann Friderich Hekel, *Dissertatiuncula de Foeminis Litteratis, qua Actum Are-*
> *talogicum Alterum* (Rudolstadt: Schulzianus, 1686), 2 [London, British Li-
> brary, 12301. m. 15 (12)]
> *Helenae Lucretiae (quae et Scholastica) Corneliae Piscopiae Virginis Pietate, et*
> *Eruditione Admirabilis, Ordine S. Benedicti Privatis Votis Adscriptae, Opera*, ed.
> Benedetto Bacchini (Parma: Ippolito Rusati, 1688), 138 (taken from Hekel)
> [London, British Library, 4405. f. 55]

Linguarum Omnium Praeconia Merentem Reverend. Patrem Iacobum Lubranum e
Societat. Iesu Scientiae Multiplicis, Pluriumque Palmarum Concionatorem, Sincera,
nec Bilinguis, Illustrissima D. Helena Lucretia Cornelia Piscopia, Septilingui Lauda-
tione Commendat: [Latin poems] 'Quae, Lubrane, iacis divino è pectore, verba',
'Ecquis ubi ardentes Laurentius insidet Aras'

> *Edition*: Elena Lucrezia Cornara Piscopia, *Seconda corona intrecciata da varii*
> *letterati co' fiori de' loro ingegni, per coronar di nuovo il molto reverendo padre*
> *Giacomo Lubrani, della Compagnia di Giesù, predicatore nella chiesa del vener-*
> *ando monistero di San Lorenzo, e corifeo tra gli oratori sacri di Venezia nell'anno*
> *1675* (Venice: Antonio Bosio, 1675), 47–62 (pp. 48, 49) [Vatican City, Bib-
> lioteca Apostolica, Chigi IV. 2132]

In Celebrem Academiam Infoecundorum Romae cum Epigraphe, GERMINABIT, *Epi-*
gramma: 'Infoecunda nives inter, gelidasque pruinas'

> *Edition*: *Poesie de' signori Accademici Infecondi di Roma, dedicate all'eminentis. e*
> *reverendis. sig. il Signor Cardinal Felice Rospigliosi, protettore dell'Accademia*
> (Venice: Nicolò Pezzana, 1678), 341 [Vatican City, Biblioteca Apostolica,
> Chigi V. 2307]

Ad Excellentissimum D. D FAELICEM ROSPILIOSUM, *Eiusdem Academiae Principem, nunc S.R.E Cardinalem, Dictae Academiae Protectorem, Epigramma eiusdem*: 'Infoecundorum quae dicta Academia portat'

Edition: Ibid. 341

Epigramma: 'Quicquid habet natura tibi, et fortuna dederunt'

> *Edition*: *Orazione di Antonio Dragoni e componimenti di altri soggetti, in lode dell' ecellentissimo Giovanni Cornaro, luogotenente generale della patria del Friuli* (Udine: Schiratti, 1683), 139 [Venice, Biblioteca Marciana, Misc. 2810 (9)]

Domina Helena Cornelia Piscopia anno ante Obitum Arentem Cupressum Succidens Funeri suo Destinat: 'Præscia succisae redolentia ligna Cupressum'

> *Edition*: *Le pompe funebre celebrate da' signori Accademici Infecondi di Roma per la morte dell'illustrissima Signora Elena Lucrezia Cornara Piscopia, accademica detta 'L'Inalterabile'* (Padua: Cadarino, 1686), 162 [Padua, Biblioteca Museo Civico di Padova, BP. 583]

Domina Helena Cornelia Piscopia in Matrimonium Quaesita Constanter Resistit, Obtenta Licet per Diploma Pontificum Dispensatione a Voto Castitatis: Epigramma eiusdem: 'Quae se cælesti dicaverat innuba Sponso'

Edition: ibid. 162

Pittori, Crispolita (Sassi)
s. xviii Assisi/Cagli (Italy)
'una lunga ed eloquente Elegia Latina, ed. Giuseppe Leonardi, 1764, in fogl. volante'

> Attested by Ginevra Canonici Fachini, *Prospetto biografico delle donne italiane rinomate in letteratura* (Venice: Tipografia di Alvisopoli, 1824), 204 [Vatican City Biblioteca Apostolica, Z. 2350 5.C.2]

Plotia Capitolina
Rome (Italy)
'Ta[m] cito pictor acu Stygia[s] delatus ad umbras'

> *Inscription*: *CIL*, vi. 6182
> *CLE*, ii. 533 (1150)

Polla Argentaria

s. i AD   Rome (Italy)

No work survives

She is mentioned as a poet by her contemporaries Martial (*Ad Pollam*) and
Statius (*Sylvae* 2)

Proba, Anicia Faltonia

fl. late s. iv   Rome (Italy)

Epitaphium ad Sepulchrum Probi: 'Sublimes quisquis tumuli miraberis arces'

> *Inscription*: Cesare Baronius, *Annales Ecclesiastici*, 12 vols (Rome: Typographia
> congregationis Oratorii, 1593–1607), iv. 717–18 [London, British Library,
> C.109.t.2]
>
> Petrus Burmann (ed.), *Anthologia Veterum Latinorum Epigrammatum et Poema-
> tum, sive Catalecta Poetarum Latinorum in VI Libros Digesta*, 6 vols. in
> 2 (Amsterdam: Schouten, 1759, 1773), i. 322–3 (II.cxxxix) [London, British
> Library, 54.f.13]
>
> Heinrich Meyer (ed.), *Anthologia Veterum Latinorum Epigrammatum et Poema-
> tum*, 2 vols. in 1 (Leipzig: Gerhard Fleischer, 1835), i. 257 (825) [London,
> British Library, 011388.b.14]
>
> *CIL*, vi. 389 (1751–6)
>
> *CLE*, ii. 630–2 (1327)

> *Translation*: *Proba Valeria's Epitaph on her Husband*: 'To God, to Princes, Wife,
> kinred, Freinds, the poore', London, British Library, Add. 15,227 (Cam-
> bridge, 1620s–1630s), fo. 98ʳ

Proba, Faltonia Betitia[7]

fl. *c*.360   Rome (Italy)

Cento: 'Iam dudum temerasse duces pia foedera pacis' (prologue)

> *MSS* (incomplete): Vatican City, Biblioteca Apostolica, Pal. 1753, fos. 62ʳ–69ʳ
> (s. viiiˣ)
>
> St Petersburg, Saltykov-Shchedrin Library, F.xiiii (s viii)
>
> Paris, Bibliothèque Nationale de France, 13048, fos. 31–8 (s. viii–ix)
>
> Paris, Bibliothèque Nationale de France, 7701 (olim 5519) (s. ix)
>
> Laon, Laudunenses (?) 279 and 273 (s. ix)
>
> Karlsruhe, Badische Landesbibliothek, CCXVII (s. ix–x)

---

[7] I have not in this case attempted to find all these editions, and some references are only as complete
as the secondary source allowed: my list is based on Schenkl's list of manuscripts in *Poetae Christiani
Minores* (Vienna: F. Tempsky, 1888) and Ermini's list of editions in *Il centone di Proba e la poesia
centonaria Latina* (Rome: Ermanno Loescher & Co., 1909), with further additions: the listing here is
given in the interests of establishing the high and long-term level of interest in this work.

Tours, Bibliothèque du Ville, C 68 (s. x)
Munich, Bayerische Staatsbibliothek, Clm 18628
Vatican City, Biblioteca Apostolica, Reg. lat. 251, fos. 15ᵛ–27ᵛ (s. xi)
Vatican City, Biblioteca Apostolica, Reg. lat. 1666, fos. 41ʳ–44ᵛ, (s. xi)
Angers?, Angelicanus, (?) V.3.22 (s. xi)
Charleville 97 (s. xii)
Cambridge, Trinity College Library, O.7.7 (s. xii)
Venice, Biblioteca Marciana, XII.7 (s. xii)
Turin, Biblioteca Nazionale, F.IV. 7
Paris, Bibliothèque Nationale de France, 14758 (s. xiii)
Escorial, Biblioteca Real, g.III.9, fos. 62–124 (s. xiv)
Escorial, Biblioteca Real, o.III.2, fos. 88–97 (s.xiv)
Florence, Biblioteca Laurentiana, XXIII.15 (s. xv)
Escorial, Biblioteca Real, o.III.1, fos. 51ᵛ–65 (s. xv)
Milan, Biblioteca Ambrosiana, D.14 inf.
Vatican City, Biblioteca Apostolica, Reg. lat. 585, fos. 2ʳ–4ʳ (incomplete)
Vatican City, Biblioteca Apostolica, Ottobonensis lat. 560, fos. 1–26
Munich, Bayerische Staatsbibliothek, Lat. 6722 (Fris. 522), fos. 140 ff.
Munich, Bayerische Staatsbibliothek, Clm 249, fos. 217–24
Munich, Bayerische Staatsbibliothek, Clm 526, fos. 59–95

Editions (incomplete): *Ausonii Opuscula, Consolationem ad Liviam Augustam de Morte Drusi, Probae Cento*, fos. 57ʳ–67ʳ, *Calpurnii Eclogae, Publius Gregorius Tiferni de Trinitate* (Venice: Bartolomeo Girardini, 1472)

Probae Falconiae Cento Virgilianus (Basel: Michael Wensler, *c.*1475)

Probae Falconiae Virgiliocento cum Opusculis Philippi (Rome: Joannis Philippus de Lignamine, 1481)

Probae Centonae Clarissimae Excerptum e Maronis Opusculum in Tractatus Solemnis et Utilis Philippi Siculi (n.p., n.d.)

Probae Falconiae Virgiliocento (Antwerp: Gerhard Leon, 1489)

Probae Centonae Clarissimae Foeminae Excerptum Maronis Carminibus ad Testimonium Veteris Novique Testamenti Opusculum (Venice: Bernadino Benatio, n.d.)

Decimus Magnus Ausonius Opera, Probae Centonae (Venice, 1492), fo. 75ʳ

Probae Centonae Clarissimae Feminae Opusculum (Brescia, 1496)

Probae Falconiae Cento et Sulpitii Soror Historia (Venice: Aldus Manutius Sr. 1501)

Probae Faltoniae Cento, in *Poetae Christiani Veteres* (Venice: Aldus Manutius, 1502)

Centones (Salamanca: J. Gysser, 1502)

Probae Faltoniae Cento (Deventer: Richardus Pafraët, 1505)

Probae Falconiae Cento Virgilianus (Paris: Jean Petit, 1507)

Probae Falconiae Vatis Clarissimae a Divo Hieronymus Comprobatae Centonam de Fidei Nostrae Mysteriis (Lyon: Stephanus de Basignona, 1516)

Probae Virgiliocento in Homerocentona Graeca et Latina (Frankfurt: P. Bubrach, 1541)

Probae Falconiae Vatis Clarissimae a Sacto Hieronymo Comprobatae Centones (Paris: François Estienne, 1543)

Probae Faltoniae Cento, ed. Margarinus Bigneus, *Bibliotheca Patrum V* (Paris: Michael Sonnius, 1575)

Probae Falconiae Virgiliocento cum Eudociae Homerocentonibus (Paris: Henri Estienne, 1578)

Probae Falconiae Virgiliocentones et Aliorum (Helmstadt: H. Meibom, 1579)

Probae Falconiae centones, ed. Julius Roscius Hurtinus (Rome: Typographia Sanctius, 1588)

Probae Falconiae Cento ex Virgilio, in A. Massa Gallesius, *A. Massae Galesii de Origine et Rebus Faliscorum Liber* (Rome: Sanchius, 1588)

Probae Faltoniae Cento, ed. Margarinus Bigneus, *Bibliotheca Sanctorum Patrum VIII*, 2nd edn. (Paris: Michael Sonnius, 1589)

Probae Virgiliocentones, ed. Joannes Platearius (Cologne: Joannes Gymnicus, 1592)

Probae Falconiae Virgiliocentones, (Cologne, 1601)

Probae Cento, in *Poetae Graeci Christiani* (Paris: Cl. Chapelet, 1609)

Elegantes Variorum Virgilio-Ovidio-Centones, including Proba's *Cento* (A. Raphaelus Sadlerus, 1617)

Probae Falconiae Cento, in *Elegantes Variorum Virgilio-Ovidio-Centones* (Munich, 1617)

Probae Falconiae Cento, in *Bibliotheca Patrum VIII* (Paris: Gilles Morel, 1644)

Probae Falconiae Cento, in *Bibliotheca Patrum V* (Lyon: Anissionios, 1677)

Probae Falconiae Foeminae Clarissimae e Virgilio Carminibus Opusculum, in Thomas de Simeonibus, *Historica Dissertatio Romano-ecclesiastica* (Bologna: Ant. Pisaro, 1692)

Probae Falconiae Cento Virgilianus Historiam Veteris et Novi Testamenti Complexus, in Vergil, *Opera*, appendix, ed. J. H. Kromayer (Halle: 1719)

Probae Cento, in L. H. Teuchem (ed.), *Homerocentones* (Leipzig: Teubner, 1793)

PL xix, cols, 803–17

In C. Schenkl (ed.), *Poetae Christiani Minores*, CSEL 16 (Vienna: F. Tempsky, 1888), 568–609

Translations: (French) Pardoux Duprat, *Amas chrestien, ou extraict de la poésie de Virgile accomodé au Vieil et Nouveau Testament, réduict en deux livres par Proba Falconia, femme d'Adelphus, consul romain, et mis en vers français* (Lyon, 1557) [not seen: reference from François Grudé de la Croix Dumain, *Premier volume de la bibliothèque du sieur de la Croix-du-Maine* (Paris: Abel L'Angelier, 1584), 369] [Oxford, Bodleian Library, C.2.15 (1) Art.]

Elizabeth A. Clark and Diane F. Hatch, *The Golden Bough, the Oaken Cross: The Virgilian Cento of Faltonia Betitia Proba*, American Academy of Religion, Texts and Translation Series 5 (Chico, Calif.: Scholars Press, 1981)

Introduction trans. Josephine Balmer, *Classical Women Poets* (Newcastle upon Tyne: Bloodaxe Books, 1996), 113–14.

Dedicatio: 'Romulidum ductor, clari lux altera soli'

MSS: as above
Editions: as above. Dedication only:
Io. Christianus Wolf, *Mulierum Graecum quae Oratione Prosa Usae Sunt Fragmenta et Elogia Graece et Latinae* (Hamburg: Abraham Vandenhoeck, 1735), 353–4 [Vatican City, Biblioteca apostolica, Ferraioli III.931]
H. Homeyer (ed.), *Dichterinnen des Altertums and des frühen Milttelalters* (Paderborn: Schöningh, 1979) 180–1 (with German trans.)

'Puella'
s. xv
[Epitaphium] Cuiusdam Puellae ad Guarinum: 'Aoniis nutrite' (6 lines)

MS: Olomouc, Universituí Knihovna/Státní Vedecká Knihovna, M I 159, fo. 178ᵛ [not seen: reference from *Iter Italicom*. This may be a copy of Isotta Nogarola's poem on Guarini]

Quarta
classical period   Salonis [Split] (Croatia)
'Aequius hunc fuerat titulum me ponere matri'

Inscription: *CIL*, iii, suppl. 9106
CLE, ii. 535 (1156)

Quirinin, Catharina
?   ?Germany
Distichon: 'Pura fui semper virgo: Moriar quoque pura'

Editions: Georg Christian Lehms, *Teutschlands galante Poetinnen, mit ihren sinnreichen und netten Proben, nebst einem Anhang ausländische Dames so sich gleichfalls durch schöne Poesien [bey] der curieusen Welt bekannt gemacht* (Frankfurt am Main: Anton Heinscheidt, 1715), 161 [London, British Library, 11525.dd.21]

Quitsov, Ana Margareta (von Pappenheim)
s. xvii   Quitsovsholm (Denmark)
'varia arguta epigrammata, quae lucem nondum viderunt'

Attested by Albert Thrura, *Gynaeceum Daniae Litterarum: Feminis Danorum Eruditione vel Scriptis Claris Conspicuum* (Altona: Jonas Korte, 1732), 95 [Wolfenbüttel, Herzog August Bibliothek, M: Da.517]

Radegund
d.587   Thuringia (Germany)/Poitiers (France)
Lost poem

Witnessed by Venantius Fortunatus, *Venanti Fortunatis Opera*, ed. Friedrich
Leo, MGH Auctores Antiquissimi IV.1 (Berlin: Weidmann, 1881), appendix
XXXI

<*De Excidio Thoringiae*
MS: Paris, Bibliothèque Nationale de France, Lat. 13048, fos. 39ʳ–42ᵛ

Editions: *Venantii Carminum, Epistolarum, Expositionum Libri XI*, ed. Christoph
Brouwer (Mainz: Bernardus Gualtherus, 1603), 343, 2nd edn. (1617), 337 (*ex*
Leo, not seen)
Leo, app. I, pp. 271–5. and III

Ad Artachin

MS: Paris, Bibliothèque Nationale de France, Lat. 13048, fos. 45ʳ–46ᵛ

Edition: Leo, 278–9

These poems may have been written, or substantially revised, by Venantius
Fortunatus>

Radke, Anna Elisa
s. xx   Germany
Musa Exul (Würzburg, 1982). [not seen]

Reference from Josef Ijsewijn, *Companion to Neo-Latin Studies*, 2 vols (Louvain:
Louvain University Press/Peeters, 1990, 1998), i. 31

Raielia Secundina
classical period   Antipolis (France)
'Respice praeteriens, oro, titulumq[ue] dolebis'

Inscription: *CIL*, xii. 218
CLE i. 219 (466)

Rainolds, Bathsua (Makin)
1600–after 1681   London (England)
Musa Virginea Graeco-latino-gallica, Bathsuae R. Filiae Henrici Reginaldi Gymna-
siarchae et Philoglotti apud Londinienses, Anno Aetatis suae Decimo Sexto Edita
(London: Edward Griffin for John Hodgets, 1616) [Cambridge, University Library, Syn. 5.61.6¹]

Edition: in facsimile, in Donald Cheney (ed.), *Neo-Latin Women Writers* (Aldershot: Ashgate, 2000)

Ad Annam Serenissimam dei Gratia Britanniae Reginam: 'Maeonidae quondam numerosa velantina Vatis'

> *Edition*: London, University of London Library, Strong Room Box 3, ref. 6839 (engraved card): before 1619

In Mortem Clarissimi Domini Henrici Hastings: 'En duplex aenigma! senex, juvenisque beatus'

> *MS*: Henry E. Huntington Library, San Marino, California, Hastings Collection, Uncatalogued Papers, Miscellaneous literature, l5A6 (1649)

> *Edition*: H. T Swedenberg, 'More Tears for Lord Hastings', *Huntington Library Quarterly*, 16 (1952), 43–51 (pp. 48–9) (with trans. by Frederick M. Carey)

Equi Aurato, ho: Henrico Vaine, Viro Dignissimo, Illustrissimo, Litereatissimo et Optimo [Anagramma]: 'Magistre, tuum nomen verum est mensura tuarum'

> *MS*: Oxford, Bodleian Library, MS Rawl. poet. 116, fo. 75ᵛ

Τω πολυμαθεστά τω Κυριω Ροβέρτω Böïl. τιμιτάτω και λογιστάτω: 'Magnus in Heroum numero spectabere Boile'

> *MS*: London, Royal Society, Boyle Letters 4, fos. 6–7

> *Edition*: *The Correspondence of Robert Boyle*, ed. Michael Hunter, Antonio Clericuzio, and Lawrence M. Principe, 6 vols. (London: Pickering & Chatto, 2001), v. 282–3

Ad Serenissimum et Potentissimum Jacobum Dei Gratia Magnae Britanniae, Franciae, et Hyberniae Regem, Fidei Defensorem, Encomiasticon Bathsua Reginalda, Anno Aetatis suae 16, μουσηπαχευτερα Compositum: 'Maximus Albionum Caesar, Pelagique Monarcha'

> *Editions*: *Musa Virginea*, sig. A1ʳ⁻ᵛ
> Anne Leslie Saunders, 'Bathsua Reginald Makin (1600–1675?)', in Laurie Churchill, Phyllis R. Brown, and Jane E. Jeffrey (eds.), *Women Writing Latin from Roman Antiquity to Early Modern Europe*, 3 vols. (New York: Routledge, 2002), iii. 247–69 (pp. 259, 264–5) (with trans.)

Sancti Pauli Norma de Regum, Potestate, & Potestatis Dignitate: 'Ensifer alta Dei narrans oracula Paulus'

Editions: *Musa Virginea*, sig. A2^v
Saunders, 260, 265 (with trans.)

Ad Annam Dei Gratia Magnae Britannie, Franciae, et Hyberniae Reginam Longe Augustissimam, Serenissimam & Prudentissimam Epigramma Bathsuae R.: 'Fingitur antiquis Pandora habuisse Minervae'

Editions: *Musa Virginea*, sig. A3^r
Saunders, 260, 265 (with trans.)

Sancti Pauli Norma de Subditorum Obsequio: 'Pyrrhus Achillies, tam re quam nomine clarus'

Editions: *Musa Virginea*, sig. A3^{r-v}
Saunders, 260–1, 265–6 (with trans.)

Ad Carolum Longe Illustrissimum & Potentissimum, Principem Magnae Britanniae & Caledoniae, Epigramma Bathsuae R.: 'Una Caledonium spes, flos, & sydus honoris'

Editions: *Musa Virginea*, sig. A4^r
Saunders, 261, 266 (with trans.)

Ad Fridericum V.G.D. Comitem Palatinum Longè Maximum et Illustrissimum Rheni, Bavariae Ducem. Principem Electorem, et Archidapiferum Sacri Imperii Romani, et, Sede Vacante, Vicarium etc. Encomiasticum Bathsuae Reginaldae, Anno Salutis 1616, Londini: 'Italiae pars una fuit Trinacria, NEREUS'

Editions: *Musa virginea*, sig. B 1^{r-v}
Jane Stevenson and Peter Davidson (eds.), *Early Modern Women Poets* (Oxford: Oxford University Press, 2001), 219–21 (with trans.)
Saunders, 261–2, 266–7 (with trans.)

Sancti Pauli Norma de Subditorum Moribus & Obsequio: 'Esse sub imperio regum divina vetustas'

Editions: *Musa Virginea*, sig. B2^{r-v}
Saunders, 262–3, 267–8 (with trans.)

Sancti Pauli Norma de Regum Clementia & Justicia: 'Numinis aeterni custodit foedera princeps'

Editions: *Musa Virginea*, sig. B4^v
Saunders, 263, 268 (with trans.)

Rangone, Ginevra (da Correggio, Gonzaga)
*c.*1490–1540   Correggio/Mantua (Italy)
Junipera ad Blancham Rangonam matrem: 'Pingere acu teneris laus est si magna
puellis'

Editions: Girolamo Tiraboschi, *Biblioteca Modenense, o notizie delle vita e delle
opere degli scrittori natii degli stati del serenissimo signor Duca di Modena*, 6 vols.
(Modena: Società Tipografia, 1783), iv. 295 [London, British Library,
10632.v.31]

Raphais, Timandra
s. xvi   Padua (Italy)
'carmen latinum non inelegans'

Attested by personal aquaintance, Jean-Jacques Boissard, *Icones Diversorum
Hominum Fama et Rebus Gestis Illustrium* (Metz: Abraham Faber, 1591), 88
[London, British Library, 683.e.17]

Rhumann, Elisabetha (Weiser)
d. 1707   Copenhagen/Lund/Copenhagen (Denmark)
Latin verses

Attested by Albert Thrura, *Gynaeceum Daniae Litterarum: Feminis Danorum
Eruditione vel Scriptis Claris Conspicuum* (Altona: Jonas Korte, 1732), 107
[Wolfenbüttel, Herzog August Bibliothek, M: Da. 517]

Richlindis
fl. *c.*1093   Pergensee/Hohenburg/Pergensee (Germany)
*Eiusdem Rilindis Pentastychon Carmen, per Monosyllaba Ingeniose Lusum, ad Con-
gregatinem Sororum Altitonensium*: 'O pie grex, cui coelica lex est nulla dolo fex'

Editions: 'Pergensis Coenobii Annalibus' (reference from Brusch, p. 154ᵛ)
Kaspar Brusch, *Monasteriorum Germaniae Praecipuorum ac Maxime Illusrtium
Centuria Prima* (Ingolstadt: Alexander & Samuel Weyssenhorn, 1551), 97ᵛ
[The Hague, Konincklijke Bibliotheek, 549.B.6]
Georg Christian Lehms, *Teutschlands galante Poetinnen mit ihren sinnreichen und
netten Proben, nebst einem Anhang ausländischer Dames so sich gleichfalls durch
schöne Poesien bey der curieusen Welt bekannt gemacht, und eine Vorrede: Dass
das weibliche Geschlecht so geschickt zum Studieren, als das männliche* (Frankfurt
am Main: Anton Heinscheidt for Samuel Tobias Hocter, 1745; repr. Leipzig:
Zentralantiquariat der DDR, 1973), 168–9 [Cambridge, University Library,
746.17.d.95.33]

Magnoald Ziegelbauer, *Historia Rei Leterariae Ordinis S. Benedicti*, 4 vols. (Augsburg: M. Veith, 1754), iii. 508 [Vatican City, Biblioteca Apostolica, Bibliografia Folio.Benedettini I (1–4)]

PL cxciv, col. 1538

Fiona Griffiths: 'Herrad of Hohenbourg and the Poetry of the *Hortus Deliciarum*', in Laurie Churchill, Phyllis R. Brown, and Jane E. Jeffrey (eds.), *Women Writing Latin from Roman Antiquity to Early Modern Europe*, 3 vols. (New York: Routledge, 2002), ii. 231–63 (pp. 252, 262) (with trans.)

'Vos, quod includit, frangit, gravat, attrahit, urit'

> *Editions*: Brusch, 97^v
> Lehms (1745), 168–9
> Ziegelbauer, iii. 508
> *PL* cxciv, col. 1538
> Griffiths, 252, 262 (with trans.)

Rings, Maria Elizabeth
s. xvii?   Frankfurt (Germany)
'Nam tibi mellifluos antiquum est volvere versus'

> Georg Christian Lehms, *Teutschlands galante Poetinnen mit ihren sinnreichen und netten Proben, nebst einem Anhang ausländischer Dames so sich gleichfalls durch schone Poesien bey der curieusen Welt bekannt gemacht, und eine Vorrede: Dass das weibliche Geschlecht so geschickt zum Studieren, als das männliche* (Frankfurt am Main: Anton Heinscheidt for Samuel Tobias Hocter, 1745; repr. Leipzig: Zentralantiquariat der DDR, 1973), 169–71 [Cambridge, University Library, 746.17.d.95.33]

Roccati, Cristina
1732–84   Rovigo (Italy)
'Elegia latina in morte del B. Butti' [not seen]

> Attested by Ginevra Canonici Fachini, *Prospetto biografico delle donne italiane rinomate in letteratura* (Venice: Tipografia di Alvisopoli, 1824), 206 [Vatican City, Biblioteca Apostolica, Z.2350.5.C.2]

Roemers, Maria 'Tesselschade' (Croombalgh)
s. xvii   Amsterdam (the Netherlands)
Altri versi latini della medesima gentildonna a la medesima Regina [Marie de Médicis]: 'Arnus habet flores vestrae Regina iuventae'

> *MS*: Paris, Bibliothèque Mazarine, 4398, fo. 217^v

Distichon ad eandem: 'Quaternis regnis regis Regina tulisti'

MS: Paris, Bibliothèque Mazarine, 4398, fo. 217ᵛ

Rusca, Antonia (Visconti)
s. xiv   Milan (Italy)
'Lucida gemma iacet Rusca qui gente Beatrix'

> *Inscription*: tomb of Beatrice Rusca (Antonia's mother): Sant'Angelo de' Frari,
> Milan
> Vincenzo Forcella (ed.), *Inscrizioni delle chiese e degli altri edifici di Milano*, 12
> vols. in 5 (Milan, Tipografia Bartoletti di Giuseppe Prato, 1889–93), v. 8
> [Vatican City, Biblioteca Apostolica, Epigrafia II.Milano.2 (1–5)]

> *Illustrated*: Catherine E. King, *Renaissance Women Patrons* (Manchester: Man-
> chester University Press, 1998), 255

Salvidiena Hilara
?   Rome (Italy)
'V. Salvidiena Q. l. Hilara'

> *Inscription*: *CIL*, vi. 2574 (25808)
> *CLE*, ii. 758 (1570)

Sarocchi, Margherita (Biraghi)
1569–1617   Naples/Rome (Italy)
No Latin verse is known to survive

> Described as a Latin poet in *Marthae Marchinae Virginis Neapolitane
> Musa Posthuma* (Rome: Philippus Maria Mancini, 1662), 1ʳ⁻ᵛ [Rome, Bib-
> lioteca nazionale Vittorio Emanuele, 6.20.C.44] and in Johann Caspar
> Ebert, *Eröffnetes Cabinet dess Gelehrten Frauen-zimmer* (Frankfurt: Michael
> Rohrlachs sel. Wittib und Erben, 1700), 311 [Oxford, Taylorian Library, EN.
> 807. A. 1]

Saturnina
?
'Sophron hic situi est aetatis parvae

> *Inscription*: *CLE*, ii. 836–7 (1816)

<Scala, Alessandra (Marullo)
1485–1550   Florence (Italy)

Alexandrae Scalae Responsum: 'Nihil utique fuit laude à prudente viro praestantius'

> *Edition: Angeli Politiani Operum Tomus II* (Lyon: Sebastian Gryphius, 1545), 341–2 [London, British Library, 634. c. 14]
>
> Holt Parker, 'Latin and Greek Poetry by Five Renaissance Italian Women Humanists', in Barbara K. Gold, Paul Allen Miller, and Charles Platter (eds.), *Sex and Gender in Medieval and Renaissance Texts: The Latin Tradition* (Albany: State University of New York Press, 1997), 247–86

This may or may not be her own version of a Greek original: it is also possible both are by Poliziano>

Schurman, Anna Maria van

1607–78 Cologne (Germany)/Utrecht/Wiuwerd (the Netherlands)
Inclytae et Antiquae Urbs Trajectinae Nova Academia Nuperrime Donatae Gratulantur: 'Tu quae lege potens agris dominaris, et altis'

> *Editions: Academiae Ultrajectinae Inauguratio Unà cum Orationibus Inauguralibus* (Utrecht: Aegidius and Petrus Roman, 1632), sig. H 2ʳ⁻ᵛ [Wolfenbüttel, Herzog August Bibliothek, M: Pd. 335]
>
> *Nobiliss. Virginis Annae Mariae Schurman Opuscula Hebraea, Graeca, Latina, Gallica, Prosaica et Metrica*, ed. Frideric Spanheim (Leiden: Elsevier, 1648 and 1650), 262–3 [The Hague, Koninckljike Bibliotheek, M. 102. F. 6; Paris, Bibliothèque Nationale de France, Z-19198]
>
> *Nobiliss. Virginis Annae Mariae Schurman Opuscula Hebraea, Graeca, Latina, Gallica, Prosaica et Metrica*, ed. Frideric Spanheim, 3rd emended and enlarged edn. (Utrecht: Joh. a Waesberge, 1652), 300–1 [The Hague, Koninckljike Bibliotheek, 188. L. G]
>
> *Nobiliss. Virginis Annae Mariae Schurman Opuscula Hebraea, Graeca, Latina, Gallica, Prosaica et Metrica*, ed. Traugott Christina Dorothea Löberin (Leipzig: M. C. F. Muller, 1749) [Wolfenbüttel, Herzog August Bibliothek, H: P. 20619.8° Helmst]
>
> G. J. D. Schotel, *Anna Maria van Schurman*, 2 vols. in 1 's-Hertogensbosch: Gebroeders Muller, 1853), 90–1 [London, British Library, 4885.e.45]
>
> Georg Christian Lehms, *Teutschlands galante Poetinnen, mit ihren sinnreichen und netten Proben, nebst einem Anhang ausländische,Dames so sich gleichfalls durch schöne Poesien [bey] der curieusen Welt bekannt gemacht* (Frankfurt am Main: Anton Heinscheidt, 1715), 214–5 [London, British Library, 11525. dd. 21]
>
> *Algemeene Feestwijzer vor het tweede eeuwfest der Utrechtse Hoofschool, 1636–1686* (Utrecht, 1836), 3–84 [not seen]
>
> Pieta van Beek, '*Sol Iustitiae Illustra nos*: de "femme savante" Anna Maria van Schurman (1607–1678) en de Universiteit van Utrecht', *Akroterion*, 40 (1995), 145–62 (pp. 147–8)

Pieta van Beek, '*Alpha Virginum*: Anna Maria van Schurman', in Laurie Churchill, Phyllis R. Brown, and Jane E. Jeffrey (eds.), *Women Writing Latin from Roman Antiquity to Early Modern Europe*, 3 vols. (New York: Routledge, 2002), iii. 271–93 (pp. 282–3, 286–7)

In Effigiem Christinae Serenissimae Potentissimaeque Suecorum Reginae Incomparabilis: 'Ut vitrum ingentem parva' (before 1654)

Pieta van Beek (pers. comm.)

Ad D. Jacobum Catzium: 'Ut cygnum refides perhibent intendere voces'

Opuscula (1648/5), 256–7
Opuscula (1652), 294–5

Ad D. Barlaeum: 'Quas ego pro tanto persolvam munere grates?'

Opuscula (1648/50), 258
Opuscula (1652) 296

Clarissimo Viro D. Andreae Riveto: 'Tanta tuae, Rivete, viget vox inclyta famae'

Opuscula (1648/50), 258
Opuscula (1652), 296

Unioni: 'Quo te, Nympha, cui tam custodita, quousque'

Opuscula (1648/50), 259
Opuscula (1652), 297

Ad Occultum Apollonis Cujusdam ad Lucem me Provocantis, Oraculum Responsio: 'Magnum Musa virum sonat, utque ego sim quoque vates'

Editions: *Opuscula* (1648/50), 259
Opuscula (1652), 297
Hugenii Epigrammata, 92–3

Epigramma in Nobilissimi Praestantissimi Viri D. Constantini Hugensi Opus-Diurnam: 'Quaeris an haec claram mereantur carmina lucem'

Editions: *Opuscula* (1648/50), 260

Ad Illustrem Virum, Zulichemii Dominum: 'Cur me mortalem poscunt tua carmina testem'

Editions: *Opuscula* (1648/50), 260
Opuscula (1652), 298
Schotel, ii. 28

Responsio: 'Hugenio cum non sit, nomine clarior alter'

Editions: *Opuscula* (1648/50), 261
Opuscula (1652), 299

Aliud: 'Anne bonum credat, nequeam cum solvere, nomen?

Editions: *Opuscula* (1648/50), 261
Opuscula (1652), 299

Aliud: 'Quare tuum CONSTANS, nostro vis cedere nomen?

Editions: *Opuscula* (1648/50), 261
Opuscula (1652), 299

Ad Serenissimum Angliae Reginam, a Puerperis Nuper Egressam: 'Quae tibi nunc gelido miracula nata Decembri'

Editions: *Opuscula* (1648/50), 262
Opuscula (1652), 300
van Beek, '*Alpha Virginum*', 284, 288–9 (with trans.)

Magnae et Generosi Animi Heroinæ Gornacensi, Causam Sexus nostri Fortiter Defendenti Gratulatur: 'Palladis arma geris, bellis animosa virago' (probably not long after 1622)

Editions: *Opuscula* (1648/50), 264
Opuscula (1652), 303
van Beek, '*Alpha Virginum*', 284, 289 (with trans.)

In Symbolum suum: 'quis non sollicito Christum veneretur amore?'

Editions: *Opuscula* (1648/50), 264
Opuscula (1652), 303
Schotel, i. 86
van Beek, '*Alpha Virginum*', 283, 287–8 (with trans.)

Ad EXOYΣ Dousicas Provocatio: 'Quos Dousarum resonantes carmina nymphae'

Editions: *Opuscula* (1648/50), 265

Opuscula (1652), 304

Clarissimo Ornatissimoque Viro D.G. Stackmanno: 'Si veneranda docet frontem obvelare vetustas'

   Editions: *Opuscula* (1648/50), 265
   Opuscula (1652), 304

Apologia Annæ Mariæ à Schurman, contra Erroneos quosdam Rumores quibus Propter Nominis Schurmanni Homonymiam, Astræam d'Urfe è Gallico in Belgicum Sermonem Vertisse Creditur: 'Cur mea lascivis praetexi nomina chartis?'

   Editions: *Opuscula* (1648/50), 265–6
   Opuscula (1652), 304–5
   van Beek '*Alpha Virginum*', 283–4, 288 (with trans.)

Epigramma in Historiam Gelricam Domini Viri Joh. Isaaci Pontani: 'Palladias artes quondam coluere Sicambri'

   Editions: *Opuscula* (1648/50), 266–7
   Opuscula (1652), 305–6

Memoriae Celeberrimi Historici et Jurisconsulti Arnoldi Buchelii: 'Gratia dum doctæ fuerit mihi grata Minervæ'

   Editions: *Opuscula* (1648/50), 267
   Opuscula (1652), 306

Nobilissimo Doctissimoque Viri d. Andreae Riveti: 'Omnia sacrilegus tandem pervaserat error'

   Editions: *Opuscula* (1648/50), 268
   Opuscula (1652), 307
   Schotel, i. 47

Nobilissimo Doctissimoque Heroum d. Claudio Salmasio: 'Hospes ave Batavis jam tandem reddite terris'

   Editions: *Opuscula* (1648/50), 269
   Opuscula (1652), 308

Reverendo, Clarissimo, Doctissimoque Viro D. Friderico Spanhemio: 'Quid me, Spanhemi, revocas Heliconis ad amnes' (1644)

Editions: *Opuscula* (1648/50), 270–3
Opuscula (1652), 309–12
Hermann Hugo, *Pia Desideria* (Antwerp: Henniaus Aertssen, 1624), appendix,
pp. 250–1.
(London, British Library, 12305.aaa.37) Lehms, 210–13 [London, British Library, 11525. dd. 21]

In Obitum Eminentissimi Theologi D. Frederic. Spanhemii: 'Ne tibi, Lugdunum,
Spanhemi funera tantum'

MS: Leiden, Universiteitsbibliotheek [not seen]

Editions: *Opuscula* (1648/50), 270–3
Lehms 210–13
Schotel, ii. 30–1

In Obitum Nobilissimi et Venerandi Theologi Johannis Polyandri à Kerckhoven:
'Fortunate Senex, quondam dum vita manebat'

Editions: *Opuscula* (1648/50), 274
Opuscula (1652), 314
Schotel, i. 45–6

Epicedium in Obitum Doctrina et Pietatate Clarissimi Viri D. Meinardi Schotani:
'Quis Schotane sibi te non suspiret ademptum'

Editions: *Opuscula* (1648/50), 275
Opuscula (1652), 315

In Obitum Summi Viri D. Andreæ Riveti: 'Dicite, Pierides, cur tanto pectora luctu'

Editions: *Opuscula* (1652), 316–17

In Obitum Reverendi Clarissimi Viri, D. Caroli Dematii: 'Ultrajectinum, rogitas,
lugere Lyceum'

Edition: *Opuscula* (1652), 318

'Non mihi propositum est, humanam illudere fortem'

Edition: Lehms, 197

Ad Birgittam Tot: 'En Senecae magnam nunc Femina Nobilis umbram'

Editions: *Skrifter, som om saedene oc et skickeligt lefnit handler...nu paa voris danske maal opversat af... Bergiere Trolig* (Sorøe: Georg Hautsch, 1658), sig. b 8 [Uppsala, Universitetsbiblioteket, Script. Lat. Fol. [Seneca] 10 (29: 136)]

Albert Thrura, *Gynaeceum Daniae Litterarum: Feminis Danorum Eruditione vel Scriptis Claris Conspicuum* (Altona: Jonas Korte, 1732), 119 [Wolfenbüttel, Herzog August Bibliothek, M: Da. 517]

'Cernitis, hic picta nostros in imagine vultus' (distich)

Editions: *Opuscula* (1648/50), flyleaf

C. F. Paullini, *Das Hoch- und Wohl-gelahrte Teutsche Frauen-Zimmer* (Frankfurt: Johnn Cristoph Stösseln, 1705), 136; 2nd edn. 1715 [London, British Library, 10705.aa.77; Munich, Bayerische Staatsbibliothek, H. lit. p. 290]

Schotel, ii. 63, 71

'Non animi fastus nec formae gratia suasit'

Editions: Schotel, ii. 63, 71

'Divini pictoris opus coelestis imago' (quatrain)

Editions: Andreas Planer, *Tactatus [sic] de Gyneceo Docto, d.i. Von gelehrten Frauenzimmer* (Wittenberg: Johann Godfrid Meyer, 1715), 62 [Wolfenbüttel, Herzog August Bibliothek, M: Li. 7057]

Paullini, 136

Schotel, ii. 73

Ad Nobilissimum Virum Sulichemii Dominum pro Musis Ethiopici Responsio: 'Non leviter Clarias tetigisti carmine divas'

Edition: Schotel, ii. 12

Ad Illustrem Virum, D. Constantinum Hugenium: 'Publica nos pietas olim ad spectacula duxit'

MS: Leiden, Universiteitsbibliotheek [not seen]

Edition: Schotel, ii. 27

Illustro Viro Domino Constantino Hugenio, A.M. à S.: 'Ordinis et pulchri spiras sub imagine veri'

MS: Leiden, Universiteitsbibliotheek [not seen]

Edition: Schotel, ii. 28

Illustri Viro Domino Constantino Hugenio, s.p.d. A.M.à S.: 'Constanter pergis varium decus addere mundo'

   MS: Leiden, Universiteitsbibliotheek [not seen]

   Edition: Schotel, ii. 27

In Imaginem Juliae a Joh. Secundo quam Artificiosissime Exsculptam: 'Julia, cui forma vix ulla secunda, secundi'

   Edition: Schotel, ii. 13

In Triplicem Imaginem Eximii Servi Dei J. de Labadie: 'Cernis Amatoris Jesu sub imagine vultum'

   Edition: Schotel, ii. 60

Vicecomito Domino B. Bushovio: 'Quid mea Musa paras? quid seris quaeris in annis'

   MS: whereabouts unknown, offered for sale in 1994. Facsimile reproduction in *Books by and about Women: A List from Bernard Quaritch* (London: Quaritch, 1994), 113–15 (p. 114)

   Dr Pieta van Beek has a modern critical edition of the works of Anna Maria van Schurman in preparation

Scotta, Francisca
fl. *c.*1500   Piacenza? (Italy)
Nothing known to survive

   Her verse is attested by Joannes Petrus Feretrius, *Sena Vetus, per Io. Petrum Feretrium . . . Carmine Illustrata* (Siena: Simeone Rubeo, 1513), vs. 378–81

Selvaggia Borghini, Maria
1654–1731   Siena? (Italy)
Nothing known to survive

   Her verse is attested by Gilles de Ménage, 'Lezzione d'Egidio Menagio sopra'l sonetto VII di Messer Francesco Petrarca' after his *Historia Mulierum Philo-sopharum* (Lyon: Anisson, J. Posnel and C. Rigaud, 1690) (separately pagin-ated), 60 [Vatican City, Biblioteca Apostolica, Mai XI. D. 1. 64 (int. 1)]

Serena, wife of Nymphius
'Vivere post obitum vatem vis noste viator?

Inscription: Giovanni Battista Ferretti (ed.), *Musae Lapidariae*, 5 books in 1, (Verona: Rubeis, 1672), v. 336 [London, British Library, 143. e. 22]

Petrus Pithoeus (ed.), *Epigrammata et Poematia Vetera*, 2 vols. (Paris: N. Gillius, 1590), ii. 126–7 [London, British Library, 1001.e.1]

Petrus Burmann (ed.), *Anthologia Veterum Latinorum Epigrammatum et Poematum, sive Catalecta Poetarum Latinorum in VI Libros Digesta*, 6 vols. in 2. (Amsterdam: Schouten, 1759, 1773), ii. 154–6 (IV.ccvi) [London, British Library, 54. f. 13]

Heinrich Meyer (ed.), *Anthologia Veterum Latinorum Epigrammatum et Poematum*, 2 vols. in 1 (Leipzig: Gerhard Fleischer, 1835), ii. 86 (1163) [London, British Library, 011388. b. 14]

<Serena, wife of Stilicho

s. v   Rome (Italy)

De Zona Missa ab eadem Arcadio Augusto: 'Stamine resplendens et mira textilis arte'

MS: Vatican City, Biblioteca Apostolica Vat. 2809 (not seen)

Edition: Alexander Riese (ed.), *Anthologia Latina, sive Poesis Latinae Supplementum*, 4 vols. (Leipzig: B. G. Teubner, 1868–97), i. 219 [Vatican City, Biblioteca Apostolica, Lett. lat. ant. 1.1.Anthologia.1] (this may alternatively be by Claudian in her name)

'Qua sinuata cavo consurgunt tecta regressu'

Inscription: also possibly by Serena, in the church of St Nazarius, Milan. Giovanni Battista Rossi, *Inscriptiones Christianae Urbis Romae Septimo Saeculo Antiquiores*, 2 vols. (Rome: Officina Libraria Pontifica (Filippo Cuggiani), 1888), ii.1, p. 181 (14) [London, British Library, 7708. f. 16]

CIL, v (no. 6250)

CLE, i. 420 (907)>

Servilia

                                                                   Venafrum (Italy?)

'Hunc Rufum suavem amisit lectissima mater'

Inscription: Ludovico Antonio Muratori (ed.), *Novus Thesaurus Veterum Inscriptionum*, 4 vols. (Milan: Ex Aedibus Palatinis, 1739–42), ii. 1215.2 [London, British Library, 1705. b. 7]

Francesco Maria Bonada (ed.), *Anthologia, seu Collectio Omnium Veterum Inscriptionum Poeticarum*, 2 vols. (Rome 1751), ii. 419 (92) [London, British Library, 671.g.1–2]

Petrus Burmann (ed.), *Anthologia Veterum Latinorum Epigrammatum et Poematum, sive Catalecta Poetarum Latinorum in VI Libros Digesta*, 6 vols. in 2

(Amsterdam: Schouten, 1759, 1773), ii. 218 (IV.cclxxxi) [London, British Library, 54. f. 13]

Heinrich Meyer (ed.), *Anthologia Veterum Latinorum Epigrammatum et Poematum*, 2 vols. in 1 (Leipzig: Gerhard Fleischer, 1835), ii. 146 (1378) [London, British Library, 011388. b. 14]

CIL, x.1, p. 494 (4993)

CLE, ii. 576 (1230)

Seymour, Anne (Dudley, Unton), Margaret, and Jane

Anne d. 1587, Jane 1541–61   London (England)

Annae, Margaritae, Janae, Sororum Virginum, Heroidum Anglarum, in Mortem Margaritae Valesiae, Navarrorum Reginae, Hecatadistichon, ed. N. Denisot (Paris: Reginaldus Calderius & Claudius Calderius, 1550) [London, British Library, 1213. h. 32 (1)]

> *Editions*: Brenda M. Hosington, 'England's First Female-Authored Encomium: The Seymour Sisters' Hecatodistichon (1550), to Marguerite de Navarre. Text, Translation, Notes, and Commentary', *Studies in Philology*, 93 (1996), 117–63
>
> *Anne, Margaret and Jane Seymour*, ed. Brenda Hosington, The Early Modern Englishwoman: The Printed Writings (Aldershot: Ashgate, 2000) (contains both editions)

(second edition) *Le Tombeau de Marguerite de Valois, royne de Navarre, faict premierement en disticques latins par les trois soeurs princesses en Angleterre, depuis traduictz en Grec, Italien & Francois par plusieurs des excellentz poétes de la France, avecques plusieurs odes, hymnes, cantiques, epitaphes, sur le mesme subiect* (Paris: De l'imprimerie de Michel Fezandat & Robert Granlon, 1551) [London, British Library, 1073. e. 11 (1)]

> *Edition*: Georg Christian Lehms, *Teutschlands galante Poetinnen mit ihren sinnreichen und netten Proben, nebst einem Anhang ausländischer Dames so sich gleichfalls durch schone Poesien bey der curieusen Welt bekannt gemacht, und eine Vorrede: Dass das weibliche Geschlecht so geschickt zum Studieren, als das männliche* (Frankfurt am Main: Anton Heinscheidt for Samuel Tobias Hocter, 1745; repr. Leipzig: Zentralantiquariat der DDR, 1973), 251–67 [Cambridge, University Library, 746.17.d.95.33]

Sforza, Ippolita (Duchess of Calabria)

1445–84   Milan (Italy)

Carmina Edita per Dominam Ipolitam Ducissa Calabrie: 'O genitrix O sola mei luce intima cordis'

MS: Pesaro, Biblioteca Oliveriana, 454, tom. II, fo. 208ʳ⁻ᵛ

Sibille, Abbess of Notre-Dame-des-Saintes
fl. 1113   Saintes (France)
Versus abbatissae: 'Cum caro nostra lutum, vermes, cinis efficiatur'

> *Editions*: Léopold Delisle (ed.), *Rouleaux des morts du ixe au xve siècle recueillis et publiés par la Société de l'Histoire de France* (Paris: Veuve J. Renouard, 1866), 242, titulus 144 [Oxford, Bodleian Library, 2372.d.84]
> Hugh Feiss OSB, 'A Poet Abbess from Notre Dame de Saintes', *Magistra: A Journal of Women's Spirituality in History*, 1.1 (1995), 39–53 (pp. 49–59), trans. pp. 52–3

Sigea, Luisa (de Cuevas)
1522–60   Tarançon/Burgos (Spain)
Syntra: 'Est locus, occiduas ubi sol æstibus ad oras'

MS: Toledo, Biblioteca Pública, 3.38

> *Editions: Syntra: Aloisiae Sygeae Toletanae, Aliaque eiusdem, ac Nonullam Praeterea Doctorum Virorum ad eandem Epigrammata*, Denis du Prat [Dionysius à Prato], (Paris, 1566), sig. A 3ᵛ–B 1ᵛ [London, British Library, 11408. f.42]
> Francisco Cerdá y Rico (ed.), *Clarorum Hispanorum Opuscula Selecta et Rariora* (Madrid, 1781), 261–4 (from 1566 edn.) [Oxford, Bodleian Library, 40. E. 13 Art. BS]
> P. Allut, *Aloysia Sygea et Nicholas Chorier* (Lyon: N. Scheuring, 1862) (from 1566 edn.), separately paginated appendix, pp. 11–14 [London, British Library, 10631. bb. 21]
> *Apuntes*, ii. 404 (version from Toledo MS) [Vatican City, Biblioteca Apostolica, Bibliografia II.Spagna.3]
> *Translations*: (Spanish) M. Menéndez y Pelayo, *Estudios poéticos* (Madrid, 1878), 91–101
> (French) Odette Sauvage, '*Sintra*, poème latin de Luisa Sigea', *Arquivos Centro Cultural Portugues*, 4 (1972), 560–70
> Edward V. George, 'Luisa Sigea (1522–1560): Iberian Scholar-Poet', in Laurie Churchill, Phyllis R. Brown, and Jane E. Jeffrey (eds.), *Women Writing Latin from Roman Antiquity to Early Modern Europe*, 3 vols. (New York: Routledge, 2002), iii. 167–86 (pp. 171–3, 177–9) (partial, with trans.)

Loisiae Sygaeae Epigramma in Hieronymi Britonii, Elegiam de Morte Augustae: 'Dum casum Augustae defles, dum funera narras'

> *Editions: Syntra*, sig. B 1ᵛ
> Allut, 15

Cerdá y Rico, 264

Eiusdem, ad eundem Britonium: 'Inter caelicolas miris iam terra, polusque'

Editions: *Syntra*, sig. B 1ᵛ–2ʳ
Allut, 16
Cerdá y Rico, 265

In Aquilam, cui Torquem Aureum Maria Infans Parabat, L. Sygeae Epigramma: 'Desine diva, precor, mirari desine: quid me'

Editions: *Syntra*, sig. B 2ʳ
Allut, 17
Cerdá y Rico, 265

Poetica

Attested by Nicolò Antonio, *Bibliotheca Hispana Nova, sive Hispanorum Scriptorum qui ab Anno MD Floruere Notitia*, ed. T. A. Sanchez, J. A. Pellicer, and R. Casalbonus, 2 vols. (Madrid: Vidua et Heredes Joachim de Ibarra, 1783–8), i. 72b.

Silvestrina, Regina (?)
Extempore lyric production

Attested by Sauerbrei, referencing 'Gualth. Tom. 12 Chron. p. 1289'. Johannes Sauerbrei, *Diatriben Academicam de Foeminam Eruditione, Priorem Consensu Inclutae Facultatis Philosophicae in Alma Lipsiensi, sub Praesidio...M. Jacobi Thomasii* (Leipzig: Johann Erich Hahn, 1671), § 50, sig. D 1ʳ [Munich, Bayerische Staatsbibliothek, 4 Diss. 5212]

Sobrarias, Juana
s. xvi, b. 1510?   Saragossa (Spain)
Epitaph on father's tomb in Saragossa [not seen]

Attested by Nicolò Antonio, *Bibliotheca Hispana Nova, sive Hispanorum Scriptorum qui ab Anno MD Floruere Notitia*, ed. T. A. Sanchez, J. A. Pellicer, and R. Casalbonus, 2 vols. (Madrid: Vidua et Heredes Joachim de Ibarra, 1783–8), i. 781.

Southworth, Mary (Mollineux)
1651–95   Lancashire (England)
'Esuriens agnis quantum concedet in agris'

Editions: Mary Mollineux, *Fruits of Retirement, or, Miscellaneous Poems, Moral and Divine, Being Contemplative, Letters &c, Written on Variety of Subjects and Occasions* (London: Printed and Sold by Mary Hinde, at no. 2 in George-Yard, Lombard Street, 1772; 1st pub. 1702), sig. B8ʳ (with contemporary trans. by her husband) [London, British Library, 1163. b. 21]

Jane Stevenson and Peter Davidson (eds.), *Early Modern Women Poets* (Oxford: Oxford University Press, 2001), 413 (with contemporary trans. by her husband)

'Qui nocent Sanctis, Dominus locutus'

Editions: Fruits of Retirement., sig. B8ᵛ (with contemporary trans. by her husband)

Stevenson and Davidson 414 (with contemporary trans. by her husband)

'Non querit laudem Virtus, sibi debita vera est'

Editions: Fruits of Retirement, sig. B8ᵛ (with contemporary trans. by her husband)

Spolverina, Ersilia
s. xvi   Verona (Italy)
Versi Latini: 'ad illustrissimam Claram Corneliam poemata duo' (pub. Verona, 1596) [not seen]

Attested in Francesco Clodoveo Maria Pentolini, *Le donne illustre: canti dieci*, 2 vols. (Livorno: Gio. Vincenzo Falorni, 1776), ii. 152 [Vatican City, Biblioteca Apostolica, Barberini JJJ. VIII. 5–6]

Sprögel, Margareta Susanna (?)
s. xvii   (Germany)
Anmuthige Lateinische Liebes-Reim: 'Deus meus, meum cor'

Editions: Cosilia und Responsa Theologica: oder Gottsgelehrte Rathschläge und Antworten, über denen wichtigsten strücken und zuständen eches göttlichen wandels, nebenst neuen geistlichen Gedichten, der weiszheit Garten, Gewächs Genannt, gemein gemacht och Gottfried Arnold (Frankfurt: Thomas Fritsche, 1705), 883–910 [Yale Collection of German Baroque Literature microfilm, no. 1469, reel 473]

Staffel, Marguerite von (von Allendorf)
d. 1471   Rheingau (Germany)
Latin verse

Attested by Frantz Joseph Bodmann, *Rheingauische Alterthümer oder Landes- und Regiment-Verfassung des westlichen oder Niederherrheingaues im mittlern Zeital-*

ter, 2 vols. (Mainz: Florian Rupserberg, 1819), ii. 552 [London, British Library, 804. f. 10]

Staples, Sara Sarah
fl. 1650   London (England)
'Quod cum coelicolis habitas, pars altera nostra'

> *Inscription*: St Giles, Cripplegate, London
> Thomas Ravenshaw, *Ancient Epitaphs* (London: Joseph Masters & Co., 1878), 28

Stella, Caterina [Estella or Estrella, Catalina?]
c. 1600   Salamanca (Spain)
Latin verse

> Attested by Francisco Agostino della Chiesa, *Theatro delle donne letterate* (Mondovi: Giovanni Gislandi & Giovanni Tomaso Rossi, 1620), 122–3 [Paris, Bibliothèque Nationale de France, G. 21, 404]

Strozzi, Francesca (Laurentia), Suor
1514–91   Florence/Prato (Italy)
Venerabilis Laurentiae Stroziae Monialis S. Dominici in Monasterio Divi Nicholaie de Prato, in Singula Totius Anni Solemnia, Hymni. Ad illustrem, et Reverediss. D. Lactantium de Lactantiis Pistoriensem Episcopum, & Patrem suum colendissimum (Florence: Filippo Giunta, 1588; 2nd edn. Paris, D. Binet, 1601) [not seen] [Paris, Bibliothèque Nationale de France, RES P YC 996; RES P YC 1223 (7)]

In Circumcisionem Domini: 'Prima currentis celebratur anni'

> *Edition*: *Hymni* (1588), 1–2, Giovanni Bensi, *Vita di Suor Lorenza Strozzi, Innografa in S. Niccolò a Prato* (Prato: Studio Bibliografico Pratese, 1998), 18 (taken from earlier edn. in Giovanna Pierattini, 'Suor Lorenza Strozzi, poetessa domenicana (1514–1591)', *Memorie domenicane*, 59 [795], 113–15, 142–5, 177–83, 796 (1942), 60 [796], 19–25) [not seen]

In Annunciatione Virginis Mariae: 'Hanc Dei dicam, ac hominis parentem'

> *Edition*: *Hymni* (1588), 24–5, Bensi, 19 (also from Pierattini)

In Festo Francisci Assisiensis: 'Floret in mundo seraphim colendus'

> *Edition*: *Hymni* (1588), 80–1, Bensi, 20 (also from Pierattini)

In Honore Protomartyris Stephani: 'Ortus in terris hodie tonantis', 'Dum silet mundus tenebris opacis'

Edition: *Hymni* (1588), 103–6, Bensi, 21, from MS in Prato, Biblioteca Roncioniana [not seen], fos. 19–24 (nineteenth-century MS copy by Luigi Sacchi from *Hymni*)

In Pentecostem: 'Lumen e coelo rutilans sereno'

Edition: *Hymni* (1588), 40–1, Bensi, 23

In Inventionem Pueri IESU in Templo: 'Ens primum et mirabile',

Editions: *Hymni* (1588), 18–19

Jane Stevenson, 'Conventual Life in Renaissance Italy: The Latin Poetry of Suor Laurentia Strozzi (1514–1591)', in Laurie Churchill, Phyllis R. Brown, and Jane E. Jeffrey (eds.), *Women Writing Latin from Roman Antiquity to Early Modern Europe*, 3 vols. (New York: Routledge, 2002), iii. 109–31 (pp. 116–7, 124–5) (with trans.)

In Beatam Catharinam Senensem: 'Hostis humani generis, triumphat'

Editions: *Hymni* (1588), 35–6
Stevenson, 117–18, 125 (with trans.)

Ode in Eucharistiam: 'Plaudat æther orbis, atque vos fideles psallite'

Editions: *Hymni* (1588), 43
Stevenson, 118–19, 125–6 (with trans.)

Ode in Visitationem Beatæ Mariæ Virginis: 'Qui fecit orbem et æthera'

Editions: *Hymni* (1588), 52–3
Stevenson, 119–20, 126–7 (with trans.)

In Beatam Mariam Magdalenam: 'Te cœtus prece nunc prosequitur pia'

Editions: *Hymni* (1588), 55
Stevenson, 120, 127 (with trans.)

In eamdem [Martham]: 'Conditor Mundi penetraret æthra'

Editions: *Hymni* (1588), 58–9
Stevenson, 121, 127–8 (with trans.)

In Nativitatem Beatae Mariae Virginis: 'Nascitur Virgo Genetrix IESU'

Editions: *Hymni* (1588), 72–3
Stevenson, 122, 128 (with trans.)

In Beatum Michaelem Arcangelum: 'Alma lux fulget nova festa portans'

> *Editions*: *Hymni* (1588), 77–9
> Stevenson, 123–4, 129–30 (with trans.)

Stuart, Mary (Mary, Queen of Scots)
1542–87 Edinburgh (Scotland)/Paris (France)/Edinburgh/Derbyshire (England)
Distich: 'Buxtona, quae calidae celebraris nomine Lymphae'

> *MS*: Paris, Bibliothèque Nationale de France, Collections Dupuy 837, fo. 191ʳ

> *Editions*: William Camden, *Britannia, sive Florentissimorum Regnorum Anglie, Scotiae, Hiberniae et Insularum Adiacentium ex Ultima Antiquitate Chorographica Descriptio*, 3rd edn. (London: G. Bishop, 1590), 44
> George Ballard, *Memoirs of Several Ladies of Great Britain Who Have Been Celebrated for their Writings or Skill in the Learned Languages, Arts and Sciences* (Oxford: W. Jackson for the author, 1752), 161 [Oxford, Bodleian Library, DD.1.Jur]
> Anon. [Elizabeth Tollet], *Poems on Several Occasions, with Anne Boleyn to King Henry the Eighth: An Epistle* (London: John Clarke, 1724), 33 [London, British Library, 1490. k. 1]
> Elizabeth Tollet, *Poems on Several Occasions, with Anne Boleyn to King Henry the Eighth: An Epistle* (London: John Clarke, 1755; 3rd edn. 1760), 41 [London, British Library, 11531. aa. 39; London, British Library, 11631. aa. 38]
> George Ballard, *Memoirs of Several Ladies of Great Britain Who Have Been Celebrated for their Writings or Skill in the Learned Languages, Arts and Sciences*, ed. Ruth Perry (Detroit: Wayne State University Press, 1985), 174

<*Responsio Reginae*: 'Zoilus invideae rumpanturque [Ilia] Codro'

> *MS*: Paris, Bibliothèque Nationale de France, Collections Dupuy 837, fo. 191ʳ also gives an additional exchange of distichs, *responsio cuiusdam Angli* and *responsio Reginae*, which may be embroidery>

'Sunt comites ducesque alii; sunt denique reges'

> *Edition*: Walter Scott, *The Abbot*, Waverley Novels XX–XXI (Edinburgh: Cadell, 1832), note to ch. xvii, i. 277, no provenance offered.

Sulpicia (I, daughter of Servius)[8]
late s. i BC   Rome (Italy)
> *Editions*: *A Poetical Translation of the Elegies of Tibullus and of the Poems of Sulpicia*, trans. James Grainger (London: A. Millar, 1759)

---

[8] I have not in this case attempted to see all these editions: references are taken from library catalogues and are consequently only as full as the catalogues permit.

Tibulli Carmina Libri Tres, cum Libro Quarto Sulpiciae et Aliorum (Leipzig, 1768)
'The Poems of Sulpicia', in Robert Anderson, *A Complete Edition of the Poets of Great Britain*, 13 (1793)/ *The Poems of Sulpicia Translated by Grainger*, ed. A. Chalmers, The Works of the English Poets 20 (1810)/ *The Works of the Greek and Roman Poets*, 15 (1813)/ *The British Poets*, 93 (1822), trans. J. Grainger *Tibulli Carmina cum Libro Sulpicae et Aliorum*, ed. E. Raczyński, Biblioteka Klassyków Łacinsckich, IV (1837)
Tablettes d'une amoureuse, ed. and (French) trans. Thierry Sandra (Abbéville, 1822)
Tibulle et les auteurs du 'Corpus Tibullianum', ed. A. Cartault (Paris: A. Colin, 1909)
Tibulli Sulpicia, ed. Eduard Michaelis (Leipzig: Insel, 1921)
Tibulle et les auteurs du 'Corpus Tibullianum', ed. Louis Pichard (Paris: E. Champion, 1924)
Tibulle et les auteurs du 'Corpus Tibullianum', ed. Max Pouchont (Paris: Éditions des Belles-Lettres, 1924)
Erotic Elegies of Albius Tibullus with the Poems of Sulpicia Arranged as a Sequence Called No Harm to Lovers, trans. Hubert Creekmore (New York: Washington Square Press, 1966)
Sulpiciae Elegidia, trans. Gilbert Sorrentino (Mt Horeb, Wis. The Perishable Press, 1977)
Sulpicia, trans. (French) Alain Absire (Cadeilhan: Zalma, 1993)
'Sulpicia', in *Classical Women Poets*, trans. Josephine Balmer (Newcastle upon Tyne: Bloodaxe Books, 1996), 98–103
The Poems of Sulpicia, trans. John Heath-Stubbs (London: Hearing Eye, 2000)

'Sulpiciae cineres lectricis cerne viator'

Inscription: Via del Tritone (Rome), Palazzo Vacchari-Bacchettoni
Bullettino communale, Rome, 1926 (1927), 229.
L'Année épigraphique, 1927 (1928), 20, no. 73
M. J. Carcopino, 'Épitaphe en vers de la lectrice Petale', *Bulletin de la Société Nationale des Antiquaires de France* (1929), 84–6

Fragment: 'implicuit femur femini'

Quoted by Charisius, in Heinrich Keil, *Grammatici Latini*, 7 vols. (Leipzig: B. G. Teubner, 1857–80), i. 130
Hermann, 'Un nouveau fragment de Sulpicia?', *Latomus*, 23 (1964), 322–3

Sulpicia (II, wife of Calenus)
s. i AD   Rome (Italy)
Fragment: 'si me cadurcis restitutis fasciis'

Petrus Pithoeus, *Epigrammata et Poematia Vetera*, 2 vols. (Paris: N. Gillius, 1590), i. 183 [London, British Library, 1001.e.1]

Heinnch Keil, *Grammatici Latini* (Leipzig; B. G. Teubner, 1857–80)

Johann Christian Wernsdorf (ed.), *Poetae Latini Minores*, 10 vols. (Altenberg: Richter, 1780–98), iii. 96 [London, British Library, 160 k. 10–19]

Edward Courtney (ed.), *The Fragmentary Latin Poets* (Oxford: Clarendon Press, 1993), 361

Classical Women Poets, trans. Josephine Balmer (Newcastle upon Tyne: Blood-axe Books, 1996), 106

<ps-Sulpicia (II): satire. This long poem *in persona* Sulpicia, wife of Calenus, probably written in the fifth century, was rediscovered in 1493 and long believed to be genuine

Editions: *Carmina LXX*, in G. Tiferni, *Opuscula* (1498)

Opera Ausonii Nuper Reperta (Parma: Thaddaeus Ugoletus, 1499). pp. lxxiiiiv–lxxcv, Sulpicia incipit. Queritur de statu Rei publicae & temporibus Domitiani

Carmina LXX, Gregorii Tipherni Opuscula etc. (Antwerp, 1509)

Satyricon Carmen, in Petronius Arbiter, *Satyricon etc.* (Paris, 1577)

Sulpiciae *Satyricon*, in *Petronii Arbitri Satyricon etc.* (Leiden: Johannel Paetrius, 1585), 129–31 (preceded by *Vita Sulpiciae*, ex. L. Greg. Gyraldi, *De Latinis Poetis Dialogo IIII* and followed by *Iani Dousae ad Sulpiciae Satyrum Schediasma*)

D. Magni Ausonii Burdigalensis, Opera, ed. Joseph Scaliger (Heidelberg, 1588) (*Sulpiciae Carmen*, 297–300)

Carmina, in *D.M. Ausonii Opera Omnia* (Bordeaux: S. Millengius, 1590)

Sulpiciae de Statu Reipublicae, in *Ausonius, Omnia Opera* (Bordeaux: S. Millengius, 1604)

Satyra de Corrupto Statu Reipublicae Domitiani, in *Poetae Latinae Minores*, ed. Petrus Burmannus (Leiden: Conrad Wishoff and Daniel Goedval, 1731) (and other edns.)

Poetae Latinae Minores, ed. P. Burmann (Glasgow: Foulis Press, 1752)

Satyra, in *Poetae Latini Minores*, ed. Johann Christian Wernsdorf, 10 vols. (Altenberg: Richter, 1780–98), iii. 1780 (other edns.)

Satira cum Notis, in *Bibliotheca Classica Latina*, ed. N. E. Lemaire, 7 vols. (Paris: N. E. Lemaire, [XXXV], 1819)

Satira, in *Corpus Poetarum Latinorum, etc.*, ed. W. S. Walker (1828). Another edn. 1849

Sulpitiae Satira de Corruptu Statu Reipublicae Temporibus Domitiani, ed. Charles Monnard (Paris: Bretin, 1816) (and other edns.)

Satire, in *Bibliothèque latine-française*, ed. and (French) trans. C. L. F. Panckoucke (1826)

Satires de Perse et de Sulpicia, ed. and (French) trans. A.-F. Théry (Paris: L. Hachette, 1827)

Satire, in *Persius, Satires, suivies d'un fragment de Turnus et de la satire de Sulpice*, ed. and (French) trans. A. Perreau (Paris, 1840)

Satire, in *Collection des auteurs latins*, ed. and (French) trans. J. M. N. D. Nisard
(Paris: Garnier Frères, 1850)

Satire, in *Satires de Perse et de Sulpicia*, trans. (French) Mis de la Rochefoucauld-Liancourt (Paris: Morris, 1858)

Satira, les satiriques latins, ed. and (French) trans. E. Despois (Paris: Hachette,
1864), 291–5

Satires of Juvenal, Persius, Sulpicia and Lucilius, trans. Lewis Evans (New York:
Harper & Brothers, 1879; London: George Bell and Sons, 1895)

Epigrammata Bobiensia. ed. Wolfgang Speyer (Leipzig: Teubner, 1963), 42–7

Ausonius, with an English Translation by Hugh G. Evelyn White, Loeb Classical
Library (Cambridge, Mass.: Harvard University Press; London: William
Heinemann, 2 vols., 1921), 282–9

H. Fuchs (ed. and (German) trans.), 'Das Klagelied der Sulpicia', in M. Gieber
(ed.), *Discordia Concors. Festgabe für Edgar Bonjour*, 2 vols. (Basel: Helbing &
Lichtenhahn, 1968), i. 32–47

Römische Satiren, ed. Werner Krenkel (Darmstadt: Wissenschaftliche Burgesellschaft, 1976)>

Susia/Suys, Anna

fl. *c*.1540?   Utrecht/Dordrecht (the Netherlands)
'Ruga genis, et muta chelys, nec munera formae'

Editions: In Nicolas Grudius, *Epigrammata*, in Ranutius Gherus (Jan Gruter),
Delitiae Poetarum Belgicorum, 4 vols. (Frankfurt: N. Hoffmann, 1614), ii. 586
[The Hague, Konincklijke Bibliotheek, 849. D. 29]

Jacob Hoeufft (ed.), *Parnasus Latino-Belgicus, sive Plerique e Poetis Belgii
Latinis, Epigrammate atque Adnotatione Illustrati* (Amsterdam: Peter den
Hengst & Sons, 1819), 13–14 [The Hague, Konincklijke Bibliotheek, 765. F10]

Tampia Hygia

                                                              Rome (Italy)
'Tu, quicumque mei veheris prope limina busti'

Inscription: Petrus Burmann (ed.), *Anthologia Veterum Latinorum Epigrammatum
et Poematum, sive Catalecta Poetarum Latinorum in VI Libros Digesta*, 6 vols. in
2 (Amsterdam: Schouten, 1759, 1773), ii. 197–9 (IV.cclx) [London, British
Library, 54. f. 13]

Heinrich Meyer (ed.), *Anthologia Veterum Latinorum Epigrammatum et Poematum*, 2 vols. in 1 (Leipzig: Gerhard Fleischer, 1835), i. 141 (1361) [London,
British Library, 011388. b. 14]

CIL, vi. 10097

CLE, ii. 511–12 (1111)

Edward Courtney, *Musa Lapidaria: A Selection of Latin Verse Inscriptions*
(Atlanta: Scholars Press, 1995), no. 123, pp. 120–1 (with trans.)

<Taurella, Hippolyta (Castiglione)

1501–20

Hippolytae Taurellae Mantuanae Epistola ad Maritum suum Balthasarem Castilionem apud Leonem X Pontific. Rom. Oratorem: 'Hippolyta ευπράττειν iam dicit Castilioni'

This work is most probably a heroic epistle by her husband Baldassare Castiglione, but was believed authentic by Coelio Curio, and subsequently by Julius Caesar Scaliger and many others.

MSS: Siena, Biblioteca Comunale, K. V. 30, fo. 168
Mantua, Marchese Capilupi 68, fo. 174
Vatican City, Biblioteca Apostolica, 6250, fo. 339
Vatican City, Biblioteca Apostolica, Lat. 2836, fo. 353
Vatican City, Biblioteca Apostolica, Lat. 5226, fo. 373
Vatican City, Biblioteca Apostolica, Lat. 5227, fo. 374
Vatican City, Biblioteca Apostolica, Lat. 5383, fo. 375
Vatican City, Biblioteca Apostolica, Reg. lat. 1593, fo. 403
Vatican City, Biblioteca Apostolica, Barberini lat. X 2163, fo. 450
Parma, Biblioteca Parmense, 1198, fo. 554

Editions: *Olympiae Fulviae Moratae Mulieris Omnium Eruditissimae Latine et Graeca, quae Haberi Potuerunt, Monumento, eaque Plane Divino, cum Eruditorum de ipsa Iudiciis et Laudibus; cum Hippolytae Taurellae Elegia Elegantissima* (Basel: Petrus Perna, 1558) [Oxford, Bodleian Library, 8o C. 12 (2) Art. Seld.]
Second edition *Olympiae Fulviae Moratae Foeminae Doctissimae ac Plane Diuinae Orationes, Dialogi, Epistolae, Carmina, tam Latina quam Graeca* (Basel: Petrus Perna, 1562), 274–8 [Oxford, Balliol College, Special Collections 0650. a. 13]
Carmina Quinque Illustrium Poetarum (Florence: Laurentius Torrentinus, 1552), 78–82 (1st edn. Venice, 1548; other edns. Florence, 1549, Venice, 1558)
Io. Matthaeus Toscanus, *Carmina Illustrium Poetarum Italorum* (Paris: Gilles Gorbin, 1576), 68ᵛ–90 [London, British Library, 238; 38]
Aegidius Periander, *Horti Tres Amoris* (Frankfurt) [not seen]⁹
Balthazaris Castillionei . . . Poematum Liber (Paris, 1606) [not seen]
Rhanutius Gherus [Jan Gruter], *Deliciae cc. Poetarum Italorum* (Florence, 1608) [not seen]
G. A. and Gaetano Volpi (ed.), *Opera volgari e latine* (Padua, 1733) [not seen]
Georg Christian Lehms, *Teutschlands galante Poetinnen mit ihren sinnreichen und netten Proben, nebst einem Anhang ausländischer Dames so sich gleichfalls durch schöne Poesien bey der curieusen Welt bekannt gemacht, und eine Vorrede: Dass das weibliche Geschlecht so geschickt zum Studieren, als das männliche* (Frankfurt am Main: Anton Heinscheidt for Samuel Tobias Hocter, 1745; repr. Leipzig:

---

⁹ The following references are from Ludwig's article cited below: since the attribution to Taurella is almost certainly spurious, I have not pursued them.

Zentralantiquariat der DDR, 1973), 302–5 [Cambridge, University Library, 746.17.d.95.33]

Carmina Quinque Illustrium Poetarum Italorum (Bergamo, 1753) [not seen]

P. A. Serassi (ed.), *Poesie volgari e latine del Conte Baldessar Castiglione* (Rome, 1760) [not seen]

B. Maier (ed.), *Il libro del cortegiano con una scelta delle opere minori* (Turin, 1955) [not seen]

P. A. Serassi (ed.), *Lettere del Conte Baldessar Castiglione*, ii. (Padua, 1771) [not seen]

Alessandro Perosa and John Sparrow (eds.), *Renaissance Latin Poetry* (London: Duckworth, 1979), 196–9

Walther Ludwig, 'Castiglione, seine Frau Hippolyta und Ovid', in Paul Gerhard Schmidt (ed.), *Die Frau in der Renaissance* (Wiesbaden: Harrassowitz, 1994), 99–156 (pp. 111–14)

Translation: anon. [Amelia Gillespie Smyth], *Olympia Morata: Her Times, Life and Writings* (London: Smith, Elder & Co., 1836), 289–93>

Taurina

s. iv?

'Lumine virgineo hic splendida membra quiescunt'

Inscription: not extant

Editions: *CIL*, v. 6731
CLE, i. 357–8 (478)

'Terentia'

fl. AD 106   Rome (Italy)/Memphis (Egypt)

'Vidi pyramidas sine te, dulcissime frater'

Inscription: not extant, *CIL* version is taken from copy made by Otto von Neuhaus (Wilhelm of Boldensele), in 1336

CIL, iii. 21

CLE, i. 130 (270)

An independent witness is found in Felix Fabri, *Evagatorium in Terrae Sanctae, Arabiae et Aegypti Peregrinationem*, ed. C. D. Hassler, 3 vols. (Stuttgart: Societas Litterariae Stuttgardiensis, 1843–9), iii. 43 (based on a reading made in the 1480s) [London, British Library, Ac. 8963]

C. L. Grotefend, *Zeitschrift des hist. Vereins für Niedersachsen an. 1832* (1885), 251

Ludwig Friedländer, *Roman Life and Manners under the Early Empire*, 4 vols. (London: George Routledge; New York: E.P. Dutton, 1913), iv. 138

Edward Courtney, *Musa Lapidaria: A Selection of Latin Verse Inscriptions* (Atlanta, Scholars Press, 1995), no. 74, pp. 88–9 (with translation)

Translation: Emily A. Hemelrijk, *Matrona Docta* (London: Routledge, 1999), 171

Tertia, wife of Suetrius Hermes

Rome (Italy)

'Suetrius Hermes hic situs est, cui Tertia coniunx'

> *Inscription*: Giovanni Battista Doni (ed.), *Inscriptiones Antiquae, Nunc Primum Editae*, 2 parts in 1, (Florence: Ex Regia Typographia Magni Ducis Etruriae, 1731), ii. 111 (196) [London, British Library, 145. g. 5]
> Petrus Burmann (ed.), *Anthologia Veterum Latinorum Epigrammatum et Poematum, sive Catalecta Poetarum Latinorum in VI Libros Digesta*, 6 vols. in 2 (Amsterdam: Schouten, 1759, 1773), ii. 162 (IV.ccxvii) [London, British Library, 54. f. 13]
> Heinrich Meyer (ed.), *Anthologia Veterum Latinorum Epigrammatum et Poematum*, 2 vols. in 1 (Leipzig: Gerhard Fleischer, 1835), ii. 132 (1325) [London, British Library, 011388. b. 14]
> Ariodante Fabretti (ed.), *Corpus Inscriptionum Italicarum Antiquioris Aevi* (Turin: Officina Regia, 1867), 165 (III.300) [London, British Library, 7707. g. 8]
> *CLE*, i. 216 (461)

Theophanu

c.1050   Essen (Germany)

'Hoc opus eximium gemmis auroque decorum'

> *Inscription*: Gabriel Bucelin, *Germania Topo-chrono-stemmato-graphica Sacra et Profana*, 4 vols. (Ulm: Goerlin; Augsburg: Praetorius; Frankfurt: Kühn, 1655–96), ii. 1662, p. 143 [Wolfenbüttel, Herzog August Bibliothek, M. Gl 4° 95. 1: 1–4]
> Karl Strecker and Gabriel Silagi (eds.), *Die lateinischen Dichten des deutschen Mittelalters*, v: *Die Ottonenzeit* (Leipzig: Karl W. Hiersemann; Munich: Verlag des Monumenta Germaniae Historica, 1937–79), 355

'Hocce deus gemmis, Cosma Damianeque, vobis'

Strecker and Silagi, 355

Tollet, Elizabeth

1694–1754   London/Stratford/West Ham (England)

Ex Job, Cap. xxvi, v.7, De Deo: 'Ille equidem magno Boream praetendit inani'

> *Editions*: Anon., *Poems on Several Occasions, with Anne Boleyn to King Henry the Eighth: An Epistle* (1724), 68–9 (one of only three Latin poems in this edition) [London, British Library, 1490. k. 1]

Under her own name, same title (London: John Clarke, 1755; 3rd edn. 1760), 75 [London, British Library, 11531. aa. 39; London, British Library, 11631. aa. 38]

Psalm XXIX: 'Vos, debellatus quorum sub legibus orbis'

    Edition: Poems on Several Occasions *(1724), 70, (1755), 77–8*

Psalm LXXIX: 'O Deus, invadunt populi tua regna profani'

    Edition: *Poems on Several Occasions* (1755), 78–9

Psalmus cxxxvii: 'Qua celer Euphrates Babylonia rura pererrat'

    Edition: *Poems on Several Occasions* (1724), 71, (1755), 79–80

CHRISTUS ad ANIMAM: 'Porrectis quoniam lignum per triste lacertis'

    Edition: *Poems on Several Occasions* (1755), 80–1

Aldricius de Paeto. Memoriter: 'Mane ceu Paeti viret herba campis'

    Edition: *Poems on Several Occasions* (1755), 81–2

M. S. JOHANNES WOODWARD, MD: 'WOODWARDUS actis ille laboribus'

    Edition: *Poems on Several Occasions* (1755), 82–3

In parmam Woodwardianam: 'Semiaremata vides disjecta moenis saxis'

    Edition: *Poems on Several Occasions* (1755), 83

Aldricius de Paeto. Memoriter: 'Mane ceu Paeti viret herba campis'

    Edition: *Poems on Several Occasions* (1755), 83

Ad Fratrem Brugis Agentem: 'O! mihi siquis, patrioque celo'

    Edition: *Poems on Several Occasions* (1755), 84

Ex Prosa Latina Epigrammatum Delecta, in Usu Etoniensium: 'Terra parens rerum, post actos vite labores'

    Edition: *Poems on Several Occasions* (1755), 84–5

Tomkyns, Mrs

fl. 1617   Oxford (England)

'Quae tu si methodum tenuissent fata, parenti'

> *Inscription*: Antony à Wood, *The History and Antiquities of the Colleges and Halls in the University of Oxford*, ed. John Gutch, 3 vols. (Oxford: Clarendon, 1786), iii. 221 [London, British Library, HLR. 378.42574]

Torelli, Alda (Lonata)

s. xvi

Latin verse and prose delivered extempore

> According to Girolamo Tiraboschi, *Storia della letteratura italiana*, 2nd edn. 8 vols. + index (Modena: Società tipografica, 1787), vii. 1195 [Oxford, Bodleian Library]

Trivulzi, Domitilla (Torelli)

1481–*c*.1527   Milan (Italy)

Nothing is known to survive

> Her verse is attested by contemporaries, e.g. *Libro di M. Gio. Boccaccio delle donne illustri, tradotto per Messer Giuseppe Betussi. Con una additione fatta dal medesimo delle donne famosi dal tempo di M. Giovanni fino a i giorni nostri* (Venice: A. Arrivabene, 1545), 194ᵛ–196ʳ [Paris, Bibliothèque Nationale de France, G. 20205]

Ulpia Veneria

                                                             Rome (Italy)

'Hic iacet ille situs M[arcus] formonsior ullo'

> *Inscription*: *CIL*, vi. 8553
> *CLE*, ii. 550 (1179)

Uta of Niedermünster

s. x   Niedermünster (Germany)

'Virgo dei genetrix, divina pignore felix'

> *Inscription*: may survive as such

> *Edition*: Karl Strecker and Gabriel Silagi (eds.), *Die lateinischen Dichten des deutschen Mittelalters*, V: *Die Ottonenzeit* (Leipzig: Karl W. Hiersemann; Munich. Verlag des Monumenta Germaniae Historica, 1937–79), 439–41

Utenhovia, Anna

s. xvi   Ghent? (Belgium)/Heidelberg (Germany)
Annae Pallantiae et Annae Utenhoviae Acrostichon: '**IA**-ne pater cedat cui matutinus Horati' (addressed to Jan Gruter)

MS: London, British Library, Burney 370, fo. 41ᵛ

Epigramma ad Nicolaum Klopferum Amicum s[uam] Suavissimum, Abeuntem ad Munus Docendi in Pago Franciae Orientalis, UTHENHOVIA: 'Hanc vitam nihil esse, monet vox aurea Pagi'

    Editions: *Epithalamiam Conscripta in Honorem Pii et Eruditi Viri D. Nicolai Klopferi, Pastoris Utenhovi: et Pudicissimæ Virginis, Elisabethae Heslerinnæ, à Viris Probatis & Amicis, Amphiaras Vatis Laude Dignissimis* (Frankfurt am Main: Nicolas Basseus, 1573), sig. A 4ᵛ [Oxford, Bodleian Library, Antiq. e.G.40 (2)]
    Jane Stevenson, 'Johanna Otho (Othonia) and Women's Latin Poetry in Reformed Europe', in Laurie Churchill, Phyllis R. Brown, and Jane E. Jeffrey (eds.), *Women Writing Latin from Roman Antiquity to Early Modern Europe*, 3 vols. (New York: Routledge, 2002), iii. 189–215 (206–7, 214)

In idem [Monavianum *Symbolum*] *ANNÆ VTENHOVIÆ*: 'Qui dixit, fiat lux: factaq; protinus est lux'

    Editions: Jacob Monavius, *Symbolum* (Gorlitz: Johannes Rhamba, 1595), 222 [The Hague, Konincklijke Bibliotheek, 1714.F.9]
    Johannes Posthius, *Parergorum Poeticorum Libri Duo* (Heidelberg: Hieronymus Commelin, 1595), 222 [The Hague, Konincklijke Bibliotheek, 1714.D.10]

Idiem Totidem Verbis ab Anna Vtenhoviade Karolantonii F. Expressum: 'Ergon Posthiadae medicam profiterier artem est'

    MS: Paris, Bibliothèque Nationale de France, Lat. 18592, fo. 62ʳ

    Edition: Johannes Posthius, *Parergorum Poeticorum Libri Duo* (Heidelberg: Hieronymus Commelin, 1595), 339–40 [The Hague, Konincklijke Bibliotheek, 1714.D.10]

Eiusdem Vtenhoviae ad Io. Posthium: 'Iane novem Musas et amans, et amatus ab iisdem'

    Edition: Posthius, 340

Anna Utenhovia Marquardo Frehero: 'Mitto tibi en tandem Nonni Marquarte secundi'

    MS: Paris, Bibliothèque Nationale de France, Lat. 18592, fo. 52ʳ

Valente, Camilla (dal Verme)
b. *c.*1520   Italy
Not seen

> Her Latin epigrams are praised by Giuseppe Betussi, who also notes that she
> wrote other Latin verse: *Libro di M. Gio. Boccaccio delle donne illustri, tradotto
> per Messer Giuseppe Betussi. Con una additione fatta dal medesimo delle donne
> famosi dal tempo di M. Giovanni fino a i giorni nostri* (Venice: A. Arrivabene,
> 1545), 229ᵛ–230ᵛ, 2nd edn. *Libro di M. Gio. Boccaccio, delle donne illustri,
> tradotto di latino in volgare per M. Giuseppe Betussi, con una giunta fatta dal
> medesimo d'altre donne famose* (Florence: Filippo Giunti, 1596), 470–2 [Paris,
> Bibliothèque Nationale de France, G.20205; London, British Library,
> 613.d.29]
> Letters, poems, and epigrams are attributed to her in Paris, Bibliothèque
> Nationale de France, Ancien fonds français 22865, fo. 34ᵛ

Valentini, Anna
fl. *c.*1597   Lohach (Hungary)
'Anna Valentino locat haec monumenta Marito'

> *Edition*: Petrus Bod, *Hungarus Tymbaules, seu Grata ac Benedicta Hungarorum
> Quorundam Principem, Heroum, Magnatum Toga et Sago ... Feminarum Hon-
> estatis Fama ac Pietatis Studio Illustrium, ex Epitaphiis Renovata Memoria*
> (Nagy enyed, 1764), 65 [London, British Library, 11403. aaa. 34]

Valeria Ursilla
s. ii   Rome (Italy)
'Nomen qui retinens tuum, magnus Alexander'

> *Inscription*: may not be extant
> Ludovicus Antonius Muratori (ed.), *Novus Thesaurus Veterum Inscriptionum*,
> 4 vols. (Milan: Ex Aedibus Palatinis, 1739–42), iii. 1414.9 [London, British
> Library, 1705.b.7]
> Petrus Burmann (ed.), *Anthologia Veterum Latinorum Epigrammatum et Poema-
> tum, sive Catalecta Poetarum Latinorum in VI Libros Digesta*, 6 vols. in 2
> (Amsterdam: Schouten, 1759, 1773), ii. 160 (IV.ccxiii) [London, British
> Library, 54.f.13]
> Heinrich Meyer (ed.), *Anthologia Veterum Latinorum Epigrammatum et Poema-
> tum*, 2 vols. in 1 (Leipzig: Gerhard Fleischer, 1835), ii. 172 (1484) [London,
> British Library, 011388.b.14]
> *CIL*, vi.2, p. 1258 (9604)
> *CLE*, ii. 589 (1253)
> H. Geist and G. Pfohl (eds.), *Römische Grabinschriften* (Munich: Ernst Hei-
> meran Verlag, 1969), 193–4 (530)

Varano, Costanza (Sforza)

1428–47   Camerino/Pesaro (Italy)

Ad Regem Aragonium: 'Caesar magnanime princeps iustissime regum'

MSS: Florence, Biblioteca Nazionale Centrale, II X 31, fos. 61ᵛ–62ʳ
Modena, Biblioteca Estense, γ.Z.6.10 (old classmark Est. compositi append.
    172), fo. 52ʳ
Paris, Bibliothèque Nationale de France, Nouv. acq. 472, fos. 35–36ᵛ
Verona, Biblioteca Comunale, 68 (1393), fos. 45ᵛ–46

Edition: Nicola Ratti, *Della famiglia Sforza*, 2 vols. (Rome: Il Salomoni, 1794–5),
    ii. 105–6 [Vatican City, Biblioteca Apostolica, Italia VIII.Sforza.1 (1–2)]

Constantia de Varano in Honorem Urbis Camerinae: 'Exoptata dies urbi celebranda
Camerte'

MSS: Florence, Biblioteca Nazionale Centrale, II.X.31, fo. 107
Milan, Biblioteca ambrosiana, Trivulz. 774, fo. 34
Modena, Biblioteca Estense, γ.Z.6.10 (old classmark Est. compositi append.
    172), p. 52ᵛ
Turin, Biblioteca Nazionale, G.V.34, fo. 69ᵛ
Vatican City, Biblioteca Apostolica, Lat. 2951, fos. 270ᵛ–271ʳ

Editions: Domenico Michiel, *Elogio storico di Costanza da Varano, degli antichi
    principi de Camerino* (Venice: Stamperia Palese, 1807), pp. xxii–xxiii [London,
    British Library, T.2266 (4)]
B. Feliciangeli, *Giornale storico delle letteratura italiana* (Turin), 23 (1894), 56.

Constantia de Varano ad Rodulfum: 'Inclyta virum procerum de stirpe Varani'

MSS: Bern, Deutsche Staatsbibliothek, Lat. 88 431, fos. 79ᵛ–80
Venice, Biblioteca Marciana, Lat. 210/cvii.5 (4689), fos. 12ᵛ–13ᵛ

Constantia de Varono ad Reginam Angellorum et Celi: 'Insignis generosa parens, spes
unica sedi'

MSS: Florence, Biblioteca nazionale centrale, II.X.31, fo. 59
Paris, Bibliothèque Nationale de France, Nouv. acq. 472, fos. 27–8
Verona, Biblioteca Comunale, 68 (1393), fos. 43ᵛ–44

Ad Dominum Oddantonium Illu. Curioni Natum [de Montefeltro], 'O magne decus
hesperie Monsfeltria proles'

MSS: Florence, Biblioteca Nazionale Centrale, II.X.31, fo. 60ʳ⁻ᵛ

Paris, Bibliothèque Nationale de France, Nouv. acq. 472, fos. 33–34ᵛ
Verona, Biblioteca Comunale, 68 (1393), fo. 45ʳ

Edition: Ratti, ii. 106

Ad Dominum Ioannem. Lucidum de Gonzaga, 'Sepe parens, dominusque meus me scribere iussit'

MSS: Florence, Biblioteca Nazionale Centrale, II.X.31, fo. 61ʳ⁻ᵛ
Paris, Bibliothèque Nationale de France, Nouv. acq. 472, fos. 30–30ᵛ
Verona, Biblioteca Comunale, 68 (1393), fos. 44ᵛ–45ʳ

Edition: Ratti, ii. 104–5

Ad Dominam Isottam Nogarolam, 'Est Isota meo tua dulcis epistola fixa'

MSS: Florence, Biblioteca Nazionale Centrale, II.X.31, fos. 60ᵛ–61ᵛ
Paris, Bibliothèque Nationale de France, Nouv. acq. 472, fos. 29–30
Verona, Biblioteca Comunale, 68 (1393), fo. 44

Editions: Ratti, ii. 105
Isotae Nogarolae Veronensis Opera quae Supersunt Omnia, ed. Eugenius Abel, 2 vols. (Vienna: Gerold & Cie., 1886), ii. 7–8 [London, British Library, 12227.e.5]
Holt Parker, 'Latin and Greek Poetry by Five Renaissance Italian Women Humanists', in Barbara K. Gold, Paul Allen Miller, and Charles Platter (eds.), *Sex and Gender in Medieval and Renaissance Texts: The Latin Tradition* (Albany: State University of New York Press, 1997), 247–86 (p. 267) (with trans.)

Constantia Sforza ad Circumstantes demum ad Virum in Extremo Vitae: 'Sanguine clara patrum sumus quoque laudibus olim'

MS: Florence, Biblioteca Riccardiana, 924, fo. 199

CV's *Opera* are also printed by Joannes Maria Lazzarono, *Miscellanea de varie operette* (Venice, 1740–4), viii, not seen

Vaz, Joanna
s. xvi   Portugal
'Johanna Vasaea naenium [Funerary poem] scribit in Erasmi obitum'

Attested by Johann Heinrich Alsted, *Thesaurus chronologiae*, (4th edn. (Herborn: haeredes C. Coruini, 1650). 251 [London, British Library, 799.c.1]

Vegri, Caterina
1414–62   Bologna, Ferrara, Bologna (Italy)
Rosarium Antiquum, et Devotum Beatissimae Matris Dei

> The unsigned work of a nun of Corpus Christi, Ferrara [not seen], attributed to
> her by Antonio Libanori, *Ferrara d'Oro imbrunito dall'abbate Antonio*, 3 vols.
> in 2 (Ferrara: Alfonso and Gio. Battista Maresti, 1665–74), iii. 73 [Vatican
> City, Biblioteca Apostolica, Barberini H.V.15]

Vettia Prima
classical period
'Fato crudeli siqua est erepta puella'

> *Inscription*: Petrus Burmann (ed.), *Anthologia Veterum Latinorum Epigrammatum
> et Poematum, sive Catalecta Poetarum Latinorum in VI Libros Digesta*, 6 vols. in
> 2 (Amsterdam: Schouten, 1759, 1773), ii. 86 (IV.cxxxiii) [London, British
> Library, 54.f.13]
> Heinrich Meyer (ed.), *Anthologia Veterum Latinorum Epigrammatum et Poema-
> tum*, 2 vols. in 1 (Leipzig: Gerhard Fleischer, 1835), ii. 111 (1260) [London,
> British Library, 011388.b.14]
> *CIL*, ix. 294 (3122)
> *CLE*, ii. 568–9 (1213)

Victoria
                                                                Rome (Italy)
'Si quis forte velit tumuli cognoscere fatum'

> *Inscription*: *Dissertatio Glyptographica* (Rome, 1739), 115 [London, British Li-
> brary, 141.c.15 (2)]
> Scipione Maffei (ed.), *Museum Veronense hoc est Antiquarum Inscriptionum atque
> Anaglyptorum Collectio* (Verona: Typis Seminarii, 1749), 174 [London, Brit-
> ish Library, 743.d.21]
> Petrus Burmann (ed.), *Anthologia Veterum Latinorum Epigrammatum et Poema-
> tum, sive Catalecta Poetarum Latinorum in VI Libros Digesta*, 6 books in 2 vols.
> (Amsterdam: Schouten, 1759, 1773), ii. 157–8 (IV.ccix) [London, British
> Library, 54.f.13]
> Heinrich Meyer (ed.), *Anthologia Veterum Latinorum Epigrammatum et Poema-
> tum*, 2 vols. in 1 (Leipzig: Gerhard Fleischer, 1835), ii. 130 (1320) [London,
> British Library, 011388.b.14]
> *CIL*, vi.4, p. 2545 (25427)
> *CLE*, ii. 528–9 (1142)

Vigoli, Maria Porcia
1632–82   Rome/Viterbo (Italy)
Latin verse

Attributed by Bandini Buti, ii. 350–1

Virula
late antiquity   Chusirensen (Byzacena [Tunisia])
'Iulius Ingenuus obit in Gallia morte'

> *Inscription*: *CIL*, viii, suppl. 12128
> *CLE*, i. 251 (522)

Wagenseil/Vagenseila, Helene Sibylla (Moller)
1669–1735   Altdorf (Germany)
'Est ubi juncta HELENAE LUCRETIA. Nomina miror'

> *Edition*: *Composizione per la morte di Elena Lucrezia Cornaro Piscopia, dedicate a
> Gianbattisto suo padre, procuratore di S. Marco dal Co. Alessandro ab. de
> Lazaro, principe dell'Accademia* (Padua: P. M. Frambotto, 1684), 81 [Padua,
> Biblioteca museo civico di Padova, BP.473.VIII]

'Arbore succisa quod ego ramus modo succi' (1705)

> *Edition*: Georg Christian Lehms, *Teutschlands galante Poetinnen, mit ihren sinn-
> reichen und netten Proben, nebst einem Anhang ausländische Dames so sich gleich-
> falls durch schöne Poesien [bey] der curieusen Welt bekannt gemacht* (Frankfurt
> am Main: Anton Heinscheidt, 1715), 141; (1745), 71 [London, British Li-
> brary, 11525.dd.21; Cambridge, University Library, 746.17.d.95.33]

Verses to Theodoor Jansson van Almeloveen, written 1696

> Attested by Theodoor Jansson, in a Latin letter written in reply: J. G. Schelhorn,
> *Amoenitates Literariae, Quibus Variae Observationes, Scripta item Quaedam
> Anecdota et Rariora Opuscula Exhibentur*, v, 14 vols. (Frankfurt: Daniel Bartho-
> lomaeus, 1726), 200–1 (German Baroque Literature, Harold Jantz Collection
> 2216 (457–58)) [Wolfenbüttel, Herzog August Bibliothek XFilm 1: 457–458]

Walburg, Judoca, Gravin van Leeuwenstein-Rochefort
d. 25 October 1683   Maastricht (Netherlands)
'Quisquis ades, qui morte cades, sta, respice mortem'

> *Inscription*: Grafmonument Hermann, Graaf von den Berch, d. 29.03.1669 St
> Servaaskerk, Maastricht

Wasenthau, Magdalena Brigitta

Germany?

'Si pietas, Candor, virtus, doctrinaque, mortem' (distich)

> *Edition*: Johann Caspar Eberti, *Eröffnetes Cabinet dess Gelehrten Frauen-zimmers* (Frankfurt: Michael Rohrlachs sel. Wittib und Erben, 1700; 2nd edn. 1706), 374 (facsimile edn. Munich: Iudicium, 1990) [Oxford, Taylorian EN.807.A.1; London, British Library, 10603.aaa.2]

Weber, Sophia Elisabeth (Brenner)

1659–1730

Stockholm (Sweden)

Epitaphium Plurimum Reverendi Doctissimique Viri dm. Isaaci Henrici Brenneri, Ecclesiae Stor-tyro in Botnia Orientali Pastoris quondam Vigilantissimi, qui Obit a 1670: 'Hoc cubat in tumulo Brenneri corpus Isaci'

> *Edition*: *Johannes Paulinus, Memoria Plurimum Reverendi Doctissimique Viri Dn Isaaci Henrici Brenneri, etc.* (Stockholm: Johann Georg Ebert, [1670]), 6 [Helsinki, Universitets Bibliothek, Rv Henk.Kirj.2(4)]

Reprinted as single sheet, no place, no printer, no date [in or after 1680] [Helsinki, Universitets Bibliothek, Rv.Henk.Kirj.2 (2)]

> *Edition*: *Uti åtstillige Språk / Tider och Tidfällen författade, Poetiska dikter* (Stockholm: Julius Georg Matthias, 1713), 82 [Wolfenbüttel, Herzog August Bibliothek, M: Lr.27 (1)]

De Duobus Ursis a Carolo XI S.G.Vque Rege in Venatu Stratis: 'Quid mirare adeo Regis fortissima facta?'

> *Edition*: *Poetiska dikter* (Stockholm: Julius Georg Matthias, 1712), 15 [Wolfenbüttel, Herzog August Bibliothek, M: Lr.27 (1)]

'Felices, blandae subeuntes vincla Cythereae'

> *Edition*: ibid. 44

Nuptiis Reverendi et Clarissimi Dn. Wilhelm Lemmini, Ecclesiae Spantekauensis in Pomerania Pastoris Vigilantissimi et Lectissimae Virginis Elisabethae Margarethae Brahe… 1705, Ad Dominum Sponsum: 'vis LEMMINE. Tuis ne desim carmine Taedis'

> *Edition*: ibid. 72

Cum Vir Clarissimus Mag. Carolus Andreas Zellinus Stockholmiae Anno 1676 Debito Honore Tumulo Interretur: 'Heu! quod tam tirus raptus PRÆCEPTOR ab undis'

> *Edition*: ibid. 81

Epithaphium Pie Defunctae [Margarethe Stiernmarck]: 'Conditur hoc tumulo probitas, patientia juxta'

    Edition: ibid. 148

Ad Antiquis Moribus et Studiis Juvenem Nicolaum Kederum: 'Svecia te Juvenem o modo novit, et ipsa' (1687)

    Edition: ibid. 195

Ad Virum Perillustrem Amplissimum Experientissimumque Dn. Urbanum Hierne: 'Hierniades, Physicis semper venerabile nomen'

    Edition: ibid., 242–3

Nobilissimo et Amplissimo Viro Dn. Joanni Nicolao Pechlino: 'Non nescimus, in arte quid valemus' (1698)

    Edition: *Poetiska dikter* (Stockholm: Johannes L. Horrns, 1732), 106–7 [not seen] [Copenhagen, Kongelige Bibliotek]

    There is also a later edition of Brenner: *Samlade Poetiska Dikter* (Uppsala, 1873) [not seen]

Webster, Augusta ('Cecil Home')

1837–94   Poole/Cambridge/London (England)
Diaboli Ambulatio Matutina, quae Vidit, quae de Visis Cogitavit [translation of S. T. Coleridge, 'The Devil's Walk']

    MS: *Diaboli Ambulatio Matutina, quae Vidit, quae de Visis Cogitavit: 'The Devil's Walk', by Democritus Oxoniensis* (Oxford: J. Vincent, 1848) [not seen] [Austin, Texas, Harry Ransom Humanities Research Center]

    A MS letter from Augusta Webster to Sara Coleridge, 20 May 1851, also in Texas, establishes authorship: 'it was commenced for the amusement of myself and a Pupil whom I was preparing for Oxford, and finished in the course of my lonely walks to distant parts of my Parish'

Weston, Elizabeth Jane (Leon)[10]

1582–1612   ?Oxfordshire (England)/Prague (Czech Republic)
In Symbolum Georgii Carolidae à Carlsperga P.L.C. Memineris Tui: 'Quam pia Carolides sibi legit symbola vates'

---

[10] References to Weston are based on the bibliographical work of Brenda Hosington and Donald Cheney, in their edition of Weston's *Collected Writings*, with some additions. I am also grateful to Susan Bassnett, Alison Shell, and Arnold Hunt for sharing Xeroxes of texts in Prague with me.

Editions: Jiří Carolides, *Parentalia . . . Carolo Mielniczky a Karlsberga, Patricio Pragensi, . . . Opera Filii Georgii Carolidae a Karlsperga . . . Celebrata*, (Prague: Johann Schumann, [1601]), *Epigrammatum Liber Secundus*, nos. xxiii–xxv, xxix, epig. II. 23 [Prague, National Museum Library (KNM), 49. E. 18, přív. (1)]

Parthenicon, ii, sig. B 8ᵛ (see below)

Kalckhoff (see below), i. 67

Elizabeth Jane Weston, *Collected Writings*, ed. and trans. Donald Cheney and Brenda M. Hosington (Toronto: Toronto University Press, 2000), 154–5 (with trans.)

In idem: 'Si bene te noris, si toto pectore constes'

> *Editions*: Carolides, *Parentalia* epig. II.24
> *Parthenicon*, II, sig. B 8ᵛ
> Kalckhoff, i. 68
> Cheney and Hosington, 154–5 (with trans.)

In idem: 'Nemo alios novit, nisi qui se noverit ipsum'

> *Editions*: Carolides, *Parentalia*, epig. II.25 (dated 19 Mar. 1601)
> *Parthenicon*, ii, sig. B 8ᵛ
> Kalckhoff, i. 68
> Cheney and Hosington, 156–7 (with trans.)

'Sis precor, Abdias meus, Invictissime CÆSAR'

> *Editions*: *Carmen ad Invictissimum et Potentissimum Principem ac Dominum Dominum Rudolphum II Sacri Romani Imperii Imperatorem semper Augustum &c. Scriptum* (Oberursel: Cornelius Sutorius, 1601) [Berlin, Staatsbibliothek, Preussischer Kulturbesitz, Ar. 10071ᵃ]
> *Poemata*, i, sig. a 2ᵛ
> *Parthenicon*, i, sig. A 2ᵛ
> Kalckhoff, i, 2–3
> Cheney and Hosington, 4–7

'Quod iustas, Hellere, foves, causasque tueris'

> *Editions*: *Carmen ad Invictissimum* . . .
> Cheney and Hosington, 323–4 (with trans.)

Elegia Consolatoria ad Nob. Opt. Virum D. Bartolemæum Havlichium Srnovecium à Varvaziova, Novæ Pragæ Civem, Consularem & Secretarium Adfinem & Collegam Meritó Observandum, Obitum Filiolæ Dorotheæ, Puellæ Elegantissimæ . . . (Prague:

Schumann, 1604): 'Heu, quis Sicelidas dubitet nunc plangere Musas?' [Prague, Strahov Library, U.K. 50. G. 126 přív. 13.]

> *Edition*: Cheney and Hosington, 332–35 (with trans.)

Meditatio, Cum Gratiarum Actione, in Diem Nataliae Salvatoris nostri IESU CHRISTI, Carmina Expressa ab Elisabetha Joanna Westhonia, Virgine Angla (Prague: Georgius Nigrinus, 1601): 'Festa dies hilari (mortales plaudite!) cælo' [Prague: Strahov Library, A.M. IX. 100]

> *Editions*: *Poemata*, ii, sig. a 2ʳ
> *Parthenicon*, ii, sig. A 1ᵛ–3ʳ
> Kalckhoff, ii. 74–8
> Cheney and Hosington, 100–7 (with trans.)

Poemata, Elizab. Ioann. Vestoniae Anglae, Virginis Nobilissimae, Poëtriae Celeberrimæ, Linguarum Plurimarum Peritissimæ, ed. G. Martinii à Baldhoven (Frankfurt: Eichorn, 1602) [London, British Library, 11408 aa 13]

> *Critical edition*: Cheney and Hosington, 310–21

'Serenissime ac potentissime . . .' (Prague, 1603)

> *MS*: not seen; reference from Z. A. Truhlár and Karel Hrdina, *Enchiridion Renatae Poesis Latinae in Bohemia et Moravia Cultae*, 5 vols. (Prague: Academiae Scientiarum Bohemoslovacae, 1966–82), v. 477

In Obitum Nobilis et Generosae Foeminae, Dominae Ioannae p.m. Magnifici et Generosi Domini Edovardi Kellei de Imany, Equitis Aurati Sacraeque Caesarae Maiestatis Consiliarii, Derelicta Viduae, Matris suae Honorandissimae Charissimaeque Lachrymaebunda Effudit Filia:. 'Mortis inexpletae quae vis, & quanta potestas' (Prague, 1606) [Prague, Czech Academy of Science, Cabinet of Greek Studies, estate of K. Hrdina, envelope 55]

> *Editions*: Cheney and Hosington, 336–41 (with trans.)
> Jane Stevenson and Peter Davidson (eds.), *Early Modern Women Poets* (Oxford: Oxford University Press, 2001), 135–9 (with trans.)
> Brenda M. Hosington, 'Elizabeth Jane Weston (1581–1612)', in Laurie Churchill, Phyllis R. Brown, and Jane E. Jeffrey (eds.), *Women Writing Latin from Roman Antiquity to Early Modern Europe*, 3 vols. (New York: Routledge, 2002), iii, 217–45 (pp. 231–4, 242–4)

Parthenicon, ed. G. Martinii à Baldhoven (Prague: Paulus Sessius, 1608) [London, British Library, C. 61. d. 2]

Editions: Leipzig, 1609, poss. ghost edn. [not seen]

Amsterdam, 1712 [not seen]

Johann Christoph Kalckhoff (ed.), *Elisabethae Joannae Westoniae, Nobilis Anglae et Poetriae Longè Celeberrimae, Opuscula, quae Quidem Haberi Potuerunt* (Frankfurt: Bertram Cramer, 1723; reissue 1724) [London, British Library, G. 17483; London, British Library, 238. m. 7]

Facsimile edition: *The Early Modern Englishwoman in Print*, ed. Donald Cheney (Aldershot: Ashgate, 2000)

Critical edition: Cheney and Hosington, 1–303 (with trans.)

In Symbolum M. Bathasaris Exneri Sil. P.L. Spero Meliora: 'Qui meliora sibi ruituro sperat in orbe'

Editions: Balthasar Exner, *Anchora Utriusque Vitae, hoc est, Symbolum Spero Meliora* (Hanau: Wechel, 1619), 41 [Vatican City, Biblioteca apostolica, Racc. I.V.1145]

Poemata, i, sig. c 7^v

Parthenicon, ii, sig. C 1^r

Kalckhoff, i. 68–9

Cheney and Hosington, 156–7

In eandem: 'Quid speras meliora? Quid est, extrema quod inter'

Editions: Exner, 41–2

Poemata, i, sig. c 8^r

Parthenicon, ii, sig. C 1^{r-v}

Kalckhoff, i. 69

Cheney and Hosington, 156–9 (with trans.)

In Palmam Illustriss: Sponsorum, quorum Nomina & Cognomina Acrostichis Præno-tantur: 'Ecquid (Apollo refer) palmarum denotat icon'

Editions: *Vota pro Felicibus & Secundis Nuptiis Illustriss. et Generosiss. Domini, Domini Ernesti Comitis Mansveldiae, Nobilis Domini Heldrungiæ, Seburgæ & Scraplæ ... et Illustris ac Generosæ Dñæ, Dñæ Annæ Sibyllæ de Warten-berg ... 22. Septembris Pragae Celebratis Anno 1608* (probably Prague, 1608) [with contributions from Weston, Nicolaus Maius, and Georgius [Jiři] Car-olides] [Zwickau, Ratsschulbibliothek, 5.3.29/8]

Cheney and Hosington, 344–9 (with trans.)

Elisabethæ Ioannæ Westoniæ Nobilis Britannæ Joannis Leonis Iureconsulti: in Aula Imperiali Causarum Patroni Uxoris, ad Dominum Michaelem Pieczek Smrziczky á

Radosticz Civem NeoPragensem: Libelli Autorem Epigramma: 'Quid mea, quid Michael, muliebres carmina, nugas'

> *Editions*: Mihal Pěčka Smržiczky z Radostic, *Akcí a řozepre mezi filozofem, v lékařství doktorem a orátorem aneb prokurátorem, třmi vlastními bratry, který by z nich obci a vlasti své neiplatněši a nejužitečnějši bý ti a tak vedle kšaftu otcovského dvou dílu statku po něm dostati měl, jac učený m a moudrý m, tak i prokurátorum vejmluvný m a všechněm lidem, obci a vlasti své sloužícím milá, prospěšná užitečná* (Prague: Paulus Sessius, 1609) [Prague, UK 54. F. 319, 54. K. 5683]
> Cheney and Hosington, 350–1 (with trans.)

In Opuscula Medica Oswaldi Crolii: 'Crollius invidiae quia sese audentius offert'

> *Editions*: Oswald Croll, *Basilica Chymica* (Frankfurt: Claudius Marnius and Heredes Joannis Aubrii, 1609), 50–1 [Oxford, Radcliffe Science Library, RR. w. 190]
> Cheney and Hosington, 60–1

AD LECTOREM: 'Omnia praesenti; Lector, quaecunque libello' (after 1610)

> *MS*: London, British Library, copy of *Parthenicon*, C. 61. d. 2, second fly-sheet r–v; Prague, National Museum Library (KNM), 49. E. 38, flyleaf. The handwriting of the Prague copy is apparently that of the owner, Christoph Girsner of Nuremberg

> *Editions*: Louise Schleiner, *Tudor and Stuart Women Writers* (Bloomington: Indiana University Press, 1994), 264–5
> Stevenson and Davidson, 141–2 (with trans.)
> Cheney and Hosington, 304–7 (with trans.)

'A nostris aufer modulis tua scripta, Georgi'
'Ut mea scripta tuis confundas, mutua dicis'
'Cur tua scripta meis misces? effare Georgi'

> *MSS*: London, British Library, copy of *Parthenicon*, C. 61. d. 2, sig. D 2v
> Prague, National Museum Library (KNM), 49. E. 38, sig. D 3r, D2v
> Cheney and Hosington, 306–7 (with trans.)

'*Ille* potens belli MACEDO genitore *Philippo*'

> *Editions*: *Ad Serenissimum, Potentissimum, ac Invictissimum Principem ac Dominum, Dn. Matthiam Secundum, Hungariæ & Bohemiæ Regem, Archiducem Austriæ, &c. XIII Julii Anno 1612 in Romanorum Imperatorem Francofurti*

Electum et Coronatum, &c. Ab Elisabetha Joanna Leonis VVestonia, Angla (Leipzig: Valentin am Ende, 1612) [Wittenberg, Evangelisches Predigerseminar, Varia 255/80]

Corona Imperialis: hoc est, Vota et Congratulationes Diversorum Auctorum, in Electionem et Coronationem ... D. Matthiae, Rom. Imp. semper Augusti, ed. Bernhard Praetorius (Nuremberg, 1613), 21–2 [Prague, Strahov Library, A.N. IX. 114]

Cheney and Hosington, 358–61 (with trans.)

De Ebrietate, ex Jussu Matris: 'Crimina, vix magni versu taxanda Maronis'

Editions: Sebastianus Hornmoldus, *In Crapulam pro Sobrietate de Vitanda et Fugienda Ebrietate, Redintegratum, Auctum et ex Diversis Authoribus Decem Epigrammatum Centurii Celebratum* (Basel: Johann Jacob Genath, 1616), 80–2 [Wolfenbüttel, Herzog August Bibliothek, 104.5 Poetica]
Sebastianus Hornmoldus, *In Crapulam, Pro Sobrietate: seu Votum Posthi-Melissæum, de Vitanda et Fugienda Ebrietate, Redintegratum, Auctum, et ex Diversis Authoribus Decem Epigrammatum Centuriis Celebratum à Sebastiano Hornmoldo, Tubing. ... 1619* (Basel: Johann Jakob Genath, [1619]), 80–2 [London, British Library, C.104.e.14]
Cheney and Hosington, 362–65 (with trans.)

Cum Ebrio non Litigandum: 'absenti nocuit praesens, qui laeserit illum'
Editions: Poemata, ii, sig. b 2ᵛ
Parthenicon, ii, sig.B1ᵛ
Hornmoldus (both editions), 130
Cheney and Hosington, 130–1 (with trans.)

Elisabetha Joanna Westhonia, Angla, Uxor Johannis Leonis, in Aula Imperiali Negociorum Agentis, &c. Christian-Theodoro Schossero: 'Carmina perlegi doctum signantia VATEM'

Editions: Chrystian Teodor Schosser, *Lauri Folium sive Schediasmatum Poeticorum Libri*, iv (Freiburg: Georg Hoffman, 1622), sig. F 4ʳ⁻ᵛ [Prague, Strahov Library, UK. 52. G. 76, přív. 3]
Cheney and Hosington, 370–3 (with trans.)

'Rex Jacobe, Pater patriae de sanguine Regum'

MS: given as London, Public Record Office, SP fos. 257–8 by Ryba [not seen; classmark is obviously incorrect, and it is not to be found in the State Papers under James]

Editions: *Parthenicon*, iii, sig. A 2ᵛ–3ᵛ

Georg Christian Lehms, *Teutschlands galante Poetinnen, mit ihren sinnreichen und netten Proben, nebst einem Anhang ausländischer Dames so sich gleichfalls durch schöne Poesien [bey] der curieusen Welt bekannt gemacht* (Frankfurt am Main: Anton Henscheidt, 1715), 327–8 [London, British Library, 11525. dd. 21]

Bohumil Ryba, 'Westoniin blahopřejný list anglikému králi Jakubovi I', *Listy filologické*, 59 (1932), 387–8

Cheney and Hosington, 170–5

Ad Nobilissimum et Excellentissimum Dominum Philippum de Monte, Sac. Caes. Mtis Capellae Magistrum Musicum hoc nostro Seculo Principem: 'Te quoque, cui nomen de Monte, Philippe, Camenae'

Editions: *Poemata*, i, sig. B 5ʳ–6ʳ

Parthenicon, i, sig. B8ʳ–C1ᵛ

Kalckhoff, i. 42–4

G. van Doorslaer, *La Vie et les œuvres de Philippe de Monte* (Brussels: Académie Royale de Belgique, 1921), 271–2

Cheney and Hosington, 50–3 (with trans.)

De Pulice et Milite: 'Pulicis interdum est audacia magna pusilli'

Editions: *Poemata*, sig. b 6ᵛ

Parthenicon, sig. B7ᵛ–8ʳ

Schleiner, 212–13 (with trans.)

Cheney and Hosington, 152–3 (with trans.)

Leo ac Rana: 'Vox Ranae fuerat delapsa Leonis ad aures'

Editions: *Poemata*, ii, sig. b 5ʳ

Parthenicon, ii, sig. B 6ʳ

Schleiner, 213–14 (with trans.)

Cheney and Hosington, 146–7 (with trans.)

Ad eundem [Nicolaum Majum] cum Periculoso Pragae Affligeretur Morbo: 'Non equidem immerito miraris candide Maje'

Editions: *Poemata*, i, sig. B 6ʳ

Parthenicon, i, sig. B 4ʳ–ᵛ

Schleiner, 214–15 (with trans.)

Cheney and Hosington, 38–9 (with trans.)

Virgini Nobili, Margarethae Baldhoveniae, B. Martin à Baldhoven &c. Senioris Filiae: 'Margari, quae monitu Fratris tibi carmina promam?'

Editions: *Poemata*, i, sig. C 3ᵛ
Parthenicon, i, sig. C 7ʳ⁻ᵛ
Schleiner, 215–17 (with trans.)
Cheney and Hosington, 72–5 (with trans.)

Ad eundem [Joanne Leoni]: 'Quid tibi pro donis, LEO concelebrande, refundam?'

Editions: *Poemata*, i, sig. C 6ʳ
Parthenicon, i, sig. C 4ᵛ
Schleiner, 217 (with trans.)
Cheney and Hosington, 66–7 (with trans.)

Illustrissimo Principe et Dno, Dno Petro Wock à Rosenberg ac Mecænati suo Gratio-sissimo: 'Inter minora sidera'

Editions: *Poemata*, i, sig. A4ʳ⁻ᵛ
Parthenicon, i, sig. A3ᵛ⁻4ʳ
Schleiner, 218–19 (with trans.)
Cheney and Hosington, 10–11
Hosington, 224–5, 234–5 (with trans.)

In Hortos eiusdem [Ioanni Barviti]: 'Hortus odoratis hic est cultissimis herbis'

Editions: *Poemata*, i, sig. B2ʳ⁻ᵛ
Parthenicon, i, sig. A8ʳ
Donald Cheney, 'Westonia on the Gardens of Barvitius', *American Notes and Queries*, 5 (1992), 64–7
Cheney and Hosington, 24–5
Hosington, 225, 235 (with trans.)

Nobili & Clarissimo Viro Erico Lymburch, I.V.D, Consiliario Comitis ab Oldenburg: 'Clare vir; & Themidos cultissime cultor, ERICE

Editions: *Poemata*, i, sig. B7ᵛ⁻8ʳ
Parthenicon, i, sig. C2ᵛ
Cheney and Hosington, 58–9
Hosington, 225, 235–6 (with trans.)

Ad Eundem [Ericum Lymburch]: 'Non ego Praxillam, Sappho, doctamque Corinnam'

Editions: *Poemata*, i, sig. B8ʳ
Parthenicon, i, sig. C3ʳ
Cheney and Hosington, 58–61
Hosington, 225, 236 (with trans.)

> *Translation*: Jane Stevenson, 'Women and Classical Education in the Early
> Modern Period', in Yun Lee Too and Niall Livingstone (eds.), *Pedagogy
> and Power: Rhetorics of Classical Learning* (Cambridge: Cambridge University
> Press, 1998), 83–109 (p. 94)

Nobili et Clarissimo Viro G. Martin à Baldhoven, Silesio &c Amico suo Singulari:
'Ecquis ad officium Musas revocabit itinere'

> *Editions*: *Poemata*, i, sig. C 5ᵛ
> *Parthenicon*, i, sig. C 5ʳ⁻ᵛ
> Schleiner, 220–1 (with trans.)
> Cheney and Hosington, 66–9 (with trans.)

Epigrammata

> *Editions*: *Poemata*, ii, sig. b 7ʳ–c1ʳ
> *Parthenicon*, ii, sig. B 4ʳ–5ʳ
> Schleiner, 221–3 (with trans.)
> Cheney and Hosington, 38–42 (with trans.)
> Hosington, 229, 239 (with trans.)

Dominica Lazari Jacentes ante Fores Divitis: 'O aeterne DEUS mirandi rector
Olympi'

> *Editions*: *Parthenicon*, ii, sig A 4ʳ⁻ᵛ
> Schleiner, 223–4 (with trans.)
> Cheney and Hosington, 114–15 (with trans.)

Mortem non Gustabunt: 'Non fratres inter tantus fuit ardor amantes'

> *Editions*: *Poemata*, ii, sig. a 6ʳ
> *Parthenicon*, ii, sig. A 6ʳ⁻ᵛ
> Schleiner, 224–5 (with trans.)
> Cheney and Hosington, 116–17 (with trans.)
> Hosington, 229, 239 (with trans.)

Dissolvi Cupio: 'Quid mea mendosae laceratis pectora curae?'

> *Editions*: *Poemata*, ii, sig. a 6ᵛ
> *Parthenicon*, ii, sig. A 6ʳ⁻ᵛ
> Schleiner, 225
> Cheney and Hosington, 116–19

De Nomine Jesu: 'Verte stylum, mea Musa, procul mundana recedant'

> Editions: *Poemata*, ii, sig. a 4ʳ–6ʳ
> *Parthenicon*, ii, sig. A 3ʳ–5ʳ
> Kalckhoff, ii. 79–82
> Schleiner, 226–30 (with trans.)
> Cheney and Hosington, 108–13 (with trans.)
> Hosington, 226–9, 236–8 (with trans.)

In Symbolam Westoniae Auctoris: 'In te, CHRISTE, mihi spes derivata recumbit'

> Editions: *Poemata*, i, sig. C 2ʳ
> *Parthenicon*, ii, sig. B8ʳ
> Schleiner, 230–1 (with trans.)
> Cheney and Hosington, 152–5 (with trans.)

De Inundatione Pragae ex Continuis Pluviis Orta, Anno 96: 'Evocat iratos Caeli inclementia ventos'

> Editions: *Poemata*, ii, sig. c 1ᵛ–2ʳ
> *Parthenicon*, ii, sig. C 1ᵛ–2ʳ
> Stevenson and Davidson, 134–5 (with trans.)
> Hosington, 231, 241 (with trans.)

In 2. Ovidii Trist.: 'Sors tua, Naso tuae praecium artis, plurima mecum'

> Editions: *Parthenicon*, i, sig. C5ᵛ–6ᵛ
> Cheney and Hosington, 70–3 (with trans.)
> Stevenson and Davidson, 139–40 (with trans.)
> Hosington, 230–1, 240–1 (with trans.)

Willetrudis
s. xii/xiii   Germany?
Versus de Susanna: 'Cum sint conscripta iustorum circiter acta'

> *MS*: Munich, Bayerische Staatsbibliothek, Clm 12513, fos. 23–35, (s. xiii)

Winkler, Elisabet (Weigler)
*c.*1525–1613   Wrocław (Poland)/Prague (Czech Republic)
'Tu datus est nobis, tu missus ab aethere summo'

> Edition: Ambrosius Moibanus, *Catechismi Capita Decem, Primum Quibusdam Thematis, Deinde Etiam Colloquiis Puerilibus Illustrata, Iuventuti Wratislaviensi Proposita. Accessit et Puellae cuiusdam Oratiuncula in Nativitate Ihesu Christi*

Publice Dicta (Wittenberg: Hans Weiss, 1538); another edn. (Wrocław: Andreas Vinglerus, 1546), 95–6 [Wolfenbüttel, Herzog August Bibliothek, H: C 154.8⁰ Helmst. (4); London, British Library, 3505.cc.35]

Winstrup,—
*c.*1600   Denmark
'Winstrupi Frater, Sum Sponsa. Venito. Valeto.'

> *Edition*: Albert Thrura, *Gynaeceum Daniae Litterarum: Feminis Danorum Eruditione vel Scriptis Claris Conspicuum* (Altona: Jonas Korte, 1732), 126 [Wolfenbüttel, Herzog August Bibliothek, M: Da.517]

Witte, Alheit von der
s. xvi?   Germany
'Candida cum pulcro dicar cognomine, cuncta'

> *Edition*: C.F. Paullini, *Dos Hoch- und Wohl-gelahrte Teutsche Frauen-Zimmer* (Frankfurt: Johnn Cristoph Stösseln, 1705), 20; 2nd edn. 1715 [London, British Library, 10705.aa.11; Munich, Bayerische Staatsbibliothek, H.lit.p. 290]

Zambeccari, Cornelia
d. 1601   Bologna (Italy)
Latin verse composition

> Alleged by Bandini Buti, ii. 365

Anonymous Latin verse probably written by women (arranged, as far as possible, chronologically)

Anonymous Vestal Virgin
                                                                                           Rome (Italy)
'Felices nuptae: morior nisi nubere dulce est'

> Single line quoted in Seneca, *Controversiae* 6. 8

> *Translation*: Emily A. Hemelrijk, *Matronae Doctae* (London: Routledge, 1999), 177

Anonymous widow
                                                                                   Tarragona (Spain)

'Manes si saperent, miseram me abducerent coniugem'

Inscription: Petrus Burmann (ed.), *Anthologia Veterum Latinorum Epigrammatum et Poematum, sive Catalecta Poetarum Latinorum in VI Libros Digesta*, 6 books in 2 vols. (Amsterdam: Schouten, 1759, 1773), ii. 153–4 (IV.cciv) [London, British Library, 54.f.13]

Heinrich Meyer (ed.), *Anthologia Veterum Latinorum Epigrammatum et Poematum*, 2 vols. in 1 (Leipzig: Gerhard Fleischer, 1835), ii. (1591) [London, British Library, 011388.b.14]

Ludovico Antonio Muratori (ed.), *Novus Thesaurus Veterum Inscriptionum*, 4 vols. (Milan: Ex Aedibus Palatinis, 1739–42), iii. 1428. 3 [London, British Library, 1705.b.7]

CIL, ii (no.4427)

CLE, i. 259–60 (542)

Anonymous widow

s. iii   Rome (Italy)

'Heu, cui miseram linquis, karissime coniunx'

Inscription: H. Geist and G. Pfohl (eds. and German trans.), *Römische Grabinschriften* (Munich: Ernst Heimeran Verlag, 1969), 35 (32)

Dronke (trans.), *WWMA*, 24.

Anonymous mother

Rome (Italy)

'Hoc Epios tumulo Cin[y]ra est cum fratre sepultus'

Inscription: Petrus Burmann (ed.), *Anthologia Veterum Latinorum Epigrammatum et Poematum, sive Catalecta Poetarum Latinorum in VI Libros Digesta*, 6 vols. in 2 (Amsterdam: Schouten, 1759, 1773), ii. 292 (IV.ccxcii) [London, British Library, 54.f.13]

Heinrich Meyer (ed.), *Anthologia Veterum Latinorum Epigrammatum et Poematum*, 2 vols. in 1 (Leipzig: Gerhard Fleischer, 1835), i. 148 (1388) [London, British Library, 011388.b.14]

CIL, vi. (no.14831)

CLE, ii. 469 (1017)

Anonymous mother

Solentia (Solta) (Croatia)

' . . . infelicissima mater'

Inscription: A. and J. Šašel (ed.), *Inscriptiones Latinae quae in Jugoslavia inter Annos mcmii et mcmxl Repertae Sunt* (Ljubljana: Narodni Musej, 1986), 413 (2940)

Edward Courtney (ed. and trans.), *Musa Lapidaria: A Selection of Latin Verse Inscriptions* (Atlanta: Scholars Press, 1995), 180–1 (191)

Anonymous widow

Ecija (Spain)

'Uxor cara viro monumentum fecit amanti'

Inscription: *CLE*, ii. 1138

H. Geist and G. Pfohl (eds. and German trans.), *Römische Grabinschriften* (Munich: Ernst Heimeran Verlag, 1969), 41 (47)

Mother of L. Comagius Firmus

Milan (Italy)

'Parcae te miseris rapuere parentibus urna'

Inscription: *CLE*, ii. 537

H. Geist and G. Pfohl (eds. and German trans.), *Römische Grabinschriften* (Munich: Ernst Heimeran Verlag, 1969), 125 (329)

Wife of L. Petronius

Seville (Spain)

L. Petronius L.P. Primus hic Situs Est: 'Uxor cara viro monumentum fecit amanti'

Inscription: Martinus de Roa, *Historia Astici (Astigi) sive Esciiae* (Seville, 1629), 42 [not seen]

Giovanni Battista Doni (ed.), *Inscriptiones Antiquae, nunc Primum Editae* (Florence: Ex Regia Typographia Magni Ducis Etruriae, 1731), 399 (xii.29) [London, British Library, 145.g.5]

Ludovico Antonio Muratori (ed.), *Novus Thesaurus Veterum Inscriptionum*, 4 vols. (Milan: Ex Aedibus Palatinis, 1739–42), iii. 1386 [London, British Library, 1705.b.7]

Petrus Burmann (ed.), *Anthologia Veterum Latinorum Epigrammatum et Poematum, sive Catalecta Poetarum Latinorum in VI Libros Digesta*, 6 vols. in 2 (Amsterdam: Schouten, 1759, 1773), ii. 156–7 (IV.ccvii) [London, British Library, 54.f.13]

Heinrich Meyer (ed.), *Anthologia Veterum Latinorum Epigrammatum et Poematum*, 2 vols. in 1 (Leipzig: Gerhard Fleischer, 1835), ii. 130 (1319) [London, British Library, 011388.b.14]

CIL, ii. 204 (1504)

CLE, ii. 525 (1138)

Anonymous mother

Salona [Split] (Croatia)

' "Crudeles Parcae, nimium!" matercula dicit'

Inscription: *CLE*, ii. 564 (1204)

H. Geist and G. Pfohl (eds. and German trans.), *Römische Grabinschriften* (Munich: Ernst Heimeran Verlag, 1969), 197 (537)

Mother of Romanus
Christian   Rome
   Inscription: *CLE*, ii. 667–8 (1404)

Widow of Q. Oppius Secundus
'Tempore quo sum genita'

   Inscription: *CLE*, ii. 756–7 (1567)

Widow of P. Aufidius Epictetus
s. iii   Ostia (Italy)
'Hic iam nunc situs est quondam praestantius ille'

   Inscription: *CIL*, xiv. 636
   CLE, i. 231 (487)

Anonymous mother

                                                                                                        Rome (Italy)
'Verius hunc titulum matri tu, nata, dicasses

   Inscription: Petrus Pithoeus (ed.), *Epigrammata et Poematia Vetera*, 2 vols. (Paris: N. Gillius, 1590), ii. 134 [London, British Library, 1001.e.1]
   Janus Gruter (ed.), *Inscriptiones Antiquae Totius Orbis Romanae*, 2 vols. (Heidelberg: Commelin, 1602–3), plate dccviii.1(there are also reissues 1603, 1616, 1707) [London, British Library, C.75.i.3]
   Giovanni Battista Ferreti (ed.), *Musae Lapidariae*, 5 books in 1 (Verona: Rubeis, 1672), iii. 163 [London, British Library, 143.e.22]
   Petrus Burmann (ed.), *Anthologia Veterum Latinorum Epigrammatum et Poematum, sive Catalecta Poetarum Latinorum in VI Libros Digesta*, 6 vols. in 2 (Amsterdam: Schouten, 1759, 1773), ii. 194 (IV.cclvi) [London, British Library, 54.f.13]
   Heinrich Meyer (ed.), *Anthologia Veterum Latinorum Epigrammatum et Poematum*, 2 vols. in 1 (Leipzig: Gerhard Fleischer, 1835), ii. 140 (1358) [London, British Library, 011388.b.14]
   CIL, vi.4, 2919 (30110)
   CLE, ii. 535 (1155)

Anonymous widow

                                                                                                        Rome
'Suscipe me sociam tumulis dulcissime coniux'

Inscription: Petrus Pithoeus (ed.), *Epigrammata et Poematia Vetera*, 2 vols. (Paris: N. Gillius, 1590), ii. 181 [London, British Library, 1001.e.1]

Janus Gruter (ed.), *Inscriptiones Antiquae Totius Orbis Romanae*, 2 vols. (Heidelberg: Commelin, 1602–3), plate dccxliii.4 (there are also reissues 1603, 1616, 1707) [London, British Library, C.75.i.3]

Giovanni Battista Ferreti (ed.), *Musae Lapidariae*, 5 books in 1 (Verona: Rubeis, 1672), iv. 233 [London, British Library, 143.e.22]

Petrus Burmann (ed.), *Anthologia Veterum Latinorum Epigrammatum et Poematum, sive Catalecta Poetarum Latinorum in VI Libros Digesta*, 6 vols. in 2 (Amsterdam: Schouten, 1759, 1773), ii. 59 (IV.ccx) [London, British Library, 54.f.13]

Heinrich Meyer (ed.), *Anthologia Veterum Latinorum Epigrammatum et Poematum*, 2 vols. in 1 (Leipzig: Gerhard Fleischer, 1835), ii. 131 (1321) [London, British Library, 011388.b.14]

CIL, vi (no.30115)

CLE, ii. 625 (no.1338)

Anonymous female friend
before s.x

Responsum Puellae: 'Conspicua primum specie quam fata bearunt'

MS: Paris, Bibliothèque Nationale de France, 8440, fo. 1ʳ (s. x)

Editions: Petrus Burmann (ed.), *Anthologia Veterum Latinorum Epigrammatum et Poematum, sive Catalecta Poetarum Latinorum in VI Libros Digesta*, 6 vols. in 2 (Amsterdam: Schouten, 1759, 1773), i. 690 (III.cclxxiii) [London, British Library, 54.f.13]

Heinrich Meyer (ed.), *Anthologia Veterum Latinorum Epigrammatum et Poematum*, 2 vols. in 1 (Leipzig: Gerhard Fleischer, 1835), ii. 44 (1010) [London, British Library, 011388.b.14]

Alexander Riese (ed), *Anthologia Latina, sive Poesis Latinae Supplementum*, 3 vols. (Leipzig: B. G. Teubner, 1868–97), ii. 186

Anonymous woman
s. x/xi

'Nam languens amore tuo'

MS: Cambridge, University Library, Gg.5.35, fo. 436ʳ

Editions: K. Strecker (ed.), *Die Cambridger Lieder* (Berlin: Weidmann, 1926), no. 14

W. Bulst (ed.), *Carmina Cantabrigiensia* (Heidelberg: Carl Winter Universitätsverlag, 1950), 34

MLREL, i. 275–6 (with trans.)

J. M. Ziolkowski (ed. and trans.), *The Cambridge Songs (Carmina Cantabrigiensia)* (Tempe, Ariz.: Medieval and Renaissance Texts and Studies, 1998)

Anonymous woman

s.x/xi
'Levis exsurgit zephirus'

MS: Cambridge, University Library, Gg.5.35, fo. 441ʳ

Editions: K. Strecker, *Die Cambridger Lieder* (Berlin: Weidmann, 1926), no. 40
F.J.E. Raby, *A History of Secular Latin Poetry in the Middle Ages*, 2 vols. (Oxford: Clarendon Press, 1934), i. 304
W. Bulst (ed.), *Carmina Cantabrigiensia* (Heidelberg: Carl Winter Universitätsverlag, 1950), 65–6
J. M. Ziolkowski (ed. and trans.), *The Cambridge Songs (Carmina Cantabrigiensia)* (Tempe, Ariz.: Medieval and Renaissance Texts and Studies, 1998)
Helen Waddell (trans.), *Medieval Latin Lyrics* (Harmondsworth: Penguin, 1929), 168–9

Translations: George F. Whicher (trans.), *The Goliard Poets: Medieval Latin Songs and Satires* (Westport, Conn.: Greenwood Press, 1949), 26–7
James J. Wilhelm (trans.), *Lyrics of the Middle Ages: An Anthology* (New York: Garland, 1990), 11–12

Anonymous woman

c. 1100   France?
'In me, dei crudeles nimium'

MS: Florence, Biblioteca Laurentiana, Aedil. 197, fo. 130ʳ

Editions: Maurice Debouille, 'Trois poésies latines inédites', in *Mélanges Paul Thomas* (Grent: A. Buyens/New York, G. E. Stechart & Co., 1930), 176
Peter Dronke, 'Profane Elements in Literature', in Robert L. Benson and Giles Constable (eds.), *Renaissance and Renewal in the Twelfth Century* (Cambridge, Mass.: Harvard University Press, 1982), 569–92 (p. 571)

Anonymous female friend

s. xii   France
Puella ad Amicum Munera Promittentem: 'Gaudia Nimpharum, violas floresque rosarum'

MSS: Liège, Bibliothèque de l'Université, 77 (47), fos. 72ᵛ–73ʳ (presented to Marbod of Rennes) (s.xi/xii)

Paris, Bibliothèque Nationale de France, Lat. 14193, fo. 1ᵛ

Editions: *Liber Marbodi quondam Nominatissimi Presulis Redonensis* (Rennes: Johannes Baudouyn and Johannes Mace, 1524), sig. B 3ʳ [Paris, Bibliothèque Nationale de France, Rés. P.YC.1533]

Walther Bulst (ed.), 'Liebesbriefgedichte Marbods', in Bernhard Bischoff and Suso Brechter (eds.), *Liber Floridus. Feschrift Paul Lehmann* (St Ottilien: Eos, 1950), 287–301 (p. 290)

Walther Bulst (ed.), *Carmina Leodensia*, vi: *Sitzungsberichte der Heidelberger Akademie der Wissenschaften*, 1 (Heidelberg: Carl Winter Universitätsverlag, 1975), 16

Walther Bulst (ed.), *Lateinisches Mittelalter. Gesammelte Beiträge* (Heidelberg: Carl Winter Universitätsverlag, 1984), 185

Translation: Constant Mews, *The Lost Love Letters of Heloise and Abelard: Perceptions of Dialogue in Twelfth-Century France* (New York: St Martin's Press, 1999), 95 (also text n. 60, p. 336)

Anonymous nuns

s. xii^in

Verses from Regensburg (text of incipits follows Dronke)

'Advolat et stillat, pugnat Vulturnus et undat'

MS: Munich, Bayerische Staatsbibliothek, Clm 17142, fo. 93ʳ

Editions: Wilhelm Wattenbach, 'Zwei Handschriften der K. Hof- und Staatsbibliothek', *Sitzungsberichte der Bayerischen Akademie der Wissenschaften*, Phil.-hist. Klasse, III (1873), 685–747 (p. 715) [London, British Library, Ac.713.8]
MLREL, ii. 422–3 (with trans.)

'Mittit vestalis   chorus ad vos xenia pacis'

MS: Munich, Bayerische Staatsbibliothek, Clm 17142, fo. 94ᵛ

Editions: Wattenbach, 716
MLREL, ii. 424 (with trans.)
Carmina Ratisponensia, ed. A. Paravicini (Heidelberg: Carl Winter Universitätsverlag, 1979), 19

'Corrige tibi quos presento, magister'

MS: Munich, Bayerische Staatsbibliothek, Clm 17142, fo. 95ʳ

Editions: Wattenbach, 716
MLREL, ii. 424 (with trans.)
Paravicini, 19

'Mens mea letatur   corpusque dolore levatur'

MS: Munich, Bayerische Staatsbibliothek, Clm 17142, fo. 96ʳ

Editions: Wattenbach, 716
MLREL, ii. 424
Paravicini, 20

'Hunc mihi Mercurius   florem dedit ingeniosus'

MS: Munich, Bayerische Staatsbibliothek, Clm 17142, fo. 96ᵛ

Editions: *MLREL*, ii. 426–6 (with trans.)
Paravicini, 23–4

'Explorare mei te credo munia uoti'

MS: Munich, Bayerische Staatsbibliothek, Clm 17142, fo. 97ʳ

Editions: Wattenbach, 720
MLREL, ii. 427
Paravicini, 24

'Fedus quod narras   nutrix mea nescit Honestas'

MS: Munich, Bayerische Staatsbibliothek, Clm 17142, fo. 101ᵛ

Editions: Wattenbach, 721
MLREL, ii. 428
Paravicini, 26

'Munere donatis   Cesar vixisse tabellis'

MS: Munich, Bayerische Staatsbibliothek, Clm 17142, fo. 105ʳ

Editions: Wattenbach, 722–3
MLREL, ii. 430–1
Paravicini, 28–9

'Quod me collaudas'

MS: Munich, Bayerische Staatsbibliothek, Clm 17142, fos. 105^{r-v}

Editions: Wattenbach, 724
MLREL, ii. 432–3
Paravicini, 30–1

'Quid tibi precipue   scribam nequeo reputare'

MS: Munich, Bayerische Staatsbibliothek, Clm 17142, fo. 106^v

Editions: Wattenbach, 28
MLREL, ii. 435
Paravicini, 34–5

'Si puer est talis   quo iungi me tibi gestis'

MS: Munich, Bayerische Staatsbibliothek, Clm 17142, fo. 106^v

Editions: Wattenbach, 728–9
MLREL, ii. 435–7
Paravicini, 35

'Sed quid certa meis   non das responsa lituris'

MS: Munich, Bayerische Staatsbibliothek, Clm 17142, fo. 107^r

Editions: Wattenbach, 730
MLREL, ii. 438
Paravicini, 37 (he interprets the poem as beginning with two more distichs
   which Dronke prints p. 446: poem thus begins 'Nomine quod resonat')

'Ut valeas animo   quamvis irata rogabo'

MS: Munich, Bayerische Staatsbibliothek, Clm 17142, fo. 107^r

Editions: Wattenbach, 730
MLREL, ii. 438
Paravicini, 37

'Me quia fecisti   letari sede decenti'

MS: Munich, Bayerische Staatsbibliothek, Clm 17142, fo. 107^r

Editions: Wattenbach, 731
MLREL, ii. 438–9
Paravicini, 38

'Vos proficiscentes   prohibetis nos fore tristes'

MS: Munich, Bayerische Staatsbibliothek, Clm 17142, fo. 107ᵛ

Editions: Wattenbach, 731
MLREL, ii. 439
Paravicini, 38

'Nobis Pierides   ferrent si vota fideles'

MS: Munich, Bayerische Staatsbibliothek, Clm 17142, fo. 107ᵛ

Editions: Wattenbach, 734
MLREL, ii. 439–40
Paravicini, 39

'Nos quibus ornatum   dominus ddit et dabit aptum'

MS: Munich, Bayerische Staatsbibliothek, Clm 17142, fo. 109ʳ⁻ᵛ

Editions: Wattenbach, 734–5
MLREL, ii. 440
Paravicini, 39

'Me tibi dantis amor   quasi dulcis ros fluat in cor'

MS: Munich, Bayerische Staatsbibliothek, Clm 17142, fo. 110ʳ

Editions: Wattenbach, 440–1
MLREL, ii. 440–1
Paravicini, 40

'Pulverulenta novis   bene verritur area scopis!'

MS: Munich, Bayerische Staatsbibliothek, Clm 17142, fo. 111ᵛ

Editions: *MLREL*, ii. 441

'Sum tibi cara gene   pro sede ruboris amene'

   MS: Munich, Bayerische Staatsbibliothek, Clm 17142, fo. 111ᵛ

   Editions: Wattenbach, 441
   MLREL, ii. 441

'Hesperidum ramis   hec mal recepta superbis'

   MS: Munich, Bayerische Staatsbibliothek, Clm 17142, fo. 111ᵛ

   Editions: Wattenbach, 736
   MLREL, ii. 441–2
   Paravicini, 41

'Nunc autem non re   sed in astu vis agitare'

   MS: Munich, Bayerische Staatsbibliothek, Clm 17142, fo. 112ʳ

   Editions: Wattenbach, 736
   MLREL, ii. 442
   Paravicini, 42

'Iam felix valeas   letusque per omnia vivas'

   MS: Munich, Bayerische Staatsbibliothek, Clm 17142, fo. 112ᵛ

   Editions: Wattenbach, 737
   MLREL, ii. 442–3
   Paravicini, 42

'Non constat verbis   dilectio, sed benefactis'

   MS: Munich, Bayerische Staatsbibliothek, Clm 17142, fo. 112ᵛ

   Editions: Wattenbach, 737
   MLREL, ii. 443
   Paravicini, 43

Anonymous woman (nun?)
s. xi
'Cantant omnes volucres'

   MS: Sankt Florian, Stiftsbibliothek, XI.58, fo. 83v (s. xi)

Edition: Dronke, *MLREL*, ii. 352–3

Anonymous woman (nun?)

Tegernsee (Germany)

'Accipe scriptorum, o fidelis, responsa tuorum'

MS: Munich, Bayerische Staatsbibliothek, Clm 19411, fos. 69ʳ–70ʳ

Editions: *MLREL*, ii. 474–5 (with trans.)

Jürgen Kühnel, *Du bist mîn, ih bin dîn. Die lateinischen Leibes-(und Freundschafts-) Briefe des Clm 19411* (Göppingen: Kummerle, 1977) (with German trans.), 68–71

<Anonymous female friend

Puella ad Amatorem: 'Noctu me queris, sed habet me nocte maritus'

MSS: Bern, Bürgerbibliothek 211, fo. 153 (s. xv)

Vatican City, Biblioteca Apostolica, Urbin. lat. 402, fo. 244ᵛ (s. xv): more probably by Aeneas Silvius Piccolomini>

Anonymous nun

1076

'. . . precibus qua poscimus iste fruatur' [from fragmentary rotulus for Foucard of Saint-Amand]

Edition: Léopold Delisle (ed.), *Rouleaux des morts du ixᵉ au xvᵉ siècle recueillis et publiés par la Société de l'Histoire de France* (Paris: Veuve J. Renouard, 1866), titulus 1, p. 136 [Oxford, Bodleian Library, 2372.d.84]

Anonymous nun

s. xii or earlier

'Abbatissa timens, ne laederent ille sorores'

MSS: Paris, Bibliothèque Nationale de France, 11867 fo. 131, (s. xiii)

Vendôme 61 (xii), flyleaf

Anonymous woman

s. xii   France

'Laudis honor, probitatis amor, gentilis honestas'

MS: London, British Library, Add. 24199

Editions: André Boutemy, 'Recueil poétique du manuscrit Additional British Museum 24199', *Latomus*, 2 (1938), 31–52, (pp. 42–4)

Gerald A. Bond, *The Loving Subject: Desire, Eloquence and Power in Romanesque France* (Philadelphia: University of Pennsylvania Press, 1995), 166–9 (with trans.)

Constant Mews, *The Lost Love Letters of Heloise and Abelard: Perceptions of Dialogue in Twelfth-Century France* (New York: St Martins Press, 1999), 164–6 (with trans.): he suggests, pp. 167–8, that Heloïse may be the author>

See also under Heloïse

Anonymous female friend
De Amico Infido: 'Cuius totus eram, cuius me cura regebat'

Edition: Hermann Hagen (ed.), *Carmina Medii Aevi, Maximo Parte Inedito* (Bern, 1877), 200

Anonymous female friend
early s. xii
Ad Fugitivum: 'Omnia vilescunt, artusque dolore liquescunt'

MS: Zurich, Stadbibliothek, C 58, fo. 11ᵛ

Editions: Jakob Werner, *Beiträge zur Kunde der lateinischen Literatur des Mittelalters*, 2nd edn. (Aarau: Sauerländer, 1905; repr. Hildesheim: Georg Olms Verlag, 1979), 45–6

Constant Mews, *The Lost Love Letters of Heloise and Abelard: Perceptions of Dialogue in Twelfth-Century France* (New York: St Martin's Press, 1999), 106, 342 (with trans.)

<Anonymous female friend
Puelle Carmina ex Florentia Romam Missa: 'Sum nuda in thalamo nec me formosior ulla est'

MS: Munich, Bayerische Staatsbibliothek, Clm 18910, fo. 136 (s. xv): probably *in persona*>

Anonymous wife
Questio Sponsi ad Maritum: 'Quid si non fueram Chanichido digna'

MSS: Augsburg 128, fos. 100–3 (s. xv)
Munich, Bayerische Staatsbibliothek, Clm 418, fo. 140 (s. xv)
Munich, Bayerische Staatsbibliothek, Clm 459, fo. 188 (s. xv)
Munich, Bayerische Staatsbibliothek, Clm 8482, fos. 54–7 (s. xv)

Anonymous woman (nun?)
s. xii?
'Foebus abierat   subtractis cursibus'

    MSS: Oxford, Bodleian Library, Bodley 38, fos. 56ᵛ–57ʳ
    Vatican City, Biblioteca Apostolica, Vat. lat. 3251. fo. 178ᵛ

    Edition: *MLREL*, ii. 334–7

Anonymous woman (nun?)
s. xii/xiii
Inc. 'Quia sub umbraculum'

    MS: Prague, UL Germ. XVI.G. 23, fo. 46ᵛ

    Edition: *MLREL*, ii. 364

Anonymous nun
s. xvii
'Accipe summe pater contentae vota puellae'

    MS: Bergamo, Biblioteca Civica, I – 11 – 29, fo. 8ʳ

Appendix of Corrections to the Checklist and Additional Verse

Abuja, Elisa

Remove: the author was not a woman, but a rabbi called Elisha ben Abuia. See Paul Fagius, *Sententiae vere elegantes, piae, mireque... utiles veterum sapientum Hebraeorum... id ist capitula patrum nominati* (Württemberg: s.n., 1541), p. 86 [Aberdeen, University of Aberdeen, Bies pi 1 765]

Accoramboni, Vittoria (Peretti, Orsini)

d. 1585   Rome, Padua

Victoria Accorambona ad ill. Rev. Domin. Episcopus Forosemproniensem, fratrem-suum: 'Non dies, eadem patria, idem [], et [ ]'

MS: Milan, Biblioteca Ambrosiana R 105 sup.
Bandini Buti, I, between pp. 16 and 17 (photograph)

Eadem ad lectorem (distich)

MS: Milan, Biblioteca Ambrosiana R 105 sup.
Bandini Buti, I, between pp. 16 and 17 (photograph)

Barbansona, Maria, later Thou

Ingrid de Smet attributes this poem to Jacques Auguste Thou (pers. comm).

Blocklandt, Anna van (Boy)

s. xvii   Dordrecht, Netherlands

Described as 'een goed Latijnsch en Nederduitsch dichter' by G.D.S. Schotel, 'Vermaarde Vrouwen, die te Dordrecht, in de xvi en xvii eeuw, geboren werden of geleeft hebben', *Letter- en oudheide avondstonden* (Dordrecht: Blessé & Vanstraen, 1841), 142–65, p. 146 [London, British Library 12258.d.17]

Buchwald/Bockwold, Anna von

fl. 1471   Schleswig

'Hunc librum edidit per se Diva Priorissa'

Edition: Johann Moller, *Cimbria Literata, sive scriptorum ducatus utriusque Slesvicensis et Holsatici quibus et alii vicini quidam accensentur, historia literaria tripertita*, 3 vols (Copenhagen: sumptibus a typis orphanotrophiis Regis, 1744), I, pp. 75–6. [London, British Library, 125.1.8]

Confienzi, Antonia (Pechius)

fl. 1533   Sardinia

Antonia Conflentia eximiae laudis Femina Elogia hoc Isac Pechium Virum alloquitur: 'Te sequar, O conjux Isac dulcissime tandem'

Inscription: originally in church of S. Lorenzo, Sardinia

Ed: 'Epigramma copiata in S. Lorenzo paviment da un pilastro mezzo rovinato per la nuova fabbrica della chiesa nel 1658', anon, *Poesie e memorie di Donne Letterate che fiorono negli stati si SSRM Il Re di Sardegna* ([Turin?], 1769), p. 95 [London, British Library, T.2282(9)]

Corbiniana, Sophiana (Bernharda)

fl. 1655   Germany (Leipzig), Poland

Panegyric in honour of Frederic William Hohenzollern, published Königsberg, 1641 [Not seen]

Attested by Karolina Targosz, *La cour savante de Louise-Marie de Gonzague et ses liens scientifiques avec la France, 1646–1667* (Wroclaw, Warszawa, Krakow, Gdánsk, Lodź: Akademi Nauk, 1982), p. 175

Tributum Laudis to Christina of Sweden, printed at Rome [not seen: attested Targosz, *La cour savante*, p. 182]

Acrostic on Wiśniowiecki published 1669 [not seen: attested Targosz, *La cour savante*, p. 182]

ECHO LAUDUM Sanctissimi Domini Nostri ALEXANDRI VII: 'Quem Virum Solis comitata currum'

MS: Città del Vaticano, Chigi D III 40, f. 46^r–48^r

ENCOMIUM Munificentiae Sanctissimi Domini Nostri ALEXANDRI VII: 'Non ergò frustrà credimus aureis'

MS: ibid., ff. 48^r–49^r

Poem on the rainbow: quoted Ján Kwiatkiewicz, SJ, *Eloquentia reconditior: ubi pleraque mira ab argumento, rariora pleraque per varia admirabilis eloquentiae specimina tractantur* (Poznan: typis collegii S.J., 1689), pp. 507–8 [Paris, Bibliothèque Nationale de France, Tolbiac, Rez de jardin magasin, X-18037, not seen]

Other writing in Latin implied by Josef Ijsewijn, *Companion to Neo-Latin Studies*, 2 vols (Leuven: University Press/Louvain: Peeters, 1990, 1998), I, p. 31, no references given. Note also the existence of A. Wisaeus, *De literatis virginibus tribus nostri saeculi, Schurman, A.M., Memorata, A., Corbiniana, S.A.* (Wroclaw: np, 1642)

Godewijk, Margareta
1627–1677   Dordrecht (Netherlands)

MS collection of Latin verse, 'Poemata', Dordrecht, Gemeente Archief 1025

> *In Historiam restaurationis Celsissimi et invictissimi Principis Caroli II, Magnae Britanniae, Franciae, et Hyberniae Regis, a doctissimo viro Lamberto Sylvio descriptam*: 'Vir praestans, quondam, nobis funesta dedisti'

MS: 'Poemata', Dordrecht, Gemeente Archief 1025, pp. 11–12 (original pagination)

> *Ed: Konincklijke Beeltenis of Waerachtige Historie van Karel de II*, trans. Lambert van Bos, Dordrecht, Abraham Andriesz, 1661, sig. *5^r–^{v}
> [London, British Library G 96 1]

'Interdum ad Cytharae cantans agit ocia nervos' (Distich)

> *Ed*: In a copy of Caspar van Baerle's *Poemata*, recorded by P. S. Schult & A. van der Hoop, *Bijdragen tot Boeken en Menschenkennis*, 7 vols (Dordrecht: J. van Honterijve, jr, 1832–36), III.3, p. 340 [London, British Library, 102354.f.4, not seen], according to G.D.S. Schotel, 'Margareta van Godwijk', *Letter- en oudheide avondstonden* (Dordrecht: Blessé & Vanstraen, 1841), 44–119, p. 101 [London, British Library 12258.d.17]

> *In Delphi descriptionem, a nobiliss. Clarissimoque D.D. Theodoro à Bleyswyk, J.C. consulari*, 'Cernite praeclaro Calamo, depingere Delphin'

MS: 'Poemata', Dordrecht, Gemeente Archief 1025, p. 52

Edition: Dirck van Bleyswijk, *Beschryvinge der stadt Delft* (Delft: A. Bon, 1667) [London, British Library, 10270 c 3, not seen]

> *In Dordrechti Descriptione a viro clarissimo Matthia Balen accurate editam*, 'Qui Patriam servat, meruit gestore Coronam'

MS: 'Poemata', Dordrecht, Gemeente Archief 1025, p. 51

Edition: Matthys Balen, *Beschryvinge der Stad Dordrecht* (Dordrecht: S. onder de Linde, 1677) [London: British Library, 10270 e 12, not seen]

In Symbolum meum, Deus nostrum Asylum: 'Seu morior seu vivo, meum sit Christus Asylum'

MSS: 'Gedichten', Dordrecht, Gemeente Archief 1024, p. 210

Den Haag, Konincklijke Bibliotheek 128 F 10, f. 51^r

Ad Cives Dordracenos: 'Vos, qui Dordrechti sedetis'

MSS: 'Gedichten', Dordrecht, Gemeente Archief 1024, pp. 248–50
Den Haag, Konincklijke Bibliotheek 128 F 10, f. 56^{r-v}

In furentes et fanaticos Anglos, Bellum gerentes adversus Batavos: 'Angli veniunt destruentes'

MSS: 'Gedichten', Dordrecht, Gemeente Archief 1024, p. 251–3 (original pagination)

Den Haag, Konincklijke Bibliotheek 128 F 10, f. 56v– 57^r

Responsio ad Parentum meum charissimum, D. Petrum Godewyck, quum nuper ad me dedisset versus suos Latinos rhythmicos: 'Pater chare cum legissem'

MSS: 'Gedichten', Dordrecht, Gemeente Archief 1024, pp. 239–43
Den Haag, Konincklijke Bibliotheek 128 F 10, f. 59r–60^v

In Creatorem Mundi: 'Sancta manu condedisti'

MSS: 'Gedichten', Dordrecht, Gemeente Archief 1024, pp. 242–47
Den Haag, Konincklijke Bibliotheek 128 F 10, f. 60v–61^r

In laudem Doctissimi viri clarissimique Johannis Beverovicii scabini et doctoris medicinae primarii, apud Dordracenos: 'Quid jam scribo, si vis scire'

MSS: 'Gedichten', Dordrecht, Gemeente Archief 1024, p. 254–7
Den Haag, Konincklijke Bibliotheek 128 F 10, f. 61^r

Memorata, Anna

Note also the existence of A. Wisaeus, *De literatis virginibus tribus nostri saeculi, Schurman, A.M., Memorata, A., Corbiniana, S.A. (Wroclaw: np, 1642)*

Nuns of Trier?

Mid- s. ix   Trier

Epitaphium Warentrudis: 'Hic Warentrudis nimium veneranda quiescit'

Editions: Christoph Brouwer, *Antiquitatum et annalium Trevirensium libri XXV*, 2 vols (Lüttich: Jo. Mathiuas Hovius, 1670), I. 404 [Cambridge, Cambridge University Library, X.1.17–18]

Ludwig Ernest Dümmler, *Poetae Latini Aevi Carolini* II (Berlin: Weidmann, 1884), p. 661

'Hulindim retinet pulchram locus iste sepultam'

Editions: Christoph Brouwer, *Antiquitatum et annalium Trevirensium libri XXV*, 2 vols (Lüttich: Jo. Mathiuas Hovius, 1670), I. 404 [Cambridge, Cambridge University Library, X.1.17–18]

Ludwig Ernest Dümmler, *Poetae Latini Aevi Carolini* II (Berlin: Weidmann, 1884), p. 661

Owen, Jane
?c. 1600–after 1628   Oxford (England)

In Laudem Autoris: 'Quod fuit, est et semper erit sollemne poetis'

Ed: Epigrammatum Libri Tres autore Joanne Owen Cambro-Britanno, Novi Collegii Oxonienses nuper socio, London, John Windet for Simon Waterson, 1606,

sig. A 2v (in first three editions); 3rd ed. Humfrey Lownes for Simon Waterson, 1607
[London, British Library, 1489 f 68 (3rd ed.)]

Trans: Praise-worthy verses of Learned Mistris Iane Owen of Oxford, in praise of my Iohn Owen, translated out of her Latine: 'It was, and is Poets quaint property' Robert Hayman's *Quodlibets, lately come over from New Britaniola, or New-found-Land. Epigrams and other small parcells both Morall and Divine, the first*

four bookes being the Authors owne: the rest translated out of that Excellent Epigrammatist, Mr. Iohn Owen, and other rare Authors: with two Epistles of that excellently wittie Doctor, Francis Rablais: Translated out of his French at Large. All of them Composed and done at Harbor-Grace in Britaniola, anciently called Newfound-Land, by R.H, Sometimes Governor of the Plantation there. London, Printed by Elizabeth Allde, for Roger Michell, Pauls Church-yard, at the signe of the Bulls-head, 1628. Part II, p. 40.
[Oxford, Bodleian Library Mal. 716 (4 & 5)]

In mortem charissimorum fratrum Ludovici Owen gener. et Griffini Owen: 'Carmina cogit amor, sed amor disjungere fratres'

Inscription: St Aldate's Church, Oxford.
Ed: Antony à Wood, *The History and Antiquities of the Colleges and Halls in the University of Oxford*, ed. John Gutch, 3 vols (Oxford: Clarendon, 1786), III, p. 135
[London. British Library HLR 378.42574]

Schurman, Anna Maria van

Epigramma Latina

Ed: Not seen. Said to be in André Rivet, *Apologiae pro Maria Virginae*, (Leiden: Franciscus Hegerus & Franciscus Hackius, 1639), by Johann Moller, *Cimbria Literata, sive scriptorum ducatus utriusque Slesvicensis et Holsatici quibus et alii vicini quidam accensentur, historia literaria tripertita* (Copenhagen: sumptibus a typis orphanotrophiis Regis, 1744), I, p. 805–17 [London, British Library, 125.1.8]

Epigramma Latina

Ed: Not seen. Said to be in Johannes Isacius Pontanus, *Historiae Gelricae* (Hardwijk: Nicol. À Wieringen, 1639), by Johann Moller, *Cimbria Literata, sive scriptorum ducatus utriusque Slesvicensis et Holsatici quibus et alii vicini quidam accensentur, historia literaria tripertita.* (Copenhagen: sumptibus a typis orphanotrophiis Regis, 1744), I, p. 805–17 [London, British Library, 125.1.8]

Two volumes which I have not seen may also preserve verse, but in any case, underline her cultural significance. A. Wisaeus, *De literatis virginibus tribus nostri saeculi, Schurman, A.M., Memorata, A., Corbiniana, S.A.* (Wroclaw (Breslau), np, 1642), Giberto da Cesena, *La fama trionfante panegirico alla bellissima, castissima e dottistima signora Anna Maria Schurman* (Rome, np. 1642)

Seymour, Anne, Margaret, and Jane

Translation: in Demers, Patricia. 'The Seymour Sisters: Elegizing Female Attachment', *Sixteenth Century Journal* 30 (1999), 343–65

Marg. S [i.e. by Margaret Seymour]: 'En consumptum corpus natura est: Vnio dici'

Edition: *Le Tombeau de Marguerite de Valois, Royne de Navarre, faict premiere-ment en Disticques Latins par les trois soeurs Princesses en Angleterre, depuis traduictz en Grec, Italien & Francois par plusieurs des excellentz Poétes de la France, avecques plusieurs Odes, Hymnes, Cantiques, Epitaphes, sur le mesme subiect* (Paris: de l'imprimerie de Michel Fezandat & Robert Granlon, 1551), sig. k viii^v [London, British Library 1073 e 11 (1)]

Taurina
s. iv?   Vercelli
'Lumine virgineo hic splendida membra quiescunt'

Inscription (not extant): 'Che sul principio del v. secolo professarono in Vercelli monastica vita esistentie già in una Capella di. M.V. nell' antico Coro di S. Eusebio' (*Poesie e memorie*, p. 84)

Ed: CIL v, 6731
  CLE, i. 357–8 (478)

Mons. Ferrero, ediz. *Della Vita Latina di S. Eusebio in Vercelli*, 1609 [not seen: cited in *Poesie e memorie*]

Marc' Aurelio Cusano, *Discorsi Historiali concernenti la vita et attioni de' vescovi di Vercelli* (Vercelli, 1676)
  [Cambridge, Cambridge University Library, Acton. b.12.121, not seen]

Poesie e memorie di Donne Letterate che fiorono negli stati si SSRM Il Re di Sardegna, 1769, pp. 85–6
  [London, British Library, T.2282(9)]

Valeria Fuscilla
Late antiquity   Coimbra (Portugal)
Epitaph on her son: 'Scribi in titulo versuculos volo quinque decenter'

Inscription: may not be extant
Edition: CLE, i, no. 485, p. 231 (485)

Walburg, Judoca, Comitissa de Leeuwenstein
d. 25 October 1683   Maastricht

This entry should be under **Leeuwenstein-Rochefort, Judoca Walburg, Gravin von**

Willetrudis
s. xii/xiii, ? before 1122   ?Wilton (England)
Versus de Susanna 'Cum sint conscripta iustorum circiter acta'

   MS: München, Bayerische Staatsbibliothek clm 12513 (s. xiii), ff. 23–35.

Witt, Maria de (Houffslaper)
1622–44   Dordrecht

   A friend of Jacob Cats, who claimed to have seen Latin verse composed by her: 'Cats noemt haar, in zijn antwoord, 'eene eerbare, tonstrijke Jonckvrouw'— het blijkt, dat zij ook Latijsche gedichten heeft vervaardigt'. G.D.S. Schotel, 'Vermaarde Vrouwen, die te Dordrecht, in de xvi en xvii eeuw, geboren werden of geleeft hebben', *Letter-en oudheide avondstonden* (Dordrecht: Blessé & Vanstraen, 1841), 142–65, pp. 147–8 [London, British Library 12258.d.17]

Bibliography

PRIMARY SOURCES (INCLUDING WORKS ON WOMEN PRE-1800), ANTHOLOGIES, FINDING AIDS, AND COLLECTIONS OF WOMEN'S WRITING

AA, A. J. VAN DER, (ed.), *Parelen uit der lettervruchten van Nederlandse dichteressen* (Amsterdam: L. F. J. Hassels, 1856).

AGRIPPA, HENRICUS CORNELIUS, *De Nobilitate et Praecellentia Foeminei Sexus* (Antwerp: Michael Hillenius, 1529).

—— *De Nobilitate et Praecellentia Foemini Sexus*, ed. Roland Antonioli, Charles Béné, and Odette Sauvage (Genevea: Droz, 1990).

—— *A Treatise of the Nobilitie and Excellencye of Woman Kynde*, trans. David Clapam (London: Thomas Berthelet, 1542).

—— *On the Nobility and Preeminence of the Female Sex*, trans. Albert Rabil, Jr. (Chicago: University of Chicago Press, 1996).

ALCINA, JUAN F., *Repertorio de la poesía latina del Renascimento en España* (Salamanca: Ediciones Universidad de Salamanca, 1995).

ALDHELM, *Opera*, ed. R. Ewald (Berlin: Weidmann, 1919).

—— *Aldhelm: The Prose Works*, trans. Michael Lapidge and Michael Herren (Ipswich, D. S. Brewer; Totowa, NJ: Rowman & Littlefield, 1979).

ANDREAS, VALERIUS, *Biblioteca Belgica in qua Belgicae seu Germaniae Inferioris Provinciae, Urbesque Viri item in Belgio Vita Scriptisque Clari, et Librorum, Nomenclatura* (Louvain: Ap. Henricus Hasternius, 1623; 2nd edn., 2 vols., Louvain Jacob Zegers, 1643–4).

ANJOS, FREY JUIS DOS, *Iardim de Portugal, enn que se la noticia de algunas sanctas e outras malheres illustres en virtude, an quãs nascaras ou viverão ou estão sepultadas neste reino* (Coimbra, 1626).

ANTONIO, NICOLÁS, *Bibliotheca Hispana, sive Hispanorum qui Usquam sive Latine sive Populari sive Alia quamvis Lingua Scripto Aliquid Consignaverunt Notitia*, 2 vols. (Rome: Nicolaus Angelus Tinussius, 1672).

ANTONIO, NICOLO, *Bibliotheca Hispana Nova, sive Hispanorum Scriptorum qui ab Anno MD Floruere Notitia*, ed. T. A. Sanchez, J. A. Pellicer, and R. Casalbonus, 2 vols. (Madrid: Vidua et Heredes Joachim de Ibarra, 1783–8).

—— *Bibliotheca Hispana Vetus, sive, Hispani Scriptores qui ab Octaviani Augusti Aevo ad Annum Christi 1500 Floruerunt*, ed. F. Peregio Bayer, 2 vols. (Madrid: [?Vidua et Heredes Joachim de Ibarra], 1788).

ARISIO, FRANCISCO, *Cremona Literata*, 3 vols. (Parma: Alberto Pazzoni & Paolo Monte, 1702–41).

ASCHAM, ROGER, *The Whole Works*, ed. J. A. Giles, 3 vols. (London: Library of Old Authors, 1865).

AUSONIUS, *The Works of Ausonius*, ed. R. P. H. Green (Oxford: Clarendon Press, 1991).

—— *The Works*, ed. and trans. Hugh G. Evelyn White, 2 vols. Loeb Classical Library (Cambridge, Mass.: Harvard University Press; London: Heinemann, 1921).

AVITUS OF VIENNE, *Opera*, ed. R. Peiper, MGH Auctores Antiquissimi 6.2 (Berlin: Weidmann, 1883).

BAEHRENS, E. (ed.), *Poetae Latini Aevi Carolini*, v (Berlin: Weidmann, 1883).

BALDWIN, BARRY, *An Anthology of Later Latin Literature* (Amsterdam: J. C. Gieben, 1987).

BALEN, MATTHYS, *Beschryvinge der Stad Dordrecht* (Dordrecht: S. onder de Linde, 1677).

BALLARD, GEORGE, *Memoirs of Several Ladies of Great Britain Who Have Been Celebrated for their Writings or Skill in the Learned Languages, Arts and Sciences* (Oxford, privately printed, 1752).

—— *Memoirs of Several Ladies of Great Britain* ed. Ruth Perry (Detroit: Wayne State University Press, 1985).

BALMER, JOSEPHINE (trans.), *Classical Women Poets* (Newcastle upon Tyne: Bloodaxe Books, 1996).

BARTHOLINUS, ALBERT, *Alberti Bartholini de Scriptis Danorum Liber Posthumus*, ed. Thomas Bartholinus, (Copenhagen: Matthias Godecchenius, 1666).

BAYLE, PIERRE, *Dictionnaire historique et critique*, 2nd edn., 3 vols. (Rotterdam: Reimier Leers, 1702).

BECCATELLI, ANTONIO (Panormita), *Hermaphroditus*, ed. F. C. Forberg (Coburg, 1824).

—— *Antonio Beccadelli and the Hermaphrodite*, trans. Michael de Cossart (Liverpool: Janus Press, 1984).

BELLAY, JOACHIM DU, *Joachimi Bellaii Audini Poematum Libri Quatuor* (Paris: F. Morel, 1558).

BERCHER, WILLIAM, *A Dyssputacion off the Nobylyte off Wymen* (1559), ed. R. Warwick Bond, 2 vols. (London: For the Roxburgh Club, 1904).

BERNAND, A., and BERNAND, E. (eds.), *Inscriptions grecques et latines de Colosse de Memnon* (Paris: Institut Français de l'Archéologie Orientale, 1960).

BETUSSI, GIUSEPPE, *Libro di M. Giovanni Boccaccio delle donne illustri, tradotto di Latino in volgare, e un'altra nuova giunta fatta per M. Francesco Serdonati, d'altre donne illustre* (Florence: Filippo Giunta, 1596).

BEVERWYCK, JAN VAN, *Van de Wtnementheyt des vrouwelicken geslachts* (Dordrecht: Hendrick van Esch, 1643).

BILLON, FRANÇOIS, *Le Fort inexpugnable de l'honneur du sexe femenin* (Paris: Jan D'Allyer, 1555).

BOCCACCIO, GIOVANNI, *De Mulieribus Claris*, ed. Vittorio Zaccaria (Milan, 1967).

—— *Concerning Famous Women*, trans. Guido Guarino (New Brunswick, NJ: Rutgers University Press, 1963).

BOGIN, MEG (ed.), *The Women Troubadours* (London: Paddington Press, 1979).

BOISSARD, JEAN-JACQUES, *Poemata* (Metz: Abrahamus Faber, 1589).

—— *Icones Quinquaginta Virorum Illustrium Doctrina et Eruditione Praestantium ad Vivum Efficiae, cum eorum Vitis Descriptis*, 4 vols. (Frankfurt: T. de Bry, 1597–9).

BOURDEILLE, PIERRE DU, Seigneur de Brantôme, *Œuvres complètes*, ed. Ludovic Lalanne, 11 vols. (Paris: Veuve Jules Renouard, 1864–82).

BRIQUET, FORTUNÉE B., *Dictionnaire historique, littéraire, et bibliographique des françaises et des étrangères naturalisées en France* (Paris: De Gillé, 1804; facsimile repr. Paris: Indigo et Côté-femmes Éditions, 1997).

BROSCIUS, JOANNES, *Apologia pro Sexu Foemineo ad Dei Gloriam et Sacri Conjugii Honorem Scripta per M. Ioan. Ireneum* (Frankfurt: Petrus Brubachius, 1544).

BRUSCH, KASPAR, *Monasteriorum Germaniae Praecipuorum ac Maxime Illustrium Centuria Prima* (Ingolstadt: Alexander and Samuel Weyssenhorn, 1551).

BRUSCH, KASPAR, *Sylvarum Gasparis Bruschiii Slaccenvaldensis Liber* (Leipzig: Michaelis Blum, 1543).

BRUTO, GIOVANNI MICHELE, *La institutione di una fanciulla nata nobilmente* (Antwerp: C. Plantain for Jehan Bellere, 1555).

—— *The Necessarie, Fit, and Convenient Education of a Yong Gentlewoman, Written Both in French and Italian, and Translated by W.P.* (London: Adam Islip, 1598).

BUCHANAN, GEORGE, *Georgii Buchanani Scoti Poemata* (Amsterdam: Henricius Wetstenius, 1687).

—— *Georgii Buchanani Scoti Poetae Eximii Franciscanus et Fratres* (with Carolus Utenhove, *Xenia*) (Basel: T. Guarinus Nervius, 1568).

BULST, WALTHER (ed.), *Carmina Cantabrigiensia* (Heidelberg: Carl Winter Universitätsverlag, 1950).

CAFFIAUX, PHILIPPE-JOSEPH, *Defenses du beau sexe, ou mémoires historiques philosophiques et critiques pour servir d'apologie aux femmes*, 4 vols. (Amsterdam: Aux dépens de la compagnie, 1757).

CAMDEN, WILLIAM, *Reges, Reginae, Nobiles et Alii in ecclesia Collegiata B. Petri Westmonasteriii Sepulti, usque ad Annum Reparatae Salutis 1600* (London: E. Bullifant, 1600).

—— *Reges, Reginae, Nobiles, et Alii en Ecclesia Collegiata B. Petri Westmonasterii Sepulti usque ad Annum Reparatae Salutis 1603* (London: Melchior Bradwood, 1603).

CAPACIO, JULIO CESARE, *Illustrium Mulierem, et Illustrium Litteris Virorum Elogio* (Naples; Io. Iacobus Carlinus and Constantinus Vitale, 1608).

CAPELLA, GALEAZZO FLAVIO, *Della eccellenza et dignità delle donne* (Venice: Gregorio de Gregorii, 1526).

CARUSO, FRANCESO, *Dialogo delle nobiltà delle donne* (Naples: Gioseppe Cacchi, 1592).

CELTIS, CONRAD, *Fünf Bücher Epigramme*, ed. Karl Hartfelder (Berlin: S. Calvary, 1881; repr. Hildesheim: Olms, 1963).

CERDA Y RICO, FRANCISCO, *Clarorum Hispanorum Opuscula Selecta et Rariora* (Madrid, 1781).

CORSO, RINALDO, *Vita di Giberto III di Correggio, detto il difensore* (Ancona: Astolfo de Grandi, 1566).

COSTA, JUAN, *Govierno de la Ciudano* (Saragossa: Juan de Altarach, 1584).

COSTE, HILARION DE, *Les Eloges et vies des reynes, princesses, ames et damoiselles illustres en pieté, courage et doctrine* (Paris: Sebastien Cramoisy, 1630).

CURIO, COELIUS SECUNDUS, *De Liberis Pie Christianeque Educandis*, in his *Araneus seu de Providentia Dei, Libellus Vere Aureus, cum Aliis Nonnullis eisdem Opusculis Lectu Dignissimis* (Basel: Oporinus, 1544).

DA BISTICCI, VESPASIANO, *Vite di uomini illustri del secolo xv*, ed. Ludovico Frati (Bologna: Romagnoli-Dall'Acqua, 1892).

D'AUBIGNÉ, AGRIPPA, *Œuvres complètes*, ed. E. Réaume and F. de Caussade (Paris: 1843–92).

DE L'ANGLOIS, PIERRE, Sieur de Bel-Estat, *Discours des hieroglyphes aegyptiens, emblemes, devises et armoiries* (Paris: 1584).

DE L'ARIENTI, JOANNE SABADINO, *Gynevera, de le clare donne* [1483], ed. Corrado Ricci and A. Bacchi della Lega (Bologna: Romagnoli-Dall'Acqua, 1888).

DELISLE, LÉOPOLD, *Rouleaux des morts du ixe au xve siècle recueillis et publiés par la Société de l'Histoire de France* (Paris: Veuve J. Renouard, 1866).

DELLA CHIESA, FRANCISCO AGOSTINO, *Theatro delle donne letterate con un breve discorso della preminenza e perfettione del sesso donnesco* (Mondovì: Giovanni Gislandi & Giovanni Tomaso Rossi, 1620).

—— *Catalogo de' scrittori piemontesi, savoiardi, e nizzardi* (Carmagnola: Bernardino Colonna, 1660).

[de Ravisy, Jean Tixier] *De Memorabilibus et Claris Mulieribus aliquot Diversorum Scriptorum Opera* (Paris: Simon Colinaeus, 1521).

DEZA, MASSIMILIANO, *Vita di Helena Lucretia Cornara Piscopia* (Venice: Antonio Bosio, 1686).

DÍAZ Y DÍAZ, M. C., *Index Scriptorum Latinorum Medii Aevi Hispanorum*, Acta Salmanticensia Filosofia y Letras 13, 1–2 (Salamanca: Universidad de Salamanca, 1958–9).

DOMENICHI, LODOVICO, *La nobiltà delle donne* (Venice: Gabriel Giolito, 1549).

—— (ed.), *Rime diverse d'alcune nobilissime e virtuosissime donne* (Lucca: Busdrago, 1559).

DOUZA, JAN, *Iani Douze à Noortuuyck Poemata* (Leiden, 1609).

EBERTI, JOHANN CASPAR, *Eröffnetes Cabinet dess Gelehrten Frauen-zimmers* (Frankfurt: Michael Rohrlachs sel. Wittib und Erben, 1700; 2nd edn. 1706).

ELLIS, HENRY (ed.), *Original Letters Illustrative of English History*, 3 vols. (London: Harding, Triphook and Lepard, 1824).

ERASMUS, DESIDERIUS, *Opus Epistolarum Des. Erasmi Roterodami*, ed. P. S. Allen and H. M. Allen, 12 vols. (Oxford: Clarendon Press, 1906–58).

—— *Erasmus on Women*, trans. Erika Rummel (Toronto: University of Toronto Press, 1996).

ERYTHRAEUS, IANUS NICIAS, *Pinacotheca Imaginum Illustrium, Doctrinae vel Ingenii Laude, Virorum* (Cologne: Judocus Kalcovius, 1645).

EVELYN, JOHN, *Memoirs of John Evelyn ... to Which is Subjoined the Private Correspondence*, ed. William Bray, 5 vols. (London: Henry Colburn, 1827).

FACHINI, GINEVRA CANONICI, *Prospetto biografico delle donne italiane rinomate in letteratura* (Venice: Tipografia di Alvisopoli, 1824).

FANTUZZI, GIOVANNI, *Notizie degli scrittori bolognesi*, 8 vols. (Bologna: Stamperìa di San Tommaso d'Aquino, 1784–8).

FONTE, MODERATA [pseudonym of Modesta da Pozzo] *Il merito delle donne* (Venice: Dom. Imberti, 1600).

—— *Donne e società nel Seicento Lucrezia Marinelli e Arcangela Tarabotti*, ed. Ginevra Conti Oderisio, Biblioteca di cultura 167 (Rome: Bulzoni, 1979).

FORESTI, JACOPO [Bergomensis], *Opus de Claris Selectisque Plurimis Mulieribus* (Ferrara: L. de Rubeis, 1497).

FROES PERYM, DAMIÃO DE (pseudonym of Frei João de S. Pedro), *Theatro heroino, AB-Cedario historico, e catalogo das mulheres illustres em armas, letres, acçoens heroicas e artes liberaes*, 2 vols. (Lisbon: Oficina da Musica de Theotonio Antunes Lima (1), Regia Oficina Sylvania e Academia Real (2), 1736–40).

G., C. [Gerbier, Charles], *Eulogium Heroinum, or the Praise of Worthy Women* (London: T.M. & A.C., 1650).

GARCIA MATAMOROS, ALFONSO, *De Asserenda Hispanorum Eruditione, sive de Viris Hispaniae Doctis Narratio Apologetica* (Madrid: Joannes Brocarius, 1553).

GEIST, H., and PFÖHL, G. (eds. and German trans.), *Römische Grabinschriften*, 2nd edn. (Munich: Ernst Heimeran Verlag, 1976).

GINANNI, PIETRO PAOLO, *Memorie storico-critiche degli scrittori ravennati*, 2 vols. (Faenza: Giosettantonio Archi, 1769).

GOETHALS, F.-V, *Dictionnaire généalogique et héraldique des familles nobles de Belgique*, 4 vols. (Brussels: Polack-Duvivier, 1849–52).

GOURNAY, MARIE DE [de Jars], *L'Égalité des hommes et des femmes* (Paris: 1622).

GRUDÉ DE LA Croix Dumain, François, *Premier volume de la bibliothèque du sieur de La Croix-du-Maine* (Paris: Abel L'Angelier, 1584).

GUASCO, GIOVANNI, *Storia letteraria del principio e progresso dell'Accademia di belle lettere in Reggio* (Reggio: Ippolito Vetrotti, 1711).

[Guasti, Cesare], *Bibliographia Pratense* (Prato: Giuseppe Pontecchi, 1844).

HAENDEL, CHRISTOPH CHRISTIAN, *Dissertatio de Eruditis Germaniae Mulieribus* (Altdorf: Heinrich Meyer, 1688).

HALE, SARAH JOSEPHA, *Woman's Record, or Sketches of All Distinguished Women from the Creation to A.D. 1854, Arranged in Four Eras* (New York: Harper & Brothers, 1860).

HAMILTON, ADAM (ed.), *The Chronicle of the English Augustine Canonesses Regular of the Lateran at St Monica's in Louvain, 1625–1644*, 2 vols. (Edinburgh: Sands & Co., 1906).

HATTON, EDWARD, *A New View of London*, 2 vols. (London: R. Chiswell, R & J. Churchill, T. Horne, J. Nicholson, and R. Knaplock, 1708).

HEKEL, JOHANN FRIEDRICH, *Dissertatiuncula de Foeminis Litteratis qua Actum Aretalogicum Alterum* (Rudolstadt: Schulzianus, 1686).

HOEUFFT, JACOB, *Parnasus Latino-Belgicus, sive Plerique e Poetis Belgii Latinis, Epigrammate atque Adnotatione Illustrati* (Amsterdam: Peter den Hengst & Sons, 1819).

HOFILLER, V., and SARIA, B., *Antike Inschriften aus Jugoslavien* (Zagreb: Dissertationes Musei Nationalis Labacensis, 1938).

HOMEYER, H. (ed.), *Dichterinnen des Altertums und des frühen Mittelalters* (Paderborn: Schöningh, 1979).

IJSEWIJN, JOZEF, *Companion to Neo-Latin Studies*, 2 vols. (Louvain: Louvain University Press Peeters, 1990, 1998).

ITTER, JOHANN CHRISTIAN, *De Honoribus sive Gradibus Academicis Liber*, (Frankfurt: Friderici Knochius, 1698).

JEROME, *Epistolae*, ed. I. Hilberg, 3 vols. CSEL 54–6 (Vienna: F. Tempsky, 1910, 1912, 1918).

JUNCKER, M. CHRISTIANUS, *Schediasma Historicum, de Ephemeridibus sive Diarii, Eruditorum, in Nobilioribus Europae Partibus Hactenus Publicatis, in Appendice Exhibens Centuria Foeminarum Eruditione et Scriptis Illustrium* (Leipzig: Joh. Friedrich Gleditsch, 1692).

KAISER, LEO M. (ed.), *Early American Latin Verse, 1625–1825: An Anthology* (Chicago: Bolchazy-Carducci, 1984).

KING, M. L., and RABIL, ALBERT, Jr. (trans.), *Her Immaculate Hand: Selected Works by and about the Women Humanists of Quattrocento Italy* (1983; Asheville, NC: Pegasus Press, 1997).

KNOX, VICESIMUS, *Liberal Education: or, a Practical Treatise on the Methods of Acquiring Useful and Polite Learning*, 10th edn. (London: Charles Dilly, 1789).

KORTHOLD, SEBASTINAN, *Disquisitio de Poetriis Puellis, Missis ab Adriano Bailleto* (Keil: Barthold Reuther, 1700).

L.-P., *Répertoire universel, historique, biographique des femmes célèbres*, 2 vols. (Paris: Achille Désauges, 1826).

LANGSCHMIDT, JUSTUS HENRICUS, *De Feminis Prima Aetate Eruditione ac Scriptis Illustris* (Wittenberg, 1700).

LATZ, DOROTHY L. (ed.), *'Glow-Worm Light': Writings of Seventeenth-Century English Recusant Women from Original Manuscripts* (Salzburg: Institut für Anglistik und Amerikanistik, 1989).

LAURENS, PIERRE, and BALAVOINE, CLAUDIE (ed. and French trans.), *Musae Reduces: anthologie de la poésie latine dans l'Europe de la Renaissance*, 2 vols. (Leiden: Brill, 1975).

LE BLANT, EDMOND (ed.), *Inscriptions chrétiennes du Gaule antérieures au xiiie siècle*, 2 vols. (Paris: Imprimerie Impériale, 1856).

LEGATI, LORENZO, *Musei Poetriarum Laurentii Legati Primitiae, ad Sapientissimum Virum D. Ovidium Montalbanum* (Bologna: Heredes Vittore Benaccio, 1668).

LEHMS, GEORG CHRISTIAN, *Teutschlands galante Poetinnen mit ihren sinnreichen und netten Proben, nebst einem Anhang Ausländischen Dames so sich gleichfalls durch schöne Poesien bey der curieusen Welt bekannt gemacht* (Frankfurt am Main: Anton Heinscheidt, 1715; (facsimile edn. Darmstadt: Josef Gotthard Bläschke Verlag, 1966).

—— *Teutschlands galante Poetinnen mit ihren sinnreichen und netten Proben, nebst einem Anhang ausländischer Dames so sich gleichfalls durch schöne Poesien bey der curieusen Welt bekannt gemacht* (Frankfurt au Main: Samuel Tobias Hocter, 1745).

LE MOYNE, PIERRE, SJ, *La Gallerie des femmes fortes* (Paris: Antoine de Sommaville, 1647).

LEVATI, AMBROGIO, *Dizionario biografico cronologico, divido per classe, degli uomini illustri V: donne illustre*, 3 vols. (Milan: Nicolò Bettoni, 1821–2).

LIRUTI, GIANN. GIUSEPPE, *Notizie delle vite ed opere scritte da' letterati del Friuli*, 3 vols. (Venice: Modesto Fenzo, 1760).

LOTICHIUS, PETRUS, *Gynaicologia, id est, de Nobilitate et Perfectione Sexus Feminei contra Mastigas* (Rinteln: Petrus Lucius, 1630).

LUPIS, ANTONIO, *L'eroina veneta, overo la vita di Elena Lucretia Cornara Piscopia* (Venice: Per il Curti, 1689).

MABILLON, JEAN, *Acta Sanctorum Ordinis Benedicti*, 9 vols. (Paris: Louis Billaine, 1668–1701).

MACCHIAVELLI, CARLO ANTONIO, *Bitisia Gozzadina, seu de Mulierem Doctorata, Apologia Legalis, Historica Dissertatio Caroli Antonii Macchiavelli Jurisconsulti Bononiensis, ad Illustrissiman Juriumque Cultricem Clarissimam Mariam Victoriam Delphinam Dosiam* (Bologna: G. B. Blanco, 1722).

MAFFEI, SCIPIONE, *Verona Illustrata*, 5 vols. (Milan: Società tipografica de' classici italiani, 1825).

MARINELLA, LUCREZIA, *La nobiltà et eccellenza delle donne co' difetti et mancamenti de gli huomini*, (Venice: G. B. Ciotti, 1600; edns. 1601, 1621).

—— *The Nobility and Excellence of Women and the Defects and Vices of Men*, ed. and trans. Anne Dunhill (Chicago: Chicago University Press, 1999).

MARINEO, LUCIO [Siculo], *Lucio Marinei Siculi Epistolarum Familiarum Libri Decem et Septem* (Valladolid: A. G. Brocar, 1514).

—— , *Opus de Rebus Hispaniae Memorabilibus* (Madrid: M. de Eguia, 1533).

—— *Obra compuesta de las cosas memorables de España* (Alcalá de Henares, 1553).

MATAMOROS, ALFONSO GARCIA, *De Asserenda Hispanorum Eruditione, sive de Viris Hispaniae Doctis Narratio Apologetica* (Madrid: Juan Brocar, 1553).

MELISSUS, PAULUS [pseudonym for Paul Schede], *Melissi Schediasmata Poetica* (Frankfurt: Corvinus, 1574; (2nd edn. Paris: Arnold Sittart, 1586).

—— *Mele sive Odae ad Noribergam et Septemviros Reipub. Norib.* (Nuremberg: Haeredes Montani, 1575).

—— *Ode Pindarica ad Serenissimam Elizabetham* (Augsburg, c.1582).

MEURSIUS, JOHANNES, *Athenae Batavae, sive de Urbe Leidensi et Academia Viriique Clavis*, 2 vols. (Leiden: Andreas Cloucquius a Elzevirs, 1625).

MODIUS, FRANCISCUS, *Poemata* (Würzburg: H. Aquensis, 1583).

—— *Francisci Modii Brugi Novantiquae Lectiones, Tributae in Epistolis Centum quod Excurrit* (Frankfurt: Andreas Wechel, 1584).

MONAU, JACOB [Monawius], *Symbolum Jacobi Monawi ipsi Faciat Variis Variorum Auctorum Carminibus Expressum et Decoratum* (Görlitz: Johannes Rhamba, 1595).

MONDOSIO, PROSPERO, *Bibliotheca Romana, seu Romanorum Scriptorum Centuria*, 2 vols. (Rome: Francisco de Legaris, 1692).

MORATA, OLIMPIA, *Olympiae Fulviae Moratae Foeminae Doctissimae ac Plane Diuinae Orationes, Dialogi, Epistolae, Carmina, tam Latina quam Graeca* (Basel: Petrus Perna, 1562).

MUSONIUS RUFUS, *Musonius Rufus, the Roman Socrates*, ed. and trans. Cora E. Lutz, Yale Classical Studies 10 (New Haven: Yale University Press, 1947).

NEUMEISTER, ERDMANN, and BROHMANN, FRIEDRICH, *De Poëtis Germanis, hujus Seculi Praecipuis, Dissertatio Compendicaria, Additae et Sunt Poetriae* (Leipzig: For the Author, 1695; modern edn. Bern: Francke, 1978).

OELRICHS, JOHANN CARL CONRAD, *Historisch-diplomatische Beyträge zur Geschichte der Gelahrheit* (Berlin: Buchhandlung der Realschule, 1768).

ORLANDI, PELLEGRINO ANTONIO, *Notizie degli scrittori bolognesi, e dell'opere loro stampate e manoscritte* (Bologna: Constantino Pisarri, 1714).

PARADA, DIEGO IGNACIO, *Escritoras y eruditas españolas* (Madrid: Librerías de A. de San Martín, 1881).

PARAVICINI, A. (ed.), *Carmina Ratisponensia* (Heidelberg: Carl Winter Universitätsverlag, 1979).

PASCHIUS, JOHANNIS, *Gynaeceum Doctum, sive Dissertatio Historico-literaria, vom Gelehrten Frauenzimmer, antea Wittebergae Ano 1686 Publice Exposita* (Wittenberg: Christian Finkel, 1701).

PAULLINI, CHRISTIAN FRANZ, *Das Hoch- und Wohl-gelahrte Teutsche Frauen-Zimmer* (Frankfurt: Johann Christoph Stösseln, 1705; augmented edn. 1712).

PENTOLINI, FRANCESCO CLODOVEO MARIA, *Le donne illustre: canti dieci*, 2 vols. (Livorno: Gio. Vincenzo Falorni, 1776).

PEREZ DE MOYA, JUAN, *Varia historia de sanctos e illustres mugeres en todo genero de virtudes* (Madrid: Francisco Sanchez, 1583).

PHILLIPS, EDWARD, *Theatrum Poetarum, or a Compleat Collection of the Poets, Especially the Most Eminent, of All Ages* (London: for Charles Smith, 1675).

PIO, GIOVANNI MICHELE, *Delle vite gli huomini illustri di S. Domenico libri quattro* (Bologna: Sebastiano Bonomi, 1620).

PLANER, ANDREAS, *Tactatus [sic] de Gyneceo Docto, d.i. Von gelehrten Frauenzimmer* (Wittenberg: Johann Godfrid Meyer, 1715).

POCCANTIUS [Poccianti], MICHAEL, *Catalogus Scriptorum Florentinorum Omnis Generis, quorum et Memoria extat, et Lucubrationes in Literas Relatae Sunt ad nostra Tempora 1589* (Florence: F. Giunta, 1589).

POSTHIUS, JOHANNES, *Iohannis Posthii Germershemii Parergorum Poeticorum Pars Prima et Pars Altera* (Heidelberg: Hieronymus Commelin, 1595).

QUETIF, JACOBUS, and ECHARD, JACOBUS, *Scriptores Ordinis Praedicatorum*, 2 vols. (Paris: Christophe Baillard and Nicolas Simart, 1721).

REISE, ALEXANDER (ed.), *Anthologia Latina* (Leipzig: Teubner, 1868).

RHODIGINUS, LUDOVICUS CAELIUS, *Lectionum Antiquarum Libri xvi*, bk. VIII: 'mulieres in Doctrinam Celebres' (Basel: J. Frobenius, 1517), 369–70.

RIBERA VALENTIANUS, PIETRO PAOLO DE, *Le glorie immortali de' trionfi et heroiche imprese d'ottocento quarantesime donne illustri* (Venice: Evangelista Benchino, 1609).

RICHERIUS see Rhodiginus

ROUILLARD, SÉBASTIAN, *Vita Laurentiae Stroziae Sacri Ordinis Dominicani* (Paris: Plantin, 1610).

ROVERSI, GIANCALVO (ed.), *Donne celebre della Emilia-Romagna e del Montefeltro* (Bologna: Edizione Grafis, 1993).

RUTINGIUS, PAULUS, *Anagrammatum Pauli Rutingii Rostochiensis Centuria* (Rostock: Stephanus Myliander, 1606).

SANDERUS, ANTONIUS, *Flandria Illustrata sive Descriptio Comitatus istius per Totum Orbem Terrarum Celeberrimi III Tomis Absoluta* (Cologne: Cornelius Egmondt & Co., 1641).

ŠAŠEL, ANNA, and ŠAŠEL, JARO, *Inscriptiones quae in Iugoslavia inter Annos MCMXL et MCMLX Repertae et Editae Sunt*, Situla 5 (Ljubljana: Dissertatio Musei Nationalis Labacensis, 1963).

SAUERBREI, JOHANNES, *Diatriben Academicam de Foeminam Eruditione, Prirem Consensu Inclutae Facultatis Philosophicae in Alma Lipsiensi, sub Praesidio...M. Jacobi Thomasii* (Leipzig: Johann Erich Hahn, 1671).

SCALIGER, JULIUS CAESAR, *Julii Caesaris Scaligeri Viri Clarissimi Poemata*, dedicated to Constance of Aragon, (n.p., 1574; 2nd edn. Petrus Santandreanus, 1591).

SCARDEONE, BERNADINO, *De Antiquitate Urbis Patavii et Claris Civibus Patavini Libri Tres* (Basel: Nicolaus Episcopus, 1560).

SCHECHT, MATTHEUS, 'Schediasma, Exhibens Specimen de Eruditis Mulieribus Daniae', *Nova Literaria Maris Balthici et Septentrionis* (Lübeck, 1700), 209–19.

SCHELHORN, J. G., *Amoenitates Literariae, quibus Variae Observationes, Scripta item quaedam Anecdota et Rariora Opuscula Exhibentur*, 14 vols. (Frankfurt: Daniel Bartholomaeus, 1725–30).

SCHENKEVELD-VAN DER DUSSEN, RIET, et al., *Met en zonder lauwerkranz: Schrijvende vrouwen uit de vroegmoderne tijd, 1550–1850* (Amsterdam: Amsterdam University Press, 1997).

SCHÖNAU, FRIEDRICH CHRISTIAN, *Samling af Danske lærde Fruentimer*, 2 vols. (Copenhagen: J. W. Bopp, 1753).

SCRIVERIUS, PETRUS (ed.), *Dominico Baudii Amores* (Amsterdam: Ludovicus Elzevir, 1638).

SIDONIUS APOLLINARIS, *Letters and Poems*, ed. and trans. W. B. Anderson, 2 vols. Loeb Classical Library (Cambridge, Mass.: Harvard University Press; London: Heinemann, 1965).

SNYDER, JANE MCINTOSH, *The Woman and the Lyre: Women Writers in Classical Greece and Rome* (Bristol: Bristol Classical Press, 1989).

STARCK, JOHANN DIETRICH, *De Feminis Prima Aetate Eruditione ac Scriptis Illustrissimis et Nobilissimis* (Wittenberg: Gerdesianus, 1703) (with Justus Henricus Langschmidt, *Responsio*).

STEVENSON, JANE, and DAVIDSON, PETER (eds.), *Early Modern Women Poets, 1520–1700* (Oxford: Oxford University Press, 2001).

STIERNMAN, ANDERS ANTON VON, 'Gynæceum Sveciæ Litterarum eler Anmärkningat om Lärde och Namnkunniga Swenska Fruentimmer', *Stockholms Magazin for 1780* (Stockholm: Magnus Swederus, 1780), 207–54.

STRECKER, KARL (ed.), *Poetae Latini Aevi Carolini*, iv. 2, MGH (Berlin, Wiedmann, 1914).

—— and SILAGI, G. (eds.), *Poetae Latini Medii Aevi*, v: *Die Ottonenzeit*, MGH (Berlin: Wiedmann, 1937–79).

STRYPE, JOHN, *Annals of the Reformation and Establishment of Religion and Other Various Occurrences in the Church of England*, 2nd edn., 4 vols. (London: Thomas Edlin, 1725).

SWEERTIUS, FRANCISCUS, *Athenae Belgicae, sive Nomenclator Infer. Germaniae Scriptorum* (Antwerp: Gulielmus à Tongres, 1628).

TANNER, THOMAS, *Bibliotheca Britanno-Hibernica, sive de Scriptoribus qui in Anglia, Scotia et Hibernia ad Saeculi xvii Initium Floruerunt* (London: William Bowyer, 1748).

TASSO, TORQUATO, *Discorso della virtù femminile, e donnesca* (Venice: Bernardo Giunta, 1582).

THIÉBAUX, MARCELLE (trans.), *The Writings of Medieval Women: An Anthology* (New York: Garland, 1987).

THRURA, ALBERT, *Gynaeceum Daniae Litterarum: Feminis Danorum Eruditione vel Scriptis Claris Conspicuum* (Altona: Jonas Korte, 1732).

TIRABOSCHI, GIROLAMO, *Storia della letteratura italiana*, 2nd edn., 8 vols. + index (Modena: Società tipografica, 1787).

—— *Biblioteca Modenense, o notizie delle vita e delle opere degli scrittori natii degli stati del serenissimo signor Duca di Modena*, 6 vols. (Modena: Società tipografia, 1783).

TOMAI, TOMASO, *Historia di Ravenna, divisa in quattor parti*, 2nd edn. (Ravenna: Francesco Tebaldini da Osimo, 1580).

TOMASINI, IACOBUS PHILIPPUS, *Bibliothecae Patavinae Manuscriptae Publicae et Privatae* (Udine: Nicola Schiratti, 1639).

—— *Elogia Virorum Literis et Sapientia Illustrium ad Vivum Expressis Imaginibus Exornata* (Padua: Sebastiano Sardi, 1644).

TOPPI, NICCOLÒ, *Biblioteca napoletana et apparate a gli huomini illustri in lettere di Napoli e del Regno . . . per tutto l'anno*, 2 vols. (Naples: Antonio Bulifon, 1688).

TRAVERSARI, AMBROGIO, *Epistulae et Orationes* (Florence: Typ. Caesareas, 1757).

UTENHOVE, KAREL, *Caroli Utenhovii F. Patricii Gandavensis* XENIA *seu ad Illustrium Aliquot Europae Hominum Nomina, Allusionum (Intertextis Alicubi Ioach. Bellaii eiusdem Arumenti Versibus), Liber Primus* (Basel: T. Guarinus Nervius, 1568).

VAN SCHURMAN, ANNA MARIA, *Nobiliss. Virginis Annae Mariae à Schurman Opuscula Hebraea, Graeca, Latina, Gallica: Prosaica et Metrica* (Leiden: Elsevier, 1643; 2nd edn. 1648).

VEDOVA, GIUSEPPE, *Biografico degli scrittori padovani*, 2 vols. (Padua: Tipi della Minerva, 1832).

VERMIGLIOLI, GIOVANNI BATTISTA, *Bibliografia degli scrittori perugini*, 2 vols. (Perugia, Francesco Baduel, 1828).

VERNEY, FRANCES PARTHENOPE, and VERNEY, MARGARET M. (eds.), *Memoirs of the Verney Family during the Seventeenth Century*, 2 vols. (London: Longmans & Co., 1925).

VERTRON, M. DU [Claude Charles Guyonnet], *La Nouvelle Pandore, ou les femmes illustres du siècle de Louis le Grand*, 2 vols. (Paris: Veuve C. Mazuel, 1698; 2nd edn. Paris: Nicolas Le Clerc, 1703).

VIVES, D. JOSÉ (ed.), *Inscripciones cristianas de la España romana y visigoda*, 2nd edn., (Barcelona: Monumenta Hispaniae Sacra, Serie Patristica II, 1969).

WARREN, F. E. (ed.), *The Antiphonary of Bangor: An Early Irish Manuscript in the Ambrosian Library at Milan*, 2 vols. (London: Harrison and Sons for the Henry Bradshaw Society, 1895).

WEBER, E. (ed.), *Virorum Clarorum Saeculi xvi et xvii Epistolae Selectae* (Leipzig: B. G. Teubner, 1894).

WESTON, ELIZABETH JANE, *Elizabeth Jane Weston: Collected Writings*, ed. Donald Cheney and Brenda Hosington (Toronto: Toronto University Press, 2000).

WILSON, KATHARINA M. (trans.), *Medieval Woman Writers* (Athens: University of Georgia Press, 1984).

XIMÉNEZ, FRANCISCO, *Le libre de las dones* (Barcelona: n.p., 1495) (Spanish trans. from Catalan, *Carro de las donas* (Valladolid: Juan de Villaquiran, 1542)).

ZIEGELBAUER, MAGNOALD, *Historia Rei Leterarie Ordinis Sancti Benedicti in IV Partes Distributa* (Augsburg M. Veith, 1754).

SECONDARY SOURCES

ADDEO, PIERO, *Eva Togata* (Naples: Editrice Rispoli anonima, 1939).

ALENIUS, MARIANNE, 'Learned Scandinavian Women in the Seventeenth and Eighteenth Centuries', in Alexander Dalzell et al., (eds.), *Acta Conventus Neo-Latini Torontoniensis* (Binghamton, NY: Medieval and Renaissance Text Society, 1991), 177–88.

—— 'Love at First (W)ink: A Fragment of Otto Sperling's Neo-Latin Correspondence', in Graham de Caie and Holger Nørgaard (eds.), *A Literary Miscellany Presented to Eric Jacobsen* (Copenhagen: University of Copenhagen Publications of the Department of English 16, 1988), 164–84.

—— and ZEEBERG, PETER (eds.), *Litteratur og Laerdom. Dansk-sveske nylatindage april 1985* (Copenhagen: Museum Tusculanum Forl., 1987).

ALIC, MARGARET, *Hypatia's Heritage: A History of Women in Science from Antiquity to the Late Nineteenth Century* (London: Women's Press, 1986).

ALLEN, PRUDENCE, *The Concept of Woman II: The Early Humanist Reformation, 1250–1500* (Grand Rapids, Mich.: William B. Eerdman, 2002).

ALLUT, PAUL, *Aloysia Sygea et Nicolas Chorier* (Lyon: N. Scheuring, 1862).

ARDOUIN, PAUL, *Maurice Scève, Pernette du Guillet, Louise Labé: l'amour à Lyon au temps de la Renaissance* (Paris: A.-G. Nizet, 1981).

ARMSTRONG, ELIZABETH, *Robert Estienne, Royal Printer* (Cambridge: Cambridge University Press, 1954).

BAKER, DEREK (ed.), *Medieval Women*, Studies in Church History, Subsidia I (Oxford: Basil Blackwell, 1978).

BARDON, HENRI, *En lisant le Mercure galant: essai sur la culture latine en France au temps de Louis XIV*, Quaderni della Rivista di cultura classica e medioevale 5 (Rome: Edizioni dell'Ateneo, 1962).

BASTIAENSEN, MICHEL (ed.), *La Femme lettrée à la Renaissance: actes du colloque international, Bruxelles, 27–29 mars 1996*, Travaux de l'Institut Interuniversitaire pour l'Étude de la Renaissance et de l'Humanisme XII (Brussels: Peeters, 1997).

BAUR, A., *Maurice Scève et la Renaissance lyonnaise* (Paris: Champion, 1906).

BECKER-CANTARINO, BARBARA, 'Die "gelehrte Frau" und die Institutionen und Organisationsformen der Gelehrsamkeit am Beispiel der Anna Maria von Schurman (1608–1678)', in Sebastian Neumeister and Conrad Wiedemann (eds.), *Res Publica Litteraria: Die Institutionen der Gelehrsamkeit in der frühen Neuzeit* (Wiesbaden: Otto Harrassowitz, 1987), 559–76.

—— *Der Lange Weg zur Mündigkeit: Frau und Literatur (1500–1800)* (Stuttgart: J. B. Metlersche, 1987).

BELL, DAVID, *What Nuns Read: Books and Libraries in Medieval English Nunneries* (Kalamazoo, Mich.: Cistercian Publications, 1995).

BELL, SUSAN GROAG, 'Christine de Pizan (1364–1430): Humanism and the Problem of the Studious Woman', *Feminist Studies*, 3 (1975), 173–84.

—— 'Medieval Women Book Owners: Arbiters of Lay Piety and Ambassadors of Culture', in J. Bennett et al. (eds.), *Sisters and Workers in the Middle Ages* (Chicago: Chicago University Press, 1989).

BENNETT, J., et al. (eds.), *Sisters and Workers in the Middle Ages* (Chicago: Chicago University Press, 1989).

BENSON, PAMELA JOSEPH, *The Invention of the Renaissance Woman: The Challenge of Female Independence in the Literature and Thought of Italy and England* (University Park: Pennsylvania State University Press, 1992).

BERRIOT-SALVADORE, EVELYNE, *Les Femmes dans la société française de la Renaissance* (Geneva: Librairie Droz, 1990).

BIAGIOLI, MARIO, *Galileo, Courtier: The Practice of Science in the Culture of Absolutism* (Chicago: Chicago University Press, 1993).

BINNS, J. W., *Intellectual Culture in Elizabethan and Jacobean England: The Latin Writings of the Age* (Leeds: Francis Cairns, 1990).

BIRNBAUM, MARIANNA D., *Humanists in a Shattered World: Croatian and Hungarian Latinity in the Sixteenth Century* (Columbus, Oh.: Slavica Publishers, 1986).

BLAMIRES, ALCUIN, *The Case for Women in Medieval Culture* (Oxford: Clarendon Press, 1997).

BLOCH, R. HOWARD, *Medieval Misogyny and the Invention of Western Romantic Love* (Chicago: Chicago University Press, 1991).

BLUMENFELD-KOSINSKI, RENATE, ROBERTSON, DUNCAN and WARREN, NANCY (eds.), *The Vernacular Spirit: Essays on Medieval Religious Literature* (New York: Palgrave, 2002).

BOND, GERALD A., '*Iocus Amoris*: The Poetry of Baudri of Bourgeuil and the Formation of an Ovidian Subculture', *Traditio*, 42 (1986), 143–93.

—— *The Loving Subject: Desire, Eloquence and Power in Romanesque France* (Philadelphia: University of Pennsylvania Press, 1995).

BOUWSMA, WILLIAM J., *The Waning of the Renaissance, 1550–1640* (New Haven: Yale University Press, 2000).

BOZZETTI, CESARE, et al. (eds.) *Veronica Gàmbara e la poesia del suo tempo nell'Italia settentrionale* (Florence: Leo Olschki, 1989).

BRADNER, LEICESTER, *Musae Anglicanae: A History of Anglo-Latin Poetry* (New York: Modern Language Association of America; London: Oxford University Press, 1940).

BRIDENTHAL, RENATE, KOONZ, CLAUDIA and STUARD SUSAN M. (eds.), *Becoming Visible: Women in European History*, 2nd edn. (Boston: Houghton Mifflin, 1987).

BRINK, J. R. (ed.), *Female Scholars: A Tradition of Learned Women before 1800* (Montreal: Eden Press Women's Publications, 1980).

—— (ed.), *Privileging Gender in Early Modern England*, Sixteenth Century Essays and Studies XXIII (Kirksville, Mo.: Sixteenth Century Journal Publishers, 1993).

BRINKER-GABLER, GISELA (ed.), *Deutsche Literatur von Frauen*, 2 vols. (Munchi, C. H. Beck, 1988).

BROWN, JUDITH C., and DAVIS, ROBERT C. (eds.), *Gender and Society in Renaissance Italy* (Harlow: Longman, 1988).

BUYZE, JEAN, *The Tenth Muse: Women Poets before 1806* (Berkeley: Shameless Hussy Press, 1980).

BYNUM, CAROLINE WALKER, *Jesus as Mother* (Berkeley and Los Angeles: University of California Press, 1982).

CAMERON, AVERIL (ed.), *History as Text* (London: Duckworth, 1989).

CANNON, MARY AGNES, *The Education of Women during the Renaissance* (Washington: Catholic Education Press, 1916).

CHADWICK, NORA K., *Poetry and Letters in Early Christian Gaul* (London: Bowes & Bowes, 1955).

CHAMBERS, DAVID S., *Italian Academies of the Sixteenth Century* (London: Warburg, 1995).

CHOJNACKI, STANLEY, *Women and Men in Renaissance Venice* (Baltimore: Johns Hopkins University Press, 2000).

CHURCHILL, LAURIE, BROWN, PHYLLIS R. and JEFFREY, JANE E. (eds.), *Women Writing Latin from Roman Antiquity to Early Modern Europe*, 3 vols. (New York: Routledge, 2002).

CLANCHY, M. T., *From Memory to Written Record: England 1066–1307* (London: Edward Arnold, 1979).

CLARK, GILLIAN, *Women in Late Antiquity: Pagan and Christian Lifestyles* (Oxford: Clarendon Press, 1993).

CLARKE, DANIELLE, *The Politics of Early Modern Women's Writing* (Harlow: Pearson Education Ltd., 2001).

—— and CLARKE, ELIZABETH, (eds.), *This Double Voice: Gendered Writing in Early Modern England* (London: Palgrave; New York: St Martin's Press, 2000).

CLOKE, GILLIAN, *'This Female Man of God': Women and Spiritual Power in the Patristic Age, AD 350–450* (London: Routledge, 1995).

CLOUGH, CECIL H., 'Daughters and Wives of the Montefeltro: Outstanding Bluestockings of the Quattrocento', *Renaissance Studies*, 10.1 (Mar. 1996), 31–55.

COLEMAN, DOROTHY GABE, *The Gallo-Roman Muse: Aspects of Roman Literary Tradition in Sixteenth Century France* (Cambridge: Cambridge University Press, 1979).

COLIE, ROSALIE L., *Paradoxia Epidemica: The Renaissance Tradition of Paradox* (Princeton: Princeton University Press, 1966).

COLTHEART, LEONORE, 'The Virago and Machiavelli', in B. Garlick, Suzanne Dixon, and P. Allen (eds.), *Stereotypes of Women in Power*, Contributions in Women's Studies 125 (Westport, Conn.: Greenwood Press, 1992), 141–55.

CONTE, GIAN BIAGIO, *Latin Literature: A History*, trans. J. B. Solodow (Baltimore: Johns Hopkins University Press, 1994).

COOLEY, ALISON (ed.), *The Afterlife of Inscriptions: Reusing, Rediscovering, Reinventing & Revitalizing Ancient Inscriptions* (BICS Supplement 75) (London: Institute of Classical Studies, 2000).

CORTON, HENRI, *Histoire des femmes écrivains de la France* (Paris: A. Dupret, 1886).

COX, VIRGINIA, 'The Single Self: Feminist Thought and the Marriage Market in Early Modern Venice', *Renaissance Quarterly*, 48.3 (1995), 513–81.

CRESSY, DAVID, *Literacy and the Social Order: Reading and Writing in Tudor and Stuart England* (Cambridge: Cambridge University Press, 1980).

CURTIUS, E. R., *European Literature and the Latin Middle Ages*, trans. W. R. Trask (London: Routledge & Kegan Paul, 1953).

DA COSTA RAMALHO, AMÉRICO, *Para a história do humanismo em Portugal* (Coimbra: Instituto Nacional de la Investigação Científica, 1988).

DAVID, DEIRDRE, *Intellectual Women and Victorian Patriarchy* (London: Macmillan, 1987).

DAWSON, RUTH, P., *The Contested Quill: Literature by Women in Germany, 1770–1800* (Newark: University of Delaware Press, 2002).

DELEN, MARIE-ANGE, 'Frauenalben als Quelle, Frauen und Adelskultur im 16. Jahrhundert', in Wolfgang Klose (ed.), *Stammbücher des 16. Jahrhundert* (Wiesbaden: Otto Harrassowitz, 1989), 75–93.

DE RENZI, SALVATORE (ed.), *Storia documentata della Scuola Medica di Salerno*, 5 vols. (Naples: Tipografia del Filiatre Sebezio, 1852–9; 2nd edn. 1857–9).

DE SMET, INGRID A. R., ' "In the Name of the Father": Feminist Voices in the Republic of Letter', in Michel Bastiaensen (ed.), *La Femme lettrée à la Renaissance*, Travaux de l'Institut Interuniversitaire pour l'Étude de la Renaissance et de l'Humanisme XII (Louvain: Peeters, 1997), 177–96.

DOGLIO, M. L., *Lettera e donna: scrittura epistolare al femmile tra Quattro e Cinquecento* (Rome: Bulzoni, 1993).

DOODY, MARGARET ANN, *Frances Burney* (Cambridge: Cambridge University Press, 1988).

DOWLING, MARIA, *Humanism in the Age of Henry VIII* (Beckenham: Croom Helm, 1986).

DRONKE, PETER, *Poetic Individuality in the Middle Ages: New Departures in Poetry, 1000–1150* (Oxford: Clarendon Press, 1970).

—— *The Medieval Lyric*, 2nd edn. (London: Oxford University Press, 1978).

—— 'The Song of Songs and Medieval Love-Lyric', in *The Medieval Poet and his World* (Rome: Edizioni di storia e letteratura, 1984), 209–36.

DURRANT, C. S., *A Link between Flemish Mystics and English Martyrs* (London: Burns and Oates, 1925).

D'UVA, ORAZIO, *Un'erudita del secolo xv, y falsa leggenda de' suoi amori* (Trani: V. Vecchi, 1904).

ECKENSTEIN, LINA, *Women under Monasticism* (Cambridge: Cambridge University Press, 1896).

EISENSTEIN, ELISABETH, *The Printing Press as an Agent of Change*, 2 vols. (Cambridge: Cambridge University Press, 1979).

ELKINS, SHARON K., *Holy Women of Twelfth Century England* (Chapel Hill: University of North Carolina Press, 1988).

ENNEN, EDITH, *The Medieval Woman*, trans. Edmund Jephcott (Oxford: Basil Blackwell, 1989) trans. of *Frauen im Mittelalter* (Munich: C. H. Beck'sche Buchverhandlung, 1984)).

ENRIGHT, MICHAEL J., *The Lady with the Mead-Cup: Ritual, Prophecy and Lordship in the European Warband from La Têne to the Viking Age* (Dublin: Four Courts, 1996).

ERLER, MARY, and KOWALESKI MARYANNE, (eds.), *Women and Power in the Middle Ages* (Athens: University of Georgia Press, 1988).

ERMINI, FILIPPO, *Il centone di Proba e la poesia centonaria Latina* (Rome: Ermanno Loescher & Co., 1909).

EVANS, R. J. W., *Rudolf II and his World: A Study in Intellectual History, 1576–1612* (Oxford: Oxford University Press, 1973).

EZELL, MARGARET, *Writing Women's Literary History* (Baltimore: Johns Hopkins University Press, 1993).

—— *The Patriarch's Wife: Literary Evidence and the History of the Family* (Chapel Hill: University of North Carolina Press, 1987).

FABER DU FAUR, CURT VON, *German Baroque Literature: A Catalogue of the Collection in the Yale University Library* (New Haven: Yale University Press, 1958).

FAHY, CONOR, 'Three Early Renaissance Treatises on Women', *Italian Studies*, 11 (1956), 30–55.

FARRELL, JOSEPH, *The Latin Language and Latin Culture from Ancient to Modern Times* (Cambridge: Cambridge University Press, 2001).

FERGUSON, MARGARET W, QUILLIGAN, MAUREEN and VICKERS, NANCY J . (eds.), *Rewriting the Renaissance: The Discourses of Sexual Difference in Early Modern Europe* (Chicago: Chicago University Press, 1986).

FERRANTE, JOAN M., 'The Education of Women in the Middle Ages in Theory, Fact and Fantasy', in P. H. Labalme (ed.), *Beyond their Sex* (New York: New York University Press, 1980), 9–42.

—— *To the Glory of her Sex: Women's Roles in the Composition of Medieval Texts* (Bloomington: Indiana University Press, 1997).

FEUGÈRE, LÉON, *Les Femmes poètes au xvie siècle* (Paris: Didier et Cie., 1860).

FLANAGAN, SABINA, *Hildegard of Bingen, 1098–1179: A Visionary Life* (London: Routledge, 1989).

FORSTER, LEONARD, *Janus Gruter's English Years* (Leiden: Leiden University Press, 1967).

FOWLER, R., 'On Not Knowing Greek: The Classics and the Woman of Letters', *Classical Journal*, 78 (1983), 337–49.

FRANKLIN, J. J., 'Literacy and the Parietal Inscriptions of Pompeii', in Mary Beard (ed.), *Literacy in the Roman World* (Ann Arbor: University of Michigan Press, 1991), 77–98.

FRINGS, THEODOR, *Die Anfänge der europäischen Liebes-Dichtung im 11. und 12. Jahrhundert*, Sitzungsberichte der Bayerische Akademie der Wissenschaften (Munich: Verlap de Bayerische Akademie der Wissenschaften [Beck], 1960).

FUSCO, NICOLA, *Elena Lucrezia Cornaro Piscopia (1646–1684)* (Pittsburgh: United States Committee for the Elena Lucrezia Cornaro Piscopia Tercentenary, 1975).

GARDINER, DOROTHY, *English Girlhood at School: A Study of Women's Education through Twelve Centuries* (Oxford: Clarendon Press, 1929).

GARDNER, JANE F., *Women in Roman Law and Society* (Beckenham: Croom Helm, 1986).

GARLICK, BARBARA, DIXON, SUZANNE and ALLEN, P. (eds.), *Stereotypes of Women in Power*, Contributions in Women's Studies 125 (Westport, Conn.: Greenwood Press, 1992).

GEORGE, JUDITH, *Venantius Fortunatus: A Poet in Merovingian Gaul* (Oxford: Clarendon Press, 1992).

GIBSON, WENDY, *Women in Seventeenth-Century France* (London: Routledge, 1989).

GOLD, BARBARA K., MILLER, PAUL ALLEN, and PLATTER, CHARLES (eds.), *Sex and Gender in Medieval and Renaissance Texts: The Latin Tradition* (New York: State University of New York Press, 1997).

GRAFTON, A., and JARDINE, L., *From Humanism to the Humanities: Education and the Liberal Arts in Fifteenth- and Sixteenth-Century Europe* (London: Duckworth, 1986).

GRENDLER, PAUL F., *Schooling in Renaissance Italy: Literacy and Learning 1300–1600* (Baltimore: Johns Hopkins University Press, 1989).

GRUPPE, OTTO, *Die römische Elegie*, 2 vols. (Leipzig: O. Wigand, 1838).

GUTWIRTH, MADELYN, *The Twilight of the Goddesses: Women and Representation in the French Revolutionary Era* (New Brunswick, NJ: Rutgers University Press, 1992).

HANNAY, MARGARET P. (ed.), *Silent but for the Word: Tudor Women as Patrons, Translators and Writers of Religious Works* (Kent, Oh.: Kent State University Press, 1985).

HARE, CHRISTOPHER, *Men and Women of the Italian Reformation* (London: Stanley Paul & Co., 1914).

—— *The High and Puissant Princess Marguerite of Austria* (London: Harper & Brothers, 1907).

HARRIS, BARBARA J., 'Women and Politics in Early Tudor England', *Historical Journal*, 33.2 (1990), 259–87.

HAWKINS, R. L., 'A Letter from One Maiden of the Renaissance to Another', *Modern Language Notes*, 22.8 (1907), 243–5.

HEINRICH, MARY PIA, *The Canonesses and Education in the Early Middle Ages* (Washington: Catholic University of America Press, 1924).

HEMELRIJK, EMILY A., *Matrona Docta: Educated Women in the Roman Élite from Cornelia to Julia Domna* (London: Routledge, 1999).

HOLUM, KENNETH, *Theodosian Empresses: Women and Imperial Dominion in Late Antiquity* (Berkeley and Los Angeles University of California Press, 1982).

HOPKINS, LISA, *Women who Would be Kings: Female Rulers of the Sixteenth Century* (London: Vision Press; New York: St Martin's Press, 1991).

HUSKINSON, JANET, 'Women and Learning, Gender and Identity in Scenes of Intellectual Life on Late Roman Sarcophagi', Richard Miles (ed.), *Constructing Identities in Late Antiquity* (London: Routledge, 1999), 190–213.

HUTTON, JAMES, *The Greek Anthology in France and in the Latin Writers of the Netherlands to the Year 1800* (Ithaca, NY: Cornell University Press, 1946).

ILSLEY, MARJORIE H., *A Daughter of the Renaissance: Marie de Jars de Gournay, her Life and Works* (The Hague: Mouton & Co., 1963).

JAEGER, C. STEPHEN, *Ennobling Love: In Search of a Lost Sensibility* (Philadelphia: University of Pennsylvania Press, 1999).

JANSON, TORE, *Latin Prose Prefaces: Studies in Literary Convention*, Studia Latina Stockholmiensia 13 (Stockholm: Almquist and Wiksell, 1964).

JANSSEN, JOHANNES, *History of the German People at the Close of the Middle Ages*, trans. M. S. Mitchell and A. M. Christie, 2 vols. (London: Kegan Paul, Trench, Trübner & Co., 1896).

JANSSEN, WILLEM, *Charles Utenhove: sa vie et son œuvre* (Maastricht: Van Aelst, 1939).

JARDINE, LISA, *Worldly Goods: A New History of the Renaissance* (London: Macmillan, 1996).

JED, STEPHANIE, 'Chastity on the Page: A Feminist Use of Palaeography', in M. Miciel and J. Schiesari (eds.), *Refiguring Woman: Perspectives on Gender and the Italian Renaissance* (Ithaca, NY: Cornell University Press, 1991), 114–30.

JENSEN, ELISABETH MØLLER (ed.), *I Guds Namm: 1000–1800*, Nordisk Kvinnolitteraturhistoria 1 (Höganas: A. B. Wiken, 1993).

—— (ed.), *Liv och verk*, Nordisk kvinnolitteraturhistoria 5 (Malmö: Bra Böcker, 2000).

JENSEN, MINNA SKAFTE (ed.), *A History of Nordic Neo-Latin Literature* (Odense: Odense University Press, 1995).

JOHNSON, PENELOPE D., 'Mulier et Monialis: The Medieval Nun's Self-Image', *Thought*, 64 (1989), 242–53.

—— *Equal in Monastic Profession: Religious Women in Medieval France* (Chicago: University of Chicago Press, 1991).

JONES, ANN ROSALIND, *The Currency of Eros: Women's Love Lyrics in Europe, 1560–1620* (Bloomington: Indiana University Press, 1990).

—— 'Contentious Readings: Urban Humanism and Gender Difference in *La Puce de Madame Des-Roches* (1582)', *Renaissance Quarterly*, 48.1 (1995), 109–28.

JONES, RICHARD FOSTER, *The Triumph of the English Language: A Survey of Opinions Concerning the Vernacular from the Introduction of Printing to the Restoration* (London: Oxford University Press, 1953).

JORDAN, CONSTANCE, 'Feminism and the Humanists: The Case of Sir Thomas Elyot's Defence of Good Women', *Renaissance Quarterly*, 36.2 (1983), 181–220.

JUGÉ, CLEMENT, *Nicolas Denisot du Mans (1515–1559): essai sur sa vie et ses œuvres* (Le Mans: Bienamé-Leguicheux, 1907).

KALLENBACH, JOSEPH, *Les Humanistes polonais* (Fribourg: Consociatio Sancti Pauli, 1891).

KAMM, JOSEPHINE, *Hope Deferred: Girls' Education in English History* (London: Methuen, 1965).

KAUFMAN, GLORIA, 'Juan Luis Vives and the Education of Women', *Signs*, 3.4 (1978), 891–6.

KEATING, L. CLARK, *Studies on the Literary Salon in France, 1550–1615* (Cambridge, Mass.: Harvard University Press, 1941).

KELSO, RUTH, *Doctrine for the Lady of the Renaissance* (Urbana: University of Illinois Press, 1956; repr. 1978).

KENDRICK, T. D., *Mary of Ágreda: The Life and Legend of a Spanish Nun* (London: Routledge & Kegan Paul, 1967).

KERSEY, SHIRLEY NELSON, *Classics in the Education of Girls and Women* (Metuchen, NJ: Scarecrow Press, Inc., 1981).

KING, CATHERINE E., *Renaissance Women Patrons* (Manchester: Manchester University Press, 1998).

KING, MARGARET L., 'Thwarted Ambitions: Six Learned Women of the Italian Renaissance', *Soundings*, 59 (1976), 276–304.

—— 'Goddess and Captive: Antonio Loschi's Epistolatory Tribute to Maddalena Scrovegni (1389)', *Medievalia et Humanistica* (1988), 103–27.

—— 'Isotta Nogarola, umanista e devota (1418–1466)', in Ottavia Niccoli (ed.), *Rinascimento al femminile* (Bari: Laterza, 1991), 3–33.

—— *The Death of the Child Valerio Marcello* (Chicago: University of Chicago Press, 1994).

—— *Women of the Renaissance* (Chicago: Chicago University Press, 1991).

KLOEK, ELS, TEEUWEN, NICOLE, and HUISMAN, MARIJKE (eds.), *Women of the Golden Age: An International Debate on Women in Seventeenth-Century Holland, England, and Italy* (Hilversum: Verloren, 1994).

KLUGE, O., 'Die neulateinische Kunstprosa', *Glotta*, 23 (1935), 18–80.

KOHL, BENJAMIN G., *Padua under the Carrara 1318–1405* (Baltimore: Johns Hopkins University Press, 1998).

KRISTELLER, P. O., 'Learned Women of Early Modern Italy: Humanists and University Scholars', in P. H. Labalme (ed.), *Beyond their Sex* (New York: New York University Press, 1980), 91–116.

KROL, STEFAN, *101 Kobiet Polskien: slad w historii* (Warsaw: Książka i Wiedza, 1988).

LABALME, PATRICIA H. (ed.), *Beyond their Sex: Learned Women of the European Past* (New York: New York University Press, 1980).

LATTIMORE, RICHMOND, *Themes in Greek and Latin Epitaphs* (Urbana: University of Illinois Press, 1962).

LAVAND, JACQUES, *Un poète de cour au temps des derniers Valois: Philippe Desportes (1546–1606)* (Paris: E. Droz, 1936).

LAVRIN, ASUNCIÓN (ed.), *Latin American Women: Historical Perspectives* (Westport, Conn.: Greenwood Press, 1978).

LEACH, EDMUND, *Culture and Nature, or La Femme Sauvage* (London: Bedford College [The Stevenson Lecture], 1968).

LEANROY, ALFRED, 'Boccace et Christine de Pisan, le *De Claris Mulieribus*: principale source du livre de la Cité des Dames', *Romania*, 48 (1822), 92–105.

LEE, SIDNEY, *The French Renaissance in England* (Oxford: Clarendon Press. 1910).

LEGARÉ, ANNE-MARIE, 'Reassessing Women's Libraries in Late Medieval France: The Case of Jeanne de Laval', *Renaissance Studies*, 10.2 (1996), 209–36.

LENZI, MARIA LUDOVICA, *Donne e madonne: l'educazione femminile nel primo Rinascimento Italiano* (Turin: Loescher, 1982).

LEVIN, CAROLE, *Political Rhetoric, Power and Renaissance Women* (New York: State University of New York Press, 1995).

LEWALSKI, BARBARA K., *Writing Women in Jacobean England* (Cambridge, Mass.: Harvard University Press, 1993).

LEYSER, HENRIETTA, *Medieval Women: A Social History of Women in England, 450–1500* (London: Weidenfeld and Nicolson, 1995).

LISS, PEGGY K., *Isabel the Queen: Life and Times* (New York: Oxford University Press, 1992).

LOADES, DAVID, *The Reign of Mary Tudor* (London: Ernest Benn, 1979).

LONSDALE, ROGER (ed.), *Eighteenth-Century Women Poets* (Oxford: Oxford University Press, 1990).

LOUGEE, CAROLINE, *Le Paradis du femmes: Women, Salons and Social Stratification in Seventeenth-Century France* (Princeton: Princeton University Press, 1976).

LYNN, CARO, *A College Professor of the Renaissance: Lucio Marineo Siculo among the Spanish Humanists* (Chicago: University of Chicago Press, 1937).

MCCASH, JUNE HALL (ed.), *The Cultural Patronage of Medieval Women* (Athens: University of Georgia Press, 1996).

MCCONICA, J. K., *English Humanists and Reformation Politics* (Oxford: Clarendon Press, 1965).

MACFARLANE, I. D., *Buchanan* (London: Duckworth, 1981).

MCKITTERICK, ROSAMOND, *The Carolingians and the Written Word* (Cambridge: Cambridge University Press, 1989).

MACLEAN, IAN, *Woman Triumphant: Feminism in French Literature, 1610–1652* (Oxford: Clarendon Press, 1977).

—— *The Renaissance Notion of Woman* (Cambridge: Cambridge University Press, 1980).

MCLEOD, GLENDA, *Virtue and Venom: Catalogs of Women from Antiquity to the Renaissance* (Ann Arbor: University of Michigan. Press, 1991).

MCMANAMAN, JOHN M., *Funeral Oratory and the Cultural Ideals of Italian Humanism* (Chapel Hill: University of North Carolina Press, 1989).

MACMULLEN, RAMSAY, *Roman Social Relations* (New Haven: Yale University Press, 1974).

MAGGIOLO, ATTILIO, *I soci dell'Accademia Patavina, dalla sua fondazione (1599)* (Padua: Accademia Patavina di scienze lettere ed arti, 1983).

MARROU, H. I, *A History of Education in Antiquity*, trans. G. Lamb (London: Sheed & Ward, 1936).

MARSHALL, SHERRIN (ed.), *Women in Reformation and Counter-Reformation Europe: Public and Private Worlds* (Bloomington: Indiana University Press, 1989).

MASCHIETTO, FRANCESCO LUDOVICO, *Elena Lucrezia Cornaro Piscopia (1646–1684), prima donna laureata nel mondo* (Padua: Editrice Antenore, 1978).

MATTER, E. ANN, and COAKLEY, JOHN (eds.), *Creative Women in Medieval and Early Modern Italy: A Religious and Artistic Renaissance* (Philadelphia: University of Pennsylvania Press, 1995).

MATTHEWS, JOHN, *Western Aristocracies and Imperial Court, AD 364–425* (Oxford: Clarendon Press, 1975).

MATTINGLY, GARRETT, *Catherine of Aragon* (London: Jonathan Cape, 1942; repr. 1963).

MAZZANTI, MARINELLA BONVINI, *Battista Sforza Montefeltro: una 'principessa' nel Rinascimento* (Urbino: Quattroventi, 1993).

MEALE, CAROL M. (ed.), *Women and Literature in Britain, 1150–1500* (Cambridge: Cambridge University Press, 1993).

MERRIM, STEPHANIE, *Early Modern Women's Writing and Sor Juana Inés de la Cruz* (Nashville: Vanderbilt University Press; Liverpool: Liverpool University Press, 1999).

MERTON, CHARLOTTE, 'The Women who Served Queen Mary and Queen Elizabeth: Ladies, Gentlewomen and Maids of the Privy Chamber, 1553–1603', Ph.D. diss. (Cambridge, 1992).

MEWS, CONSTANT, *The Lost Love Letters of Heloise and Abelard: Perceptions of Dialogue in Twelfth-Century France* (New York: St Martin's Press, 1999).

MIGIEL, MARILYN, and SCHIESARI, JULIANA (eds.), *Refiguring Women: Perspectives on Gender and the Italian Renaissance* (Ithaca, NY: Cornell University Press, 1991).

MOHLER, S. L., 'Feminism in the *Corpus Inscriptionum Latinorum*', *Classical Weekly*, 25 (1932), 113–17.

MOLLEDA, DOLORES GOMEZ, 'La cultura femenina en la época de Isabel la Católica', *Revista de archivos, bibliotecas y museos*, 61 (1955), 137–95.

MOMIGLIANO, ARNALDO (ed.), *The Conflict between Paganism and Christianity in the Fourth Century* (Oxford: Clarendon Press, 1963).

MONSON, CRAIG (ed.), *The Crannied Wall: Women, Religion and the Arts in Early Modern Europe* (Ann Arbor: University of Michigan Press, 1991).

MOORE, CORNELIA NIEKUS, *The Maiden's Mirror: Reading Material for German Girls in the Sixteenth and Seventeenth Centuries*, Wolfenbütteler Forschungen 36 (Wiesbaden: Otto Harrassowitz, 1987).

MOORE, MICHAEL J. (ed.), *Quincentennial Essays on St Thomas More* (Boone, NC: Appalachian State University Press, 1978).

MÖRNER, BIRGER, *Maria Aurora Königsmarck: en Krönika* (Stockholm, P. A. Norstedt & Söners Förlag, 1914).

—— *Maria Aurora Königsmarck, eine Chronik*, German trans. (Munich: Georg Müller, 1922).

MORRIS, PENNY, et al., 'Bibliographical Guide to Women Writers and their Work', in Letizia Panizza and Sharon Wood (eds.), *A History of Women's Writing in Italy* (Cambridge: Cambridge University Press, 2000), 282–337.

MYERS, SYLVIA HARCSTARK, *The Bluestocking Circle: Women, Friendship and the Life of the Mind in Eighteenth Century England* (Oxford: Clarendon Press, 1990).

NADER, HELEN, *The Mendoza Family in the Spanish Renaissance, 1350 to 1550* (New Brunswick, NJ: Rutgers University Press, 1979).

NATIVEL, COLETTE (ed.), *Femmes savantes, savoir des femmes: du crépuscule de la Renaissance à l'aube des Lumières: actes du Colloque de Chantilly, 22–24 sept. 1995* (Geneva: Droz, 1999).

NELSON, JANET, 'Women at the Court of Charlemagne: A Case of Monstrous Regiment?', in John Carmi Parsons (ed.), *Medieval Queenship* (Stroud: Alan Sutton, 1993), 43–62.

NEUMEISTER, SEBASTIAN, and WIEDEMANN, CONRAD (eds.) *Res Publica Litteraria: Die Institutionen der Gelehrsamkeit in der frühen Neuzeit*, 2 vols. (Wiesbaden: Otto Harrassowitz, 1987).

NEWCOMB, ANTHONY, *The Madrigal at Ferrara: 1579–1592*, 2 vols. (Princeton: Princeton University Press, 1980).

NICCOLI, OTTAVIA, *Rinascimento al feminile* (Bari: Editore Laterza, 1991).

NOLHAC, PIERRE DE, *Un poète rhénan ami de la Pléiade: Paul Melissus*, Bibliothèque Littéraire de la Renaissance, NS 11 (Paris: H. Champion, 1923).

O'DONNELL, ANNE M., 'Contemporary Women in the Letters of Erasmus', *Erasmus of Rotterdam Society Yearbook*, 9 (1989), 34–72.

OETTEL, THÉRÈSE, 'Una cathedrática en el siglo xvi, Lucía de Medrano', *Boletín de la Real Academia de la Historia* (1935), 310.

ONG. WALTER J., 'Latin and the Social Fabric', in *The Barbarian Within and Other Fugitive Essays and Studies* (New York: Macmillan, 1962), 206–19.

—— 'Latin Language Study as a Renaissance Puberty Rite', *Studies in Philology*, 56 (1959), 103–24.

ONG, WALTER J., (ed.), *Rhetoric, Romance and Technology: Studies in the Interaction of Expression and Culture* (Ithaca, NY: Cornell University Press, 1971).

ORTEGA COSTA, MILAGROS, 'Spanish Women in the Reformation', in Sherrin Marshall (ed.), *Women in Reformation and Counter-Reformation Europe: Public and Private Worlds* (Bloomington: Indiana University Press, 1989), 89–119.

OZMENT, STEVEN, *When Fathers Ruled: Family Life in Reformation Europe* (Cambridge, Mass.: Harvard University Press, 1983).

PANIZZA, LETIZIA (ed.), *Women in Italian Renaissance Culture and Society* (Oxford: European Humanities Research Centre, 2000).

—— and WOOD, SHARON (eds.), *A History of Women's Writing in Italy* (Cambridge: Cambridge University Press, 2000).

PARSONS, JOHN CARMI (ed.), *Medieval Queenship* (Stroud: Alan Sutton, 1993).

PATTEN, ELIZABETH, 'Second Thoughts of a Renaissance Humanist on the Education of Women: Jean Luis Vives Revises his *De Institutione Feminae Christianae*', *American Notes & Queries*, 5, 2.3 (1992), 111–14.

PAZ, OCTAVIO, *Sor Juana: Her Life and her World* (London: Faber and Faber, 1988).

PERRY, RUTH, *The Celebrated Mary Astell* (Chicago: University of Chicago Press, 1986).

PEVSNER, NIKOLAUS, *The Buildings of England: Cumberland and Westmorland* (Harmondsworth: Penguin, 1967).

POLHEIM, KARL, *Die lateinische Reimprosa* (Berlin, 1925).

POLLOCK, LINDA, ' "Teach her to Live under Obedience' ": The Making of Women in the Upper Ranks of Early Modern England', *Continuity and Change*, 4 (1989), 238–44.

POWER, EILEEN, *Medieval English Nunneries, c.1275 to 1535* (Cambridge: Cambridge University Press, 1922).

PRIOR, MARY (ed.), *Women in English Society 1500–1800* (London: Routledge, 1985).

QUENTIN BAUCHART, ERNEST, *Les Femmes bibliophiles de France*, 2 vols. (Paris: Damascène Morgand, 1886).

RABY, F. J. E, *A History of Christian-Latin Poetry from the Beginnings to the Close of the Middle Ages* (Oxford: Clarendon Press, 1927).

—— *A History of Secular Latin Poetry in the Middle Ages*, 2 vols. (Oxford: Clarendon Press, 1934).

RAPLEY, ELIZABETH, *The Dévotes: Women and Church in Seventeenth-Century France* (Montreal: McGill-Queen's University Press, 1990).

RATEL, SIMONNE, 'La Cour de la reine Marguerite', *Revue du seizième siècle*, 11 (1924), 1–29, 193–207; 12 (1925), 1–43.

REYNOLDS, L. D., and WILSON, N. G., *Scribes and Scholars: A Guide to the Transmission of Greek and Latin Literature*, 2nd edn. (Oxford: Clarendon Press, 1974).

—— et al., *Texts and Transmission: A Survey of the Latin Classics* (Oxford: Clarendon Press, 1983).

RICHARDSON, BRIAN, *Printing, Writers and Readers in Renaissance Italy* (Cambridge: Cambridge University Press, 1999).

RICHARDSON, LULU MCDOWELL, *The Forerunners of Feminism in French Literature, from Christine of Pisa to Marie de Gournay* (Baltimore: Johns Hopkins Studies in Romance Literature and Language 12, 1929).

RICHÉ, PIERRE, *Education and Culture in the Barbarian West*, trans. J. J. Contreni (Columbia: University of South Carolina Press, 1976).

RIGOLOT, FRANÇOIS, 'Écrire au féminin à la Renaissance: problèmes et perspectives', *L'Esprit créateur*, 30 (1990), 3–10.

ROBIN, DIANA, 'Women, Space and Renaissance Discourse', in Barbara K. Gold, Paul Allen Miller, and Charles Platter (eds.), *Sex and Gender in Medieval and Renaissance Texts: the Latin Tradition* (New York: State University of New York Press, 1997), 165–87.

ROELKER, NANCY LYMAN, *Queen of Navarre: Jeanne d'Albret, 1528–1572* (Cambridge, Mass.: Belknap Press, 1968).

ROELKER, NANCY L., 'The Appeal of Calvinism to French Noblewomen in the Sixteenth Century', *Journal of Interdisciplinary History*, 2 (1972), 391–418.

—— 'The Role of Noblewomen in the French Reformation', *Archiv für Reformationsgeschichte*, 63 (1972), 168–95.

ROPER, LYNDAL, *The Holy Household: Women and Morals in Reformation Augsburg* (Oxford: Clarendon Press, 1989).

ROSE, MARY BETH (ed.), *Women in the Middle Ages and the Renaissance: Literary and Historical Perspectives* (Syracuse, NY: Syracuse University Press, 1986).

ROUSSELOT, PAUL, *Histoire de l'éducation des femmes*, 2 vols. (Paris: Didier et Cie., 1883).

SÁNCHEZ, MAGDALENA S., *The Empress, the Queen, and the Nun: Women and Power at the Court of Philip III of Spain* (Baltimore: Johns Hopkins University Press, 1998).

SCHAMA, SIMON, *The Embarrassment of Riches: An Interpretation of Dutch Culture in the Golden Age* (London: Collins, 1987).

SCHIANCHI, LUCIA FORNARI, *Correggio* (Florence: Scala, 1994).

SCHLEINER, LOUISE, *Tudor and Stuart Women Writers* (Bloomingto: Indiana University Press, 1994).

SCHMIDT, PAUL GERHARD (ed.), *Die Fraue in der Renaissance* (Wiesbaden: Otto Harrassowitz, 1994).

SEALY, ROBERT J., SJ, *The Palace Academy of Henry III* (Geneva: Librairie Droz, 1981).

SEGEL, HAROLD B., *Renaissance Culture in Poland: The Rise of Humanism, 1470–1543* (Ithaca, NY: Cornell University Press, 1989).

SELLA, DOMENICO, *Italy in the Seventeenth Century* (London: Longman, 1997).

SEYMOUR, WILLIAM, *Ordeal by Ambition: An English Family in the Shadow of the Tudors* (London: Sidgwick and Jackson, 1972).

SHARP, TONY, *Pleasure and Ambition: The Life, Loves and Wars of Augustus the Strong, 1670–1707* (London: I. B. Tauris, 2001).

SHATTOCK, JOANNE, *The Oxford Guide to British Women Writers* (Oxford: Oxford University Press, 1994).

SMITH, HILDA L. (ed.), *Women Writers and the Early Modern British Political Tradition* (Cambridge: Cambridge University Press, 1998).

SOCOLOW, SUSAN MIGDEN, *The Women of Colonial Latin America* (Cambridge: Cambridge University Press, 2000).

SOLTERER, HELEN, *The Master and Minerva: Disputing Women in French Medieval Culture* (Berkeley and Los Angeles: University of California Press, 1995).

STAFFORD, PAULINE, *Queens, Concubines and Dowagers: The King's Wife in the Early Middle Ages* (London: Batsford, 1983).

STALLAERT, CHARLES, and VAN DER HAEGEN, PHILIPPE, 'De l'instruction publique au Moyen Âge du viiie au xvie siècle', in *Mémoires couronnés et mémoires des savants étrangers publiés par l'Academie Royale des Sciences, des Lettres et des Beaux-arts de Belgique*, 23 (Brussels: Académie Royale, 1850).

STEPHENS, WINIFRED, *Margaret of France, Duchess of Savoy, 1523–74* (London: John Lane, Bodley Head, 1912).

SURTZ, RONALD E., *Writing Women in Late Medieval and Early Modern Spain: The Mothers of St Teresa of Avila* (Philadelphia: University of Pennsylvania Press, 1995).

SYME, RONALD, *The Augustan Aristocracy* (Oxford: Clarendon Press, 1986).

SZÖVÉRFFY, JOSEPH, *Secular Latin Lyrics and Minor Poetic Forms of the Middle Ages: A Historical Survey and Literary Repertory from the Tenth to the Late Fifteenth Century* (Concord, NH: Classical Folia Editions, 1992).

THOMPSON, JAMES W., *The Literacy of the Laity in the Middle Ages* (Berkeley and Los Angeles: University of California Publications in Education 9, 1939).

TOO, YUN LEE, and LIVINGSTONE, NIALL (eds.), *Pedagogy and Power: Rhetorics of Classical Learning* (Cambridge: Cambridge University Press, 1998).

TRUHLÁR, Z. A., and HRDINA, KAREL, *Enchiridion Renatae Poesis Latinae in Bohemia et Moravia Cultae*, 5 vols. (Prague: Academiae Scientarum Bohemoslovacae, 1966–82).

USHER, M. D., *Homeric Stitchings: The Homeric Centos of the Empress Eudocia* (Lanham, Md.: Rowman & Littlefield, 1998).

VAN DORSTEN, JAN, *The Radical Arts* (Leiden: Thomas Brown Institute; London: Oxford University Press, 1970).

VEDOVA, GIUSEPPE, *Biografica degli scrittori padovani*, 2 vols. (Padua: Tipi della Minerva, 1832).

VISSAC, J.-A., *De la poésie latine en France au siècle de Louis XIV* (Paris: A. Durand, 1862).

WAQUET, FRANÇOISE, *Latin: Or the Empire of a Sign*, trans. John Howe (London: Verso, 2000).

WARNICKE, RETHA M., *Women of the English Renaissance and Reformation* (Westport, Conn.: Greenwood Press, 1983).

WATSON, FOSTER, (ed.) *Vives and the Renaissance Education of Women* (London: Edward Arnold, 1912).

WATT, DIANE (ed.), *Medieval Women in their Communities* (Cardiff: University of Wales Press, 1997).

WEAVER, ELISSA, 'Spiritual Fun: A Study of Sixteenth-Century Tuscan Convent Theater', in Mary Beth Rose (ed.), *Women in the Middle Ages and the Renaissance: Literary and Historical Perspectives* (Syracuse, NY: Syracuse University Press 1986), 173–206.

WIESNER, MERRY, *Gender, Church and State in Early Modern Germany* (London: Longman, 1998).

WILL, S. F., 'Camille de Morel: A Prodigy of the Renaissance', *PMLA* 51 (1936), 83–119.

WILSON, KATHARINA M., and WARNKE, FRANK J. (eds.), *Women Writers of the Seventeenth Century* (Athens: University of Georgia Press, 1989).

WILSON-KASTNER, PATRICIA, et al., *A Lost Tradition: Women Writers of the Early Church* (Washington: University Press of America, 1981).

WOODWARD, WILLIAM HARRISON, *Vittorino da Feltre and Other Humanist Educators: Essays and Versions* (Cambridge: Cambridge University Press, 1905).

WUNDER, HEIDE, *He is the Sun, She is the Moon: Women in Early Modern Germany*, trans. Thomas Dunlap (Cambridge, Mass.: Harvard University Press, 1988).

WYKE, MARIA, 'Written Women: Propertius's *Scripta Puella*', *Journal of Roman Studies*, 77 (1987), 47–61.

YATES, FRANCES, *The French Academies of the Sixteenth Century* (London: Warburg Institute, 1947; repr. London: Routledge, 1988).

ZARRI, GABRIELLA, *Recinti: donne, clausura e matrimonio nella prima età moderna* (Bologna: Il Mulino, 2000).

INDEX

Note to readers

The preparation of this index has presented major difficulties. Conventions differ from nation to nation; and it is to be remembered that my information about any particular individual has not necessarily been derived from a text written in his or her native tongue. Readers are therefore advised that toponyms involving 'da', 'de', 'di', 'of', 'van', 'von', etc., are listed under first name if the individual is pre-1300, otherwise, except in the case of queens, normally under the final element. The form in which I came across a name may not be the most correct one; therefore readers looking to see if I reference a particular woman whom they know of from other sources are asked to bear this in mind, and try alternatives. Some women's names appear in Latinized form if I have seen no other (e.g. 'Corbiniana'); but where the vernacular form is recoverable, I use it ('Weston' not 'Westonia', 'Deshoulières' not 'Hulleria', 'von Druppach' not the semi-Latinized 'à Druppach'): similarly, where I have seen a German name only with the feminine termination –in (e.g. Calwerin) I give this form, but when the surname is recoverable I use it (Möller, not Möllerin or Mölleria).